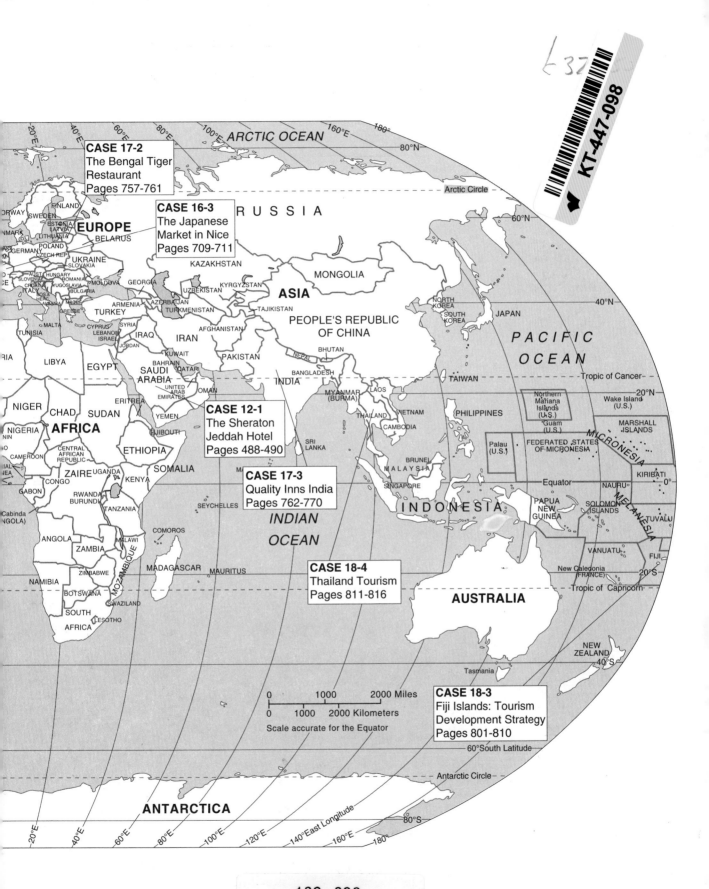

CASE 17-2
The Bengal Tiger
Restaurant
Pages 757-761

CASE 16-3
The Japanese
Market in Nice
Pages 709-711

CASE 12-1
The Sheraton
Jeddah Hotel
Pages 488-490

CASE 17-3
Quality Inns India
Pages 762-770

CASE 18-4
Thailand Tourism
Pages 811-816

CASE 18-3
Fiji Islands: Tourism
Development Strategy
Pages 801-810

ARCTIC OCEAN

Arctic Circle

RUSSIA

EUROPE

FINLAND
NORWAY
SWEDEN
DENMARK
ESTONIA
LATVIA
LITHUANIA
BELARUS
POLAND
GERMANY
CZECH REP.
UKRAINE
SLOVAKIA
AUST.
HUNGARY
SLOVENIA
CROATIA
ROMANIA
MOLDOVA
BOS.
HER.
YUGOSLAVIA
BULGARIA
ITALY
ALBANIA
MAC.
GREECE
TURKEY

KAZAKHSTAN

MONGOLIA

ASIA

PEOPLE'S REPUBLIC
OF CHINA

NORTH
KOREA
SOUTH
KOREA

JAPAN

PACIFIC
OCEAN

60°N

40°N

MALTA
TUNISIA
CYPRUS
LEBANON
ISRAEL
SYRIA
JORDAN
IRAQ
ARMENIA
AZERBAIJAN
GEORGIA
UZBEKISTAN
TURKMENISTAN
KYRGYZSTAN
TAJIKISTAN
AFGHANISTAN
IRAN
KUWAIT
BAHRAIN
QATAR
PAKISTAN
NEPAL
BHUTAN
BANGLADESH

LIBYA
EGYPT
SAUDI
ARABIA
UNITED
ARAB
EMIRATES
OMAN
YEMEN

INDIA

MYANMAR
(BURMA)
LAOS
THAILAND
VIETNAM
CAMBODIA

TAIWAN

PHILIPPINES

Tropic of Cancer

20°N

Northern
Mariana
Islands
(U.S.)

Wake Island
(U.S.)

Guam
(U.S.)

MARSHALL
ISLANDS

MICRONESIA

NIGER
CHAD
SUDAN

AFRICA

NIGERIA
BENIN
CAMEROON
CENTRAL
AFRICAN
REPUBLIC
ERITREA
DJIBOUTI
ETHIOPIA
SOMALIA

EQ.
GUINEA
GABON
CONGO
ZAIRE
UGANDA
RWANDA
BURUNDI
KENYA
TANZANIA

SEYCHELLES

SRI
LANKA

BRUNEI
MALAYSIA
SINGAPORE

Palau
(U.S.)

FEDERATED STATES
OF MICRONESIA

KIRIBATI

Equator

NAURU

0°

INDONESIA

INDIAN

OCEAN

PAPUA
NEW
GUINEA

SOLOMON
ISLANDS

MELANESIA

TUVALU

Cabinda
(ANGOLA)
ANGOLA
ZAMBIA
MALAWI
ZIMBABWE
MOZAMBIQUE
COMOROS

MADAGASCAR
MAURITUS

VANUATU

New Caledonia
(FRANCE)

FIJI

20°S

NAMIBIA
BOTSWANA
SWAZILAND
SOUTH
AFRICA
LESOTHO

AUSTRALIA

Tropic of Capricorn

0   1000   2000 Miles
0   1000   2000 Kilometers
Scale accurate for the Equator

NEW
ZEALAND

40°S

Tasmania

60°South Latitude

ANTARCTICA

Antarctic Circle

80°S

20°E 40°E 60°E 80°E 100°E 120°E 140°East Longitude 160°E 180°

KT-447-098

136   360

Marketing Leadership in Hospitality

Marketing
Leadership
in Hospitality

FOUNDATIONS AND PRACTICES
Second Edition

ROBERT C. LEWIS, Ph.D.
Professor of Marketing and Graduate Coordinator
School of Hotel and Food Administration
University of Guelph, Guelph, Ontario

RICHARD E. CHAMBERS, MBA
President
Directional Marketing
New York, New York

HARSHA E. CHACKO, Ph.D.
Associate Professor
School of Hotel, Restaurant and Tourism Administration
University of New Orleans, Louisiana

NORWICH CITY COLLEGE LIBRARY

Stock No	136360	
Class	647.940688 LEW	
Cat.	Proc.	

 VAN NOSTRAND REINHOLD
I(T)P A Division of International Thomson Publishing Inc.

New York • Albany • Bonn • Boston • Detroit • London • Madrid • Melbourne
Mexico City • Paris • San Francisco • Singapore • Tokyo • Toronto

Copyright © 1995 by Van Nostrand Reinhold

I(T)P   A division of International Thomson Publishing Inc.
       The ITP logo is a trademark under license.

Printed in the United States of America
For more information, contact:

Van Nostrand Reinhold
115 Fifth Avenue
New York, NY 10003

International Thomson Publishing GmbH
Königswinterer Strasse 418
53227 Bonn
Germany

International Thomson Publishing Europe
Berkshire House 168-173
High Holborn
London WC1V 7AA
England

International Thomson Publishing Asia
221 Henderson Road
Henderson Building
Singapore 0315

Thomas Nelson Australia
102 Dodds Street
South Melbourne, 3205
Victoria, Australia

International Thomson Publishing Japan
Hirakawacho Kyowa Building, 3F
2-2-1 Hirakawacho
Chiyoda-ku, 102 Tokyo
Japan

Nelson Canada
1120 Birchmount Road
Scarborough, Ontario
Canada M1K 5G4

International Thomson Editores
Campos Eliseos 385, Piso 7
Col. Polanco
11560 Mexico D.F. Mexico

All rights reserved. No part of this work covered by the copyright hereon may
be reproduced or used in any form or by any means—graphic, electronic, or
mechanical, including photocopying, recording, taping, or information storage
and retrieval systems—without the written permission of the publisher.

1 2 3 4 5 6 7 8 9 10 EDW-AA 01 00 99 98 97 96 95 94

Library of Congress Cataloging-in-Publication Data

To
Peg, Richard and Meagan, and Elen

and

John Levak,
the archtypical hospitality consumer,
and those like him

Contents

Preface   xv

I. Introduction to Hospitality Marketing

   1. The Concept of Marketing   3

     Foundations and Practices   4
     The Concept of Marketing   4
     Solving Customers' Problems   8
     Management Orientations   10
     The Marketing Concept   14
     Marketing Leadership   16
     Marketing Is Everything   17
     Summary   18

       Case 1-1   We Do It All For You   19
       Case 1-2   The Glorious Hotel   22
       Case 1-3   Ritz-Carlton Changes Its Orientation   25

   2. Nontraditional Marketing in Hospitality   29

     Services vs. Goods   29
     Components of the Hospitality Product   30
     Why the Marketing of Services Is Different   32
     Keeping Hospitality Customers   41
     Internal Marketing   41
     Relationship Marketing   46
     Summary   54

Case 2-1   Sojourn in Jamaica   56
Case 2-2   Packing 'em In!   59
Case 2-3   Houston's   61

II. Managing the Marketing System

3. The Strategic Marketing System   65

Marketing Management vs. Strategic Planning   65
The Concept of Strategy   66
The Concept of Strategic Planning   66
The Strategic Marketing System   68
Using the Strategic Marketing Systems Model   76
Strategy Selection   89
Summary   89

Case 3-1   Keihan's Palace Side Hotel   91
Case 3-2   The Riverside Restaurant   93
Case 3-3   Johnson Hotels   97

4. The Marketing Plan   103

Requirements for a Marketing Plan   103
Development of a Marketing Plan   104
The Marketing Budget   117
Marketing Controls   120
Summary   120

Case 4-1   The Luxury Hotel   122
Case 4-2   Le Marquis de Napoleon   126
Case 4-3   The Superior Inn and Conference Center   131

5. The Marketing Environment, Competitive Analysis, and Marketing Research   137

A. Environmental Scanning   137
Macro Competition   139
Types of Environments   140
B. Opportunities, Threats, and Competitive Analysis   155
Market Opportunities   155
Market Threats   156
Competitive Analysis   156
Micro Competition   158
Finding Marketing Opportunities   166
Market Feasibility Studies   169
C. Marketing Research   169
Formal Marketing Research   171
The Need for Research   174
The Research Process   175
Summary   180

Case 5-1   Butler's Hideaway   182
Case 5-2   Empire Szechuan   184

Case 5-3   Westin Hotel of Stamford   187
Case 5-4   Taco Gourmet   196

III. The Hospitality Customer

6. Customer Behavior and Customer Markets   199

A. Characteristics of Hospitality Customers: Needs and Wants   200
The Buying Decision Process   202
B. Types of Hospitality Customers   215
The Business Traveler   215
The Pleasure Traveler   222
The Package Market   227
The Mature Traveler   231
International Travelers   232
Free Independent Travelers (FIT)   234
Summary   235

Case 6-1   Little Things Mean a Lot   237
Case 6-2   Nightmare at the Resort   239
Case 6-3   Weekend at the Ritz   241

7. The Organizational Customer and Planner   243

The Generic Organizational Market   243
The Organizational Customer Buying Process   245
The Corporate Travel Market   254
The Corporate Meetings Market   259
Conference Centers   261
The Incentive Market   263
Association, Convention, and Trade Show Markets   267
Convention Centers and Convention and Visitors Bureaus   271
Airline Crews   273
The SMERF and the Government Markets   275
The Group Tour and Travel Market   276
Summary   279

Case 7-1   The Government Market   280
Case 7-2   The Airline Market   281
Case 7-3   Hawthorne Inn & Conference Center   283

IV. Defining the Market

8. Differentiation, Segmentation, and Target Marketing   291

Differentiation   291
The Process of Market Segmentation   301
Segmentation Variables   308
Segmentation Strategies   320
Target Marketing   322

Target Markets of One   325
Summary   326

Case 8-1 Hedonism II   327
Case 8-2 Cafe DiCarlo   332
Case 8-3 Holiday Inn Chattanooga   337

9. Market Positioning   343

Objective Positioning   343
Subjective Positioning   346
Effective Positioning   350
Repositioning   356
Developing Positioning Strategies   358
Salience, Determinance, and Importance   360
Competitive Positioning   363
Multiple Brand and Product Positioning   366
Internal Positioning Analysis   371
Summary   375

Case 9-1 Hotel Inter-Continental/Toronto   377
Case 9-2 The Upper Crust Restaurant   379
Case 9-3 Forte Hotels' Rebranding   383

V. The Marketing Mix

10. The Marketing Mix and the Product/Service Mix   393

The Hospitality Marketing Mix   394
The Hospitality Product/Service Mix   395
The Product Life Cycle   405
Stages of the Product Life Cycle   406
Developing New Products/Services   413
Summary   414

Case 10-1 The Mt. Hiei Hotel   417
Case 10-2 Carbur's Restaurant   420
Case 10-3 Sheraton Lakeside Inn   424

11. The Hospitality Presentation Mix   427

Physical Plant   428
Location   434
Atmospherics   437
Employees   443
Customers   445
Price   449
Summary   451

Case 11-1 Le Chateau Frontenac   452
Case 11-2 Hot Tomato's   453
Case 11-3 Holiday Inn Enters Salzburg   457

12. Pricing the Hospitality Product   463

    Pricing Practices   465
    The Basis of Pricing   469
    Pricing Objectives   470
    Cost Pricing   476
    Competitive Pricing   480
    Market Demand Pricing   481
    Customer Pricing   483
    Common Mistakes in Pricing   486
    Summary   487

        Case 12-1   The Sheraton Jeddah Hotel   488
        Case 12-2   The Mooring Restaurant   491
        Case 12-3   The Nikko Hotel/Atlanta   496

    Chapter 12 Appendix. Yield Revenue Management   498

    What Yield Management Is   498
    Why Hotels are Different   499
    Effective Use of Yield Management   500
    The Customer   504

13. The Communications Mix: Foundations and Advertising   505

    The Communications Mix   505
    Communications Strategy   507
    Target Market Stages   511
    Research for the Communications Mix   512
    Word-of-Mouth Communication   517
    Customer Complaints   519
    Customer Complaint Research   522
    Database Marketing   525
    Advertising   528
    Summary   546

        Case 13-1   The Berkshire Place Kaffee   548
        Case 13-2   The Customer's Complaint   550
        Case 13-3   Letter to the Executive Vice-President   552
        Case 13-4   Andiamo's   553

14. The Communications Mix: Sales Promotions, Merchandising,
    Public Relations, and Publicity   559

    Principles and Practices of Sales Promotion   559
    Principles and Practices of Merchandising   576
    Public Relations and Publicity   582
    Summary   589

        Case 14-1   Promoting Sunday Brunch   590
        Case 14-2   The Real Road Warrior   591
        Case 14-3   Merchandising Power Breakfasts   595
        Case 14-4   Hilton International/Toronto   601

15. The Communications Mix: Personal Selling   607

  The Sales Process   609
  Sales Management   624
  Sales and Operations   635
  Summary   636

      Case 15-1   Raise the Goal!   638
      Case 15-2   Raise the Numbers!   639
      Case 15-3   Winning Back the Customer   641

16. Channels of Distribution   647

  Hospitality Distribution Channels   648
  Owning and/or Managing   650
  Franchising   653
  Other Distribution Channels   663
  Consortia, Affiliations, Reservations Companies, and
      Representation Companies   663
  Incentive Houses   680
  Travel Agents   680
  Tour Operators and Wholesalers   691
  Strategies for Distribution Channels   695
  Channel Management   701
  Summary   703

      Case 16-1   The Sheraton Parc Central   705
      Case 16-2   Savage House Pizza Parlours   707
      Case 16-3   The Japanese Market in Nice   709

VI. The International Market

17. International Marketing   713

  The International Hospitality Industry   714
  Economic Environments   718
  Social and Cultural Environment   721
  Political, Regulatory and Legal Environments   723
  Demographic Environments   723
  The International Marketing Mix   724
  Segmentation   740
  Positioning   744
  Marketing Research   746
  Summary   748

      Case 17-1   The Plaza Hotel in Buenos Aires   750
      Case 17-2   The Bengal Tiger Restaurant   757
      Case 17-3   Quality Inns India   762

18. International Tourism Marketing   771

  International Tourism Today   771

The Role of NTOs   780
Summary   788

    Case 18-1   Creole Christmas in New Orleans   790
    Case 18-2   Tourism in Corfu   793
    Case 18-3   Fiji Islands: Tourism Development Strategy   801
    Case 18-4   Thailand Tourism   811

Glossary   819

Index   831

World Maps   845

Preface

In the past 20 years, the world has witnessed a massive explosion in the hospitality industry. Today the industry only vaguely resembles a second cousin of the one that existed 20 years ago. Not only has there been a proliferation of hotels and restaurants and airlines, but the way they do business has also changed drastically. Concurrently, there has been a massive change in the hospitality customer. The link between these two phenomena is marketing. This book is about that link.

Much of today's hospitality industry is made up of sophisticated organizations. This is less true in parts of the world where travel and tourism are still developing, but as more companies go global, that scene is also rapidly changing. Independent operations have become increasingly fewer, and their number will continue to dwindle. This is more true with hotels than with restaurants, but even the latter are forming more strategic alliances, if not outright expanding. The transition is not unlike that of the industrial revolution that began over two centuries ago. Cottage industries still exist and so do the individual entrepreneurs in hospitality. It is these same entrepreneurs, however, who have led the way in the growth explosion.

E.M. Statler, Conrad Hilton, Howard Johnson, Kemmons Wilson, and Ray Kroc were some of the early entrepreneurs whose legends and legacies survive today. All these men were marketers, *par excellence,* albeit by a different standard than that of hospitality marketing today. No doubt, words and terms like *segmentation, positioning, marketing mix, consumer needs and wants, product life cycle, distribution systems,* and many others you will find in this book, were not even part of their vocabulary. Nevertheless, these entrepreneurs all had one thing in common: They solved consumers' problems—and that is what marketing is all about.

It was only natural that the legacies of these individuals, and others like them, would evolve in one form or another into large organizations. Growth inevitably comes from continued solving of consumers' problems. Growth, however, also brings with it growing pains—the pains of organization, management, financing, distribution, and finally, competition.

The emphasis during these heavy growth years was on operations and costs. The person who could run a good operation and control costs was likely to be successful. In hotels, many general managers rose through the ranks in food and beverage departments. In restaurants, the emphasis was primarily food, beverage, and labor costs.

There were still (and always will be) the grand hotels and the grand restaurants, usually owned and run by entrepreneurs in the classic *mein host* style. By and large, customers took what they got for what they paid. There wasn't too much choice. Little attention was paid to selling and advertising, *marketing* was a foreign word.

Marketing in *any* industry, in fact, did not truly begin to evolve to its present state of growth and recognition until the 1960s. It was another 15 to 20 years before it began to evolve in the hospitality industry. When this first happened, moreover, marketing was not recognizable in its present form. With the growth of chain operations and regional, nationwide, and global distribution, organizations began advertising more extensively. Hotels began to fill out their sales staffs. When marketing became an accepted word in the hospitality lexicon, advertising and sales activities were largely what marketing meant; merchandising and promotion were added later.

Thus, until approximately 15 years ago, marketing consisted largely of what we know today as the communications mix, a subset of marketing. Today, outside personal selling is a major portion of the marketing mix in percentage of time and effort, although a small portion of marketing strategy. Extensive advertising is affordable by relatively few, although merchandising and promotion are quite common in operations of all sizes. Hospitality marketing today, like the industry itself, only vaguely resembles a second cousin of what was practiced 20 years ago.

Marketing has evolved similarly in academic programs in restaurant and hotel management. The early subjects were primarily merchandising and selling. Marketing was thought by many to be something intuitive—either you were good at it, or you weren't—but there wasn't much point in spending an entire semester learning it. Hospitality marketing texts were largely non-existent. What did exist concentrated primarily on merchandising, promotion, and selling.

In the early 1980s, hospitality marketing began to acquire recognition. This came about primarily as a result of two forces. The first was the recognition of marketing in other industries and its increasingly frequent mention in the business press. Individuals who had degrees from business schools and/or came from other industries entered the hospitality industry and recognized the need for marketing. Former sales departments became marketing departments. By and large, however, much of the industry was unaware of the difference between sales and marketing.

The second force occurred in the marketplace. As competition intensified, it was no longer a case of "building another better mouse trap" and letting the people come; one had to fight to obtain the business that the competition was also seeking. The customer had also changed. Demographic lines began to blur. Customers became "educated," more demanding—after all, they now had alternatives as properties sought to differentiate from each other.

This pattern has increased one hundred-fold in reaching its present state. The hospitality marketing trend that began in the United States is now in the heavy growth stage internationally. Businesses are now being challenged as never before to improve their marketing capabilities worldwide. Marketing in hospitality is coming of age.

Coming of age, however, does not signify expertise. The transition has been slow, if not painful, it seems, and there is still much to be learned. On the other hand, when one considers a 15-year span in the course of the long history of hospitality, the movement has been rapid—almost to the point of mind-boggling. It is the marketing-oriented operation that survives today and in the future—not the sales- or cost-oriented one. This is the state of the hospitality industry that exists today and that this book addresses.

This Edition

Previous books on hospitality marketing served the purpose of identifying "what is going on out there," but did not deal with the theoretical and conceptual foundations of *why* it was going on. This was a natural evolution, ongoing when the first edition of this book was published in 1989. In the short time since then, however, hospitality marketing has soared in practice and the proper foundations become even more necessary.

The second edition of *Marketing Leadership in Hospitality: Foundations and Practices* attempts to bring all of this together. It is filled, as its subtitle indicates, with both marketing *foundations* and *practices*. Our thesis is that the same situation rarely happens twice in the same way. Thus, a known practice is of minimal help when faced with a situation that only *appears* to be similar but may be radically different. It is at these times that solid foundations lead the way to marketing leadership. Deceptive appearances happen because factors in marketing are based on human behavior; there is nothing we know that is more complex than the unpredictable human being. Human behavior does not offer the concrete, factual, and ascertainable solutions that are presented by manufacturing goods, financial equations, accounting manipulations, or even flights to the moon.

Nevertheless, there is a logic and a system to marketing that greatly increases its probability of success—and these can be learned. There are ways that we can better understand the vagaries of customer behavior. There are ways to get at the issues and to reveal the substance of marketing problems. There are underlying principles that appear time and time again.

Although marketing's elusiveness is frustrating to many on first exposure, we have no choice in the hospitality industry today but to study marketing. Marketing is the umbilical cord that connects the business to the consumer. It is the means by which the organization adjusts to the ever-changing needs of the marketplace. It is the force of change and growth and the exploration of new opportunities. It is the strongest weapon there is in fighting the competition. It is, in fact, the substance of survival in a dog-eat-dog business world.

This book takes a leadership approach to the study of marketing in hospitality organizations.

Our target audience includes those in introductory marketing courses, marketing management courses, and strategic marketing courses. It also includes managers and marketers now operating in the real world of the hospitality industry, at any level, who feel a need for a more foundational view of marketing with applied examples.

This book also takes a realistic approach. We call it as we see it, but we don't do this lightly. Examples used come from many sources and have been checked and rechecked. Foundations presented are based on accepted principles and solid research. We editorialize and give opinions. These occasions should be clear to the reader, who should feel free to disagree. We will never claim that marketing is an exact science or that we have all the answers, but we will claim a reason and rationale for most marketing decisions. That's why marketing is also fun—we can all disagree as long as we have foundations on which to base our decisions.

A final note: Examples used, and the ads used to illustrate examples, are largely those of well-known and international hotel companies. These should not be construed as implying that these companies do things any better or more poorly than any other company. Rather, we have used them because they are well-known and many readers, worldwide, will be familar with their names and better able to identify with them. For students not that familiar with the industry, we have used these ads to create awareness as well as to demonstrate examples related to the text. Further, the use of ads does not contradict our thesis that advertising is but a small subset of marketing—used here, the ads are simply the best sources available to graphically demonstrate our points.

This edition, unlike the first, includes case studies at the end of each chapter. Although some of these have problem orientations, their main purpose here is to be descriptive of the chapter context and to give life to it in a real-world situation. All the cases are based on actual events, although in some instances names, places, and figures may be disguised. Dates have been removed from most because we believe that the situations are timeless—they continue to exist and apply, even if in different settings.

Why a Second Edition?

Just as we believe that the first edition of this book was the first definitive text on hospitality marketing, we believe that the second edition makes a giant leap forward. About two-thirds of the total content is new—including 59 case studies, only six of which have been previously published (four by us); about 265 illustrations (not counting those in the cases), of which only 15 were used in the first edition; numerous new anecdotes and examples; and a revision and restructuring of chapters. New sections have been added on *target markets of one, yield management, database marketing, pricing,* and new chapters on *personal selling* and *international tourism marketing.* Other parts of the first edition have been substantially revised or edited, while some parts have been dropped.

In the five years the first edition has been in use we have received much feedback from users. While this has been helpful and insightful, it has also been somewhat conflicting. Some had found the book to be too "high-level" or too long for introductory courses, while others were pleased to use it at the community college level. Many used it at the graduate level, while still others believed it was not up to that level.

These contradictions made it quite difficult to know how to position the second edition. The senior author has successfully used the first edition at both the introductory and senior levels, in some cases with the same students, as well as at the graduate level and in executive seminars in North America and abroad. The junior author has used it at the intro level, but only about 15 chapters; this seems to be the case with other instructors at that level—that is, the first edition was too long.

Our task then, for this edition, was to maintain the book at a level above the competition, but at the same time ease its use for those who will choose it over the competition for its greater depth, writing style, real-world examples, cases, and more comprehensive coverage.

This strategy meant fewer chapters, a lightening up on vocabulary, and removal of some theoretical models and narrative. We cautioned ourselves not to remove too much, but to keep the book lively and easy to read. This version, like the first, will for some courses have more chapters than can be covered in one semester, depending on how heavily the case studies are used and the level of the class. The book has been arranged so that marketing teachers can readily adapt it to their classes by using those chapters they feel appropriate, as one does with the better generic marketing texts, most of which run around 1,000 pages, including cases.

The net result is a shorter text(!) to which are added illustrations and cases. The number of chapters has been reduced from 22 to 18. With two new chapters added, this means that the others have been cut down and combined. While total content and number of pages is longer, this is caused by the addition of cases—all of which are never expected to be used in one semester—and heavier use of illustrations. The text itself is about 20 percent, or 100 pages shorter. All of these changes allow the second edition to be used in different ways at different course levels.

We have responded to many users' and reviewers' comments as follows:

- Chapter 1 has been shortened and sharpened.
- Chapter 2 combines the previous edition's chapters 2 and 3 in a shortened version. The customer complaint section has been moved to Chapter 13.
- Chapters 3 and 4 are former chapters 20 and 21. Many asked for these chapters to be moved forward to provide a framework for the rest of the book.
- Chapter 5 combines previous chapters 4, 5, and 19, again in a shortened version, with the marketing intelligence section of former chapter 19 deleted. Chapter 5 is divided into three parts (as opposed to making it three short chapters) for those who do not want to use it all.
- Chapter 6 combines former chapters 6 and 9. Theoretical discussion has been removed, shortened, or footnoted.

- Chapter 7 is former chapter 7 revised.
- Chapter 8 is the same chapter as before and Chapter 9 is the former chapter 10.
- Chapters 10 to 16 cover the marketing mix, previously chapters 11–18. They have been combined and shortened and Chapter 15, "Personal Selling," added.
- Chapter 17, "International Marketing," previously chapter 22, has been greatly revised. We have also added many more international examples throughout the text because (1) we think that students everywhere need to be more globally aware, and (2) over 40 percent of the first edition's sales were overseas.
- Chapter 18, "Tourism Marketing," is new for instructors who wish to put more emphasis on this area. This chapter is relatively short, but it contains the four longest cases in the book—cases that pick up on many of the elements of the first 17 chapters and tie them to a tourism perspective.
- The first edition's epilogue has been deleted. It is interesting to note, however, that in the first edition epilogue we made ten forecasts for the future direction of hospitality marketing, all of which have come true—some more, some less—in the ensuing five years. —We believe these trends will continue as hospitality managers become ever-more "marketing-savvy."
- Bill Hulett, when President of Stouffer Hotels & Resorts, ordered 50 copies of the first edition for his staff and managers—not a bad coup when considering that his own senior vice-president of marketing had also written a hospitality marketing text! While we can't take credit—because Bill Hulett was a marketing-oriented hotelier if there ever was one—we have noted that many of today's Stouffer hotels (maybe all) have replaced 60-watt bulbs with three-way ones (50/100/150); have placed at least two comfortable chairs and sometimes a couch in bedrooms, plus a place to put your feet up; have priced room service beverages at only about 100 percent markup; have installed desks even large enough for two people to work on; and have chosen to leave complimentary coffee at your door with just a knock (so you don't have to worry about time and state of dress), among other things. At the same time, Stouffer has reduced extravagant bathroom amenities that no one needs. All of these items—price/value and knowing-the-customer examples pointed out in the first edition and, still, in this one—have for years been major traveler gripes that even some deluxe hotels haven't caught on to yet. While the high-tech facilities going into hotel rooms today (even in some budget properties) are needed by *some,* too many basics needed by *almost all* are still being ignored, even at the upscale level. We continue, in this edition, to emphasize these points.
- World maps, as an Appendix, have been updated. (Some users wondered why they were even there in the first edition.) We believe, once again, that students everywhere need to be globalized, and we direct them to the maps when international examples come up in the text and cases. Sometimes we give continental map quizzes, with cities and/or countries to be filled in. (Don't laugh until you see London put in Italy and Rome in France!)

Usage of the Book

This book has been designed for use at different levels of expertise, background, and experience for the student, the instructor, and the practitioner. All chapters have been used, at one time or another, in the classroom at various levels and/or in industry seminars at the line-, middle-, upper-management, and executive levels.

We are acutely aware of the different class and instructor levels existing in academic institutions. For example, some programs require the introductory marketing course in the business school be followed by a second course in the hospitality program; some teach the intro course in the hospitality program. Some instructors have Ph.D.s in marketing; others, in smaller programs where there is more diversity in subjects taught, may be simply "assigned" the marketing course for a given semester. As much as possible, we have tried to accommodate all these needs.

Each chapter is followed by three or four cases. We have included this many for the following reasons, as much as possible given our resources: to provide short and intermediate choices, to offer simpler and more complex issues, to provide both hotel and food-service options, to have extra cases for quizzes or exams, and to permit use of different cases in subsequent semesters, to avoid repetition.

The cases are intended, primarily, to be explicative of the issues in the chapter that they follow. Because most are not that finely defined, however, you will find many adaptable and useable with other chapters as well. They are descriptive cases more than they are decision cases for these reasons. This is not to say, however, that they cannot be used with a decision focus. In our opinion this depends on the class level. For example, at the intro level you may want to put the emphasis on the chapter content, with perhaps a short case for illustration. At advanced levels—and this is also how we do it —the chapter content becomes review, with deeper discussion and more chapters assigned per week, and the emphasis is on the longer cases and the decision process. Thus, there is much flexibility in the use of the cases, and it is incumbent upon the instructor to advise students how they are to be handled.

Acknowledgments

Many people—friends, colleagues, and even enemies—both advertently and inadvertently, have contributed to this book and, especially, to the cases. Those who have directly contributed to a case are noted on the first page of that case, and we especially thank them. Others will never realize how helpful they have been—we can only mention a few—and we are grateful to these and to many others who are unmentioned.

We are especially thankful to Susan Morris and Ursula Geschke, each of whom contributed to Chapter 15 on personal selling and sales management. Kaye Chon, professor at University of Nevada/Las Vegas, is the sole author of Chapter 18 on international tourism, and we are extremely grateful for his contribution. Ellen Krentzman Schuster of Hyatt Hotels was most helpful in sorting out some of the confusion of the distribution mix in Chapter 16, as were Jackie Beatty of Utell International and Caroline van der Drift of Supranational. Margaret Shaw reviewed various chapters and sections and made meaningful contributions throughout, as did several reviewers—Kaye Chon, Chekitan Dev, Susan Gregory, John Bowen, Katie Wiedman, Alan Paret, William Greathouse, Marlene Larson, and Ron Cox.

The efforts of many who contributed to the first edition, and thus the second, are also noted here—Mike Leven, Venkat Chandrasekar, Siew Ang, Steve Weisz, Chekitan Dev, Jim Nassikas, and many others.

There were also many sub-rosa contributors—executives, managers, sales and marketing people, and others from numerous hotel companies, restaurant chains, individual hotels and restaurants—and former students, as well as many, many customers.

We have used numerous printed sources as indicated by footnotes throughout the text. We thank all of them for their gracious consideration in furnishing and allowing us to use these materials, as well as the companies that gave permission to use their ads.

Inevitably, we are responsible for any errors, oversights, or deficiences that remain herein—and we welcome any specific comments about this edition or recommendations regarding the future of our work.

Robert C. Lewis
Richard E. Chambers
Harsha E. Chacko
Summer, 1994

PART I
Introduction to Hospitality Marketing

CHAPTER 1

The Concept of Marketing

Everyone knows McDonald's. Even in Moscow, where 40,000 customers a day stood by the hundreds in long lines, McDonald's is a household word. Why is this? Some will say it is the products—the Big Mac or the Chicken McNuggets or the french fries and milk shakes. Others might repeat the McDonald's slogan, "QSC—quality, service, cleanliness." All would be wrong. McDonald's has no monopoly on any of these features, yet its competition cannot catch up with it. The reason McDonald's is a household word around the world is because its lifeblood is filled with the concept of marketing and it practices it in nearly everything it does.

Practicing the concept of marketing means recognizing the relationship between marketing and management. Marketing and management in a service business, such as the hospitality industry, are one and the same. Practicing the concept of marketing means marketing leadership, which recognizes that it is marketing forces that shape the total organization.

It is said that some fast-food chain manuals instruct management that the front windows must be washed every six hours, but the McDonald's manual states, "The front windows will never be dirty." In fact, some believe that the most innovative thing done by Ray Kroc, founder of McDonald's, was to put large windows in front of every store. It was not enough that a McDonald's was clean inside; it was important that people could look in and see that it was clean. Before McDonald's, customers took their chances when they walked into a low-priced restaurant. Kroc went one step further. He insisted not only that the outside of McDonald's be litter-free, but also the space next to them, even if McDonald's employees had to do the cleaning.

What do clean windows and clean sidewalks have to do with marketing? In hospitality, everything that management does affects the customer and everything that affects the customer is marketing, good or bad. We cannot repeat that enough, because it may be the most important thing that you will ever learn about marketing. *Marketing* is

communicating to and giving target market customers what they want, when they want it, where they want it, and at a price they are willing and able to pay.

This book is about marketing leadership in the hospitality industry. More specifically, it is about the causes and effects of marketing leadership, about why people such as Ray Kroc and companies such as McDonald's succeed while others don't succeed or succeed less well. It is about what it takes to succeed in the hospitality marketplace. Most important, this book is about hospitality customers, because it is with the customer that marketing leadership begins.

After reading this chapter, you will understand why this is true. In short, you will understand the concept of marketing, the marketing philosophy, and the elements of marketing leadership. You will also understand why these factors are critical to the future of the hospitality industry. In the chapters that follow, you will learn how marketing leadership works.

Foundations and Practices

Marketing-oriented companies and marketing-oriented people are the ones who are truly successful in the highly competitive hospitality marketplace. Does this mean that marketing has replaced operations and accounting? Of course not. The operations career individual will take fewer marketing courses, but must learn to apply marketing in his or her operations courses. When a menu is designed, the first question to be asked is, "How will the customer react to it?" When a hotel room is configured, the first question is, "How will the customer use it?" When prices are established, the first question is, "How will the consumer perceive the risk and the price/value relationship?" When engineering is taught and electric consumption is measured, the first question is, "Is the lighting appropriate for the customer?" When food, liquor, or labor cost controls are taught, we must ask how they impact upon the customer. The foundation is the concept of marketing; the application is its practice.

No company can continue to operate without a profit. But, let's put first things first. No company can begin to operate without customers. For many years the hospitality industry operated under the saying, "We are in the people business." Today we are in the "customer business." Without customers, we are dead. And the way to create and keep customers is to satisfy their needs and wants and solve their problems.

This, then, is the foundation of marketing. Its practice starts at the highest level by deed and action, not just words, and it permeates to the lowest level of the organization. Concern and responsibility for marketing are the concerns and responsibilities of every person in a hospitality enterprise. At the highest level, marketing shapes the corporate effort; at the lowest level, it means the porter doesn't mop where the customer is walking.

The Concept of Marketing

For many, the term *marketing* conjures up images of selling and advertising. Because of this long-standing and common belief, we call selling and advertising *traditional* marketing. Restaurant management advertises, so they think they are marketing. Hotel management has four salespeople selling, so they think they are marketing. Actually, however, selling and advertising are only two subsets of the broad range of marketing. While they are important, they are only subsets. Marketing is a philosophy or umbrella under which these communications are used to reach the customer.

All phases of marketing, both foundations and practices, derive from the customer. Sales- and advertising-oriented management may think in terms of the virtues of their product and how they can persuade the customer to buy. Consciously or unconsciously, they may be selling the operations or physical end of the business. They often think in terms of what they have to offer the customer. *Nontraditional* marketing-oriented management thinks in terms of customer needs when designing the service or product before the sale or advertisement, when delivering the service after the sale, while the customer is consuming the service, and after the sale is over. They think in terms of what the customer wants.

The Twofold Purpose of Marketing

It is accepted without question that any business that fails to operate at a profit will eventually cease to exist. If goods and services cannot be offered at a price exceeding their total cost, then they should be removed from the market.

Although essential to survival, however, profit is not the purpose of marketing, but rather a way of measuring the success of management decisions made by a company. As well-known management guru, Peter Drucker, has stated:

> Profitability is not the purpose of but a limiting factor on business enterprise and business activity. Profit is not the explanation, cause, or rationale of business behavior and business decisions but the *test of their validity* . [emphasis added].[1]

The only valid definition of *business purpose,* says Drucker, is to create a customer.

> It is the customer who determines what a business is. For it is the customer, and he alone, who through being willing to pay for a good or for a service, converts economic resources into wealth, things into goods. What the business thinks it produces is not of first importance—especially not to the future of the business and to its success. What the customer thinks he is buying, what he considers "value," is decisive—it determines what a business is, what it produces and whether it will prosper.[2]

Creating a customer does not mean simply making a sale. It means creating a relationship wherein a buyer wants your product or service instead of that of the competition. In addition to creating a customer, the purpose of both marketing and business is also to *keep* a customer. A business' purpose and marketing's purpose, in fact, are really one and the same. Any definition of marketing must emphasize that creating and keeping customers is of primary importance.

In the early 1970s there were more customers than hotel rooms or restaurant seats in many markets. The idea of retaining customers was secondary. As competition increased in the 1980s and operators became more aware of this need, the era of mints on pillows and fancy bathroom amenities arrived. But these were shallow appeals for loyalty, in spite of claims by their manufacturers, still being made in the 1990s (Figures 1-1 and 1-2). The 1990s are a very different type of environment, one in which each customer has a multitude of hospitality options. The marketing challenge of the decade is a two-pronged approach: creating new customers while maintaining existing ones by establishing true relationships. The finest cost controls, the highest profit margins, the most highly-trained management, the most innovative products, and the most efficient production lines do not produce revenue and, ultimately, profit, if there are no customers. We will discuss the concept of relationship marketing in Chapter 2.

There are only three ways to create and keep customers:

1. Get new ones.
2. Steal them from competitors.
3. Build true loyalty in those you have and get.

Creating new customers is difficult. A wine festival or a murder mystery weekend may bring in customers who have had no need or desire to visit a restaurant or hotel; however, developing new products for nonusers is a limited activity and can be very expensive. In a stagnant or overbuilt market, stealing customers from competitors is the first marketing challenge. The second challenge is keeping them. Thus, the first consideration of any management decision should be, "Will it create and/or keep customers?"

Often, decisions are made that are in the best interests of the customer. Such decisions may, in fact, create satisfaction, like mints and shampoos, but may not contribute to creating or keeping a customer. Although we certainly must satisfy customers to create and keep them, as we will shortly demonstrate, marketing means something more than simply "satisfying" them. It means understanding customers' needs and wants and solving their problems. It is not difficult to satisfy a customer if you want to give the store away. However, satisfaction alone will not necessarily ensure that customers will return if that satisfaction does not serve their needs and wants or solve their problems. As a case in point:

> Two focus groups—the executive committee of a hotel and meetings customers—were given the as-

---

[1]Peter F. Drucker, *Management: Tasks, Responsibilities, Practices,* New York: Harper & Row, 1974, p. 60.

[2]Peter F. Drucker, *The Practice of Management,* New York: Harper & Row, 1954, pp. 37–39.

FIGURE 1-1   The 1980s and 1990s argument for building loyalty with mints

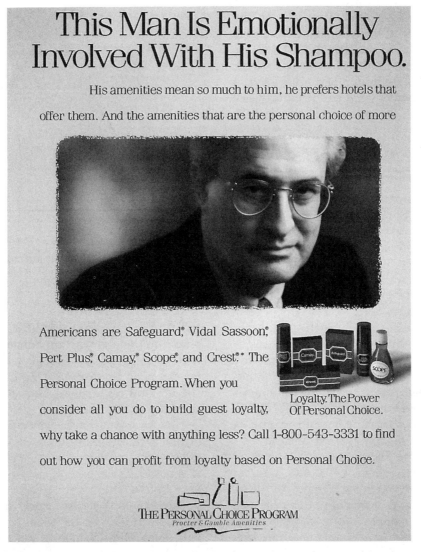

This Man Is Emotionally Involved With His Shampoo.

His amenities mean so much to him, he prefers hotels that offer them. And the amenities that are the personal choice of more

Americans are Safeguard,® Vidal Sassoon,® Pert Plus,® Camay,® Scope,® and Crest.®* The Personal Choice Program. When you consider all you do to build guest loyalty, why take a chance with anything less? Call 1-800-543-3331 to find out how you can profit from loyalty based on Personal Choice.

Loyalty. The Power Of Personal Choice.

THE PERSONAL CHOICE PROGRAM
Procter & Gamble Amenities

FIGURE 1-2 The 1980s and 1990s argument for building loyalty with bathroom amenities

signment to *design* the "perfect" coffee break for a meeting *set-up*. The executive committee diligently set out to design the "mother of all coffee breaks," including tri-level presentations, mirrors, ice carvings, lighting, flavored coffees, and so on. When costed out, the break had to be priced at $27 per person to make a profit. The meetings customers then turned in their "perfect" coffee break design: a simple coffee break with the table holding the break positioned about ten feet from the back wall. The purpose, they explained, was to alleviate the congestion caused by a single line break. Their meetings could resume more quickly if the table were simply moved a few feet!

This example shows how far management can be from the real needs and problems of customers.

But, you might add, there are many ifs, ands, and buts to this scenario. For one, will the company achieve a sufficient profit in order to satisfy its owners and survive? That will be the test of the validity of the company's decisions and the extensions of marketing that will be discussed in the remainder of this book. First, let's go back to the definition of marketing and look at what customers want and what they are willing to pay.

Solving Customers' Problems

There is a basic premise of marketing that we must understand: Simply put, consumers do not buy something unless they have a problem to solve and believe that a purchase will provide the solution to the problem. An example, attributed to Charles Revson, founder of Revlon cosmetics, is: "In the factory we make cosmetics; in the store we sell hope."

In this sense, customers buy solutions, nothing else. If we can think of goods and services as solutions that we want to sell, we are a long way along the road to successful marketing. Thinking this way forces us to stand in the customer's shoes, to think like the customer thinks, and to understand what it is the customer wants, as well as when, where, and at what price.

This point can be illustrated as follows: Perhaps you are driving down a highway and you become hungry or you need a place to sleep. These are needs, and basic ones at that. Needs create problems—namely, how to satisfy them—so what you do next is to seek a solution. You know that solution will have a cost. You have to give up something or make a sacrifice in order to obtain the solution. What emerges is a trade-off situation, like that portrayed in Figure 1-3.

This is the trade-off thought process that a consumer faces when contemplating a purchase. In general, the decision-making process is more complicated with the increase in cost of the item to be purchased. A consumer may spend months selecting a honeymoon destination and seconds selecting a can of soda. Nevertheless, the process takes place and the depth of deliberation depends on numerous factors, which will be discussed in Chapter 6.

For the moment, let's continue the illustra-

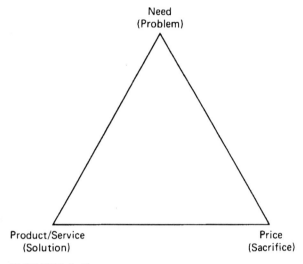

FIGURE 1-3   The trade-off of problem solutions

tion and assume that a solution presents itself: A sign on the highway announces a hotel ahead, with rooms at $59.50. Rooms provide a solution for the need to sleep, and $59.50 is a sacrifice you are willing to make. You decide to head for the hotel rather than continue driving.

Now the situation becomes complicated. You *expect* that the solution is at hand (i.e., you *expect* that you can get a good night's sleep at this hotel). You *expect,* of course, that there will be a bed in the room, a bathroom, and other appointments. You also expect that the bed will be comfortable and the room quiet, so that you will sleep well. You may not verbalize these expectations, but subconsciously they exist. You also have, consciously or unconsciously, made another decision: You have decided that spending $59.50 is worth the *risk* that your expectations will be met, the solution will solve your problem, and the value you receive will be worth the sacrifice. The trade-off model now looks like that in Figure 1-4.

Obviously, consumers buy expectations at the same time that they buy solutions, both of which require a sacrifice. It then follows that the greater the sacrifice, the greater the risk, the greater the expectation, and the more demanding the customer is of the solution. To put it another way, if the solution meets the expec-

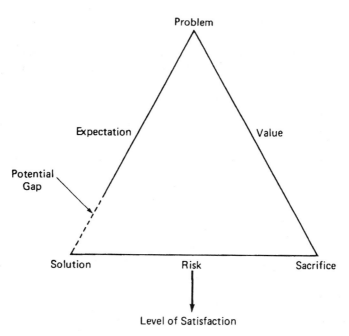

FIGURE 1-4   Expansion of the trade-off model

tation and the value justifies the sacrifice, the risk becomes more justifiable, and a higher level of satisfaction becomes more likely. The result is a higher likelihood that a customer has been created. To put this in realistic terms, consider each element of Figure 1-4 in terms of going to eat at McDonald's vs. Lutece, a French restaurant in New York City where luncheon checks average over $150 per person.

Notice now what happens when the solution does not meet the expectation—this is the "potential gap," represented by the dotted line on the left-hand side of Figure 1-4. (We have made the dotted line "Pizza Hut length." We could have made it a hair shorter for "McDonald's length," but for "Lutece length" it might run almost to the peak of the triangle.) The point is obvious: The greater the expectation, the greater the potential that it will not be fulfilled. We will explore this point in more detail in later chapters. For now, you can see very clearly why marketing and management are one and the same. If management cannot fulfill customers' expectations, it won't create and keep customers; when it does, it is marketing.

Now notice in Figure 1-4 where satisfaction

occurs—at the bottom of the triangle. This places satisfaction clearly as an end product of marketing, *not* as part of the process, in creating and keeping the customer. If the gap is too great between expectation and fulfillment (i.e., between problem and solution), or the sacrifice is too high, there will be a low level of satisfaction. Now you should understand why it is expectations and solutions to problems that marketing must serve, not just satisfaction. While mints on pillows and bathroom amenities may create satisfaction in themselves, if they aren't expected and don't solve problems for the sacrifice made, the purchase may not be worth the risk or provide the overall level of satisfaction expected.

In essence, Figure 1-4 represents the concept and definition of marketing—giving the customers what they want, when they want it, where they want it, and at a price they are willing and able to pay (or a sacrifice they are willing to make). Each step in Figure 1-4 can also be shown to represent the process of marketing, as we will now explain.

Marketing, of course, does not create the needs or problems associated with hunger or the need to sleep.[3] However, it does identify the needs associated with *what to eat* and *where to sleep*. Marketing differentiates between the available solutions through the creation of expectations. On the other side of the equation, having created expectation, marketing needs to reduce perceived risk so that the prospective customer perceives the expectation as being worth the risk.

This means not only that pricing is an important marketing tool, but also that marketing must persuade the customer that the solution is worth the price. The bottom line in the marketing model is not profit; it is the level of satisfaction felt by the customer after making the sacrifice (Figure 1-4). If the satisfaction level is positive, a customer has been created and kept. Keep in mind, of course, that the same tenets hold whether we apply them to a budget motel or a five-star hotel, a McDonald's or a Lutece.

Naturally, the solution to any problem rarely exists in a vacuum. That's why marketing becomes more complex than the example presented. If a solution to the problem of needing a night's sleep were only a room and a bed at the right price in the right place, then there would be little need for marketing. Solutions aren't that simple and include many needs other than a simple bed in a simple room. The instant one motel provides something different than another motel, competition is created and the mettle of marketing is tested. Instead of "here's *a* bed" (solution to problem), marketing creates "here's *this* bed," the *only* solution to *your* problem.

The goal for marketers is *to present the best solution to the problem at the lowest risk.* Marketing, however, does not stop there, especially in the hospitality industry. The creation of expectations might be classified as traditional marketing. There are, however, those who believe that marketing does end there, and that it then becomes operations management's job to assure that those expectations are fulfilled. (Figure 1-5 depicts some marketing views of solutions to customers' problems.)

_____

[3]This is not totally true. A billboard or television commercial depicting a steaming pizza, or a radio commercial describing an elegant dinner, can literally cause salivation. For our purposes of illustration, however, the assumption is normally true.

While the fulfillment of expectations is surely operations management's responsibility, it also means that operations management is totally involved in the marketing effort: Traditional marketing only brings the customer to the door; it is up to nontraditional marketing to *keep* the customer.

The trade-off model is critical to the understanding of marketing. The concept will be developed further in the chapters to follow, but first we need to see how marketing influences the total picture.

Management Orientations

All companies, firms, organizations, and other business entities operate under a basic philosophy or orientation. This philosophy may be spoken, written, or simply implied. An organization's philosophy is the part of its corporate culture—it emphasizes that "this is the way we do business around here." It is what drives the firm, what makes it work.

Orientations in the Hospitality Industry

The hospitality industry encompasses many philosophies and orientations at various times and places. These orientations may be an operations, a product, a service, a selling orientation, or some combination of these four.

Operations Orientation An operations orientation is categorized by its emphasis on a "smooth operation," as symbolized by the anonymous wag who once stated, "This is a great business to be in, if only the customers didn't get in the way." Operations manuals provide prescriptions for direction and behavior for almost every conceivable possible occurrence—until the customer decides to do something differently.

Operations-oriented hotels and restaurants sometimes forget the customer in the interest of a smooth operation. Although these facilities run well, customers are fickle and procedures cannot be written for every kind of demand or problem. This does not mean that manuals are not desirable for operations purposes. In fact, in today's large chains, it would be impossible to obtain consistency in service delivery without some of them.[4] Problems occur, however, when the manual becomes the "be all to end all" and there is no room for deviation on the customer's behalf. Or, what may be even worse, sometimes the manual is written only from an operations efficiency or cost perspective and without consideration for the customer.

Operations philosophies, like all philosophies, come down from top management. When the company or the company's executives are bottom-line or profit-driven, they tend to follow procedures based mainly on cost considerations, overlooking their impact on customers.

Consider, for example, the restaurant that has a slow night. Typically, management will send wait personnel home and close part of the dining room. The section that gets closed is often the exterior section, near the windows or with the view, because it is farthest from the kitchen and takes more effort to serve. It is also the most desirable from the customer's perspective. The part that remains open, of course, is closest to the kitchen because it is most convenient to serve. Similarly, you may have had the experience of saying to a dining room hostess, "Can we have that table over there?" (instead of the one you were led to), and receiving the response, "I'm sorry, but it's not that waiter's turn."

These types of procedures are established in the name of operational or cost efficiency. Perhaps a better phrase might be, "customer-blindness efficiency." Hotels and restaurants that operate by these kinds of procedures pride themselves on their operational efficiencies, rather than on their solutions to customers' problems. Obviously, such efficiencies may well cause problems instead of solving them for guests seeking a hassle-free experience.

Product/Service Orientation Hospitality properties that operate under this orientation place their emphasis on the product or service. These properties market according to the concept of "build a better mousetrap and the world will beat a path to your door." They trumpet that their property has the best food, the finest chefs, the ultimate in service, designer-decorated lobbies, or even the best location. Consider, for instance, the previous example of the coffee break design or the ads in Figure 1-6.

Properties may have all the attributes they claim; sometimes they do not. Regardless, the claims, like the coffee break design, often fail to consider whether these factors are solutions to customers' problems. In the marketing sense, products and services should be defined only in terms of what they do for the customer. Whatever they do, they should not create even more problems.

Selling Orientation A selling orientation in hotel and restaurant companies is one in which the effort to obtain customers emphasizes finding someone who will come through the doors, as opposed to marketing a solution to a designated market's needs. Hotel companies with this kind of orientation often have large sales forces and large advertising budgets. They are very conscious of their "open" periods, and they push their salespeople to "go out and fill them" and to meet their sales quota. Or, as in the case of restaurants, these properties may run frequent promotions and special offers. Whatever, everything is based on the "sell, sell, sell" edict rather than on identifying customers' needs and wants.

There is obviously nothing wrong with running a good operation, having a good product/service, or having an effective sales force. Well-run and successful companies accomplish all these and do them well. A truly marketing-oriented company, however, views these achievements as subsets of marketing—that is, they are accomplished with the customer as the focal point. The operations manager says, "I run a tight ship," but only after making sure that the customers' needs and wants have been considered. The service manager considers first what the service will do for the target market.[5] And the sales manager sells those benefits that

---

[4]Interestingly, when Bass Plc. of England took over Holiday Inn in 1990, they reduced the stack of operations manuals from about three feet to about three inches.

[5]Cf. Robert C. Lewis and Michael Nightingale, "Targeting Service to Your Customer," *Cornell Hotel and Restaurant Administration Quarterly,* August, 1991, pp. 18–27.

A fax that takes five minutes to travel 2000 miles shouldn't take an hour to get to your room.

When a fax arrives for you at Westin, it won't gather dust at the front desk, you'll get it immediately. That's the high level of service you

can expect from everyone you do business with at Westin. It's all part of our

You can count on Westin for quick check-in, express check-out and prompt, reliable room service 24 hours a day.

commitment to continuous improvement. We're constantly looking for new ways to eliminate hassles and make things easier for you. For reservations, call your travel consultant or (800) 228-3000.

WESTIN
HOTELS & RESORTS®

FIGURE 1-5   Hotels addressing consumers' problems

We Offered Our
Unconditional Support When
The Account Executive In 415
Came Unglued.

At the Marriott Eaton Centre, a broken heel won't turn into
a catastrophe, even an hour before your meeting. Because we'll
take care of getting it repaired. That's one example of the service
you'll enjoy at the Marriott Eaton Centre, downtown Toronto's
newest hotel. For reservations, contact your travel agent, or
Marriott, where service is the ultimate luxury. Call (416)597-9200,
or toll-free, 800-228-9290.

TORONTO
Marriott.
EATON CENTRE
525 Bay Street, Toronto, Ontario M5G 2E1

FIGURE 1-5   (continued)

Dip into a billion dollars.

Plunge into luxury, poolside at a Sheraton Hotel. It's one way to take advantage of ITT Sheraton's billion dollar improvement. And across the country, enjoy our new health clubs, guestrooms, restaurants, lobbies and enhanced services. For reservations, call your travel professional or 800-325-3535. We spent a billion to make you feel like a million.

ITT Sheraton

Courtesy of ITT Sheraton Corporation

FIGURE 1-6   Ads with product and service orientations

will solve customers' problems and make their experiences hassle-free.

The Marketing Concept

If a firm adopts the marketing philosophy as its orientation, then the development and implementation of that philosophy is based on what has come to be known as the marketing concept. The marketing concept is based on the premise that the customer is king, the customer has a choice, and the customer does not have to buy your product. Thus, the best way to earn a profit is to serve the customer better.

According to the marketing concept, an organization should try to provide products [and services] that satisfy customers' needs through a coordinated set of activities that also allows the organization to achieve its goals.... The organization must continue to alter, adapt and develop products to keep pace with customers' changing desires and preferences.... The marketing concept stresses the importance of customers and emphasizes that marketing activities begin and end with them.

OUR LEVEL OF SERVICE ISN'T NEW TO THE WORLD. JUST TO ATLANTA.

*In more than 80 cities
on six continents,
millions have experienced our
uncompromising dedication
to personal service
and luxury.
In September,
it can be experienced
in Atlanta.*

HOTEL INTER-CONTINENTAL ATLANTA
AGAIN AND AGAIN.

FIGURE 1-6   (continued)

In attempting to satisfy customers, businesses must consider not only short-run, immediate needs but also broad, long-term desires. Trying to satisfy customers' current needs by sacrificing their long-term desires will only create future dissatisfaction.

...To meet these short- and long-run needs and desires, a firm must coordinate all its activities. Production, finance, accounting, personnel and marketing departments must work together.

...The marketing concept is not a second definition of marketing. It is a way of thinking—a management philosophy guiding an organization's overall activities. This philosophy affects all efforts of the organization, not just marketing activities.... The marketing concept stresses that an organization can best achieve its goals by [fulfilling customer expectations and solving customer problems].[6]

The marketing concept does not consist of advertising, selling and promotion. It is a willingness to recognize and understand the consumer's needs

---

[6]Adapted from William M. Pride and O.C. Ferrell, *Marketing: Concepts and Strategies,* 7th ed., Boston: Houghton Mifflin, 1991, pp. 13–14.

and wants, *and* a willingness to adjust any of the marketing mix elements, including product, to satisfy those needs and wants.[7]

Let us translate this definition into simpler language.

Having a marketing orientation is necessary but not sufficient. We can believe that we are in the business of solving consumers' problems and serving their needs and wants, and we can have this philosophy permeate the entire firm, but until we do something about it—put it into practice—it will not suffice. Perhaps a better way of stating this is: "You have to put your money where your mouth is." Practicing the marketing concept does exactly that.

There is a fine but important distinction in the phrase, *a company can have one without the other.* A company's having a marketing orientation without practicing the marketing concept is a good start, but it will not succeed in the long run. When the company dies, it will be said, "They were such nice people, I wonder why they didn't make it." On the other hand, practicing the marketing concept without a marketing orientation is like giving lip service to marketing; it constructs marketing as a company policy without permeating the firm as a shaper of the corporate effort. Both a marketing philosophy and the marketing concept must exist before we can define the firm as a true marketing company.

Practicing the marketing concept means putting yourself in the customer's shoes. It means selecting market segments that can be served profitably. This translates into profitable products and services that the company can produce. Practicing the marketing concept means making the business do what suits the customer's interests. For management, it has implications of integrating and coordinating the research, planning, and systems approach of the firm. Practicing the marketing concept is a management approach to marketing that stresses problem-solving and decision-making responsibilities to enhance the objectives of the entire firm. Philip Kotler, a noted marketing author and educator, says the following about

the marketing concept: "Marketing is not the art of finding clever ways to dispose of what you make. Marketing is the art of creating genuine customer value. It is the art of helping your customers become better off."[8]

Marketing Leadership

The guiding philosophy in any firm is established by its top management, which provides the leadership and direction for the organization. These leaders must believe in the marketing philosophy and the marketing concept and ensure that they pervade all levels of the organization. Marketing leadership accepts change as a constant. It not only recognizes the needs and wants of the customer, but it also recognizes that the customer changes. The customer is not in a static state, and any successful company must change with, if not before, its customers. Business obituaries are replete with companies that failed to recognize changes in the marketplace.

On the other hand, take the example of Jan Carlzon. In 1981, he was picked by the Scandinavian Airways System (SAS) Board of Directors to be its President, with the challenge of turning around an ailing company. In what were tough times for the airlines, most other companies were cutting back. Carlzon went the other way—he poured it on. In a little over a year Carlzon took SAS from an $8 million loss to a gross profit of $71 million. He did it by going to the trenches, where the customer was.

Carlzon initiated the marketing concept and a marketing philosophy at SAS and, along with his top executives, literally hit the road and personally visited all front-line management of the airline and many of its line employees. He convinced employees that customer loyalty could be developed if employees fulfilled the needs and demands of travelers quickly and efficiently. SAS soon became one of the industry's leading

---

[7]Franklin S. Houston, "The Marketing Concept: What It Is and What It Is Not," *Journal of Marketing,* April, 1986, p. 85

[8]Philip Kotler, Professor of Marketing at Northwestern University, cited in *Marketing News,* July 19, 1985, p. 1, on notification that he would receive the first American Marketing Association Distinguished Educator Award.

and most profitable international airlines.[9] In 1993, Carlzon led SAS into a merger with KLM, Swissair, and Austrian Airways to better serve a new European Community and common market. Carlzon understood the importance of the marketing concept, advocated it, and provided the leadership to permeate the marketing philosophy throughout the organization.

And everyone knows about McDonald's. Ray Kroc initiated a marketing leadership that permeated the company so deeply that it has continued to this day under his successors.

Marketing Is Everything

"The 1990s will belong to the customer. And that is great news for the marketer."[10] We repeat these words from Regis McKenna because they relate so well to what the rest of this book is about. (At times you may think that we are on a different subject. Now you know.)

Technology, as McKenna says, is transforming choice, and choice is transforming the marketplace. Almost unlimited customer choice, accompanied by new competitors, is seen as a threat by many marketers. But the threat of new competitors is balanced by the opportunity of new customers.

> These new customers don't know about the old rules, the old understandings, or the old way of doing business—and they don't care. What they do care about is a company that is willing to adapt its products or services to fit their strategies. This represents the evolution of marketing to the market-driven company.[11]

The alternatives to traditional marketing approaches are what McKenna calls *knowledge-based* and *experience-based* marketing. Knowledge-based marketing includes mastering the technology in which a company competes with knowledge of competitors and customers, the

competitive environment, and its own organization, capabilities, and way of doing business. With this knowledge, companies can integrate the customer into the process to guarantee a product or service that solves consumer problems, to identify segments of the market that the company can own, and to develop an infrastructure of suppliers, partners, and users to sustain a competitive edge.

Experience-based marketing means spending time with customers, constantly monitoring competitors and developing a feedback system that turns this information into new product/service intelligence.

We have talked, and will talk more, about creating and keeping a customer and about customer loyalty. But today, with so much choice, customer loyalty may be short-lived. The only way to keep a customer may be to integrate him or her into the company and to create and sustain a relationship between the customer and the company. This will be marketing's job. In the 1990s, "marketing will do more than sell. It will define the way a company does business."[12]

The old notion of marketing was based on certain assumptions and attitudes, but:

> Marketing today is not a function. It is a way of doing business.... Marketing has to be all-pervasive, part of everyone's job description.... Its job...is to integrate the customer into the design of the product and to design a systematic process for interaction that will create substance in the relationship.[13]
>
> ...Technology permits information to flow in both directions between the customer and the company. It creates the feedback loop that integrates the customer into the company, allows the company to own a market, permits customization, creates a dialogue, and turns a product into a service and a service into a product.[14]
>
> ...In the 1990s, the critical dimension of the company—including all the attributes that together define how the company does business—are ultimately the functions of marketing. That is why marketing is everyone's job, why marketing is everything and everything is marketing.[15]

---

[9]Cf. Jan Carlzon, *Moments of Truth*, New York: Harper & Row, 1989 .

[10]Regis McKenna, "Marketing is Everything," *Harvard Business Review,* January–February, 1991, p. 65. Copyright © by the President and Fellows of Harvard College; all rights reserved.

[11]*Ibid*, p. 66.

---

[12]*Ibid*, p. 68.

[13]*Ibid*, p. 69.

[14]*Ibid*, p. 78.

[15]*Ibid*, p. 79.

Better yet, we might add, the customer is everything. The rest of this book is about customers.

Summary

This chapter has introduced marketing as a philosophy and a way of life for the hospitality firm. We have defined marketing in terms of the customer, and we have demonstrated how a marketing orientation, or the lack of it, impacts the entire organization. We have examined the concepts of internal (employee) and relationship (customer) marketing (although without using those terms), which will be discussed in detail in Chapter 2.

We have shown that marketing is far more than selling and advertising, the traditional concepts of the field. In fact, it has been shown that advertising and selling, equated with the term *marketing* by some people, are only subsets of marketing. The philosophy of marketing is needed before these communications vehicles are employed. In some cases, these activities may not even be necessary to marketing, as demonstrated by the many successful establishments that never advertise or practice direct selling.

The operations side of this coin should also be apparent. You don't have to have a marketing title to engage in marketing. Marketing is an integral part of management and the day-to-day business of running an operation.

Those readers for whom this chapter is their first real introduction to marketing may, in fact, be a little bewildered by this concept of marketing. Do not worry. In service industries, of which the hospitality industry is certainly a part, more than 80 percent of marketing may be nontraditional marketing. In Chapter 2 we will explain why.

Discussion Questions

1. A very successful restaurateur says, "Who needs marketing? That's for big corporations and business students. I operate by hunch and common sense." Discuss this statement.

2. Give examples of hospitality operations that you are familiar with or have read about that seem to operate by the different philosophies discussed in this chapter. Relate their philosophy to their success or lack of it.

3. From some of your own experiences, apply the consumer trade-off model. How do you balance sacrifice against problem solution? How does this affect your price/value perception and your expectations? Develop a scenario for how a hospitality customer might do the same thing.

4. This chapter states that "having created expectation, marketing needs to reduce perceived risk." Discuss the ways in which marketing might do this in the hospitality industry.

5. Discuss the application of the marketing philosophy and why it is needed before utilizing advertising and sales efforts.

6. Read Case 1-1, "We Do It All For You." Apply what you have learned in this chapter to how McDonald's practices the concept of marketing.

7. Read Case 1-2, "The Glorious Hotel." Does this company/hotel practice the concept of marketing? How? How not? Does it have a marketing orientation?

8. Be prepared to discuss Case 1-3, "Ritz-Carlton Changes Its Orientation," in the context of this chapter. Are the new goals realistic?

✔ Case 1-1
We Do It All For You[16]

In 1995, McDonald's celebrated its 40th anniversary. It has long been the largest food-service organization in the world, and its success story is unparalleled in the food-service industry. In 1993, McDonald's sold its 100 billionth hamburger. In 1984, the American Marketing Association awarded McDonald's its supreme accolade of "marketing company of the year." How did McDonald's get this way? The answer to that question demonstrates the concept of marketing.

Ray Kroc, McDonald's founder, probably never heard of the marketing concept. Yet Kroc and McDonald's is probably the best example we have in the hospitality industry of a successful marketer.

McConcept

Kroc found a particularly successful restaurant in San Bernardino, California, and approached the owners (the McDonald brothers) with the idea of franchising their fast-food (then an unknown term) concept. When they finally and reluctantly agreed, Kroc converted a product orientation into a marketing orientation that has since spelled out the reasons for McDonald's success.

Major demographic shifts were taking place in the American landscape in the 1950s and early 1960s. First, there was a massive movement of the middle-class population to the suburbs. This population was families, typically with 2.7 children, a wife and mother who stayed home, a casual lifestyle, and many trips to shopping centers and other suburban locations with the children in the back of a station wagon. There was also a perceptive increase in discretionary dollars for these families.

Kroc saw in these demographic movements a need for food-service establishments that provided uniformity and cleanliness, wherever and whenever a family might choose to eat, at affordable prices. Typically, in those days, one of a mother's most frustrating experiences was to enter a restaurant with children. Enduring the long wait for service was a harrowing experience, not to mention the usual "greasy spoon" ambience and the unreliability of the product.

Recognizing these problems, Kroc developed the concept of " QSC—quality, service, cleanliness." Quality meant that the food was hot and tasted good. Rigid standards were established as to the beef used in hamburgers, the potatoes used for french fries, and the recipe used for milk shakes. Service meant that it was served quickly and courteously and produced without hassle. Cleanliness meant that the surroundings would be clean and neat, both inside and out. This included personnel, equipment, and product presentation. Perhaps Kroc's greatest coup in this respect was the use of large windows in the front of his stores that revealed everything inside. Cleanliness not only existed, it was there for all to see. In 1955, this concept was totally unique.

Kroc initially identified his market as the large number of families across the United States who wanted budget-priced hamburgers produced fast in clean surroundings. Early advertising was targeted at this market, and McDonald's research revealed that over three-fourths of the company's sales were to families influenced by children. The early McDonald's sales pitch was aimed almost entirely at these children.

According to Kroc, McDonald's success was derived from finding something the market wanted that was basic and simple and that could be sold fast and in volume. "What could be more natural than meat and potatoes—that's what we sell at McDonald's," he said. McDonald's initial emphasis was on the customer, and it still is.

---

[16]Adapted from Robert C. Lewis, *Cases in Hospitality Marketing and Management*, pp. 13–16. Copyright © 1989 John Wiley & Sons, New York. Reprinted by permission of John Wiley & Sons, Inc.

McProgress

Of course, menu expansion occurred. The market changed and McDonald's changed with it. There was the Big Mac in 1968 and the Quarter Pounder in 1972. There was the Filet-O-Fish sandwich, hot apple pie, McDonald Land cookies, Egg McMuffin, Chicken McNuggets, Mc-D.L.T., and in 1991 the McLean Deluxe burger for the calorie-conscious. Innovative packaging was developed for takeout orders. Some of these innovations succeeded and some did not, but almost all new menu items originated with franchisees who got the ideas from their customers. They then went through extensive testing in McDonald's cooking labs as well as in the field. It was McDonald's that changed America's habits when it rolled out "Breakfast at McDonald's."

In 1993, McDonald's struck again. It initiated McChannel, which broadcasts "the latest on what's cookin' at McDonald's." Patrons tune in their car radios as they pull into the parking lots (signs give the FM frequency, which can only be heard within about 100 feet of the restaurant). It begins by saying that the station is intended "to make your visit even quicker and easier by telling you some specials before you order." These are quickly recited as "McTheme music" tinkles in the background.

McDonald's stuck with its original strategy and its continued reverence for the principles of Ray Kroc. Consistently, in good times and bad, McDonald's has been able to maintain, if not increase, market share against its rivals, who "do or die" to catch the leader. More than that, McDonald's has never taken its eye off the customer. This strategy led to overseas expansion, although it was initially unprofitable, while other chains concentrated on saturating the domestic scene.

In 1975, McDonald's inaugurated its "At McDonald's We Do It All For You" campaign on the premise that McDonald's offers people more than just "quality, service, cleanliness." The campaign was designed to communicate that McDonald's was an experience that was the sum total of the food, folks, and fun found there. That theme, although not in those words, has

continued, and the emphasis remains on the experience that one has at McDonald's each and every visit.

In addition to national programs, local operations frequently participate in community development and local programs developed from local concerns, such as safety, ecology, and nutrition. When communities suffer hardships, McDonald's is the first one there giving coffee to firemen, feeding victims, raising relief funds, and contributing to the cause. Ronald McDonald Houses, supported by local McDonald's restaurants, the medical community, and volunteer groups, serve as homes away from home for nearly 100,000 family members whose children are being treated at nearby hospitals in the United States, Canada, and Australia.

A strong marketing research department conducts ongoing surveys to measure the company's strength with consumers and to provide direction for marketing strategy. In 1970, research found that most of McDonald's customers were young married couples with small children, children who led their parents to McDonald's. In the 1990s these children, and those of the baby-boom generation that preceded have all been weaned on McDonald's and led their own children in that direction. From sponsoring Saturday morning cartoons on television, McDonald's now sponsors the Olympics and major golf tournaments.

McFuture

McDonald's has always had plenty of competition. (The stories of those who have come and gone, or hung on, would fill a few books.) But for years they were largely copiers or imitators. On McDonald's 40th anniversary, they were merely alternatives.

Fast food, and not-so-fast food, has come a long way. What's a McDonald's to do? Burger consumption has dropped, and the entire fast-food industry is slowing down. New rivals are dividing and conquering. Some are beating McDonald's on price, and some even on speed. At a company, which some say owes its success to a religion of standardization, McDonald's is rethinking all of the rules that Ray Kroc devised.

This means new, ambitious experiments in food and decor and new formats, from self-service to cafes, to dinner menus, to serving McDonald's fare on airplanes, to contracting to provide 24-hour room service in upscale hotels. It means experimentation with more than 150 menu items, from lasagna to corn on the cob to egg rolls, all of which threaten the much-copied operating system that produces the company's signature consistency and speed. And items such as pizza and chicken fajitas put McDonald's up against well-entrenched competitors.

It's a far cry from Ray Kroc's "by-the-book" days. At a chain that would give you anything you wanted as long as it was "two all-beef patties, special sauce, lettuce, cheese, pickles, and onions on a sesame seed bun," there's a new message: "Do whatever it takes to make a customer happy," according to Michael Quinlan, CEO.

In another break with its principles of standardization, Quinlan has asked every restaurant to analyze its customers' expectations and then customize their responses to the local market. TV commercials starring real crew members promise, "Whatever it takes, that's McDonald's today."

On its 50th anniversary in 2005, will McDonald's still "Do It All For You"?

✔ Case 1-2

The Glorious Hotel[17]

The $100-million-plus, 650-room Glorious Hotel, originally budgeted at $80 million, was under construction in Chicago when management decided to plan marketing strategy a year in advance of opening with a two-day session led by a hotel strategic marketing consultant. Plans for the session were scrapped, however, when management decided that (1) the consultant's fee of $2,000 a day was too high, and (2) management already knew what its strategy would be.

The Glorious Hotel in Chicago was, after all, joining a prestigious line of luxury hotels bearing the Glorious name in San Francisco, San José, New York, Dallas, and New Orleans. Like those hotels it would be a member of the prestigious reservations network, *Leading Hotels of the World*. All of these hotels were considered luxury properties, with some holding the AAA Five-Diamond Award and some the Mobilguide Four-Star Award. The Chicago property, like the others ranging in size from 550 to 750 rooms, would also have strong meeting and convention facilities.

In fact, Glorious corporate considered itself to be a premier operator of large luxury hotels. Richard Smith, Chairman and Chief Executive Officer of the Glorious Hotel Management Company, responded to an interview as follows:

Q How do you accomplish a high level of personal service in hotels large enough to host major conventions? Doesn't "large hotel" contradict "personal service"?

Smith Not when you put yourself in your guests' shoes. Our hotels are designed to attract people of quality. Therefore you put into effect the services you believe persons of quality want.

Q Do customers understand what they're getting when they stay at "luxury" properties?

Smith This is very confusing. The only thing "luxury" about a new hotel may be that it's new. This doesn't make a luxury hotel. It takes a lot of years, a lot of experience.

Q Is the size of your hotels in this age of "trendy" and "boutique" properties a detriment to selling?

Smith By being a large hotel, most people don't think it's possible to give personalized service to guests. I disagree. It's no harder to keep 500 rooms clean than 100.

Q How can you deliver personalized service to individual travelers and cater to groups at the same time?

Smith To us, every guest coming into the hotel is recognized as an individual traveler. We don't look at anyone as being a member of a convention. They're all individual people who want luxury service.

Q How involved do you get in the fine details of running Glorious Hotels?

Smith I get right into what tablecloths are put in a restaurant, the china, the stemware. I read all the menus before they're put in a room. I go through every detail, but everybody's ideas are listened to.

Q How do you keep yourself from becoming insular in your hotel business?

Smith I don't think any ideas are new, just repeats from years ago. All you do is take other people's ideas, convert them to match your own ideas and philosophies, and try to accomplish the same thing.

The Glorious Experience

An attendee at a convention held at the Glorious in Chicago stayed at the hotel over a year after it opened and related the following experience:

I checked into the hotel at around 10:00 P.M. From the doorman on through the desk clerk and the bellman, the personnel were very efficient and friendly. Riding up in the elevator, I asked the bellman where I could still get something to eat. His answer was the Primavera Restaurant. Suggesting that I didn't want a full

---

[17]Names have been disguised.

dinner but more of a snack, he said I should go to the Primavera Bar, where a snack would be available until 11:00 P.M. I set my bag in my room and headed straight for the bar.

The Primavera Bar was separated from the restaurant by a ten-foot corridor. Coming from the elevator or escalator from the lobby floor, one came first to the bar. One could go around the outside of the bar to reach the restaurant, or could go through the bar, out the other end, across the ten-foot corridor, and into the restaurant. I went straight into the bar, which had about 125 seats plus about a dozen bar stools.

I had hardly entered the bar when, walking in front of a large-screen television, I was jarred by the noise of the Denver Broncos engaging the Buffalo Bills in the weekly Monday Night Football event. I noticed two people sitting at the bar and a couple in the far, far corner at a table. The bar and lounge area were otherwise empty and none of the four was watching the football game. This emptiness surprised me since I had already ascertained that the hotel was full.

There were a waitress and bartender on duty. I stood for awhile until they finished a conversation, and the waitress came over and asked if she could be of help.

"I understand," I shouted over the football game, "that I can get a snack here."

She reached to a table, picked up a menu, and handed it to me.

"Sit anywhere," she said, then returned to the bar.

I sat at a table behind a large pillar so as to block out the television screen, but not the noise. After about ten minutes, the waitress came to my table to take an order.

"The menu says wine by the glass," I said. "What wine is it?"

"I'll find out," was the reply.

She returned in about five minutes. The wine was a cheap Italian at $8 a four-ounce glass. I ordered it along with some shrimp and pasta. She left and I looked around. There were bowls of peanuts on some of the tables, so I got up and retrieved a bowl from another table. Unfortunately, the peanuts were too soggy for my taste. The waitress came back with the wine.

"Do many people come in to watch the football game?" I asked.

"Do you mean employees or guests?" she responded.

"Are you ever busy here?" I asked.

"Well, yeah, sometimes," she replied.

While enjoying my wine—and eventually my snack—I saw about 20 people walk into the lounge and look around. Two stayed, one of whom watched the football game.

I returned to my room and made a number of observations. The bedside light and radio were on. What a nice touch, I thought. The radio later went off by itself. The bed, of course, was turned down. This was no small feat since the covering quilt was a heavy and expensive one that had been placed in one of the two plush and comfortable chairs by the desk/side table. There were four pillows on the queen bed, two feather and two standard, and they seemed to be of high quality as well. On the night stand next to the bed was a chocolate basket—yes, a basket *made out of chocolate*—which contained six rich and expensive, albeit delicious, chocolates. I estimated this to have cost at least five dollars. There was also a card from the General Manager welcoming me.

The room itself had an excellent layout, unlike any I had seen, and was quite large—I estimated over 400 square feet—in the shape of a parallelogram, with a large desk, two comfortable chairs, a long dresser, and a separate, well-built television table. It was all of high quality and in very good taste. There was a full vanity section, a bathtub and basin section, a large walk-in shower, and finally a toilet section. Each section could be shut off from the others. There was an automatic light in the closet and, bless it, removable hangers! I couldn't have been more delighted and wasn't surprised when I read on the back of the door that the room rate was $240 single, $280 double, even though I was only paying the convention rate of $115.

In fact, the room was loaded with additional amenities: Over the washbasins was a tiny TV on which, unfortunately, I was never able to get clear reception. There was no pay TV, and no special movies were offered. Two gorgeous terry-cloth robes hung in the closet. The room had a phone by the bed, plus a "state-of-the-art" one on the desk that looked like you could place a conference call to Congress on it. Being unsophisticated about these things I didn't try; the only problem I had was, when trying to give the hotel's number to my daughter who lived in Chicago, it was nowhere to be found.

There was a stand-up electric shoe-polisher, plus an offer of a free shoeshine if you hung your shoes on the doorknob between 11:00 and 6:00. (I tried it and it worked!) There were three large, pink bars of soap, one each in the basin, tub, and shower, a "French Mill" soap, along with "Glorious" shampoo, hair conditioner, body lotion, and a shower cap. (I took most of these amenities home in my suitcase.) The large bars of soap, although hardly used, were replaced daily. One minor annoyance was that, in the large walk-in shower, there was no place to put the soap other than on the floor. There were also a sewing kit and a notice of the number to call if you wanted anything more.

At 8:30 the next morning I went to the Primavera Restaurant for breakfast. This time I walked around the lounge, which was immediately adjacent, dark and empty, to the restaurant. About ten people were waiting in line, and a jovial maitre d' kept asking things like how many in your party, are you having a nice stay, sorry for the delay, have a nice day, to those departing, and similar friendly expressions. The reservation phone rang frequently. The maitre d' was quick to answer, "Thank you for calling Primavera. This is Daryl Patten. How may I help you?"

After about ten minutes I was seated at a table for four, complete with table linen, silver, service plate, and crystal. After about seven minutes a waiter came and removed the other three place settings. Five minutes later, he came back for my order—orange juice and coffee.

The conference was a great success and the luncheons that went with it were excellent, although perhaps more than I normally eat in the middle of the day. One minor annoyance was that in the middle of each "eight round" [table] was a beautiful and expensive flower arrangement, such as birds of paradise. These made it impossible to talk, eye-to-eye, with people directly opposite you at the table.

Oh, yes, there was one other thing. The second night I decided to work in my room and order room service. I couldn't quite understand why a three-quarter-liter bottle of Smirnoff vodka was $52 and a grilled steak was $22, so I ordered a Beck's and sent out for a pizza.

All in all, the Glorious is a great hotel for $115. It was interesting to read in a trade publication, after I returned home, that the Glorious was barely doing 50 percent overall occupancy, in a city running almost 70 percent overall, and might have to be "repositioned as second-tier luxury" property. In the same article the GM of the Glorious was quoted: "Tiers are establishing themselves. Only some hotels will get top rates. It will depend on name recognition and the strength of their marketing programs." To boost occupancy levels, the article stated, many high-end hotels in Chicago were charging "rates significantly lower than what is needed to pay their debts" with a "backing off from published rates...and heavy discounting off rack rates on commercial group business." One industry spokesman was quoted in the article as saying, "[It] is difficult if not impossible for large luxury hotels to deliver the personal services that guests who pay $200 or more for a room expect."

✔ Case 1-3
Ritz-Carlton Changes Its Orientation[18]

Mr. Horst Schulze, President and Chief Operating Officer of Ritz-Carlton Hotel Company, was contemplating the fact that Ritz-Carlton had just been named the top hotel company in the United States for the second year in a row. "That's good," he thought, "but not good enough. *We're* not good enough and we have to get better."

Horst Schulze had come to Ritz-Carlton as Operations Vice President because it was a quality company. Now, as President and COO, he wanted to make it a company of even higher quality. He knew there were still plenty of customer complaints, and he knew they were still losing customers.

To Horst Schulze, one complaint was one too many, and one complaint could mean one customer lost, not to mention all the others to whom that dissatisfied customer might talk. Multiply that by a few dozen, he felt, and Ritz-Carlton could be losing thousands of customers a year.

Ritz-Carlton was making money at a time when some of its competitors in the luxury category were not. Its experienced management knew how to run hotels, and some of its hotels had the best product and the best restaurants in the business. "Great food, great product, great service, and great costs," thought Mr. Schulze, "but that's not good enough. We have to find a way to be even better. Real quality means zero defects and 100 percent customer retention. Those are the goals we have to shoot for."

Horst Schulze knew that other upscale hotels weren't going to stand by and let Ritz-Carlton walk away with their customers. They would be trying to steal customers, especially those with complaints. And they would try to do it with product, service, and price—especially price. Ritz-Carlton couldn't afford to rest on its laurels—it had to go out and steal their customers, and keep them. "If we're 'five' on a ten-point scale," he thought, "we're just lucky they're '4.9.' And that means that some others are rating them 'number one.' Our goal has to be to be 'number one' to everyone in our product class, and a few that aren't. And the way we do that is give each and every target customer what they want, when they want it, at a price they are willing to pay—and let them know about it. In other words, we (1) get them in the door, and (2) we give them a 'zero defect' performance every time. That leads to 100 percent retention—no lost customers and plenty more coming when they hear about it."

The Ritz-Carlton Hotel Company

The Ritz-Carlton Hotel Company was a management firm that developed and operated luxury hotels worldwide. It operated over 30 hotels, mostly in North America, but had expansion plans in Europe, Asia, and Australia, with hotels either under development or in the planning stage, and it was actively seeking other international sites. Ritz-Carlton had become the standard of independent rating organizations as the only hotel company that consistently met their highest standards. This wasn't good enough for Horst Schulze.

In Pursuit of Quality

Ritz-Carlton's history was one of reliance on the product and service provided to drive the company effort. According to Jim DiChiara, Vice President–Sales, "In the hotel industry, the '80s were a time to make a buck as fast as you could, to heck with quality—just put it out, sell it to a big investor, and move on."

---

[18]This case is largely drawn from a personal interview in November, 1993 with James P. DiChiara, Vice President–Sales, Ritz-Carlton Hotel Company. The starting point of the case is about seven years earlier and moves to the date of the interview. Quotations are paraphrased from the interview. In 1992 Ritz-Carlton earned the Malcolm Baldridge National Quality Award, established by the United States Congress in 1987 to recognize companies that had achieved excellence through adherence to quality improvement programs. Ritz-Carlton was only the second company in the service sector to win the award.

The people at Ritz-Carlton felt differently. Ritz-Carlton needed to go from being a product-driven company to being a market-driven company. Jim DiChiara summed it up: "The reality of life is that if you don't put the ingredients in the soup, you're not going to have a great soup. You ask people what they want in the soup, you make the soup, and then you ask them if they like the soup. It's pretty simple, but we tend to create our own boll weevils in business. We make it more difficult.

"Luxury hotels," he continued, "will become dinosaurs if our service isn't better—and remarkably better—than that being provided by lower-level hotels. A room is a room is a room—a bed, a light, a carpet. We have to do something much better than that and let people know they can count on it. Luxury has become a rejected term. We need to focus on reliability. Successful companies don't just have great products; they do the best job in conveying values and what they have to offer to their markets.

"Take the room service delivery problem we had at the Buckhead Hotel. We tracked it, and it all seemed to work as it should. The orders got taken quickly, the trays got put up quickly, and the room service waiter left promptly. But we couldn't figure out why it took so long to get to the room. In the old days we'd fire somebody for slow delivery, but that's not the answer anymore. Today, we have to find out why the system doesn't work.

"We'd never tracked these complaints. In fact, I'd go so far as to say we never knew we had a problem. That's what comes from being 'number one.' That's a problem. That's a problem when someone is spending $300 a night. That's a problem when people see us as unbelievable because of the image we've created. We sent them all this collateral, we established dress codes—all those things that people saw as a little unbelievable.

"We hadn't gone to our customers to find out what they really wanted—from a message standpoint. What was really important to them in selecting a hotel? We needed to put a more rational spin on the way we did business—tie in the fact that we're reliable to the fact that we have some system of guaranteeing to cus-

tomers that we will deliver on their expectations. We needed to give people a feel for what they will get when they get there. We were image-driven. When the market changes, it becomes a problem.

"People talk about the beauty of our hotels. But, you know, I'll bet when they get back home they don't talk about the carpets and the chandeliers. I'll bet they talk about their experience—because that's what they're really paying for. Did we deliver on our commitment? If we're going to the great expense of putting these hotels together, are we making them user-friendly?

"We wondered if we really knew our customers. How often did we go out and meet them? Were we treating different customers differently according to the things they want most? Maybe everyone doesn't want incredible personal service. Maybe we tied too much to the sales effort. Thus, the system dictates the outcome.

"So, with Mr. Schulze's urging and strong backing, we began to look at the major issues in our business. First, what do customers want? Second, how do we ensure that we deliver this to them? Third, how do we make the system work, for sure? Marketing does not stop at bringing guests in—it is continuous—and how guests are treated is a marketing tool. Fourth, how do we communicate this to the market?

"This gave us another thought. What about our reservation system? You know these games that people play. They call the hotel, they call the 800 number, they call the travel agent. For some hotels, not necessarily ours, they get different quotes from each call. This must get both confusing and frustrating, especially when they get to the hotel and find still different rates.

"Another thing was to look at complaints. How do we handle them, for example a late room service breakfast? Of course we apologize. The GM would call them and repeat the apology; then we'd send them a fruit basket. If it was really bad, we gave away a room-night.

"I don't think a fruit basket would compensate me for being late to an 8:00 A.M. meeting because of room service, or missing breakfast altogether. I think the days are over when we can pass on our inefficiencies to the customer. Not to mention the costs and confusion that we put into soothing a customer in a way that has no correlation with his or her problem. Our figures showed that it cost us about $250,000 a year *per hotel* to handle these kinds of problems.

"Finally, the luxury market is a thin market—and getting thinner every day. We wanted to know how we could attract more of the top-end buyers just below that market—and I don't mean by cutting product, service, or prices. Let's call them the 'step-up buyers.' How could we make ourselves attractive to a wider audience? Should we just chase after the luxury buyer? What about those who are bombarded by Hyatt, Hilton, Westin, and Marriott? They're conditioned to stay in those products. Maybe some of them don't know any better. How could we do a better job of reaching them? Could we define ourselves better?"

Summary

"TQM [*total quality management*] is our game," said Jim DiChiara. "To us it means continuous improvement. It comes down to what you can do that the competition is not doing to give yourself a competitive advantage. TQM forces you to analyze your business process. How do you get from point A to point Z? You focus on the middle.

"You know," he continued, "when you get right down to it, maybe TQM should be called TQS, with the 'S' standing for Sense. We've always done what we did intuitively—what we thought was important. We rushed to solutions to make decisions—we *fixed* the problem. If we're not having the right impact on the customer, internally or externally, we're wasting our time. I think what we needed was some Total Quality Sense.

"But let's not forget, as Mr. Schulze says, the founding reason for us to exist is to make money. We sell excellent service, but the purpose is to make money. You have to charge for the service, for the friendly employee. When we capture a guest, that guest is willing to pay more than at another hotel because they receive value for the dollar. We want to accomplish simply the highest occupancy at the highest rate, the highest top line. We want consistent, good business in slow times or good times and, consequently, a high return on investment. We clearly understand that we will not have investors if we don't deliver returns on investments."

CHAPTER 2

Nontraditional Marketing in Hospitality

Today, people doing knowledge work and service work account for three-fourths, if not four-fifths, of the workforce in all developed countries—and their share is increasing. In 1955 these people formed less than one-third of the workforce.[1] In the United States the service sector provides over three-fourths of the gross domestic product and a similar percentage of total employment.

The hospitality industry is generally conceded to be a "service" industry. This suggests the need for special examination of hospitality-marketing activity to contrast the marketing of "services" with the marketing of "goods." The basic concept of marketing will not change, however, since it is concerned with the fulfilling of needs and wants in any industry.

It was argued in Chapter 1 that in the hospitality industry every act of management is also an act of marketing. When this notion is contrasted with the management of a manufacturing plant and the marketing of the goods produced by that plant, it can be seen that many differences exist between the two types of industry. These differences and the differences between services marketing and goods market-

ing are worth examining before we proceed to the special case of hospitality marketing.

Services vs. Goods

Services are often differentiated from goods by a notion of intangibility. Yet, there is no such thing as a pure good without some elements of service attached to it. For example, an automobile is a manufactured good, but few of us are strangers to the service aspects of buying and owning a car. Thus, even the purchase of a manufactured good will have some element of intangibility. Similarly, most services contain some element of tangibility. Airlines are considered part of the service sector, but the seat you sit in is very tangible. What concerns us here is the marketing of the intangible aspects of the product, namely the service that accompanies it. Services have special problems when it comes to marketing them.

Essentially, the goods component of a product is different from the service component because you can see and feel goods, while services provide you with an experience. A car is a good that can be driven and tested before being purchased. A hotel stay or a restaurant meal is a service, since the room or food cannot be tried before

---

[1]Peter Drucker, *Post-Capitalist Society,* New York: Harper Business, 1993.

purchase. A car-buyer leaves with a car, a service-buyer leaves with an experience. This explanation is somewhat simplistic. What we need to do is break the product down into its various components. Customers tend to view each component in tems of the problems it solves.

As the state of the art of marketing services has developed over the past 15 years it is clear not only that services are different from goods, but that services are different from services. The professional services of a doctor, lawyer, or accountant are not the same as those of a hospital, a dry-cleaning service, a barber, or a hairdresser. Similarly, the hospitality product is different. Its components can be both tangible and intangible, as well as be both services and goods. It is all of these elements that make the marketing of hospitality products a special case of nontraditional marketing.

Components of the Hospitality Product

There are three major elements that concern customers, in relatively equal proportion, when purchasing and using the hospitality product: tangible goods, environment, and intangible services.

Goods   Goods include the mostly physical factors over which management has direct, or almost direct, control and they encompass management decisions or practices that directly affect goods. In some cases management expertise determines the quality level of goods, as in the case of a chef. Alternatively, quality of goods may depend on management's willingness to spend or not spend money in pursuit of the target market it wishes to serve. In this category we place beds, food, room size, furnishings, location, bathroom amenities, elevator service, heating and air-conditioning, TVs, things that don't work, and so forth. We also define price as tangible, although it is a cost of services as well as goods. (To the consumer, price is very tangible in any purchase decision.) In hospitality it is the goods components that, generally speaking, satisfy or don't satisfy the *basic* needs of cus-

tomers, as illustrated in Chapter 1. They provide solutions to basic problems.

Environment   In the category of environment, we place those items over which management may also have some control, but not as directly and not as easily. While environmental items may or may not be tangible, they are something the customer feels. And what we are marketing is that feeling. For example, putting electronic locks on bedroom doors is something very physical and tangible, but we do not sell the electronic lock to the customer. What we sell, instead, is the benefit of the feature—a feeling of security, a very important but intangible attribute for many hotel customers. Other attributes in this category are decor, atmosphere, comfort, ambience, architecture, and so forth. These attributes fall more in the "want," as opposed to the "need," category. They solve extended problems.[2] A hotel room, for example, satisfies a basic need; a luxurious room satisfies a "want."

Services   The third category, services, includes nonphysical, intangible attributes that management clearly does, or should, control. Items in this category depend heavily on the personal elements provided by employees, such as friendliness, speed, attitude, professionalism, and responsiveness. But there are other factors as well: There are those that may depend on employee aptitude, but that may also depend on the system, such as the handling of reservations. Then also, there are those that may strictly depend on management decisions, such as whether to offer a service. Room service is an example of this. In fact, we can use room service to demonstrate the complexity of the interrelationships among the three components of the hospitality product.

Management must first decide to offer room service. Obviously, this decision is relevant to many things, including the particular property and the target market. The first question to be answered, of course, is whether offering room

---

[2]The same argument can be made, of course, for a car—we need a car but we want a Mercedes. The difference lies in the intangibility and nonpossessiveness of the hospitality environment.

service will solve a problem for customers at this property. If an alert management decides that the answer is yes, it will then analyze demand, cost, resources, and facilities. If customers expect room service and it is not offered, there will be dissatisfaction.

Deciding to offer room service does not end there—in fact, it leads inevitably to many related opportunities to fulfill or not fulfill expectations. First, there is the service element. How many times does the phone ring before the room service department answers it? What is the attitude of the person who does answer? Is it delivered when promised?[3] What is the attitude of the room service waiter? Did he remember the rolls, the sugar, and enough cream for the coffee? When the meal is finished and the tray is put out in the hallway, how long does it stay there before someone takes it away?

Now, let's look at the goods element. Is the orange juice fresh, the coffee hot? Is the silverware clean? Is the bacon crisp or the toast soggy? Is the price fair?

What about the environment? Is there a table to put the food on without rearranging the bedroom? Are there chairs to sit on that enable occupants to reach the table? Is the tray well-presented?

If all these things are done well, consistent with the target market that determines what "well" is, do guests say, "Boy, this is a well-managed hotel!"? Probably not. But if one thing is *not* done well, guests may well say the opposite. Why should this be? Because , whatever it is, it is *expected* to be done well. That is the solution to the customers' problem. That is how the customer measures the price/value relationship. This is why the "risk" was taken. *All* these lead to the ultimate level of satisfaction. There is no opportunity to return room service for another room service in the same way a good can be exchanged.

You can see now that room service, like all parts of hospitality operations, is *marketing*—it

solves or causes problems, it can keep or lose a customer. Look now at Marriott's 1993 ad in Figure 2-2. Comparing it to Figure 2-1 you can see that Marriott went from a stance of timely delivery to having your breakfast "perfect in every way."

Now you can see why marketing the hospitality product is not exactly like marketing tires, stereo sets, a doctor's services, a hospital room, or a haircut. In the room service case, the person who answered the phone, the person who took the order, the person who fixed the breakfast, the person who delivered the meal, the person who designed the room, the person who retrieved the tray, the china, the silver, and the room itself are all part of the product. More important, they are all part of the marketing effort.

In this chapter our concern is with the special case of nontraditional marketing of hospitality products, with special attention to the services element. We should bear in mind, however, that whether we call the hospitality product a good (steak), environment (decor), or service (service), in essence hospitality product in its entirety can be classified as an intangible service.

This is true for two reasons: First, the hospitality product is personal. The customer interacts with all phases of the product at a very personal level and judges them on the basis of personal experiences. Judgment is usually based less on the quality that the manufacturer puts into the product, than on the personal relationship of the customer to the product.

Second, the hospitality product is always "left behind," that is, customers do not take it with them and it can never be redone. The moment has passed forever. They go away empty-handed, with nothing to show for their money. Even the services of a doctor or a barber, considered by many to be more pure services than hospitality, have some elements that you can take with you. You can show your friends the scar left by the surgeon's knife and, generally, your hair will grow in again. The hospitality product is unique in that there is no cure or second chance. This has incredible implications for hospitality marketing and operations, as we will now explain.

---

[3]Failure to deliver room service when promised (i.e., a nonsolution to a customer's problem) is such a frequent complaint that some companies put all their emphasis on delivery. See Marriott's 1991 ad in Figure 2-1; Marriott's promise was based, however, on ordering the night before.

You can't be late for
your business appointments,
and neither can we.

At Marriott, if your breakfast doesn't show up on time, it won't show up on your bill.
That's because we take our business just as seriously as you take yours. And our business
is service. This commitment is what makes Marriott the business traveler's first choice.
See for yourself. Call **1-800-228-9290** or your Travel Professional.

SERVICE. THE ULTIMATE LUXURY.℠

Courtesy of Marriott Hotels & Resorts

FIGURE 2-1   Emphasizing timeliness of room service delivery

Why the Marketing of Services Is Different

Writers on the services marketing scene have noted a number of important differences between services and manufactured goods. Four of these differences have found general agreement among most marketers and are those most frequently mentioned in discussions of services: intangibility, perishability, heterogeneity, and simultaneous production and consumption. It is important to understand these differences because they have major implications for marketing. For each difference, we will discuss the implications for marketing from the perspective of both the consumer and the marketer.

"I'M A REAL
STICKLER ABOUT
BREAKFAST.
SO IF YOURS
ISN'T JUST RIGHT,
I'LL PAY
FOR IT MYSELF."

Bill Marriott

We want your breakfast to be perfect in every way –
preparation, presentation, service and timing. If everything isn't
just so, it's on us. Call your travel agent or 1-800-228-9290.

HOTELS · RESORTS · SUITES

WE MAKE IT HAPPEN FOR YOU.

Not available at Courtyard by Marriott, Residence Inn by Marriott or Fairfield Inn. ©1993 Marriott Corp.

Courtesy of Marriott Hotels & Resorts

FIGURE 2-2   Emphasizing all elements of breakfast

Intangibility

In describing services, the term *intangibility* is best defined by the following thoughts: Services are experienced, rather than possessed. One cannot grasp a service with any of the five senses—that is, one cannot taste, feel, see, smell, or hear a service, and one cannot easily grasp it conceptually. There is no passing of title when a service is purchased. Buyers have nothing to be displayed, to be shown to friends or family, to put on the shelf, or ever to use again. In sum, buyers go away empty-handed. They do not, however, go away empty-*headed*. They have an experience to remember and to talk about. Although services will differ in some of these respects (and it is obvious that this description is not appropriate to the hospitality product in all cases), we will continue to use the term as described, violating it now and then only with discretion.

The Consumer   The intangibility of services has profound implications for consumers, and thus for marketers. In the extreme, buyers are not sure what they are buying, or what they will get. Even if they have bought it before, they cannot go back and say, "I want one of the same" and show the seller what it is that they want. Buyers cannot kick the tires, turn up the sound, smell the aroma, measure the size, or taste the flavor before buying. They are buying a "pig in a poke."[4]

A buyer's first service experience creates expectations for future experiences—which is why each experience of a service rendered is a marketing effort. It is the only true way consumers have of valuing the purchase and determining if it is worth the sacrifice. Even then, they are not sure if it will be repeated in an identical fashion, increasing the sense of risk for customers. When buyers have not previously had the same experience, they may have to rely on similar experiences. If there have been none, then they may choose to rely on the experiences of others, either with the same or similar experi-

ences. Or, they may rely on traditional marketing advertising. Any of these sources create perceptions and expectations.

For hospitality marketing, creating the right customer perception and expectation is critical. This is why traditional marketing may be counterproductive. A Howard Johnson hotel may advertise itself as a "Hotel and Conference Center." Similarly, a dedicated conference center such as Arrowwood in Westchester County, New York may also advertise itself as such. Consumer perception and expectation, based on the ads, may be the same, however the service levels in these two "conference centers" will be vastly different. Further, a customer who has just held a meeting at the Arrowwood Conference Center would be very disappointed at the Howard Johnson version. And, conversely, the Howard Johnson customer could be overwhelmed by the cost of holding a similar meeting at the Arrowwood Conference Center. Buyers who have only the advertising or the promise of the seller on which to rely, may truly be buying blind.

Business centers are another service that is offered to hotel customers, through various means. Hotel A may in fact have a state-of-the-art business center, with secretarial help, fax machines, computers, copiers, etc. Hotel B's business center, however, may turn out to be the administrative assistant to its general manager. Both "market" business centers as an amenity to their guests, but offer very different levels of service.

Words like "conference center" and "business center" create perceptions that may be far from the reality when encountered. Good marketing seeks to make perception and reality equal because perception *is* reality for the consumer. Thus, word-of-mouth, nontraditional marketing may be the most potent force in creating a customer.

The Marketer   The intangibility of services creates several other challenges for marketers. It is not easy to display and communicate intangible services. Marketers must convince the prospective buyer that they offer the right solution to the buyer's problem. The first step is to

---

[4]This phrase is derived from the Scotch language and, in turn, farmers of the American Midwest, where a poke is a bag or sack; it means that one cannot see what one is buying.

develop the expectation. Traditional methods of doing this are through advertising, personal selling, and public relations. In many cases hospitality companies use these methods, but there are inherent problems: How do you advertise or sell an intangible service? You can use words (e.g., "the finest," "the ultimate"), but often these are as abstract as the service itself and may serve only to compound the service's intangibility. Or, you can use tangible clues. Refer again to Figure 2-1 to see both of these approaches in use, and to Figure 2-2 for an updated version that promotes total expectation. We will discuss these further in the chapters on positioning and advertising.

What we really do is make promises; the greater the intangibility, the greater the promise—and the greater the risk to the buyer in terms of the sacrifice that has to be made. Customers have no choice but to believe us and take our word, or not believe us and go somewhere else where they will likely get the same promise and be faced with the same dilemma. It is because of this quandary that we say that traditional marketing is only a small part of hospitality marketing.

In fact, there are some who have raised serious questions about the value of advertising hospitality services except for the purpose of creating awareness. Research has shown that, barring firsthand experience, buyers of services rely on word-of-mouth more than any other source of information. We have now come full circle. If we want to create positive word-of-mouth, it is obvious that we must create positive experiences for customers.

Refer back to the example of room service and it is clear that one of the most important elements of marketing a service lies in the handling of a customer's experience, which compounds the situation even further. The typical customer who experiences poor room service will complain not only about room service, he or she will complain in general about the service in that hotel. The same analogy can be made for restaurants.

Intangibility also makes pricing decisions difficult. How much more will a customer pay for "excellent" service versus "good" service? In addition, do you price a service while totally accepting the notion that buyers of services are likely to equate higher prices with better quality? Consider this example: Prospective attendees of large conventions are sent a list of hotels and their rates for the city in which the convention is to be held. If one does not have any previous experience in that city, room rates may be the only indicator of quality. Buyers may speculate that lower room rates indicate a bad location, or poor upkeep, or any other unfavorable reason. After all, the buyer cannot experience the service before making the choice.

Marketers are also affected by the fact that intangible services, unlike tangible products, cannot be protected by patents. No organization has the exclusive right to provide excellent service; additionally, any new service that a hotel might introduce can be copied by its competition. The intangibles of customer satisfaction derived from intangible services are far more elusive, as shown in Figure 2-3.

Perishability

The second primary characteristic of services is their perishability. It has often been said, for example, that there is nothing as perishable as an airline seat or a hotel room. If not sold on a particular flight or for a particular night, that opportunity to sell is gone forever. Initially, the impact of this characteristic appears to be a major problem of management rather than of the consumer. That is undoubtedly true, but the repercussions are felt by the consumer as well. A hotel has a fixed number of rooms available for sale on any given day and it is the task of management to create demand for these rooms.

The Consumer Just as hotel room-nights cannot be stored, other services provided also cannot be stored. A front desk clerk may be swamped during a busy check-in period and humanly incapable of providing good service to all customers. An hour later, however, he may be standing around with nothing to do. This fluctuating demand can cause services provided to customers to be uneven. The same is true, of course, in restaurants.

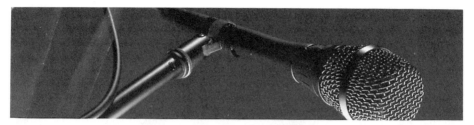

Details, details, details, details, details, details, details, details, details, details,

details, details, details, details, details, details, details, details, details, details,

details, details, details, details, details, details, details. In short...

Simply everything.   Simply.

hotel nikko san francisco

Union Square West
222 MASON STREET
415 · 394 · 1111

FIGURE 2-3   The intangibility of customer satisfaction

The Marketer Just as inventory management and control are important to a goods-manufacturing company, so management and control of "inventory" (i.e., a capacity to satisfy) are critical to a service company. In essence,

however, the service company—if it wants to be able to satisfy demand from its "inventory"—must have the capability of producing satisfaction *when demand occurs.*

Hotels and restaurants are limited in their

ability to increase this service capacity in the short run. Not having enough rooms at certain times offers problems, as does having too many rooms available. Often a hotel's management will see that it has many rooms available, one week in advance; it will decide to "panic price" the inventory in an effort to fill the empty rooms. Customers traveling to this destination, however, unaware of the hotel's "gap" period, may phone ahead; and, willing to accept a higher price but quoted the "panic price," they become further confused because of the pricing decision.

A 500-room hotel cannot sell more than 500 rooms in one night even though there may be a great additional demand for rooms that night. On the other hand, if demand does not occur, that capacity and capability are lost and wasted, causing excessive costs. The result has been to push many hospitality managements into an operations mode and orientation to restrict costs in the event of unused supply.

The emphasis on operations and cost control, while necessary in many cases for survival, may have an adverse effect on the customer relationship. Housekeeping staff, front desk staff, dining room staff, and other staff who serve the customer directly become the instruments of control. If overstaffing occurs, there is a high cost ratio and the labor cost percentage becomes too high. Bottom-line management may resist this potential by understaffing, but when unexpected demand occurs, the service becomes inadequate.

One alternative has been to charge prices that are high enough so that overstaffing does not become a serious problem. Four Seasons Hotels, during strong economic times, followed this strategy and became known for their high level of service regardless of the level of demand, but not without serious impact on the bottom line. In poor economic times, many competitive hotels discounted severely and Four Seasons was unable to sustain a price advantage. Many hotels and restaurants, however, could not afford to discount, and the result was often irate customers.

While there is no easy solution to the problem, it is one in which, once again, marketing and management are inextricably intertwined. What this means is that reduction of staff is both a marketing decision and a management decision. The impact on the customer must be the first consideration. If service is an element that is being marketed, then service is an element of customer expectation that should be provided because service is being offered as a solution to the customer's problem. It is part of the value for which a sacrifice is made and the risk taken.

Finally, while it is popular to talk about the perishability of the hospitality product, the often-forgotten flip side of that characteristic is its perpetuability—the product can be sold over and over again. Doing this, of course, depends upon demand—and nothing maintains constant demand better than keeping customers.

Heterogeneity

Heterogeneity of service is concerned with the variation and lack of uniformity in the service being performed. The service received by a guest at the front desk of a hotel may be much better (or much worse) than that received at the restaurant in the same hotel. Here we mean something different from lack of service caused by insufficient staff; instead we mean fluctuations in service caused by the human element, individual differences among employees and among customers themselves, as well as customers' perceptions of these differences.

On any given day, a hotel guest may come in contact with at least 25 different employees. The switchboard operator, front desk clerk, restaurant manager, housekeeper, all are likely to have some contact with the guest. To have 25 different contacts all go well for, perhaps, as many as 300 guests in one day, is a marketing task that is truly a special case.

Consistency of service may be very difficult if only because of the human-intensive nature of providing service. Manuals may well prescribe exactly what every employee in a large restaurant is supposed to do in any given situation, but they can never predict what various individuals with various backgrounds, orientations, and personalities will actually do in a given situation.

The Consumer   Understanding customers' problems can mean a lot more than smiling at the customer and believing "the customer is always right." First of all, customers themselves are heterogeneous; they are not exactly alike. Consider, for example, an elderly woman at a hotel's front desk who needs considerable help in understanding where things are in the hotel, how to work the electronic key in her door, and how to get assistance when she needs it. The service-oriented desk clerk patiently and graciously explains these things to the woman, who will depart from the hotel to tell all her friends how nice the employees are. Unfortunately, the person waiting in line behind this woman may be a businessperson anxious to get to a meeting. As a frequent traveler, this individual knows the ropes and only wants to register, get the key, and be on the way. This person will depart from the hotel and tell friends about the wait in line and poor service.

Another aspect of service heterogeneity is that the knowledge, experience, and proficiency of the customer affect the quality of consumption. One customer says, "Look at the full glass of wine they give you!" Another says, "Don't they know that a glass of wine should never be more than half full?" One customer says, "Boy, this Veal Oscar is good!" Another says, "Don't they know that Veal Oscar should be served with Bearnaise sauce, not Hollandaise?" Obviously, there is a wide variation in the consumers' measurements of quality, and what satisfies one may very well not satisfy another. Regardless, what consumers experience, they pay for; they cannot exchange that experience for another one.

The Marketer   Marketers of services who make promises to customers have two strikes against them. The first is the question of how the employee with whom customers come face-to-face will handle the situation. The second is the customers themselves. What is appropriate treatment of one is inappropriate to another; service to one customer may affect service to

another. The consequence is that good service may equal bad service.

For the marketer, the heterogeneity of services constitutes a lack of assurance that the product you market is what you actually sell or produce. For the consumer, it means risk and a lack of assurance that what you buy is what you get. In the hospitality industry, the consumer often perceives the personnel as the service, so that one unpleasant interaction with personnel can result in criticism of the entire experience. Customers' problems are infinite in number and diverse in scope but, petty or significant, they are real to the customer and a problem to the marketer.

Many companies have attempted to overcome the difficulties of heterogeneity through what Theodore Levitt has termed the industrialization of service.[5] Levitt sees these problems as special opportunities, and so they may well be. (Certainly they should be analyzed closely with that possibility in mind, but the customer must be knowlegeable about service improvements—technological advances, such as utilizing electronic door locks and receiving your bill in your room on television, fall into this category.) Some fast-food restaurants provide an excellent example of industrializing a service to near-uniform performance. Little room is left for human judgment or error. Salad bars in other restaurants and budget motels are other examples.

Budget motels and salad bars are only two examples of a phenomenon to be pondered by the hospitality marketer: When is less service more service, and vice versa? Or, to put it another way, when should service be more personal and when should it be less personal? Numerous studies have shown that salad bars are very popular with a majority of the eating-out public because you can "do it yourself." Yet, the salad bar is actually less service, since you have to get your own food. Whether in this case less service is more depends on the individual customer's perception of salad bars, and clearly

---

[5]Theodore Levitt, "The Industrialization of Service," in Theodore Levitt, ed., *The Marketing Imagination*, New York: Free Press, 1986, pp. 50–71.

what satisfies one customer does not necessarily satisfy another.

Are budget motels offering service when they sometimes, literally, just throw the key at you and make sure you pay first? For some, yes, you get what you pay for; for others, no. On the other hand, a friend told us how impressed he was when he came downstairs the first morning at a five-star hotel and was greeted by name by all the staff. By the third day, however, he had become irritated at having to go through this interchange of pleasantries every morning.

It is not hard to see that the marketer faces many problems when trying to cope with the heterogeneity of services, or even when trying to provide solutions to consumers' problems. The answer, at least partially, lies in knowing your market and your customers and the custom-tailoring of services. This means the emphasis should be on the customer, not on the service.[6] We will address this subject in more detail in later chapters.

Simultaneity of Production and Consumption

The service characteristic of simultaneous production and consumption is somewhat unique among service characteristics. It is also the strongest foundation for the premise that management *is* marketing in the hospitality industry. This is so because, in the case of services, the buyer must be present to experience (consume) the service provided (produced) by the seller. Thus, production and consumption occur simultaneously. These close interactions often result in interpersonal relationships between the buyer and seller that may supersede the service itself.

The Consumer Personal interactions in the marketplace are not new, of course. We have them at the supermarket, the department store, the automobile dealership, and other places where intangible services sell very tangible products. The difference between intangible services and tangible goods, however, is critical. Unless a marketplace situation is totally unacceptable, people are still likely to visit the same store to buy goods even if their relationship with the salesperson is not the best. This is because they are buying something other than the service. If goods-seeking customers respond to an advertisement for a brand of sneakers, they go to purchase the sneakers. Regardless of whether their experience in the store is less than satisfactory, the clerk not knowledgeable about the product, the check-out lines too long, in any case the customers purchase the sneakers, take them home and "consume" them. If the sneakers fall apart, the maker is far away, perhaps even in some foreign country.

In hospitality, that is not the case. The entire product—service *and* goods—is consumed on premise with the seller (producer) on hand. The customer is buying the service. One individual can totally personify the service of a particular establishment and cause a customer not to return. Being merely a smiling, call-you-by-your-name clerk is not enough in a service environment in which each employee is literally part of the product, in which each employee is producing while the customer consumes.

Another facet of the simultaneous production/consumption characteristic of a hospitality purchase is that you don't know what you are buying until after you have consumed it. When you think about it, that seems like a pretty stupid thing to do, but that's what we do when we buy a service, even if we have bought the same service before. The heterogeneity principle of services supports this premise. Obviously, there are exceptions to this rule in services: If we have been to the same doctor 20 times, we pretty well know what to expect. In some cases this will also be true in hotels and restaurants, but to a lesser extent because of the heterogeneity principle. In most cases, however, every time we purchase a service, we assume a new risk.

The Marketer The interaction of marketing and production is inescapable in the hospitality business, so let us go back to the friendly and smiling employee. The customer cannot

---

[6]Cf. Robert C. Lewis and Michael Nightingale, "Targeting Service to Your Customer," *Cornell Hotel and Restaurant Administration Quarterly,* August, 1991, pp. 18–27.

consume what the employee cannot produce. Employees may be given "smile training," but still be restricted in their ability to solve consumers' problems; smiles in these cases are of little avail. Thus, the marketer must be able to produce *while* the customer consumes and in a way that solves the customer's problem on the spot.

To add insult to injury, another aspect of the simultaneous production and consumption of hospitality services is that the buyer is subject to the seller's rules for usage, and these rules become an element of the service. Some rules are necessary in hospitality premises; but many rules are operations-driven and formulated to prevent the customer from "getting in the way," serving only operational efficiency. Other rules may be totally frivolous or archaic, but management doesn't stop to question why they exist or if they should. For example, such rules as "Sorry, that section is closed," or "The pool doesn't open until 10:00," or, on a menu, "No substitutes allowed" become part of the service because they restrict the consumer's consumption. It wouldn't hurt for every hospitality operation to periodically review rules that affect the customer and question why they exist.

Tying together the above four elements of service, we have come up with the following definition of the *hospitality product:* The hospitality product is *something that prospective buyers, for the most part, cannot fully grasp with the senses before buying. Consumers do not know if they will get what they think they are buying. After they buy it they must wait until the seller produces it before they can consume it, sometimes after having paid for it. It may be available today at $50, but not tomorrow at $150. The seller is not totally sure that he or she can produce it, and the buyer must consume it at the same time according to the seller's rules. What's more, if buyers don't like what they get, they can't take it back, get an exchange, or, in most cases, get their money back.*

Although this definition may appear to be a little extreme, perhaps we can better understand the problems of hospitality marketing if we consider the product in this light. After all,

this does describe the position in which the buyer is placed.

Other Aspects of the Service Component

There are a number of other aspects of the service component of the hospitality product that impact on the marketing effort. One of these is that the needs of buyers may be totally unrecognized by them; thus, they do not notice it until it is missing. This factor places a burden on the marketer to anticipate buyers' needs. There is really only one way to do this and that is by putting yourself in the customer's shoes and thinking like a customer. Mike Leven, President of Holiday Inns Worldwide, tells a story demonstrating this point by recounting what took place when he was Senior Vice-President of Americana Hotels:

> I was waiting in the lobby of our Jamaica property with some other of our executives about 6:00 A.M. one morning, waiting for the limo to take us to the airport. Also waiting for the same limo to catch the same flight were half a dozen guests who had just checked out. Suddenly, down the hallway came the F&B manager and a waiter wheeling a cart with fresh orange juice, coffee, and Danish. I thought to myself, "Now here's a management that knows how to take care of its customers," until I watched them wheel the cart right past the guests and in front of us.
>
> I immediately grabbed the cart, turned it around, and wheeled it back in front of the guests. I couldn't help but think, "If only we treated our customers as well as we treat ourselves."

The absence of the coffee cart might have had no effect on the guests' perception of the hotel's service quality. After all, coffee is not what they came to Jamaica to buy. On the other hand, the presence of the coffee cart could have had considerable impact, because the customer leaves with a warm feeling about the concerns of this hotel for its customers. If they return to this hotel and the same situation and there is no coffee cart, they may then question the service quality.

Another critical aspect of the hospitality product are the additional services that affect the basic product of rooms, meals, and so on.

TABLE 2-1   Functional Differences Between Services and Goods

Functional Characteristics	Goods	Services
Unit definition	Precise	General
Ability to measure	Objective	Subjective
Creation	Manufactured	Delivered
Distribution	Separated from production	Same as production
Communications	Tangible	Intangible
Pricing	Cost basis	Limited cost basis
Flexibility of producer	Limited	Broad
Time interval	Months to years	Simultaneous or shortly after
Delivery	Consistent	Variable
Shelf life	Days to years	Zero
Customer perception	Standardized—what you see	Have to consume to evaluate
Marketing	Traditional, external	Nontraditional, largely internal

Source: Adapted from a talk by Thomas Fitzgerald, Vice-President, ARA Service, Ltd., American Marketing Association Services Conference, Orlando, 1981.

Although the customer reserves only a room or a table, an almost endless number of peripheral services are expected to accompany that room or table. In the extreme, such as at a resort hotel in Jamaica, this could even include whether the sun shines. Certainly it includes the beach, the pool, the entertainment, the sports facilities, and many other features that accompany the resort image. In a restaurant, it includes the lighting, the noise level, the print size on the menu, water glasses filled and ashtrays emptied, and even, perhaps, where you have to park your car. The marketer and management cannot escape the responsibility for all of these surrounding attributes. The more obvious tangible components of the purchase bundle, however, may lead management to concentrate on those elements to the detriment of the peripheral or intangible elements. For a service firm the intangibles are an integral part of the total product bundle. Thus, the service delivery system must be designed with the presence of the consumer in mind.[7]

---

[7]Conversely, management may neglect the tangible components because they don't have the presence of the guests in mind. Hotels, even the four-star ones for example, are infamous for having only one comfortable chair in a room that is sold to a couple on a weekend package; or having 60-watt bulbs on desks for business travelers.

Table 2-1 summarizes what has been said about the differences between services and manufactured goods, and depicts some of the problems of the hospitality marketer.

Keeping Hospitality Customers

The fact that management and marketing are inseparable in hospitality creates unique problems for the keeping of customers. This is because most of what hospitality products *do* for the customer takes place at the property. The solutions to those problems require an extension of nontraditional marketing, which can be broken down into two major categories: internal marketing and relationship marketing, mentioned at the end of Chapter 1. We will discuss each in turn.

Internal Marketing

Internal marketing means applying marketing principles to the people who serve the customers. The emphasis of internal marketing is on the employee as the internal customer who also

FIGURE 2-4 Keeping employees means keeping customers. One of a series
of Four Seasons ads

CHARLES IS THE CONSUMMATE
AMBASSADOR. HE CAN USHER
YOU FROM CHAOS TO COMFORT
IN MERE MOMENTS.

He will relieve you of all cares as well as your luggage. By welcoming you to a serene enclave where requests are carried out with distinction and dispatch, meals may be enjoyed in your room at any hour, and you are courteously awakened with the day's forecast, thus properly prepared for the elements. Invariably, Charles greets you with a good word and winning smile. Perhaps because no one knows better than our front-line ambassadors the warm, comfortable realm that awaits you behind the Four Seasons door.

Four Seasons
Hotels·Resorts

FIGURE 2-4   (continued)

has needs, wants, and problems. What this customer is buying is his or her job. Thus, the job is the product that satisfies the needs and wants of these internal customers so that they, in turn, will better satisfy the needs and wants of the external customer.

At first glance, this may appear to be a strange way to look at marketing; it is certainly not the way that we look at the marketing of goods. However, a closer look makes the case obvious: One of the first tasks of marketing and management is to have the employees believe in their job, which is the product that they represent to the customer. The successful hospitality firm must first sell its jobs to employees before it can sell its services to its customers. If this is not done, we end up with disgruntled employees who will, one way or another, express their dissatisfaction to paying customers. Paying customers, in turn, find that their problems are not adequately solved, so they go elsewhere. Clearly, this is not the way to keep customers. Thus, what is practiced in the creation and keeping of customers needs also to be practiced in the creation and keeping of employees. An example is shown in Figure 2-4.

Management Practices

Keeping good employees leads to keeping good customers. The quality of services depends in large measure on the skills and attitudes of the people producing the services. An acceptable product is necessary to appeal to the external market. The same is true of the internal market. Employees, an integral part of the product in hospitality, must also be marketing-oriented. Unless a firm has something to offer to its employees, it should not expect marketing-oriented behavior. Just as we select customers whose needs we can best meet, we must select employees whose needs can be met through a job in our organization.

Understanding the simultaneous production and consumption nature of services is helpful in understanding what has just been stated. Many companies conduct employee courses in customer handling, including what trainees have dubbed "smile training." Smile training, as we

have said previously, is not enough. Consider the room service waiter who arrives an hour late with breakfast, a big smile, and a "How are you folks today?" instead of a somber "I'm sorry." (Does a smile, or lack of one, make up for an hour's wait for breakfast?) Or, the following anecdote, told by a front desk clerk of a large convention hotel:

> A large convention was checking into the hotel all day, and we never had a chance to get away from the desk and take a break for coffee, or even for lunch. We were smiling our damndest, dealing with all the problems, and things were going fairly smoothly considering the circumstances. After a while, however, it began to get to us, so we devised a little sing-song communication and banter among ourselves, which helped to keep our sense of humor and keep us going. While all this was going on, our supervisors were sitting in a room behind the front desk, talking and drinking coffee. Occasionally, one would step out and, seeing that all was going well, would go back to the room and leave us to carry on. When they heard our banter, however, things changed. One of us was called into the back room and told to tell the others to cut it out. Our attitudes changed immediately. We kept on working, but we couldn't have cared less about the customers and it showed.

The impact of this anecdote is that marketing principles have not been applied to these employees' jobs. Customer satisfaction has been given token attention rather than being treated as a philosophy. Employees will not "buy" the product, customer service, when it appears that management is not willing to deliver on its promise of what it is "selling." The anecdote demonstrates that the old expression "practice what you preach" is also the essence of internal marketing.

There is a natural conflict between company policies and the ability of the employee to satisfy customers. The very nature of the service business implies that it is impossible to anticipate all the needs and wants of customers. Obviously, there must be policies to guide employee actions, and no one is suggesting that there are easy solutions to these conflicts; but it is just as obvious that there must be flexibility. Instead of binding employees into "nega-

Dear Guests:

Welcome to Guest Quarters Suite Hotels and Guest Quarters Magazine — an informative guide to this hotel's community, as well as interesting and entertaining reading on a variety of subjects.

I would like to take this opportunity to share something with you that is new and exciting at all Guest Quarters Suite Hotels. It's not a new amenity or special promotion — in fact, you can't touch or see this at all. But, when you stay at any Guest Quarters, you will sense what we are calling employee empowerment.

Employee empowerment means that at Guest Quarters, all of our employees have been trained and authorized to handle your inquiries on-the-spot. Whether it be a concern over our quality levels or a special request, Guest Quarters employees have been given the tools to make your stay flawless, without having to find a supervisor. (Of course, there are special situations which require the attention of a manager.)

Employee empowerment takes our award-winning service levels one step higher. It provides you with a more efficient and effective staff that is eager to serve you. Just as importantly, empowerment further demonstrates our confidence in our company's most valuable asset — our employees.

The results? I can't express how proud I am of how our employees have utilized empowerment. Rather than just exercise their decision-making privileges to address negative guest situations, Guest Quarters employees are going "above and beyond the call of duty" to provide unexpected touches and unanticipated acts of kindness. This is the true meaning of hospitality.

As we move forward in this decade which has been designated the "Decade of Customer Service," I am confident that Guest Quarters will continue to be one of the hotel industry's shining stars. I invite you to visit any of our 30 locations nationwide to experience impeccable service, coupled with the luxury of a suite.

Sincerely,

Richard M. Kelleher
President Guest Quarters Suite Hotels

FIGURE 2-5   Employee empowerment for the customer

tive guest situations," progressive companies, like Guest Quarters, are embracing the concept of employee empowerment (Figure 2-5), in which line employees are allowed to make decisions that address guests' immediate prob-

lems, without seeking prior approval of their supervisors.

The Peabody Hotel in Orlando, Florida and the Opryland Hotel in Nashville, Tennessee are two properties that have managed to "break the mold" for customer service. Visiting these hotels, both of over 1,000 rooms, one is completely impressed with the level of service offered by *everyone*. Each hotel has over 800 employees continuously interacting with guests. Every employee verbally and visually engages the customer and is empowered to satisfy that customer's needs and ask questions later. Ritz-Carlton employees are empowered to spend up to $2,000 to satisfy a customer. According to Patrick Mene, head of quality control at Ritz-Carlton, "To us, empowerment means giving the employees responsibility for solving guests' problems."[8] This leads Ritz-Carlton to run ads like that in Figure 2-6.

Customers have a wide variety of expectations. Although the customer is *not* always right, there is not much to be gained in proving the customer wrong. Employees, instead, must be empowered to make the customer "feel right." This constitutes marketing to both the customer and the employee—that whatever influences customers must be marketed to all employees.

The Internal Marketing Concept

Motivating employees is not a new management task but neither is it solely a function of the organization's personnel department. The effort that supports the concept of internal marketing starts with top management and involves management at every level of the organization. Lower-level employees, whether they are customer contact or not, cannot be expected to be customer conscious if management above them is not similarly involved. Management style and decisions must support this orientation, not counteract it. Personnel policies, likewise, must reflect this orientation and practice it in the form of job-filling, recruiting, and promotion. We can take this one step further: If internal marketing is not incorporated into the management culture, the direction of the firm may make implementation of internal marketing difficult or even impossible at lower levels.

[8]Charles G. Partlow, "How Ritz-Carlton applies TQM," *Cornell Hotel and Restaurant Administration Quarterly,* August, 1993, p. 20.

The comments of the general manager of a large hotel, recorded in Table 2-2, are worth noting in this regard. Two other views of the internal marketing culture are given in Table 2-3. Successful internal marketing considerably eases the task of implementing the second element of nontraditional marketing, relationship marketing, or the primary task of keeping customers, to which we now turn.

Relationship Marketing

Customers are assets. They are the most important assets a company can have. It is good business management to protect your assets, but assets like buildings, or a warehouse of goods, do not produce profits; the customer that buys the goods does. Relationship marketing is defined as marketing to protect the customer base. It sees the customer as an asset. Its function is to attract, maintain, and enhance customer relationships.

Relationship marketing should be practiced in all industries. Consider, for example, Whirlpool's "hot line" for customers who buy its appliances and have problems or need help. Perhaps no one has been more cognizant of this need than the computer and software industries, many members of which provide toll-free service to help their customers become "friendly" with their user-friendly products. Simon Cooper, President of Delta Hotels in Canada, and the GM of *each* Delta Hotel, have their personal phone numbers in every hotel room.

Nowhere is relationship marketing more applicable than in service industries in general and the hospitality industry in particular. Relationship marketing is most applicable when

1. There is an ongoing and periodic desire for service by the customer.
2. The service customer controls the selection of the service supplier.
3. There are alternative supplier choices.
4. Customer loyalty is weak and switching is common and easy.

AFTER A DAY OF COMPETITION, YOU DESERVE A HOTEL THAT HAS NONE.

We take the hassle and hustle out of being away from home on business. At The Ritz-Carlton, Buckhead you can expect all your business needs to be granted. You can also expect impeccable service in surroundings that are always comfortable and productive. So you'll be rested, relaxed and ready for the next day of competition. For information or reservations, please call 800-241-3333, 404-237-2700 or your travel professional.

THE RITZ-CARLTON®
BUCKHEAD
The Leading Hotels of the World

FIGURE 2-6   Ritz-Carlton defies the competition

TABLE 2-2   The Internal Marketing Culture I

The solution to this dilemma [between employee and management] lies with responsibility at all levels of management. Once the leadership role has been established, line employees will follow suit. To change the way an organization works, each manager must assume that she or he is 100 percent responsible for everything that happens in the work environment. To step this concept down, imagine the post-convention analysis of a front office manager: "The lines were too long because housekeeping didn't have the rooms ready on time, the VIP checked in one hour before she was supposed to, and checkout was screwed up because the sales office didn't tell me that it was a package plan."

The result? A convention that will never come back to the hotel again. You can rest assured that the front office manager in no way feels responsible for the problem. Queries to the housekeeper and sales director will reveal similar conclusions. Line employees pick up on this attitude and begin to transfer the feelings to the next customer.

Contrast this with the front office manager who checked the room status, prepared for the VIP's possible early arrival, and went to the sales office to discuss billing. This manager has taken control of the situation, satisfied the convention, and exemplified the intangible leadership necessary for internal marketing. Internal marketing will never be executed properly until the department head understands the concept of 100 percent responsibility.

TABLE 2-3   The Internal Marketing Culture II

[S]ervice of exceptional quality can be delivered only by highly motivated people.... Managers either succeed in creating a climate in which people are encouraged to release their inbuilt motivation or they create a climate which stifles it....[C]reating the right climate for our employees is as important as creating the right climate for the client. Success in one reinforces and enhances the other.[a]

Service providers treat customers similar to the way they, as employees, are treated by management.... The employees in turn convey the identical message to the customer. If management treats employees' concerns with indifference, then employees will not care about the customers' complaints. Managers must provide services to the employees in a friendly, helpful and efficient manner that will enable those employees to better serve the customers. Customers thus become the beneficiaries of high-quality service that mirrors the organization's inner working.[b]

[a]John Sharpe, "The Challenge of Effectively Managing," *Foodservice and Hospitality,* October 1985, pp. 58, 60. 1987, p. 20.
[b]Robert E. Kelley, "Poorly served employees serve customers just as poorly," *Wall Street Journal,* October 12, 1987, p. 20.

5. Word-of-mouth is an especially potent form of communication about a product.[9]

These conditions are obviously quite prevalent in the hospitality industry. We don't sell one-time services, and the consumer has many choices, especially today. In an era of heavy hotel building and restaurant openings, any hotel or restaurant is especially vulnerable to new competition. Most everyone likes to try a new place. The question is, will they come back? Do we offer a competitive product on dimensions that are meaningful to customers, solve customer problems, and are difficult for competi-

[9]Adapted from L. L. Berry, "Relationship Marketing," in *Emerging Perspectives on Services Marketing,* L. L. Berry, G. D. Shostack, and G. D. Upah, eds., Chicago: American Marketing Association, 1983, p. 25.

tors to duplicate? This is what relationship marketing is all about, and when the above conditions pertain, the opportunities to practice it are abundant.

Ongoing Relationships

In relationship marketing, moreover, the process doesn't stop there. The relationship marketer works to maintain the relationship long after the formal production/consumption process has ended, seeking not only to keep customers but to bring them back as well. Levitt compares the relationship to something like a marriage:

> The sale merely consummates the courtship. Then the marriage begins. How good the marriage is depends on how well the relationship is managed by the seller. That determines whether there will be continued or expanded business or troubles and divorce, and whether costs or profits increase.
>
> …It is not just that once you get a customer you want to keep him. It is more a matter of what the buyer wants. He wants a vendor who will keep his promises, who'll keep supplying and stand behind what he promised. The age of the blind date or the one-night stand is gone. Marriage is both more convenient and more necessary.… In these conditions success in marketing, like success in marriage, is transformed into the inescapability of a relationship.[10]

Service is not an event any more than a marriage is. It is a process creating an environment of information, assurance, and comfort for the customer. It has its focus on building loyal customer relationships.

Building Loyalty

The true sense and purpose of relationship marketing is to maintain the customer relationship and build loyalty. To offer special attractions and rewards to obtain customers, and to continue to give those rewards to keep customers

are in the vein of traditional marketing. Frequent-traveler programs do not constitute relationship marketing in the true sense. These programs are really "buying" customers and "buying" their repeated patronage; they are not creating or keeping customers in the marketing sense of creating loyalty. Most frequent-traveler beneficiaries are unfaithful; they will go where the grass looks the greenest, without remorse. The reason for this is readily apparent: Frequent-traveler programs do not solve consumers' problems or satisfy needs and wants. Instead, they provide something for nothing; in the long run, someone has to pay for it.[11]

So-called "twofer" programs (two for the price of one) and other types of restaurant promotions also have the trappings of relationship marketing but have been found lacking. Those who take advantage of these promotions often would not come to the restaurant otherwise, and won't come back.

Relationship marketing means getting and keeping the customer because of his or her relationship with you. It should not be necessary to give away something that you would not otherwise give away—an observation that Stouffer Hotels trumpeted in a 1993 advertising campaign when Bill Hulett was its president and Stouffer was a Nestlé company (Figure 2-7). In fact, if the relationship is strong, the customer may be willing to pay even more because of it. The view of marketing as only an external activity is both shortsighted and self-defeating.

Relationship marketing means thinking in terms of the customers we have, rather than just in terms of the ones we hope to acquire. This is crucial in the hospitality industry. Competition is standing by, all too ready and willing to take the customers you can't keep.

Attracting new customers is only the beginning of marketing in the hospitality industry.

---

[10]Theodore Levitt, "Marketing Intangible Products and Product Intangibles," *Harvard Business Review,* May–June, 1981, pp. 94–102. Copyright © 1981 by the President and Fellows of Harvard College; all rights reserved.

[11]As we predicted in the first edition, "Some hotel frequent-stay plans may be next on the endangered list…. [S]ome chains may be finding frequent-stay plans too expensive, costing about $350 million annually." Radisson Hotels ended its plan in 1989, Inter-Continental Hotels in 1993. Only 12 percent of business travelers, in a survey in April, 1994, said such plans influenced their hotel decision. Jacqueline Simmons, "Tracking Travel," *Wall Street Journal,* June 28, 1994, p. B1.

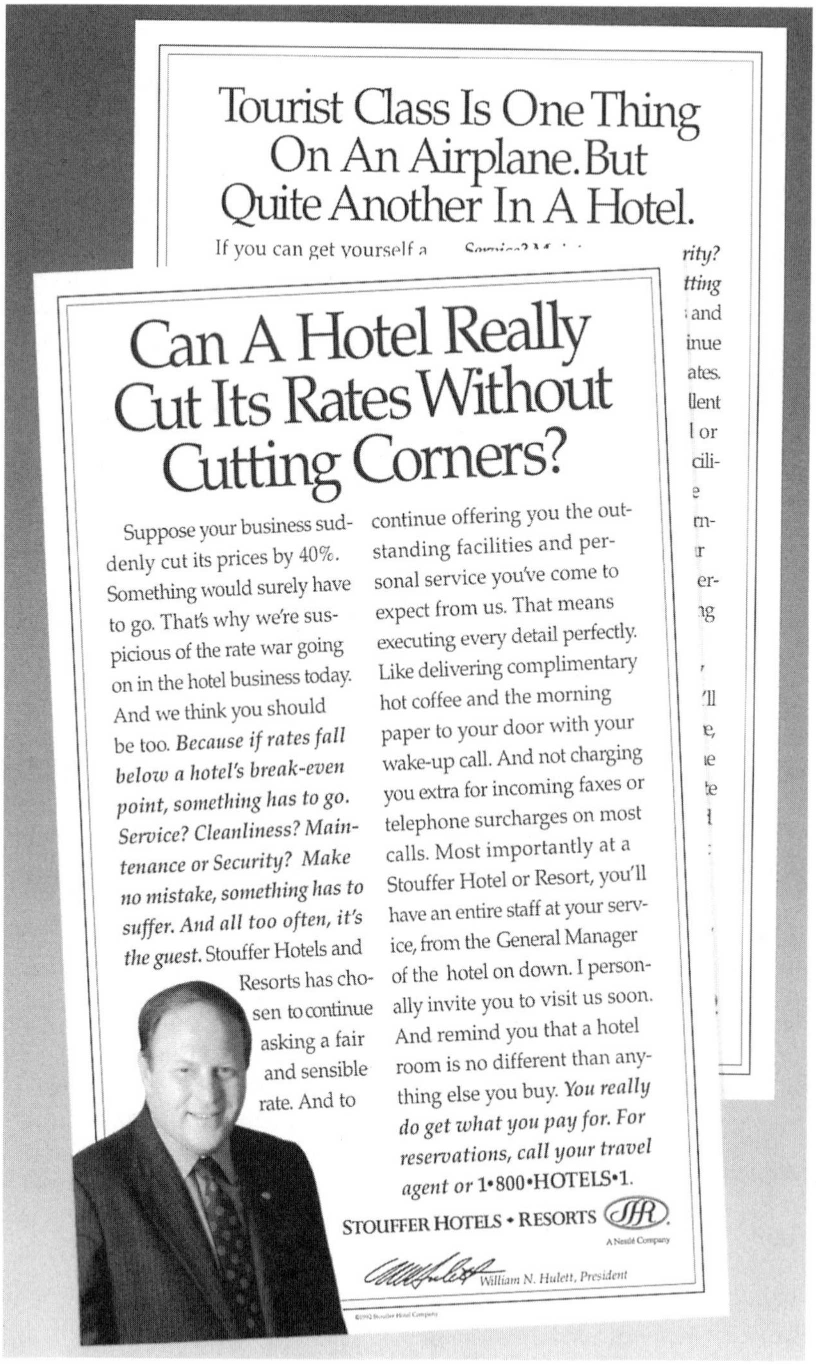

Tourist Class Is One Thing On An Airplane. But Quite Another In A Hotel.

If you can get yourself a ... Service? M... ...rity?
...tting
...and
...inue
...ates.
...lent
...l or
...cili-
...e
...m-
...r
...er-
...ng

Can A Hotel Really Cut Its Rates Without Cutting Corners?

Suppose your business suddenly cut its prices by 40%. Something would surely have to go. That's why we're suspicious of the rate war going on in the hotel business today. And we think you should be too. *Because if rates fall below a hotel's break-even point, something has to go. Service? Cleanliness? Maintenance or Security? Make no mistake, something has to suffer. And all too often, it's the guest.* Stouffer Hotels and Resorts has chosen to continue asking a fair and sensible rate. And to continue offering you the outstanding facilities and personal service you've come to expect from us. That means executing every detail perfectly. Like delivering complimentary hot coffee and the morning paper to your door with your wake-up call. And not charging you extra for incoming faxes or telephone surcharges on most calls. Most importantly at a Stouffer Hotel or Resort, you'll have an entire staff at your service, from the General Manager of the hotel on down. I personally invite you to visit us soon. And remind you that a hotel room is no different than anything else you buy. *You really do get what you pay for. For reservations, call your travel agent or 1•800•HOTELS•1.*

STOUFFER HOTELS • RESORTS
A Nestlé Company

William N. Hulett, President

Courtesy of Stouffer Hotels & Resorts

FIGURE 2-7   Paying more for the right relationship

Marketing must also include building lasting relationships, creating loyal customers, and serving customers as valued clients. L.L. Berry has noted five specific strategies for doing this.[12] We elaborate on each of these below.

Core Services   Core services are based on central rather than peripheral market needs. They are the services around which the customer relationship is built, because they attract new customers by meeting their needs, cement the business through their quality and enduring nature, and provide the means for offering additional services over time. An example of offering a new core service is the suite hotel concept—a suite, including breakfast and drinks, for the price of a regular room.

Customizing the Relationship   Because hospitality services are flexible to a large degree, they can often be customized. Here, hospitality businesses have a considerable advantage over goods manufacturers because they have the customers in-house, on premise, where there is tremendous opportunity to learn about particular customers and their specific problems and to tailor the service to solve those problems. At Caneel Bay Resort on St. John in the Caribbean, guests are allowed to store for their *next* vacation anything that they do not want to carry back home, including such things as suntan lotion, swimsuits, and snorkel gear. For their next visit, these belongings are placed in their rooms before arrival. Figure 2-8 shows some more recent methods of delivering amenities that build relationships but cost little.

Service Augmentation   Service augmentation means building "extras" into services, especially those that are difficult for the competition to copy. These extras must be genuine, extras that have meaning and value for the customer. Fancy bathroom amenities and mints on pillows, although introduced in this sense, do not fill the criterion unless they are something

the customer genuinely values. When the customer simply packs them to take home, they do not add value, only cost.

On the other hand, consider Little Dix Bay Resort on Virgin Gorda in the Caribbean. Accessibility to this island requires several changes in flights on small commuter airlines; therefore, guests often arrive at the resort before their baggage. This resort assigns one person the responsibility of tracing and retrieving lost baggage. In addition, these guests are given a free "survival" kit of essential toiletries in a bag with the hotel's logo on it.

In a hotel or restaurant, it is not easy to add amenities or augmented services that the competition cannot duplicate, but this should not deter the effort when it serves a need. Recalling an earlier comment—that one problem with services is that they are not noticed until they are *missing*—in many cases, just the presence of a service becomes a service augmentation.

An example that demonstrates this point is the pull-out clothesline that many hotels, even older ones, have installed in bathrooms to solve a traveler's laundry problem. When a national chain's new 1,200-room hotel opened recently, the housekeeper was asked why such clotheslines had not been installed. The response was, "They're too much trouble." This management didn't understand service augmentation.

There are many ways that today's hotels and restaurants can augment, or personalize, service. One way to find out what they are is to talk to customers, something the relationship marketer will do on a regular basis. Customers will always have problems that need solving.

Relationship Pricing   Hotels commonly give "quantity discounts" to companies that agree to book so many room-nights a year. They also discount rooms for large groups. Frequent traveler plans were discussed earlier, but relationship pricing can go far beyond these practices, which ignore a large part of the market and should deal with rewarding loyalty.

Suppose, for example, that regular hotel customers were allowed to order wine or liquor room service, by the bottle, without paying the

---

[12]L.L. Berry, "Services Marketing Is Different," *Business*, May–June, 1980, p. 25.

To make your stay more enjoyable,
we have the following special amenities
available upon request:

Conditioner	Body Lotion
Emery Board	Talc
Fabric Wash	Sewing Kit

Lint Brush

*Please call Housekeeping for delivery
at Ext. 35*

Holiday Inn
CROWNE PLAZA®
WHITE PLAINS

Dear Guest,

We know you had a choice and, we thank you for choosing Holiday Inn Crowne Plaza,® White Plains.

If we can be of any assistance during your stay, please feel free to give me a call by dialing "O".

Thank you.

Stephen P. Mitchell
General Manager

3m 4/90

The "Sorry You Couldn't Wait" Card

294 Adelaide Street West, Toronto, Ontario M5V 1P6

FIGURE 2-8   Amenities that build relationships without the cost

SHR

*Your freshly brewed beverage
and this morning's newspaper
have arrived with our compliments.*

A Stouffer Hotels and Resorts Tradition

Today's Weather Forecast

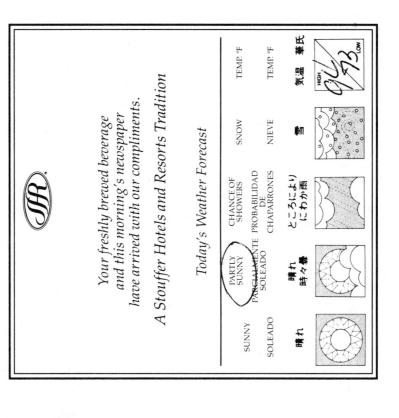

SUNNY	PARTLY SUNNY	CHANCE OF SHOWERS	SNOW	TEMP. °F
SOLEADO	PARCIALMENTE SOLEADO	PROBABILIDAD DE CHAPARRONES	NIEVE	TEMP. °F
晴れ	晴れ時々曇	ところにより にわか雨	雪	気温 華氏

SHR

*As a courtesy
to our guests, we
offer free overnight
shoeshine service.*

*Shoes turned in
by 9:00 P.M. will
be brilliantly shined
and returned to your
door by 7:00 A.M.*

*Please call
the bell captain
to take advantage
of this service.*

FIGURE 2-8 (continued)

Courtesy of Signature Inns, Inc. and Lord, Sullivan & Yoder Agency, Columbus, Ohio

FIGURE 2-9   Relationship pricing

300 to 500 percent markups that appear on most room service lists. Not only would customers feel privileged, they wouldn't feel taken advantage of. The hotel would also benefit, not just from the customers' loyalty but also from the service's being purchased in the hotel instead of at the package store across the street, where many hotel guests now go. All customers have pet peeves about "extras" they have to pay for; they prefer feeling they are getting something "free." Figure 2-9 shows some of both.

Internal Marketing   Internal marketing is the fifth strategy suggested by Berry. Because it has already been discussed in this chapter, there is no need to go into further detail here. We should not, however, overlook the fact that internal marketing may be the most critical phase of relationship marketing.

Summary

The U.S. economy can be broadly divided into manufacturing and service sectors. The hospitality industry is part of the service sector, which has grown to become three times larger than its manufacturing counterpart. In this chapter, it was argued that the differences between the nature of services and manufactured goods require different approaches to their marketing. Services are essentially intangible, heterogeneous, and perishable. In addition, services are produced and consumed at the same time. Of course, hospitality services are also different from other services (such as health care, education, banking, and insurance) and require different marketing strategies. The inseparability of marketing and management creates numerous challenges for marketers and requires the use of both traditional and nontraditional marketing.

Two techniques of nontraditional marketing are internal marketing and relationship marketing. The principle of internal marketing is to market hospitality jobs to employees just as we market hotels or restaurants to customers. Relationship marketing creates good customer relations, an integral part of any company's sustenance and growth. Relationships must be developed and sustained. In a services business, this is hardly possible without developing and sustaining similar employee relations.

Discussion Questions

1. Discuss the argument that the marketing of services is different from the marketing of goods. Give examples, both pro and con, from your experiences.
2. Discuss and explain the goods/environment/services trichotomy of the hospitality product. When is one more/less important than the other?
3. What is the difference between "selling" a job to a prospective employee and "marketing" it?
4. How can you tangibilize the intangible in hospitality marketing?
5. Analyze Cases 2-1 and 2-2 in terms of nontraditional marketing as discussed in the chapter.
6. Analyze Case 2-3 from the perspective of internal and relationship marketing.

✔ Case 2-1
Sojourn in Jamaica[13]

It was a balmy evening in March when the Air Jamaica 727 touched down at the Montego Bay airport in Jamaica. As Mr. and Mrs. Saltzer stepped off the flight they marvelled at the 75-degree weather, the short-sleeve shirts everyone was wearing, and the bright moon in the sky. They had boarded the plane at John F. Kennedy Airport in New York, where the temperature was ten degrees above zero, the ground was covered with snow, and the wind was howling. They were happy to leave all this behind and planned to totally forget it for the next two weeks as they enjoyed a sojourn in Jamaica.

It was a short taxi ride to the Elegant Hotel just outside of Montego Bay, which they had chosen from an ad in a popular magazine (Exhibit 2-1-1). They were soon there, checked in, and unpacked. Having had dinner on the plane, they went downstairs to explore the hotel, after which they stopped for a drink at the circular bar off the lobby. "Wow," they thought, "this is going to be neat. We really made the right decision!" They then retired to bed so as to get an early start in the morning.

The Next Morning

The Saltzers were up bright and early and looked out over the grounds from the balcony of their room before going downstairs for breakfast. The hotel was shaped like a "U" facing the ocean and, from their room in the center, they had a broad view of the ocean with extensions of the "U" projecting out on either side of them. Immediately below them, the Saltzers could see a large, inviting pool with a pool bar with the bar stools in the water. To the right of the pool was a large dining area with about 30 round tables with umbrellas, about ten of which were occupied. In this section, and closer to the hotel, was an extensive breakfast buffet set-up. Farther out, beyond this area and the pool, was a

beach house where sports facilities were offered and, beyond this, the sandy beach with sailfish, other boats, and water sports equipment.

The Saltzers headed for the outside dining area as soon as they got downstairs. Although they only wanted juice and coffee and not the buffet (they were on European plan), they wanted to sit out in the sun, watch the ocean, and forget the New York weather. The maitre d' quickly seated them as close to the ocean as possible. He then suggested that they partake of the buffet at their leisure.

"We only want juice and coffee," they responded.

"Oh," he said, "in that case you can't sit here."

"What do you mean we can't sit here?" said Mrs. Saltzer.

"This is only for people having the buffet," replied the maitre d'.

"Then where can we sit?" said Mr. Saltzer.

"You have to go inside to the coffee shop," was the reply.

Reluctantly, the Saltzers got up and went inside to the coffee shop. They found a booth on the outside of the room by a window. There was no sun shining on them, but they could peer out and see the ocean in the distance.

"Oh, well," they said, "we'll be out there soon enough."

A waitress came and handed them two menus.

"Just orange juice and coffee," they said.

"Oh," she replied, "if you just want orange juice and coffee, you can't sit here."

"Why not?" they said.

"This room is only for people ordering from the menu," was the reply.

"Then where can we sit?"

"You can sit in the other room at the counter."

The Saltzers went into the other room. There was no sun, no ocean, no windows, and no view. "How do we know we're not still in New York?" they wondered. They decided to skip breakfast and head for the waterfront.

At lunchtime, the Saltzers ran into the same

---

[13]Names have been disguised.

Exhibit 2-1-1   Ad for the Elegant Hotel

WHERE ADULTS GO WHEN THEY RUN AWAY FROM HOME.

If you're looking for Jamaica's most spectacular vacation setting, no other place comes close.

FEATURES:

-Located on a historical 400 acre sugar plantation.

-500 guest rooms, all with private balcony views.

-5 exquisite dining options.

-7 lighted tennis courts.

-Challenging 18-hole championship golf course.

-Refreshing swim-up pool bar.

-Non-motorized watersports.

-10,000 sq. ft. of meeting space.

-10 minutes from the airport.

problem. There again was a buffet outdoors, of which 30 or 40 people were partaking, and they were told they had to go into the bar restaurant if they didn't want the buffet. They found this restaurant to be empty except for one other couple. They sat down and waited about 20 minutes for the waitress. When she came they ordered two club sandwiches. These came about 45 minutes later; the delay almost causing them to miss their planned train trip into the interior of Jamaica to visit the Appleton rum distillery.

That Evening

The train was not air-conditioned and, although the Saltzers enjoyed the trip, they returned to the hotel at 5:00 P.M. very hot and perspiring from the 90-degree weather. They went straight to their room, put on their bathing suits, and headed for the pool.

On one side of the pool was the pool bar, on the other side were lounge chairs. The Saltzers put their robes, towels, reading materials, etc., on two lounge chairs and jumped into the pool. After swimming a few minutes, they swam up to the pool bar and sat on two of the stools that were otherwise empty. They ordered two of the hotel's signature rum drinks.

"Sorry, the bar is closed," said the bartender, pointing to a sign that stated the bar closed at 6:00 P.M.

"But it's only 5:35," they protested, pointing to the clock above the back bar.

"I know, but it takes us time to check out and close up."

"Come on!" they pleaded, "We just got here. Give us a break."

"Well, okay, let me see your chits."

"What chits?"

"The small cardboard piece you got when you checked in that show that you're a registered guest and can charge to your room."

"Oh, yeah," they said. "They're in our room. We didn't think of them. Besides, if we had them in our bathing suits, they'd be soaking wet by now."

"Well, I have to have your chits," said the bartender.

"Do you think we just parachuted into the pool?" said Mrs. Saltzer.

The bartender finally agreed to call the front desk and verify that the Saltzers were guests of the hotel. After this he served them their drinks and proceeded to close up the bar.

At about 6:00 the Saltzers, still hot, went back into the pool. At the end of the pool was a large sign that another swimmer called to their attention. The sign read, "POOL CLOSES AT 6:00."

"That's ridiculous," thought Mr. Saltzer as he kept on swimming. "No one closes a pool at 6:00 in Jamaica when the temperature is 90 degrees, especially at an expensive resort like this."

At about 6:05 a hotel employee walked along the end of the pool where Mr. Saltzer was swimming and where the sign was located. Catching Mr. Saltzer's attention, the employee called to him, "Do you see that sign?"

"No, I can't read," Mr. Saltzer pretended.

The employee went away, but about ten minutes later he returned carrying two large buckets in each hand. He dumped them into the pool, about five feet from Mr. Saltzer, who quickly realized that the pool was being chlorinated! He got out quickly.

The Saltzers had dinner in the hotel dining room that night. They weren't sure if it was a good dinner or not. By this time they were so upset that they just picked at their food. After a brief discussion they decided to leave the hotel the next day, although they didn't know where they would go.

The next morning they packed their bags and carried them downstairs to the lobby, where they found about 40 people waiting in line to check out. There was one desk clerk handling these check-outs. Also behind the desk, however, were three other employees engaged in conversation but not helping with the check-outs. After about an hour the Saltzers reached the head of the line.

"Why are you checking out today when your reservation is for two weeks?" asked the desk clerk.

"This place stinks!" Mr. Saltzer replied.

"Gee, that's what a lot of people are saying," said the desk clerk. "Why do *you* say that?"

"Just give us our bill," said Mr. Saltzer.

As they rode in the taxi toward Ocho Rios, about 50 miles down the northern coastline, looking for a place to finish their vacation, the Saltzers discussed the comments they had heard from others while standing in line to check out.

"I guess we were lucky," they said, "even if it did cost us $320 for two nights."

✔ Case 2-2
Packing 'em In![14]

Situated in a striking re-creation of an eighteenth-century French farmhouse, La Caille at Quail Run, Utah's priciest restaurant, is peddling its number one commodity—romantic evenings—at a fast and furious pace.

The 20-year-old, 310-seat restaurant, nestled within 22 acres of vineyard and lush gardens about 20 miles from downtown Salt Lake City, enjoys a per-person average of $58 and annual sales of more than $3 million. "La Caille is the highest-priced restaurant in Utah," says an industry observer, "but they do a whale of a business in a state where theme restaurants, with average per-person charges in the mid-teens, have done the best job of attracting customers in recent years." La Caille's ability to sell $20 and $30 entrees supports his belief that it is "the elite of the white-tablecloth restaurants in our state."

How It Works

La Caille's theme concept works, observers say, because its restaurateur–creator, David Johnson, and his partners, Steven Runolfsen and Mark Haug, strive to captivate customers from the moment they hit the property line—a philosophy they say they learned by studying Johnson's idol, Walt Disney. Success is attributed to "setting the tone from the time you turn in through those big iron gates and wind up the cobble drive.... It's not the sort of place you go every week, but it is such an awesome sight the first time you go there—almost like going to Disney World as a small child—that you have to go back because you're afraid you might have missed something."

The three Utah restaurateurs go to considerable trouble and expense to maintain and improve their make-believe world. "We put in 18,000 tulip bulbs every year and 1,000 flats of

bedding plants each spring," Johnson says, outlining just a portion of the planting done annually around the restaurant. Patrons often precede summer meals by strolling through gardens scented and splashed with the colors of begonias, bougainvillea, calla lillies, geraniums, tulips, and such tropical species as banana trees. An assortment of birds, including swans and peacocks, contributes graceful movement and sound.

In the winter, when snow brings out the cuddling instincts of guests, large fireplaces warm the dining rooms on three levels. At times, the icicles that hang from the eaves and from the fountain at the center of the circular drive reflect the twinkling of thousands of electric lights; the lights, when viewed directly, can appear as a miniature galaxy with plenty of stars on which to pin wishes.

Regardless of the season, the restaurant's spire-topped towers, sod roof, and vine-covered walls—complete with "weathered" faux finish—create a visual link to the past. Inside, the wenchlike wardrobe worn by the mostly female waitstaff puts cleavage on parade in the best tradition of *Tom Jones*.

La Caille's menu is a mixture of traditional and contemporary dishes, with entrees such as Utah lamb stuffed with onions and peppers and coated with mustard and parmesan ($30.50), rosette of fresh salmon baked in parchment ($31.50), and boneless breast of duckling with a brandy-fruit sauce ($34). The dessert list is a sampling of true restaurant classics, and its showcase flaming fare (e.g., Baked Alaska at $8) would make a firefighter feel at home.

Maintaining the Image

A good portion of La Caille's profits and energies is annually plowed back into the business. For example, the cobble drive, meandering almost a half mile from the main road to the front door, took a whole summer and 298,000 bricks to finish. Other recent projects were the plant-

---

[14]Paraphrased from Alan Liddle, "Disney touch packs 'em in at Utah's priciest eatery," *Nation's Restaurant News,* January 22, 1990, p. 1. Used with permission.

ing of the vineyard, the construction of an enclosed garden dining room, and the development of a large greenhouse where a tropical rain forest can be produced.

The site was formerly that of a family restaurant operated by Johnson's father. "When we decided to make the move and change the concept," Johnson says, "we wondered how we could keep the old clientele but still let people know the new place was really different." The name was changed from Quail Run to La Caille—*quail* in French—at Quail Run.

The biggest challenge in operating La Caille, Johnson says, is "people: getting them, keeping them, training them, and keeping them trained."

✔ Case 2-3
Houston's[15]

Houston's Restaurants, Inc. is a privately-owned company, with headquarters in Atlanta, Georgia, that has been in business since 1977 when its president, George Biel, opened the first restaurant in Nashville, Tennessee. By 1995 the company had grown to over 25 locations. Continued growth was planned at two restaurants a year.

Although a small company by most chain standards, the restaurants average over $4.5 million a year in sales, probably the highest average sales per unit of any restaurant company in the country. Why does a relatively small company in Atlanta enjoy such incredibly high sales volume and a nationwide reputation for quality food and service? To understand that, you need to understand the philosophy of the company.

Houston's Philosphy

In the 1970s George Biel identified a need for a restaurant concept uniquely positioned between the traditional theme dinner house and the bar-oriented "fun food" segments of the market. Houston's never features trendy menus, arcade games, or artificial antiques in any of its restaurants. What it features are traditional American dishes prepared from "scratch," a handsome understated decor, and a management team with an extreme sense of pride and professionalism.

Houston's is committed to a quality- rather than quantity-oriented growth plan. Its mission is never to compromise the quality of the food, service, or atmosphere in order to open more restaurants. Houston's buys the best possible ingredients, hires the best staff, and uses the best construction materials for all its restaurants—a " Commitment to Excellence " that has enabled Houston's to grow and become one of the nation's outstanding restaurant companies.

Houston's has never opened a restaurant ahead of schedule or before they had the capacity to manage it properly. It has been deliberate, building success on success with nothing held back. A Houston's executive agrees: "Some public restaurants get put on a certain earnings treadmill, and we don't want that. Our existing restaurants are our focus; the growth is an offshoot of that."

Houston's managers represent a diverse range of backgrounds, but they have certain characteristics that are universal. First is a commitment to excellence. Managers must be able to recognize quality and never be willing to compromise the customers' dining experience. A sense of urgency and an ability to implement and enforce standards are essential.

While demanding strict standards of performance and conduct, Houston's also believes in creating a pleasant work environment. Maturity and empathy in dealing with employees is extremely important—that they be treated fairly and with respect at all times. The restaurant industry is an intense experience. Managers with Houston's need a strong work ethic and a willingness to be "hands-on." "Managers do not hesitate to help bus tables or jump behind the line and help out. You will never see a manager standing idly by as cook times mount and customers grow impatient."

While Houston's entry training program is longer and more intense than many other companies', and quality performance is absolutely demanded, Houston's is willing to pay for it. Starting salaries for a college graduate are over $30,000 a year, plus relocation costs, paid health, dental, and life insurance, and all meals. General Managers of a Houston's earn an average base pay of over $75,000 and can earn over $100,000 with bonus.

What It All Adds Up To

A successful restaurant must have a consistent product, perfect execution, and a properly man-

---

[15]Adapted from Houston's corporate recruiting brochure and other sources.

aged program of innovation, according to one industry consultant. Houston's boasts of attaining all three. "Houston's works very hard on its food, and people perceive they are getting a very good food value. The public feels they are getting a better experience at Houston's than at other casual-themed restaurants. They're willing to wait 20 minutes extra for the experience."

Another source, however, offers a different perspective on Houston's: "To insure that its execution is razor-sharp, Houston's management is brutal. Management is very demanding and adheres to all the rules. If one of the waitresses comes in and her oxford pastel shirt has a wrinkle in it, she's sent home." Another restaurateur says that Biel is a "hands-on man who watches the details. He's a sharp operator who works very hard. He gets into the details and makes sure they're done right every time. He's there always checking to see they train their people so the product is always consistently high-quality."

A Houston's executive agrees. "We are very demanding and difficult. We have extremely high standards and expect the best out of everyone. It's a demanding business and you have to lead people to perfection." While he doesn't deny that burnout occurs, he also points out that many general managers are longtime employees.

Houston's has changed its menu somewhat over the years, but basically the look, service, and atmosphere are maintained. "They stick to their knitting," says a competitor. "They're deliberate and careful."

In a tight restaurant market, Houston's stable menu may be one of its most valuable assets. "There are too many restaurants and a shakeout is occurring," says an analyst. "Those that are doing well have evolved a concept and been successful with it; they're not the innovators, they just do it better. Restaurants don't win on concept, price points, or locations. Restaurants succeed by their execution and operation style."

Houston's executives agree. "There's no secret trick to the restaurant business. You just have to work extremely hard. We pride ourselves on being among the best managers in the business. We found a good formula and we haven't changed it. Most restaurants are experiencing lower sales. The business has been down the past five years, but we're not. We just opened our third restaurant in Houston and it's doing great. Nobody is opening anything in Houston."

Houston's also doesn't want their competition copying their look too closely. All the lampshades and lighting fixtures are especially designed and made for Houston's exclusive use. A local craftswoman who makes planters for Houston's says she agreed not to sell any to Houston's competitors.

As for advertising or name-awareness activities, one observer remarked, "They don't have to. Restaurants advertise themselves because they can't separate themselves from the competition. The best advertising in the restaurant business is word-of-mouth. Houston's is one of the rare, lucky restaurants that has word-of-mouth."

Says Houston's, "We're just plodding along but, then, we're three yards ahead and everyone else is in a cloud of dust."

PART II
Managing the Marketing System

CHAPTER 3

The Strategic Marketing System

Today's complex hospitality industry environment requires that organizations be better prepared to anticipate and proact upon internal and external changes. Successful achievement of a firm's objectives depends on the ability of management to respond to opportunities in an ever-changing environment. Strategic marketing includes all the decisions and actions used to formulate and implement strategies designed to achieve the marketing objectives of an organization.

In this chapter we will clarify the use of the word *strategy* in the marketing or management context. We will then enlarge upon the process of strategic marketing planning and demonstrate its importance in any marketing context. A strategic framework will be presented to show how all of the various elements fit together. In Chapter 4 we will explain how an annual marketing plan that includes these strategies is developed.

Marketing Management vs. Strategic Planning

First, we need to differentiate between marketing management and strategic marketing.

Some people place *strategy* largely at the corporate or *strategic business unit* (SBU) level and *management* at the local level; we believe that both belong at both levels when good marketing leadership is practiced.

Strategic marketing takes an overall view, allocating resources and setting objectives after defining the market; marketing management develops the product/service, prices it, tells the customer about it, and gets it to the customer. This is why strategy must precede management. A restaurant, for example, cannot be appropriately designed without first correctly designating the market it is to serve.

Strategic marketing deals with the long-term view of the market and the business to be in; marketing management stresses running that business and the implementation of the strategies on a daily basis. We emphasize this distinction for a specific reason. Far too many annual marketing plans fail because they are based on the wrong strategy, or fail to flow from the right strategy. An excellent example of this is the strategy of a hotel that targets an upscale market when that market does not exist, is already overcrowded, or the product is not adequate to serve it. A marketing plan is then developed to implement the strategy, and fails.

If the strategy cannot be implemented, it is

65

the wrong strategy. Too often a marketing plan is developed with the final conclusion drawn before the work begins, and the data collected are summarily "fitted" to the conclusion. The result is a marketing plan that is both unrealistic and unworkable.

The Concept of Strategy

We begin with the standard textbook definition of strategy vs. tactics, which is directly derived from the military: Tactics are the way to win the battle; strategy is the way to win the war. In a simplistic example, we could demonstrate this as follows:

Objective: Surround the enemy.
Strategy: Take one area at a time.
Tactic: Use armored tank divisions.

Actually, marketing is not much different. The objective is to increase revenues. Strategy is the way to gain and keep customers; tactics are the step-by-step procedure of how to do it. For example:

Objective: Increase revenues by being perceived as the hotel of choice.
Strategy: Give customers better value.
Tactics: Always have their reservations and rooms (tables) ready; call them by name; make sure they receive their wake-up calls; have full-length mirrors and good bathroom lighting in their rooms; offer fresh-brewed coffee as soon as they sit down for breakfast; have room service delivered on time; have the print on the menu large enough to read; offer a selection for those who are light eaters; and so forth.

From this example it can be seen that tactics flow from strategy. This means that the first thing we have to do is develop the appropriate strategy. It is the strategy that drives the firm and specifies the direction in which it is going.

If that is the case, you might ask, if no strategy has been developed, then what drives the firm? The answer is that there is always a strategy, in one way or another. If there is no *explicit*

strategy, then there is an *im*plicit one. In fact, too often strategies exist by default. Here's a simple example:

> One of the basic tenets of marketing strategy is market segmentation, which involves dividing the total market into smaller groups of customers who have similar needs. We then select those markets that we can serve best. Suppose no one has even given this a thought, much less developed a strategy. The result is, "We'll take any customers we can get." The strategy, by default, is to take anyone as a customer. Along comes a bus tour group; we take it and it fills the lobby. The result may be our corporate customers saying, "What's going on here? We thought this was a businessperson's hotel. Let's go somewhere else next time."

The default strategy in this case is counterproductive. That is why strategy should never be left to chance. It should be both planned and executed very carefully.

The Concept of Strategic Planning

The essence of strategic planning is "how to get from here to there." Although it is not quite that simple in execution, it is that simple to understand. It naturally follows that there are two things inherent in such a statement: If you want to get from "here," you have to know where "here" is; if you want to get to "there," you have to know where "there" is. In strategic planning, the first is called a "situation analysis," or "where we are now"; the second is called "objectives," or "where we want to go." Strategic *planning* fills the gap: How do we get from where we are now to where we want to go? Strategic thinking is the synthesis that brings it all together.

In a more formal sense, strategic planning is concerned with the setting of business objectives, the match between products and markets, the choice of competition, the allocation of resources, and the proactive planning to reach the objectives. Although some people believe that strategic planning is complicated and difficult to understand, it is really an everyday, basic concept. We'll explain this with another simple example:

> Consider a high school graduate. Where is he now? Seventeen years old, no real skills, no profession, and certainly little chance for professional growth in a solid career path. Where does he want to be? A solid candidate for a good job in a firm that will offer opportunities for growth and advancement. Strategy? Get a good education and enhance capabilities and potential in the business world. Tactic? Go to college.

Although most strategic planning is done at the higher levels of a business organization, this should not necessarily be the case. *Strategic marketing planning is appropriate at any level.* We repeat this because of the common perception to the contrary. In fact, this has been one of the major failings of strategic planning: It often takes place only at higher levels and doesn't filter down to strategic management, which focuses on implementation of the strategic plan. Actually, strategic *thinking* is an asset at any level of management, and the best strategic marketing occurs when the decision process is primarily bottom-up.

To use the same example as above: Giving the customer better value can be a strategy at any level. If this is the actual corporate strategy of a 300-property hotel chain, let's see how it translates to the strategic management of a coffee shop in only one of those 300 units.

> The manager, a recent college graduate, thinks, "If that's the corporate strategy, then how does it affect me—how do I give better value?" She looks around and says, "Right now (situation analysis) we're just another coffee shop. What we'd like to be (objective) is the best coffee shop in town. The answer is (strategy) to give the customer better value. How that is done (tactics) is always to have fresh orange juice and fresh-brewed coffee, offer coffee as soon as a customer is seated for breakfast, never close off the most desirable part of the dining room no matter how slow it is, don't "push" customers so we can turn the tables over, don't put singles next to the kitchen door, and be sure that prices are competitive.

In contrast, a fast-food operation works on volume. The objective is to maximize patronage and turnover. The strategy is to give the customer every reason to move on quickly. The tactics are to have all food ready, accept pay for food when it is picked up, and minimize table-setting so the table can be ready for another party almost immediately.

This, then, is the concept of strategic planning: Decide where you are now, decide where you want to go, and develop and implement the strategy that will get you there. From that strategy, let flow everything else that you do, including all tactics.

The strategic marketing planning and management process has many interrelationships between the various elements and requires a systems perspective. The strategic framework for this perspective is illustrated in Figure 3-1; we will discuss it step-by-step here and cover each step in more detail in later chapters.

The Strategic Marketing System

Any strategic planning process begins with the firm's mission statement. This is true whether you are Hilton Hotels or Joe's Diner. Both Hilton and Joe have specific objectives and missions. Hilton's may be put together by an executive committee of senior vice-presidents. Joe may carry his around in his head and, if you asked him, might be unable to articulate them. It doesn't matter; objectives are still there and they will drive the operation of the diner, for better or for worse, every bit as much as Hilton's will guide the operation of that large corporation. The mission statement usually includes the broad, long-term goals of an organization.

The Mission Statement and Objectives

Any firm has certain financial objectives and we will not dwell on them here, keeping in mind that profit is the test of the validity of decisions. In addition, the firm has competitive objectives, consumer objectives, and company objectives, all of which are related. These objectives are

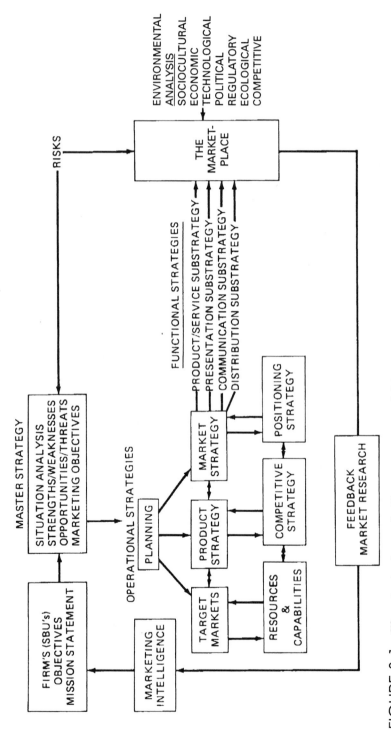

FIGURE 3-1   The strategic marketing systems model

68

brought together in what constitutes the business mission statement.

The business mission statement defines the purpose of a business. It states why it exists, who it competes against, who its market is, and how it serves its constituents—those who have an interest in what it does. These include customers, employees, owners, financial backers, and the local community.

Mission statements exist not only at the corporate level, but also at the level of every strategic business unit (SBU) within the firm. A strategic business unit is a unit within a business that serves a clearly defined product-market segment with its own strategy, its own mission, and its own identifiable competitors, but in a manner consistent with the overall corporate strategy.

As Marriott Hotels and Resorts has a mission, so too does the Courtyard by Marriott division, the Fairfield Inns division, and the Residence Inn division. The same is true of the Marriott Long Wharf and the Marriott Copley Place, both in Boston. These hotels not only have their individual competitors but also compete against each other, not to mention three other Marriotts in the Boston area. By the same token, each restaurant and lounge at the Marriott Copley Place should have its own objectives and mission, and its own identifiable competitors.

It is the corporate mission statement, however, from which all other mission statements in the organization flow, as shown in Figure 3-1. Figure 3-1, on the other hand, can be applied just as well to any strategic business unit. Thus, in the case of the Marriott Copley Place, we could replace "Firm's" objectives with "Hotel's" objectives; and, by the same token, we could replace "Hotel's" objectives with "Restaurant's" objectives. Strategic planning occurs at every level where a strategic business unit exists. We should bear that in mind as we discuss the remainder of the strategic marketing systems model.

A firm's (or SBU's) objectives may include growth, return on investment, profit, leadership, industry position, or other factors. These are included in the mission statement. Thus,

developing the mission statement is a crucial assignment. Since the mission statement indicates the purpose of the business, and is a statement of why the business exists, it drives all subsets of the business. Most importantly, mission statements must be realistic. For a mission statement to say, as some do, "we will be known as the leader in the hotel industry," when such a possibility is not realistic, only leads to confusion at lower levels of the organization.

The mission statement should be something in which all employees can believe. It sets goals and it urges everyone in the organization to meet those goals. Properly, it is communicated throughout the organization for all to follow. That, in fact, is one of its purposes—to unify the organization. When the response at lower levels is "Who are they kidding?" the entire effort becomes a meaningless and self-defeating endeavor. An effective mission statement, nothing less than an overall strategy statement, should fulfill the criteria shown in Table 3-1.

Figure 3-2 contains the mission statement of Holiday Inn Worldwide. However, it doesn't go very far. The purpose should be to gain total commitment at all levels. Consider, in contrast, the mission statement of Kraft General Foods, in Figure 3-3. You should evaluate both these mission statements in light of the criteria in Table 3-1.

Master Strategy

Developing the master marketing strategy is the next stage in the strategic marketing system, as shown in Figure 3-1. The master strategy is designed to be long-term, not short. This does not mean it will never change; if conditions change, then so too should the master strategy.

Consider, for example, Marriott, which was initially founded as a food-service organization. In the 1980s, Marriott's restaurant division pursued a master strategy of growth and acquisition. To implement this, one sub-strategy aimed at creating a midpriced restaurant chain (named Allie's) to complement Marriott's fast-food branch (Roy Rogers). The long-term objective of

TABLE 3-1   Criteria of an Effective Mission Statement

1. It states what business the company (or SBU) is in, or will be in. This goes considerably beyond being in the hotel, restaurant, or food business. Instead, it is more specific and states how we serve our customers and specifies who they are. For example:

   Hotel XYZ is in the business of providing the traveling and price-sensitive public with modern, comfortable, and clean accommodations at a very reasonable price.

   Accordingly, it recognizes the basic needs of travelers as well as the need for a pleasant and hassle-free experience, but without the amenities for which this market is unwilling to pay. Hotel XYZ wants to be known as the best buy at the moderate price level, satisfying all essential needs for the motoring public.

   You can see that this statement has numerous ramifications, such as how, what, when, and where. These are enumerated later in the strategic plan, but the answers will be driven by the mission statement.

2. It identifies the special competency of the firm and how it will be unique in the marketplace.

   XYZ hotel company is and will continue to be a leader in its field because of its special identification with the budget-minded traveling public and its needs. By continuous communication with its market and regular adaptation to the changing needs of that market, Hotel XYZ will maintain its position as the hotel of choice of its customers.

   Again, it can be seen that the mission statement has committed the firm to a definite course of action. Its competency and uniqueness is special knowledge of the target market and a commitment to maintain and implement that knowledge.

3. In a market position statement it defines who the competition will be—that is, it actually chooses whom it will compete against and does not leave this to chance.

   Hotel XYZ's niche in the market will be between the full economy, highly price-sensitive market that chooses accommodations almost solely by price, and the middle-tier market that will pay $20 more for additional amenities and services. Accordingly, XYZ competes only tangentially against ABC and DEF, on the one hand, and GHI and JKL on the other hand. XYZ competes directly for the same market against MNO and PQR, as well as other companies that choose to enter this market.

   As Burger King knows it has to beat McDonald's and Pepsi Cola knows it has to beat Coca-Cola, XYZ knows it has to beat MNO and PQR and will watch these competitors very closely.

4. It identifies the needs of its constituents.

   Customers: XYZ will conduct ongoing research of its customers' needs, both at the corporate and unit levels. It will continuously seek to satisfy those needs within the constraints of its mission.

   Employees: XYZ recognizes all employees as internal customers with their own varying needs and wants. Accordingly, it will attend to those needs and wants with the same attitude it holds toward its paying customers and will maintain an open line of communication for that purpose.

   Community: XYZ recognizes its position in the economic, political, and social communities. Thus, it will maintain a role of good citizenship in all endeavors and efforts.

   Owners: XYZ has committed itself to a 15 percent ROI for its investors, as well as a positive image of which they can be proud. XYZ will function both in the marketplace and in its operations to maintain these commitments.

5. It identifies the future.

   Hotel XYZ will develop and expand through controlled growth in suitable locations. Its strategy will be to develop regional strength as a gradual development toward national strength, with the objective of reaching that goal by the year 2000.

WORLDWIDE

A Global
Perspective

Mission Statement:

▲ To be the preferred hotel brand by guests and the travel industry, the preferred hotel company by employees and the preferred hotel business by developers, financial institutions and franchisees.

▲ To build on the strength of the Holiday Inn® name utilizing quality and consistency as the vehicle to enhance its perceived "value for money" position in the middle market.

▲ To maximize distribution throughout the world by aggressive expansion of existing and new products through owned, managed and franchised developments.

▲ To employ our resources and investments so as to yield premium returns.

Goal For The 90s:

▲ To build the Holiday Inn brand into an unassailable position in the global hotel industry.

Focus Of Future Activity:

▲ Launch Holiday Inn Crowne Plaza® hotels in major cities around the world.

▲ Expand into the resort market with the introduction of the Holiday Inn Crowne Plaza Resorts brand.

▲ Continue the expansion of Holiday Inn Garden Court℠ hotels in Europe.

▲ Sponsor the development of the Holiday Inn Express® brand.

▲ Offer the first 'branded' resort hotel experience for the mid-market through Holiday Inn Sunspree Resort® hotels.

▲ More than double the number of Holiday Inn hotels in Europe, Middle East and Africa.

▲ Commit $1 billion to acquire CMH Properties.

▲ Commit $60 million to acquire a competitive edge through state-of-the-art technology.

Company Managed Hotels   Human Resources

Courtesy of Holiday Inn Worldwide

FIGURE 3-2   The mission statement of Holiday Inn Worldwide

WHY A MISSION?

A mission statement defines what we want our company to be.

It sets forth our business objectives and provides our strategic planning process with an overall direction and coordination.

A clear mission also gives us a sense of purpose and a set of values that we can all share, so that we're all pulling together in the same direction.

Our KGF Mission...

♦ *Sets a long time horizon.* Its goals stay the same over a very long period of time — at least ten years and perhaps even for the lifetime of the Company.

♦ *Allows flexibility and room to maneuver.* It enables us to navigate through change — in market conditions, in the economy, in the competition, and in the management of the Company itself.

♦ *Describes qualities, not quantities.* Rather than setting specific financial targets, it says what our company stands for, what we believe about ourselves, and how we want to be perceived.

♦ *Projects a vision.* It's not just a prediction of what the business will be, given the historical financial trends. It's also a vision of what the business could be if it were to achieve its highest and fullest potential.

When we all give our full support and commitment to the KGF Mission, we not only promote our Company's success; we also make KGF a place where each of us can enjoy the rewards of meaningful, stimulating work and of professional and personal growth.

Mission

Kraft General Foods' Mission is to be the leading food company in the world, recognized as such because of its:

♦ Outstanding overall quality of people, products, and business plans and execution.

♦ Commitment to the superior understanding and service of customer and consumer wants and needs.

♦ Excellent financial performance, as measured by growth and return on investment.

♦ Unsurpassed reputation for honesty, integrity, and responsibility in all aspects of operations.

The pursuit of this mission is intended to benefit our shareholders, our customers and consumers, our employees, and the communities in which we operate.

Customers

KGF business will be built on the fundamental concept of achieving superiority versus competition in:

♦ Identifying the wants and needs of customers, both end user consumers and the trade.

♦ Providing high quality products and/or services to meet those wants and needs in unique or advantageous ways.

♦ Marketing those products/services to reinforce their appeal and achieve superior acceptance.

Courtesy of Kraft General Foods, Inc.

FIGURE 3-3 The mission statement of Kraft General Foods and strategies to achieve it

Industries / Markets / Channels of Distrbution

KGF will compete in any segment of the food business, in any geographic market, and in any channel of distribution, where:

♦ Participation can make a material long-term contribution to sales and income, while generating returns at or above corporate targets.

♦ The combination of product quality, management quality, innovation, synergy and productivity provides us with a sustainable competitive advantage, or the prospect of same within a reasonable time frame.

Competition

KGF has mass and resources that enable it to compete with any company in the world, and will utilize these strengths to the fullest legal, ethical and moral extent.

♦ KGF will engage any competitor in any geographic market, category, or channel of distribution of interest, where:

♦ The combination of product quality, management quality, innovation, synergy and productivity provides us with a sustainable competitive advantage, or the prospect of same within a reasonable time frame.

Such engagement can result in a material long-term contribution to sales and income, while generating returns at or above corporate targets.

♦ KGF will defend its established businesses ferociously.

People / Organization

KGF recognizes that the quality of its people is *the* critical element in achieving its mission.

KGF's human resources policies and practices will be built on:

♦ A standard of excellence.

♦ A dedication to assisting every employee in reaching his or her highest level of individual achievement.

♦ A total commitment to equal opportunity and fair treatment.

KGF will promote based on merit, and from within wherever possible.

Business Style

KGF business style will be characterized by:

♦ Overarching Commitment to Quality

♦ Legal, Moral and Ethical Conduct

♦ Openness, Honesty

♦ Initiative

♦ Innovation

♦ Aggressiveness

♦ Competitiveness

♦ Superior Analysis and Planning

♦ Action Orientation

♦ Risk Acceptance

♦ Synergy and Productivity

♦ A Standard of Excellence in People

Courtesy of Kraft General Foods, Inc.

FIGURE 3-3   (continued)

Overall Strategies

KGF

To achieve its Mission, KGF will:

1 Focus resources on countries, categories and brand franchises with significant profit and return potential, and where KGF has or can develop a sustainable competitive advantage, and thus a leadership position.

Avoid or exit/harvest other businesses.

2 Protect and grow our business while categorizing and analyzing new business development activities to control risk and financial exposure.

Focus on profitability and return in addition to volume potential.

Defend established businesses ferociously.

(Remember that the best defense is a strong offense.)

3 Identify and leverage all possible synergies among KGF units (and other P.M. companies, as appropriate)

that will strengthen our operating effectiveness or efficiency.

4 Pursue optimum "qualitivity" (quality and productivity) in all business units on a continuing basis, using Total Quality Management (TQM) principles including formalized and documented:

♦ Quantified goal setting,

♦ Project identification,

♦ Implementation plans (specifying accountability, responsibility, authority, and timing), and

♦ Performance tracking.

5 Manage all aspects of KGF's business with a global perspective; seek and leverage business system opportunities on an optimum source basis.

6 Be organizationally flexible, to allow adjustments necessary to leverage synergies and maximize productivity.

Courtesy of Kraft General Foods, Inc.

FIGURE 3-3   (continued)

the division was to have 3,000 Allie's units after ten years; 600 of these were to be completed in three years at a budgeted cost of $250 million.[1] By the end of 1989, however, and after completing another situation analysis, Marriott decided to divest its entire restaurant division. A company that was founded on food service had to face the realities of the environment. It changed its corporate master strategy and placed its emphasis where its strengths and opportunities lay—in hotels and institutional feeding.

The original intention, however, of master strategies is that they will endure for some time. This means that they take a long-range perspective of the environment, as opposed to the short-range perspective of the marketing

plan (discussed in Chapter 4), even though many of the issues are the same.

The master strategy shapes objectives after developing and weighing alternatives. It specifies where the firm is going and thus is the framework of the entire marketing effort. Derived from the mission statement and objectives, the master marketing strategy turns to the marketing emphasis to fulfill those missions.

The mission statement of the hypothetical hotel company XYZ in Table 3-1 noted that it wanted to be perceived as the best buy at the moderate price level. The master marketing strategy, then, would deal with that accomplishment to make it happen.

The master strategy begins with a situation analysis, again asking the questions, "Where are we now?" and "Where do we want to go?" It is the "where" of the strategic marketing system that shapes objectives and overrides all decision

---

[1]Christopher Muller, "The Marriott Divestment: Leaving the Past Behind," *Cornell Hotel and Restaurant Administration Quarterly,* February, 1990, pp. 7–13.

aspects. A master strategy deals with such issues as new markets, growth sectors, customer
loyalty, repeat business, quantity vs. quality,
cheap vs. expensive, best vs. biggest, high or
low markups, quick turnover, product/service
range, building brand name, consumer awareness and perception, and a host of other factors
that guide operational strategies. Marketing
objectives are identified in the master strategy
in these contexts.

To address these issues it is clear that one
must first know their current state. We begin
with the environmental analysis, looking especially at the long-range trends and effects.
These trends could be economic (the state of
the international, national, or local economy);
sociocultural (the graying of America, Generation X); lifestyle (interest in fitness and health);
legal (employment laws, such as the Family
Leave Act of 1993); ecological (a greater awareness of environmental hazards); political (eastern Europe), technological (teleconferencing),
and competitive (growth of all-suite hotels).
The major purpose of environmental analysis
is to identify external opportunities and threats
to the organization. This will be discussed further in Chapter 5.

An opportunity is a favorable trend in the
environment such as an emerging market segment, or a need or demand for certain specialized services.

On the other hand, a threat is an unfavorable
trend, such as reduced demand or new competition. External opportunities and threats will
evolve when various questions are asked about
the organization, along with its internal
strengths and weaknesses, in a situation analysis. Examples are shown in Table 3-2.

The distinctive competency of an organization
is more than what it can do; it is what it can do
particularly well. It often takes a great deal of
self-analysis to understand this and to abide by
it. Objective situation analysis is the tool to lay
bare the facts. Abiding by it is sometimes more
difficult. Holiday Inns[2] learned this when it diversified into over 30 different businesses in the

1970s in which it lacked strength or distinctive
competency. In many cases, failure to recognize
strengths and weaknesses results in targeting
the wrong markets. Strategically speaking, a
firm should do only what it has the competency
and resources to do well. Ignoring this fact may
result in a colossal strategic error.

Solid strength and weakness analysis may
be the most neglected phase of strategic planning in the hospitality industry. Without a
doubt, this lack was a major contribution to
the failure of Howard Johnson's in the early
1980s,[3] the stages of which are shown in Table
3-3. In less than ten years Howard Johnson's
went from boom to bust. In 1985 it was broken
up and sold off in pieces, all because management failed to understand its strengths and
weaknesses or to see its opportunities and
threats.

Opportunity analysis is the matching of
strengths to opportunity while counteracting,
when possible, the threats caused by weaknesses.[4] Many opportunities and threats spring
from the changing environment, as seen in the
case of Howard Johnson's in Table 3-3, as well
as from consumers' problems, which will be discussed in Chapters 6 and 7, but which you can
also conjecture from Table 3-3.

Using the Strategic Marketing Systems Model

Rather than discourse further on the model in
Figure 3-1, we will make it come alive by illustrating the stages with excerpts from the actual
strategic marketing plan of a hotel in India. The
mission of this hotel was to be the top upscale hotel of choice in the city for the international traveler. Without enclosing the full situation analysis, covered above, that forms the basis of the
strategy, we have placed some key questions in

---

[2]Today called Holiday Inn Worldwide under new ownership.

[3]Today known as Howard Johnson (without apostrophe and s)
under new ownership.

[4]Analysis of Strengths, Weaknesses, Opportunities, and Threats
is often called **SWOT** analysis.

TABLE 3-2   Elements of a Situation Analysis

EXTERNAL—Opportunities and Threats

Generic Demand   Why do people come here and why do they use this product? Where else do they go? What do they need, want, demand? Are there unmet needs? What do users/nonusers look like? What are the segments for this product category? What are the alternatives? What are the trend patterns—cyclical, seasonal, fashionable?

Brand Demand   Who is our customer? Why? What is our position? Who are our market segments and target markets? To which do we appeal the most? What use do they make of our product/service? What benefits do we offer? What problems do we solve or not solve? What are the levels of awareness, preference?

Customer Profile   What do they look like—demographically, psychographically, socially? Are they heavy users or light users? How do they make decisions? What influences them? How do they perceive us? What do they use us for? Where else do they go? What needs and wants do we fulfill? What are their expections?

Competition   Who are they? Where are they? What do they look like? How are they positioned against us? In what market segments are they stronger/weaker? Why do people go there? What do they do better/poorer than us? What is their market share? What are their strengths and weaknesses? What are their expectations?

INTERNAL—Strengths and Weaknesses

Organizational Values   What are the values that guide us? What is the corporate culture? What drives us in a real sense? Do these limit alternatives?

Resources   What are our distinctive capabilities and strengths? What do we do particularly well? How do these compare with the competition? What are our physical resources? Are there any conflicts among our resources, our values, and our objectives?

Product/Service   What is it? What benefits does it offer or problems does it solve? How is it perceived, positioned? What are the tangibles/intangibles? What are our complementary lines? What are our strengths and weaknesses?

Objectives   Where do we want to go? What do we want to accomplish? How do we want to be perceived? What are the long-/short-range considerations?

Policies   What rules do we have now? How do we operate? What guides us? Are any rules conflicting?

Organization   How are resources, authority, and responsibility organized and implemented? Do we proact rather than react? Does the organization enhance the strategy or does the organization need to be changed?

---

brackets. Three years after this strategic plan was drawn, this hotel was devastated by new competition. Examine its analysis and plan and see if you can understand why.

Objectives and Master Strategy

Marketing Objectives   To be perceived as a premier, super-deluxe hotel marketed to the connoisseur consumer.

Master Marketing Strategy   To create an image of exclusivity and uniqueness with premium-quality facilities and services.

Strengths
Personalized and professional service
Prime, strategic location
Part of chain that has already made its mark
High standards of food and service
Newly refurnished outlets

TABLE 3-3   Chronology of the Howard Johnson's Failure Due to Lack of SWOT Analysis

[1979]   Daiquiris, discos, and candlelight dinners: that's what Howard Johnson's is serving up these days.... The bastion of the highway travel market is out to change its image. Says [Howard] Johnson, "We know where our operations will be in the 1980s, but the question is 'will we be in the right spot?'...I still don't think the food business is a marketing business.... I'm sure that we're making the right long-term moves."[a]

[1983]   The wraps are slowly coming off a new strategic business plan at the Howard Johnson Co. Key to the sluggish giant's assault on its problems is a carefully planned, major reorganization of the way the company manages and markets its restaurants and lodges.... "It's just a case of reorienting the thinking under new leadership."[b]

[1983]   "Everybody has a theme restaurant, but I think Ground Round [a restaurant concept division of Howard Johnson's] has a unique niche among them. Both families and singles are comfortable with us. We have done the one thing older chains have failed to do: marry the family trade with strong liquor sales."[c]

[1984]   Bettering the chain's infamously undependable service has suddenly become a priority.[d]

[1985—after the fall]   Howard Johnson's restaurants had become over-priced and understaffed purveyors of pallid food, hamstrung by outdated ideas.... Howard Johnson's troubles [were blamed] on everything but incompetent management.... Howard Johnson stood fast with a diversified menu while it was being "segmented" to death...for two decades, what an opportunity was blown![e]

[a]"The Howard Johnson Team: Razing the Orange Roof," *Restaurant Business,* February 1, 1979, pp. 123–134.
[b]"Hojo Unveils New Strategy to Overcome Sluggish Sales," *Nation's Restaurant News,* January 17, 1983, p. 1.
[c]"Welcome Back, Howard Johnson's," *Restaurants and Institutions,* December 28, 1983, p. 88.
[d]"Howard Johnson: Is It Too Late to Fix Up Its Faded 1950s Image?" *Business Week,* October 22, 1984, p. 90.
[e]"The Sad Case of the Dwindling Orange Roofs," *Forbes,* December 30, 1985, pp. 75–79.

Renowned shopping arcade on premise
Wide variety of excellently appointed suites
[Do these strengths represent unique competitive differences perceived by the customer that build defenses against competitive forces or find niche positions in the market?]

Weaknesses
Higher room and F&B rates, making it difficult to secure international conference business
Market sensitivity that we are more pro-foreigner and have less identification with local community
Lower percentage of national clientele
Marketing being more product-oriented than customer-oriented
Lack of exclusive executive club
Absence of well-located properties in chain that reduces chain utilization

[Are these weaknesses, or problems that need to be solved?]

Opportunities
Commercial market in the city very active; our location strategic
Development in this area strong; has strong affiliation with our hotel
Entrepreneurial market growing; most locating in this area
[Is this a matching of strengths and competencies to opportunity?]

Threats
Foreign traffic dependent on political stability of country
Corporations developing own facilities to encourage privacy and reduce expenditures
Renovated rooms at biggest competitor
Some corporations moving to suburbs

[Are these threats caused by weaknesses? Can they be avoided? Can resources be better deployed?]

Operational Strategies

Referring back to Figure 3-1 it can be seen that the next stage in strategic marketing, and one flowing from the master strategy, is the planning stage, or what are called the operational strategies. Operational strategies are the "how" of strategic marketing—that is, "how" we're going to get from "here" to "where" we want to go. Strategies at this point are more easily measurable and may have time and performance requirements.

This is the stage at which the organization acts in advance, rather than reacts, by planning for change. It is here that the organization shapes its own destiny. It is at this stage that the company attempts to minimize risk, maintain control, and allocate resources to keep in focus and reach its objectives.

The planning stage is also the stage of specific matching of the product to the market, of understanding where the business is going to come from, of developing new products and services, and of influencing demand. We continue to take excerpts from the marketing strategy of the Indian hotel. You should take special note of the interrelationship among the various elements of the operational strategies.

Target Market Strategy Target market strategy clearly depends on, among other things, resources and capabilities. To target a market with similar needs and wants is grossly insufficient, if not fatal, when the resources and competencies are not there to serve that market. The appropriate strategy is to target not just markets that appear to have the most opportunity, but also those that the firm can serve best and, one hopes, better than the competition.

A common failing in this respect is the hotel that targets the upscale market and prices accordingly. If the firm does not have the re-

sources and capabilities to sustain an advantage in that market, such strategies often fail. The hotel then has to accept lower-rated business while management continues to vehemently maintain that it is in the upscale market. The result is a confused image and failure to fulfill potential. Such strategies are often built on egos and wishful thinking rather than on unbiased analysis.

Another area of weakness in target market strategy is targeting too many different markets—a strategy of providing something for everyone, which results in confusion for anyone.

Target market strategy means defining the right target market within the broader market segment. The strategy of the Indian hotel we have been discussing is to target the following market:

Age: 35-plus
Income: High
Lifestyle: Result-oriented, professional business-person, aristocratic, with a modern outlook on life, respected in the community, voices an opinion, a leader, an active socializer
Desired consumer response:
Rational—I like staying here because the rooms are spacious and beautiful. I like the computerized telephone exchange with its automatic wake-up call and direct international dialing. The executive club with computers and word processors is time-saving, smooth, and trouble-free. Check-in/check-out is fast and efficient. Because the hotel is so exclusive I don't encounter undesirable people. Service is smooth, courteous, and efficient.
Emotional—I like staying here because everyone knows me and takes care of me. I feel very much at home with the room service and restaurants. They know my likes and dislikes and make it a point to remember. It is so exclusive, I like to be seen here.

Target marketing will be discussed further in Chapter 8.

Product Strategy Product strategy is concerned with the offering of different products and services to satisfy market needs. It deals with the benefits the product provides, the problems it solves, and how it differentiates from the competition. Product strategies should be based on opportunities in the environment and customer needs rather than be based on owners' or management's concept of what the product should be. For example, it is quite common in southeast Asia for upscale hotels to have as many as five formal dining rooms. These will inevitably be Chinese, Japanese, and French, plus one native to the country. The other is likely to be Italian or American. The reasoning, of course, is that all these geographic markets are served by the hotel. Each room usually seats 100 or more and in most cases is fortunate when it is 50 percent occupied.

The low patronage does not occur because there is no market need. Demand exists for all these ethnic foods, but at varying levels. Further, there are numerous freestanding restaurants in the city also filling these needs—at least the Chinese, Japanese, and native. Instead of strategically analyzing the market and the competition, owners simply insist on the variety of restaurants.

The essence of marketing is to design the product to fit the market. When, however, the product already exists, the situation is reversed: The market must be found that fits the product. A not uncommon failing are renovated hotels that try to position "upscale," when the product simply does not fit the upscale market or compete effectively against newly constructed upscale hotels. Product strategy will be discussed further in Chapter 10.

Competitive Strategy   In developing competitive strategy, the firm actually chooses its competition and also when and where it will compete. This is realistic, provided the choice is realistic and based on an objective situation analysis. Take, for example, the case of Wendy's Restaurants:

In the early 1970s, when McDonald's and Burger King were already well established, industry experts did not think that there was room for another hamburger chain to enter the market and

grow to any substantial size. However, in less than ten years since opening their first restaurant in 1969, Wendy's had grown to a chain of 1,000 units. Wendy's did not compete head-to-head with McDonald's or Burger King, but rather it selected a special niche in the crowded hamburger market. It went after the young adults in their 20s and 30s. Surveys showed that over 80 percent of Wendy's business came from those over 25 years old. Compare this with McDonald's, which derived 35 percent of its business from those under 19 years.

The secret to a successful competitive marketing strategy is to find a market where there is a clear advantage or a niche in the market that can be defended. The trick, then, is to match the firm's product strengths with the market or niche. It does not matter whether this niche occurs in the high or low end of the market. Consider examples on both ends of the spectrum.

Ritz-Carlton Hotels is positioned at the top of the market. Their product is "top drawer" and it is almost never compromised. On the other hand, Days Inn has maintained its position in the budget segment. Both these companies chose their competition, stuck to it in the marketplace, and were realistic about the choice. This is the essence of formidable competitive strategy. These are single-product companies that compete in a single niche, although Days is owned by Hospitality Franchise Systems, which also owns three other lodging product lines including Ramada and Howard Johnson, in its latest reincarnation, all of which are marketed separately. In a converse situation, today's Howard Johnson has six product lines all carrying the Howard Johnson name. This serves to blur both its image and who it is competing against.

Other companies, like Choice International, choose their competition in different niches with different product lines—Clarion, Quality, Comfort, and Sleep Inns—and market them together, giving the customer a choice. Ashok, in India, does likewise with Elite, Classic, and Comfort (Figure 3-4), while Groupe Accor of France has four product lines—Sofitel, Novotel, Ibis, and Formule1, plus Motel 6 in the United States—but markets them separately.

Some of our hotels are priceless. Some are thoughtfully priced.

The Ashok Group gives a new dimension to hospitality with a multiple choice of hotels.

Ashok ELITE HOTELS

- Ashok Hotel, New Delhi
- Hotel Samrat, New Delhi
- Hotel Ashok, Bangalore
- Hotel Airport Ashok, Calcutta
- Kovalam Ashok Beach Resort
- Lalitha Mahal Palace Hotel, Mysore

Ashok Classic HOTELS

- Hotel Kanishka, New Delhi
- Qutab Hotel, New Delhi
- Hotel Janpath, New Delhi
- Ashok Country Resort, New Delhi
- Hotel Agra Ashok
- Bharatpur Forest Lodge
- Hotel Kalinga Ashok, Bhubaneswar
- Hotel Bodhgaya Ashok
- Hotel Jaipur Ashok
- Hotel Jammu Ashok
- Hotel Khajuraho Ashok
- Hotel Madurai Ashok
- Temple Bay Ashok Beach Resort, Mamallapuram
- Hotel Manali Ashok
- Hotel Pataliputra Ashok, Patna
- Laxmi Vilas Palace Hotel, Udaipur
- Hotel Varanasi Ashok

Ashok Comfort HOTELS

- Hotel Ranjit, New Delhi
- Lodhi Hotel, New Delhi
- Ashok Yatri Niwas, New Delhi
- Hotel Aurangabad Ashok
- Hotel Lake View Ashok, Bhopal
- Hotel Brahmaputra Ashok, Guwahati
- Hotel Hassan Ashok
- Hotel Donyi Polo Ashok, Itanagar
- Hotel Japfu Ashok, Kohima
- Hotel Pondicherry Ashok
- Hotel Nilachal Ashok, Puri
- Hotel Ranchi Ashok
- Hotel Pinewood Ashok, Shillong

The Ashok Group

India's host to the world

FIGURE 3-4   Ashok offers three product lines

On the other hand, poor strategic planning leads to choosing the wrong competitors to compete against, and with the wrong product. When Omni Hotels took over the New York Sheraton on 7th Avenue and refurbished it in the mid-1980s, management chose as its competition upscale hotels such as the Essex House and the Parker Meridien, coming not even close to offering a comparable product and almost losing its management contract. Gross operating profit doubled when new management chose instead to compete against the lower-scale hotels in the marketplace.

In some companies with widely varied product carrying the same name, each property has to choose its own competition. This is sometimes difficult when the brand name is carried on all products. For example, Sheraton operated the deluxe Sheraton St. Regis in New York City, the convention hotel Sheraton New York a few blocks away, franchised a midscale Sheraton Inn in Bordentown, New Jersey (50 miles away), and a basic low-tier Sheraton Inn in Westchester County (since disenfranchised), half an hour from New York City. Each of these properties has markedly different competition and customers, but all were marketed together under the Sheraton flag.

Conversely, Marriott, Westin, Stouffer, CP Hotels, and Hyatt have all maintained similar competitors in all markets. When Marriott decided to go "downmarket," it followed the Choice and Groupe Accor lead with new products, Courtyard and Fairfield Inn, and aimed at different markets with very different competition.

Market Strategy Market strategy is concerned with reaching the market with the product. In the final analysis, if you can't reach the market, the best product and the most well-defined strategy will fail. Some hotels, hotel companies, and restaurants have failed or done poorly for just that reason.

For the hospitality industry, reaching the market can be looked at in two ways. The first is taking the product to the market; the second is bringing the market to the product. By contrast with manufactured goods, taking the product to the market is a major commitment and, in some cases, a major capital investment.

For multiunit hotel and restaurant companies, taking the product to the market is part of the distribution system. This is the area where location becomes a major factor. The strategy involved concerns the appropriate markets to enter.

For multiunit companies that seek growth, the case is multiplied many times. When McDonald's saw its growth limited in freestanding, drive-up stores, it changed its market strategy. Soon McDonald's appeared in inner-city locations, office buildings, universities, and almost anywhere else one looked. It then headed overseas to both the European and Asian markets. In Singapore, on Orchard Road, the main road of the city and right next to the Hilton International, sits what became the highest-grossing McDonald's in the world, later supplanted by the one in Red Square, Moscow. Market strategy has been a major factor in McDonald's success.

Ritz-Carlton Hotels has a single-market strategy at the top end of the market, where it seeks to find a unique niche, avoid confrontation with large competitors, and dedicate itself to serving the one market. Venture Inns of Canada does likewise in the "luxury budget" market but faces far more competition there, albeit a far larger market demand. Choice International and Groupe Accor of France have total-market strategies, with hotels aimed at every level of the market, as we have pointed out.

Hilton International's market strategy was to locate in major capital cities throughout the world. Inter-Continental aimed for cities where Pan American Airlines, its former owner, flew. Le Meridien Hotels chose to enter primary cities like Boston, New York, and San Francisco when it expanded into the United States. Marriott likes to saturate an area with multiple units, as it has done in Boston, Washington, D.C., and other cities. Multiple market strategies are covered further in Chapters 9 and 16.

Getting the market to the product involves a new set of strategies. When resources are scarce, as they usually are, the market strategy must designate where to use those resources. A restaurant may choose the surrounding neighborhood and concentrate on word-of-mouth. McDonald's, on the other hand, uses national television to cover the entire United States, as well as other countries. The Stanhope Hotel in New York City uses the *International Herald Tribune* in Europe to attract the European market. Hyatt concentrates heavily on airline magazines, meeting-planner journals, and travel agent indexes. Marriott concentrates on its frequent-traveler program and business publications. Many hotels, especially in Asia and southern Europe, rely heavily on tour operators to get their customers for them.

Positioning Strategy The last, but by no means least, of the operational strategies is the positioning strategy. Market positioning means to create an image in the consumer's mind. Positioning strategy is no less than the presentation of the product strategy directed at the target markets, consistent with the resources and capabilities of the firm, aimed at specific markets, vis-a-vis the competition. It is important to note the relationship between positioning and the other operational strategies, as shown in Figure 3-1. Positioning will be discussed in greater detail in Chapter 9.

The strategic plan for positioning the Indian hotel to its market is specified as follows:

> The hotel will be positioned as a super-deluxe property for the "up" market. It will be positioned to image-conscious elitists and high-flying business executives. All marketing will be geared to the top-brass, higher-echelon bracket of both the social and business circles, for whom facilities, specialties, and personalized attention are the main criteria for selection. The exclusive executive club, the businessman's club with business equipment, and the rooms with antiques, objets d'art, and special butler service, will symbolize luxury-plus.

Functional Strategies

Functional strategies (refer again to Figure 3-1) are the "what" of the strategic system—that is, the "what" we are going to do to get "where" we want to go. The important thing to remember is that these are still strategies, not tactics, which come immediately afterward. It is this set of

strategies that flows directly to the consumer. For example, in the Indian hotel situation the communication strategy might be to portray luxury, the presentation strategy to price exclusively, the product/service strategy to render personal attention (e.g., butler service), and the distribution strategy to use exclusive referral systems and select travel agents. The functional strategies are the substrategy implementation of the operational strategies. They are commonly referred to as the marketing mix, which will be discussed in detail in Chapters 10 to 15.

Strategies at this level of the hierarchy represent shorter-term and more flexible strategies.

Product/Service Substrategy The product/service mix is

> [The] combination of products and services, whether free or for sale, aimed at satisfying the needs of the target market.[5]

In the better-known "Four Ps" (product, price, place, promotion) developed for goods marketing, this is the product. Ritz-Carlton Hotels has a top-of-the-line product/service strategy at the master and operational strategy levels. At the functional strategy level, strategic decisions must be made on the level of service to offer, and when and how to offer it. The same criteria, of course, apply: What is important to the target market? What does the target market expect? What problems does the target market have?

Let's say the product/service substrategy is to provide luxury. This would be a natural derivation from the master strategy and the operational strategies. The question is how to put it into practice. These are the tactics. Consider terry-cloth bathrobes in each room: Is this important to the market? Does the market expect it? Does it solve a problem for the customer? For Ritz-Carlton the answer may be yes, and the customer is willing to pay the additional cost. For most other hotels, however, the answer is probably no. We carry this further in Chapter 10.

---

[5]Leo M. Renaghan, "A New Marketing Mix for the Hospitality Industry," *Cornell Hotel and Restaurant Administration Quarterly,* April, 1981, p. 32.

FIGURE 3-5   Ad illustrating product/service strategy

The Oberoi Hotel chain in India changed its master strategy in 1986 and decided to aim at the luxury market. Into the rooms went antique desks, personalized stationery, beautiful brass ashtrays, and terry-cloth bathrobes, among other things. The rooms themselves weren't much different; it was the symbols of luxury that made the difference and the product/service strategy had to change. Many other changes were also made in the hotel's marketing mix to carry out this strategy. Figure 3-5 provides an example of advertising elements of the product/service strategy.

Presentation Substrategy   The presentation mix is defined as

[All] elements used by the firm to increase the tangibility of the product/service mix in the perception of the target market at the right time and place.[6]

---

[6]*Ibid.,* p. 32.

These include the physical plant, atmospherics, employees, customers, location and price, all to be further elaborated later in the book. The same rules apply to this strategy as to the product/service strategy. Much of what we have said above could also be applied here—that is, this strategy is no less than a carryover of the product/service strategy. This mix has no true counterpart in the Four Ps but includes the price category.

Physical plant and *atmosphere* must be consistent with the product/service. This means they shouldn't be overdone or underdone. There are many beautiful hotels and restaurants that remain largely empty because they were built and designed without an underlying, valid strategy that emanated from valid master and operational strategies.

Employees must be hired and trained accordingly. Certainly we expect a bigger smile and quieter maids at a four-star than at a two-star hotel, and better service at a three-star than at a one-star restaurant. But we expect something more—an emphasis on the customer rather than on the service. This difference, in fact, is why Ritz-Carlton does so well at what it does. The reverse is also true: At McDonald's we expect service to be consistent with the product strategy, for example, McDonald's expects you to empty your own tray when finished!

The *customer* mix strategy is very important. In some four-star deluxe hotels in Paris and London, men don't get in the door without a coat and tie. At other places you may be an "oddball" if you have them on. There is a basic strategy here that really applies in almost all cases: Don't mix incompatible markets if you can possibly help it; if you have to deal with incompatible markets, keep them separated in both time (e.g., seasonally) and space (e.g., separate dining rooms).

Location strategy means being where the customer can get to you or you can get to the customer. Again, McDonald's, in its infinite ubiquitousness is a prime example of this element being located in just about every conceivable facility or location one can imagine. We will discuss these elements further in Chapter 11.

Pricing strategy, in our experience, represents the greatest potential for confusion in the marketing mix. In too many cases, in fact, there seems to be no strategy at all. Prices seem to be set totally independent of all other strategies and without regard to their interrelationship. Price creates many expectations. Consider the airline passenger who pays $2,000 to fly first class vs. the one who pays $600 in economy. They leave and arrive at the same time and travel at the same speed. What does $1,400 tell you? That's an easy one. What does $200 in a hotel room tell you? Or $100, or $75, or $35? In Toronto we found a hotel that charged $150 for a room service imperial quart (40 ounces) bottle of liquor, plus tax and tip, that sold in the liquor store for under $30. The room cost $89. Although the customer is the same for both, there is clearly no relationship between the pricing strategies. As S.C. Jain states,

> Increase in price should be considered for its effect on long-term profitability, demand elasticity and competitive moves. Although a higher price may mean higher profits in the short run, the long-run effect of a price increase may be disastrous. The increase may encourage new entrants to flock to the industry and competition from substitutes. Thus, before a price-increase strategy is implemented, its long-term effect should be thoroughly examined. Further, an increase in price may lead to shifts in demand that could be detrimental.[7]

All of the possibilities mentioned by Jain have happened in the hotel and restaurant industries in recent years, because of overpricing in the short run. We will spend all of Chapter 12 on this subject so it will not be belabored here. Suffice it to say that pricing is both a powerful and a dangerous strategic tool. In our Indian hotel example the following points have been considered in developing the pricing strategy: the special features of the product, the spending power of the market, the traffic movement of the market, the possibility of losing

---

[7]Subash C. Jain, *Marketing Planning and Strategy,* 4th ed., Cincinnati: South-Western Publishing, 1993, p. 452.

At Delta Hotels, we're dedicated to making your meeting great, from beginning to end.

Our **Great Meetings Assured** program means you deal with one meeting arranger, right from your very first phone call. For reservations and information, call **Good Meetings Express, 800-387-1265.** In Toronto call **927-1133.**

Delta Hotels & Resorts
You'll appreciate the Delta Difference.

FIGURE 3-6   Ad illustrating presentation strategy

regular users of high-rate rooms to lower-rate rooms, pricing of the competition, and management policy to avoid discounted business and group business (especially low-budget).

Figure 3-6 gives an illustration of communicating a presentation strategy.

Communication Substrategy   The communications mix is

[All] communications between the firm and the target market that increase the tangibility of the product/service mix, that establish or monitor consumer expectations, or that persuade customers to purchase.[8]

The communication mix replaces promotion in the Four Ps.

The issue here is obviously the strategy to be used to communicate all of the above to the marketplace. The strategic issue is what to say,

---

[8]Renaghan, *op. cit.,* p. 32.

not how to say it. The "how to say it" requires exceptional creativity in many cases and is often best left to those with that kind of expertise. The "what to say," however, is a strategic management decision and should not be left for advertising agencies to decide without extensive consultation.

Management's failure to clarify its strategy will not stop the agency from being creative. But it could, and too often does, result in advertising that does not clearly communicate the desired or appropriate message. The finished ads, the "how to say it," should always be checked back against the strategy to be certain of what is really being said.

An example that happens quite frequently is advertising copy that places a hotel or restaurant at a higher level than its positioning strategy calls for. The property may be at three-star level and aimed at the corresponding target market. The "creative" agency, however, gets carried away with terms like "luxurious," "elegant," etc. The appropriate target market feels it cannot afford it, and the upscale market, which is attracted, is disappointed. The result is a net loss for everyone.

Advertising, of course, is not the only part of the communications mix strategy. The strategy will also dictate the methods of communication. Under the umbrella of the overall communications strategy is the mix of personal selling, public relations, promotion (including frequent traveler programs), merchandising, and direct mail. The strategy will indicate where the emphasis and what proportion of budget will be placed on each. All these will be discussed further in Chapters 13 and 14.

An excerpt from the strategic plan of the hotel in India follows:

Objective: To creatively highlight the uniqueness of the product.
Strategy: To convince customers, especially the FIT [*foreign independent traveler*] and corporate segments, that we have a unique hotel in terms of its being traditional in decor, equipped with the most modern business aids, and a greater accent on personalized service. To create awareness of the new F&B outlets.

Mix: [This is followed by an extensive list including advertising media, in-house materials, sales materials, direct mail, publicity materials, brochures, sales trips and blitzes, research, personal invitations, travel agencies, and other strategic and tactical plans.]

Figure 3-7 provides an example of advertising fulfilling the communication strategy.

Distribution Substrategy The distribution mix is

[All] channels available between the firm and the target market that increase the probability of getting the customer to the product.

Strategies for distribution deal with channels and, in the case of most hospitality services, how to move the customer physically to the product. These include travel agents, tour brokers, wholesalers, referral services, reservations systems, airlines, travel clubs, and so forth. Strategies involve the emphasis placed on each (or none) as well as the channels used. Distribution replaces "place" in the Four Ps.

Destination hotels and resorts will place special emphasis on utilizing these channels. Distribution systems have become increasingly complex in the hotel industry and for many companies require far more attention today than they did ten years ago.

Club Med presents a somewhat unusual situation. The Club Med vacation is generally all-inclusive (meals, transfers, hotel room, and sometimes airfare are packaged on a per-person pricing basis). Accordingly, Club Med tended to act largely as its own travel agent. This strategy was less-than-optimally effective in penetrating the American market. The revised strategy was to cultivate specific markets and select travel agencies. Club Med personally trained these agencies in the "Club Med concept" and made them "Club Med specialists." This strategy established a special distribution channel that turned out to be very effective.

The Indian hotel in our example belongs to a consortium that advertises as a group but represents many hotels and hotel chains in the world in a similar product class. This enables it

THE LEGEND OF PARIS

The heart of Paris. Scintillating and alive. Legendary. The magic of the Etoile and of the Champs Elysées. The chic of the Faubourg Saint Honoré and the most exclusive shops in the world. □ An encounter between history and modernity . . . the calm elegance of the Hotel Royal Monceau. A hotel that combines the traditional refinement of Parisian architecture and furnishings with modern facilities and a quality of service which is second to none. □ Savour the superb French haute cuisine of "Le Jardin," and feast on the finest Italian fare served in the sumptuous "Ristorante Carpaccio." □ Relax in a spa, in the ancient Roman tradition, "Les Thermes." The best equipped water therapy and fitness centre you could ever imagine. □ Whether you are on business or for pleasure, the excitement of Paris is right on your doorstep, when you stay at the Hotel Royal Monceau.

HOTEL ROYAL MONCEAU

FIGURE 3-7   Ad illustrating communications strategy

to benefit from international advertising that it otherwise cannot afford.

Restaurants are also involved in distribution channels. Restaurants in New Orleans, where there is heavy convention and tourist traffic, work closely with tour operators and incentive travel planners to bring in customers. There are other special cases, too. Many restaurants utilize the services of concierges at hotels to make recommendations to out-of-town guests. This distribution channel in many cases is worked every day, with financial rewards to the concierges who send the most business to certain restaurants.

Figure 3-8 illustrates a distribution network that is part of a distribution strategy. Chapter 16 will elaborate more on this strategy.

Feedback Loops

There are two feedback loops in the strategic marketing systems model in Figure 3-1. One is

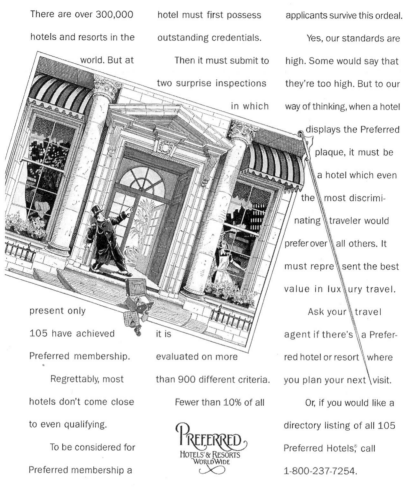

"WE MADE IT IMPOSSIBLE TO JOIN. THAT'S WHY EVERY HOTEL WANTS TO GET IN."

There are over 300,000 hotels and resorts in the world. But at present only 105 have achieved Preferred membership. Regrettably, most hotels don't come close to even qualifying.

To be considered for Preferred membership a hotel must first possess outstanding credentials. Then it must submit to two surprise inspections in which it is evaluated on more than 900 different criteria. Fewer than 10% of all applicants survive this ordeal.

Yes, our standards are high. Some would say that they're too high. But to our way of thinking, when a hotel displays the Preferred plaque, it must be a hotel which even the most discriminating traveler would prefer over all others. It must represent the best value in luxury travel.

Ask your travel agent if there's a Preferred hotel or resort where you plan your next visit. Or, if you would like a directory listing of all 105 Preferred Hotels, call 1-800-237-7254.

PREFERRED HOTELS' & RESORTS WORLDWIDE

Courtesy of Preferred Hotels & Resorts Worldwide

FIGURE 3-8 Ad illustrating distribution strategy

the risk loop. Feeding back to the master strategy, this loop questions the risks if the strategy is pursued. Some of the risk questions to be asked are: "What can happen? Will it work? What if it doesn't? How will competitors react? What are the economics? Does it meet objectives? Does it match capabilities? Does the organization support it?" These are critical questions that *must* be asked. If answers are negative, reevaluation must take place. This is far better than following hunches that often end in failure.

The second loop is the feedback on whether the strategy is working once it is in place. Marketing research is fed into the marketing intelligence system. This is the control that warns management to act before the possibility arises of the system's being out of control.

Strategy Selection

As we have progressed through the strategic marketing systems model illustrated in Figure 3-1, we have provided a framework on which we can later expand. We have probably raised more questions than we have provided answers. That is because there is no single "right" marketing strategy for any situation; there are simply right alternatives. The situation analysis, if done objectively, should lay bare the facts. The environmental analysis provides the bases for assumptions. From these sources, the strategic planner develops alternative courses of action.

Which one should be chosen? That is a simple question that has no simple answer. When you consider that there are also alternatives at every step of the strategic planning process, you find that you have dozens, perhaps hundreds, of choices to make as the possible combinations increase exponentially. That seems like a formidable task and it may well be. Some are better at it than others. Good common sense, wisdom, judgment, and intuition still have their place. Interpreting information, while objective, is not mechanical. The functions of strategic planning are to define objectives in terms other than profit, to plan ahead, to influence and not just react to change, and to inspire organizational commitment. Once your strategy has been formulated, it should be evaluated. Here is a checklist for that purpose:

Is it identifiable and clear in words and practice?
Does it fully exploit opportunity?
Is it consistent with competence and resources?
Is it internally consistent, synergistic?
Is it a feasible risk in economic and personal terms?
Is it appropriate to personal values and aspirations?
Does it provide stimulus to organizational effort and commitment?
Are there indications of responsiveness of the market?
Is it based on reality to the consumer?
Is it workable?

Summary

Strategic planning is a difficult but essential process. At the highest level of the firm, it drives the firm. At the lowest management level, it drives day-to-day activities. It is an essential phase of marketing and management leadership. In the short term, however, it is the annual marketing plan, to which we turn next, that makes the strategic plan work.

Good strategic planning rests on knowing where you are now and where you want to go, and finding the best way to get there. Its success rests on objective analysis, knowing what business you are in, understanding markets, integrating within the firm, and creating an organizational structure that will provide the implementation. In essence, there is no substitute for strategic planning and execution in today's competitive environment.

At the same time, we want to mention once again that all strategic thinking and planning need not take place solely at the corporate or higher levels of management. Unit managers have to be involved in strategic planning, as has been pointed out. We have given numerous examples of what happens when strategic planning is not done, or is done poorly, or is poorly executed. At the least, every manager should be thinking strategically at every level.

Strategic planning occurs at the functional level following the strategies set forth at the higher levels. It may occur for a 60-seat coffee shop or a 20-unit motel. Regardless, it is strategy that drives tactics and that, when done and executed properly, optimizes marketing performance. Even Joe at Joe's Diner will sell more hot dogs when he plans strategically. The functions of strategic planning are to define objectives in terms other than profit, to plan ahead, to influence and not just react to change, and to inspire organizational commitment.

Discussion Questions

1. Discuss the key differences between strategies and tactics. List three examples of each

as they apply to the hospitality industry. Do the tactics flow from the strategies?

2. Discuss why a mission statement and objectives are needed at the highest and lowest levels of management.

3. How is product strategy related to target market strategy in strategic planning?

4. What are the most critical factors in strategy selection? Discuss why.

5. Why does marketing strategy have to come before the marketing plan?

6. Discuss the strategy, or lack of it, in Cases 3-1, 3-2, and 3-3. Apply the strategic systems model (Figure 3-1) to these cases. How can each improve their strategic planning?

✔ Case 3-1
Keihan's Palace Side Hotel[9]

"This is an efficient hotel, I believe," said Mr. Kawarabayashi, General Manager of the Palace Side Hotel in Kyoto, Japan. "I don't know what else I can do within the boundaries of my assignment as General Manager—and the resources given to me by the parent company. My whole work career has been as a hotelman. The bosses at the railway just don't understand this business."

Background

The Palace Side Hotel was well located opposite a major entrance to the Imperial Palace grounds in Kyoto, Japan's capital for 11 centuries until 1865. The hotel, built in a Spartan contemporary style in 1968, sat on an inviting and shady street. It was owned by Keihan Railway Company, one of Japan's private railway companies, and was one of three Keihan hotels in the Kyoto area. The three properties were all completely different in style from each other and catered to different market segments. Each was run independently of the others, a not uncommon practice in Japan.

The Palace Side Hotel had done well since its inception but several factors had caused its profitability to suffer. The supply of Western-style hotel rooms in Kyoto had grown in number. These hotels were also of higher quality, commanded higher rates, and were attracting an increasing share of the Kyoto market. The Palace Side was unable, competitively, to raise its prices and thus had been forcibly positioned at a lower level in the marketplace. Although its location was excellent and considerably better than its nearest neighbor, the Kyoto Brighton Hotel, its average room rate of about US$ 90 was essentially half that of the Brighton.

Additionally, Keihan's strong railway unions had helped raise the hotel's wage structure.

When labor costs reached 45 percent and room rates could not be increased correspondingly, Keihan took strong action. The Palace Side reduced its labor cost to 11 percent by leasing out the restaurant, contracting for the maid service, and eliminating bellboys and room service. The full-time staff was cut to six persons, including the General Manager. The resulting poor service, despite the presence of service standards, contributed to the hotel's inability to maximize its pricing and profit potential. The owning company, however, which was primarily concerned with maximizing its return on investment and not willing to add to it, was satisfied with the current gross operating profit.

Marketing the Palace Side

The Palace Side Hotel had 120 rooms, all Western-style. Its market was 60 percent Japanese and the balance mainly Southeast Asian; 60 percent of occupancy was group business and two-thirds of this was Japanese. The average stay was less than two nights. American and European travelers tended to go to more upscale properties. "This is a business-class hotel," said Mr. Kawarabayashi. "It is what we called 20 years ago 'a five-dollar hotel.'"

Average occupancy was usually between 70 and 75 percent, although it could be higher when there were major events in Kyoto. Gross operating profit was 20 percent, and 60 percent of total revenue was from the Rooms division.

When Mr. Kawarabayashi was asked what changes had occurred in the hotel since its inception, he replied, "No changes. Everything is just the same. Same people, same types of businessmen and sightseers all these years. [We do] zero marketing. I've been in this hotel since it opened and I've done everything: bellboy, room service, maid, front desk, Manager. The bosses just don't understand the need for marketing. If it was my choice, the first thing I would do is marketing. Part of my job as General Manager

---

[9]We gratefully acknowledge the contribution of this case by Professor William Kaven, School of Hotel Administration, Cornell University.

here is to be the salesperson, although there is some slight help from our sister hotel. I contact the tour operators and I get the bulk of the business into the hotel."

"It's true," he added, "that we derive 60 percent of our revenue from rooms, while the major Tokyo hotels run 20 percent rooms revenue. That means that our banqueting hall is quite underutilized; we get only modest wedding and banqueting business. But what can one man do? I don't even get all my days off or whole vacations."

✔ Case 3-2
The Riverside Restaurant[10]

It had been a cold and blustery day and the weatherman was forecasting a blizzard. Reservation cancellations had begun flooding in to the Riverside Restaurant by late afternoon, and by 7:00 o'clock it was obvious that the evening's business would be negligible.

Manager Joseph Cantone took advantage of this rare opportunity to leave the floor and retire to his office. He began reviewing financial records and was pleased to see that the Riverside had continued to increase its sales volume in each of the past three years. On a less encouraging note, he realized that the restaurant had not produced the substantial profits necessary to achieve its financial objectives.

Background

The Riverside Restaurant was located in North Caldwell, Idaho, approximately 20 yards off the heavily trafficked Route 44. Caldwell had once been a familiar way station for east-west travelers on the Old Oregon Trail as early as the mid-seventeenth century. It was approximately 15 miles from Boise, Idaho, the state capital, and just off Interstate 84 that crossed the state. Transportation access to Caldwell was excellent and probably the area's greatest asset for retaining present industry and attracting new businesses.

The town's approximately 25,000 citizens had increased by about 12 percent in the last five years, growing at a rate one-and-one-half times that of the state. Statisticians predicted that the population would jump by another 11.5 percent over the next four years. The events of recent years had tended to decentralize the community and progressively change its character from a self-sufficient manufacturing town to a bedroom community.

The Riverside Restaurant had been solely-owned by Orly Cantone. Cantone started his

restaurant career as a busboy at the competing Lafayette House and was eventually promoted to head waiter. He decided to create a roadside restaurant specializing in Prime Rib. The Riverside became known for its superior Prime Rib, a reputation it still held. Orly also had owned the Riverside Pub in South Caldwell. His sons, Joseph and Robert, purchased the two restaurants from him when he retired. Joseph managed the Riverside Restaurant, while Robert managed the Riverside Pub.

Word-of-mouth advertising had always been responsible for the growth of the Riverside. Orly Cantone had never advertised the restaurant or promoted his specials in any way, and Joseph felt the same way. "When people walk into our restaurant," he said, "we try to take care of them. Customers do not want their guests to be dissatisfied. Food has to be good. Service has to be polite. At lunchtime, it has to be fast. We do our best to provide a relaxed and comfortable dining experience with quality food and genial service while providing an acceptable price/value relationship. People who have dined with us have had a favorable experience and tell their friends and relatives—it's as simple as that."

The Restaurant

The Riverside Restaurant was a stately, old mansion that had been the showplace of North Caldwell in the mid-1800s. It was a three-story, white Victorian structure with four dining areas and a cocktail lounge. The main dining room, called the Lounge, was decorated in a pink and maroon motif and seated 70 people. The main dining area was adjacent to the cocktail lounge, which seated 30 and was for cocktails only, except when customer requests or dining room overflow necessitated serving dinner in this room.

The non-smoking dining room, also decorated in pink and maroon, had a capacity of 40 and was located next to the stairway leading to

---

[10]Names and location have been disguised.

the second floor. This area, separated from the other dining rooms and hallways, was most popular. The River Room, a 125-seat function room located behind the non-smoking area, was used for a la carte service on Saturdays and holidays only. Done in blue and gold, the River Room was an ideal spot for rehearsal parties and wedding receptions. Finally, there was the 15-seat private dining room, located on the second floor; it was increasingly popular with business groups, particularly in the spring.

The Riverside had existed for almost 40 years and had witnessed the rise and fall of many area restaurants. Five years ago, there were at least a dozen pizza parlors in North Caldwell, each of which had a long waiting line. Now only a handful remained. There were also many Chinese restaurants in the area, but most also eventually failed.

The Riverside menu featured Prime Rib, steak, and various seafood items. Dinner prices ranged from $10.50 to $18.95 and included a selection of relishes, crackers, and homemade cheese, as well as a house salad. The best-selling entree had long been the Prime Rib, available for as little as $18–$20 with beverage and dessert. Upon request, the house policy was to offer an additional serving of Prime Rib, but few customers requested seconds since the entree was a generous portion.

The restaurant's luncheon menu was in the $6–$10 range and offered smaller portions of some of the dinner items, as well as soups, sandwiches, and salads. A banquet menu was available for parties of 25 or more.

Joseph Cantone was hesitant to embrace "trendy" cuisines, since he feared that they would lead to his restaurant's downfall. Although he had agreed to revise the Riverside menu a few years before in response to the strong demand for seafood, beef remained a popular selection. Nonetheless, seafood soon overtook beef as the top seller.

The Riverside tried to position itself as a moderately priced meat and potatoes restaurant that did not attempt "gourmet" preparations. Joseph remarked, "I don't want to be perceived as an elegant restaurant which only the well-to-do can afford. I also have no intention of

expanding to a chain operation, which would require more managerial and financial capabilities than we currently have. I want to improve what we are doing. Wouldn't it be great to see the whole restaurant reserved by 12:00 on Saturday?"

Customers

According to Joseph Cantone, the Riverside attempted to appeal to everyone. "When you do that," he said, "what you have is wholesome food which is served nicely at a reasonable price." For some reason, however, the restaurant was not popular among residents of North Caldwell. Cantone suggested that perhaps they were afraid to try the restaurant because of its "ritzy-looking" building.

Demographically, the Riverside customers were predominantly male, with over 75 percent of all female diners accompanied by a male companion. More than half were in the 40–60-year-old age bracket. One-third of all sales volume was generated by corporate bookings. Cantone cultivated this patronage with membership in various social and civic organizations. Credit card sales represented 60 percent of total sales.

At lunchtime, approximately 80 percent of the clientele were businessmen, whereas that percentage dropped to 20 percent at dinner. For the most part, dinner regulars were residents of the surrounding communities who had patronized the Riverside for many years. These guests were set in their ways and the waitresses frequently complained about their demanding natures.

Financial Performance

The restaurant's peak periods were predictable, with Tuesdays and Wednesdays generally proving to be the slowest nights. The restaurant served an average of 150–250 covers on Sundays through Thursdays, 450 on Fridays, and approximately 600 on Saturdays.

Joseph Cantone had targeted a 14 percent profit margin when he established his price structure, yet he considered his product to be severely underpriced relative to the market. He chose not to raise his prices since he felt they reflected the financial attitude of what he considered to be an economically depressed community. Joseph alluded to his current situation with the following comment: "Our dollar volume has increased every quarter for the last three years. However, the increase in volume did not keep pace with the inflationary trend. Additionally, we did not achieve the desired return on gross sales."

Management

When he first purchased the restaurant from his father, Joseph immersed himself in the minute details of operating the establishment and interacted personally with everyone from the dishwashers to the vendors. Recently, however, he had begun to delegate more of the operational details to his unofficial assistant manager, Veronica Terinese. Veronica was a veteran waitress who had gradually taken over the hiring and scheduling of the wait staff. She had begun at the Riverside ten years before and had become a go-between for Joseph and the service personnel. She kept track of the daily performance of the restaurant by recording the number of covers and the average checks on her personal computer. She also compiled sales abstracts for use in future menu planning.

A strong emphasis was placed on quality control of service. Joseph established the service standards, monitored their execution, and actively solicited feedback from his customers. He also held frequent staff meetings to discuss service-related problems. Veronica Terinese was proud of the Riverside staff. "You just have to make sure you don't lose any of your good people," she said. Many of the waitresses had been at the Riverside for 10–15 years, although an increasing percentage of the staff were college students and young mothers.

The Riverside had no sales or marketing staff per se, since Joseph did not feel that employing a salesperson would prove cost-effective. As a result, a considerable part of the sales effort was made by Joseph himself.

"Our base is too limited to support a major marketing program," he said. "In order to attract the Boise market, we would have to go out and hire professionals who are knowledgeable of that specific market. Our business simply does not warrant that type of activity." On a local level, Joseph acknowledged that it would be relatively inexpensive to advertise in the area media. However, he contended that it might change the restaurant's image.

Competition

Joseph Cantone considered everyone in food service—from a McDonald's to a Chinese restaurant—to be his competitor. However, he was not concerned about those who offered two-for-one specials as a means of attracting new business. "They will steal your customers for a while," he said, "but they are not building loyalty. Our customers return when their specials end."

Of the 22 restaurants in North Caldwell and the several others within 10–20 miles, only a few could be identitfied as direct competitors. There was no other restaurant in North Caldwell that was comparable in level of service and atmosphere, although a similar new establishment was slated for construction across the street within the next year. The primary competitors were identified as the Riverside Pub, the Lafayette House, and Benjamin's.

The Riverside Pub The Riverside Pub was a "sister restaurant" to the Riverside and was located five miles away in South Caldwell. When it was opened in 1979, the establishment attracted many of the Riverside customers since it was closer to Boise and therefore more convenient for many.

Except for minor variations in decor, the two facilities were similar. Menu, prices, and level of service were virtually identical. The customer base of the Pub was primarily businessmen, with some local residents and college students as well.

The Lafayette House The Lafayette House first opened in 1784, a popular tavern on the Old Oregon Trail. It was located on Route 44 in North Caldwell, five miles north of the Riverside, and was easily accessible from all directions. The facility had six dining rooms and a cocktail lounge.

The Lafayette House attracted businesspeople and locals on the strength of its word-of-mouth advertising. With a somewhat rustic atmosphere, the establishment was known for its excellent facilities for small or large banquets accommodating up to 200 people.

Entree prices ranged from $14 for shrimp scampi to $18.50 for filet mignon, with Prime Rib prominently featured at $16.50. As at the Riverside, entrees included fresh relishes, tossed salad, and assorted rolls.

Benjamin's Benjamin's was 12 miles from the Riverside. Since opening in 1979, the restaurant's seating capacity had been increased to 650 people. Presently, there were three dining areas, a lounge, and a ballroom that accommodated 250 guests. After dinner, many of the guests enjoyed dancing in the Library Lounge, which featured live entertainment five nights a week.

The best-selling entree at Benjamin's was the Prime Rib at $16.95. Other items included poultry, seafood, and beef, with filet mignon at $20.95 as the most expensive. Side dishes were offered a la carte with prices for salads or vegetables ranging from $2.25 to $4.50.

The major markets for Benjamin's were the businesspeople and the special-occasion diner. The establishment's reputation had been built on its ability to provide either intimate dining for families and friends or a large-scale business function. There were many repeat customers, who had generally become acquainted with Benjamin's through word-of-mouth, although some were first attracted by infrequent newspaper ads.

Conclusion

Despite the fact that sales volume had increased over each of the last three years, Joseph Cantone was not altogether satisfied. His restaurant had not kept pace with inflation and his real profit was declining. Cantone wondered if this was the case with his primary competitors and pondered this dilemna as the snow outside continued to fall.

✔ Case 3-3
Johnson Hotels[11]

Roger Johnson expressed concern over the increasing number of luxury hotels under construction in Denver. Nevertheless, Johnson believed that the oversupply of upscale hotel rooms would actually strengthen the position of Johnson Hotels within the market. As Johnson explained, "By next year 77 percent of the available rooms in Denver will cost more than $150 per night. Of the 23 percent of rooms left, 50 percent of those in the $125 range or below will be our three properties."

Background

The Tremont Square, oldest of the three Johnson hotels, was purchased in 1973, followed by the Lenox in 1983. In December of 1986, Roger Johnson bought the old Statler Hotel and renamed it the Denver Park Plaza. With the acquisition of the Statler, Johnson Hotels boasted three hotels in downtown Denver.

The Tremont Square The Tremont Square Hotel was built in 1891 and was the oldest continually operating hotel in Denver. The hotel afforded guests easy access to the Insurance Center as well as to business and shopping districts. The 153-room property was described as having a European atmosphere. Twenty-nine of the rooms had no private bath, but these economy rooms were nonetheless popular with tourists. Conference space was limited with only one small meeting room. In addition to The Sports Saloon and the hotel's restaurant, Dad's Place, the building also housed the well-respected Cafe Vienna. Known for its fine European cuisine, Cafe Vienna was leased on a profit-sharing basis.

When Johnson acquired the hotel in 1973, it was described as a disaster. He proceeded to undertake a major facelift and worked at changing its dubious reputation. Renovations

continued over the years, with the most recent lobby renovation due for completion early next year.

The Lenox The Lenox was built as a railroad hotel in 1905. The hotel's choice location was a primary attraction. This nine-story 221-room structure featured high ceilings, wide corridors, and individually designed Colonial-style rooms. The ninth floor had been converted into an executive floor with a concierge to better serve the needs of the business traveler. Other facilities included Delmonico's, a fine-dining restaurant and piano bar, and a pub called The Olde London Grille. The hotel also had five small meeting rooms with a maximum capacity of 300 people.

At the time of the acquisition, considerable work was required in order to modernize the facilities and renovate outdated features. The most recent overhaul included the installation of distinct, blue awnings over the first and second floor windows in an attempt "to make the Lenox a more visible product and to give it a landmark identity."

The Denver Park Plaza Built by Ellsworth Statler in 1927, the Denver Statler was a 1,350-room landmark, located in the heart of the stockyard district, which catered to the cream of Denver society. Extremely successful in the early years, the Statler was adversely affected by its deteriorating neighborhood in the 1960s and 1970s. Unable to maintain even a 40 percent occupancy, it was sold to Hilton in 1976. Hilton milked the hotel until there was nothing left and slated it for demolition in 1986.

Roger Johnson, a longtime admirer of the old Statler, began immediate negotiations to purchase it. The hotel reopened in January of 1987 under its new name, the Denver Park Plaza and Towers. A complete facelift of the property began about a year later and continued for five more years.

Once assured of the hotel's survival, the Denver Urban Renewal Agency proceeded with

---

[11]Jyothi Murthy and Michelle Alten researched and contributed to this case. Names and places have been disguised.

plans for major redevelopment of the surrounding area. The undesirable parking lots and sleazy nightclubs had been cleared to make way for new construction, most notably the Four Seasons Hotel, due to open next year, and the massive Department of Transportation headquarters. To commemorate the changes, the area previously called Park Square was renamed Park Plaza.

Overlooking Denver Common and the Public Gardens and located between the government and insurance centers, the hotel was within walking distance of chic Park Street boutiques, stockyard eateries, and the theater district. The city's Grayline sightseeing tours departed from the front of the hotel.

Renovations had expanded the size of rooms by combining smaller "salesman singles," thus pruning the number of rooms down to 880. As a result, many of the rooms sported two bathrooms, popular with families and conventioneers sharing rooms. Room interiors were completely redone, stripped down to the plaster, and a new telephone system was installed. Other improvements included new kitchen and laundry equipment, boilers, and computers.

The Denver Park Plaza housed four restaurants in addition to 22 small meeting rooms, 13 larger ones, and a grand ballroom seating up to 2,000 people. The restaurants included the four-star Stockyards, the Cafe Bison, which was often frequented by theater people, Denver Seafoods, which was a popular seafood restaurant operating on a lease agreement, and a coffee shop.

The fifteenth floor of the hotel was called the Denver Park Plaza Towers. It had been converted into 82 richly-appointed rooms and suites, "a luxury hotel within a hotel." Manager Lee Matson said, "We offer a very personalized service. Our customers come back because they like it."

Designed for the discerning upscale traveller, the Towers had its own registration desk and was serviced by a private express elevator. Amenities in each room included a terry-cloth bathrobe, electric blankets, safes, and refrigerators. A complimentary continental breakfast and concierge service were also provided.

The Marketing Organization

The marketing division of Johnson Hotels was headed by Frank Hughes, who had been with Sheraton's marketing division for 11 years before joining Johnson. Hughes was assisted by seven account executives responsible for soliciting specific markets—two for sales and national convention groups, four for corporate travelers, and one for travel agent and tour sales. This sales-oriented team represented the entire chain but focused primarily on the Park Plaza.

The Lenox also had one sales representative on its staff. The Tremont Square had no sales or marketing staff; these areas were handled by Robert Johnson, Roger's son and Manager of the Tremont Square.

Market Segments and Advertising

The Tremont Square Tourists and tour groups accounted for approximately 65 percent of the business at the Tremont Square Hotel, with 30 percent of tourists originating in Europe or Latin America. Another 20 percent of the business was conventioneers, with the remaining 15 percent a mix of middle managers and sales representatives. The hotel benefited from convention overflows at other hotels "about 10–15 times a year," according to Robert Johnson. The Tremont Square also tied in with small commuter airlines in offering a discounted rate for passengers.

Airport courtesy phones accounted for approximately 300 calls and 150 bookings per month, at an estimated cost of $7,700 each year. All three Johnson hotels were on the worldwide reservations systems of Utell and Golden Tulip, although the Tremont Square Hotel gained more business from these services than either the Lenox or the Park Plaza.

The Lenox Commenting on the Lenox clientele, Gary Johnson, Roger's other son and Manager of the Lenox, said, "We're more likely to get the middle manager or the self-employed individual." The Lenox also actively pursued the small-meeting business to fill its five meeting rooms and subsequently its hotel rooms. "Small meetings of 40–50 represent a substantial group size for a hotel of our size," Johnson continued. "There has been a 300–400 percent increase in our wedding business in the last three years and our sales team aggressively pursues this market."

Food and beverage sales accounted for one-third of total revenue. Management was proud of this high ratio since it indicated that Denverites, who might be asked to recommend a local hotel, were familiar with the property and its facilities.

The hotel's previously-mentioned blue awnings were prominently featured in all print advertisements. This practice was consistent with the goal of establishing a "landmark identity."

The Denver Park Plaza With its 36 meeting rooms, the Park Plaza had the most square footage of all hotels in Denver competing for the Class A major convention market. However, the opening of a new Marriott would drop the Park Plaza to second place among the four major convention hotels in the city. In addition, the Park Plaza was the only hotel of the four not located within easy walking distance of the Denver Convention Center. Although positioned in the major convention market, the hotel was also marketed to corporate travelers, tour operators, conference business, airlines, and government officials. The Denver Park Plaza was actively promoted as a hotel with a Denver flavor. In justifying this stand, Johnson said, "We're trying to make the Park Plaza the Denverite's hotel and we have an opportunity to do that better than anyone else in the city. We're Denverites, we are Denver operated. It is more than physical value of the building, it's our people, ownership, and involvement in the community politically, socially, and economically."

Pricing Policy

In order to establish room rates, general managers met with their respective Rooms division and sales managers and then forwarded recommended rates to Roger Johnson for approval. Prices depended on competitors' room rates and anticipated cost increases and were deliberately set below those of the competition in order to encourage the potential customer to take a risk

and try a hotel without a nationally known name.

Management felt that its ability to offer an attractive price/value relationship gave the hotels, particularly the Park Plaza, a distinct advantage in the increasingly competitive Denver market. Frank Hughes explained the ability of the Park Plaza to offer rates lower than the competition: "We have a property that was bought at the right price. It has been paid for mostly out of cash flow and its overhead is minimum in terms of debt service." It was believed that the Johnson Hotels could be very flexible in their pricing and could offer a similar product/service at lower rates essentially because of low overhead as compared to the newer competitors.

Rack rates (minimum single to maximum double) and average rates and occupancies are shown in Table 3-3-1 for the last 12 months.

Denver Area

Greater Denver had a variety of pleasurable attractions for locals and visitors alike. Aside from being a major financial and commercial center, Denver was world-renowned for its fine university, hospitals, and medical research centers. The city was also the home of many historic sites and art museums, with the Denver Museum of Fine Arts leading the pack. Performances in the theater district, as well as concerts by the Denver Symphony Orchestra, drew large, enthusiastic audiences. The Insurance Mall, Tremont Place, Park Plaza, and Stockyard Marketplace were all popular shopping areas. Everything in Denver was within convenient walking distance, a fact appreciated by budget-conscious visitors to the city.

Convention and Exhibition Centers

Although Denver had long been a popular choice as a convention destination, the city had difficulty attracting major national conventions due to its inadequate facilities. As a result, considerable development and expansion in both convention space and exhibition halls had begun.

The Denver Auditorium, located at the Insurance Center, was the Rocky Mountain's largest

TABLE 3-3-1   Rack Rates, Average Rates, and Occupancies

	Park Plaza		Lenox		Tremont Square	
Rack Rates	$95–$132		$62–$126		$78–$105	
Towers	$120–$15					
	Occ.%	ADR$	Occ.%	ADR$	Occ.%	ADR$
September	70	94	83	99	96	83
October	90	98	95	99	94	82
November	57	91	65	96	69	79
December	36	87	38	93	38	76
January	39	90	38	94	38	74
February	42	92	47	92	47	74
March	47	93	56	79	67	77
April	64	99	71	97	85	81
May	72	99	79	99	92	82
June	74	97	79	98	94	83
July	47	95	71	94	90	82
August	63	96	82	97	97	82

and most utilized convention center. It was the focus of renovation and expansion, with plans to make it one of the most modern facilities of its type in the country. The facelift would double the existing space from 150,000 square feet to 310,000.

The Northside Exposition Center had 200,000 square feet of exhibition space and meeting facilities for 3,000 people. The Center was able to accomodate conventions, gate shows, and trade shows.

DENCOM, the third high-technology trade center to have been built in the United States, was still under construction and due to open next year. When completed, the facility would have 160,000 square feet of exhibit space and 600,000 square feet of permanent showrooms featuring the latest in advanced computers and communications technology. DENCOM also included its own dining facilities.

The Hotel Market

Thirteen new hotels had opened in the city since Roger Johnson bought the Statler Hilton, adding 5,000 rooms to the existing 6,000. This expansion was all the more pronounced because the 1970s and the early 1980s had marked an era of little or no hotel construction in the city. At the same time, a string of older, obsolescent, and unprofitable establishments had been shuttered and padlocked.

Statistics showed a continuing increase in the number of luxury hotel rooms. The Marriott Tremont Place (1,000), a Ritz-Carlton (280), a Vista (250), and a Holiday Inn (250) were all scheduled to open in the next two to three years, which would change the present ratio of rooms in Class A (luxury), Class B (moderate), and Class C (inexpensive). Compared to other western American cities, Denver had the second smallest percentage of inexpensive rooms, thus forcing many potential customers to go to other parts of the metropolitan area. Projections indicated that the number of Class A hotel rooms would greatly exceed demand. According to the Denver Redevelopment Authority, when the Auditorium reopened, supply and demand would be as shown in Table 3-3-2.

Until the Colorado Legislature acted to authorize expansion of the Denver Auditorium, there had been fear that overconstruction, cou-

TABLE 3-3-2 Projected Supply and Demand in Denver

	% Room Sales	% Class A		% Class B		% Class C	
		Supply	Demand	Supply	Demand	Supply	Demand
Business	44	70	68	26	27	4	5
Tourist	26	47	40	40	41	13	19
Convention	30	83	64	15	32	2	4

pled with the lack of a large, modern convention center, would result in low occupancy levels. The Greater Denver Convention and Tourist Bureau predicted that the city's overall occupancy could slip ten percentage points from the current 58 percent before rising again when the Auditorium reopened. The total number of people visiting the Denver area had been declining for the past three years.

Competition

The management of Johnson Hotels believed that the three hotels had different competitive markets. In describing the Park Plaza, Johnson said, "Our competition is everybody. In an 880-room hotel, we can't deal with just one segment. We've got to deal with every segment. Downtown first-quality hotels are the Towers and the Sheraton Denver for convention groups, the Quality or Tremont Square for tours, and the Denver House for airlines. They are all our competition."

Management was confident that distinct differences existed that set the Park Plaza apart from the competition. The Park Plaza was primarily concerned with the convention market. Price/value was the key to differentiating from the competition, with the pricing flexibility of the newer hotels being limited by a high debt

service. Location, guest relations, and service quality were also cited as differentiating factors.

The Plaza Towers competed with the Sheraton Towers, the Denver House Towers, the Hyatt Regency, and the Tremont Plaza. The new hotels were expected to offer further competition.

Competition for the Lenox was considered to be the Denver House, Summit, and the existing Marriott. "Even the Park Plaza competes with the Lenox for some segments," commented one salesperson. In management's opinion, the Lenox had the advantage of location and also price/value due to its ability to undercut the competition and still realize a profit.

In the case of the Tremont Square, Johnson said, "There is really no competition for this hotel. One could say that the Uptown Motor Inn competes with us, or maybe the Beaver Hotel to a certain extent. But they don't compete in terms of the quality offered or location."

Jeffrey Johnson commented that the Uptown was a property with higher rates located in a less-desirable section of town. The fact that the Uptown was owned by the Church of the Latter-day Saints and, therefore, not serving liquor, was also considered a disadvantage. However, he felt that the Beaver would effectively compete if the hotel's facilities were improved.

CHAPTER 4

The Marketing Plan

The marketing plan is the working document that the hospitality enterprise develops for action during the forthcoming year. Although sometimes marketing plans are written for future years, and in fact often give at least some brief mention to the next two to five years for the sake of continuity, they are usually written for just one year at a time.

The marketing plan of a business unit flows from its own strategy and mission statement that, of course, derive from the corporate strategy and corporate mission statement. In many hospitality firms the corporate level and the business unit level are one and the same. This does not negate the need for strategic planning. On the other hand, many hospitality firms do not do strategic planning or develop annual marketing plans. This can be a mistake. Marketing plans are quite common in chain hotels and large restaurant companies, but not so common in smaller companies or individual properties, especially restaurants.

Requirements for a Marketing Plan

There are two key elements to a successful marketing plan: (1) that it is workable, and (2) that

it is realistic. Too many plans fail in one or both of these respects.

The marketing plan has to remain simple and easy to execute. Two-hundred-page marketing plans with a list of one-hundred action steps may be impressive, but unproductive. Too many hospitality enterprises confuse activity with productivity. The result is poorer performance and frustration. The marketing plan that is the simplest, with a few key items to be completed, will be the most focused and successful.

The marketing plan must also be flexible.

A road map is useful if one is lost in a highway system, but not in a swamp whose topography is constantly changing. A simple compass that indicates the general direction and allows you to use your own ingenuity in overcoming difficulties is far more valuable.[1]

The topography of the hospitality industry changes rapidly these days. Marketing plans, even more than strategic plans, should always be adaptable to changes in the business topography. Thus, marketing plans must constantly be reviewed and reevaluated. This is not to say that they should be changed at the sign of the slightest aberration; a good marketing plan has

---

[1]Robert H. Hayes, "Why Strategic Planning Goes Awry," *New York Times,* April 20, 1986.

a certain stability to it. This simply means that you mustn't be locked into a position when you later encounter evidence that this position will no longer be the most effective.

The marketing plan must be appropriate for the business in terms of capacity, image, scope, and risk, as well as being feasible in terms of time and resources. This would seem to be a fairly obvious statement but it is often violated. Owners' demands, corporate and management demands, and other factors may sometimes lead to marketing plans that simply have little or no chance of success. Although a marketing plan will have objectives, they should be based solely and entirely on the characteristics of the market and the resources to implement the plan. Wild-eyed dreams and wishful thinking will not overcome these realities just because someone higher-up says, "Raise the numbers" (a hotel industry expression meaning increase occupancy and average rate).

The marketing plan should assign specific responsibility, with times and dates for accomplishment. Continuous follow-up assures that these responsibilities will be met. This provision requires that the plan be thoroughly understood by everyone in the organization. A good plan indicates how marketing activities are integrated with all other activities of the operation. What this means is that the marketing plan doesn't stop at the door of the marketing office. Although the details of the plan will not go to every person in the workforce, the essence of the plan should do exactly that.

A Bangkok hotel, for example, planned to attract a market segment of German families with children on vacation at a package rate. The promotion was a success and the families came, but no one had made adequate plans, as promised in the promotion, for children's activities, baby-sitters, or even extra beds to be placed in the rooms. Any plan that succeeds in attracting the market but fails to fulfill its promises, explicit or implicit, to that market will in the long term be self-defeating. Personnel cannot deliver what marketing promises if they don't know what those promises are or don't have the tools to deliver on them.

A good marketing plan provides direction for an operation. It states where you are going and what you are going to have to do to get there. It builds employee and management confidence through shared effort and teamwork toward common goals. It recognizes weaknesses, emphasizes strengths, and deals with reality. It seeks and exploits opportunities. And last but certainly not least, a good marketing plan gets everyone into the act.

Some marketing plans are no more than a description of the facility, a list of possible competitors and their facilities, an advertising and sales plan, and a forecast and budget. These are necessary but not sufficient elements of a marketing plan that succeeds. Like everything else we have said in this book, the test of the marketing plan is embodied in the question, "How will the customer be served?"

Development of a Marketing Plan

As in strategic planning, the marketing plan begins with a situation analysis. Here, however, we are dealing with greater specifics. Our goal is to decide how our marketing resources will be used to best attract and serve designated markets.

It is well to begin, then, with a restatement of the firm's philosophy, the master strategy, and the mission statement of the property. This will establish the context within which the marketing plan will be developed. The next step is to complete the first major portion of the plan, data collection.

Data Collection— The External Environment

Data collection can be divided into two parts, external and internal. External data deals with the environment, including international and domestic trends that were mentioned in Chapter 3. These will be further explained Chapter 5. There are also numerous industry trends to be considered, such as growth or decline of various market segments, building trends affecting future supply, room occupancy and eating-out trends, and new-concept trends.

Then there are external impacts such as state, regional, or national tourism promotions, major new tourist attractions, new industries in the area, new office buildings being built, airline routes added or removed, plant closings, companies merged and moved, new sources of visitor origin, and new convention centers being built. Every factor does not affect every operation; the key is to recognize those that may affect yours. The marketing plan has to deal with these factors, prepare for them, and, whenever possible, capitalize on them or counteract them.

For example, we know of one restaurateur who had operated a very successful restaurant for a number of years until business began declining drastically in the late 1970s. Because this operation was in the country and off a main highway, the operator concluded that people were simply not traveling as often or as far, because of the recent increase in the cost of gasoline due to the sudden increase in oil prices. Closer analysis, however, revealed that his competition was doing better than ever. In fact, the tastes of the market had changed and new markets had emerged. Instead of adapting to the market (e.g., he refused to change his menu because his remaining old customers "loved it as it is"), he watched his business gradually disappear.

Data Collection—The Competition

The second area of external data collection is concerned with the competition. It is important that the local marketing team collect data on all feasible competitors within logical boundaries. Understand that "logical boundaries" may mean the hotel or restaurant across the street or it may mean the one 3,000 miles away. The competition for the convention market for the Hotel del Coronado off the coast of California includes the Homestead Hotel in Hot Springs, Virginia, the Greenbriar Hotel in White Sulphur Springs, West Virginia, the Cloisters Hotel in Sea Island, Georgia, the Breakers Hotel in

Palm Beach, Florida, and the Hyatt Regency in Maui, Hawaii, not to mention many others.

The motel in North Overshoe, Maine, competes with the motel in South Skislope, Maine, even though they are 30 miles apart. The Club Med in Eleuthera in the Bahamas competes with the all-inclusive Couples in Jamaica.[2] The restaurant in the city competes with the one in the suburbs. And McDonald's competes with the convenience store but, by the same token, neither one competes with the French restaurant located between them. *Competition,* as defined in the marketing plan, *is anyone competing for the same customer with the same or a similar product, or a reasonable alternative, that the customer has a reasonable opportunity to purchase at the same time and in the same context.*

As in everything, of course, there may be exceptions. We may even want to expand from this perspective of competition in a highly competitive environment, or from the perspective of a period of slow economic growth, when it may be necessary to reach downmarket from the current level of product in order to maintain acceptable profit margins.

These different views of who the competition is will be discussed in the next chapter on competitive analysis. Let it suffice here to say that the marketing plan should include data on any competitor that, in the forthcoming year, we can reasonably expect to take customers from, or to which we could conceivably lose customers.

The marketing team must take an objective stance when it comes to evaluating the competition. While we all like to believe we have the best product to sell in our product class, this may lull us into a false sense of security, and the competition can move by us very quickly. The marketing plan must be truly objective and realistic about the products evaluated, for the best results. After making a list of all competitors for your product, the information shown in Table 4-1 will be needed.

In the development of the marketing plan, it is also critical to keep in mind the fact that you want new customers and that you are looking

---

[2]An "all-inclusive" resort contains all products/services, e.g., food, drink, lodging, sports activities, in one all-inclusive price.

TABLE 4-1   Competitive Information Needed in the Marketing Plan

Description: A brief description of the physical attributes of the competing hotel or restaurant or lounge (or nation, country, state, or city, etc.). Emphasize good points as well as bad. Determine such things as when the product was last renovated, plans for upgrading in the near future, physical facilities, and all features that compete with yours—that is, the product/service mix. The description includes quality and level of both tangible and intangible features, personnel, procedures, management, reservations systems, distribution networks, marketing efforts and successes and failures, promotions, market share, image, positioning, chain advantages/disadvantages, and so forth. All of these items will be important in the final analysis. A physical description—number of rooms, meeting space, F&B outlets and so on—is simply not enough. All strengths and weaknesses need to be defined.

Customer Base: Who are their customers? Why do these customers go there? Are they potentially your customers? Part of the marketing plan will focus on creating demand for your product. Most of the plan will focus on taking customers directly from your competitors. It will be difficult to take customers from your competition if you do not know who these customers are. In a restaurant situation, for example, do your competitors have a high volume of senior citizens eating at traditionally quiet times, a group that you desire? Does their lounge have a successful "happy hour" that you could augment for your lounge and, if so, what type of people go there? Does your competitive hotel have a higher percentage of transient guests than your own? What particular market segments does the competition attract?

Price Structure: Where is your competition in relation to price? While food and beverage prices are relatively easy to obtain, the product delivered for the price is also important. Is their $6.95 chef's salad as large as yours for $7.95? When analyzing prices it is important to compare "apples with apples." Published guestroom prices are relatively easy to discover. Negotiated prices with volume producers take a little more effort but can usually be obtained from purchasers.

Future Supply: It is important to determine if there are any new projects that will affect your competitive environment in the future. This information can normally be obtained from the Chamber of Commerce or other local sources. The fact that a new 300-room hotel is scheduled to break ground soon is very important in the development of the marketing plan. Likewise, if the building that houses a major food and beverage competitor is scheduled for demolition to make way for a new office park, this could also influence your decision-making process for the following year.

Once again, keep in mind that competition is all relative. Traditional boundaries of location may no longer apply. For a restaurant in New York City the competition may encompass a three-block radius that is less than one-quarter square mile. For a five-star resort hotel the competition might be located thousands of miles away. When determining who your competition is, the question must be asked, "Where else do/might my customers/potential customers go?"

for opportunities to get them. This means that sometimes you have to break the "rules" of competition. For example, a Hilton property might normally be positioned against Sheraton, Hyatt, and Westin as competition. In good times this might be correct. However, when occupan-cies are low the Hilton Hotel might consider customers whom it could capture at a profit from other competition. If rooms are going vacant, a "normal" Holiday Inn customer might be a target of the marketing plan of the hypotheti-cal Hilton. A Holiday Inn customer, paying $50 for a room that costs $25 to produce, may be a good customer to have when the room might otherwise be vacant. In addition, there might be a synergistic effect in being able to retain this person as a regular customer. On the other hand, the Red Roof Inn customer, who can only afford a room at $39, would not be considered as an alternative target.

Data Collection—Internal

The third area of data collection is internal. One hopes that accurate and adequate records have been kept, and much of this information will be readily at hand. Once you have prepared your first marketing plan you will have said, at least a dozen times, "I wish I knew that." Thus, you will have set up procedures so that next year you will know "that."

Hotels and/or restaurants should have current data at all times on occupied rooms, occupancy ratio, revenues, average rate (totally and by market segment), market segments served, restaurant covers, seat turnovers, menu abstracts, average check, food- to beverage-check ratios (totally and for each outlet), and ratios as a percentage of gross revenue. These figures should be broken down by month, seasonally, and by days of the week.

These are the "hard" data and the easiest to obtain, but not the place to stop. List now what you know about the markets. Who are they, what do they like, what are their needs and wants? Why do they come here? Where would they go if they didn't come here? What are their complaints? Describe their characteristics, attitudes, opinions, and preferences. What is the market's perception and awareness? If you don't know the answers to these questions, it is time to start doing some research. At the minimum, start talking to your customers. Have personnel in every single department keep logs on all customer comments—good, bad, and otherwise.

Formal research is even better. The basic tenet of all marketing is to know your market. It is surprising how few hospitality establishments do. This is why so many marketing plans, rather than discuss what they will do for

the customer, deal with bricks and mortar, physical facilities, inaccurate definition of competition, broad market segments (e.g., the business traveler), vague budgets and forecasts, and undirected advertising.

The second category of internal data collection is the objective listing of resource strengths and weaknesses—including the bricks and mortar. What is the condition of the property? Where is it weak and where is it strong? How can/should it be improved? What does it offer in terms of facilities? How effective is the location?

Then, the hardest part: How strong is management? The marketing staff? Personnel training, experience, and attitude? How are guests being treated? What do complaints look like? How are they handled? How successful have marketing efforts been in the past? What is the consumer image of the property? What is the position in the marketplace? This is the time for realistic objectivity, not glossing over or wishful thinking. Finally, make a list of what you do not know—that is, what research is needed.

To give an idea of how all this comes together, some abstractions from the data collection portion of the actual marketing plan of a hotel in Belgium are shown in Table 4-2.

Data Analysis

Thus far, we have been engaged only in the collection of data. It is wise to complete this stage first without attempting to analyze the data, because you want to obtain the complete picture. Analyzing different factors in isolation can be misleading.

Analysis follows the same flow as the data-collection process. Essentially, we want to draw some conclusions about market position, market segments, customer behavior, environmental impacts, growth potential, strengths and weaknesses, threats and opportunities, performance trends, customer satisfaction, resource needs and limitations, and other factors that will be pertinent to the marketing plan.

Environmental Analysis   Look first at environmental trends. Are they positive or negative? How will/can they affect us? How can we

TABLE 4-2   Data Collection Abstracts from a Belgian Hotel Marketing Plan

Economy : Despite the economic recession and the bad position of the Belgian franc (which favors our incoming business), business is showing a slightly increasing trend. The percentage of international tourists is increasing. On the other hand, Belgian companies have substantially reduced or canceled budgets for meetings, seminars, and travel.

External Impacts: There are severe occupancy problems in winter. Bad weather conditions and lack of activities in the city center have strong negative impact on travel patterns. Competition is coming down hard on prices. There are a large number of good a la carte restaurants downtown offering attractive weekend menus at good prices. Our location away from the center of town is a disadvantage.

Internal Impacts: Customers are more and more cost-conscious, especially on F&B expenses. We are receiving many complaints on lack of color TV sets and on the lack of soundproofing on the first, second, and third floors. Quality of food is not up to standard, especially for groups. Budgets were not finished until the end of last year and were not ready or effective at the beginning of this year. Communication between departments is poor. The entire staff is not sufficiently motivated.

Future of Our Markets: There is an increase of short-holiday tourists and weekenders from the Netherlands and Germany. There is an increase of the European tour series. There is an increase of package bookings, especially during the summer. There is a decrease of company individual bookings. A new 230-room hotel will open next spring near the city center.

---

take advantage of, or compensate, for them? What are our alternatives? How long will they last? What courses of action are possible and feasible? How do these fit together?

Competitive and Demand Analysis   What are the potentials and opportunities in the marketplace? This requires a close analysis of all the demand factors, various market segments, and target markets—for instance: What are the strongest market segments? What is their potential for further growth? Are they steady, growing, or in decline? What is their contribution in room-nights, covers, revenue? What can be done to accelerate a growing trend, begin growth in a steady trend, or reverse the direction of a declining trend? What other segments are there, perhaps untouched, that could be developed?

How do these segments affect our market mix? Are they compatible? Can they be expanded to fill gaps such as seasonal or day-of-the-week fluctuations? What types of business would complement these segments? What types of action could be taken to attract more business during low-occupancy periods? How does the competitive situation affect all these factors?

Property Needs Analysis

A property needs analysis is a thorough review of major profit areas to see what gaps have to be filled. These gaps could be in occupancy, market share, average room rates, market segments, food sales, beverage sales, seasonal needs, and many other areas. In other words, instead of looking at where we can cut costs, we want to look at where we can obtain business. When we have done that, we can match property needs with market needs to determine target markets and how to reach and serve them.

Needs analysis also means identifying other marketing problems. These might be, for example, marketing strategies that aren't working, image changes that are needed, ineffective advertising or promotion, pricing problems, losing business to a particular competitor (perhaps because of a new facility, new product or service, or even just better marketing), or changing needs of a market segment that we can't meet.

In short, needs analysis is an identification of problems to be overcome. It makes the case clearer if we can apply some quantitative measurements to our analysis, which is no more than a best estimate based upon all of the data assembled. To demonstrate this we will use a simplified case to determine what the overall increase or decrease for the product will be for the forthcoming year. Ideally, this would be done by market segment. In this example, we will say that we are anticipating an increase of two percent in demand for both group and transient hotel rooms in the product class category. From the data collected, a competitive universe can be compiled as shown in Table 4-3. Assume, also, for the purpose of this discussion, that a Holiday Inn Crowne Plaza of 200 rooms is opening in the following year with a projected occupancy of 55 percent. Its forecasted market mix is 50 percent group and 50 percent transient.

Now, for the purpose of developing the marketing plan, we have some quantitative data with which to work. One thing is immediately obvious: ABC Hotel has a relatively low occupancy and is barely getting fair market share. After analyzing all the data collected in the situation analysis, two main areas of concentration are ready to be addressed: creating new business and capturing competitors' business.

Creation of New Business

Given the current situation, what plans can be developed to create a new demand for the product? McDonald's created a new demand for its product by opening for breakfast. Package weekends have created new demands for hotel products in the past. Creating a new demand in the hospitality industry, however, may be the toughest part of marketing. The important point to remember is that we are creating demand that until now did not exist for a product. This usually means creating a new use.

The "Murder Mystery Weekend" is an example (Figure 4-1) of a promotion to create new business. In this case, the target market is couples with a sense of adventure who may be bored with alternatives. They might have stayed home for the weekend except for this exciting opportunity, or they may have been enticed from a competitor offering the standard weekend package. The objective of the hotel, of course, is to build weekend business. This is different from, for example, selling a corporate meeting package, where meeting planners have already decided what they want to do, their only question being "where." That constitutes direct marketing against the competition, rather than creating a new use for the product. The rest of the marketing plan will carry out and specify the implementation of the murder weekend concept in terms of the specific target market, as discussed later.

Capturing Competitors' Business   Most efforts of the marketing plan will concentrate in this area. Specifically, let's return to the competitive universe depicted in Table 4-3. ABC Hotel's main competitors are Westin, Hyatt, and Hilton, plus the new Crowne Plaza being built.

TABLE 4-3   Hypothetical Competitive Universe of ABC Hotel

Hotel	Number of Rooms	Avail./Year	FMS[a]	% Occ.	Rooms Sold	AMS[b]	% Var.	Rank
ABC Hotel	200	73,000	20%	67	48,910	20%	0	3
Westin	350	127,750	35%	73	93,258	38.2%	3.2	1
Hyatt	250	91,250	25%	72	65,700	26.9%	1.9	2
Hilton	200	73,000	20%	50	36,500	14.9%	(5.1)	4
Total	1,000	365,000	100%		244,368	100%		

[a]FMS (Fair Market Share) is the number of available rooms per hotel divided by total available rooms.
[b]AMS (Actual Market Share) is the number of rooms sold per hotel divided by the total number of rooms sold.

Courtesy of Buck Hill Inn and Greenwald/Christian Agency, Philadelphia

FIGURE 4-1   Advertising a murder mystery weekend

A demand analysis for these five hotels, two of which are capturing more than fair market share while ABC and Hilton are not, might appear as shown in Table 4-4.

A red flag should be raised with this scenario. Although the forecast is an increase in demand for the hotel product, the increase in supply will be greater than the increase in demand. Each hotel will now be fighting for a smaller piece of the pie. If ABC Hotel does everything the same as the year before, they will be drawing on a smaller pool of rooms and occupancy will drop lower. In fact, ABC and its four competitors are now competing for 209,105 rooms vs. the 244,368 of the previous year, after the new Crowne Plaza takes its share.

ABC's marketing team can now see the task that lies before it. In order just to maintain the occupancies of the year before, it will have to create new demand for the product, aggres-

TABLE 4-4   Hypothetical Demand Analysis

	Total	Group Segment	Transient Segment	New ABC FMS	@20% AMS
Rooms Sold Previous Year	244,368	146,231	98,137		
Next year projection with 2% increase in demand	249,255	149,156	100,099		
New Supply Crowne Plaza	40,150	20,075	20,075	16.7%	49,851

sively attack competitors for new business, and maintain its own customer base, which the competition will be trying to lure away with their own marketing plans. It will also have to exceed its new FMS by 2.95 percentage points, something it hasn't been able to do in the past. ABC's strength may be as a transient hotel, while this may be a weakness of the other properties. In this case, ABC might choose to direct its major marketing effort at that market.

Another possibility is that ABC has neglected the group market and needs to direct greater effort in that direction. Then, of course, it may have to make major efforts in both directions. Let us assume, for the sake of argument and because it is easier to demonstrate, that there is high price sensitivity in the market in either one or both of these segments. In either case, specific marketing plans must be made to attack the competitive hotels in order to capture rooms from them. The plans might, perhaps, be directed at lowering prices on specific days of the week or times of the year when ABC's occupancy suffers the most.

The ABC example is clearly an oversimplified one. There are innumerable other factors affecting any similar situation, and numerous alternative approaches. In fact, we haven't even mentioned the consumer in this discussion, and that database would be the first one to consider! The point we want to make is that there is an absolute need for complete and adequate data and information, followed by thorough analysis of all possible considerations. It is only through

such methods that workable, realistic, and effective marketing plans can be developed.

Internal Analysis

We now turn to the internal analysis (not that we would have done the preceding without doing the internal analysis first!). Using the realistic and objective data we have gathered, we start by asking questions such as those shown in Table 4-5.

Once again, the list could go on indefinitely. Once again, we have to state that workable, effective, and realistic marketing plans can be developed only through the gathering of complete and adequate information and its thorough and objective analysis.

Market Analysis

Our final step in analysis is the market itself, the customer. Because this entire book is about the hospitality customer, it would be redundant to repeat here all that we will say about this strange individual who is the reason for the existence of any hospitality enterprise. For purposes of developing the marketing plan, this step means determining where the gaps are, where needs are unfulfilled, where problems are not being solved, and where the niches are that the competition is not filling.

This analysis must be matched with the environmental trends, the competitive and demand analysis, the property needs analysis,

TABLE 4-5   Internal Analysis Questions

What is the gap between what your customers want and need, what you promise them, and the product/service that is provided?

How well do you meet or exceed customer expectations?

How does the market's estimation of your product/service agree with yours? What makes you think so?

What items, product improvements, or services are needed to improve customer satisfaction?

Are you actually delivering what you think you are?

What patterns are appearing in guest comments? What types of problems seem to recur? What areas seem to need improvement?

Do you have the proper organization to accomplish what you are trying to? For instance, although the manager is a strong operations person, does he or someone else understand the customer?

Do you reward your staff strictly on bottom-line results? If so, does it show up in matters affecting the customers?

Do you know, identify, and deal with your real strengths and weaknesses?

and the internal analysis. We would, of course, combine all these analyses by segment and target market. We are then ready to develop a mission statement for the property, determine opportunities, establish objectives, and begin the actual marketing plan, which will include a plan and course of action for each segment or target market.

The Mission Statement

Earlier we discussed developing a mission statement for strategic planning. The mission statement of the marketing plan flows from the strategic mission statement and differs only in that it applies at the unit level (this could be an individual hotel or restaurant, or even an F&B outlet within a hotel).

The general guideline of the strategic mission statement may serve the purpose. In multiunit organizations, however, there can be great variety. Many chains have diversified products selling in diversified markets for diversified uses. Corporate strategies established in corporate headquarters in Atlanta, Memphis, New York, Hampton (NH), Paris, or Tokyo, do not necessarily fit the situation in India, Germany, Kuwait, New York City, Minneapolis, or Los Angeles. It is

the situation analysis of the marketing plan that provides the test of the strategy and may necessitate rewriting the local mission statement. Thus, only after the situation analysis has been completed do we recommend writing the marketing plan mission statement and, if necessary, adjusting the strategic mission statement. Recall, moreover, that the latter is the long-term mission; the marketing plan mission is designed for one year at a time.

Opportunity Analysis

If a thorough job of data collection and analysis has been done, we should now be able to determine the opportunities available. The section heading is self-explanatory and can best be discussed by example. Therefore, we abstract from the marketing plan of the Belgian hotel previously mentioned, as shown in Table 4-6.

The opportunities in Table 4-6, although perhaps too general, have been derived after analysis of the market, market segments, the competition, trends, the needs of the property, and so forth. Its brief form belies the groundwork that goes into identifying opportunities. Sometimes this groundwork is not done—that is, someone says something like, "How about the incentive

TABLE 4-6   Marketing Plan Opportunity Analysis of Belgian Hotel

A. Market segments relating to existing customer mix:
   1. Company groups
   2. Company residential seminars
   3. Company individual bookings
   4. Leisure tours
   5. Leisure clubs and societies
   6. Weekend packages
   7. Travel agents
   8. Walk-ins
B. New markets:
   1. Winter packages for individual travelers
   2. Netherlands bank travel agencies
   3. Incentive market
   4. Magazine holiday or mini-trip packages
   5. Incoming travel agencies
C. Image:
   1. More professional and colorful F&B promotions
   2. Improved reputation of service and cuisine
   3. Provide better background information about the city
   4. Renovations to improve image of bar, sauna, and swimming pool terrace
   5. Professional advertising to improve hotel image

market? We don't have any of that business. That's an opportunity! Let's put it down." Of course, a thorough study of the incentive market, its needs and wants, and the organization's ability to serve it is necessary first. Opportunities, in the true sense, are not just something that's "out there"; they are, instead, a match between consumer needs and an organization's competencies and, one hopes, a lapse in the competition.

Objectives

The next step in the marketing plan is to establish the objectives and how they are to be accomplished. Again, this is better explained by doing, so we continue to abstract from the marketing plan of the Belgian hotel as shown in Table 4-7.

The objectives listed in Table 4-7 are specific and fairly typical of hotel marketing plans. Action plans are designed to carry out each one. There could be many other kinds of objectives, including strategic ones, particularly those that

derive from the identification of market needs, such as the following:

Changes in marketing direction
Defensive or offensive marketing moves
New opportunities
Other specific product line objectives
Market share objectives—overall and by market segment, such as geographic, demographic, psychographic, group, FIT, package, etc.
Pricing objectives
Sales and promotion objectives
Advertising objectives
Channel, distribution, and intermediary objectives, such as travel agents
Research objectives
Awareness, perception, image, and positioning objectives
Double occupancy objectives
Customer loyalty and repeat business objectives
Customer satisfaction objectives

TABLE 4-7   Objectives and Methods from Belgian Hotel Marketing Plan

A. To increase yearly occupancy:
  1. Review annual forecast on a monthly and weekly basis to ensure an overall and continuous view of occupancies and early actions in case of problem periods or days.
  2. Orient the room rate structure to the market.
  3. Conduct permanent hard and aggressive sales actions to increase:
      a. company and commercial rate business
      b. seminars and conferences, especially in summer and winter
      c. winter and summer weekend business with families
      d. incentive travel year-round
      e. tour business and stopovers, especially in off-season
B. To keep up with the competition:
  1. Provide color and cable television.
  2. Hospitality service and well-trained staff.
  3. Continuous sales follow-up on existing clients.
  4. Continuous sales calls to potential new customers.
  5. Improve restaurant image.
  6. Offer clients "just a little more" in rooms and restaurant, which will make their stay with us different from the others.
  7. Refurbish bar (if possible enlarge).
  8. Develop more creativity in sales and F&B.
C. To level out occupancy throughout the year:
  1. Develop attractive (but not bargain) offers during weak periods for seminars and conferences.
  2. Develop winter packages for individuals.
  3. Provide seasonal rates for bus tours.
  4. Develop new initiatives, such as room here and lunch in Bruges.
  5. Develop incentive tour arrangements.
  6. Promote Sunday night business to tour operators and wholesalers.
D. To level out occupancy over the week:
  1. Lower rate for winter seminars during the week.
  2. Develop packages for individuals to be distributed to German and Netherlands travel agents with special commission rates.
  3. Create special activities for tour operators to sell in United Kingdom, Germany, and the Netherlands.
E. To increase average rate:
  1. Increase company rates.
  2. Increase bus tour rates.
  3. Increase rates in the commercial business market.
  4. Appeal more to walk-in guests with roadside advertising.
  5. Build higher rate in luxury rooms through luxury room amenities.
  6. Try to reduce low-rate contracts during high season.
  7. Charge supplement on group rates on special event weekends.
F. To increase F&B sales by:
  1. Appeal more to in-house guests through:
      a. promotional material in rooms, lobby, reception, and other guest service areas
      b. vouchers for first drink in bar at reduced rate
      c. food promotion frames inside and in front of elevators

(continued)

TABLE 4-7   (continued)

      d. sales-trained people in bar, restaurant, and coffee shop
      e. dinner dance twice a week during winter
      f. more eye-catchers in restaurant and coffee shop
      g. training desk clerks to ask at check-in if guests want to reserve table in restaurant
  2. Develop the local market through promotions:
      a. candlelight dinner dance promotions
      b. Sunday family brunch
      c. wedding promotions
      d. charity dinners
      e. promotions for staff parties
      f. funeral banquet promotions through funeral agents
      g. attract companies in the neighborhood, e.g., with a sandwich bar
      h. more organized activities

We caution again not to try to do too many things at once. Make objectives reasonable, so they can be accomplished and can be done well.

A marketing plan needs to be employed for existing customers as well. These customers may, in fact, be the best opportunity and the target of the most important objectives. This part of the plan addresses current patrons, and should be designed to make them "competition proof." Because the main emphasis of the marketing plan will be on capturing competitors' business, so too will be the emphasis of competitors' marketing plans. If the focus is entirely on bringing in new customers and the present customers are forgotten, then the marketing plan is simply going to be one of robbing Peter to pay Paul. Replacing current customers with new customers is never cost-efficient.

A documented plan to keep guests coming back and to reduce exposure to competitors' attempts to steal customers should be an integral part of any marketing plan. Once again, however, this does not necessarily mean giveaway programs. The basic task of marketing is to fulfill its promises, not give away the product.

Action Plans

Action plans dictate how the marketing plan will be carried out. They assign specific responsibility to individuals and dates for accomplish-ment. An action plan is a detailed list of the action steps necessary for carrying out the strategies and tactics for reaching each objective. One format for an action plan is shown in Table 4-8, but there are numerous variations on the theme.

Action plans deal with the various parts of the marketing mix which, of course, is the implementation of the marketing plan. For example, the action plan for the communications mix would incorporate advertising, direct mail, personal sales efforts, promotions, merchandising, and public relations campaigns. Each of these is coordinated for maximum impact of the strategies derived from the conclusions drawn from the creation of the business- and competitive-strategies section of the plan.

The action plan should be developed for a full year, with all products and actions for new business, keeping current business, and strategies for taking business from competitors outlined in time frames that reflect achievable goals.

In the previous example of the murder mystery weekend, advertising support may be necessary in designated months to create awareness and requests for more information. An ad in a meeting magazine might be in support of a special meeting package, designed to counter a competitor's offering during the traditionally slower months in the fall. An advertisement in a travel agency index might be intended to offer

TABLE 4-8   Marketing Action Plan

XYZ HOTEL MARKETING ACTION PLAN

NAME: _____ Quarter: _____

BOOKING GOALS

1,000 MONTH   250 WEEK   50 DAY

NEW ACCOUNTS OPENED

20 MONTH   5 WEEK   1 DAY

Action Plan by Week: **Person Responsible:**

Week 1 _____ begin advertising campaign, corporate group _____
Week 2 _____ trade show schedule, third quarter _____
Week 3 _____ direct mail, corporate transient_____
Week 4 _____ good accounts function, associations _____
Week 5 _____ public relations for catering _____
Week 6 _____ public relations for catering _____
Week 7 _____ focus groups, meeting planners_____
Week 8 _____ focus groups, travel agents_____
Week 9 _____ image advertising campaign begins _____
Week 10 _____ strategy session, tour and travel_____
Week 11 _____ direct mail, past users _____
Week 12 _____ develop co-marketing partners _____

an alternative to competition, at present more frequently utilized by travel agencies.

Yearly schedules of the communications mix's other support mechanisms are needed to coordinate the entire plan. A direct mail campaign might be used in conjunction with the advertising for the murder mystery weekend to generate the highest volume. Without action plans, too many things are forgotten too often, or are done too late to be effective.

There are other concerns as well. The communications mix is expensive to execute. The aggressive marketing executive will constantly be looking for ways to maximize communications mix dollars. Co-advertising is possible with related travel industries. Airlines are increasingly willing to work with hotels to generate business through collective advertising and direct mail.

Credit card companies are continually doing dual promotions with restaurants and lounges to differentiate their products and combine resources. All these efforts require considerable advance planning and specific, timely action.

Except for forecasts and budgeting, the marketing plan is now complete. Remember, this should be a "fluid" document, ready to be changed with shifts of the marketplace. This is not to suggest that the entire marketing plan be rewritten every time there is a shift in the market; if the situation analysis is done properly, the conclusions drawn should not change dramatically.

Some opportunities, however, that present themselves during the year should be incorporated into an effective marketing plan. If an opportunity arises to do a combined direct mail piece to selected guests of a reputable credit card company, it should not be passed up just because it's not in the marketing plan. If necessary, the plan should be re-analyzed and resources reallocated.

The Marketing Forecast

Making accurate marketing forecasts is one of the most difficult stages of the marketing plan. Regardless, the best attempt possible is essential. Forecasts are ventures into the unknown that are subject to any number of alterations in the marketplace. The answer to accuracy lies in the best available information, thorough analysis, and the best judgment of the forecaster.

Many hotel marketing plan formats require the projection of room-nights for every day of the forthcoming year to forecast, by segment and day of the week, the upcoming year's business. It is not uncommon for forecasters to use some figure, say five percent, as the projected increase in sales over the previous year. Such a method is purely arbitrary and of little advantage. It is better to start with a zero base each year and build according to the marketing plan. In this way, room-nights, covers, and other sources of revenue are based on the marketing objectives that have been realistically established. Monetary amounts such as average room rate per segment, average breakfast, lunch, and dinner check, and so on are used as the multipliers to forecast revenue.

Table 4-9 illustrates a forecast form used by one hotel company. Again, there are many variations on the theme according to the particular situation or needs of the operation.

The Marketing Budget

Industry-wide averages for marketing budgets of U.S. hotels are between six and seven percent of total sales. (There are no reported averages for restaurants except a general figure of two to three percent of sales spent on advertising for an individual sit-down mid- to upper-scale operation.) As a rule of thumb, the marketing payroll expenses are normally about one-half of the marketing budget. Traditionally, resorts have slightly higher marketing expenses. The overall trend in the industry has been toward increasing the marketing budget as a total percentage of sales.

Internationally, the expenses for marketing average slightly lower, at between four and five percent of total sales. Latin American and Caribbean hotels spend over six percent of sales for their marketing budget, while hotels in Europe and Africa spend under four percent of their total sales.[3]

Unfortunately, these industry averages mean very little in the increasingly competitive environment that has been created in the hospitality industry. The traditional five percent of hotel sales allocated to marketing was sufficient for a property to consistently maintain its market share and occupancies in the days when the increase in demand for hotel rooms was exceeding the number of rooms being built.

While demand continues to be strong for the lodging product, supply of the product in many markets has eclipsed the growth curve. Some markets have seen a 20-plus percent increase in supply of hotel rooms, with a five percent increase in demand. More important, for marketing planning, what is taking place is a shift in the market into different product classes. To attack a problem of this kind with a traditional marketing budget of five percent of total sales would be like David fighting Goliath. (Recall, however, that David won—with a better strategy.)

The marketing budget should be a natural extension of the marketing plan—no more and no less. Once a strategy has been developed to create, steal, or keep customers, the funds need to be allocated to ensure success.

The budget will normally include the following categories in some degree, regardless of the size or type of the operation. This even includes a case in which, for example, the manager of a restaurant (chain, individual, or within a hotel) performs all the marketing and sales duties.

---

[3]Percentages are from *Trends in the Hotel Industry USA Edition* and *Trends in the Hotel Industry International Edition*, published annually, Houston, TX: Pannell Kerr Forster.

TABLE 4-9 Hotel Occupancy Forecasting Form, by Month

	Last Year Actual Rooms Occupied	Last Year Actual Average Rate	Last Year Actual Revenues	Budget Revenues	Budget Average Rate	Budget Rooms Rented	J	F	M
Pure/Transient									
Meeting/Convention									
Tour & Travel									
Individual									
Wholesaler									
Group									
Total Tour & Travel									
Contract									
Charter									
Other									
Total Contract									
Commercial									
Preferred Company									
Preferred Guest									
Other									
Total Commercial									
Special Programs									
Weekend Package									
Other									
Other									
Other									
Other									
Totals									
Rooms Available									
% of Occupancy									

Parts of that person's salary and expenses should be allocated to the marketing budget.

Payroll will include all marketing and sales time plus any secretarial or related work.

Communication includes all advertising, promotion, direct mail, public relations, collateral, and related items.

Travel includes all related travel.

Office Expenses include telephone and related office supplies.

Research includes all research expenses.

Entertainment includes entertainment of clients or prospective clients both in-house and out.

The above are broad and fairly obvious categories. Further breakdown depends on the needs of the operation. What is important is that marketing expenses be clearly and appropriately assigned. As with any other budget items, they are a cost of operating a particular department. Table 4-10 shows one hotel's monthly spreadsheet for allocating particular expenses to a given month.

The budget should be carefully prepared, not done haphazardly or by guesswork. If you are not your own boss, you will probably have to have it approved by someone. In that case, you may have to justify each cost item as one that will produce tangible results.

The marketing budget should also be a fluid tool, reacting to the changes in the marketing plan. It is critical to protect the integrity of the budget and plan throughout the planning year.

TABLE 4-10   Monthly Spreadsheet for Allocating Expenses

	Date	Market Segment	Costs
Sales Trips / Trade Shows			
Washington (WSAE)	5/95	Group	
Atlanta/Delta & Agents	5/95	T&T/Whlslrs.	
Incentive House Trip	5/95	T&T	
Advertising			
Hotel Trvl. Index 1 pg 4C	Quarterly	T&T	
Fla. Resident Ad 2 col 5"	1 week	Special	
Southern Living 4" ad	Monthly	Trans.	
Travel Agent Mktplc.	Bi-monthly	T&T	
Trvl. Weekly 20" 4C	6×	T&T	
F&B Advertising			
Fla. Tour News	6×	F&B	
Orlando Mag. 1/2 pg BW	Monthly	F&B	
Dining Out 1 pg BW	Monthly	F&B	
Orlando Sentinel	5×	F&B	
Local News	1×	F&B	
Special Promotions			
Mother's Day Coll. & Menu	Annual	F&B	
Samantha's Calendar	Monthly	F&B	
Direct Mail			
Bus. Reply	Ongoing	Group	
Samantha's Mailing	Monthly	F&B	
Mother's Day Mailing	Annual	F&B	
Collateral Proration			
5,000 Rack Brochures	Ongoing	Group	
5,000 IT Brochures	Ongoing	T&T	
7,000 F&B Brochures	Ongoing	F&B	

The plan and budget should be changed if results are falling short of forecasts. For instance, the murder mystery weekend might be considered cost-effective if it produced 50 rooms for a given Friday and Saturday night. If after three or four attempts, the demand never exceeds 35 room-nights, the responsive marketing team will reevaluate the feasibility of the project.

The decision might be to try the promotion again at a later date, or to scrap it altogether and allocate the funds elsewhere. When cutting the marketing budget, the difficult decisions occur when managers think only in short-term objectives (i.e., improving short-term financial performance by cutting costs) rather than execute longer-term strategies to increase and retain customers.

This type of situation occurs frequently in the careers of sales and marketing professionals. Although there is no clear-cut answer to the dilemma, the need to create and keep customers should be the paramount consideration for any successful organization. Short-term rewards are gained too many times at the expense of future business.

Marketing Controls

There is a final step and an important one: monitoring the marketing plan throughout the year and evaluating it at the end of the year.

The first step, of course, is to continuously match performance against the desired results and to detect when and where deviations occur. The extent of each deviation should be measured and the worst ones addressed. The cause of each deviation should be determined and dealt with, either by bringing it into line or by adjusting the plan.

Yardsticks are set up in advance. These could include any of the following as well as others: market share, occupancy figures, covers served, seat turnovers, check averages, F&B ratios, revenue per guest room, average room rate by market segment, product mix, business mix by segments, advance bookings, advertising results, return per marketing dollar, customer sat-isfaction, complaints/compliments, repeat business, revenue, and profit.

A feedback system should be established to synchronize with the yardsticks. You should be able to answer questions such as the following:

Is the product meeting needs of the market segment(s)?
Is the segment growing, static, or declining?
Is the segment profitable?
Is customer perception as intended?
Is your positioning correct?
How are you doing vis-a-vis the competition?
Are you solving consumers' problems?
Are weaknesses showing?
Are strengths being exploited?
Is there price resistance?
Are you having selling problems?
What are the reasons for the variances?

You may have to make changes where necessary and/or introduce contingency plans. You may have to re-analyze your strategy or your plan, or perform a new situation analysis. Marketing plans are not static, but dynamic; they operate under dynamic conditions and must be monitored in the same way.

A final word: The marketing-driven organization must not be susceptible to a short-term mentality that will eventually lose customers. The marketing budget and plan should be adjusted according to the customers, not the accountants. To do otherwise is not unlike deferring maintenance to improve short-term bottom-line figures, and then having to buy new equipment at some time in the future. Even so, accountants must have their say. Thus, plans and budgets must ultimately stand the test of concrete cost-effective results and proven revenues.

Summary

The marketing plan and the marketing budget are fluid tools designed to create, capture, and retain customers. The process begins early in the year and continues until fall. It is based on a sound and realistic situation analysis, which requires good data collection, research where necessary, and acute analysis. Instead of relying on traditional methods to deal with unique situations, the marketing team needs to develop innovative strategies based on solid information. The funding of these strategies must then be realistic, to get the job done.

Discussion Questions

1. Discuss the key differences between strategic marketing and marketing management in the development of the marketing plan.
2. Formulate a situation analysis for a restaurant or hotel where you have worked or with which you are familiar. Analyze the internal and external factors.
3. Construct a detailed property needs analysis for the same restaurant or hotel that will form the basis of a marketing plan.
4. Develop an internal marketing plan for a real or hypothetical hotel or restaurant.
5. Why is the realistic and objective analysis of the data collection critical to a successful marketing plan? Discuss. What happens when this is lacking?
6. Write a mission statement for the restaurant or hotel analyzed in Question 2.
7. Develop mini-marketing plans for the properties in Cases 4-1, 4-2 and 4-3.

✔ Case 4-1
The Luxury Hotel[4]

Luxury Hotel tradition originated in the late-nineteenth century with a Swiss hotelier named Andre Luxury. As a hotelman, and befitting his name, Luxury strove for uncompromised excellence in all his professional endeavors. In 1898 he opened the Luxury of Paris and, in doing so, initiated the tradition of the deluxe European hotel.

Luxury established stringent standards that would be the foundation of any hotel bearing his name. He demanded that the location be central, the rooms comfortable, and the food and beverage quality second to none. Most importantly, Luxury recognized that impeccable service would be the crucial ingredient in creating his version of an ideal hotel. Few hotels would attain the rigid standards of Andre Luxury.

On May 18, 1927, the first Luxury Hotel in the United States opened for business at its present location in Dallas. The owner/operator, Edward Williams, was a local businessman who obtained the rights to the Luxury name and desired to provide his city with a deluxe hotel. His intention was to operate the hotel by the same standards as those established by Andre Luxury. The hotel was managed much like a private club catering to the elite and famous. Williams stressed impeccable service by his staff and required appropriate dress and demeanor from his guests. In many respects, the Luxury was the trendsetter among exclusive, "luxury" hotels.

The Changing of the Guard

In June 1988, E.B. Phillips Properties Inc. bought the rights to the Luxury name in North America along with the Luxury Hotel property in Dallas. E.B. Phillips was a Dallas-based real estate development company dabbling in the hotel business. The company owned E.B. Hotels, which managed eleven Holiday Inns and two Marriott Hotels under franchise agreements. E.B. Phillips also owned Magnificent Hotels, a drawing-board and development-stage hotel chain based in Dallas. Upon purchase of the Luxury name, the Magnificent Hotel Company became known as the Luxury Hotel Company.

The Luxury Company opened three new Luxury properties in late 1989 and 1990—the Luxury Chicago, the Luxury Atlanta, and the Luxury Newport Beach in California, which would be the first resort hotel. The Luxury Company planned to continue to expand. In essence, according to the company president, "What we have accomplished by acquiring the Luxury name will save us several years of effort as far as gaining a reputation." He believed that the Luxury name provided instant identity.

When the Luxury Company purchased the Luxury Dallas, the Phillips management desired to maintain the traditions the Luxury had established, but it also wanted to infuse new blood into the Dallas institution. The president was an experienced hotelier who had previously served as CEO of the Kyoto International Corporation and general manager of the Kyoto Regency–Chicago. He installed a new general manager in the Dallas property, along with other new, key management personnel. With the new management came a new philosophy emphasizing the maintenance and respect of the traditions of the Luxury, while incorporating fresh ideas through qualified, experienced people.

The Luxury Dallas

The Luxury Dallas had 250 rooms. The decor and rooms in the original building reflected the old-fashioned elegance for which the Luxury was known. The overall appearance of the hotel was one of simple, genteel comfort.

Since the hotel had been well-established as a Dallas landmark and tradition, the new management wanted to expand its current facilities

---

[4]Charles Augur and John Neville researched and contributed to this case. Names and locations have been disguised.

to better serve the needs of its guests. As a result, the Luxury opened an extension to its original structure in 1993, a contemporary duplication of the older hotel containing 80 guestrooms. An elegant ballroom and several small, private dining and function rooms were also included.

Primarily, the addition was designed to improve the facilities for guests, create more rooms available for sale, and compete in the attractive executive conference market. Although the addition improved business volume, the increase in the number of rooms available caused the occupancy ratio to drop.

The Dallas Hotel Market

For several years there had been little hotel construction in Dallas, but all that changed in the 1980s. In 1987 and 1988, four new hotels and one addition to an old hotel were completed. By the mid-1990s four more hotels had been built. The additional hotels increased the number of rooms by over 50 percent in the last ten years.

This development reflected expectations of continued growth of the local economy, an increase in tourism, and the expansion of the city's convention facilities. However, with delays in expanding these facilities, limited funding for promoting visitor-related facilities in Dallas, and a weakened economy, there was concern about prospects for the hotel industry in the next five years.

Hotels in downtown Dallas had increased to 12,000 rooms in the first quarter of 1995. Over 70 percent of these rooms were classified as luxury, one-fourth were moderately priced, and the remainder were inexpensive. Fifty percent of guests were business visitors, a group that accounted for much of the demand for luxury accommodations. Thirty percent of the hotel guests were conventioneers and 20 percent were tourists. In the next two years there would be an estimated 10,000 luxury rooms in all of the Dallas area. The Redevelopment Authority projected demand would be only 6,000 luxury rooms.

Target Markets

The Luxury Dallas viewed its social clientele as the high-end social traveler from Texas, Chicago, and the East and West Coasts. This market was the vacationer, college visitor, or shopper interested in Dallas's sophisticated offerings and desirous of staying at a high-quality hotel. The weekday target market was high-level executives who appreciated the comfort, service, and central location of the property. The weekday occupancy rate was significantly higher than on weekends.

Management believed its customers to be 35–50 years old. According to Sales Director Paul Goodrich, "The Luxury aims to cross markets; we do not want to be limited—honeymooners to people on their 50th anniversary and the high-end business traveler. We want anyone who can appreciate the amenities we offer at the Luxury."

Goodrich also felt the amenities and services offered kept the clientele returning. "We don't need to promote due to tremendous loyalty." As part of a recent study by the marketing department of the Luxury (a telephone survey of 200 people with incomes greater than $100,000 per year), people were asked the question, "What hotel would you stay at in Dallas?" Forty-five percent named the Luxury, ten percent said the Fairmont, eight percent named the Hyatt Regency, and the remainder were spread among twelve other hotels. An outside researcher had conducted a consumer study of the Dallas hotel market. The Luxury was rated as the most luxurious hotel in Dallas, offering the best service. A Luxury study of its own customers yielded the profile shown in Table 4-1-1.

Competition

The Luxury Dallas was in a city with a high concentration of luxury hotels, 17 in all as classified by the Dallas Redevelopment Authority, including two under construction. Paul Goodrich, Director of Sales, and Tom Bullsworth, Director of Marketing, narrowed the list down to eight that they seriously considered to be competition. These are shown in Table 4-1-2

TABLE 4-1-1   Profile of Luxury Customers

Business travelers	57%
Pleasure travelers	43%
Average age	49
Male	74%
Average annual income	$100,000
When in Dallas, stays at the Luxury	67% of the time
Business travelers on expense accounts	85%

TABLE 4-1-2   Hotels Viewed As Prime Competition

	Rooms	Corporate Rate	% Occupancy
Dallas Hunt	153	180	76.3
Hyatt Regency	478	175	74.2
Marriott West	400	155	88.7
Four Seasons	295	—	—
Inter-Continental	500	—	—
Fairmont	960	165	56.2
Le Meridien	328	175	69.0
Summit	450	165	74.2
Luxury	330	220	65.0

with their room counts, corporate rate, and last year's occupancy. Both Goodrich and Bullsworth felt that their main competitors were the Dallas Hunt, Le Meridien, the Four Seasons (right around the corner), and the Inter-Continental, although the latter two had yet to open. These hotels catered to the same clientele as the Luxury and also stressed impeccable service, comfort, and outstanding food. All four competing properties would be considerably newer than the Luxury.

Goodrich and Bullsworth felt the Summit and the Marriott West were secondary competition; and further, they dismissed the Hyatt Regency and the Fairmont as direct competition, for they felt these hotels catered to a different clientele.

The Marketing and Sales Directors believed that the Luxury tradition for the finest service, exceptional food, and comfort had created a loyal clientele over the years. They were confi-

dent that, although new hotels might open with high occupancies and some Luxury customers, the clientele would return to the Luxury after sampling the newer hotels.

Problems and Strategies

When the Directors of Sales and Marketing were posed the question, "What is the major problem with which the Luxury is faced in view of declining occupancies and new competition?" Goodrich and Bullsworth responded as follows:

Goodrich How to maintain our position with the new competition.

Bullsworth How to expand our market while maintaining our position.

Goodrich Don't cheapen the image, keep the aloofness.

Bullsworth How to be a five-star hotel where people are smiling.

Goodrich Blend Magnificent's youth with the Luxury tradition.

Bullsworth How to integrate new blood with Luxury traditions.

Overall, both felt the challenge would be to capitalize on the rebirth of the hotel.

The marketing strategy was to aggressively pursue the target markets, position the Luxury as the best hotel in Dallas, expand the executive conference market, and maintain the traditions. Bullsworth also felt that higher-level executives were younger than in the past and that the Luxury needed to change the perception of its being for older, "stuffy" people. Plans were also made to pursue more of the pleasure market, the new generation of travelers coming to Dallas. An additional strategy was to never discount, but rather to market the high-level services and amenities that were expected of the Luxury.

✔ Case 4-2
Le Marquis de Napoleon[5]

The Napoleon Hotel was a deluxe four-diamond (AAA rating) hotel located in the heart of downtown Philadelphia, owned and operated by a French hotel chain. It was within short walking distance of the financial district, the government center, the main business district, Liberty Market, and cultural and historical landmarks. It was also attached to Napoleon Place, a 175-store shopping mall that included boutique as well as major department stores, and a food court with 25 counter-style service restaurants.

The hotel, with a distinct European atmosphere, contained 500 rooms constructed around four atria, with about 130 guestrooms in each atrium. All rooms were furnished in a combination of antiques and classic European-designed furniture. Room service was available around-the-clock, and evening turn-down service with a French chocolate was standard in all rooms. The hotel had a large indoor swimming pool with a sun terrace and a fully equipped health and fitness club. There were also 16 function rooms and a grand ballroom seating 600. The hotel averaged 65 percent occupancy the previous year with an ADR of $160.

The Napoleon Hotel had two restaurants and one bar. The Lobby Bar was a large lounge/bar located off the 'hotel lobby. It was very open, comfortable, and inviting. Entertainment was provided. Cafe Rouge was an informal dining room/coffee shop that specialized in French Bistro cuisine and American food. It had a light, casual atmosphere and was open from 7:00 A.M. through 11:00 P.M. Cafe Rouge was especially popular among hotel guests at breakfast; at lunch and dinner guests came from both inside and outside the hotel.

Le Marquis

Restaurant Le Marquis de Napoleon was the hotel's flagship award-winning restaurant. The food was French nouvelle cuisine. A sample menu is shown in Exhibit 4-2-1. Other details are given below.

- Winner of Mobil Four-Star Award award
- 17 Gault Millau Toques
- Best of City Award for four straight years
- *Philadelphia* Magazine Hall of Fame Restaurant
- American Express/Travel Holiday Award
- *Esquire* Magazine's 100 Best New Restaurants Award
- *Philadelphia Eagle* Four-Star Award
- Open every night except Sunday, 6:00–11:00 P.M.
- Seats up to 90 people
- Private dining room seats up to 14 people

The Le Marquis menu was created by a world-renowned French chef and changed on a quarterly basis. Press releases were sent to local newspapers announcing the changes; any other advertising was by word-of-mouth. No promotion was done in-house for the restaurant except for a small ad on the back of the room service menu in each room, plus placards in the hotel elevators.

Le Marquis employed a full staff of seven chefs, seven waiters, five buspersons, and a manager; all were nonunion employees, skilled professionals in their fields. All were on duty every night, although some would be sent home on slow nights.

The average customer at Le Marquis was over age 30, was not a hotel guest, and was dining there for a special occasion, business or pleasure, but usually to celebrate an event.

The main competition for Le Marquis came from restaurants located in other Philadelphia hotels, all of which were relatively nearby. This was because there was a dearth of first-class, freestanding restaurants in the downtown area. Le Marquis management felt that it was distanced from the competition because of its physical facilities, both the restaurant and the hotel, the quality of its food, and its excellent

---

[5]Emily Hartman researched and contributed to this case. Names and places have been disguised.

EXHIBIT 4-2-1   Sample menu of Le Marquis

Les Hors d'Oeuvre

Rouleau de Printemps de Thon aux Pousses de Soja Marinées, Wasabi Vinaigrette 9.00
Raw Tuna in a "Brick", Marinated Bean Sprouts, Wasabi Vinaigrette

Salade de Crevettes et Topinanbour à l'Huile de Curry et Graines de Vanille 13.50
Louisiana Shrimp on Jerusalem Artichoke Salad and Curry Oil

Ravioli de Confit de Canard, Salade d'Epinards Nouveaux au Foie Gras, Vinaigrette au Jus de Viande 16.00
Confit of Duck in a Crisp Potato Slice, Spinach and Foie Gras Salad, Meat Juice Vinaigrette

Salade Fantaisie aux Asperges 9.50
Seasonal Salad with Fresh Asparagus, Enoki Mushrooms and Truffle Dressing

Chaussons de Sarasin aux Crabes, Huile de Crustacés 11.00
Buckwheat Pancakes with Crabs and Shellfish Oil

Les Potages

Soupe de Moirilles Fraîches aux Herbes de Printemps 7.50
Morel Soup flavored with Fresh Herbs and Asparagus

Bouillon de Galanga et Shiitake, Quenelles de Crevettes 8.50
Galanga and Shiitake Broth with Shrimp Dumpling

Les Mets de la Mer

Dos de Sandre Poché au Jus de Celeri en Branche 26.50
Yellow Pike Poached in Celery Juice

Saumon en Coque de Shiitake, Jus au Champignons 29.00
Salmon in Shiitake Caps with a Light Mushroom Juice

Homard du Maine à la Polenta Liquide, Vinaigrette au Miel et Romarin 34.50
Maine Lobster with a Liquid Polenta, Honey and Rosemary Vinaigrette

Flétan Poêlé au Hachis de Fèves, Artichaut et Olives Noires à l'Huile de Corriandre 28.00
Halibut topped with Fava Beans, Artichokes and Black Olives

Les Entrées

Côtelettes d'Agneau dans une Pomme en Robe, Vinaigrette au Basilic 32.50
Lamb Stuffed Potatoes, Goat Sour Cream, Basil Vinaigrette

Lapereau Mitonné au Jus d'Oignons Nouveaux, Pâtes Croustillantes 28.00
Young Rabbit with Fried Pasta and Onion Juice

Noisettes de Veau aux Huiles de Poivrons Rôtis 33.00
Veal Saddle with Roasted Pepper Oil

Terrine de Boeuf et Pommes de Terre, Bouillon de Légumes au Paprika 29.50
Beef and Potato Terrine, Vegetable and Paprika Broth

Crotin Chavignol Gratiné et sa Salade d'Endive 8.00
Glazed Crotin Chavignol with Endive Salad

TABLE 4-2-1 Comparison with Competition's Signature Restaurants

Hotel	Daily Avg. Covers		Avg. Food Check $		Avg. Time Spent		Dinner Choice %	
	Lunch	Dinner	Lunch	Dinner	Lunch	Dinner	a la carte	Menu
Le Meridien	40	60	26.00	47.00	90	120	70	30
Ritz	40	60	24.00	45.00	90	160	100	0
Adam's Mark	40	55	20.00	42.00	60	120	70	30
Marriott	79	80	11.32	30.29	50	90	50	50
Philadelphian	55	75	14.00	40.00	60	120	100	0
Liberty House	35	50	20.00	35.00	60	120	40	60
Napoleon	NA	46	NA	50.04	NA	150	60	40

reputation. Table 4-2-1 shows comparative figures among these restaurants.

On average, Le Marquis did about 46 covers a night with an average food and beverage check of $71.69. Top management, however, was not at all happy with the current situation, which last year showed a loss of $204,000. Jean Claude, the Food and Beverage Manager, felt his job was on the line and was searching for solutions including opening for breakfast and lunch. He acknowledged that the restaurant had some weaknesses, namely location (the hotel was two blocks from the city's "war zone"), high prices, high employee turnover, and a general unawareness among potential customers. He examined last year's financial statement for further clues (Table 4-2-2), keeping in mind that management was adamant about positioning the restaurant as "the finest dining room in the city of Philadelphia."

TABLE 4-2-2 Financial Figures for Le Marquis

	JAN	FEB	MAR	APR	MAY	JUN	JUL	AUG	SEP	OCT	NOV	DEC	TOTAL
Food $	61,160	61,829	67,313	68,623	64,749	61,025	48,472	42,433	57,246	66,523	56,684	67,365	723,422
Beverage $	19,856	24,814	27,760	29,274	30,662	27,885	22,020	21,242	26,416	31,080	24,437	27,488	312,934
Total Revenue $	81,016	86,643	95,073	97,897	95,411	88,910	70,492	63,675	83,662	97,603	81,121	94,853	1,036,356
Food Cost $	23,614	23,619	25,646	26,557	33,151	28,743	22,249	18,017	22,555	26,674	24,771	27,499	304,095
Beverage Cost $	6,715	7,866	9,105	9,631	9,808	9,035	7,002	6,925	8,506	9,915	7,991	9,263	101,762
Total Cost of Sales $	30,329	31,485	34,751	36,188	42,959	37,778	29,251	24,942	31,061	37,589	32,762	36,762	405,857
Gross Profit $	50,687	55,158	60,322	61,709	52,452	51,132	41,241	38,733	52,601	60,014	48,359	58,091	630,499
Total Payroll and Benefits $	59,299	61,214	57,815	61,052	57,301	51,694	48,725	54,255	47,404	55,270	55,185	65,544	673,758
Total Other Expense $	14,231	14,976	10,593	13,922	12,688	13,410	15,434	11,412	15,702	12,707	11,152	14,606	160,833
Departmental Profit $	(22,843)	(21,032)	(8,086)	(13,265)	(17,537)	(13,972)	(22,918)	(26,934)	(10,505)	(7,963)	(17,978)	(21,059)	(204,092)
Dinner Covers #	1,141	1,185	1,381	1,340	1,312	1,231	949	862	1,139	1,338	1,167	1,412	14,457
Average Daily Dinner Covers #	47	49	57	55	54	51	39	36	47	56	48	45	46

(continued)

129

TABLE 4-2-2 (continued)

	JAN	FEB	MAR	APR	MAY	JUN	JUL	AUG	SEP	OCT	NOV	DEC	TOTAL
Average Food Revenue per Cover $	53.60	52.18	48.74	51.21	49.35	49.57	51.08	49.23	50.26	49.72	48.57	47.71	50.04
Average Beverage Revenue per Cover $	17.40	20.94	20.10	21.85	23.37	22.65	23.20	24.64	23.19	23.23	20.94	19.47	21.65
Average Total Revenue per Cover $	71.00	73.12	68.84	73.06	72.72	72.23	74.28	73.87	73.45	72.95	69.51	67.18	71.69
Average Cost of Sales per Cover $	26.58	26.57	25.16	27.01	32.74	30.69	30.82	28.94	27.27	28.09	28.07	26.04	28.07
Average Payroll per Cover $	51.97	51.66	41.86	45.56	43.67	41.99	51.34	62.94	41.62	41.31	47.29	45.71	46.60
Average Other Expenses per Cover $	12.47	12.64	7.67	10.39	9.67	10.89	16.26	13.24	13.79	9.50	9.56	10.34	11.12
Average Total Cost per Cover $	91.02	90.86	74.70	82.96	86.09	83.58	98.43	105.11	82.68	78.90	84.92	82.09	85.80
Net Revenue per Cover $	(20.02)	(17.75)	(5.86)	(9.90)	(13.37)	(11.350)	(24.15)	(31.25)	(9.22)	(5.95)	(15.41)	(14.91)	(14.12)
Room Occupancy %	40.1	39.1	67.0	67.4	68.6	77.4	71.2	80.4	78.8	87.2	61.7	39.0	65.0

✔ Case 4-3
The Superior Inn and Conference Center[6]

It was a beautiful morning in February when Susan Newton replaced Howard Creel and assumed the position of Director of Marketing of the Superior Inn and Conference Center in Omaha, Nebraska. Howard had already reviewed the competitive situation with Susan and presented her with a marketing plan that covered the rest of the year. Although he sincerely wished her the best of luck, Howard was anxious to return home and await his movers. True to character, Susan wanted to talk.

The Superior Inn was a 25-year-old property that had averaged a 64 percent occupancy the year before at a $63 average rate in a highly competitive market. This level of business represented an actual market share of 9.8 percent, which fell far short of the property's fair market share of 14.29 percent. The question foremost in Susan's mind was this: "What would it take to improve the overall occupancy picture to at least the point where the hotel received its fair market share of the potential business?"

The City of Omaha

Omaha, Nebraska was a fast-growing metropolis located at the crossroads of the nation. It was considered to be the agricultural capital of the world as well as its largest livestock market and meatpacking center. Omaha was one of the nation's largest producers of quick-frozen foods and was notable as a transportation, communication, and insurance center. The city was presently in the midst of a diversification and expansion program with the goal of lessening its dependence on agriculture.

Omaha was readily accessible by all means of transportation. It was situated at the intersection of Interstate 80, which ran across the United States from the East Coast to the west,

and Interstate 29, which ran north-south. Several major airlines operated a total of more than 100 daily flights in and out of Omaha, and Eppley Field was about 12 miles from the downtown area. Eight railroads made Omaha the fourth largest railroad center in the country.

History of the Superior Inn and Conference Center

The Superior Inn and Conference Center was built in 1970 by the Kraus Corporation. Initially, the Hotel Kraus was the showplace of the area. Unfortunately, however, the cumulative effect of successive owners and franchisers eventually took its toll on the hotel. A series of investors proceeded to bleed the property, rather than reinvest in capital improvements. As a result, the Hotel Kraus became sorely in need of extensive renovation.

In 1983, the Innstar Corporation purchased the facility. Innstar decided that the existing franchise had a poor image that was not unlike that of a truck stop. A new franchise agreement was signed but business remained poor. In 1993 Ozark Innkeepers assumed ownership of the hotel and converted it to a Superior Inn franchise that, with the change in ownership, was hoped to be a real shot in the arm for the hotel's momentum. Ozark Innkeepers spent $1 million renovating 100 of the 185 guestrooms, the lobby, and some of the meeting space, but there was a great deal more to be done. Most disheartening, however, was the fact that the expected surge in business due to the renovation failed to materialize. Nonetheless, Susan Newton was enthusiastic about the impact the renovation would have on her clients.

The Superior Inn and Conference Center was a "U"-shaped low-rise building with 185 sleeping rooms. The 100 rooms in the "Executive Wing" had been completely renovated. The hotel was located in the southeast section of town and was easily accessible from either Interstate

---

[6]Bharath M. Josiam researched and contributed to this case. Names and places have been disguised.

80 or US Highway 275. The hotel did not provide limousine service to the airport, which was about 12 miles away.

There was a private courtyard adjoining a spacious and canopied patio between the two wings of the building. Features included an olympic-sized, heated outdoor pool, patio bar, and barbeque pit. The landscaping and groundswork had been partially redone in recent months and quotations were being received on the remainder of the project. This area was conveniently located near the lower lobby, ballroom, and lounge and was extremely popular from May through October for parties and receptions.

The main lobby was large and had been renovated within the last year. It lent itself well to convention groups for either mass registration or just plain congregating. The lower lobby was connected to the main lobby and also served as a registration area. In addition, the lower level could also be utilized for either coffee breaks or as a display area.

Guestrooms ranged in price from $73 to $83 single, and from $78 to $90 double, depending on bedding. Suites were available for either $115 or $155 per night. Each room or suite included a Touch-Tone telephone as well as cable TV hookup, complete with remote control. The hotel did not offer room service.

Meetings and Banquets

Meeting facilities at the Superior Inn were well-conceived, with a good balance of various sized rooms and one of the largest ballrooms in the area. The Omaha Ballroom seated 650 guests for a banquet and could accommodate a maximum of 900 people theater-style, although its room dividers were not soundproof. There were a total of 13 meeting rooms in all, and most were in urgent need of renovation. A charge was assessed for room rental if no meal was served at the function.

Meeting room equipment was generally dated and in need of replacement. The approximately 500 chairs and 30 banquet tables were in particularly bad condition, and the audio-visual paraphernalia was not remotely state-of-the-art.

Banquets at the hotel were noted for their good food and service. However, the lack of proper equipment created problems when it necessitated the "borrowing" of crockery and cutlery from the restaurant when Banquets was busy. Meetings and banquets accounted for about 20 percent of total revenue.

Effie's

The restaurant at the Superior Inn was named in remembrance of its first manager, Effie Hathaway. Effie's had a maximum capacity of 75 and was comfortably decorated with overstuffed chairs and well-cushioned banquettes along the walls. However, the room had not been physically improved in many years and the wear and tear was pronounced. Effie's was located in between the lounge and the kitchen.

The menu consisted of basic American fare with an emphasis on the agricultural products native to the region. Beef was well-represented along with a wide variety of vegetables, but fish and seafood items were noticeably scarce. Management generally attempted to offer a middle-of-the-road selection since Effie's was the hotel's only restaurant.

The market for the restaurant varied significantly by meal period. Breakfast business originated almost entirely in-house, and only five percent of breakfast customers were not registered at the Inn. Lunchtime business was about a 50/50 mix, and dinner patrons were 70 percent guests of the hotel. Effie's represented about 18 percent of total revenue.

Harry's

The lounge at the Superior Inn was warm and friendly, with a forest green and pale yellow decor accented by polished brass. Unfortunately, Harry's had not aged well and was seriously in need of major renovation. At present, the lounge seated 58 people and was open from the hours of 11:00 A.M.–1:00 A.M., seven days a week.

There was a small alcove off the lounge that was regularly used as a serving station. A cook was scheduled to man this area during each weekday lunch period, hand-carving the meats for overstuffed delicatessan sandwiches. The alcove was also staffed during cocktail hour when complimentary hors d'oeuvres were available.

Harry's boasted live entertainment on weekend nights when a three-piece band played Top 40 hits. There was a 8' × 8' dance floor in the center of the room, which was generally crowded.

Approximately 30 percent of the lounge's clientele was drawn from the local market, with the remaining 70 percent originating in-house. Business was particularly strong when conventioners arranged to congregate in the lounge. Harry's sales accounted for about ten percent of total revenue.

The Mission Statement

Howard Creel had prepared the hotel's new mission statement as follows:

> We are a highly successful, full-service conference center providing the finest service, highest quality of food, and the cleanest, most comfortable rooms in all of Omaha. Because of our excellent reputation, location and value, we cater not only to a strong association/convention market but to the corporate and transient market as well.
>
> In order to remain successful and to maintain our strong, positive image, we must continue to provide the finest food, beverage, and entertainment in the area at the best value. We must continue ongoing renovations and keep abreast of the changing marketplace. We must be trendsetters and not trend-followers, and must strive to keep our employees motivated and well-trained. A good attitude is the answer.
>
> If we are able to achieve all of this and continue our strong public relations efforts, we will reach new markets and will in turn increase revenues in all areas of the hotel.

Market Segments

Susan Newton disagreed with Howard Creel's feeling that the Superior Inn could not afford to pick and choose its guests, particularly in response to the highly competitive environment. Creel had attempted to increase sales by targeting virtually all segments, but Newton felt that the property should create a niche for itself rather than attempting "to be all things to all people," as she put it. The rooms revenue and occupancy by segment is shown in Table 4-3-1.

Susan was particularly interested in the corporate market, which currently represented only 16.4 percent of total rooms revenue. Creel's one assistant had been assigned to this segment for the past two months and had spent a great deal of time making initial contacts with potential corporate clients. A special rate was offered to those area businesses that produced more than 50 room-nights per month, and the secretaries who reserved the room-nights were invited to a private party. Susan also wondered about the Superior reservations system, which generated about eight percent of total rooms occupancy.

Susan Newton felt that the hotel was well-positioned in the association market, where most of the groups were voluntary organizations on limited budgets. Howard Creel had focused on this segment personally and counted many associations as regular, repeat guests of the hotel. The good reputation of the Food and Beverage department was an added "plus" in appealing to this segment.

The Superior Inn periodically received inquiries in regard to bus tours and their room requirements. Susan Newton was not interested in pursuing this market since it conflicted with the many associations that also required weekend rooms. Exhibit 4-3-1 illustrates day-of-week average occupancies, which were fairly consistent throughout the year.

TABLE 4-3-1   Revenue and Occupancy Percentages

	Revenue	Occupancy
Transient	42.8%	37.6%
Social	1.8	1.5
Tour	3.4	4.6
Association	34.1	41.2
Corporate	16.4	12.3
Military/Govt.	1.5	2.8

EXHIBIT 4-3-1   Day of week occupancies

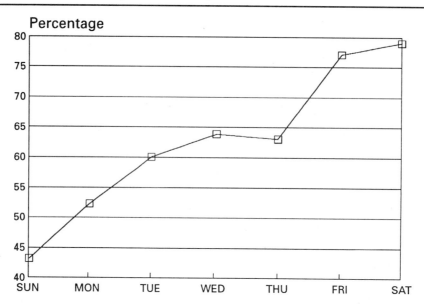

Finally, there was the transient market, which accounted for 42.8 percent of revenue. Newton was dissatisfied with the current system for identifying the sub-segments of this market and was committed to instituting a better tracking system in the future. In the meantime, however, defining the unique characteristics of this market would continue to be a highly subjective proposition.

Advertising

All advertising for the Superior Inn–Omaha was handled by the general manager. At the moment, advertising was restricted to spots on the local radio stations and a few print ads in the local and area newspapers. Almost all of these ads featured the lounge and/or the restaurant.

The Superior Inn headquarters handled the advertising intended to build and promote the "Superior Inn image" on the national level. These advertisements appeared in major newspapers and periodicals and on national television.

Competition

As evidenced by its occupancy and average room rate (Exhibit 4-3-2), the Superior Inn was challenged by competitors on all fronts. Susan Newton was convinced that the only way the hotel could hold its own against intense competition was to offer good food and service and clean, well-maintained rooms at a reasonable price. She was optimistic about the future since renovations were proceeding on schedule.

Susan Newton considered the competition to be both the full-service establishments such as the downtown Marriott, the Ramada right across the road, and the no-frills properties like the Susse Chalet. Table 4-3-2 provides pertinent information about competitive properties in the same approximate price range.

Newton was firmly of the opinion that the only way the property could hold its own in the face of such intense competition was to offer good food, prompt and courteous services, and clean and well-maintained rooms at a reasonable price. She was optimistic about the future since the renovations were progressing at a good pace.

EXHIBIT 4-3-2 Average occupancies and room rates

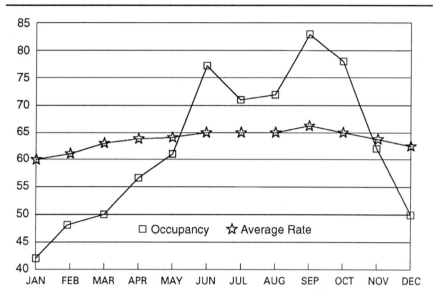

Conclusion

Whereas Susan Newton was trained in marketing, Howard Creel was an "old school" salesman who believed that you can sell anything if you are aggressive enough. Newton recognized that a hard sell was not the answer and believed a policy of segmentation and diffentiation was desirable.

The question to Newton was this: How to develop a marketing plan in order to increase market share by smoothing the peaks and valleys of the hotel's recent performance. With this in mind, Susan Newton sat back to plot her strategy.

TABLE 4-3-2 Competitive Property Comparison

Hotel	Single Rack Rate	Rooms	Outlets[a]	Banquets[b]	Location	Other
Superior	73–83	185	1R, 1L	13 Rms, 900	Off Hwy	No Limo
Susse Chalet	55–62	86	1R, 1L	5 Rms, 1,000	Off Hwy	Billboards
Ramada	75–88	120	1R, 1L	4 Rms, 200	Off Hwy	Billboards
Sheraton	88–108	263	1R, 2L	15 Rms, 900	Rte. 29	Limo
Hilton	82–92	178	2R, 1L	7 Rms, 450	Airport	Undercuts
Holiday	76–85	168	2R, 1L	8 Rms, 700	Highway	Renovated
Best Western	75–85	181	1R	17 Rms, 375	Highway	Limo
How. Johnson	78–88	114	1R, 1L	3 Rms, 100	Highway	No Limo

[a]Number of restaurants and lounges
[b]Number of banquet rooms, maximum capacity theater-style

CHAPTER 5

The Marketing Environment, Competitive Analysis, and Marketing Research

Every organization is part of a larger environment that includes many forces beyond the control of any one firm. As discussed in Chapters 3 and 4, a careful assessment of these environmental forces is necessary before any strategic plans can be implemented. As the world's economies become more intertwined, the environment of a company becomes larger and more complex than ever before. Events in faraway places have an impact close to home. Customer needs and wants are ever-changing, creating an environment that is dynamic and demanding.

Environmental impacts, such as the recession of the 1990s, change the buying habits of consumers just as the boom days of the 1980s did. The customer today is looking for "value-added" in every purchase, from cars to homes to hotel rooms to fast food. As one hotel executive stated, off the record, "During the '80s, we just provided the product. The '90s is a service decade. Unless we are able to provide the service, we cannot compete."

These demands create opportunities to serve customers in new and better ways. There is no other choice. Yesterday's idea is as obsolete as yesterday itself. The right choice means reading the environment, understanding that change is

constant, and developing the product that anticipates customers' problems, as shown in Figure 5-1. Yesterday's success is tomorrow's failure, if there is no constant adaptation to the environment. Opportunities lie in the environment and in the future. Success in the future requires being alert to that environment and those opportunities, while understanding the competition. This calls for constant and careful scanning and analysis. It also often calls for solid, scientific research.

These areas—environmental scanning, opportunities, threats, competitive analysis, and research—are so closely interrelated that they are included here in one chapter. To make them easier to digest, however, we have broken the chapter into three parts: environmental scanning; opportunities, threats, and competitive analysis; and research.

A. Environmental Scanning

Marketing leadership means planning for the future. Trying to determine what the future holds in store has come to be known as environmental scanning, which simply means, "What is

137

Hyatt Business Services

WHO'D HAVE THOUGHT YOU'D HAVE TO SEND A FAX WITH NO PANTS ON?

At Hyatt, we know just because you've left the office doesn't mean you've left work. Which is why we offer Hyatt Business Centers and Services. Where you can get everything you need—like typing and copying services, computer hook-ups and fax machines. Right where you need them. And the nice thing is, it doesn't matter what you wear to work. To find out all the details about Hyatt Business Centers and Services, call your travel planner or Hyatt at 1-800-233-1234.

HYATT. WE'VE THOUGHT OF EVERYTHING.℠

FIGURE 5-1   Anticipating customers' future problems

going on out there in the environment that is going to impact on our business?" Of course, the environment didn't suddenly start changing. What has occurred, instead, is a new awareness of the need to proact, rather than react, and the need to constantly scan the environment to perceive what is happening and to anticipate what will occur. Environmental scanning as a systematic approach is an essential leadership tool.

Any organization is a creature of its environment. Scanning is an organization's method of improving its ability to deal with a rapidly changing environment. All of this, of course, is relative to the competition. First, we have to know who the competition is. Because it is too easy to identify the wrong competition, or to fail to identify the right competition, it occurs often.

Macro Competition

How do we define competition? There are actually two broad forms of competition, *macro,* or industry competition, and *micro,* or product class competition. We will discuss the macro here and the micro later.

In a macro sense, competition is anyone competing for the same consumer's dollar. This means that any restaurant represents competition to any other restaurant, at least in the same area, and any hotel is competition to any other hotel. We can carry it even further: We can say that any supermarket is competition to any restaurant, or that a new car is competition to a two-week cruise.

Several changes take place in the competitive environment as an industry reaches the "mature" stage of its life cycle. Some that have particularly impacted the hospitality industry are:

- Competition for market share has become more intense as firms are forced to achieve sales growth at one another's expense.
- Firms are selling increasingly to experienced, repeat buyers who are making choices from known alternatives.
- Competition has become better oriented to cost and service as knowledgeable buyers expect similar price, product, and service features.
- New products and services and new applications are harder to come by.

Tablecloth restaurant operators are threatened by the competition they are getting from supermarkets (especially prepared dinners), take-out services, catering services, and casual dining. Hotel and motel operators are threatened by the competition they are getting from campers, recreational vehicles, and the hospitality of friends and relatives. Condominiums that didn't sell during the 1980s have been marshalled to accommodate transient guests at resorts, leaving hotel rooms empty. (Notice one thing about services: that one can readily substitute one for another, often at a much lower price.) All are examples of environmental changes that are taking place, in which the macro competition is moving in to fulfill a need.

Why are these other businesses competition? Because they are satisfying the same needs, only with different wants. The customer wants the product or service more cheaply, quickly, easily, or conveniently, with less hassle. The hospitality industry is not, of course, totally oblivious to this. McDonald's, Burger King, Wendy's, and others have gone back to drive-up windows. Many tablecloth restaurants have gone into catering and/or casual dining. Marriott, Choice International, and Groupe Accor of France have bought, built, or franchised into every tier of the hotel industry. All-suite and luxury budget hotels have become commonplace. All these started out as opportunities as the environment changed, and someone saw an opportunity—a niche, if you will—in the marketplace left void by the competition.

Environmental changes should not be confused with fads, although there is no reason not to make an opportunity out of a fad. Fads tend to be short-lived, whereas environmental changes are major shifts in the environment and society. The point at which a fad ends and a shift or trend begins can be problematic; marketing can take advantage of either. The risk lies in making substantial investment in what turns out to be a fad. A food item may be a fad, but this should not inhibit the opportunity to make a few menu changes that can easily be reversed. On the other hand, fantasy mega-resorts in Hawaii, with multimillion dollar investments, may turn out to have been fads, since some have been sold for less than half the cost of building them.

Types of Environments

There are environmental forces other than competitive forces. They can be broadly classified as technological, political, economic, sociocultural, regulatory, and ecological environments. We will discuss some of the impacts of these environments upon the hospitality industry.

Technological Impacts

In the technological environment, when we think about scanning from a marketing viewpoint, we need to think about the impact of technology upon the customer. In the restaurant business, the improvement in credit card processing technology has prompted even quick-service chains such as Burger King and Pizza Hut to provide that convenience to their customers. In addition, many U.S. restaurants provide customers with a fax number for placing orders, according to a survey conducted by the National Restaurant Association.[1]

Computers have certainly been one of the greatest technological advances. Awareness of this fact in environmental scanning leads to analysis of its uses—that is, leads to asking how this advance can be used to customer and competitive advantage.

Until recently, most hospitality firms viewed computer technology from the perspective of how it could be used to improve operations. There is nothing wrong with this. In fact, computerization soon became a necessity to many operations, but from a marketing perspective it did not deal with the needs of the consumer. As one example, when first introduced, electronic cash register or computer receipts from both restaurants and hotels, which provided a listing of all charges, were almost undecipherable by the consumer; many still are.

Let's analyze the computer revolution from a marketing standpoint. We could say something like, "Okay, here's this great new technology. How can we use it to make life better for the customer?" One answer might be at the front desk of a hotel. Here, computers have improved operational control immensely, but often leave the customer standing in line just as long, if not longer, to check in. To make matters worse, employees have had their eyes glued to the computer screen instead of looking at the customer, creating a more sterile environment for the traveler. Things are better today, especially in the check-out area where it is possible to do this from the TV screen in a guest's room (Figure 5-2). Computers are also becoming more useful in the check-in area (Figure 5-3), perhaps even with guests checking themselves in, eventually, but this has been a long time coming. Figure 5-4 shows a software company addressing hotels' needs to serve guests better.

The latest trend in TV technology is its use as a high-tech concierge. Guests at the Sheraton New York Hotel & Towers can watch video channels describing local attractions, shops, and restaurants to see what, for example, the restaurant looks like and hear about its specialties. Press another button and guests learn not only the address of Saks Fifth Avenue but also what the cab fare should be for the ride over. Another channel provides information on special exhibits at museums and hard-to-get theater tickets. Guests can also order breakfast in advance in six different languages. Stouffer Hotels & Resorts is developing a system through which guests can buy theater tickets and shop at local merchants directly through their in-room televisions.

Guest databases have been a major product of computer technology, although they have been greatly underutilized. (The "data" needs to be converted to more useful "information.") New, integrated guest history databases connect the central reservations office to the front office property management system (PMS). Some advantages are:

- Databases speed the taking of reservations.
- A guest's record can be located quickly.
- Guest history reports can be reviewed and rooms prepared accordingly. A guestroom can be stocked with a guest's preferences.

---

[1]National Restaurant Association, Table Service Operator Survey, Chicago, Illinois, 1992.

Welcome to our Hotel. Our Associates have been looking forward to providing you with exceptional service in a World Class Facility.

We want to exceed your expectations inclusive of your departure. When checking out, there is a potential for line ups and some delays at the Guest Service Desk.

We have a solution! If you are paying your account by credit card this will allow you to use the following service and avoid any delay in your departure.

> o   *On the morning of your departure a copy of your charges and credit card voucher will be placed under your door for you to review. Simply tell Guest Services when you have checked out of your room.*

> *or*

> o   *Use our Video Check Out Services. Touch Channel "88" on the free TV Keys; follow the simple instructions and you will have checked yourself out without having to say anything or stop off anywhere! (You will already have a copy of your account from under your door).*

Our check out time is 1pm. Taking advantage of Sunday Shopping and wish to check out later than 1pm? Just call the Guest Service Desk (Dial 3) and let us know.

Thank you for staying at the Toronto Marriott Eaton Centre Hotel. It has been a pleasure to serve you; and have a safe trip home.

Sincerely,

TORONTO MARRIOTT EATON CENTRE

William J. Saitta
Front Office Manager

WJS/gv

FIGURE 5-2   Using technology to enhance check-out

One minute check-in at any Delta.

Or your room is free.

Your Privilege reservation assures our service commitment.

Toronto, Ottawa and Montréal are each recognized for unique qualities and character, but they all share one great feature – the exceptional value available at Delta Hotels. Three of the finest hotels in Delta's national chain are situated right downtown in these outstanding cities. Each offers first-rate accommodation and convenient in-house business services. And busy schedules are easily accommodated with *free* Privilege membership that ensures one minute check-in upon greeting at our Privilege desk. Travellers who appreciate quality and value, appreciate the Delta difference.
Ask about our corporate rates.

Call for Reservations and a free Delta Privilege Membership

1-800-268-1133

or contact your travel agent

Canada

 The Delta Chelsea Inn
Downtown Toronto

 Delta Ottawa
Downtown Ottawa

Delta Montréal
Downtown Montréal

FIGURE 5-3   Using technology to enhance check-in

In the world of Front Office Systems, Fidelio sets the pace of innovation in improving service and ease of use. It's no wonder that Fidelio is the world's best selling front office system in the last three years.

The unique graphical checkout, the most elegant method of handling even the most complicated cases. The graphical room rack, just as intuitive as the traditional rack with online access to all guest information. A sophisticated groups module – perfectly designed for everything from seaside resorts to the largest convention hotels. The revolutionary rate management – the only fully integrated yield system on the market. Comprehensive guest history providing you with all the information for marketing and personalized service – and last but not least Fidelio's famous customer-definable screens and reports which do more than customize the way your product looks – they optimize the way Fidelio works for your staff and guests.

That's why such renowned chains as Hilton International, Inter* Continental, Steigenberger, Ramada International, ANA, Mandarin Oriental, Shangri La, The Hongkong & Shanghai Hotels, Red Roof, Beaufort, Rafael, Kempinski, The Ritz, CIGA, Regent, Robinson Clubs, Taj, Forte, Accor and many others use Fidelio in all areas of Hotel Management.

How to improve guest and staff satisfaction

FIDELIO S O F T W A R E

Courtesy of Fidelio Software

FIGURE 5-4   A software company addresses the guest satisfaction problem

- Guest preferences in the aggregate can be reviewed to see if guests have a common need that the hotel is not providing.
- Profiles of frequent guests can be established. Mailing lists of names that match the profile can be purchased.
- Sales and marketing can track the effectiveness of advertising campaigns and promotional rates.
- Hotels in a chain can fulfill guests' needs on the first visit when that guest has stayed at other hotels in the chain.

Database marketing is discussed in more detail in Chapter 13.

Political Impacts

Politics impacts upon the hospitality industry vary both with the stability of governments and with the interest of governments in developing tourism. In the United States there has been relatively little interest at the federal level in developing tourism.[2] This has placed a far greater burden on the states and industry to develop international trade. In other stable governments, such as Singapore's and Bermuda's, positive interest in developing tourism has been a tremendous asset to the industry. Even some unstable governments, such as the Philippines', make strong political efforts to boost tourism.

Political uprisings, of course, can kill tourism in destination areas. Contrarily, political change such as in Cuba—where new hotels are being built and Canadians are flocking—can greatly boost tourism. Political differences between countries, such as an airline route squabble between the United States and Canada (at this writing there are still no direct flights between Ottawa and Washington, D.C., the two national capitals), can also impede tourism. Positive arrangements, on the other hand, can enhance it, such as the agreement between the United States and China.

The political environment is particularly critical for large and multinational companies in many areas of the world. The opening of the People's Republic of China to trade has led to many opportunities for both hotel and fast-food companies, as has economic change in Russia. One of the most successful Kentucky Fried Chicken restaurants is now in Tiananmen Square, Beijing, and the largest McDonald's is in Red Square, Moscow.

Globalization has so predominated in the hospitality industry, in fact, that no company so involved can remain aloof from international politics. Formerly American companies like Holiday Inn, Omni, Westin, and Motel 6 have been bought by British, Hong Kong, Japanese, then Mexican, and French companies. Sydney-based Southern Pacific Hotels, owned by the Pritzker family of Chicago (Hyatt Hotels), oper-

ates a floating hotel in Calcutta and is opening Travelodge properties (an American brand owned by Forte Hotels of England, which also managed Ciga Hotels of Italy) in India in agreement with Shri Tribura Sundari Hotels of that country. Queens Moat Houses of England owns HI Management, a French hotel management company. Reso of Sweden manages the Royal Classic Hotels of Denmark. Thousands of other hotels are operated in countries other than those of their owners, like Sol Hotels (Spain) which operates in Australia, Indonesia, Malaysia, Thailand, Singapore, Andorra, Venezuela, Colombia, Cuba, Mexico, Moscow, Brazil, and the Dominican Republic; or Sheraton (Boston) in 65 countries; or Radisson (Minneapolis) in 33 countries (Figure 5-5).[3] All of these international moves have had political implications.

Other political impacts occur within a nation's borders and are either to be taken advantage of or counteracted. Within the United States, both the National Restaurant Association and the American Hotel & Motel Association maintain lobbyists in Washington, D.C. to fight taxes and minimum wage laws and lobby for a greater emphasis on tourism. State and provincial politics can be equally important. Florida (United States), Ontario (Canada), Loire Valley (France), Algarve (Portugal), Costa del Sol (Spain), and the Bosphorus (Turkey) are examples of locations where state and provincial politics have had major impacts in helping or impeding tourism.

State and provincial politics can be equally important, and often critical at the local level. At the even more local level, politics—village, town, or city—controls such things as liquor licenses, zoning variances, building permits, and hours of operation. When the state of Louisiana licensed a casino in New Orleans, the local restaurant association lobbied to prevent the casino from having any substantial food and beverage services that would compete with existing local restaurants.

---

[2]In 1993 the U.S. federal government allocated $15.3 million to market to international visitors, placing the United States twentieth in the world behind such countries as Korea, Malaysia, and Greece. Reported in *Hotels*, March 1993, p. 3.

[3]World maps are provided in an appendix to this book so you can become familiar with the location of these countries where you may be working some day!

Courtesy of Radisson Hotels International

FIGURE 5-5   The globalization of Radisson

Economic Impacts

There are many obvious economic factors affecting any business—recessions, inflation, employment levels, interest rates, personal discretionary income, and so forth. Foreign exchange rates affect international travel. If the U.S. dollar is weak relative to other international currencies, Japanese tourists, for example, can purchase more dollars with their yen, thus making the United States a more attractive place to visit.

All the above factors and many more must be analyzed and considered in environmental scanning, even at the local level. In the early 1990s the New England economies were suffering while Houston was well on the way to recovery, the exact opposite of the late 1980s. In Seattle the economy rises and falls based on the fortunes of Boeing Aircraft. But in little Orem, Utah, where WordPerfect is located, there is a boom on as WordPerfect sales soar. In depressed Toronto in 1993, with at least five major hotels in receivership, Delta Chelsea management successfully practiced "marketing in a downmarket" to maintain market share (Figure 5-3 shows one way) while other hotel managements simply complained about the economy—which didn't help much when lenders wanted their money.

Among other economic factors affecting the hospitality industry is price resistance, strong in many world areas. In the United States the expense account customer, whom many hoteliers had classified as "nonprice sensitive," is resisting higher prices. Corporate controllers have forced cutbacks in expense accounts, and organizational travel-planner buyers are seeking reduced price contracts with both airlines and hotel companies. Recent tax laws have further decreased the deductibility of meals from corporate expense accounts and tax increases have deterred travel. In 1993 the Professional Convention Management Association (PCMA) started a boycott of New York City, protesting the additional tax on hotel rooms of over $99.99 a night, which is the vast majority of them, making a total rooms tax of 21.25 percent. (The added tax was repealed in 1994.) Even fast-food companies are affected: The 1993 introduction

of the "Value Menu" by Wendy's was a result of extreme price sensitivity at the low end of the food-service industry and belatedly followed the lead of "value pricing" by Taco Bell in 1988.

As some companies choose to ignore these trends, others capitalize on them—the best use of environmental scanning. Marriott found a niche in the market at the $59-a-night level in the early 1980s and designed Courtyard by Marriott rooms to sell at that price and, later, Fairfield Inns rooms to sell for $10 less. In the late 1980s Choice International developed Sleep Inns, a downsized guestroom concept to sell at $25 a night. Groupe Accor of France had earlier developed Formule1 to sell for 119 francs.

The economic impacts of the environment, as in the examples just given, are of course the main reason behind the tier structure of the hotel industry today, started by Quality Inns, now Choice International, in 1981. This "reading" of the environment—by Robert Hazard of Choice, and others who soon followed—gave these companies a large head start and competitive advantage. They grouped hotels into different categories based on the price levels that customers would be willing to pay. Choice developed Comfort Inns for the luxury-budget traveler, Quality Inns for the middle tier, and Clarion Hotels for those customers willing to pay a higher price, added Sleep Inns for the low budget, and then bought Econolodge, Friendship, and Rodeway to fill out the budget categories (Figure 5-6). Many other hotel companies have followed suit.

Sociocultural Impacts

Because hospitality is a personal business and of a personal nature to everyone who buys its product, it is extremely vulnerable to social and cultural change. As S.C. Jain states, "The ultimate test of a business is its social relevance. This is particularly true in a society where survival needs are already met. It therefore behooves the strategic planner to be familiar with emerging social trends and concerns."[4]

---

[4]Subhash C. Jain, *Marketing Planning and Strategy*, 4th ed., Cincinnati: South-Western Publishing Co., 1993, p. 146.

1.

In the beginning, there was Quality. But we've changed with the times. Since 1981, more than half of the original Quality Inns have been eliminated for failure to meet our new, stricter standards. Yet today there are nearly three times as many properties as there were in 1981, including our beautiful all-suites hotels. And nearly 60% of the chain has achieved a three-diamond or better rating.

2.

In 1981, we entered the luxury-budget hotel market with Comfort Inns. Since then, Comfort has grown to over 850 properties, becoming the fifth largest lodging chain in the U.S. in its own right. But we didn't stop there. Comfort is still one of the fastest-growing chains in the country. And with good reason. We've earned three times as many three-diamond or better ratings than our nearest economy competitor.

3.

In 1981, we introduced our first luxury hotel chain. Since then, Clarion has grown into a worldwide network of distinctive upscale hotels. Today, there are over 80 Clarion hotels open or under development around the world, from our convention hotels to our quaint Clarion Carriage House Inns, all meeting the highest standards in the industry.

4.

Sleep Inns are Choice's newest lodging concept. The all new construction, limited-service hotels offer travelers amenities such as oversized showers, large desks, and color televisions with VCRs at a budget rate. At the same time, they offer hotel owners the opportunity to build an attractive property for an affordable price. In just two years, 50 Sleep Inns are open or under development, and there's no end in sight.

5.

The Friendship Inns chain includes over 100 budget hotels nationwide. Friendship strengthens our presence in the super-economy segment, making us the number one choice for the price-conscious traveler.

6.

With about 800 hotels open or under development in the U.S. and Canada, Econo Lodge gives Choice the strongest presence in the economy segment. Econo Lodge has a national average room rate of about $35 a night, and continues to grow very quickly as the most recognized name in the economy segment.

7. RODEWAY

Rodeway is an economy chain with 160 hotels in the U.S. and Canada. For years it has courted a loyal following of economy travelers. Its affiliation with Choice brings it the marketing muscle and services necessary to compete on a national scale.

FIGURE 5-6   Choice International's stable of hotels covering the market range

Today, more people are searching for basic values, are less cynical than in the '80s. The self-gratification of that decade has been replaced with more diverse, yet simplified lifestyles. Two-income families, later marriages, higher divorce rates, AIDS, fewer children, female careerism, physical fitness and well-being, escape from monotony and boredom, return to nature, greater sophistication, and many other social changes have affected the hospitality industry in recent years, and many hotels and restaurants have reflected these changes—some sooner, some later.

The sociocultural environment includes demographics (e.g., aging of the population), socioeconomics (increasing dual-income households), cultural change (the changing role of women), and consumerism (certain "rights" like full information, safety, and environmental health). Many of these trends started in the United States and have moved abroad; others have been imported. The hospitality operator doing international business in the United States or abroad must be knowledgeable of these changes, as well as the political and economic ones.

Contained within the sociocultural environment is the marketplace itself and the characteristics of a society. While the hospitality industry has not been oblivious to sociocultural trends, it is sometimes slow in catching up with them. This is hardly surprising, since so many have come so quickly, but the organization that is constantly alert, that adapts to these changes, will have a lead on the others.

Let's consider some examples of change. The single woman traveler, now 38 percent of the U.S. market, says, "I want to be treated the same way as men." Her wants include special hangers, full-length mirrors, better lighting around mirrors (never fluorescent!), irons, softer colors, and a myriad of other amenities that never occurred to men. Electronic door locks have become critically important to the security-conscious (Figure 5-7), as have lobby lounges that are out in the open, and room service, to avoid going to restaurants.

In restaurants, sociocultural changes are affecting menus and food concepts. Trends to-ward healthier foods have increased the consumption of salads, fish, pasta, and chicken at the expense of red meat. Interesting food and presentation are replacing quantity. Decaffeinated coffee, tea, substitutes for sugar and salt, truth-in-menu, and nonsmoking sections are "in." Consider Dunkin' Donuts doughnuts *without* egg yolks, to make them cholesterol-free, and dealcoholized wines and beers. Moderately priced, casual restaurants are succeeding at the expense of high-priced gourmet restaurants.

Consider the baby boomers, a term applied to those born in great numbers immediately following World War II and now in their forties. They won't tolerate old product or poor service. They are taking many short vacations, they are eating out frequently; they are more sophisticated than their parents, they have more choices, and they are demanding. They want five-star standards in four-star hotels at three-star prices. They want personal service, and they don't want excuses for inferior performance. They want added value—a superior product and better service at a reasonable price.

Many of the baby boomers were labeled not long ago as "yuppies," young, urban, professionals with high incomes on the fast track, who never worried about tomorrow but spent for today. More recently, we have the "dinks," double income, no kids, with high discretionary dollars; and the "dewks," dual earnings with kids. Dewks, who don't get to see much of their children, now take them with them but still want escape. Other acronyms will no doubt arise to categorize particular population segments as they develop.

This is the sociocultural environment facing the hospitality industry today, and it continues to change. The "can you top this?" policies of coupons, "twofers," concierge floors, frequent-traveler giveaways, pillow mints, and extended bathroom amenities are not going to satiate these social changes or take the place of better price-value relationships. The industry has worked hard at increasing customer expectations; now it has to deliver. Michael Diamond, when Senior Vice-President of Marketing at the

FIGURE 5-7 Electronic door locks especially desired by women travelers

Boca Raton Hotel and Club in Florida, a five-star resort hotel, stated it this way:

[W]hatever their needs, business travelers want those needs met. You can have all the amenities you want, but unless there's a friendly, knowledgeable, caring person to make those amenities work, you have nothing.... It's knowing what travelers need and want in a hotel and then providing it that keeps us in the travel business. If we lose sight of that, then we might as well forget the concierge floors, special menus and technologies. We're here to serve our customers' needs.[5]

Contrast this with the case of Holiday Inns, which in 1987 faced a system occupancy below 60 percent for the first time in its history:

> The tale shows a company can fall victim to its own success, how a business that rode up on the demographics and developments of one time can be laid low by those of another.... With their wall-to-wall carpeting and Danish furniture, Holiday Inns were on the cutting edge of '50s modern. They were cookie-cutter standard for the masses.... By the mid-1960s, these standard, two-story U-shaped motels were being stamped out at a rate of one every two and a half days, or one room every 30 minutes. Holiday Inns had an 80%-plus occupancy rate.... [But] Holiday was also vulnerable because it hadn't much changed and consumers had. They were more sophisticated and widely traveled. They demanded more—and instead of getting better, many Holiday Inns had gone downhill.[6]

Holiday Inn Worldwide, its name today, is now owned by Bass Plc of England where marketing-oriented Bryan Langton, CEO, and Mike Leven, President, are taking it on a different track.

The sociocultural environment is also changing, of course, in different parts of the world. International cable television provides viewers direct access to the latest trends and has a great influence on people all over the world. As has been stated,

> Social changes occurring in foreign countries which mirror the changes in the United States during the 1970s and 1980s are expected to lead to a greater demand for meals away from home, and global interest in American popular culture continues to create a demand for American food-service establishments.[7]

The major difference, in fact, at least as regards the more developed countries, is in the education of the consumer. Consumerism has had no small part in the movement of social change affecting business in the United States. The same is true of marketing itself. Marketing, particularly as evidenced by advertising (as you can see from the ads in this book), has conditioned consumers to greater and greater expectation. When consumers don't get what they expect or have been promised, they are not hesitant to make an issue of it.

Regulatory Impacts

Regulations tell restaurateurs to whom they can sell liquor and when. They tell hoteliers what information they must obtain from a guest; in many countries, such information includes a passport number, where the guest came from, where the guest is going, how and when, and a multitude of other details. Regulations tell us how much tax to add to a bill, what can be said on a menu, how much to charge for a room, how much to pay employees, what to do with waste, how to provide accessibility for the disabled, where to smoke, and whom to accept as a customer. This is not to mention the mass of paperwork required to comply with city, state, and national government information requirements, or the taxes to be paid.

In fact, costs and profits can sometimes be affected as much by regulations as by management decisions or customers' preferences. This, of course, is why hospitality professional associations have lobbyists in Washington, D.C., as well as in state capitals. In many countries there is no such luxury as lobbyists—if the government decides it wants to do something, it simply does that thing. Wherever regulations come from, including the smallest town's local ordinance, opposing, supporting, or dealing with regulations is a science of its own. We are more concerned here, however, with the marketing implications derived from scanning environments.

Aside from fighting proposed regulations that will affect a business, scanning the environment means preparing for an event if and

---

[5]Presentation at World Hospitality Congress III, Boston, March 9, 1987.

[6]John Helyar, "The Holiday Inns Trip: A Breeze for Decades, Bumpy Ride in the '80s," *Wall Street Journal,* February 19, 1987, pp. 1, 23.

[7]"1993 Foodservice Industry Forecast," *Restaurants USA,* December, 1992, p. 23.

when it materializes. A good example is the somewhat recent and continuing banning of "happy hours" with reduced drink prices in various American states and municipalities. While there has been no definitive evidence, before or after, that banning happy hours would decrease drunk driving, the climate (or social environment) was ripe for such action. (There was, and is, actually no concrete evidence that banning happy hours hurt business either; nor evidence that people drank at that time of the day because of them.) Astute operators read the writing on the wall and, before the laws were passed, turned to other promotions such as free happy hour snacks that have been just as succssful. If people drink less now it is because of society and driving laws, not the banning of reduced drink prices.

On a national scale, a similar event occurred with the passage of the 1986 U.S. tax law allowing only 80 percent (reduced to 50 percent in 1993) of meal expenses as a business deduction. Many restaurant operators, especially those who count heavily on the expense account customer (Who else could afford to pay the prices?), seemed to go into panic. More astute operators, however, quietly went about their business, adjusted their menus, and provided other inducements. Most realized that few good businesspeople would jeopardize a business relationship by *not* taking a customer to lunch to save a few dollars in tax benefits. Some, wisely, began to target other market segments that they had previously ignored.

Regulatory impacts are bound to be with us for a long time to come. There is no way that they can be successfully ignored. The marketer's task is to be aware of them, prepare for them, and develop a contingency plan before they occur.

Ecological Impacts

As consumers become more aware of the fragility of our natural environment, issues relating to ecology have risen to the forefront. In fact, one of the buzzwords of the travel industry in the 1990s is "ecotourism." Belize, a small country nestled between Mexico and Guatemala, is trying to create an image of an ecotourist paradise. With many unspoiled natural resources ranging from tropical mountains to the second largest barrier reef in the world, Belize is approaching tourism with caution and has positioned itself to attract the growing number of environmentally conscious travelers.

Among environmental concerns, waste disposal, recycling, and pollution are all attracting attention, not only from customers but regulators as well. Cruise ships are not allowed to dump their wastes into the sea, and some even provide biodegradable golf balls so that their customers can practice from an on-board driving range without polluting the sea! Golf courses are looking for new strains of grass to minimize the use of pesticides and hotels are slowly moving toward recycling of solid wastes. McDonald's Corporation, once committed to the use of styrofoam containers, realized that customers' attitudes had changed and switched to paper wrappers. Increasingly, the hospitality industry will be expected by the public to incorporate ecological concerns into their decision making. Some have already started and found it profitable.

It is interesting that so much of the progress in ecological management at hotels and restaurants has been made outside the United States. Steigenberger Hotels of Germany now places unwrapped soap in guestrooms and saves 50 percent. When it changed from portion packs for butter and jams, it estimated the saving at 40 percent. The Crowne Plaza in Wiesbaden, Germany uses low-energy lightbulbs and a central switch to make it easy to turn them all off. The Thai Wah Group of Thailand won the International Hotel Association 1992 Environmental Award for converting an abandoned, denuded former tin-mining area into the luxurious Laguna Beach resort on Phukat Island, with a total commitment to the physical, cultural, and social environment. Wood was not used as a structural material in the hotel. All organic waste is composted. Treated sewage is cycled into a chemically-treated system and recycled into the gardens.[8] Figure 5-8 shows how other

---

[8]Reported in *Hotels*, February, 1993, pp. 21–22, 57–58.

Our program ...

In 1990, Canadian Pacific Hotels & Resorts undertook the development of a green program for our hotels in Canada. Our aim was to institute the highest possible standards of environmental responsibility throughout the chain.

Environmental Committees were formed at every one of our properties to lead the green program in-house. An Environmental audit was conducted in all our hotels in Canada, looking for areas where we could introduce more nature-friendly products and practices.

We asked professional environmental consultants for ideas on "going green." And most importantly, we asked our 10,000 employees in Canada how they felt about introducing a green program. Our employees gave us an overwhelming vote of support as well as lots of great ideas on where to start greening our hotels....

Exciting results...

- Each year the Royal York collects over 496,000 bottles.
- We also collected and recycled over 24,000 aluminum cans!
- Last year, over 224,000 pounds of paper were recycled – a savings of 2,128 trees!
- Organic waste from the kitchen has been cut by approximately 2,000 pounds per day through the use of a Hobart Press waste disposal system!
- A $25,000 program of replacing leaky steam traps and fixing leaks brought stream consumption levels down from 160 million to 130 million pounds per year, with corresponding energy production savings.

Other achievements...

- Extensive recycling program for aluminum, metal, glass, cardboard, newsprint, paper and plastic have resulted in the reduction of over 1 million pounds of waste annually.

- Our discard bedding, linens, hand soap and unused portions of hotel amenities are distributed to a variety of local relief agencies and Third World Countries.
- Guest laundry bags on Business Class floors are made from discarded bedding, thereby eliminating quanties of plastic bags.
- Unused portions of facial and toiletry tissue are placed in staff locker rooms.
- Blue boxes are in all guest rooms to encourage hotel guests to participate in the hotel's recycling program.
- Conversion is in all guest rooms to energy efficient light bulbs throughout the hotel is in progress.
- Installation of a freon management system recaptures old freon gas when chillers are being repaired.
- Our kitchens supply local organizations such as Second harvest with leftover baked goods and hot food.
- Our food and beverage outlets are phasing in recycled paper with environmentally friendly coatings on all menus.
- All office stationery and paper suppies are being converted to products that are made from 100% recycled paper with a high post-consumer content.
- Elimination of all aerosols within the hotel.

The Royal York is "Toronto's most advanced hotel" on the environmental front.
– Meeting & Incentive Magazine, Spring 92

Toronto Region of Canadian Pacific Hotels and Resorts are winners of the 1992 Lieutenant Governor's Conservation Award.

What some of our sister hotels have been doing....

CHATEAU WHISTLER

Commercial pesticides on its rose bushes have been replaced by lady bugs, which are equally effective in controlling aphids and similar pests. They also have a reforestation program whereby Christmas trees used in the hotel over the holiday season are kept in pots, and are replanted locally in the summer.

LE CHATEAU MONTEBELLO

Two particularly interesting projects undertaken at this hotel are the construction of a compost site to fertilize the hotel's own herb garden and natural fish fertilizer being used on the golf course!

LE CHATEAU FRONTENAC

Every month, two metric tons of cardboard are sold to a local recycler for $60 per ton. Proceeds from this sale help a local charity, Reves d'enfants (Children's Wish) which raises money for terminally ill children.

HOTEL NEWFOUNDLAND

Without the support of recycling programs which exist in other areas of Canada, ingenuity was the key here. They now work with a local wine supply store. The hotel sends its glass and plastic bottles (over 70 cases per month) to the store, which in turn recycles them to their customers who make home-made wine!

HOTEL VANCOUVER

One of the hotel's most successful environmental moves took place in the hotel laundry. The engineering department installed 82 steam guards in the laundry, and in just 3 weeks, saved 1.25 million pounds of steam.

SKYDOME HOTEL

The hotel was the first hotel in the chain to start a blue box program, a program which helped inspire Canadian Pacific Hotels & Resorts to make this a chain-wide project.

BANFF SPRINGS HOTEL

All non-refundable cans are being collected both within the hotel and in staff accommodations, and shredded in the hotel's new Rabco recycling machine. Every month over 1,000 pounds of cans are recovered in this way, and sent to a recycling plant in Calgary.

L'HÔTEL

The most striking example of L'Hôtel's environmental program success is in the area of energy conservation. With the involvement of Ontario Hydro, L'Hôtel switched its 40-W fluorescent tubes to 34-W tubes, an investment of $10,000 which paid off swiftly; the first energy year saving was over $25,000, and to top it off, L'Hôtel qualified for an Ontario Hydro conservation rebate of $1,900!

FIGURE 5-8 Dealing with guests' ecological concerns

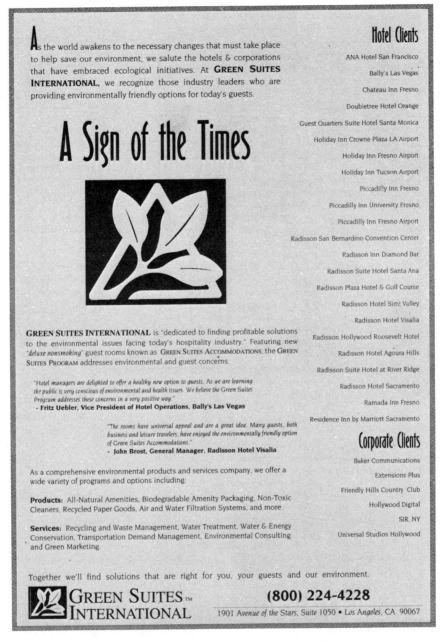

FIGURE 5-8   (continued)

hotel companies are dealing with ecological concerns.

So far, we have discussed the different components of the environment and how they affect the hospitality industry. However, it must be noted that these components are dynamic and often tied to each other. The major task of environmental scanning is not only to identify those elements that will affect the firm but also to assess the nature of the effect. A favorable effect

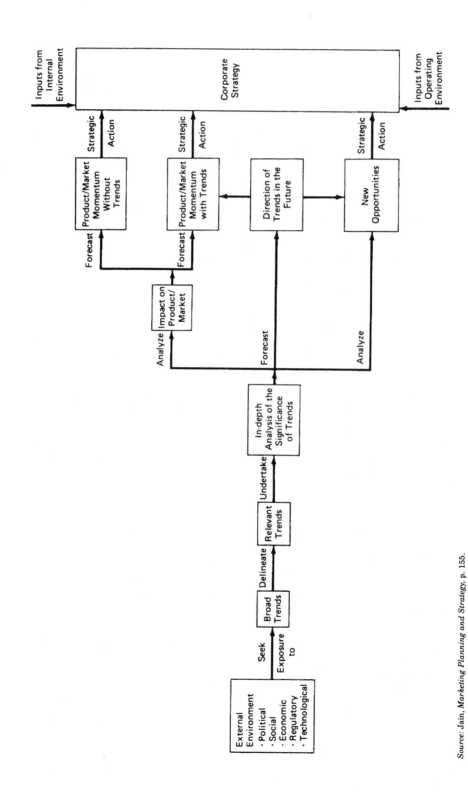

Source: Jain, *Marketing Planning and Strategy,* p. 155.

FIGURE 5-9 Linking environmental scanning to corporate strategy

is an opportunity while an unfavorable effect is often a threat. Figure 5-9 is a self-explanatory model for using environmental scanning to develop corporate strategy.

B. Opportunities, Threats, and Competitive Analysis

In marketing, opportunity and competitive analysis go hand-in-hand. This is so because opportunity means being where the competition *isn't,* or being where the competition is weak. Someone once said that marketing opportunity is "the niche that cries out to be filled." That statement may be a little melodramatic but it does make the point. The only problem is that most opportunities don't cry out; in fact, they can be very well hidden. Perhaps it would be better to say that opportunity in marketing is "the niche that cries out to be found."

There are other opportunities that don't necessarily involve competitive weakness. These are the ones right under our noses, connected with improving our own product and making our customers' lives easier. These opportunities usually come under the rubric of new product development or "upselling"—selling more to the same customers. Or, they may simply involve policy or procedural changes. Obviously there is some overlap, but here we will be more concerned with market (customer) opportunities, those that exist in the marketplace (where the customers are). We will first discuss what market opportunities are, as well as their counterparts, market threats. We will then look at competitive analysis and finally, in section C, at marketing research and its use in discovering market opportunities.

Market Opportunities

Let us begin with a basic premise that never hurts repeating: Finding marketing opportunities means finding customers, creating customers, and keeping customers. By contrast, many financial opportunities begin with the "chance to make a lot of money." Many defunct multimillion dollar projects have been based on that premise, and many supposedly great ideas have failed for lack of customers. Here we are concerned with customer opportunities.

Ray Kroc's original and continuing McDonald's concept remains a classic case of seized market opportunity, as we saw in Chapter 1. Kroc saw families moving to the suburbs, with discretionary income and children, having a real hassle in finding a place to eat that was quick, clean, and dependable. Howard Johnson (the founder) saw an opportunity in nationwide consistent restaurants; Kemmons Wilson saw the same thing with motels for Holiday Inns. More currently, developers of suite hotel and budget motel chains saw opportunities in changing needs in the lodging market. Total conference center hotels were an opportunity that grew out of companies' dissatisfaction with what they were being offered at standard hotels. Domino's saw an opportunity in home-delivered pizza, McDonald's in putting their product on airlines, in volume discount stores and hotels, Whattaburger in gourmet hamburgers, PepsiCo in Mexican food (Taco Bell), and Hyatt in in-room fax machines, as we saw in Figure 5-1. All of these opportunities occurred in areas where the competition was weak or nonexistent and where there was a consumer problem.

New markets come from only three places: They are "stolen" from the competition, they are created, or they are cannibalized (that is, we take them from ourselves). Taking markets from the competition means that we have to do something better than the competition, or we have to do something the competition isn't doing at all. Creating new markets means that we have found an undeveloped need that either wasn't recognized or wasn't being fulfilled. An example of creating a new market is McDonald's introduction of breakfast, which turned out to fill a real need that no one was really sure was there. In most of these cases, however, whether of the stolen customer or the created customer, the window of opportunity closes very quickly.

Stolen customers must be convinced to make the change—that is, they must get everything they were promised, or they will not stay stolen. This makes the task of stealing customers all the more difficult. Furthermore, competition will act quickly to get them back. (See Figure 5-10: Radisson will have to perform well to keep these customers.) Created customers, on the other hand, will soon be offered an abundance of similar products and/or services, sometimes at lower prices. The answer to this problem is to be continuously seeking new opportunities, since successes can often be short-term.

In cannibalizing, we steal from ourselves. We get customers to buy from us something instead of what they were previously buying from us. When Marriott developed its Courtyard by Marriott concept (an opportunity well filled), a major concern was whether the Courtyards might draw away too many regular Marriott customers from its higher-priced properties. A rationalization of such concern is: Usually, it is better to steal from yourself than to let someone else do it. But you don't want to rob Peter to pay Paul—new dining concepts in a hotel, for example, sometimes decimate the old ones with no net gain or loss, except for the expense of opening it.

Another way to look at opportunity is through consumer demand. *Existing* demand is demand for a good or service that is available from one or more sources. *Latent* demand is demand where there is a need but no suitable product available to satisfy it. *Incipient* demand is demand for which even the customer may not yet recognize the need as it is just beginning to exist or appear. There are opportunities at all three levels of demand but especially the latter two. Of all the opportunities we have presented in this chapter, see if you can categorize them in these three levels.

Market Threats

Threats are the other side of opportunities. Often one needs only to look at the other side of the coin. For example, computers are an opportunity. If not seized, they become a threat when a competitor adopts the new technology. Competition is only one threat in the environment, but

a powerful one. Competitive threats mean that the enemy did, or will, get there first or will soon follow. Threats also come from environmental changes, as we have shown. We hope to be able to react quickly enough to turn the threat into an opportunity, but this may not be possible; we may just be too late.

When another company can throw millions of dollars into an opportunity and you cannot, that is a threat of a different color. In this discussion, however, we will consider threats and opportunities as the same, recognizing that this may not always be the case. Take the example of changing demographics: Fast-food companies rely heavily on a teenage workforce, but as the number of teenagers decreases as a percentage of the total population, lack of workers becomes a threat. On the other hand, seeking employees from the growing number of senior citizens is an opportunity.

Now that we understand what opportunities and threats are, let us see how we can go about conducting competitive analysis in order to find opportunities and diminish threats.

Competitive Analysis

In marketing, competition is the enemy. To outmaneuver the enemy we have to know its strengths and weaknesses, what it does and doesn't do well, who its customers are, why they go there, and what they do when they get there. We would also like to know something about customer loyalty, dissatisfaction, what needs and wants are not being fulfilled, and what problems customers are having. This calls for a great deal of marketing intelligence.

Competitive analysis is not limited to investigating bricks and mortar, number and size of meeting rooms, decor, what grade beef is bought, what size drink is poured, or what prices are charged. That would amount to a product orientation, and we don't want to be any more product-oriented in analyzing the competition than we do in analyzing ourselves. Of course, if the competition itself is product-oriented, we should know that as well, for it may be our marketing opportunity.

Is it in the cards for you?

Friday, January 26th and Friday, February 2nd, every available room in the house will be on the house. And you're eligible if you're a holder of any hotel frequency card. Reservations must be made through our 800 number—no more than 72 hours in advance. Radisson's Friday Freeday. We're free on Friday. Are you?

• FOR RESERVATIONS WORLDWIDE 800-333-3333 •

Radisson Hotels International
WORLDWIDE • WORLD CLASS℠

FIGURE 5-10   Radisson makes a blatant effort to steal customers

If, on the other hand, the competition is marketing-oriented, how marketing-oriented are they? Are they creative, do they adapt quickly, will they accept short-term losses for long-term gains, do they worry about the customer, and how soon will they copy or react to what we do (or, how short-lived will be any advantage we gain)?

In other words, we have to get to know the competition. Of course, we have to know something about their facilities, product, services, and resources, but here's a basic truism that is often ignored: The competition is not simply other hotels and restaurants; it includes the people who manage and operate those hotels and restaurants. Understanding these people adds to our understanding the competition.

Like the Japanese. When Toyota wanted to learn what Americans preferred in a small, imported car, it didn't ask the people who owned Chevrolets and Pontiacs, as GM did; it asked the owners of Volkswagens what they liked or disliked about the Beetle. They looked for the "niche crying out to be found"! They identified the true competition and then addressed consumers' problems.

Micro Competition

Earlier we discussed macro competition; now we will describe the other form of competition, that of the micro level. At this level we define competition as any business that is competing for the same customers in the same product class at the same point in time—in other words, a business that is a direct competitor with a similar product in a similar context. By this definition, the gourmet restaurant does not compete with fast-food restaurants, and upscale hotels do not compete with budget motels.

Caution is necessary at this point to avoid overgeneralizing these contrasts. As mentioned above, an alternative in a different product class can become a competitor if the one product class is not fulfilling a need. In other words, we would not normally think that a three-star hotel would be a direct competitor of a four-star hotel. The situation changes, however, if the four-star hotel prices itself out of the market and consumers turn to lower-priced alternatives. Nowadays, the situation is reversed in many markets where upscale hotels with full services are offering rates almost as low as limited-service properties. Perhaps the toughest

part of competitive analysis is recognizing its realities.

Conversely, for marketing planning at a given time, a greater failing may be to consider as competition properties that are actually in different product classes. This failing can lead to major strategic errors. If the operator of a French restaurant says his competition is the Red Lobster across the street, he is probably basing his statement on geographic proximity rather than product class or customer needs, wants, and demand. Let us analyze this point in some detail to be certain that it is clear.

The people who eat at the French restaurant may also eat at the Red Lobster—they may even eat there more often, but this does not make the two restaurants direct competitors. The reason is that customers are fulfilling different needs and wants at the two restaurants. Except in rare cases, one of these restaurants would not be an alternative to the other.

Suppose these are the only two restaurants within 100 miles. Does the situation change? If the Red Lobster disappeared, would patronage increase at the French restaurant? Probably very little. At those times that people might have gone to the Red Lobster, they will now stay home.

Suppose, however, that the Red Lobster is doing volume business and the French restaurant is doing zilch. Now does the situation change? Yes, but.... The "but" is not that the Red Lobster is the competition; it is that the French restaurant, assuming it is a good operation, has misjudged the market and is not catering to the needs and wants of the marketplace. If the Red Lobster now disappears, the French restaurant will still do zilch—that is, it is not a direct competitor. These examples assume prices consistent with the product, but even at the same price level, there would be some noncompetitive separation of needs and wants.

Choosing the Right Competition

Choosing the right competition is very critical in competitive analysis because it has tremendous bearing on the marketing strategy and tactics of any hospitality operation. Choosing the "wrong" competition is an error that can be illustrated with cases of a French restaurant and a resort hotel. In the first example,

> Management of the only French restaurant in a small city was unhappy with the volume they were doing. They were at a loss to explain this, since they received very favorable customer comments. In fact, cursory research showed that they were overwhelmingly rated the best restaurant in the city in terms of food, service, and atmosphere. In final desperation, after scouting all the "competition," management decided to "do as the Romans do." They put in a prime rib buffet, added steaks and chops to the menu, and did various other things that other restaurants were doing. A little less than a year later, business had fallen to the point where ownership sold out.

What had happened, of course, was two things: First, the new menu had alienated the old clientele. Second, the restaurant had failed to attract a new clientele that still perceived them as an expensive French restaurant. Their failing was in not recognizing that their major competition was not in the same city; the competition was in adjoining cities where this restaurant lacked awareness. The appropriate strategy would have been to develop the strong niche they had, create new awareness, and pull in customers from out of town who would have been willing to go a distance for their kind of food and service.

The second case is one of a 300-room resort hotel in a remote seasonal, oceanside location:

> In an attempt to build the off-season business, management did extensive refurbishing and remodeling so as to have expansive conference facilities. It was the only hotel in the area with the capacity and the facilities to draw groups of substantial size.
>
> In a market analysis, two large cities 75 and 175 miles away were designated as the markets. The only lodging properties within 25 miles, a Holiday Inn, a Sheraton franchise, and three or four individual properties, were designated as the competition. Marketing efforts were aimed at competing with these properties. However, the effort to build off-season business failed.

Once again, management failed to recognize that the customers who went to the "competi-

tion" were neither the same ones, nor in the same market segment as the ones the property was trying to attract. The competition in this case was hundreds of miles away in similar properties that drew from diverse markets for conference and meetings business.

Managements that, in designing their properties, concentrate on the concept, rather than the customer and the competition, have what we call "conceptitis." One former food and beverage vice-president of a hotel chain was noted for his public statements that he developed hotel restaurants not just for hotel guests but for a clientele outside the hotel. This is a fine idea, provided the market is there, provided you are not at the same time losing all your hotel customers, and provided the concept fits the needs of the designated market that the competition is not filling. More than one "great" concept designed by this vice-president did poorly because these provisos were ignored.

With all the possible alternatives, then, who is the right competition? Unfortunately, there is no simple answer to that question. The answer requires thorough analysis of any given situation. We can suggest, however, two launching points: First, deliberately choose whom you want to, and can, compete against. Rarely do markets appear simply out of nowhere; most of the time you have to steal them. As Michael Porter has pointed out in his extensive writings on competition, choosing whom you want to compete against is one of the first decisions that has to be made in developing a product or business.[9] Figure 5-11 shows Renaissance's choice of competition by finding people named Hyatt, Marriott, and Hilton to appear in their ads.

Second, ask your customers where they would be if they weren't at your property. Why? Or, if you're developing a new product, research the market. Where does your target market go now? Why? The answers to these questions will tell you, at least, who the market perceives as your competition. The answers will also tell you what you have to compete against in terms of attributes and services. If the answers from the mar-

---

[9]Michael E. Porter, *Competitive Strategy: Techniques for Analyzing Industries and Competitors*, New York: Free Press, 1980.

Why the Hiltons stay at Renaissance.

"We have traveled throughout the world, and we find Renaissance Hotels rank among the best.

"The lobby areas are beautiful, the decorations and furnishings in the rooms are of high standing. The service, the cleanliness and the facilities stand out. Renaissance will certainly be our hotel of choice on future trips."

*Bruce and Carmen Hilton
from North Carolina,
while staying at the
Vancouver Renaissance Hotel.*

UNITED STATES
Arlington, VA
Atlanta Downtown
Atlanta Int'l Airport
Dallas/Richardson
Dulles Int'l Airport
East Brunswick, NJ
Jackson, MS
Long Beach, CA
Los Angeles Int'l Airport
New York City
Orlando Int'l Airport
Springfield, IL
Washington, D.C.
CANADA
Dartmouth/Halifax
Edmonton
Niagara Falls
Regina
Saskatoon
Toronto
Vancouver
CARIBBEAN
Antigua
Grenada
Ocho Rios, Jamaica
Santo Domingo, D.R.

RENAISSANCE℠
HOTELS · RESORTS

FIGURE 5-11   Renaissance chooses its competition

ket are different from the properties you have chosen to compete against, it is clear that your perception differs from the market's. It may be necessary to rethink your competitive strategy.

We can illustrate these two points with further reference to hotel F&B outlets. Astute marketers will first determine who they want as customers and what their needs and wants are. (These include in-house customers and the local market.) Then they will ask where these customers go now, or will go. Next, they will do a thorough analysis of this competition. They will then go to the architect, the F&B director, and other involved parties and say, "This is what we need to do to keep/steal these customers." Then, and only then, should concept development begin because you have now chosen whom you will compete against. You have also determined the weapons you need to compete.

Competitive Intensity

The competitive intensity in a marketplace is the fierceness with which competing companies do battle with each other. (See Figure 5-12 for an example in the airline industry.) It is an important measurement in competitive analysis because the level of intensity will often dictate the way a firm does business. In general, today, competitive intensity is very high in the hospitality industry, as shown in Figure 5-11, an ad campaign that was followed by a lawsuit. Too much intensity can lead to less-than-wise decisions to gain competitive advantage. This can be illustrated with what took place in the so-called hotel amenities wars, because it is a marketing truism that all opportunities are not necessarily competitive advantages.

The amenities wars started in the United States in the early 1980s with one hotel chain adopting the European custom of putting a mint on the pillow and turning the bed down. Other hotel chains followed suit, and the mints got better and more expensive. Then someone started with special soaps, soon followed by shampoos, body lotions, shoe horns; and then a choice of soaps, body lotions, shampoos, bubble baths, and so on. In some cases all this added well over $5 per occupied night to the cost of the room for the hotel.

No hotel company bothered to do research to determine what effect all these amenities were having on the customer, or read the research others were doing.[10] At the same time, hotel guests were filling their suitcases with the amenities and stocking their home medicine

cabinets. Finally, Michael Leven, President of Holiday Inn, Americas Division, called a halt: "Bubble bath is not [in]. We are off Vidal Sassoon and into reality."[11]

The amenities wars story demonstrates some important things about competitive intensity. First, services that can be easily duplicated offer only short-term advantage, if that, when you have aggressive competitors. When those services are not perceived as a determinative advantage by consumers and instead end up costing them more for the core product, such services may in fact become a negative factor for the entire product class. Figure 5-13 shows how one hotel company finally countered the amenities war. Second, when introducing an additional service, you need to have an idea of how your competitors will react. Third, competitive tactics should, as much as possible, be based on the customer, not on the competition, unless this is essential to the firm's self-protection.

Does this mean that a hotel or restaurant should not try to gain competitive advantage by introducing services that are easily duplicated? No, it does not, or else there would never be growth or improvement. It means, instead, that the intensity of the competition is a critical factor and should be carefully weighed before making the decision.

It also means going back to the customer first. Does introducing services or amenities create or keep customers? If yes, at what cost to them and at what cost to the hotel? Does it increase the price/value relationship, or just price? If it is to be done, in what meaningful way can it be done—that is, do we know what the customer really wants? If the competition follows suit, do we retain an advantage or just an additional cost? Competitive advantages are those that are *sustainable*.

When the needs of the market are similar, the intensity of competition is much greater because many entries in the market are competing for the same customer. Small competitive advantages can become large ones if they can be sustained. On the other hand, it may be mandatory

---

[10]In one study, for example, of 1,314 hotel guests of six hotels, amenities were found to be nonsignificant in determining their choice of hotel and nonsignificant in importance when staying at a hotel, for both business and pleasure travelers. See Robert C. Lewis, "Predicting Hotel Choice: The Factors Underlying Perception," *Cornell Hotel and Restaurant Administration Quarterly*, February, 1985, pp. 82–96. This finding has been validated by others many times since.

[11]Quoted in "Industry rethinks amenities and value," *Business Travel News*, September 27, 1993, p. 20.

After lengthy deliberation
at the highest executive levels,
and extensive consultation
with our legal department,
we have arrived at
an official corporate response
to Northwest Airlines' claim
to be number one
in Customer Satisfaction.

"Liar, liar. Pants on fire."

Okay. We lost our temper for a moment. Northwest didn't really lie. And, its pants aren't actually on fire. Northwest simply excluded Southwest Airlines from its comparison.

Fact. According to the U.S. Department of Transportation's Consumer Report for May, the real leader in Customer Satisfaction is Southwest Airlines. That means we received the fewest complaints per 100,000 passengers among all Major airlines, including Northwest.

More facts. The Department of Transportation's Consumer Report also shows Southwest Airlines best in On-time Performance (highest percentage of system-wide domestic flights arriving within 15 minutes of schedule, excluding mechanical delays), best in Baggage Handling (fewest mishandled bags per 1,000 passengers),

as well as best in Customer Satisfaction, from January through August 1992. It's all there in black and white.

Fly the real No. 1. You'll know there's no substitute for satisfaction. Call Southwest Airlines or your travel agent for reservations.

SOUTHWEST AIRLINES℠
Just Plane Smart™
1-800-I-FLY-SWA (1-800-435-9792)

Courtesy of Southwest Airlines

FIGURE 5-12   Competitive intensity in the airline industry

for one firm to copy another that is aggressively seeking an advantageous position, if it can do so, in order to eliminate the advantage.

Competitive Intelligence

As in war, one always wants to know what the enemy is doing, their position and intentions, strengths and weaknesses, where they are most vulnerable and least vulnerable, and where the best place is to attack. For our purposes, competitive intelligence goes beyond merely physical property description.

There are a number of ways to get this information, and it is well worth getting. First, there is public information. The media, annual re-

FIGURE 5-13   Countering the amenities wars' impact

ports if a publicly held company, company brochures, flyers and ads, publicity releases, and so forth are some of the sources. Then there is trade gossip—information from vendors and others who deal with the competition.

Market Share   In some areas, hotels exchange room occupancy percentages and average rate figures nightly by mutual arrangement. Many restaurant operators do likewise. (An old restaurant trick is to drive around and count cars in parking lots, but beware of employee cars!) Actually these arrangements are mutually beneficial because all they tell you is how you are doing relative to the others. The refusal of some managements to share this information, or to lie to each other, is generally self-defeating. It still remains to discover why you are doing better or worse. Comparison figures of occupancy and covers are called *market share* figures and are used to compare actual market share with fair market share, as explained in Chapter 4.

In computing fair market share it is important to be certain that you are comparing apples with apples—in other words, with other properties in the same product class competing for the same customer. To do this you divide your capacity by total capacity in the product class. The resulting figure is your percentage

of fair market share. To compute actual market share you divide your actual occupancy (or covers) by total product class occupancy. You then compare actual to fair market share as a measure of how well you are doing relative to the competition.

Consider the hypothetical example shown in Table 5-1 for one city area for one night. All the participants in the arrangement are not in the same product class. This does not mean that you are not interested in their occupancy—for instance, it would be worthwhile to know why middle-tier properties are running at higher occupancy than upper-tier properties. It might indicate that the upper-tier properties are pricing themselves out of the market, or it could mean something entirely different, for instance, concerning the type of business that was in town last night.

Now consider the market shares of the properties in your product class. Hotel C's actual share is considerably lower than its fair share. But look at the size of this hotel; it is still filling more rooms than any of the others in the product class. Perhaps this is primarily a convention hotel with widely fluctuating occupancies; perhaps it should not be included in the same product class. What this means is that one has to interpret these figures with discretion before making judgments.

TABLE 5-1   Hypothetical Example of Market Share

Hotel	Actual Rooms	Rooms Sold	Occupancy%	Fair Share%	Actual Share%
Upper-tier Hotels					
A	300	220	73.3	11.5	15.5
B	500	350	70.0	19.2	24.7
C	1,200	500	41.7	46.2	35.2
Yours	600	350	58.3	23.1	24.7
Total	2,600	1,420	54.6	100.0	100.0
Middle-tier Hotels					
E	275	220	80.0	31.3	30.6
F	425	360	84.7	48.3	50.0
G	180	140	77.8	20.4	19.4
Total	880	720	81.8	100.0	100.0

TABLE 5-2   Hypothetical Example of REVPAR

Hotel	Actual Rooms	Rooms Sold	Average Daily Rate (ADR)	Revenue	REVPAR
Upper-tier Hotels					
A	300	220	$60	$13,200	$44.00
B	500	350	65	22,750	45.50
C	1,200	500	73	36,500	30.42
Yours	600	350	70	24,500	40.83
Middle-tier Hotels					
E	275	220	$55	$12,100	44.00
F	425	360	53	19,090	44.89
G	180	140	56	7,840	43.56

As you can see, your hotel is barely getting its fair market share and would not be doing even that if Hotel C's occupancy was up. Hotels A and B, however, are substantially exceeding their fair share. What, you might ask, are they doing right? Or, are you doing wrong? This calls for an examination of their segments and marketing strategies.

REVPAR While market share is one method of measuring position in the marketplace, increasingly the calculation of *revenue per available room* (REVPAR) is being employed.[12] The fallacy of market share is that a competitor can gain actual share in the market at the expense of room rates. By dropping its rates $10, more people may buy the facility. REVPAR measures the revenue generated per available room.

This calculation more accurately measures the balance of marketing efforts, as shown in Table 5-2. The middle-tier hotels indicate better asset management. Their REVPARS are comparable to the upper-tier hotels, or better, and they undoubtedly are lower cost producers. One possible conclusion is that they are stealing business from the upper-tier hotels with lower rates. Another is that, on this particular day, the upper-tier hotels had booked lower-rate conference groups. In any case, the reason needs to be examined on a regular basis. Trends are more enlightening than single days, and other conclusions might be drawn.

Another technique for getting information is simply to talk to your competitors. You might do this one-on-one, or at industry meetings. You can also talk to your customers, who might have been *their* customers. You can talk to your employees, who might have been *their* employees, or at least might know some of their employees. Don't forget, of course, that while you are doing this, so is the competition!

In the final analysis, the management that obtains the most information will be the one that moves around, keeps its eyes and ears open, and uses good intuitive judgment. Close observation can tell you a lot about what the competition does best and why, where they are off the mark and why, what their strengths are and their weaknesses, and what they plan next. All this is good marketing intelligence and it can go a long way in helping you to develop your own marketing strategy.[13]

Beating the Competition

The purpose of competitive analysis, of course, is to use it to your best advantage. If you are

---

[12]REVPAR = room revenue ÷ number of rooms available for sale.

[13]A good analysis of gaining competitive information is given in K. Michael Haywood, "Scouting the Competition for Survival and Success," *Cornell Hotel and Restaurant Administration Quarterly,* November, 1986, pp. 81–87.

behind, you need to seek and increase competitive advantage. If you are ahead, you need to sustain and increase competitive advantage. In the first case, you need to overcome barriers to move ahead. In the second, you need to erect barriers to stay ahead.

The essence of opportunity is beating the competition. Intense competition in an industry is neither coincidence nor bad luck. It is a fact of business life. The competitive objective is to find the position where you can break down or influence the barriers, or where you can erect the best defense. This means finding what makes the competition vulnerable. Attacking vulnerability, as in the military sense, means attacking the weaknesses and avoiding the strengths in the line. The latter is as important as the former.

Wendy's is one fast-food operator that has proven the above point. Wendy's attacked where McDonald's was weak in two areas: One was the area of "adult" hamburgers. Wendy's saw that McDonald's was not really serving this market, so they set out to carve their own niche. The second area was in the product. Wendy's saw a dislike in the market for the frozen, precooked hamburger, especially among a portion of the adult market, and offered fresh hamburgers. Wendy's has survived where many others that attacked McDonald's strengths failed. The budget portion of the hotel industry has done likewise.

Competitive Marketing

Porter suggests three strategies for beating the competition: positioning to provide the best defense, influencing the balance by taking the offense, and exploiting industry change.[14]

Defensive positioning means matching strengths and weaknesses against the competition by finding positions where it is the weakest, and strengths where the company is least vulnerable. Ritz-Carlton Hotels have accomplished this by maintaining their level of service at all costs.

Influencing the balance by taking the offensive, or proacting, means attempting to alter the industry structure and its causes. It calls for marketing innovation, establishing brand identity, or otherwise differentiating the product. This has happened with suite hotels, conference center hotels and, especially, luxury budget hotels.

Exploiting industry change means anticipating shifts in the environment, forecasting the effect, constructing a composite of the future, and positioning accordingly. Robert Hazard accomplished this in his successful metamorphosis of Quality Inns (now Choice International) in the early 1980s, when he offered three different product levels to the marketplace.

A successful company must look beyond today's competitors to those that may become competitors tomorrow (a la convenience stores and take-out vs. the fast-food industry). It must also watch out for new entries in the race (e.g., conference center hotels), and the threat of substitute products (e.g., supermarket "make-your-own-meal" bars).

The key to growth, even survival, is to obtain a position that is less vulnerable to direct attack, old or new, and less vulnerable to consumer manipulation and substitute products. This can be done by relationship marketing, actual or psychological product differentiation, and constant and foresighted competitive awareness and analysis. We will discuss how to analyze competitive strengths and weaknesses in Chapter 9, on positioning.

Finding Marketing Opportunities

To be sure, all marketing opportunities begin with consumers' problems. Well-known management author Peter Drucker calls these opportunities "incongruities."[15] Incongruities here are discrepancies between what is and what ought to be. As far as the customer is concerned, this may be the difference between expectation and reality; it also may be the difference between

[14]Michael E. Porter, "Note on the Structural Analysis of Industries," Harvard Business School Case Services, 1975, p. 22.

[15]Peter F. Drucker, *Innovation and Entrepreneurship*, New York: Harper & Row, 1985, p. 57.

what the customer would like it to be and what is available. These are both true opportunities. Drucker states,

> Of all incongruities, that between perceived and actual reality may be the most common. Producers and suppliers almost always misconceive what it is that the customer actually buys. They must assume that what represents "value" to the producer and supplier is equally "value" to the customer. . . . And yet, no customer ever perceives himself as buying what the producer or supplier delivers. Their expectations and values are always different.[16]

If Drucker is only half right, it is clear that within consumer incongruities there are tremendous opportunities. Every one is familiar with the expression, "there ought to be a better way." It is in that better way that opportunities lie. Consider the case of the atrium hotel lobby, now common all over the world:

> John Portman was an architect who decided there ought to be a better way to design a hotel. At the time, hotel architecture had reached a degree of sameness that was so "commodity-laden" that no one thought hotels could ever be other than what they were, architecturally speaking. The first Portman-designed atrium hotel was opened by Hyatt in Atlanta in 1967 and the industry was shocked. Everyone criticized but the customers kept coming and Hyatt became a major chain as a result.

Was this a consumer problem solved? Was this a case of consumer expectations being unfulfilled? Of course it was. Hotels were dull, dreary places with long, dark corridors and dull lobbies with couches built around the antiquated concept of "a home away from home." Customers didn't want a home away from home; they wanted a new and exciting experience. They wanted something different, and Hyatt gave it to them. The decision by Hyatt to build an atrium lobby hotel did more than start Hyatt on its way; it started hotel architecture on its way, and today's examples are a result of that initial Portman design and Hyatt decision.

Consider the now-popular restaurant salad bar. Who knows where or when it started? Someone saw an opportunity arising from a consumer problem. Fine wine by the glass, thanks to nitrogen-filled, partially empty wine bottles, and coffee, juice, and roll carts on hotel elevators solved other consumer problems. An enterprising and successful young company in Florida calls itself "wee-bag-it." It delivers to offices hot, delicious breakfast, lunch, and dinner with considerable variety (Figure 5-14). What was the problem? What an opportunity! Environmental changes discussed earlier present other, more macro problems and opportunities. If you want to find an opportunity, look for a consumer problem.

Opportunity solutions, to be effective, have to be simple. They have to be easily understandable by the consumer. They have to avoid increased customer risk. This was the initial problem with the automatic teller machines of banks and why they took so long to catch on. Opportunities call for innovation, leadership, and a constant awareness that there ought to be a better way. Opportunities are out there crying for solutions, but innovation to fulfill them doesn't fall in your lap. Sometimes it takes hard work, sometimes just a little common sense.

The search for opportunity begins with knowing your market, knowing your customers, and understanding your customer's problems. But never forget the first rule of marketing when you get a great opportunity idea: Will it create and/or keep a customer? When you can answer yes, then and only then ask what it will cost to do it and if you can afford it.

All opportunities to create and keep a customer are not "great" ideas. Some are just common sense, as previously mentioned. A Holiday Inn in Kuala Lumpur, Malaysia offered freshly-squeezed orange juice, but you couldn't get it until after 10:00 A.M. Why not? "The juicer is in the bar and the bar doesn't open until 10:00 o'clock." The service personnel didn't tell you this, they simply served canned orange juice until 10:00 o'clock! Opportunity lost, and plain common sense lacking.

Marketing research is a critical activity in marketing and getting to know the customer. It

---

[16]*Ibid.*, p. 66.

wee-bag-it®
delivery emporiums

... is a food franchise that prepares and delivers quality "American" fare to the home and office. The franchise offers distinctive menu selections for breakfast, lunch and dinner. A typical **wee-bag-it**® is 800 to 1200 square feet, and depending upon location, may have limited seating. Opportunities in both urban and office/residential areas as well as downtown highrise locations are available. The restaurants utilize a copyrighted fully computerized food service system which keeps track of information such as customer frequency of use, packing and delivery instructions and food usage. In addition, comprehensive marketing, operations and delivery systems are in place. The initial investment ranges from approximately $70,000 to $85,000 plus working capital. Exclusive single and multi unit rights are available.

> ...Research firms predict exponential growth of delivery by the end of the decade. As long as Americans spend an increasing percentage of their food money on convenience, restaurants that don't deliver could be losing out to restaurants and others (sic) that do.
> *Restaurant Hospitality, June 1992*

> Named as one of nineteen 1990 Growth Companies -- Up-and-Comers
> *Restaurants & Institutions, November 1990*

> "Our customers always compliment us on our food quality and service."
> *Michael and Josephine Dattolico*
> *Boca Raton Franchisee*

Courtesy of David Klein, President, wee-bag-it delivery emporiums

FIGURE 5-14   Customer problem solved by wee-bag-it® with office deliveries of full meals

is a particularly vital part of environmental scanning and opportunity and competitive analysis. It is also, of course, a subject of its own. We introduce readers to a once-over-lightly treatment of the subject in section C of this chapter. We urge you to read this (if it is not assigned) and then take a marketing research course.

Market Feasibility Studies

Another form of marketing opportunity analysis differs somewhat from that in the previous discussion. Instead of looking for opportunities, market feasibility studies are conducted to verify whether an opportunity exists. When feasibility studies are conducted, someone already believes that there is an opportunity, such as to build a hotel or open a restaurant in a certain location. The purpose of the feasibility study is to verify that belief (and prove to the lender that it is a viable one). Measurement of market potential, or feasibility, is to gain knowledge of market size, market growth, market segments, profitability, demand, and type of buying decision. In essence, the feasibility study should ask these questions:

Is there a market for this property (business, concept, operation) in this location? If so, where is it, how large is it, or will it be, what are its needs, and how is it currently served? What share can be captured? Will it use our property? Who are its members? Other related questions will follow naturally.

How does the answer to the first question project into financial realities—for example, room rates or check averages, revenue, profit, return on investment, and other quantitative financial considerations?

The answers to the second question obviously depend upon the answers to the first question. Our interest here is only in the first question.

Market feasibility studies are concerned with both marketing opportunities and competitive analysis. Feasibility studies deserve an entire chapter to themselves, but that is not within the scope of this text. Instead, we place the emphasis on the analysis of the marketing opportunity. Studying markets, as we know by now, involves studying consumers or consumer groups and how they will respond (in this case) to a given offering. In other words, having decided that we would like to do something (e.g., build a new hotel or restaurant), we seek to determine whether the opportunity is there. The opportunity, of course, lies in consumers who are ready, willing, and able to buy.

The marketing opportunity depends on the consumer. If the consumer is not willing, there is no marketing opportunity. By the same token the competitive analysis of this marketing opportunity must be restricted to focus on those who are competing for the same customer under the same conditions. The six motels within a five-mile area have little to do with the competition of a proposed 300-room conference center.

A market feasibility study should have only one purpose: to show the opportunity to attract that many customers, to pay that price, to come to that property, over a period of time. That's the hard part. Once done, the easier part is to estimate revenue, subtract cost, predict net and cash flow, and determine whether the project is "feasible"—that is, a financial opportunity.

A true market feasibility study depends, totally, on customers, whether they will come, and what they will pay. This is the competitive opportunity, or lack of it. Unfortunately, most feasibility studies crunch numbers with only a remote idea of where the customers are, whether they will come, or who the real competition is. In marketing, opportunities depend on creating paying customers—and on nothing else.

C. Marketing Research

Marketing research is important in environmental scanning, competitive analysis, and opportunity analysis. We deal here largely with the last two, although all three are closely aligned with consumer problems and demands—existing, latent, and incipient.

The trick here is to find out the problems and demands customers have when using our product. What do they do when they arrive, walk in or check in, and go to their rooms or tables? What do they do the rest of their stay? To determine incipient demand you cannot always ask customers what their problems are, because they don't always know. Management has a theory about what is important to the customer, but rarely is that theory grounded in scientific research. Here is another coffee break example:

> As the time approached for the coffee break, someone in the group asked, "What factors are important in a good coffee break?"
>
> The server, the food and beverage manager, and the hotel manager all agreed that the coffee should be of the highest quality, well-brewed and served in attractive china. It should be served from a polished, elegant coffee urn on a clean, attractively arranged table.
>
> None of the people in the workshop mentioned any of these factors. They wanted to get through the line quickly. They also wanted the coffee service area to be located close to the restrooms and telephones. They thought of a total break that would take care of a variety of needs. None of them even mentioned the quality or flavor of the coffee.[17]

You can see that, in a situation like this, if we asked the customers what problems they had, they would probably reply, "None. Everything is just elegant." That is because the problems are probably in an initial stage, just beginning to exist. Problems like this are difficult to articulate, so management concludes it is doing the best job possible; because it has satisfied customers, it fails to see the opportunities.

As an example of typical, unscientific research—like the amenities studies done by their manufacturers—assume management decided to survey what was important in a coffee break. They would make up a list of items and ask respondents to indicate the importance of each one in a coffee break. One of the items would be "quality of coffee," which 98 percent would check as "very important." Voila! The most important thing in a coffee break is the quality of the coffee. Management buys the best coffee—situation taken care of, but opportunity lost.

Research is used to study how people use the product. What do they do, where do they go, how do they do it? With this kind of information, we can look for opportunities to make it all happen more easily and with less trouble. Take the example of Marriott Host/Travel Plazas, which provides food service at many airports in the United States:

> If you stand in front of one of our Host airport facilities and see all these people walk by and only a very small proportion of them actually stopping to buy something, of course the thought is, "What can we do to attract those people?" So we started looking at the research with a focus on customer needs.
>
> Host conducted over 2,000 customer interviews. We discovered that there was a relatively small number of things which we could expect to drive capture of sales. Among the items that topped the list? Convenience of location, speed of delivery and friendliness of service.
>
> Host decided to examine the convenience issue first. At an airport, customers prefer the food and beverage facility to be within sight of the gate-hold area. If they can't have that, they prefer it to be along their path from the entrance to the counter.
>
> Unfortunately, this preference isn't always factored into existing airport facility design. To counteract this limitation, Host decided to test a concept where snack bar attendants would walk the gate-hold area selling a variety of beverages and snacks. An upscale version of the traditional "hawking" found at stadiums and arena, the goal is the same: Take the product to the customer.[18]

Figure 5-15 shows a Sheraton effort to understand how customers use a hotel before building it.

[17]Karl Albrecht and Ron Zemke, *Service America,* Homewood, Illinois: Dow Jones–Irwin, ©1985, p. 59.

[18]"Empowerment Provides a 'Host' of Ways to Capture Customers on the Go," *Marriott World,* Jan/Feb/Mar, 1993, p. 10.

Introducing the Result of 600 Hours of Market Research.

Overlooking The Lake, The River And Nothing Else.

Call now to reserve your room in Chicago's newest and most exciting hotel. There may be no better time to experience business travel as it is meant to be. Situated just off Michigan Avenue, in the heart of it all where the river meets the lake in Chicago's Cityfront Center. The new Sheraton Chicago; with a spectacular view of the city from every guest room, an indoor pool, health club, five restaurants and lounges, and a service team providing the ultimate in hospitality.

After 600 hours of market research with individual business travelers and meeting and travel planners, we began our plans. So here you'll find a 1,200 room hotel with advantages that include a higher ratio of elevators to guest rooms to expedite busy travelers. And a "flying kitchen" to deliver cold breakfasts in 15 minutes and hot breakfasts in 30 minutes throughout the hotel, guaranteed. Plus, our attention to the details that make business travel easier.

For reservations call **(312) 329-7000**, your travel professional, or **800-325-3535.**

The Odyssey docked at the Sheraton Chicago Hotel & Towers.

Sheraton Sure Savers:
$169.00 A break for the Business Traveler! No advance reservations required, good for Sunday through Thursday.
$145.00 Plan ahead and get more savings! Offer good Sunday through Thursday with 14 day advanced reservations.

*Not applicable to groups. Subject to change without notice and based upon availability. Rates do not include applicable taxes and gratuities. Some restrictions apply.

"© 1992 ITT Sheraton Corporation"

Sheraton Chicago
HOTEL & TOWERS
CITYFRONT CENTER
301 East North Water Street
Chicago, IL 60611
ITT SHERATON

Courtesy of ITT Sheraton Corporation

FIGURE 5-15 Sheraton Chicago integrates the customer into the design with market research

Formal Marketing Research

Formal marketing research—and we use the word *formal* to distinguish it from the haphazard collection of data provided by comment cards—is the objective and empirical collection of information about consumers. In this same sense, it means *primary* data as opposed to *secondary* data. Secondary data are those collected for some other purpose that may be useful to our purpose. For example, the U.S. Travel Data Center and Tourism Canada gather information on national and state/provincial travel trends. This is information not specific enough for a firm's needs but useful for environmental scanning. Primary data, on the other hand, are data collected for a specific purpose and constitute what is called formal, or primary, marketing research.

Data are not necessarily information. This point is important because research is only as good as its interpretation. There is another important point about business research: Its purpose is to provide information to make decisions; if it doesn't serve that purpose, it is a waste of both time and money. As competition becomes more intense, and creating and retaining a customer becomes evermore difficult, it becomes more and more necessary to know and understand that customer prior to making decisions.

Qualitative Research

Qualitative research is concerned with obtaining information on consumer attitudes and behavior on a subjective basis. It is largely exploratory in nature and the findings cannot be generalized to a larger population. Its purpose is usually to learn more about a subject, to understand how consumers use a product, to test a new product concept, or to provide information for developing further quantitative research.

The most common form of qualitative research is the focus group. A focus group is six to ten people "typical" (obtained by screening in their selection) of the type of people expected to use the product. These people are brought together in a room where a skilled moderator leads them in discussion.

As illustration, suppose a restaurateur is considering a radically new menu. He has a mock-up of the menu made, but before he goes ahead with the change, he wants to see how his customers might react. He invites eight of his customers, on each of four different days of the week, to have a free dinner if they will agree to participate in a two-hour focus group. He hires a skilled moderator (he should not do this himself because of his lack of skill and potential bias) to lead the group in discussion. The moderator not only asks questions but also attempts to build a rapport with the group and spends a lot of time "probing." The relationship between the moderator and the group is important because a reluctant group will not provide thorough information.

It is not uncommon for focus groups to be audio- or videotaped. Thus, more complete analysis is possible after the session is over. Also, while the session is being conducted, the restaurateur and some of his staff may sit behind a one-way mirror and observe the proceedings, watching for special nuances and signs that the moderator might miss.

The other most common form of qualitative research is the personal interview. This constitutes an unstructured exchange in which the interviewer probes for specific comments and reactions.

There are a number of pragmatic reasons for using qualitative research:

- It can be executed quickly in a short period of time.
- It is relatively economical.
- The environment can be tightly controlled.
- It permits direct contact with consumers.
- It permits greater depth by probing for responses.
- It permits customers to "open up."
- It develops new creative ideas.
- It establishes consumer vocabulary.
- It uncovers basic consumer needs and attitudes.

- It establishes new product concepts.
- It interprets previously obtained quantitative data.

The major problem with qualitative research is that you cannot generalize from it—at best you can say, this is what "these people" say. Qualitative research does, however, help to "get inside the consumer's mind." It helps to define problems and it forms the basis for quantitative research to follow. Sometimes we think we understand the problem but we really don't; we are unable to put ourselves into the consumer's perspective.

At other times we simply don't know just what the problem is. Comment cards may be positive—customer comments are good and everything looks rosy—except business is declining. Through qualitative probing it may be possible to uncover some problems that, otherwise, would never reveal themselves.

Quantitative Research

Quantitative research deals with numbers. It measures, quantitatively, what people say, think, perceive, feel, and do. Descriptive quantitative research is the kind with which we are most familiar. It tells us how many, how often, and what percentage, such as how old people are, their sex, their income, their education, or whether they like or dislike something. It then tells us frequency and percentages; e.g., there are 362 females in the sample (48 percent), they ate in a restaurant 2.3 times last week, and 36 percent of them have at least a college education.

Descriptive data tell us who and what, but they don't tell us why. It might tell us how many persons in each age bracket ate out how many times and the relative percentages. From this information we could also determine, statistically, if any differences in eating-out patterns by age category were likely to have occurred by chance. But it wouldn't tell us how these factors interact, for instance: Does the age of an individual predict how many times that person will eat in a restaurant in a given week? As an example, from a comment card like the one in Figure 5-16, we might learn that an individual

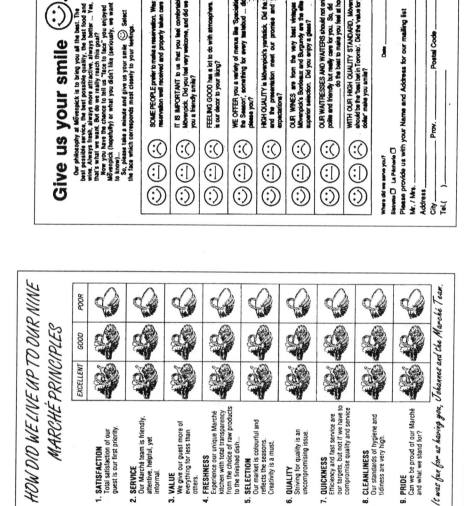

FIGURE 5-16 Mövenpick gets feedback using informal research

thought the food and service were fine, but we wouldn't be able to predict if that meant that they would return.

Descriptive research tells us one or more things at a time, but it does not tell us if there is an implied causal relationship between them. Descriptive data don't identify the real reasons consumers behave as they do and make the decisions they make. The frequency of consumers naming an attribute (for example, location) does not necessarily indicate its relative determinance in the process of choice.

Inferential quantitative research is a horse of a different color. It allows us to infer to a larger population based on the findings from a probability sample, a sample where each person in the population being studied (e.g., business travelers) has an equal chance of being selected. As it is rarely feasible to survey everyone in whom we might be interested (called a population), we have to select only a few people from the larger group (called a sample). With inferential statistics, it is possible to draw conclusions about the population on the basis of the sample data.

At the same time, inferential methods permit the analysis of the effects of interaction. An example would be the measurement of the various effects of why members of a particular market segment might choose a particular restaurant. A sample from the segment could be surveyed and asked to rate the importance their decisions on food quality, service, ambience, location, and price. In inferential analysis, each of these attributes would interact with the others. The analysis would then reveal "weights," i.e., the respective weights of each attribute in choosing the restaurant. This would reveal both the relative relationship of the various attributes as well as the predictive capability of each in choosing the restaurant.

With the findings from the above, assuming we had surveyed a representative sample of all people who choose that restaurant, we could infer to all those people (the population) as to why they make that choice. This would tell us what is important in influencing people to choose the restaurant or, perhaps, why they would not choose it. Thus, inferential data are far more powerful and useful than descriptive data. They are also more complex, take more skill to obtain, require the use of a computer, and are more expensive both in collection and analysis. Further, while more powerful, inferential data are also more susceptible to misinterpretation.

The Need for Research

Marketing research is necessary, among other things, to accomplish the following:

Lessen uncertainty
Replace intuition with facts
Stay current with the market
Determine needs and wants
Locate segments and target markets
Plan strategies and tactics
Act in advance for the future
Make business decisions

Some of the areas of marketing research that need to be pursued to accomplish the above are:

Customer perception
Customer awareness
Need for new products and services
Price sensitivity
Communication strategies—image, media, targets, frequency, content, appeals
Product strategies—service, quality, price, needs and wants, renovations, amenities
Market segments—demographics, psychographics, users, benefits, volume, motivations
Consumers—opinions, beliefs, attitudes, intentions, behavior
Demand analysis
Competitors' strengths and weaknesses

This list could easily be continued at some length but that is not necessary here; you will find many additions to it in the following chapters. The important point, however, is not the list but the identification of *why* you are doing the research. It is the answer to that question that leads to good research design.

Research Design

Developing the research design may be the most important part of all research. This is because perfectly executed and analyzed research is virtually worthless if it is not based on the appropriate design. The design is what guides the research from beginning to end. Whether you are conducting research, commissioning it, or reading it, you should understand the requirements of the research design. For that reason we will go through it step-by-step. The first four steps are the most critical ones for building the research foundation. They include specifying the research purpose, defining the research problem, establishing the research objectives, and determining what we expect to find out. The research process is shown in Figure 5-17.

The Research Process

The Research Purpose

Research design begins with establishing the purpose of the research, which derives from the management problem. For example, you might say the purpose of a research study is to find out why business is declining, which is the actual management problem. You might learn that it is declining because three new competitors have come to town and your former customers are going to them. That would be interesting, but it wouldn't tell you what to do about it. What you want to know is how to stop business from declining.

The purpose of research is what you intend to do with the findings—that is, what kinds of business decisions you plan after you have the results. You might want to develop an advertising campaign, change your menu, refurbish your decor, run a special promotion, challenge your competition, or any number of other things. Simply knowing that you had new competition, which you probably knew anyway,

would not help much in making these decisions. Knowing your purpose will lead to obtaining the information you need to fulfill that purpose. The purpose of the research establishes the parameters of everything that follows in the research design. The first of these is the research problem.

The Research Problem

The research problem means exactly that, the research problem. It doesn't mean the management problem; the existence of the management problem explains why you are doing the research in the first place. The research problem is how to provide the information that addresses the management problem.

We can utilize the aforementioned example of declining business. That business is declining is the management problem. The research problem is to answer the question, "What is causing business to decline?" or, as in the example above, "Why are our customers going to the competition?" The answer to this question will tell us what to do to stop it from declining—that is, how to fulfill the research purpose. These first two steps are so important in designing research that we will elaborate further.

Suppose we had said that the purpose of the research is to find out why business is declining and that the problem was to find out why it was declining. We discover that the answer is that our customers are going to competitors so we have the answer to the problem and we have satisfied the purpose. Instead, let us say that the research purpose is to develop a marketing strategy to stop the decline in business. That leads us directly to the problem: What needs to be done to stop the decline in business?

We now know that merely learning that our customers are going to new competition is not enough. We need to know why they are going there, or perhaps, why they are not coming here anymore—that is, we need to know what has to be done to stop this desertion. This, in turn, guides the rest of the research design. In fact, it is often useful to state the research problem even more specifically in the form of a question:

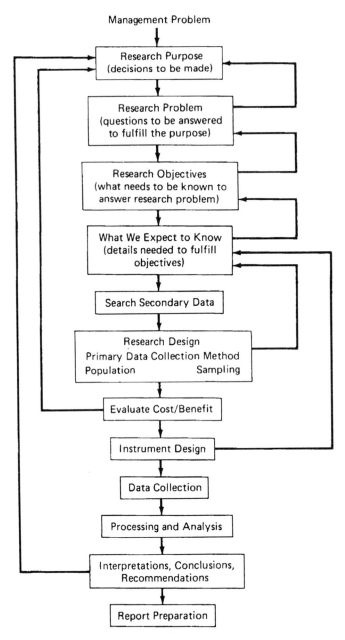

FIGURE 5-17   A flowchart of the research process

What needs to be done to stop the decline in business?

Objectives of the Research

These are the specific objectives—what we want to find out. To follow from the research problem ("What needs to be done to stop the decline in business?"), it is obvious that the sample that we survey is not going to provide the answer directly. We will need to infer that from the information we collect. The research objectives, then, might be to find out what people do and why, for instance:

What are present eating-out habits?
What are perceptions of our restaurant?
What do customers look for in a restaurant?
What would they like to see in a restaurant?

The objectives are to obtain the information we need to address the problem. From the objectives flow the answers to the question, "What do we expect to know after the research is completed?"

What We Expect to Know

What we expect to know is all the pieces of information that are necessary to fulfill the objectives, for instance:

Where do they go now?
How often do they go there?
Why do they go there?
How much do they spend there?
What do they order there?
Why do they dine out at all?
What do they think of us?
What do they seek that they can't find?
What would persuade them to go to a different restaurant?

It should be clear now that if we simply deal with the issue of why business is declining, we might not come up with answers that would be very useful in changing the pattern. That is why the above four steps are so critical to good research, and why each one must flow from the previous ones. What each step does, in turn, is simply to narrow the boundaries of the research so that it focuses directly on what is needed to make management decisions.

Research Method

The remainder of the research design is called the research method. This includes establishing the sample, the sample size, the method of data collection, the questions asked, and the type of analysis that will be applied.

Population The population is all those people in whom we are interested. This might mean all present customers, all potential cus-

tomers, or both. It might mean all people who eat at restaurants in this area, or all those who come from another area. It might be all businesspeople, or leisure travelers, or those who eat beef, or those who don't. It might be all those who use a certain restaurant category (fast-food), or a certain restaurant brand (McDonald's).

In the broadest sense, the population is all those people who might spend money to buy our product. The important criteria are that the population be as homogeneous as possible—that is, that its members have similar characteristics along the dimensions we wish to measure—and, when not, we control for the differences—called intervening variables. Consider the following example, of a restaurant operator who wishes to determine the opinions of a particular group of people concerning her restaurant operation. The populations involved could be classified in the following ways:

All people who eat out
People who like to dine out in the type of restaurant operated by this restaurateur
People who have an opportunity to dine at this type of restaurant
People who know about this particular restaurant, and
Have never dined there
Have dined there in the past but do not dine there now
Dine there now on an irregular basis
Dine there now on a regular basis

Suppose our population is the first category of the above list—all people who eat out. Our sample would contain people who fit one or more of the other categories. These are the intervening variables for which we must control in order to separate them. For example, people who have never dined there and people who dine there on a regular basis will obviously have different perceptions and feelings. We control for this so that we can separate, measure, and compare these subsets of the population.

Sample The sample is derived from the population. Because we can't survey everyone, we will have to survey only a few. From these few we hope to learn the characteristics of the many. Selection of the appropriate sample and sample size is beyond the scope of this book. There are prescribed methods for doing this that may be found in any research text. Our main concern here will be with the type of sample.

A *probability* sample is one in which every member of the population has an equal chance of being selected. This means that the sample is collected randomly without any bias as to who is selected. A simple method of randomly selecting a sample group of 50 might be to put all the names in the population in a bowl, reach in, and pick out the 50 names one at a time.

Statistically, it can be shown that a random sample will closely approximate the true characteristics of a population. This is why we can infer from a sample. It can also be shown that we can say, with a certain degree of confidence, that what we have learned could not have occurred by chance, given a certain error tolerance. It is only with probability samples that one can legitimately use inferential analysis.

A *nonprobability* sample obviously means just the opposite—that is, everyone in the population does not have an equal chance of being selected. This may be called a convenience sample, in which people are selected simply because they are convenient. We might choose to sample the first 50 people who check out of the hotel one morning. This does not allow us to generalize our findings to anyone else who stays at the hotel. People who check out later, or on another day, might have very different characteristics from these first 50.

Another kind of nonprobability sample is called a *judgmental* sample. In this case, it might be decided that some specified variation is needed, such as a mixture of sexes, age groups, travel purposes, and methods of arrival at a hotel. We might choose the first ten of each category who check out. A *quota* sample is similar. It specifies a certain quota of people or kinds of people.

A common method of creating judgmental or quota samples is what is called a "mall-intercept." This means, essentially, that we go to a shopping mall and intercept people. If they will respond (many won't), we screen them, by asking, for example, "Do you eat dinner in a restaurant two or more times a week?" If the answer is no, we move on; if it is yes, we proceed with further questions. Of course, all so-called mall-intercepts don't take place in malls; they may take place in airline terminals, restaurant entryways, or hotel lobbies.

Another type of nonprobability sample is composed of the people who fill out guest comment cards in hotel rooms. This is a biased "default" sample. Although you could argue that everyone who stays in a hotel has the same opportunity to fill out the comment card, this does not constitute a probability sample because the researcher has no means of controlling the probability. This results in a default selection. The bias comes from the fact that the sample represents only those people who are prone to fill out comment cards. These people may differ drastically from people who never fill out comment cards.

Data Collection　The data collection design comes next. However, data collection was clearly in mind when the sample was selected because the two are closely interrelated and must be coordinated.

Some written preparation is required before the data are actually collected. For example, a questionnaire has to be prepared if the data are collected by telephone, personal interview, or mail. A mailed questionnaire will require more care in its preparation in terms of format, design, appearance, and other factors that will both induce respondents to complete it and make it easier for them to do so. It is also important that the data collected be easy to tabulate or feed into the computer for analysis.

Questionnaire design is not as simple a task as it may sometimes seem. Questions must be clear and unambiguous. Each question should, as nearly as possible, have the same meaning for all respondents. This means that, if an abstract term such as "quality" is used, the word *quality* should be defined so that everyone interprets it in the same way.

The subject of questionnaire design is covered in research textbooks and will therefore not be discussed here. We only caution of the hazards involved, because if you are not measuring what you think you are measuring, you will obtain invalid data and findings. For this reason, too, it is always necessary to pretest the questionnaire. This means trying it out on people who will not be included in the sample in order to get feedback on the wording, the time it takes, the clarity, the understanding of terms, possible omissions, and other factors that might confuse respondents or invalidate the findings.

The decision as to whether to use personal interviews, mail, telephone, or other data-collection methods (such as comment cards or individual intercepts) is an important one in the research design. Each one has its trade-offs in terms of time and money. While a budget is always a limiting factor, the most important criterion is the method that will provide the most reliable data for the problem at hand. There is no one answer to this because each case is individual and must be weighed on its own merits.

Analysis   The data obtained must, of course, be analyzed very carefully. The method of analysis will have been decided beforehand, including whether it will be done by hand or by computer. Also, the analytical techniques to be used should be predetermined, since these will affect the way questions are asked, the type of response solicited, and how they are measured. Data analysis is also beyond the scope of this book; instead, we refer readers again to any good marketing research text.

Reliability and Validity

The research design, the sampling, the data collection, and the data analysis must all be rigorously controlled when doing research. Each step is critically important, none more or less so than the others. Two supreme tests are applied to research findings: reliability and validity. Because these tests are so critical we will discuss them briefly.

Reliability   Reliability in research means that the findings can be projected to a larger population if it is one of the intents of the research to do so. It means that, if we take a similar sample from a similar population, we will get similar results. It means, if we ask the same questions in a different way, we will get similar results. Even if reliable, the findings may or may not be valid.

Validity   Findings must be reliable if they are to be valid. Validity means that the data must support the conclusions. The conclusions must be valid in that they are based on whether the research actually measures what it is presumed to measure. Anyone who wants to use research for decision-making purposes should always verify its validity first. Lack of validity is the most common cause of faulty research.

Toward More Useful Research

Despite its importance, marketing research will never substitute for bad management, a bad product, poor service, or a product that has no market. Assuming none of these conditions, marketing research is appropriate when you don't know, for certain:

- Why people choose your property
- Why people choose another property
- Who your real competition is
- How many of your customers come back
- How many don't
- How people "use" your property
- What trade-offs your customers make in choosing
- How to gauge acceptance of a new concept
- Price sensitivity and how much to discount to gain competitive advantage
- Whether your product and pricing strategy is in tune with your market
- Who your target market is
- If your thinking is the same as your customers
- What are the persuasive appeals for each market and each type of customer
- Whether you are keeping up with changes in your customers' needs and wants
- Whether your customers are truly satisfied
- Whether you are keeping customers with complaint handling or losing them

- Whom your advertising is reaching and affecting—if anybody
- How your advertising is positioning your property in the market's perception
- If you are ahead of market trends or running to catch up
- Many, many other things about your market

Marketing research forms the basis for decisions, but it does not make them for you. It should be designed to provide specific information to answer the questions to which an operator needs answers. This is not a simple matter. Too much research is conducted without full understanding of what management hopes to learn. On the other hand, too much research is conducted to confirm decisions already made or to feed an ego. When the decision fails, the research is blamed.

The results of valid research should be accepted and used, even if they refute existing beliefs. Too much research ends up buried in a file drawer because it does not agree with someone's prior assumptions. Regardless of what management believes, it is customers' perceptions that count.

Summary

Today's complex and dynamic marketing environment requires hospitality firms to constantly look out for new and evolving opportunities and threats. Environmental scanning has become increasingly relevant for all businesses in this fast-moving and fast-changing world. Without it, a company is relegated to merely reacting to what happens in the environment. The basis of hospitality marketing, which was presented in the first four chapters of this book, and the application of hospitality marketing, which will be presented in the remainder of the book, lie in what is happening in the environment.

Environmental scanning looks at the big picture, the broad view, and the long range. Marketing builds on this by approaching it in an increasingly narrower perspective, resting ultimately on the individual consumer.

Environmental scanning, both in textbooks and the real world, has been largely confined to the corporate level and to strategic planning. By definition, environmental scanning presents a macro view. We believe, however, that this macro view can be given a micro perspective. In other words, we believe that every individual or unit operator, as well as corporate and higher-level management, must be conscious of and continuously analyzing the environment, and forecasting its impact upon each unit operation. The hospitality industry today is too broad-based, too diversified, and too much operated in multiple micro environments to ignore this technique at any level.

Although we tend to think of marketing as a managerial activity in reaching the customer, we have shown in this chapter that there are other elements involved. Marketing, in fact, is warfare and includes outwitting, outflanking, and outdoing the competition in the battle for consumer loyalty. Marketing does not live in a vacuum in solving consumers' problems and satisfying their needs and wants. A firm's marketing must perform these tasks better than the competitors. This is the only answer to sustained advantage and growth in the hospitality industry.

Opportunities are the bedrock of marketing, the chink in the competitor's armor. They are the unsolved consumer problem or the unfulfilled consumer need and want. Seizing upon marketing opportunities means being able to analyze the competition, understand competitive strengths and weaknesses, and being able to strike when the iron is hot. To do otherwise is to court disaster.

Marketing research must be used to get to know market needs and wants. There is a myth that marketing research is used only to make big decisions and has little to do with daily operations. While this argument might have some merit in, say, manufacturing tires, it bears little weight in an industry where brand loyalty is difficult to earn and where almost every sale requires a personal relationship with the customer.

There are, without doubt, many firms in the hospitality industry that maintain the status quo and still survive, but maintenance and survival are not the essence of marketing. Neither objective will fulfill the potential of the firm.

This chapter has examined the environment, explored the opportunities available to alert marketers, and shown that understanding the competition does not mean merely understanding bricks and mortar. Rather, understanding these things, and the actors who make them work, requires constant analysis. Without this understanding, and good research to explain it, marketing is doomed to ignore opportunity and the property is doomed to the status of "also ran" when the final count is in.

Discussion Questions

1. Consider a local restaurant or hotel. What is its competition in a macro sense? Explain. How is it affected by the three types of consumer demand?

2. Consider some current fads in eating. How long will they last? Will they turn into trends? Why/why not? If you were a restaurateur, how would you capitalize on them? What social issues have changed your restaurant purchase habits?

3. Political impacts on the hospitality business environment can be enormous. Discuss some present potential impacts.

4. Discuss some of the actions taken by hotels and restaurants to keep up with the growing ecological movement.

5. Consider a restaurant that you know. Analyze its competition under various market conditions discussed in the text. How should this restaurant react to these possibilities?

6. Explain competitive intensity. How does it impact upon marketing? Discuss.

7. How would you determine fair and actual market share for a restaurant? What would these figures tell you?

8. Analyze Cases 5-1, 5-2, and 5-3 in terms of this chapter, such as environmental impacts and competitive analysis with opportunities and threats. In Case 5-3, compute the REVPAR for each hotel. What does it tell you?

9. Describe the difference between a probability and a nonprobability sample. Be prepared to discuss when and why you would use each.

10. You, as manager of a hotel, have run a unique weekend package promotion for six weeks. It was an unqualified success. You wonder why and decide to commission some research to find out. Define the research purpose, the research problem, the objectives, what you would expect to know when done, the population, the sample, data collection, and analysis (in general terms).

11. Develop a research design and method for Case 5-4.

✔ Case 5-1
Butler's Hideaway[19]

Jonathan Butler sipped his Piña Colada on the sundeck of his terrace overlooking the Caribbean sunset and felt very pleased with his decision to create Butler's. Butler's Hideaway had opened five years before with a mission to offer the most discriminating of guests a vacation hideaway. Located on the island of Grand Cayman in the British West Indies, well known for its beautiful seven-mile beach, magnificent waters, peace and quiet, political stability, and strong economy, Butler's had been a smashing success.

Grand Cayman Island was only a 75-minute flight from Miami International Airport. This was one of its important strengths, highlighted by the feasibility study conducted by Pannell Kerr Forster before the investment was made. Mr. Butler, an investor but not a hotelier, felt that the product Butler's was offering was working very well.

An award-winning architect had been selected to design Butler's to complement the colors and rhythm of the tropics with a distinctly opulent and luxurious flavor. Butler's overlooked the magnificent seven-mile beach. The Great House included 20 rooms and 20 suites. Also in the Great House was a Cartier boutique, a Carita beauty salon, and a "sun and sundries" store. The beautiful lounge had a waterfall that cascaded down to a freshwater pool, bar, and casual restaurant called Pimms, which served breakfast and lunch. The fine-dining room was fronted by famous Chef Raoul Vertier and offered both lunch and dinner.

There were also 20 villas in the complex, some with one bedroom and a few with two bedrooms. All villas included a private pool exquisitely designed to meander through the dining terrace. A fully-equipped kitchen was concealed behind a service entrance in order that room service of the highest standard might be served with discretion. Butler's had become known as one of the great hideaways for the elite.

The finest of personalized service was offered at Butler's; all guests had a personal concierge who doubled as their driver. A water sports center chartered luxury motor yachts for those wishing to visit neighboring islands or seek well-known snorkeling or diving spots.

Current Status

Butler's had just had its best year. Its average annual occupancy was 74 percent and its average daily rate was $350 European Plan, $240 in the Great House and $750 in the villas. Although the past two years had been tough years, due to international turmoil and weak economies, Mr. Butler felt they were right back on track as he looked at the customer profile. Butler's clientele was the rich and famous, including celebrities, CEOs, private bankers, high-level executives, dignitaries, and entrepreneurs. Thirty percent came through *Leading Hotels of the World,* 15 percent through travel agents, 20 percent through selected American and European wholesalers, while ten percent were corporate bookings and 25 percent were direct. Sixty-five percent came from the United States, 20 percent from Europe, and the rest from around the world. The average length of stay was 6.5 days, five days for Americans and eight days for Europeans.

Repeat business had grown to 34 percent. Butler's prided itself on remembering all the whims and fancies of each guest staying with them. This demanding clientele seemed to be very happy with the facilities of the hotel and the services provided.

Serious competition in the region included Cap Juluca on Anguilla, La Samanna on St. Martin, and Manapany on St. Barthelemy. None of these was a large resort, and there seemed to be plenty of business for all.

Advertising for Butler's was handled by Robinson, Yesawich and Pepperdine, one of the

---

[19]Sheena Smyth provided the data to this case. Names and places have been disguised.

leading agencies in the hotel industry. Mr. Butler was very happy with their services, which included differentiated advertising, press kits and press trips, media blitzes, news releases, and special event promotions. He felt that their efforts were timely, cohesive, and targeted.

The General Manager of Butler's, Kathryn, had been there since it opened. Mr. Butler was pleased with her performance. It was not easy in Grand Cayman to find the staff profile needed to accommodate clients such as theirs. She always planned ahead and had a great sense of her customers' wants and needs, likes and dislikes.

Training was high on the list of priorities. Total Quality Management had been implemented two years before and was now working very well. Most of the staff had been hand-picked by Kathryn. Because labor costs were extremely high in Cayman, the quality of service generally found was, to say the least, "challenging." Kathryn always seemed on top of things, however. The restaurants were profitable and had a good following from lawyers, bankers, and other professionals living locally.

Future Plans

Mr. Butler was considering opening a second Butler's and was conducting research on another Caribbean island. He was, however, somewhat alarmed by some of the information being sent to him. A Pannell Kerr Forster study stated, "The status element has diminished; it is now being replaced by personal pleasure. Trading up is out!"

Peter Yesawich, President of Robinson, Yesawich and Pepperdine, had recently written, "The images of luxury, opulence, and indulgence do not play with the image of today. The consumer mindset of the '90s is extremely conservative."

Mr. Butler was disturbed by these consumer trends. He was not going to make a decision unless it was founded in fact and decided to research further. He called some of his advisors and was told, "Focus on the genuine, real, authentic—there seems to be an aversion to glitz."

He did not feel comfortable asking Kathryn to conduct focus groups with the delicate level of his clientele, but he knew she was always sensitive to their needs and wants. He asked himself if he was thinking from the customer's perspective.

Mr. Butler did not want to signal anxiety to his partners or customers, but further research informed him that the concept of luxury as a motivator no longer worked. Indeed, in the Yankelovich *National Travel Monitor,* an ongoing research study of consumer habits, he found some disturbing trends in American society.

	1989	Present*
Shopping in prestige stores	24%	15%
Wearing designer clothing	26%	14%
Driving expensive cars	39%	29%
Staying at luxury hotels	29%	15%

*Margin of error +/− 3%

All indicators on Grand Cayman, however, looked positive. His colleagues on the board of the hotel association were happy with the current situation and future forecasts for business. Mr. Butler felt that he had carved out a niche in the market that would be hard to lose, providing all services were in place and the product was desired. On the other hand, as Americans brought him 65 percent of his business, how could he afford to ignore the market mood in the States and not look at these trends?

"Are we at the top of the life cycle?" he thought. "Do we need to reposition? Can we risk it and stay as we are? Can we risk change? What should he do about his second project that he had in mind? No one pays rack anymore," he repeated to himself. "The crisis is moving from west to east."

He looked around his fine-dining restaurant and decided to discuss his concerns with Kathryn.

✔ Case 5-2
Empire Szechuan[20]

"How was your dinner here?"

"Very good, it was excellent."

"Thank you very much for coming."

After saying "Good night" to a customer, Charlie Gao, Manager of the Empire Szechuan Chinese restaurant, stepped out from behind the counter and looked through the dining room window. The street was busy, cars were passing back and forth. This had been a busy day for most people, but not for his restaurant. Seat turnover tonight was one-and-a-half, not even up to two. It had been three or four when the restaurant first opened.

Charlie recalled that the first month's business had been so busy that queues lined up along the counter waiting to get seats. Gradually, sales volume had slipped at both lunch and dinner. Now, only six months later, business was so disappointing that shares in the restaurant had been sold three times over. "Something must be wrong," he thought, but whenever he asked for feedback from customers, he always received compliments.

History

Charlie Gao was the Manager as well as the principal owner of the Empire Szechuan, holding 40 percent of the stock. Other minor partners were in New York City. Working in the restaurant industry for ten years, Charlie had obtained substantial cooking and waiting experience, as well as some management knowledge. He had been a manager in several Chinese restaurants, including Jade Beach, a Chinese restaurant in a casino in Atlantic City, and Szechuan Empire on Broadway at 97th street in New York City. After he had accumulated enough money, he decided to fulfill his fantasy of opening a restaurant of his own.

Eventually finding partners among his career friends, Charlie got his opportunity in Amherst, Massachusetts, a town of 20,000 permanent

residents known for its high involvement in education. With five colleges in the Amherst area (Smith, Mount Holyoke, Amherst, Hampshire, and the University of Massachusetts), the population was swelled by students, particularly during fall and spring semesters. The Empire Szechuan opened in the heart of Amherst featuring Hunan/Szechuan regional style cooking.

Charlie's research revealed that the average income in this area was high. He also learned that there were four other Chinese restaurants in downtown Amherst. Chinese restaurants also existed in Hadley, which was five miles away, and in Northampton, nine miles away. He considered that only Panda East in Amherst would be his immediate, main competitor. From observing Panda East's operation, Charlie was encouraged.

People in the area seemed to love Chinese food. He was surprised to learn that Amherst Chinese Food, a family-owned, family-operated restaurant—whose owner had never received proper training in the restaurant business and knew little about restaurant operations—had been successful in this little town for 15 years. The future really looked promising!

Charlie's restaurant was small, but comfortable. It had one dining room, with a seating capacity of 70. There were eight booths lining the walls. In the center were some square tables seating four or two. Both walls were decorated with glass, which made the restaurant look more spacious.

With his ten years experience, his advantages in location, plus the acquisition of a chef who used to work at nearby Panda East, Charlie firmly believed that his "empire" would conquer this town easily. Since Panda East had been successful, Charlie designed his menu after the menu of Panda East.

Competition

Panda East Panda East was one of two Panda restaurants in the area, the other being Panda

---

[20]Jane Lin researched and contributed to this case.

Garden in downtown Northampton, where it had been operating successfully for a number of years featuring four regional styles of Chinese cuisine: Hunan/Szechuan, Beijing (Mandarin), Shanghai, and Cantonese. Many customers from the Amherst area had asked the manager to open another Panda restaurant in downtown Amherst. He opened Panda East with two spacious dining rooms seating 130 people. As successful as it had been in Northampton, the restaurant drew much of the local Chinese food business to its premise.

Amherst Chinese Food Located on Main Street, not far from Empire Szechuan, was Amherst Chinese Food. After getting his Doctor's degree in Plant Science at the University of Massachusetts, Mr. Chang, the owner, opened the restaurant in 1980 with the idea of making enough money to buy a farm. His mission statement was clear: "To offer healthy, fresh, Chinese food to the community." He further stated, "We welcome everyone here to be comfortable whether in jeans or tuxedo." His farm supplied all the vegetables needed and local people perceived his restaurant as one that served healthy (no MSG), fresh family-style food. With a seating capacity of 130, this restaurant enjoyed a substantial repeat business, its sales volume increasing despite the opening of Panda East and Empire Szechuan.

Hunan Garden Hunan Garden was located on Route 9, about a mile east of Amherst. As its name indicated, it served mainly Hunan/Szechuan-style food. This restaurant had been acquired by the Ngs family in 1990 and had been successful until the arrival of Panda East and Empire Szechuan. Due to this stiff competition, it was promoted heavily among college students who had been chosen as its target market. It ran frequent-student specials, issued coupons, and served a buffet at a tempting price of $5.25 from Monday through Thursday.

Kim Toy Chinese Foods This was the oldest Chinese restaurant in the area, having opened in 1966. It was owned and run by an elderly couple. The restaurant had only 20 seats and opened only from 4:00 P.M. to 8:30 P.M. Since there was not much business, the owners handled cooking, serving, and washing dishes themselves and employed no other staff.

Other Problems

Business for Empire Szechuan had never stablized, and went down shortly after opening. One disadvantage was that the restaurant did not have a liquor license. Charlie believed that, if he got this license, business would increase greatly, but licenses were scarce and you had to "know someone." Customers could, however, buy beverages at a package store around the corner and bring them in to drink at no additional charge. Another disadvantage was that the restaurant was small; this discouraged parties of more than six people.

Most guests who tried the new restaurant did not return. Except for the above two disadvantages, Charlie Gao had no further explanations for his declining business. In fact, he believed that the food prepared in his restaurant was finer than that served in Panda East. One example of this was his Ginger Chicken from the old menu of Empire Szechuan in New York. According to the standard recipe, the main ingredient for this dish, chicken, should be slices from the breast, and Empire Szechuan prepared this dish accordingly. At rival Panda East they used ordinary chicken slices. Charlie admitted that his portions were not as large as those served at Panda East, although the price range was the same. In Charlie Gao's view, if customers sought real fine-Chinese cuisine, they would not care about this little difference.

Repositioning

Charlie Gao decided that he would not be successful by simply copying what Panda East was doing. He decided to reposition his product.

First, he redesigned the menu. He decided to bring what had been successful in New York City, Empire Szechuan-style, to this little town. On his new menu, he especially stated: "Empire Szechuan, New York Style." To differentiate from the other Chinese restaurants, Charlie designed a Special Diet Menu, which included no salt, sugar, cornstarch, or MSG.

Charlie also tried to improve the product from the service aspect. He employed experienced waiters, asked for feedback from customers, and embellished his product. Besides serving tea and ice water, as most Chinese restaurants did and as most customers expected, Charlie also offered crispy noodles while customers were waiting for their order. As a lunch special, besides serving free rice and free soup, as Panda East and other Chinese restaurants did, Empire Szechuan attached two free eggrolls to the lunch package and kept the price the same. To attract even more business, Charlie planned to convert the basement into a banquet room. He also added seasonal specials and chef's specials not on the regular menu.

The recovery was slow in coming. Overhead exceeded revenue. At this point, besides the lack of a liquor license and the size of the restaurant, Charlie concluded that another reason for his slipping business was that it was very hard to change customers' habits. He believed that, once customers went to a place to dine, they would stick to it unless they were not satisfied.

Advertising and Promotion

Prior to opening, and at the beginning of its operation, Charlie set a promotion budget of $4,000 a month and promoted heavily in the *Daily Hampshire Gazette, Amherst Bulletin, The Collegian,* and other local newspapers, trying to create awareness. After two months, the budget was cut to $2,000 per month, and then to $700 per month. Currently, after only a half-a-year of operation, Charlie did hardly any promotion except for delivering menus to some supermarkets. By this he considered that awareness had been created.

Conclusion

How, Charlie thought, was he going to rejuvenate the business? How could he boost the volume? What was the best strategy for this restaurant, open for only six months, to adopt?

Charlie Gao stepped out the door. It was a bit chilly. It was spring now. Summer was coming. When summer came, this town, with its population largely made up of students, would be empty and quiet. If he did not do something soon, he could foresee that his business would go nowhere but down and down, worse, and worse....

✔ Case 5-3
Westin Hotel of Stamford[21]

The Westin Hotel in Stamford, Connecticut first opened as a Trusthouse Forte Hotel. Two months later, Trusthouse Forte pulled out of the project and cited weak potential as the primary motive. The owners attempted to operate the hotel as an independent property with little success, because it lacked the brand recognition of competing properties. The owners were also having financial difficulties and faced a great deal of pressure from their lender to find a reputable operator. The hotel had been financed primarily through debt rather than equity and the bank was about to begin foreclosure proceedings.

Two years after it first opened, Westin Hotels and Resorts assumed the management contract on the provision that $2 million would be spent by the lender on lobby renovations. The money, however, was used to cover operating losses instead. In essence, the hotel fell far short of Westin standards, which stressed high quality in physical plant and service. Despite these many shortcomings, Westin was keen to pursue the venture.

Westin had conducted its own feasibility study prior to signing the management contract. Pro forma projections painted a rosy picture. Westin Hotels and Resorts also felt a strong need to be represented in the Stamford area, which contained a number of Fortune 500 company headquarters. Moreover, corporate objectives at the time were clearly directed toward growth at all costs in an effort to make Westin Hotels competitive with Marriott, Hilton, Hyatt, Sheraton, and other large hotel companies.

Environment

The city of Stamford is located in southwestern Connecticut, approximately 30 miles northeast of New York City and easily accessible by inter-state highway. With a population of 110,000, it was the major retail trade center of Fairfield County. The southwestern Connecticut region as a whole had become a very attractive area in which to live and work. Some of the regional strengths were:

- No state income tax
- High-quality residential environments
- Wide choice of convenient transportation modes
- Accessible government
- Highly regarded educational systems
- Urban amenities in a suburban environment
- Proximity to New York City
- Access to high-income market areas
- Nationally recognized quality of life

Stamford in particular had gained recognition as a base for approximately ten Fortune 500 companies such as Xerox, Pitney Bowes, and Olin Corporation. Companies were first attracted to the area in the late 1970s due to tax incentives. Commercial development and the influx of major corporations into the area changed the face of Stamford and the region as a whole. These trends encouraged economic growth in the early 1980s as population, employment, and area travel increased. Accompanying the growth in economic activity came the realization that Stamford, with its proximity to New York City, represented an attractive alternative to affluent individuals and families who preferred the quality of life found in the southwestern Connecticut region. The results of a feasibility study, conducted by a leading hospitality-consulting firm in 1986, had sparked numerous hotel-building projects by developers, all of whom had received the same study results. According to these, overall occupancy would reach 89 percent six years hence. A new Hyatt, Sheraton, Marriott, Crowne Plaze, and now the Westin, were the result. The market segments that would make up the total demand for the area were projected as follows:

---

[21]Denise Lieberman and Vikram Sood researched and contributed to this case. Some facts have been altered.

General Commercial (industry-related, transient commercial) demand—79 percent

Conference and Group (meetings) demand— 11 percent

Tourist and Other (pleasure, travelers, and vacationers) demand—9 percent

The study also predicted that future demand would occur from economic growth as population, employment, and area travel increased and commercial development in the area continued. All this pointed to a favorable growth climate for hotel development. On the other hand, while the study was fairly accurate in pinpointing the market segments that would constitute demand for hotel rooms, updated information revealed that the study also had its shortcomings. It failed to properly identify some of the environmental trends that would emerge and affect hotel operators in the area. Some of these trends and their impacts on area hotels are shown in Exhibit 5-3-3.

Competition

As available hotel rooms increased and demand decreased, the five major hotels, plus a small new luxury hotel, battled intensely for market share. Table 5-3-1 shows the previous year's results. Exhibit 5-3-4 gives details of the major hotels and Exhibit 5-3-1 shows their locations.

Connecticut Limousine provided transportation to and from all New York airports—Newark, La Guardia, and JFK—from its terminal permanently located at the Stamford Marriott Hotel. The company also serviced the Holiday Inn, Sheraton, and Hyatt hotels. It had been reluctant to service the Westin Hotel because its primary means of access, the Merritt Parkway, did not allow vehicles of the type used by Connecticut Limousine.

Operations

In light of the environmental trends and the increase in supply of hotel rooms in Stamford, the Westin Hotel had employed some unique tactics in both the rooms and the food and beverage areas in order to increase occupancy and *gross operating profit* (GOP). To increase occupancy, management signed a contract with IBM Corporation, which stipulated that 120 guestrooms would be used by IBM as offices during the following year. This conversion was the first step in establishing a training center in the hotel. In addition, the junior ballroom was renovated and made into three, separate meeting rooms; two were state-of-the-art classrooms complete with audio-visual capabilities and computer workstations, while the third room was set up for conference sessions. Westin entered into this venture for a number of reasons. First, the hotel would be assured of receiving $51 a night, year-round, while spending approximately $4 per office per day for cleaning, as opposed to the normal $25 per room per day. These offices needed little more than vacuuming, dusting, and changing soap and paper towel dispensers. The 120 converted rooms were used by IBM support staff for its training program based in the hotel.

Second, the hotel would benefit from the spin-off revenue generated by those attending training sessions. Approximately 120 persons would attend these sessions monthly and be housed and fed in the hotel. A buffet breakfast would be served each morning and special prices were arranged for other meals. As these meal arrangements were centered around low price and high volume, they would do little more than cover fixed costs.

TABLE 5-3-1   Results of Major Hotels in the Stamford Area

Hotel	Rooms	Occupancy (%)	ADR ($)
Westin	457	45.8	91.10
Sheraton	359	52.0	98.44
Marriott	505	64.6	86.22
Crowne Plaza	385	52.0	74.30
Inn at Mill River (new)	92	35.0	118.60
Hyatt Regency	353	62.0	104.70
Total	2,151	54.6	91.27

EXHIBIT 5-3-1   Stamford area locations of hotels and major companies

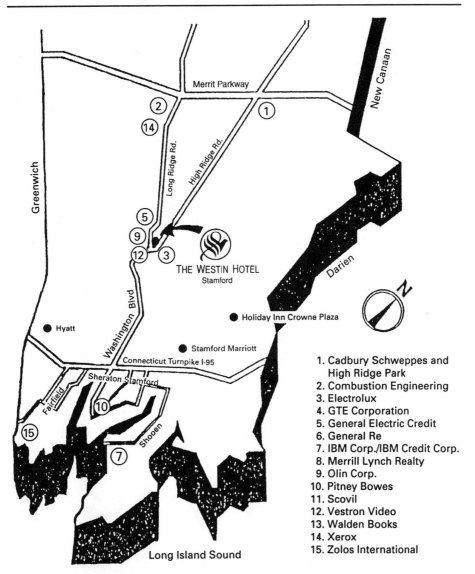

1. Cadbury Schweppes and
   High Ridge Park
2. Combustion Engineering
3. Electrolux
4. GTE Corporation
5. General Electric Credit
6. General Re
7. IBM Corp./IBM Credit Corp.
8. Merrill Lynch Realty
9. Olin Corp.
10. Pitney Bowes
11. Scovil
12. Vestron Video
13. Walden Books
14. Xerox
15. Zolos International

TABLE 5-3-2   Operating Results and Projections

	Previous Year		Next Year
	Forecast	Actual	Projection
Gross Operating Profit	$1,400,00	−$100,000	$873,000
Occupancy (%)	57.3	45.8	70.2
Average Daily Rate ($)	108.40	91.10	83.15
Rooms Revenue	$10,360,792	$6,959,738	$9,736,625
F & B Revenue	$5,800,000	$4,322,656	$5,600,000

Results for the previous year and projections for the following year are shown in Table 5-3-2.

In addition to banquet and catering facilities, the hotel had three food and beverage outlets. The Terrace was a 150-seat restaurant offering breakfast, lunch, and dinner service with a distinct menu for each meal period. The restaurant served approximately 80 covers for breakfast, 75–100 covers for lunch, and 100 covers for dinner. Customer composition for each meal varied as follows:

Breakfast—95 percent Hotel guests, 5 percent Transient

Lunch—5 percent Hotel guests, 95 percent Corporate/local offices' guests

Dinner—75 percent Hotel guests, 25 percent Transient

The shortage of labor in the Stamford area had affected The Terrace and the restaurant was not run the way it should have been. To alleviate this problem, the hotel adopted a buffet-style service for breakfast and lunch. In addition, the restaurant was poorly laid out and equipment was less than adequate. Since Westin had come in after the restaurant was completed, they had to live with these faults. While management wanted to upgrade the facilities to meet Westin standards, they were restricted by the lack of a capital budget. One of the restaurant's primary strengths had been its reputation for high food quality. For Sunday brunch, The Terrace competed against other local restaurants, as well as restaurants in the Hyatt, Marriott, and Sheraton. Aside from the IBM catering, the challenge was to keep food costs down while maintaining food quality.

The two other restaurants on premise were leased to private operators. These were Mr. Lee, a Chinese restaurant, and Le Coq Hardi, an upscale French restaurant. Neither restaurant was performing admirably. There seemed to be little demand for an upscale French restaurant in Stamford. People were not willing to pay New York City prices. Residents of Stamford who might have comprised the customer base were more concerned with finding restaurants with innovative mid-priced menus. Mr. Lee was doing somewhat better than the French restaurant because it had expanded its business to include office delivery, bar mitzvah catering, and lunch buffets, but Mr. Lee relied heavily on hotel guest patronage on the weekends.

The existence of the leased outlets on the hotel property had been detrimental to the hotel's bottom line. The original owners of the hotel had leased the space prior to Westin's involvement. The complex nature of the hotel's financial situation, coupled with difficulty with the original lease agreements, had placed the hotel's management in a delicate position. The lessees had been able to default on their lease payments without punitive action being taken by the lender or Westin Hotels. The hotel was forced to pay the restaurants' utility bills without receiving any compensation. These events caused friction between the restaurant owners and hotel management and complicated the marketing of the hotel's services. Marketing was forced to mention the existence of these two restaurants in sales literature but was hesitant to invest a great deal of time and money in promoting products that fell short of Westin Hotel standards. Food service in these outlets could enhance Westin's image, but poor service could tarnish that image and affect business in other areas of the hotel.

Other food and beverage operations included the lobby lounge, 24-hour room service, and catering. The 24-hour room service was company policy. As mentioned earlier, the hotel's banquet and catering areas had undergone some changes resulting from the agreement with IBM. The conversion of the junior ballroom to training facilities lessened the hotel's potential for accommodating small- and medium-size groups. To bolster catering and banquet revenue, the hotel had contracted with United Airlines to provide airline meals for flights departing from White Plains, New York.

Current Strategy

In light of the environmental trends and competition from area hotels, Westin's mission was to provide upscale hotel accommodations, with emphasis on service rather than on costly amenities. Service was the hotel's strongest selling point; it could not compete on the basis of its facility. Primary target markets were 75 percent transient and 25 percent group business. Weekdays, the hotel pursued travel affiliated with area firms that were visiting for purposes of training, seminars, relocations, inspections and consulting. Weekends, the hotel catered to associations and small groups comprised of extremely cost-conscious individuals. As the area was not really a tourist destination, the hotel spent little effort pursuing pleasure travelers. Also, the hotel's distance off the Connecticut Turnpike made it less conducive to the tourist traveling by car.

The hotel had utilized a number of tactics to reach its target markets. Direct mail was the most frequent means of communication. The hotel also relied a great deal on direct selling to corporations through its sales staff. Some actions were somewhat restricted by corporate directives. For example, the hotel was less inclined to utilize sponsorship of local activities to generate business because the corporate office felt it too difficult to measure the return on such investment. One of the flyers developed by the hotel's ad agency is shown in Exhibit 5-3-2.

Despite the tarnished image, Westin corporate officers had been more concerned with maintaining the management contract and its associated management fee. This preoccupation with the generation of revenue and the continuing need to be represented in Stamford had prevented them from reevaluating their original decision to enter into the Stamford contract. Now the dilemma facing Westin Hotels and Resorts was whether or not they should remove themselves from the Stamford area or continue to operate under stiff financial constraints in a very competitive market.

EXHIBIT 5-3-2   Collateral developed by Westin's ad agency

1. Looking for a place to stay in Stamford, Connecticut? The local Yellow Pages list 35 hotels, motels, inns and boarding houses that can give you a bed for the night.

2. If you want a color TV in your room, you cut the list by a third.

3. If you want more than network TV—cable and in-house movies, for instance—the majority goes. Only 8 hotels offer this.

4. And if you are like us, hating to get out of bed to change channels, the list is suddenly very short. Only one hotel in the area has remote-control TV in every room: The Westin Hotel, Stamford.

5. TV may be a detail. But how about a meal in the room? Only one place gives you room service around the clock. You guessed it, The Westin Hotel, Stamford.

6. The Westin Hotel, Stamford is also the only hotel to offer you a choice of three very different restaurants: French gourmet cuisine at Le Coq Hardi, Mr. Lee's Szechuan Chinese dining, and the all-American cafe, The Terrace.

7. And every day, there is one new sheet in the menu with fresh items of the season to give you variety. Long stays become more pleasant that way.

8. Back to the rooms. There are only 457 of them, which helps to avoid the feeling of an accommodation factory. And they are all larger than the standard American hotel room.

9. Some of them deliberately lack ashtrays. They are the designated non-smoking rooms.

10. Each room has a separate dressing area—nice when you share the room with someone, but still want some privacy.

11. Need to freshen up? 60 rooms at The Westin Hotel, Stamford are equipped with a pants presser and a hair dryer.

12. Are you, too, irritated by little details such as clothes hangers that can only hang from special brackets in the closet? At The Westin Hotel, Stamford we believe in old-fashioned removable hangers.

13. Do you like your bed turned down at night? This service is available for everyone at The Westin Hotel, Stamford.

14. Or extra maid service during the day or night? Same thing.

15. When it comes to conferences and meetings, The Westin Hotel, Stamford is also in a class by itself. It is, for instance, one of the few hotels in Fairfield county with a ballroom capacity for 1,000 persons.

16. It is the only hotel in the Northeast with two satellite dish antennas. This gives the rooms more TV channels, but more important, it gives you the possibility for rather sophisticated teleconferences.

17. The Westin Hotel, Stamford's meeting and break-out rooms are not spread out all over the

place, but concentrated in one area. This makes it easy for you to run a smooth conference.

18. Needless to say, the audio-visual equipment is state-of-the-art. And if you need quick help, the company that handles the equipment is located right on the premises.

19. The Westin Hotel, Stamford has a special conference service department. No passing the buck—the same person handles your business from booking to billing.

20. Our hotel is located halfway between the Connecticut Turnpike and Merritt Parkway. That makes it easy to get to from either one. But you don't have to listen to trucks and trains rumble by in the night.

21. And all overnight guests enjoy complimentary parking in our garage, which is directly attached to the hotel building.

22. Were you born to shop? Well, you don't even have to leave our atrium lobby to indulge in that. There is an arcade of small, independent shops for fine jewelry, gifts, antiques, flowers, real estate, skin care and hair styling. Plus your regular hotel newsstand, of course.

23. And if that isn't enough, just walk out the front door. Next to The Westin Hotel, Stamford is a shopping plaza with more than 60 stores and boutiques as well as a movie theater.

24. Change of travel plans? The Westin Hotel, Stamford is again the only hotel with

EXHIBIT 5-3-2   (continued)

in-house ticket desks for American Airlines, Eastern and Pan Am, as well as a full-service travel agency.

25. At the travel service center you can also rent a car if you need one.

26. When you stay at The Westin Hotel, Stamford you automatically earn bonus points with the United Airlines Mileage Plus program for frequent travelers.

27. All work and no play can make you a dull boy or girl. How about a game of tennis? The Westin Hotel, Stamford is the only hotel with its own courts. Or a sauna, maybe? Or a Jacuzzi? Or an exercise round on our 25 Nautilus stations (more than any other hotel)? Or a dip in the pool?

28. And why not top it off with a relaxing, professional massage and some time in the tanning salon? No hotel in the area has as many ways to make you feel like a new person as The Westin Hotel, Stamford.

29. But forget disco dancing. Our guests have a taste for other types of entertain-

ment. Soft jazz, for example. Every night we feature a group in the atrium lobby.

30. Maybe an overnight stay or a business conference is not your problem, but your daughter's wedding or your son's bar mitzvah is. The Westin Hotel, Stamford is the only hotel where you can choose anything from a small private room for a party of 6 or the outside deck for 500, to the atrium for 800 people, or the grand ballroom for 1,000.

31. Whatever you want to celebrate, we will help you create the perfect menu, including a complete selection of kosher food.

32. As much as we hate to see you leave, we provide express check-out service when you are in a hurry.

33. And, as a final example of things you won't find with anyone else, The Westin Hotel, Stamford has an express, non-stop

limousine service that takes you directly to La Guardia, JFK, or Westchester airports. Pleasant journey and welcome back!

WHEN!

Does the Westin Hotel, Stamford sound like the hotel for you?

Well, you are not alone. In an American Express Travel Holiday poll of 5,000 frequent travelers this spring, Westin Hotels and Resorts was the number one choice.

This made us proud, but, quite frankly, not too surprised. Westin is the oldest hotel management company in North America, founded in 1930. Today, no competitive chain can flaunt as many four- and five-star hotels as Westin. The Copley in Boston and the Plaza in New York, just to mention our two nearest sister hotels.

We have a policy of taking care of our employees with the same attention that we want them to take care of you. No hotel in the area matches The Westin Hotel, Stamford employee reward program. So, again it does not surprise us to find that in Levering, Moskowitz and Katz's book, "The 100 Best Companies to Work for in America," only one hotel company made the list. Yes, Westin Hotels and Resorts.

But don't take ours or anybody else's word for it. Come stay with us and see for yourself. For reservations or information, call our toll-free numbers.

It would please us to please you.

1-800-231-2042
The Westin Hotel, Stamford

1-800-228-3000
Westin Hotels and Resorts

THE WESTIN HOTEL
Stamford
2701 Summer Street, Stamford, CT 06905

THERE ARE OVER 2,500 HOTEL ROOMS IN STAMFORD. ONLY 457 OF THEM MEET THE WESTIN STANDARD.

EXHIBIT 5-3-3   Emerging environmental trends and their impact

1) Lack of affordable housing
   The demand for housing in Stamford exceeded supply. This had forced prices upward to the point that the average price of a single-family home in the region ($400,000) was six times greater than the median household income. This trend severely impacted hotels in the area. Due to the high cost of living, hotel employees had to work two or three jobs to survive. Lack of affordable housing made it difficult for the Westin Hotel to attract not only line staff but also qualified management personnel. The hotel was forced to pay salaries well above the company average to facilitate and encourage the transfer of key personnel.

2) Labor shortage
   With an unemployment rate of 2.1 percent, hotels faced an acute labor shortage. This limited the level of service they could offer. Hotels were faced with having to look outside Stamford for employees and for transportation for them. Also, the labor shortage had done little to enhance the work ethic of employees. Not only were they overworked in many areas, but there was a lack of commitment to their jobs as employment in other hotels was readily available. Westin had made a further effort to offer highly competitive salaries comparable to the competition.

3) Changing nature of corporate community
   Large amounts of available office space (27 percent) were an attraction to relocating and expanding firms. These firms were small to medium in size, not large corporations relocating their corporate headquarters to Stamford. The influx by smaller companies was attributed to the depressed prices in the commercial office market. Smaller companies necessitated a change in the way in which hotels pursued company business in Stamford.

4) Mergers and acquisitions
   Corporate mergers and acquisitions also had a strong impact on Stamford's local economy. An announced merger or acquisition could signal the exodus of a corporation from the local area, as well as wholesale staff cutbacks. Such mergers could result in the loss of large corporate accounts. Conversely, a merger could represent an additional source of business.

5) The political battleground and taxes
   Although Connecticut had managed to survive for many years without a state income tax, albeit by raising other taxes, there were clear political and economic pressures that foreshadowed one being imposed. Opposing political parties had campaigned for years on opposite sides of the issue with one party controlling the state's House and the other controlling the General Assembly. This led to numerous power plays and jockeying for position between the two parties. When the economy went into decline in the early '90s, there was little doubt about the outcome, that a state income tax would be imposed.

6) Other environmental trends
   An ongoing major shift, from a production to a service-oriented economy, was making even more acute the shortage of service-sector employees. Job growth outpaced the resident labor force, limiting expansion of some industries.
   The area population was growing older and wealthier than in the past. Household size was shrinking and the number of households increasing, fueling the demand for housing.
   The cost of doing business was the highest in the state. Salaries in the service sector were 17 percent higher than in second-place Hartford, the state capital. Growth in companies relocating to the area tended to be smaller, service-related firms and regional sales offices of larger firms.
   The region's hotel inventory was slated to peak in the next two years with over 3,500 rooms; in Stamford alone there were over 2,500 rooms. A Convention and Visitor's Bureau was planned for Stamford to advance the area as a tourist and lodging center.

EXHIBIT 5-3-4 Details of major hotels in Stamford area

Sheraton Stamford Hotel and Towers

Rates: $110—main building
$125—tower level
$150—VIP floor
$75—weekends

Facilities: 2 restaurants, lounge, health club, pool, gift shop, nightclub, grand ballroom, 8 meeting suites, Connecticut Limousine pick-up spot.

Strengths: easy access from Connecticut Turnpike (I-95), two blocks from train station, adjacent to First Stamford Place—a large office complex, largest meeting facility in the county, tower rooms offer complimentary hors d'oeuvres in the evening and continental breakfast in the morning, popular entertainment facility, strong reservation system.

Weaknesses: had to go through run-down area to get to hotel.

Stamford Marriott

Rates: $129—weekdays
$89—weekends including breakfast for two

Facilities: 2 restaurants, lounge, health club, 2 pools, gift shop, nightclub, Connecticut Limousine depot, 2 ballrooms, 7 conference rooms, 7 hospitality suites, valet parking.

Strengths: first major hotel in the area, strong customer loyalty, convenient location, strong reservation system, and nightclub.

Weaknesses: ?

Holiday Inn Crowne Plaza

Rates: $124—weekdays
$119—corporate
$146—concierge floor
$79—weekends

Facilities: 2 restaurants, lobby lounge, pool, gift shop, nightclub, Connecticut Limousine pick-up spot, 1 ballroom, 5 meeting rooms.

Strengths: good location in financial district, nightclub, concierge floor, and strong reservation system.

Weaknesses: poor physical plant and poor hotel layout.

Hyatt Regency

Rates: $154 single, $174 double—weekdays
$164 single, $184 double—Regency Club
$134 single, $154 double—corporate
$95—weekends

Facilities: 2 restaurants, bar, health club, pool, gift shop, nightclub, ballroom, meeting rooms, Connecticut Limousine pick-up spot.

Strengths: new hotel, easy access from Connecticut Turnpike, and Regency Club has strong recognition.

Weaknesses: had to go through run-down area to get to hotel.

The Westin Hotel, Stamford

Rates: $145—weekdays
$82—weekends

Facilities: 3 restaurants, lounge, health club, pool, gift shop, tennis courts, 1 ballroom, 13 meeting rooms.

Strengths: convenient to major corporations.

Weaknesses: poor access, poor physical plant, no Connecticut Limousine, and no nightclub.

✔ Case 5-4
Taco Gourmet

A successful restaurateur decided to start a Mexican fast-food chain, offering "gourmet" tacos and other Mexican foods, to cash in on the latest fast-food trend but at a higher level of quality. His pilot effort was called Taco Gourmet. The food quality was superior because he used only the best ingredients. He priced his items about 30 percent higher than the competition for the same items.

Business was excellent the first month, then started falling off. After three months it was only half of what it had been the first month. The owner noticed that few of his customers were repeaters. He inquired among his friends to see if they had heard complaints. The only complaint that seemed to appear was about the prices. The owner decided to conduct some formal research. After analyzing the situation he asked a consultant to develop a research design.

PART III
The Hospitality Customer

CHAPTER 6

Customer Behavior and Customer Markets

If the first step in marketing is to recognize customers' needs and wants, then it is obvious that we must understand how and why customers behave the way they do, as well as what leads them to behave in that manner. This is no small task.

There are no easy and definite answers to these questions. Instead, there are many theories, concepts, and models that have been developed to explain this complex being, the customer. These theories have been derived from many disciplines—sociology, psychology, social psychology, anthropology, philosophy, and economics—and these approaches must be integrated before we can approach even a limited understanding. Our ultimate goal, of course, is to be able to influence buyer behavior. We may fall far short of that goal in its full sense, but we will learn, at least, to understand some hows and whys and their causes.

It is important to begin with some basic and generally agreed-upon beliefs of consumer behavior, because effective marketing must be based on these premises. Managerial decisions that ignore these premises will tend to lead to marketing failures.

Premise 1: Consumer behavior is purposeful and goal-oriented. What may appear to be completely irrational to the outside observer is, nev-

ertheless, the action that an individual views as the most appropriate at the time. To assume otherwise is to underestimate the consumer.

Premise 2: The consumer has free choice. Messages and choices are processed selectively. The frequency of these messages is increasing daily; those not felt to be pertinent are either ignored or forgotten. Failure to realize this fundamental is a basic cause of marketing failure.

Premise 3: Consumer behavior is a process. The specific act of buying is only an intermediate stage in that process. There are many influences on consumer behavior both before and after purchase. The purchase is only a culmination of the marketing effort and its influence on the process.

Premise 4: Consumer behavior can be influenced, but only if we address perceived problems and potential needs. Properly designed research can identify and assess these problems and needs.

Premise 5: There is a need for consumer education. In all their wisdom and purposeful behavior, consumers may still behave unwisely, against their own interests. Marketers have a responsibility in this effort.

Are hospitality customers any different from customers of other goods and services? Probably not. After all, they are the same people regardless of the type of purchase they are contemplating or making at any given time. It would seem, then, that theories of basic buyer behavior would apply and we could confine ourselves to that domain. There is a difference, however, and it lies in the context of the purchase.

Buying a stereo is certainly not in the same context as buying a hotel room or a restaurant meal. The characteristics that distinguish services from products, such as intangibility, perishability, heterogeneity, and simultaneous production and consumption, create different contexts in which hospitality purchases take place. In section A of this chapter we will look at a few theories of consumer behavior that have been developed in other contexts and then apply them to the hospitality context. In section B we will look at specific types of hospitality customers.

A.   Characteristics of Hospitality Customers: Needs and Wants

Abraham Maslow was a psychologist who wanted to explain how people are motivated. What he learned was that motivations are based on different needs in different contexts. Maslow labeled his theory of motivation the "hierarchy of needs."[1] His hierarchy model has stood the test of time and is the basis of much of what we know about human behavior. The model is shown in Figure 6-1.

The thrust of Maslow's hierarchy is that lower-level needs have to be met before the higher-level needs become important. Thus, until physiological needs such as hunger and thirst are satisfied, they remain primary in human motivation. Once these are satisfied, our needs for security and protection become primary, and so forth, on up the pyramid. Of course, all of us will not act in exactly the same manner, but it has been shown, in a general sense, that the order prevails.

Maslow did not claim that the hierarchy was completely rigid or necessarily exclusive. In

fact, it should be noted, we may seek to satisfy two or more diverse needs at the same time; for instance, reserving a hotel suite instead of just a room might be an attempt to satisfy needs at opposite ends of the hierarchy at the same time.

Maslow also identified two categories of cognitive needs that he did not specifically place on the hierarchy, but that he felt belonged fairly high on the scale. These additional needs are the need to know or understand and aesthetic needs, designated as the need for things that are pleasing to the eye. These, also, certainly apply to hospitality.

It should also be noted that we may satisfy the same need in different ways, depending on the occasion, the availability, and the appropriateness at the time. This leads us into a second-level theory called behavior primacy theory. This theory holds that behavior is a reaction to the environment—that is, behavior changes as the environment changes or, to use the same term used previously, as the *context* changes.

Application of the Theories

Do we have to know a psychological theory to explain that, when we say we are "starving," the first thing we want to do is eat; or that we have higher-level needs such as belonging, esteem, and self-actualization? The reason the answer is yes will become clearer when we get to the chapter on segmentation and target marketing, both of which mean pinpointing particular customers. In the meantime, let us consider the need/context relationship.

Businesspeople who travel have the need to sleep, shower, change their clothes, and perhaps watch a little TV. These are basic needs, so almost any hotel will satisfy them. But they also may have the need for esteem and will select a hotel to fulfill that need.

At the same time, they will have other needs, such as a desk to write at, good lighting to read by, good telephone service, a timely wake-up call, and perhaps a stenographic service. These are not needs in the sense of Maslow's hierarchy; they are needs, or more likely wants, in the hospitality marketing sense, when we say, "the consumer has a problem." Customers seek solu-

---

[1] Abraham H. Maslow, *Motivation and Personality,* New York: Harper & Row, 1954.

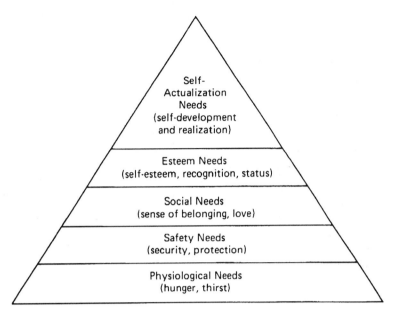

FIGURE 6-1   Maslow's hierarchy of needs

tions to problems and are willing to pay for them (or have their companies pay).

Besides these, they have other wants. They want the bed to be comfortable, the room to be large, a comfortable chair to sit in; they want to be able to see the TV while lying in bed, to have breakfast in the room, and to have their reservations and check in at the front desk without hassles.[2] They definitely do not want to stand in line, wait an hour for breakfast to be delivered, have the telephone ring 15 times before the operator answers, and hear the housekeepers yelling at each other in the hallway.

For the sake of example, the same businesspeople go home on Friday, after a very hectic week, and say to their families, "Let's get out of here. I just need to relax." Let's say they go back to the same hotel. Their basic needs haven't changed; they still need to sleep, shower, and change clothes, but now the environment or context has changed. Now, price is a factor; the

cost will come out of their own pockets. The phone is unnecessary and there is no need for a desk. They want the TV away in the corner so they won't be disturbed when the children are watching it. They still don't want housekeepers yelling in the hall, but they aren't too disturbed when their kids run up and down the hallway screaming at each other. The hotel restaurant, which was perfect for entertaining their clients, is now too expensive; besides the kids won't eat that "stuff!" and the service is too slow for them. Where's the nearest McDonald's? In short, the needs are the same whether for business or pleasure: What has changed is the wants and problems.

The upshot of all this is that we have to understand the needs hierarchy, the wants that go with each level of the hierarchy, the "problems" of given individuals, and we have to understand the context or environment in which they will consume the hospitality product. Still, needs and wants cannot be generalized across the entire population. Consider, then, what hoteliers and restaurateurs might like to know of the needs and wants of women vs. men, meeting planners vs. corporate planners, incentive planners, tour planners, and self-employed

---

[2]Marriott research found that the five "key drivers" of guest satisfaction are: the qualities of check-in speed, friendliness, cleanliness, value, and breakfast. *Trends in the Hotel Industry,* PKF Consulting, Houston, August 1993.

business travelers, just to mention a few of the broader possibilities.

Maslow's hierarchy of needs is a critical foundation of human behavior. At the same time, it is only a foundation upon which to build. Motives activate people's behavior but perceptions determine the course of that behavior.

The Buying Decision Process

It was stated at the beginning of this chapter that consumer behavior is a process and this process is influenced in many ways both before and after the act of purchase. We will now examine in some detail the buying decision process as shown in Figure 6-2. Only by under-

standing the process can the marketer hope to influence it.

Needs, Wants, and Problems

The process normally begins with needs, wants, and problem recognition or identification. Sometimes the need, want, or problem recognition will come as a response to stimuli, for example, a TV commercial, an ad, or a billboard.

First, in the case of problem recognition, consumers know or think they have a problem and begin a search for a solution. We should understand that this may be a very subtle stage. Consumers do not suddenly jump up and shout, "I have a problem." In fact, consumers may not even think of it as a problem; they might simply

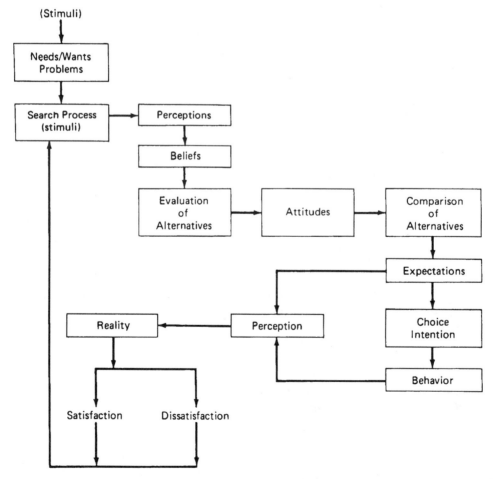

FIGURE 6-2   The consumer buying decision process

say, "I'm hungry [problem]; let's eat [solution]." On the other hand, they might think, "I'd really like to go to a quiet [want] place for a good [want] dinner [need] tonight. Where should we go [problem]?"

Search Process

They then begin the search process for a solution. They may simply search their memories, they may ask others, look to the newspaper or the telephone directory, or they may do any number of other things to obtain either new information or additional information. They may do this in split seconds if there is a suitable restaurant right around the corner, or they may take a year to search, as in planning an annual vacation. They may give the task to someone else, such as a subordinate, a secretary, a spouse, an airline, or a travel agency.

In the example given above the consumer has recognized the problem unaided. Marketing has had little, if any, impact upon that recognition. Once the problem has been recognized, however, marketing can begin to take an active role. Where consumers go for information, what they read or hear there, whether the information was already in their memories, for whatever reason marketing has had an influence on this part of the process.

At other times the problem may arise not through recognition, but through identification. In this case, consumers are unaware that they have a problem until it is presented to them and identified for them. In this, marketing has a role right from the beginning. Let us say that these same consumers plan, as usual, to eat dinner at home. They are reading the newspaper or watching television, when suddenly they see an ad for what appears to be a nice, quiet restaurant. They think, "Boy, wouldn't that be nice for a change?" Their wants and problem have been identified for them. Marketing has not created a need—that was already there. Marketing has created a want and caused a problem that needs a solution.

These simplistic examples can be applied to the beginning of any purchase decision process,

whether it be for a glass of milk or a year-long trip around the world. For simple purchases the process may be totally subconscious, or parts of it may be skipped. For similar decisions such as those made many times before, the process may be instantaneous because of what has become a learned reaction. Of course, the process could also end in a decision *not* to purchase; this might be the case when marketing has not done its job adequately. Regardless, the role of marketing is apparent even at this early stage. It is also apparent that if marketers want to affect the process at this stage, they must be aware of the complexities of the decision and the influences that will modify it.

Stimuli Selection

In the first case above, consumers determined their own problem; in the second case, it was caused by a stimulus. In either case, stimuli may affect the process at some stage. The degree of impact, as well as the intensity of the entire search process, is determined by the level of involvement the consumer has with the purchase decision.

The impact and intensity is greater in cases of *high involvement*. These are cases in which the decision has high personal importance or relevance to the consumer, such as high cost, high risk, or high effect on self-image. For example, selecting the place where customers are going on their honeymoon is usually a high-involvement decision. When *low involvement* exists (selecting a fast-food restaurant), the process is similar except that it proceeds far more quickly and some stages may be skipped, especially when information is readily at hand. Regardless, consumers are affected only by stimuli that they selectively choose.

The process of selective choice represents an hierarchy. That is, the steps are taken in sequence, or dropped at any point, as follows:

Selective attention—we attend only to that which is of interest to us. Advertisers may use graphics or headlines to get this attention.

Selective comprehension—we try to comprehend that which is still of interest.

Selective acceptance—we accept or reject that which we comprehend.

Selective retention—we retain in memory that which we have accepted.

Because consumers *selectively* attend to, comprehend, accept, and retain messages, we should be aware that much of what we direct at them does not sink in. Unless we can bombard them, a la McDonald's, we need to be certain that what we want them to select is directed in a manner that appeals to their needs, wants, and problems. This truism applies not only in advertising but also in selling, in-house merchandising, public relations, and any other way in which consumers gather information.

Perceptions

For the consumer, perception is reality. This point is so critical that it is worth repeating: *Perception is reality.* Perhaps one of the greatest mistakes we can make as marketers is thinking that what we perceive is also what the customer perceives. If the customer doesn't perceive it, it doesn't exist. If the customer does perceive it, it does exist. You cannot make something what it is *not* by simply saying so; you have to change perception. Perceptions are meanings we assign to what we see, hear, and sense around us. Our perceptions are heavily influenced by sociocultural and psychological forces. Sociocultural forces include the culture of society, social class, and small reference groups, among others. A *reference group* may be defined as people who influence a person's attitudes, opinions, and values, such as family, friends, or business associates. Reference groups are especially important in the purchase of hospitality services where word-of-mouth recommendations play a major role in the buying decision. Psychological forces that influence consumer behavior generally come from within a person and include learning experiences, personality, and self-image.

Hotels and restaurants that brag about how great they are must be able to live up to their boasts. When they promise the moon and then fail to deliver the moon (in fact, are bewildered when the customer asks for the moon), they have defeated their own purpose: they have alienated a customer. Expectations arise from initial perceptions and may be disconfirmed by subsequent perceptions.

Initial perceptions depend on stimulus factors. This is the area of traditional marketing.

A resort hotel brochure illustrates an indefinitely long ("as far as the eye can see") stretch of white sandy beach, a quiet remote setting, elegant dining on "your own" private patio overlooking the ocean, and a romantic full moon.

These are the stimulus factors and the reader's perception is, "What a perfect place for a honeymoon!"

Actual perception depends on personal factors: needs, moods, experiences, values and, most of all, expectations. We have reversed the order: Perceptions now derive from expectations. This is the area of nontraditional marketing.

You find the beach all right—it's on the other side of the island. The beach at the hotel is the size of a postage stamp. When you check in, you find that a 300-room convention is checking in ahead of you. The "remote setting" is in the flight path of the airport. The private patio overlooking the ocean is in the $800 suite, which you didn't reserve. You can eat in your room or in the enclosed dining room—which doesn't have a view because it has no windows! It rains the entire week. "What a bummer!"

Now, reality is perception; expectations were not fulfilled and your perceptions are negative.

The following week, when the convention is gone and the moon shines, you meet the couple who stay in the suite. They couldn't care less about the beach; they spend all their time in their suite, and have room service for every meal. They tell you what a fantastic place it is!

Reality is perception. These differences in perceptions create many problems for service marketers.

Perception is selective. We cannot possibly perceive all the stimulus objects that are presented to us, so we select what we want to perceive. If you are looking for a honeymoon spot, you select to perceive the beach, the patio, the quietness, and the moon from the brochures, ads, or materials presented you. If you are looking for a spot for your company's next sales meeting, you select to perceive the meeting rooms, the banquet facilities, and the sports facilities from the very same brochures, ads, and materials. When you are at a hotel, you may select to perceive the decor, elevator service, the bar, the golf course, or anything that you felt was promised you. Perceptions are images, and images influence purchase behavior.

Marketers must deal very acutely with perceptions. Marketers must create images with the stimuli pertinent to the specific target market they are trying to attract. They must use stimuli that are relevant to that market, and they must be certain that reality equals, or almost equals, expectation, so that reality doesn't negatively influence perception. Failure to do this will create a dissatisfied customer and negative word-of-mouth. Recall, in the hospitality business, that it is not enough just to create a customer; it is necessary, as well, to keep the customer.

The ads in Figure 6-3 certainly create some initial perceptions. Analyze the stimulus factors and your selective perception and then consider whether you believe that reality will meet these perceptions.

Beliefs

Belief can be defined as something we actually think is fact; it derives from perceptions. We attach a belief to an object. An object could be a restaurant, and a belief could be that it is expensive. Whether or not the restaurant is expensive is incidental to the belief. Beliefs are *cognitive;* they exist in the mind regardless of where or whom they come from. If beliefs are accurate (i.e., if the restaurant is expensive) and we want consumers to have that belief,

then we can be satisfied with the status quo in that respect.

Sometimes, however, marketers want to change or create beliefs. The restaurant is really not expensive, we say. But how can we say that? For some people it may be very expensive, and for others it may be quite inexpensive. The solution lies in the definition of the target market. These are the people we want as customers; what are their beliefs? We have to learn this before we decide whether we want to change them.

The same is true if we want to create beliefs, as for a new restaurant. Creating beliefs, however, is much easier than changing them, because essentially what exists already is a vacuum and all we have to do is fill it. When we want to change a belief, we have to get rid of the old one and replace it with a new one. This is why it is important that we try to "do things right" in the first place.

People change beliefs frequently without any effort on the part of marketers, or maybe because of lack of effort. Consider again the case of the former Howard Johnson's in the 1980s. Customers changed their beliefs over time to conclude unclean facilities, poor service, and mediocre food. This belief became so ingrained that a massive effort was necessary to change it. Howard Johnson's tried to clean up their act and then tried to persuade the public that it had done so. The persuasion effort failed, not just because they failed to clean up their act sufficiently—they also failed to understand that their orange roofs epitomized negative beliefs. People were not going to be persuaded simply because they were told that things were different.

Research by Howard Johnson's failed to uncover this problem. Howard Johnson's research analyzed attitude. They responded to this analysis with the notion that if they could change attitude they would change behavior. But the problem wasn't attitudes. People's attitudes were, and continued to be, negative toward unclean restaurants with poor service. The problem was the belief that these elements were inherent in Howard Johnson's.

Howard Johnson's then committed a major

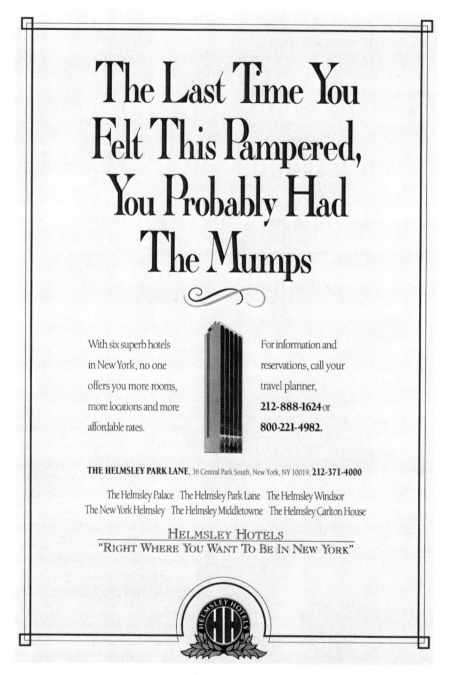

FIGURE 6-3   Ad creating initial perceptions

blunder. Their research showed that people's attitudes toward family restaurants were that they liked them to be "homelike." Based on this revelation, Howard Johnson's commenced an advertising campaign to convince the public that its restaurants were homelike. The headline of the campaign was, "If it's not your mother, it must be Howard Johnson's." Con-

FIGURE 6-3   (continued)

sider the subliminal impact: First, I still believe that Howard Johnson's is unclean and has poor service; and second, I'm insulted by your telling me that my mother has an unclean house and poor service. Of course, beliefs did not change, they only became more negative. With a better understanding of consumer behavior, the story might have had a different ending.

Alternative Evaluation

Rarely is there only one possible solution, and the consumer now has to compare the alternatives. Reference groups and other evaluative criteria have strong impact at this stage. More important, how well have the marketers done their job? Has the case been well presented? Does the solution look viable? Is the risk worth it? Is the price/value relationship appropriate? Does it cover the necessary needs and wants? What is the word-of-mouth reputation? Is it different or better than the other alternatives, and if so, why? These are the thoughts that are going through the mind of the consumer. Again, the higher the involvement, the lengthier and more deliberate the process and the greater the search for more information.

The marketer's most critical impact is probably at this stage, at least for medium- to high-involvement purchases. The level of involvement will vary with the individual. Eating at McDonald's is low-involvement, but that does not stop McDonald's from having one of the largest advertising budgets in the country. McDonald's truly wants you to have high involvement with them.

As the price gets higher and, in the hospitality industry, as the service element becomes more important, the level of involvement increases. But the involvement level in choosing a hotel is always relatively high, because the product is consumed as purchased, unlike a good, which can be returned if it doesn't work. It is also because the entire hotel experience is personal; if it's a bad experience, it affects the user personally. Alternative evaluation is the point at which the total marketing effort, including especially internal and relationship marketing, will pay off.

Attitudes

Attitudes are the *affective* component of the belief–attitude–intention triad that consumers often follow. Affective means the subjective and emotional feelings toward the belief. Attitudes are tendencies to respond toward beliefs, as in the Howard Johnson's case above. If you believe that a restaurant is expensive, how do you actually feel about going there? In a sense, this is the application of our beliefs; this is how we judge our beliefs and how we react to them.

Let's assume that our restaurant is expensive and our target market believes this. There is no point here in trying to change belief, because it is true. Yet people are not coming to the restaurant because of their response to their belief that it's too expensive. Unless, of course, we want to change the restaurant to lower prices (and research may show that to be the only viable course of action, given this market), what we have to change is attitude and affective feelings. One way to do this might be to try to persuade people that the restaurant is expensive but worth the price. If we could succeed in this effort, we will have changed attitude while maintaining the same belief.

Research contrary to that of Howard Johnson's makes this point. Coca-Cola found that a significant majority of the 40,000 people who taste-tested "new" Coke vs. "old" Coke preferred the new variety. When they switched their formula to the new Coke, the market revolted. What Coca-Cola's research did was to measure beliefs and ignore attitudes. People believed that new Coke was better, but their attitude toward changing was negative.

Alternative Comparison

Hospitality purchase choices often include many elements. There are the obvious elements such as price, location, accessibility, reputation, and quality. There are also the less obvious or anticipated elements such as service, ambience, attitude, newness, and other clientele. Researchers have developed different models to explain how consumers compare alternative choices. One assumption is that consumers will make trade-offs of one attribute for another—that is, a weakness in one attribute can be made up for by a strength in another. For example, we might select a hotel on the outskirts of town (weak in location) because the price is very reasonable (strong in price). Another model would have the consumer establish a minimum level on only one or a few attributes—for example, price. These choice models and others require consumer research to determine the target market's choice process.

Expectations

All the steps of the process, in Figure 6-2, through which the consumer has now proceeded, lead to expectations (we might even say "great expectations"). We will come back to these in a moment, when we discuss expectation gaps between perception and reality.

Choice Intentions

The final stage of the belief–attitude–intention triad is called the *conative* stage, covering what people intend to do. This is not behavior, but it may be as close to behavior as we can get, as will be discussed shortly. There is no way we can positively be assured of behavior until after it happens. Failing this, we want to know what people intend to do.

Let us assume that we have a restaurant that we believe is expensive, but worth it. We have a positive disposition to patronize this restaurant. Do we intend to go there? No! We can't afford it. Our positive attitude thus turns out to mean nothing for the marketer who wants our patronage. Of course, the specific context may change: Would you intend to go there on your tenth wedding anniversary next week? Perhaps now the answer is yes. It can be seen now how context can change behavior, or at least *intended* behavior. It can also be seen that simply asking people what they intend to do can be very misleading without also measuring belief, attitude, time, and context.

Behavior

Intention is followed by actual behavior. This may mean to do nothing, which is still a behavior. But assume that the consumer does "behave," that is, makes a choice and acts upon it. Now we have a new stage of perception—the

one that comes *after* the fact—face-to-face with reality.[3]

Perception vs. Reality

We now come back to expectations: Were they met or not? Perception, once again, is reality. The differences between what was expected and what is perception/reality, if any, are the gaps that can occur between the two, and we will now discuss them in some detail.

Expectation Gaps In Chapter 1, Figure 1-4, we considered the potential gaps in expectation that may occur between the problem and the solution. Figure 6-4 is a model that illustrates potential "gaps" in service quality and where they may occur. Gaps arise because of differences between expectations and perceptions, but they occur for different reasons. In Table 6-1 we apply this model to the hospitality industry to show the challenges that hospitality marketers face in eliminating gaps.

It is clear that all ten of these gaps may overlap and affect each other. Yet, each is critical to keeping customers and can have serious consequences. Any gap may cause a difference between expectation and reality because perception is reality. Again, all management is marketing.

Outcomes—Satisfaction or Dissatisfaction

The choice is made and the performance takes place. What is the outcome? Does performance match expectation? Is perception changed? We have managed to create a customer, but have we managed to keep one? Will he or she come back? Tell others? Is the new customer satisfied, dissatisfied, or just so-so?

We could never hope to know if every customer left satisfied or dissatisfied, but we cer-

---

[3]This discussion of consumer information processing is limited. For further study, Icek Ajzen and Martin Fishbein, *Understanding Attitudes and Predicting Social Behavior,* Englewood Cliffs, New Jersey: Prentice-Hall, 1980, is recommended.

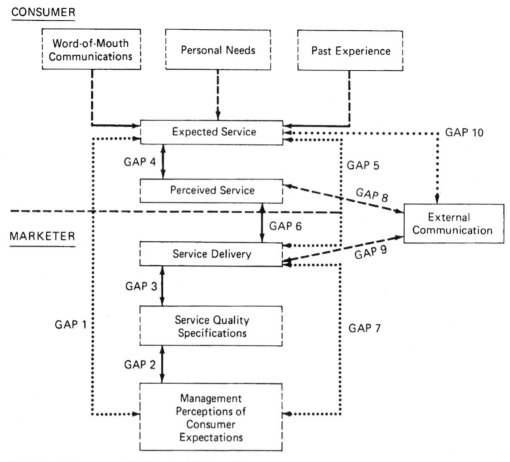

Adapted from A. Parasuraman, V.A. Zeithaml, and L.L. Berry, "A Conceptual Model of Service Qualiy and its Implications for Future Research," *Journal of Marketing,* Fall 1985, pp. 41–50, published by the American Marketing Association.

FIGURE 6-4   Potential gaps occuring between consumers' problems and solutions

tainly should have a good idea of many of them. With individuals, we will have to randomly sample to find this out; with groups and large parties, we should have some contact with each one.

Marketing hasn't stopped yet. Remember, we want to keep these new customers. As much as we can, let's follow up with them. If they are satisfied, let's find out why. Maybe it will teach us something.

If they are not satisfied, why not ? What can we do about it? Can we still get them to come back? Can we correct the problem? Perhaps they are suffering from a reality called *cogni-*

tive dissonance, a state of mind in which attitudes and behaviors don't mesh—in other words, when what we do is not the same as our attitude toward it. This state causes us to have second thoughts or doubts about the choice that we made. This is especially true when the choice was an important one pschologically and/or financially and when there were alternative choices with a number of favorable features.

Most people try to reduce their own cognitive dissonance. We can't change the behavior, so we try to change our attitude to feel better about having done it. Marketers can help cus-

TABLE 6-1   Potential Gaps in Hospitality Service

Gap 1—*between services expected by the consumer and management perceptions of consumers' expectations.* When a new hotel is opened, management has to decide the range of services to offer. A business center, concierge, round-the-clock room service, in-room computer hook-ups and an airport shuttle, are just a few of the services that may be offered, plus all the service intangibles. The gap will result if what is offered and what is received do not coincide with the expectations of the market segments that the hotel is trying to attract.

Gap 2—*between management perceptions of consumer expectations and service quality specifications.* Specifications dictate how the service will be implemented by the company. Let's say a hotel realizes that a free airport shuttle is a service that customers expect. They offer the service but vans are scheduled to leave the hotel only once every hour, causing long, inconvenient waits for customers. The gap arises from the difference between what management thinks the customer wants (free airport shuttle) and how management decides to implement the service (only once an hour).

Gap 3—*between service quality specifications and service delivery.* This is a common gap in almost any business and is caused by the failure of employees to provide services in accordance with the procedures established by the company. An example of this would be the once-an-hour airport shuttle, from above, showing up after an hour and a half.

Gap 4—*between service expected by the consumer and perceived service,* as we previously discussed, but not derived from traditional marketing. Figure 6-4 shows that expected service is affected by consumers' past experiences, personal needs, and exposure to communications such as word-of-mouth recommendations.

Thus, consumers have a certain level of expectations even before they arrive at the hotel or restaurant. This gap can be especially difficult for marketers, even with the best of intentions. Customers may have totally unrealistic perceptions that have been created in their own minds through no fault of the marketer. When customers' perceptions are unrealistic or wrong, it will be almost impossible to fulfill their expectations. As an example, a person who travels infrequently might perceive that a $100 hotel room in New York City would be a "great" hotel room; in fact, the room may be closet-sized. There are no great hotel rooms in New York City for $100. The customer has created an unrealistic perception of a $100 room. This type of scenario is important to understand when we are faced with an some "expectations not realized" customers.

Gap 5—*between service expected by the customer and the service delivered by the company when the service expected may be the same as the perceived,* but the customer really wanted something different. A customer at an expensive hotel might expect and perceive room service only from 6:00 A.M. to 12:00 midnight but really wanted it 24 hours. In this case a service is not delivered that would make a better experience for the customer.

Gap 6—*between service as perceived by the consumer and the service delivered by the company.* Again, this may be a difficult gap to overcome because customers and organizations often have different perceptions as to service quality. A well-traveled international tourist may find it unbelievable that most hotels in the United States have no currency exchange facility, a service that most American hotels consider to be unnecessary even though they consider themselves full-service hotels.

Gap 7—*between management perceptions of consumer expectations and service delivery.* Even when management has been able to monitor customer expectations, it may be difficult to provide services to meet those expectations. Heterogeneity, as described in Chapter 2, may often be the

(continued)

TABLE 6-1   (continued)

cause, even though the specifications are accurate. After all, when services are performed by humans there are bound to be fluctuations in service delivery.

Gap 8—*between perceived service and external communication.* Advertisements and other forms of external communication by a firm are intended to create perceptions regarding the services offered. However, different people read different meanings into what they see and, thus, gaps will occur between what an ad is saying it offers and what the customer perceives it to offer (e.g., Figure 6-3).

Gap 9—*between service delivery and external communication.* In their advertisements, firms often make promises that are difficult to live up to or imply something that is not fulfilled (e.g., the moon). Holiday Inn's "No Surprises" campaign of a few years ago is an example: The implication was that everything would be "right." It soon became apparent that this promise could not be delivered and the advertising campaign was dropped after angering a lot of customers. Figure 6-5, for example, has great gap 9 potential.

Gap 10—one of the most serious gaps caused by advertising claims and puffery, gap 10—*in which advertising, intentionally, builds expectations that are knowingly not representative*—is more blatant. When advertising builds expectations knowingly not representative, the customer, having no reason to expect the promise, instead enters a state of disbelief (e.g., Figure 6-3). Or, it could fail because of any or all of the other gaps.

Certainly a billion dollars spent on hotels would create great expectations (refer back to Figure 1-6 in Chapter 1). In fact, this billion dollars was spent on some of Sheraton's luxury line of hotels, of which there are about a dozen out of some 400-plus. Many Sheraton properties, especially some franchised inns, still suffered badly from lack of renovation and would disappoint many who believed this ad. Such advertising may be self-defeating. Strangely, Hilton followed with similar ads and similar problems. Figure 6-5 shows ads with potential gaps 8, 9, and 10.

---

tomers reduce cognitive dissonance by convincing them that they did, in fact, make the right choice.

Research has shown that people try to reduce dissonance by seeking or choosing to perceive information that supports the wiseness of the decision, by finding fault with the alternatives so that they look less favorable, and by downplaying the negative aspects of the choice and enhancing the positive elements. Advertising that supports the choice, or personal communication that commends the wisdom of the choice have been found to be helpful in reducing dissonance and increasing loyalty.

Now, let us apply the consumer behavior process to the hotel industry. The process shown in Figure 6-6 is one of choosing a vacation destination, but it is easily adaptable to other choices, such as for a restaurant. It is self-explanatory, so further discussion here is unnecessary, but the reader should trace the steps to see how they fit the elements of consumer behavior we have discussed thus far. This analysis will make the theory more practical. You might even attempt fitting to the model your own particular mental process on a recent or proposed purchase to see how it fits.

Figure 6-6 is an oversimplification of a very complex process. In fact, this process is so full of different variables that only one's mind can process it. The process, in an overall consumer behavior sense however, is important and marketers should understand it. Here, we tie them together so as to understand how they are interrelated.

So far we have discussed hospitality customers and their purchase behavior in a general sense. Now, in section B of this chapter, we will look at some specific types of customers, as commonly defined in the industry.

AT SHERATON LITTLE THINGS MEAN A LOT • AT SHERATON LITTLE THINGS MEAN A LOT • AT SHERATON LITTLE THINGS MEAN A LOT • AT SHERATON LITTLE THINGS MEAN A LOT • AT

We Didn't Invent The Word Satisfaction. At Sheraton, We Simply Defined It.

Sa-tis-fact-ion.
(1) At Sheratons throughout Canada, it means a commitment to making sure all your business needs are satisfied. **(2)** To be friendly. Responsive. **(3)** To anticipate even the littlest things. **(4)** And above all, to surround you with a spirit of service and a sense of well-being unlike anything you've ever experienced.

Choice-s.(1) No one else accommodates the business traveler in more ways than Sheraton. **(2)** Sheraton Hotels offer you a complete selection of exceptional services and fine amenities. **(3)** Sheraton Inns are conveniently located near highways and airports, providing a full range of services in a less formal setting. **(4)** Sheraton Resorts let you conduct business while enjoying a variety of vacation activities within a luxurious environment. **(5)** Sheraton All-Suites feature a more spacious atmosphere for added comfort.

Aer-o-plan Bon-us Points.* **(1)** If you're a member of Air Canada's frequent Flyer Programme, you'll receive 1,000 additional Aeroplan miles just for staying at a participating Sheraton hotel. **(2)** What's more, members can also get upgraded accommodations as well.

Call 800-325-3535.
(1) Sheratons have defined satisfaction in our Hotels, Inns, Resorts and All-Suites. **(2)** Call our toll-free number now. **(3)** And experience Sheraton satisfaction for yourself at these and other fine Sheratons.

ITT Sheraton
HOTELS · INNS · RESORTS · ALL-SUITES
800-325-3535

*Aeroplan Bonus Points available on Sheraton Executive Traveler. Regular or Corporate rates only at participating properties.

Courtesy of ITT Sheraton Corporation

FIGURE 6-5 A potential gap 8, 9, and/or 10 between external communication and delivery, perception and/or expectation

IF YOU'RE EXPECTING EVEN MORE FROM A HOTEL IN TIMES LIKE THESE, YOU'D BETTER WAKE UP.

Over the last few years, we've invested more than a billion dollars in our hotels to meet your changing needs. So, while other hotels may be forced to cut back and give you less, at Hilton we're giving more, doing more, and moving ahead.

DOUBLE-DIPPING ENCOURAGED HERE.

As a member of the HHonors Guest Reward Program, you won't have to choose between earning hotel points, or mileage credit on your favorite airlines. Unlike other hotel programs, Hilton HHonors lets you have both. As well as fabulous new rewards.

HERE'S A HOTEL WITHIN A HOTEL.

At select Hiltons across America, you can enjoy the very best we have to offer the business traveler—our magnificent Towers accommodations. With separate registration, private lounges, and a concierge and staff devoted to your every need.

HERE.

RENOVATIONS HERE, THERE AND EVERYWHERE.

Unlike some of our competitors, we're continuing to refurbish our hotels, like The Waldorf=Astoria and the Chicago Hilton and Towers, from lobby to penthouse. We've also added exciting new properties, like The Pointe Hilton Resorts in Phoenix.

THERE'S SOMETHING HAPPENING HERE.

We've created a new Hilton image, as evidenced by our brand-new signature, to underscore our commitment to continuous improvement. So, next time you're hoping for more from a hotel when you're on the road, wake up here. At Hilton.

Hilton

FIGURE 6-5 (continued)

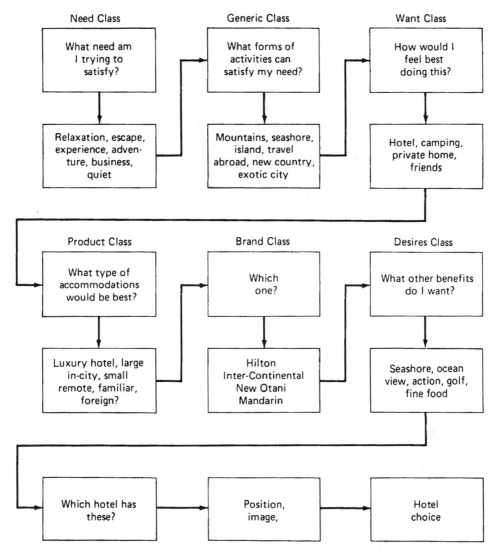

FIGURE 6-6   Consumer mental evaluation process (conscious and/or unconscious)

B. Types of Hospitality Customers

There are various ways of grouping different types of hospitality customers, based on common needs and wants. (This will also be discussed in greater detail in Chapter 8, under Market Segmentation.) Here we will try to understand customers in broad categories so that

we can make an effort to influence their purchase behavior.

The Business Traveler

The business traveler market segment is one of the most desirable for the hospitality marketer. According to the U.S. Travel Data Center, this market consists of over 36 million travelers in the United States alone.[4] Most of these travelers spend between two and three nights away from home on each trip. The business travel segment is not only the largest major segment, but it is also considered the least price-sensitive market available. The business traveler is defined as a customer who is utilizing the product because of a need to conduct business in a particular destination area. While the hotel facility or restaurant may be used during business, the facility is not the sole reason for the buy. Purposes of the business trip might include company-related business, consulting, sales trips, personal business, and trips required to fulfill managerial functions.

On the surface, the needs of this market are simple; in practice, they are far more complex and not so simple to deliver. One study revealed that the most important factors in the business traveler's selection of a hotel were cleanliness and comfortable mattresses and pillows.[5] It is important, however, to understand that these factors do not truly determine initial hotel choice; they (especially mattresses and pillows) are unknowns until one has stayed there and experienced a need factor according to his or her own expectations.

When research respondents are allowed to check everything they consider important from a predetermined list, then any number of items become important. In truth, all these factors and many others are usually most important only when they don't exist. One thing is certain: The business traveler group contains the greatest "complainers"—best explained by considering the nature or purpose of their travels. They would rather be home, they may have had a bad flight or business dealing, they are quickly in and out, and they want everything to go like clockwork.

Because the business traveler is such an important segment and the one that is researched the most, we will take some space to discuss it.

Business Traveler Needs

Perhaps 30 or so years ago, most hotel or motel rooms in the United States were by and large undependable. Rooms were often small and cramped; plumbing, heating, and air-conditioning did not always work; cleanliness was hit or miss and the bar of soap was minuscule. It was this kind of situation that Kemmons Wilson set out to correct when he opened the first Holiday Inn in Memphis in 1952.

Holiday Inns greatly improved the situation along the highways, but the real progress, especially in the cities, came a number of years later. Today, the unclean, cramped room and the minuscule soap bar are no longer the rule but the exception. Whereas travelers once complained loudly about the dirty shower and the soap bar, they now have other things to complain about. The industry has changed radically and so has the customer. In the past, a hotel served the purpose of providing a place to sleep while a customer was on a business trip. Today, a hotel has to provide the services for a *successful* business trip, and may just happen to be a place to sleep as well. So what factors do business travelers consider when choosing a hotel? In the above-mentioned study, when business travelers were asked open-ended questions about their first consideration when selecting a hotel, convenience of location received the highest response. This was followed by reputation, price, cleanliness, and service.[6] These results somewhat mirror those found in previous studies. It is useful to go through the actual decision process.[7]

First, business travelers consider location when choosing a place to stay. If a hotel's location is inappropriate, it's out of the running and the traveler looks to see what other hotels are situated within that general area. Marriott Hotels tried to circumvent the location issue by offering strong "bonus awards" to their customers. Giving the customer frequent-stay bonus "points" for choosing a Marriott, versus a competitor in a better location, the company attempted to influence the location choice of the

[4]Research conducted by the U.S. Travel Data Center, reported in "1993 Outlook for Travel and Tourism," Proceedings of the U.S. Travel Data Center's 18th Annual Travel Outlook Forum, pp. 86–89.

[5]"1990 Business Traveler Survey," *Hotel & Motel Management*, June 25, 1990, p 1.

[6]*Ibid.*, p. 30.

[7]This discussion is based on extensive research by the authors and others.

business traveler. Even these efforts, however, are suspect. *Business Travel News* research found that frequent-guest programs were rated very negatively, suggesting that such programs were not a major factor in influencing where travelers choose to stay.[8]

Second, business travelers look at rate ranges impacted by any company mandates or personal limitations. This is a determination by product class—that is, all hotels within the product class are assumed to be in the appropriate rate range, be it upscale, middle-tier, or budget. This is why descriptive research with close-ended questions often does not indicate price as an important factor—that decision has already been made and is no longer a factor. Furthermore, price is a factor only relative to what is available. If the product class desired is middle-tier (Ramada), and the only other available choice is upscale (Four Seasons), then price may be the single important factor in the decision, including location.

Most hotels have what are called corporate rates. To get them, all you have to do is ask. These are not necessarily the lowest rates, but often they are for better rooms, better furnished for the business traveler at a discount from the rack rate. Some are on concierge floors where, at a higher price, special services, a lounge, and complimentary continental breakfast are available. The concept is that the business traveler will pay more for less hassle. In other cases, corporate rates apply to specific corporations that book a certain number of room nights a year, either at a particular hotel or at any hotel of a chain.

Price is a very important factor for most business travelers today. And, in many locations all over the world, there is an alternative to high prices that includes clean, comfortable rooms and good locations, as well as security, prompt/courteous service, friendliness, and other factors. In understanding the business traveler, one has to understand the *role* of price—its role lies in designating a price range. Once that price range is determined, price is a

minor factor unless, of course, the same or better value can be found at a lower price.

Business travelers do not really think much about cleanliness when making an initial choice; they assume it exists (unless they have had a previous bad experience). Cleanliness is almost never given as a reason for choosing a particular hotel at a particular time. Cleanliness aside, what travelers want to know next is the reputation of the hotel or the chain. This will come from their own personal experiences or from conversations with others. (They have little, if any, faith in "highfalutin" hotel ad claims unless there is a promise behind it that can be backed up.)

We are now past the "threshold" items and at a level where the issues become myriad and idiosyncratic, depending on the individual, but they can be lumped together by target market—these are the service aspects. Each hotel should do its own research on these aspects, since these will often be the determining factors in a traveler's choosing among competitors in similar locations at similar rates. Again, most of these will be based on reputation and previous experience. If these are unknown, the first two items—general location and price—will prevail.

One most important factor in business travelers' wants, according to one hotel company's research, is covered by the question, "Will they have what I ordered and have it on time?" This may include things like floor level, exposure, bedroom configuration, type of bed, working space, telephone location, lighting, and so on. This is consistent with the notion that hotels today have a greater role to play in the success of a business trip, as indicated by the Westin ad in Figure 6-7. This was echoed by Nan K. Moss, Assistant Vice President of Hyatt Hotels:

> Customers tell us that they basically want what they need when they need it. They need a hotel to be flexible in meeting their needs because what they are looking for is enhanced productivity.[9]

Other concerns are check-in lines (Figure 6-8), employee attitudes, deferential treatment,

---

[8]Cited in *Trends in the Hotel Industry*, PKF Consulting, August, 1993.

[9]Reported in "1993 Outlook for Travel and Tourism," Proceedings of the U.S. Travel Data Center's 18th Annual Travel Outlook Forum, p. 94.

Some of our guests like the idea of a mouse in their room.

Now any room at Westin can be turned into a custom-tailored office.  Just tell us what you need. We'll do whatever it takes to make it easier for you

to get some work done while you're on the road. After all, giving you

Phone ahead for a computer, cellular phone, fax machine or whatever else you need. It'll be ready for delivery to your room when you arrive.

the competitive edge makes us a better business

hotel. That's 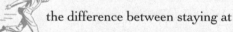 the difference between staying at a Westin, or just squeaking by. For reser-

WESTIN
HOTELS & RESORTS

vations, call your travel consultant or (800) 228-3000.

FIGURE 6-7   Westin enhances the success of a business trip

lighting, skirt hangers, mirrors, security, type of clientele, coffee makers, business services, noise (some business travelers avoid convention, atrium-lobby hotels and prefer more bou-

tique, smaller properties), operational efficiency, hotel "rules," limousine service to the airport, and a host of other things.

On the whole, business travelers who are

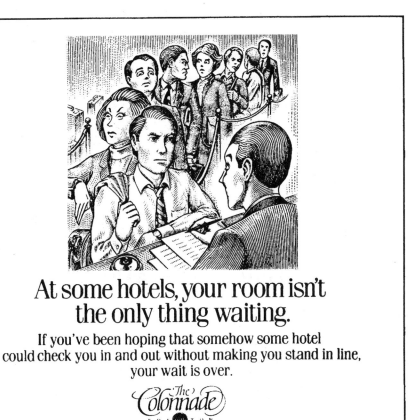

At some hotels, your room isn't the only thing waiting.

If you've been hoping that somehow some hotel could check you in and out without making you stand in line, your wait is over.

The **Colonnade**
B O S T O N

For reservations, call 800-962-3030 or 617-424-7000.

PREFERRED HOTELS

FIGURE 6-8   Ad addressing the common complaint of check-in lines

choosing a hotel do not consider bathroom amenities, shoe polishers, bathrobes, turn-down service, chocolates on the pillow, and other such factors. These are nice "extras" but not critical, and customers have come to expect certain amenities, such as a decent-size bar of soap. Goat's milk shampoo, herbal soap, and bubble bath are mostly "take home" items. Even when some are used, their absence wouldn't be considered serious. These travelers are more concerned with how the shower works.

An even better example is that of a new president of a major hotel company in India. Seeing competition increasing, he decreed that business travelers would get a box of chocolates, a bathrobe, a copy of *Time* magazine (expensive in India), and other amenities adding about $10

to the variable room cost. "Whoa!" said the director of marketing in the London office that booked many of these guests. "What our customers want is to get through the airport hassle-free," a real hassle in India but easily relieved by a little know-how. The president prevailed, but added only costs, not revenue—and he left the company soon afterward.

For many hotels superfluous amenities have become a cost they can no longer afford at the prices travelers are willing to pay. Claims like those shown in Figures 1-1 and 1-2 are pure fiction, yet they keep coming. A better way, perhaps, is the approach now taken by some hotels to provide amenities only when really needed, as shown in Figure 6-9. " 'Amenity creep'...is coming to a halt. It appears the clear winners in

Holiday Inn

HOSPITALITY PROMISE℠

Making your stay a complete success is our goal. Just let our Manager on Duty or front desk staff know if any part of your stay isn't satisfactory. We promise to make it right or you won't pay for that part of your stay.

If you have any further comments regarding your stay, let us know by calling Holiday Inn Worldwide Guest Relations at 1-800-621-0555.

FORGET SOMETHING?℠

If you forgot to pack any standard toiletry item (toothbrush, toothpaste, shaving cream, razor, or comb), just call the front desk and we'll get you a complimentary replacement right away.

FIGURE 6-9 Providing amenities when they are really needed

the future will be hotel management which is truly committed to customer satisfaction, value, and consistent provision of the basic lodging fundamentals,"[10] plus the availability of things that certain business travelers want. Hyatt, for example, reports great success with its Business Plan (Figure 6-10).

Hoteliers should also recognize that all of these items, actually unimportant to the business traveler, cost money. For all of the mints on the pillows and fancy bars of soap that do not create or keep a customer, the savings might be reallocated, for example, to front desk staffing. Having a swift, friendly check-in, with all of the information being correct the first time, solves a specific problem and greatly improves customer satisfaction.

Most business travelers visiting cities do not consider hotels' restaurants as a determining factor in their choice of hotel, simply because there are usually numerous alternatives available. A good breakfast room is assumed and a quick and easy "grazing" restaurant open all hours is desired; having other restaurants in a hotel is considered convenient, sometimes, but not totally necessary. A majority of city hotel customers, in most developed countries, eat out for lunch and dinner. (This does not mean that an upscale hotel should not have good restaurants, but that they are seldom determinant in the choice of hotel.) This somewhat contradicts the notion of convenient location, which only tends to reappear when staying at a roadside hotel. These are generalizations. As we have said, each hospitality establishment has to know its own target market.

Dealing with the Business Segment

While the corporate office is saying, "Raise the rates," the local marketing team will frequently feel that lower pricing is the means necessary

[10]*Trends in the Hotel Industry,* PKF Consulting, August 1993.

Courtesy of Hyatt Hotels Corp.

FIGURE 6-10   Hyatt's Business Plan for those who need it

for capturing new customers, or for keeping existing customers. Naturally, if a hotel is significantly higher or lower in price than its competition, a choice may be made on price, but this alone is not the answer—and there is no *one* answer. What it is necessary to know is the appropriate price range for existing market conditions. This is not an arbitrary decision, as is sometimes assumed. An inherent conflict often exists, in this regard, between the local sales department and the corporate office of hotel chains. For example:

> A 1,400-room hotel was undergoing a three-year, $100 million renovation program. This had caused considerable customer discontent and some serious loss of business at the same time that the economy had turned down. Although hotel management felt that there was no problem in selling the 600 renovated rooms at a higher rate, there was a problem with the rest of the hotel and the disruptive construction work.
>
> The corporate rate for this hotel was $104; the corporate rate of its major competitor was $99. The corporate office of the hotel under renovation, in the midst of this situation, mandated that the property increase its corporate transient roomnights sold from 60,000 to 65,000. At the same time, it mandated a corporate rate increase to $118, *while* the disruptive renovations continued. This mandate left the property sales staff in an impossible and noncompetitive situation and caused the eventual loss of a considerable amount of business, much of which was never regained.

Most business travel is affected by prevailing economic conditions. The early 1990s were difficult times for many corporations worldwide, and this resulted in declines in business travel. The number of business travelers has remained fairly steady but the numbers of trips taken by these travelers has changed according to the fortunes of their companies.[11] It is no wonder, then, that today's business travelers are price-sensitive. It is true, of course, that the business traveler who always stays at a Four Seasons or comparable hotel is probably less price-sensitive. In fact, all upscale hotels have some of

these customers. The question is: Are there enough of them? For most hotels, the basic premise is simple: If a hotel is providing what the customers want at a reasonable price, then market share will be obtained.

For the restaurant industry, business travelers mean expense account travelers. Like hotels, a sizable number of restaurants would not be in business today were it not for these customers. Although, restaurant meals became only 50 percent tax-deductible in 1993, this issue is not the primary factor in the eating-out decision and restaurants that serve well the needs of this market will prosper even if the tax laws are changed. No logical businessperson would decide not to take a good customer to lunch because of a $10 deduction in expenses. On the other hand, restaurants have needed to adjust menus and prices creatively, to charge lower prices and/or create greater value perception. In the long haul, no business can go wrong by "treating the customer right."

The hospitality industry, worldwide, cherishes the business travel segment—which, today, is simply not large enough to go around. The major competition in the travel marketplace is for this segment. The property that gets its fair market share, and more, will be the one that truly understands the needs, wants, and problems of this market. It will not be the one that tries to win it by giveaways and gimmicks. The business traveler segment is not homogeneous. All of its members want convenience of location and cleanliness. The irony is that some want price, some want service, some want room appointments (like a large desk with good lighting), and some want a number of other things. Separating the "somes" is the essence of target marketing.

The Pleasure Traveler

The leisure market is comprised of travelers who—individually, in couples, in families, or in small groups—visit a hotel or restaurant for nonbusiness purposes. They may be traveling on vacation but often are not. Many, of course, are weekend, or other, package users. Others

---

[11]Research conducted by U.S. Travel Data Center, reported in "1993 Outlook for Travel and Tourism," Proceedings of the 18th Annual Travel Outlook Forum, pp. 86–89.

travel to cities for shopping, visiting friends, going to the theater, "just for a change," personal business, and various other purposes.

Increasingly, many pleasure travelers and business travelers are becoming the same person. With significant airfare reductions being offered for Saturday night stayovers, many business people do just that, to see the sights of the destination. One recent survey of a Wall Street (New York City's financial district) hotel's weekend guests found that 95 percent were originally there because of business. Among the idiosyncracies of this market, as described at the beginning of this chapter, the same individual has different needs at different times. Figure 6-11 shows some research results on these differing needs.

In the restaurant business, this segment includes a very large market of those who eat out just for pleasure. In many cities, both large and small, the pleasure traveler is a powerful segment with many diverse needs and wants. Not as constrained as the business customer by having to "get back to the office," the pleasure diner tends to be more relaxed and casual. At the same time, since the primary purpose of being there is to eat and socialize, these diners have more time to be critically conscious of the product/service delivery.

Some pleasure travelers use the best hotels and visit the best restaurants. In recent years, however, there has been a growing trend toward short pleasure trips and frequent dining out at less-expensive properties by those with limited budgets. This has considerable impact on the hospitality industry both in expanding the industry and in the need to better serve this market.

Many destinations have recognized the value and significance of tourism and there is intense competition among countries and states to attract the pleasure traveler. For example, residents of New Orleans are exposed to advertising campaigns from the states of Texas, Arkansas, Mississippi, and Tennessee, all of which compete heavily for visitors from that area. Malaysia seeks Singaporeans and vice versa. Advertising campaigns, such as that shown in Figure 6-12, have raised the awareness of customers as to

their many vacation choices. Thus, demand for hospitality services is being created and spurred on by foreign, state, and local governments, which reap their share from taxes levied on visitors. The international tourism market has grown huge and is still growing with many different needs and wants. We will discuss this further in Chapter 18.

The pleasure market is a high-growth potential market. While the business market remains relatively stable, and travels and eats out when it has to, a large portion of the pleasure market stays home and has yet to be developed. It *chooses* to travel or eat out. This is even more true in countries other than the United States. Many countries have only recently seen a large growth in the so-called middle class with more discretionary income. Since they are not "big spenders," however, they are often closed out of a market that caters and prices to the expense account customer. Lower-cost options of hotels and restaurants in some countries have expanded this market.

A major part of the pleasure market is made up of family travelers. Even despite tough economic times, a family vacation has become an essential part of many lifestyles. This market is more price-sensitive than the business segment and is more fickle about choices of destinations and hotels. Just as hotels must learn the needs of business travelers, however, they must also determine the underlying reasons and needs of pleasure travel. Peter Mason, Travel Marketing Director of *Better Homes and Gardens* magazine, revealed the results of research on the family vacation market:

> The number one reason is *To Be Together as a Family.... The* next most important reason is *The Need to Get Away from the Stress of Balancing a Home and a Career.... Rest and Relaxation* is number three. This all boils down to the fact that the Boomer Generation, the two income households, who are so important to the travel industry, are stressed out. They feel that they have got to get away.[12]

---

[12]Reported in "1993 Outlook for Travel and Tourism," Proceedings of the U.S. Travel Data Center's 18th Annual Travel Outlook Forum, pp. 107–108.

Comparison of determinance attributes for business and pleasure travelers (on a standardized ten-point scale after multiple regression of 15 factors derived from 67 attributes)

Business travelers		Pleasure travelers
	10	
Services quality		Quiet
	9	
	8	
	7	
	6	
Security	5	Security
Quiet		Image Room and bath condition
	4	Price-value
Reservations, front desk	3	Services quality
Room and bath condition		
Image	2	
Amenities Upscale services		Aesthetics
Food and beverage price and quality	1	Health facilities
Location		Reputation Reservations, front desk
Reputation Aesthetics	0	
Health facilities		
Room attributes Price-value	−1	Food and beverage price and quality
	−2	Room attributes Amenities
		Upscale services
	−3	Location
	−4	

Comparison of importance attributes for business and pleasure travelers (on a standardized ten-point scale after multiple regression of 14 factors derived from 67 attributes)

Business travelers		Pleasure travelers
	10	
Security		Services quality
	9	
Services quality		
	8	
Room and bath furnishings and condition	7	Restaurant quality and price options
	6	
	5	
Restaurant quality and price options		
Reputation Image	4	Building aesthetics
		Quiet
Location	3	Room and bath furnishings and condition
		Security
Quiet	2	Location
Amenities and conveniences		Amenities and conveniences
Price-value	1	Food and beverage service
Food and beverage service		Price-value
VIP treatment and extra luxury	0	
Health facilities		
Building aesthetics	−1	VIP treatment and extra luxury
		Reputation Image
	−2	
	−3	
		Health facilities
	−4	

Source: Robert C. Lewis, "Predicting Hotel Choice," *Cornell Hotel and Restaurant Administration Quarterly,* February, 1985, p. 91.

FIGURE 6-11   Relative differences in important and determinant attributes of hotels for business and pleasure travelers

FIGURE 6-12   Creating awareness of vacation choices

Another important pleasure market is made up of people traveling to visit friends and relatives. Although many of these travelers stay with friends and relatives at their final destination, they often seek out lodging along the way. This is a value-conscious market attracted to budget hotels and eating places like McDonald's and family restaurants. In these lower-tier markets, pleasure travelers are actually less demanding than customers in almost any other market. One reason for this is the lack of experience. Travelers may not realize just what is available, or they may simply not know how to voice a demand. (The exceptions, of course, are business travelers turned pleasure travelers.) They do, however, have long memories. These customers are prone simply to walk out of a bad experience without complaining, never to return. They also are prone to spread negative word-of-mouth. They are and will become, however, more demanding as their travel experience increases.

Resorts   The resort leisure market is also unique from the consumer viewpoint. Business travelers stay at a hotel because they have business to do. The resort leisure market, however, travels to resorts because it wants to be there, and to get away from it all. This has led to a proliferation of both mega-resorts, where you can fulfill almost every fantasy (a fad?), and quiet country inns, where you can spend a week in a rocking chair on the front porch. Again, the wants and needs of these customers are different from those of the usual traveler. We showed the decision process of these customers in Figure 6-6 but the possibilities are almost endless, as shown in Figure 6-13. Resort leisure guests need to fulfill their idea of a vacation. Whether it be total, quiet relaxation or a sports/recreation schedule busier than their job back home, they must feel satisfied that their idea of relaxation was met.

The complexion of resort guests is different from that of guests at commercial hotels. Almost two-thirds may be pleasure travelers, while the rest are attending a conference, or vice versa, participating in an incentive junket or on business, depending of course on the hotel and the location. This varied market poses inherent problems, especially when it comes together at the same time, which should be avoided when possible. The hotel staff must be trained to deal with the diverse needs of the leisure traveler on vacation, at the same time that it executes complicated conferences with infinite details. The needs of the meeting planner and the leisure resort market come into conflict. The hotel that mixes them has to be prepared to serve them both.

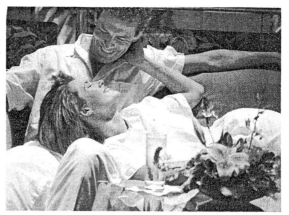

Courtesy of Stouffer Hotels & Resorts

FIGURE 6-13   Endless possibilities for the resort leisure market

For example, a major conference at the hotel may want to use the pool area for a cocktail reception, worth $20,000 to the resort. Should the manager shut down the pool area to leisure guests to accomodate the needs of the conference? This integration of diverse customers is more amplified in the resort setting. Many times, the exclusive nature of the facility lends itself to these conflicts, as, for example, when there are so many conferees on the golf course that it is impossible for an individual to get a tee time. The marketing-driven manager will understand the needs of both customers, develop operating standards for both, and sell the facility so that revenues will be maximized without losing guests.

Weekend escape travel is another part of the pleasure market. Dual-income households provide better incomes for people, but make the scheduling of vacations much harder. There is a trend toward shorter, more frequent vacations, taken by travelers who will be more demanding during the use of their precious vacation time. Much of this is part of the package market.

There is a large market in pleasure travel, even if it comes in small pieces. The hotel that can segment and serve this market appropriately will reap the rewards.

The Package Market

This increasingly popular method of attracting customers during low-demand periods is becoming more crowded with offerings every day. In the *New York Times* Sunday Travel Section, hotels from the famous Ritz-Carlton on Central Park and the Carlyle on the upper East Side, to the Waldorf-Astoria on Park Avenue, to the convention-type Hotel Pennsylvania in the gar-

ment district, and the Milford Plaza on Broadway, are all offering weekend packages. The same is true in major cities throughout the United States, at resorts, and in London, Paris, Rome, Athens, Singapore, Bangkok, and just about any other place you look. Figure 6-14 shows an example.

The hotel package market is defined as the offering of a combination of room and amenities to consumers for an inclusive price. While normally these packages are designed to boost occupancy during low-demand time periods, such as weekends and off-seasons, cases exist where packages are used to maximize revenues at all times.

An example of this might be a resort where a package includes three nights' accommodations and breakfast and dinner daily. The purpose of this combined package is to ensure that, while the hotel is full, the guests are required to make use of the food and beverage facilities. Also, the three nights are sold at once, ensuring their occupancy over the period. If sold individually, one night might sell out before the others, eliminating longer, more desirable bookings. Naturally, the hotel would have to forecast some sig-

FIGURE 6-14 Seducing the weekend package customer

nificant demand to be able to force the customer to purchase that type of package.

We define a package as bundling of goods and services, be it food and beverage, coupons to a nearby retailer, or a welcome gift upon arrival. Often the term is misused to describe blatant discounting. Offering a guestroom at a significant discount is nothing more than that; it certainly does not package anything for the consumer.

An example of this "bundling" of services is Le Meridien Hotel in Boston. The hotel worked closely with a famous retailer, Filene's Basement, on joint marketing promotions as shown in Figure 6-15. The result was satisfied customers and significant business increases for both parties.

First, the needs and problems of the customer must be understood in order to succeed in developing the target package market. What works in one section of the country, or the world, may be completely foreign in another market.

Once the needs of the target package consumer have been identified, the competition needs to be analyzed. As was mentioned earlier, there are very few places left that do not have a myriad of packages for the consumer to buy. Again, the key is the differentiation of the product to the target market. With so many different packages available—and plenty of availability on weekends, or in off-season, or midweek, for some resorts—the creative package must, to capture the market, clearly be better from an offering or price advantage.

From the customer's point of view there are four different advantages to packages, assuming the initial motivation exists from the needs and wants perspective. (In other words, why buy a package when you can do the same thing on your own?) The first advantage is price. The implication with package prices is that the sum is cheaper than the individual parts. This is usually but not always true, and depends heavily on the quality of the parts. A low-rated, ob-

FIGURE 6-15   Hotel weekend packaging with retailers

scure room and an inexpensive split of champagne might be bought cheaper on your own, but many people don't know this, and either don't want or don't know how to take the trouble to find out, so they buy on price. Even when the price is not less, there is a *perception* of value in packages.

The second reason is that packages offer something that people want but probably would not request—for example, breakfast in bed. "It's too expensive, but look, it's included." Or perhaps it's something like horseback riding: "I always wanted to do that but never would have thought of it." Packages remove the worry of "how to," and make it easier for the customer to do whatever it is.

The third reason, and sometimes the greatest, is that packages tend to be more hassle-free. The customer doesn't have to make decisions about where to eat, where to dance, where to go to the theater, how to get there, and so on. This is particularly true for the inexperienced traveler. It is also why carefully thought-out packages can be priced at more than the sum of their parts. The package removes much of the hassle for customers, and they will pay for that, even though they probably think they are getting it cheaper. Packages make the multiple-purchase decision much simpler.

Club Med has become a master at this art by offering a total week's experience at their resorts, including airfare, ground transportation, all food, wine, and sports activities. All you pay for is drinks and you do that with beads, for which you are charged on departure. In fact, Club Med is an excellent example of a marketing-oriented packaging company (Figure 6-16).

When Club Med was first conceived, packages appealed to the younger single set that wanted to get away and meet members of the opposite sex. There was a definite hedonistic overtone to the advertising messages. The market has since changed. Consumers are more conservative, and many of today's Club Med customers are older and married with children. Club Med's product has changed with them, offering a much more wholesome package including a staff pediatrician.

Other companies have taken this one step further to what is called the all-inclusive resort—for instance, Sandals in Jamaica. These packages don't include airfare but they include everything else—all you can drink, for instance, and cigarettes. The price is high but is paid only once. The customer feels that a problem is solved: "I can do whatever I want and don't have to worry about what it costs." Figure 6-17 is an example.

The fourth appeal of some packages is that buyers get something they would not get without the package. That something appeals to a particular interest. One example is the "murder weekend" package that started in England and had mixed success in the United States. With these packages, a couple went to a hotel for the weekend and, with other couples, tried to solve a murder that was literally enacted before their eyes, with all the appropriate clues. With the package, of course, came room, food, and beverages (refer back to Figure 4-1). Murder mystery nights are now sometimes available at restaurants. Other packages of this type are designed for "buffs." For example, there are rock buffs, seashell buffs, bird-watcher buffs, and others. Special activities are planned for these buffs, who know they will be sharing the experience with others of like interest.

There is an important warning about packages that too often is violated: Provide what you promise in the package! This advice is obvious, but is not always followed, resulting in negative feedback for the property. For example, we know one small city hotel that offered the usual weekend package. The main appeal of this package, in the winter in New England, was the indoor pool and lounge area. People from only a few miles away bought the package for that reason. More often than not, the hotel had a wedding party every Saturday afternoon that was held by the pool. Including set-up and break-down time, package customers could not use the pool for much of their stay.

Too often hotels do not deliver on the promises made with their packages. The main reasons for this seem to be that they do not plan for packages and consider them secondary, low-rated business. This is self-defeating and re-

This Summer Join A Health Club, A Golf Club, A Beach Club, A Sailing Club, A Tennis School, A Scuba Class And A Circus Act.

It's all there, all-inclusive and all waiting for you at Club Med. And never before has a summer holiday been a better value.

Select villages throughout the Caribbean, Mexico, French West Indies and Bahamas are being offered starting at $1399. Two new programs are also available at Club Med: "**The Family Dream Vacation**", an irresistible offer for **Parents With Children 2-11 years old** and "**Forever Young**" at selected villages especially for **guests 60 years and over** with savings of $150 per person.*

Summer Dreams for Everyone starting at $1399

For details on the new summer programs, call your travel agent or Club Med at: **(416) 960-3279** or **1-800-268-1160** toll free.

*Certain restrictions apply.

Club Med provides return airfare, village accommodation, 3 gourmet meals a day with unlimited wine and beer at lunch and dinner, a complete sports program with all the equipment and professional instruction, a diverse range of nightly entertainment including cabarets, theatre and discos.

Club Med
If only the real world were this real.

FIGURE 6-16   The Club Med package

"Hey sleepyhead, wake up…"

there's a big, beautiful beach waiting right outside the door.

Mmmm. It'll be there later, trust me.

We're booked for later. We're going to snorkel or windsurf or maybe play volleyball.

Wait a minute. I came down here with my husband Jerry the accountant and I wake up with Superjock?

OK, after breakfast we'll just lounge around in the swim-up pool bar and then we'll devour…

Don't tell me. Lunch.

Hey, at least I worked it off yesterday in the fitness center. All you did was veg out in the whirlpool, putting away those endless cocktails.

I was saving my energy for later.

Now that was a workout.

Get used to it. I meant the romantic candlelight dinner, the wine, the dancing.

Yeah…

And that's why I'm staying right here in this big beautiful bed.

Move over…

Sandals

Exclusive features found only at Sandals Resorts.
Rooms and suites right on the beach. King-size beds, hair dryers, clock/radios in every air-conditioned room • Elegant full-service evening dining • Specialty dining by reservation • Snacks anytime • At least 2 freshwater pools and whirlpools
At least four bars including swim-up pool bars serving unlimited name brand liquors.

Jamaica's #1 All-Inclusive Resorts for Couples Only
Stay at one, play at all four resorts. Sandals Royal Caribbean • Sandals Montego Bay • Sandals Ocho Rios • Sandals Negril
Contact your travel agent or call toll-free in North America **1-800-SANDALS**

FIGURE 6-17   All-inclusive packaging at a resort

sults in extremely negative word-of-mouth. Research on customer complaints has revealed a disproportionate number of complaints about package "promises."

There is another kind of package—the tour group package that includes air and accommodations. This will be described in Chapter 16 on the distribution mix.

The Mature Traveler

The mature traveler market, actually a subsegment of the pleasure market, is another important growth segment for both the hotel and restaurant marketer. Usually defined as aged 55 and over, this market's size is on the increase as people tend to live longer and better. This segment is important to the hospitality industry not just for its size but for two other reasons—mature travelers have time and money. They travel extensively, spending over 50 percent more of their time away from home than the younger pleasure segments. It has often been reported that members of this market are living longer, healthier, and more vigorous lives, are better educated, and have wider interests and activities. Their children are grown, their mortgages are paid, and they have the time, energy, and inclination to travel.

The needs and wants of the senior citizen market are different from those of other segments discussed in this chapter. A recent study reported that "to visit new places" was the number one reason for trips taken by mature travelers, followed by "to visit friends and family."[13] Many mature travelers are price-sensitive and getting a discount is an important attraction. Because they have the flexibility to plan trips any time, they can take advantage of the lowest prices. These travelers use hotels of all price ranges, from luxury to budget, but hotels must be able to provide those attributes that are important to this segment. Some of these attributes include increased security, well-lit public areas, legible signage, no-smoking rooms, easily

---

[13]Senior Traveler Study, *Hotel and Motel Management,* September 9, 1991, p. 31.

maneuverable door handles, grab-bars and supports in bathrooms, and wide doorways to accommodate wheelchairs and walkers.[14]

The senior citizen market is not homogeneous, as recent research has revealed. This market can be segmented in a variety of ways:

Travel habits of mature travelers differ depending on retirement status.
Travel habits are likely to be affected by travelers' life stages as they grow older and encounter physical restrictions.
Mature travelers may prefer to travel as part of a group while others travel in pairs.[15]

Many hotel chains are aggressively pursuing this market (Figure 6-18). Choice Hotels features famous but active seniors in its television advertising. Hilton has a Seniors Honors Program where members can receive up to a 50 percent discount on room rates. Best Western provides the following advertising guidelines to hotel members who want to target this market:

Keep ads and collateral pieces upbeat and positive.
Always depict older customers as active, healthy, and involved.
Use language that is sensitive to mature audiences.
Emphasize convenience.
Show price/value relationship.
Stress service, reliability, and savings.

Restaurants also tap into this market. Active senior citizens spend a large proportion of their food budgets on food away from home and most prefer mid-scale restaurants. Today's seniors are bargain hunters who are conservative in their eating habits. Restaurants should have good lighting to avoid safety hazards, and menus should be easily readable with enough variety to satisfy senior citizens' nutritional needs. Service staffs should be trained to recognize changes in vision and hearing so that people with special needs can be provided better

service without calling attention to their impairments.

The restaurateur can fill some seats early in the evening, since seniors tend to eat dinner earlier. In fact, "sunset dinners" or "early-bird specials" have become quite popular in attracting diners from 5:30 to 7:30 P.M., before the regular patrons arrive. These menu offerings normally include beverage and dessert at an attractive price.

The needs of the senior citizen are basically simple. They are not, as a group, a demanding one. They want rooms close to the lobby, they want help with luggage, and they want information. Like most customers they want clean rooms, convenient location, and value. They do not want to be publicly singled out for service, but at the same time hospitality employees must recognize their special needs and provide them in a subtle way. This market tends not to be rushed through their stay like conferees or businesspeople.

Senior citizens tend to travel outside such traditional times as the businessperson's Monday-through-Thursday, or the weekend package guest's Friday and Saturday. They are also more flexible in rearranging their schedules. Senior travelers can often check in on a Thursday and stay through Monday, making their stay attractive to the hotelier.

As the baby-boom generation in the United States matures, it is quite possible that the needs of this market will further evolve and change. It is up to hospitality corporations to research these needs as they evolve so that this market can be better served.

International Travelers

Tourism is already reputed to be the world's largest retail industry and travel between nations is expected to continue to grow. The U.S. Travel and Tourism Administration estimates 50 million international arrivals spend $85 billion in the U.S.[16] International visitor spending

[14]M. Ananth, F.J. DeMico, P. Moreo, R.M. Howey, "Marketplace Lodging Needs of Mature Travelers," *Cornell Hotel and Restaurant Administration Quarterly,* August, 1992, pp. 12–22.
[15]*Ibid.*

[16]"1993 Outlook for Travel and Tourism," Proceedings of the U.S. Travel Data Center's Annual Travel Outlook Forum. pp. 25–35.

10 to over 50% AARP discounts.

15% AARP discounts.

15% AARP discounts.

15% AARP discounts.

Four Marriott discounts worth checking into.

AARP members can save from 10% to over 50% off the regular room rates at Marriott's family of hotels and resorts nationwide.

Like Marriott full service hotels, moderately priced Courtyard, Residence Inn for extended stays or the economy priced Fairfield Inn. Wherever you're going, there's a Marriott hotel to suit every need. Which means you'll be staying with the name that has become synonymous with quality lodging and dependable service.

For reservations and purchase requirements, call: Marriott Hotels, Resorts & Suites, 800-228-9290; Courtyard, 800-321-2211; Residence Inn, 800-331-3131; Fairfield Inn, 800-228-2800 or your travel agent.

Discount based on availability and cannot be used in conjunction with any other discounts. Important restrictions may apply. Call for complete details. ©1992 Marriott Corporation

AARP is the acronym for American Association of Retired Persons.
Courtesy of Marriott Corporation

FIGURE 6-18   Seducing the mature market

in the U.S. is growing each year and may now account for 25 percent of total tourist spending in the U.S.

Canada and Mexico provide the most tourists to the U.S. because of their contiguous borders. Overseas visitors are led by the Japanese, followed by Europeans from the United Kingdom, Germany, France, and Italy. Growth markets in the future are visitors from Argentina and South Korea which have shown huge increases. In Singapore they target Australians and Japanese. In Thailand they target Germans. In Portugal, Spain, and Turkey they target the British. And so it goes.

The international market is staggering in its size and complexities. Over 400 million people travel outside their own countries every year. This market is obviously not homogeneous and hospitality marketers must be sensitive to the cultural differences of visitors from different nations. Since it is expensive and risky to try to directly market to individual international visitors, hospitality operators often seek out an intermediary, such as a consortium, reservation system, referral network, or tour operator (discussed in Chapter 16) with which to establish marketing relationships.

International trade shows like the Travel Industry Association's Annual POWWOW are also essential for reaching this market. This show brings together tour operators from all over the world who meet with hospitality industry representatives to conduct business. These people account for almost 70 percent of all international tourist arrivals to the U.S. As the number of international travelers has increased, hospitality corporations and tourist destinations have become more user-friendly. However, there is much that can be done.

Not long ago, most U.S. hospitality companies, both small and large, could disregard the international market unless they deliberately chose to enter it. This situation is changing quickly. To this day, foreign visitors to the United States can go to only a very few select hotels in major cities like New York and expect to find someone who speaks their language and exchanges their money, not to mention understanding their needs. The situation is even

worse in restaurants; the only hope for a foreign speaker in this case is to go to a purely ethnic restaurant or hope to have an immigrant waiter or waitress who speaks the same language.

On the other hand, an American can travel almost anywhere overseas and find hotels and restaurants in which at least someone will speak English, or make an honest attempt at it. The overseas hospitality enterprise has long recognized the value of the American market. Even in some remote European or Asian villages it is possible for Americans to communicate basic needs and wants. Contrarily, foreign visitors to the United States are too often greeted with a "Huh?" when trying to communicate in an American hospitality enterprise. This problem goes far beyond the problem of language difficulties; it extends into the area of basic consumer needs and wants. Because many foreign visitors to the United States are able to speak some English, Americans are relieved of the burden of understanding another language, but this does not relieve them of the burden of understanding the customer.

Free Independent Travelers (FIT)

There is a final category of individual travelers that is somewhat of a catch-all for everyone that is left over. In fact, in many hotels' segment breakdowns of their customer base, this may be quite a substantial proportion. That is because everyone that is not known to fit some other category will fall into this one.

The FIT traveler is a "non-organized" visitor who does not belong to a group. While these travelers may well participate in tours during their visit, they essentially come on their own and do as they please. Unidentified business travelers will also be lumped into this category. Hotels catering to the FIT market will usually set aside a block of rooms a year in advance, and fill them in as reservations are made. The lead time may be three to six months in advance. The hotel releases the unused blocked space according to its buy-time schedule.

Both wholesalers and retail agents (who will be discussed in Chapter 16 on distribution) handle the FIT. This segment is normally willing to pay higher rates than group customers. However, a conflict arises with this situation. While the FIT is willing to pay a higher rate because of a lack of volume, the wholesaler and retailer are able to negotiate large discounts due to aggregate FIT bookings.

The resulting savings are not always passed on to the traveler. Therefore, the guest may pay a high price while the hotel receives a relatively low room rate. Often the FIT booked by an intermediary may get the poorest room in the house based on the rate being paid to the hotel. The traveler is at a disadvantage in these situations, and is surprised at the accommodations. This can hurt the hotel that is caught in the middle.

Summary

There is a tremendous amount of research on the topic of consumer behavior and it is impossible to review all of it in any one chapter. However, we have tried to show how some of these theories can be applied to understand the behavior of hospitality customers. This chapter has also shown that it is very difficult to do this because we cannot be sure what goes on in a person's mind. Maslow's hierarchy of needs forms a foundation but perceptions and expectations play an important role. Differences between perceptions and expectations create many challenges for hospitality marketers as seen in the gap model.

Perceptions lead to beliefs, which in turn affect attitudes and much of marketing deals with attitudes and the changing of attitudes. Positive attitudes toward a product or service are required before customers will include it among their choices. Consumer behavior is a complex process, and the different stages are need or problem recognition, search, stimuli selection, alternative evaluation, alternative comparison, and choice.

The key to marketing today is to understand the customer. Good theory provides the basis for that understanding. Applying it will put you light years ahead of those who are still selling when they should be marketing.

In the latter part of this chapter we reviewed the most common broad market segments that are encountered in the marketing of hospitality. There are numerous other segments, as well as more specifically defined target markets. The most important point to remember is that market segments represent groupings of customers with similar needs and problems. Ideally, the scenario would be to operate a hotel or restaurant that catered to one market segment year-round. Unfortunately, this is not often realistically possible. In fact, different segments will often be on premise at the same time, making service and execution of the product difficult. The marketing-oriented team responds to this challenge by truly understanding the needs of the customer, and communicating these needs to the staff that will deliver the product promised.

Discussion Questions

1. Consider Maslow's hierarchy in terms of a hotel and of a restaurant. In each case, name as many attributes as you can that fit each level of the hierarchy. Be prepared to discuss.
2. From a recent paper or magazine, collect a half-dozen hotel or restaurant ads. Discuss them in terms of perception, expectation, beliefs, attitudes, and intentions.
3. List the reference groups that you belong to and how they have shaped your choices of hospitality facilities.
4. Explain the relationship among beliefs, attitudes, and intentions. Discuss how all these interrelate in hospitality consumer behavior.
5. Prepare one example for each of the ten gaps in service quality as applied to the restaurant business.
6. Consider Figure 6-6. Take an example of something you have done or might want to do in terms of a hospitality purchase. Apply the model.
7. What are the major factors that business travelers consider when selecting a hotel?
8. We do not sell hotel rooms to business

travelers, we improve their productivity. Discuss.

9. What role can a hotel play in fulfilling the need for stress reduction that leisure travelers seek.

10. Cases 6-1 and 6-2 consider the negative side of Maslow's hierarchy, perceptions, gaps, beliefs, attitudes and intentions that could quickly stop short the buying decision process. What is going wrong at these hotels? Explain it in terms of the gap model and the customer.

11. Mature travelers' needs will change as the baby-boom generation ages into this market. Discuss.

12. Case 6-3 provides a chance to develop a unique weekend package. Do this applying the concepts discussed in the chapter.

✔ Case 6-1
Little Things Mean a Lot

"Eureka!" cried Jim Jackson to his wife Joan. "We won a free weekend from the drawing at that party we went to last week! A weekend at the Meadow Lodge Resort with deluxe accommodations in a Signature Service room. We also get a free Sunday brunch. All we have to do is call the concierge. Let's go next week, I need a break."

The Meadow Lodge Resort was not far from where Jim and Joan Jackson lived. Next to it was a modern athletic center with, among other things, four tennis courts. Because tennis was the Jacksons' favorite sport, they had often talked about going there for a weekend, just to get away from the "rat race." The resort also featured indoor and outdoor swimming pools and other health center amenities.

Friday Night

The Jacksons arrived at Meadow Lodge about 5:00 P.M. on a Friday afternoon in early June. They planned to play some tennis, do a little swimming, take a whirlpool and sauna, drink wine at the outside pool patio cafe, catch up on some reading, watch a recent movie and, in general, just relax. They arrived in their room full of anticipation.

"Uh-oh, " said Jim, as they entered the room. "There's only one comfortable chair in the room for reading." He called housekeeping and another one was delivered promptly. There was still, however, only one reading lamp for the one chair. He tried to position the desk lamp for the other chair, but it didn't provide enough light. Also, there wasn't any table for either chair on which to put a drink or a coffee cup. "So much for reading," he said, as he positioned the desk chair so at least one of them had a "table."

The Jacksons proceeded to unpack and put their clothes in the two dresser drawers—not that easy since the drawers had no runners and kept sliding askew and falling out. "I wonder where they got this furniture," said Joan.

Jim picked up the TV program to see if he could catch the French Open Tennis Tournament. "Darn! This TV program is for next week," he said. "They've already replaced this week's." He called housekeeping again, but the same program was delivered by a houseman, who then said, "I think I know where there's this week's." The houseman departed quickly and got one.

"Let's play tennis," said Jim. After tennis, they decided to have a drink on the outdoor pool patio, but found it closed. When they returned to their room the phone rang; it was a friend of the Jacksons who lived nearby. They agreed to meet him for a drink at 8:00. "Meet you in the piano lounge," said Jim. "The room directory says it's open until 10:00; it should be nice and quiet."

They went downstairs, met their friend, and went into the piano lounge, which was part of the lobby but sectioned off with comfortable chairs and couches. There was no one else there. As they sat down the piano player said, "The bartender just went home. If you go in the bar and ask, they'll bring you a drink."

The three got up and went into the bar. "We can't stay here," observed Jim. A small TV in one corner of the bar, as well as a large-screen TV in the center were blaring some nonsense, although there was only one other couple in the room who were not watching it. The Jacksons tried to find a corner to get away from the TV, but there was no escaping, so they asked the bartender to serve them in the piano lounge. He replied that he couldn't do that but offered to give them drinks to take out themselves. Jim signed the check and, as they walked out, they picked up some munchies on a table by the bar. "Do you want that charged to your room?" said the bartender.

"We thought they were free snacks," they said.

"Oh, that's okay," said the bartender. "Go ahead and take them. I won't charge you."

They went back to the piano lounge to have their drinks and enjoy the music, but the piano player left at 9:00, about the time they got there.

At 9:45 the Jacksons' friend left and they headed for the Meadow Lodge's "casual" restaurant, which closed at 10:00. The hostess greeted them with, "We close in 15 minutes."

"Does that mean you'll throw us out at 10:00?" Joan asked.

"No, but we close in 15 minutes," responded the hostess as she led them to a table, where she repeated the admonishment a third time. There was only a party of two in the restaurant that looked like it could seat 150. The hostess seated them in a dark corner, close by the kitchen entrance. "Do you have another table?" they asked, and were led to a table near the door. They ordered light and ate quickly.

The Jacksons went back to their room and turned on a pay movie. It was too fuzzy to watch, so they turned it off and went to sleep. The next morning the desk clerk removed the pay TV charge from their bill and told them, if it happened again, to call maintenance.

Saturday

The Jacksons got up at 7:00 A.M. and made some coffee in the in-room coffee maker. They found orange juice and cream in the mini-bar, but it was so warm they were hesitant to use it.

"Let's go for a swim," said Joan.

"Better check first to see if it's open," said Jim.

Joan looked in the room directory and saw that the pool opened at 7:00. "But it's closed from 8:30 to 9:00," she said. "What's the point in going, it's already after 8:00. I wonder why they do that with all these people in the hotel on weekend packages?"

They decided to spend the day driving around the countryside instead.

Later in the day, back in their room, the Jacksons had a glass of wine and tried to decide where to go for dinner. Not wanting to get back in the car and drive again, they decided to go back to the Meadow Lodge's restaurant. This time they went earlier, about 8:00. There was a party of six and another couple in the dining room. Again, they were seated in the dark corner, next to the party of six, and once again they asked to move. They were moved again near the

door, right in front of where the buffet was being set up for Sunday brunch. "What's the use?" they said.

The hostess, a different one, overheard them and came back to ask if they would like to move. "Yes," they said. "We'd like to sit near a window."

The hostess departed and talked to the waitress who, shortly after, came to take their order.

"The hostess said we could move."

"Well," was the reply, "she talked to me, but I'm the only one on tonight and that section is closed."

The pained expression on the Jacksons' faces then must have moved the waitress, so with a "Well, all right," she took them to a window table. She wasn't too pleasant, however, the rest of the meal. The Jacksons finished dinner and went to their room, where they finally found a movie to watch that was clear.

Sunday

Sunday, the Jacksons slept late, then packed their bags before going downstairs to have their "free" Sunday brunch in the same dining room where they had been twice for dinner. This time there were about 20 people in the room, but again they were led to the same dark corner table. As they muttered, the waitress overheard them.

"Would you like to move?" she asked.

"We'd really like to sit by the window on such a beautiful day," they replied.

"Fine," she said, "but I'll have to set up the table because that section is closed."

"Never mind," the Jacksons surrendered, "we'll stay here."

After brunch, which turned out to be delightful, the Jacksons checked out. As they pulled out of the driveway, Jim said, "Well, that's the last time for that place—even if it was free."

"Not really," said Joan, as she looked at the bill. "We spent over $200, but it wasn't so bad. It's a nice hotel and at least some of the people were certainly nice and responsive when you asked."

"I know," said Jim, "but it's the little things that make the difference."

✔ Case 6-2

Nightmare at the Resort[17]

John Sessions and his family drove up in front of the well-known Super Resort Hotel for a long-anticipated two-week stay, but a puzzling series of events curtailed it. Their car was parked by resort personnel, which they later learned meant a 15- to 25-minute wait each time they wanted to pick up the car. This became a daily ordeal despite repeated pleas that somehow the service be speeded up.

John and his wife, two sons, 13 and 14, their daughter, 19, a girlfriend, 20, and John's mother and sister had reserved four concierge-floor rooms. Although the reservations, confirmed by the hotel, had been made months in advance for four concierge-level rooms (with an inside door connecting two of these rooms and two double beds in three of them), they were forced to accept no connecting rooms, two rooms with king beds, and one boy had to sleep on a roll-away cot.

Using the Resort's Facilities

On the first day, the daughter and her friend went to the highly-touted health club to see the exercise facilities, but they were told they would have to pay $15 each just to look, even though their group was paying well over $1,000 a day for their rooms. They did not pay and thus did not see the facilities.

On the second day, the family needed some laundry done. It was left outside the door, early, for guaranteed pickup, as requested. Returning after breakfast, they found the laundry still there. A phone call to housekeeping brought an apology, an immediate pickup, and an emergency delivery to an outside laundry service. John's confidence in the hotel's reliability suffered another dip.

On day three, the family decided to eat lunch at one of the resort's nicer restaurants. They were told, "Sorry, we're closed for the week. Please go to another restaurant." They did go to another restaurant where they could sit outside on a warm, sunny day. "Sorry," they were told, "outside seating is only available in the summer." They went inside where they were seated in the back, facing the wall, rather than the empty front area with a beautiful water view.

The two boys became ill. The hotel called a doctor who charged $150 each to examine them, would give no prescription, and told them to come to his office in two days for $50 each. Thanks, but no thanks, they said, and the boys recovered on their own.

On the fourth day, one of the boys walked into the concierge lounge for a soda and was told he was not allowed in without a parent. John then accompanied his son to the lounge for a soda.

On the sixth morning, John walked into the concierge lounge for breakfast with his two sons. "Sorry," he was told, "rules and regulations. Nobody under 18 is allowed to eat here," although they had been eating there for almost a week.

"You should rethink your policy," suggested John to the attendant, who assured him, "Your children have been perfectly behaved and are no problem, but we must enforce the policy."

The following day, that attendant's superior encountered John, severely upbraided him, and said the policy would be enforced under all conditions with no exceptions.

Now You Want Me!

Not too surprisingly, John called a nearby competing resort, obtained guarantees that he would encounter no such problems there, and checked his family out of the first resort. As they left, the hotel's general manager pleaded with them to stay, apologized profusely, and admitted that everything they had suffered had been due to the hotel's negligence. He also offered to waive the lounge policy for children

---

[17]Adapted with permission from an editorial by Charles Bernstein, Editor, *Nation's Restaurant News*, February 5, 1990, p. 27. Copyright 1990, Nation's Restaurant News. Names have been disguised.

under 18. John thanked him, drove two miles to the other hotel, and enjoyed a great week's vacation at a far lower price.

A busy and harried staff? Hardly. The hotel was at 20 percent occupancy when all this occurred.

On returning home, John's wife wrote to the general manager of the hotel, related the incidents, and asked how they could call themselves a hotel geared for family-type holidays. The general manager replied immediately:

Please accept our apologies for not properly communicating our concierge lounge policy and for the subsequent frustration and embarrassment experienced by your family. As an expression of our good faith, and in the hope that you will one day return to our hotel, we are enclosing a $1,814.40 check.... We also invite you to enjoy a complimentary brunch for six people.... We want you to be assured that your experience was a gross exception to the norm. Your letter has been shared with the appropriate personnel and corrective action has been taken.

✔ Case 6-3
Weekend at the Ritz[18]

The Ritz Hotel on Place Vendome in Paris, France has long been considered one of the super-deluxe hotels of the world. It first opened in 1898 under the ownership and management of Cesar Ritz with the famed Auguste Escoffier as chef in the kitchen. A long line of celebrities, down to the present day, have enjoyed its grandeur and stayed at the Ritz, for it is known to cater to even the slightest whim of its guests. This does not mean, however, that the hotel has not had its ups and downs.

The Ritz in the 1980s

The Ritz Hotel had become somewhat run-down and was badly in need of a capital infusion. Egyptian Mohammed Fayed bought the hotel for US$29 million. Fayed wanted to own the finest hotel in the world and an unlimited budget was supplied in refurbishing the hotel; $150 million was eventually spent in renovations of the 142 rooms, 45 suites, and all public spaces as well as service areas. An additional $50 million was spent to install a luxurious, large swimming pool, lounge, and state-of-the-art health spa in the basement of the hotel.

Occupancy was 50 percent at an ADR of $360. The goal set for the next year was 67 percent occupancy with an ADR of $407. Rack rates were set at a minimum of $306 for a single to a maximum of $7,538 for the Imperial Suite, per night. There were 540 staff to serve the 187 rooms and the food and beverage outlets, or about 2.83 staff per room.

The hotel had a two-star Michelin-rated restaurant with 125 seats.[19] As a matter of practice, however, only 75 to 80 seats were sold at a time in order to be able to provide the maximum in fine service. The restaurant did extremely well with very high check averages. There were

also three bars that served food. There was the world-famous Hemingway bar, a pool (indoor) bar, and one other bar. There also was a nightclub with 150 seats, serving a limited dinner with a check average of $50. This nightclub had members as well, 300 of them who paid 5,000 French francs each for the privilege of going there.

The Ritz was a member of the referral and reservation system of Leading Hotels of the World, a group of about 200 fine, independent hotels worldwide. This service produced 30 percent of the Ritz' business, with about 65 percent of that coming from the United States. Another 45 percent of the business came direct, through mail or personal calls, and the other 25 percent came through travel agents.

Targeted markets of the Ritz were the international elite, high corporate business, and other well-to-do individuals who didn't meet either of those criteria. Segments were 70 percent FIT individual, 20 percent corporate, and ten percent "elite." Geographical sources of business were 45 percent United States, 35 percent Europe, 12 percent Japan, and eight percent other.

The Ritz marketing department analyzed its competition and gave each hotel a rating on location and image. This analysis is shown in Table 6-3-1.

To fill in soft periods, the Ritz developed a cooking school program promotion that proved quite successful. One could attend a demonstration for $46, a Master Class demonstration for $90 (held four times a month), a weekly program for $615, or a six-month program for $8000.

The Ritz Weekend

The marketing department saw the weekend market as one answer to their low-occupancy problem. Weekends normally ran only about 45 percent occupancy, and marketing looked for some way to boost this percentage. Both the

---

[18]Sylvain Ercoli provided the information for this case. All dollar amounts are in U.S. currency.

[19]Michelin's highest rating is three stars; normally, fewer than a dozen restaurants in France are given this rating.

TABLE 6-3-1   Rating the Ritz Competition

	Rooms	Occ	ADR	Location	Image
Ritz	187	50%	$360	7	10
Bristol	200	64	277	7	8
Plaza Athenee	246	60	270	9	7
Le Crillon	200	67	246	8	6
George V	300	49	200	8	4

Note: All hotels are French government-rated four-star luxe, the highest rating in France, except the Crillon, which is four-star.

George V and the Plaza Athenee offered standard weekend packages. Other hotels, such as the Inter-Continental Grand, were known to offer weekend packages, but one had to be clever to get them. For example, at its front desk, the Grand offered a minimum rate of $250, with a promised upgrade, but if one called and asked specifically for a weekend package, the rate given was $125 per room.

The Ritz marketing staff wondered if they should offer a weekend package. If so, what should it look like?

CHAPTER 7

The Organizational Customer and Planner

The organizational planner is defined as the purchaser of hospitality products for a group or organization that has a common purpose. This customer's needs are somewhat different from those of the individual customers described earlier. Although all of the basic principles are the same as described in Chapter 6—stimuli, search, perceptions, beliefs, attitudes, etc.—organizational planners are essentially buying for someone else who is the actual user. Although both the planner or arranger and the user are organizational customers, we will use the term *customer* for the actual user who is not the buyer. We will use the term *planner* for the buyer who is not the end-user. Planners seek to satisfy all the needs and wants of the users, as a group, which is why this is often called the group market. Planners are intermediaries. They may "sell" to the organizational customer, just as travel agents, tour operators, and incentive travel planners do; or, as is the case with meetings and convention planners, they may organize and plan on demand of the organizational customer.

Although there are a number of target market categories in the organizational market, we can define them in seven major segments: the corporate travel market; the corporate meetings market; the incentive market; the association, convention, and trade show market; the airline crew market; the *social, military, education, religious, and fraternal* (SMERF) and government markets; and the group tour and travel market. The planners for each of these categories of customers purchase hospitality services for a group of people with a common purpose.

For marketing purposes, as we have said, there is a difference between planners' needs and the needs of individual customers. The planner is not, in the true sense, the end-user of the product. When a couple books a hotel room on a weekend package, it knows what its expectations will be: The expectations are their own. Similarly, business travelers may choose to be close to their business location for the next day, sometimes at the expense of comfort. The needs and purpose of these customers are individualized; the similarity, of course, is that in either case if expectations are not met, the customer may go somewhere else the next time.

The Generic Organizational Market

The planner intends to satisfy, perhaps, 25 to 5,000 individual needs. Although the group may have a common purpose, such as a corporate business meeting, a computer industry convention, or an insurance salespeople's incentive trip, each member of the group may have somewhat different individual needs. This makes the overall task for planning somewhat more formidable for the planner.

The problem has grown greater in recent years due to the corporate trend toward "downsizing." Large corporations have trimmed their workforces by tens of thousands of employees. Many meeting planners have been included in the downsizing, leaving meeting planning tasks to administrative assistants who lack experience in this field. This gives the meetings marketer an even more critical task—a need to understand the buyer. This has also led to more independent professional meeting planners, who do not work for just one company but plan meetings for any number of company clients.

Specifically, the planner must try to anticipate the needs of the group, as well as to select the proper facilities to accomplish its common purpose. For example, the meeting planner of a corporation may be given the task of planning a sales conference for the international division. The planner must understand the needs of that particular department within the company, with which he or she normally has very little contact, as well as the needs of the individual members.

At times, planners may not even visit the hotels or restaurants to which they send their organizational group. Thus, to make the right decision, the planner needs to rely on a different set of stimuli from those used by other customers. Various research studies have shown that word-of-mouth from fellow planners ranks first as probably the predominant factor in choosing facilities. Recommendations from others within the organizational group rank second in the decision-making process, with direct sales efforts by suppliers ranking third. Advertising ranks far down the list of possible influences on the planner. Regardless, hotels are heavy advertisers in publications such as *Meetings & Conventions, Successful Meetings,* and *Corporate Meetings and Incentives.*

Planners rely on hotel salespeople far more than do individual customers. Also, conference coordinators of the hotel, who handle the details, become extremely important in the decision to book, and to re-book after the event is over. Even the chef, who is going to be serving perhaps 300 attendees three meals a day, becomes critical. The organizational customer is at far more risk from a bad meal than the weekend package customer who is not pleased with an individual meal.

There is evidence, however, that as planners gain more experience on the job, they are less influenced by the salespeople. In the case of the incentive buyer, it has been found that only about 25 percent of those planners with more than five years' experience are greatly influenced by salespeople.[1] These people and many other planners want to see for themselves, and will visit the property before booking it. There is an increased professionalism among experienced planners, evident in the way they go about inspecting properties and setting up meetings.

> The smart salesperson moves the selling session away from price and toward service and the benefits of using the service. All planners, no matter what their depth of competence, are most concerned that the hotel and its staff perform so that their meetings are successful. Quite often a planner's promotion—or even her job—is on the line.
>
> Even if the hotel was entirely at fault, it is ultimately the responsibility of the planner who chose the wrong site for the meeting.[2]

Some planners have said,

> You can have the most gorgeous facility in the world....I still need professional staff to augment what I do....I often follow the same people as they move from hotel to hotel.
>
> The people I do meetings for like to be pampered a little bit. A property may be less than desirable, but if they can provide service and if the food is good we can overlook the other things.

---

[1]Robert C. Lewis, "The Incentive Travel Market: How to Reap Your Share," *Cornell Hotel and Restaurant Administration Quarterly,* May, 1983, pp. 19–27.

[2]Margaret Shaw, *The Group Market: What It Is and How to Sell It,* Washington D.C.: The Hotel Sales and Marketing Association International Foundation, 1985, p. 9.

What's important to me is…that everything I've ordered is there.

Problems occur when hotels don't deliver what they say they can deliver.[3]

Figure 7-1 shows site selection criteria of association and corporate meeting planners.

The Organizational Customer Buying Process

To begin to understand the needs of the organizational customer and planner, it is important to see how the planning process should go for a meeting or function. Understanding this, the sales and operations departments of a hotel can anticipate problems before they happen, perhaps preserving the success of an entire meeting.

Buy Time   Each segment of customers purchases its hotel product at various stages of the decision-making process. A corporate traveler may make reservations one week in advance of an upcoming trip. The convention planner is booking business as far as ten years in advance. A weekend package user may buy on impulse within a few days or a few hours of check-in. The tour operator will have routes calculated a year in advance. Some lead times required for different corporate meetings groups, in the United States, are shown in Figure 7-2.

Knowing the timing of the purchase is important in selecting potential market segments. In order to maximize revenues, the ideal business mix of segments may include a variety of customers. With the different room rate potential of each customer grouping, managing the inventory becomes critical.

For example, a 400-room hotel may have an opportunity to sell 350 rooms to a midweek convention three years in advance at a rate of $75. At first glance, this would appear to be a good decision. The hotel will likely be sold out during this period, and the sales department can spend its time trying to fill other, less busy time periods. More careful analysis, however, shows that this hotel has an average of 200 rooms per night occupied by business travelers during the week. The rate this year is $100, and in three years is expected to be at $125. Few business travelers plan business trips three years in advance. These travelers will be calling the hotel one to three weeks in advance for their room reservations, unaware of the convention that is being held there at that time. If all patterns hold, the hotel will lose $50 per room on the 150 rooms that it should have held for the segment that pays a higher rate, but books the shortest lead time. Mistakes like this are very subtle, because the hotel "appears" sold out, yet the revenues are decreased by $7,500. The hotel may also alienate some regular customers who cannot get rooms. It does not take many miscalculations like this to bring home the importance of the lead time of market segments. Dealing with this has led to a practice called yield management, which will be discussed in detail in Chapter 12.

On the other hand, another buy time variable is the use of a property at different periods of time. City hotels generally target business travelers and conventions during the week and pleasure travelers on weekends. The same variation occurs between summer and winter. Thus, many hotels offer "package" meetings at special rates during slow periods, just as they do for individual travelers, as shown in Figure 7-3. Resort hotels have similar situations, depending on the season of the year. At one time, many of these hotels simply closed during the "off-season." Now most stay open year-round but seek different markets, such as meetings and conventions.

Assess the Needs   Each body of people with a common purpose has different needs as an organization. The Elks Club (the *F* in SMERF) certainly has a different reason for meeting than does the new product development team for Eastman Kodak Co., yet both of these organizations may meet in the same meeting room, in the same hotel, at the same

---

[3]Quoted in Kathy Seal, "Staff, service, top priorities for planners," *Hotel & Motel Management,* July 20, 1987, pp. 40, 42, 43.

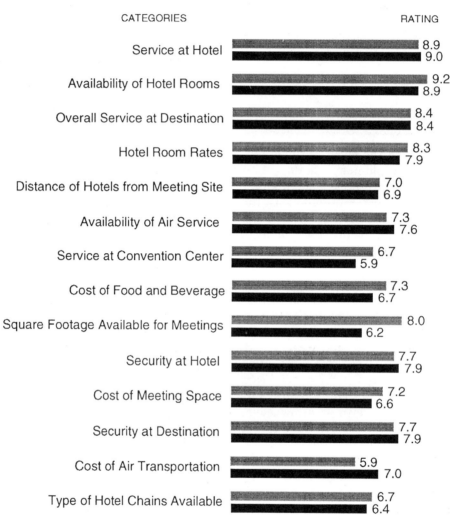

Site Selection Criteria
(Rated On a Scale Of 1-10)
1992

CATEGORIES	RATING
Service at Hotel	8.9 / 9.0
Availability of Hotel Rooms	9.2 / 8.9
Overall Service at Destination	8.4 / 8.4
Hotel Room Rates	8.3 / 7.9
Distance of Hotels from Meeting Site	7.0 / 6.9
Availability of Air Service	7.3 / 7.6
Service at Convention Center	6.7 / 5.9
Cost of Food and Beverage	7.3 / 6.7
Square Footage Available for Meetings	8.0 / 6.2
Security at Hotel	7.7 / 7.9
Cost of Meeting Space	7.2 / 6.6
Security at Destination	7.7 / 7.9
Cost of Air Transportation	5.9 / 7.0
Type of Hotel Chains Available	6.7 / 6.4

■ Association Planners
■ Corporate Planners

Base: Association 176, Corporate 525

Source: Successful Meetings, July, 1993, pp. 60–61. Reprinted with permission.

FIGURE 7-1   Site selection criteria of association and corporate meeting planners

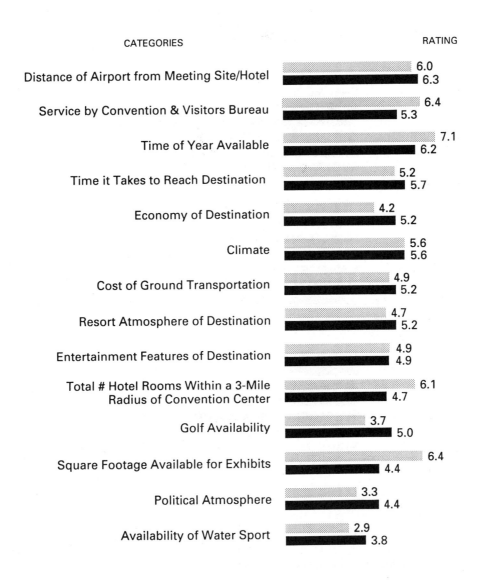

CATEGORIES	RATING

- Distance of Airport from Meeting Site/Hotel — 6.0 / 6.3
- Service by Convention & Visitors Bureau — 6.4 / 5.3
- Time of Year Available — 7.1 / 6.2
- Time it Takes to Reach Destination — 5.2 / 5.7
- Economy of Destination — 4.2 / 5.2
- Climate — 5.6 / 5.6
- Cost of Ground Transportation — 4.9 / 5.2
- Resort Atmosphere of Destination — 4.7 / 5.2
- Entertainment Features of Destination — 4.9 / 4.9
- Total # Hotel Rooms Within a 3-Mile Radius of Convention Center — 6.1 / 4.7
- Golf Availability — 3.7 / 5.0
- Square Footage Available for Exhibits — 6.4 / 4.4
- Political Atmosphere — 3.3 / 4.4
- Availability of Water Sport — 2.9 / 3.8

1=NOT IMPORTANT
10=EXTREMELY IMPORTANT

FIGURE 7-1   (continued)

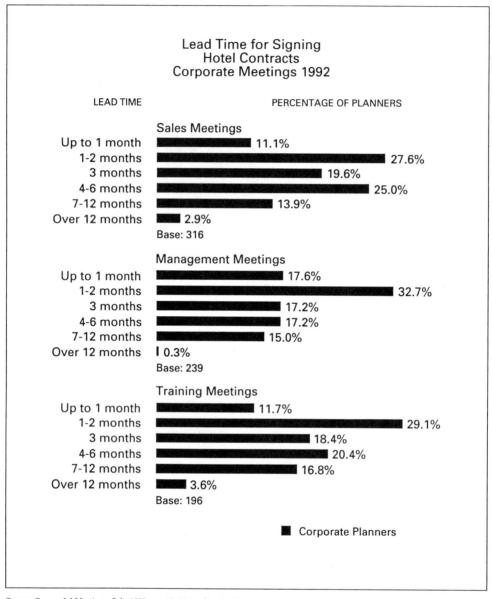

Source: Successful Meetings, July, 1993, pp. 41, 43, 51. Reprinted with permission.

FIGURE 7-2   Lead times for signing hotel contracts before the event

time of the year. Both the planner and the hotel employees must understand the purpose of the meeting. If, in fact, the meeting is purely a social one, theme parties, golf outings, fashion shows, and so on are expected and welcomed. If, however, the purpose of the meeting is to devise strategies that will bring a corporation out of bankruptcy, the entire agenda will be altered accordingly. These are obvious differences; there are many far more subtle ones.

The most common complaint planners have about hotel salespeople does not relate either to high-pressure selling or to cold calls—although they don't particularly like either one. It is that the salesperson has not taken the time to find out about their business. Often they are pitched by a

Lead Time for Signing
Hotel Contract
Incentive Travel 1992

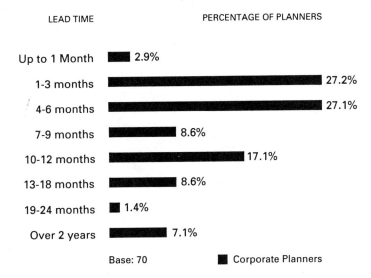

LEAD TIME   PERCENTAGE OF PLANNERS

Lead Time	Percentage
Up to 1 Month	2.9%
1-3 months	27.2%
4-6 months	27.1%
7-9 months	8.6%
10-12 months	17.1%
13-18 months	8.6%
19-24 months	1.4%
Over 2 years	7.1%

Base: 70   ■ Corporate Planners

Lead Time For Signing
Hotel Contract
International Meetings & Incentives 1992

LEAD TIME   PERCENTAGE OF PLANNERS

Lead Time	Association Planners	Corporate Planners
Up to 1 month	5.3%	5.8%
1-3 months	10.5%	30.4%
4-6 months	10.5%	17.4%
7-9 months	0%	7.3%
10-12 months	26.3%	26.1%
More than 12 months	47.3%	13.1%

Base: Association 19, Corporation 69   ▨ Association Planners
                                             ■ Corporate Planners

FIGURE 7-2   (continued)

FIGURE 7-3   Promoting meeting packages in the off-season

property wholly unsuited to their needs and resent the fact that their time is being wasted by someone who didn't even make the effort to find out what they were like.[4]

Set Measurable Goals   For the planner, nothing can be managed if it cannot be measured. It is critical that the needs of the meeting be translated into measurable results. Corporate planners can measure results from their agenda. If the meeting purpose is to brainstorm for a new product, the success of the meeting can be judged on whether the product is ever developed. For the incentive planner, post-trip evaluations are helpful. The goal may be that 90 percent of the winners of the incentive would return next year if given the opportunity. From the hotel side, if the planner does not set measurable goals, success for the meeting becomes subjective rather than objective and minor discrepancies are susceptible to magnified scrutiny.

---

[4]Shaw, *The Group Market,* p. 15.

Develop a Plan   The plan needs to be concise and to lead directly from the goals and needs of the organization. The plan should include hotel and non–hotel-related activities. Airline tickets, ground transportation to and from the airport, excursions and transportation of materials are all items that must be incorporated into the plan. An organizational planner without a plan is one who must be helped through the process by the hotel marketer.

It is the responsibility of the hotel that wants satisfied customers to assist inexperienced planners with all phases of the meeting. Earlier in the chapter the changing profile of the planner, in the wake of corporate downsizing, was discussed. Many hotels, accustomed in the past to working with meeting professionals, now find these duties in some cases assigned to staff with little or no experience in this area. For example, the bylaws of the organization may stipulate that the secretary of the group is responsible for the annual convention. If the newly elected secretary has no prior planning experience, the hotel staff needs to give assurance that all phases of the meeting will be accommodated. It will do the hotel no good to have a disorganized function come to fruition. Once the salesperson senses an absence of knowledge, a different selling scenario should be employed.

During the planning process, it may be found that the planner did not allow the proper timing between sessions for the group to move from the meeting rooms to the ballroom for lunch. In such a situation, the conference coordinator must be knowledgeable enough to steer the planner toward realistic timing of events. An example occurred in the city of Boston, where two hotels formed a strategic alliance to market themselves. The "Copley Connection" combined the guest rooms of the Marriott Copley Place and Westin Hotel (Figure 7-4). Together their facilities offered the planner 1,500 guestrooms committed to groups with 100,000-plus square feet of function space. The hotels were marketed together, as one big place to have a meeting. Although the hotels were connected by a skywalk, planners soon found that it took 30 minutes to move a group from the ballroom of the Marriott to a function room at the Westin. Experienced planners adjusted their agendas accordingly; others found the spaces and distances to be problematic.

On the other hand, professional planners are also becoming better educated as to what is best for their meetings. For example, a hotel salesperson might book another group into the meeting room next to the general session of the conference. The planner might, in this instance, insist that the space be utilized for his or her luncheon, thereby preventing any unanticipated interruptions from the group next door.

Resolve Conflicts   Planners have to work in tandem with both the hotel and their own organizations to anticipate and resolve potential problems. While planning may alleviate possible conflicts, the hotel may be only half of the problem. The organization itself presents problems that must be addressed before the function occurs. There may be a hierarchy within the organization that needs suites, first-class travel, and seats at the head table. Failing to accommodate these needs can cause conflicts that ruin the meeting through no fault of the hotel. A hotel staff can anticipate these needs by asking to review the VIP list and discussing its needs.

There are numerous other potential issues: Non-smoking guestrooms and meeting rooms are entering into the spectrum of worries. Individual special meals during a banquet are no longer limited to just kosher meals. Many banquet meals now require low-salt or vegetarian plates to satisfy the needs of attendees.

The best way to resolve possible conflicts for both sides is to have a preconference meeting. (The term *preconference* is generic, and can be applied to incentive trips as well as to corporate meetings.) At this meeting, the planner reviews the details of the meeting with each department to ensure that communications have not been distorted through the conference coordinator. The front office and banquet managers, and general manager if the situation warrants, should be in attendance with the salesperson and conference coordinator to ensure that all potential conflicts are discussed and remedied before the function occurs.

BOSTON

The Copley Connection

"PROUD TO HOST PCMA '91"

TWO HOTELS WORKING TOGETHER IN WAYS YOU NEVER THOUGHT POSSIBLE

Boston's always been a proven draw for meeting attendance. Now this great city offers you "The Largest Complete Meeting Facility on The East Coast...The Copley Connection."

The Copley Connection is a joint venture of two world class hotels and an outstanding shopping facility. The Westin Hotel Copley Place, the Boston Marriott Copley Place and The Copley Place Shopping Galleries... three luxurious properties all under one roof. It's the ultimate convenience for meeting planners, delegates and conventioneers.

The Copley Connection makes it easy for you, the meeting planner, to schedule a major convention using two hotels while you and your delegates receive the services associated with one luxury facility. It is truly one of the most innovative ideas in the group meeting industry today. Other hotels are promoting themselves together, but no other hotel partnership provides meeting planners and delegates the exceptional combination of services, accommodations, and conveniences unique to The Copley Connection.

COPLEY PLACE

THE WESTIN HOTEL COPLEY PLACE

FIGURE 7-4 A strategic alliance to attract large groups

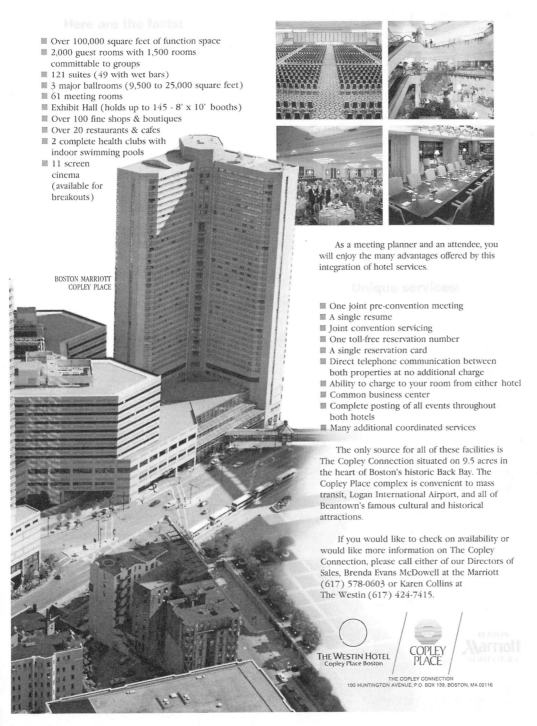

Here are the facts:

- Over 100,000 square feet of function space
- 2,000 guest rooms with 1,500 rooms committable to groups
- 121 suites (49 with wet bars)
- 3 major ballrooms (9,500 to 25,000 square feet)
- 61 meeting rooms
- Exhibit Hall (holds up to 145 - 8' x 10' booths)
- Over 100 fine shops & boutiques
- Over 20 restaurants & cafes
- 2 complete health clubs with indoor swimming pools
- 11 screen cinema (available for breakouts)

BOSTON MARRIOTT
COPLEY PLACE

As a meeting planner and an attendee, you will enjoy the many advantages offered by this integration of hotel services.

Unique services:

- One joint pre-convention meeting
- A single resume
- Joint convention servicing
- One toll-free reservation number
- A single reservation card
- Direct telephone communication between both properties at no additional charge
- Ability to charge to your room from either hotel
- Common business center
- Complete posting of all events throughout both hotels
- Many additional coordinated services

The only source for all of these facilities is The Copley Connection situated on 9.5 acres in the heart of Boston's historic Back Bay. The Copley Place complex is convenient to mass transit, Logan International Airport, and all of Beantown's famous cultural and historical attractions.

If you would like to check on availability or would like more information on The Copley Connection, please call either of our Directors of Sales, Brenda Evans McDowell at the Marriott (617) 578-0603 or Karen Collins at The Westin (617) 424-7415.

THE WESTIN HOTEL
Copley Place Boston

COPLEY
PLACE

Boston
Marriott
COPLEY PLACE

THE COPLEY CONNECTION
100 HUNTINGTON AVENUE, P.O. BOX 139, BOSTON, MA 02116

FIGURE 7-4   (continued)

Execute the Meeting This may be the simplest phase of the planner's job, if all the previous steps were followed. If they were not, this is certainly the hardest portion of the process. The execution of the meeting could occur without the planner being in attendance. The needs of the planner are now being transferred onto the group.

Sometimes, even if the organizational planner is on the site, the end-users' needs are not met. For example, the association planner may want the general session set up theater-style, with the room's chairs facing the podium for a guest speaker. The guest speaker might demand that the room be set up classroom-style, with each chair having a desk in front of it so that participants can write in conjunction with the presentation. Two of the authors once attended a function in Chicago where the meeting specifications called for a podium on the platform. At the last minute it was decided by the meeting organizers that a sit-down panel format would be more appropriate. It really did not matter how many times the organizers changed their mind about the set-up of the room. The hotel was responsible for making the changes; the flustered set-up man clearly was annoyed.

These are classic examples of how the planner is not the end-user, and the needs of the group change right up to the last minute. The hotel that adjusts accordingly will be the one that receives the future business. There are no right and wrong sides to this scenario. The task must be completed to satisfy the needs of both the end-user and the organizational planner.

Evaluate the Results Based upon the goals of the organization, was the meeting a success? The hotel should be interested in the results as much as is the planner. The evaluation process can take place in a post-conference meeting held shortly after the conclusion of the function. Department heads and the planner can review face-to-face all the things that went right, as well as those that went wrong. The marketing-oriented organization will take immediate steps to correct the malfunctions and to reinforce the positive aspects. Some details of meeting rights and wrongs are

revealed in a critical incident study by Rutherford and Umbreit that is recommended for additional insight into this critical process.[5]

The evaluation process is also critical for the planner. When customers are buyers who may not be present at the actual event, it may be difficult for them to understand exactly what took place. Even when the hotel delivers as promised, the organization may not have accomplished its goals. The planner will need to assess the results before starting to plan the next similar function, and should be made aware of the problem areas. We will now discuss each of the various organizational market categories mentioned at the beginning of the chapter.

The Corporate Travel Market

The planner for the corporate market plans the travel and entertainment for a corporate group. The term *group* needs to be interpreted loosely here. Corporate travel planners are different from corporate meeting planners (discussed in this chapter's next section) in that they plan for a group of people with a common purpose, although with individual travel schedules. A common purpose still exists, since the corporate entity is relatively homogeneous. In some organizations, the travel planner and the meeting planner are the same person.

The size of the corporate travel market is very large, running into tens of millions of business travelers. About half of these end-users are directed or influenced by the corporate planner who plans, controls, mediates, negotiates, evaluates and/or approves their travel expenditures. This market is very desirable for hotels because it tends to pay good rates, is large in size, and travels consistently throughout most of the year. Executive clubs like that shown in Figure 7-5 are popular with this market.

The corporate planner in this case needs to find the correct products for the entire corporate entity. Once the product is identified, the

---

[5]Denney G. Rutherford and W. Terry Umbreit, "Improving Interactions between Meeting Planners and Hotel Employees," *Cornell Hotel and Restaurant Administration Quarterly,* February, 1993, pp. 68–80.

*We make sure that
you always have
reason to say "Cheers".*

The Executive Club makes eminent business sense. Not only because it's the finest business address in town.

But also because of the exclusive privileges that Executive Clubbers enjoy.

...An exclusive express check in.

A work table with an extra phone. And the Club Lounge, with the Club Hour every evening.

The piece de resistance, however, is the way we look after you - indulgently, but without intrusion.

For the discerning business traveller.

IN NEW DELHI, BOMBAY, MADRAS & BANGALORE. AND NOW OPEN, RAJPUTANA PALACE SHERATON, JAIPUR.

ITC-WELCOMGROUP
Hotels, palaces and resorts

FIGURE 7-5 Executive club for corporate travelers in India

best rates are negotiated. The supplier needs to understand the culture of the organization to fulfill its needs. For example, some companies go to the top of the line for their hospitality and service needs. From first-class airplane seats, to limousines for ground transport, to the best hotel in the area, some companies spare no expense when entertaining themselves or their customers.

Some corporate cultures are just the opposite. They use hotel rooms sparingly, have meetings in their own offices, and use cabs or airport shuttles to reach hotels. Negotiations with a large corporate planner at an Embassy Suites Hotel revealed such a culture. After renovation, the hotel approached a major customer for a rate increase. During the sales call, the customer did not disagree that the hotel was improved, and worth more money, but simply said that the company at this time would not pay more than $45 for a hotel room, even in a Ritz-Carlton. The Embassy Suites lost the business.

Most companies are somewhere in between the cultures described above, despite hotel ads that seem to assume that all corporate customers expect Rolls Royces to whisk them to the hotel. Typically, corporate executives get the best treatment and company trainees the least. It mostly comes down to examining the purpose of travel, who is traveling, and what is their position.

Only recently have many companies come to realize the extent of their travel and entertainment budgets, in some cases as much as 25 percent of an organization's costs. Today, a majority of corporations are tightening the screws on travel costs. As one corporate travel planner told us, "You can't believe what $5 a night means over a year's time." Figure 7-6 shows a hotel company advertising to this need.

Digital Equipment Company in Boston is a case in point. During the high-flying 1980s, the company sponsored a customer event called "DecWorld." Every hotel room within 50 miles of the city was sold out for two weeks. Banquet rooms, restaurants, and limo companies shared the wealth. Digital even brought in the Queen Elizabeth cruise ship to house some VIPs. Total cost was about $33 million.

DecWorld 1991, however, was a very different event. The theme for this customer event was education, not entertainment. The city of Boston again sold out, but that was all. Entertaining took on a serious tone, real business was conducted, and the Queen Elizabeth never made it to Boston for this event—total cost, about $17 million. Lesson learned, the "no holds barred" expense accounts of the 1980s have given way to the well-planned customer educational programs of the 1990s.

The way corporations spend their travel and entertainment dollars significantly affects the revenues of the hospitality industry. The emergence of corporate travel buyers is a result of this cost control effort. Essentially, such people's task is to control the cost without losing the quality of the product. Corporate travel buyers first ascertain the level and service of product that the organization is willing to accept; they then negotiate the prices and proceed more or less as follows.

Know the Volume   It is difficult to negotiate anything without knowing the parameters within which both parties are dealing. A hotel might give a discount based upon expected volume, only to find that the volume never materializes. A corporation, on the other hand, might be unaware of its true rooms volume at a destination and be paying more than it could negotiate at that volume. The same is true with airline travel, where companies can often negotiate volume discounts.

With hotel rack rates at their present heights, the planner has come to expect a discount no matter what the volume. One of the authors once received a call from a corporate travel department asking for an additionally-discounted rate. The company, which happened to sell shoes, claimed its volume would be about 100 room-nights annually. The hotel happened to enjoy high occupancies and rarely further discounted rooms, even for 1,500 room-nights a year. The shoe company planner was not convinced that his perception of volume did not apply in this case. Finally, the author asked if he could get a discount on shoes if he bought three pairs a year. The response was, "Of course

An appeal to those who set corporate per diems on behalf of those who must sleep with your decisions.

Corporate per diems have always been viewed as a necessary evil.

Those who guard the company purse strings consider them necessary. While those who travel on a shoestring just consider them evil.

However, there's actually hope for a true meeting of the minds. Hope that comes in the form of a Hyatt Hotel.

In short, Hyatt, the hotel where most business travellers would prefer to stay, is surprisingly no more expensive.

This preference for Hyatt can be attributed to the fact that everything at our hotels is geared to making a trip easier, more productive and more relaxing. Our sweeping atriums instantly inspire lofty feelings and a sense of well-being. We've designed our guest rooms to be as conducive to work as they are to sleep.

And, to take the edge off a long day, there are relaxing lounges. Plus the added comfort of finding your bed turned down and your pillow fluffed up.

To make the thought of returning to Hyatt even more attractive, there are a host of privileges available through the rewarding Hyatt Gold Passport® Frequent Traveller Program.

All of which enables business travellers to do something long thought to be impossible: maintain their dignity. Without ever having to violate their per diems.

We invite you to compare our competitive corporate rates.

	New York	Washington, D.C.	Dallas	Chicago	Minneapolis	Los Angeles	Seattle
HYATT	$185.00 Grand Hyatt New York	$145.00 Grand Hyatt Washington	$119.00 Hyatt Regency Dallas	$150.00 Hyatt Regency Chicago	$103.00 Hyatt Regency Minneapolis	$105.00 Hyatt at Los Angeles Airport	$75.00 Hyatt Seattle
MARRIOTT	$195.00	$162.00	$125.00	$152.00	$107.00	$114.00	$90.00
WESTIN	$225.00	$155.00	$125.00	$155.00	$110.00	$130.00	$110.00

Above are sample occupancy comparison rates for Hyatt and the major Hyatt and Marriott hotels in each city.
National corporate rates from Westin. Rates in effect October 27, 1987, for November 1, 1987, reservations.

THE HYATT TOUCH

HYATT ● HOTELS & RESORTS™

Courtesy of Hyatt Hotels Corp.

FIGURE 7-6 Hotel addressing the need of the corporate travel planner

not! You have to be a big retailer to command a discount!" The point was finally made.

Hotel room rates are negotiated initially from the published or rack rates. Rarely, today, do customers pay the rack rate unless they are uneducated enough not to ask for the myriad of other rates available, or are traveling during peak demand periods. From rack rates come corporate or commercial rates usually at least 10 to 15 percent lower than the rack rate, or even drastically lower, depending on how inflated the rack rates are in the first place. This practice is discussed further in Chapter 12.

Hotels now negotiate individual corporate rates with corporations. Volume corporate planners recognize the widescale availability of corporate rates for anyone, and demand their own corporate rate relative to their volume. These rates can run 15 to 35 percent below the rack rate. This, of course, makes the rack rate a ridiculous pretension, so hotels raise the rack rate, say ten percent, in order to raise the corporate and volume rates. With the few people who do pay rack rate, hotels thus manage to increase average rate about two percent each time, even if occupancies decrease.

Large travel agencies, or consortiums, offer mega-purchasing power for their corporate customers. Woodside Travel in Boston, American Express in New Jersey, or Rosenbluth Travel in Philadelphia are all considered consortiums, or a large umbrella under which smaller agencies can access the technology and buying power of larger entities by combining the volume of a number of corporations to get the best rate for all.

A recent study also found that corporate travel managers would like hotel chains' representatives to negotiate rates that will apply chain-wide. The study suggested that a chain that provided the convenience of "one-stop shopping," or one place where corporate travel managers could negotiate room rate agreements for all hotels in the chain, would have a competitive advantage in this market.[6]

---

[6]Russell A. Bell, "Corporate Travel-Management Trends and Hotel-Marketing Strategies," *Cornell Hotel and Restaurant Administration Quarterly,* April, 1993, pp. 31–39.

Understanding Travel Patterns   The corporate planner uses knowledge of corporate travel patterns to negotiate with hotel suppliers; the supplier responds in kind. For example, if the corporation has people traveling to a given city mainly when occupancy is already high, the planner will have far greater difficulty in negotiating preferred rates. On the other hand, if travel can be planned during low-occupancy periods, the planner may obtain not only high discount rates but also preferred availability during periods of high occupancy. The corporate planner tries to anticipate travel patterns, reserve in advance, and not just react to travel trends.

Controlling the Costs   When low room rates are negotiated, the corporate planner tries to ensure that they are used. If rates were negotiated on the basis of volume, then lack of volume may forfeit the rate. This stipulation is often inserted by the hotel. Of course, if lower rates are negotiated and company personnel don't utilize them, the cost savings are not realized.

Some companies develop policies to enforce their negotiated rates. The corporate planner might go into a marketplace and negotiate with hotels at various levels of product class and cost. For example, in Denver a company might have three preferred hotels: Holiday Inn, Sheraton, and Hyatt. Who stays at which depends upon the management level of the employee. To enforce compliance, the company may not reimburse the employee for hotel bills at alternative hotels unless the others are sold out.

Recently, there has been a trend by companies to hire outside professionals to handle this phase of the business. As rates for hotels and airlines become more complicated, along with the benefits of frequent-traveler programs, the task of managing individual travel for corporations has become increasingly complex.

One solution has been the hiring of "in-plants" by companies with large travel budgets. An "in-plant" is a division of a travel agency that is located within the corporate offices of an organization. The equipment and employees belong to the travel agency, but their utilization is dedicated to the one company's needs. These employees become the planner, although they technically work for the travel agency. The in-plant receives either straight fees, commissions on bookings, or a combination of both for services rendered.

The in-plants offer unique resources to the corporation that would likely be inaccessible in any other way. Specifically, the in-plant can leverage its business with the one corporation through other companies also served by the agency, to negotiate even lower rates. For example, XYZ company may be using 500 rooms annually in Denver. This volume might justify a ten percent discount off rack rates. The in-plant agency, however, might also represent four other companies with equal room usage in Denver. Thus, the in-plant can negotiate on the basis of 2,500 room-nights to receive a 25 percent discount for all, the same as the travel agent consortiums mentioned above.

The Corporate Meetings Market

The title of corporate meeting planner covers a wide range of organizational customers. This market represents some 700,000 meetings annually, with total expenditures, including travel, of $21.5 billion for U.S. corporations.[7] Although a part of a large market, individual corporate meetings are relatively small, requiring an average of 60 hotel rooms at an average rate of $96 in 1992 in the United States.[8] The meetings are organized with an average lead time of five to six months.[9]

The most common type of corporate meeting is a management meeting, where executives meet to discuss company business. Another kind of meeting is the sales meeting, which is usually organized once a year to discuss and review company sales goals and strategies. Training meetings and seminars provide corporations avenues to exchange information and improve their personnel's performance.

To understand the needs of the meeting plan-

ner, one must review all the components of the organizational customer. In a nutshell, meeting planners need to "look good." They need to look good to their boss, to the person whose meeting they organize, and also to the hotel, if they want to continue to look good to the first two people. At least two hotels try to appeal to this need of meeting planners, as shown in Figure 7-7.

Meeting planners need to match the requirements of the organization with the site of the meeting, and then feel confident that all of the arrangements that were discussed are executed. In the end, they need to evaluate their own organization, together with the performance of the hotel, to determine whether the meeting was a success.

What meeting planners do not need is for hotels to mislead them in regard to the capabilities of the physical plant and the personnel. The often short-term thinking of the hotel business sometimes lends itself to this undeliberate type of misrepresentation, and eventual loss of the customer. With as much as a 70 percent annual turnover in many hotel sales offices, and bonuses based on room-nights sold, the reward system essentially mandates how fast you can make your quota to increase your income or get promoted. Sales offices are told to "book it, not cook it," meaning get the signed contract and go find more business.

Many experienced planners, however, have little need for the salesperson, requiring instead the attention of a professional conference coordinator, who works for the hotel, to service the meeting. All of the detail work will be done with a conference coordinator who, like salespeople, may also be on a "fast track," often leaving the meeting planner in the hands of inexperienced new people.

Conference coordinators are the on-site need-fulfillers. Meeting planners need meeting rooms that will suit the purpose of the event. They also want a quiet room. Often, hotel ballrooms are divided by thin, movable walls that allow noise from the meeting next door to filter through. One of the authors recently gave an all-day seminar on research methods directly across a narrow hallway from a national convention of gospel singers. Guess what?

---

[7]State of the Industry, *Successful Meetings*, July, 1993, pp. 32–33.
[8]*Ibid.*, pp. 7, 23.
[9]*Ibid.*, p. 7.

Make yourself look good in San Francisco.

By impressing your group with a smooth-running conference at a truly French hotel. By far the nearest of the great luxury hotels to the new Moscone Center as well as downtown business, Union Square shopping and Chinatown. 700 deluxe rooms and suites, plus flexibly expansive meeting facilities for up to 1,400 persons. Brilliant cuisine developed by Michelin-starred chefs. Attentive service far beyond the call of duty. Located at Third and Market. Call David Marten, Director of Sales and Marketing, at (415) 974-6400. They'll feel good. You'll look good.

HOTEL MERIDIEN SAN FRANCISCO
Travel Companion of Air France

"The Claremont makes me look good."

Hal Grice, First Interstate Bank, Los Angeles

PREFERRED HOTELS WORLDWIDE

THE
CLAREMONT
RESORT AND CONFERENCE CENTER

Ashby & Domingo Aves., Oakland, CA 94623
(415) 843-3000

FIGURE 7-7   Hotels need to make meeting planners "look good"

Hotel employees may also be a source of disruptive noise. While it is operationally convenient to have the kitchen next to the ballroom, meeting attendees are disconcerted when the kitchen crew bangs pots and pans throughout a meeting. Doors that bang when people go in and out of meeting rooms are another source of high irritation.

The meeting planner needs an efficient front desk that will assign rooms to the right people: the VIPs in the suites and the attendees in the regular rooms. The billing needs to be right: Some rooms may be billed to the organization, some attendees may have to pay for their own. The meeting planner needs meeting rooms to be set up on time, and coffee breaks to arrive when ordered. The audiovisuals need to be in the meeting room at the right time, and in working order. The spare bulb for the projector should be on the cart, not locked in a closet at the other end of the building.

Meeting planners, like all customers, do not need excuses. It is not their problem that the banquet manager did not show up for work, or that the linen was supposed to be delivered at 10:00 A.M., or that they should not have scheduled the break so close to lunchtime. The hotel staff assumes all responsibility for the "well-being" of the meeting.

In short, meeting planners expect all of the details to be handled absolutely professionally so that they "look good." If a hotel is able to provide planners not only with what they think they need, but also with what they don't realize they need, the planners will return. The above concerns, and much else, fall on the shoulders of the conference coordinator assigned to service a group.

From the hotel's side, there are problems with the corporate meetings market. While attendance at these meetings is usually compulsory, thus assuring the planned rooms and meal counts, cancellation of the entire meeting is often a threat. At the last minute, a corporation can cancel a meeting for hundreds of people that has been in the planning stage for months. Economic conditions, failure to develop a new product on schedule, or simply whim may provoke such a decision. This has led to more large up-front nonrefundable deposits. Corporate meetings also have shorter lead times but often demand what they want when they decide that they want it.

Corporate meeting planners may be spending only a small portion of their time on meeting planning. They thus need as much help as they can get and may require a great deal of guidance in accomplishing their company's objectives. The hotel staff that provides that guidance will often secure the business. Figure 7-8 shows part of a tongue-in-cheek letter that Hilton International sent to corporate meeting planners to address their concerns and offer "value" rates.

Conference Centers

Today there is a multitude of hotels from which meeting planners can choose. With this additional supply in most marketplaces, the need to attract meeting planners' business has grown. Hotels that offered mediocre service in the past now find that there are willing competitors to match rates and offer service to win over and keep these customers.

One way the industry has responded to the unique needs of the meeting planner is by developing "dedicated" conference centers, reserved mainly for meetings and doing an excellent job specializing in this market. Some hotels claim to be conference centers by adding the words to their name, believing they can establish a new identity (i.e., XYZ Motor Inn becomes XYZ Motor Inn and Conference Center). These properties are not, however, conference centers in the true sense. In fact, many are far from it and may, in the long run, be hurting themselves with this pretension.

Pure conference centers are interested primarily in meetings. Scanticon Conference Center in New Jersey or Arrowwood Conference Center in Westchester, New York are pure conference centers. IACC (International Association of Conference Centers) sets a criterion that at least 60 percent of business come from meetings or conferences to qualify as a "legitimate" conference center. (See Figure 7-9 for descriptions and examples.) Even this may be suspect, however, unless the appropriate facilities exist and transient business is not allowed to interfere with conference participation. The needs of the meeting attendee are very different from those of leisure guests or business travelers. Figure 7-10 shows an example of a dedicated resort conference center.

FERRET, INC.

Expert Detection
Suite 3B, The Buena Vista
Yonkers, NY 11463

Dear Mr. Lewis:

You weren't kidding when you said this job wouldn't be easy.
My head is still spinning from trying to make sense of all
those hotel brochures. First class. World class. Attention
to detail. Impeccable service. State-of-the-art facilities.
Spectacular scenery. If I had to deal with this mumbo jumbo
every day, I'd get fed up, too.

Not everybody can be telling the truth. (There aren't that
many pristine white beaches in the world). But hey, I love a
challenge and I've already made some progress. I've been
snooping around keeping my ears open and have heard a lot
about a program called "Value Days" offered by Hilton
International.

Get this: A choice of luxury hotels all over the world.
Internationally trained meeting staff, supposedly the best in
the business. Food and beverage quality that's apparently
superior -- someone said "no rubber chicken", whatever that
means.

And now, here's where it gets really interesting. These guys
at Hilton International are letting the word out they're
willing to deal! That's what Value Days is all about.

See, if you have a meeting in one of their hotels during a
time when it's not too busy (and I hear their sales reps have
these handy-dandy 18 month calendars for each hotel to help
you plan it all out), they're willing to negotiate, and you
still have the famous quality and service of Hilton
International.

FIGURE 7-8   Addressing concerns of corporate meeting planners

According to the IACC the big difference between a combined hotel-and-conference center and a legitimate conference center is not just technical services but human services. The IACC claims that the business of the typical hotel is transient, limiting the attention and service it can give to every meeting, and that conference centers have a stronger commitment to conferences as essentially the only market they have.

In some cases, the combination of hotel and conference center works well when the markets are separated by time of the week or season. In other cases conflicts are created that can be detrimental. The ballroom that is ideal for weddings, or for trade shows, may be entirely inappropriate for meetings. For example, in the first case, wedding guests would probably not hear noise coming from the kitchen. During a meeting sales presentation, however, those noises can break the concentration of the speaker and ruin the meeting.

The dividing walls of the same ballroom may be ideal for the separation of a cocktail reception and a dinner, while too porous for the holding of two meetings simultaneously. There are very few facilities that are ideal for all markets.

True conference centers attempt to serve one market only, the meetings market. They offer strictly meetings in controlled environments. With soundproof meeting rooms, dedicated audiovisual rooms with state-of-the-art equipment, and conference coordinators whose sole job is to facilitate the needs of the meetings, these properties offer a serious environment for conducting meetings. Most are located outside and away from major cities so that distractions are held to a minimum.

Many conference centers offer a full package rate that includes all the necessary services for one per-person price. These centers are dedicated to the needs of the meeting planners and serve them well. At the same time, some are having a difficult time making ends meet. High occupancy occurs during selected time periods and the shoulder and low periods incur very high costs without compensating revenues. For this reason most dedicated conference centers do attempt to fill in with the social transient market.

The Incentive Market

The incentive planner has a unique problem (need) when compared with other customers of the hospitality product. The incentive planner has to provide not only for the accommodation of the group, but also for the group's idea of "fun." This is a difficult task. When you think of your own idea of a good time, it is probably quite different from that of some people you know. This problem of disparity is one with which the incentive planner is challenged.

The incentive planner organizes travel as a reward for superior performance within a group. For example, the sales team of a computer manufacturer may have exceeded its sales quota by 30 percent. The reward is a trip to the Caribbean for a week, with spouses. Managers of a retail store chain may be eligible for

travel incentives if their profit margins are above a certain quota.

The Society of Incentive Travel Executives, SITE, defines incentive travel as follows: "Incentive travel is a modern management tool that motivates salespeople, dealers, distributors, customers, and internal employees by offering rewards in the form of travel for participation in the achievement of goals and objectives."[10]

The United States incentive travel market generates almost $8 billion a year, including airfare and ground service. Over 50 percent is hotel related. Trip sizes range from 2 to 2,000 people, with an average of over 100 people per trip. Most trips include spouses. About 50 percent of locations are resorts.[11]

Travel certainly is not the only method of incentive reward, but it is one that projects an image of excitement and relaxation away from the job. When this is done in the group format, teamwork and morale increase with the sense of accomplishment. Merchandise rewards, such as television, stereos, and cash bonuses, are the competition to travel rewards. Travel rewards are preferred by many companies, and managing that travel becomes an important task.

This has led to the growth of "incentive houses," companies that provide professional incentive planning and hope to assure no-hassle, successful, and satisfying trips. As the value of the incentive travel market has become recognized by the hotel industry, companies are trying to better meet this market's needs. According to J.J. Gubbins, Vice-President of Sheraton:

Incentives really taught the hotel industry to be creative. It got us to focus on the idea of travel as entertainment. Through servicing incentives we learned how to develop the creative aspects of our own industry, which has affected nearly every aspect of our operation—even in the way hotels and resorts are designed.[12]

---

[10]Quoted in Shaw, *The Group Market*, p. 45.

[11]State of the Industry, *Successful Meetings*, July, 1993, pp. 7, 30.

[12]Quoted in Vincent Alonzo, "A Wider World for Winners," *Meetings and Conventions*, August, 1991, p. 101.

BURT CABAÑAS TALKS ABOUT EFFECTIVE MEETINGS.

A CANDID CONVERSATION WITH AN INDUSTRY LEADER

BURT CABAÑAS
PRESIDENT AND CEO
BENCHMARK HOSPITALITY, INC.

■ IN A NUTSHELL, WHAT DIFFERENTIATES A CONFERENCE CENTER FROM A TRADITIONAL HOTEL?

"To begin with, conference centers are designed, built and managed with one primary purpose in mind . . . maintaining the balanced environment of "Living, Learning and Leisure"™ in order to ensure productive meetings. Unlike hotels, this means that everything from the physical facilities to the operating policies to conference services maintains the meeting planners' needs as the number one priority."

■ ARE THERE GUIDELINES THAT A PROPERTY MUST FOLLOW TO BE CONSIDERED A "CONFERENCE CENTER"?

"While the term 'conference center' is not protected, IACC (International Association of Conference Centers) has worked hard to identify the criteria for inclusion. Membership in IACC–of which we are one of the founders–is usually a good indicator that the property is getting at least 60% or more of its business from meetings and conferences and its facilities and operating focus are geared toward the service of conferences."

■ WHAT KIND OF MEETINGS ARE BEST SUITED TO A CONFERENCE CENTER?

"Any time the ultimate goal of a meeting is information retention and learning, a conference center–with its more focused environment–is an ideal setting. Management training meetings

THE WOODLANDS EXECUTIVE CONFERENCE CENTER & RESORT
The Woodlands, Texas (Houston Area)

• 268 rooms and suites
• 59,000 square-foot executive conference center
• 30 conference rooms for groups of 10 to 400
• Indoor arena that seats 2,000 for banquets
• Two restaurants, including The Glass Menagerie for fine cuisine
• Two championship 18-hole golf courses, including TPC, site of the Shell Houston Open; 24 tennis courts; swimming pools; executive health spa; bike and hike trails
• Located 30 minutes from Houston Intercontinental Airport

CHAMINADE EXECUTIVE CONFERENCE CENTER
Santa Cruz, California (Monterey Bay)

• 152 guest rooms
• 12,000 square-foot executive conference center
• 12 conference rooms for up to 250 people, plus 10 parlors for smaller groups
• Two restaurants, including gourmet specialties at The Library
• Tennis; heated swimming pool; jogging and hiking trails; extensive 14,000 square-foot fitness center
• Located 80 miles south of San Francisco, 30 miles from San Jose Airport

THE NORTHLAND INN & EXECUTIVE CONFERENCE CENTER
Minneapolis, Minnesota

• 231 suites, each featuring spacious bedroom and living area
• 33,000 square-foot executive conference center, including 8,100 square-foot ballroom; 4,200 square-foot junior ballroom and 138-seat amphitheater
• Two restaurants, including fine dining at Wadsworth's
• Executive health club and indoor lap pool on-site; nearby tennis, racquetball and golf
• Located 30 minutes from Minneapolis/St. Paul International Airport

FIGURE 7-9 Conference center descriptions and some pure and quasi conference centers

to teach managers about new products or management methods . . . or meetings focusing on marketing and financial strategies . . . are well suited to conference centers where the average group size is less than 50 people."

■ DO CONFERENCE CENTERS PROVIDE RECREATION?

"Conference centers are not designed for all work and no play. Benchmark understands how critically important the "leisure" aspect of a meeting is—not just for relaxation but as an important way to foster interaction among the conference attendees. As a pioneer of the "conference resort" concept, Benchmark offers worldclass recreation that ranks with the nation's best. Championship golf, Olympic-calibre skiing, tennis, swimming, hike and bike trails, and extensive executive fitness centers featuring state-of-the-art exercise equipment and spa facilities all help attendees unwind."

■ IS THE CONFERENCE CENTER DINING EXPERIENCE FLEXIBLE?

"The conference center dining concept—three meals per day served 'kiosk' style—provides the quality of first-class dining. Our "America's Harvest" approach to menu planning offers guests tremendous variety at each meal as opposed to pre-set banquet menus and allows meetings to break at a time that's convenient for the planner. It also includes flexible continuous coffee breaks with an abundance of choices."

■ THERE'S A MYTH THAT CONFERENCE CENTERS ARE NOT AESTHETICALLY APPEALING. IS IT TRUE?

"In generations past, conference centers were more utilitarian than luxurious, but that's not the case today. Baby Boomers expect a higher level of comfort. At a Benchmark property, you will find recreational facilities, guest room amenities and customer service delivered at a four-star level."

■ WHAT ABOUT PRICE? IS IT COMPETITIVE?

"Myth versus reality . . . the conference center's value to a meeting goes beyond dollars and cents. The fact of the matter is that conference centers are not only competitive, but when you take advantage of the Complete Meeting Package (CMP), which generally covers in excess of 90% of the total meeting costs, there are no surprises at check out."

■ WHAT IS CMP AND IS THERE ANY ROOM FOR NEGOTIATION?

"The Complete Meeting Package (CMP) includes the meeting space, refreshment breaks, all meals, guest room, most audio-visual equipment, conference services and concierge and some recreational activities. Negotiations are based on supply and demand coupled with our strong desire to meet the meeting planner's objective and to establish a long-term working relationship. In general, our pricing varies as much as 30%."

RESORT AT SQUAW CREEK
Squaw Valley USA, California
(Lake Tahoe)

• 405 deluxe guest rooms and suites
• 33,000 square-foot executive conference center, including 10,000 square-foot grand ballroom; 5,200 square-foot junior ballroom
• Three restaurants, including acclaimed continental fare at Glissandi
• Ski-in, ski-out access to Squaw Valley slopes; 18-hole Robert Trent Jones, Jr. golf course; tennis center; executive fitness center and spa; equestrian center; skating rink; three swimming pools; hike and bike trails
• Located 45 minutes from Reno Cannon Airport

LANSDOWNE CONFERENCE RESORT
Lansdowne, Virginia
(Washington, D.C. area)

• 305 guest rooms and suites, many with Potomac River views
• 45,000 square-foot executive conference center
• 25 conference rooms; 9,525 square-foot grand ballroom and 124-seat amphitheater
• Three restaurants and one lounge
• 18-hole Robert Trent Jones, Jr. golf course; four-court tennis center; executive fitness center; squash and racquetball courts; indoor/outdoor swimming pools; jogging and nature trail
• Located just 8 miles from Dulles International Airport

SADDLERIDGE AT BEAVER CREEK
Beaver Creek, Colorado
(Vail Valley)

• 27 exquisitely appointed guest rooms in 12 mountain villas, each with 2 or 3 bedrooms.
• High-level conference facilities for up to 50 attendees
• Access to the exclusive private dining club and apres-ski lounge
• Ski-in access to downhill and cross-country trails at Beaver Creek Mountain; indoor/outdoor swimming, whirlpool spas and steam rooms; nearby championship golf course
• Located 15 minutes from the legendary resort town of Vail

FIGURE 7-9 (continued)

FIGURE 7-10   A dedicated resort conference center

The nature of incentive trips has also changed in the 1990s. With an ailing world economy, incentive trips are shorter and less elaborate.

Incentive Planners

The incentive planner often becomes involved in the development of criteria for incentive success. In order to have winners to send on trips, the framework of the incentive must be established.

In order to have a successful incentive, the reward must be different and worth wanting.

Once the framework of the incentive has been developed, the incentive planner must formulate the appropriate travel prizes. Even if incentive planners do not specifically design the promotion, it is critical for them to have a full understanding of the composition of the group and its achievements. Incentive planners need to establish the perceived level of incentive, and plan accordingly.

The Incentive Trip

The actual incentive trip can take three forms: pure incentive, incentive-plus, and incentive weekends. The pure incentive trip is dedicated to having a good time without any business-related activities.

The incentive-plus is a more popular form of incentive trip and is used in over 70 percent of the cases. Incentive-plus trips combine pleasure with some form of meetings or new product introductions. In this way, companies maximize use of their incentive travel dollars. The company can disseminate valuable information without having another meeting elsewhere.

Incentive weekends are increasingly being used as rewards for good, but less-than-superior, performance. Companies recognize that while incentive trips are productive, they also take time away from the workplace. Three-day weekend incentives are more cost effective from a time management viewpoint.

The incentive planner has a multifaceted job when planning the actual trip. Specifically, all phases of the excursion must be minutely planned to enhance the end-user experience. This is different from planning corporate or association meetings or conventions, in which cases the planner plans the functions but leaves it to the individuals to get there and participate. The incentive planner, on the other hand, arranges for literally everything: air and land travel, hotel, food, excursions, sight-seeing, entertainment, sports, and anything else that might take place during the trip. Each and every one of these categories can be critical to the success of the trip.

This is why incentive planners have almost always visited the site, and the hotels and restaurants at the site, before developing the package. They want to make sure that everything is up to par, that every detail will be taken care of; they or their representatives go on the trip as final security. Therefore, a hotel has a special challenge in booking and handling incentive travel. We know of one case, for example, when the planner ruled out a hotel on an inspection trip because the sand urns had cigarette butts in them and facial tissue was missing in some of the rooms. "If they can't take care of the little things, they'll never take care of the big ones," was this planner's comment.

Incentive trip planning also differs from that of other organizational customers in that the destination is of primary importance. The corporate customer or meeting planner may choose a facility because of the hotel itself or because of its proximity to business-related activities; for the incentive planner, the choice of hotel comes after the choice of destination.

Many companies are not large enough or skilled enough to develop incentive trips through their internal organization. A company may have a full-time corporate travel manager and a meeting planner, but the complexities of the incentive purchase are entirely different. For example, staying familiar with different destination areas and necessary ground arrangements is incredibly time-consuming.

Incentive houses are a popular intermediary for the companies that need the dedicated attention of a professional. The incentive house is more than a travel agent; its professional incentive planners help in all phases of incentive management. Broad experience with specialized organizational needs supplements seasoned knowledge in even first-time attempts.

Overall, the incentive organizational planner has a unique job. The "fun" aspect of the planning can be anything but that. Hotels that want a greater share of the incentive market must be extremely flexible in their approach to this marketplace. Standardized approaches to capturing this market are likely not to be fruitful.[13] An ad aimed at this market is shown in Figure 7-11.

Association, Convention, and Trade Show Markets

Association and convention planners have similar needs, although they are somewhat different types of groups. Both tend to have large

---

[13]For more explicit details of the needs, wants, and satisfactions of incentive planners, and how to market to them, see Lewis, "Incentive Travel Market."

The world's most rewarding incentive destination.
Combine the myriad sights of an ancient culture with a rich variety of beach
and city hotels; add sunshine, theme parties, shopping and nightlife; and you
have the perfect incentive: Thailand

FIGURE 7-11   Ad aimed at the incentive market

guestroom and function space requirements. These organizational planners are, in many cases, full-time employees or executives of the associations they represent. In general, they are becoming more sophisticated and more professional in their jobs. Association meetings, often connected with trade shows or conventions, account for over $32 billion a year in the United States.[14]

An association meeting can comprise a group of people convening on a social basis to elect officers, have social functions, and organize activities on a regional and/or a national basis. This category of organizational customer also tends to meet throughout the year in smaller groups, and social contacts are a major reason for attendance. There are, of course, innumerable professional (e.g., American Medical Association) and business (e.g., National Association of Manufacturers) associations that meet both

---

[14]State of the Industry, *Successful Meetings,* July, 1993, p. 33.

regionally and nationally to present papers, have board meetings, and set policy.

Conventions are more focused on annual activities, such as annual meetings of delegates for a political caucus. Other examples are union gatherings to decide policies for the coming year and a fishermen's convention to plan lobbying efforts. The participants may or may not meet throughout the year, and dissemination of information, not social contacts, is the primary objective. A convention solicitation showing different capacities is illustrated in Figure 7-12.

Finally, the main purpose of trade shows is to sell products. This takes wide-open space, as shown in the advertisement in Figure 7-13. The hotel's task in booking trade shows is to provide the space, ease of access for products to be brought in, and the facilities, such as electric power and lighting, to display the products. This requires a great deal of work, which can be disruptive to other guests. In addition, the hotel sells rooms and meals to exhibitors and those who attend. Exhibitors also make wide use of "hospitality suites" where they entertain customers. This puts heavy pressure on the hotel's room service division, although at high cost to the exhibitors.

While each of these three planners (association, convention, and trade show) has a different reason for purchasing the hospitality product, the needs are similar. At times, an entire facility will be purchased for a two- or three-day period. Usually, the planner arranges for guestrooms to be held, but reservations are made individually by the participants. The organizer will have a list of VIPs, but the majority of guestrooms are booked by direct calls or through the use of reservation cards.

Reservations cards are essentially order forms provided by the hotel and designed specifically for the use of attendees. Attendees, of course, are always free to stay somewhere else if they prefer; through reservation cards, the hotel sales department tries to make it conducive for them to stay at the host hotel. Handling reservations in this manner can make coordination difficult. The hotel must be flexible to the needs of the attendees, many of whom are buying the hotel sight unseen. Strict inventory control is necessary. If, for example, the hotel accepts more king-size bedroom requests than it can accommodate, it may have many unhappy customers.

Food and beverage is also a unique problem for hotels in these markets. The organizational buyer tries to be as precise as possible in the number of people who will attend meal functions, but the actual attendance can vary widely. If there are alternatives, as in a large city, many attendees will go out for meals. Attendance at different meal functions can also vary widely, even within the same meeting. The first night's award banquet might attract close to 100 percent attendance; the following night, perhaps featuring a boring speaker, might send half the attendees elsewhere.

Association, convention, and trade show planners need extremely good coordinators within the hotel to execute all phases of the event. These coordinators are far more important than the salespeople in delivery of the final product. Rutherford and Umbreit found that convention-services managers of hotels had the greatest number of encounters with meeting planners during the process of planning and executing an event, more than any other personnel.[15] This may be true for any meeting of size, but it is especially true for these large, complex ones. Technical details such as the voltage in the main ballroom, the delivery space for exhibits, and the audiovisuals for the speakers are all critical to the success of the function.

The hotel staff also needs to have good relations with the unions involved in handling large affairs. Not only are union members within the hotel utilized, but often there are members of other unions who set up booths, deliver products to the display area, and so forth. A meeting planner working at too much of a distance will be unaware of the vagaries of local unions. A mistake in procedures can ruin the set-up or break-down of a function very easily.

Delegates to these kinds of functions often will not stay for the duration of the meeting. They may book for three nights and stay two, and not give any notice of doing it. Many are employees of small businesses, people who are

---

[15]Rutherford and Umbreit, "Improving Interactions."

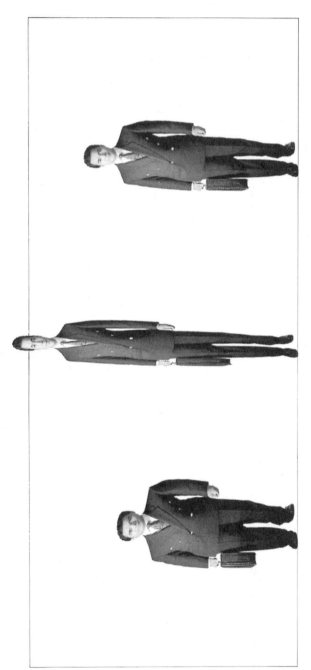

BECAUSE PEOPLE COME IN *ALL* SHAPES AND SIZES, SO DO OUR CONVENTION ROOMS.

At the Equatorial Penang, our rooms are designed to accommodate all kinds of conventions. Our ballroom is the largest on the island, and it has no pillars. So you can easily divide it up any way you like. It is supported by 14 function rooms that are conveniently close to each other. You'll of course have the back up of state-of-the-art AV equipment like multiple spectrum ceiling lights, and a simultaneous translation system as well as the usual facilities. So no matter what kind of crowd you're expecting, we're flexible enough to fit you in.

Equatorial
Penang

 HOTEL EQUATORIAL INTERNATIONAL

FIGURE 7-12 Ad soliciting convention business

We've got 299,999 more of these.

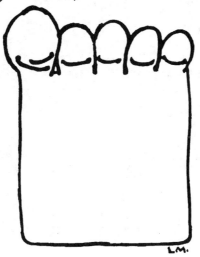

So if you need a lot of square feet to make your trade show work, call the Opryland Hotel.

Whatever your trade, the Opryland Hotel has the spaces to show it off–including 145,000 square feet of dedicated exhibit space on one level. The Opryland Hotel has the square footage and more...superior service, outstanding facilities, state-of-the-art technology and spaces that work hard to make your trade show work:

□ 145,000 square feet of exhibit space, all on one level
□ 300,000 total square feet of magnificently designed public space
□ 1,900 deluxe guest rooms, including 120 suites
□ three expansive ballrooms, totalling 68,000 square feet–each divisible into smaller areas
□ the new Cascades–a 2½-acre indoor water garden with dancing waters, brooks, waterfalls and fountains
□ the Conservatory–a two-acre, year-round tropical garden under glass

□ 29 front desk stations–more per room than any other hotel our size in the nation
□ conveniently adjacent to the 4,400-seat Grand Ole Opry House
□ part of Opryland USA, including Opryland, America's Musical Showplace, the *General Jackson* showboat and The Nashville Network.

We invite you to discover the superb spaces and facilities of the Opryland Hotel. Please call George Aguel, Vice President/Marketing, or Jerry Wayne, Director of Sales, at (615) 889-1000. Or write Opryland Hotel, 2800 Opryland Drive, Nashville, TN 37214.

OPRYLAND HOTEL

FIGURE 7-13   Ad soliciting trade show business

called away by changes in plans; others will simply feel they've had all they want and decide to leave.

Delegates to these functions also tend to be price-sensitive. The organizer who wants to keep the delegates happy looks for low rates and for low-cost or free meeting space. All three of these markets—association, convention, and trade show—are tough to sell and tough to service, but they can represent lucrative business, especially if booked during slow business periods.

Convention Centers and Convention and Visitors Bureaus

There are two external bodies, often closely involved in the handling of association, convention, and trade show marketing, that require brief mention.

The first is the freestanding convention center, such as that shown in Figure 7-14. Most major and many secondary cities in the world

WE'RE EXPANDING OUR WIDE OPEN SPACES.

We offer 1,500,000 square feet of dedicated exhibit space, with half of it in the Dallas Convention Center alone. And effective January 1, 1994, we will have an additional 225,000 square feet of exhibit space. So plan your next event in Dallas, where you'll find room, with room to spare. Call (214) 746-6630 for your convention planner's package. Dallas Convention and Visitors Bureau • 1201 Elm Street • Suite 2000 • Dallas, TX 75270

FIGURE 7-14   A free-standing convention center

have such convention centers. Everywhere, it is the "main event" that takes place in the convention center, which is usually publicly owned but privately operated, and/or the trade show or convention itself is handled by a private trade show organizing firm.

The National Restaurant Association (NRA) trade show in Chicago or the annual computer show in Las Vegas are examples of trade shows held in convention centers. Either booths or space are sold to purveyors, and attendees peruse the offerings under one roof. Although informational seminars may be given during the show, the main purpose of the event is to display products and take orders. The trade show organizer makes money from the booth or space sales. In turn, the purveyors hope to write enough business to make their expenses worthwhile.

The convention center works closely with its city's hotels and restaurants to coordinate lodging and feeding. In New York City, for example, the annual AH&MA (American Hotel & Motel Association) trade show is held in the Jacob Javits Convention Center. The collateral sent out by the show operator includes hotels' locations and rates, free bus schedules, and restaurant and theater ads to make it easier for attendees to plan their stay. Hotels may get individual groups and functions from this event, but they are not the main center of focus.

Many such events are arranged, at least initially, through convention and visitors bureaus (CVBs). These organizations are publicly and privately supported by those they serve—convention centers, hotels, restaurants, merchants, theaters, airlines, and so forth. A *Successful Meetings* annual study shows that CVB services are used about 31 percent of the time by associations and 22 percent of the time by corporations.[16]

CVB organizations are nonprofit, serving their constituents. They exist in both large and small cities. Their main mission is to promote the city as a destination area. Hotels and restaurants need to work very closely with CVBs. If the CVB can sell the city to a group, it then provides information on hotel accommodations, restaurants, and other attractions that are part and parcel of the overall enticement. An example is shown in Figure 7-15.

Airline Crews

As the hotel industry faces increased competition to fill hotel rooms with a trailing demand, alternative target markets are needed to fill guestrooms. To this end, the airlines have pro-

vided a reasonable alternative to traditional sources of business for many properties.

The airline market is defined as the housing of airline employees and crew members on a contract basis. When an airline's employees fly for over a designated number of hours, as established by government aviation bodies, the airline has to provide a place for the crew to rest, also for a designated number of hours. In the past, hotels chosen for this purpose were low-priced and located near the airport, for reasons of reduced transportation costs. Two factors have changed the traditional scenario, however: one is the supply/demand ratio in the hotel marketplace, and the other is unions, participating in the bargaining process on behalf of their members.

In the first case, as more hotels have been built in relatively stable demand centers, the competition for customers has increased. This has put pressure on hotels to find new customers to fill their hotel rooms. In the second case, although airline unions were forced to accept lower wages after the bad economic times of the industry, they were successful in keeping and improving other benefits for their members, such as housing.

The net result has been that the local airline station manager, who negotiates for crew accommodations, finds a number of better products to choose from, with pressure from the unions to make the best possible facilities available to their members. On the hotel's part, however, facilities alone will not hold the contract. Unless the hotel understands these customers and their unique needs, it will not be able to deliver the product and will eventually lose the business to the hotel that understands airline and crew members' problems.

Airline crew members have entirely different needs and problems from those of the corporate traveler or the weekend package guest. Due to tight flight schedules, for instance, there are sometimes as few as 12 hours available to rest between flights. Airline crews must have all of their rooms available and assigned before they arrive. To ask each crew member for identification and credit cards may cut into 12 precious hours of rest. Unusual situations need to be

---

[16]State of the Industry, *Successful Meetings,* July 1993, p. 62.

Our high-level support staff is there when the big guns come to meet.

Chances are, the fate of the free world isn't hanging on the outcome of your next meeting or convention.

But that doesn't mean you're any less important to us.

In fact, because we're a little smaller than most, we rarely have to juggle several schedules at one time. So every meeting in High Point – from 2 to 2,000 – gets the attention it deserves.

Our support staff is there to make sure of it.

This time, try High Point, one of the Carolinas' fastest growing convention cities. Call Director of Sales Charlotte Young at 919-884-5255 to arrange a site inspection.

HIGHPOINT
NORTH CAROLINA
Convention & Visitors Bureau
101 West Green Drive • P.O. Box 2273
High Point, NC 27261

FIGURE 7-15 A convention and visitors bureau (CVB) solicitation

discussed with the airline captain—always in charge of the crew, even off the plane—before any decisions can be made.

Once in their rooms, airline crews do not prefer street views! (Here is a market segment that would gladly take rooms facing an inner courtyard or another building.) Some airline crews sleep at unusual hours; for instance, some international flight crews check in at 8:00 A.M. and need to sleep immediately. Heavy black-out shades are necessary to enable crew members to sleep during the day, a feature that would not affect most other customers of the hotel.

Coordination in behalf of airline crews is needed in all phases of the operation. For the corporate client who is at a meeting, 11:00 A.M. may be the best time to have a houseman vacuum the hallways, but this is not true for the crew that checked in at 8:00 A.M. Wake-up calls are critical. Flights delayed because an operator making $6.50 per hour forgot to make wake-up calls at 3 P.M., can cost an airline thousands of dollars. There are numerous other seemingly small details that are critical for crew members, such as locating them away from elevators and ice machines, and putting female crew members into adjacent rooms that have only other crew members next door.

Finally, integration of the food and beverage offerings needs to occur. Recognizing that crews are not on expense accounts (like many government employees, they are on *per diem*—a fixed daily allowance), the lunch menu with an $18 average check will probably not be utilized by them. However, there is potential in these extra customers, and special menu discounts can provide additional revenues and profits.

How much is too much? Airline crews in the past tended to be contracted on a yearly basis for a set number of rooms, but this is changing as the airlines insist on short-term contracts to give them more flexibility. Rates can sometimes be very low (as little as 40 percent) in comparison to the printed rack rates, or even the corporate rates. In fact, airline crew rates were the same in New York City in 1993 as they were in 1985. In the late 1980s many hotels displaced their crew rooms because demand was so strong from more lucrative market segments. The pendulum has now swung back to where almost every hotel is looking for the airline segment of business.

Some managers shy away from airline business because of a low average rate or because they think it gives a negative image to a hotel. Airline crews may not be considered "appropriate" in the lobby of a luxury hotel in the United States; overseas, however, in many countries they are accepted as adding prestige to the hotel. Besides the image factor, the real test of accepting airline business depends on the net revenue generated by the business and the compatibility with the segment mix.

To determine the profit margins of an airline contract, a displacement study needs to be done. First, management must estimate how many nights during the contract period the hotel will run a high general occupancy that it

could not accommodate under the crew contract; for example, if an airline wants 100 rooms in a 500-room hotel, how many nights is the hotel likely to have between 80 and 100 percent occupancy? The number of possible lost nights becomes the basis for revenue displacement. In other words, how many nights could the guestrooms be sold to a non-airline guest at a higher rate?

Revenue can be calculated for both scenarios—with and without the crew contract. From this should be deducted variable cost. For example, if the variable cost to service a room is $20 and the airline contract is for $40 a room, and the otherwise obtainable rate is $80, the hotel has to sell three airline rooms to make the same gross margin as one regular room. It may also be wise to calculate additional margins such as from food and beverages, on which crews tend to spend very little. If the gross margin earned from an airline crew contract is greater than the gross margin from the displaced rooms, then the airline business should be considered.

The SMERF and the Government Markets

Until recently, the SMERF market was not solicited by many major hotels. Their inventory was being used by more upscale corporate customers and associations. Given the current supply/demand position most hotels experience now, SMERF customers are being called on by almost everyone. For the first time, the SMERF market is being considered a "segment" by the Professional Conference Managers Association.[17]

SMERF customers are comprised of all organizational customers that do not fit into the other categories, a "catch-all" market. Major sub-markets of SMERF—social, military, religious, education and fraternal—cover most of the complexion of the market.

So what is a SMERF market? It is a price-sensitive, nonprofit organization market. All

[17]Peter Shure, "Sustained Recovery Necessary to Boost Attendance," *Convene Magazine*, March, 1993, pg. 35.

social-related business is considered SMERF. Wedding parties needing overnight accommodations, rehearsal dinner parties, society events, fundraisers, etc., are all considered within the social market. So are gospel singers. Military customers use hotel rooms for reunions and travel on business. The education subsegment consists of groups such as faculty and school sports groups. Religious groups, rising in popularity with large Baptist conventions filling cities, or the Order of the Rising Star, are meeting in hotels. Finally, fraternal orders such as the Elks Clubs or the Benevolent Order of Moose all fall into the SMERF segment.

Although the SMERF segment has the reputation of being low-rated, customers nevertheless fill guestrooms, ballrooms, and local restaurants, especially during slow periods. The "Head Buffalo" of an Elks group may be no less important a customer to a hotel than a corporate meeting planner.

The government market is also low-rated, but in the United States it is a $7 billion market, and is large in other countries as well.[18] Again, the international slump in bookings is leading hoteliers to see government as an attractive market. This market is a reliable source of incremental revenue for many budget and mid-level properties. Upscale properties also cannot ignore the upper end of this business.

Government at all levels is engaged in many activities that tend to be travel-intensive: research, regulation, investigation, enforcement, oversight, litigation, education, and coordination. They travel anywhere and everywhere people are to be found.

Although government employees may be end-users, they may not be the customers to whom to make the sale. Government travel planning is a bureaucratized affair. A program manager or travel coordinator is probably responsible for their reservations and per diem rates are set by state or national capitals. As with airline crews, hotels can target this market for rooms that might otherwise be left empty. Careful planning and marketing is needed.

The Group Tour and Travel Market

This market is defined as leisure travelers who travel in groups, with or without an escort. This is a wide-ranging market that has changed dramatically in recent times and is no longer characterized by hordes of ignorant travelers visiting five countries in four days. Tour groups may range from trekkers in the Himalayas to whale-watchers in the Pacific; from a ladies' garden club touring Japan to high school seniors "seeing" Spain. Group tour travelers have different motivations for selecting this form of travel, most important being the convenience of having all arrangements made for them. Other motivations include companionship (especially among mature travelers), lower travel costs, and planned itineraries that ensure that travelers will not miss the "must-see" places. Regardless of motivation or type of tour, hotel accommodations are the most important part of a group tour package. As Stanley Plog states:

> An adequate hotel room is important in travelers' itineraries because it becomes a stable base for almost everything that vacationers want to do, whether they are the venturesome types or the more timid souls. They do not want to worry about making wrong choices, in terms of quality or price, because so much of an always short vacation can be ruined by the discomforts and indignities that accompany the wrong choice of hotel. The assumption exists that the travel organizer, whether an airline or a tour wholesaler, can obviate the need for the vacationer to go through the learning curve on how to select hotels of adequate quality and that they will do this for a relatively reasonable price because of the buying power of large organizations.[19]

Hotels and restaurants will have to deal with these travel organizers who may be tour opera-

---

[18]Victoria Dunn, "You can capture a fair share of the $7 billion government market," *HSMAI Marketing Review*, Winter, 1992/1993, pp. 25–28. It should be noted that in some countries outside the United States (for example, Saudi Arabia), much government business is akin to royalty and is *top-rated*.

[19]Stanley C. Plog, *Leisure Travel-Making is a Growth Market Again*, New York: John Wiley & Sons, 1991, p. 98.

tors, travel agents or both. Although there are many kinds of tours a common type is the motorcoach travel market. Other markets in this category will be discussed in the Chapter 16 on distribution.

A recent study showed that there are over 1,600 tour operators in the United States, and they conducted half a million tours in 1992.[20] Total expenditures were over $5.4 billion, of which 80 percent was spent on multi-day tours requiring hotel accomodations. Tour operators usually belong to trade associations such as the National Tour Association, American Bus Association, or the United Bus Owners of America. Member directories provide useful information and are a good starting point for hospitality marketers interested in pursuing this type of business. Although there are many kinds of tours, the most common are the escorted motorcoach tour and the Group Inclusive Tour (GIT), which will be discussed further in Chapter 16, arranged by wholesale tour brokers.

Motorcoach Tour Travelers

In the United States, this market segment was traditionally set aside for older travelers. In other parts of the world, however, where owning cars is not as prevalent, motorcoach tours have long been a popular mode of getting around. As most of the trends in the industry indicate, things have changed in the United States. Many younger travelers are utilizing motorcoach tours to see domestic sights inexpensively.

The motorcoach tour market for hotels and restaurants can be defined as ten or more travelers arriving at a hospitality establishment by motorcoach, as part of a total tour package. This market really has to be separated from other travelers arriving at the hotel by bus, simply because of their original reason for the purchase. A group of corporate business people could arrive at a hotel by bus, yet their sole purpose for the visit would be a corporate meeting, making them a corporate group. A convention could have an entire delegation from a similar geographic area arrive by bus, but again the reason would be to attend the convention, not to visit local attractions.

The size of the motorcoach tour market is expanding. Although the majority of these trips occur within one day, almost 40 percent stay overnight in a lodging establishment. Motorcoach tours from the United States to Canada generate over $1 billion a year in Canada, according to the National Tour Association.[21] Every "bus night" (average of 40 passengers) generates C$8,000. More than one-fourth of this went to hotels. Figure 7-16 shows how Venture Inns goes after this market.

Motorcoach tours are arranged in two formats, series and ad hoc groups. A tour series is a prearranged link of stopovers, usually carrying a theme. An example is a motorcoach tour to see the New England autumn foliage. Stopovers include country inns and landmark restaurants, with occasional visits to local museums.

An ad hoc group has a specific destination in mind; for example, Disney World. A group arranges to travel there by motorcoach and stay several nights to take advantage of the attraction. While ad hoc groups might also have another stopover, this is normally just a stopover, not the initial reason for the trip.

When soliciting the motorcoach market segment, responding to its specific needs makes the marketing more successful. Tours employ tour leaders responsible for the well-being of the group as well as the satisfaction of its individual members. Tour leaders are also, in essence, sales representatives for the tour company. The hotel salesperson sells the hotel to the tour company, but the tour leader is the one who has to travel with the group and ensure their satisfaction. As with most other products, there are many similar tours available to the consumer, and often the tour leader develops a following of repeat customers.

The group requires special room keys, all being preassigned before the bus arrives. The

---

[20]*1992 Leisure Traveler & Tour Expenditure Report,* published by the National Tour Association/International Association of Convention Bureaus, Lexington, Kentucky, p. 16.

[21]*Ibid.*

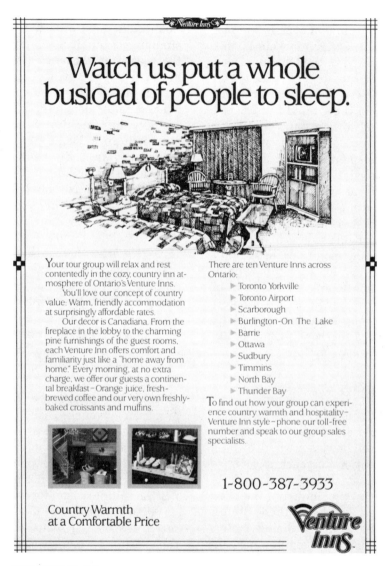

FIGURE 7-16   Soliciting the bus tour market

keys are distributed by the tour leader, and the baggage is unloaded and tagged. The luggage is a critical need for motorcoach customers. It is unacceptable to have to wait over half an hour for luggage to arrive in the rooms, after a long day on the road and before an inflexible dinner time. Whether luggage is carried to the rooms by bellmen, or by the customer directly, this relatively simple yet unusual situation can, if not handled correctly, cause many dissatisfied customers.

Although the median age of motorcoach tour travelers is dropping into the 50s, generally such travelers prefer rooms that do not require the use of stairs. They prefer rooms with views, they like being close to each other, and they want the correct bedding configuration—areas in which misunderstanding this market may arise. A weekend package user might ask for a double room and be completely satisfied with a queen bed assignment. The same double room for the motorcoach guest indicates a need for two beds in the same room—and a roll-away is not an acceptable substitute.

Motorcoach tour groups are a viable market for many hotels; in fact, some hotels survive on them. The warning here is the one we have mentioned before: The motorcoach tour segment may not mix well with some other market segments, and special care is needed to see that this mix is not a problem. Motorcoach tour operators traditionally seek out medium-priced hotels, but a recent study by one of the authors showed that tour operators used four-star hotels for 31.5 percent of their business.[22]

Regardless of their budget, these travelers' needs come all at once. An average normal busload of 46 means 46 bags at once, 46 luncheons at once, and 46 breakfasts at once. Staffing to handle this is critical, especially when these customers don't tip well and employees are not eager to serve them. Disgruntled tour groups make a great deal of noise!

Summary

Organizational planners are unique to the hospitality industry in that they plan travel for others in groups, but not for themselves. These planners/customers are responsible to the organizations they represent. They have to anticipate the wide variety of needs that members of these organizations represent.

Overall, organizational planners are better educated and have more experience in the hospitality industry than the individual purchaser of the hotel and restaurant product. The single most important factor in their decision-making process remains the word-of-mouth of their fellow professionals. Second, references from someone within their organization help steer organizational planners toward a hotel choice.

The conference coordinator at the hotel is probably more significant than the salesperson, in most cases, in creating and keeping customers. Advertising ranks low on the scale of influence. The organizational customer is a special case for the hospitality industry.

Discussion Questions

1. What is the essential difference between the organizational customer and other customers discussed earlier in this book?
2. Why do hotel convention and conference coordinators play a more important role in the decision-making process of the organizational customer?
3. How do the corporate travel planner/customer and the corporate meeting planner/customer differ?
4. Describe the three types of different incentive trips. How would each of these affect the choice of destination and hotel?
5. Why is the post-conference evaluation process critical for organizational customers?
6. Describe the differences between the association, the convention, and the trade show segments in terms of the end-users.
7. In Case 7-1, "The Government Market," discuss what you would do to make a decision about accepting/rejecting this market and/or what rates you would set.
8. In Case 7-2, "The Airline Market," do a displacement analysis and decide whether you would or would not accept the contract based on the subsequent gross margins and other factors discussed in the text.
9. In Case 7-3, "Hawthorne Inn & Conference Center," what are the problems facing Mr. Biden? What would you do to resolve them?

[22]Harsha E. Chacko and Eddystone C. Nebel, "The Group Tour Industry: An Analysis of Motorcoach Tour Operators," *Journal of Travel & Tourism Marketing,* Vol. 2(1), August, 1993, pp. 69–83.

✔ Case 7-1
The Government Market[23]

Le Meridien Hotel, a four-star, 600-room hotel in Montreal, Quebec, Canada, is located in the Complex des Jardin. The locale is shown in Exhibit 7-1-1. Government offices in this complex, and surrounding area, accommodate 150,000 people a day during weekdays. These offices also attract many government visitors who stay overnight in the immediately surrounding area.

The previous year, in fact, Le Meridien Hotel did 23,500 room nights from government employees at a rate of C$82, in spite of the fact that these government employees had a per diem

allowance of only C$72. Fifteen percent of occupancy came from this source. Another two percent of occupancy, 3,000 room nights, came from Quebec Hydro, the government-owned utility company whose employees were on the same per diem.

In December, the Budget Hotel opened up around the corner from Le Meridien. This hotel, in the two-star category with 200 rooms, was targeting the government market. Rooms and baths were small and contained only single beds. There was no room service. The rack rate was C$65. For the forthcoming year Le Meridien management wanted to increase its government rate by five percent. Should they?

---

[23]Georges Torrani provided the information for this case.

EXHIBIT 7-1-1   The Locale in Montreal

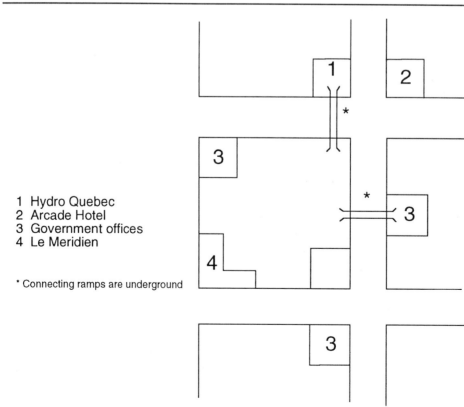

1 Hydro Quebec
2 Arcade Hotel
3 Government offices
4 Le Meridien

* Connecting ramps are underground

✔ Case 7-2
The Airline Market[24]

"I will give you my position in about a week," said Jean Valjean, General Manager of the Le Chateau Hotel, and he put down the phone and looked at the letter before him. The letter was from SKS Airlines requesting a one-year contract for 40 rooms each night at $48 per night. The problem facing Jean was a simple one: Does he take SKS and fill the 40 rooms for 365 days at $48, or does he refuse the business so that he can sell the rooms up to the full rack rate of $115? Last year the hotel had 95 percent occupancy or above for 135 nights; overall occupancy was 68 percent with an ADR of $72, but on nearly full or sell-out nights, the hotel could usually get rack rate on incremental room sales. This year was expected to be about the same.

Background of the Hotel

Le Chateau Hotel was located in the downtown area of a Canadian city. It was viewed as a four-star corporate/convention hotel. It had 800 rooms including the Towers—a prestigious five-story hotel within a hotel. The Towers had its own check-in facilities, lounge, and special amenities and contained 140 rooms, including 16 suites. The balance of the hotel offered a choice of king, queen, and double beds, with an additional 24 suites and six rooms especially equipped for the handicapped.

The hotel operated three restaurants. Le Mistral on the 37th floor offered gourmet French cuisine and an exceptional wine list. It had a seating capacity of 84. Le Shoppe on the third floor was open for breakfast, lunch, and dinner and had a seating capacity of 260. L'Expresso, a European-style "express" restaurant on the promenade level, was for people in a hurry. It had a seating capacity of 60. In addition to the restaurants, the hotel had five

lounges. Other features of the hotel included a five-story glassed-in atrium, glass-enclosed year-round pool, and health club with gymnasium, sauna, whirlpool, and massage. The hotel had a multilingual staff.

Competition

For airline crews, all hotels in the area were Le Chateau's competitors, because airlines historically chose hotels based on price and location, as long as they met a minimum level of comfort and services. SKS, however, preferred four-star hotels near shopping and entertainment facilities. This made competitive about ten properties located in the downtown area, so the decision would be made based on price and service. Jean was well aware that a number of competitors had expressed interest in the SKS business. He was also aware that, if he took the contract and satisfied the SKS crew, he would have more negotiating power when the contract came up for renewal next year, when the room rate could be increased. In the hotel business, it was always easier to renew existing room contracts than to solicit new ones.

The Proposal

Le Chateau's target market included all forms of corporate groups, professional associations, and conventions. The SKS proposal appeared to be a good opportunity for Le Chateau because it guaranteed 40 rooms per night (two overseas flights a day) for the entire year, plus potential clients from their flights. The contract, if accepted, would require the hotel to have clean rooms immediately upon check-in and to control the crews' wake-up calls. These services were standard tasks for Le Chateau. However, because of the late departure of aircraft toward Europe, check-out time for SKS would be between 4:00 and 6:00 P.M., while the inbound crews would be arriving between 9:00 and 10:00 P.M. the same night. This meant the

---

[24]This case was originally prepared by Professor W.M. Braithwaite, University of Guelph. It has been revised and disguised for use here.

hotel had to have extra maids on duty to have these rooms ready within two to four hours. In addition, when flight schedules were changed, this meant changes in wake-up calls. This extra service posed a problem during the summer months, when the hotel was full of regular guests and the staff was reluctant to provide extra service to the crews at the expense of the other guests, who were paying the full rack rate.

Experience with other airlines had shown that airline crews spent less money in the hotel than other guests during their stay, an average of only about $10 each. This was because their usual stay was only one night. If they had leisure time, if grounded for additional days, they preferred to explore the city; hence, food and beverage purchases were largely made outside the hotel.

Sales and Cost Data

Jean knew he would have to work fast on this proposal. He called in his assistant, Colette Chabot, and asked her to collect all the data required to estimate the comparative revenue and costs that would be involved to make a decision whether to accept the SKS offer.

Colette began with an analysis of room statistics for the previous year. These showed that, if the proposal had been in place, the number of regular guestrooms that would have been lost was equivalent to 105 nights sold-out and 30 nights at an average of 97 percent occupancy. Analysis of the food and beverage statistics, not including banquets, for the previous year showed food revenue of $22 per occupied room and average beverage revenue of $15. The hotel's standard cost percentages were 36 percent for food and 32 percent for beverages. In analyzing the probable effect on operating costs, Colette found that, on about 150 nights, the SKS contract would require the equivalent of one additional front desk clerk for eight hours at an average hourly rate of $12.20. Fringe benefits were calculated at 35 percent of all payroll costs. In addition to this cost, Colette estimated the following variable costs per occupied room.

Housekeeping: one-half hour per room at $10.60 per hour for the evening shift (part-time maids were available at this rate)
Laundry and linen: $1.25 per occupied room
Utilities: $1.50 per occupied room
Amenities: $2.50 per occupied room

Colette turned this information over to Jean for final analysis and a decision. As Jean sat in his office contemplating this information, he was reminded of a discussion at a recent meeting of general managers of all Le Chateau hotels, when they were told that one of the company's objectives for the coming fiscal year was a 12 percent return on investment. He was also very aware of the serious cash flow problem facing his hotel at that time. For the last fiscal year cash flow was negative by more than $2 million. With a $50 million long-term mortgage at floating rate interest and $4.2 million in annual municipal taxes to pay, the SKS business promised a steady and certain cash flow every week.

✔ Case 7-3

Hawthorne Inn & Conference Center[25]

According to John Phillips, CEO and President of Hawthorne Conference Services, the typical meeting planner devotes only 20 percent of his time to planning meetings. In most cases, the individual responsible for the organization of the meeting is also a participant who finds it difficult to both host the event and make a suitable contribution. "He's not a 'pro'," explains Phillips, "so we try to take the worry away from him to let him concentrate on the business at hand. Our aim is to make him look like a hero."

A consulting firm profiled this industry segment, based on a small sampling of executive conference centers, as shown in Table 7-3-1.

Hawthorne Conference Services

A large and highly developed marketer of meetings at conference centers was Hawthorne Conference Services, Inc., operating nine properties around the country. The emphasis at Hawthorne Conference Centers was on self-contained meeting packages with exceptional services to enhance the productivity of meetings. As opposed to a hotel in a major metropolitan area complete with all the distractions, Hawthorne Conference Centers were located in natural settings away from the hustle and bustle of the city.

The centers offered extensive recreational activities that invigorated the body as well as the mind. The advantage of the self-contained facility was that meeting participants tended to discuss related business matters while enjoying the leisure activities, thus increasing the overall productivity of the meeting. Hawthorne Conference Services catered to Fortune 500 companies, which normally demanded first-class dining, accommodations, and amenities and looked toward executive conference centers to improve the productivity of their meetings.

Hawthorne Conference Services performed most external marketing functions at the re-gional and national level, rather than at each of the individual properties. Hawthorne Conference Services believed this was beneficial for the company because interested parties could contact one central office to obtain information on any or all of the properties.

All of the centers operated by Hawthorne Conference Services were closed to transient guests, with the exception of the Hawthorne Inn at Hawthorne Village. This facility was open 365 days a year to the general public (the "social market") whenever rooms were available and not used by conferences.

The Hawthorne Inn

The Hawthorne Inn at Hawthorne Village was conveniently located close to the major metropolitan areas of the Northeast, yet completely removed from the noise and distractions of city life. The Inn itself was located in Hawthorne Village, a self-contained community that also boasted a 3,000-unit condominium complex, a shopping bazaar, a professional building, and a bank. The physical structure of the Inn reinforced the natural atmosphere.

The meeting rooms of the Inn, and the very heart of its business, were fixed in size and soundproof—they were not the retractable walls that were trademarks of many downtown convention hotels and allowed for greater flexibility. The meeting rooms were equipped with comfortable chairs, table space, screens, and state-of-the-art audio-video equipment that, along with coffee breaks, were included in the price of the room.

The 121 guestrooms were also fitted in the rustic mold, with a camp-like firmness to the beds and custom furnishings in the bright and airy rooms. Most of the rooms had two twin beds, although more and more were being converted to include queen-sized beds and private sitting areas in response to customer requests. Deluxe facilities at the Inn included a golf course, outdoor swimming pool, tennis courts,

---

[25]Scott Flagel and Karl Grover researched and contributed to this case.

health club with saunas, billiard room with connecting pub, and a beautiful restaurant and lounge called Woody's.

The Hawthorne Inn was owned by the Hawthorne Village Developers and operated by Hawthorne Conference Services, Inc. Joseph Biden, the General Manager of the property, believed that there were problems inherent in this type of arrangement. For example, plans for an expansion of 80 rooms and an indoor fitness facility—consisting of a swimming pool, racquetball courts, and an improved health club—had been discussed again and again, with no definite decision being made. Biden felt that the expansion would not only be beneficial in the long run, but actually essential if they intended to maintain their competitive position in years to come.

The pricing strategy of the hotel was to offer an all-inclusive price that included a room, three meals a day, coffee breaks, meeting facilities, and use of all recreational facilities, with the exception of golf, where there was a minimal greens fee. The convention rack rate was $185 per person double occupancy and $229 single occupancy, which was comparable to city hotels offering the same services separately priced.

The hotel split its markets into two categories: conferences, which had a 50 percent repeat factor, and transient social customers, who returned 60 percent of the time. The conference markets comprised almost three-fourths of all business and were diverse demographically. The conference market also generated the greatest percentage of the Inn's revenue.

Organization

The conference manager of the Inn served as the liaison between the regional sales office and the property's clients. There was no sales department for conferences on the premises. When arranging with a future meeting planner, the conference representatives acted as consultants to the company planner. This was beneficial to the client because the representatives were experienced in meeting particular meeting requests.

The operations manager had created strategies to encourage better utilization of the food and beverage outlets, such as promoting sports-oriented theme nights in the lounge to the mostly male guests. Woody's restaurant catered to the local market and also those social guests not on a meal plan, in addition to the American Plan conference guests. Business was brisk on the weekend nights, and Sunday brunch was also popular with the locals.

The General Manager, Mr. Biden, was the final member of the executive staff. He was pleased with the performance of the hotel, but would have liked to add an on-site sales position to the budget. All executive committee members agreed that a salesperson based at the Inn would be better equipped to make a sale than one who was geographically distant.

The Competition

Because of the success of hotel concepts similar to the Hawthorne Conference Centers, there had been an increase in competition from two separate sectors. The first form of competition was from hotels that had shifted their marketing efforts toward executive conferences when they recognized the potential for revenue.

The second form of competition was from companies invading the niche that Hawthorne had carved out. An example of this was the Arrowwood facility, located not far away in Rye, New York. Arrowwood was built at an average room cost of $220,000 and boasted the latest in audiovisual equipment and indoor recreational facilities, although at a higher price than Hawthorne. More competition like this was expected as more and more companies attempted to jump on the executive conference bandwagon.

Demand

The occupancy rate for the Hawthorne Inn at Hawthorne Village had hit a peak two years before at 73 percent. Mr. Biden believed that the occupancy rate was still well above the industry average, but was nonetheless concerned with the negative trend in occupancy.

TABLE 7-3-1   Profile of Executive Conference Centers

Meeting Types: Executive conference centers were most often used for training sessions (44% of all meetings, with a mean group size of 28), management planning (27% of meetings, with a mean of 23), and sales meetings (16% of meetings, with a mean of 44.)

Sources of Business: Most conference center meetings were sponsored by business organizations (82%), although trade and professional associations accounted for 9% of the business at participating centers, and academic institutions and government bodies occasionally met at the centers.

Occupancy: Although some conference centers did play host to transient traffic in order to boost business during slow periods, average annual occupancy among the centers was still low at 59%. December and January were the slowest months; March and October the busiest.

Traffic Patterns: Conference centers reported that meeting participants most often arrived on Sunday or Wednesday and stayed through Friday. An earlier trend toward weekend meetings appeared to be reversing, except in resort areas where a Friday arrival was common. Conference centers handled an average of 5 to 12 meetings each week.

Recreational Facilities: Most executive conference centers offered tennis, swimming, golf, an exercise room, and a game room; some also boasted facilities for bowling and horseback riding. (Although most centers allowed meeting participants unlimited access to these facilities, some derived additional revenue from recreation.)

Operating Statistics: Revenues and operating expenses of executive conference centers, compared with those of convention hotels, found most operating ratios to be similar. At 8.5% of sales, however, marketing costs at executive conference centers were almost twice those of convention hotels (4.9%)—presumably reflecting the need to communicate both the existence of a new facility and a fairly new concept to prospective clients.

He was convinced that decisions by the developers had triggered this downward spiral, stating, "Not adequately renovating the existing facility and not proceeding with the expansion/addition has contributed to the occupancy problem. The addition of 80 rooms would help meet the demand of weekday requests for conferences and the indoor facility would attract more winter guests."

For the conference market, January and February had the lowest weekday occupancy, but the remaining months were consistently higher. Weekend occupancies, however, fluctuated drastically due to special packages and other incentive plans. The impressive weekend occupancy rates for January and April were a little misleading because room rates were discounted considerably in those months.

For the social market, the biggest demand fluctuations occurred between summer and winter months, and between weekdays and weekends. The hotel had much more to offer the social guest in the summer. Although overall weekend occupancy had improved over the last five years, it still ran a poor second to weekday occupancies. Occupancy information is shown in Table 7-3-2 for the previous year.

The Marketing Function

Mr. Biden was concerned about the negative trend. He had done what he felt was necessary at the local level, but any long-range actions were subject to the approval of both Hawthorne Village and Hawthorne Conference Services.

A problem, however, existed among Hawthorne Village Developers, Hawthorne Confer-

TABLE 7-3-2   Occupancy Information

Social Market			
Month	Weekday	Weekend	Total
January	8.0	23.5	12.8
February	9.9	27.3	16.1
March	9.8	37.7	17.9
April	13.3	26.9	18.3
May	17.7	49.7	28.0
June	7.3	56.8	20.5
July	17.3	59.6	33.6
August	13.8	44.7	21.8
September	15.7	53.1	30.4
October	9.8	50.4	25.5
November	8.9	47.4	19.0
December	5.1	22.4	18.6
Average	11.4	41.6	21.9

Conference Market			
Month	Weekday	Weekend	Total
January	57.0	33.3	49.4
February	49.6	6.6	34.2
March	61.5	8.2	46.0
April	61.2	19.5	45.9
May	61.9	5.1	43.6
June	71.8	13.8	56.4
July	65.1	5.6	42.1
August	59.8	3.1	45.2
September	74.0	5.0	54.6
October	83.4	10.0	59.8
November	68.5	9.5	46.2
December	72.0	2.2	37.6
Average	65.5	10.2	46.8

Note: Weekday occupancy is Sunday night through Thursday night and weekend occupancy is Friday and Saturday night.

ence Services, and the management of Hawthorne Inn in terms of short-range versus long-range objectives. Management had felt constraints in having to set objectives that adhered to short-term goals while also keeping long-range objectives in mind.

The marketing function of Hawthorne Inn was somewhat diversified. First, there was the corporate marketing department that handled all but local group sales, advertising, and corporate strategy. In fact, 88 percent of conference bookings went through the main sales office at corporate, which handled all but on-the-spot arrangements. This was designated corporate procedure even to the point that, if the Inn received inquiries, it was required to refer them to the corporate office.

Then, there was the network of interaction

between the corporate marketing department and the Inn's catering and conference sales force, which sometimes became tense. Finally, operations management had the responsibility of marketing the restaurant and lounge, both internally to in-house guests and conferees, and externally to the local community. The overall marketing function was covered by all three of these divisions, but there was no one person involved and responsible for the mass marketing activities of the Inn.

Mr. Biden noted that, in spite of the decline, the customer repeat rate was over 50 percent of the total business. He wondered if this was good or bad; if the Inn was losing customers, or potential customers; if the overall market was declining—or a combination of all three. He summed up the situation by saying, "Our bottom line is fantastic in terms of profit, but we have to correct the problems at hand. Only then will we be able to make meeting planners look like heroes."

PART IV
Defining the Market

CHAPTER 8

Differentiation, Segmentation, and Target Marketing

In previous chapters we have talked about differentiation, segmentation, and target markets without really explaining those concepts in detail. It is time that we did so, since each is a vital and integral part of marketing. Accordingly, each deserves the extended treatment given in this chapter.

Differentiation, segmentation, and target marketing are each critical marketing concepts and tools that help us to understand and analyze the market. They are tools by which the marketer hopes to outflank the competition, seize marketing opportunity, maximize marketing efforts, and satisfy customer needs and wants. They are separate concepts and tools but, at the same time, they are highly interrelated—that is, all three are almost always involved in the marketing of the same product. We will first define how they are different, then how they work together.

Differentiation

Differentiation in its simplest form means differentiation of your product or service from those of other firms for the entire potential market. This means you are distinguishing your product/service from that of the competition, so that demand will come your way.

The assumption is that the customer will perceive greater utility, better price/value, and better problem solution in your product/service. Notice the use of the word *perceive,* a word that we expanded on at some length in Chapter 6; it is not necessary that there be an actual difference, only that the market perceives there to be one. It is just as important to note the converse situation: If the market does not perceive a difference, then for all intents and purposes it doesn't exist. It is clear, once again, how important knowledge of the customer is in marketing a product.

The objective of the marketer in practicing differentiation is to convince consumers that a particular product is different, or better, so they will choose it over all others. There are numerous examples of this strategy in the hospitality industry, including that of the Peabody Hotels, which differentiate in a unique way. A family of ducks is housed in each hotel, and they are brought down in an elevator each morning to spend the day at a fountain in the hotel lobby. In the evening the ducks troop back into the elevator to return to their quarters. This ritual attracts many spectators to the Peabody lobbies. The lobby bar does a roaring business every evening as people wait to see the ducks march into the elevator. In fact, the logo of the Peabody Hotels is a duck (Figure 8-1). Does this make the Peabody a better hotel? Probably not, but it certainly makes it different.

Bases of Differentiation

The bases for differentiation are often minor product features. In themselves, they may be

*Blending in with
the American Cotton Council*

*Swinging with
the Professional Golfers Association*

*Breaking out
with Federal Express*

The versatile Peabody duck.

(Hotelius meetingus spectacularis)

Our trademark mascot may look like a duck. Walk like a duck. And quack like a duck. But he's a true chameleon when it comes to adapting to your group's needs.
Because here at The Peabody Hotels, we believe each meeting we host is the most important meeting ever. And we're committed and equipped to provide every foot, and feat, needed to make yours the best one yet.
Your attendees will feel right at home, too – whether steeped in legendary elegance and white glove hospitality at the Peabody Memphis, or pampered with warm personal service and a surplus of resort amenities at the Peabody Orlando.
No matter what size gathering is next on your agenda, give us a call at 1-800-42 DUCKS and let us help you make it magic. Even if that means teaching our old duck some new tricks.

*Showing his colors
at the Century 21 convention*

*Attending to the Johns Hopkins
School of Medicine meeting*

The Peabody

ORLANDO · MEMPHIS
America's Only 5-Duck Meeting Hotels℠

FIGURE 8-1   The Peabody Hotels differentiate on ducks

unimportant, but they can be very effective when (1) they cannot be easily duplicated, (2) they appeal to a particular need and/or want, and (3) they create an image or impression that goes beyond the specific difference itself. (Like ducks?)

Consider the Plaza Hotel or the Waldorf-Astoria, both in New York City. Both are eminent hotels with a great deal of history behind them, which have been frequented in the past by international celebrities. These hotels' histories cannot be duplicated by other hotels in New York. This "product" has considerable appeal for consumers who like the old world and the feeling of blending with the past. Finally, there is an image or impression that these hotels, because of their past, will have great service and unmatched elegance. In sum, companies that differentiate products must also face the need to instill an image in the minds of customers that distinguishes their products from others, and causes the customer to react more favorably toward them.

Differentiation of Intangibles

Because the hospitality product is so largely intangible, differentiation in traditional marketing needs to center largely on "tangibilizing the intangible," an expression commonly used in services marketing to mean making a concrete representation out of something abstract, such as using an atrium lobby (concrete) to represent an "exciting" (abstract) hotel. Some hotels try to differentiate on the basis of better service quality. However, this is very difficult to prove since customers must experience the service first before deciding if it is indeed better. If credible proof is offered, then differentiating on the basis of service quality can be successful. For example, the Windsor Court Hotel in New Orleans is perceived to have the best service in town. Proof? The Windsor Court is the only five-diamond hotel in New Orleans. As we showed in earlier chapters, consumers need tangible evidence to support intangible claims. An example is shown in Figure 8-2.

The Roger Smith Hotel has differentiated itself in the New York City marketplace by creat-

WE GUARANTEE YOUR MEETING WON'T MISS.

• Too easily, a successful meeting can become hit or miss. That's why every Radisson resort hotel offers an Assured Meeting℠ guarantee. An exclusive performance agreement that guarantees your satisfaction or you'll be promptly compensated. • Plus a Conference Service Manager will help plan and execute your meeting. Without a slip-up.

• Call your nearest Radisson International Sales Office today.

CHICAGO	NEW YORK	WASHINGTON, D.C.
312-263-3690	212-826-3590	202-898-0182
MINNEAPOLIS	LOS ANGELES	TORONTO, ONTARIO
612-540-5526	213-322-1600	416-675-7755

• FOR RESERVATIONS WORLDWIDE 800-333-3333 •

 Radisson Hotels International
WORLDWIDE • WORLDCLASS℠

FIGURE 8-2   Tangibilizing the intangible

ing an artistic guest experience. The exterior, lobby and restaurant all feature original art designed by the owner and others. This "thinking man's" boutique hotel is unique in a city full of medium to large commercial hotels.

Differentiation as a Marketing Tool

Differentiation is an important marketing tool, whether the differences are real or merely perceived. For one thing, differentiation helps to create awareness and trial by the consumer.

Atrium lobby hotels certainly did that for Hyatt, Ronald McDonald did it for McDonald's, boxcars did it for Victoria Station restaurants, mega-swimming pools with waterfalls did it for mega-resorts, orange roofs did it for the original Howard Johnson's, a musical waterfall did it for the New Otani Hotel in Singapore, and "We'll keep the light on for you" commercials did it for Motel 6. Internally, personnel attitude has done it for the Opryland Hotel in Nashville, cleanliness has done it for McDonald's, and extra personal service has done it for the Oriental in Bangkok (Figure 8-3), the Peninsula Hotel in Hong Kong, and Ritz-Carlton Hotels, which won the coveted Malcom Baldridge National Quality Award in 1992—the first and, so far, the only hotel company to receive it (Figure 8-4).

As we shall see later in this chapter, sometimes the only thing we can do when we compete with others in the same market segment is attempt to differentiate the product. As pointed

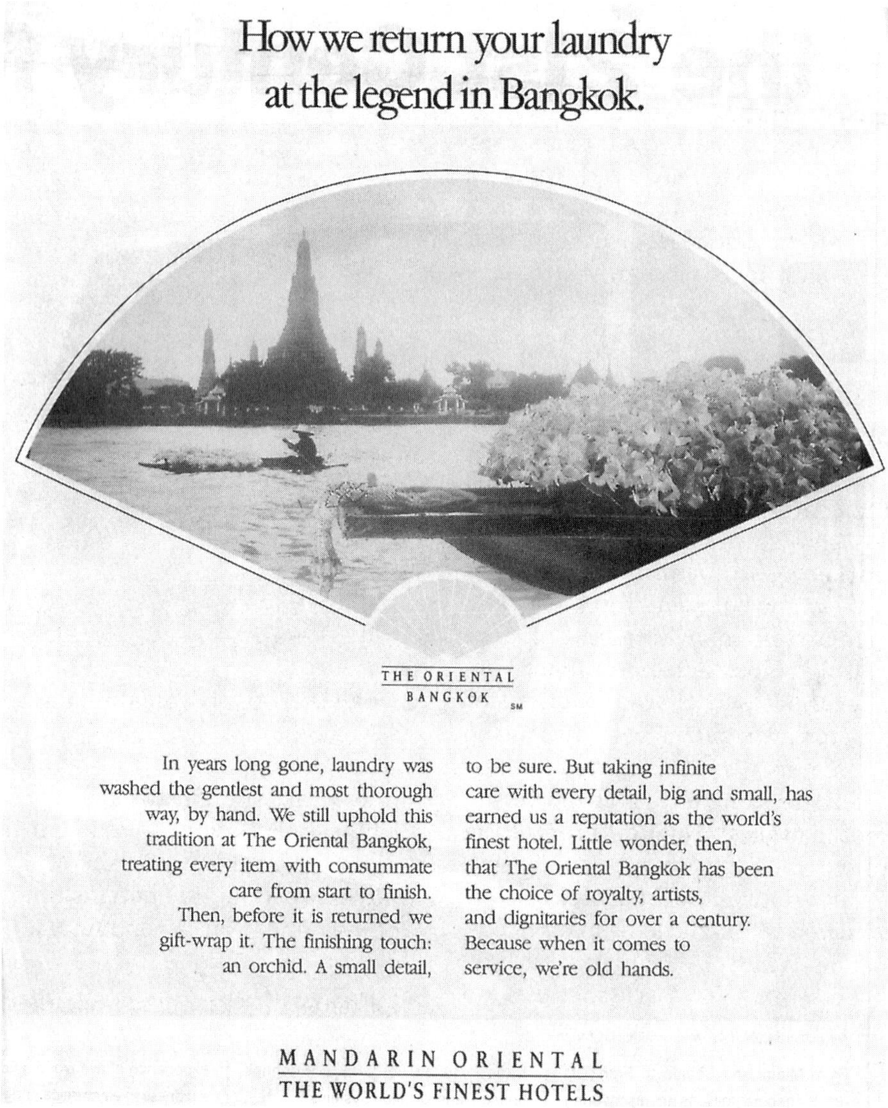

FIGURE 8-3 The most frequently top-rated hotel in the world

The Ritz-Carlton won the 1992 Malcolm Baldrige Quality Award. So stay with us. And you win.

The Malcolm Baldrige National Quality Award, created by Congress in 1987 and managed by the U.S. Department of Commerce, reflects our commitment to service, consistency *and reliability. Comforting thought next time you're considering hotel accommodations for your associates. The Ritz-Carlton Hotel Company. 800-241-3333. CRS access code: RZ.*

THE RITZ-CARLTON®
HOTEL COMPANY

FIGURE 8-4   Ritz-Carlton differentiates on the Baldridge Award

out in Chapter 5, it is a world of limited opportunities, in this respect, in that the product approaches commodity status and differentiation may occur only in the marketing or, unfortunately, sometimes in the pricing.

Attempts to differentiate also have another drawback. When they are vulnerable to easy copying by the competition, there are two possible negative effects. The first is obvious and has already been mentioned: As in the case of extensive bathroom amenities, when the competition quickly follows suit, the differential advantage is lost, and the cost of the differential becomes a burden without producing additional revenue. The second negative effect is the creation of expectation in the consumer, who comes to expect a differential even after the competition has done the same thing. This might be called the "what have you done for me lately" syndrome. The property is now caught in a cycle of being unable to fulfill expectations—reality does not match expectation for the consumer.

There is a way out of this, however, and it lies in marketing in its true sense, rather than in essentially giving things away. This means, of course, going back to the customer.

> Days Inn research revealed that guests prefer in-room coffee service over such basic amenities as shampoo, lotions, and shower caps: 87 percent indicated they would even pay an increased room rate if rooms were supplied with such a service; 78 percent indicated an in-room coffee system would influence their selection of a hotel the next time they traveled.[1]

Differentiation, to be effective, must be meaningful. There's still nothing like asking the customer. In-room coffee service, of course, can be duplicated and has been. Days, however, set itself apart by inaugurating this service in budget hotels. They created an impression that goes beyond the service itself.

Food-service establishments actually have greater opportunity to differentiate than do hotels. Although some food-service product classes may be somewhat close to commodity status, there is a wide variety of ways that restaurants can differentiate their product; in other words, it is much easier to be creative, economically, with a menu and decor in a restaurant than with a hotel room. Lettuce Entertain You Enterprises has been very successful with its creativity in Chicago, as shown in Figure 8-5. In spite of this potential, however, restaurant advertising tends to be blandly and boringly the same (Figure 8-6). Figure 8-7 shows an exception to this.

Hotel managements have also begun to realize the need to differentiate restaurants in recent years and have developed more creative concepts, although many still tend to ignore the customers' needs, as pointed out in examples in previous chapters. The traditional hotel had a coffee shop, a fine dining room, and a lounge, often with little imagination or creativity and often not fulfilling customers' needs. Rather than be creative and seek new opportunities, it was simply accepted that food and beverage departments would hopefully operate at a small profit and there wasn't much that could be done

---

[1]Tony Lima, "Updating Amenities to Meet Changing Lifestyles," *Lodging Hospitality*, June, 1987, p. 118.

about it. The frequent customer reaction was, "That's hotel food.... Let's go out to eat."

The situation is quite different outside the United States. Both in Europe and Asia it is not uncommon for hotel dining rooms to be the best restaurants in the city. Both hotel guests and the local populace patronize them heavily. In France, for example, one can find a two-star hotel with minimal rooms that includes a dining room superior to most in New York City. In Japan, where eating out is such a common practice, F&B can contribute as much as 70 percent to a hotel's revenue.

One of the first to break the "hotel food" mold and take a different approach was Jim Nassikas, when he opened The Stanford Court Hotel in San Francisco in 1971. Nassikas opened Fournou's Ovens restaurant within the hotel, but didn't tell the hotel guests. There was no mention of the restaurant in the guestrooms or within the hotel. To get there, guests were instructed to go out the front door and around the corner. In fact, one of Nassikas' favorite stories is of the hotel guests who hailed a cab in order to get to the restaurant. Nassikas' strategy not only added a mystique to the restaurant, it also differentiated it in the perception of nonguests who fastidiously avoided "hotel food." The result was a very successful, differentiated hotel gourmet restaurant, now well-established and no longer a secret.

Today there are hotels with "fast-break" bars for juice, coffee, and rolls; lounges with deli bars as well as liquor bars, lobby lounges with entertainment, "grazing" restaurants, and so forth. When the basic hotel room doesn't change much, these areas present excellent opportunities to differentiate because they are not as susceptible to copying and can offer unique and distinct advantages.

Differentiation...of Anything

Goods manufacturers seek competitive difference through features that may be seen and measured or sometimes just implied. For example, people still prefer brand-name drugs over the generic kind, even if the drugs are exactly

Avanzare®
Setting the standard for Northern Italian dining, this elegant restaurant features classic and innovative modern dishes. Reservations recommended. 161 E. Huron St., Chicago, 337-8056.

Scoozi!®
In Chicago's art gallery district. Recalls an art studio; serving rustic, country Italian featuring pasta, antipasti, thin crust pizza, and house specialties. 410 W. Huron Street, 943-5900.

Everest™
Spectacular 40th-floor views, 4-star reviews. Acclaimed chef-owner Jean Joho creates personalized French cuisine. Reservations accepted. Valet parking. 440 S. LaSalle St., Chicago, 663-8920.

The Pump Room™
World famous as Chicago's #1 celebrity haunt since 1938, this Gold Coast favorite serves renowned American dishes. Live entertainment nightly. 1301 N. State Pky., Chicago, 266-0360.

Shaw's Crab House®
Chicago's premier seafood house is really two restaurants in one: a classic East Coast dining room and the Blue Crab Lounge, an authentic oyster bar. 21 E. Hubbard Street, Chicago, 527-2722.

Bub City®
Huge, lively "joint" famous for Southern B-B-Q dinners and sandwiches, plus fresh fish and seafood. Adjacent to Club Bub, with real country music. 901 W. Weed St., Chicago, 266-1200.

Hat Dance®
Adventurous Mexican cuisine including fresh seafood in a dramatic white-on-white setting. Featuring wood-oven roasted chicken and tuna asada. 325 W. Huron St., Chicago, 649-0066.

Tucci Milan®
An open kitchen and original artwork create a comfortable atmosphere in this Italian trattoria. Featuring an antipasti table, homemade pastas, rotisserie specialties and much more. 6 W. Hubbard St., Chicago, 222-0044.

Tucci Benucch®
Rustic Italian food in a warm country-home setting. Limited reservations accepted. Free parking after 5 p.m. in 900 N. Michigan Avenue Self-Park. 900 N. Michigan Avenue, 266-2500.

Maggiano's Little Italy™
A classic Italian dinner house. Large platters of pasta, chicken, veal, steaks and fish. Great for big parties. 516 N. Clark, Chi., 644-7700. 240 Oakbrook Center, Oak Brook, (708) 368-0300.

Ambria®
Extraordinary cuisine Légere of our renowned Chef Gabino Sotelino noted for four-star reviews. Art Nouveau decor. Reservations required. 2300 N. Lincoln Park West, Chicago, 472-5959.

Un Grand Café®
Authentic Parisian café famous for steak frites, poulet rôti, and bouillabaisse. Outdoor dining overlooking Lincoln Park in spring and summer. 2300 N. Lincoln Park West, Chicago, 348-8886.

Cafe Ba-Ba-Reeba!®
It's like a brief trip to Spain! Enjoy our famous tapas, the very popular, tasty hot and cold "little dishes of Spain"—plus great paella. 2024 N. Halsted Street, Chicago, 935-5000.

Papagus™ Greek Taverna
Feast on hearty regional Greek fare in a warm, friendly rustic taverna that features great bite-sized appetizers called mezedes. 620 N. State Street (at the Embassy Suites), Chicago, 642-8450.

The Original A-1™
Boisterous, Western-style restaurant featuring lip-smacking BBQ dinners, sandwiches and more. Set amidst the excitement of North Pier. Gringos welcome. 401 E. Illinois Street, Chicago, 644-0300.

The Eccentric®
Oprah Winfrey invites you to dine at this cosmopolitan American restaurant serving Chicago's finest prime rib, plus a wide variety of home-cooked specialties. 159 W. Erie Street, Chicago, 787-8390.

The Mity Nice Grill™
This friendly neighborhood grill serves steaks and burgers, salads, simply grilled fish, homemade pies, etc. Great people watching at the classic bar, too. Water Tower Pl., 835 N. Michigan Ave., 335-4745.

foodlife™
A revolutionary food forum that serves a multitude of ethnic and healthy food choices. Setting is like a park-within-the-city. Water Tower Pl., 835 N. Michigan Ave., 335-3663.

We have great restaurants sprinkled all around.

For over 20 years, we've been moving and shaking Chicago with our delicious diversity of cuisines. What's more, with our choice of locations, you can count on one of our restaurants being close to you.

So get shaking and let us shower you with impeccable service and memorable dining. And don't forget the American Express® card, the card used by seasoned travelers.

Don't leave home without it.®

LETTUCE ENTERTAIN YOU ENTERPRISES, INC.
©1993 Lettuce Entertain You Enterprises®, Inc.

Courtesy of Lettuce Entertain You Enterprises, Inc.

FIGURE 8-5   One organization that differentiates its restaurants

"Always unique among Little Italy restaurants

remains the area sophisticate"

OF LITTLE ITALY

Let us help plan your very special rehearsal dinner.

PRIVATE ACCOMMODATIONS
for up to 50 people

Our goal is to provide the finest, most
innovative and satisfying foods from the cuisines of
Italy, France & America.

(410) 539-1965

On the corner of Albemarle St. and Eastern Ave. in Little Italy
OPEN DAILY LUNCH & DINNER

Capriccio

Northern Italian and Continental Cuisine

Experience our tableside magic...
Featuring Steak Diane, Famous flambée
coffees, & desserts.
Fresh seafood, veal & pasta prepared in
Northern Italian fashion.

Private Rooms for Rehearsal Dinners

846 Fawn St. Balt. MD. 21202
(410) 685-2710

Boccaccio
Northern Italian Cuisine In Little Italy

*Giovanni Boccaccio, one of
Italy's most renowned XIV
century authors, is said to
have been born in Florence in
1313. Boccaccio, a
contemporary of Francesco
Petrarca and Dante
Alighieri, is most famous for
his literary masterpiece the
"Decameron". In literary
history, the "Dacameron" has
represented a true spirit of
greatness. It is in this spirit
of greatness we honor
Boccaccio by serving you the
very finest of Italian cuisine.*

BUON APPETITO

Giovanni Rigato

925 Eastern Avenue
Baltimore, MD 21202
410-234-1322

FIGURE 8-6   The sameness of restaurant advertising

FIGURE 8-7   Creative restaurant advertising

the same. This is also true, says Levitt, with services.

> Commodity exchange dealers trade in totally undifferentiated generic goods such as pork bellies and metals; what they sell is the claimed distinction of their execution, their efficiency, their responsiveness to customers' buy and sell orders.... In short, the "offered" product is differentiated, although the "generic" product is identical. When the generic product is undifferentiated, the offered product makes the difference in getting customers, and the delivered product in keeping them.[2]

Product differentiation, then, is any perceived difference in a product when compared with others. It is what makes Smirnoff a premium vodka when it is fairly well established that all American vodkas are, by legal specifica-

tion, very much the same. It is what makes Stolichnaya or Absolut vodka even more "premium" than Smirnoff, even when used in a mixed drink where the subtle difference is indistinguishable to most. It is what makes a McDonald's hamburger better than Burger King's (or vice versa). It is what makes a person respond, "I just like it there," when asked why he or she goes to a particular restaurant. And, it is what makes one hotel appear more friendly, another more efficient.

In short, the marketer seeks differentiation whether perceived or real. The differentiation may be product-specific or it may be brand-specific. The latter is more difficult to achieve in the hospitality industry because of the heterogeneity of services but, because of that, even more desirable for chain operations.

Levitt states the case for differentiation as follows:

> To attract a customer, you are asking him to do something different from what he would have done in the absence of the programs you direct at

---

[2]Theodore Levitt, "Marketing Success through Differentiation—Of Anything," *Harvard Business Review,* p. 73, Jan–Feb, 1980. Copyright © 1980 by the President and Fellows of Harvard College; all rights reserved.

Hospitality at the Pahk Plaza.

Service with a Boston accent.

The native accent is one of the first things guests notice at the Boston Park Plaza. Not just the manner of speech. But the manner of style. A decorative accent that enters into every room and suite, creating an ambiance that's as Bostonian as the Swan Boats below and the State House beyond. An accent on service that emphasizes promptness, courtesy, neatness, and the extra things that make a hotel memorable. Why, we'll even pahk your cah overnight. Free, of course.

The Boston Park Plaza Hotel & Towers.
A Saunders Hotel
Arlington Street at Park Plaza, Boston, Mass. 02117. (617) 426-2000. Outside Mass., 800-225-2008.

Courtesy of The Boston Park Plaza Hotel & Towers

FIGURE 8-8   Differentiation—of Anything

him. He has to change his mind and his actions. The customer must shift his behavior in the direction advocated by the seller.... If marketing is seminally about anything, it is about achieving customer-getting distinction by differentiating what you do and how you operate. All else is derivative of that and only that.... To differentiate an offering effectively requires knowing what drives and attracts customers. It requires knowing how customers differ from one another and how those differences can be clustered into commercially meaningful segments. If you're not thinking segments, you're not thinking.[3]

Differentiation separates product classes. The luxury hotel is different from the budget hotel. Choice International tries to differentiate Sleep from Comfort from Quality from Clarion.

[3]Reprinted with permission of The Free Press, a Division of Macmillan, Inc., from *The Marketing Imagination* by Theodore Levitt, p. 128. Copyright 1986 by The Free Press.

Within the same product class, differentiation separates the competition. Days Inn strives to be different from La Quinta, and Wendy's differentiates from McDonald's and Burger King. In traditional marketing, differentiation is essentially a promotional or advertising strategy that attempts to control demand. In nontraditional marketing, it is an internal strategy that attempts to satisfy demand. Differentiation provides an opportunity in competitive strategy, as discussed in Chapter 5, and it forms the basis of positioning strategy, as shown in Figure 8-8 and to be discussed in Chapter 9.

The Process of Market Segmentation

Differentiation and market segmentation are not competing but complementary strategies. It is useful to clarify this point.

In its purest form, product differentiation is the effort by competitors to differentiate their offerings across the total market. It is based on an assumption that customers' needs are quite alike and that the products offered are quite similar. Thus, the offering company sees demand arising from one big marketplace and tries to offer a product that is different from the competition.

Segmentation, on the other hand, assumes that the market is made up of customers whose needs are different. The product must be defined for specific market segments based upon basic differences in users' needs and wants. This calls for a more precise adjustment of the product to the requirements of specific market segments. Market segments are no more than groups of people who are in some way alike— that is, who have the same needs or wants on one or more dimensions. We will discuss these groups further later in the chapter.

Which to Use

Although differentiation and market segmentation are complementary and may be applied

either simultaneously or sequentially, Peter Yesawich suggests some general guidelines as to which one to use, as shown in Figure 8-9 and Table 8-1.[4]

When an establishment cannot be easily classified as definitively belonging to one of these two categories, says Yesawich, the situation probably calls for a combination of differentiation and segmentation strategies. Coca-Cola and Pepsi Cola, for example, both market to a number of the same segments. Each, of course, tries to create a perceived, if not real, difference in its products from the other's in each of the segments, and not just based on taste.

Which Comes First

Differentiation can lead to market segmentation, and market segmentation can lead to product differentiation. In the first case, the product differentiates for essentially the same market— that is, the product does the segmenting (termed product segmentation). In the second case, the market is segmented first and then followed by differentiation of the product among competitors in the same segment, based on needs and wants (termed market segmentation).

An excellent example of this process is the genesis of the current "product segmentation" trend in the hotel industry. Since 1981, this trend has resulted in hotel companies featuring a number of product lines such as budget, economy, suite, middle-tier, and upscale properties. As an analogy, this is no different from General Motors' offering five different product lines of automobiles, which started out as market segmentation that succeeded in the 1920s, but in the 1980s became primarily product segmentation that failed.

Product segmentation in the hotel industry actually started as product differentiation. It had its inception in 1981, when Robert Hazard

---

[4]Peter C. Yesawich, "Post-Opening Marketing Analysis for Hotels," *Cornell Hotel and Restaurant Administration Quarterly*, November, 1978, pp. 70–81.

	Market Composition	Market Sensitivity	Establishment Age	Product Distinctiveness	Competition	Competitors Strategy
Differentiation Strategy	Similar	Very Sensitive	Relatively New	Distinctive	Few	Differentiate
Segmentation Strategy	Diffused	Not too Sensitive	Relatively Old	Not Distinctive	Many	Segment

Source: Peter C. Yesawich, "Post-Opening Marketing Analysis for Hotels," Cornell Hotel and Restaurant Administration Quarterly, November, 1978, pp. 70–81.

FIGURE 8-9 Classification to determine differentiation or segmentation strategy

TABLE 8-1   Differentiation vs. Segmentation

A differentiation strategy is probably most appropriate when:

1. The total market is demographically, geographically, and psychologically similar.
2. The market is sensitive to differences between establishments.
3. The establishment is relatively new.
4. The establishment is distinctive.
5. There are few competing establishments.
6. Most competitors employ a differentiation strategy.

A segmentation strategy is probably most appropriate when:

1. The total market is demographically, geographically, and psychologically different.
2. The market is not too sensitive to differences between establishments.
3. The establishment has been in operation for several years.
4. The establishment is not distinctive.
5. There are several competing establishments.
6. Most competitors employ a segmentation strategy.

Source: Adapted from Peter C. Yesawich, "Post-Opening Marketing Analysis for Hotels," *Cornell Hotel and Restaurant Administration Quarterly,* November, 1978, pp. 70–81.

became Chief Executive of Quality Inns (now Choice International), a hotel franchisor. Hazard inherited a wide variety of franchisees with diverse properties, ranging from the barely adequate to the middle tier of quality. The result had been a very confused image with mixed consumer expectations and high risk. To counteract this, Hazard differentiated the product into three categories: Comfort Inns, Quality Inns, and Quality Royale (now called Clarion), and advertised to create different perceptions of each category. What resulted was a market segmented by the product. Hazard's concept was highly successful and other operators soon jumped on the bandwagon. A new term, *segmentation,* became common jargon in the hotel world. Eventually, true market segmentation evolved in some, but not all, cases.[5]

True market segmentation practices the marketing concept. In fact, a major reason for studying consumer behavior is to aid in the development of segmentation strategies. Segmentation distinguishes groups of customers, their needs and wants, and develops the product specifically for them. The essence of this development is Marriott's "Courtyard by Marriott" product line. What Hazard had started as product differentiation became product segmentation; Marriott developed the concept as market segmentation. Marriott went to self-employed, independent, restricted, or non-expense account customers, and asked what they wanted in a relatively low-cost hotel room, what trade-offs they would make, and what they would give up in order to pay less. The product was then designed to fit the demand

[5]Eventually, more confusion evolved as product lines began to overlap each other and owners and franchisees became greedy. Studies have shown that consumers see broad price ranges greatly overlapping so-called product segments. One of the authors, in fact, was "socked" a late-evening $100 for a Comfort Inn (luxury budget) Murphy-bed mediocre room in Erie, Pa., after leaving the Chicago Hyatt Regency at $105 (group rate), when down the highway Holiday Inn was selling a better room for $63. This subject is discussed

further in Chapter 9 where Figure 9-13 shows the current Choice brand positioning. It seems the hotel industry, like General Motors, has come full circle. A year later (1994) he paid $63 for an "upscale" Quality Inn Suites room with all-suite amenities in Burlington, Vt.; $60 for a noisy "budget" Friendship Inn room in Hadley, Mass.; $42 for an Econolodge "economy" room in Plattsburgh, N.Y., which was the best room of the bunch, except Quality Suites, and the best service of them all.

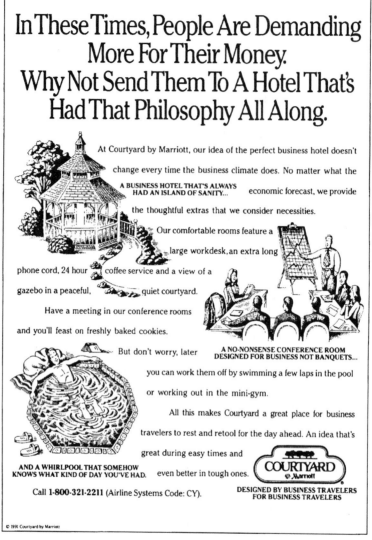

Courtesy of Courtyard by Marriott

FIGURE 8-10   Market segmentation—the product designed to fit the market

(Figure 8-10). This is true market segmentation.[6]

The result, of course, was much copying by others. In fact, some hotel chains blatantly to trade press usage, segmentation most definitely occurs with one product line. A trade journal (*Hotels*, September, 1987, p. 40) subheads "Stouffer Steers Away from Segmentation" by operating only upscale properties. William Hulett, then President of Stouffer Hotel Co., is quoted as saying, "There's no need for us to segment." What Stouffer actually did was to segment. They have segmented on one end of the market and designed the product to fit it. Four Seasons Hotels, Ritz-Carlton, and others have done likewise. Super 8 and La Quinta have done the same in the budget category. These so-called non-segmenters are, in truth, the strongest segmenters of all. This is exactly what Levitt means when he says (above), "If you're not thinking segments, you're not thinking."

---

[6]The industry's common use of the term *segmentation* is that, if a company has different levels of product class, they are segmenting. This may or may not be true (i.e., it could be simple differentiation, product line extension, or product segmentation). However, contrary

stated that their new products would be copies of Marriott's Courtyards. Today, there are many hotel companies competing in the same market segment as Courtyard. The astute marketer now must turn back to differentiation within that market segment.

Another example is the all-suite hotel concept pioneered by Granada Royale Hometels in the late 1970s. The all-suite hotel was designed for the extended-stay business traveler who wanted a little more room to spread out. At the time the all-suite was a differentiated product; today it is a full-blown market segment with a number of individual target markets, with upscale and downmarket offerings.

Granada Royale Hometels evolved into Embassy Suites, and some then spun off as a direct competitor, Crown Sterling Suites. Positioned above Embassy Suites is Guest Quarters and, to some extent, Radisson and Sheraton Suites. An alternative to Embassy Suites, focusing more on the long-term stay market, is Residence Inn. Below Embassy Suites are Quality Suites, Plaza Suites, and Homewood Suites.

Segmentation Comes First

At first glance, it may appear that we have really been saying the same thing in different ways. Who cares if first we segment, then differentiate, or vice versa? The difference, of course, is in customers' needs and wants. Numerous cases exist where attempts to differentiate have been less than fulfilling and failure to recognize market segments has resulted in loss of market share. In some cases this has been carried to the extreme, when a company tries to be "all things to all people," the antithesis of market segmentation.

Strategies of segmentation and differentiation may be employed simultaneously, but more commonly they are applied in sequence in response to changing market conditions.

The Process of Market Segmentation

With all of the above in mind, let us proceed through the market segmentation process. The basic assumption, once again, is that the mar-ketplace is heterogeneous; customers have different needs and wants. If we are to establish a more precise definition of the needs and wants of the marketplace, it is clear that we will need to locate those segments of the market with similar needs and wants—in other words, we need to break the market down into smaller homogeneous segments. Our need is better served if we take this in stages, since there are a number of elements that we will need to consider along the way.

Needs and Wants of the Marketplace In an oversimplification of the problem, we could conduct a giant research survey in which we asked consumers what it was they wanted in a hotel or restaurant. The complexity of this question is immediately apparent: Where? When? With whom? For what purpose? At what price? It is clear that we will not get very far with this approach, so the first thing we will have to do is to set some parameters. Let us proceed with a hypothetical example.

We are considering opening a restaurant in a city whose population is a million people, including the environs. We have decided that this will not be a fast-food restaurant but could be anything from an inexpensive family restaurant to a very expensive gourmet restaurant. We analyze what already exists and find that there is no high-quality French restaurant in the area. With this existing void, we could go this route and, without too much difficulty, clearly differentiate our restaurant and its French cuisine from the competition.

But what if no one wants French cuisine? We would be in serious trouble. Already we see the hazards of differentiating before segmentation. Instead, at this stage, let's ignore the competition and what already exists because, even if it exists, we really don't know if it is satisfying the needs and wants of the marketplace. Maybe it is not as successful as it looks; maybe it is successful only because there is no alternative.

So, let us reset the parameters. To simplify the example, let's say we have found a location and we have decided to open for lunch and dinner. Otherwise, there are no restrictions. Now we can conduct our survey.

Assume that we can survey the entire population (actually, we would take a random sample), of those with household incomes of $20,000 or more per year (50 percent of the population). The questions we could ask are almost unlimited, but we will have to narrow them down: How often do you go out for lunch/dinner? Where do you go? What do you order? Are you satisfied with the offering? What would you like to have instead? How much do you spend? How far do you travel? Do you like the atmosphere? Would you like a different atmosphere? What? Where would you like to go? How often? How much would you be willing to spend? What would you order? and so forth.

Our survey shows that six percent of the population with incomes greater than $20,000 (those with incomes over $40,000) would go or are going to a gourmet restaurant with some frequency. They will go there an average of five times a month for lunch with an average of two other persons, and twice a month for dinner with an average of one other person. They would spend $12 per person for lunch and $24 per person for dinner.

Of course, the other 94 percent of the same population is saying something else that, having open minds, we could not ignore. For purposes of illustration, however, let us concentrate on this six percent. This is a market segment: a relatively homogeneous segment of the market that likes, and will patronize, a gourmet restaurant. Armed with this information, we proceed to the second stage.

Projecting Wants and Needs into Potential Markets

This stage is called demand analysis. Demand analysis includes needs and wants plus willingness and ability to pay. Willingness and ability to pay are critical and we cannot afford to overlook them. For example, we may truly need a car to get to work every day, and we may truly want a Mercedes, but if we are unwilling to pay the price of a Mercedes, we are clearly not in the demand segment for that car. On the other hand, if we are willing but unable to pay, we are also not in the appropriate demand segment. Demand analysis means projecting needs, wants, and willingness and ability to pay into a potential market.

Our survey has shown that we have needs, wants, and willingness and ability to pay. What does this mean in terms of potential market? If we can believe the figures (again, this is an oversimplification to make the point and we are ignoring beverage sales), we can quickly calculate that 30,000 people in the area (six percent of 500,000) would be interested in the restaurant. If we take the worst case scenario and assume that those who would accompany them are also in the population surveyed, we calculate 50,000 [(30,000/3) × 5] lunches a month for a gross of $600,000 (50,000 @$12). For dinner we calculate 30,000 covers [(30,000/2) × 2] a month for a gross of $720,000 (15,000 @$24). The total potential of this market is perceived to be approximately $1,320,000 gross per year in food sales. This appears to be sufficient, so we proceed to the third stage.

Matching the Market and Capabilities

Recall that, when we surveyed the market, we had open minds about the type of restaurant we would open. Now that we have found an effective demand, the question is, do we have the capabilities to meet that demand? In this case, because we are starting from scratch, we have to consider dollar resources and all the financial implications of a major undertaking; designing and equipping a gourmet restaurant is not the same as designing and equipping a family restaurant. But we also have to consider the expertise in the firm: Who will manage it? What is their experience? Is this our mentality or philosophy? Does it fit with other things we are doing? Do we need outside help? and so forth. It is important, but often overlooked, that a firm's capabilities be matched to the market it is trying to serve.

There are many examples in industry of failures due to lack of understanding of a different market. City Investing Corp. had purchased the Motel 6 chain. By exercising strong cost controls and positioning the property at the low-cost, no-frills end of the budget motel market, City Investing succeeded where others had failed. It then took on Sambo's Restaurants and applied the same strategies and tactics, not recognizing the personal relationships of the restaurant business or the consumers' different perspective. In short, City Investing lacked the capabilities to operate restaurants, and Sambo's ended up in bankruptcy court.

If we have successfully passed the first three stages, we can proceed to stage 4.

Segmenting the Market   We have determined the needs and wants of the marketplace, projected them into potential markets, and matched them with our capabilities. But "gourmet" is a very broad category; in fact it is quite heterogeneous in composition. Not only does gourmet mean different things to different people, there are also many forms of gourmet. So we turn to further segmentation. To simplify the case, let's assume that we found a strong preference for French food in our survey; we decide to segment the market on those who have a high preference for French food. Now we have to go back through stages 2 and 3, and reevaluate the situation once more.

Selecting Target Markets from Identified Segments   Just as all gourmet food is not the same, neither is all French food. To take an example, this fact was learned the hard way by a restaurateur in a midsized New England city:

> An operator opened a French restaurant because "there weren't any around." He managed to build a small, loyal, steady clientele as well as an infrequent special-occasion following. When he closed, unsuccessful, two and a half years later his comment was, "The people in this city think French cuisine is quiche Lorraine."

So we have to select specific target markets from the broader market segment. This will be discussed in more detail later, but we might target on occasion, on nouvelle French, on income bracket, on age, on business entertaining, or any number of other things.

Tailoring the Product to the Wants and Needs of the Target Market   Now we see the advantages of segmenting and target marketing in terms of the marketing concept. Let's look at these advantages more specifically.

- *We are better able to identify and evaluate opportunities in the marketplace.* By knowing our target market, we can track it, identify what is missing, find niches, and discover consumers' problems.
- *We can better mesh our product with the needs of the market.* Consider the survey we did of the entire population, an expensive and time-consuming chore. Now we can be more specific as to who the market is. We can ask more specific questions and get higher response rates because we now have people interested in the subject. We can identify better who those people are. We can have a much better idea of the acceptance of any innovation.
- *We can optimally allocate and direct our resources.* As in the case described above, we wouldn't build a fancy French restaurant for a market that wanted quiche, nor would we need the same level of manpower and expertise. Perhaps we could determine that there is a takeout market for quiche and develop that end of the business. In short, the potential for wasting resources is greatly decreased.
- *We can use relevant market intelligence to sense change and to change strategies.* Because we now have a smaller market and are closer to it, we can keep in touch with it better. We have more opportunity to "talk" to the customer. We are better able to determine cultural and reference group influences, understand beliefs and attitudes, recognize and influence perceptions, use tangible evidence of intangible constructs, understand the information processing of the consumer, and give more "control" to both consumers and employees.
- *We have greater ability to tailor our behavior, promotion, logistics, distribution channels, and marketing mix to the market.* Essentially, this means we are better able to reach customers both by knowing where they are and what appeals to them, what they pay attention to, what they react to, and what media they use.
- *We are better able to be unique and to differentiate from the competition.* We can deter-

mine more readily what the competition is doing for this segment or target market. We know better what to copy, what not to copy, and what we do that will be copied. We have more opportunity to find competitive advantage and exploit the weaknesses of the competition.

- *We are better able to determine strategies to develop and enlarge the core market.* Take again the example of takeout quiche. Initially, we might not think this was a viable opportunity at all; by knowing our market, however, we might learn that it was and start offering take-home quiche to our customers. Eventually we could expand this market by selling it to non-customers—those who would not come to eat but would come to take it home.

Segmentation Variables

There is no one best way to segment the market, but there is no shortage of different ways to do it. What's more, they are certainly not mutually exclusive. First, we will discuss some of the more commonly used segmentation variables and then we will take a look at how they overlap.

Geographic Segmentation

Geographic location is probably the original segmentation variable and one of the most widely used. It has its strengths and its weaknesses.

Geographically speaking, we can segment by country, city, town, part of city, or even neighborhood. The essence and the substance of geographic segmentation is that certain geographic locations are the major sources of our business. A hotel in San Francisco might draw most of its business from Los Angeles and New York. A hotel in Singapore might draw most of its business from Australia and Japan. A restaurant in New York City might draw most of its business from the upper East Side. A restaurant in Hartford, Connecticut might draw most of its business from suburban towns.

If geographic segments can be pinpointed,

then the problem of reaching those segments is greatly facilitated, especially if they are in concentrated areas. Both direct mail and media forms of communication are more easily specified. It is also possible to utilize available resources to learn more about the denizens of these areas.

The U. S. federal government defines large metropolitan areas in terms of supposed economic boundaries called *standard metropolitan statistical areas* (SMSAs—for example, the New York City SMSA). The government produces reams of data on these areas—population, ethnic mix, growth, income, discretionary spending, household size, occupations, and so forth. The use of SMSAs in hospitality marketing is probably greatest when the market is being segmented on certain demographic variables. SMSAs can be analyzed for the existence of these variables.

Another geographic division is the *designated market area,* or DMA, developed by the A. C. Nielsen research company. These designations are based on geographic areas served by television stations. Their data also include demographic characteristics that can be used for reaching specific audiences by television. Fast-food chains such as McDonald's and Burger King use these designations.

A final, widely used geographic designation is the ADI, or *area of dominant influence.* These designations are also based on television coverage but are used as well by newspaper and magazine media for distribution of their regional editions. Thus, one could use ADIs for print communication as well as television.

Geographic segmentation is the easiest segmentation to define, but it is also the most fallible for the hospitality industry. The local neighborhood eatery doesn't have to employ SMSAs, DMAs, or ADIs to know where its business comes from. Broader-based operations draw from a wide variety of geographic locations and need to use more specific and economical means to reach their markets. In fact, one of the problems of individual restaurants is that they cater to numerous small segments that are difficult and prohibitively expensive to reach through traditional advertising media.

The other problem with geographic segments is that such definitions tend to arise largely after the fact. Once we have determined where our customers will or do come from, we then establish that area as the target of our marketing efforts. This may help in developing the area, but it may ignore other areas and does not necessarily influence buyers—that is, just because they are from that area does not mean they will come to our property, and it does not tell us what their needs and wants are.

On the other hand, geographic segmentation can be very useful in concentrating resources. The tourism board of Bermuda knows that most of Bermuda's tourism comes from the northeastern United States, eastern Canada, and the United Kingdom, and their advertising dollar is concentrated in those three areas. The New York City restaurant that knows most of its business comes from within a five-block radius can use direct mail and flyers to reach that market. Singapore can spend a major share of its marketing resources in Australia and Japan.

While all this is both true and helpful, it only helps us to reach the market; it is not of much assistance in determining the needs and wants of the market, because geographic segments, unless they are very small ones, are still heterogeneous in terms of consumer profiles, needs, and wants.

Demographic Segmentation

Demographic segmentation is widely used in almost all industries. One reason for this is that, like geographic segments, demographics are easily measured and classified. Demographic segments are segments based on income, race, age, nationality, religion, sex, education, and so forth. For some goods, demographic segments are clearly product-specific—for instance, children's clothes, lipstick, Rolls Royces, and denture cleaners.

For the hospitality industry, however, these segments may be somewhat moot. Knowing that someone is 30 years old, earns $40,000 a year, is married, and has a child may not be too helpful in separating a truck driver, a college professor, and an accountant. Each of these people will have different needs and seek different benefits, but for a large majority of hotels and restaurants the demographics will not distinguish between them.

There was a time, not that long ago, when this was not the case. You could open an expensive French restaurant and you didn't have to worry about what the customers' incomes were, what part of town they came from, what kinds of cars they drove, or whether they would wear coats and ties. Such a restaurant, by default, would define its own market segment.

This is no longer the case because demographic lines have, in many cases, become blurred and fuzzy. Plumbers may have higher incomes than accountants with MBAs. Everyone wears jeans, regardless of social standing. Executives check into hotels on weekends looking as if they had just finished mowing the lawn. Some of the wealthy get wealthier by eating cheaply, staying at budget motels, and fighting over the last nickel on their check. In fact, demographic lines have become so blurred that it is hard to tell what they mean anymore—unless, of course, you operate something like a specific neighborhood ethnic restaurant.

For the hospitality industry today, one of the most useful demographic parameters may be age—age in the sense of attracting children who bring their parents with them, a la McDonald's, or age in the sense of senior citizens, a vast and rapidly growing market with distinctive needs and wants, not to mention discretionary income.

Another demographic variable that may be useful in some operations, particularly restaurants and resorts, is the family life-cycle stage. The cycle runs, of course, from the single young person, to the married couple, the married couple with children, the married couple with grown children, to the widow or widower. In between there are, increasingly today, couples who don't have children and both have incomes; single parents and non-parents; and second and third marriages. Each of these stages contains, for most people, its own level of discretionary income, personal time/freedom, specific buying

FIGURE 8-11   Attempt at demographic segmentation

needs, and patterns of behavior. Marketers can tap into this information, as has been demonstrated by singles resorts, early-bird dinners, special tours, and packages.

Demographic market segments, like geographic ones, are also largely nonpredictive because they too are post hoc, that is, after the fact. We may know that older people with high incomes come to our property, but we still need to find out why—What needs and wants of these people are/are not being satisfied? Age, income, education, nationality, and other demographic or sociodemographic characteristics are limited in informing us of the needs and wants of these segments.

Does this mean that demographics are an unimportant segmentation variable? No, it does not. It means that we have to understand the meaning of those demographics and how they relate to other segmentation variables. Demographics serve as gross parameters within which are found more specific subsegments, as shown in Figure 8-11.

Psychographic Segmentation

Psychographic segments are segments based on *attitudes, interests, and opinions* (AIO), self-concepts, and lifestyle behaviors. AIOs are personality traits and the word *psychographic* actually means the measurement of personality traits. This view of segmentation is relatively new, having arisen mostly in the early and mid-1970s. Today, psychographic segmentation is very popular with some and totally disdained by others. There is good reason for both points of view.

First, we need to understand what psychographics are. According to Joseph Plummer, an advertising executive and one of the leading proponents of lifestyle segmentation, the concept is defined as follows:

Life style [sic] as used in life style segmentation research measures people's activities in terms of (1) how they spend their time; (2) their interests, what they place importance on in their immediate surroundings; (3) their opinions in terms of their

TABLE 8-2   Lifestyle Dimensions

Activities	Interests	Opinions	Demographics
Work	Family	Themselves	Age
Hobbies	Home	Social issues	Education
Social events	Job	Politics	Income
Vacation	Community	Business	Occupation
Entertainment	Recreation	Economics	Family size
Club membership	Fashion	Education	Dwelling
Community	Food	Products	Geography
Shopping	Media	Future	City size
Sports	Achievements	Culture	Life-cycle stage

Source: Plummer, "Life Style Segmentation," p. 34.

view of themselves and the world around them; and (4) some basic characteristics such as their stage in life cycle, income, education, and where they live [i.e., demographics and geographics].[7]

Lifestyle dimensions, as defined by Plummer, are shown in Table 8-2.

Those who are strong advocates of psychographic segmentation argue that lifestyle patterns combine, as can be seen in Table 8-2, the virtues of demographics with the way people live, think, and behave in their everyday lives. Psychographers attempt to correlate these factors into relatively homogeneous categories using classification terms such as homebodies, traditionalists, swingers, loners, jet-setters, conservatives, socialites, yuppies, and so forth, as well as the previously mentioned acronyms for certain couples, DINKS (double income, no kids) and DEWKS (dual employed, with kids). The classifications are then correlated with product usage, desired product attributes, and media readership and viewing. This has led to the VALS approach.

The VALS™ Approach   SRI International, a major research firm, is responsible for introducing the *values and lifestyles* (VALS) approach, a consumer psychographic segmentation tool. It has proven effective for categorizing

Americans into various lifestyles using values, beliefs, and lifestyles to do this. For example, Merrill Lynch replaced its "Bullish on America" herd of bulls with one bull after analysis revealed that the target market that Merrill Lynch wanted to attract saw themselves as self-made visionaries rather than as part of a herd.

VALS 2, introduced in 1989, presented eight segments of adult consumers and three major categories or "orientations" (as shown in Table 8-3)—principle-oriented, status-oriented, and action-oriented. Within each, people's resources were ranged, from abundant to minimal. Orientations classify three different ways of buying: 1) principles or beliefs rather than feelings, events, or desire for approval; 2) status or other people's actions, approval, or opinions; and 3) action prompted by a desire for social or physical activity, variety, and risk-taking. Resources include education, income, self-confidence, health, eagerness to buy, intelligence, and energy level (ranging from minimum to abundant, increasing through middle age and decreasing with extreme age), depression, financial reverses, and physical or psychological impairment. VALS defines these segments with different attitudes and distinctive behavior and decision-making patterns.

The assumption is that product attributes can be tailored to psychographic segments and that the product will thus have special appeal to those segments. The greatest proponents and

[7]Joseph T. Plummer, "The Concept and Application of Life Style Segmentation." Reprinted from the *Journal of Marketing*, January, 1974, pp. 33–37, published by the American Marketing Association.

TABLE 8-3   VALS™ 2 Psychographic Segments

1. *Actualizers*—successful, sophisticated, active, "take-charge" people with high self-esteem and abundant resources. They are interested in growth and seek to develop, explore, and express themselves in a variety of ways. Their possessions and recreation reflect a cultivated taste for the finer things in life.

Principle-oriented:

2. *The Fulfilled*—mature, satisfied, comfortable, reflective people who value order, knowledge, and responsibility. Most are well-educted, well-informed about world events, and professionally employed. Fulfillers are conservative, practical consumers; they are concerned about value and durability in the products they buy.
3. *Believers*—conservative, conventional people with concrete beliefs and strong attachments to traditional institutions—family, church, community, and nation. As consumers they are conservative and predictable, favoring American products and established brands.

Status-oriented:

4. *Achievers*—successful career- and work-oriented people who like to, and generally do, feel in control of their lives. Achievers live conventional lives, are politically conservative, and respect authority and the status quo. As consumers they favor established products and services that demonstrate success to their peers.
5. *Strivers*—people who seek motivation, self-definition, and approval from the world around them. They are easily bored and impulsive. Money defines success for strivers, who lack enough of it. They emulate those who own more impressive possessions, but what they wish to obtain is generally beyond their reach.

Action-oriented:

6. *Experiencers*—young, vital, enthusiastic, and impulsive. They seek variety and excitement and combine an abstract disdain for conformity and authority with an outsider's awe of others' wealth, prestige, and power. Experiencers are avid consumers and spend much of their income on clothing, fast food, music, movies, and video.
7. *Makers*—practical people who value self-sufficiency. They live within a traditional context of family, practical work, and physical recreation and have little interest in what lies outside that context. They are unimpressed by material possessions other than those with a practical or functional purpose (for example, tools, pickup trucks, or fishing equipment).

8. *Strugglers*—people whose lives are constricted—chronically poor, ill-educated, and low-skilled. They lack strong social bonds; aging strugglers are concerned about their health; they are focused on meeting the urgent needs of the present moment. Strugglers are cautious consumers who represent a very modest market for most products and services but are loyal to favorite brands.

Source: Adapted from *Values and Lifestyles™: The VALS™ 2 Typology.* Menlo Park, Cal.: SRI International, © 1994.

users of psychographics are advertising agencies, which use the classification elements to reach the segments via specific media, and to communicate the product attributes via lifestyle factors. Lifestyle research provides advertisers with insight into the setting, the type and appearance of the characters, the music, the tone, self-perceived roles, and the rewards people seek. Thus, in the past we saw on television the "typical" housewife, whose main concern was taking care of her family, standing by the washing machine extolling the virtues of a laundry detergent. Today, there is a different kind of woman, as well as a man, washing clothes.

Psychographics are, in fact, very useful in developing advertising messages but have been little used in the hospitality industry, other than in broad categories such as "business traveler." Clear exceptions to this are national advertisers such as McDonald's and Burger King. Another exception has been Club Med resorts, which for years promoted a hedonistic, singles lifestyle for the swinger segment. More recently, Club Med has been trying to reposition for both family groups and conferences and has incorporated some of these segments' lifestyles into their advertising. In some cases, however, it has been found that lifestyle variables themselves are more important than media exposure in planning vacations, and that media exposure alone may be an inadequate influence.

More commonly, however, hotel and restaurant advertising has stayed with the ubiquitous appeals of location, edifice, pool, or sterile pictures of dining rooms or hotel bedrooms. There may be good reasons for this, the best probably being that no substantial research has been conducted to classify hospitality customers in definitive lifestyle segments. Even resort advertising has not progressed far, when it pictures a beautiful woman in a bathing suit on the beach or by a pool. Presumably, these advertisers believe that this is the desired lifestyle criterion by which people choose a resort hotel.

One of the authors attended a Le Meridien Hotels sales conference where advertising was being discussed for the North America division. The company had chosen a very different image approach for their hotels, using artist Ken Maryanski to sketch various French scenes to convey the image of upscale and European lifestyles. The director of marketing of one Le Meridien resort complained loudly that her hotel did not have a picture of its pool in their brochure.

Critics of psychographics express concern whether these variables can be defined, are valid, and are stable. Lifestyle variables not only are difficult to define but also overlap greatly. Because of this there is considerable room for error/variance in establishing the classifications. Furthermore, people change, and do so rapidly, in today's society: Today's lifestyle may not be tomorrow's.

Regardless of the criticisms and failings of psychographic segmentation, it remains a rich area for marketing effectiveness in the hospitality industry. New hotels and restaurants are sometimes designed and built, and old ones refurbished, by architects, designers, and developers who pay little attention to consumers and how they "use" a property. Architects and designers want their creations to be artistic, developers want them to be built at minimum cost, and operators wants them to be functional. It is possible that psychographic research can tell us a great deal about what the customer wants and how to build and market to those wants. Research by both Hyatt and Marriott revealed that resort goers were fantasy seekers and incorporated this into their marketing strategies. As Joe Garvey, when Vice President–Marketing of Hyatt Hotels, argued, "Market segmentation through psychographic research is the future path for true customer satisfaction and supplier profitability."[8] Figure 8-12 shows an example.

Usage Segmentation

Usage segmentation is a broad umbrella that covers a wide range of categories that probably apply more specifically to hospitality businesses than any other type of segmentation. Although we often accept these categories as givens, some are not always well-utilized in market segmentation strategies. We will discuss them one at a time.

Purpose   Purpose is a common segment category in hotels. Often market breakdowns of occupancy are kept on a daily basis and categorized by purpose. Approximately 80 percent of urban hotel occupancy in the United States, on average, derives from business travelers who obviously constitute a major market segment. The business expense account customer is also

8Joe Garvey, "Outlook and Opportunities in Market Segmentation," in R. Lewis et al., eds., *The Practice of Hospitality Management II*, Westport, Ct.: AVI, 1986 p. 455.

You have arrived.   Vous êtes arrivé.

FIGURE 8-12   Attempt at psychographic segmentation

a source of sizable patronage in many restaurants. Business purpose can be broken down into submarkets such as conventions, associations, corporate, expense account, non-expense account, and so forth. These subcategories are important because each one will have somewhat different needs and wants and should be marketed to accordingly. These were discussed in Chapters 6 and 7.

The other major purpose category is called social, pleasure, or leisure. This market actually has a number of specific purposes, and a better term would probably be, simply, nonbusiness. For restaurants this segment will represent a larger proportion of business than for hotels.

Frequency   Frequency segments obviously have to do with regularity of usage. Repeat business is well recognized as highly desirable, and programs like frequent traveler plans are geared to this element. Some might call it loyalty. Again, however, there are subsegments that should not be ignored. High frequency might mean once a week to a restaurant, once a month to a commercial hotel, and once a year to a resort hotel. Low frequency can also be an important segment, especially if it occurs with regularity. A restaurant might have certain customers who come only once a year on an anniversary date. A few hundred of these, however, constitute an important segment that needs special attention.

Purchase Size We might call the important members of this segment "big spenders." The high check average in a restaurant, the expensive wines, even the big tippers can be a vital segment. In hotels this segment might use the better rooms or suites, eat in the hotel's restaurants, or order expensive room service. Obviously, this type of behavior should be encouraged by marketing.

Timing Timing deals with days, months, or seasonal periods of the calendar. The Monday night customer can be icing on the cake for a restaurant, the weekend customer for a hotel, and the off-season customer for a resort. These segments may include people who don't like crowds, or simply those on different schedules. Of course, those who come at busy times also represent a timing subsegment.

Timing segments also can be based on when the customer buys, as explained in Chapter 7. For a wedding anniversary dinner, it might be two weeks ahead; for a simple dinner out, two hours. A meeting planner may buy one or more years in advance; the business traveler, two days in advance.

Nature of Purchase Consumer behaviorists often categorize buyers as convenience (buy a particular product because it's convenient to do so), impulse (buy products on impulse without much forethought), and rational (buy only after careful consideration). Each of these subsegments is susceptible to a different approach.

Convenience buyers, for example, are probably more apt to utilize in-room refrigerator bars, or room service if it is convenient to get it. Impulse buyers are highly subject to suggestions such as menu clip-ons, wine carts, the server's dessert suggestions, and a higher-priced room with a view. Rational buyers need more information; they are more apt to be influenced by descriptions on wine lists, in-room descriptive materials, and ads or brochures with more detailed information.

Where They Go These segments go to certain destinations on a regular basis. For vacation, they might always go to the Caribbean; for a hotel, they might always go near the theater district; for a restaurant they might always go to the suburbs. They can be marketed to according to these inclinations.

Purchase Occasion These may be special-occasion segments. They go to restaurants for birthdays and anniversaries, or use hotels for the same occasions. Alternatively, they may use hotels only for business and never for pleasure, or vice versa.

Heavy, Medium, and Light Users These segment categories usually get special attention from marketers. An old marketing shibboleth states that 80 percent of the purchases are made by 20 percent of the people (often referred to as the 80/20 rule). Any marketing research needs to pay special attention to separating these categories. As a total group, customers might have a mean of 2.5 on a scale of five when evaluating an attribute. Broken down, scores might show that light users have a 1.7, medium users a 3.2, and heavy users a 4.4. Changes made to please heavy users might alienate light users, a consideration that management must evaluate before making changes.

There tends to be a heavy concentration in marketing circles on the so-called heavy user. This is probably advisable, but at the same time it should not distract from the light user or, to coin a new phrase, the "other-user." Hypothetically, let's suppose the heavy user represents 80 percent of an establishment's patronage while the other 20 percent represents a mix of various segments. That 20 percent may well represent five more percentage points of occupancy or, in a volume-sensitive business, its spending may come 90 percent down to the bottom line. These are crucial figures that are too often unrealized. Frequent-traveler programs tend to be biased against these customers.

It would not be too difficult to suggest even more user segments than those mentioned above. The point that has to be made is that each of these segments has some different needs and wants. They may also have many needs and wants in common, but it is catering to the different, special needs and wants that creates and keeps customers.

A given restaurant or hotel may well have every segment mentioned above as customers or potential customers. This is not as impossible a situation as it may at first seem; it is simply the nature of the hospitality business and demonstrates why paying attention to only broad segments such as business/pleasure may constitute falling into a trap. With few exceptions, a hotel or restaurant that wants to maximize its potential simply cannot afford to treat all people the same.

The Saturday night hotel guest is simply not the same as the Wednesday night one—even when it is the same person. Likewise, the Monday night restaurant customer is not the same as the Saturday night one. The anniversary dinner is not the same as the business dinner. One restaurant of one author's acquaintance had a heavy weekday lunch patronage of businessmen but wondered why they never appeared for dinner or on weekends. Subsequent research revealed that these men found the restaurant convenient for lunch but did not find it satisfactory as a place to bring their wives for dinner.

User segments have an advantage over geographic, demographic, and psychographic segments. By their nature and narrowness they are more predictable. In other words, if we know what influences them (i.e., why they constitute a segment), the chances are good that they can be influenced. This is not necessarily the case simply because we know someone's age, income, sex, or geographic origin. In fact, Holiday Inn claims that, "Today, 'purpose of trip' and 'experiences desired' are the prime reasons for choosing a hotel. Though a mid-market consumer always retains the same mid-market val-

ues and demographics, her or his 'ideal hotel' concept changes depending on the occasion of travel.... The future lies with innovative customer-focused lodging concepts that serve the needs of specifically defined segments of traveling customers."[9]

Benefit Segmentation

Benefit segments are based on the benefits that people seek when buying a product. Benefits are very akin to needs: comfort, prestige, low price, recognition, attention, romance, quiet, and safety are just a few of the possible benefits sought in a hospitality purchase. Like psychographic segments, benefits have the disadvantage of being more difficult to measure. Similarly, they are subject to whimsy and change. On the other hand, when measurement is reliable, benefit segments may be the most predictable of all segments and the ones to which we should pay closest attention.

The strength of this statement lies in the fact that benefits are also akin to need satisfaction. Knowing what benefits people seek provides a basis for predicting what people will do. Benefit segmentation is a market-oriented approach consistent with the marketing concept.

The classic article on benefit segmentation was written by Russell Haley in 1968 and has stood the test of time. In this article, Haley states:

> The benefits which people are seeking in consuming a given product are the basic reasons for the existence of true market segments. Experience with this approach has shown that benefits sought by consumers determine their behavior much more accurately than do demographic characteristics or volume of consumption[10]

Haley suggested that market segments be determined first by the benefits people seek. From these segments can be derived other characteristics such as demographics, psychographics, usage patterns, and so forth; in other

---

[9]Standards Manual: Holiday Inn Sunspree Resort, January 1, 1993, p. 6.

[10]Russell I. Haley, "Benefit Segmentation: A Decision-oriented Tool," *Journal of Marketing*, July, 1968, pp. 30–35.

words, benefit segments can be used to identify relevant descriptive variables and consumer behavior.

Benefit segmentation is concerned with why consumers seek and purchase a particular product or service. Benefit segmentation is also concerned with total satisfaction from a service rather than simply individual benefits. This phenomenon has been termed the benefit bundle and is the significant factor in segmenting markets by benefits. The sense of the benefit bundle is that people buy a service in order to receive a group of benefits rather than a single one. A study of mid-scale restaurant chains revealed three benefit dimensions, food-service quality, family price/value, and time/convenience.[11]

A group of Finnish researchers studied the benefit segments of Scandinavian hotel business customers. They found that business customers do not evaluate hotels homogeneously. Six distinct segments emerged, plus a seventh one that the authors called the "idiosyncratics." Benefits sought by the six different segments varied primarily on the use of business services, efficiency, friendliness, quiet, restaurants, image, clientele, interior decor, and location. These benefit segments were related to background data for each segment: travel-related attributes, company-related attributes, demographics, geographics, hotel-related attitudes, and behavior. This study demonstrated both the power of benefit segmentation and the error of treating business travelers as one homogeneous segment.[12] In fact, some of today's middle-tier hotel product is based on the business traveler's desire for facility, as opposed to service. In spite of industry claims, all travelers are not seeking better service.

In a study of restaurant benefits sought, different segment characteristics were distinguishable for three types of restaurants—gourmet, family, and atmosphere. The identified benefits were related to advertising appeals that could be used for each type of restaurant.[13]

There are two important distinctions between benefit and other forms of segmentation. Benefits *are* the needs and wants of the consumer. More than that, benefits are what the product/service does for the customer. Other segmentation strategies only assume a relationship between the segment variables and consumer needs and wants. We all know that McDonald's makes a special effort to appeal to children, a strong demographic segment. The next time you go to a McDonald's, look around at the people and see if you can place them into a segment category. Chances are it will be a benefit segment—quick, clean, cheap. Actually, McDonald's returned to cheap after leaving it for awhile. From 1990 to 1992 prices for two parents and two children were over $20, not cheap, and drew strong price resistance. McDonald's started packaging and bundling specials, as Taco Bell had done some time before them, to bring value back to the purchase.

Second, understanding benefits enables marketers to influence behaviors. (Consider the discussion of selective perception in Chapter 6 to see how it pertains to benefit segments.) Other segmentation variables are merely descriptive. The marketer can only try to appeal to what exists and its assumed relationship. Consider the singles category, a fairly large market segment: Is it relatively homogeneous, so that it can be treated as one major segment? Not at all, but break it down by benefits sought and you will find high degrees of similarity.

In summary, benefit analysis can be a powerful segmentation tool. Its best utilization lies in good research that can pay off in terms of understanding customers and what motivates them, such as that shown in Figure 8-13. For example, Taco Bell research found wide variation in U.S. geographic areas. For instance, "[C]ustomers in Minneapolis don't care how

[11]Michael S. Morgan, "Benefit Dimensions of Midscale Restaurant Chains," *Cornell Hotel and Restaurant Administration Quarterly,* April, 1993, pp. 40–45.

[12]K. E. Kristian Moller, et al., "Segmenting Hotel Business Customers: A Benefit Clustering Approach," in T. Bloch et al., eds., *Services Marketing in a Changing Environment,* published by the American Marketing Association, 1985, pp. 72–76.

[13]Robert C. Lewis, "Benefit Segmentation for Restaurant Advertising That Works," *Cornell Hotel and Restaurant Administration Quarterly,* November, 1980, pp. 6–12.

It's hard to raise a growing boy in a tiny home in a crowded city like Tokyo. The faster Yukio grew, the harder I mopped and scrubbed. Anything to keep his small room neat as a pin.

Does he appreciate it?

Mrs. Ichro Kimura
Mother of Yukio Kimura

FOR RESERVATIONS, CALL 1-800-424-2900.

FIGURE 8-13   Segmenting on benefits

long it takes as long as employees are courteous. In New York City, they don't care how courteous you are, they want it fast."[14]

---

[14]From a speech by Blaise Mercadente, Taco Bell Research Director, at the American Marketing Association Conference on Customer Satisfaction, Sheraton Palace Hotel, San Francisco, May, 1993.

Price Segmentation

Price segmentation is actually a form of benefit segmentation, only more visible and more tangible. Ten years ago it would have been included in the benefits category. Because the hospitality industry today essentially sees itself as seg-

GUEST QUARTERS®
SUITE HOTELS

FIRST-CLASS SERVICE. WITH THE ROOM TO ENJOY IT.

FIGURE 8-13   (continued)

menting on price, it now deserves separate consideration. There are two ways to look at price segments: One is within the product class, the other is between product classes.

Five-star hotels and budget motels both provide lodging, but they are each a different product class. Gourmet restaurants and fast-food restaurants are also separate product classes. The inference is that one product class does not truly compete with another on the same occasion, given the same circumstances. If we go to New York City, we do not choose between the Waldorf-Astoria and Days Inn.

Price segments within the product class, at

least in hospitality, are limited. A lower price may increase the value of the benefit bundle, other things being equal, but customers will generally not make major trade-offs for a small gain in price; that is, they won't accept a poor location or poor service just to save a few dollars. It is difficult to develop segments based solely on price within the same product class, although it has been done.

Between product classes is a different story. The initial determination by the customer may be based on price range; it is the other elements of the bundle that will influence the final choice. As with Scotch whiskey and wine, there are high-priced, medium-priced, and low-priced segments. These segments are based on expectation. No one rationally pays more for something without expecting to get more. In cases like these, markets are segmented within broad price ranges.

In the hotel industry, although there have obviously been shades of difference and exceptions, for many years the consumer has had little choice other than top, middle, and bottom. The expectation of what was chosen was fairly clear because there were definite lines of distinction. Today we have low budget, middle budget, upper budget, and luxury budget, and the same four classifications apply to the middle- and upper-tier categories.

Amazingly, with today's modern construction, the physical product is not all that different, within ranges, and in some cases neither is the price. In many cases lower prices have been obtained by lower construction and operating costs and through elimination of public space and food and beverage facilities. Surely, as one moves up the ladder, the furniture gets better, the walls and the carpet get thicker, the atrium gets higher, and the bathroom (sometimes) gets larger and has more amenities. No longer, necessarily, does the bed sag in a budget motel, or is the furniture scratched, broken, and torn, or the soap in the bathroom minuscule. In other words, the basic needs are still fulfilled.

Why, then, are customers willing to pay more for relatively little more? And is this really market segmentation? Well, in many cases they are not, and in many cases it really isn't. Those

cases in which customers are willing to pay more constitute market segmentation. Customers are willing to pay more largely because of the intangibles that they receive in return: service, prestige, professionalism, and others. These are benefits, and the net result is actually benefit segmentation, not price segmentation. Price is the risk the customer is willing to take to obtain the benefits.

The success of hotel industry segmentation did not mean that customers suddenly joined a lower-priced segment; they simply found an alternative for expressing dissatisfaction with the high prices they had been paying.

This brings us to the question of whether prices do indeed constitute market segments in the hotel industry. (Refer back to footnote 5 in this chapter, commenting on Comfort Inns. One hundred dollars at a Comfort Inn totally confuses the entire concept of price segmentation.) The answer is somewhat ambiguous because, for most, price is a major consideration in any purchase, and varying price sensitivities will stratify any market. In the final analysis however, other than at the bottom of the market, it is rarely price alone that determines the segment. Price is only the risk that the willing and able buyer will take, based on the intensity of the problem and the perceived value and expectation of the solution. This analysis applies to both the hotel and restaurant industries. See Figure 8-14 for an example.

Segmentation Strategies

No segments exist in isolation, and there is considerable overlap and sharing of the variables. Also, few hotels or restaurants today can survive on only one market segment. It is likely that there will be numerous segments and numerous segmentation strategies. The foundation of any segmentation strategy is behavioral differences. No segment is meaningful if it does not behave differently from another segment—the same factor that leads to conflict between segments. Whether you use geographics, demographics, psychographics, benefits, or usage, the test of the segment is the differentiation of

FIGURE 8-14   An attempt at price segmentation

behavior. Thus, in the final analysis, it is the behavior of segments that is the true test of their validity. Consider the following example:

A suburban hotel suffering from slow weekend occupancy surveyed the market for new sources of business. Two distinct segments were discovered, but neither one was large enough to create the desired weekend occupancy. It was decided to market to both, and separate strategies based on the needs and wants of each segment were developed and implemented. The segments were romantic couples who wanted to get away for a peaceful and quiet weekend, and families who wanted to take their children for a mini-vacation with lots of activities. It wasn't long before the two segments collided head-on. The potential damage is obvious.

Knowing this, and already knowing how consumer behaviors change, it is readily apparent that segments also change over time. We have already argued that one of the advantages of segmentation is the ability to stay closer to the customers and understand them better. This advantage should never be neglected and a constant alert must always be maintained for changing, merging, or dividing segments. Too much segmentation can lead to too many markets and an inability to serve anyone well, or profitably. To avoid this, each market segment should be subjected to the tests in Table 8-4.

In the final analysis, market segmentation is a scientific procedure requiring scientific analysis. It cannot be a casual or haphazard exercise. Hotel management engages in strategic thinking to seek the "ideal business mix." Figure 8-15 shows the relationship between analysis and segmentation and marketing strategies to help to do this.

The necessity of market segmentation in the hospitality industry has become increasingly critical due to the intense competition that has occurred over the last ten years. In many cases, market segmentation may be a prerequisite to growth. In some cases, large or major segments may have reached their level of fulfillment. As the airlines have learned, smaller segments, unimportant individually but critical in the aggregate, may be the next wave.

Product differentiation, as a singular market strategy, may have seen its day in the hospitality industry. As has been pointed out numerous times in this book, product differentiation can be a high-cost method of obtaining or maintaining market position. Market segments are more stable and enduring because they go to the heart of customer satisfaction.

Target Marketing

Target markets are drawn from segments. They might be called subsegments, but the word *target* has a more active connotation that is important. Once we have segmented the market and examined the market potential, we must select those markets that we can best serve by designing our products and services to satisfy the selected markets.

There are three strategies for selecting target markets: undifferentiated, concentrated, and multi-segment targeting. An undifferentiated targeting strategy assumes that customers have similar needs, so only one type of product or service is offered to all customers. Examples of this are rare in the hospitality industry of the 1990s.

More common is a concentrated targeting strategy, where a firm selects one market segment and pursues it aggressively. For example,

TABLE 8-4   Tests for Segmentation

1. Is it homogeneous? Homogeneity of every aspect is not possible or even necessary, but certain key aspects should be identified. These aspects form the basis of the segment.
2. Can it be identified? Certainly we can identify segments based on sex or geographic origin, but other measures are not so easy. For example, suppose we wanted to segment on the psychographic dimensions of conservative, moderate, and liberal. The segment would be of little value if we could not identify those who fit those dimensions.
3. Can it be measured? Suppose we could identify a conservative segment. We would then need to be able to measure the level of conservatism and the accompanying needs and wants.
4. Can it be reached economically? The segment will not be much use to us, beyond present customers, if we cannot build upon it. Through media, direct mail, or even internal marketing, we need to be able to get to the segment.
5. Can a differential in competitive advantage be maximized and preserved? In the hospitality industry this is one of the toughest tests of segmentation, but one that should be constantly sought, if not always reached.
6. Finally, is the segment large enough and/or profitable enough? There is a large bus tour segment for hotels that many would find unprofitable. There is a very small segment of visiting royalty that a few hotels may find very profitable. The cost and effort of serving each segment must be weighed against the return.

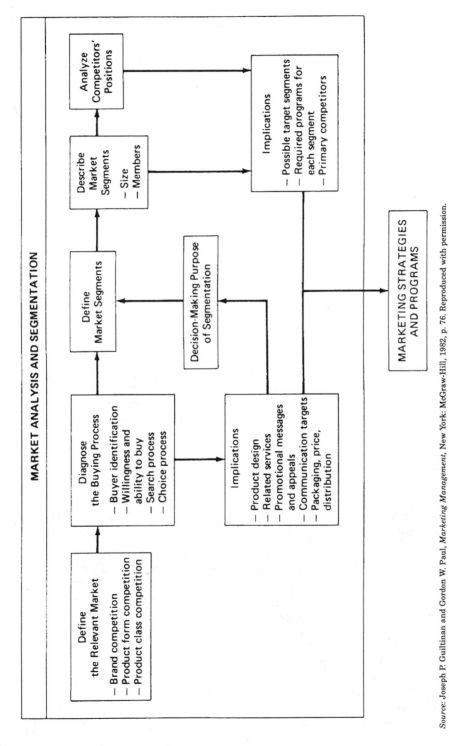

MARKET ANALYSIS AND SEGMENTATION

Define the Relevant Market
— Brand competition
— Product form competition
— Product class competition

Diagnose the Buying Process
— Buyer identification
— Willingness and ability to buy
— Search process
— Choice process

Implications
— Product design
— Related services
— Promotional messages and appeals
— Communication targets
— Packaging, price, distribution

Define Market Segments

Decision-Making Purpose of Segmentation

Describe Market Segments
— Size
— Members

Analyze Competitors' Positions

Implications
— Possible target segments
— Required programs for each segment
— Primary competitors

MARKETING STRATEGIES AND PROGRAMS

Source: Joseph P. Guiltinan and Gordon W. Paul, *Marketing Management,* New York: McGraw-Hill, 1982, p. 76. Reproduced with permission.

FIGURE 8-15 Relationship between market analysis and segmentation and marketing strategies and programs

TABLE 8-5　Vacation Target Markets

The Carriage Trade—desire a change of scene but not of style; secure in wealth and position, they play golf and tennis year around and, when traveling, tend to vacation as a family.

The Comfortables—the largest group, insecure, they seek social and psychological comfort, like recommended restaurants, guided tours, and organized activities.

The Venturers—want to see new things, have a thirst for fresh ideas, information, and education; they seek the new and the different, don't travel in groups, collect experiences.

The Adventurers—the venturer advanced one step—*adventurers* seek risk, danger, and the unknown.

The Inners—jet-setters, they go somewhere because of who is there rather than what is there; they "make" destinations like Acapulco, Majorca, Costa del Sol.

The Buffs—strongly subject-oriented, they travel because of a particular interest or hobby.

The Activists—not content to sit by the pool and bask in the sun, they want constant activities.

The Outdoorsers—they enjoy camping, hiking, bird-watching, bicycling, and other outdoor recreations.

The Restless—travel for something to do, tend to be senior citizens, retired, widowed; they collect travel experiences, travel all the time including off-seasons.

The Bargain Hunters—can afford to travel but compulsively seeks the best deal.

---

the Ritz-Carlton chain targets customers who want luxury hotel experiences, while Motel 6 goes after customers at the opposite end.

The third strategy is multi-segment targeting, very common in the hotel industry. Marriott Corporation is the perfect example, with Marriott Hotels, Courtyard by Marriott, Fairfield Inns, and Residence Inns all trying to serve different markets and doing without the confusion that Choice International has created with its products. Within hotels, multi-segment strategy is in effect. High-rated, midweek business travelers are replaced by low-rated, pleasure customers on the weekends. Numerous hotels have "towers"—a hotel within a hotel—or concierge floors with special services that market to the higher-rated, expense account business traveler.

Target marketing means aiming specifically at one portion of a market. One travel researcher found, for example, that the vacation market segment could be broken down into ten target markets. Each one represents an isolation of interests based on benefits, usage, demographics, and psychographics. Each one has different needs and wants, and each requires a different package, a different positioning, and different communication. These target markets

and some of their specific characteristics are shown in Table 8-5.

As with segmentation criteria, there are criteria for choosing target markets. They overlap the segmentation criteria but are a little more precise. These are shown in Table 8-6.

Target marketing is practiced at the unit level also. A hotel may use concentrated targeting and select one market and serve it well. For example, the Delta Queen Steamboat Company, which operates three-day to one-week cruises on the Mississippi River, effectively targets, attracts, and serves the mature traveler market. There is a risk in concentrated targeting, however, in that all our eggs are put into one basket. If environmental or other changes negatively affect the demand for our service, we may not have any market left to serve. On the other hand, a hotel may select several markets to serve, but there are risks to this strategy too, as we noted above. These markets must be compatible and seek similar benefits from our establishment.

Take the case of one very successful resort, on a small, remote island in the Virgin Islands. One of its target markets was honeymoon couples and the other was high-income senior ex-

TABLE 8-6   Target Market Criteria

1. What is the potential revenue and market share?
2. What are the demand characteristics? Are they able and willing to buy?
3. How are they currently being served by the competition?
4. Are they compatible with the objectives of the firm?
5. Are they compatible with each other?
6. Do they fit the resources of the firm?
7. Do they fit the tastes and values of the firm?
8. What is the feasibility of exploiting them?

ecutives and their spouses, usually over 55 years old (employees referred to these markets, tongue-in-cheek, as newly-*weds* and nearly-*deads,* respectively). At first glance, these segments do not appear to have much in common, but in reality they complemented each other. Both segments wanted isolation, peace, and quiet. The resort—its rooms without air-conditioning, radios, television, or telephones—pursued these two markets aggressively and ran an annual occupancy rate of over 85 percent. In order to increase low season occupancy rates, the resort decided to book group leisure travelers from Italy. These guests on holiday rightfully sang and danced until the wee hours of the morning—alienating the resort's traditional market segments. Needless to say, this experiment was quickly ended.

Target Markets of One

While we have talked about criteria for market segments and target markets, such as homogeneity, size and so forth, modern technology is bringing us closer to target markets of one, at least in the hotel industry. This is because of the computer databases that contain vast amounts of guest histories. According to Terry Ortt, President of Journey's End Hotels, "You take your orientation to the customer from a very broad brush down to the individual."[15]

Often considered the domain of upscale hotels with their frequent traveler plans and finicky customers (feather pillows, special amenities, etc.), computer power is now coming down to the budget-level properties such as Journey's End. When Ortt took over as President in 1992, he ordered a search of ten million guest registration cards that had been kept, but never read, in an old warehouse. Instead of the presumed 72 percent of guests who were supposed to be city-based, it was found that 45 percent came from rural areas or small towns. This brought a change in marketing efforts[16] and led to more surveys to find out how customers at the 120 properties really thought and acted. These surveys, in turn, led to a range of changes, from how employees are paid to what guests are offered for breakfast. The next step was to the chain's check-in counters, compiling a database to track every guest, every stay, every wake-up call. "Eventually, Journey's End will be able to pitch its specials to guests by name, reward them for stays at other properties in the chain, and perhaps remember to turn up the thermostat to just the temperature they requested last time."[17]

Marketers are taking the database far beyond the simple electronic Rolodex of names and addresses. It is possible to talk to custom-

---

[15]John Southerst, "Customer Crunching," *Canadian Business,* September, 1993, p. 28. Journey's End hotels are now "Comfort Inn, or Quality Inn, by Journey's End."

[16]Similar market research was done in an upscale hotel in Philadelphia. The executive committee was asked, "Where do your weekend customers come from?" The answer was Boston, New York, and Washington, D.C. A review of 1,000 registration cards of weekend guests indicated that 945 came from the Greater Philadelphia area.
[17]*Ibid.*

ers as individuals, then reconstruct the product/service to aim at target groups and to reward repeat customers. Databases can measure what the customers do, not just what they say they do. This information can drive the entire marketing strategy. Much of this, of course, is based on the heavy user segment that accounts for a large proportion of sales.

Hotel databases have not yet reached their potential. Data are often collected *en masse* without first knowing what will be done with them. Customer loyalty is the ultimate goal. Knowing *why* you want to know the customer better, you know what questions to ask. Databases are rich sources when they combine demographics with buying habits. These will become even more potent marketing tools in the future.

Once target markets have been determined, the next step is to tailor the marketing effort to the needs and wants of each market. In Chapter 9, we will discuss this under the term *positioning*. In subsequent chapters, we will discuss it in terms of the product/service, the presentation, and the communication effort. And in Chapter 13 we will discuss database marketing further.

Summary

Differentiation, market segmentation, and target marketing are alternate and complementary marketing strategies. In a highly competitive marketplace, each one alone and together are critical to the marketing effort.

Differentiation is used to create real or perceived differences between products and services offered by hospitality organizations. The objective is for the customer to perceive a positive difference between our hotel and the competition and thus react more favorably toward us.

The differences among customers is the basis for using segmentation. Segmentation is the way in which the firm attempts to match its marketing effort to the unique behavior of specified customer groups in the marketplace, through the use of segmentation variables.

Several criteria guide the process of segmentation and differentiation. It is necessary first to identify the bases for segmenting the market.

Profiles of the resulting segments are then determined and matched with the firm's capabilities, followed by the projection of potential markets and segment attractiveness. The market is then segmented and target markets are selected from the identified segments. Positioning is developed for each target market as well as the tailoring of the marketing mix.

Each segment or target market must be examined competitively. Where others are targeting the same market, as will often be the case, a final differentiation strategy is needed.

Discussion Questions

1. Distinguish between product differentiation and market segmentation. Discuss how they relate. Which would you use, and how, if your product was a pure commodity? Why?

2. Consider a restaurant with which you are familiar. Apply Yesawich's guidelines for differentiation and segmentation. Discuss.

3. Using the same restaurant, discuss the various segmentation variables. How do they fit? Apply? How would you recommend that restaurant segment its market? What does it do now?

4. The text argues that price segmentation is really benefit segmentation. Explain and discuss.

5. What is the difference between a target market and a market segment? Give some examples and explain them.

6. Considering your answers to questions 2 and 3, how would you develop this for a marketing program for the restaurant?

7. In Cases 8-1 and 8-2 consider the market segments, target markets, and the idiosyncracies of each. How can Gary Williams and Bonni DiCarlo use segmentation to plan their marketing strategies?

8. In Case 8-3 consider the target markets and the preparation for them. Are these the right target markets? Or, is the Holiday Inn simply differentiating within the same product class as its competition? What would you suggest to Mr. MacLeod?

✔ Case 8-1
Hedonism II[18]

Gary Williams, General Manager of Hedonism II, enjoyed the sunset from the deck of the resort's Rick's Cafe as he thought about yesterday's board meeting. The discussion at the meeting centered around expanding the resort's rooms and adding a swimming pool for nudists. Gary's concern was what this would do to their position in the marketplace and their perceived image. He had been noting for some time how Club Med was changing its image from a place for "swinging singles" to one for families. Hedonism II had been patterned after Club Med. "Was it now time," Gary wondered, "to follow a different path? What would this do to our market? What would it do if we don't and follow Club Med instead?"

Hedonism II was situated on 22 acres of landscaped gardens at the northern end of the Seven Mile Beach in Negril, a resort community on Jamaica's western tip, famous for its Caribbean sunsets. By law, there are no buildings taller than palm trees in Negril. The resort had 280 rooms located in a multitude of two-story buildings. It had just about every known Caribbean resort amenity with the exceptions of golf and cruises. Hedonism II was one of the Super-Clubs. SuperClubs was a marketing organization that promoted five resorts in Jamiaca and one in St. Lucia. It operated a network of sales representatives and ran advertising campaigns across North America to market the resorts. It was innovative in the sense that each property was marketed to a separate target market. Couples Jamaica and Couples St. Lucia attracted couples seeking romance; Jamaica Jamaica targeted couples, singles, and families (with children over 16); Boscobel Beach drew families of all ages; Grand Lido was aimed at the sybaritic market; and Hedonism II targeted fun-loving couples and singles. Only Couples St. Lucia and Boscobel Beach did not offer a nude beach or nude sunbathing.

---

[18]Kate Taylor and Judy Atkin researched and contributed to this case.

The Hedonism II Package

Originally, the Hedonism II package was an all-inclusive holiday that included everything except drinks. Similar to Club Med, guests purchased plastic sharks' teeth, which were strung around the neck, to buy drinks. This idea, however, had recently been dropped in favor of a total all-inclusive package at this and other SuperClubs.

Hedonsim II attracted over 45 percent repeat guests. To encourage this, many "perks" were offered. For example, there were weekly repeat guest cocktail parties, yearly reunions, and three free nights for all guests who had paid for 14 or more nights in the previous year. Some guests had been known to stay there as many as ten times a year. This strong and loyal customer base was continually acknowledged.

The Marketing Plans

The original marketing strategy developed by Hedonism II was to position against Club Med, a well-established, worldwide, and original all-inclusive resort concept started in 1950. There were more than 100 Club Meds in over 30 countries but none in Jamaica, because Club Med rotated its staff every six months and Jamaican law required hiring a certain number of Jamaicans. Club Med staff came from all over the world and were unable to obtain Jamaican work permits.

Generally, although their resorts varied, Club Med targeted office workers, executives, and professional people. In the 1980s, some Club Meds gained a reputation for wild, sex-oriented vacations. In the late 1980s a new attitude was developing in North America about the negative aspects of promiscuity. Club Med rethought its positioning and started to focus more on sports and family vacations in order to evolve in response to changing times and needs. Club Med was a formidable competitor and had locations on other Caribbean islands that drew 80 percent of their market from the United States and Canada.

Hedonism II's first strategy was to "piggyback" Club Med. Brochures identified it as an alternative to Club Med. A later marketing strategy called for a breakaway from Club Med. Hedonism II marketed on the intangibles of the resort by using pictures and language that stressed the hedonistic approach. Another change was to advertise the clothes-optional aspect of the resort. Brochures showing nudity in its photographs indicated there was a nude beach.

Still positioned against Club Med but without mentioning it in the advertising or brochures, Hedonism II's emphasis was on the intangibles, such as shown in Exhibit 8-1-1. Billboards, newspapers, and magazine ads featured a half torso with sharks' teeth strung

EXHIBIT 8-1-1   Hedonism II stresses the intangible in words

On Pleasure:

The dictionary will tell you that Hedonism is the seeking of pleasure as a way of life.

Not a bad definition, but not very imaginative. And we wish the word "pleasure" was a verb rather than a noun.

We believe that pleasure—the feeling of pleasure—is the most normal and natural of all states and that it is a great deal more natural than its opposite alternative!

We believe, too, that pleasure comes in many forms and that it is most gratifying when it involves all your parts—mind, body, spirit, soul.

It is holistic, not secular.

This is what sets Hedonism II apart from any other Caribbean experience and why we don't consider ourselves as an hotel. We don't look like one. We don't act like one.

Hedonism II is a tropical village by the sea where adults share the pleasures of mind, body, spirit, soul.

There are no children. No formality. No need for money of any kind. And it is the freedom from money, beads, signing chits, etc., that forms an important element of the Hedonism II experience: it breaks down the barriers that usually exist between the guest and the traditional hotel.

around the neck, shown in Exhibit 8-1-2. This was designed to create curiosity and encourage people to contact their travel agents for information. Currently, there was less of a focus on nudity and more focus on sports, but the clothes-optional aspects were still identified.

The original target market for Hedonsim II was singles between the ages of 20 and 40, affluent and adventurous, fun-loving and casual. Presently, it was couples and singles between 25 and 45, with the same characteristics, who wanted excitement, relaxation, and an array of activities. The actual breakdown was as follows: 65 percent singles, 35 percent couples,

60 percent males, 40 percent females, average age—summer 28, winter 39.

Occupancy

From the mid to late 1980s Hedonism II ran year-round occupancies in the 80 to 86 percent range. Around the turn of the decade, shortly after Club Med changed its target market strategy, occupancies began falling into the mid to low 70s. Occupancy ran highest from January to May and slumped lowest during the hurricane season from September into December, but rarely fell below 50 percent. Management and

EXHIBIT 8-1-1   (continued)

Freedom from any concern for money also liberates your mind; it frees your spirit and does wonders for your soul! You simply enjoy <u>everything</u> we have to offer without a second thought. And the absence of commerce allows natural friendships to develop freely between guest and guest and guest and staff.

Hedonism II is <u>the</u> place to meet kindred people who <u>expect</u> life to be enjoyable. Because there is no formality the sharing of the experience occurs naturally as it is happening. People who come together as couples rekindle their relationship and mingle easily with singles. And with singles many a lasting romance has found its beginnings here.

Hedonism II can engage you in enough activity to keep you on the go all day and most of the night. In this respect we follow the dictum of Oscar Wilde that ''Nothing succeeds like excess.'' But we also believe you should be able to take it all in at your own pace. It's your holiday, not ours, and we never forget it.

Please consider this to be your passport to the best holiday of your life. Above all, enjoy, enjoy.

Manager,
Hedonism II, Negril, Jamaica.

EXHIBIT 8-1-2   Hedonism II photographically stresses
the intangible

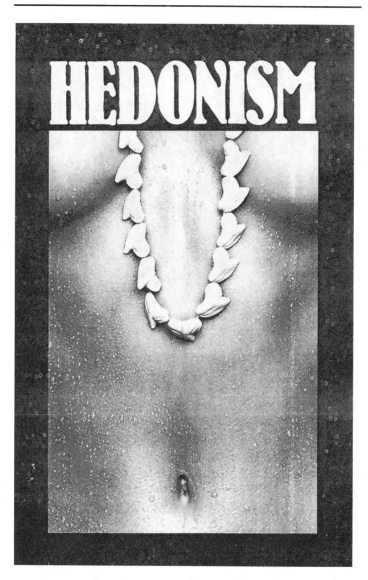

the board of directors had become concerned
about the overall decline.

Future Plans

Hedonism II, like Club Med, had kept in touch
with its customers' changing needs and wants.
In response to these it was planning a full-service restaurant for those who desired a sit-down
meal (presently, there was only a buffet). Sales
managers in the United States and Canada
were continually creating new travel incentives
for customers and travel operators, such as Canadian dollars at par with the U.S. dollar and
all-inclusive airfare similar to Club Med packages. It also planned 70 more rooms on the
"nude side" of the hotel, plus a nude swimming
pool. With the high prices of all-inclusive holi-

days, and more and more of them coming on the market, Hedonism II was constantly trying to add extras that would maintain and enhance the value perception. A long-term plan was to copy the Hedonism concept on another Caribbean island.

Gary Williams wondered what all this meant in terms of the future.

✔ Case 8-2
Cafe DiCarlo[19]

"Call it being in the wrong place at the wrong time. The building was being offered to me and I didn't know what to do with the space. So, I decided to put up some sort of dining establishment, just for the fun of it."

Bonni DiCarlo was the sole proprietor of the Cafe DiCarlo restaurant, located in the center of Amherst, Massachusetts, a town of 20,000 permanent residents and 30,000 college students. Bonni began her career in the food-service business by developing a "pizza joint." With the University of Massachusetts (UMASS) and Amherst College close by, the restaurant was an immediate success with students as the major market. After almost seven years of catering to a "loud and obnoxious group," Bonni felt that she needed a change. This was when the concept of Cafe DiCarlo was born, an upscale Italian restaurant.

This change involved not only a makeover in menu but also in facility, design, staffing, management philosophy, and market positioning. The layout and design of Cafe DiCarlo was conducive to a warm and intimate fine-dining experience. Entering the below-street level restaurant, one immediately took comfort in the warm wooden floors, tables and seats, the brick columns, and the wide array of artwork displayed. All the artwork was provided by local artists who exhibited their work for six weeks at a time in hopes of selling it. In the background a wide range of music, jazz to opera to new age, could be heard. On the whole, Cafe DiCarlo could be described as a creative, artsy interior design catering to the intimate dining experience. The dining area consisted of 13 tables of varying sizes, seating a total of 40.

The design of Cafe DiCarlo was such as to promote privacy and a sense of being one-on-one. "I want the customer to feel as if he or she is walking into their friend's dining room...they

should feel relaxed and enjoy the fine dining atmosphere and experience," said Bonni.

Bonni had the intention of catering to the UMASS and Amherst College market, but she did not want to attract the "pizza and beer" crowd. Instead, she hoped to attract students who preferred to dine in a classier place, where they could take their parents, and generally have a pleasant and quiet evening out—a place where they could relax, dine unhurriedly, and enjoy good food, good wine, and efficient service. Bonni believed that students would be eager to come to a "more casually elegant restaurant such as this one."

EXHIBIT 8-2-1   Cafe DiCarlo ad to attract students

CAFE DICARLO

Fine Italian Dining...

When where to dine is the question...we provide the classic answer

Students
Wednesday night is Pasta Night!
Choose from a variety of additions to create your own pasta dinner.

starting at
$4.95

71 N. PLEASANT ST.
AMHERST   MA.
253-9300

---

[19]Nicole Panlilio, Alice Tse, Shari Aloni, and John Griffin researched and contributed to this case.

EXHIBIT 8-2-2   Cafe DiCarlo awareness ad

The Realization

Bonni closed the pizza operation right after she bought the building. Four months later, Cafe DiCarlo–Fine Italian Dining, opened its doors in the same space. To Bonni's surprise and disappointment, the students were neither anxious nor excited about the new restaurant. In fact, Cafe DiCarlo's actual patrons were mostly professors, graduate students, foreign students (mostly European), and a few local, elderly couples, most of whom came for dinner.

To counter this, Bonni initiated a promotional "Pasta Night" on Wednesday evenings

EXHIBIT 8-2-3   Cafe DiCarlo theater-goer ad

Fine
Italian
Dining...

CAFE
DICARLO

Featuring Daily Luncheon
Specials plus an extensive
list of wines from Italy
and California.

*Try us for dinner before or after the theatre...
and bring your program in for a complimentary
cup of cappuccino.*

71 N. PLEASANT STREET
AMHERST, MA • 253-9300

when students could "choose from a variety of additions" to create their own pasta dinners, starting at $4.95. She ran an ad in the local, daily student newspaper for one month (Exhibit 8-2-1). The purpose of the promotion, Bonni said, was "not to make money but to let the restaurant be known." The promotion, however, was unsuccessful. Bonni decided to scrap the idea and be happy with her present patrons and regulars, about 70 percent of whom were repeat customers.

Competition was not a major concern for Bonni. She viewed as her major competitors a nearby "gourmet" continental restaurant with comparable atmosphere, which also focused on the non-college market, and two other nearby Italian restaurants that had more traditional family-oriented concepts and drew from all segments of the local market. In Northampton, eight miles away, there was one Italian restaurant somewhat similar to Cafe DiCarlo and drawing from a more sophisticated population of 40,000. Bonni had not tried to reach this market so didn't consider this restaurant as competitive.

Marketing Efforts

Bonni embarked on another promotion, this time geared toward the senior citizen market. Bonni wanted to increase the poor luncheon and afternoon sales by offering senior citizens a daily special of two entree choices (pasta), including freshly baked bread, a house salad, and

EXHIBIT 8-2-4   Cafe DiCarlo dinner menu

ENTREES
all entrees are served with vegetables or roasted potatoes

GAMBERI alla DIAVOLA
shrimp in a peppery tomato sauce with cherry tomatoes
and sauteed fresh spinach
16.95

CAPE SANTE con VERDURE alla GRIGLIA
scallops with braised greens in a sherry cream sauce with fresh herbs
15.75

PESCE del GIORNO
Fish of the Day
Priced Accordingly

GALLETO al FORNO
Rock Cornish Game Hen
roasted with olive oil, fresh rosemary
and white wine, served with potatoes
12.25

PETTO di POLLO con CARCIOFI e FUNGHI
Breast of Chicken
sauteed with mushrooms and artichoke hearts
in a tangy vermouth and butter sauce
12.95

CASSOULET TOSCANA
Tuscan Stew
a rich stew made of fresh vegetables, kidney beans
and plum tomatoes with sweet Italian sausages
10.95

SCALLOPINE di VITELLO con SPEZZIE
Veal Scallopine
in a rich white wine and butter sauce with minced fresh herbs
16.75

COSTOLETTE d'ABBACCHIO DORATO
Prime Lamb Chops
marinated in fresh herbs with lemon - breaded - then baked
16.95

BISTECCA AL PEPE
sirloin steak with cracked black pepper in a
rich red wine mustard glaze
18.95

a beverage. These were served for only $5.95 and only between the hours of 11:00 A.M. and 4:00 P.M. The promotion was successful in that it somewhat boosted luncheon and afternoon turnover. It also made more people aware of the restaurant.

Other efforts at increasing market awareness were ads run in various publications, at the beginning of each semester, for about two weeks to a month (Exhibit 8-2-2). Other ads ran during the semester to attract theater-goers (Exhibit 8-2-3). Both these ads introduced a somewhat lighter fare at lunch. The restaurant continued to serve as an art gallery, and walk-throughs and browsing were encouraged in the afternoon.

When asked whether or not her target market had changed, Bonni DiCarlo replied, "No. We still want and are attempting to attract the UMASS and Amherst College students. We believe that placing ads in the college newspapers is sufficient enough to accomplish this." Bonni really did not put much effort and thought into marketing, aside from these ads. In fact, she had a very small budget for it—about $500 a month. Most ads were "fun" ads for special promotions, changes in menu, and holiday specials. The ads focused on food, rather than the creative concept and the dining experience.

The Future

Eighteen months later, Cafe DiCarlo—still an unknown commodity to the general public—offered a new seasonal menu. A new chef who, for the past ten years, had lived in Italy and worked in a family-style restaurant in Tuscany, was hired. This, Bonni hoped, would help to project a family-style image for the restaurant. While most Italian restaurants seemed to bow to customer demand, Cafe DiCarlo was dedicated to educating the customer. The menu was not Italo-American but actual dishes as they were prepared in homes in Italy. Price-wise, the menu was far-ranging (Exhibit 8-2-4).

The next summer Bonni expanded the operation to include a fifty-seat outdoor area at the back of the restaurant. A slightly different menu was offered outside. Bonni also planned to expand into the second level of the building. She was a little hesitant because of the possibility of losing the privacy and personable atmosphere that Cafe DiCarlo possessed. Further, she wasn't sure just who would be her market, especially when she wasn't yet able to fill the first floor.

Bonni DiCarlo wanted to classify her restaurant as a fine dining establishment. On the other hand, she also liked to attract the college students, as long as they were not "rowdy and obnoxious." Essentially, they were the largest group of people in Amherst for nine months of the year. As things were, Bonni was barely breaking even and needed to increase her market share or attract new markets.

✔ Case 8-3
Holiday Inn Chattanooga[20]

Graham MacLeod, General Manager of the Holiday Inn Chattanooga, was staring out of his tenth-floor, makeshift office overlooking the city when the telephone rang. He listened as his secretary responded to the call: "Good morning, Holiday Inn Chattanooga.... No, this isn't the Skyline Inn.... No, we haven't been reinstated by Holiday Inn, we're owned by a different company now.... I know this used to be a Holiday Inn before it was Skyline, but Pavilion Hotels purchased the property over six months ago...."

For the past three months, MacLeod had become increasingly aware of the uphill battle he faced to overcome the negative image inherited from the Skyline Inn. He was fully confident, however, that his brand new, renovated and refurbished hotel would prove successful, since it would be the only true businessperson's hotel in Chattanooga. The only question that remained in MacLeod's mind was how long it would take to bury the Skyline connection.

Background

In 1978, the hotel was built by the Holiday Inn Corporation, which owned the property until it was sold in 1988. Holiday Inn had begun striving to upgrade its image as well as increase its profitability. The run-down Chattanooga property did not fit the corporation's plans. The decision was made to sell the hotel rather than refurbish it.

The hotel was purchased by Dr. Robert Chung, who created the Skyline Inn. Dr. Chung was a multimillionaire computer engineer turned hotelier. Chung was a brilliant man, but his talents were not well-suited to a service industry. During his stint as owner, he was known for his unwillingness to finance renovations. As a result, the hotel's reputation suffered. The perception of the Skyline Inn grew progressively worse and occupancy levels fell to 40–45 percent. Robert Chung finally sold the hotel when he acknowledged the deteriorating reputation of the property.

Pavilion Hotels was chosen as the management company for the property under the franchise, once again, of Holiday Inn. The new owners planned to invest $10.5 million in improvements to the property. The intended result would be a first-class, quality facility.

Chattanooga was a city of about 200,000 in the southeastern part of Tennessee. It was well-situated near the intersection of Interstate 75 and Route 24, and Chattanooga Airport was only ten miles to the south. Downtown Chattanooga had been revitalized significantly over the past several years and was clearly on the upswing. It boasted numerous newly constructed office towers and rehabilitated buildings. There were over 500 specialty shops located within a 30-mile radius of Chattanooga, and the Mid-America Mall, the largest shopping mall in Tennessee, was just five miles from downtown. Chattanooga's urban facelift was further assisted by increasing industrial growth. Six new major industrial sites would eventually accommodate the area's strong demand for commercial expansion. These sites were located beween one-half mile and eight miles from the hotel.

The most significant current development was the $150 million Monarch Place, which would include a 26-story office tower and a 12-story atrium-lobby Sheraton Hotel. This building included 350,000 square feet of office space in addition to the 300-room first-class hotel that Sheraton would operate there. The property would have convention facilities for 1,500 people as well as an executive boardroom, four hospitality suites, a complete health club, and a full-scale business center.

Consultant Christopher Griffin summarized the city's potential by stating, "Chattanooga has the potential to some day be the mecca of Tennessee—if we cultivate it and not get greedy and choke. There is enough for everybody, and

---

[20]William Romeo researched and contributed to this case. Names and location have been disguised.

we have so much going for us. Chattanooga will have the brightest red carpets you have ever seen. Believe me, Memphis will know that Chattanooga is here."

Pavilion Hotels

Pavilion Hotels was an individually owned company that had expanded from one original hotel to ten properties. Pavilion operated properties extending from Little Rock, Arkansas to Raleigh, North Carolina under a variety of franchises. Within the next two years, Pavilion planned to add ten more hotels to its portfolio, for a total of 20 hotels.

The company had recruited many top leaders in the hospitality field, all of whom were young but experienced, and the group had developed a reputation as an up-and-coming company. Pavilion Hotels was a people-oriented organization that recognized the attitude of its employees was the key to success. Its philosophy was to listen to employees of the hotel because they were its representatives. One Pavilion executive summed up their philosophy by stating, "Theory-wise, people are inherently good by nature, and with a little pat on the back, they will perform to the best of their ability."

Holiday Inn Chattanooga

The Holiday Inn Chattanooga was located in the north end of the city at the intersection of Interstate 75 and Route 24. Although the facility was still in the midst of major renovations, the Director of Sales, Ray Flynn, was optimistic. He believed that the completed project would produce an upscale, corporate transient facility that would have no equivalent in the area. "We're brand new," he said. "Everything's been redone. By June 1st, no other hotel will be able to say that. When businesspeople arrive, they will know that there's new plumbing, wiring, lighting fixtures—everything from stem to stern. They won't have to worry about a thing."

Once completed, the 12-story hotel would consist of 250 first-class rooms. Each would contain such amenities as a state-of-the art tele-

phone system, a computer connection modem, a fax machine, and a VCR video component. The rooms were all to be furnished with nongeneric, walnut furnishings and a large, well-lit workstation. Two hundred rooms would have king-sized beds. All were to be decorated in good taste with only top-quality furnishings.

The eleventh floor of the hotel would offer three executive suites and two executive boardrooms. The Presidential Suite, which overlooked the entire city of Chattanooga, was the largest on the floor and consisted of three full-sized rooms as well as a kitchenette. The remaining two suites were the Governor's Quarters, each consisting of two rooms. All of the property's suites were positioned on a corner of the building in order to provide maximum visibility.

The Holiday Inn Chattanooga would also provide guests with an olympic-sized indoor swimming pool and a full-facility health club featuring a Jacuzzi, sauna, and Nautilus system.

Business Facilities

Management considered that the hotel's Business Center would be one of its major differentiating points. The Holiday Inn Business Center was to be truly "an environment designed for results." As the customer entered the hotel, the Business Center would be immediately visible through smoked-glass doors. This effect intentionally emphasized the commitment of the hotel to the business customer.

The Center would contain three high-performance state-of-the art PCs attached to top-quality printers. There would also be a facsimile machine, telex machine, and dictaphone. Complete secretarial services and a Federal Express office would be available, plus three private consultation rooms. Holiday Inn had fully committed to the Business Center in the hope of wooing the business traveler, particularly the one who appreciated the attention to detail.

Function space at the Holiday Inn would be less extensive than that of competitive hotels. One room would accommodate a maximum of

100 people and seven small conference rooms would hold up to 20 people each. The hotel's marketing plan anticipated that most function business would originate locally. It was planned that room rentals would require a sleeping room commitment, except during off-season periods. Weekend banquet business was expected to consist of weddings, reunions, and association business.

Other Facilities

The rooftop restaurant, which once rotated atop the hotel, had received a facelift along with the rest of the hotel. The dining room no longer revolved and the entire top of the hotel was currently in the process of being squared off. "The Squared Circle" had been selected as a name reminiscent of the past.

The restaurant, which seated 112 guests, offered a casual and relaxed atmosphere. It was a multi-purpose facility serving breakfast, lunch, and dinner with an emphasis on traditional Southern cooking. Graham MacLeod did not anticipate that the restaurant would see much activity on the weekends, but he was philosophical. "What the Squared Circle does on the weekends is a bonus," he said. "Our main concern is to take care of the individual corporate traveler."

Adjacent to the restaurant was the Squared Circle Lounge. The 104-seat lounge was planned to feature live entertainment each evening with various local pianists at the baby grand. The decor focused on brass and mirrors that encouraged eye contact, and there was an abundance of stand-up space. Management described the lounge as "fun, yuppie, and conducive to meetings."

The Corporate Travelers Club constituted another extra to be provided by the hotel. This amenity was especially geared toward the individual corporate traveler and included the following:

- The Manager's Table—For purposes of comaraderie, guests would receive an invitation to the Manager's Table, to dine with other club members.

- Pre-ordered Breakfast—The club's members would be offered the option of utilizing door-knob menus to request breakfast for the next morning.
- Complimentary newspapers were to be delivered each morning.
- Beds would receive turn-down service every night.
- Use of the health club was to be complimentary, as was each eleventh night as a guest of the hotel.

The Pricing Policy

The establishment of rates at the Holiday Inn was in direct relation to the occupancy of the hotel. When demand was high and there was a major attraction in the city, only the rack rate would be available. At other times, when the city was quiet and occupancy was low, a potential guest could negotiate with the front office manager in order to obtain a bargain rate.

Management recognized that a hotel room was a perishable commodity, and every effort would be made to prevent a potential customer from bypassing the Holiday Inn and patronizing the competition. Forecasted average rates were as follows:

Corporate	$ 90.00
Rack	$115.00
Group	$ 80.00
Suites	$155.00

Occupancy percentages were estimated to be 56 percent, 62 percent, and 73 percent respectively for each of the first three years. The hotel's private consultant was not concerned about occupancy during the slow periods. "There's an old saying: 'Let's schedule it for January or February because it's quiet.' Well," he said, "we've changed our tune. If it's quiet, let's not meddle with it. Bring them in here when it's busy. Bring them in when the hotel is full. Because when you're doing that, you are telling people that you care enough about them to pay for rooms at another hotel when we are booked. Why bring them in when the place is a morgue?"

Competition

According to General Manager MacLeod, the Holiday Inn Chattanooga currently had only two direct competitors, the Marriott and the Hilton West. The marketing plan, however, included the Holiday Inn Chickamauga, the Quality Inn Lookout Mountain, and the Ramada Inn South on the list of competitors.

The Marriott was located in the heart of downtown Chattanooga and catered to both the corporate traveler and the convention market. The Hilton West was situated off Interstate 75, five miles north of the downtown section. This hotel catered to essentially the same two markets as the Marriott. MacLeod acknowledged that the proposed Sheraton convention hotel, upon completion, would become the third major competitor. Table 8-3-1 gives details on the competition. Presently, the fair market share of the Holiday Inn Chattanooga was 20 percent in relation to its five competitors. Once the new

Sheraton opened, the percentage would drop to 16 percent.

Management Philosophy

Graham MacLeod and other members of the management team planned to operate the hotel with an exciting, aggressive, and innovative style. They believed that their positive energy and enthusiasm would rub off on the entire staff, thus distinguishing the Holiday Inn Chattanooga from the competition.

The management team also attempted to instill a caring attitude in the employees. They felt it imperative to constantly remind the guest that he or she was welcome, and they planned to instruct their staffs to follow through with this approach from the second the guest set foot on the property until the moment of departure.

Mr. MacLeod stated that the Holiday Inn aspired toward two primary objectives: First, to achieve an occupancy of 70–75 percent and, second, to be perceived as a quality, yet reasonable businessperson's hotel.

TABLE 8-3-1   Holiday Inn Chattanooga Competition

Hotel	Rooms/Suites	Rates	Meeting Space*	Location	Amenities
Holiday Inn Chattanooga	250/3	$80–115	100	Downtown	Full business center/ indoor pool, health club
Marriott	265/9	95–125	1,000	Downtown	Indoor pool/health club Concierge floor
Sheraton West	268/5	90–120	900	5 miles north	Indoor pool/VIP floor
Quality Inn	185/0	70–90	600	6 miles east	Outdoor pool
Holiday Inn Chickamauga	154/2	85–100	350	9 miles north	Indoor/outdoor pool and health club
Ramada Inn	124/1	80–100	200	5 miles east	Outdoor pool
Sheraton	308/8	120–140	1,500	Downtown	Indoor pool, full health club, racquetball courts, concierge floor, business center

*Number of people

The marketing plan defined the mission statement as follows:

Our product is unique to the Chattanooga area and we have arrived at the ideal time in terms of demand. The location is superb and we must now begin to concentrate on guaranteed satisfaction of service. Both the professionalism of the staff and the consistency of the service will be critical if the previously held opinions of the facility are to be erased.

A version of the mission statement was also distributed to all employees so that they would be repeatedly reminded why the hotel was in business. A burgundy card with decorative gold lettering was inscribed with the following:

Our mission is:
To be metropolitan Chattanooga's BEST at providing FIRST CLASS GUEST SERVICE and price/value satisfaction to the traveling executive.
To become known as an organization whose managers direct the staff with dignity and respect.

Our Staff is:
Dedicated to the individual guest's comfort level.
Committed to impeccable excellence in product quality.

Marketing

Because of the limited meeting/function space, management recognized the need to target markets different from either the Marriott or the Hilton West. Holiday Inn's management identified the individual business traveler market as the prime niche for the hotel. They also agreed that it would not be a group-oriented property. Thus, the hotel's target market was defined to include corporate transients, airline crews, and the weekend traveler, although convention overflow business would certainly be welcomed.

Since Chattanooga was not considered to be a weekend destination, minimal interest was anticipated from the leisure traveler. This particular segment generally visited the city because of specific Civic Center activities, and MacLeod was optimistic that some of this business would come his way due to his past support of the Civic Center. Four weekend packages had been developed to lure whatever weekend business existed, with special focus on lovers, singles, shoppers, and country/western enthusiasts.

Within the next month, the Holiday Inn would begin negotiations with various airlines. It was hoped that this would lead to several contracts that would produce 8–10 percent of the hotel's customer base. According to MacLeod, airline revenue was a highly desirable means of increasing guaranteed cash flow during the uncertainty of the first year.

The Holiday Inn Chattanooga positioned itself as a mid-priced, upper-middle market property. In order to ensure that the customers' perceptions outweighed their expectations, the hotel was priced just below the Marriott while offering a higher quality property.

The focus of the hotel's advertising would be to reach the corporate travel market. Therefore, it would be concentrated in the larger air carrier magazines and with popular car rental agencies. Piedmont and Delta (airlines) and Budget and Hertz (car rentals) were to receive the bulk of the advertising dollars. MacLeod was investigating the possibility of installing a direct telephone line from the airport to the hotel.

Three weeks prior to the re-opening, the Chattanooga Holiday Inn had done very little advertising. The only significant piece was small and appeared in the Travel section of the major Tennessee newspapers. However, advertising was expected to increase once the hotel opened. Additional efforts to reach the corporate traveler would be via newspapers, billboards, and trade and business journals. The sales staff had already initiated frequent direct mailings.

It was estimated that the Holiday Inn Reservation System, Holidex III, would account for 20 percent of all reservations. The Holiday Inn Chickamauga was expected to lose 8–10 percent of its market base to the refurbished hotel.

Conclusion

Graham MacLeod realized that he had a lot to do before the Holiday Inn Chattanooga opened its doors. Most importantly, it was essential that he develop a reasonable plan of attack to overcome the hotel's image problem. He sat back in his chair and sighed, "I only wish that we had never become a Holiday Inn franchise; then things would be much easier."

CHAPTER 9

Market Positioning

Market positioning is the natural follow-through of market segmentation and target marketing. In fact, it is upon those strategies that positioning is built because they define the market to which the positioning is directed. Essentially, market positioning means creating an image in the consumer's mind. Therefore, it is necessary to select and understand our target markets before effective and efficient positioning strategies can be developed. The objective of positioning is to create a distinctive place in the minds of potential customers; a place where customers know who we are, how we are different from our competition, and how we can satisfy their needs and wants.

If we do not create this distinctive place for ourselves, there are several pitfalls:[1]

1. The firm is forced into a position of competing directly with stronger competition. For example, an independent midscale hotel may be pushed into a losing competition with a new Courtyard by Marriott.
2. The firm's position is so unclear that customers do not know who the target markets are and what needs can be fulfilled. This

often happens when a property or chain tries to be all things to all people.
3. The firm has no position in customers' minds and no one has really heard of it and/or there is no customer demand there.

There are actually two kinds of positioning in marketing: objective positioning and subjective positioning. Each has its appropriate place and usage. Each is concerned with its position vis-a-vis the competition.

Objective Positioning

Objective positioning is concerned almost entirely with the *objective* attributes of the physical product. It means creating an image about the product that reflects its physical characteristics and functional features. It is usually concerned with what actually is, what exists. For example, let's take the statement, "The car is red." We can all see that it is red, and it will be a rare person among us who will disagree that it is red. If the company that makes this car makes only red cars, we might call it "the red car company." We would carry an image of these cars as opposed to those made by "the green car company."

[1]Christopher H. Lovelock, *Services Marketing,* 2nd ed., Englewood Cliffs, NJ: Prentice-Hall, 1991, p. 112.

That's a little simplistic, so let's apply it to the hospitality industry. Econolodge is a low-cost motel; the Cerromar Beach Hotel is on the beach; Ponderosa Steak House sells steaks; the Chicago Hilton is a big hotel. All of these businesses conjure up specific images based on their product. In three of the cases the image comes from the name itself. Almost no one would argue with our image because it derives from an objective, concrete, specific attribute. If we know anything about the product, we know at least that much.

Objective positioning need not always be concrete, however. It may be more abstract than these examples. Maseratis are not only red; they also go fast. The Ritz-Carlton is a luxury hotel; the Chicago Hilton is a convention hotel; McDonald's is a clean place; Lutece serves gourmet meals and fine wines. A few perhaps, but not too many, would argue with us on these images. Again, they derive from the product itself.

Objective product positioning can be very important and is often used in the hospitality industry. Many hotels still position on their atrium lobbies, which do exist. Haagen Dazs positions on the richness of its ice cream, which it has. Red Lobster positions on seafood and Olive Garden on Italian food, which they have. The Plaza Hotel in New York City positions on the important people who do go there.

You begin to get the picture. If your product has some unique characteristic or unique functional feature, that feature may be used to objectively position the product, to create an image, and to differentiate it from the competition.

Less successful objective positioning occurs when the feature is not unique, as shown in Figure 9-1. This is why many hotel ads with pictures of the hotel fail to create an image or to differentiate the product. Other unsuccessful approaches include a picture of two people in a

FIGURE 9-1   Ineffective positioning on non-unique features

hotel room that looks like six million other hotel rooms, or people seated in a restaurant, or, worse, a picture of an empty restaurant with tuxedoed waiters standing at attention. Perhaps an even better example of poor positioning is that shown in Figure 9-2. One of the first rules of effective positioning is good taste as well as uniqueness. We will come back to that, but first we need to explain subjective brand positioning.

Palace Hospitality

Overheard at the Palace:

"The roast beef here is the best I've ever tasted."

"Yes, but if anything, the Beef Burgundy is even better."

Long years of dedication to the finest in food and wine earn us compliments like this.

And at the Palace, there's nothing we'd rather hear.

The Palace Hotel. A simply unique experience.

Palace Hotel

1-1-1 Marunouchi, Chiyoda-ku, Tokyo, Japan
Tel: (03) 3211-5211 Telex: 0222-2580 Palace J
Cable: PALACEHOTEL TOKYO Fax: (03) 3211-6987

Our Representatives for reservations & information:
UTELL INTERNATIONAL: U.S.A. toll free 800-448-8355
LOEWS REPRESENTATION INT'L: U.S.A. only toll free 800-223-0888
ROYAL PALACE INC: New York Tel. (212) 808-5550
WESTIN HOTELS & RESORTS: U.S.A. toll free 800-228-3000

▣ Associate Member of CIGA HOTELS: any CIGA HOTELS offices
Ⓖ Member of GOLDEN TULIP HOTELS: call your local Golden Tulip office

FIGURE 9-1   (continued)

A workout at our poolside health spa should leave you short of breath. *If not, the view certainly will.*

the
Regent

BEVERLY WILSHIRE

AUCKLAND. BANGKOK. BEVERLY HILLS. FIJI. HONG KONG. JAKARTA. KUALA LUMPUR.
LONDON. MELBOURNE. SINGAPORE. SYDNEY. TAIPEI.
HONG KONG: 366-3361. SINGAPORE: 737-3555. TOLL FREE: USA & CANADA (800) 545-4000. UK (0800) 282-245.
GERMANY 0130-85-2332. FRANCE (05) 35-04-97. JAPAN 0120-001500. AUSTRALIA (008) 022-800.

FIGURE 9-2   A luxury hotel chain uses poor taste in positioning

Subjective Positioning

Subjective positioning is concerned with *the subjective* attributes of the product or brand.

Subjective positioning is the image, not of the physical aspects of the product, but other attributes as perceived by the customer—they belong not necessarily to the product but to the customer's mental perception. These perceptions and the resulting image do not necessarily reflect the true state of the product's physical characteristics. They may simply exist in the customer's mind, and it is possible that we could find many who would disagree with particular perceptions and images. What the marketer hopes is that the people in the target market will agree on a favorable image, whether or not the image is true. This is the test of effective subjective positioning.

Hilton Hotels' former ad campaign, "When American business hits the road, American business stops at Hilton," and its slogan "America's Business Address" are examples of attempts at subjective positioning. The desired image, obviously, is that businesspeople prefer Hilton Hotels. One reason that people might not have accepted the campaign's attempted positioning was because it lacked uniqueness and did not differentiate from the competition. This failing was compounded by the pictures in the ads. For example, one picture was of an empty conference room with a conference table surrounded by chairs. These are objective product characteristics that clearly are no different from characteristics at thousands of other hotels.

Tangible Positioning

There are two very important differences in the types of positioning when they are used in the hospitality industry. The first occurs because the industry's product has almost reached commodity status; in other words, many of the rooms in hotels of the same product class are almost exactly alike. We need to understand what this means for positioning.

Consider the ultimate commodity, salt. How would you use positioning to create a unique image and differentiate your salt from someone else's salt? Morton tries it with the positioning statement, "When it rains, it pours." This is intended to imply that Morton salt is free-flowing even when the weather is damp, whereas other salts are not. It is not necessarily true that others are not, but if you buy into it you do so because you differentiate Morton's salt from other salts based on the physical characteristic

of its being free-flowing. Salt is a very tangible good; it would be difficult to argue that salt is exotic, tantalizing, or romantic.

Those arguments, however, could be made for cosmetics, and they certainly are, as we all know. Cosmetics are mostly tangible. However, their successful marketing is based on mental perceptions of intangible results. As Charles Revson, founder of Revlon, said, "In the factory we make cosmetics; in the drugstore we sell hope."

Now let's get back to hospitality and see if the same strategy will work with the hospitality product. If we are selling a near-commodity product like a hotel room that is mostly tangible, then we need to develop intangible mental perceptions that may or may not actually belong to the product. Thus arose the expression "Sell the sizzle, not the steak."

Consider again the hotel ad showing a picture of a couple in a hotel room. A hotel room is very tangible. It looks like thousands of other hotel rooms. As with salt, it is very hard to develop a mental perception of a hotel room that creates an image and differentiates from other hotel rooms. Two people in the room are also tangible. What's more, they are no different from two people in any other hotel room. Now you see the problem that hotel advertisers have been struggling with for years: How do you position a tangible product that has very little means of differentiation or intangibility?

It's difficult but not impossible. What, for example, is more dull, plain, ordinary, and undifferentiated than a hamburger? But notice the next McDonald's commercial that you see. Notice the emphasis on people, fun, good times, convenience, or whatever.

Le Meridien Hotels, as we mentioned in Chapter 8, has used sketches by a famous artist to "intangibilize" a tangible product. This campaign, featuring artwork by Ken Maryanski, conveys French service with a flair. Customers can imagine the experience through the caricatures of the advertising campaign (Figure 9-3).

Intangible Positioning

The second important difference in the types of positioning for hospitality products resides in the converse situation. What we are largely marketing is not tangible, it is intangible. Some would say that is nonsense, because what's more important than the room or the meal? They would be right, but that's what we're selling, and not what we're marketing. If we were selling rooms and beds, or steaks and salad bars, what difference would it make where the customer went, assuming a comparable level of quality? And that is an assumption we have to make within the same product class, so it doesn't get us very far.

What we are marketing, of course, are intangibles. The tangibles are essential and necessary, but as soon as they reach a certain level of acceptance, they become secondary. Because they are so difficult to differentiate, to be competitive we have to market the intangibles. Hospitality products are mostly intangible. Even when tangible (e.g., a steak) they have a measure of intangibility because they are consumed rather than taken home to be possessed.

If hospitality products are mostly intangible, we have to market them with tangible evidence. This is what is referred to as "tangibilizing the intangible." We have noted that most of the tangible aspects of the hospitality product (within the same product class) have a high degree of sameness. The rooms of the Marriott, Sheraton, Hilton, and Hyatt are almost the same everywhere. The intangible elements are abstract. To emphasize the concrete elements is to fail to differentiate from the competition. To emphasize the abstract (e.g., with words like "escape to the ultimate") is to compound the intangibility. Thus, hospitality positioning needs to focus on enhancing and differentiating the abstract realities through the manipulation of tangible clues. Consider, for example, the intangibility of Merrill Lynch investment services and the tangibility of the bull featured in its television commercials and ads.

Hyatt has done likewise with its atrium lobbies. People don't buy atrium lobbies; they buy what the lobbies tangibilize. We might not all agree, but some would say atrium lobbies are exotic, full of grandeur, majestic, or exciting. These are intangible images and nothing more than mental perceptions. The good part (for

Hyatt) is that these perceptions carry over to the brand. Hyatts are exciting, exotic, and majestic hotels; anyone can see that things happen here! Of course, check-in may be just as slow, and the rooms may be no different from those in other hotels, but the image is there, not just the physical characteristics. Today, many other hotels also have atrium lobbies but Hyatt got there first and the image is still maintained for many people.

Unfortunately, being aware of this need does not greatly ease the problem. It is still difficult to find meaningful tangible evidence that supports intangible constructs. What we want to do is create a subjective "position" in the consumer's mind. You can see now why positioning follows so closely on target marketing—we need to know what mental constructs are held by the consumer in the target market, and what tangible evidence sustains them.

Return for a moment to the steak-and-sizzle argument. If we want to sell the steak, this argument goes, we need to market the sizzle. But our steak is just like all the others, so what we have to do is sell the sizzle, the intangible. How do we tangibilize the sizzle? If we knew, we'd be millionaires. But you see the problem, and it is not totally insoluble. It is best explained by example.

There is probably no better example, even 20 years later, than what Jim Nassikas did at the Stanford Court Hotel in the 1970s. In fact, this was so successful in positioning the Stanford Court that Nassikas virtually stopped advertising and still ran one of the highest occupancies and ADRs in San Francisco, until he sold the hotel to Stouffer Hotels in 1988. Examples of the ads Nassikas ran are shown in Figure 9-4, along with a current comparison of Ritz-Carlton.

Note the positioning statement in the Stanford Court ads, "For people who understand the subtle differences." Note the tangible evidence in the picture. Finally, note the caption, "You're as finicky about choosing a fine hotel as you are about.... We designed the Stanford Court for you." For an example in the restaurant industry, see Figure 9-5.

Positioning, then, is a relative term. It is not

Les Hôtels Meridien d'Europe
Au Cœur
Des Villes Qui Battent Plus Fort.

Au pied de l'Acropole, entre Regent Street et Piccadilly, sur la promenade des Anglais, à deux pas du Marché aux fleurs de Nice, entre La Défense et l'Étoile, à quelques minutes du vieux Porto... les hôtels Meridien rayonnent au cœur des villes qui battent plus fort.

Tout près des centres d'affaires, trouvez les boutiques les plus chics ou les plus typiques, les musées les plus réputés ou les théâtres les plus en vogue.
Ainsi en Europe, les courants de mode et d'affaires passent toujours par les hôtels Meridien.

Athènes, Casablanca, Lisbonne, Londres, Marrakech, Nice, Paris, Porto, Tours, Tunis et dans plus de 50 villes de New York à Tokyo en passant par Rio et Le Caire, Dakar et Les Seychelles.

Le
MERIDIEN
COMPAGNON
DE VOYAGE D'AIR FRANCE

FIGURE 9-3   Intangibilizing hotels

just how the brand is perceived alone but how the perceived image stands in relation to competing images. It is the consumer's mental perception, which may or may not differ from the actual physical characteristics. It is most important when the product is intangible and there is little difference from the competition on physical characteristics.

Courtesy of the Stanford Court Hotel and Norman R. Tissian, Spiro & Associates, 100 South Broad St., Philadelphia, PA 19110

FIGURE 9-4   Tangibilizing the intangible for hotels

Effective Positioning

Our discussion so far has dwelled largely on *image,* the mental picture the consumer has of the product or service. We have also discussed the need for the image to *differentiate* the brand from the product class. These are two essential criteria for effective positioning, but there is one more.

This will take us back to the basic marketing concept, the notion of needs and wants and problem solutions—the promise we make to the customer. It also takes us back to Chapter 6, on consumer behavior in terms of customer attitudes. Images and differentiation mean creat-

Auguste Renoir: *La fin du déjeuner.*

"There, there is nothing else but grace and measure, Richness, quietness and pleasure." Charles Beaudelaire

With words a poet creates images. On canvas a painter causes color to speak and sing. Each in his own way transforms reality – organizing and embellishing it.

The art of living also is concerned with transforming reality – organizing and embellishing it.

In this respect a great hotel is elevated to the level of a work of art.

RITZ-CARLTON
MONTRÉAL
1228 Sherbrooke St. W., Montreal, Quebec H3G 1H6
Telephone : (514) 842-4212 (800) 363-0366 Telex : 05-24322 Fax : (514) 842-3383

FIGURE 9-4   (continued)

ing beliefs. Next we have to develop the affective reaction, the attitude toward the belief, and the action that will create the intention to buy.

Thus, effective positioning also must *promise the benefit* the customer will receive, it must create the expectation, and it must offer a solution to the customer's problem. And that solution, if at all possible, should be different from

Named after . . .

the great Armagnac District of France --

home of Armagnac, the world's finest brandy,

truffles, foie gras, roquefort cheese and

D'Artagnan, Captain of the Three Musketeers.

Chef Lucien Robert invites your company to dine at his Maison.

FIGURE 9-5   Tangibilizing the intangible for restaurants

and better than the competition's, especially if five of one's competitors are already offering the same solution.

David Ogilvy, a longtime advertising guru and former head of the international firm, Ogilvy and Mather, states in his classic book:

> Advertising which promises no benefit to the consumer does not sell, yet the majority of campaigns contain no promise whatever. (That is the most important sentence in this book. Read it again.)[2] [His parenthesis]

Here are some better-known positioning statements of the past with which many of us are familiar. As you read each one consider the image, the differentiation, and the promised benefit as well as the tangible and intangible aspects.

Toyota—*I love what you do for me.*
Hyatt—*Feel the Hyatt touch.*
McDonald's—*We do it all for you.*
Burger King—*Have it your way.*
Harvey's—*We make you spoiled for char-broiled.*
United Airlines—*Fly the friendly skies.*
General Electric—*We bring good things to life.*
Microsoft—*Making it easier.*
Holiday Inn—*Stay with someone you know.*
Marriott—*Service. The ultimate luxury.*
Embassy Suites—*Twice the hotel* (Figure 9-6).
Hilton International Hotels—*Take me to the Hilton* (Figure 9-7).

Most positioning statements are not so short and simple as these short advertising lines. Examine the La Quinta ad in Figure 9-8. The image presented by the ad is that you don't have to forsake the elements of a quality motel in order to obtain a low price. The ad differentiates La Quinta from similar properties; it gives you what they give you but at a lower price. Also, it promises a benefit—quality at a low price. This ad clearly positions to the target market: the self-employed or non-expense account business traveler who wants a reason-

---

[2]David Ogilvy, *Ogilvy on Advertising,* New York: Vintage Books, 1985, p. 160.

IF YOU THINK THERE'S NOTHING NEW TO EXPERIENCE IN TORONTO, THINK TWICE.™

Now there's one hotel that can turn any business or pleasure trip to Toronto/ Markham into an exceptional experience. Embassy Suites. Twice The Hotel.™

TWICE THE ROOM. Enjoy a large, luxurious two-room suite. Each includes a coffee maker and a mini bar/ refrigerator.

TWICE THE EXPERIENCE.
Relax in our breathtaking sunlit atrium. Dine in one of our outstanding restaurants. Or enjoy our exclusive health club.

TWICE THE VALUE.
As with every Embassy Suites hotel, enjoy our complimentary cooked-to-order breakfasts and manager's reception† nightly.

If you're looking for a welcome change in the Toronto/Markham area, Think Twice.™ Then call your travel agent or 1-800-EMBASSY.

EMBASSY SUITES™
8500 Warden Avenue
Markham (Toronto), Ontario L6G 1A5
(416) 470-8500
Formerly the Markham Suites hotel †Subject to applicable law.

FIGURE 9-6   Embassy Suites positioning statement

able level of amenities without paying an arm and a leg for them.

Positioning's Vital Role

We have dealt with positioning so far in the context of advertising only because it is easier to illustrate that way. This is by no means, however, the only context in which positioning should be used. Positioning should be a single-minded concept, an umbrella from which everything else in the organization flows. Bill Dowling, a noted hotel marketer, states, "Properly targeted, single-minded positioning affects

IN BUSINESS, WHERE YOU'RE STAYING SAYS EVERYTHING ABOUT WHERE YOU'RE GOING.

It can say that in business travel, as well as in business, you always establish your own ground.

And that while you like your surroundings to have every comfort, you expect every business tool to be on tap.

To help them achieve their aims, more business travellers check into the Hilton than any other hotel.

Because as business takes them further, they just don't stay at the Hilton.

They stay with the Hilton.

To make a reservation at any Hilton International in Puerto Rico or anywhere in the world, call Hilton Reservation Service at 1-800-HILTONS or your nearest Hilton.

HILTON
PUERTO RICO
San Juan, Ponce & Mayagüez

"Take me to the Hilton."

La Milla de Oro, San Juan, Puerto Rico

THE HILTON · THE HOTEL

FIGURE 9-7   Hilton Hotels International positioning

everything a hotel [or restaurant] does or stands for—not only advertising but also all of its promotions, brochures, facilities—even its decor."[3]

Dowling stops short, however. Positioning also affects policies and procedures, employee attitudes, customer relations, complaint handling, and the myriad of other details that combine to make a hospitality experience. Positioning plays a vital role in the development of the entire marketing mix, which we will discuss in

---

[3]William Q. Dowling, "Creating the Right Identity for Your Hotel," *Lodging,* September, 1980, p. 58.

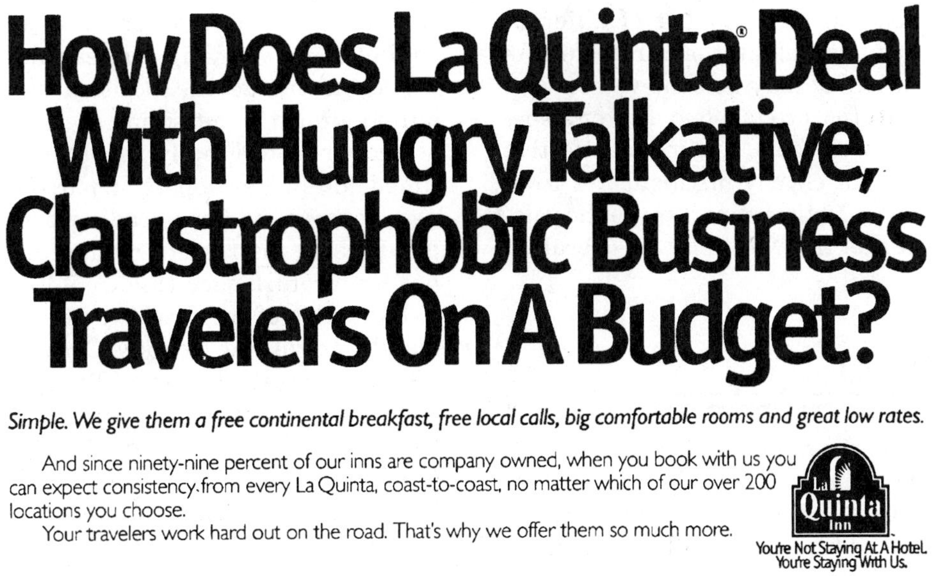

How Does La Quinta Deal With Hungry, Talkative, Claustrophobic Business Travelers On A Budget?

Simple. We give them a free continental breakfast, free local calls, big comfortable rooms and great low rates.

And since ninety-nine percent of our inns are company owned, when you book with us you can expect consistency from every La Quinta, coast-to-coast, no matter which of our over 200 locations you choose.

Your travelers work hard out on the road. That's why we offer them so much more.

La Quinta Inn

You're Not Staying At A Hotel. You're Staying With Us.

Courtesy of La Quinta Inns, Inc.

FIGURE 9-8   Positioning lodging with words

the next few chapters. Hospitality services compete on more than just image, differentiation, and benefits offered. There must be a consistency among the various offerings, and it is the positioning statement that guides this consistency. Likewise, although positioning can be applied for a given unit, or a specific service, chain operations should develop a consistency if the company desires to use one unit to generate business for another.

Kyle Craig, former President and CEO of S&A Restaurant Corp., then a subsidiary of Pillsbury Company and operators of the Steak & Ale, Bennigan's, JJ Muggs, and Bay Street chains, says:

When we talk about a marketing niche we are really talking about positioning. You must position your concept as offering a unique product or service. The key is to understand the consumer decision and then use it to your advantage to successfully stimulate sales. Once you understand what the customer wants and match that against what your chain has to offer, you have a better chance of success.

...Finding a niche is tough but delivering the restaurant experience the niche demands is

tougher.... Once the concept matches consumer needs there are two litmus tests. First, your position must be believable in the consumer's mind. Second, you must deliver on the promise on a consistent basis. [Craig also warns us to] watch out for a niche that is restaurant-driven rather than consumer-driven.[4]

Subjective positioning is a strategy for creating a unique product image with the objective of creating and keeping customers. It exists solely in the mind of the customer. It can occur automatically, without any effort on the part of the marketer, and any kind of positioning may result. Two very dissimilar products may be perceived as the same; two similar products may be perceived as different. What the marketer hopes to do is to control the positioning, not just let it happen. Failure to select a position in the marketplace and, moreover, to achieve and hold that position may lead to various consequences, all undesirable, as pointed out earlier.

---

[4]Quoted in Denise M. Brennan, "Niche Marketing," *Restaurant Business,* May 1, 1986, pp. 186, 189.

One may position in a number of different ways, all related to segmentation strategies. As discussed, positioning may be achieved on specific product features, product benefits, or a specific usage or user category. In sum, an effective position is one that clearly distinguishes from the competition on factors important to the relevant target market in everything an operation does.

Repositioning

Repositioning, as the name implies, constitutes changing a position or image in the marketplace. The process is the same as initial positioning with the addition of one other element—removing the old positioning image.

There may be a number of reasons for wanting to reposition: One reason may be that you are occupying an unsuccessful position in the first place. Another is that you may have tried and failed to fully achieve a desired position. Also, you might find that competitors, too many and too powerful, have moved into the same position, making it overcrowded. Another reason could be that you have perceived a new niche opportunity of which you wish to take advantage.

All of these situations are relatively common in the hospitality industry. Hamburger chains have tried repositioning as "gourmet" hamburger restaurants. Friendly's, originally an ice cream and sandwich chain, tried to reposition as a family restaurant. Dunfey Hotels shed its weaker units and changed its name to Omni Hotels in order to reposition as an upscale hotel chain. Club Med, as we have noted, has repositioned with a family image. Howard Johnson's, among other things, tried repositioning from being only a family restaurant to being that plus a young adult restaurant with bar and live music; this served only to confuse an already tarnished image. Repositioning fails, of course, when the promise is not delivered and/or the old image is not removed.

Repositioning might also be used to appeal to a new segment, to add a new segment while trying to hold on to an old one, or to increase the size of a segment. Another reason to use it could be that new ownership desires a new position or wishes to merge the position of a newly acquired property into that of other properties already owned. Finally, repositioning would be called for in developing a partially or totally new concept, or downgrading a property that has become distressed, or upgrading one that has been refurbished (Figure 9-9).

Examples of the first two statements immediately above are Holiday Corporation's going into its upscale Crowne Plaza line, Howard Johnson going into the suites line with Plaza Hotels, and Marriott going downscale with the Courtyard line. Quality Inns (now Choice) initially introduced three product lines in place of the previous one, in order to increase the segment size, create a new position, and downgrade distressed properties. Developing suite hotels is an example of repositioning for a new concept.

Stouffer Hotels is a good example of a successful repositioning that took place because ownership wanted a new image, and confusion that resulted from a new ownership:

Stouffer Hotels had been little more than a sideline for the Stouffer restaurant company. When William Hulett was brought from Vice-President of Operations for Westin to be President of Stouffer Hotels, the owners, the Nestlé company of Switzerland, wanted to change that. Hulett established what the identity should be and defined the company's niche in the upscale market. Refurbishing followed, some properties were eliminated, including franchises, and a one-segment successful market repositioning was instituted.

Unfortunately, a new affiliation clouded Stouffer's vision of positioning. The company was sold in 1993 to a Hong Kong firm, New World Development, that also operated previously named Ramada Renaissance Hotels. The Ramada name portion of the Renaissance brand was eventually dropped to better position Renaissance Hotels as upscale. New World decided to market both Stouffer and Renaissance together, but under their separate names.

The Renaissance brand name had a long-term affiliation with Ramada Hotels, the opposite of the upscale image that Renaissance wanted to convey. This had thwarted its upscale positioning

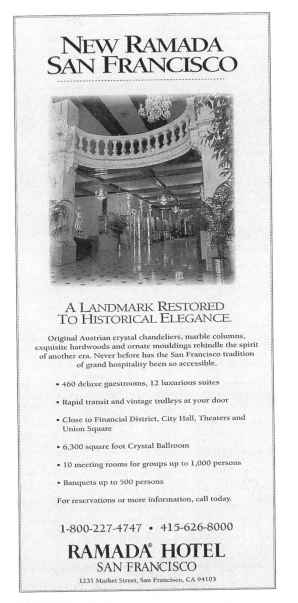

NEW RAMADA SAN FRANCISCO

A LANDMARK RESTORED TO HISTORICAL ELEGANCE.

Original Austrian crystal chandeliers, marble columns, exquisite hardwoods and ornate mouldings rekindle the spirit of another era. Never before has the San Francisco tradition of grand hospitality been so accessible.

- 460 deluxe guestrooms, 12 luxurious suites
- Rapid transit and vintage trolleys at your door
- Close to Financial District, City Hall, Theaters and Union Square
- 6,300 square foot Crystal Ballroom
- 10 meeting rooms for groups up to 1,000 persons
- Banquets up to 500 persons

For reservations or more information, call today.

1-800-227-4747 • 415-626-8000

RAMADA® HOTEL
SAN FRANCISCO
1231 Market Street, San Francisco, CA 94103

FIGURE 9-9   Attempt to reposition a refurbished property

effort. The Renaisance name was clouded with the prior Ramada affiliation, while the well-known Stouffer name was also clouded by the confused affiliation.[5]

Renovating old hotels has become a common practice. As an example, Dunfey Hotels (now called Omni) based a strategy on this practice in managing, first, the Parker House in Boston, then the Ambassador East in Chicago, the Royal Orleans in New Orleans, and finally Berkshire Place in New York City. These were all old, "classic" hotels that Omni refurbished and repositioned as historic, classic hotels in the upscale market.

Stephen Taylor describes the problem:

Today an increasing number of hotel industry leaders as well as smaller owners/developers are finding themselves with properties in distress situations. Even downtown luxury hotels, the workhorse giants of the business, are failing along with roadside independents. Fortunately for the industry, the art of repositioning is coming into its own. Repositioning, the economic [marketing] revival of troubled properties and the renovation and revitalization of old/outdated ones, can provide an alternative to the more traditional routes taken when hotels stop making good economic sense.[6]

Renovating old properties is not the only time for repositioning, as has been indicated. Since Taylor put the case so well, however, we continue to quote from his article.

The task of repositioning is not as simple as creating a market slot for a brand-new hotel. A repositioner has to deal with two consumer images—the existing one and a new one that must be projected.

Repositioning is a two-pronged effort. In most cases, a negative image and consumer ill-will must be overcome before a new impression can be created. In some cases, the added burden of a market shift must be carried....

...Winning back customers is a function of the type of expert marketing, promotion, and public relations procedures.... To achieve the goals which define the success of a repositioning effort...it needs to be finely tuned to fit the specific situation, and it takes thought, perceptiveness, and careful planning.... The successful repositioning of any hotel property begins with an intensive examination of the market the repositioner intends to enter.[7]

---

[5]As of 1994, the hotels are marketed as Renaissance ♦ Stouffer.

[6]Stephen P. Taylor, "Repositioning: Recovery for Vintage and Distressed Hotels," *HSMAI Marketing Review,* Fall, 1986, pp. 12–15.
[7]*Ibid.*

TABLE 9-1   Procedure for Repositioning

1. *Determine the present position.* It is essential to know where you are now, before you determine how you are going to get to where you want to go. In repositioning, this is absolutely critical because the consumer's image may not be at all what you think it is. Before trying to change a perception, you have to know what that perception is.
2. *Determine what position you wish to occupy.* This calls for thorough and objective research of both the market and the competition, as well as your resources and ability to occupy that position. One has to be very realistic at this stage and not simply engage in wishful thinking.
3. *Make sure the product is truly different for the repositioning.* Telling a customer that the product has changed, and is therefore now attractive, had better be followed through operationally.
4. *Initiate the repositioning campaign* based on the three criteria of effective positioning formulated from the research of the target market: image, differentiation, and promised benefits.
5. *Remeasure to see if the position has significantly changed in the desired direction.* This too is critical. It is naive to assume that perceptions have changed simply because you expected them to. Do not simply measure this in terms of sales or profits; changes there may be due to other causes. What you want to know is whether perceptions have truly changed.

The Art of Repositioning

Repositioning rests on a change of image. The appropriate procedure for doing this is shown in Table 9-1.

The application of the first four criteria in Table 9-1 is evident in the effort of the Waldorf-Astoria Hotel to reposition, as shown in Figure 9-10. The Waldorf was perceived as the hotel of U.S. presidents, royalty, and top business executives, and as being very expensive even though it was in the same price range as its competition. Management wanted to position to customers at the middle-management level. Research revealed lifestyles of this level of the Waldorf's customers. The repositioning campaign emphasized these lifestyles as well as the attributes and the affordability of the Waldorf.

There are pitfalls to repositioning of which one should be wary. The short-run effect may be a loss of sales while the repositioning is being accomplished. A gain in sales, on the other hand, may occur only because people are "giving it another chance." There may be a sales drop because the new position was a poor choice and the market is too limited or already dominated by a competitor. It is important to find out why something has happened; it is never good business sense to assume that you know why.

Developing Positioning Strategies

Lovelock suggests the model shown in Figure 9-11 as appropriate for developing market positioning strategies. This model is no different than one might use for selecting target markets. A major distinction, however, would occur in the thrust of the research. In this case we would need to know a great deal more about perceptions, what they mean and what they reflect. A benefit is not a benefit unless it is perceived to be one.

Once again, positioning is not in the product, in the brand, or even in the advertising; it is in the consumer's mind. It is definitely and positively not in management's mind. This is why it is so important for management to understand true positioning. It can be a perilous trap to assume that customers position in the same way as management.

Aaker and Shansby suggest that there are six major positioning approaches.[8] These are listed in Table 9-2 with our comments added.

---

[8]David A. Aaker and J. Gary Shansby, "Positioning Your Product," *Business Horizons*, May–June, 1982, pp. 56–62.

THE WALDORF REGULARS

Curran Croskeys
Director Product Marketing
Mary Kay Cosmetics
Dallas, Texas

"The last set is always the best. I get tense from all the traveling I do. And a hard game of tennis when I get home lets me really unwind. When I go to New York, I can even feel the tension building on the way. Then I arrive at the Waldorf=Astoria, and I know that everything will be all right.

I always stay at the Waldorf. The people are really nice and warm, not what you'd expect from New York. And the rooms are fantastic; so different from the other cookie-cutter rooms in town. When I meet people from the cosmetic business here...being at the Waldorf makes a statement in itself. And the Waldorf costs about the same as an ordinary hotel. Amazing."

For reservations and information, call (212) 872-4534 or 1-800 HILTONS, or call your travel agent.

The Waldorf=Astoria
Hilton Hotel
Park Avenue at 50th Street, New York, NY 10022.

Courtesy of the Waldorf-Astoria and Kaufman & Maraffi, Inc., Agency

FIGURE 9-10 Repositioning the Waldorf-Astoria

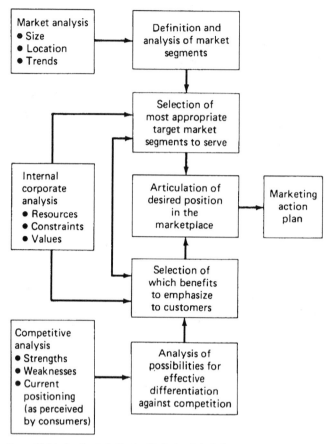

Source: Christopher Lovelock, *Services Marketing,* 2nd ed., Prentice-Hall, 1991, p. 112. Reprinted by permission of Prentice-Hall, Inc., Englewood Cliffs, NJ.

FIGURE 9-11   Developing a market positioning strategy

A checklist for developing positioning strategies is presented in Table 9-3.

Salience, Determinance, and Importance

There is another issue in regard to developing effective positioning that must be kept in mind. This is the differentiation among salient, determinant, and important product attributes or benefits. One might position on a salient benefit with poor results because those benefits are not necessarily determinant or important in the consumer choice process.

Salience

Salient attributes are those that are "top of the mind." They are the ones that readily come to mind when you think of an object. Because of this, a list of strictly salient attributes obtained from customers may be totally misleading in describing how they make choices. If you were asked, "Why did you buy that shirt?" you might

TABLE 9-2   Positioning Approaches

1. *Positioning by attribute, feature, or customer benefit.*
   For this strategy, we try to emphasize the benefits of particular features or attributes of the service or product. American Express created the first travelers' checks that can be signed by two people and emphasizes this benefit by showing that couples on vacation do not always have to stick together. Guest Quarters Suite Hotels brings out their differentiating feature (all-suites) with the statement, "What you do with the extra room you get at Guest Quarters is your business." The Loews Anatole in Dallas asks, "Where else can you promise a party for 4,000 without bursting anyone's balloon?" referring to the size of their banquet space.

2. *Positioning by price/quality.*
   We have already stated that price is not, by itself, a true segment category in many cases, particularly within the same product class. Between product classes, however, price can segment a market that is able and willing to pay from one that is not. In either case, price is a powerful positioning tool because it is perceived to say a great deal about the product.
   To use a simple and singular product example, many restaurant customers would perceive a $300 bottle of wine as an excellent bottle of wine. A wine connoisseur, on the other hand, might not agree and might be able to pick out a $50 bottle that is as good or better. Thus, we would need to know the perception of the target market vs. the benefit of an excellent wine list.
   The power of price positioning is one reason that upscale hotel chains maintain high rack rates and then discount them severely. To lower the published price is perceived as lowering the image and positioning downscale. Many hotels are finding that their "rack rated" business has dwindled to less than five percent of total sales. Of course, it works the other way as well: Potential customers who call Reservations and are quoted only the highest rack rate perceive the hotel's position as out-of-reach and hang up, not realizing they could bargain for a much lower rate.

3. *Positioning with respect to use or application.*
   Here a service is positioned on the reasons for using it. Often hotels will direct this positioning toward specific markets that have been segmented by purpose of use. Hilton Hotels called themselves "America's Business Address," clearly seeking people traveling for business purposes. Harrah's in Lake Tahoe goes after incentive travel business with "Tell your best people to go jump in the lake." The Ventana Canyon Golf & Racquet Club in California sets itself apart as a place for meetings that require golf as an essential amenity.

4. *Positioning according to the users or class of users*
   In this case, positioning features the people who use a particular product. Choice Hotels' decision to pursue senior citizens prompted advertising showing famous, but active senior citizens as users of their hotels. Fisher Island, a luxury residential development in Florida, positions itself as the place "where people who run things can stop running."

5. *Positioning with respect to a product class.*
   This technique is often used when we want to position a product in a certain product class. Preferred Hotels, a referral group of independent hotels, tries to show their exclusivity with the statement, "We made it impossible to join. That's why every hotel wants to get in." Or the Beverly Wilshire Hotel that says,"If Hollywood is indeed ruled by czars, the Regent Beverly Wilshire is their palace."

6. *Positioning vis-a-vis the competition.*
   This approach is used when it is necessary to take on the competition head-on to bring out differences between services. Visa credit cards competes with American Express by showing examples of places all over the world where they do not accept American Express, and only Visa cards are accepted. Ritz-Carlton is a little more subtle when they say, "After a day of competition, you deserve a hotel that has none."

TABLE 9-3   Checklist for Developing Positioning Strategies

1. Company: What are strengths and weaknesses, resources, management capabilities, present market position, values, objectives, and policies? Where are we now? Where do we want to go?
2. Product/Service: What are facilities, location, attributes (salient, determinant, important), physical condition, level of service? What is it? What does it do, in functional terms? Why do/should people come?
3. Brand Position: What is awareness, loyalty, image? How does it compare to the competition? What are the market segments? What are the perceived attributes and how are they distributed among the segments? Where are we positioned?
4. Customers: What are their segments and needs and wants? What benefits do they seek? What is the optimal position of attributes for each segment?
5. Competition: Who is their customer and why does he or she go there? What do they do or not do better? How are we differentiated? What positions do they occupy?
6. The Marketplace: Where is it? What are the segments? What is the generic demand? What is our market share? How are the segments reached?
7. Opportunities: What needs are unmet? Can we meet them? Can we improve on them? What innovations are needed? Are they worth going after? Are there new uses, new users, or greater usage?
8. Decision: What is the best overall position?

say because it was on sale. If we then assumed that the next shirt you buy will be one on sale, we could be making a completely erroneous assumption. What really determines your choice could be the style of the shirt; the sale price was just an inducement.

Salient factors might also be determinant factors, but they are not determinant when they are not the true differentiating factor the consumer is looking for, or when they are common throughout the product class. In the first case, let's go back to the chocolates on the pillow. This could be salient and be remembered by customers, but it is doubtful that they would base their choice of hotel on chocolates.

In the second case, an excellent example is location. Take a survey of almost any set of hotel customers and ask what is important to them in choosing a hotel. At the top of the list will almost always be location, as we have previously discussed and as descriptive, multiple-answer questionnaires will always reveal. Location is a salient attribute, but if four hotels are within two blocks of each other, as is the case in so many cities today, location is not likely to be a determinant factor.

Determinance

In one study, 81 percent of respondents said location was salient in choosing a hotel, 82 percent said it was determinant, but only 18 percent said location was the reason they chose the hotel at which they were staying.[9] The frequency of consumers' naming an attribute does not necessarily indicate its relative determinance as the true differentiating factor in their choice process.

Determinant attributes are those that actually determine choice, such as a restaurant's reputation, price/value, or level of service. These are the attributes most closely related to consumer preferences or actual purchase decisions—in other words, these features predispose consumers to action. These attributes are critical to the consumer choice. The research problem, as indicated above, is that consumers do not always know exactly what it is that forms the basis of their choice.

An example here is the same one we have used before, bathroom amenities. Bathroom

---

[9]Robert C. Lewis, "The Basis of Hotel Selection," *Cornell Hotel and Restaurant Administration Quarterly,* May 1984, pp. 54–69.

amenities may not be salient, but they could be important after we have become used to having them. If every hotel in the product class has them, however, they are hardly determinant any more, if they ever were. There is a caveat here, however: If we were now to remove the extended line of bathroom amenities, they might become negatively determinant—people might say, "I won't go there because they don't have good bathroom amenities." The implication is that perhaps hotels in this product class should now have the amenities, but promoting them or positioning on them would be to little avail.

This is also true of location and cleanliness, supposedly the main reasons that people choose hotels. People don't choose hotels simply because of location and cleanliness; they do choose against specific hotels because of their lack of location and cleanliness.

Importance

Importance attributes are those that are important to the consumer in making a choice, or after having made a choice. The example above of bathroom amenities demonstrates this. It is important that they be there, once the customer is accustomed to their being there, but they are still not determinant. Once the choice has been made, what was salient or determinant fades into the background unless, of course, they are found not to exist. *Now* it is important that the room be clean and the bed comfortable.

Salience, determinance, and importance are complementary concepts, and they are all significant in the positioning effort. It is critical to understand the place of each. Recall the discussion in Chapter 6 of selective perception, selective acceptance, and selective retention. Salient factors may cause all three to operate. Determinant and important factors are more likely to cause selective retention, but determinant factors are most vital in the actual choice process. Much positioning that is done only on salient factors—for instance, location or atrium lobby—is less than successful when these factors are not determinant. The uses and interpretations of each concept depend highly on the nature of the target market.

Competitive Positioning

In developing positioning strategies, a critical element is the positioning vis-a-vis the competition. It is necessary first to examine images and positions of all entities that may compete. One should then try to anticipate the effects of the proposed positioning and the reactions of competitors. Examining strengths and weaknesses of competitive positioning can identify positions to adopt, to stay away from, and areas of dissatisfaction where a new positioning could generate new customers or lure others from the competition. If the segment is expanding, this process can also identify a growth opportunity.

Many hospitality entities today focus *too* closely on their immediately adjacent competition, as we pointed out in Chapter 5. As the economy becomes more global, newer markets and competitors must be sought to effectively market a hotel. There is a temptation to judge success by looking at the competition down the street, for example:

A Marriott-franchised hotel in east Cleveland, Ohio was concerned about its rate structure for the upcoming year. After doing a quick review of local hotel offerings, it was found that the hotel was competitive ratewise.

The subtle determination of the pricing should not have come from the local competition, but from the target markets.

Research indicated that a majority of customers at this hotel could be segmented on similar characteristics and came from certain East Coast cities. Travel agencies from these "feeder cities" were booking thousands of room nights per quarter.

These customers were used to paying $200-plus per night in New York, $150 in Boston, and $135 in Chicago. Why, then, $59 in Cleveland? By positionig the hotel vis-a-vis its local competitors, money was being lost. When the hotel positioned itself against other destinations, the results improved dramatically.

Focus groups (small groups of consumers gathered together for the express purpose of analyzing a product's image and gaps) can be very useful at this point of exploration. Similarly useful are positioning maps. Mapping is used to place various competitive positions on a two-dimensional scale, along with an "ideal" position, in order to locate the gaps and niches or, conversely, the crowded areas. This technique may involve simple plotting on an arbitrary scale, or sophisticated statistical methods known as multidimensional scaling or discriminant analysis, which are far beyond the scope of the discussion here. A hypothetical output of the process, however, is shown in Figure 9-12.

The hypothetical positioning map in Figure 9-12 shows the results of customer research on how customers position, in their own minds, various restaurants on the two dimensions of service quality and price. It also shows how they would position an "ideal" restaurant, the "ideal" in this case having fairly high service quality and fairly high prices. There is no one restaurant that actually fits this ideal in the customers' minds. Restaurant A is perceived as

having even better service, but also higher prices. The customers' ideal would be to have less service, at less cost. Restaurant E is at the other extreme, with low service and low price. This target market wants lower prices than A, but it wants more service than E has to offer at that price. You can compare these two, in the same manner, against restaurants B, C, and D.

Which restaurant has the best opportunity in this hypothetical situation? Probably B. If B can raise its service level, or the perception of its service level, just a little, it can raise its prices quite a bit (assuming, of course, that all other things are equal). On the other hand, to get closer to the ideal, A would have to lower its perceived prices, but could also give up some service refinements.

In analyzing the position of the competition, marketers also want to be able to protect the position they hope to establish. This means anticipating possible competitive reactions and

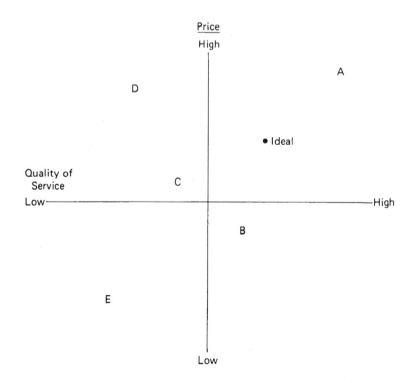

FIGURE 9-12   Hypothetical perceptual map of restaurant positioning on dimensions of service quality and price

taking measures to reduce their impact. One method would be to use hard-to-duplicate product forms such as Hyatt's atrium lobby. As history has shown, of course, sooner or later duplication will occur, but getting there first can always be an asset.

In Figure 9-12, restaurant B could raise its prices "very cautiously" so that A would have to come down substantially to match them. If B knew its competitors, it might "know" that this is something A would be reluctant to do.

Positioning Hotel Restaurants   A case in point, in a general sense, is hotel restaurants, which for years have been perceived as overpriced. At the same time, they have been perceived as offering "hotel food." The current trend is to reposition hotel dining rooms by offering different food types. Although the change in hotel restaurant concepts is apparent everywhere, the change in the prices, in many cases, is not. In fact, it appears that customers are against paying almost the same prices for trendy food with less service that they used to pay for a "fine dining" experience. While some hotel restaurants concentrate on the neighborhood customer, their own house guests continue to go out. In this sense, hotel restaurants, generically speaking, are positioned against non-hotel restaurants.

We once had cocktails with the controller of a major hotel in New York City, in a beautiful, very expensive new lounge that seated over 100 people, off the main lobby of the hotel. The hotel was full, but the lounge was empty and it was cocktail time. We discussed the problem as well as a similar problem with one of the hotel's dining rooms. "What are your liquor and food cost percentages," we asked. "Fourteen percent and 24 percent," he proudly answered. The emphasis was on cost, and the lounge and dining room were inadvertently positioned as far too expensive.

This same hotel had a coffee shop in which one could obtain juice, coffee, and a roll for $8.95 plus tax and tip. Across the street, one could obtain juice, coffee, roll, two eggs, bacon, and hash browns for $2.79, plus tax and tip. Obviously, there was a big difference between the two operations, but the waitresses were as surly in one as in the other, and both operations paid the same un-

ion wages. The $2.79 restaurant also had to pay its own rent, heat, light, and power. One was definitely cleaner and you had to wait for a hostess to take you to your table. But the food, for breakfast, was comparable. The example was a good case for positioning.

People who stayed in the hotel, mostly on expense account, surely could afford to have breakfast there, and many did. A great many also went across the street. This was not price segmentation, but benefit segmentation. Some liked the "benefit" of staying in the hotel in cleaner and more prestigious surroundings; others liked the "benefit" of feeling they got their money's worth. The two restaurants were subjectively positioned on benefits, and value was the positioning tool. As the GM of a Boston hotel once said, "Then there's the guest who takes a suite, has rack of lamb and fine wine for dinner, and goes across the street to Dunkin' Donuts for breakfast."

In another hotel in New York City, a new restaurant concept was designed to appeal to the local neighborhood. Seating 125, it averaged 40 to 50 covers a night and most house guests ate elsewhere. A quick look at the menu made one imagine a check average of around $35, although there were a few lower-priced items available. The actual check average was about $14, which should tell somebody something. To counter this, menu prices were raised! This is a case, as mentioned above by Kyle Craig of S&A Restaurant Corporation, where the positioning was restaurant-driven rather than customer-driven.

Some hotel restaurants have a major repositioning to undertake and many are doing it. They not only need to be more realistic about current eating trends, but they have a major job to do in changing consumers' perceptions. Products must be matched with their market segments. Positioning makes a statement of what the product is and how it should be evaluated. True positioning is accomplished by using all the marketing mix variables. This includes the products and services offered, how they are presented to the customer, the price, and all the methods used to communicate to the customer. Not a single one can be ignored, because it is there whether or not a conscious effort is made to use it.

TABLE 9-4 Positioning Checklist

1. Does it say who you are and what you stand for? Does it create a mental picture?
2. Does it set you apart and show how you are different?
3. Does it preempt a benefit niche and capitalize on an advantage?
4. Does it turn any liability into an asset?
5. Does it have benefits for the target market you are trying to reach?
6. Does it provide tangible evidence or clues?
7. Does it feature the one or two things that your target market wants most?
8. Is it consistent with strategy—for instance, does it expand or exchange usage patterns? Create new awareness? Project the right image?
9. Does it have credibility?
10. Does it make a promise you can keep?

Once the positioning goal has been established, every effort must be made to be certain that the product or brand actually achieves the position. Even with all the necessary ingredients of good positioning, there is no assurance of success until "share of mind" is achieved. This is where promotional strategy comes into play. Whether it is implemented through advertising or in-house, desired positions do not wait to be discovered. Success here means the realization of all positioning efforts. Table 9-4 provides a checklist for your positioning or desired positioning.

Multiple Brand and Product Positioning[10]

Hospitality companies develop multiple brands for growth purposes. Sometimes this is through development of a new concept, sometimes through acquisition, and sometimes through both. Marriott, for example, developed the Courtyard (midprice) and Fairfield Inn (budget) lodging concepts to develop new segments, purchased Residence Inns for quick entry into mod-

erate-price all-suite properties, developed Marriott Suites as luxury all-suites, and initiated J.W. Marriotts as upscale luxury hotels.

While development of multiple brands provides growth, it also provides protection from the competition against a single brand. Marriott saw other chains moving into lower-tier markets and threatening the middle to upper tier in which Marriott hotels were positioned. Marriott felt it might as well steal its own customers (also called cannibalization) as let someone else steal them. It also realized that there were markets that the existing concept was neglecting.

Multiple brands, of course, are common practice in other industries, for instance, Procter & Gamble and General Motors. The restaurant industry has long had multiple brands, as in the case of General Mills, which owns Red Lobster, Olive Garden, and their new Chinese restaurant concept, China Coast. PepsiCo owns Pizza Hut, Taco Bell, and KFC.

The issue here is one of positioning each brand. In the case of PepsiCo, positioning Pizza Hut, Taco Bell, and KFC is not much different from positioning against an outside competitor in terms of positioning strategy, with one exception: It would be self-defeating for the parent company if these three chains cannibalized each other. What they want to do, instead, is to position to different market segments.

The different market segments may include many of the same people. People belong, how-

---

[10]The usage of the terms *brand, product,* and *product line* can be confusing. As commonly used and used here, a brand is a brand name that identifies a set of products called the product line. Thus, Chrysler Corporation has four car brands—Chrysler, Dodge, Plymouth and Eagle. The brand Chrysler has a product line with different products, such as New Yorker, Fifth Avenue, and Le Baron.

ever, to a different segment when they use restaurants for different purposes, in different contexts, or at different times. Thus, the positioning of each chain should be managed so that they do not steal from each other, and then the standard positioning rules can be applied.

This is easier to do when your chains are named Pizza Hut and Taco Bell, and when many people don't even know they belong to the same company, than when they are named Ramada Inn, Ramada Hotel, (Ramada) Renaissance, Ramada Plaza, Ramada Suites, and Ramada Resorts, often leading to multiple confusion. This was actually one brand (Ramada) with six products in its product line.

Ever since Quality Inns was successfully broken into Comfort Inns, Quality Inns, and Quality Royale (now Clarion) there have been a number of hotel chains with properties under the same or similar name, each trying to position to a different market segment. This is commonly referred to as brand proliferation.

Quality Inns subsequently created Sleep Inns and renamed itself Choice International Hotels with four brands. Management claims that there is no question about the difference between the four brand names. This may not be the case when a Comfort Inn (so-called luxury budget segment) charges $100, as we previously noted, denying the positioning of that brand name. Further, the purchase addition of Rodeway, Friendship, and Econo Lodge to the Choice fold may have created some very confused customers, particularly as all brands answer to the same 800 number. Choice now has seven brands with 13 different products, as seen in Table 9-5. The overlap is obvious, as shown in their own brand positioning portrayal (Figure 9-13).

This is exactly how General Motors lost its positioning distinctiveness for Chevrolet, Pontiac, Buick, and Oldsmobile, when these four brands started changing engines and parts and greatly overlapping their price ranges. Hospitality Franchise Systems (HFS), whose CEO specifically disagrees with Robert Hazard of Choice, maintains that customers want separate brand identities with separate 800 numbers (Figure 9-14).

A *Cornell Quarterly* article contains some comments on this situation:

> Yesawich [President of the hospitality advertising firm Robinson, Yesawich & Pepperdine] said that the success of brands depends on creating a clear differentiation in the minds of customers. With only few exceptions, the advertising and promotion that has been initiated on behalf of new product concepts has failed to communicate clearly or convincingly the basis of the differentiation. Consumers are quick to discern the availability of free drinks or free breakfasts, but it takes much more to constitute a new product in consumers' minds.... If advertising doesn't communicate the perception of a new product, then maybe the product isn't really new at all.
>
> Some observers are concerned that consumers may be confused by a chain that has one name on a variety of hotels. Yesawich noted that chains pursuing diversification by introducing new products under different names have so far met with greater success.

TABLE 9-5   Choice International Hotels' Seven Brands and 13 Products

Sleep Inns: limited-service, economy hotels
Comfort Inns and Suites: upper-economy, limited-service hotels and all-suite hotels
Quality Inns, Hotels and Suites: mid-priced, full-service inns and limited-service all-suite hotels
Clarion Hotels, Suites, Resorts, and Carriage House Inns: upscale hotels, all-suite hotels, resorts and boutique inns
Rodeway Inns: limited- and full-service, upper-priced economy hotels
Econo Lodges: limited-service, mid-priced, economy hotels
Friendship Inns: lower-economy, limited-service hotels

Source: Choice International Hotels' franchise brochure, 1993.

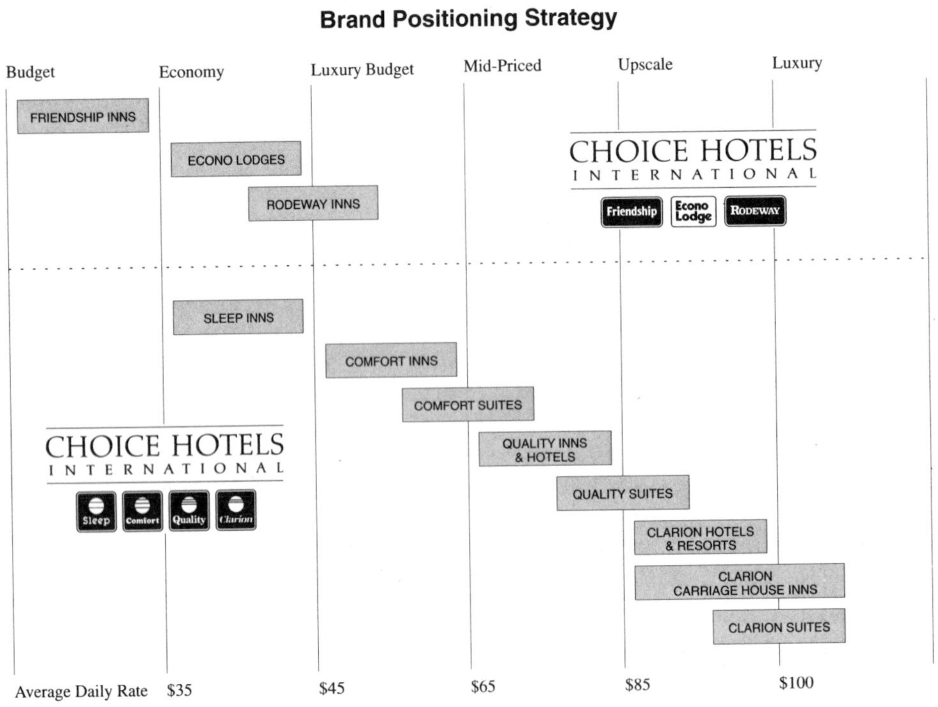

Brand Positioning Strategy

Courtesy of Choice International

FIGURE 9-13   Choice International's self-positioning

"In general terms, a brand name is an asset, as long as it stands singlemindedly for a specific package of value and benefits. Call it a personality," said Bloch [then Senior Vice-President for Marketing at Four Seasons]. "Leaving a midprice brand name on an upscale property, as some operators are doing, may confuse some customers."[11]

Ramada had the same problem with Renaissance and Holiday Inn with Crowne Plaza, which it positioned upscale, but not luxury, at the top of its product line. But notice in Figure 9-15 how a franchisee tries to position the basic Holiday Inn product.

Even worse is what Howard Johnson did, as shown in Figure 9-16. After this, and fol-lowing its sale to HFS when its parent Prime Motor Inns went into bankruptcy, Howard Johnson developed still another brand and opened 165 HoJo Inns, limited-service properties. In late 1993, expansion of HoJo Inns was aborted. Eric Pfeffer, President of Howard Johnson, reported:

[R]esearch shows that 80 percent of American travelers believe the name HoJo is synonymous with Howard Johnson, so when they show up at a HoJo Inn "their expectations are fried clams, 28 flavors of ice cream and a full-service lodging facility, complete with meeting rooms and swimming pool," not a budget motel...as many as 55 percent of the properties will eventually convert.[12]

[11]Glenn Withiam, "Hotel Companies Aim at Multiple Markets," *Cornell Hotel and Restaurant Administration Quarterly,* November, 1985, pp. 39–51.

[12]Ed Watkins, "The Forum," *Lodging Hospitality,* September, 1993, p. 2.

HOSPITALITY
FRANCHISE
SYSTEMS, INC.

339 JEFFERSON RD. P.O. BOX 278, PARSIPPANY, NEW JERSEY 07054-0278
PHONE (201) 428-9700
FAX (201) 428-6057/8

TRUTH IN ADVERTISING

Mr. Robert C. Hazard, Jr.
Chairman and CEO
CHOICE HOTELS INTERNATIONAL

Dear Bob:

No, Bob, we don't specialize in negative advertising -- instead we are committed to the truth.

Fact: All three of the franchisees you mentioned in your advertisement in this publication who converted from Choice to Days Inns, Howard Johnson and Ramada have made or have committed to make significant investments in their properties in order to upgrade to meet their new franchisor's standards. These licensees informed us that they were unwilling or unable to make the investment under their former Choice flags due to, among other reasons, their concern about reservation volume being split among seven brands.

Bob, what we are saying in our advertising is that our policy of separate brand identity for Days Inns, Howard Johnson and Ramada is our **comparative difference** with Choice. It is what our customers tell us they want - **separate brands**, each with a clearly articulated **impact policy** and with **distinct marketing/advertising programs** and **different 800 numbers.**

Fact: Smith Travel Research merely points out various chains' market share of travelers based on total rooms in the chain*. Of course your market share went up: you increased the size of your systems. HFS could make the same claim; since 1990 our three brands have grown by more than 20%. Our customers, however, could care less; what they are solely interested in is how we are doing **for them.** As long as our **call volume** and **room nights booked per available room** continue to **increase** every year, as they have, then we're on the right track.

Bob, if you will allow me to have the last word, we're not being negative but rather we're running a comparative advertising campaign. It's the kind of advertising that makes a distinction between companies and allows buyers to make a choice. It's a highly respected tradition in the advertising world and one that's particularly appropriate in our industry today. We're happy to offer customers real choices, not manufactured statistics, and let them decide.

Best regards.

Sincerely yours,

Henry R. Silverman
Chairman and CEO

---

* Source: Smith Travel Research letter dated May 6, 1992.

FIGURE 9-14 Two opposing CEOs disagree on separate brand identity: An open letter published as a paid advertisement

GO FROM PLANE TO LUXURIOUS AT THE HOLIDAY INN- JFK AIRPORT.

In a matter of minutes. The Holiday Inn - JFK Airport offers luxurious rooms, exquisite dining, spectacular meeting rooms and state-of-the-art health facilities, without Manhattan prices or hassles. Shouldn't luxury be a convenience?

1-800-HOLIDAY

Holiday Inn

JFK AIRPORT
114-02 135th Ave., Jamaica, NY 11436
718-659-0200

Stay With Someone You Know.

FIGURE 9-15   Positioning a Holiday Inn above its product class

The folly of not doing their homework has plagued Howard Johnson for years and illustrates the importance of proper positioning.

Sheraton and Hilton have wrestled with a similar image problem for the past decade. The vast difference between the Sheraton Wayfarer Motor Inn in Bedford, New Hampshire and the Sheraton St. Regis in Manhattan is about the same difference as the Berkshire Hilton Inn in Pittsfield, Massachusetts and the Waldorf-Astoria, two hotels sporting the Hilton name brand. Customers can be very confused with what position the brand name actually conveys. A Sheraton example is shown in Figure 9-17. The addition of the word "Inn" on the franchise brand name was done to try to rectify this situation.

Marriott debated long and hard, when developing the Courtyard concept, as to whether to call it a Marriott. The final decision was to call it Courtyard by Marriott, with the "Marriott" in smaller letters. Today, the "by" has been dropped. Thus, Courtyard can trade on its famous brand name without creating expectations of the same product/service. The same was done with their Fairfield Inn brand line. (See Figure 9-18.) Regardless, our point here is a different one. The problem is not merely in the name (only a possible compounding of the problem), but in the positioning.

Can hotel concepts under the same or similar names make the same claim? In other words, is each brand or product positioned to a different specific target market, each with specific needs that relate to the positioning? Second, if the first case is true, can these markets differentiate the positioning of each brand or product name so that they (the markets) know which one "belongs" to them? This is the case in point and is the concern of positioning any multiple

FIGURE 9-16   Howard Johnson confuses its brand name image

brands, more so when the problem is compounded by similar names. Forte Hotels of the United Kingdom went through a complete rebranding of its entire product line in 1991 for this very reason. If the answers to the above questions are negative, then there will be a clear case of cannibalization and customer confusion.

Multiple brand positioning can be done successfully, as Marriott has shown. Groupe Accor, a French firm, has developed lodging concepts called Formule1, Ibis, Novotel, and Sofitel and now owns Motel 6 in the United States. By French government rating, these are one-, two-, three-, and four-star properties respectively. Each is based on the needs of a specific target market. Each is clearly differentiated from the other three; in fact, you could say that no customer would ever choose one when he or she wanted the other. In at least one place, in Paris, a Novotel and Sofitel sit side-by-side with a common wall dividing them, but separate entrances; the traveler has a choice in the same location. Each is clearly positioned to its own market segment. This is true segmentation and good positioning of multiple brands. Accor has

had difficulty, however, positioning its Sofitel and Novotel products in the crowded American market.

Internal Positioning Analysis

Positioning maps, mentioned above, help to determine positioning strategies vis-a-vis the competition. They are also useful methods for analyzing one's position on a number of different attributes or benefits. As has been said so often, internal marketing is critical in the hospitality industry. If this is true, then it is obvious that internal positioning is also critical.

Figure 9-19 illustrates another use of perceptual mapping, in the case of an actual restaurant. Respondents were asked to rate the importance of certain attributes in choosing an upscale restaurant at which to have dinner; some of these are shown in the figure. Respondents were also asked to rate this particular restaurant on a scale ranging from poor to excellent. No one rated it poor, but Figure 9-19 shows the quadrants in which are located those who rated it Fair (F), Good (G), and Excellent (E).

Most inns give you a good price.
We just make it worth more.

More service is what you'll find at Sheraton Inns. Besides affordable
rates, we have room service, meeting space, restaurants, pools, comfortable rooms
and of course, ITT Sheraton quality.
If you join ITT Sheraton Club International, you can enjoy late check-out,
upgrades when available and earn ClubPoints. ClubPoints can
be redeemed for awards and free travel. And right now we have SureSaver Business
Rates that are 5%-30% off of our regular rates. They're available
Sunday through Thursday with no advance reservation or purchase requirement. As
you can see, we're making it very easy to find a good value.
Simply contact your travel professional or **800-325-3535.**

A whole lot of Sheraton   **Sheraton** *Inn*   *at just a slice of the price.*

ITT Sheraton

Courtesy of ITT Sheraton Corporation

FIGURE 9-17   Sheraton tries to differentiate the positioning of its franchises by calling them "inns"

In the same quadrants can be seen the reasons or attributes that were significant in determining the ratings. For example, those who
rated the restaurant Fair did so largely because
it was intimidating. Those who rated it Good
saw it as a special occasion restaurant. Those
who rated it Excellent did so for the reasons
shown, with the length of the lines (vectors)
indicating how important each attribute was in
the rating (e.g., quality of food and service were

Marriott...
The Right Choice

Whenever you travel, there's a Marriott that's right for you.
Each of our chains is unique. And they
all offer the hospitality and service you've come to trust.
Marriott. The Right Choice Every Time.

Full Service Accommodations
1-800-228-9290

Moderate Priced Lodging
1-800-321-2211

Extended Stay Lodging
1-800-331-3131

Economy Lodging
1-800-228-2800

Courtesy of Marriott Corporation

FIGURE 9-18   Marriott positions its four brand name products with different 800 numbers

the most important determinants). While the last case is not totally revealing, the reasons for the Fair and Good ratings were revealing and led the restaurant to initiate a campaign showing that it was not intimidating, that it was a place to go at times *other* than special occasions, and that it was indeed worth the price.

Internal analysis not only helps to determine internal positioning, but it also indicates where the operation may be failing both internally and relative to the competition. Further, it aids in the best use of resources by indicating where they will count the most for the customer.

The hard questions that have to be asked are these:

1. What is important to the target market?
2. How does the target market perceive us?
3. How does the target market perceive the competition?
4. What should we differentiate on, so as to make best use of our limited resources?

The reality is that if the target market doesn't perceive the image, it doesn't exist; if the target market doesn't believe that what you have to offer is a benefit, it isn't a benefit; if customers do not believe that you can deliver the benefit, your promises are meaningless; if the benefit isn't important to the target market, it isn't important; if your benefit is not perceived as different from that of the competition, you haven't differentiated.

In short, images, benefits, and differentiation are solely the perception of the consumer, not management. (We keep repeating these state-

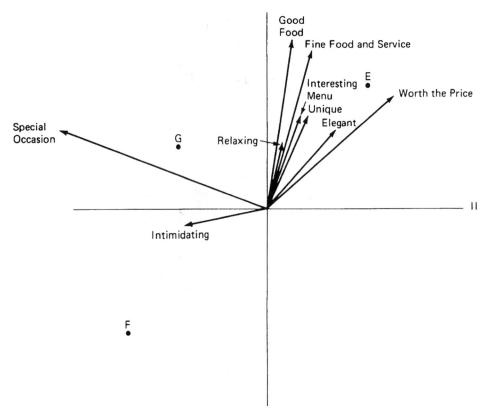

FIGURE 9-19   Perceptual mapping of restaurant attributes

ments intentionally—they are the most often forgotten or neglected truths of marketing.) Let us also repeat, as a reminder: These statements are especially pertinent to hospitality marketing because of the intangibility of the services offered and the simultaneous production and consumption of the offering, which permits evaluation only after the purchase.

Hospitality research too often fails to identify the vital elements of benefits. Comment cards, for example, ask customers whether they liked certain features of the property or operation. What those features do for the customer or how important they are, even when satisfactorily rated, is not revealed.[13]

The architecture of a property, the decor, and the furnishings are examples of attributes that may produce a benefit, or may be tangible representations of an intangible benefit, but are not themselves the benefit. The benefit itself is what the attributes do for the customer—for instance, give a sense of security, a sensation of grandeur, an aura of prestige, or a feeling of comfort. The credibility of these benefits may diminish rapidly if an expectation is not fulfilled. Decor is soon forgotten if the service takes an hour. The impression of security loses credibility if the guest encounters slovenly characters in the restroom. It is this fulfillment of expectations, or lack of it, that creates the perception of deliverability for the consumer.

Finally, as previously mentioned, competing properties may be seen to offer the same senses of security, grandeur, prestige, and comfort. The

[13]See, for example, Robert C. Lewis and Abraham Pizam, "Guest Surveys: A Missed Opportunity," *Cornell Hotel and Restaurant Administration Quarterly,* November, 1981, pp. 37–44.

tangible attributes have lost their ability to differentiate and, at the same time, are no longer determinant in the consumer choice process.

Benefits, then, like positioning, exist in the mind of the consumer and are determinable only by asking the consumer. This information is essential to proper positioning analysis.

Positioning is the ultimate weapon in niche marketing. Stripped of all its trappings, positioning analysis answers the following questions:

1. What position do you own now? (In the mind of the target market.)
2. What position do you want to own? (Look for positions or holes in the marketplace.)
3. Whom must you outposition? (Manipulate what's already in the mind.)
4. How can you do it? (The attributes or benefits that are salient, determinant, and important to the target market and that the firm can deliver.)

Summary

Market positioning is a valuable weapon for hospitality marketers. To position successfully requires recognizing the marketplace, the competition, and consumers' perceptions. Positioning analysis on a target market basis provides the tools to identify opportunities for creating the desired image that differentiates from the competition, and for serving the target market better than anyone else.

Positioning may be objective, where images of the physical characteristics of the product are used, or subjective, where customers' mental perceptions play a greater role. Positioning of a tangible good is often accomplished through association with intangible notions, but it is better to position intangible services with tangible clues.

Repositioning may be necessary when a hospitality firm is in an unacceptable position or when trying to appeal to a new market segment. Old hotels with poor images are often renovated, and repositioning them is crucial to their success. Six approaches to positioning

were discussed, and marketers may select the ones that will be most effective after selecting the desired position.

The differences between salient, important, and determinant attributes must be considered especially if the firm is being positioned by benefit or attribute. All three are complementary and it is crucial to understand their place.

As many hotel and restaurant chains grow by adding new brands and concepts, multiple brand positioning becomes important. Marketers must prevent one brand from cannibalizing the other and also be able to create separate images and benefits for each one. Finally, internal positioning analysis can be used to examine one's own position to see if it is perceived by its customers.

Discussion Questions

1. What are the different kinds of hospitality positioning? Give examples of when and why you would use each one.
2. Discuss the problems a product can incur with a weak or undefined position.
3. Identify a hotel or restaurant you know that is in need of repositioning, and outline the steps needed to achieve the repositioning.
4. Take two competing hotels you are familiar with and position them using the six approaches to positioning.
5. Discuss the salient, determinant, and important attributes of the same hotel or restaurant.
6. Develop a list of questions that you would pose to a focus group of customers of a cocktail lounge that seeks to establish a position in the marketplace.
7. How does competition affect the positioning of a product? Discuss.
8. Draw a positioning map like that in Figure 9-12 for a group of restaurants or hotels with which you are familiar, based on your own perceptions.
9. In Case 9-1, how should the Inter-Continental Hotel be positioned to best advantage? Why? Draw a competitive position-

ing map for the case. Recalculate market share figures after you have determined ICH's best position and its key competitors.

10. In Case 9-2 what are the problems facing the Upper Crust Restaurant? What does management need to do?

11. In Case 9-3, evaluate Forte Hotels' rebranding. Why did they do it? Have they established clear positions for their brands? Discuss.

✔ Case 9-1
Hotel Inter-Continental / Toronto[14]

Rex Rice, General Manager of the Toronto Hotel Inter-Continental, wondered how he could increase occupancy and raise prices to their original level. The hotel had opened with a single corporate rate of $195 but only a 22 percent occupancy during the first four months. Occupancy increased to 55 percent when the rate was dropped to $169 after the first summer.

Background

The Inter-Continental Hotel (ICH) was owned and operated by the parent company of the same name, which was owned by the Saison Group of Japan. It claimed to be the world's leading deluxe hotel chain. ICH contended that 85 percent of its customers were business travelers, 40 percent of all guests at a specific hotel were repeat visitors to that hotel, and it was the first choice of frequent international business travelers, according to an in-flight survey.

The chain had 105 properties located in 48 countries around the world. Eighty-six of these were deluxe, first-class Inter-Continental Hotels; 17 were high-quality, moderately priced hotels known as Forum hotels; three were executive conference centers called Scanticon. Over the past 40 years, the company had achieved a reputation for personalized service, luxury product, and geographic scope, making it a recognized name among international business and leisure travelers. ICH had a strong foreign presence, but the image in the North American market was considerably weaker.

The Toronto property was built for about $50 million and was fully owned by ICH. It was one of Toronto's premier boutique hotels and was located in the upscale downtown area of the city, also known for expensive restaurants and boutique shops. There were 213 guestrooms, including 12 suites plus seven meeting rooms, a

business center, a fitness center, an indoor rooftop lap pool, and a sundeck. There was also an upscale lounge and dining room. Guest services included laundry, valet and shoe shine service, 24-hour pressing, twice-daily maid service and turn-down, 24-hour room service, concierge, guest-relations service, and valet parking.

Competition

The Inter-Continental Hotel had five competitors in the same product class. All were in the same approximate area, except for the King Edward, which was farther downtown. A comparison of these properties for the past year—on price, number of rooms, average occupancy rate, and market share—is shown in Table 9-1-1. Mr. Rice, however, felt that not all of these properties were competing for the same customer.

Mr. Rice felt that the main competitive advantage for the ICH was its facilities. The hotel was less than a year old and had a very high-quality product with exclusive guest services. Mr. Rice asked his Marketing Director, John Visconti, to rank the competition based on the condition of the facility and the guest services offered for the corporate market. His report follows:

The Four Seasons has the same guest services and competes for the same business market segment. It is a luxurious facility with an image of the best upscale hotel chain in North America. The Toronto property has a refurbished lobby and front desk but the rooms are beginning to look tired and run-down. (Mr. Visconti rated it as an eight out of ten.)

The King Edward and Sutton Place has refurbished facilities, but each lacks essential customer services for the corporate transient segment. (He rated Sutton Place a six but downgraded King Edward to a five because of its location.)

The Park Plaza has two towers. One has been recently refurbished but the other is very run-down. (It also lacks essential guest services, so

[14]David Blake and Paul Kuno researched and contributed to this case. All rates are given in Canadian dollars which, at the time of writing, was equal to about .85 U.S. dollar.

TABLE 9-1-1

Hotel	Rooms	Occ%	Corp. Rate$	FMS%[a]	AMS%[b]
Inter-Continental	213	55	169	12.4	11.2
Four Seasons	382	87	230	22.3	31.8
King Edward	318	75	175	18.6	22.8
Sutton Place	280	65	160	16.4	17.4
Park Plaza	264	45	130	15.4	11.4
Renaissance	256	22	125	14.9	5.5[c]
	1,713	61%		100.0	100.0

[a]FMS(fair market share) is the number of rooms of each hotel divided by the total number of rooms.
[b]AMS (actual market share) is the number of rooms occupied of each hotel divided by the total number of rooms occupied.
[c]The Renaissance periodically closed rooms for refurbishing during the year.

was rated a four.) The Renaissance is being refurbished and promises an upgraded facility next year. (It also lacks essential guest services and was also rated four.)

The ICH has superior facilities with a lavish marble entryway, mahogany paneling, and rooms that cater specifically to the business traveler with oversized desks, and a separate shower and bathtub in each bathroom. Extensive guest services also rank the ICH higher than the competitive properties, except the Four Seasons which has the same services. (ICH was rated a nine out of ten.)

Mr. Visconti felt that the area drew four major market segments. They were the tourist/entertainment, corporate transient, government, and upscale conference segments. Major attractions for the tourist/entertainment segment were in the farther downtown core except for the very upscale boutique shop buyer. The ICH area was home to most of the large businesses in the downtown area and attracted the corporate transient market. Government was a large segment because of Queens Park, just to the south and home of the provincial government. The upscale conference market was attracted to the area because of its quality and upscale hotels.

ICH targeted the corporate transient and corporate group markets specifically. The Four Seasons, King Edward, and Sutton Place were competing for these same segments. The Park Plaza and the Renaissance, because of their lower prices, were getting a majority of the government segment. The tourist/entertainment market, because of its diversity, was spread among all downtown hotels.

Mr. Rice wondered how to position the Inter-Continental Hotel for the future. If they stayed at their present price level, other hotels might steal their present customers. If he raised prices to attract the upscale business market, he was afraid that occupancy would drop as it had before.

✔ Case 9-2
The Upper Crust Restaurant[15]

Rick Maple, the General Manager of the Howard Johnson Newton Hotel, sat at his desk and breathed a deep sigh of frustration. He had just received the month end figures for the hotel's main food and beverage outlet, the Upper Crust Restaurant, for April. Sales for the month were about $61,000. This figure was substantially less than the $71,000 that had been budgeted. Figures for previous months showed similar discrepancies.

Madison Simpson, the restaurant Manager, walked into Mr. Maple's office and acknowledged the disappointment showing on Rick's face.

"We have to do something," Mr. Maple said to Madison. "The restaurant is simply not generating enough volume."

Both Maple and Simpson had earned B.S. degrees in hotel and restaurant administration. They now knew they faced a major challenge to what they had learned, in attempting to generate higher volume for the Upper Crust Restaurant.

History and Background

The Upper Crust was an upscale restaurant specializing in seafood and New England-style cuisine. The name was used for the signature restaurants in the Sheraton Tara Hotel chain. There was an Upper Crust Restaurant located in eight Sheraton Tara Hotels in Braintree, Danvers, Framingham, Springfield, and Newton, Massachusetts; in Nashua, New Hampshire; in Portland, Maine; and in Parsippany, New Jersey.

Tara Hotels was the largest franchisee of the Sheraton Corporation in the New England area. The hotels were owned and operated by The Flatley Company, based in Braintree, Massachusetts. They were positioned in the marketplace as upscale properties, catering to higher-rated groups and corporate travelers. The

physical hotel product was above that of average Sheraton standards.

The Howard Johnson Newton was a 261-room property located literally above the Massachusetts Turnpike in Newton, Massachusetts, six miles west of Boston, but carefully sealed away from the noise, traffic, and congestion of the turnpike. The turnpike was the main interstate highway into Boston from suburban areas and western Massachusetts. The hotel was formerly managed by Dunfey Hotels under the same Howard Johnson franchise. Although the property was now owned by Flatley, it still carried the Howard Johnson sign on its exterior, as well as the Tara sign, and would continue to do so for two more years because of the franchise agreement. Until the Howard Johnson sign was removed from the exterior of the property, the hotel would continue to cater to lower-rated market segments such as mid-range commercial travelers, airline crews, and sports teams, which were attracted to the Howard Johnson name by its low prices.

After purchasing the property, The Flatley Company began to renovate the interior of the hotel in order to bring it up to Tara standards. The front desk area, the lobby, 50 percent of the rooms, and the Upper Crust Restaurant had been renovated.

At the time of the purchase, the main food and beverage outlet in the hotel was known as Oscar's, the third "name" on the restaurant in the past five years. Prior to Oscar's, it had been a Red Coach Grille, a subsidiary product line of Howard Johnson. Oscar's was an independently owned, mid-scale restaurant. Flatley eventually had purchased Oscar's and run the restaurant as such for a year. The concept was then terminated and the restaurant closed for renovation. It reopened six months later as the Upper Crust. The decision had been made by the Flatley Company to renovate and open the Upper Crust despite the fact that the hotel had not yet become a Tara. Since the lobby and the front desk area were being renovated at the time,

---

[15]Eric Jhanji and Felix Mou researched and contributed to this case.

management believed that it was in the best interest of the property to also renovate the restaurant at the same time, prior to the forthcoming name change of the hotel.

Problems Faced by Management

From a marketing perspective, management faced the following problems with the Upper Crust:

1. The Upper Crust was an upscale restaurant situated in a property that catered to low-rated group segments, and would continue to do so for another two years.
2. How would upper-middle class customers from the Newton area communities be attracted to an upscale restaurant located in a hotel still perceived to be a Howard Johnson?
3. How would lower-rated hotel guests be attracted to an upscale hotel restaurant?
4. Attached to the north end of the property, and accessible through the lobby of the hotel, was an independently owned "pub-like" restaurant known as Appleby's. This restaurant specialized in light, lower-priced foods such as hamburgers, chicken wings, and sandwiches. Appleby's operated under a ten-year contract with the owner of the entire Gateway Plaza property, which included the hotel. Its business boomed because it attracted the in-house, lower-rated market segments staying in the hotel.
5. Financial data indicated that the business of the Upper Crust Restaurant was not meeting The Flatley Company's expectations.

The Restaurant

The guiding principle of the Upper Crust was stated on the cover of the lunch and dinner menus:

> Once upon a time the custom of the land was for kings and nobles to entertain frequently at court. Guests from far and near were invited and the gaming and feasting lasted for a week. Huge banquets were held and every night the great halls of the castles rang with the sounds of celebration.
>
> The feasting boards were set up in the shape of a "T", with the king and his ranking nobles occupying the head table. And, when the occasion called for a very special feast, the cooks were commanded to prepare giant meat pies, concocted from choice mutton, pork, or beef. These giant pies were carried steaming from the galley directly to the king. He and his royal followers were served the choicest parts of the meat pie...the upper crust. And so it came about that those who receive special treatment are called the Upper Crust. We chose it as the name of our restaurant because we believe that our patrons are something special and deserve royal treatment.

A newly renovated restaurant with luxurious surroundings and a warm and inviting atmosphere, the Upper Crust was divided into three main sections: the Lounge, the Tapas, and the main dining room.

The Lounge In the lounge area there was a large sit-down bar, as well as a big screen TV that regularly displayed major sporting events. Light snack foods, as well as pizza, were available. A monthly calendar of events for the lounge was displayed at the bar, as well as in the lobby of the hotel. Some of these events included BBQ Nite, Deli Nite, the Mexican Fiesta, and the Oriental Express.

Tapas The Tapas section was a Spanish concept. Spanish-style appetizers were available in this section, which could be seen at the end of the main aisle upon walking into the restaurant. Very attactively decorated, it contained a long, "L"-shaped counter with eight seats. (In Spain, the *tapas* is known as "a traditional Spanish appetizer that originated when city and town people congregated together for conversation and good times.")

Main Dining Room The main dining room consisted of 145 banquette seats, attractively covered. The room was elegantly designed, the carpeting and drapes plush. In one corner of the dining room was a grand piano for live entertainment during dinner hours; in another corner, a harp, played during the Sunday brunch. In addition, a small private dining room, which could accommodate up to 14 people, was situated at the back of the main dining room. This was ideal for small meetings and private dinners.

The Upper Crust had a total of 60 employees, including an executive chef, two sous chefs, and five line cooks. Newly hired employees were required to study staff and service manuals prepared by the restaurant manager. In addition, they were required to pass a written exam and familiarize themselves with all aspects of the operation. The restaurant had recently experienced problems relating to a high rate of employee turnover. This was due to the low volume of business, as well as to the numerous employment opportunities available in the surrounding areas.

Menu Description

Breakfast at the Upper Crust was a traditional, American-style offering. Prices ranged from $5.95 for a continental breakfast to $7.75 for bagels and lox. In addition, an a la carte selection was available.

Lunch at the Upper Crust offered a diverse array of tempting foods. In addition to New England-style appetizers, soups, salads, burgers, and sandwiches, a wide variety of entrees were available. Some of these included Chicken Citrone ($8.25), Seafood Frittata ($7.95), and Stir Fry Chicken ($8.95). A special lunch treat was the Carvery Buffet, which included a variety of several meats, salads, seafood dishes, and fruits for $9.95.

Dinner at the Upper Crust included an excellent selection of entrees, as well as an appealing variety of appetizers, soups, and salads. Appetizers included Veal Ravioli ($6.50), Escargot Tara ($8.95), and Oysters Bienville ($8.95). Soups included Clam Chowder ($3.50), Seafood Gumbo ($3.95), and Onion Soup ($4.50). Entrees ranged in price from $14.95 for Chicken Zinfandel to $18.95 for Grilled Tournedos Aux Fine Herb. Some popular favorites were Boston Schrod ($13.95), Veal Pomeroy ($16.75), and Filet of Salmon ($17.95).

The Upper Crust was open seven days a week for breakfast, lunch, and dinner. The lounge was open nightly until 1:00 A.M.

Marketing—Current Strategies and Tactics

Madison Simpson identified his main markets by meal period as follows:

Breakfast Predominantly an in-house market with very few people from outside the hotel.

Lunch Much of the lunch business came from local companies in the Newton area. Individuals, as well as small groups of businessmen, formed a large portion of this market. In addition the retired, elderly community in the Newton area also was considered a part of the lunch market.

Dinner Much of the dinner business stemmed from the surrounding communities, especially Newton. This clientele was generally upper middle class in terms of socio-economic status. They ate out quite often and were quite fussy and demanding in terms of their expectations.

The in-house business generated by the Upper Crust was quite small. Management felt that this was because it was an upscale restaurant located in a hotel that still attracted lower-rated market segments. Madison Simpson anticipated about a 25 percent increase in the restaurant's volume, once the hotel officially became a Tara. This assumption was based on the fact that the property would then be catering to higher-rated market segments who would frequent the Upper Crust more often, thus increasing the in-house business.

In the meantime, however, Madison emphasized that much of the marketing being utilized revolved around creating awareness of the restaurant in the outside area, communities outside Newton. In order to achieve this, various marketing and promotional tactics had been employed.

Competition

Management felt that the Upper Crust competed against other food-service operations in the Newton area, as well as in the nearby suburbs of Boston. It did not compete against restaurants located within the city of Boston, where there was of course an array of restaurants from which to choose.

The assumption could be made that any operation that sold food, beverage, and/or liquor in the Newton area was a competitor. Management, however, perceived three hotel restaurants as their primary competition. These restaurants were located in the Sheraton Needham, the Marriott Newton, and Embassy Suites in Cambridge, four, two and six miles away, respectively. The Upper Crust, however, was very reasonably priced compared to these competitors.

Advertising

Various advertisements had been run in local area newspapers, *The Newton Graphic, The Wellesley Townsman,* and *The Needham Times.* A general advertisement introducing the restaurant to the community also provided some descriptive information on the cuisine. This ad was run frequently. Another frequently run advertisement was one that offered a $10 discount off a second entree, if the first were purchased at full price.

During the summer, a Grand Opening party had been held in the restaurant. Prominent politicians, area business leaders, and media people were invited. The purpose of this event was to gain exposure for the restaurant in the Newton area.

Another promotional tactic utilized the Sunset Dinner. This was a complete dinner including soup, salad, entree, beverage, and dessert for a price of $8.95, $9.95, or $10.95. These dinners were served from 5:00 P.M. to 6:30 P.M., Sunday through Thursday. This was a form of discounting designed to attract guests from the outside. The emphasis was on price/value.

A separate telephone line, independent of the hotel, was established for the restaurant in order to separate its identity from Howard Johnson. When customers called to inquire about the restaurant, they were told that it was located in the Howard Johnson Hotel, which would soon become a Tara Hotel.

A large sign was placed above the Massachusetts Turnpike, as a way to capture the attention of commuters. The high volume of traffic made this an appealing tactic.

Special promotions were run throughout the year, as part of a company-wide Upper Crust promotion, for all eight restaurants of the same name in different Flatley Hotels. For example, a "Seafood Festival" was run in February. Seafood dishes such as Gulf Shrimp, Red Drumfish, and Stone Crab Claws were offered.

Conclusion

Rick Maple and Madison Simpson both understood that it was largely their responsibility to attract more customers from the outside community to the Upper Crust. Although they knew that business would improve once the hotel become a Tara, this alone was not enough. "In order to generate the kind of volume desired by the corporate office, we must think of new ways to attract people from the area communities," said Mr. Simpson.

✔ Case 9-3
Forte Hotels' Rebranding[16]

Trusthouse Forte (THF), of the United Kingdom, was formed in May 1970 when Forte Holdings Limited merged with Trust Houses. Trust Houses was originally a large chain of traditional inns but, before the merger with Forte Holdings Ltd., they had acquired Gardner Merchant (industrial caterers), started to build the Posthouse chain, and had a financial interest in the Travelodge chain in the United States. Forte Holdings went public in 1962 and operated hotels, restaurants, and large-scale catering enterprises.

The merger of the two companies gave Trusthouse Forte a relatively large coverage of the hotel market in the United Kingdon, but the hotel business grew further with the acquisition of 35 hotels with 6,438 bedrooms from J. Lyons and Co. in 1977. This gave THF a preeminent place in the U.K. hotel industry. Also in the 1970s the U.S. Travelodge chain was purchased. This included 500 hotels under franchise, joint venture, and full ownership.

THF continued to expand its hotel operations, mainly through acquisitions. These included Imperial Catering and Hotels from Hanson Trust in 1986 (30 hotels) and Kennedy Brookes hotels and restaurants in 1988 (24 hotels). In May 1990 they acquired Crest Hotels from Bass Plc (43 hotels). Throughout the 1970s and 1980s, THF had also acquired hotels overseas. A number of prestige international hotels were purchased in a variety of locations.

The U.K. Travelodge chain expanded rapidly in the late 1980s and grew to around 100 hotels. Travelodge in the U.K. was based on organic growth, and most Travelodges were built new. THF thus became one of the largest hospitality groups in the world but, as a result of growth through acquisition, it had a largely heterogeneous mix of hotels.

---

[16]We gratefully acknowledge the contribution of this case by John Connell, Professor at the School of Hospitality, Tourism and Leisure Management, Glasgow Caledonian University. 1992 © Glasgow Caledonian University. Used by permission. The case has been modified slightly for use in this text.

THF performed well in financial terms over the years. The hotel business, although smaller than the catering business in terms of turnover, consistently achieved higher margins of profitability. The U.K. hotel business outperformed American operations with higher sales and higher profit margins. In 1990, London hotels contributed 57 percent of U.K. hotel profits, but represented only 30 percent of U.K. hotel rooms. A long-term goal was to achieve a 50/50 split between profits from U.K. hotels and hotels abroad, but this was less likely in the short term. One aim was to move into continental Europe and to compete with the new North American entrants in that market by offering an alternative product. At the time, Forte had only a few luxury hotels in continental Europe, as opposed to around 320 hotels in the United Kingdom.

Economies came through the cost-effectiveness of mass media advertising, which in turn made branding more cost-effective. The same principle applied to a wide range of marketing activities. For example, the central reservation system was so heavily used that it could immediately increase occupancy by ten percent in newly acquired hotels.

Branding Background

THF was the first U.K.-based hotel company to offer a national and highly consistent hotel chain in the form of Posthouse. First-generation Posthouses were modern, functional hotels offering value for the money to the business and leisure user. Most Posthouses were built new to offer a standard range of facilities and services. A second generation was added in the 1980s that reflected more sophisticated customers' needs. With the exception of Posthouse and Travelodge, brand names had been given to hotels for internal management purposes only. The company had not tried to create an easily discernible or differentiated product range.

In 1988, when most other hotel groups were

branding their hotels, THF advertised theirs as "the finest collection of hotels in the world." THF admitted that it had a diverse range of hotels, but its philosophy was to "blend with the environment rather than to slavishly follow a set product design for a hotel." Company research showed that individuality was a strength in the five-star and English country house-style units. The same was not thought to be the case for the four-star market and the Forte hotel brand was chosen to address this. This brand was to include Viscount hotels (20) in the United States, some European hotels, and enough "new builds" and acquisitions to achieve 200 Forte hotels in continental Europe by 1992.

In 1989 the company announced six main product lines described as three brands and three collections, as shown below:

Five-star	THF exclusive hotels	collection
Modern four-star	Forte hotels	brand
Modern three-star	Post House hotels	brand
Budget hotels	Travelodges	brand
Older four-star hotels	Forte classic	collection
Older three-star hotels	Heritage Inns	collection

This broad range of hotels was seen as a problem since customers required recognizable standards and values. One hotel analyst pointed out that THF's branding problem was related to the differences in hotel size, level of market served, location, architecture, rates, and facilities. THF, however, felt that it should not go into full branding until they had the critical mass to make it successful. This was achieved in 1990 with the acquisition of 43 Crest hotels in the U.K. from Bass.

The purchase of Crest enabled THF to create brands within the hotel division, brands that would be large enough to compete in the marketplace. The name Crest also provided a high-quality four-star brand name that was known throughout Europe, since Bass had previously operated 50 hotels on the continent under the Crest name. These were sold by Bass prior to the sale of Crest to THF and rebranded. THF, however, was able to capitalize on the Crest identity with new properties. Crest hotels consisted mainly of modern, purpose-built properties trading within the three-star and four-star classification. They were located in city centers and on main motor routes.

Rebranding

Corporate Name The decision to rebrand hotels led to the change in corporate name, Forte Hotels, a more "snappy" name for Europe (*forte* means strength in Latin), and easier to pronounce. The reasons given for the corporate rebranding were many and varied. One was to capitalize on the diversity of products, which Forte saw as a competitive advantage. They had not done this before because of the difficulty in identifying the wide variety. Another was to develop internationally. A third reason was to develop responsibilities for each division as the company grew larger.

Forte claimed the following benefits from rebranding:

- The ability to exploit to the full the unique competitive strength
- The ability to offer a clear position in an expanding international market
- The ability to develop a common purpose by creating a closer association between group and core business
- The ability to create opportunities for cross-selling and more effective marketing
- The ability to make it easier for people at all levels of the organization to be clear about the contribution they could make
- The ability to ensure the continued success of the business and increased profitability

Hotel and Product Branding

Hotel and product branding was to enable the company to capitalize on size and market presence and more easily communicate the differences among brands to make it easier for customers to choose the hotel they wanted. Three brands and three "collections" were identified (Exhibit 9-3-1). Branded hotels had more clearly defined, shared characteristics than "collection" hotels. Hotel groupings were identified as follows:

Physical characteristics	modern or traditional
Service style	formal or informal
Location	city center or out of town
Principal use	business or leisure

"Product brand" logos were used to define what customers received and the level of service for distinct segments of the market. These were claimed to be simple, easy to buy, easy to understand, and delivered in a style of hotel at a location and at a price to suit all needs by setting prices to match individual hotel locations. Product brand logos are shown in Exhibit 9-3-2.

Defining the Brands

Forte management redefined Posthouse and Crest brands by focusing on the needs of different groups of consumers, obtained through extensive research using a wide range of segmentation variables to define market segments. Operations management, headquarters specialists, and outside consultants were involved in drawing up specifications for all aspects of the brands. Working with research staff, they examined how new services could be produced and delivered in line with customer requirements. Within Crest, for example, 20 brand standards were identified.

Forte regrouped hotels into the new brands using the groupings given above. For Crest and Posthouse, for example, both of which had consisted of more functional older hotels and more sophisticated newer hotels, this provided the rearrangement shown in Exhibit 9-3-3. This permitted each brand to compete against its more similar competition. In some cases it was recognized that hotels could not be physically upgraded and made more consistent in a short

period of time and that this would need to be a longer-term objective. Management considered service range and quality as the most effective way to keep customers loyal. The need for staff development was emphasized as was the need to monitor service quality and general levels of customer satisfaction.

The research also highlighted the need to give value for money. The use of highly visible fixed prices had been very successful for the Travelodge brand and so was extended to the Posthouse brand. Traditionally, U.K. hotel companies priced hotel services on the basis of individual hotel quality and demand. This meant that published prices varied considerably and, to cause further confusion, were often discounted. Posthouse became the only middle-market brand in the U.K. that was prepared to offer a fixed price across all its hotels. This price was highly competitive and its fixed nature helped to reduce customer confusion. It was felt that, by standing firm on price, the integrity of the Posthouse brand would be enhanced.

The provision of more distinctive brands for the business market narrowed the customer base in some hotels that had not previously carried the Crest name. These hotels were able to cater more directly to the business traveler without having to cater to other more diverse and sometimes conflicting segments during the week. On weekends, Crest offered the "leisure breaks" product when it did not interfere with the main business segment.

Product brands (Exhibit 9-3-2) produced an additional level of product consistency, since all hotels had to meet the standards set. Product brands were grouped within three price bands to reflect the location of hotels where the product brand was used. Intermediaries serving the business market welcomed the clear product features of product brands, since these made the task of selling to end-users easier and more effective.

The use of brand specifications and higher levels of service standardization also meant that services could be costed more accurately. This led to better budgetary control, since cost comparisons were easier to make between and within hotels. This allowed more time for quality assurance and marketing activities. Service quality had to be maintained whether the hotel was full or empty. Thus, it was not possible to reduce service levels or to "trade down" in order to improve short-term profitability. If necessary, the product could be enhanced to compete at the local level.

The final branding (Exhibit 9-3-1) produced the following brand characteristics (final positioning is shown in Exhibit 9-3-4):

EXHIBIT 9-3-1   Forte rebranding

The new strategy for our hotels

OUR BRANDS *will consist of purpose-built modern hotels, each brand catering for a different set of customer needs by providing a different level of facilities and service.*

Forte Travelodge: our roadside budget accommodation brand offering simple, modern rooms conveniently situated along major routes. It will encompass the existing Travelodge networks in the UK and North America, as well as new properties on the Continent where construction begins this year.

Forte Posthouse: our branded UK chain of accessible, modern hotels offering comfortable rooms and providing good restaurant and meeting facilities at highly competitive prices. It will comprise many of the three star properties presently trading under the Post House and Crest names.

Forte Crest: our branded chain of high quality modern business hotels specialising in personal recognition and service. Most of the properties will be situated in major city centres throughout Europe. Forte Crest will incorporate some of the best existing Crest and Post House hotels as well as a number of other properties in our portfolio.

Courtesy of Forte Hotels

Forte Travelodge Two-star budget with 90 hotels in the U.K. and fixed price of £29.95 per room. Newly built, situated near roadside services. Rooms-oriented and limited service.

Forte Posthouse Three-star mid-market with 53 hotels in the U.K. and fixed price of £49.50 per room. Modern hotels (mostly built in the '70s and '80s) located in or near towns and cities and often on main motor routes. Free room for children under 15. Offer parking and dog and baby-listening services. About half offer swimming pool, health facility, or sauna. Sixty to 208 rooms and conference capacities to 650.

Forte Crest Four-star up-market with 41 hotels in the U.K. and four overseas. Largely in major city centers and directed toward business market with business support services and personal recognition. Prices fixed at £95 in London and £70 or £80 elsewhere in the U.K. depending

EXHIBIT 9-3-1   (continued)

OUR COLLECTIONS *will be different from our brands insofar as they will bring together a range of individual properties, each with its own name, style and character. Like the brands, each collection will appeal to a particular set of customer needs.*

Forte Heritage: our collection of traditional British inns offering a unique combination of comfort, personal hospitality and character. Forte Heritage will include properties such as The White Horse at Dorking and the Black Swan at Helmsley.

Forte Grand: our collection of first class international hotels offering traditional European standards of comfort, style and service. Forte Grand will include hotels such as The Waldorf in London, The Randolph in Oxford and the Grand Hotel in Nuremberg.

Exclusive hotels: the Exclusive portfolio presently includes sixteen hotels such as the Hyde Park Hotel in London, the Georges V in Paris, the Ritz in Madrid and the Plaza Athénée in Paris and New York. These internationally renowned names represent the finest hotels in the world, and will continue to be promoted in their own right with subtle Forte endorsement.

FORTE
Heritage

FORTE
GRAND

FORTE

Courtesy of Forte Hotels

on location. Offer parking, 24-hour room service, dog and baby-listening service. About half have swimming pool and/or other leisure facilities. Seventy to 560 rooms and conference capacities to 1,000.

Forte Heritage Hotels Traditional British Inns with 93 in the U.K.

Forte Grand Hotels First-class international with 17 in the U.K. and two in continental Europe.

Forte Exclusive Hotels Exclusively named, elegant hotels with three in the U.K., nine in continental Europe, and four in the United States.

EXHIBIT 9-3-2   Forte product brand logos

Courtesy of Forte Hotels

EXHIBIT 9-3-3   Forte rearranges its hotels

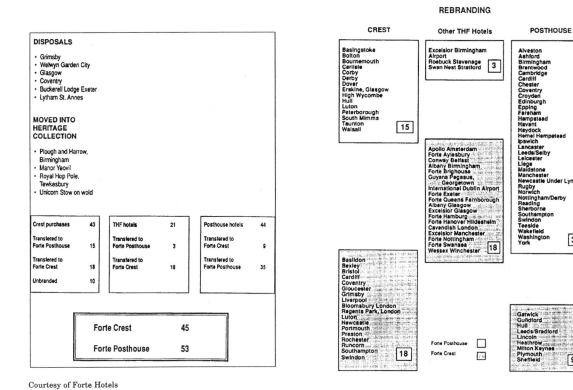

DISPOSALS

- Grimsby
- Welwyn Garden City
- Glasgow
- Coventry
- Buckerell Lodge Exeter
- Lytham St. Annes

MOVED INTO HERITAGE COLLECTION

- Plough and Harrow, Birmingham
- Manor Yeovil
- Royal Hop Pole, Tewkesbury
- Unicorn Stow on wold

Crest purchases	43	THF hotels	21	Posthouse hotels	44
Transferred to Forte Posthouse	15	Transferred to Forte Posthouse	3	Transferred to Forte Crest	9
Transferred to Forte Crest	18	Transferred to Forte Crest	18	Transferred to Forte Posthouse	35
Unbranded	10				

Forte Crest	45
Forte Posthouse	53

REBRANDING

CREST

Basingstoke
Bolton
Bournemouth
Carlisle
Corby
Derby
Dover
Erskine, Glasgow
High Wycombe
Hull
Luton
Peterborough
South Mimms
Taunton
Walsall
[15]

Other THF Hotels

Excelsior Birmingham
Airport
Roebuck Stevenage
Swan Nest Stratford
[3]

Apollo Amsterdam
Forte Aylesbury
Conway Belfast
Albany Birmingham
Forte Brighouse
Guyana Pegasus, Georgetown
International Dublin Airport
Forte Exeter
Forte Queens Farnborough
Albany Glasgow
Excelsior Glasgow
Forte Hamburg
Forte Hanover Hildesheim
Cavendish London
Excelsior Manchester
Forte Nottingham
Forte Swansea
Wessex Winchester
[18]

Basildon
Bexley
Bristol
Cardiff
Coventry
Gloucester
Grimsby
Liverpool
Bloomsbury London
Regents Park, London
Luton
Newcastle
Portmouth
Preston
Rochester
Runcorn
Southampton
Swindon
[18]

POSTHOUSE

Alveston
Ashford
Birmingham
Brentwood
Cambridge
Cardiff
Chester
Coventry
Croydon
Edinburgh
Epping
Fareham
Hampstead
Havant
Haydock
Hemel Hempstead
Ipswich
Lancaster
Leeds/Selby
Leicester
Liege
Maidstone
Manchester
Newcastle Under Lyme
Rugby
Norwich
Nottingham/Derby
Reading
Sherborne
Southampton
Swindon
Teeside
Wakefield
Washington
York
[35]

Gatwick
Guildford
Hull
Leeds/Bradford
Lincoln
Heathrow
Milton Keynes
Plymouth
Sheffield
[9]

Forte Posthouse ☐
Forte Crest ☐

Courtesy of Forte Hotels

EXHIBIT 9-3-4   Forte's rebranded positioning map

Hotel Positioning

Formal

EXCLUSIVE PORTFOLIO

FORTE CREST

FORTE GRAND

Modern — FORTE HOTELS — Traditional

FORTE Posthouse

FORTE Heritage

FORTE Travelodge

Informal

Courtesy of Forte Hotels

PART IV
Defining the Market

CHAPTER 10

The Marketing Mix and the Product/Service Mix

The marketing mix involves developing and implementing an appropriate mix of marketing activities directed toward market segments and target markets. These activities include the creation and presentation of products and services; the methods used to get the customer to these products and services (or vice versa) for an appropriate price; and the various techniques employed to communicate with customers. We briefly mentioned these activities in Chapter 3. We will now elaborate further. In this chapter we will define the marketing mix, especially as it relates to the hospitality industry, and then discuss in detail its first element, namely the product/service mix. The other elements will be discussed in future chapters.

The marketing mix is the stage of marketing management and strategy that directly affects the customer, but it is also a stage where the company has the most control. We can decide what kind of products and services to offer, or the kinds of hotels and restaurants we want to build. We can also select the magazines or radio stations to carry our message and, of course, we determine the price. Naturally, all these activities will take place only after we have studied the external environment and learned the needs and wants of our target markets and determined our positioning. The marketing mix is

the ultimate outcome of the company's philosophy and mission statement—it is the delivery of the company's offering to the marketplace. It is the culmination of everything we have discussed so far, including both traditional and nontraditional marketing.

The "Four Ps"

The marketing mix was originally developed by Professor Neil Borden of Harvard in what have come to be known as the "Four Ps" through subsequent alteration.[1] Borden's six original elements—product planning, pricing, distribution, promotion, servicing, and marketing research—were later reduced to four elements by Jerome McCarthy—product, price, place (distribution), and promotion.[2] Although we will change the names of these elements to better fit the hospitality industry, it is necessary to understand the concept.

The elements of the marketing mix represent a delicate balance of resources of the firm in providing the product, pricing it, getting it to

---

[1]Neil Borden, "The Concept of the Marketing Mix," *Journal of Advertising Research,* June, 1964, pp. 2–7.

[2]E. Jerome McCarthy, *Basic Marketing: A Managerial Approach,* Homewood, Ill: Richard D. Irwin, 1975, pp. 75–80.

the customer, and telling the customer about it. In effect, the marketing mix is the output of all marketing decisions and the target of the marketing mix is the customer.

The problem that we have with the "Four Ps" in hospitality marketing is not their concept, but the elements of the mix that are essentially based on the marketing of goods. Consistent with our previous arguments in Chapter 2, we believe that the marketing of hospitality services is different from the marketing of goods and thus requires a different approach to the marketing mix. The point in redefining the mix elements for this purpose is not to change their meanings (essentially, they remain the same) but to make the concept of the marketing mix more useful and applicable for hospitality marketing decisions.

The Hospitality Marketing Mix

The first attempt at developing a new marketing mix for the hospitality industry was undertaken by Leo Renaghan.[3] The hospitality marketing mix, according to Renaghan, contains three major submixes: the product/service mix, the presentation mix, and the communications mix. To this trio we add back one of the original elements defined by Borden—distribution. We repeat here the definitions given in Chapter 3.

The Product/Service Mix

The *product/service mix* is the *combination of products and services, whether free or for sale, that are aimed at satisfying the needs of the target market.*[4] The product/service mix is what customers see and get when they go to a hotel, restaurant, or other hospitality entity.

This definition is consistent with our discussion of the hospitality product in Chapter 2. An important addition here, however, is the word *free.* This, again, is an important distinction

between the marketing of manufactured goods and the marketing of hospitality services. We can infer "free" as including those supporting goods that the customer does pay for, but indirectly. In this category would be placed swimming pools, exercise facilities, complimentary airport transportation, linen tablecloths, china and silverware, fresh flowers on the table, and so forth. These are items over which management has control, that thus become part of the offering decision process.

There are other "free" features over which management may have little or no control but that are part of the consumer's expectation. These items include such things as the sun, the moon, the stars, the ocean, the beach, and the weather.

The product/service mix will be discussed in detail later in this chapter.

The Presentation Mix

The *presentation mix* is *all of the elements used by the firm to increase the tangibility of the product/service mix in the perception of the target market at the right place and time.*[5] The presentation mix is how the product/service is presented for the customer to sense.

Renaghan describes the presentation mix as an "umbrella concept covering those elements under the firm's control that act in concert to make the total product/service offering more tangible to the consumer." He goes on to state, "The presentation mix is also the means by which the firm differentiates its product/service offering from competitive offerings."

There are six elements of the presentation mix that can be utilized to make tangible the product/service mix and to differentiate from the competition. These elements include the physical plant, location, atmospherics, price, employees, and customers. The presentation mix will be discussed in detail in Chapter 11.

Some would argue that price does not belong in this mix but should stand by itself, as it does in the original "Four Ps." Although there is some merit to this argument (and we will dis-

---

[3]Leo M. Renaghan, "A New Marketing Mix for the Hospitality Industry," *Cornell Hotel and Restaurant Administration Quarterly,* April, 1981, pp. 31–35.

[4]*Ibid.,* p. 32.

[5]*Ibid.,* p. 32.

cuss it later), we include it here because price is a highly tangible element that increases the tangibility of the product/service mix in the perception of the target market. For example, if you believe that the check average at a certain restaurant is $50, or the price of a hotel room is $25, you immediately sense how the product/service will be presented. Because price is such a dominant factor in marketing, however, we will discuss it at length in Chapter 12.

The Communications Mix

The *communications mix* is *all communications between the firm and the target market that increase the tangibility of the product/service mix, that establish or monitor consumer expectations, or that persuade consumers to purchase.*[6] This is how marketing people tell customers what to expect when they buy a product/service.

This area is similar to that of traditional marketing, although with some new twists due to the intangibility of the product. Except for these new twists, this part of the marketing mix is no different from the promotion element of the "Four Ps" The word *communication,* however, covers a far broader expanse than the word *promotion.* In fact, we will show that promotion is but one subset of communications. The communications mix will be discussed in detail in Chapters 13 and 14.

The Distribution Mix

The *distribution mix* is *all channels available between the firm and the target market that increase the probability of getting the customer to the product.* This is how the customer can buy and use the services offered.

The general concept of services, as opposed to goods, is that the customer must *come to* the services, whereas goods are *taken to* the customer (e.g., through retail outlets). Thus, a hotel or restaurant chain that has 500 locations nationwide is "distributing" the product so that the customer can come to it.

The "Four Ps" approach typically assumes that decisions relative to product design and distribution are largely independent of one another. In hospitality, a customer must come to the place where a service is produced in order to experience it, making production and distribution largely inseparable. The complexities of selling the hospitality product, however, especially in the case of hotel rooms through telephone 800 numbers, global distribution systems, wholesalers, tour brokers, travel agents, and others, have become so confounding that location itself is no longer adequate to describe this phenomenon. We will treat distribution as a separate element of the marketing mix and discuss it in detail in Chapter 15.

The Hospitality Product/ Service Mix

We have defined the product/service mix in general terms as the combination of products and services, whether free or for sale, aimed at satisfying the needs of the target market. We need now to be more specific. From here on we will use the word *product* as a generic term to describe product/service or the offering of a hospitality entity.

A *product* is *an offering of a business entity as it is perceived by both present and potential customers.* It is a bundle of benefits designed to satisfy the needs and wants and solve the problems of specified target markets. A product is composed of both tangible and intangible elements; it may be as concrete as a chair or a dinner plate, or as abstract as a "feeling." The value of a product derives from what it does for the customer.

The key terms in this definition are *perceived* and *what it does for the customer.* Both are critical to the discussion that follows. "Perception is reality," as we pointed out in Chapter 6. *Perceived* means that if the customer doesn't see it, it isn't there; that is, something is not what management says it is, but what the customer perceives it to be. This notion is so critical and basic, yet so often overlooked, that one cannot

---

[6]*Ibid.,* p. 32.

be an effective marketer without grasping it. A simple example is the case of the restaurant that advertises "finest food." If that judgment is not consistent with the target market's perception, the advertising dollar is wasted.

What it does for the customer is an even more critical notion. We have covered this ground before but it bears repeating. Recall Theodore Levitt's analogy: "People don't buy quarter-inch drills, they buy quarter-inch holes." It is what the drills *do,* not what they *are.* Carry this thinking to the intangibility of the hospitality product—for instance, an expensive and beautifully decorated room. Such a room should make a hotel guest feel warm, comfortable, secure, or whatever. If the room doesn't actually do whatever it is supposed to do for the target market, then the decor and the cost are inconsequential. Recall that we are in the business of solving consumers' problems, as abstract as they may be. Solving problems, then, is what the product does for the customer.

Designing the Hospitality Product

If a product is defined in terms of what it does for the customer, then it becomes immediately obvious that the design of a product begins with what the customer wants done. In the case of goods, that is often easier to determine. People who buy tires want safety and endurance. People who buy stereos want good sound reproduction. People who buy a Mercedes want prestige. But what do people want when they buy hotel rooms and restaurant meals? A comfortable bed and a good meal? Of course this is what they want, but we know that it goes far beyond those basic minimums.

An important feature of the product/service mix is the *bundle purchase* concept. Consumers do not purchase individual elements of the offering; rather, they purchase a bundle or unified whole. When buying a hotel room, the customer is also buying the bed, bathroom, restaurant, wake-up call, and many more bundled items. The restaurant customer is buying food, as well as the service and atmosphere of the restaurant. It is clear that a delicate balance exists in the mix and that management

must be aware of how the various elements of the bundle interact. Every element of this bundle is an integral part of the product, and a change in one element can affect the perception of the entire product. Thus, it is useful to break the bundle down into its component parts: the formal product, the core product, and the augmented product.

The Formal Product

The formal product can be defined as what customers think they are buying. This may be as simple as a bed or a meal, or it may be as elusive as quality or elegance; it may be as intangible as environment or class, or as specific as location. The formal product, in fact, might be defined as what the customer can easily articulate. Because of this, it is easy to be misled by what the customer does articulate.

It has been noted that hotel and restaurant customers frequently name location and good food as their primary reasons for choosing a particular hotel or restaurant. In many cases, however, this is only because location and good food are elements that can be easily articulated. In fact, if these were really major reasons for choices, we could dispense with the bundle concept and concentrate on these elements alone. Such, of course, is not the case and it would be a serious mistake to believe that it is.

The Core Product

The core product is what the customer is really buying. This often consists of abstract and intangible attributes. Some examples of core products are experience, atmosphere, relaxation, celebration, and convenience. These are actually core benefits rather than product attributes. By now, of course, we know that what the customer is buying is, in fact, benefits rather than product attributes. In understanding the core product, we come closer to understanding problem solutions.

Understanding the core product—what the customer is really buying—means understanding the customer's problems. This has two very important implications. First, understanding the customer's problems is where product design should begin. Too often it begins, instead, with management's problems.

Consider, for example, the case of large banquet rooms that can be divided into smaller meeting rooms through the use of folding accordion doors. The innovation of doors of this kind came about some years ago because of a critical management problem: how to accommodate both large and small groups in the same space. The solution solved the problem for management, but caused one for the customer. In many hotels, one can sit in a small meeting room and listen not only to what is occurring in that room, but also to what is occurring in the rooms on either side, not to mention the banquet kitchen. This is an aggravating and ongoing problem for meeting attendees. Today, better folding or collapsing doors are built that almost eliminate this problem, but they can be found only in the newer and more expensive hotels.

Meeting rooms need doors that can be secured, but are safe for quick exiting. Architects have solved this problem by installing large bar-levered doors with massive catches. Conference meetings, however, often have frequent comers and goers. Each time someone comes or goes, the door closes on its massive catch with a sound that resounds throughout the room, annoying almost everyone present. Lighting continues to bedevil hospitality customers. The ballroom is needed for both sales meetings and weddings. The lighting needs are entirely different. In many cases, neither customer is satisfied.

Although it may be true in some cases, not much has been written about meetings planners who "buy" the folding doors that separate meeting rooms, or doors that close meeting rooms, or lighting for ballrooms. The formal product—what customers think they are buying—is the meeting room and the seating capacity, and that's what the hotel is selling. The core product, what they are really buying, is a quiet, controlled, hassle-free, successful meeting. That's what the hotel should be marketing.

These examples demonstrate the complexities of the hospitality product. More important, they demonstrate the need for hospitality management to understand the product bundle, the customer's problems, and the design of the product.

The second important implication of understanding the core product is the awareness of what one should be marketing. Just about every hotel management in the world that has meeting facilities composes elaborate collateral describing and picturing the hotel's meeting facilities, sizes, and capacities. Rarely does one hotel differentiate substantively from the others in the same product class.

The formal product, of course, is the meeting space and, unless it meets a minimum standard, it will be unacceptable. This is also the salient product. The core product, that which is also determinant and important, is how the entire facility deals with the meeting planner's problems.

The Augmented Product

The augmented product is the totality of all benefits received or experienced by the customer. It is the entire system with all accompanying services. It is the way the customer uses the product. The augmented product may include both tangible and intangible attributes. These attributes range from the manner in which things are done, the assurance that they will be done, the timeliness, the personal treatment, and the no-hassle experience, to the size of the bath towels, the cleanliness of the restrooms, the decor, and the honored on-time reservation.

The augmented product even includes the sun and the moon. As any resort manager can testify, there is nothing worse than three or four rainy days with all your guests locked inside on their vacation, or a ski area with unskiable conditions. The frequent effect is that customers go away mad over something management can do nothing about. Or can it? For a marketing-oriented management the answer is yes. This is a customer problem that management anticipates and for which it prepares by developing alternative activities.

The augmented product is the total product bundle that should solve all the customers' problems, and even some they haven't thought of yet. In designing the product, it is critical to understand the concept of the augmented product and its basis in consumer problems. This is different from simply augmenting for the sake of augmenting. Mints on pillows don't make up for poor service, as Marriott points out in its ad in Figure 10-1. Elaborate bathroom amenities don't make up for a businessperson's having no place to write, or for a couple not having two chairs to sit in.

The success of the all-suite hotel concept is based on the augmented product. This concept provides guests with a total living experience rather than simply meeting their basic needs. The success of McDonald's is based on the augmented product, which includes, among other things, cleanliness and fast service. In fact, the success of any hospitality enterprise begins with an understanding of the core product and its augmentation to solve consumers' problems.

WE DIDN'T GET TO BE #1 WITH BUSINESS TRAVELERS JUST BY LEAVING MINTS ON YOUR PILLOW.

Those little touches are sweet, but it's crackerjack performance that business people savor most. That's why a recent survey in USA TODAY reported Marriott the first choice among business travelers. We believe efficient, warm, respectful service always leaves the best taste of all.

SERVICE. THE ULTIMATE LUXURY.℠

Courtesy of Marriott Hotels & Resorts

FIGURE 10-1   Marriott downplays the pillow mint

Examine the ad in Figure 10-2, which was used previously (as Figure 8-10) to illustrate segmentation. What do you consider to be the formal, core, and augmented products?

The Complexity of the Product/Service

Now that we understand what a product is and what it does, it should be easy enough to go out and design a hotel or restaurant that will solve consumers' problems. Ah, if only life were that simple! Obviously, we have a multitude of consumers with a multitude of problems, and we can never hope to satisfy all the consumers or solve all the problems. We narrow the problem down, of course, by segmentation and target marketing, which is why these strategies are so critical to effective marketing. Even within these submarkets, however, we can never hope to be all things to all people.

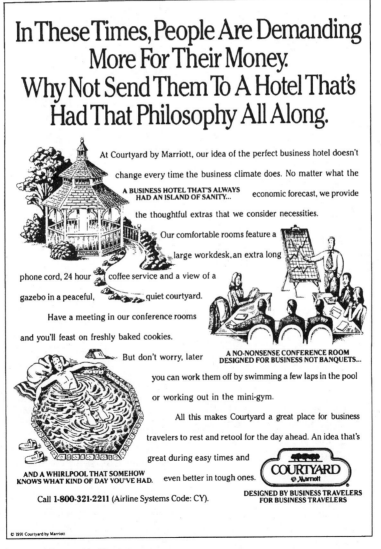

Courtesy of Courtyard by Marriott

FIGURE 10-2   The formal, core, and augmented products

It is clear, however, that we need to go beyond the basic and formal product when designing the hospitality product/service. Consider the following comment of three decades ago by Nelson Foote, former Manager of Consumer Research for General Electric, a company widely recognized for its marketing acumen:

> ...certain characteristics of products come to be taken for granted by consumers, especially those concerned with basic functional performance.... If these values are missing in a product, the user is extremely offended. But if they are present, the maker or seller gets no special credit or preference, because quite logically every other maker or seller is assumed to be offering equivalent values. In other words, the values that are salient in decision-making are the values that are problematic—that are important, to be sure, but also those which differentiate one offering from another.[7]

Today's hospitality customers are much more well-traveled and sophisticated than previous generations. Thus, the basic functions served by a hotel are taken for granted. Customers expect a good location, clean room and bath, comfortable beds and pleasant service from all hotels. However, customers look for other benefits that may be unique to a particular hotel, benefits that differentiate one hotel from others. For example, business travelers will look for a hotel that offers services that will increase their productivity, as Westin advertises (Figure 10-3). A family on vacation will look for services that allow them to be together as a family but, perhaps, also separate to enjoy their own activities, as Hyatt has provided (Figure 10-4).

Another way to look at a product offering is as a standard product, a standard product with modifications, or a customized product. S.C. Jain suggests two questions to answer when deciding which to offer.[8] The first question is "What are our capabilities?" Without a clear perspective of the firm's capabilities, there is a danger of overstating them or having unrealistic notions about them. This may result in unfulfilled expectations and disappointed or irate customers. For example, consider Howard Johnson's former ill-fated advertising caption, "If it's not your Mother, it must be Howard Johnson's." Probably no restaurant chain, much less Howard Johnson's at that time, has the capability of fulfilling such an expectation. The result for Howard Johnson's was, as could have been anticipated, irate customers.

The second question to be answered is "What business are we in?" This is a strategic question that needs to be asked about any business, as was discussed in Chapter 3. Both these questions either have not been asked or not accurately answered by some midscale hotel chains that have attempted to go upscale and have ignored the required capabilities that did not exist in their core business.

Standard Products

Standard products have the advantage of providing a cost benefit derived from standardization. They are also more amenable to efficient national marketing. Holiday Inn's original motels are an example of a successful standardized product. No matter where in the country customers stayed at a Holiday Inn, they could just about find their way blindfolded to the front desk, their room, the lounge, or the dining room.

A problem with standardized products, however, and one that befell Holiday Inns for awhile, is the emphasis placed on cost-savings so that needed, and sometimes more expensive, variations in the product in certain markets are ignored. Eventually this results in a loss of customers who either want something different or want a more customized product. Even McDonald's, which has been incredibly successful with a highly standardized product, allows its franchisees to make variations on the theme. McDonald's does this because it is a marketing-

---

[7]Cited in James Myers and Mark Alpert, "Determinant Buying Attitudes: Meaning and Measurement," *Journal of Marketing,* October, 1968, p. 14.

[8]Subhash C. Jain, *Marketing Planning and Strategy,* Cincinnati: South-Western Publishing, 1993, pp. 397–398.

FIGURE 10-3   Westin helps business travelers increase productivity

FIGURE 10-4   Hyatt offers peace of mind to parents

oriented company; the effect has been a major contribution to their success.

Standard Products with Modifications

The standard product with modifications is a compromise between the standard product and the customized product. An example is the concierge floor of a hotel. In such cases, the scale economies of building and furnishing a standard room remain unchanged; the modifications are easily added only to those rooms requiring them, and an additional charge is extracted for them.

This strategy has one considerable advantage: The modifications, or added amenities, are easily added, removed, or changed as the market changes. Thus, the property maintains a flexibility that in itself may be perceived as a desirable attribute because the property can more easily meet customer requirements and encourage new uses of the product. Another advantage that accrues is differentiation within the product class, while maintaining the same strategic position. An example is shown in Figure 10-5.

In restaurants, one example of a standard product with modifications is a small but mounting trend in restaurants to offer different-size portions of their menu items. Such a policy has a high level of flexibility as well as the ability to cater directly to changing market needs.

Customized Products

Customized products are based on the premise of designing the product to fit the specific needs

FIGURE 10-5   Hyatt offers the standard product with modifications

of a particular target market. Price may not be a large consideration for the buyer of customized products, because he or she expects to pay a premium price to have it exactly the way it is wanted. On the other hand, Marriott has demonstrated with Courtyard a customized product for the price-conscious.

The growth of all-suite hotel concepts has led to both modifications in the standard product and some degree of customization. Free breakfasts and free cocktail hours have been two of the modifications, while the perceived price/value of the suite is still maintained with rates in the $70–$90 range. One all-suite in San Francisco, however, charges over $200 a night. This property stocks the suite with cooking and eating equipment, foods and snacks, liquors and wines, stereo, cassette recorders, and a VCR with a choice of movies and free exchange for other ones. The concept is customized to a very specific target market.

Making the Product Decision

Standardizing, modifying, and customizing are important marketing decisions in designing the hospitality product/service. Although the examples used here have been on a fairly large scale, these decisions also apply to all facets of the product. To illustrate this point, let's examine a relatively minor product decision in the light of the criteria that have been proposed.

If a restaurant has Rack of Lamb on its menu, or Dover Sole, or Caesar Salad, does it carve, bone, or mix these in the kitchen or at tableside? To do it in the kitchen is to standardize it. This provides cost efficiencies, and presumably the finished product offered to the customer is identical to the one offered when the work is done at tableside.

The decision, however, is a marketing one, not a cost one. To perform the work at tableside has elements of both the core and augmented product in it. First, we would have to identify the target market. Does this market expect, want, and appreciate the additional effort and cost to customize the product at tableside? Is it willing to pay an additional price for it?

What does the modified or customized product do for customers? Does tableside service make customers feel better and more prestigious? Does it impress their guests, add perceived quality, or add romance or mystique to the product? Or, does it simply delay the service delivery?

What business are we in? Are we in the business of serving quality food at a fair price, or providing a dining experience? Are we providing elegance, flair, or entertainment?

Finally, do we have the capabilities? Is the staff properly trained, or can they be trained? If trained to do the carving, boning, or mixing properly, can they do it with flair and finesse? If not, we may defeat the entire purpose.

The hospitality product/service includes everything we have to offer the guest, whether "free" or for sale. It contains the basic elements of what guests think they are buying, what they really hope to get, and the total augmentation of the product that constitutes the entire experience in purchasing it. From the budget motel in North Overshoe to the Bristol Hotel in Paris, from the hot dog vendor at Fenway Park to Freddie Giradeau's widely acclaimed restaurant in Switzerland, the hospitality product/service determination is a marketing decision based on the target market. The problem for the marketer is to determine the effective demand for the various product features and the total benefit bundle.

Table 10-1 is a marketer's checklist for analyzing an existing hospitality product. Answers to the questions will give the marketer the necessary tools to market the product. When applying the list, keep in mind the two critical definitions of a product: How is it perceived, and what does it do for the customer? See if you can apply these criteria to the ad in Figure 10-2. Is the product standardized or customized?

There is one more thing to be said about designing the hospitality product, which has been said before but bears repeating: No matter how successful your product is now, never forget that the customer changes. The hospitality product requires constant evaluation and re-evaluation. We will discuss this in more detail in the next section, on the product life cycle.

TABLE 10-1   Analyzing the Hospitality Product/Service

As Seen by the Target Market:
What is it in terms of what it does for the customer?
How does it solve problems?
What benefits does it offer?
How does it satisfy demand?
Who uses it? Why?
How does it compete?
What are the occasions for its use?
What are its attributes?
What is the perception of it?
How is it positioned?
Which attributes are salient? Determinant? Important?

The Product Life Cycle

The concept of the *product life cycle* (PLC) is basic to the marketing literature. It rests on the premise that a product goes through various stages during its lifetime, much as individuals do. There is the introduction, or embryonic stage, followed by the growth stage, the mature stage, and the stage of decline. Each stage calls for different strategies and tactics. The product life cycle may be applied in three ways. It may refer to all products within a product class, such as all fast-food restaurants. On the other hand, the product life cycle may be used in reference to one particular brand, such as McDonald's or Burger King. Finally, it may apply to one specific product line, such as Burger King's Whopper or McDonald's Egg McMuffin. The traditional and widely-used perspective of the product life cycle is shown in Figure 10-6.

The Nature of Product Life Cycles

Life cycles of products can vary widely in time span. Researchers have identified some as long as 100 years (Ivory soap) and some as short as six months (hula hoops). The life cycle of the fast-food industry, which is now considered to be in the mature stage, had its introduction in the 1950s. In retrospect, products with very short life cycles are usually referred to as fads.

Product life cycles do not always follow the familiar "S"-shaped curve shown in Figure 10-6. An example of a variation of the curve is the

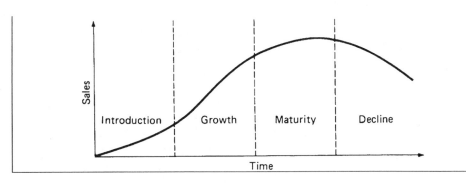

FIGURE 10-6   Stages of the product life cycle

growth of the highway motel. This product had a fast growth period following World War II and the end of gas rationing. It then fell into disrepute (as well as disrepair) and went into decline, to finally emerge on a new growth curve as the motor inn with full hotel facilities. Today, there is another new growth curve in the motel life cycle caused by the boom in budget motels without full facilities.

Product life cycles may be in different stages in different parts of the world. The hotel industry is considered mature in the United States but is still in its introductory stage in China. Upscale hotels are in the mature stage in India, while middle-tier properties (budget in the U.S.—Days Inn and Holiday Express) are in the growth stage, and budget brands like Sleep Inn are still emerging. In Sweden, due to overbuilding, hotels are in the decline stage. Similarly, the fast-food industry is considered mature in the U.S. but is in a growth phase in Russia.

Regarding brands, Rodeway Hotels had been in the decline stage for some time, which took it through six owners. Now franchised by Choice Hotels International, it is being revitalized as senior citizen hotels with special senior citizen pre-tested amenities.

With regard to product modifications, mints and fancy bathroom amenities are in decline, while Business Centers and large working desks are in the growth stage. In restaurants, similar examples apply. Nouvelle cuisine came and grew fast and is now all but dead. Hard liquor is in decline and bottled water is in growth.

All these examples should make clear how products, brands, and product lines go through life cycle stages. How this relates to marketing is the issue that now needs to be addressed.

It is well to keep in mind that the introductory, growth, and decline stages of the product life cycle must, at some point in time, come to an end. The mature stage, at least theoretically, could go on forever. Our argument, then, is that the mature stage is the most critical to the marketer. It is at this point, or that of early decline, that the introductory and/or growth stage must be reincarnated if the product is to survive in some form. S.C. Jain argues,

...the growth of a product is to some extent a function of the strategy being pursued. Thus, a product is not necessarily predestined to mature as propounded by the traditional concept of product life cycle, but can be kept profitable by proper adaptation to the evolving market environment.[9]

As an analogy, Crest toothpaste has been re-introduced several times—with special plaque fighters, mint flavors, and a "new improved" dispensing cap. Consider, as well, the McDonald's hamburger and its various incarnations. On the other hand, there are many products that just decline and die and are replaced with something else.

Perhaps what is most important, then, is to recognize the stage in which the product presently resides—for instance, to see that one's product is in the mature stage. Too often, management may be unaware of the product's stage, believing that growth will go on forever.

Stages of the Product Life Cycle

The Introductory Stage

The introductory stage of a product is its entry into the marketplace; the new restaurant that opened down the street, or the new hotel that was just built in Las Vegas are entering the introductory phase of their product life cycles.

As well, some products in the later years of their product life cycles begin anew with new names. The Park Suites Hotel in Boca Raton, Florida entered the decline stage with decreasing occupancies and revenues. By re-flagging the hotel with the Embassy Suites name, and investing capital for refurbishment, the existing real estate structure entered a new introductory stage of its life cycle.

The very nature of the hospitality product often makes test-marketing prohibitive before introduction. Ideally, then, the product should be developed on the basis of as much consumer research as possible. Frequently, however, this is not done, and a new hotel or restaurant is opened on the opinions of the owner, developer,

---

[9]Jain, *Marketing Planning and Strategy*, p. 258.

and/or management. An exception was the Courtyard by Marriott concept introduced in 1984. Extensive consumer research was conducted before three Courtyards were built in the Atlanta area to test the concept before further expansion ensued. If the property is truly innovative, the marketer holds a two-edged sword: The product will be easier to differentiate, but may create more resistance to achieving trial and acceptance.

The introductory stage may also be one of high costs. Before McDonald's could open its first restaurant in Moscow, the company had to build a 100,000-square-foot distribution center that included a meat plant, a bakery, a potato plant, and a dairy. McDonald's even had to work with Russian farmers to raise the appropriate breed of cattle, from which the meat would be obtained.

Whereas goods manufacturers will shroud their new products in secrecy as long as possible before introduction, hotels and restaurants do not have the same luxury. Construction time may be as long as three to four years and is often preceded by publicity due to zoning changes, financial arrangements, and other events that must occur long before the actual opening. This may be considered an advantage to the property because it is all free publicity.

Whereas goods manufacturers may work with only two or three months lead time to promote the introduction of their product, hotels seek two to three years of lead time and restaurants may use up to a year. For hotels, extensive lead time is needed because groups, conventions, corporate accounts, and others must be solicited far in advance of actual purchase and usage. Thus, the property's marketing team arrives well ahead of the opening.

Introduction begins with a "soft" opening, maybe a few days to a few weeks before the official opening. Word-of-mouth brings some customers, small groups (sometimes large ones) are booked, and various dignitaries are invited to "test" the facility. This is the shakedown period, when management hopes to get a smooth operation going before the expected deluge.

Marketing's concern is very different with hospitality than with a manufactured good. The

good has been built to specification and tested; so many units have been produced and distributed, and one hopes they will be sold.

Hospitality marketers have a different problem. Instead of producing just so many units to be sold, they must produce on demand. They hope they can "handle the crowds," that the staff is trained and ready, that everything has been thought of, and that there are no major snafus. Chances are that the product is not even totally complete, since construction never seems to finish quite on time, and not all the furniture and equipment arrives on time. Hospitality products depend on repeat purchases. Business may boom initially; the question is, "Will they come back?"

In the marketing sense, initial hospitality customers are less innovative than are new goods buyers, although initial hospitality customers may be more innovative with restaurants. More likely, people who try new hotels or restaurants are variety-seekers who want to try something different and may not be too willing to forgive when everything doesn't go right the first night. Also, competitors may be many and customers can always go back to where they came from.

The same factors apply, only to a lesser degree, to the introductory stage of a new cocktail lounge or restaurant concept. The lead times will be shorter, more publicity and advertising will be needed to create awareness, but the same concerns pertain. This is also true for a new service, menu item, or other smaller part of the product mix. Obviously, advance time is less, if it exists at all, and the risk is far lower, but the elements are the same. The marketing objectives at this stage include creating product awareness, inducing trial, and establishing a position in the marketplace. When the property is part of a known chain, this is easier to do than if it is an independent entity. However, brand name alone is insufficient to establish a firm position because of the often wide variations between properties, especially in the case of hotels. Research has shown that businesspeople, at least, judge far more by the individual property than by the chain name.

There is still a far more important marketing

objective in the case of introducing the hospitality product—the use of recognizing the stages of the product life cycle concept. It is critical and essential that for a product to enter the growth stage, the customer must be persuaded in the introductory stage. Awareness and trial will come, relatively easily, through advance publicity, advertising, and word-of-mouth if the demand forecast is accurate. It is what happens to the customer during trial that determines the slope of the growth curve. Although selling and advertising to get new customers is important, it is secondary to the critical need for relationship marketing.

Consider a case in point. A new, large hotel opened in Atlanta with existing ample competition and wholesale rate-cutting being practiced. The corporate office of the hotel company was so convinced that they had a winner, and that there would be a deluge of demand to stay at the new hotel, that it issued orders not to offer discounts to get business. Advance bookings remained minimal, however, and the sales staff was literally laughed at. After six months, corporate rescinded the order. The sales staff was laughed at again; they had alienated a major part of the market. The hotel survived because it was one of a large national chain with an excellent reputation, but hundreds of thousands of dollars in revenue may have been lost in the process.

New product introductions rarely go perfectly, especially when they are major products such as a hotel or restaurant. This is the high-cost, low-profit stage of the life cycle. It is the stage when the customer has to be wooed and won at any cost. Failure to recognize this can be suicidal. Most of all, the emphasis must be on internal and relationship marketing.

The Growth Stage

Many newly developed manufactured goods, in fact most, fail in the introductory stage and never reach the growth stage. This is not as true in the hospitality world, where there is large investment capital. If a new menu item does not sell, of course, it can be discontinued with minimal loss. McDonald's twice pre-tested

pizza in selected restaurants and withdrew it from the market when it did not receive a favorable reception. If the new product is a $50 million hotel or a $5 million restaurant, however, it is more difficult simply to "discontinue" it. Generally, the property will find a new owner who buys it at the right price and has pockets deep enough to ride out the slow growth period. It may also emerge in a new form, such as condominiums. There is an old saying in the restaurant industry that it is the third owner who succeeds, having bought it at the right price after two failures. But even the high rate of restaurant failures occurs mostly in the growth stage.

The growth stage of a hospitality entity is one of excitement and pitfalls. Sales may be growing monthly, there may not be enough seats in the restaurant, or the hotel is filled on many nights. Customers who tried the facility in the introductory stage have told others who are now trying them. Business may be booming, but there are many marketing issues at hand.

Survivors of the introductory stage will proceed into a period of slow or rapid growth, or somewhere in between. It is during the growth stage that previous relationship marketing pays off. Customers come back and they tell others. This is what the growth stage of a hospitality product is all about. Although, like goods, new customers are needed for rapid growth, the hospitality product depends far more on repeat customers. Good relationship marketing must, of course, continue. The hospitality customer is fickle and management must be ever-alert, unlike the following, which was written about the trendy Aurora restaurant in New York City, which closed a few months later:

If the evening is ruined and the dinner a disaster, if all the complaining—oral and written—is to no avail, the offended customer still might get some consolation from the certain knowledge that at least some of this month's most popular and crowded restaurants will, soon enough, be empty has-beens. "The trendy places take success for granted, and that hurts many of them eventually," says Paul Emmett, who manages Jake's Restaurant in New York. "You see places that were hot a year ago become lackadaisical, then sales drop precipitously and they fold."[10]

The growth stage is also the time of product refinement. Continuous customer research and feedback should result in both elimination of flaws and fine-tuning of the product to the target market. This is by no means a time to rest on one's laurels over the introductory stage having been a booming success. Products must be improved and ways must be found to serve the target markets better than ever before. A frequent mistake made with hospitality products is for management to assume that initial fast growth gives them automatic license to raise prices. In the short term, this means higher profits; in the long term, it can mean disaster. The growth stage is the time for building loyalty, not for gouging the customer.

Here are some of the things that management can do to alienate the market after a successful introduction:

- Charge for coffee formerly included with the meal
- Raise prices of alcoholic beverages
- Raise prices of menu entrees that are selling well
- Stop taking reservations or fail to honor them on time
- Move tables closer together to fit more people in
- Refuse to serve arrivals who come at closing time
- Not provide rooms requested
- Raise room rates
- Overbook and have to "walk" too many customers[11]
- Dismiss complainants as a nuisance
- Overcharge for small extras or room service items
- Fail to honor special requests like bedboards

Consider the above list. It is operations that makes these decisions 99 times out of 100, but

you can see that they are really marketing decisions. Every one affects the customer. It is poor management that would make such decisions without a marketing perspective. Once again, hospitality management is inseparable from hospitality marketing. Typically, instead, while these decisions are being made, management is exhorting its sales people, "Get out there and get more customers." And, believe it or not, when decline comes the only question management can ask is, "What happened?" Many will answer, "overbuilding," "too much competition," "everyone's going to Europe these days," or, "they rerouted the highway."

The growth stage of a product is the time for fortification and consolidation. It is the time to plow back both money and good will, not take them away—it is the time to sow, not reap. It is the time to reward your good staff, to keep them enthusiastic and motivated. It is the time to listen to your customers and your employees for constant improvement of the product. It is the time to steal customers from the competition.

The marketing objectives at this stage are to solidify, to price for penetrating the market, and to keep customers. Every customer you keep at this stage will create other customers. This is the stage when you not only have to do things right; you also have to do the right things. This is the stage that will make or break the product. Finally, it is the time to start planning, if you haven't already, for extension of the mature stage.

The Mature Stage

The mature stage of the product life cycle, as we have already said, can continue for a long period of time. It can also end very abruptly. Once more, complacency is a bitter foe. If the product has successfully and correctly traversed the introductory and growth stages, the market should now be pretty well in place. The product's positioning should be established, its niche carved out, and its target market steady and loyal. There is a temptation at this stage to say, "We've got it made!" Nothing could be further from the truth. Never forget that fickle cus-

---

[10]Kathleen A. Hughes and Laura Landro, "A Lot of Restaurants Now Serve Rudeness with the Rigatoni," *Wall Street Journal,* November 12, 1986, p. 22.

[11]"Walking" a customer is industry jargon for not having a room available for someone with a confirmed reservation, forcing him or her to go elsewhere.

tomer out there, the one who says, "What have you done for me lately?"

The characteristics of the mature stage are usually easy to diagnose: leveling off of sales levels, good repeat business, and general settling down of the operation. Things finally seem to be getting easier, but now is the time for marketing management to be at its best.

At the mature stage, the product sometimes begins to get a little frayed around the edges—not just the furniture, carpet, and drapes, but also the concept and the execution. All elements need refurbishing. Too frequently, management thinks that a face-lift is all that is needed, and then wonders why business continues to slip.

Consider a 1,400-room hotel in a large city, for years the largest hotel and the major convention property in town. Occupancy in the hotel began slipping when other chains started to move into the city with brand-new, state-of-the-art properties. The corporate office's decision was to put $27 million into refurbishing the property. Instead of putting the money into renovating guestrooms where customers sleep, two-thirds of the monies went into building an exterior carriageway.

This hotel essentially had the market to itself for a number of years, with relatively little effort. It had stayed in the mature stage largely because there was no serious competition to stop it. It did need refurbishing, but probably could have done what was necessary for less than half the amount spent—but that wasn't the real problem. The real problem was that management didn't communicate with the customer. It virtually ignored complaints or dismissed them with trite responses. It was notorious for snafus at the front desk—lost reservations, overbooking and walking, putting people in rooms not made up, making people wait until 5:00 P.M. to get into a room, long lines and waiting, incredibly slow room service, lost telephone messages, overpricing, and other related problems.

The hotel also had waited too long for refurbishment because management thought it had a captive market. Instead of building customer loyalty at the right time, according to many who stayed there, the hotel seemed to delight in alienating customers, even to the point of refusing such simple requests as to split a shared room bill on two credit cards. One large group that occupied a very sizable block of rooms four times a year, had

been complaining for years, to no avail, about both the services and the prices. This group, for one, moved en masse as soon as another hotel opened that could handle it.

The above example is a classic case of a management not understanding the ramifications of having reached the mature stage of its life cycle, of not having prepared for that stage, and of not taking the appropriate actions when it reached that stage. Even a customer-research study, showing that this hotel was perceived as the poorest in the city in its product class, failed to daunt management. The hotel survived because of its size, location, and membership in a large chain, but it took years and new management to recover its former position.

In the mature stage of the product life cycle, the product has to run harder just to stand still. Competition abounds, market segments have been tapped, and the product and product concept are old hat. The best defense at this stage is to have built the loyalty and fortification in the growth stage, but this alone will not be enough to contend with the newcomers on the block. One must also go on the offensive.

The best offenses are innovativeness, staying close to the customer, finding new markets, seeking and solving consumers' problems, and doing this better than the competition. McDonald's, for example, reached this stage around the mid-1970s. It developed the breakfast concept and Egg McMuffin. It researched its market to see what it could do better. It went overseas, into malls, office buildings, museums, and other unsuspected places to find new markets. It developed new products such as styrofoam takeout containers to solve consumers' problems—and it did these better than the competition.

You don't have to be a McDonald's to survive in the mature stage. You can be Joe's Bar and Grill on the corner. The concepts, principles, and practices are the same; the difference is only a matter of scale. Sales growth slows down in this stage; that is to be expected. This is a maintenance stage, not of creating interest, but of maintaining it. This is a stage of developing new users and new uses, and new variations on the theme. It is a stage when product quality is paramount, and to slip now is to court disaster. This is a stage when customers have gotten to know us well and will not tolerate our blunders. This is the time to augment the product. This is the stage when *total quality management* (TQM) proves itself. TQM is a classic example of the principle that, in services, management and marketing are the same.

If the product is not maintained during the mature stage, it will enter into the decline stage. In some cases, when the product was a short-lived fad and has run its course, this is a natural and appropriate occurrence. Menu items lose their freshness, tastes change, the customer changes, and it is time to go on to bigger and better things. When the product is something like a hard piece of real estate, however, the situation is somewhat different. To avoid decline, sooner or later the product must be re-analyzed, refurbished, renovated, reformatted, redesigned, repositioned, and/or remarketed. This is the time to reverse the curve before it heads south with abandon.

McDonald's did it with innovativeness and new markets. Burger King did it with head-on competitive advertising. Marriott did it with Courtyard and Fairfield Inn. Holiday Inn Worldwide is trying to do it with upscale Crowne Plaza hotels, downscale Holiday Express, and a new corporate philosophy. Days Inn did it with new leadership.

Hyatt was not sure how it was going to do it, having publicly eschewed new market segments and frequent-traveler programs, but the company changed its mind on both and is still struggling. The Greenbriar and Homestead Resorts in West Virginia and Virginia did it by targeting convention business instead of primarily the leisure market. Pinehurst Resort, in the golf capital of North Carolina, did it by repositioning from a golf resort to a family sport resort. Club Med is doing it by targeting families instead of singles and yuppies, its target in the past.

Although all this may sound fairly easy, it is not. It takes real marketing leadership to know which way to go, to understand the market, and to take the risk involved. Often it demands a change in attitude, as with the case of the 1,400-room hotel previously discussed above. The main point is that the mature stage is the critical stage: Sooner or later it will end in decline if something isn't done, and done right.

Howard Johnson's failed because it waited too long, couldn't change its attitude, was too solidified in a negative position, and didn't understand the customer. Its third owner is now trying to revitalize it. Victoria Station and Valle's Steak House failed because they waited too long, didn't understand what was happening, and didn't know what to do. Sambo's Restaurants disappeared because they took away management's incentive and didn't understand its employees. Many restaurants fail simply because they allow product quality to slip. When the product slips and business declines, some hotels fail because management thinks the way to survive is to raise prices and cut costs. These responses only serve to grease the skids.

The Decline Stage

Decline has a tendency to accelerate even faster than growth. Actually, some of the above examples of reversing the life cycle curve have occurred in, or very close to, the decline stage. Alert leadership does not wait that long; it knows when it is in the mature stage and that something has to be done. Even more alert leadership starts planning before it reaches the mature stage. We use the term *decline stage* here, then, to mean that the end is near. Although there may be a rebirth in some other form, for all intents and purposes the product, as we know it, is finished. Howard Johnson, Valle's Steak House, and Victoria Station were all close to this state for a number of years. They live today in reincarnated forms.

The signs of the decline stage should be obvious, but too often are ignored. Declining sales, disgruntled employees, poor comment cards, and overall business malaise become the way the hotel or restaurant operates. Figure 10-7 shows a simple schematic, called the product death spiral, of what can happen in the decline stage of the product life cycle.

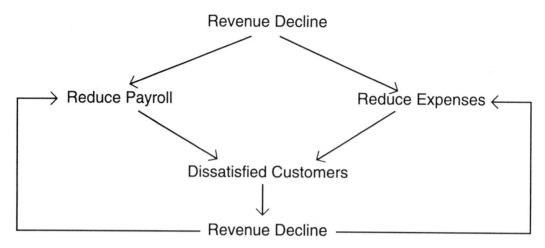

FIGURE 10-7   The product death spiral in the decline stage

Management, faced with declining revenues, takes the easiest course of action, reducing expenses. This is done by reducing the number of desk clerks, housekeepers, servers in the restaurant, telephone operators, and others. Other reductions follow: no new carpet for the ballroom, cheaper shampoo in the bathroom, and smaller shrimp on the menu. Customers begin to notice the decline in service and product. With so many options in the marketplace, they begin to go to competitors. The results are more revenue decline, leading to more dissatisfied customers and resulting in further revenue declines. The product death spiral continues until someone finally wakes up and says, "Hey, let's do some marketing to bring in customers instead of cutting costs." Of course, by that time it may be too late.

Some products, of course, should die. They have lived their time and served their purpose. We may even push them into oblivion to make room for new products. Others, like many fast-food franchises of the 1960s and 1970s, simply become extinct. When demise is not natural, not anticipated, and not desired, however, marketing probably has not done its job.

Locating Products in Their Life Cycles

How do you know what stage the product is in at any given point in time? Such an evaluation is highly subjective, prone to error due to irregularities in the "S"-curve, and inconclusive. There are guidelines that, along with good management acumen, marketing leadership, and willingness to objectively accept reality, make determining the life cycle stage for hospitality products not as difficult as it might seem.

The first step in locating a product in its life cycle is to study its performance, competitive history, and current position and match this information with the characteristics of a particular stage of the life cycle. Past performance can be analyzed as follows:

- Sales growth and market share progression in comparison with the best-fitting curve that one would expect for the particular product
- Alterations and enhancements that have to be made to the product
- Sales and profit history of similar, related, complementary, or comparable products
- Casualty history of similar products in the past
- Customer feedback
- Repeat- and new-business ratios (heavy repeat business with declining overall business being a sign of maturity or decline)
- Competitive growth and decline
- New competition and new concept introduction

- Number of competitors and their strengths/weaknesses
- Industry life cycle progressions
- Critical factors for success of the product

S.C. Jain also suggests that, in addition,

...current perspectives may be reviewed to gauge whether sales are on the upswing, have leveled out for the last couple of years, or are heading down; whether any competitive products are moving up to replace the product under consideration; whether customers are becoming more demanding vis-a-vis price, service, or special features; whether additional sales efforts are necessary to keep the sales going up; and whether it is becoming harder to [work through the distribution network].[12]

Such an analysis is not a task for amateurs; managerial intuition and judgment are critical. As our thinking tends to be strongly tainted or biased after the fact, a wise move would be to develop a model, based on the above, prior to introduction of the product. The model will then serve as a yardstick for future measurement.

Developing New Products/Services

It is clear by now that the development of a new product or service should start with customers' needs and wants and problems. This does not prohibit someone with a stroke of genius from shouting, "Eureka, I've got it!" and coming up with just the right new idea that customers will love.

It also does not necessarily mean that finding new ideas comes from *asking* customers what they want. In fact, research has long shown that customers are really not very good sources for new product ideas if we ask them directly. Customers have difficulty articulating just what it is they would like to have in a new product. Nevertheless, it is around the customer that most new products should be developed.

Having said that, we hasten to add that this is often not the case in the hospitality industry.

It is doubtful that anyone has ever asked customers whether they wanted a mint on their pillow or their bed turned down. If they had, of course, the reply would no doubt be a unanimous "Yes." Why not? It doesn't hurt, and it's "free."

When the bathroom "amenities wars" started, no one asked customers what amenities they wanted; management made that decision. Since then, it is true, customers have been surveyed as to which ones they use. One company found, to no one's surprise, that soap is the most frequently used bathroom amenity. No one has yet scientifically determined, to our knowledge, which of the amenities people take and use at home.

When frequent-traveler plans are developed, how often are customers asked what should be included? When a hotel is built, how many ask customers how they "use" it? (Actually, today, some chains do ask.) How often is the market asked what items it would like to see on a menu? (Some restaurant chains do ask.) Or how it would prefer the seating and lighting in a restaurant? Or whether it really likes that loud music or blaring TV in the lounge (often the preference of the employees who work there), especially when the lounge is empty most of the time?[13]

The point of all these questions is to emphasize that too many new hospitality products originate from the mind of someone other than the customer—yet their purpose is usually to enhance the product, increase satisfaction, create and keep a customer, and generally to fulfill the customer's needs and wants. With these objectives, the customer should be consulted more often. There is, however, the definitely emerging trend of more and more companies conducting consumer research.

Those operators who do, in fact, introduce successful new products are usually those who have based the product on solving consumers' problems. Adding more fish to menus came in-

---

[12]Jain, *Marketing Planning and Strategy*, pp. 258–259.

[13]An insight into new-product development in restaurants, as well as an excerpt on the development of Courtyard by Marriott, can be found in Tom Feltenstein, "New-Product Development in Food Service: A Structured Approach," *Cornell Hotel and Restaurant Administration Quarterly*, November, 1986, pp. 63–71.

itially from customers' problems with high cholesterol. No-smoking sections came from an obvious consumer problem even though, in most cases, it had to be mandated by law before restaurants would offer a solution. All-suite hotels came from consumers' problems of where to stay on extended stays. Directories in hotel rooms came from problems of guests' wanting information, and keyless door locks came from consumers' problems with security.

But mints on pillows, turn-down service, the extravagance of bathroom amenities, and TVs in bathrooms (but not telephones) were ideas that originated from management. Frequent-traveler plans were designed to solve management's problem, not the customers'. The utility of all of these products in bringing the customer back, in many cases, is questionable at best. Perhaps the worst part of this kind of product development is that, once the competition does the same thing, the differential advantage is lost, and what remains is a higher cost structure, as hotel managements have learned. Montreal's Bonaventure Hilton learned that "most guests can climb into bed at night without the help of hotel staff." It found that "evening turn-down service was a cost to the hotel and an annoyance to a lot of customers."[14]

What we are saying is not that a new or improved product should not be developed to try to gain a marketing edge and differentiate from the competition. What we are saying is that products and services should be developed for the purpose of creating and keeping a customer and that, if you are in the new-product development game, the best place to start is with the customer. Figure 10-8 demonstrates this point.

What Succeeds?

Many new products fail, as we have previously said. What about those that succeed? Researchers have found the following factors most likely to be associated with successful new products:

- The ability to identify customer needs
- Use of existing company know-how and resources
- Developing new products in the company's core markets
- Measurement of performance during the development stage
- Screening and testing ideas before spending money on development
- Coordination between research and development and marketing
- An organizational environment that encourages entrepreneurship and risk-taking
- Linking new-product development to corporate goals

New-product development is a total company effort: McDonald's has proven that, if no one else has. Successful new products very often come from the bottom up, rather than the top down. This is especially true in the hospitality business, because it is the bottom line of employees that is closest to the customer. It is often these people who can best tell you what the customers' problems are. Of course, you can always ask customers as well; do not ask what they would like to see, but what their problems are. For example, Marriott Suites Hotel in Downers Grove, Illinois has a General Manager's breakfast every Tuesday, Wednesday, and Thursday morning, when 15 guests of the hotel are treated to a complimentary buffet. Each is asked to bring questions and concerns of the hotel operation to discuss.

Summary

The marketing mix consists of various activities directed toward the customer. Most day-to-day marketing efforts take place in the implementation of this stage of the marketing effort. The importance of the marketing mix is evident in the marketing of any goods or services. Because of this, Borden's original marketing mix and McCarthy's popularization of it have made the "Four Ps" common terms in the language of

---

[14]Carolyn Leitch, "Cutting the Fat in Tough Times," *The Toronto Globe and Mail,* February 22, 1994, p. C1.

FIGURE 10-8 The relationship between product and need

marketers. The "Four Ps" have survived for many years, and it has been difficult for marketers to break away from this constraint in terms of marketing services. Renaghan, however, has shown that traditional marketing-mix concepts have limited utility for hospitality marketers because they reflect strategies for marketing goods and ignore the unique complexities of marketing hospitality services.

The product/service mix represents what the hospitality firm has to offer to the consumer, both tangible and intangible, both "free" and for sale. The product/service mix drives the other elements of the marketing mix; in some cases it may even drive the strategy of the firm. Accordingly, it is not just the marketer's job to "sell" the product/service. More important, it is the marketer's job to design in accordance with the needs and wants of the target markets.

A product/service has three elements: the formal element, the core element, and the augmented element. These elements are closely related to the concepts of salience, determinance, and importance discussed in Chapter 9. The astute marketer will develop products/services with these relationships in mind.

The product life cycle is concerned with the various stages of a product's growth in the marketplace. The best use of the product life cycle is not so much to predict the future, but to recognize its existence and pre-plan for it, and to recognize the product's present stage and the appropriate actions necessary.

Product innovation is a characteristic of marketing leadership. The place to look for new product ideas is in consumers' problems. Too many new products are designed without considering the customer's real needs.

Discussion Questions

1. Discuss the virtues of the hospitality marketing mix against those of the "Four Ps." Do you think, as some do, that the "Four Ps" are adequate for the hospitality market? Argue why they are or are not.
2. List the formal, core, and augmented products of an all-inclusive resort hotel in the Caribbean.
3. Give examples of various hospitality products that are in various stages of the product life cycle. How do you define which stage they are in? What specific implications does this have for marketing them?
4. Discuss the following: Hospitality customers really have no choice in product determination. They can't articulate what they want until they have it. Therefore, there really is no alternative to determining the product for them.
5. Consider a common customer complaint—for instance, waiting for the elevator, waiting at the front desk, hearing the telephone ring 15 times before the operator answers. Develop a new, economically feasible "product" to solve these customers' problems.
6. Which part of the hospitality product is most important to the customer—the tangible or the intangible? Discuss.
7. Read and analyze Cases 10-1, 10-2, and 10-3. Identify the product/service in each—what it is and what it might be. Where are these properties in their product life cycle? What should management do?

✔ Case 10-1
The Mt. Hiei Hotel[15]

The Mt. Hiei Hotel was about a 20-minute drive, at an uncrowded hour, east of Kyoto, Japan, adjacent to a national park and an important shrine. Lake Biwa, Japan's largest lake, was off to the east. The southern-exposure rooms had useable balconies from which one could view Kyoto in one direction and Lake Biwa in the other. The northern-exposure rooms on the front of the hotel were more modest and faced the park and shrine in the near distance. The hotel was surrounded by tended lawns and gardens, but not the ornamental shrubbery so popular in Japan.

The hotel was built in 1959 as an upscale resort for wealthy Japanese families. The surrounding area of Kyoto, Kobe, and Osaka was well-known for many years as a wealthy market. Some smaller, nearby cities were likened to Beverly Hills, California for per capita income. The hotel had 74 rooms, 69 in the traditional Japanese style. The rooms were large, especially considering the time of construction and the customary Japanese hotel room size.

When the hotel opened, the disparity between rich and poor in Japan was greater than in the 1990s. The initial room rate of 9,000 yen per person, double occupancy, was equal to 45,000 yen, or about US$335 per person, in the early 1990s, prohibitive to most then and now. Occupancy, however, although it varied by season, was about 80 percent. Customers were mainly Japanese families who stayed more than just a few days, especially in the summer when they enjoyed the escape from the oppressive hot and sultry lower elevations.

General Manager of the hotel was Mr. Kusano, who began his career at Mt. Hiei as a page boy. According to him, "The rich and influential guests came in the early 1960s. They were elegant people who met with each other, chatted, and walked about in a relaxed environment, enjoying just being here. The hotel was a wonderful vacation haven, especially since there were currency restrictions for Japanese traveling abroad. Now that I am General Manager, I'd like to bring back the wealthy and elegant clients of those early days. I want to relive that grandeur at firsthand—as the GM."

Mt. Hiei Hotel Today

Changes in Japanese disposable personal income had brought changes in Japanese tastes and spending. Lake Biwa and its major city, Otsu (700,000 population), had high-rise hotels, marinas, amusement parks, and excursion boats not unlike Mississippi River paddlewheelers. Many new resorts were being built around Japan, and over 11,000,000 Japanese traveled abroad annually.

Present occupancy at Mt. Hiei was about 42 percent, with July and August over 88 percent. Summer business was mainly families with an average age for adults of over 40 years. The average stay was one night.

The rest of the year the customer mix at Mt. Hiei included about 60 percent individual travelers. The other 40 percent was composed of incentive groups, corporate training groups, and junior high school student groups on escorted trips to see Kyoto's historic sights.

The average rate for the individual travelers was 9,000 yen per person per night (18,000 yen per couple or US$135), which was the nominal rate that Mt. Hiei charged when it first opened. Eighty percent were from the surrounding area, and the rest were from the Tokyo area. The group travelers provided an average rate of 9,500 yen (US$70.40) per person, three to a room, with breakfast and dinner included. The meal segment of the price was valued at 1,600 yen for breakfast and 5,000 yen for dinner. This left 2,900 yen (US$21.50) per person for the room.

---

[15]We gratefully acknowledge the contribution of this case by Professor William Kaven, School of Hotel Administration, Cornell University. At the time of the case, the exchange rate was about 135 yen per U.S. dollar.

Incentive group customers, being rewarded by their employer, usually stayed two nights. Corporate training meetings and conferences, held by firms such as Matsushita, could last as long as 15 nights. The high school students usually came in April and stayed two nights. This was an annual Kyoto phenomenon, when motorcoaches brought thousands of exemplary, polite, uniformed students from all over Japan for a two-day whirlwind tour of palaces, shrines, temples, and gardens. This annual deluge caused a competitive pricing frenzy among Kyoto area hotels and ryokans (traditional Japanese inns or small hotels whose floors are covered with tatami).

The food and beverage department played a strong role at Mt. Hiei, as was common in most Japanese hotels. This resulted from the Japanese custom of entertainment away from home, and the importance that the Japanese placed on eating and drinking with families, friends, and colleagues. At Mt. Hiei food and beverages accounted for 60 percent of revenue, rooms accounted for 25 percent, and other services for 15 percent.

In addition to the main dining room, grill room, and bar in the hotel, there were two additional special facilities. The first was a large, covered and glassed-in Bar-B-Q area adjacent to the hotel and useable year around. The local definition of Bar-B-Q was for each customer to grill his or her own steak over charcoal braziers installed in the middle of round tables, which seated about eight people, while chatting and drinking at the same time. The Bar-B-Q area was used by groups on outings or business meetings as well as by in-house guests.

The second facility was a detached building, the Eizankaku Japanese Inn. The Inn contained a few Japanese-style rooms that could serve as private dining rooms or sleeping rooms, but the building was used mainly for Japanese banquets. The building was small, but the atmosphere was inviting for the Japanese traditional style of entertainment. The customers were usually male and from organizations, clubs, or firms on a special outing. Most were transported to and from the hotel on a chartered bus. They first enjoyed a hot public bath, then dressed in cotton kimonos provided by the hotel and sat around having a good time chatting, drinking, singing, eating, and relaxing. The sameness of the attire and the convivial atmosphere served to eliminate rank and rancor; old wounds were often erased. Such outings were common in Japanese organizations.

Plans to Improve the Operation

The hotel's owner was determined to improve profitability. The physical plant was upgraded at substantial cost by renovating the lobby and reception area, adding new rugs and wall hangings. Guestrooms were refurbished and refurnished, but hallways and stairways were not included in the renovation. Upon completion, a six-person promotion department set out to increase guest traffic and make the hotel profitable.

The promotion effort was short-lived and unsuccessful, so a different direction was pursued. Payroll costs and expenses were reduced. Contracts were let to outside suppliers for all possible labor functions of the hotel, including food and beverage operations, housekeeping, and maintenance.

The leasing of the food and beverage operation presented several problems. The hotel was in a sparsely populated area that did not allow for outside customers other than the booked banquets. Also, qualified employees were scarce in the area. This made it difficult to use part-time staff. Further, public transportation up Mt. Hiei was infrequent and costly for the few hours of work that part-time employees might get. Finally, and most important, was the status of the head chef, whose entire career had been tied to Mt. Hiei Hotel. He was an influential top executive with an excellent reputation whose replacement was not feasible even under the best of circumstances.

When profit did not return after renovation, promotion, and cost-cutting, a contract was let for the selling function to an outside professional sales organization. This organization, active in contacting group buyers, produced an increase in the numbers of guests such as the junior high schoolers, incentive groups, and training meetings, but all at low rates. This further decreased the average room rate.

Mr. Kusano was deeply concerned about the hotel and its decline in customers, revenue, and profit. He very much wanted the hotel to be popular, full, and profitable. He felt the hotel was efficiently run; it only needed the customers to make it profitable. Mr. Kusano yearned for the return of the elegant clientele and the wonderful feeling of customers enjoying their stay with him as General Manager.

"I think that the hotel may need some added attractions to bring back those elegant custom-ers," said Mr. Kusano. "But the owner is not interested in adding anything to the hotel, as it is losing money anyway. The pity is, people have changed; they don't know how to be real guests in a fine hotel. I see people now coming into this hotel in their designer label clothes and carry-ing plastic sacks. They sit down on our chairs, open their sacks, and bring out Bento[16] and eat it right here. There is nothing I can say, as I am not here to teach them manners."

---

[16]Bento are small Japanese wooden box lunches consisting gen-erally of rice with pickled vegetables and fish or meat.

✔ Case 10-2
Carbur's Restaurant[17]

Once upon a time, two frustrated knights (their codpieces rusted shut) were searching over hill and to no avail for a better way to make a buck.

Seated at their usual round table in the village tavern over their usual roast dragon (rare) on Bunny Bread, Baron Burr grumbled, "I've had it with the same old thing day in and day out."

Count Carl clanked to his feet. "Electrolux," he cried, "I've got it! We'll open a tavern all our own. We'll offer so many choices no one will ever have to tire of the same old thing."

"I believe you've got it," the Baron sang in. "How's this sound? We'll offer five basic sandwiches on 95 different kinds of bread!"

"Great!" agreed the Count, "and we'll sell 'em so cheap we'll lose money on every one we sell."

"But we'll go broke!" blurted the Baron.

"Naw," countered the Count. "We'll pack 'em in and make it up in volume." (They didn't call him the no-count Count for nothing.)

The rest is history....

Background

In September of 1978, Carl Capra and Burr Vail, graduates of Cornell's School of Hotel Administration, opened the first Carbur's in Burlington, Vermont. Seeking to develop a new concept that would appeal to an "offbeat market," the Burlington location proved to be successful. Plattsburgh, New York was chosen as the next site. It was felt that Plattsburgh was similar to Burlington in that it was a college town and was on a major thoroughfare. When the Plattsburgh property also succeeded, Capra and Vail realized the potential of the Carbur's concept and examined a location in the old port district of Portland, Maine, then undergoing a major renovation. Carbur's–Portland opened its doors in 1981 and experienced the strongest takeoff thus far.

In the fall of 1981, Chuck Bowles joined the company and became the third partner. Although lacking practical restaurant experience, Bowles was an MBA from the University of North Carolina who brought a strong background in sales and marketing to the team. At this point in the organization's expansion, Capra and Vail recognized the wisdom of bringing a trained marketer into the thus-far operations-oriented company.

Carbur's of Portland

The Carbur's facility in Portland was located between two universities on Route 9, a major two-lane thoroughfare, in a mini-mall strip. Upon acquisition, the Portland location was "Carburized" in both decor and furnishings. All Carbur's were uniformly outfitted with authentic antiques, stained glass, brass railings, and lots of barn board and memorabilia from the 1920s and 1930s. Most of the actual furnishings were purchased by the owners themselves on weekend jaunts to New England auctions and antique shows.

Carbur's of Portland consisted of Carbur's, a "fancy sandwich place," the Carburet, a lounge and sometimes function room, and the Rib-It-Room, a more formal dining area.

The Carbur's Room

The Carbur's Room had a seating capacity of 96 and was located on the ground floor and to the left of the main entrance. Distinctly furnished in rustic decor, there were lining the walls seven booths with such names as the Clare Loose Booth, the Cabooth, John Wilkes Booth, Booth Bay Harbor, Emerson Booth, Shirley Booth, and Big Bootha.

Carbur's had a 26-page, 110-sandwich menu, presented in booklet style. It emphasized sandwiches and salads with fun, trendy names that were a play on words. A sample page is shown in Exhibit 10-2-1. As the specialty of the house, Carbur's offered the Two College Club for $7.95, "the State of Maine's only five-decker sand-

---

[17]Nancy Charves, Shari Aloni, and John Griffin researched and contributed to this case. The location has been disguised.

EXHIBIT 10-2-1   Sample page of Carbur's menu

- **THE WHAT'S YOUR CRAB?**
  (And is that what Pales you?)
  Seafood salad, baked ham, bacon, tomato, avocado spread and melted swiss

- **BURR'S BLUNDER**
  (You can't win 'em all)
  Seafood salad, turkey chest, bacon, lettuce, tomato and tarragon mayo club

- **THE CAMEL'S HUMP**
  (Just doin' what comes naturally)
  Seafood salad, turkey bosom, bacon, lettuce and tomato with Sunshine Sauce club

- **THE CARBURATOR**
  (What do you call somebody who ate at Carbur's?)
  Seafood salad, chest of turkey, tomato and lettuce with tarragon mayo club

- **THE BAGGY THIGHS**
  (Once the knees go, there's no stopping it)
  Seafood salad, sliced ham, avocado spread, lettuce and tomato with ever-loving tarragon mayo club

- **SOCKET TOOMY**
  (Buzz word in Insertiveness Training course)
  Seafood salad, sliced ham and Sunshine Sauce, topped with melted swiss cheese

- **THE MENAGE A TROIS**
  (A triple decker, of course. The middle layer subject to change.)
  Seafood salad, bacon, avocado spread, lettuce and tomato with blue cheese dressing club

- **THE SUNSHINE OF YOUR LIFE**
  (To keep the moonshine from your wife)
  Seafood salad, avocado spread, lettuce, turkey slices, tomato, swiss cheese, and of course, Sunshine Sauce club

- **THE MARQUISE de SOD**
  (Hang in there while we whip one up)

  Seafood salad, sliced bacon, tomato and sharp cheddar. All broiled

- **CHARLES OF THE RITZ**
  (A wheeler-dealer and fast-talking entremanure)
  Seafood salad, roast beef, lettuce and tomato club

- **THE MURPHY BED**
  (Making a comeback, but as Mrs. Murphy said "It's news to me.")
  Seafood salad, shrimp salad, lettuce and tomato club

wich." Upon presentation, the server was accompanied to the table by fellow employees who formed a marching band complete with tuba, washboard, bass drum, and sparklers. This performance, like the sandwich descriptions, was intended to entertain the customers and create a lighthearted, fun atmosphere.

The Rib-It-Room

The Rib-It-Room, which had a seating capacity of 74, was located on the lower level of the establishment. The concept was initially offered as an alternative to the Carbur's sandwich menu, for those seeking a full dinner in a more formal dining room atmosphere.

Entrance to the Rib-It-Room was through the main doorway and down a curved stairway to the right. The original brick walls were decorated with framed "frog prints." Antiques, hanging plants, Tiffany lamps, and stained glass pieces were placed throughout. Many of the tables were secluded in little alcoves or behind assorted wicker and wooden dividers, and all were set with linen and contrasting placemats.

The menu at the Rib-It-Room offered a selection of steaks, seafood, and chicken entrees, as well as frog legs and prime rib. Each entree included relish tray, choice of salad, potato/rice or vegetable, and warm bread and butter. The prices ranged from $6.95 to $14.95. Diners could also choose from a selection of appetizers (or "rib ticklers") and five different desserts ("If you haven't croaked yet....").

Lounges

Bar customers at Carbur's could choose between the first-floor lounge or the upstairs Carburet. Despite a combined seating of 130 plus limited standing room, the lounges at Carbur's reached capacity each Friday and Saturday night, with a waiting line outside the main entrance.

Both the lounge areas were Carburized in decor, with antiques, memorabilia, and barn board. The second-floor Carburet, which opened in September of 1985, could be reached by a staircase inside the main entrance and directly to the right. Although Carburized, this room was intended to be more eclectic, with an actual cabaret flavor. There were striped awnings over the bar and matching curtains and fixtures. The furniture varied in size and shape from sink-in couches to high-backed bar stools, to a pair of authentic barber's chairs. Low-hanging lights and brass railings completed the decor. Both lounges featured a large specialty drink list.

The original lounge, on the first floor to the left of the main entrance, was furnished with deep leather couches and three tabletop video games. Prior to the lounge promotion (and the opening of the Carburet), this room served only as a holding tank for dinner guests. Recognizing the underutilization of the first-floor lounge, Bowles tried a "bold and bullwash" approach to transform the lounge into a revenue-producing area.

In the spring of 1984 Carbur's began promoting two "happy hours," offered seven days a week. Both "happy hours" offered double-sized drinks for the price of one, and Carbur's also gained the distinction of being the first in the area to offer a late-night "happy hour." Less than one year after the lounge promotion kicked off, Carbur's was voted the best "happy hour" in Portland by the *Valley Advocate* newspaper. The "happy hours" were very successful until the state legislature passed a law in 1988 banning drink price-reduction promotions.

The original target market was a relatively casual one, geared solely to the Carbur's Room. However, with the opening of the Rib-It-Room and the Carburet and the promotion of the first-floor lounge, Carbur's began to offer products appealing to a blend of markets. The customer base was comprised one-half of locals and one-half of students, two groups not necessarily compatible. As a result, there was not a loyal customer following and, in the 1990s, what had been a slow customer decline accelerated into a steep one.

Summary

Carbur's was modeled after the largely successful chains of the 1970s, such as TGIF (Thank

God It's Friday), Bennigan's, and Fitzwilly's. The concept had been successful from the start and survived well into the '80s. In the late '80s and early '90s, however, problems arose and business started falling off.

Business had improved steadily since Carbur's first opened in Portland in 1981, but it stabilized in the late 1980s. In 1991 revenue peaked at $1.2 million, partly reflected in menu and drink price increases, and then decreased each year thereafter.

Contemplating this situation and noting that 75 percent of his revenues came from the Carbur's Room and the lounges, Bowles was concerned. He felt that Carbur's had a monthly potential of $125,000. He was particularly concerned about the seasonal fluctuations, as well as the fact that he could no longer promote special "happy hour" drink prices.

One major problem at Carbur's was the high costs involved with operating this kind of restaurant. Kitchen costs were especially high due to high inventory costs and the large number of kitchen employees needed. Another major problem was in the market mix.

Management attempted to address this problem by using the downstairs dining room for more formal dining, largely for the locals, and keeping the main floor for the more casual dining off the 26-page menu, largely for the students. These two segments, however, did not sort themselves out the way management had expected they would.

Increasing costs and declining sales led, eventually, to new ownership and new management, which was instructed to make recommendations for the future and to turn the restaurant around.

✔ Case 10-3
Sheraton Lakeside Inn[18]

The Sheraton Lakeside Inn opened during the early 1970s as a Sheraton franchise property in Kissimmee, Florida. It was one of the first hotels built in the area following the completion of Disney World, less than two miles away. It was conveniently located within 15 minutes of all the major attractions in the area. The property took pride in offering fine quality service at a reasonable price. The clientele tended to be vacationing families with one or more children. The length of stay ranged from five days to two weeks.

The Inn was visible from the highway, but set back at a comfortable distance so guests were not disturbed by the traffic. There were several restaurants within walking distance of the Inn, ranging from McDonald's and Burger King to more elite and expensive dining facilities. There were also several convenience stores within walking distance. An 18-hole miniature golf course and several tourist shops were nearby.

The Property

The Inn was a 651-room, two-story complex on 27 acres with a man-made lake that offered complimentary paddleboats for its guests. There were three swimming pools within the complex—two large pools, each with its own gazebo bar, and one smaller pool. Recreation activities were centered primarily around the two larger pools. There were four lighted tennis courts, a nine-hole miniature golf course for guests at a small charge, as well as game rooms for children.

Most rooms within the hotel were designed as doubles. They were of basic quality and design, comparable to those you would find in a Days Inn or Ramada. Each was equipped with an in-room refrigerator. Average room rate was approximately $100 per room per night, a reasonable and competitive rate for the area. The

hotel had always been successful and, in the 1990s, with many newer hotels in the area, year-round average occupancy was about 85 percent, a figure of which management was proud.

The Inn employed a full-time recreation director responsible for organizing guest activities for both adults and children. One recent program, for example, was a poolside barbeque, offered three to four times a week when, for a small price, guests were served hot dogs and hamburgers by the pool. This had produced very low response and was generally unsuccessful.

Food and Beverage

A delicatessen, which offered homemade baked goods, deli sandwiches, and assorted snacks for takeout, was the only outlet that offered luncheon service. Most of its business, however, came from the sale of convenience store items since most guests were visiting area attractions at lunchtime.

Two restaurants were located within the complex. The Greenhouse seated 150 people and offered both breakfast and dinner in buffet-style for both meals. The menu changed nightly and featured themes such as "seafood buffet" and "Italian night." Cost for the buffet was $5.95 for breakfast and $9.95 for dinner for all you could eat. Children under 12 ate free at both meals. The Greenhouse was almost always seated to capacity for breakfast, but had few dinner covers. Overall, it fell well short of breaking even.

The Sunset Grille was open only for dinner and seated up to 75 guests. The atmosphere was bright and comfortable, but more formal than the Greenhouse. The restaurant offered table service, linen tablecloths and napkins, and a beautiful view of the lake. The cuisine was classified as upscale American. Prices were expensive compared to other restaurants in the immediate area. The restaurant was rarely full

[18]Shane Hammond and Susan MacArthur researched and contributed to this case.

and guests had no trouble walking in without a reservation. Business remained low regardless of the efforts of a puzzled management.

The Sheraton Lakeside also had a lounge facility known as Hurricane Sam's. This was a very comfortable and cozy room with a tropical atmosphere. Unfortunately, it was usually empty, even though its drink prices were quite reasonable. Management had recently brought in live entertainment, but this failed to significantly increase business.

Management turnover in the food and beverage department had been high in the past year. In the past six months alone the food and beverage director, three of the four food and beverage managers, the executive chef, and the sous chef had all been replaced. The position of assistant food and beverage director had been eliminated. This turnover had contributed to the lack of implementation of plans developed by management to produce additional revenue in this department.

There was an increasing amount of competition in the area. Along the immediate four-mile stretch of highway alone, 15 hotels of comparable style and price now existed. Some of these properties were more upscale than others; the rest were equipped with facilities similar to the Sheraton Lakeside. All operated their own restaurants. Also along the highway numerous freestanding restaurants sought the family market with comparable prices. Many hotel guests also took advantage of dining facilities at the area attractions.

Conclusion

Sheraton Lakeside management was quite satisfied with its above-average occupancy percentage, but was troubled by significant losses in the food and beverage department. It was puzzled by the low patronage and revenue produced. Several suggestions on how to increase revenue had not been implemented.

Extensive renovations had recently been completed in the main complex, including large windows, redesign, and softer colors in the restaurants, as well as completion of a number of special bedrooms aimed at the honeymoon market. Management hoped these renovations would not only sustain high occupancy, but also aid in increasing the revenue generated by the food and beverage department so it could at least operate at a break-even point.

CHAPTER 11

The Hospitality Presentation Mix

The second part of the hospitality marketing mix is the presentation mix. It is helpful to repeat the definition of the presentation mix given in Chapter 10: *All elements used by the firm to increase the tangibility of the product/service mix in the perception of the target market at the right place and time.*

First, we need to clear up what may be a source of confusion to some. Traditional marketers, or goods marketers, would likely tell us that this definition has done nothing more than describe the product/service mix in a different way. In a sense they would be correct. Discussion of the product/service mix in the previous chapter included some of the elements of the presentation mix. It would be difficult to argue that the physical plant, location, atmospherics, and employees are not part of the product.

It would also be difficult to argue that price is not part of the product. Yet, traditional marketers establish price as a separate entity in the "Four Ps." Why this difference? The answer is that price says something about the product. Price is a separate part of the marketing mix, or the "Four Ps," because it can be changed without materially affecting the formal, core, or augmented product itself. For this reason we include price as part of the presentation mix in

recognition of the fact that price makes the product tangible.

At the same time, we recognize that the development of pricing strategy, as a powerful marketing tool, deserves much fuller treatment than just as a tangible reflection of the product/service. To provide this fuller treatment, albeit still limited, we devote all of Chapter 12 to further discussion of price.

The hospitality presentation mix is the way we *present* the core product, or what the customer is really buying. It increases the tangibility of the product/service mix in the *perception* of the target market at the right place and time. This is not to say that there will be no overlaps between the product/service mix and the presentation mix; there will be.

Our purpose is to provide marketing *tools* so that we can do a better job of marketing. Once we understand the mind and decision-making process of the hospitality customer, we can see why the presentation mix is such an important tool in that task. It is also important that the successful hospitality marketer be able to conceptualize this distinction. This chapter will proceed with that understanding and will consider the six elements of the presentation mix: physical plant, location, atmospherics, employees, customers, and price.

427

Physical Plant

The term *physical plant* represents everything physical and quickly perceptible to the senses in the hospitality property. It is bricks and mortar, marble columns, potted plants, wallpaper and paint, chandeliers, flowers, gardens, sand urns, and a multitude of other things. That should make life easy; all we have to do is hire a good architect and a good interior designer, and the problem takes care of itself.

What is so easy to forget (although we assume that, after finishing this book, you will never forget it) is that all of this must begin with the customer. Did you ever inspect a factory before you bought the stereo produced there? Did you care what the factory looked like after you bought the stereo? Of course not—but in hospitality things are different.

We will carry the analogy further because contrast helps in understanding the differences. Do you suppose the marketing department of the stereo company was consulted before building the plant? Why not? Because, of course, it has nothing to do with the customer.

Does this mean stereos are built without regard to the customer? Again, no. Knowledge of what the target market wants in a stereo is taken back to the design team and the engineers. The stereo is built. If the research is well done, the marketing team can take over. The job is relatively easy because the product has been built to the specifications of the customer. All that is needed now is basic traditional marketing and assurance to customers that this stereo does what they want better than the competition's. But because sound also cannot be seen, even the stereo company has to do some tangibilizing to create expectation and reduce risk. This is done with packaging. In the final analysis, however, the customer listens to the stereo and judges by the sound, before buying.

Developing the Physical Plant Package

The physical plant element of the hospitality presentation mix is nothing more than packaging, only in this case the customer has to largely consume and judge after buying. Packaging helps in attracting and creating the customer, and good packaging will help to bring the customer back; this is nontraditional marketing.

There are numerous examples of what we are saying. Atrium lobbies, elegant chandeliers, marble columns, luxurious bathrooms, all are statements about a property and are tangible entities in the presentation mix. (So, too, are dingy lobbies, burned-out lightbulbs, chipped columns, and stained sinks.) Rarely are these design decisions based directly on consumer needs and wants, nor would it be too feasible if they were. For example, we would never be able, even if consumers had the knowledge, to get a consumer consensus on the appropriate chandelier or wallpaper. We have little choice but to rely on the expertise of architects and designers for these decisions. Their judgments, in turn, are strongly influenced by the owner's "gut feeling" and personal likes and dislikes.

When this happens, the consumer sometimes gets left out. Marketing plays little if any direct part in decisions about the physical plant but is left with the job of selling the property in order to pay for the cost of those decisions. It is little wonder that a product orientation develops.

Although it is not feasible to ask customers to make all these decisions, it is feasible to ask, "What will this do for the customer? How will the customer use this property? What kind of tangible presentation does this make of what our product really is?" Architects and designers don't always ask these questions. Owners or developers, especially in the case of hotels, are probably even less knowledgeable. They only know what *they* like. In the case of some "grand" hotels, they may only want to build a monument of which they can be proud.

Some Examples   Although drawn from the "grand" end of the market, the principles in the following examples are the same for a budget motel, a pizza parlor, or a McDonald's:

(1) The Four Seasons Hotel in New York City was built at a cost of $1 million per room. Al-

though now managed by Four Seasons for an upscale market, the hotel may never pay for itself. The ad in Figure 11-1 capitalizes on the presentation mix and the physical plant, as well as location, aided by research that showed that an important component of high-priced hotels is luxurious bathrooms.

(2) A relatively new hotel in a major U.S. city has a beautiful lobby and two-story waterfall. So as not to impose on the aesthetic sense, the front desk is tucked into a corner on the second floor. What does the lobby and waterfall tangibilize for the new customer who spends five to ten minutes wandering around trying to find the front desk?

(3) Another new hotel in the same city has rooms with wall-to-wall windows covered by expensive drapes about two inches too narrow. If the drapes are drawn to the middle, they leave a narrow slit on the ends, and vice versa. If you were to have such a room on the east side, on a sunny morning you would never need to leave a wake-up call.

(4) There are any number of hotels targeting the business market that have desks in the rooms hardly large enough for two pads of paper, never mind the telephone, lamps with low-watt bulbs, and other paraphernalia. What does this say about the problems of the targeted business purpose? Or, targeting the weekend market, a new upscale hotel in Toronto had only one comfortable chair in each room. When queried, the general manager said, "That was a big mistake. Now we're trying to find the money to buy the chairs."

(5) A real estate developer of our acquaintance decided to get into the hotel business. He bought a 300-room resort that was in the decline stage of its product life cycle, and he planned to refurbish it. As sometimes happens, his wife became the interior designer and set up three beautifully refurbished rooms as prototypes. However, no one stopped to think how a guest would use such rooms. Here were some of the problems:

- The television was hidden in the bottom level of a console across from the end of the bed. It was impossible to lie in bed and see the television.

- The exquisite bedside lamps were about a foot tall. It was impossible to read in bed without leaning over the side to get enough light.
- The bed headboards were covered with a fine satin that absorbed hair stains, giving the appearance of uncleanliness.

(6) At the same time, consider The Stanford Court Hotel in San Francisco. Here, too, guests could not readily find the front desk; in fact, there was nothing in the lobby to let customers know that they were in a hotel lobby. The decor deliberately said, "We don't want to look like a hotel." There was an antique Napoleonic clock in the lobby. There were always fresh flowers in both public places and bedrooms. The cocktail lounge and dining rooms were hidden away in corners. All of this made a tangible presentation that the highly repeat business target market loved.

(7) Once again, it has been said that the greatest contribution Ray Kroc made to the success of McDonald's was the large windows that surround McDonald's. For the first time, people could look into a restaurant and immediately see if it was clean. It took away the unknown; it reduced the risk. Kroc's windows were a tangible presentation of his concept.

We have cited mostly negative examples of the physical plant element of the presentation mix only because they make the point more clearly. In fact, there are thousands of examples of physical plant elements making a positive presentation: lobbies, dining rooms, spacious seating, room arrangements, grounds, decor, space, lobby, cocktail lounges, and so forth.

Considering Marketing The point that we want to make, once again, is that the physical plant is an integral part of nontraditional marketing. When it "works," it makes a strong and positive statement about the property and the product it has to offer. When it doesn't work, it makes the opposite statement—in fact, it becomes a major source of customer complaints. Marketing should be involved in initial management decisions; management should be

Courtesy of Four Seasons Hotels Ltd.

FIGURE 11-1 The Four Seasons Hotel in New York City advertises to support a million-dollar per-room property

practicing marketing in subsequent operational decisions. There are always two lines of inquiry to be considered:

1. What statement does the physical plant make to the target market—that is, how does it tangibilize the core product? Will it help to create customers?

2. How does/will the customer use it—in other words, does it solve problems? Will it keep customers?

Pursuing these two lines of inquiry, we should make note that physical plants do not necessarily always have to be top-drawer facilities. We have used those kinds of examples be-

Only Here
will you find the first I.M. Pei-designed hotel
on this continent.

Only Here
are you on 57th Street, between Madison and Park.
The crossroads of civilization.

Only Here
is your 600-square-foot room rich in silk,
marble and rare English sycamore.

Only Here
can you gaze down at three states and one ocean
from your room.

and

Only 60 Seconds To
fill your ergonomically designed steeping tub and ponder all
or none of the above.

You've never experienced anything quite like it.
Even in New York.

Four Seasons Hotel
NEW YORK

57 EAST 57 STREET BETWEEN MADISON AND PARK.
TELEPHONE (212) 758-5700. OPENING SPRING 1993.

FIGURE 11-1   (continued)

cause they are more familiar and help to make the point. A physical plant can also say to the right target market, "Relax, don't worry; throw your peanut shells and your cigarette butts on the floor."

Consider the example of Caneel Bay, a very successful resort in the Virgin Islands, where room rates are over $400 per night. The resort is set on land now part of a national park, and its core product is peace, quiet, prestige and total relaxation. The physical plant consists mostly of one- or two-storied units that blend in with the environment, with the 168 units spread out over 170 acres. The rooms are very simply, but elegantly decorated and, surprisingly, they do not have air-conditioning, radios,

In Orlando, The Real Magic Is Booking A Hotel Like This At A Reasonable Rate.

When you're planning a meeting in Central Florida, cost-effectiveness can be quite an attraction. Especially when combined with the excellent service, amenities and location offered by the Clarion Plaza Hotel. Here you'll find 59,000 sq. ft. of meeting space, 18 versatile breakout rooms and 810 oversized guest rooms, including 42 suites. Plus a location that puts you right next to Orlando's Convention Center, just minutes from all the attractions. It's not magic. It's the Clarion Plaza. If you want Orlando's best convention value, be our guest.

Clarion Plaza Hotel
Orlando

FIGURE 11-2   How do these ads tangibilize the properties?

Courtesy of Forte Hotels

FIGURE 11-2   (continued)

television, or telephones. Peace, quiet, and re-laxation is effectively tangibilized. The resort solves the problems of the mostly urban, highly successful professionals who lead hectic lives and need a place to get away from it all.

Consider and contrast the ads in Figure 11-2. What do they tangibilize for the properties?

Location

Location is a limited but useful element of the presentation mix. Its limitation lies in three factors. First, location is inflexible once the property has been erected. A hotel is on the beach or it isn't. Second, location is a minimum threshold attribute. By this we mean that loca-tion is in a somewhat black-or-white category with little gray in between. If the location is desirable, it then becomes secondary as a deter-minant or important factor, and other factors take over in the decision process. If the location is not desirable, other attributes may have little meaning.

The third limitation of location is that it tan-gibilizes only one attribute of the product—namely, convenience. There is no other reason for location to be a determining factor in choos-ing a hotel or restaurant.[1] This means that lo-cation must play a smaller role in the market-ing bag of tricks, if we accept the benefit bundle concept.

In spite of these limitations, location plays a major role in the minds of many hospitality marketers as well as hospitality customers. Ex-ploring why this is so will provide some insight into the use of location in the presentation mix.

Location's Role

E.M. Statler, legendary founder of the Statler Hotel chain in the 1920s, is purported to have said that the three most important elements of a hotel were location, location, and location. No doubt, that was true in the 1920s, when existing hotels may have been many blocks or many miles apart. Also, if one were staying at a hotel some distance from where one wanted to be, it was no easy task to travel the distance in be-tween. Today, of course, that situation is greatly changed and Statler's comment needs reevalu-ation.

The major role of location for hospitality cus-tomers derives from its salient nature. Almost any survey will show location as one of the most frequently mentioned attributes in choosing a hotel or restaurant. This response is strongly related to the tangible nature of location as well as its salience. When we think of choosing a restaurant or staying in a city away from home, we immediately think of what is most conven-ient. That tends, in many cases, to become the first consideration. Whether it is the final con-sideration depends on two factors. First, cus-tomers look at what else is available in rela-tively the same location. Second, customers examine any other criteria that are important to them. Research has shown that when a num-ber of different variables are considered at the same time in relation to each other, location is a far less important variable (e.g., Figure 6-10).

The most important use of location in mar-keting is obviously in its initial selection rele-vant to target markets and competition. To build a hotel or restaurant where no one ever goes would not be too wise unless, of course, one could then get people to go there. Twenty years ago no one went to Cancun, Mexico, because there was nothing there but a large sandbar. Today, after massive effort, there are thousands of hotel rooms and accompanying facilities, and Cancun is a major destination for those who like to frolic in the sun and sand. Cancun, how-ever, does have an advantage of location. It is attractive to Americans because it is not too far or "too foreign." Some Americans choose desti-nations such as Bermuda and Cancun because they can experience a "foreign" culture with as little discomfort as possible.

On the other hand, very few would ever go to Hot Springs, Virginia, or White Sulphur Springs, West Virginia, except for the hotels

---

[1]There are, of course, exceptions to this rule. A location may be quite inconvenient but will be desirable as regards privacy, seclu-sion, vista, prestige, or other intangible elements (an example is Caneel Bay, from above). This, however, falls outside the common usage of the word location. We use the word here in its more common usage.

that are there: The Homestead and The Greenbriar, respectively. It is true that both hotels are in beautiful country settings, but it is also true that there are other beautiful country settings in that part of the country. People go there specifically because of The Homestead and The Greenbriar; in other words, location is not a strong, tangible presentation of convenience for these hotels.

A similar but converse situation is the Banff Springs Hotel in the Rocky Mountains in Alberta, Canada. This hotel is also in beautiful countryside and people go to Banff because of that feature. While there, they stay at the Banff Springs Hotel because it is there. For the Banff Springs Hotel, location is a strong, tangible presentation of convenience.

These examples are given to demonstrate the increasing or diminishing importance of location. Location today, as opposed to E.M. Statler's day, has been strongly affected by modern methods of transportation. Because of major expansion of air travel, for example, very few destination locations at this time can be considered "bad," as far as reaching them is concerned. While some are clearly more desirable, modern transportation has diminished location's importance.

The same thing applies within a city. Few go to the Millenium Hotel in New York City for reasons other than its being the only deluxe hotel in the Wall Street area. Those who go to the Waldorf-Astoria on Park Avenue, however, have many other choices and choose the Waldorf for reasons other than location. In fact, some of them endure the long taxi ride to Wall Street by choice.[2]

We have a similar situation with restaurants. Fast-food restaurants tend to cluster on so-called fast-food rows. These rows are where the heavy traffic is and where the target markets for these restaurants prevail. Location is critical for fast-food restaurants because of the need for population density, which is why so many of them group together, giving the fast-food customer a choice in the same area. Many contend that all the good fast-food locations in the United States are now gone. Paradoxically, once established, location has little marketing value for a fast-food restaurant and one rarely sees it emphasized in their advertising.

Upscale restaurants face a different situation. Locating an upscale restaurant on fast-food row would probably be its kiss of death. Remoteness can well be an asset for these restaurants. In fact, there are many successful ones in the country in small towns that have no other claim to fame. Many upscale restaurants strive to be a destination unto themselves. Durgin Park Restaurant in Boston was famous as a restaurant long before the development of the Faneuil Hall area as a major tourist attraction near it. One of the authors remembers vividly being brought there by his grandfather in the 1960s, when the area was run-down and unsafe. The restaurant was always full, despite its poor location. Now the restaurant is full and has a superior location.

One of the most successful restaurants in the United States is Anthony's Pier 4 in Boston ("You haven't been to Boston if you haven't been to Anthony's"). Although it is on the waterfront, that factor has little appeal once you are inside. Enduring the long wait for a table, when you get to it, will place you elbow-to-elbow with hundreds of others. Anthony's is also not that easy to get to from downtown Boston, and is situated among several abandoned warehouses. There are better restaurants in Boston with lower prices, better atmosphere, easier-to-find locations, and shorter taxi rides. Is location an important attribute for Anthony's? Not at all. Its target market doesn't much care where the restaurant is.

Location as a Marketing Tool

Let us go back now to the three limitations of location in the presentation mix to see when and how location can be an important attribute.

We said, first, that location, once decided, is

---

[2]At the same time, there is another location aspect that may be important only because it exists in the consumer's mind. For example, hotels in New York City may sell a location advantage as little as two blocks apart. A hotel on the East Side of town traditionally commands higher room rates than those of comparable quality on the West Side. It is unimportant that the East and West Sides are separated by a street only 150 feet wide.

inflexible. This means that marketing must enter into the decision process at the first step. The importance of the decision at this stage is directly related to the target market; if location is not important to the target market then it isn't important. The presentation element comes in "being there." As we have said in the case of fast-food operators, it would be of little use for them to promote location, but being in the right location itself makes the tangible presentation of convenience.

For the Banff Springs Hotel the situation is reversed. Its major attraction is its location. Thus, the location becomes the tangible presentation of the product/service, is a very important factor in its promotion, and should be used as a marketing tool. This is also true of remote island resort hotels located in areas of great natural beauty, as seen in Figure 11-3.

The second limitation is that of minimum threshold. This limitation is more relevant to immediate competition. If you have a motel in North Overshoe, Maine, the nearest motel being 25 miles away, and if your market wants to do business in North Overshoe, it may not mat-

ter too much what else you do. Location is your major asset and possibly the sole criterion in the market's choice of your motel—that is, it is a determinant attribute.

On the other hand, a hotel in Boston faces a different situation. Like business travelers in North Overshoe, people who go to Boston to do business in the downtown area don't want to stay at a hotel 25 miles away. Given, however, that a particular hotel, among 20-plus others, is located within a five-mile radius in Boston, it has passed the minimum threshold—for most it is "close enough." Location is salient but not determinant. This does not mean that if, for example, you intended to do business in the Prudential Center, it wouldn't be most convenient for you to stay at the Sheraton next door. It means that you would introduce other, more determining criteria in making your choice. In such cases, where competition possesses relatively the same location, location goes from being salient to being minimally determinant in the process of choice.

The third limitation of location is its singular tangible presentation of the attribute of conven-

FIGURE 11-3   Remoteness as a location advantage

ience. To turn this to advantage, we again must examine the target market. If convenience is a determining attribute for the target market, location should be stressed; otherwise, it has little appeal.

Location is a significant but somewhat overrated variable in hospitality marketing. While salient, it has limited use. Hospitality customers today have many other choices and many other reasons for choosing a property. The strength of location in the presentation mix—the tangibilization of the product—lies in knowing when and how to use it in marketing, as shown in Figure 11-4.

Atmospherics

The third element of the presentation mix is a powerful one: atmosphere. While most of us are fully aware of this element—we often say that we like or don't like the "atmosphere" somewhere—marketers often do not take full advantage of it. Atmosphere is a quality of the immediate environment recognized by all the senses except taste, although taste can be influenced by the other senses. Thus, wine or food may seem to taste better when other atmospheric dimensions are positive.

Atmosphere constitutes a sensory experience, a core product of many hospitality experiences, that can be obtained in a number of ways. Visual sense is influenced by color, light, size, and shape. The sense of hearing is influenced by volume and pitch, sense of smell by scent, and sense of touch by texture and temperature.

We have previously stated that hospitality customers buy a total bundle of benefits. Atmospherics is one element of that bundle. It is often the atmospherics that tangibilize all those intangible benefits that are sought—comfort, good feeling, excitement, serenity, contentment, romance, or any number of others. In the hospitality industry, atmospherics are a critical part of the marketing mix. In fact, the atmosphere itself may be the core product that consumers buy. If not, it can at least greatly influence the purchase decision. Marketers can use atmospherics as consciously and skillfully as they use other tools of marketing.

What Atmospherics Do

Atmospherics should have an emotional effect on buyers that will increase the likelihood of purchase. This is especially true in the hospitality industry. The hospitality customer learns to expect certain atmospheric conditions and often makes a purchase decision based on those expectations. A convention hotel is crowded, noisy, and boisterous; avoid it for a quiet weekend. A certain restaurant is dark and quiet, another is bright and happy. The task for the marketer is to create the atmosphere that it is hoped will be perceived.

This is not as easy as it may sound, if only because of the individuality of customers. Many people will not equate the intended atmosphere with the perceived atmosphere simply because we all react differently to lighting, colors, sounds, and temperatures. Once again, this tells us that it is important to understand the target market.

The dimly lighted restaurant is romantic for a young couple; for an older couple it makes reading the menu difficult. The air-conditioned restaurant is refreshing for the waitstaff, cool for the man with a jacket on, and freezing for those in short-sleeved shirts. The finely decorated restaurant is elegant for some; for others, it looks too expensive. The large hotel is "where things happen" for some; for others it is noisy and intimidating. Club Med is where many find there is never a dull moment; others wonder "Why don't they shut up and leave me alone?" The more heterogeneous the customers, the more varied their perceptions will be. Selecting and knowing target markets that are compatible become critical in this situation.

Atmospherics as a Marketing Tool

There are a number of situations where atmospherics can be particularly important as a mar-

The 45-story Chicago Marriott stands just about where it ought to be—right in the middle of things.

The right hotel is never hard to find

The Marriott Hotel people have built their reputation on doing things right.

And one of the things they do most consistently right is to be, somehow, in just the right location for the business you want to conduct, in any given city.

In New York, for instance, Marriott's Essex House is right on Central Park. In Chicago? Right on Michigan Avenue (photo)—and also at O'Hare International Airport. In Kansas City, Cleveland, Miami, L.A. and Rochester, also conveniently right near the airport. In Philadelphia? Right at the edge of the Main Line. Some cities already have several Marriotts.

Atlanta, four. Houston, three. Five in Washington, D.C. And new Marriotts are blooming worldwide. Marriott can now do it right for you in Saudi Arabia, Kuwait, Holland. Even right on the beach in resorts like Acapulco, Barbados, Santa Barbara, and Marco Island.

To reserve at a Marriott where you're headed, call a professional, your travel agent. Or dial toll-free 800-228-9290.

WHEN MARRIOTT DOES IT, THEY DO IT RIGHT.®

Marriott Hotels.

Courtesy of Marriott Corporation

FIGURE 11-4   Emphasising location to affect consumer choice

keting tool. The following pertain especially to hospitality establishments:

1. In situations where the product is purchased and consumed on premise

2. In situations where the seller has numerous design options

3. In situations where atmospherics help to create or increase the buyer's rate of consumption

4. In situations where there are a number of competitors, and atmospherics can be used to differentiate the product
5. In situations where the objective is to attract and hold a particular target market segment
6. In situations where product and price differences are small for products that are very similar
7. In situations where one wants to create a price difference for products that are very similar

Probably nowhere else in the presentation mix does a hospitality marketer have as much opportunity to manipulate tangible clues to increase the tangibility of the product/service mix in the perception of the target market. The decor in a hotel creates perceptions as to the atmosphere of the hotel. The Windsor Court, a five-diamond hotel in New Orleans, has fresh flowers in the lobby and numbered, limited-edition prints in guestrooms (Figure 11-5), while the Travelodge has simply colorful wallpaper. Each does its own job of tangibilizing. The Mirage Hotel in Las Vegas uses atmospherics as a major differentiating feature in the following message in its ads geared toward meeting-planners:

> Undoubtedly, people are influenced by the location of your meeting. What you call distractions, they call attractions. And the Mirage has plenty of them. Here, they can wander through our tropical rainforest to the most elegant casino on the strip. Visit our white tigers, sharks or dolphins.... Or just relax near [our] waterfall, poolside. All between your meetings, of course.

Thus, atmospherics can be used to get attention, create retention, and manipulate perception. Accordingly, atmospherics are a message-creating medium by which marketers say certain things about the establishment. By this means they can communicate to the target market what they intend to offer. They can differentiate from other establishments. Affective states are enhanced by arousing sensations that create a desire for goods, services, and experiences. In this role, atmospherics help to convert behavioral intentions into actual buy-

FIGURE 11-5 Atmospherics in a hotel

ing behavior. Well-orchestrated atmospherics can move buyers into action.

Over approximately the last 20 years there has been a greater emphasis on atmospherics in restaurants. Before that, restaurants tended to be plain and basic in their decor. Almost total emphasis was on prices and the quality of food. There is no doubt that today, given a moderate level of food quality and the right price range, atmosphere can often make or break a restaurant. Even institutional dining rooms have been caught up in the trend and few now look like the army dining halls they used to resemble.

There is a very important warning here, however. Restaurants' atmospheres are likely to have a very fast growth period, early maturity, and quick decline. "Fern bars" (loaded with ferns just as the name implies), for example, which were extremely popular in the 1980s, are becoming obsolete. The public is extremely fickle in this respect and today's "in" decor is tomorrow's "out" decor. Most vulnerable seem to be those restaurants that are also called "theme" or even "atmosphere restaurants," in which the decor follows a particular theme such as Nautical, Western, or Early American. Victoria Station restaurants were an early example of this, with their boxcar theme.

Atmospheres must be continually reevaluated in relation to the changing market, new possibilities, and competitive developments. Its effectiveness can decline because of imitation or changing styles. Management, therefore, must be constantly alert to the need for refreshing or revising atmospheres.

Using atmosphere as a marketing tool for restaurants thus becomes a tricky proposition. This is one area where you really cannot go out and ask customers what their needs are because they can tell you what they like only after they see it.

In hotels, a prime example of the use of atmospherics is the atrium lobby (Figure 11-6), that began with Hyatt Hotels. The story of Hyatt is an excellent, albeit not typical example of the power of atmospherics as a marketing tool:

John Portman, a relatively unknown Atlanta architect, designed the first modern atrium lobby hotel with open-air space, glass elevators, and the accoutrements that are relatively common today. Portman tried to peddle his idea to a number of the large hotel chains. No one bought, and one reason was the cost of heating and cooling such a physical plant. When Portman approached the Pritzkers, owners of Hyatt, they had both the capital and the imagination to support the potential.

The first Hyatt atrium hotel opened in Atlanta to "rave reviews" and international press coverage. Others soon followed and Hyatt was on its way to being a major force to be reckoned with in the hotel industry. Unfortunately for Hyatt, they didn't "own" Portman and Portman didn't own a patent on atrium lobbies. He was soon designing hotels all over the world, as were others who copied the idea.

Atmosphere-Planning

There are numerous other facets of atmospherics that the reader should have no problem identifying, including music, color, lighting, and design. We need, however, to take a more general approach to discussing the marketing elements of atmosphere-planning.

If atmospherics play an important role in the buying process, then we need to apply the same regimen to their planning as we would to any other process of consumer behavior. What atmospherics do, naturally, is create a feeling; that is, the best atmosphere is one that makes the customer "feel good." Feeling good, of course, can take on many dimensions, depending on the purpose and the use of atmosphere— for instance, it can mean exciting, romantic, or relaxed. Our first criterion, then, as usual, is to recognize who the target market is, for example, by asking the following questions:

What is the target market seeking from the buying experience?
What atmospheric variables can fortify the beliefs and emotional reactions buyers are seeking?
Will the resulting atmosphere compete effectively with competitors' atmospheres?

The focal point of each Embassy Suites hotel is a beautiful atrium with lush landscaping, fountains and waterfalls, providing a pleasant environment for free breakfast and complimentary cocktails*. With all suites overlooking the atrium, there are no long walks down dark hallways.

*subject to state and local laws.

FIGURE 11-6   Atrium lobby that creates atmospherics

These are necessary questions, but not easy ones to answer. It is often for lack of answers to these questions that some "great" atmospheres fail (atmospheres considered "great" by the owner or management, the architect, the designer, and often their spouses and friends). Even customers come in and say, "Boy, is this great!" But somehow it doesn't capture the right feeling, create the right emotional reactions, or compete effectively with the competition.

Also, a "failed" atmosphere just may not suit the target market—not an excusable mistake given today's marketing consciousness. Probably the most frequent reason for this occurring is that marketing had minimum input into the decision, that no one took the time to fully analyze the target market.

Another typical case is the one mentioned before of a hotel in New York City:

The new management team refurbished the hotel, including what had been a successful coffee shop. The food and beverage vice-president developed the concept of an authentic French Brasserie, with menu prices at least double what they had previously been. Here, in a 1,400-room hotel, a hamburger was not available to airline crews and other mid-market segments of customers. Although the conception was good, the restaurant turned out to be totally out of touch with the hotel's market and did poorly.

The restaurant was out of touch with the local environment as well. This neighborhood, in Manhattan in the mid-1980s, was awash with T-shirt shops, Irish pubs, and pizza parlors, not upscale restaurants. Local customers were perplexed by the setting.

As in any type of marketing planning, the more homogeneous the target market the easier it will be to design the appropriate atmosphere, and the more heterogeneous the market, the more difficult the task. With more than one target market, as is often the case, there is always the risk of pleasing one while alienating another. Two examples of this are provided in Table 11-1.

It is important to keep in mind that hospitality customers are not just buying, they are also consuming on-premise. "Living" with an atmosphere for two or more hours can provoke reactions very different from those experienced simply walking in and out. After a period of time, noise can seem louder, colors can be annoying, and decor can be distracting. Thus, one must recognize what experience the customer is seeking, not only immediately, but over a period of time. It must also be recognized that emotional reactions can change over the same period of time.

Pre-testing and Research   It would be nice if one could construct an "atmosphere" and pre-test it on the target market. Although scale models are recommended, they are not overly effective for pre-tests simply because one has to live with an atmosphere in order to experience

TABLE 11-1   Examples of Incompatible Market Segments

Different customers with different needs:
During the 1970s the Dunfey Hyannis Hotel on Cape Cod hosted a disparity of customers using the same facility. The hotel was appealing to an upscale transient and meetings customer. The room rates were positioned at the top of the destinations market. The same vice-president of food and beverage who developed the French Brasserie in a New York hotel's coffee shop (described in the text) had a hand in the development of the lounge concept at this resort: Tingles, one of the first "fern bars" of the mid-1970s. Developed to attract young singles, this high-energy lounge was successful from the beginning, drawing hundreds of young partiers on a nightly basis—young partiers very different from the upscale customers in the hotel. Management had a difficult decision to make: Should they reduce profits by closing the lounge to appease the hotel customers?

Luckily, perhaps, the problem solved itself. Fern bars were eclipsed in popularity by discos, and Tingles died a slow death, much to the delight of the rooms customers. Coincidentally, other upscale properties opened on Cape Cod, and many prior Dunfey customers, who remembered the Tingles experience, moved to other accommodations.

Similar customers with different needs:
The Omni Berkshire Place in New York City had a multifaceted food and beverage operation wherein the Rendez-Vous lounge and restaurant occupied the same room. The Rendez-Vous was *the* place for Madison Avenue advertising executives to meet after work. The lounge portion of the room generated large profits for the hotel, at the expense of the customer that wanted a quiet dinner. Again, profits from the lounge were too lucrative for management to make a significant change. Customers desiring a quiet evening went elsewhere. In an attempt to satisfy these customers, management created Le Gallery, a well-appointed dining room toward the back of the current restaurant.

Le Gallery failed miserably. Not because it didn't create a quiet atmosphere (it did), but because it did not make the decision to dine in peace easy. Customers still had to come to the front of the restaurant, observe the raucous behavior of advertising executives drinking in the lounge, and "find" their way to the quiet of Le Gallery.

it realistically. Some hotel companies, notably Marriott and Holiday Inn, have constructed full-size models of prospective hotel rooms and have utilized actual customers to provide feedback on the rooms' utility, not so much for atmospherics as for room content, design, and arrangement.

Although full pre-testing is usually prohibitively expensive for individual units (not necessarily for multiple units of the same theme, such as hotel rooms or multiple restaurants), and customers are unable to articulate what an atmosphere should be, it would be a critical mistake to ignore customer feedback. Presenting a new atmosphere should be followed by immediate research on customer reaction, rather than waiting until the concept has failed. Small changes, such as lighting or sound, can often turn a disaster into a triumph.

In one example, a restaurant chain hired a research firm to survey its customers before and after a major change in decor. The research firm planned to conduct the "after" survey in the first two months after the work was completed. The chain's management, however, disagreed and said, "Let's wait six months and let them get used to it." Of course, by that time the people who liked the change would still be there, those who didn't like it would be long gone, and the research would have lesser value.

Atmosphere is always a factor in a purchase situation, whether it be at the local pub, a ski lodge, or a resort in the Caribbean. It is not only a presentation of the offering but also a powerful competitive tool. More research is needed to understand just how different atmospheric elements work and what messages they communicate. Atmospherics call for conscious, not casual, planning because they represent tremendous potential for differential advantage when there are few other ways to achieve it.

Employees

It should be more than obvious that employees are an important part of the presentation mix. In some cases they may be the most important part. The hospitality industry is one in which

management, the entire property, the service, and the quality of the product can be judged in the consumer's mind by employee contact, sometimes even by a single incident.

In Chapter 2 we discussed the important concept of internal marketing and the notion of "selling" the job to employees. We will not repeat that discussion here, although it is pertinent to the subject. Instead, the thrust of the present discussion of the topic will lie in the definition of the presentation mix: the tangibilization of the product/service mix at the right place and time.

The initial tangibilization is in the presentation itself—the appearance of employees. Not much argument is encountered when one says that public-contact employees in a hotel or restaurant should be neat, well-groomed, personable, and appropriately dressed or uniformed. This is usually paramount. Customers arriving at the front door of an establishment are no longer looking at the architectural design. What they see is the employees who greet them: the doorman, parking valet, bellhop, desk clerk, host or hostess, waiter or waitress.

On the other hand, as with the physical plant and atmospherics, there are many times when the staff's being well-groomed not only is unnecessary but also is not expected. A guest at a budget motel doesn't really expect to see a smiling "Hyatt girl" in uniform behind the desk. A family-run neighborhood restaurant gains much of its charm from family members working in various forms of dress. Tangibilization sets no standards; it simply implies the presentation, in whatever form, of the desired product to the target market.

What this means is that employees should "fit" the presentation mix. For example, the French Brasserie, in the hotel example given earlier, was staffed with 15-year veteran, unionized coffee shop employees. The result: surly waiters from a coffee shop posing as young people in the "brasserie" model of service. The staff didn't fit the concept or the intended market.

These people immediately became, if only temporarily, the product itself. They were the physical manifestation of what the establishment had to offer. Most people accept this premise. What many don't realize is that it is not just that employees should "look good," it is also that they are part of the marketing team, and this means they should also "look right." Looked at this way, employee appearance takes on a slightly different perspective and should receive more attention than it does sometimes.

What about casual or noncontact employees, such as maids, engineers, servicepeople, maintenance workers, chefs and cooks? How does their presentation affect the tangibilization of the product? Consider the following analogy:

Few airline passengers see the cockpit crew except for a goodbye when deplaning or when walking through the terminal. The crews almost always look neat and well-groomed and have all the other desired qualities. So far, so good.

Now, suppose you stop for dinner at a restaurant on the way home. While waiting in the cocktail lounge, you see an airline captain—neat, well-groomed, and all the rest—sitting at the bar and drinking what looks like a double martini on the rocks. How would you feel? Chances are you might never fly that airline again. Perhaps he is only on his way home as well; perhaps he is only drinking ginger ale while waiting for someone. It wouldn't matter, would it? The tangibilization of airline safety just became "something else." This, of course, is why airline crews are forbidden to drink alcohol beverages when in uniform.

The point made by this analogy is the same one we have made numerous times before. It is the perception that counts, not the reality, because for the consumer, perception is the reality. Think back to a hotel or restaurant situation, where every single employee is part of the marketing team. Some managers allow employee appearance to slip when business gets bad. They want to save on the cost of uniforms as well as laundry and cleaning. The man who comes to fix the TV is in jeans and a torn shirt, and the maids slough around in old slippers—these are signs of the beginning of the product death spiral described in Chapter 10.

"Smile training" plays a role in the presentation mix as well. Greeting guests, calling them by name, offering to help, and all the rest that goes with generally accepted public contact is important. It is not always easy to extend this practice to noncontact employees. Frequently these people are of different ethnic backgrounds and may speak limited English. But smiling is an international language—often, all it takes—and it is nothing short of amazing what a smile can do for a tired, irritable, unhappy, or discontented customer. While not sufficient, smiling is a necessary requisite in employee presentation.

Employees as a Marketing Tool

With the acceptance of *total quality management* (TQM) principles by some of the leading hotel companies such as Ritz-Carlton and Marriott, the importance of the role of all employees in marketing is being recognized. TQM and employee empowerment require a change in the culture of an organization and include total employee involvement, a customer focus, continuous improvement of operations, and a spirit of teamwork. One company that does this well is described in Table 11-2.

Employees are one of the most powerful parts of the presentation mix and can be used to tangibilize the product, as shown in Figure 11-7. This is commonly accepted wisdom in the hospitality business. The only problem seems to come in its execution. Management needs to be constantly aware of this critical aspect of the marketing concept and to understand the motivations of employees. For example,

In one case, a waiter received the "employee of the month reward" because he came in during a snowstorm, slept in the hotel, and worked long hours to compensate for the shortage of other employees. When asked privately why he did this, he said, "I knew there would be a shortage of help and I could make lots of money. I made $600 in two days."

In another case, an uneducated maid with three children and an absent father, who had trouble paying the rent, also won the employee of the month award. Her reward? An IBM Selectric typewriter!

Understanding employees' needs is every bit as important as understanding customers' needs!

TABLE 11-2　Peabody Hotels Gets Employee Involvement

A small chain of hotels in the United States has taken a dramatic lead in the level of service offered by its employees. Peabody Hotels, with locations in Memphis and Orlando, has taken the term "service" to a new level. Faced with increased supply in both markets, and limited name-brand recognition (as opposed to Hyatt, Marriott, etc.), Peabody Hotels made a strategic decision to invest in its employees. Instead of cutting costs (product death spiral), or spending money on advertising and promotions, Peabody Hotels gave the customers what they wanted—good service.

Peabody Hotels faced the same labor problems that everyone else does—turnover, multi-ethnic staff, limited educations, etc. Across the board, all employees went out of their way to satisfy the needs of customers. Repeated stays in these hotels showed similar results—impeccable service.

One common theme comes from repeated employee interviews—the company cares. Many companies have "smile" programs, where everyone wears a button for two weeks and management feels they are addressing customers' needs. Peabody Hotels have gone further. Its management trained employees not only to be nice to customers, *but to be nice to the other employees!* The good will naturally flows to the customers.

There are thousands of first-class hotel rooms in the Orlando area. The transient and group customer has hundreds of options of similar products from which to choose. Peabody Hotels has differentiated from the competition by offering superior service and, incidentally, runs some of the best occupancy and average rates in the area, without a national brand affiliation.

Customers

How can customers constitute a marketing tool? Think about it. When you go into a restaurant or bar, do you look to see who else is there? Of course you do, and not just to see whether there is someone you know. You look at the type of people, how they are dressed, how they behave, and how they look.

This is an area where hospitality truly departs from manufactured goods. We buy goods without too much concern for who else is buying them, unless we want an opinion on a major item like a computer. When we buy a hospitality product, we are concerned because we share space, noise, atmosphere, and other elements with people who are there to consume the same product or service.

Consider two extreme cases to make the point:

The Ritz-Carlton in Boston once did not allow in its dining rooms or lounges men without coats and ties, or women in slacks. In fact, if dressed too casually, it was about all you could do to walk through the lobby without feeling out of place. The Ritz-Carlton wanted only a certain class of people in its hotel, and one of their means of discriminat-

ing was through clothing requirements. They have since relaxed these stringent rules, but still expect conservative dress. The presentation of the customers is clear.

The other extreme is at the opposite end of the scale, a blue-collar bar. If a man goes there in a three-piece suit, regular patrons will look at him in a way that will make him feel out of place, if he doesn't already.

In between, there are many variations on the theme. No longer, in the vast majority of places, do hospitality establishments discriminate by dress. People who wear jeans drive Mercedes, and people who wear three-piece suits may not be able to afford them. So we use other means to judge the patronage and to see if we "belong." In effect, the *customers become part of the product.* They are a tangible manifestation of the product/service being offered. We can tell a great deal about that product/service by looking at the people who use it. In effect, we are asking, "Are we in this target market?"

Positioning the Customer Mix

Does this mean we "kick out" those who don't fit the right image? Not necessarily. What it means

OUR MAIDS ARE WOMEN. OUR BUTLERS ARE WOMEN.
EVEN OUR DOORMEN ARE WOMEN.

Heaven forbid, but have the women taken control of our hotel?

We think not, although, that wouldn't be a bad idea. After all, if women can run rings round men, they can easily run a hotel.

Which is why, at The Pan Pacific: we've engaged rather a lot of them. *(Never a dull moment here!)*

The truth is, our female butlers tend to be just that bit more attentive than their male counterparts elsewhere.

Our maids seem to add that feminine touch to caring for your clients' rooms.

As for our Doorwomen?

Well, put it this way, your clients will never have to wait around too long for a taxi.

And, as for you; we guarantee that 48 hours after your clients check out, your commission cheque is on the way.

The women in our Accounts Department will make sure of that.

THE PAN PACIFIC HOTEL
Singapore

FIGURE 11-7   Employees' part in the presentation mix

is that by our positioning, the level of the product/service, or the target markets we designate, we establish the types of customers we expect to come to our establishment. Would you expect to see a bus tour unloading at a Ritz-Carlton hotel as you were checking in yourself? Consider the following incident:

A couple went to a resort in the Bahamas for their honeymoon. They chose this destination because the brochures had pictured it as a quiet, remote place on the ocean, with individual bungalows and a romantic setting. When they arrived they found 85 percent of the rooms occupied by a tour group that was drinking heavily, carousing most of the day and night, and making an incredible amount of noise. When they went to the dining room for dinner, they found that it looked like a university dining hall. They had to wait an hour before reaching the front of the line. They were then told they would have to share a table with a couple from the tour group. It is not surprising that they checked out the next morning and found another resort.

Today, except at the highest and lowest ends of the scale, we are accustomed to seeing people of all kinds in hotels and restaurants. Yet it is a task of marketing to attempt to sort out these groups so as to establish specific target markets and cater to their needs and wants. It does this, in fact, by catering to the needs and wants of the specific target markets and not to the needs of those not targeted. A business travelers' hotel doesn't feature cribs, baby-sitters, or entertainment for children, although it may have them available for select instances. A family hotel doesn't feature conference rooms. A gourmet restaurant doesn't offer children's portions. McDonald's, at least in the United States, doesn't serve alcoholic beverages.

At the root of market segmentation is the question of what sorts of customers should be served. Although many hotels and restaurants would like to cater to one customer segment, economics dictate other action. If the property is unable to obtain enough of the most desired target customers, a decision must be made: either accept other customers or don't pay the mortgage.

Once a decision is made to accept alternative market segments, marketing needs to be involved. For example:

A midsized hotel decided to accept an airline crew contract, to provide a base of business for the next few years. The introduction of the crew business could have been traumatic for both employees and costumers. The hotel was insightful,

however, from a marketing perspective. A separate airline check-in desk was created to alleviate congestion at the front desk during busy periods. Airline floors were established, separating the crew from other customers. An airline crew lounge was carved out of an existing suite, creating a separate area for crews to wait for their airport transportation. The result, two segments of customers using the same hotel with no negative interaction.

The customer mix is an issue that must be addressed if an establishment hopes to avoid conflict between market segments, as in the honeymoon example above. The hospitality industry is a high public-contact business, where even the customers interact and share services. These customers contribute to the atmosphere of the establishment. As such, they should be aware of some of the rules regarding dress, decorum, behavior, and courtesies. Management cannot mandate these rules, but it can create awareness by careful selection of the target markets.

Refusal to admit people, as was done in the "old days," is today both unethical and illegal in most countries. Today customer presentation is done by good marketing that identifies to the marketplace the positioning of the property and the kinds of people who go there (Figure 11-8). This takes careful planning.

Market segments that are fully compatible are not easy to find, and an even greater problem for hotels and restaurants that are large in size. With many rooms to fill, low demand for the rooms, and a perishable product, many properties have to respond to two or more different segments, which may or may not mix well. When they do not mix, it is wise to keep them separated. For example, a hotel might have primarily business customers during the week and families on the weekend, with children who love to run around the hotel.

Sometimes it is possible to separate by using different sections of a restaurant. Some hotels try to separate by using different floors, as in the airline case above. This doesn't always work because sooner or later the two groups are likely to come together in the public spaces.

We know who you are at The Lafayette Hotel in Boston.

When you frequent The Lafayette, we may get a bit familiar and start calling you by name.

While such personal attention could be deemed a minor mark of manners, we deem it a matter of major importance.

Because as a Swissôtel, we strive to pursue perfection down to the last detail.

That's why we'll deliver your favorite newspaper *before* you awake. Why we'll take note of your favorite foods and snacks and remember to offer them when you return.

And why—especially when home is far away—our familiarity with your name will breed a comforting sense of contentment.

For reservations, call 617-451-2600 in Boston. Outside Boston, call 800-621-9200 or your travel agent.

Other fine hotels of the Swissôtel group in the United States:
The Drake Hotel, New York
The Swiss Grand Hotel, Chicago

THE LAFAYETTE HOTEL
BOSTON
swissôtel

FIGURE 11-8   Emphasizing the customer mix

Pricing is another, and simpler, method to separate groups, as long as it doesn't lead to the alienation of a desired segment.

The best customer mix, sometimes called the ideal business mix, varies from one establishment to another. The important point is that it shouldn't be allowed to "just happen."

Hospitality marketers need to be concerned about who their customers are because customers help to define the character of the organization. Selective targeting is mandatory for the most potentially successful operation. The customer is tangible representation of the product/service.

*He offered me
his red leather chair and said
"Congratulations, Mr. Chairman."
We were in the boardroom.*

Or was it The St. Regis?

The St. Regis
NEW YORK

AN ITT SHERATON LUXURY HOTEL

FIFTH AVENUE AT 55TH STREET, NEW YORK, N.Y. 10022•TEL 212.753.4500, TELEX 148368, FAX 212.787.3447
FOR RESERVATIONS CALL TOLL FREE 800.759.7550 OR YOUR TRAVEL SPECIALIST

Courtesy of ITT Sheraton Corporation

FIGURE 11-8   (continued)

Price

Prices are the most visible and flexible part of the presentation mix. This is of critical importance. Flexibility means, at least in the United States, where prices are not regulated, that prices can be changed at any time—on a whim, in response to competition, to make a deal, or just to fill more rooms or sell more steaks. Visibility means that the use of price to influence the consumer is rapid; in some cases, instant. This flexibility and visibility provides management with a versatile and useful sales tool.

The flip side is that price flexibility can lead to misuse. Using price flexibility strictly as a revenue generator or a financial tool ignores the fact that pricing is best used as a marketing tool. The visibility of prices makes them the most tangible aspect of the presentation mix. Prices undeniably say something about the product. Prices are a critical factor in the risk/return trade-off and the value/expectation relationship discussed in Chapter 1. This means that prices should invariably be consumer-based according to the target markets.

The development of pricing strategies will be discussed in Chapter 12. Here we extract only minimally from that discussion to place pricing in its appropriate place in the presentation mix. What we need to keep in mind is that the ultimate objective of pricing strategy, from a marketing viewpoint, is to present the desired tangible surrogate of the product/service. Chapter 12 deals with how we go about doing that, along with the financial ramifications of pricing. The discussion here deals only with the end result.

One of the objectives of pricing concerns how we want to influence the customer—that is, what tangible presentation we wish to achieve. Because customers use price to make judgments too readily when other information is unavailable, price is a potent force in creating perception. That perception represents reality to consumers until they learn otherwise. Because price is so visible, it may be the only variable on which a judgment is made. If that judgment is negative, there is a good chance that consumers will go no further and will not buy, and that their negative judgment will be a lasting one. Our first decision, then, is what it is that we want price actually to say to the marketplace.

In the above sense, price is a potent force in positioning either a product or a brand in the marketplace. Because of this, much of the hotel industry has segmented the market by price. What this strategy says is that there are segments of the market that buy hotel rooms based on price. This is a product-oriented strategy

seeking a market. Thus, if price says something about product, the effect is to position a low-priced property as an inferior product.

No one, admittedly or intentionally, buys an inferior product. On the other hand, we can utilize price as the tangible symbol of the "bargain" or "good value" that our product represents. This is the appropriate use of price in the presentation mix. Instead of segmenting by price, we segment by benefit bundle and use price to represent that bundle. This is a fine but an important distinction: It is the difference between being product-oriented and marketing-oriented. Take the example of Motel 6 and their radio advertising:

> "Hi. Tom Bodett here for Motel 6 with a comparison. You know, in some ways, a Motel 6 reminds me of one of those big, fancy hotels. They've got beds; we've got beds. They've got sinks and showers; by golly, we've got 'em too. There are differences, though. You can't get a hot facial mud pack at Motel 6 like those fancy joints. And you won't find French-milled soap or avocado body balm. You will, however, find a clean, comfortable room, and the lowest rates nationwide. Under 21 bucks in most places. A lot less in some, a little more in others, but always the lowest price of any national chain. And always a heck of a deal.
>
> "Motel 6 has 400 locations from coast to coast. And we operate every darn one of 'em, which means they're always clean and comfortable.
>
> "Oh sure, it'll be rough to survive one night without avocado body balm or French-milled soap, but maybe the money you save'll help you get over it. It always works for me.
>
> "I'm Tom Bodett for Motel 6."
>
> Occupancy rates rose dramatically after the successful advertising campaign that effectively showed the price/value advantage of Motel 6.[3]

Another customer objective of pricing is to use it to differentiate the product from that of the competition. This is something more than price segments because it assumes that the competition is competing for the same market segment. Customers use price to make a judg-

---

[3]Mark W. Cunningham, Chekitan S. Dev, "Strategic Marketing: A Lodging 'End Run,'" *Cornell Hotel and Restaurant Administration Quarterly*, August, 1992, pp. 36–43.

ment about value; they use price to develop expectations; they use price to assess risk. All these uses are part of the trade-off decision process of the consumer. Realizing this, marketers or price-setters have a complex situation on their hands. The tools for dealing with this situation are discussed in Chapter 12.

Summary

The presentation mix of the hospitality product makes a statement to the marketplace. It consists of the physical plant, location, atmospherics, employees, customers, and price. Especially where the product is abstract and intangible, as it is with services and as it is with customer experiences, the presentation mix may be all the customer has to "hang on" to.

As with products, the presentation mix is the hospitality marketer's major tool for communicating with the customer in the sense of nontraditional marketing. Using tangible aspects to communicate with the customer in the sense of traditional marketing is part of the communication mix, which will be discussed in later chapters.

Discussion Questions

1. How is the physical plant different for hospitality presentations than for consumer goods? Give some examples from personal experience.
2. Discuss the limitations and roles of location in the presentation mix.
3. Define and discuss how atmospherics would influence your choice of a restaurant.
4. Describe how the customer integrates with the product/service mix. Give positive and negative examples.
5. What is the role of pricing in the presentation mix?
6. Establish the advantage of recognizing the customer in the design of the physical plant of a hospitality product.
7. Case 11-1 describes a decision on customer mix. Evaluate the variables involved that impact upon this decision.
8. Evaluate Case 11-2 in terms of the presentation mix for a restaurant.
9. Case 11-3 concerns a decision on how to position in the marketplace for a new hotel. Consider the alternatives and the impact of each on the presentation mix.

✔ Case 11-1
Le Chateau Frontenac[4]

Le Chateau Frontenac Hotel in Quebec City, Quebec, Canada was a classic "grande dame" hotel. Built in 1893 it had always epitomized elegance, architectural beauty, and the grandeur of what a hotel could be before modern construction overtook the industry. Simply standing in the lobby with its high atrium and regal tapestries, one could feel the charm of another era.

The main competition for Le Chateau Frontenac were the more modern, convention-type hotels of Loew's Concorde (450 rooms), Hilton International (540 rooms), Radisson (375 rooms), and Holiday Inn (300 rooms). All of these had been built in the last 15 years and none had the charm of the Frontenac, but they did have more efficient facilities and physical plants. While they all targeted the business traveler, summer tourists, and group business, as did the Frontenac, the more modern hotels did not attract the "traditionalist" who was drawn to the Frontenac.

Le Chateau Frontenac had undergone numerous refurbishings in its lifetime and was due for another. A decision was made, at the same time, to add 66 more rooms to the existing 544. The refurbishing and addition were done over a six-year period at a cost of $50 million with the new rooms replicas of the old ones. Le Chateau Frontenac now stood in its finest glory—but with a sizeable debt, 610 rooms, and a need to fill them.

Hotel Demand

Hotel demand, mainly from May through October, came largely from tourists and tours to Quebec City, the most classic French city in North America, steeped in history and tradition, as was Le Chateau Frontenac. For culture buffs, there was much to see, including great antique stores and outstanding restaurants. Convention season was September and October, with the rest of the year mostly business travel. Le Chateau Frontenac had 85 to 98 percent occupancy during the tourist and convention seasons at $145 ADR, and 50 to 55 percent the remainder of the year at $125 ADR.

With 66 more rooms now, management wondered how to increase revenue to pay their cost. November to April offered little hope since the market was static at that time. From May through August the hotel took only upscale tour groups, at an average rate of $130 to $150. Anxious to fill its extra rooms during high season, management contacted a group of tour operators. These contacts revealed that the hotel could capture additional tour groups and easily fill the hotel in high season if it offered a $99 rate. This meant about 75 rooms sold per day for the 100 days—rooms that otherwise would likely remain empty. Management called an executive staff meeting to discuss the wisdom of this decision.

---

[4]Alex Kassatly, Executive Assistant Manager at Le Chateau Frontenac at the time, contributed the information for this case.

✔ Case 11-2
Hot Tomato's

"I'm becoming very frustrated," admitted Assistant Manager John Daniels of the trendy new Northampton, Massachusetts restaurant, Hot Tomato's.

"On the one hand, I see a very innovative concept that has proven both successful and profitable and shows tremendous potential for growth in the future. Then I see a company that has succeeded despite its trial-and-error approach. You should see how decisions get made around here, totally on a whim without any substance to back them up. This is really beginning to bother me. If we don't do something soon, we'll start to lose our market to other restaurants in town. I've had a suspicion over the last few months that things are beginning to slide. The worst part is that the owner is not concerned about a decrease in the number of covers. He almost seems oblivious to anything but his past successes and is only motivated by his ego."

History

An entrepreneur named Tomas Renarro once purchased a pizza parlor on Ann Street in Hartford, Connecticut. The owner's goal was to create a small, Italian restaurant that offered a limited number of unique and unusual dishes in addition to the ever-popular pizzas and calzones. Renarro was confident of the quality of his cuisine since he had spent many years perfecting his technique in establishments around the world.

Renarro opened the new establishment under the name "Hot Tomato's," based on a friend's suggestion at a party one night. The interior of the restaurant was left essentially untouched and the original formica booths remained in place. Hot Tomato's opened in Hartford quietly, without fanfare, and met with great success. Many customers returned to the restaurant, which now sported funky pink walls and an outrageous collection of tomato prints.

Tomas Renarro soon realized that he had a success on his hands. He was pleased to see customers line up outside his 44-seat restaurant, and was encouraged by the rave reviews he heard when circulating among the guests each evening. Renarro had learned to refine his menu concept by soliciting customer feedback and eliminating unpopular menu items. Eventually he decided that he had perfected his concept and set out to find another location to test his idea further.

Hot Tomato's–Northampton

Renarro discovered a bankrupt Italian restaurant in Northampton, in western Massachusetts, a town of some 30,000 population. He purchased the building and began renovation to accommodate his plans, including the creation of the new 38-seat Cafe Pomodoro. Naturally, the facility was decorated with the trademark hot pink walls and tomato print motif.

Renarro decreased the size of the original kitchen by 50 percent and renovated the unfinished basement to increase his overall capacity. The new level housed a private dining room with separate kitchen, storage closets, and employee changing areas. The majority of the basement was converted into a manufacturing base for the production of homemade pastas and sauces to supply both the Hartford and the Northampton restaurants.

Hot Tomato's quietly opened its second restaurant in Northampton two years later and quickly became popular with locals and visitors alike. With Tomas Rennaro cooking and continuing to perfect his recipes, Hot Tomato's slowly evolved from its pizza parlor beginnings into a more sophisticated establishment. Along with the growth in the menu, the wine list expanded from six to almost 60 selections as the restaurant's popularity continued to grow. As in Hartford, Renarro fine-tuned the Northampton operation while cooking in the kitchen each night and by checking with the customers personally to ensure that all was satisfactory.

As time progressed, Renarro found a chef who was considered extremely talented. To Renarro's relief, he quickly mastered the proven recipes and turned his expertise with seafood and French preparations toward solidifying the chain's budding reputation as a producer of new and intriguing dishes.

Atmosphere

By any assessment, the interior design of Hot Tomato's was a major contributor to the success of the establishment. Upon entering the cafe, the customer was forced to recognize that Hot Tomato's was "different"—hot pink walls and wacky tomato wall prints accentuated by overflowing flower boxes and dark green ceilings that gave the area the ambiance of an outdoor cafe. An actual awning hung from the ceiling to separate the kitchen from the cafe, and oversized windows exposed the cafe to passersby.

The cafe seated 26 people at 13 tables, although the capacity was easily increased by producing additional red vinyl-covered aluminum chairs. The floors were carpeted in dark red and the tables were clothed in matching linen under individual glass tops.

There was an antipasto bar and a wine and dessert display to the left of the front entrance. The kitchen area was beyond these displays and completely exposed, indicating perhaps that the chef had nothing to hide. To the right, patrons passed a coat rack and a bench that served as the waiting area. On busy weekend nights, this space proved drastically inadequate to accommodate the long lines of diners who spilled out into the service aisles, and many guests waited to be paged at the bar next door.

The decor of the dining room was very similar to the cafe, although somewhat upgraded. A more formal place setting including two glasses and a linen napkin, plus white vinyl chairs. High-gloss wooden floors completed the transformation from cafe to restaurant.

The dining room waitstaff wore traditional black and white, while the cafe servers sported Hot Tomato's T-shirts. In the kitchen, everyone wore the colorful T-shirts, with only the chef dressed in traditional kitchen whites.

To say that ambiance was key to the success of the restaurant would be an understatement. Without discounting the quality of the food, Hot Tomato's was undoubtably trendy, upbeat, and fun. In more ways than one, Hot Tomato's left its customers with a good taste in their mouth.

Hours of Operation

Hot Tomato's opened its doors at 5:00 P.M. each evening and closed the dining room at 9:00 P.M. and the cafe at 10:00 P.M., from Sunday through Thursday nights. On Fridays and Saturdays, the dining room closed at 10:00 P.M. and the cafe an hour later. The cafe was originally open for lunch with a limited menu, but Renarro discontinued it for what he deemed a lack of interest.

The establishment's reservation policy was confusing to almost everyone. Simply stated, the restaurant accepted reservations for parties of six or more, from the hours 5:00–7:00 P.M. only. Although well-intentioned, the specifics as well as the intent of this policy were unclear to both employees and customers alike.

The Menu

After cooking for many years in kitchens around the world, Tomas Renarro was confident of his culinary skill and creativity. The Hot Tomato's menu offered a few of the traditional Italian favorites such as lasagna, but Renarro was more proud of some of his unique creations. The restaurant's booming success was also credited to the fact that many of the local residents had never before sampled this somewhat nouvelle-style Italian cuisine.

There were two separate menus for the dining room and the cafe, respectively, although some items overlapped. Guests in the cafe were presented with both, but dining room customers could not order from the cafe menu. Despite this confusion, the system helped identify those agreeable to a $5 minimum and those just looking for a snack.

After a while, Renarro changed the system. When he realized that the overwhelming demand on weekend nights had created a seller's market, he discontinued the cafe menu on Fridays and Saturdays and served from the dining room menu in both rooms. The regular cafe clientele was not pleased, since they had grown accustomed to the cafe menu, and the regular dining room customers were confused if they happened to be escorted to tables in the cafe. The staff was not overly enthusiastic about the weekend change, but the cafe servers were noticeably cheered by the promise of increased tips due to higher menu prices.

Renarro eventually decided to reprint the menus, since they were mounted on a piece of oaktag that had proven less than durable and costly to reproduce. He also used this opportunity to eliminate slow-moving items and replace them with new inspirations. The revised menu prices ranged from $9.50 for a complete pasta dinner, including garden salad and Italian bread, to a high of $18 for some of the more costly specials created by the chef. The menu was a bit more expensive than the area competition, but Renarro justified this by preparing all his food from scratch.

Hot Tomato's did not have a full liquor license, but offered an extensive selection of beers, wines, and bottled waters, with a strong emphasis on Italian products. The staff was surprisingly adept at suggesting suitable wines, and the list itself was both extensive and reasonable, although Renarro did stock a small supply of special bottles in the $100–$200 price range.

Clientele

The Hot Tomato's clientele was a diverse crowd with a strong following among baby boomers. Assistant Manager John Daniels felt that many people visited Hot Tomato's on a whim, attracted by the bright neon. He thought that others had opted to take a friend's recommendation and become enchanted with the unusual ambiance and cuisine. Some customer research determined that diners hailed from throughout the county, although a surprising number were from the eastern part of the state. Understandably, cafe customers were observed to be younger than dining room guests.

The Competition

There were a number of different restaurants in the Northampton area. The local Yellow Pages listed 47 establishments in Northampton alone, not one of which featured a menu even remotely similar to that of Hot Tomato's. However, 13 offered a comparable level of service and a high-quality food product, as well as their own unique atmosphere.

In addition to the 13 competitors, three additional establishments were slated to open before the end of the year. The first new restaurant planned to feature grilled items and was located just off Main Street in the downtown area. This 98-seat facility had targeted the substantial yuppie market and was aiming for a September grand opening. The second restaurant was on Main Street and was to be an Italian restaurant operated by the owners of two successful pizza parlors in neighboring Amherst. Many particulars such as capacity and menu focus were not yet known, but it was expected that the new facility would be more likely to compete with the cafe, if it competed at all. The final restaurant would be located in the now-vacant Northampton train station. The establishment was designed to be part of a marketplace including apartments and was actively supported by the town of Northampton as a future source of employment. Specifics of this proposed facility were also unknown.

Promotional Activities

Thus far, the promotion of Hot Tomato's had been limited at best. The opening of both the cafe and the dining room had been intentionally low-key, but the customer traffic continued to increase as the staff became more efficient. Newspaper and radio advertising had been kept to an absolute minimum in accordance with the owner's policy. However, an occasional commercial was heard on one of the local radio stations, and print advertisements appeared infrequently.

Management felt that the restaurant's reliance on word-of-mouth advertising had proven most successful and that advertising dollars could be better spent elsewhere. However, Daniels believed that the majority of the potential market was unaware of Hot Tomato's.

Tomas Renarro did agree to finance the production of a small brochure, although no effort was made to distribute it other than as an in-house giveaway. The brochure contained no menu information, although it did publicize the hours of operation and the availability of catering facilities.

Conclusion

Later that day, Daniels continued his musings.

"I keep seeing things happen at the restaurant that I know are confusing the customer, and yet the owner and everybody else don't seem to care. A couple of weeks ago, Mr. Renarro walked in after not being around for a while and decided to make major additions to the number of chairs in the dining room. Now the customers down on the floor are squeezed into the next table.

"Next, he decided not to offer the cafe menu on weekend nights anymore. On the last four Fridays I have worked, I've turned away 10–15 parties because they couldn't get the cafe menu. This usually happens when the cafe is empty, making the situation even worse. I know that revenues have increased, but how many people do we have to offend just to make a few extra bucks? And once we've turned them away, do they ever come back?

"There have been a lot of little changes, but the biggest has got to be the new menu Mr. Renarro is introducing in a month or so. I'm all for a new menu, but he has discontinued some of our best sellers and added some personal favorites that have not done well as specials. He doesn't bother to reference the sales abstracts and won't even ask the cooks what sells and what doesn't.... Each month the financial sheets reflect an increase in revenue, but I'm not sure that these increases are the result of the changes that Mr. Renarro made in the last few months. What really worries me is this: What will happen when Mr. Renarro runs out of things to change or our market becomes bored with our product?"

✔ Case 11-3
Holiday Inn Enters Salzburg[5]

Walter Foeger looked at the stack of information before him. His new Holiday Inn, now under renovation, would open in about a year in Salzburg, Austria. Who would be the market and what would be the positioning of the hotel were at the top of his mind. He had to make a decision soon, before the renovation went much further.

Walter had negotiated an "open" management contract with Holiday Inn Worldwide (HIW), based in Atlanta, Georgia, USA. "Open" meant that he had the option to position mid-market as a Holiday Inn, or up-market as a Holiday Inn Crowne Plaza. He was fully aware that HIW preferred a Crowne Plaza, the upscale hotel in its product line. But Walter had no illusions. He had observed the positioning problems of some of the other Crowne Plazas in Europe, such as the one in Amsterdam, and wasn't sure that an upscale position was the right one for the Holiday Inn in Salzburg. He was investing a lot of his resources in his first hotel and wanted to be sure of its success.

As a Crowne Plaza—which tries to be a five-star property in Europe, although a three- to four-star in the United States—Walter knew he would have to build a better product with more amenities. He was willing to commit the resources to do this if the market called for it, but that wasn't his greatest worry. As a man who had made his money in importing and exporting, he was well aware of the need to reach the right market segments and to position to offer the best value in the product class.

Walter had calculated that renovating to a basic Holiday Inn would cost him about 1,200,000 ATS per room, while a Crowne Plaza would cost him about 1,600,000 ATS per room, in order to compete in the upscale market.[6]

The size of the hotel was already established and configured for 199 rooms, including seven suites. What was still in doubt were the choice of room furnishings and the quality and type of public space, food and beverage outlets, meeting rooms, recreation facilities, and other services. The difference in construction cost of $7,000,000 meant to Walter Foeger a higher average ADR of at least $35.[7]

"Can I do this in this market?" he wondered, as he pondered the information that had been collected for him.

Location

Salzburg, Austria was located in the heart of Europe, no more than a two-hour flight from the farthest major European city, London (Exhibit 11-3-1). It was in the middle of Austria, capital of the Salzburg province, and had a population of about 135,000.

Salzburg was an interesting area for tourism because of its historical and cultural significance. The city also contained 12 conference or exhibition centers. Approximately 30 fairs occurred in the city each year, but only four really affected the hotel business. Salzburg also had very heavy motorcoach traffic, but very few stopped overnight. There was an excellent variety of tourist packages and a large choice of cultural highlights, such as all-day excursions in "Salzburger Land" and Mozart events.

The Salzburg economy was generally strong, with unemployment less than three percent. Approximately 120 companies in Salzburg had annual gross revenues of over $6,000,000.

The soon-to-be Holiday Inn's location in the city center, opposite the Congresshall and the Mirabellgarden, was considered to be a unique selling point. It was one kilometer from the train station and seven kilometers from the airport. The downtown area was within easy walk-

---

[5]Karsten Rosel, Manager–International Sales, Holiday Inn Worldwide, Wiesbaden, Germany at the time, contributed the information for this case. Some facts have been altered to facilitate the use of the case.

[6]At the time of writing, 100 ATS (Austrian Schilling) equalled approximately 8.8 US$, 14.2 German DM, and 5 GBP. For ease in using the case, other figures are given in U.S. dollars converted at .088 US$ = 1 ATS or, conversely, 11.36 ATS = 1 US$.

[7]Walter used the old rule of thumb of $1 per $1,000 construction cost.

EXHIBIT 11-3-1   Salzburg, Austria

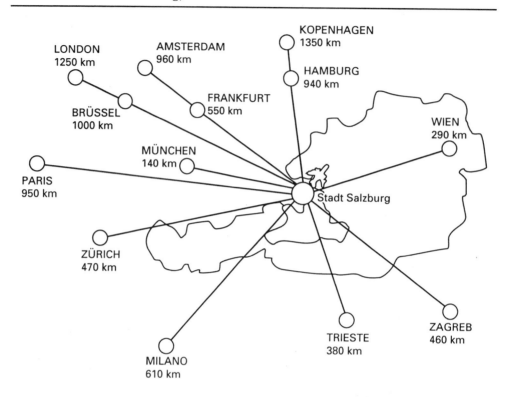

ing distance. The property had originally been the long-standing 208-room Hotel Pitter, a well-known three- to four-star hotel that had fallen on hard times. Walter Foeger had maintained the existing frame of the building but had gutted the interior for renovation.

The Hotel

The preliminary plans for the renovated and refurbished five-story hotel showed the following configurations:

Rooms:
7 suites
36 standard
  double/double
7 executive standard
61 queen
8 executive queen
5 king
15 executive king

58 single
2 wheelchair accessible

Recreation:
1 ballroom
Indoor swimming
  pool
Sauna, steam bath,
  solarium

Outlets:
2 restaurants
  a) 2,400 sq. ft.
  b) 900 sq. ft.
  Both served by
  one kitchen
Cocktail bar
Lobby bar

Meeting Facilities:
4 conference rooms
1 boardroom
Capacity: 10–300
(All on same floor
  and adjacent)
Ample parking avail-
  able outside

Walter still had time, but not much, to change these configurations.

The Market

The Salzburg market was essentially divided into low, medium, and high seasons. January, February, October, and November were low seasons, when city occupancy usually ran 20 to 30 percent. Medium season was March to June, September, and the first half of December, when occupancy ran about 50 percent. High season was July, August, and the last half of December, when there were numerous festivals, Christ-

TABLE 11-3-1   Hotels Considered Competitive in Salzburg

5-Star

Sheraton Hotel   165 rooms, 8 years old; rack rate $135–$445

Advantages	*Disadvantages*
next to Congress Hall (city center)	no swimming pool or leisure facilities
has established position	
in market	
well-known cuisine	
aggressive sales force	
international reservation system	
listed in company directories of Hoechst, Siemens, BASF	

Radisson Hotel   62 rooms, opening in 6 months; rack rate $167–$600

Advantages	*Disadvantages*
magnificently restored houses	no pool or leisure area
very luxurious	no parking
Old Town district	limited banquet capacity
international reservation system	

Osterreichischer Hof   120 rooms, first opened in 1866; rack rate $141–$431

Advantages	*Disadvantages*
downtown location	no pool or leisure facilities
very traditional hotel	no parking space
loyal clientele for many years	no sales force
major renovation 2 years ago	
belongs to famous Hotel Sacher in Vienna	

Goldener Hirsch   70 rooms, converted baroque; rack rate $229–$572

Advantages	*Disadvantages*
baroque center of city	no parking
Ciga Hotel chain	limited meeting facilities
Leading Hotels of the World	no pool or leisure facilities
famous bar for celebrities	
Gault et Millau Award restaurant	
furnished with authentic folk art masterpieces	

4.5-Star

Penta Hotel   257 rooms, 1 year old; rack rate $141–$343

Advantages	*Disadvantages*
spacious banquet capacity	bad location, out of city center
550 parking places	no cosy atmosphere
local sales force	price-dumping advocate
pool, gym, sauna	

Best Western Kaserhof   110 beds, converted manor house; rack rate $116–$310

Advantages	*Disadvantages*
lovely garden	limited conference space
3 restaurants	city outskirts

(continued)

TABLE 11-3-1   (continued)

4-Star

Novotel   140 rooms, 4 years old; rack rate $110–$189

Advantages	*Disadvantages*
good parking space	weak product quality
local sales force	no pool or leisure facilities
city location	
works closely with local companies	

Dorint Hotel   140 rooms, 4 years old; rack rate $97–$185

Advantages	*Disadvantages*
sauna, gymnasium	no swimming pool

mas, and strong tourism. The city ran at close to 100 percent occupancy during high season, and hotels typically did one-third of their annual occupancy at that time.

Overall, about 20 percent of the market was transient corporate, 15 percent groups and congress, the balance being tourism. The top four feeder markets were the United States, Germany, Italy, and Great Britain, followed by France, Spain, Switzerland, and Japan. Eighty percent of these markets were tourism. A feeder market for commercial business was also Vienna.

Fifteen companies in Salzburg had subsidiaries or mother companies in other countries and were considered major potential commercial accounts:

Aqua Engineering	Porsche GmbH
BMW Austria	Puma GmbH
Brenntag Austria	Raab Karcher
Conoco Austria	Schosswender Werke
Ford Motor Company	Teekanne GmbH
Melitta GmbH	Wacker Chemie
Mercedes Benz GmbH	Wrigley Austria GmbH
Mannesmann Demag	

Competition

Walter Foeger's staff had completed a competitive analysis. Ten hotels were found to be in the five-star category and 22 in the four-star. Many were quite small, locally owned, and with limited facilities. Although all these were in some way competitive, for reasons of location, condition, size, facilities, reputation, and international affiliation, Walter's group decided that the Holiday Inn's positioning should be weighed against only eight. Brief descriptions of these eight are given in Table 11-3-1. All eight hotels offered room service and had computer reservation systems (CRS). More details appear in Table 11-3-2, on the five hotels presently operating and considered, in the final analysis, to be the main competitors.

Walter analyzed these figures one more time before he called in his executive team to make a final decision.

TABLE 11-3-2   Final Competitive Analysis in Salzburg

	Sheraton	Oster. Hof	Penta	Novotel	Dorint
Rooms	165	120	257	140	140
Building	modern	traditional	modern	modern	modern
Renovations	ongoing	2 years ago	new	none	none
Parking	indoor	none	indoor	in & outdoor	outdoor
Hotel Staff	157	220	230	60	75
Sales Staff	5	0	4	1	1
Reservations Staff	1.5	2	3	1	1
Rooms Quality (1–10)	8	7	5.5	4	4.5
Rooms					
doubles	144	65	247	137	120
singles	—	45	—	3	—
Suites	21	10	10	—	20
Restaurants	2	5	2	1	1
appearance (1–10)	1. 8	6–8	1. 7	4	4.5
	2. 6		2. 5		
capacity	1. 100	80–150	1. 140	80	120
	2. 40		2. 85		
cuisine	1. traditional	1. traditional	1. continental	standard	standard
	2. bistro	5. rathskeller	2. coffee shop		
Bars	1	2	1	1	0
appearance (1–10)	8	8	6	4	—
capacity	50	80	100	25	—
Banquet Rooms	4	6	15	3	3
appearance (1–10)	7	6	5	3	3
maximum capacity	150	300	1000	260	140

NEXT YEAR'S RACK RATES (off-season rates discount at least 50%)

	Sheraton	Oster. Hof	Penta	Novotel	Dorint
single $	158–282	172–268	191–268	110–136	97–150
double $	205–335	229–308	229–308	136–189	132–185
max. comm'l. discount	50%	20%	60%	30%	30%
group rate $	137 pp	negotiable	negotiable	55 pp	63 pp
suite $	400–700	352–660	negotiable	—	160–238
Forecasted Year Occ. %	65	65	45	70	60
Forecasted Adr ($)	169	184	157	145	138
Estimated Mix %					
individual	40	55	25	45	60
business	35	25	20	25	20
group	15	10	35	15	10
congress	10	10	20	15	10

CHAPTER 12

Pricing the Hospitality Product

Price is of unique importance to marketers for a number of reasons. It is the matching of supply to demand so that financial objectives can be achieved. It is also a powerful force in attracting attention and increasing sales. As such, price must be based on a thorough decision-making process by the seller that will communicate the worth of the total offering, a worth that is consistent with the market's perception of the offering's value. The importance of price in the marketing mix, stated by Martin Bell in 1971, still holds true today:

> Price is a dangerous and explosive marketing force. It must be used with caution. The damage done by improper pricing may completely destroy the effectiveness of the rest of a well-conceived marketing strategy.... As a marketing weapon, pricing is the "big gun." It should be triggered exclusively by those thoroughly familiar with its possibilities and dangers. But unlike most big weapons, pricing cannot be used only when the danger of its misuse is at a minimum. Every marketing plan involves a pricing decision. Therefore, all marketing planners should be equipped to make correct pricing decisions.[1]

Product and price decisions are inseparable because of the importance that buyers place on price in relation to value. The buyer uses price to estimate value received even when competitive prices are the same. This means that, with the proper pricing decision, there is a real opportunity to enhance the product's acceptance. In the hospitality industry (and some others), however, pricing practice remains largely intuitive and routine, or cost-based.

We have said it before and we will say it again: Without customers, nothing else matters. If the customer won't pay the price, it matters little how high or low your costs are or what your profit goals are. Price, like product, flows from the consumer; the integration of product and price is critical. Notice how this is done in Figure 12-1.

Setting prices is a complex exercise, with any number of strategic and tactical implications. The hospitality industry has fixed physical-plant products and locations. Sometimes we have to work with the product we have and set prices accordingly. In other words, rather than set the price to the target market, we may have to find the target market that will accept a given product at a given price. The given price is the price we can obtain for the given product. This is called product-driven pricing,

---

[1]Martin L. Bell, *Marketing: Concepts and Strategy,* Boston: Houghton Mifflin, 1971, p. 857.

FIGURE 12-1   The integration of price and product

but it is still the customer who will determine the acceptable price.

In the final analysis, pricing, like product, is consumer-driven. It is this thesis that we will pursue in this chapter. First, we will set the stage by discussing recent pricing history in the restaurant and hotel industries.

Pricing Practices

Restaurant Pricing

The concept of consumer-based pricing has sometimes been ignored in the hospitality industry. The first to learn this was the restaurant industry. When inflation became rampant in the 1970s, the restaurant industry responded by continuously increasing prices. Whenever the cost of staples of the industry (e.g., butter, beef, sugar, coffee) went up, restaurant prices quickly followed suit. The result was that the consumer eventually said, "Whoa!" and turned to other alternatives, including staying home.

Eventually, the industry caught on. It found new ways to do things, new items to put on menus, new ways to prepare menu items, and new ways to serve them (e.g., the salad bar) to cut labor costs. The consumer is the final decision-maker on prices; in the restaurant industry the reaction can be very swift, if only because it is relatively simple for someone else to enter the market with a new idea and/or a better price.

In the 1990s, the most successful restaurants are those that use a concept called "value pricing." Value pricing in food service had its inception, nationally and scientifically, at Taco Bell in 1988. It is based on research originally conducted by the Dutch economist, Peter H. Van Westendorp. It was further developed, as the *price sensitivity measurement* (PSM), by Kenneth Travers and others,[2] but had been largely ignored in the hospitality industry until Taco Bell picked up on it. The process, explained briefly in Table 12-1, puts a price value on a product as determined by the perception of the target market, which, in the final analysis, is the only way to set prices. Its success at Taco Bell, and later at McDonald's, Burger King, and a few others, has not yet led to its wide acceptance, although that is gradually emerging.

Through value pricing, Taco Bell learned to bundle its products (for example adding sour cream, including a soft drink, etc.) in a way and at a price wherein the consumer perceived "value."[3] For the fast-food industry giants, value pricing and bundling have largely reduced the former standard practices of discounts, coupons, and direct mail as the key weapons in the fast-food wars.

Hotel Room Pricing

The hotel industry fell into the same trap as the restaurant industry. Throughout the 1970s and early 1980s, average hotel rates increased at a pace considerably exceeding the increase in the *consumer price index* (CPI). Rack rates increased even faster, average rates being held down only by heavy discounting. A major factor was the demand by owners, who were rarely hoteliers, for greater profits through higher prices. Due to highly favorable tax laws before the U.S. 1986 tax act, many hotels were built with little regard to customer demand or customer needs. Almost all hotel owners were financially oriented, which has had considerable impact on hotel pricing and has severely strained its relationship to marketing. Of course, by 1989, the slide in national occupancy rates was accelerated, and the early 1990s saw some of the worst years the hotel industry had ever experienced. For the first time in many years, U.S. hotel room rates grew at a slower rate than that of the CPI. Customers became more aware that they were in a buyer's market, and discounting hotel rooms became rampant. Consider the following description of a frequent business traveler (*page 468*):

[2]Kenneth Travers, "PSM: A New Technique for Determining Consumer Sensitivity to Pricing," Los Angeles: Plog Research, no date.

[3]From a speech by Blaise Mercadente, Taco Bell Research Director, at the American Marketing Association Conference on Customer Satisfaction, Sheraton Palace Hotel, San Francisco, May, 1993.

TABLE 12-1   PSM—Price Sensitivity Measurement

PSM is based on psychological and sociological principles and aims to examine price perception by determining levels of customer resistance as they relate to quality perceptions and the market range of acceptable prices for a specific product or service. For each specific product or service, four questions are asked. The first two questions determine the *indifference point* (IDP, Graph I). This is the price at which an equal number of respondents feel the product or service is cheap as feel it is expensive.

1. At what price on the scale do you consider the product or service to be cheap?
2. At what price on the scale do you consider the product or service to be expensive?

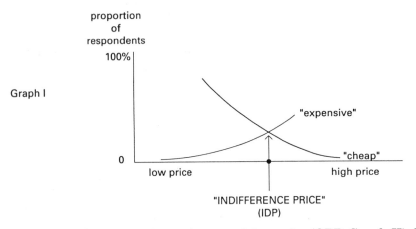

The second two questions determine the *optimum pricing point* (OPP, Graph II). This is the price at which consumer resistance to purchase is at its lowest—that is, an equal number feel the product or service is too cheap as feel it is too expensive.

1. At what price on the scale do you consider the product or service to be too expensive, so expensive that you would not consider buying it?
2. At what price on the scale do you consider the product or service too cheap, so cheap that you would question the quality?

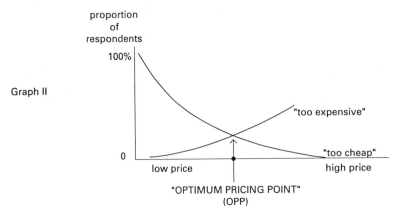

When the four cumulative distributions are combined, it can be determined if there is "stress" in price-consciousness (Graph 3). The closer the OPP is to the IDP, the less price-conscious are the respondents. As the gap widens, the greater is the number of consumers who feel the "normal" price is too high—that is, they are more sensitive to price.

TABLE 12-1   (continued)

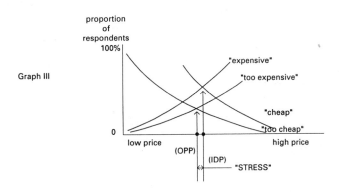

The final manipulation gives the *range of acceptable prices* (RAP, Graph IV). The "too cheap" and "too expensive" curves are graphed with the *reversed* cumulative distributions of the "cheap" and "expensive," which are then labelled "not cheap" and "not expensive." The intersection of these two curves is the *point of marginal cheapness* (PMC). This is the point where the number of respondents who feel the product or service is too cheap is equal to the number of respondents who feel it is not cheap.

The intersection of the "not expensive" and "too expensive" curves is the *point of marginal expensiveness* (PME). This is the point where the number of respondents who feel the product or service is too expensive is equal to the number of respondents who feel it is not expensive.

The *range of acceptable price* (RAP) has the PMC as its lower price limit and the PME as its upper price limit. It would be unwise to price outside this range unless there is real change in the perceived value or positioning of the product or service. Thus, for example, Taco Bell found that it could move price up (i.e., create great price value) by adding sour cream to tacos and changing the perceived value.

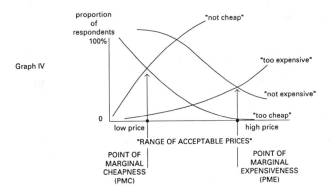

Source: Kenneth Travers, "PSM: A New Technique for Determining Consumer Sensitivity to Pricing," Los Angeles: Plog Research, no date; and Karen Krim, "Measuring the Price Sensitivity of Consumers: A Study in the Hospitality Industry," unpublished manuscript, Amherst: University of Massachusetts, 1990.

[She/he] is part of a burgeoning group of price-conscious customers who exasperate hotel marketing executives. Taking their cue from years of discounts and giveaways by the hotel industry, these travelers know how to bargain, and they cheerfully pitch brand loyalty out of the window if the place down the street is offering a better deal. [He] gleefully recalls nabbing a choice room at Boston's Ritz-Carlton for $185, a steep discount off the full rate of $350.[4]

It was 1960 when Ted Levitt said, in his classic article, that businesses fail "not because the market is saturated. It is because there has been a failure of management" that the following mistaken assumptions occur:

There is a never-ending, ever more affluent population that will sustain increasing demand for an industry's major product.
There is no competitive substitute for a product.
There is preoccupation with a product that lends itself to improvement and cost reduction.[5]

Thirty-three years later Peter Drucker was saying about the same thing in his first three of five "deadly business sins":

The past few years have seen the downfall of one once-dominant business after another…. But in every case the main cause has been at least one of the five deadly business sins—avoidable mistakes that will harm the mightiest business.

- The first and easily the most common sin is *the worship of high profit margins and of "premium pricing."*
- Closely related to this first sin is the second one: *mispricing a new product by charging "what the market will bear."*
- The third deadly sin is *cost-driven pricing.* The only thing that works is price-driven costing.

[Cost-driven pricers argue] "We have to recover our costs and make a profit."

This is true but irrelevant: Customers do not see it as their job to ensure manufacturers a profit. The only sound way to price is to start out with what the market is willing to pay—and thus, it must be assumed, what the competition will charge—and designing to that price specification.[6]

Worse than the restaurant industry, the hotel industry did more than pass on its cost increases, and then some, to the customer. In the 1970s and 1980s, many companies automatically raised rack rates quarterly or semiannually regardless of occupancy ratios or business trends. In the wake of this practice, what followed was a multiple-discount process that was, at best, unsophisticated, naive, myopic, confusing to the customer, and, in the final analysis, self-defeating. We have already related the common story of the hotel salesperson who reports that the market "won't pay the price," and the response from corporate: "Raise the numbers."

The upscale end of the hotel industry literally forced the growth of the middle-tier properties and spawned the growth of the budget and all-suite chains. As a result of this, only the budget hotels were showing any signs of growth during the early 1990s and many luxury hotels were hemorrhaging money. Budget hotels offered what many travelers were looking for—clean rooms, convenient locations, and an alternative to high prices. As of this writing, the upscale hotel industry had still not learned the concept of value pricing. Instead, it sought to

[4]"Industry hooks travelers on bargain rates," *Wall Street Journal,* July 27, 1992, p. B1.

[5]Theodore Levitt, "Marketing Myopia," *Harvard Business Review,* July/August 1960. Copyright © 1960 by the President and Fellows of Harvard College; all rights reserved. Reprinted in Theodore Levitt, *The Marketing Imagination,* New York: The Free Press, 1986, p. 141, 147.

[6]Peter F. Drucker, "The Five Deadly Business Sins," *Wall Street Journal,* October 21, 1993, p. A20.

A good example is recent (although not new) trade press and business articles on excessive wine pricing in restaurants. Operators who mark up their wines 300–400 percent argue that the customer has to understand the cost of the sommelier, the glasses, the presentation, etc., and that they have to make their margin on wine because of the high cost of food for which they can't charge higher prices, especially when business is slow. They myopically ignore two basic factors: The customer who sees a wine in a retail store for $15 is not willing to pay $50 for it in a restaurant; and regular wine drinkers, who may be willing to pay the food prices but not the wine prices, have a competitive substitute—they stay home.

eliminate costs, guessing at what the customers "wouldn't miss," in order to compensate for its heavy discounting from rack rates that were too high.

The hotel industry was, however, arguing over the merits of "value-added services" (not scientifically established like Taco Bell) versus discounting. Different views were apparent and often based on guesswork. Some of these are reported in Table 12-2.

The Basis of Pricing

The marketing discipline grew out of the economic discipline. The basic theory of economics, simplistically stated, is that the economy responds to the consumer. The basic theory of marketing is that the consumer calls the shots. When it comes to setting prices, these basic theories need to be remembered. Prices need to be established with the long-term customer, not the short-term margin, in mind.

The case on which we will follow up is well stated by Elliot Ross of the well-known consulting firm McKinsey & Co.:

> [I]mproving pricing performance without the risk of damaging market repercussions [rests on understanding how the industry's pricing works and how customers perceive prices, based on] information about market and customer characteristics, competitor capabilities and actions, and internal capabilities and costs.... Proactive pricers...time price changes to the anticipated reactions of customers and competitors rather than to...their own analysis of costs.[7]

Marketing and pricing strategies must be developed on a supply and demand basis. Supply deals with the number of hotel rooms available in an area—that is, the competition. Demand is created by customers and their need for hospitality services. Pricing decisions should be based on solid "market research and thorough understanding of the economics of price changes," rather than "intuitive judgments of what the market will bear."[8]

The hotel industry in the United States suffered several bad years in the late 1980s and early 1990s, followed by similar trends in most parts of the world. In 1991, the average occupancy rate in U.S. hotels was around 60 percent, and most hotels were not making a profit. Rack rates became even more of a myth, in fact a joke, as we have previously noted. Average room rates had been declining since 1988 and three factors were responsible for this trend. These factors show how important is the influence of supply and demand in determining prices. First, individual hotels could not raise rates as customers had many choices and competition was fierce. This was especially true of the upscale properties (Figure 12-2). Second, the economy or limited-service hotels showed the most growth during this period and accounted for 30 percent of hotel rooms in the United States, and growing rapidly in other parts of the world. Third, many older, upscale properties were being converted and repositioned at lower levels to help them remain competitive, providing even more choices to customers.[9] Of course, the bad times of the early 1990s were not experienced by all hotels. Those hotels that had focused, clear target markets whom they served well, continued to prosper. For most, however, it will be some time before the industry "shakes out."

There are five major categories to be considered in developing pricing strategies: pricing objectives, costs, competition, market demand, and customers. We will discuss each in turn, but will not go into depth on those areas that are traditional financial concerns, mainly because this chapter is not on pricing in and of itself, but on the role of pricing in marketing. Financial concerns receive heavy treatment in economics and traditional marketing texts.

---

[7]Elliot B. Ross, "Making Money with Proactive Pricing," *Harvard Business Review*, November–December, 1984, pp. 145–155. Copyright © 1984 by the President and Fellows of Harvard College; all rights reserved.

[8]James Abbey, "Is Discounting the Answer to Declining Occupancies?" *International Journal of Hospitality Management*, Vol. 2, No. 2, 1983, pp. 77–82. Similarly, when business is bad it is folly simply to follow a knee-jerk reaction and lower prices.

[9]"Lodging industry turnaround is forecast for 1993," *Hospitality Directions*, Vol. 1 No. 1, p. 7.

TABLE 12-2   Hotelier Views of Discounting versus Value-added Services

Thomas Lattin, Hotel Accounting Consultant for Coopers & Lybrand in Houston, opposed discounting. "A guestroom should not be worth less on weekends than it is on weekdays," [an opinion that goes totally against common wisdom and reality because it ignores the two different markets].

Frank Camacho, Vice President–Marketing, North America and Research Director, ITT Sheraton Hotels, also opposed discounting but added, "The direction is now going toward 'value-engineering'— that is, offering very selective added benefits," such as coffeemakers in guestrooms. Camacho recommended "price sensing" to segments such as "senior couples, people on vacation alone, individual business travelers and others."

Robert Dirks, Vice President–Marketing, Hilton Hotels, "[V]alue-marketing is the way to go."

Barry Parrish, Vice President–Marketing, Howard Johnson, believes in "action incentives" such as their Business Traveler Club that offers discount coupons with retailers, room upgrades, vacation and airline discounts.

Jeff Angus, Vice President–Sales, Red Lion Hotels, "...discounting not value-added marketing, is a more effective way to boost business. Customers want to know what their bill will be in the morning. They are not as concerned with what they received during their stay."

Mark van Hartesvelt, Senior Vice President–Marketing, Guest Quarters, "People are still into price." Guest Quarters found that a promotion that added breakfast and a Polaroid camera at a $15 premium did not work well.

Geof Rochester, Vice President–Marketing, Radisson Hotels, says to use both, but under different circumstances: discount to bring in new customers and use the value-added approach to upsell a room to loyal customers.

Bob Gilbert, Vice President–Marketing, Richfield Hotel Management, recommends "packaging, in which value-added services are offered to business travelers who are willing to pay a premium."

William Watson, Senior Vice President–Marketing Best Western, "Discounting works best and makes the most sense at the luxury end, while value-added promotions are best at middle range or lower properties."

Raymond Lewis, Jr., Executive Vice President–Marketing, Holiday Inn Worldwide, "You need to provide the right price for the right customer at the right time. Discounting and value-added approaches can both be useful, but you don't want to give the value-added benefit to the price-oriented person."

[*Note:* It appears that the hotel industry has not progressed too far in its knowledge of pricing. Perhaps it should talk to Taco Bell?]

Source: Laura Koss, "The Great Marketing Debate: Discounting vs. Value-Added Services," *Hotel & Motel Management,* November 1, 1993, pp. 57–58.

Our light treatment is not intended to indicate that financial concerns are insignificant. On the contrary, they are critical. We maintain, however, that the role of pricing must be, first and foremost, consumer-based. Cost and profit considerations follow under the heading of "Can we afford to do it?" as has been indicated earlier. Recall that profit should be the test of the validity of management decisions, not the cause or rationale for them, and that "the only thing that works is price-driven costing."

Pricing Objectives

Objectives are what we want to accomplish. Without them it is hard to determine where we are going or how we are going to get there.

How we appear to our guests.

How we appear on their bill.

No matter which Fairmont you choose,
you'll find the royal treatment is much more reasonable than you'd expect.

Most planners know that a stay at The Fairmont is about as luxurious as it gets. What you may not realize however, is that our rates are extremely competitive. As a matter of fact, they're even negotiable. And our rates aren't all we arrange specially for business people. Each of our over-sized guestrooms is conveniently equipped with PC dataports and dual line phones. Although chances are, our fitness facilities, fine restaurants and attentive staff will make you forget you're there on business at all. So before you settle for merely adequate accommodations, give us a call. You won't find a more luxurious hotel anywhere – only a more expensive one. For reservations, please call your travel agent or The Fairmont at 1-800-527-4727.

THE FAIRMONT HOTELS

Chicago   *Dallas*   *New Orleans*   *San Francisco*   *San Jose/Silicon Valley*

FIGURE 12-2 Influence of supply and demand on poorly focused upscale hotels

Pricing objectives fall into three major categories: financial, volume, and customer objectives.

Financial Objectives

Financial objectives are probably the most dominant, widespread, and enduring pricing objectives in the hospitality industry. Although absolutely essential to success, or even survival, the heavy emphasis on financial objectives tends to overwhelm all other considerations. In some cases this can actually lead to failure; in others, even in successful firms, it can lead to the inability to maximize potential.

Financial objectives take different forms, all interrelated. Profit is the one that usually comes to mind first. We call this pricing for profit maximization, whether the emphasis is on gross profit or net profit. The first problem with the heavy emphasis on profit in pricing is that it tends to ignore many other considerations—in particular, the customer. The second and related problem is that a built-in profit determination may be hard to achieve in the hospitality industry.

In other industries, the relationship between cost, price, and profit is more direct and obvious. In the hospitality industry it is indirect and vague. Product-makers can calculate very closely both their variable and indirect costs; from that basis they can add on a profit margin per unit. If they are good forecasters, they will do well because the product they don't sell today they will sell tomorrow, even if they have to discount it and reduce their profit margin.

In hotels and restaurants, the room or the seat not occupied tonight cannot be sold tomorrow even at a discount.[10] Yet a large part of the fixed and semi-variable cost of selling that room or seat exists, regardless. Even with these problems, there are tools for calculating desired profit margins, which go beyond the scope of this section.

Instead, we are more concerned with the setting of prices based on the thesis that the higher the price, the greater the profit. That thesis will hold true if the price has no effect on patronage. For example, airline terminal bars are notorious for overpricing and operating with a cost of sales under 15 percent. It is doubtful that this practice has much effect on volume, given the nature of the captive market; in most other instances, however, this will not hold true.

High prices alone will reduce volume in most cases. Thus, after setting high rack rates, hotels discount to get back the volume at a lower price. From a marketing point of view, something else

occurs in the process—the hotel loses customers who are turned off by the high prices, don't know how to negotiate a discount, or simply don't like being gouged. Even in times of high demand, prices that are too high force many travelers to seek alternatives. Communication technologies are making this even more possible. These customers not only don't come, or don't come back, but they also tell many others. It is because of this common practice by upscale hotels that we say that they have spawned the growth of the middle- and lower-tier properties.

The airlines learned this lesson even though it was forced upon them. Greater competition and declining airfares induced many people to fly who had never flown before, and others to fly more often, and the airline industry had increased its customer base. In a business in which the variable cost is so low, as in hotels, this is a significant factor for the long term and a lesson to be learned by the hotel industry. Essentially, pricing for profit maximization by maximizing prices ignores marketing forces.

Other financial objectives in pricing are target *return on investment* (ROI), stabilization of prices and profit margins, and cash flow pricing (to maximize short-run sales to generate cash). All of these objectives have their place in pricing and, in fact, are necessary. Problems arise when one of them becomes the sole pricing objective.

Volume Objectives

Volume objectives, a second set of pricing objectives, take a number of forms. These objectives are particularly prevalent in the hotel industry because it is such a highly *volume-sensitive* business—that is, fixed costs are high but variable costs per room can run as low as 15 percent to 25 percent of departmental income. Once fixed costs have been surpassed, a small gain in volume supports a large increase in profit, as with the airlines. In the restaurant business, a *price-sensitive* business (i.e., a small increase in price supports a large increase in profit), variable costs can run as high as 35 percent to 65 percent of sales. Both industries, of course, seek volume (with some noted exceptions, where

---

[10]This is, as previously noted, referred to as the perishability of services. To counteract this, prices are set accordingly. This practice, unfortunately, ignores the seldom-mentioned and also previously-noted ease of renewability of these services—the unique ability to sell the same product over and over. To do so means, among other things, setting the price correctly the first time.

high prices are designed to promote exclusivity). Lower variable costs, however, provide hotels with the ability to discount deeper to promote volume. Hotel restaurants also are in the unique position of "paying no rent," by contrast with their freestanding competitors.[11]

One major and commonly used measure of volume is market share. Alternatively, this objective may simply be stated as the desired sales growth rate. Market share is the percentage or dollar volume share of the total business that an individual business is able to obtain within a competitive group. For example, for the business traveler segment, Hotel A may have a 20 percent market share, Hotel B may have a 35 percent market share, and Hotel C may be the leader with a 45 percent share of the business traveler market. Market share has been shown in other industries to be a leading indicator of profit. It also measures how well one is doing vis-a-vis the competition and also how well in terms of one's own fair share.

To increase market share, a property has to do something better than the competition. This can be a better product, better service, better location, or better perceived value. One can also be "better" by lowering prices. This may or may not be self-defeating. For a restaurant, a quickly calculated break-even analysis can indicate at which point increased volume will overcome the lost revenue due to lower prices. For a hotel, it is more likely that competition will follow suit and market share will soon return to where it was before. It is probably foolish, in most cases in the hospitality industry, to lower prices for the sole purpose of increasing market share.

Another volume objective is to build business by increasing the customer base, as occurred in the airlines case above. With this strategy, prices are usually lowered, either temporarily or in special promotions, to attract more customers with the hope that they will become permanent customers. This also can backfire, as it usually does with restaurants that run "twofer" promotions (two meals for the price of one). The reason it backfires is that many consumers who take advantage of the promotion will never return to the property when they have to pay the regular price.

There can be much merit, however, in using price to build the customer base when doing so will build customer loyalty, especially during normally slow periods. For hotels, more customers in the rooms can also mean more customers in the food and beverage outlets.

Another objective is to increase occupancy or seat turnover. This is really no different from talking about increasing sales by lowering the price. Higher occupancy or seat turnover helps to cover relatively fixed labor costs and overhead. Again, for hotels it can mean more customers in the food and beverage outlets. Hotel management personnel are also judged on their occupancy ratios and are often rewarded accordingly, so there is high incentive to price with the objective of increasing occupancy.[12]

A final volume objective is the contribution to fixed costs that is made by any incremental business. If the variable cost of a bottle of wine is $15 and the wine is sold for $25, then $10 is available as a contribution toward fixed costs. This is better than zero if the wine is normally sold for $50 but can't be sold. The high fixed costs and volume sensitivity of hotels make this objective even more viable.

---

[11]In many hotels this creates an interesting paradox that is counterproductive. The following scenario is common: A sales manager books a large group at a favorable (to the hotel) room rate. To do so, she has to heavily discount the meals. The food and beverage manager and the chef scream—the prices will ruin their food cost percentage—oblivious to the overall profit to be gained from the booking. In most cases, these F&B managers' bonuses are tied into producing a satisfactory food cost. This type of reward/compensation forces managers to choose between customers and their own pockets. Some hotels counter this "F&B mentality" by assigning a portion of room revenues to F&B revenues.

[12]This is changing. ITT Sheraton Hotels, for example, was long noted for its "bottom-line mentality" in awarding bonuses. Now, bonuses as high as 40 percent of salary for general managers are awarded on four criteria: *employee service index* (ESI), *customer service index* (CSI), *gross operating profit* (GOP), and *revenue per available room* (REVPAR). Sheraton found that ESI can account for 50 percent of the variance in CSI, which can account for 50 percent of the variance in REVPAR. From a speech by Frank Camacho, Vice President–Marketing, North America, and Research Director, ITT Sheraton Hotels, at the American Marketing Association Conference on Consumer Satisfaction, Sheraton Palace Hotel, San Francisco, May, 1993.

This observation is even more apt when one considers the disadvantage that hotel restaurants face when contrasted with their free-standing competitors. The disadvantage is that higher fixed costs are incurred because outlets must be kept open for guest convenience. Local restaurants can close on days when business is slow; hotels do not have the same option. Many hotels must also offer room service in spite of its unprofitability.

Volume and profit objectives in pricing often go hand-in-hand, but this is not always the case. Volume objectives tend to be more oriented to the long term and, when done wisely, to building the customer base.

Customer Objectives

The term *customer objectives,* as used here, means influence of the customer in a favorable way; this is truly the marketing objective of pricing. There are many ways that pricing can be used to do this simply because it is the most visible part of the presentation mix. We will suggest a number of those ways.

One customer objective is to instill confidence in the customer by price stability. However, in the inflationary times of the 1970s, the public became accustomed to continuously increasing prices. The hotel industry in the United States also increased its prices at a rate that was even greater than the rate of inflation. Customers started to trade down to more inexpensive alternatives. In the 1980s, a major portion of the hotel industry believed it could still ride the waves of inflation even when inflation did not exist. This destroyed a great deal of consumer confidence and built business for those properties that didn't follow the practice. In the 1990s, the hotel industry finally realized that prices may actually have to be reduced in order to get customers.

The hotel industry is aware of the need for some price stability. One way this is accomplished is through what are known as "corporate rates." In some cases this has been done on a broad scale, except that these rates, too, increase on a regular basis. On a more narrow scale, hotel companies have negotiated rates with other corporations that remain constant for some period of time. The rates are usually based on the guarantee of a certain number of room-nights during the same period. This allows corporations to better budget their travel expenses when they are confident of a stable price.

Another customer objective is "inducement to try." Restaurant "twofers" are designed for this purpose, as are other special promotions. Restaurants run loss leaders (items on which they take a loss or lower margin with the hope of making up the profit on other items) just as retail stores do. Individual and new menu items may also be priced lower for this purpose.

"Opening specials" represent a specific case of inducement-to-try pricing. Hotels used to open at the highest price they thought the market would bear and avoided initial discounting on the assumption that natural demand would fill the rooms. The objective in this situation, rather than inducement to try, is another customer objective called "enhancing the image." The attempt was to make the property appear so special, new, and different that it was worth the higher price. Unless that is really the case, the net result is often lost customers in the long run. Figure 12-3 is inducement-to-try pricing, after refurbishing, to regain lost customers.

In most marketplaces, new demand is not created because a new hotel is opened.[13] The meetings or business traveler market already exists, in another hotel. Opening pricing is extremely important; the idea is to get existing customers in competitors' hotels to try the new product, not to scare them away.

The practice of initial high pricing is also called "price-skimming." The term derives from the notion of skimming the cream off the top, before the competition comes in and forces prices down. Price-skimming is sometimes profitable when a company introduces a new product into the market. Price-skimming was a

---

[13]There seem to be some noted exceptions such as Orlando, Las Vegas, and Hong Kong. Although new hotel building in these areas has sometimes gotten ahead of demand, the additional capacity has helped to increase demand; this is especially true for large convention business. It should be noted, however, that these three locations may have some of the greatest demand generators in the world.

The restoration of Toronto's historic landmark hotel, the Royal York, is now complete. Experience a return to an era of gracious hospitality served in the grand hotel tradition. At this rate it's a priceless experience. Enjoy luxury accommodation in a newly renovated guest room. Complimentary morning coffee or tea. A morning newspaper and Canadian Plus Points. All for just $79.00.* Thursday through Saturday. Or $89.00* Sunday through Wednesday. Perhaps you'd prefer the exclusive service and special amenities of our Business Class, offered at a special $119.00* rate.

Take advantage of these priceless rates. Our new health club and indoor pool opens May 1. Why stay at a standard hotel when you can get a decent price at a priceless hotel? For reservations please call: in Toronto **(416) 863-6333** or call toll-free, **1-800-268-9411.**

Canadian Pacific Hotels & Resorts

Royal York

100 Front Street West. Toronto. Ontario M5J 1E3

FIGURE 12-3 Price inducement "to try" after refurbishing

popular pricing strategy for computers: The model that came out one year at $4,000 could be had a year or so later for $1,999. For hotels and restaurants, price-skimming usually creates the negative, and often lasting, image of being overpriced, and is to be avoided.

"Enhancing the image" is better used when the product is truly unique and special. Four Seasons and Ritz-Carlton are hotel chains that followed this practice. The Stanford Court in San Francisco did likewise and maintained some of the highest average rates and occupancies in the city. Some very special restaurants also successfully price high for the same reason, under the philosophy, "If you have to ask the price, you shouldn't be here." These are excellent examples of tangibilizing the product through pricing, but there are very few of these opportunities in the marketplace. When these practices are based on ego rather than reality, they are self-defeating.

Another consumer objective in pricing is to "desensitize" the consumer to the price. Outstanding examples of this practice are Club Med and the all-inclusive resorts of Jamaica. Club Med started the trend with its "one price covers all" policy, sometimes even including airfare. Alcoholic drinks and incidentals are extra, however, but you "pay" for them with colored beads that you buy (they go on your bill) at the front desk and wear as a necklace. You are desensitized until you check out—but it works.

The all-inclusives have no extra charges; everything is "free" after you have paid one price (substantial) per week. An example of attempts to desensitize in restaurants is the use of fixed price menus, with one inclusive price.

A good price/value relationship is another pricing objective that is aimed at by many hospitality companies (see Figure 12-2). This is another form of image enhancement, since the market is generally conceded to be very price/value-sensitive, except for the high expense account customer. Restaurants in the middle to lower price ranges use this technique all the time in their advertising. Hotel companies are frequent proponents. In 1986, for example, the "new" Howard Johnson, then a new division of Prime Motor Inns, announced the opening of its first Howard Johnson Park Square Inn. The announcement was accompanied by this statement:

> "It's a unique product. It's something no one else can offer...." The target is between $45 and $60. Bean [Vice-President of Franchising] says that Howard Johnson's competitors, who are geared for the midpriced segment, have lost focus. "I see us as being in that very niche to a more sophisticated traveler, and to a businessman who wants a quality room and is still looking for price and value in a room."[14]

Howard Johnson's performance after that indicates that the above statement was nothing more than wishful thinking.

Two other customer objectives are worth mentioning. One is to use pricing to differentiate the product, usually with higher prices. If the product appears essentially the same, then price can be used as a consumer perception mechanism to differentiate one product from another: The 12-ounce prime New York Sirloin for $16.95 certainly must be better than the same item for $12.95 somewhere else. Another objective in the same vein is to introduce or promote added services and/or physical facilities. Concierge floors in hotels are priced in this manner, as are flambé desserts at tableside in restaurants. While it is difficult to justify the price differences for these services in the formal product, other core elements such as "prestige" may justify the cost to the buyer.

Cost Pricing

Cost-oriented pricing comes in a number of versions in the hospitality industry. Most popular among these are cost-plus pricing, percentage or markup pricing, break-even pricing, contribution margin pricing, and $1-per-thousand pricing. We will cover each of these briefly.

Cost-plus Pricing This method involves establishing the total cost of a product, including a share of the overhead, plus a predetermined profit margin. Its common use in pricing food and beverages is to relate the profit margin to the selling price. Thus, if desired profit is 20 percent of selling price, an item that costs $4, plus $2 labor and $2 overhead, would be priced at $10. This results in $2 of profit for that item. Each product or product line is allocated an appropriate share of every type of expense as well as its own variable cost. The intent is that every product should be profit-generating.

The method ignores the notion that total income is a combined effort in which some products will not generate as much profit as others but will contribute to the whole. It is also subject to misallocation of costs such as depreciation, maintenance, and so on. Cost-plus pricing does not allow for flexibility in pricing decisions nor does it take into consideration consumers' perceptions of a product's value. It is totally cost-oriented and ignores demand. Attempts to apply different gross margin percentages to different menu items to account for different labor costs have done little to overcome the deficiencies of this method.

Cost Percentage or Markup Pricing This method is heavily favored by the restaurant industry. It features either a dollar markup on the variable-ingredient cost of the item, or a percentage markup based on the desired-ingredient cost percentage, or a combination of both. A bottle of

---

[14]"Howard Johnson's New Market," *Restaurants & Institutions*, December 10, 1986, pp. 122–123.

wine that costs $10 might be subject to a $5 markup, making the selling price $15. The markup percentage would give a 66.6 percent cost percent to the selling price ratio. If, on the other hand, a 50 percent wine cost was desired, the bottle would be marked up by $10 to make the selling price $20. A common combination of both would be to mark the wine up 100 percent plus $2, making the selling price $22.

The food-service industry appears to be enamored of this method of pricing. Food cost and liquor cost percentages become the standard by which results are measured. The major fallacies of this method are: (1) It is totally cost-oriented; (2) it ignores consumer perceptions of value, particularly in times of widely fluctuating costs; and (3) it tends to price high-cost items up to a level that customers are unwilling to pay.

Break-even Pricing   Break-even pricing is used to determine at what sales volume and price a product will break even, where costs are equal to sales. It distinguishes between fixed costs and variable costs. The break-even point is graphically plotted for several prices using the same fixed and variable costs. By plotting the revenue generated at various prices, a comprehensive picture of profit can be created if the demand is known at various levels.

Figure 12-4 demonstrates the process of break-even pricing. Figure 12-4(a) shows a hypothetical break-even analysis for price-sensitive restaurants. In this case fixed costs are relatively low and unit variable costs are relatively high. Because of these factors, sales quickly pass the fixed cost line, but the profit margin remains relatively narrow regardless of the quantity sold. This leaves relatively little room for discounting for purposes of increasing volume.

Figure 12-4(b) shows the break-even point for several different prices. If demand at a certain price is equal to or greater than the break-even point, then that price would be profitable.

Figure 12-4(c) demonstrates a break-even analysis for *volume-sensitive* hotels. The fixed cost line in this case is higher, and it takes longer for the sales line to pass it. Once past it, the profit margin widens quickly since variable costs remain a relatively small percentage of unit sales. There is more room for discounting to increase volume once the fixed and variable cost lines have been passed by the sales line.

Break-even analysis is a fairly efficient method of determining profit margins at various price levels if—and this is a big "if"—sales volume can be accurately predicted at the different price levels. To predict this volume, knowledge of consumer perception and demand is still needed.

Contribution Margin Pricing   This method is depicted in Figure 12-4(d). By contrast with (a) and (b), the variable cost line is interjected into the plot at the same place as the sales line, starting at the zero intersection. This demonstrates the concept of "contribution," showing that, if the product sells at a higher price than its variable cost, then it makes a contribution to fixed cost even when sales are not high enough to produce a profit.

The technique is very useful for hotels in soft periods of demand. Room prices can be discounted substantially, if that is what it takes to have them occupied. Even though no profit results, a portion of the fixed cost that would occur if the room was not occupied would be covered. The success of this technique must be assessed by examining the total revenues from rooms sold. After all, selling more rooms at discounted prices may have the same effect as selling fewer rooms at higher prices.

Contribution margin pricing is also another version of markup pricing that can be used beneficially in pricing food and beverages to overcome the problem of overly high prices on high-cost items. To use a previous example, a bottle of wine that costs $50 could be priced with a contribution margin of $25, for a selling price of $75. Wine cost percentage would then be 67 percent, a very high and forbidding percentage by industry standards. However, the contribution margin would be higher than on two $10 bottles sold at $20 each with a 50 percent wine cost. There is a saying that goes, "You bank dollars, not percentages." Figure 12-5 is an example of this.

$1-per-thousand Pricing   This is a unique method for establishing the selling price of hotel rooms. Although it should serve strictly as a rule

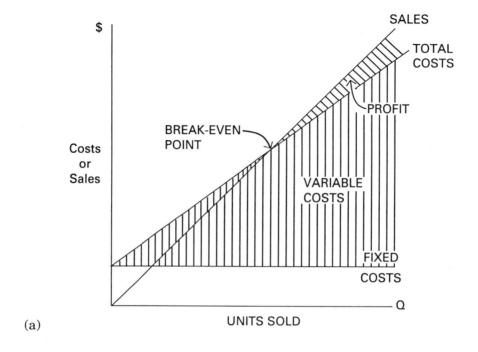

(a)

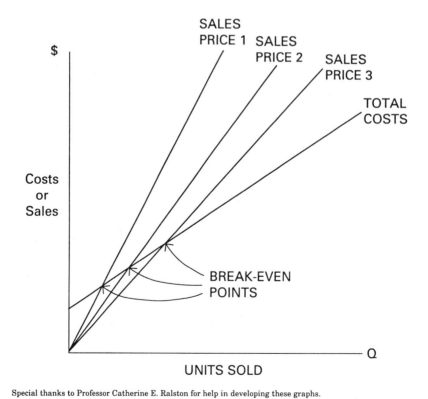

(b)

Special thanks to Professor Catherine E. Ralston for help in developing these graphs.

FIGURE 12-4 Break-even and contribution margin analysis for pricing decisions

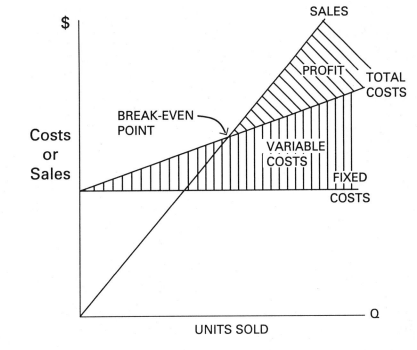

(c)

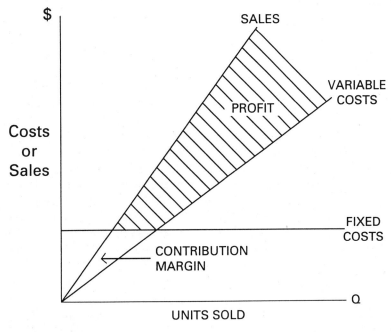

(d)

FIGURE 12-4   (continued)

FIGURE 12-5 Discounting prices to maintain contribution margins

of thumb, it is a widely proclaimed measure in the hotel industry (as in Case 11-3). The rule is that the average room rate in a hotel should be $1 per every $1,000 of construction cost per room. Thus if a hotel cost $80,000 per room to construct and furnish, the average selling price of the rooms should be $80.

This rule of thumb is somewhat archaic in today's world and totally ignores consumer perception and demand. It should be used more as a starting point than anything else. After the hotel is built, the rates are adjusted according to other factors.

Competitive Pricing

One of the most direct methods of determining price is to base it on what competitors charge. One has little choice but to stay in line with other properties offering *the same product in the same product class*. It is difficult to get higher prices, and lower prices will probably be met by competitors. Competitors' prices are readily available, making it easy to use them as a benchmark. For example, the New Orleans Hilton, because of its size and location next to the convention center, is the price leader among convention hotels in New Orleans. All other convention hotels are priced below the Hilton to remain competitive.

Competitive pricing is viable as long as there is no consumer perception of significant differences among the entities, as long as one's cost structure allows pricing at that level, and assuming competitors' prices are set correctly at the beginning. This means that the market must be willing and able to buy at that level or, better, it means determining what the customer thinks is a fair value for the price.

For example, a new upscale hotel will price its rooms competitively with existing upscale hotels. That seems to work fine as long as the demand exists. If, however, present upscale hotels are running at low occupancy and the market has largely traded down, this may be sheer folly. It might be advantageous to position by pricing somewhere in-between the two tiers, with the advantage of a better product than one competitor and a lower price than the other. If existing upscale hotels react by meeting this lower rate, the consequences will be the same. A positive effect, however, would be that at least the upscale properties together might take business back from the lower tier.

The other side of competitive pricing is that the *augmented* product is rarely the same, even in the same product class. This will make little difference—*unless* the customer perceives it to be so. One way to create that perception is with pricing as a tangible aspect of the product/service mix. When one prices above the direct competition, a statement is made that a better product is being offered. The reverse is true if one prices below. In the final analysis, this is only a starting point; the market will make the final decision. Thus, it is inherently foolish to attempt to bait the customer with pricing if the product is not there to support it.

A good example is a hotel in New York City that was running an average room rate of $86. New ownership and management took over and decided to go upscale after slightly refurbishing the hotel. Rack rates of $149 and $169 were posted. The market quickly perceived that the refurbishing was inadequate to justify this kind of price increase and occupancy dropped. Not until rates were dropped to $109 did the hotel regain its market share. The same situation can also work in reverse: The same company opened a refurbished smaller hotel in a different location, and priced rooms at $95. The market saw an incredible value, since comparable hotels in the area were already at $125. Rates were successfully increased to $150. These two situations in the same company are examples of ignoring the market when setting prices, an all-too-common mistake in the hotel industry.

In restaurants there is far more variation in the product relative to the same product class. Atmospherics—along with the menu items, the chef's preparation, the quality of food and drinks, and other variables—are probably more important. Nevertheless, the need to maintain a strong pricing relationship with competitors is important. Restaurants have more opportunity to differentiate their product and should price accordingly, provided the market perceives that differentiation and is willing and able to pay for it.

Both restaurants and hotels will sometimes set low prices initially to create awareness and trial, steal customers, and build volume. This strategy is called *penetration pricing* because it is designed to penetrate the market. Once the business is established, it is not unusual for prices to be increased. Sometimes this works, and sometimes it backfires and business is lost, at which point it is far more difficult to lower prices and recapture the business. The image of being overpriced or having poor price/value is an enduring one with the consumer.

In setting prices, the marketer must always make conscious predictions about competitive reactions. Will they meet the prices? What will be the effect if they do/don't? A classic textbook case is that of Peoples Express Airlines. By drastically reducing airfares, Peoples captured enormous market share until the bigger carriers met them at the same price levels with a superior product. This eventually led to the demise of Peoples. On the other hand, Southwest Airlines has remained one of the most profitable carriers, with low costs and low prices that the large carriers have been largely unable to combat. It has done this by carefully focusing on the markets and segments it serves, which Peoples did not, and by practicing price-driven costing. (See Figure 5-12.)

The decision of whether to meet, ignore, or undercut a competitor's price moves is one that is situation-specific. We can only caution here that the marketer should conduct a thorough analysis of the complete situation—the product, the market, and the competition—before establishing prices or reacting to the prices of others. This is not a time for seat-of-the-pants judgments.

Market Demand Pricing

The term *market demand* covers a broad range of factors to be considered in any pricing decision. The appropriate term for the consideration of all these factors is *demand analysis*. Demand analysis should be a major portion of any feasibility study because it is the most critical element in establishing a market. Demand analysis means more than demand for a product; it means, instead, asking whether there is a market sufficient in size that is willing and able to buy this product. This is also the foundation of yield management, which we will discuss later.

Sufficient demand means that there is a large enough market that wants the product. Let's simplify the problem and say the product is a Rolls Royce automobile. Able to buy means those who actually have the means to buy it. For a Rolls Royce the market is now considerably smaller. Willing to buy means that those who are willing are also willing to *buy* it. Now we have a very small market.

With this information (and much else, of course) the makers of the Rolls Royce can make a pricing decision. The target market is very small, so large quantities will not be sold, eliminating economies of scale. To make a reasonable profit or return on investment, the car will have to be priced considerably higher than its variable cost. Will the target market pay this inflated price? The willingness and ability exist. In fact, for this market, another $10-, $20-, or $30,000 is not going to make much difference. The car can thus be priced at the appropriate level.

The same process applies to steak dinners, lobsters, flambé desserts, vacations, hotel rooms, suites, or any other product that is put out to market. If there is not sufficient market willing and able to buy, the product is doomed to failure. It doesn't matter what the costs are, how much advertising you do, what the guarantee is, or anything else. The critical question is simply, "What is the market acceptance level of price?"

The answer is not the simplest to find. Many don't find it until after the product has been marketed, for better or worse, but a careful analysis of the market beforehand can make life a great deal easier when the pricing decision is being made. The example was given above of a hotel in New York that tried, and failed, to price above the market. This is the same hotel described in the discussion on atmospherics in Chapter 11 as having made the same mistake in putting in a French brasserie restaurant. In these cases the market was relatively easy to identify, but management chose to ignore it and go with its own whim.

There is another concept of demand analysis that is called demand or price elasticity. The concept is covered fully in economics texts so it will not be discussed in detail here.[15] Generally speaking, high elasticity means that the higher the price, the lower the demand, and vice versa. In the case of the Rolls Royce, we could say that *within* the target market, the product is inelastic—a few more thousand dollars is not going to affect demand. We cannot ignore the elasticity

concept and we cannot ignore that this concept must be applied to the appropriate target market. This is especially true in the cases of hotels and restaurants where there are numerous alternatives. Alternative options increase the elasticity of the product. This is exactly why hotel rooms are subject to major discounting in order to obtain sufficient business.

The situation is further convoluted by what people say and what they do. In a study conducted on hotel attributes as perceived by hotel guests in six major hotels in an eastern city, 19 percent of business travelers and 31 percent of pleasure travelers at one hotel (small, upscale) indicated that price was a determining factor in choosing a hotel. At another hotel (large, convention-type), 51 percent of business travelers and 72 percent of pleasure travelers said that price was a determining factor. Yet—and this is an important "yet"—only 1 percent of all travelers at the first hotel and only 9 percent of those at the second hotel, said that price/value was the reason they chose *that* specific hotel.[16] The reason for this kind of price discrepancy is the price/value bundle, to be discussed in a moment.

There are a number of other points in regard to market demand that affect pricing, that we will not discuss in detail, but will mention briefly. The list is not all-inclusive but only suggests elements of the identified and appropriate target markets that must be considered:

Usage How is the product used? Business purposes, pleasure, or personal? What are the users' lifestyles? Do they use it because it is convenient or do they make a special effort to come here? Do they buy on price? Do they shop for the best price? Is it the main usage in this area or an alternative? Do they use it regularly or just for special occasions? Do they use the whole product or just part of it? Do they use it seasonally, cyclically, at certain times, on certain days, during certain periods? Are there different target markets? How

---

[15]The simplest and most common equation for elasticity is percent change in price divided by percent change in quantity sold equals degree of elasticity, that is, the proportionate change in demand relative to the change in price represents the degree of elasticity.

[16]Robert C. Lewis, "The Basis of Hotel Selection," *Cornell Hotel & Restaurant Administration Quarterly,* May, 1984, pp. 54–69.

many are on expense accounts? Use credit cards? Come through agents who receive commissions?

Alternatives What are the competitive options? Upscale, downscale? Other locations? What are nonprice alternatives such as staying with friends, or staying home?

Demand Satisfaction Is there unfulfilled demand or is the market saturated? What is the market acceptance level? Is the quality level satisfied? What is the generic demand as opposed to the brand demand? Are the available product/service mixes appropriate? How many customers are in the market? Is the number increasing, decreasing? Do demand differentials reflect differential costs?

Economic Conditions Good? Bad? Inflationary? Is promotional and discount pricing in vogue? Will we have to compete?

Customer Pricing

Here, again, we refer to the target market. Because we have discussed the customer in some detail earlier, we will not reiterate all the elements that need to be considered in pricing the product. The reader knows by now that, in using any marketing tool such as pricing, the customer is the first consideration.

Price/Value In establishing prices there are some elements that are particularly pertinent in regard to the customer. The first of these is the perceived price/value relationship, as it is commonly called. Given that the customer is willing and able to buy, this is the first price consideration in a purchase decision. It may not be articulated in exactly those words, but whatever words and by whatever criteria, it is this element that will establish the correct pricing levels.

There are many criteria to serve the customer in the price/value appraisal. Each customer will have different tastes and preferences. Each customer will make different trade-offs such as location for price, prestige for price, service for price, quality for price, and so forth. All will evaluate in terms of the quality of the entire experience (i.e., the total product), but each will evaluate the price/value bundle by different criteria.

The hospitality industry places special emphasis on the term "price/value." It is not at all uncommon for an executive or a manager to state, "We give price/value," or "Our distinction is the price/value we give," when asked to identify their marketing strength. Often, however, the concept of price/value is in the mind of management or in the product quality level (e.g., the Fairmont Hotel ad in Figure 12-2) rather than in the mind of the consumer.

Price/value is a complex consumer construct that needs to be better understood, because it includes three other constructs. First is quality, which may be objective or perceived quality. Second is sacrifice, which includes both monetary and non-monetary sacrifice. Third is perceived value—the perceived relationship between quality and sacrifice—the final perceived value on which decisions are made at McDonald's or Lutece, at Ritz-Carlton or Comfort Inn. These relationships are shown in Figure 12-6.

In practice, quality is most often operationally or physically defined by management, and is objective in nature, giving rise to such statements as "Our service is the best" or "Our atrium lobby is the highest in the world." Perceived quality by the consumer, on the other hand, is more likely to be the result of customer experiences, especially in the case of hospitality services. The objective quality of the atrium lobby may be negated by the perceived quality that is experienced by the noise that resounds across the atrium. Or, a rude desk clerk or waiter can, instantaneously, change a "fair" objective price to an "unfair" perceived price.

As shown in Figure 12-6, sacrifice is both monetary, where money is paid, and non-monetary, as with inconvenience, time, and experience. Thus, the meal or room, and their respective objective qualities, may justify the monetary price. The perceived quality, on the other hand—such as an experience with a rude employee, a noisy atrium, a long wait for the elevator, the raucous music in the lounge, or

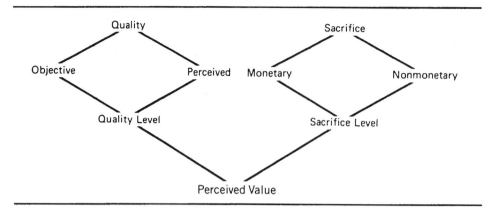

FIGURE 12-6   The relationship between quality, sacrifice, and value

the menu with print too small to read—may well not justify either the monetary (price) or the nonmonetary (experience) sacrifice. If management can truthfully say, "Our unique difference is greater *perceived* value" (at any price), then and only then has the ultimate objective been reached, as Figure 12-6 shows.

There is much talk in the hospitality industry about quality, as we have discussed. Too often, however, quality is not measured by guest perception. Only by using guest perception as the standard—and matching objective quality to perceived quality—can management establish the right price resulting in the right so-called price/value relationship. This in turn will lead to information on how to add value, in a true sense, that increases the price/value relationship and/or truly justifies the raising of prices (as done by Taco Bell).

Expectation Pricing   As we know from Chapter 1, consumers purchase problem solutions based on expectations. Let's turn that around and say that consumers also have in mind a price they expect to pay for a given solution. Reactions to prices will vary around this expected price—an important concept with which to deal.

We know from the research on customer satisfaction that satisfaction occurs when the actual experience is equal to or greater than that which is expected. Thus, contrarily, consumers

would also be satisfied when the price paid is the same or less than that which they expected to pay for what they got. The old adage, "You get what you pay for," has been proven incorrect too many times but, nevertheless, still forms a basis for consumer expectations. Satisfaction occurs when the customer feels he got what he paid for.

As explained earlier in this chapter, research has also shown that consumers, in some arbitrary fashion, establish an upper price level at which they deem the product to be too expensive, and a lower price level below which the quality of the product would be suspect. This is based on expectations. In between is the "indifference" price, the price perceived as normal for that product in a given market, given one's expectations. There are certain hotels and restaurants at which we would expect to pay different prices. When we are "surprised" by an unexpected price, we may tend to become somewhat irate. Thus, it is the responsibility of the price-setter not to surprise the customer, such as by charging $100 for a night at a Comfort Inn.

Expectations should be built into the pricing decision. Research can determine what the market thinks the product should cost. This can be especially useful in the pricing of services where a cost basis is lacking for developing an expectation. Findings may indicate that the service can be priced higher; contrarily, a lower-than-expected price may offer competitive advantage. Knowledge of price expectation can help avoid both overpricing and underpricing, such that the quality is suspect, or that the product is positioned as "cheap" and retains that position later when the price has been increased, thus later appearing overpriced.

Psychological Pricing   Prices cause psychological reactions on the part of consumers, just as atmospherics do. As noted, high prices may imply quality and low prices may imply inferiority. This is especially true for services because of their intangibility. Thus, higher-priced services may sell better, whereas lower-priced services may sell poorly, contrary to the standard economic model. Psychological reactions, however, do not necessarily correspond to reality, and it is not unusual for consumers to feel that they have made a mistake.

This is also true in the hospitality industry because of the "visibility" factor. Being "seen" at an upscale restaurant or hotel is very important to some customers. For example, a businessman might buy inexpensive furniture for his apartment and drink ordinary wine at home. This same businessman, trying to make an impression on peers and customers, will rave about the antique furniture in the lounge and the expensive wine ordered with dinner—in other words, he wants to be seen with the product that offers the highest affordable visibility factor.

Buyers and nonbuyers of products also have different perceptions of price. This contrast can be demonstrated best with the case of upscale restaurants. Many such restaurants are perceived by those who have never been to them to be far more expensive than is actually the case. Commander's Palace, one of New Orleans' finest restaurants, used large advertisements in the local paper detailing their attractively-priced lunch specials to counteract this perception. In pricing it is important to understand the price perceptions of nonusers as well as of the users.

Another psychological pricing technique is called *price-lining*. This technique clumps prices together so that a perception of substantially increased quality is created. For example,

a wine list might have a group of wines in the $8–$10 range and have the next grouping in the $14–$16 range. The perception is a definitive increase in quality, which may or may not be the case.

Still another version of psychological pricing is called *odd-numbered pricing*. This is a familiar tactic to all of us. Items sell at $6.99 rather than $7 to create the perception of a lower price. Sometimes this is carried to extremes, such as a computer that sells for $6,999.99 or a car advertised at $22,999. This tactic is often used in menus and hotel room pricing.

All these differences in consumers' perceptions might seem to make pricing an impossible task. Perhaps that is why so often hotels and restaurants tend to ignore the customer and price according to other factors! Consumer-based pricing is not impossible, however. Target marketing allows us to select relatively homogeneous markets for whom the product and the price are designed.

The marketer should also be very aware of how the customer uses price to differentiate competing products and services. This is a key to positioning with price. Value perception is always relative to the competition, whether the value perceived is real or imagined. It is the marketer's job to understand this process.

As an example of what we have just said, consider the case of a major hotel chain that conducted price research in one of its major market areas. Following are some of the findings and conclusions of the research:

The research revealed a steady loss of regular-rated room-nights and revenue—that is, there was enough increase in discounted transient room-nights to make published rack rates virtually meaningless. Moreover, many of these rooms were being sold at rates below the corporate rate. This trend had led to declining average rates over-all, with almost half the room-nights being sold at deep discounts. Although published and corporate rates had been increased dramatically, discount rates had remained flat.

In regard to customers, this research also had some interesting findings. For one, the pricing strategy was building loyalty and repeat business with the "wrong" target markets. Customers were found to have a high degree of rate awareness that influenced their value perception and intention to return; corporate- and regular-rate customers felt the hotels were overpriced. The indifference price was found to be as much as $25 lower than the regular or corporate rates being charged. For discount customers, however, it was slightly higher than what they were paying. In addition, corporate- and regular-rate customers gave the hotels lower value ratings, and the higher the rate they paid the less likely they were to return. Market share of high-rated customers was being lost to competitors. Furthermore, reservation incentive systems designed to obtain higher rates from customers were, in fact, damaging long-term profitability by alienating customers. One important conclusion of the findings was that by reducing high rates and raising discount rates, the market mix could be changed so as to produce increased profits in the long run.

Common Mistakes in Pricing

The following list summarizes the pitfalls of pricing that have been found to occur most frequently. Because pricing is the most flexible part of the presentation mix, it requires constant evaluation. Those who evaluate pricing should check their pricing strategies against this list:

1. Prices are too cost-oriented. They are increased to cover increased costs and don't allow for demand intensity and customer psychology.
2. Price policies are not adapted to changing market conditions. Once established they become "cast in cement."
3. Prices are set independent of the product mix rather than as an element of positioning strategy. Integration of all elements of the marketing mix is essential.
4. Prices ignore the customer psychology of experience, perception of value, and the total product. These are the true elements of price perception that will influence the process of choice.
5. Prices are a decision of management, rather than marketing.

In the final analysis, the best price is the one that makes the best overall contribution.

Consumer Price Search

In an appendix to this chapter we discuss *yield management,* a current practice in the hotel industry, especially in chains, in pricing its rooms. While this practice—attempting to maximize revenue on each room sold at each point in time—may be efficient in price-setting, it has also added to the confusion of the customer seeking hotel room prices.

The confusion started in the 1980s with rack rates that eventually became virtually meaningless, except to a few poor souls who didn't know how to get a better rate. (This was essentially the case in the United States, but it has now spread overseas.) Today, in the middle and upper ends of the market in the large chains, there may be at least seven rates for any given room at any given point in time: the rack rate, the 800 number rate, the call-the-hotel rate, the membership rate, the corporate rate, the rate of the travel agent (who may have as many as 20 different rates on a monitor), and the rate you negotiate at the front desk. Which rate you get may depend on how good you are at ferreting out the lowest rate—something many hotels won't tell you without a great deal of effort even when they spend a great deal of money advertising it. Unlike the airlines, which have the same practices but quote only one rate at a time, the hotel industry has yet to get its act (or its computers) together.

The retail industry went through the same cycle. "List price" no longer has any meaning—it's the discount price and/or the sale price but again, like the airlines, it's the same price. Some large retailers such as Sears, Wal-Mart, and K-Mart, have gone to what they call "everyday low pricing," with limited success, to try to counter the consumer-learned experience of "wait for the sale price." The hotel industry needs to do something similar. (Interestingly, while a restaurant may have "specials" on certain days of the week, one does not go in, or call, to negotiate a price.)

First, "fair" prices need to be set based on value pricing as discussed earlier in this chapter. These may change seasonally or under certain conditions, but need to be consistent regardless of who is quoting the price. Second, these prices should not be discounted (or raised) other than for specific reasons (such as seasonal, weekends, large groups), and at those times they should also be consistent. Finally, the value must be in the price—that is, not in a lot of unnecessary amenities and services that the target market doesn't want and for which it isn't willing to pay.

The hotel industry, especially the upper tier, operates under the short-term profit syndrome and is choking on it. Until stability and reasoning come to hotel pricing, hotels will remain at the mercy of customers, will continue to lose and irritate them, and will continue to debate the virtues of discounting; revenue maximization will never be achieved under these conditions.

Summary

Pricing is a complex marketing tool but it is, first and foremost, a marketing tool. Thus, by definition, pricing is customer-based and customer-driven. Pricing is also a tangible aspect of the product/service offered. As such, it can be utilized to change and manipulate customer perception. The effective marketer must understand this process.

The first step in establishing prices is to identify the target market objectives in terms of financial objectives, volume objectives, and customer objectives. The marketing mix strategy should be based on these objectives and the customers' needs and wants. Cost and competitive pressures establish constraints but cost-oriented methods of pricing—such as cost-plus, cost percentage, break-even, and contribution margin pricing—ignore the need for price-driven costing. Prices must also take into account overall market demand for the industry's products and services.

Finally, it is the customers themselves who will determine the appropriate pricing strategy and actual setting of the pricing schedule. Marketers must understand customers' expectations and how they perceive the price/value relationship.

Discussion Questions

1. What pricing lessons should the hospitality industry have learned from the boom times of the early 1980s followed by the tough times of the early 1990s?
2. Discuss the three types of pricing objectives, how they are different, and how they overlap.
3. Why is using only cost percentage pricing methods not recommended as a marketing-driven option, especially in the hospitality industry?
4. Discuss why it is possible for the hotel industry to have room rates that can change on a daily basis. How would you deal with a guest who complains about her room rate because she has found that her friend is paying $20 less per night for the same type of room?
5. Discuss your personal pricing elasticity in terms of restaurants, i.e., at what point in the price/value mode will you trade down?
6. Discuss how psychological pricing can make a product seem to have a higher price/value relationship.
7. Choose two common mistakes in pricing and apply them to a real life hospitality establishment.
8. Case 12-1 concerns a hotel threatened by new competition. What should it do about its pricing strategy?
9. Analyze Case 12-2. Develop a strategy that will help this restaurant to be more successful. Consider all the variables.
10. In Case 12-3, what should be the pricing strategy of the Nikko Atlanta ten months before its opening?

✔ Case 12-1
The Sheraton Jeddah Hotel[17]

The Sheraton Jeddah Hotel overlooked the Red Sea in Jeddah, Saudi Arabia. It was just two years old and was built as an upscale luxury hotel. Exhibit 12-1-1 provides some descriptions, including the rack rates, from the hotel's brochure.

The hotel had 145 rooms and suites, and 17 villas. Its annual occupancy was 84 percent with an ADR of US$158. Government business accounted for over half of occupancy and was top-scale, including princes who rented the suites at rack rate or better. Meetings business was minimal since the largest meeting space accommodated only 50 persons. This was not uncommon in Saudi Arabia where large business meetings were few.

The Sheraton Jeddah was the market leader in Jeddah in both average rate and occupancy. It was the superior hotel in the marketplace and was considered to have no direct competition. In the first-class category there was only a 275-room Marriott in the commercial center with a rack rate of $110 single, an ADR of $93, and a 74 percent occupancy. Also existing was a 280-room Holiday Inn with a $95 single rate, an ADR of $82, and an occupancy of 66 percent.

All this, however, was about to change. Within six months a new 375-room Inter-Continental Hotel would open in Jeddah. This hotel would be equal in standards to the Sheraton, and its rack rates would be approximately the same. It would also have the advantage of a better location, nearer the commercial center of Jeddah. It would not, however, have the large rooms and suites of the Sheraton. In fact, the rooms would be somewhat limited in size. It would also have no beach or bay view. Inter-Continental management was projecting its first year's occupancy at 55 percent with an average rack rate of $180 single.

Sheraton management projected the business mix of the four Jeddah hotels for the year after the Inter-Continental opened, as shown in Table 12-1-1, keeping their own mix as it had been the past two years. It also rated the hotels on four attributes from "1" (poorest) to "4" (best), also shown in Table 12-1-1. As the hotel market in Jeddah was static, management felt definitely threatened by the new hotel. One consideration was to lower rates, but there was fear of starting a rate war if they did this. How else, they thought, were they going to protect their market share?

[17]Joerg Heyer, Director of Marketing at the Sheraton Jeddah at the time, contributed the information for this case. All currency except that in Exhibit 12-1-1 is in U.S. dollars. At the time of this case's writing, one U.S. Dollar was equal to about two Saudi Riyal.

EXHIBIT 12-1-1   Sheraton Jeddah brochure descriptions and rack rates

Sheraton Jeddah
HOTEL

TARIFF SHEET

Sheraton Jeddah Hotel situated on North Jeddah Corniche, enjoys panoramic views over the Red Sea and Jeddah City, offering luxurious accommodation, 15 kms. from Downtown, and 10 kms. from king Abdul Aziz Airport.

All Hotel Rooms and Suites enjoy spectacular views over the Red Sea, the Corniche and Jeddah City and are fitted with Individual A/C Controls, Radio, T.V. in-house movies. Direct Dial Telephones, Mini-Fridge and key Card System.

Hotel facilities include, unique shaped Outdoor Swimming Pool with Whirlpool, Two Tennis Courts, Squash Court, Gym, Aerobic Room, Sauna, Steambath Jacuzzis and Massage.

Business Centre: offers Secretarial Assistance, Typing, Photocopying, Translation, (Arabic, English, French and German), Personal Computers, Computer Telex and Facsimile.

Private Beach: featuring 17-Villas, Two Tennis Courts, Volleyball, Basketball, Swimming Pool, Children's Pool, Sand Beach, Scuba Diving and Snorkling facilities.

Rates:

Single	SR. 350.00
Double	SR. 455.00
Superior Single	SR. 375.00
Superior Double	SR. 485.00
Business Suite	SR. 1,000.00
Executive Suite	SR. 1,000.00
Ambassador Suite	SR. 1,500.00
Amiri Suite	SR. 1,750.00
Royal Suite	SR. 3,000.00
Family Apartment (1 BR)	SR. 650.00
Family Apartment (2 BRS)	SR. 900.00
Extra Bed	SR. 75.00

Above rates are subject to 15% service charge.

Family Plan:
Children under 12 years of age sharing same parents room are accommodated free of charge.

P.O. Box: 14315 Jeddah 21424
Tel. 699 2212, Fax: 699 2660
Telex: 607229 JEDSHE SJ.

Sheraton Jeddah
HOTEL

From the Presidential, Ambassador, Amiri Executive suites to the deluxe bedrooms, every room has magnificent panorama views of the Red Sea coastline. Supreme in comfort and facilities – all bathrooms are fitted with whirlpools. There are superior bedrooms in two wings alongside the Esplanade, all furnished in impeccable taste by the world famous Cassina of Italy

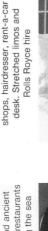

The Skytop lounge accommodates meetings and private parties, up to 50. In the evenings the terrace gardens may be reserved for parties up to 300. Shaped swimpool with light refreshments, 2 open tennis courts, squash, basketball, gym, executive meeting room, business center, Reuters, shops, hairdresser, rent-a-car desk. Stretched limos and Rolls Royce hire

The Al Waha international restaurant offers all day dining. Alongside, on the swimpool terrace, barbeques are held on many nights. Glass elevators will sweep you up to rooftop restaurants. The Al Ta'ee serves Arabian cuisine. The Xian Gong is a refined Chinese restaurant with a Mandarin welcome and ancient Chinese drums. All the restaurants have windows facing the sea

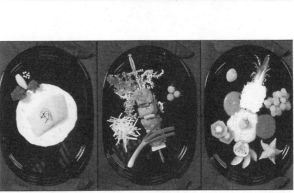

489

TABLE 12-1-1 Projected Business Mix and Subjective Attribute Ratings

	Sheraton	Inter-Continental	Holiday	Marriott
Corporate Individual	20%	30%	70%	60%
Transient Leisure	20%	20%	10%	20%
Government	60%	40%	0	0
Crew/airline	0	10%	20%	20%
Location	3	4	2	3
Service	4	4	2	3
Rooms	4	3	1	2
Resort Facilities	4	4	1	2

✔ Case 12-2
The Mooring Restaurant[18]

The Mooring Restaurant was located in the Mystic Hilton Hotel in the southeastern Connecticut shore-town of Stonington. It was approximately 130 miles from New York City and 90 miles from Boston. This prime location made it easily accessible by boat, Amtrak, by car off Interstate 95, and by plane via the Groton–New London Airport. The hotel used location as a convenience aspect in marketing the hotel to many business clients and families, as shown in Exhibit 12-2-1.

The Town of Stonington was a small, seaside lower-middle class town of 17,000 inhabitants with an average yearly per capita income of $18,536 and an average age of 40. Its seaport charm and history, along with that of its somewhat larger sister city, Mystic, attracted many tourists during the summer season, when the population tripled, who came to visit the famous Mystic Seaport, Olde Mistick Village, and Mystic Marinelife Aquarium, located across from the Hilton. Also located in and around the Mystic area were a number of large companies, such as Dow Chemical, Pfizer, and General Dynamics.

The Mystic Hilton

The Mystic Hilton was a relatively new franchise property of Hilton Hotels. It was operated under management contract by the Fisher Hotel Group, which also operated the deluxe Bostonian Hotel, located in the Faneuil Hall marketplace in Boston. Frank Fisher's overall mission for his hotels was to operate "small urban luxury hotels, such as the Bostonian."

The Mystic Hilton was the only major hotel in the area, with 184 rooms and a year-round occupancy of 76 percent. Occupancy was greatly higher in the summer tourist season and much lower in the winter season. Winter weekends were close to full occupancy, however, as the hotel aggressively promoted winter weekend

getaways. In addition, the hotel hosted many business clients and conventions, which made up approximately 40 percent of hotel revenues. The average age of the hotel guests was between 30 and 50 years.

Every hotel, motel, bed and breakfast, and lodging place in the area offering a place to sleep was considered competition. In a micro sense, however, the Old Mystic Motor Lodge and a Comfort Inn were the only product class competitors for the Hilton.

Frank Fisher did not believe in having any small, coffee shop-style restaurants in his hotels. He believed that a hotel restaurant must draw people in from the outside and that it must be an integral part of the overall package to help market the hotel. Fisher hotel restaurants must be high-quality, service-conscious, fine dining establishments. Fisher Group was experienced in running these types of hotel restaurants and had been very successful with their four-star Seasons Restaurant in the Bostonian Hotel.

The Mooring Restaurant

The Mooring was one of two restaurants located in the Mystic Hilton. It was easily accessible through the hotel lobby entrance, but there was no separate entrance to the restaurant from the outside. The only physical evidence of the restaurant on the outside of the hotel was the Mooring logo on the Hilton sign at the beginning of the driveway entrance. The other outlet in the hotel was the Soundings Lounge, which offered a limited menu consisting mostly of appetizers and sandwiches.

The Mooring was initially modeled after the inside of a ship. It sported wood floors and tables and an overall nautical appearance. This design, however, created a dark, noisy atmosphere that was not conducive to the luxury restaurant that Frank Fisher had imagined, so it was remodeled. The physical plant and atmospherics of The Mooring were exemplified in a

---

[18]Kevin Durfee and Melissa Pappas researched and contributed to this case.

EXHIBIT 12-2-1   Location of the Mystic Hilton Hotel

brightly lighted room with large windows over-looking a small courtyard plaza. Linen table-cloths, fine china and silver, a wine table dis-play, carpeted floor, soft background music, and comfortable upholstered chairs made up The

Mooring's atmosphere to appeal to a more dis-criminating diner. Through the use of atmos-pherics, the Fisher Group created an environ-ment that they hoped would affect the buyer and increase the purchase probability.

EXHIBIT 12-2-2   Sample lunch and dinner menus

THE MOORING

Starters

Grapefruit & Avocado Medley	3.50
Crab and Corn Fritters with Lemon, Chive Mayonnaise	4.25
Potato Pancakes Grilled Apples & Sour Cream	4.25
Angel Hair Pasta with Littlenecks and Tomatoes	4.50
New England Fish Chowder	2.25
A Winter Soup of Sausage and Rices	2.50

Salads

Chef's Salad	5.50
Grilled Duck and Spinach with Spiced Pecans	6.50
Pasta Salad with Crabmeat	5.75
Mixed Greens with Baked Goat Cheese Croutons	2.75

Specialties

Chicken and Veal in Puff Pastry	6.75
Sauteed Ocean Catfish, Creole Sauce	6.25
Shirred Eggs with Your Choice of Link Sausage or Smoked Salmon	5.50
Vegetable Lasagna	6.25
Traditional Boston Schrod Filet	6.50
Whale-of-a-Burger with Bacon and Cheddar, Bleu Cheese or Swiss	4.75
Stir Fried Scallops with Vegetables and Spiced Orange Sauce	7.75
A Belgian Waffle with Walnuts and Bacon	4.75
Chef's Sandwich Board Roast Beef, Genoa, Ham and Swiss, Liverwurst	5.75
Half Board	3.00

THE MYSTIC HILTON

The Mystic Hilton Grill

Rib Veal Chop	18.25
12 oz. New York Sirloin	18.75
Atlantic Swordfish	17.75
Roast Chicken	16.75
1-1/2 lb. Lobster, Steamed	21.75
Filet of Sole, Meuniere	17.50

Served with Potato, Winter Vegetables and a Dinner Salad

Dinner Specialties

Breast of Duck, Cranberry Bread Pudding	18.50
Sauteed Scallops & Shrimp with Crisp Potatoes	17.75
Rack of Lamb, Port Sauce and Winter Vegetables	19.75
Three Tournedoes — Beef, Veal, Lamb with a Selection of Mustards	20.75
Seared Filet of Norwegian Salmon with a Sauternes Cream	18.75
Loin of Rabbit with White Beans and Marjoram	19.50
Sauteed Red Snapper with Basil	19.25

Your Entree Includes a Dinner Salad

Your Server Will Present a Selection of Dessert Specialties.

Erik Anderson, Executive Chef

The restaurant seated approximately 108 people and served three full-service meals a day. Lunch and dinner menus varied in respect to both entrees and price. The average lunch item was $6, while the average cost of a dinner entree was $19. Through the use of price the restaurant positioned in the upscale market, differentiated itself from the competition, and created a perception of its product. Exhibit 12-2-2 shows samples of lunch and dinner menus.

The restaurant served 120 to 150 covers per day, midweek, almost on a year-round basis: 20–30 breakfasts, 60–70 lunches, and 40–50 dinners. On weekends it served about 40 breakfasts, 40 lunches, and 120 dinners.

Management marketed the restaurant to a variety of segments. The primary market for lunch was business clientele, attracted by the guaranteed 30-minute Express Lunch consist-

ing of soup and sandwich. The dinner crowd was a varied mix with no specific market segments. The restaurant did not attract many families. The front desk often suggested to price-sensitive families staying in the hotel that they eat at the more moderately priced Skipper Jack's nearby.

The Mooring was a very good restaurant in keeping with Frank Fisher's desires. The restaurant had received many favorable reviews from local newspaper and magazine critics regarding the food preparation and service. These accolades were displayed prominently in various locations throughout the hotel, including several at the restaurant entrance and the front desk area. Exhibit 12-2-3 shows samples of reviews.

The restaurant also did a fair amount of advertising, including special holiday promotions.

EXHIBIT 12-2-3 Accolades for The Mooring Restaurant

"Chef Erik Anderson is truly talented and (has) been given his leave to produce delicious departures from the ordinary."

— Elise Maclay,
Connecticut Magazine

IN THE MYSTIC HILTON

20 Coogan Boulevard, Mystic, CT 06355
Phone (203) 572-0731.
Reservations suggested.

"...the venison could not have been better... the salmon dish looked as elegant as it tasted. Not to negate the tournedos of beef, nor the marinated breast of pheasant..."

— Patricia Brooks,
The New York Times

IN THE MYSTIC HILTON

20 Coogan Boulevard, Mystic, CT 06355
Phone (203) 572-0731.
Reservations suggested.

"...creatively conceived and adeptly executed ... tradiitional dishes prepared in a seductively stylish manner..."

— C.C.B. Bryan
and M. Simonds,
The Hartford Courant

IN THE MYSTIC HILTON

20 Coogan Boulevard, Mystic, CT 06355
Phone (203) 572-0731.
Reservations suggested.

"I'd dine at The Mooring at least twice a week even if I had to pay."

— Richard Hertz, Owner,
The Mystic Hilton

IN THE MYSTIC HILTON

20 Coogan Boulevard, Mystic, CT 06355
Phone (203) 572-0731.
Reservations suggested.

494

This was done locally from May to August, as well as in Connecticut, Rhode Island, and New England monthly magazines, and in the newspapers of nearby cities, Hartford, New London, and Providence.

Frank Fisher wanted to use The Mooring Restaurant as a prime marketing tool for the hotel. The restaurant, however, was not attracting much business despite its excellent reputation, and was losing money.

✔ Case 12-3
The Nikko Hotel/Atlanta

Nikko Hotels, a subsidiary of Japan Air Lines, planned to open a new 440-room property on Peachtree Road in the Buckhead area of Atlanta in November. This was just after Swiss Hotels was to open a new 300-room property just down the road, in August. Management's quandary was to adjust the opening rack rates as it marketed the property ten months before the opening.

The city of Atlanta, Georgia encompassed three distinct areas: the downtown area; the Buckhead area in the north, about six miles (as the crow flies) from downtown; and the Perimeter area, another six miles farther north. Each area had its own market and did not compete directly with the other two areas. Thus, each hotel thought, competitively, of its own particular market area.

The Buckhead area was well-known for industrial parks and corporate offices, lots of executive "power," and shopping centers with very fine and expensive shopping. In the immediate center of this area, and adjacent to the well-known Lenox shopping center, the largest in the Southeast, there were four major hotel properties, with the Nikko and Swiss to join them. All except the Westin were on Peachtree Road within a short distance of each other; the Westin was around the corner on Lenox Road, an equally short distance in the other direction.

The major hotels had performed as follows during the past year:

	Rooms	Occ%	Sgl Rack	ADR
Ritz-Carlton	553	75	139–185	120
Westin	371	55	130–170	100
Embassy Suites	311	70	119–139	85
Holiday Inn	221	52	78–109	75

Except for Embassy Suites, the spread between single and double was $20. Rack rates, in traditional hotel industry fashion, were expected to go up five to ten percent during the

current year. Average rates, however, especially with the two new hotels competing for customers, were expected to show an increase of only two to three percent, at best.

Rooms-Pricing at the Nikko

Klaus Mennekes, the new GM at the Nikko/Atlanta, had just been transferred from the Nikko Essex House on Central Park South in New York City. He was fully aware that pricing in Atlanta was a different ballgame than in New York. Pondering how to price into the Buckhead market and forestall a threat from Swiss Hotels, he ran across an article in *Hotel & Motel Management* headlined, "Added Properties in Buckhead May Create Occupancy Squeeze."

"Just what I need," thought Klaus as he started to read the article.

The addition of the Nikko and Swiss hotels, said the article, would nearly double the luxury hotel segment in Buckhead, already showing a few signs of strain, making it the scene of fierce competition. The Westin Lenox Hotel had recently been taken over by its lender, the First National Bank of Boston, although it remained under Westin management with little or no operating changes. A senior principal at PKF's Atlanta office had this to say: "The Westin Lenox may not have had a terrible first year, but it was still difficult for them. In a new luxury hotel it's always difficult in the first few years because of the high costs per room; it puts the hotel in a difficult situation." After several months of pre-marketing under the Inter-Continental flag, the hotel switched marquees just a few days before opening. A vice president at First Bank of Boston stated, "Westin came in at a real disadvantage. They didn't have 12 months to do pre-marketing."

"The troubles at the Westin may be symptomatic of a Buckhead slump spanning all hotel segments. This slump provides a textbook case of what happens when rooms are added to an area without a correspondingly significant addition to existing demand generators," continued the article. According to the Atlanta office of PKF, occupancy rates in the Buckhead area over the past four years were 74 percent, 72 percent, 66 percent, and 65 percent last year. During the same period, the number of rooms increased from 1,325 to 2,293 and would approach 3,400 by the time the Nikko and Swiss open.

Poised above the fray was the highly successful Ritz-Carlton. "We feel we have the jump on the competition because we are very focused on our mission of achieving high occupancy," said Manager John Arnett. "We sell one commodity, and that is service." It is that level of service that will give the Ritz and the Westin an advantage even after the Nikko and Swiss are open, according to an industry observer. "The Ritz and Westin are going to have a real advantage because they will have had several years of opportunity to earn market identification." He also noted that rate structures for slightly older properties were based partly on recovering construction costs that, by current standards, seemed inexpensive.

Price wars are typical hotel strategies during a supply glut, but Arnett said the Ritz' reputation as a five-star hotel may well make price reductions unnecessary. "We are very sensitive to what the competition is offering, but we are not going to slash rates as a reaction to what they might or might not charge," he said.

The PKF principal offered a mixed forecast for discounting in Buckhead. "Many new properties seek to achieve penetration rate by discounting," he said. "At the same time others feel that they have an established clientele. They think diluting rates dilutes quality." Other local analysts seemed to agree on a good news/bad news prognosis for Buckhead—tight in the short term, but bright over the long run.

PKF's Atlanta office was optimistic about the long term. It saw the Buckhead ratio as 34 percent group business to 54 percent commercial business with more swing to the group side. From a group standpoint, Buckhead had food, beverage, and prestigious retail—everything but a central meeting facility, although the hotels had fairly sizeable meeting space. The Buckhead Business Association reported that they receive about 60 calls a year asking if there is a conference center in Buckhead able to handle small conventions.

"Okay," thought Klaus, "short-term, long-term, we aren't even open yet. What do we do now?"

Chapter 12 Appendix

Yield Revenue Management

In 1988 some players in the hotel industry introduced a pricing concept called *yield management,* now often called *revenue management.* This concept was copied from the airlines, which, it is claimed, change rates as many as 80,000 times in a single day through central computer reservation systems.

Under the yield management system, discount prices are opened and closed based on fluctuating demand and advance bookings. Like airline passengers, hotel customers under this system pay different prices for the same room depending on when their reservation is made. Through the sophistication of a central computer, different prices are set depending on demand, day-by-day or hour-by-hour.

For example, when demand is soft, discounts requiring advance bookings remain available or are reopened for sale shortly before the dates that are not fully booked. When demand builds, the discount rates are removed so that customers then booking will pay higher rates. In other words, all levels of pricing are controlled by opening and closing them almost at will, with any variation in demand. It is said that the competitive advantages of yield management are enormous:

Yield management can dramatically increase revenues; maximize profits; greatly improve the effectiveness of market segmentation; open new market segments; strengthen product portfolio strategy; instantly improve cash flow; spread demand throughout seasons and times of day; and allow management to price according to market segment demand.[19]

Seven years later, yield management in hotels has not quite lived up to all those rosy predictions. Although all sizeable hotel chains, and even some individual properties have yield management systems in some form or other [*property management systems* (PMS) to *computer reservation systems* (CRS)], the practice in the hotel industry has been far different from that with the airlines. In this appendix we will briefly discuss the practices and some of the reasons for differences. In one form or another, yield or, better, revenue management is here to stay, and it is well to be aware of its nuances.

What Yield Management Is

Yield management is a systematic approach to matching demand for services with an appropriate supply, to maximize profits. Until 1988 this was largely limited to balancing group with individual demand, based on complementary

---

[19]James C. Makens, "Yield Management: A Major Pricing Breakthrough," *Piedmont Airlines* (in-flight magazine), April, 1988, p. 32.

booking times. Today, through computer technology, the attempt is to juggle all bookings and rate quotations so that on any given night the maximum revenue potential is realized.

There are several factors that make the use of yield management suitable to the hotel industry. First, a hotel room is a perishable product, so it is sometimes better to sell it at a lower price than not to sell it at all, because of low marginal production costs and high marginal capacity costs (i.e., contribution margin pricing). Second, capacity is fixed and cannot increase to meet more demand. Third, hotel demand is widely fluctuating and uncertain, depending on the days of the week and seasons of the year. Fourth, market segments have different lead times for purchase. A convention group might reserve hotel rooms three years in advance, a pleasure traveler two months, and a businessman a week ahead. Fifth, hotels have great flexibility in varying their prices at any given time.

These factors are very similar to the airline industry and represent the requisite conditions for a successful yield management program. Although an operational tool, yield management requires hotels to be market-oriented. Knowledge of market segments, their buying behavior, and the prices they are willing to pay is essential for maximum success.

Why Hotels are Different

Only certain aspects, however, of the airline-based yield management techniques can be used in hotels. Commonalities exist, to be sure. The premise of airline yield management is that each seat has a certain level of demand. Obviously, when demand is high, the price for the seat should be also, and vice versa. While this may seem to be an ideal scenario for hotel pricing, other factors intervene.

A hotel room is very different from an airline seat. The configuration of a hotel room inventory could have 20 different categories of rooms, for example, rooms that face the water, some near the elevator, others on high floors, some facing the parking lot, as well as different types of beds. The differentiation in available rooms within a hotel can thus be immense. On the other hand, an airplane has only economy or first class—even window, middle, or aisle seats are priced the same, and you don't necessarily get what you want. Hotel customers aren't as amenable.

There is a wide range of service choices among hotels at the same destination. Ritz-Carlton is right down the street from Days Inn. Each offers very different levels of service. Consumers say something about the image they want to convey by their choice of venue as well as about the price they are willing and able to pay. There is no such choice among domestic carriers in the United States. On Continental, American, Delta, United or TWA, the experience is similar. Airlines, at least in North America, have yet to differentiate themselves from each other in any outstanding way. Passengers choose airlines for where they are going when they want to go (other than some diversion due to frequent-flyer mile rewards). In contrast with impersonal airline seats, a hotel room is a personal experience. As well, hotel guest nights are often multiple. They may span both low-yield and high-yield nights, rather than one flight. Thus, a high-yield rate one night may be a low-yield one the next.

Hotel guests have choices. If they don't like the rate at one hotel, they can usually easily switch to another. Airlines, however, can match a competitor's rates instantly. Airline choices are very limited and often non-existent at the same place and time. Hotels have many competitors; airlines have few.

Hotels may charge rack rates, which they rarely get at other times, during busy time periods. The customer has little choice, and while the yield could be very high for a particular period, the long-term impact can be disastrous. Paying $275 for a room that is normally $150, the customer may not return again, until perhaps during the summer when the hotel offers the same room for $100. With airlines, there is little choice. Hotels practicing yield management, unlike the airlines, also reopen lower rates as the reservation date comes closer with rooms remaining unfilled (which is most of the time). Thus, the room buyer can often call the day before and get a lower rate than quoted a month before. For these reasons, yield management in hotels is a far more sensitive practice than with airlines.

Effective Use of Yield Management

The essential rules of this process for hotels have been said to be as follows:

- Set the most effective pricing structure.
- Limit the number of reservations accepted for any given night or room type, based on profit potential.
- Negotiate volume discounts with groups.
- Match market segments with room type and price needs.
- Obtain more resources from current and potential business.
- Enable reservations agents to be effective sales agents rather than merely order-takers.[20]
- We have added: Provide reasons for discounting, such as advance purchase time, payment in advance, nonrefundability, length of stay, etc. Marriott has done this deliberately to put the trade-off decision in the hands of the customer (Exhibit 12.A-1).
- Be consistent across CRS, property reservationists, travel agents, and other intermediaries so that quoted rates are the same.

The actual practice of yield management is far more complex than this, of course. We have only touched on the rudiments which are sufficient for an introduction to the process. Now we will look at the benefits.

Yield Yield is the ratio between actual and potential room revenue. Actual revenue is that received from room sales. Potential revenue is what a hotel would have received if all their rooms were sold at full price or rack rates. Keep in mind, of course, that for this to be realistic, the full price rates must be realistic. Rack rates that are rarely achieved have little meaning for true yield ratios. Also realize that, unlike the example in Table 12.A-1, a hotel will have any number of different rates, including suite rates. All these must be calculated to determine a true yield ratio. Table 12.A-1 also ignores incremental reve-

---

[20]W. Lieberman, "Debunking the Myths of Yield Management," *Cornell Hotel and Restaurant Administration Quarterly*, February, 1993, pp. 34–41.

TABLE 12.A-1   Calculating Yield

Hotel A has 400 rooms and a rack rate of $120. On August 1st it had an occupancy of 70% or 350 rooms sold, at an average rate of $80.

$$\text{Yield} = \frac{\text{Revenue Realized}}{\text{Revenue Potential}} \times 100$$

Revenue Realized = $80 × 350 rooms sold = $28,000
Revenue Potential = $120 × 400 = $48,000

$$\text{Yield} = \frac{\$28,000}{\$48,000} = 58.33\%$$

The same yield can be realized if Hotel A sold fewer rooms at a higher rate or more rooms at a lower rate:

Average Rate	Rooms Sold	Revenue Realized	Yield
$100	280	$28,000	58.33%
$ 70	400	$28,000	58.33%

Note: REVPAR calculations produce the same percentage.

EXHIBIT 12.A-1   Discounting for advance purchase and payment—no changes, no cancellations, no refunds (in the fine print)

"I DON'T THINK YOUR TRAVEL PER DIEM SHOULD STAND BETWEEN YOU AND A MARRIOTT."

You may be able to afford the Marriott you thought you couldn't.
Just purchase your room 7, 14 or 21 days in advance and save up to 30% off
our regular corporate rate. Call your travel agent or 1-800-228-9290.

Marriott
HOTELS · RESORTS · SUITES

WE MAKE IT HAPPEN FOR YOU.

Non-refundable credit card purchase for the entire stay is required. No changes or cancellations are permitted on 14 or 21 day rates. (7 day rate is 50% refundable if cancelled.) Some black out dates and important restrictions apply. Available in limited quantities at participating properties. Not available with other offers and discounts or to groups of 10 rooms or more. Rates are not available at Courtyard by Marriott, Residence Inn by Marriott or Fairfield Inn. ©1993 Marriott Corp.

Courtesy of Marriott Corporation

nue of food and beverages that, unlike the airlines, cannot be ignored. Yield takes into account both occupancy and room rates and can be illustrated by the example in Table 12.A-1.

Note that a hotel can reach the same yield through different combinations of average rates and occupancy. Effective yield management requires hotels to have access to many kinds of information, but the most basic element is *demand forecasting*. Hotels must be able to forecast the demand for rooms from each of its market segments for any date in the future (the near future, at least). Thus, customer purchase behavior must be well understood—especially the lead time for purchase and price elasticity.

Generally speaking, business travelers as a group are willing to pay more for lodging, and their bookings are usually made in the days immediately preceding their trip. On the other hand, tourists will make reservations well in advance of their trip and will expect lower rates. The yield management system should be able to estimate the number of rooms that will be demanded by each segment for any given day. It is then up to hotel management to set prices accordingly.

Yield Management and Pricing Yield management systems provide information on how many rooms to sell at differing prices. They help hotel managements to decide what rate classes to open and close, and they provide information on whether pricing structures should be revised. Although there are several approaches to adjusting room rates, a common element is the comparison of actual demand versus forecasted demand. Consider the example of an August 1st, four months away, for a 500-room hotel. The yield management system should establish a trend (based on reservations history, estimates of demand, etc.) for reservations for that day. Table 12.A-2 is a simplified example of the process.

The room sales for August 1 are forecasted to be 500. On April 1, the forecast shows that 300 rooms should have been reserved, but actual reservations are only 250. Since reservations are lagging, that hotel can introduce price discounts to spur demand. On July 1, the actual reservations are greater than forecasted, so it is time to close the availability of lower rates.

This is a simple example. Just imagine the complexity of systems that keep track of every future date, numerous rate categories, continuous changes in the environment, various sources of reservations, and different market segments.

The large number of variables required to forecast demand accurately make it essential that computer systems be used. Hotels must select software that is suitable to their unique needs and must remember that final decisions are made by marketers, not by a computer.

Yield management, if used effectively, allows a hotel to manage its limited inventory better in order to maximize revenues. Short-term gains, however, must not substitute for long-term profits. Loyal and repeat customers will not appreciate the lack of room availability or special rates to which they are accustomed. They are likely to be more interested in consistent pricing, so it may be a mistake not to honor a long-term customer's request for special rates. Hotel employees who are affected by yield management systems, especially in reservations, sales, and front office departments, must be involved in the process so that they understand the objectives of yield management, that is, to maximize revenues per available room (REVPAR) while keeping customers loyal.

TABLE 12.A-2   Adjusting Prices to Market Demand

	Dates Forecasted				
	April 1	May 1	June 1	July 1	August 1
Room Reservations	300	340	400	440	500
Actual Room Reservations	250	305	380	450	500
Difference	−50	−35	−20	+10	0

EXHIBIT 12.A-2   What's fair (and what ain't fair)

Part of the economic theory of supply and demand suggests that as an item becomes more scarce, its price should go up. Like so many other economic theories, however, this one fails when applied to many real-world situations. For the World Series, major-league baseball sets a ticket price too low to dampen demand for a relatively small supply of tickets. Instead of raising the price to cut down the demand, the baseball leagues allocate tickets among the various teams and allow fans to line up. Restaurants and airlines often end up fully booked (with customers standing by for a table or seat), but rather than raise prices, they turn away business.

Three researchers contend that these pricing strategies, which do not reflect economic theory, are based on meeting a popular notion of fairness. In an article in *American Economic Review,* Daniel Kahneman, Jack L. Knetsch, and Richard Thaler suggest that fairness in pricing is, in fact, a constraint on profit-seeking.[a] Working in Canada, the three researchers presented thousands of respondents with hundreds of hypothetical situations that involved the question of when a price is fair, and when it isn't. In one of the situations, for instance, respondents were asked whether a store was justified in raising the price of snow shovels the day after a blizzard. Such a price increase was overwhelmingly condemned as unfair.

"We concluded that scarcity was not a fair excuse for raising the price of an item," Thaler told participants in a seminar at Cornell University's School of Hotel Administration. "The timing of a sale transaction is also not viewed as a fair reason to increase the price. We think this is why restaurants do not raise their prices on Saturday night, even though it is generally their busiest time."

On the other hand, eliminating a discount is widely viewed as fair. (Nearly 60 percent of the respondents agreed with this proposition.) "What this means," Thaler suggested, "is that you should always make your stated price the highest price you *ever intend to charge* for an item. Then you can offer discounts from that price as appropriate."

He related the story of a ski-resort operator who wanted to charge higher rates in February, when the snow was ideal. Rather than add surcharges when the snow conditions were good, the operator set all rates at the February price, giving discounts when the skiing was poor. Another justification for raising prices is increased costs. "Passing on cost increases is always perceived as fair," Thaler said, "although double-ticketing—marking up items that are already on the shelf—is considered unfair." If a restaurant simply increases its prices on Saturday night, for example, people will think that's unfair. But if the same restaurant adds a small musical combo, and then raises prices with an entertainment charge, that will be viewed as properly passing on increased costs."

Inefficiency. Thaler argued that those results show an inverse correlation between fairness and economic efficiency. He noted that people view queues as more fair than lotteries or "market-clearing" prices for the sale of scarce goods.

The perception of fairness probably also interferes with the pricing of strongly seasonal items such as rooms in a seasonal resort. Thaler said: "In a market with strong periodic fluctuations in demand, a fixed supply, and cost variability, price variations will be insufficient to clear the market. Most resorts use in-season pricing and off-season pricing as a means of optimizing their profit. But a price that is high enough to clear the market during the peak season—setting demand equal to supply—will probably be viewed as unfair, because scarcity is not a fair reason for price increases."

"On the other hand," he continued, "demand may also be relatively inelastic during off-peak times. It may not make any difference that, in April, Vail's or Aspen's price is low and the skiing is wonderful: people may just not be able to get away then. Moreover, an appropriately low off-peak price—one that fills the resort—may make the peak prices seem just that more unfair."

(continued)

EXHIBIT 12.A-2   (continued)

So what? The real question, however, is one of punishment, Thaler explained. If individuals perceive a business as being unfair, will they punish that business, even at a cost to themselves? If a person thinks the laundry around the corner acted unfairly, for instance, will that person pay the cost of driving to a more distant laundry to punish the first one?

"We set up two research studies to test the premise that people would punish unfair sellers at a cost to themselves," Thaler said. "We asked psychology students and business students to play a game in which one person was asked to be a 'judge,' who could deprive other persons of money, if they were perceived as being unfair to a third person. But to take the money from the first person, the judge had to give up a certain amount of money as well. We found that people would, for instance, pay $2 to deprive a person who was unfair of $8," Thaler said. "We found support for our idea that people would incur expense to punish someone who had dealt unfairly with someone else."

—Glenn Withiam

[a]D. Kahneman, J.L. Knetsch, and R. Thaler, "Fairness as a Constraint on Profit Seeking: Entitlements in the Market," *American Economic Review*, Vol. 76, No. 4 (1986).
Source: Glenn Withiam, Editor, *Cornell Hotel and Restaurant Administration Quarterly*, February, 1994, p. 25. Copyright © Cornell University. Used by permission. All rights reserved.

The Customer

The customer's reaction to yield management practices in hospitality is a quite complex one and not fully known by scientific research at the time of this writing. It is, however, one that needs to be thoroughly examined. Combined with the unscientific pricing practices of the hotel industry that we have discussed in Chapter 12, it is certain that the customer is confused and frustrated by the dickering process and never really knowing "I got the best deal." As one news item reported, "For travelers in search of bargains, the recession of the nineties is hotel heaven. Getting a great deal, however, takes bargaining."[21]

The restaurant industry does not yet practice yield managment, with possibly the exception of "early bird" dinners. But, maybe it should. Many restaurants are booked to capacity on Saturday nights, with empty tables abounding on Monday nights. Why not raise prices on Saturdays? How would the customer react? We don't know the answer to that one, but it seems only fair that if hotels can do it, so too can restaurants. Perhaps it would help spread out the business.

The ultimate question, of course, lies in the customer's perception—it might be sheer folly to attempt such a course of action without first learning what the customer's reaction might be. One might surmise that, if the customer was asked, the response would be negative. The issue, we suspect, is embedded in what is perceived as "fair." This is the same issue that the hotel industry is already grappling with but, perhaps in too many cases, is ignoring from the customer's perspective.

Sheryl Kimes of Cornell Hotel School has provided the most recent case of addressing this issue of perceived fairness. For those interested in the subject, a vital one we believe, reading of her article is a good place to start.[22] Exhibit 12.A-2 is an excerpt from the editor of the *Quarterly* that appeared in the same article and was adapted from an article that originally appeared in the November, 1986 *Quarterly*. Not totally applied to the hospitality industry, it forms an excellent basis for initial discussion.

[21]Andrew Allentuck, "Dickering Can Save You Dollars," *The Toronto Globe and Mail,* February 23, 1994, p. D5.

[22]Sheryl E. Kimes, "Perceived Fairness of Yield Management," *Cornell Hotel and Restaurant Administration Quarterly*, February, 1994, pp. 22–29.

CHAPTER 13

The Communications Mix: Foundations and Advertising

The third part of the hospitality marketing mix is the communications mix. This is what we have come to know as traditional marketing. Again, it is useful to repeat the definition given in Chapters 3 and 10: *All communications between the firm and the target market that increase the tangibility of the product/service mix, that establish or monitor consumer expectations, or that persuade customers to purchase.*

Some elements of this definition need further explanation. Note the phrase "between the firm and the target market": This tells us that communications are a two-way street. It is not simply what the firm does to communicate, but it is also the feedback from the target market that tells the firm how well it is communicating and how well it is providing the services promised.

Second, the definition says that communications "increase the tangibility of the product/service mix." As we have seen, the presentation mix does the same thing. The difference is that the presentation mix does this with tangible physical evidence of the product; communications do it with words and symbols, not facets of the product itself.

Third, communications "establish or monitor consumer expectations." Not only do communications create expectations, but they also provide warning when expectations change or are not being met.

Finally, marketing communications "persuade customers to purchase"—we hope. Although interim communications, particularly in advertising and public relations, may have other specific purposes, such as to create awareness, enhance a corporate image, and so on, the ultimate goal of all marketing communications is to induce purchase.

The Communications Mix

The communications mix contains five elements: advertising, sales promotion, merchandising, public relations and publicity, and personal selling. We will discuss each of these in turn. First, we relate an example to demonstrate the elements of the mix:

Jim and Paula Johnson saw a news item in the paper that a new restaurant was going to be created in a long-abandoned, historic, old stone mill

505

down by the river. "It's about time," they thought, "that this town had a new restaurant. This one sounds intriguing. Any restaurant in an old stone mill has to be an exciting concept and it would have to have good food."

Jim and Paula forgot about the restaurant, except when someone mentioned it during a bridge game or in casual conversation, until about six months later. Then they saw a half-page ad in the newspaper. The ad announced the grand opening of the Old Stone Mill Restaurant on the next Friday night, featuring fine cuisine and excellent service. There was an enticing picture of the old stone mill by the river. They couldn't go Friday, but immediately made reservations for the next night, Saturday, when the grand opening special drink prices and hors d'oeuvres would still be featured.

On Saturday night they drove with some friends to the restaurant. They had difficulty finding it because the roads down by the river were confusing and not clearly marked. They finally found the restaurant but couldn't find any nearby parking spaces. It was a clear night with almost a full moon, however, and they found the walk to the restaurant invigorating. They looked forward to a great meal and a great experience.

When Jim and Paula got to the restaurant they found a long line waiting to get in. Because they had reservations, they passed by the line and went into the cocktail lounge. They had come early to take advantage of the special offer. They found the lounge packed, with no seating space available. The special hors d'oeuvres had all been devoured. They tried to find someone to take their drink order, to no avail, so they went looking for the hostess. They were 30 minutes early for their reservation, but the hostess told them there would be a two-hour wait for their table. "What the heck," they said, "it's always this way on Saturday night anywhere," and decided to wait. They were seated an hour and 45 minutes later.

They waited a long time for a waiter. The waiter suggested a menu item that he said was a special and unique creation of the restaurant's owners. Jim and Paula both decided to order it. They then waited a similar length of time, until the waiter explained that the special dish required extra care and time to prepare. On the table, however, was a table tent featuring a carafe of house wine and some shrimp canapes at a special price. They ordered this to have while waiting for their dinner, and it came quickly.

By the time the meal came, they were filled up on the canapes, salad, bread, and cheese, and were not very hungry. The meal was delicious, but they had lost their appetites. They wanted to have another wine with dinner but were never brought a wine list, so they didn't order it. Later, they were just as happy that they hadn't. They didn't complain but, as they left, vowed never to go there again and to tell their friends what kind of experience they'd had.

A month later, the ad rep from the local paper visited the same restaurant to solicit some advertising. The owners were glad to see him because they were having real problems. The restaurant had opened to rave reviews, although one restaurant critic mentioned the slow and inefficient service. At first, there had been so much business that they couldn't keep up. Lately, however, business had dropped off dramatically. There had been very few complaints; in fact, almost everyone praised the food, the decor, and the concept. The owners figured that what they needed now was a good advertising campaign.

This story dramatizes the kinds of problems that arise in marketing communication. The Johnsons were not satisfied with the restaurant and felt frustrated—they wished they had complained to the management. In that wish, they were typical of consumers who feel reluctant and frustrated in not communicating their true feelings to business organizations.

The restaurant owners also felt frustrated. Apparently people were not returning to the restaurant, and there had to be some reason why. On the other hand, the owners knew their food was superior and their atmospherics were unique. They wished that they had spent more time talking to their customers to see what they liked and disliked about the restaurant. In that wish, they were typical of business owners who feel they could do a better job of communicating with their customers.

The example illustrates a lack of effective marketing communication. The restaurant has frustrated its customers by not being responsive to their needs. Customers complain to each other by word-of-mouth but don't communicate their feelings to the restaurant management. Both parties would like to have a favorable relationship with the other but don't know how to go about it.

The anecdote also demonstrates all the elements of the communications mix: public relations and publicity, advertising, promotion, personal selling, and merchandising, as well as word-of-mouth and complaint behavior. If the restaurant owners had understood communications, they could have made the necessary adjustments and prevented the business drop-off. The lack of communication in business causes conflicts with employees and consumers. This chapter will explore those conflicts and their resolution, after which you should be able to advise the Old Stone Mill Restaurant's owners what they should have done.

Communications Strategy

Communications strategies are concerned with the planning, implementing, and control of persuasive communication with customers. Strategies are the plan and tactics are the action, as discussed in Chapter 3. This is an important distinction because it is very easy, in implementing marketing communications, to get bogged down in the tactics. When this happens, our communication tactics are often not consistent with our strategic objectives.

For example, in personal selling we might call on a client hoping to convince him to book his next group meeting at our hotel. Knowing when his next meeting will be held, we might try to persuade him to book that period. That's a tactic. But he has already reserved at another hotel for that meeting. The result is no sale, and we will have to go through the same process for his subsequent meeting.

Instead, we might use strategic persuasion. Our strategic objective is to persuade the client that our hotel, of all hotels, can best serve his meeting needs and solve his meeting problems. We don't mention dates, we don't "sell" our product; we address his needs. Instead of a "no sale," we receive this response: "I've already booked our next meeting, but I'll get in touch

with you for the one after that." If our persuasion has been successful, he will.

In advertising, the same concept applies. We really like the ad copy, but what is its objective? What will it accomplish? Does it address the needs of the target market? Take a familiar example, we used previously (Figure 9-2): The ad copy illustrates a beautiful, well-proportioned woman in a bathing suit by a pool. What is the objective? What needs does it address? We're sure you can think of lots of them, but are they the needs of the target market? Are they what we expect the ad to accomplish? Will they persuade the customer to buy?

The first step of our communications strategy is to decide what our objectives are and what we hope to accomplish. These are broad objectives that will serve as an umbrella for all our communications efforts; they will permeate our advertising, selling, promotion, merchandising, and public relations. Some, or all, of these elements may also have sub-objectives, but they will all be subsumed under the main objectives. Similarly, we may have more than one objective at a time. In any case, we want the objectives to be congruent and not in conflict with each other.

There are many possible main objectives. Here, we list just a few: to create an image, to position (both objectively and subjectively), to provide benefits, to offer solutions to problems, to create awareness, to create belief, to stir emotions, to change attitudes, to create expectation, and to move to action. These are all strategic objectives, one or more of which will guide the communications process.

The communications process has five broad stages. The first of these stages is "whom to say it to." This stage sets the guidelines in terms of featured attributes, positioning, benefits offered, promises made, and so forth. Consider the ads for two different hotels and two different restaurants for the purpose of relating the communications process to an actual strategy (Figure 13-1). Each ad has a different strategic objective. Before reading further, look at each ad. What is the message you are receiving—what do you think they are trying to say other than, of course, to buy? Now see if the message

...AND ON THE SEVENTH DAY, HE RESTED. NOW YOU KNOW WHERE.

Lana'i has changed little from the time of creation. Since the 141-square-mile island was forged of nature's tidal, tropical, and volcanic forces, we've added two luxury hotels, the impeccable seaside Manele Bay Hotel and the lavish upland Lodge at Koele, each offering award-winning cuisine. For golfers, we've added a course that golf writers call one of "America's Best," *The Experience at Koele*. And new this year, Jack Nicklaus' *The Challenge at Manele*, a stunning coastal course carved into a lava cliff 150 feet above the crashing surf.

Aside from the temptations of croquet and snorkeling,

horseback riding and tennis, you'll discover seclusion and relaxation unheard of this side of Paradise.

For further revelations on Lanai's heavenly meetings, call: Honolulu (808) 545-3913, Los Angeles (310) 348-9373, New York (212) 765-5950, Florida (407) 394-4433, or Lana'i (808) 565-3600.

 ROCKRESORTS

HAWAII'S PRIVATE ISLAND

FIGURE 13-1 Ads illustrating the communications process ads

---

you receive is the same as the objectives of the ad. Are you the target market?

Whom to Say It To

The first stage is to define the target market. First, the appropriate research must be done and the needs and wants of the target market clearly identified. If you read the copy in the Lana'i ad, you will see that it is aimed at meeting planners, but what meeting planners? This appears to be a fine-tuned target market within the meeting planner segment. Define this target market.

For the La Quinta ad, the target market is the more cost-conscious vacationer, with a special appeal to members of the American Automobile Association (AAA), who are looking for hotels of reasonable quality (three-diamond ratings), but at a very affordable price. The Bijou Cafe ad, on the other hand, seems to target upscale diners looking for value. Is this the same target market as that of the Myrtles Plantation, which also offers candlelight dinners?

What to Say

The "what to say" strategic objective of the RockResorts on Lana'i ad is to position its hotels as totally out of the mainstream but with all the amenities a luxurious resort would have. Without looking at the ad, consider the many different ways that this might be accomplished. Pretend that the ad does not yet exist. Given the objective and the creative minds of the advertising agency and the marketing department, go to work.

The objective of the La Quinta ad is quite different. The intent is to create a picture of inexpensive hotels without sacrificing basic needs. Again, there are many ways that this could be said. Now look at the two restaurant ads and do the same analysis. What are they trying to say? Do they say it? If you flip back, you can apply this same test to any of the ads in the book.

How to Say It

Once the first two stages have been absorbed, the creative juices of everyone involved start

Some People See A Muffin.

Some People See A Free Continental Breakfast.

Some People See A Great Place To Stay.

Some People Have Excellent Vision.

Sure, it looks like your ordinary muffin. But look a little closer and you can see there's not a single ordinary thing about staying at a La Quinta. Each of our over 200 inns has money-saving AAA rates starting at $39*. And every day starts off with a free continental breakfast. Plus, our on-site management teams help make your vacation as comfortable as possible. AAA seems to agree. We've received a three-diamond rating at over 90% of our inns. All of which, we're sure you'll agree, makes that muffin anything but ordinary. For reservations, call our AAA member line at 1-800-221-4731.

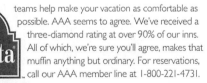

You're Not Staying At A Hotel.
You're Staying With Us.

Courtesy of La Quinta Inns, Inc.

FIGURE 13-1   (continued—*and see next page*)

FIGURE 13-1   (continued)

flowing in the direction of the advertising copy, the appeals to the customer, the execution stage. Of the many, many options, which one will work best? Which one most precisely accomplishes the objectives consistent with the identified target market?

The Lana'i ad uses a biblical reference to get its point across. Can you doubt it? The only thing that has changed since the time of Creation is two luxury hotels and two golf courses. Do you buy that? Sure you do, because this is subjective positioning of the intangible—an image, a benefit, and a differentiation. On the other hand, the La Quinta ad uses the lowly muffin to attract attention. It has resorted to the mundane to get its message across. Is it any less effective? Consider, again, the consumer trade-off model in Chapter 1: How does the ad fit this model? What expectations does it create, what problems does it solve, what is the price/value relationship and the risk?

Consider all four ads in terms of the definition of the aims of the communications mix:

- Establish communications between the firm and the target market
- Increase the tangibility of the product/service mix
- Establish or monitor consumer expectations
- Persuade consumers to purchase

Have these things been accomplished? Consider the ads also in terms of selective perception, selective attention, selective comprehension, selective acceptance, and selective retention, which we discussed in Chapter 6.

How Often to Say It

The next stage, "how often," is both a consumer-driven and a budget-driven one. Repetition has been shown to help selective retention. It has also been shown to increase "wear-out"—that is, the tendency of the consumer to ignore it after having seen it so often. Therefore, this stage requires careful consideration of when to say it (e.g., television times, newspaper placement, inflight magazines), as well as how often, which will always have a budget limitation.

Where to Say It

"Where," as used here, applies to the various components of the communications mix. The examples used above were advertisements, but only for ease of illustration. If we use advertising, then we must select the appropriate medium, electronic or print. Electronic media include television, radio, and now the growing home computer on-line services. Print media include newspapers, magazines, billboards, and direct mail. Demographics, geographics, psychographics, annual incomes, and a multitude of other determining factors are reviewed before the selection of "where to say it."

We might also, of course, use personal selling, promotion, and/or public relations ("Who goes there?"). For Lana'i, collateral or brochures might be appropriate to send to meeting planners; for La Quinta and the restaurants, brochures would probably be ineffective. Instead, selected publications would be chosen. Radio or TV? La Quinta might emulate the success of the Motel 6 radio commercials, described in Chapter 11. The two restaurants might well use local newspapers (Bijou Cafe), radio advertising, direct mail, or a city's "What To Do" magazine (The Myrtles Plantation).

Target Market Stages

As with everything in marketing, target markets are integral in developing the communications mix. There is not much more to say except this: "Know your target market."

There are three basic rules of persuasion, and they were laid down by Aristotle centuries ago:

- *Logos*—logic and reasoning (e.g., "where your meetings run like clockwork")
- *Pathos*—emotions (e.g., "where a waterfall cascades down through the lobby")
- *Ethos*—source credibility (e.g., "respected restaurant critic gives it four stars")

Which one(s) will persuade your target market? We will not discuss these rules and all their offshoots here because they consume chapters in advertising texts and their proper treatment is too extensive for this book. For the marketer, however, they represent commonsense treatment in communicating with the target market. Logos, pathos, and ethos are a refinement in stage three of communications strategy, "how to

say it"—that is, what is the most effective means of persuasion for the target market?

The other thing we need to know about the target market is what "stage" it is in. Robert Lavidge and Gary Steiner have suggested that people move up through a series of seven steps to actual purchase of a product.[1] The steps are not equal: Some may be climbed quite rapidly, or even simultaneously, but when there is more psychological and/or economic commitment involved in the purchase (called high involvement), it will take consumers longer to climb the steps, and each step will be more important. The steps the consumer progresses through, as suggested by Lavidge and Steiner, describe the consumer's state of mind, as follows:

1. Has complete unawareness of the existence of the product or service
2. Has mere awareness of the existence
3. Knows what the product has to offer
4. Has favorable attitudes toward the product
5. Has preference for the product over other possibilities
6. Has a desire to buy and is convinced that it would be a wise decision
7. Actually purchases the product

An adapted version of the Lavidge and Steiner model is shown in Table 13-1. This model points up the need to know the existing stage of the target market.

Figure 13-2 shows an ad aimed at the cognitive stage; Figure 13-3 aims at the affective stage; Figure 13-4 is aimed at the conative stage.

Analyzing the target market in terms of this model is critical to development of communications strategies. Good strategies may prove useless if they address the market at a stage other than the one that exists.

Another model that is useful in planning communications strategy mirrors the Lavidge and Steiner model and is called the "adoption process model." This model of consumer behav-

---

[1]Robert J. Lavidge and Gary A. Steiner, "A Model of Predictive Measurements of Advertising Effectiveness," *Journal of Marketing*, October, 1961, pp. 59–62, published by the American Marketing Association.

TABLE 13-1   A Model of Consumer Stages and Their Impact on Communications

Consumer Stage	Effect Stage	Strategy
Cognitive: the stage of thoughts/beliefs	Create awareness, beliefs, interest; differentiate	Provide information, get attention
Affective: the stage of emotions	Change attitudes and feelings, get involved, evaluate	Position, create benefits and image, stir emotions
Conative: the stage of motivation and intention	Stimulate and direct desires, adopt	Move to action, reinforce expectation

Adapted from Robert J. Lavidge and Gary A. Steiner, "A Model of Predictive Measurements of Advertising Effectiveness," *Journal of Marketing,* October, 1961, published by the American Marketing Association.

ior contends that adoption, or purchase of a product, is a process. The process starts with awareness, because obviously consumers cannot buy something if they are not aware of it. Awareness can develop simply from walking down a street and seeing a restaurant entrance. It can also develop from seeing a billboard on the highway and, of course, from word-of-mouth. Apart from word-of-mouth, awareness in the hospitality industry is usually created by advertising and public relations.

Once the consumer is aware, the next step in the process is "interest." If consumers are interested, they seek further information and details about the product, such as the quality, the cost, how to buy it, and so forth. This information may, and often does, come via advertising. In many hospitality cases, however, it may come through the consumer's own initiative—that is, consumers will pay to use the telephone or mail to obtain more information on their own. Personal selling also plays an important part in providing information when marketing to groups and meeting planners.

The third step of the model is "evaluation." At this stage consumers ask themselves a number of questions: "Does this fulfill my needs? Does this solve my problems? Does this product do it better than someone else's? Is it worth the risk?" Advertising, personal selling, and public relations can play important roles at this stage. If the evaluation is favorable the consumer moves on to the next stage, "trial."

As we have seen in Chapter 2, trial of the hospitality product usually means the same as purchase; there is really no other way to try it. The promotion and merchandising parts of the communications mix are often used to induce trial, beyond that induced by the other mix elements.

If the trial is favorable, the consumers "adopt." They become repeat customers and tell others, thus becoming sources of awareness, information, and evaluation for others who are at various stages of the process. Marketers can influence adoption through performance and relationship marketing, which is why the quality of those two factors is so critical to successful marketing.

Like the Lavidge and Steiner model, marketers should know at what stage of the adoption model their target market is. This knowledge will strongly influence the communications strategy and objectives.

Research for the Communications Mix

If we have to know the target market in order to develop the optimal communications mix and strategy, it follows that the best results will be obtained through research. In the long run, good research will save communications dollars.

We recognize that many properties, particularly individually owned restaurants, will not have such involved communications mixes as those described here. Even these properties, however, will most likely engage in merchandising, sales promotion, and some advertising, if

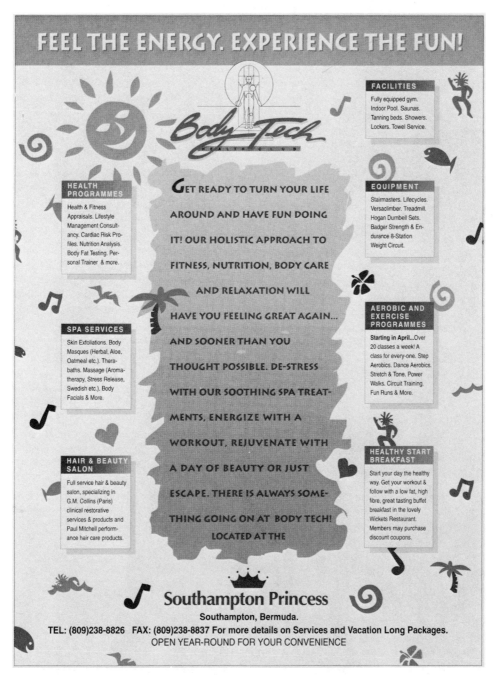

FIGURE 13-2   Ad aimed at the cognitive stage

not personal selling; and good public relations can be used by any business. Research is done both internally and externally. The following guidelines apply to even the smallest business, if in somewhat modified form.

Communications are designed to establish and monitor consumer expectations and to persuade consumers to purchase. To accomplish this, we need to know not only about the target market but also about our property and how we

FIGURE 13-3 Ad aimed at the affective stage

FIGURE 13-4   Ad aimed at the conative stage

are perceived. Research is one form of communications that comes the other way. There are five major questions to be answered.

Where Are We Now?

This means not what we ourselves think, but what the target market thinks. In other words, how are we perceived? Examples might be "expensive," "luxurious," "good service," "good food," "full facilities," "atmospheric," "cheap," "unfriendly," "rundown," "old and tired," or any number of other things.

We seek to understand perception through the eyes of the target market, but more than one research effort has revealed that the market segment being reached is not even the one that management thought it was reaching. Thus, the first thing we may need to learn is who our actual target market is, using all the principles laid out in Chapter 8.

Here are other questions to be asked:

How do we compare with the competition?
What do their customers think of us?
Are they aware of what we have to offer?
Have they tried us? If not, why not? If so, do they return? Why? Why not? What are their attitudes and feelings?

In short, the research question at this stage is, "How are we seen now?" Our management may believe that we have the finest food in town, but if the market doesn't believe this, it really doesn't matter whether we do or not. It is hard to go anywhere if you don't know from where you are starting.

Why Are We There?

This research step calls for an evaluation of the product and previous communications efforts. To embellish on the example above, suppose analysis shows that our food is really not that good. If the objective is to be perceived as having the finest food in town, the product will have to be altered and a new communications effort initiated. If, in fact, we do have the finest food in town, then the communications objective will be to change perceptions.

Besides product evaluation, here are other aspects to be researched:

Are prices too high or are they perceived as too high?
What is the real quality level of our service?
Is the competition doing the same thing, only better?
Are our attributes and benefits what we think they are?
Do we really solve consumers' problems? The right ones?
What puts us in this position?
What are our strengths and weaknesses?
What are the users' dissatisfactions?
What is the profile of users?
What is the usage pattern of users?
Have we communicated what we want to communicate?

The research questions at this stage are: "How is our product perceived? How is it used?" If where we are now is not where we want to be, then we have to find out how we got there. Even if it is where we want to be, we still need to know how we got there. There is nothing like knowing what you are doing right and why.

Where Could We Be?

If where we are now is not where we want to be, then where could we realistically be? Let's say we are not perceived as having the best food in town, but that is where we would like to be: Is that realistic? Do we have the right staff in the kitchen? Can we afford to buy the finest ingredients without raising prices? Would we have to raise prices to achieve the "finest food" objective? Is there a market for it?

That's the product point of view. Perhaps we do have the finest food in town, just what we want to be, but the market doesn't see it that way. Then we would have to ask whether it is realistic to believe that we can change perceptions that, in this case, would be vis-a-vis the competition. Here are some other issues in this stage:

What market position could we achieve?
Are there new buyers and users out there?
Can we increase awareness?

Can we change beliefs or create new ones?

Can we increase benefits and solve other problems?

Do we have the right target markets? Are there others?

Can we create new target markets?

Can we steal from the competition?

The answers to these questions will establish our communication objectives. The major research question at this stage is: "What unmet needs, wants, and problems are there that we have the capability of fulfilling?"

How Can We Get There?

Now comes the creative thinking. When this is based on good, solid research, it comes easier and is more likely to work. The first and most obvious question is, "What do we have to change?" This could be any part of the product/service mix, or of the presentation mix that is tangibilizing the product/service to the marketplace. Thus, we might have to change the product, the service, the price, the atmospherics, facilities, employees, or, if we can, the location. We might also have to change the distribution network, or the target markets.

Once we have the product right, and not until then, we can commence with what we have to change, via the communications mix. The Howard Johnson's case described earlier gives an example of trying to persuade with communications before the product is corrected. Howard Johnson's ad campaign, "If it's not your mother, it must be Howard Johnson's," stretched consumer credibility to a limit that very few restaurants could hope to achieve, and which Howard Johnson's never did. Such actions are often fatal—the customer doesn't like to be fooled twice.

Are We Getting There?

This is probably the most neglected stage of communications research. It really means starting over again at the beginning, except that now the field is narrower because we know what we are looking for. This is research to measure results. It asks, "What have we, or haven't we, changed?"

If the objective was to be perceived as having the best food in town, are we now so perceived? The campaign may have brought people, which can be temporary and misleading, but what we want to know is whether we have changed perception, which will have a long-lasting effect.

Some years after the Howard Johnson's campaign, after Marriott had bought Howard Johnson's and resold the lodging properties to Prime Motor Inns (which changed the name to Howard Johnson, went into bankruptcy, and later sold them to Hospitality Franchise Systems), another communications campaign took place. This story is told in Table 13-2 to illustrate all of the above points.

Word-of-Mouth Communication

The most powerful form of communications, especially in the hospitality industry, is word-of-mouth. This is particularly true of many individual restaurants and small, exclusive hotels that do not formally use any portion of the communications mix.

Elements of the communications mix can, of course, influence word-of-mouth behavior. We may see an ad, read or hear publicity, or talk to a salesperson, and from any one of those experiences develop a perception and expectation. We may then communicate that perception to someone else via word-of-mouth, even though we really have no actual experiences with the product. In this sense, the communications mix affects word-of-mouth and, indirectly, may persuade someone to purchase or not to purchase.

By and large, however, word-of-mouth behavior originates in actual experience or the word-of-mouth of others who have had an actual experience. Thus, we control behavior more by what we do (relationship marketing) than by what we say. Word-of-mouth is familiar to all and needs no further discussion here. A strong foundation for good word-of-mouth communication, however, is built by fulfilling the needs and expectations of our customers. When this is not done, an important factor in recapturing a repu-

TABLE 13-2   The Howard Johnson Repositioning Ad Campaign

Where are we now?

Prime Motor Inns conducted research to answer this question. According to the trade press, Prime's research determined that the negative image accorded Howard Johnson's was due solely to the restaurant division; the lodging division was perceived as having a positive image.

We are not familiar with the actual research, but let's consider what it *should* have done. First, referring to Lavidge and Steiner's seven steps, awareness was not a problem; just about everyone knew Howard Johnson. Step three is knowing what the product has to offer. Howard Johnson's early motel units were notorious for thin walls, noise, poor maintenance, dark hallways, depressing lobbies, and other negative factors. This generates a research question: Did the consumer now know that at least some of the properties did not fit this image?

Step four is favorable attitude toward the product. If the answer to step three—knowing what the product has to offer—was "No," then the answer here is "No." If the answer to step three was "Yes," then the question is, "Do some units with positive conditions create a favorable attitude toward the entire product line?" If the answer was "No," then the first step of the campaign should be to create a favorable attitude—after the problems were corrected, of course.

This would mean repositioning. Recall from Chapter 9 that repositioning can mean removing negative images while creating positive ones. One way to help do this would have been to change the name and paint Howard Johnson's famous orange roofs another color.

Prime's research answer, as we have indicated, was "Yes"—some units with positive conditions created a favorable attitude toward all units. Prime therefore retained the name and the orange roofs. Frankly, we doubt the validity and reliability of this finding. We think that Prime had some doubts about it too because, as we will soon see, they went to great effort to change the image.

From this point, the research would address the issues in Lavidge and Steiner's steps five to seven—that is, how do we actually create preference, the desire to buy, and the actual purchase? If Prime had believed what they said they believed, this is where they would have commenced the communications campaign, in stage three, the conative stage, of the Lavidge/Steiner model in Table 13-1. Instead, they commenced it in the affective stage.

Why are we there?

Howard Johnson had a long history that provided many answers to this question. Even if given a positive answer to "Where are we now?" fresh research would have proven very enlightening. If the positive answer was, in fact, incorrect, this would have come out at this step and signalled a change in direction. If it was, in fact, correct, Howard Johnson could have learned at this step why it was correct. This would form the basis of the new communications campaign.

Where could we be?

The answers to this question for this example deal largely with positioning. What position could Howard Johnson fill? Did it have to change beliefs to do that? Did it have the right target markets, and so forth? This stage of research is designed to bring realism to the campaign, as opposed to wishful thinking.

How can we get there?

This is the ultimate question, the answer to which will drive the communications campaign. For Howard Johnson, in our opinion, it meant a total repositioning possibly aided by a name change. In Prime's opinion, apparently, it also meant repositioning, but with the same name and without any

(continued)

TABLE 13-2   (continued)

real effort to destroy any previous negative image; in other words, they said, "Believe us when we tell you that 'we're turning Howard Johnson upside down,'" as shown in the ad in Figure 13-5 aimed at travel agents who were, and remained, reluctant to book their clients at a Howard Johnson.

Here's what a Howard Johnson spokeman said about the estimated $5 million advertising campaign:

> Howard Johnson wants to inform the public that the company has changed dramatically...to position itself solely as a lodging chain. "What we're saying is, 'Hey, folks, we've got a really good product here and don't be discouraged by what we were in the past. Now we're strictly in the hotel business. If you try us, chances are you're going to like us and want to come back.'...[W]e wanted a campaign that would cut through all the clutter out there. We wanted our customers to know that something is changing at Howard Johnson."
>
> The new ad campaign is based on research that indicated..."A lot of the negative image of Howard Johnson *is* related to the restaurants."[a]

Note: Another reason Howard Johnson failed was because it failed in its communications strategy. Today, it has gained somewhat in stature. Under new ownership it has divested many of its inferior properties, has built or converted a number of new ones, and has expanded internationally where it does not have to fight a previous image. Overall, Howard Johnson is a much better product today. The roofs, however, are still orange and much of the negative image lingers on in the United States, particularly with the older generation who can still remember.

[a]Steven J. Stark, "HoJo 'Dusts Off' its image with a $5M Ad Campaign," *Business Travel News,* June 9, 1986, pp. 1, 50.

tation is the way customer requests and complaints are handled. This is worthy of some discussion.

Customer Complaints

In a business where word-of-mouth communications is so very important, there is one place where internal marketing (marketing to our employees), relationship marketing (establishing personal relationships with guests), and the communications mix come together. This place is the handling of customer complaints. Customer complaints are a special case and deserve special treatment in this chapter because they are one of the most misunderstood and mishandled areas of the communications mix in the hospitality industry. Let us look first at what customer complaints are.

- *Inevitable* Nothing is perfect. The diversity of the hospitality customer and the heterogeneity of the hospitality product absolutely ensure that there will be complaints. This will be true even when everything goes according to plan. Of course, when everything doesn't go according to plan, and this is bound to happen, there will be additional problems and there will be complaints.

- *Healthy* The old army expression is, "If the troops aren't griping, look out for trouble." An absence of complaints may be the best indication management has (along with declining occupancies or covers) that something is wrong. Hospitality customers are never totally satisfied, especially over a period of time. Instead, they are probably not talking to you or you are not talking to them. The communication process is not working; the relationship is deteriorating. By the time it explodes, it will be too late. Some say, "If it isn't broken, don't fix it." First, you have to know if it's broken. The ones who know first are your customers. And, incidentally, the ones they tell first are your employees, which means that you had better listen to your employees as well.

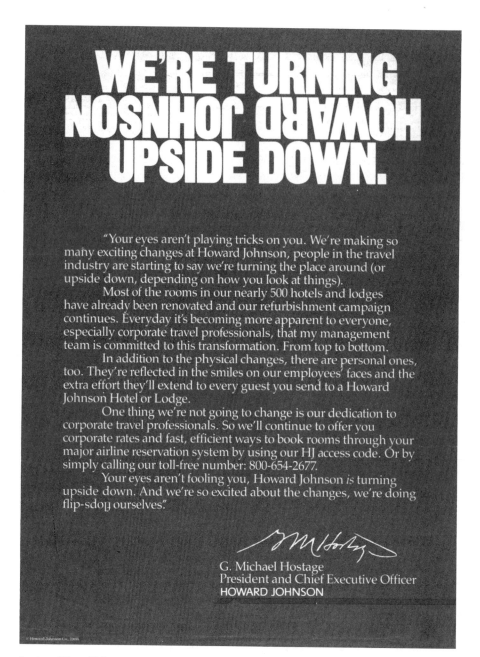

Courtesy of Howard Johnson

FIGURE 13-5   Ad with objective of converting negative image to positive

- *Opportunities* Customer complaints are opportunities to learn of customers' problems, whether they are idiosyncratic or caused by the operation itself. If it's broken, you have an opportunity to fix it. If it's not broken, you have an opportunity to make it better, to be creative, to develop new product, to learn new needs, and to keep old customers.
- *Marketing Tools* If marketing is to give customers what they want, then marketing

must know what they want. All the customer surveys in the world won't tell you as much as customer complaints will tell you.

- *Advertising* Yes, advertising. The advertising is negative if you don't resolve the problems, and there is nothing more devastating in the hospitality business than negative word-of-mouth. Problems, however, can be positive if you fix them. Research has shown

that one of the best and most loyal customers is the one who had a complaint that was satisfactorily resolved. And this customer loves to tell others about it.

Table 13-3 shows a letter received in response to a letter of complaint to a famous four-star resort where the complainer paid $280 a night and was there to consider whether to book

TABLE 13-3   Management Response to Complaint at Four-Star Resort

Dear Mr. Smith:

Your letter of January 12 has been referred to me for reply. I am amazed to learn that you encountered so many difficulties during your brief stay with us.

Each of our guestrooms is provided with a stationary folder containing notepaper and pen. The previous guests in your room must have taken the folder with them upon departing and our maid neglected to replace it, for which we apologize.

We also apologize for the delay in providing a crib. We can offer no excuse for this other than our housekeeping department must have been extremely busy on your day of arrival.

We have very little call for room service before seven o'clock. The hours of operation for all food and beverage outlets are displayed prominently throughout the hotel.

We are fortunate to have an excellent Executive Housekeeper and we receive many favorable comments about the cleanliness of our rooms. I am surprised that you found it to be to the contrary.

The lamp shade in the room that you occupied has been repaired. When our hotel is running at full capacity, it is sometimes difficult to accomplish these minor repairs at once.

I reiterate my earlier statement that we are proud of our housekeeping. The carpets most certainly are vacuumed daily.

Again, an oversight on the part of our maid. There should have been a room service menu in the room and the soap replaced.

I cannot understand the Express Cafe being out of food. We offer a limited menu in this room and it is just a matter of calling to the kitchen for additional supplies. No children's menu is offered in this room because of the nature of the restaurant.

There are always two rolls of toilet paper in the room so that our guests are not inconvenienced by running out. Again, the maid must have overlooked this as well as the Kleenex and this has been brought to her attention.

We have just had every window in the hotel cleaned. If the window in the dining room appeared dirty, it may be because of the abundance of rain. In any event, we will certainly see that they are cleaned.

We attempt at all times to relay messages received as quickly as possible. I cannot explain the delay you experienced.

I apologize also for the delay in your room service order. The service in this department is normally quite good.

In closing, I am enclosing some recent complimentary letters we have received from satisfied guests.

(signed) General Manager

TABLE 13-4   Comment Card Complaint and Management Response at a Holiday Inn

Complaint

Your hotel is somewhat run-down to say the least. It is tired and tawdry. You should really do something about it as I, for one, will not return. Especially bad are those old bedspreads which are straight out of the '60s, not too mention being torn and soiled. Also, your coffee is horrible! This has nothing to do with the '60s because there is certainly better coffee on the market today. I would expect better from a Holiday Inn.

Phyllis Rupert
Fargo, North Dakota

Response

Dear Ms. Rupert:

Thank you for filling out your in-room guest comment card for your recent stay with us. Your comments and concerns are very important...and true by the way. As a matter of fact, our hotel is slated for renovation beginning the second week of next month. We are extremely excited about our renovation as I know our guests will be too. Of course, those old bedspreads will soon be a thing of the past...none too soon.

Additionally, I am in the process of changing our brand of coffee. Just last week I participated in a blind coffee taste testing and found that the coffee we have been using is not of sufficient quality.

I am only sorry that these positive changes had not been implemented by the time of your visit. I can assure you though that you will be pleasantly surprised upon your return. I only hope that you will give us another chance to let you know that you are our first concern.

Thank you again, Ms. Rupert. If you are ever in Dallas again, please call on me.

(signed) General Manager

---

the hotel for a large group. Table 13-4 shows a comment card complaint received by a Holiday Inn, where the complainer paid $59 a night, and the manager's response. Consider the inevitable, the healthy, the opportunity, and the advertising aspects of these complaints and responses.

Because customer complaints are so critical to internal and relationship marketing, as well as word-of-mouth marketing, the results of some research will be presented.

Customer Complaint Research

One hundred twenty previous guests of a specific hotel who had communicated with the hotel were surveyed by mail as to their feelings, actions, and behaviors. About 50 percent of those surveyed had written only complaints, 20 percent had written only compliments, and 30 percent had written both to complain and to compliment. Of the complainers, 60 percent had complained to management in person before leaving the hotel.

Of the guests who had complained, 71 percent said they never used guest comment cards to register their complaints. Thirty-eight percent of those who complained said they would never return, while 25 percent were unsure. For those who would choose to return, the major factor in their decision was the way the complaint was handled. Of those who complained, 63 percent were highly likely to make a point of telling others about their complaint, and 21 percent were unsure if they would; 47 percent were

TABLE 13-5   Word-of-Mouth Behavior of Hotel Complainants

Likely to tell others outside family about the complaint?

Highly likely   62%
Undecided   18%
Number of people actually told (average)   12

If the complaint was not resolved?

Highly likely   75%
Not sure   15%

Likely to tell others not to use the hotel?

Highly likely   43%
Not sure   13%
Number of people actually told (average)   8

If complaint was not resolved?

Highly likely   71%
Not sure   11%

Source: Susan Morris, "Complaint Handling and Consumer Behavior."

highly likely to tell others not to use the hotel, and 12 percent were unsure if they would.

These percentages were even higher when the complaint was not handled satisfactorily. On the other hand, the percentages decrease substantially when the complaint was handled satisfactorily; as few as 14 percent would tell others not to use the hotel under this condition. From these findings it could also be inferred that for every ten complaints received there were 25 that were not expressed.

This research shows that, once the cause of a complaint has occurred, the level of distress becomes a function of the handling of the situation. The disturbance level can be reduced if the complainant actively believes in management. This means that it is important for management to direct its efforts toward creating an attitude that will minimize the negative effect of the complaint.

Complainants want to feel that management cares and will make a sincere attempt to correct the situation. If this belief is supported, they will probably choose the same hotel again; the tendency of complainants, however, is not to believe. Interestingly enough, 29 percent of the still-unsatisfied complainants in the study indicated they would have been satisfied simply with a proper response from management rather than what they felt were token gestures.[2]

In another study, 479 of those people who had written complaints to managements of nine hotels in a 21-hotel chain over a two-month period, were surveyed by written questionnaire.[3] Sixty-four percent had made their complaint in person at the time of the incident; 66 percent said they were extremely disturbed at the time.

Of the respondents, 50 percent said it was highly unlikely that they would ever stay at the same hotel again. Of those who had been in the area of the hotel since their complaint, 75 percent had purposely not returned to the hotel; 32 percent had purposely not returned to other hotels in the chain. An analysis of their word-of-mouth behavior is shown in Table 13-5.

[2]Robert C. Lewis, "When Guests Complain," *Cornell Hotel and Restaurant Administration Quarterly,* August, 1983, pp. 23–32.

[3]Susan Morris, "The Relationship Between Company Complaint Handling and Consumer Behavior," Master's thesis, Hotel Restaurant & Travel Administration, Amherst: University of Massachusetts, 1985.

Fifty-eight percent of the respondents in this study reported that they were led to complain by an entire series of problems or incidents. This indicates that the hotel managements involved had a number of opportunities, if they had known of them, to resolve difficulties for the same customer. After the complaints were received, management had additional opportunities, which it failed to take advantage of in 61 percent of the cases.

This 61 percent indicated that they believed their complaint could have been better handled. How? Only 19 percent felt that they should have received a rebate or complimentary rooms or meals. Thirty-four percent thought the situation could have been better handled at the time the incident occurred. A whopping 47 percent stated they would have been satisfied with a better response from management in terms of more detailed and speedier communication or a more pleasant tone.

These studies demonstrate the opportunities inherent in the proper handling of consumer complaints. Appropriate complaint handling just may be relationship marketing at its finest; certainly it is a tremendous marketing opportunity, which is why a marketing-oriented management should actually seek out complaints.

What to Do About It

Practicing relationship marketing through consumer complaint handling is not the easiest task in the world. We have already seen that many discontented customers will not take the trouble to complain, yet complaints may provide some of the best opportunities. Actually encouraging complaints becomes the necessary objective.

Research has shown that people do not complain for three primary reasons:

It is not worth the time and effort.
They don't know where or how to complain.
They believe that nothing will be done even
   if they do complain.

Marketing's task is to overcome these obstacles by making it easy to complain, making it known where and how to complain (see, for

example, Figure 13-6), and truly doing something about the complaint if it is reasonable, and over three-fourths of all complaints appear to fall into that category. This means setting up specific procedures.[4] Such an action will also constitute internal marketing; when employees see management taking complaints seriously, they will feel more inclined to do likewise.

Consider the following anecdote from Eddystone C. Nebel, who followed and observed ten hotel general managers as part of a qualitative research study:

> This general manager tries very hard to communicate what is important to his employees. He's developed a series of sayings to help guide the thinking and actions of the entire hotel staff. His first saying, which he preaches with missionary zeal to his staff of 850 employees and executives, is, "Talk to the guests." Talking to the guest is meant to convey a number of things. It means that a pleasant hello from all the staff is a sign of hospitality, even in a 1000 room hotel. But talking to the guests means much more; it means finding out from the guests if things are going well or if they need anything. In short, "Talk to the guests" means constant and total communication, one-on-one, between as many employees and as many guests as possible. How is your stay? What do you need? Are there any problems? How can I help? These are the kinds of questions his staff is continuously asking the guests....[His] goal is to not only talk to the guest but also to get the *guest talking* [emphasis added].[5]

The benefits are clear: long-term profit from loyal customers and more positive, less negative word-of-mouth advertising. There are other ancillary benefits, such as new product ideas, new product information, improved image, better-educated customers, and higher productivity and service. For line employees there are also the benefits of less customer conflict, better image and word-of-mouth about the company, and

---

[4]For more discussion of this subject, see Robert C. Lewis and Susan V. Morris, "The Positive Side of Guest Complaints," *Cornell Hotel and Restaurant Administration Quarterly,* February, 1987, pp. 13–15.

[5]Eddystone C. Nebel, *Managing Hotels Effectively: lessons from outstanding general managers,* New York: Van Nostrand Reinhold, 1991, p. 37.

ITT Sheraton Corporation
WORLDWIDE HOTELS, INNS, RESORTS & ALL-SUITES

Dear ITT Sheraton Guest:

At ITT Sheraton, we are committed to ensuring the satisfaction of each and every guest. Our goal is to provide a consistent, high quality guest experience at Sheraton Hotels, Inns and All-Suites worldwide.

To help us meet this goal, we are asking you to evaluate our performance using the enclosed questionnaire. Your comments will be shared with each property's General Manager, and I will personally review the overall results.

You were selected to participate in this survey based on your reservation records at the Park Central (Dallas, TX) property. If, in fact, you did have a recent stay at this Sheraton, your response regarding their service will be of great value.

Although we often ask these same questions during a guest's stay, our efforts to continuously improve the Sheraton guest experience depend on your feedback over a period of time.

Thank you for letting us know your thoughts. We appreciate your patronage and hope to serve you in the near future.

Cordially yours,

John Kapioltas
Chairman, President and
Chief Executive Officer

FIGURE 13-6   Soliciting customer complaints

better respect for the company and the product. Each company must devise its own system for soliciting and handling complaints. Handling satisfied customers is easy; handling dissatisfied customers is the acid test of marketing and management.

Thus far we have looked at the communications mix from a broad, overall view. In this and the next two chapters, we will now look at each of the five parts of the mix individually.

Database Marketing

Database marketing is a subset of the communications mix. Essentially, databases are decision-support systems. The information in the systems includes internal data on customers and purchased data (list sources) on customers and prospects. The information can be used to generate mailing lists and prospect lists for salespeople and to identify market segments. A direct communications channel with customers and prospects is provided through a computerized customer database.

Database information enables companies to target individuals or small microsegments of people. This is very useful for sales and sales management support and for direct marketing programs. Database marketing has three main benefits: It provides a strategic advantage through the more effective use of marketing information internally; it improves the use of customer and market information; and it forms a basis for developing long-term customer relationship marketing, especially with those who account for a large portion of a firm's business.

Proprietary marketing databases are those developed by an individual company for its own use. They provide a competitive advantage in enabling a company to focus on a particular market segment. Examples in the hotel industry are guest history information and frequent-guest programs. Preferred room type, pillows, amenities, and other services enable a hotel to be ready to satisfy a customer upon arrival and without hassle. This is a powerful force in relationship marketing. Some systems, such as Ritz-Carlton's, enable any Ritz-Carlton in the world to tap into these preferences after a customer has stayed at any other Ritz-Carlton at another location. Direct mail contact is also facilitated when an event is planned that coincides with certain guests' particular interests. The same is true for restaurants, although databases have not yet seen widespread use in these operations.

Customized marketing databases are used to profile prospective customers. Data obtained from outside sources are customized to fit the property's customer profile. Customer information is obtained before the customer is actually contacted so that product information can be customized in advance. Also, contacts can be made with potential customers who have profiles similar to present customers, thus being those who have a greater probability of becoming future customers. Known media use, for example, enables a company to better target its markets through the proper advertising chan-

nels. In fact, several customized versions of a promotion or advertisement can be specifically designed for particular market segments.

Database Marketing Components

Database marketing begins where all other communications vehicles begin, with the customer. Database marketing has four fundamental components: strategy, data, information, and knowledge.

Strategy begins with the objectives of the marketing program. Who are the target customers, where do they live, what do they buy, where else do they go? Once the strategy is conceived and integrated with the other marketing vehicles, such as advertising and public relations, the data is assembled.

Data start with the actual names, addresses, telephone numbers, dates of departures, preferences, purchase habits, credit card usage, etc. The initial database should contain data on past customers. New customer prospects, obtained from list sources, can then be added.

The *information* portion of database marketing is the analysis of the data. Demographics and psychographics of customers need to be analyzed. Other factors, such as why they use a particular hotel or restaurant, can be added.

The *knowledge* stage of a database marketing program includes segmentation, clustering, and modeling. Segmentation, as discussed in Chapter 8, includes gathering similar customers together. For example, a hotel might have a list of customers who buy weekend packages segmented under a "leisure" code. A restaurant might have a list of customers who attend Sunday brunch. These segments are then clustered. For example, the leisure traveler may also be a brunch-goer at the same property. Or, the leisure customer might come to New York City on weekends in April and live in northern New Jersey, another cluster.

Once customers are clustered, the search for new lists (and potentially new customers) begins by modeling. The assumption is that if non-users have clusters similar to current customers, such a list source will have a higher yield.

Using the Database

Database marketing should first be employed to "talk to" past customers. Many *property management systems* (PMS) in hotels have extensive data on customers that have used the hotel in the past and are familiar with the property. The first step in a database marketing campaign is to assemble the list of past customers. This list may come from the PMS, registration cards, old invoices, credit card companies, or business cards.

The list of past customers is then put on some type of computer program. Simple lists can be assembled on traditional software such as WordPerfect or Lotus. More complex lists need to be built on d-base programs such as Paradox. Once the list of past customers is organized, certain fields are established to allow the organization to segment the customers. A field is an indication on the database that one characteristic is different from another. Fields can be established for location, date of check-out, market segment, amount spent per visit, etc.

For example, in a hotel there is a major difference between corporate and leisure customers. To make the example simple, a hotel determines that most customers checking out Monday through Friday are corporate, and customers checking out Saturday and Sunday are leisure. These are two different types of customers with two different sets of needs. Fields are set up within the database to allow the marketer to choose corporate and leisure customers to contact.

The hotel then decides to "talk to" both its corporate and leisure customers. Two different collateral pieces are developed, one aimed at the corporate customer, the other at the leisure customer. The advertising agency creates two mailers designed to thank the past customers for their business and encourage future usage. For the corporate customer, a newsletter is created to inform them about the different programs within the hotel. The leisure customer is mailed a promotion encouraging return during certain slow weekends.

Once the collateral is developed, the piece is "dropped," or mailed to the customers. To track the database marketing effort, a "trigger" or response mechanism is placed in the collateral to measure success. A trigger might be a special telephone number for the promotion or a certificate to be redeemed in the hotel's restaurant. Advertising campaigns work similarly. Database marketing is unique in its ability to be tracked and documented.

Once a facility covers its past customers, new customers can be obtained through database marketing. New customers can be found by profiling past customers. The theory behind profiling is that similar customers buy similar facilities. By analyzing the fields of the past customers, a good picture of new customers begins to emerge. Past customer fields can yield age, location, income, type of car driven, purchase habits, media usage, local business contacts, number of visits to restaurants in a month, etc. Given this information, the savvy database marketer seeks lists of similar customers.

Examples A hotel in Stamford, Connecticut built a database of existing customers and sent collateral to encourage repeat usage. The marketing team then wanted to find new customers through database marketing. By profiling its past customers, a picture of new customers emerged. The past customer for the leisure segment was a married couple earning a $75,000 household income, 49 years of age with two cars; they stayed one night, ate breakfast and dinner in the hotel, and lived within 45 miles of the hotel. The hotel conducted several focus groups of past customers to determine the psychographic reasons for the weekend package purchase. In brief, the customers were looking for a quick getaway for a night.

Armed with this information, the hotel marketing team began to research list sources for similar customers. "Let's fish where the fish are," proclaimed the marketing director. They felt that pockets of similar customers were available for new business. Lists were purchased that matched the current customer base. A new collateral piece was developed, aimed more at the potential customer and encouraging trial of the hotel, rather than repurchase. The trigger was a coupon for an upgrade to better accommodations upon check-in. This feature allowed the management of the hotel to measure response. The database marketing was successful and was continued as an integral portion of the communications mix.

Many times marketing partners share databases for mutual marketing needs. A hotel in Atlanta approached an area attraction to do some combined marketing. The attraction was busy on weekends, when the hotel was slow. Conversely, the hotel was busy in the middle of the week, the attraction's slowest time period. The two organizations shared customer lists and both received additional business by database marketing to each other's customers. There is no doubt that good database marketing will provide a strong, competitive edge in the future.

Advertising

Advertising is mass communication that is paid for. It is the most visible element and has the broadest potential reach of all the components of the communications mix—that is, it can reach the largest mass of people. Advertising can also be the most expensive component. The question is, how effective is it? That is a question that researchers, especially those connected with advertising agencies, have been trying to answer for years. It is an especially pertinent question in the hospitality industry, where word-of-mouth is such a potent force.

We include in advertising all those things that are part of the public media, such as newspaper and magazine ads, television and radio commercials, billboards, airplane streamers, train, bus, and taxi cards—in other words, any advertising paid for by a specific sponsor. We also include collateral, such as hotel brochures, flyers, pamphlets, and direct mail, which are not exactly public media but fit into the same genre.

The Roles of Advertising

Advertising, of course, performs the same general role as all communications: It informs, cre-ates awareness, attempts to persuade, and reinforces the buying behavior of present customers. It also can play a major role in positioning, as we have shown. Advertising is subject to the same guidelines that we discussed in the first part of this chapter, the major difference being that it is *paid* mass communication.

For the hospitality industry, the most important objective function of advertising may be to create and maintain awareness of the property or some particular component of the property, such as a new addition or a new service. The most important subjective function is to position the property. See, for example, the Regent ads in Figure 13-7: The Beverly Wilshire positions itself as a luxury hotel, catering to the upper echelons of society. The Regent in Melbourne, on the other hand, makes readers aware of its high-technology capabilities, in addition to a promise of high-quality service in an attractive setting.

Advertising also informs, although much hospitality print advertising is not very informative because its constant sameness (Figure 13-8) often fails to differentiate one property from another in the same product class. Figure 13-9 tries to do differently. Figure 13-9 and the Regent ads function more in the cognitive stage, creating awareness and beliefs and developing interest. The ad shown in Figure 13-10 functions in the affective stage. It attempts to persuade by stirring emotions. The ad in Figure 13-11, on the other hand, attempts to reinforce behavior and expectation. Much of hotel chain advertising is done for this purpose. Companies like Marriott, Westin, Hilton, Holiday, Hyatt, etc., do chain advertising as constant reminders to their customers (called maintenance advertising) and, of course, they create awareness for potential new customers who may switch. Figure 13-12 also intends to induce switching and move the customer to action.

What Advertising Should Accomplish

Major advertising campaigns in the hospitality industry are conducted only by very large companies that have the resources. And, in the restaurant industry, we are all familiar with the

When sailing through Beverly Hills, stay at the flagship of luxury. _The Regent Beverly Wilshire, a harbor of high society._

6.40pm. _Back at the Regent of Melbourne, the auditorium lights dim for a satellite transmission from Milano._

Every aspect of your day is attended to, leaving you free for other matters. Such as finding a good seat for the Melbourne sunset.

FIGURE 13-7   Positioning Regent hotels

FIGURE 13-8 Ads that fail to differentiate

THIS IS AN AD FOR A HOTEL.
The likes of which you've never seen before.

*We've all seen luxury hotels. They have the requisite
doormen, bellmen and marble lobbies. But how many
boast renowned tennis and racquetball pros, personal
trainers and Olympian instructors? They'll have fine
restaurants, lounges and maybe a pool. But indoor
jogging, full-court basketball, tons of weights and a
private TV at every Stairmaster? You'll only see it at
The Houstonian. Newly renovated, in the heart of
the city and absolutely one of a kind.*

THE HOUSTONIAN HOTEL
111 North Post Oak Lane • Houston, TX 77024
713/680-2626 • Reservations 800/231-2759
Owned & operated by Redstone Hotels

FIGURE 13-9   Trying to differentiate a hotel in an ad

television commercials that emanate from McDonald's (one of the largest advertisers in the country), Burger King, and other large fast-food chains.

On the other end of the continuum are the individual restaurants or motor inns that do almost no advertising. In between these two extremes lies a vast group of hospitality operators who do limited advertising on very limited budgets. For these operators, the "more bang for the buck" principle is especially appropriate: Advertising dollars have to be carefully allocated to where they will do the most good.

To do the most good, the ideal hospitality advertisement will accomplish five objectives:

1. It will tangibilize the service element so the reader can mentally grasp what is offered.
2. It will promise a benefit that can be delivered and/or provide solutions to problems.
3. It will differentiate the property from that of the competition.
4. It will have positive effects on employees who must execute the promises.
5. It will capitalize on word-of-mouth.

We can demonstrate these accomplishments by referring to the Marriott ad in Figure 13-13. Marriott is a national advertiser, but the same principles apply even if you are only advertising in your local newspaper.

The Marriott ad promises a benefit and a solution to one of the most common complaints of hotel guests, slow room service. It differentiates from the competition by promising that room service will be on time, a promise that few hotels make. The ad also says that Marriott will keep that promise because (1) there's CEO Bill Marriott himself putting his name on the line, and (2) if they don't keep the promise, you don't have to pay for the breakfast.

The ad also tangibilizes the service. It shows the room service cart arriving, and it shows Bill Marriott checking his watch. The reader has no trouble conceptually grasping what the benefit

FIGURE 13-10   Ad stirring emotions

will be. The ad has a positive, inspirational effect on employees because it makes a commitment from the President of the company that he is prepared to back up what he says.

Finally, the Marriott ad capitalizes on word-of-mouth. Even though a reader may not have yet experienced the service, he can talk about it: "Hey, did you hear Marriott promises your room service on time or you don't have to pay for it?" Of course, this word-of-mouth will be even more positive once the actual experience has occurred.

FIGURE 13-11   Ad reinforcing behavior and expectation

Note that the Marriott ad is also informative and creates awareness (of a new service). It reinforces the Marriott image for present customers ("See, we're always doing something to make your stay with us better."), without coming right out and saying it. Many ads strain so hard at doing this that they lose credibility. The ad positions Marriott as service-oriented, as al-

One smart business call.

That's all it takes to put you in touch with over 60 Doubletree Hotels from coast to coast, where you'll enjoy the luxuries you like at rates that will let you rest easier.

And at every Doubletree, you'll find the kind of personal service and special attention that will bring you back again and again. And it begins the very first night with our welcoming chocolate chip cookies.

So. You don't have to give up the great restaurants, swimming pools, and health clubs that make business trips bearable. Because now, you've got the right connection. Doubletree Hotels. It's a smart call.

DOUBLETREE
H O T E L S

We're waiting to welcome you at over 60 Doubletree Hotels from coast to coast.

FIGURE 13-12   Ad motivating to action

ways trying to do something more for its customers. It shows that management cares—Bill Marriott cares about the details of your stay. Finally, the ad is persuasive. It addresses an issue of frequent concern and says, "We've taken care of that particular problem for you."

It is seldom easy to get all these elements into one advertisement; often we have to settle for less. Even then, however, one should strive to differentiate with something other than the grandiose claims that characterize so many hotel and restaurant ads, such as that in Figure 13-14. Unless there is something truly unique about the hotel, this kind of ad achieves none of the objectives given above. It does, however, create location awareness and, thus, may build upon word-of-mouth experience.

Another typical hotel ad scene shows a couple in a room, usually with the woman sitting on the bed and the man standing in a sliding doorway; or, the couple may be in a swimming pool, at a golf course, or in a lobby, as in Figure 13-15. While the room, the pool, the golf course, and the lobby are all part of the product, they probably do not differentiate from other hotels in the same product class. In most cases, they don't position the property, they promise no special benefit or problem solution, they don't tangibilize the service or provide reinforcement, they don't have positive effects on employees or generate positive word-of-mouth, they are not very informative, and they hardly persuade the consumer to choose this hotel. Inter-Continental's claim of uniqueness is hardly apparent from its ad.

So much for graphics. How about the wording of the ads, the copy? The same rules apply. Ads that simply list the physical facilities of the

Courtesy of Marriott Corporation

FIGURE 13-13   Ad demonstrating the five major accomplishments of good hospitality advertising

THE INTERNATIONAL SUBSIDIARY OF HILTON USA

Dublin

Mexico (1991)

Brussels (1992)

Gold Coast, Australia

Mexico (1992)

St. Martin, Caribbean

Mexico

Monte Carlo

London

Hong Kong

Toronto (1992)

Istanbul (1991)

The finest hotels in the world all share the same first name.

In the tradition of Conrad Hilton and his famed Waldorf Towers comes
Conrad Hotels. Our dedicated staff of meeting and incentive experts is eager to serve you.
Call Lynne Partridge at 212 867 1400.

The International Symbol
For Service.

FIGURE 13-14   Creating location awareness, but otherwise not giving a reason to buy

FIGURE 13-15 An undifferentiating and contradictory ad by word and picture

property (e.g., number of rooms, pools, restaurants, bars, etc.) also do not fulfill the criteria we have given. True, it may sometimes be necessary to provide this information, depending on the target market, but this does not exempt the remaining copy from saying something different. Apply the above criteria for a good ad to the copy in Figure 13-16. Does it do the job?

The Use of Advertising Today

Advertising is traditional marketing. It is so traditional in the hospitality industry that it has lost much of its creativity. If you cannot make an impact upon the market with advertising—other than to create awareness and provide information as shown in a number of ads throughout this text—it might be better

to save your dollars and put them to better use (for instance, in the product or in lower prices, which will generate positive word-of-mouth, a far more powerful force than most advertising). This is not to say that ad agencies are not creative; it is just that they don't always stick to the basics we have discussed. For example, contrast the ads in Figure 13-17. Which, if either, do you believe would be ineffective, or effective? Why? You will find many ads in this text that do follow the rules and are quite effective.

The consumer today is constantly bombarded with advertising messages from all directions. The human mind is not capable of paying attention to all these messages. Instead, the mind will selectively perceive, attend to, comprehend, accept, and retain that

FIGURE 13-16   Differentiating with copy

After taking the plunge in the cool water the city's pulse slowed and I began to unwind. Escaping to a rooftop pool in the very centre of New York was not what I had in mind when I had arrived. But the experience was one that could only be described to the uninitiated as swimming over Manhattan.

THE PENINSULA
NEW YORK

SHARE THE EXPERIENCE

The Leading Hotels of The World Tollfree: (800) 223 6800   Preferred Hotels & Resorts Worldwide Tollfree: (800) 323 7500
The Peninsula New York, 700 Fifth Avenue at 55th Street, New York NY 10019, U.S.A. Tel: (212) 247 2200 Fax: (212) 903 3949 Tollfree: (800) 262 9467
The Peninsula: Hong Kong • Manila • New York • Beverly Hills • The Palace Hotel Beijing • The Kowloon Hotel Hong Kong

FIGURE 13-17   Creative advertising

to which it is most responsive. What the mind is most responsive to are those things we have outlined.

Hospitality properties and services are very similar in the same product class; some would say that they have reached commodity status. The competition is selling the same thing, unique niches are harder and harder to find, services are easy to copy, and aggressive competitors are using innovative positioning strategies—it is difficult to gain advertising advantage. In many cases, it may be too expensive to

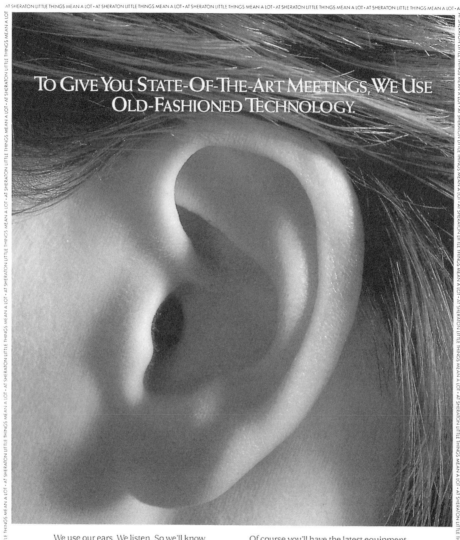

Courtesy of ITT Sheraton Corporation

FIGURE 13-17   (continued)

TABLE 13-6   Expectations of an Ad Campaign for Weekend Packages

Step One	
Ad Preparation	$ 2,000
Media and Agency	15,000
Total Communications Expense	$17,000
Step Two	
Weekend Package Room Rate	$ 100
× Departmental Profit	70%
Net Room Rate	$ 70
Step Three	
Total Communications Expense	$17,000
÷ Net Room Rate	$ 70
Room-nights Needed	243
÷ 10-week Media Placement	10
Room-nights Needed per Weekend	24
÷ 2 Nights per Weekend (Fri/Sat)	2
Additional Room-night Sales per Weekend Night to Return Advertising Investment	12

TABLE 13-7   Expectations of an Ad Campaign for Sunday Brunch

Step One	
Ad Preparation	$ 2,000
Media and Agency	15,000
Total Communications Expense	$17,000
Step Two	
Sunday Brunch Price	$ 20
× Departmental Profit	15%
Gross Margin per Cover	$ 3
Step Three	
Total Communications Expense	$17,000
÷ Gross Margin per Cover	$ 3
Covers Needed	5,666
÷ 10-week Media Placement	10
Covers Needed per Sunday Brunch	567

FIGURE 13-18   Brochure panels from four different hotels

achieve effective awareness and persuasion levels by this means.

All this shows that advertising must be approached with extreme care. Successful advertising is not just copy and graphics, not even just clever copy and graphics, but it derives from a well-planned strategy. Yet there is a strong tendency to look just at the copy and ignore the strategy. Many copy decisions in all industries, in fact, are based on what someone likes rather than how it affects the customer. It is no wonder they say that only half of advertising is effective but no one knows which half!

Like everything else in marketing, there is only one criterion for measuring advertising effectiveness—the customer.

Evaluating Advertising

After all of the above described phases of the advertising process are employed, the ultimate question is: Does it work? Although some advertising firms may disagree, advertising can be measurable. With more sophisticated computers in hotels and restaurants, an advertising

For authentic American food — made great again every day, we proudly present MAX'S CAFE • Food • Spirits • etc.... The atmosphere is casual, the service anything but. Open daily for breakfast, lunch, and dinner or for light hors d'oeuvres and your favorite cocktails. A special room service menu is also served daily.

FIGURE 13-18   (continued)

campaign's effect on business levels can be tracked.

First, an estimate needs to be made of the cost of the program, including all of the components. Ad design, creative work, copy, production, and other costs are combined under the terms "ad preparation." These are added to the media and agency costs and the total costs are compared to expected results.

Table 13-6 shows a calculation for weekend package advertising for a 400-room hotel: In order to evaluate the potential return on investment for advertising a weekend package for this hotel, the total communications expense is calculated. Step one combines all of the ad preparation with the actual media and agency expense.

Step two determines the net room rate generated by the sale of each weekend package room. Although the price is $100 per room, there is the cost to service the room, pay the travel agent, run the air-conditioning, etc. For this example, a typical cost of 30 percent of the sale price of the room was established.

The final step matches the advertising cost with the results expected. In this case, the hotel has to generate an additional 12 rooms sold per weekend night in order to return the investment. Each additional room sold generates an incremental gross margin of $70 for the property. In this case, the hotel decided that there was a good chance that 12 more rooms per weekend night could be sold. With this type of tracking in place, both the advertising agency and the hotel management have clear expectations of the campaign and the net result after it's over.

Let's look at a similar model for the hotel's restaurant. Sunday brunch covers have been

Canadian Pacific ◼◀ Hotels & Resorts
_____

Deerhurst Resort

Robert C Lewis
Robert C Lewis Assoc Inc
65 Wilsonview Ave Ste 2
Guelph ON   N1G 2W5

Read how Deerhurst plans to help you feel more relaxed while you're working.

Dear Robert C Lewis,

I often wonder whether Mr. Murphy was thinking about meetings and conventions when he formulated his famous law! After all, what other activity provides so many opportunities for things to go wrong?

But Mr. Murphy had obviously never experienced a Deerhurst convention.

You see, we've been in the hospitality business for almost a century. And in that time, we've learned to avoid the problems before they happen.

And now, with all that experience behind us, we are uniquely placed to introduce something new to the world of meetings and conferences:

The Convention without Tension.

Deerhurst is the one lakeside resort that boasts every facility you would expect to find in a major city convention centre. That means you get the best of both worlds.

Our on-site coordinators are there to help you work out both the business and the leisure side of things. And your clients get to enjoy the country atmosphere and sporting facilities of Ontario's most famous resort.

I've enclosed a brochure that tells you more. But to help you plan your own conventions without tension, you'll want all the details — and I'll be happy to send them to you. All I ask in return is that you provide some general information about the kinds of conferences you plan.

Simply take a few moments of your time to fill out the questionnaire below. Return it to me today — by fax or in the reply paid envelope provided — and I'll send

Over please...

FIGURE 13-19   A direct mail example

declining for some time. The advertising agency designs a similar campaign to advertise the Sunday brunch. Table 13-7 shows the results of the potential return on investment.

In this case, the hotel wisely declined. The restaurant had only 200 seats, and the return on the advertising investment could never be recovered.

There is no guaranteed way to measure advertising results. This method, however, reduces the risk of spending money unwisely.

Collateral

The same rules discussed above also apply to brochures, direct mail, and other forms of ad-

you your own copy of our Convention Kit by return mail.

Why not do it now? You owe it to your clients — and to yourself — to start planning meetings you can really feel relaxed about.

Sincerely,

John Bullock
Director of Sales & Marketing

P.S. Whether it be a corporate meeting, small meeting, conference, convention — I think you'll find we can accommodate your client requirements.

QUESTIONNAIRE

Here's my information, now please send me yours.

Robert C Lewis   SM
Robert C Lewis Assoc Inc
65 Wilsonview Ave Ste 2
Guelph   ON
N1G 2W5

❏ YES, send me my own copy of the Deerhurst
Conference Kit by return mail. And as my part
of the deal, here is the information you wanted.

1) Approximately how large are your conferences?
Number of people:
From _____ To _____
Number of bedrooms:
From _____ To _____

2) Who else in your company is specifically responsible for conference planning?
a) Name _____
b) Name _____
c) Name _____

3) Have you ever arranged a conference at Deerhurst?
❏ Yes   ❏ No
If yes, when?
_____

4) When do your conferences usually take place?
_____

5) When is your next conference?
_____

002982

FIGURE 13-19   (continued)

vertising called collateral in the industry. We do not reiterate them here. We add, however, a commentary. Some hotel print advertising has progressed considerably in the past few years beyond the stereotyped ads we have described. Hotel collateral, on the other hand, has progressed only in rare instances and consists of essentially contrived, unreasonable depictions, and standardized copy, both dull and boring. We guess that if you changed the name, address,

and picture of the hotel, in at least 75 percent of all hotel brochures you couldn't tell one hotel from another.

Because collateral is a common form of advertising for hotels, we recommend you evaluate the brochure pages from four different hotels shown in Figure 13-18. Do the rules apply?

Direct mail is another special form of advertising and/or special promotion. In many instances direct mail can be a far more influential medium than other forms of advertising. The reason is that one is much better able to directly address the target market. This is especially true for single-unit restaurants that have limited market reach.

Direct mail is also easier to track. While "image" advertising can develop awareness, a direct-mail piece with a "call for action," such as redemption of a coupon, can provide almost immediate feedback for a campaign. An example of direct mail is shown in Figure 13-19. With the growing use of direct mail, consumers are getting tired of "junk mail," and the effectiveness of this method is debatable. For those interested, the subject is well-covered in numerous books, although not much has been written on direct mail for hospitality. This could be a fertile research area, but the same rules we have given above will apply.

Summary

In this chapter we have discussed the foundations of the communications mix and two of its components, advertising and word-of-mouth. The foundations apply to all aspects of communications, and successful implementation depends critically on knowing the target market and conducting the appropriate marketing research, two factors that complement a more recent phenomenon, database marketing.

In small firms, all the parts of the communications mix will often fall within the domain of one person, or one department, thus easing their coordination. In larger firms, there may be both an advertising and public relations firm on retainer, with only personal selling handled mostly in-house. In these cases, a special effort is needed to be certain that all the elements of the communications mix are synchronized. In either case, the mix should emanate from the marketing need of the firm and be consistent with its overall marketing strategy.

Word-of-mouth communications are a potent force in the hospitality industry, and recommendations from persons who have experienced a service play an important role in the customer choice process. Complaints are a way that customers choose to communicate, and how these complaints are resolved has a great impact on customer satisfaction.

Database marketing allows for customization of the communications effort. It provides a knowledgeable and responsive marketing system that helps to personalize the customer relationship and focus marketing efforts, to allow target marketing to achieve its ultimate goal of addressing customers' needs, wants, and problems.

It should be clear that good advertising is not simple to orchestrate. While it is easy to employ advertising techniques, it is difficult to do so successfully. The common theme in the development of advertising is that its success depends upon the needs of the customer. Advertising should have clear goals and should be developed after asking the right research questions.

This chapter offers a foundation and a methodology for successful execution of advertising. The most common reason for failure in delivering these subsets of the communications mix is lack of research and planning. With a strong planning process in place and a good research evaluation mechanism, both revenues and customer satisfaction can be maximized. In the next chapter, we continue with the communications mix and four of its other elements: sales promotions, merchandising, public relations, and publicity.

Discussion Questions

1. Discuss word-of-mouth communications and how they are affected by the communications mix. Give specific examples. How does this affect the need, or lack of a need, to advertise?
2. Spot the five elements of the communications mix in the anecdote given in the beginning of the chapter. How could the restaurant have communicated better? How could the couple? Is the answer to the restaurant's problem now to advertise? Discuss.

3. Evaluate the ads in Figure 13-1. Discuss the strategy and tactics of these ads and how they are/are not implemented.

4. Select a local restaurant and ask the five major questions that must be answered by market research to develop the communications mix.

5. Why is it so critical to understand the target market before developing the communications mix? Discuss this in detail, with specific examples.

6. Discuss a complaint you have made in a hotel or restaurant. How was it handled? How would you have handled it? Or, write a letter of complaint to any business and evaluate the response.

7. Consider a special case of database marketing from your own experience. What information would you want in the database?

8. Develop a communications mix for Case 13-1. Consider "whom to say it to, what to say, how to say it, how often, and where to say it."

9. Write responses to the customers' letters in Cases 13-2 and 13-3.

10. In Case 13-4, what should be Andiamo's communications mix? Consider "where are we now, why are we there, where could we be, and how do we get there."

✔ Case 13-1
The Berkshire Place Kaffee

Philip Georgas, Managing Director of the 400-room Omni Berkshire Place, was struck by the number of afternoon "high teas" being served in the New York City marketplace by upscale hotels. The Omni Berkshire Place, located at 52nd and Madison, had for years also offered this traditional tea and pastry service in its atrium lounge. In spite of its excellent location, the hotel experienced declining revenues for this feature over the years. Competition was omnipresent in the City, and there was little differentiation between "high tea" at the Waldorf-Astoria, The Plaza, The Palace, or the Omni Berkshire Place. Mr. Georgas decided that it was time for a change.

Rather than expanding his tea offering to try to make it different, or closing it altogether, Georgas decided to offer his guests something different. He recognized a new trend in the industry; namely, special coffees were becoming a big seller, primarily on the West Coast. Coffee bars were springing up everywhere, and upscale coffee house chains, such as Starbucks, were coming to the East Coast. The specialty gourmet coffee segment had grown by 30 percent per year over the past three years and was forecasted to account for 50 percent of all coffee sales by the turn of the century. Along with this growth in coffee sales was a dramatic increase in the number of coffee houses and stand-up coffee bars, predicted to increase to 10,000 nationwide in the same period, up from 200 in 1989. Georgas decided to provide an upscale version of the coffee theme.

First, he surveyed his customers to find out what they thought. Almost all loved the idea. While "high tea" was interesting to the American customer, it was perceived as more of an event, rather than a regular experience. So far, tea had not become a significant part of the American culture. Coffee most certainly was, and it was growing as a national trend.

Georgas began to design his version of "high coffee." Everything about the change in concept was authentic. His choice of a coffee vendor,

Oren's Daily Roast Coffee, was ideal. Oren's specialized in various coffees and was strict in its quality control: Each pot had to be made at a certain water temperature and special equipment was ordered to ensure high quality. Various coffees from around the world were selected for the new experience, now named the Berkshire Place Kaffee. Together with the authentic coffees came authentic accompaniments: Turkish coffee came with the types of food that Turks ate with their coffee; the same was true for the Belgian, Colombian, and Ethiopian blends. Following are some of the details:

Coffees Selection of 13 different coffees provided daily by Oren's Daily Roast and grouped according to body (dark roast, full bodied, medium bodied). Included were two flavored coffees, two decaffeinated coffees, and one flavored decaffeinated coffee. All decaffeinated coffees produced by Swiss water process. Espresso, cappuccino, and a selection of teas also were available.

Accompaniments A selection of 13 international accompaniments were offered, including traditional English scones, Halvah & Loukoumi, Biscotti, Colombian rice pudding, Linzertorte, Sachertorte, and fresh raspberries with Devonshire cream.

Service Beans roasted and delivered to hotel daily. Coffee individually prepared at the table in French presses. Available in 2, 3-1/2, 5-1/2, and 8-cup pots. Coffee served with complimentary chocolates. Fresh cream, sugar sticks, as well as white and brown sugar, accompany each order. Served on round, marble cafe tables from early morning to early evening.

Setting Comfortable and inviting European-style drawing-room setting in skylit atrium with large, beautiful cascading plants. Bevelled mirror walls set off by an Oriental lacquered screen and lavish floral centerpiece. Rich, tapestry-patterned carpeting in shades of taupe, ivory, and forest green. Accommodates up to 50 persons in plush settees and armchairs in shades of wintergreen.

After creating the theme and product offering, Georgas began to form his target markets.

First were the in-house guests: All Omni Berkshire Place guests needed to be aware of the new offering. Second, the local business community needed to be alerted. Georgas' research had shown that there were many businesspeople who wanted an upscale meeting place to discuss business, without the time and expense of a typical business lunch. Also, with the trend of outplaced executives beginning their own consulting businesses, many did not have offices in which to meet their customers; the Berkshire Place Kaffee provided them with the right upscale meeting place to join colleagues and customers. There were also the area residents and shoppers who visited nearby upscale retail stores such as Saks Fifth Avenue, Tiffany's, and Bloomingdale's, all within a short walking distance of the hotel. Finally, Georgas saw the Berkshire Place Kaffee as an alternative to the traditional cocktail lounge.

With his research completed, target customers identified, and product defined, Georgas was ready to communicate his new Berkshire Kaffee to the public.

✔ Case 13-2
The Customer's Complaint[6]

===

123 Main Street
Boston, Massachusetts
Gail and Harvey Pearson
The Retreat House on Foliage Pond
Vacationland, New Hampshire

Dear Mr. and Mrs. Pearson:

This is the first time that I have ever written a letter like this, but my wife and I are so upset by the treatment afforded by your staff that we felt compelled to let you know what happened to us. We had dinner reservations at the Retreat House for a party of four under my wife's name, Dr. Elaine Loflin, for Saturday evening, October 11. We were hosting my wife's brother and his wife, visiting from Atlanta, Georgia.

We were seated at 7:00 P.M. in the dining room to the left of the front desk. There were at least four empty tables in the room when we were seated. We were immediately given menus, a wine list, ice water, dinner rolls, and butter. Then we sat for 15 minutes until the cocktail waittress asked us for our drink orders. My sister-in-law said, after being asked what she would like, "I'll have a vodka martini straight-up with an olive." The cocktail waittress responded immediately, "I'm not a stenographer." My sister-in-law repeated her drink order.

Soon after, our waiter arrived, informing us of the specials of the evening. I don't remember his name, but he had dark hair, wore glasses, was a little stocky, and had his sleeves rolled up. He returned about ten minutes later, our drinks still not having arrived. We had not decided upon our entrees, but requested appetizers, upon which he informed us that we could not order appetizers without ordering our entrees at the same time. We decided not to order appetizers.

Our drinks arrived and the waiter returned. We ordered our entrees at 7:30. When the waiter asked my wife for her order, he addressed her as "young lady." When he served her the meal, he called her "dear."

At ten minutes of eight we requested that our salads be brought to us as soon as possible. I then asked the waiter's assistant to bring us more rolls (each of us had been served one when we were seated). Her response was, "Who wants a roll?", upon which, caught off guard, we went around the table saying yes or no so she would know exactly how many "extra" rolls to bring to our table.

Our salads were served at five minutes of eight. At 25 minutes past the hour we requested our entrees. They were served at 8:30, one and one-half hours after we were seated in a restaurant which was one-third empty. Let me also add that we had to make constant requests for water refills, butter replacement, and the like.

In fairness to the chef, the food was excellent and, as you already realize, the atmosphere delightful. Despite this, the dinner was a disaster. We were extremely upset and very insulted by the experience. Your staff is not well trained. They were overtly rude, and displayed little etiquette or social grace. This was compounded by

---

[6]"Talkback Answering the Customer's Complaint: A Case Study," *Cornell Hotel and Restaurant Adminsitration Quarterly.*
Copyright © Cornell University. Used by permission. All rights reserved. The names of the people and the restaurant have been disguised.

the atmosphere you are trying to present and the prices you charge in the dining room.

Perhaps we should have made our feelings known at the time, but our foremost desire was to leave as soon as possible. We had been looking forward to dining at the Retreat House for quite some time as part of our vacation weekend in New Hampshire. We will be hard-pressed to return to your establishment. Please be sure to know that we will share our experience at the Retreat House with our family, friends, and business associates.

Sincerely,
Dr. William E. Loflin

✔ Case 13-3

Letter to the Executive Vice-President

===

Mr. John Sharpe, Executive Vice-President, Operations
Four Seasons Hotels Limited, Toronto, Ontario M5S 9Z9

Dear Mr. Sharpe:

I was pleased to stay at the Four Seasons in downtown Toronto the night of March 3. As I would have expected, treatment was beyond reproach and the entire staff was not only friendly and helpful, but totally efficient. After all, this is the Four Seasons reputation.

As the hotel industry, however, continues to put more and more emphasis on service, service, service, I sometimes find that little nuances that don't show up on guest comment cards, or are not significant enough to "complain" about, make a considerable difference in a guest stay. (I still call them service albeit without personal contact.) In fact, in this case, had I been staying longer I would have picked up the telephone and, I'm sure, all would have been rapidly corrected. As you well know, most guests don't complain; they simply don't come back. Of course, much of this comes from the high expectations that one has when staying at a Four Seasons. So, I thought I would pass on to you how Four Seasons failed to meet my expectations on a one-night stay.

The room, 2707, was large, delightful, understated and in excellent taste, on a corner with two large windows. In front of one window, a perfect place for reading, was a coffee table and *one* comfortable chair. There was plenty of room for a second chair, but one of us had to use the not-so-comfortable desk chair to sit there, much to our surprise. The overhead light had a lightbulb missing and the total wattage made reading somewhat difficult. The desk light had two 60-watt bulbs, better than too many hotel rooms that have only one, but two 75s or 100s would have been far preferable for someone doing close work, or with 60-year-old eyes.

I have read somewhere that Four Seasons was the first to introduce shampoo to bathroom amenity packages. My own research has shown me that people, especially women, are very reluctant to put a shampoo in their hair when they don't know what it is. Generic shampoos are out, brand names are in, and a no-name is a surprise at any first-class hotel.

I am a regular sauna user and can easily stay 20 minutes or better in a sauna at usual temperatures of 160–200 degrees Farenheit. But 230 degrees drove me out in five minutes and there was no control to change it. I have only seen a sauna that hot, once before, and that was in Bangkok where the sauna was also empty in spite of the large contingent of Japanese using the health club.

Yours truly,
James E. Watts

✔ Case 13-4
Andiamo's[7]

"I don't believe in advertising," John Quinn, co-owner of Andiamo's stated. "You need lots of money to advertise and it's better to promote things in-house. Andiamo's has done the same amount of business since we stopped advertising. If I had the money to spend again, I would build a banquet room to increase our capacity to do business."

Andiamo's was a small, moderately priced restaurant featuring northern Italian cuisine. It was located on a side street in the college town of Ithaca, New York. The decor was "simple, high-tech, and New York chic."

Andiamo's had two storefronts: One featured a deli decor where passersby could observe fresh pasta being made, the other exposed the restaurant. As guests entered Andiamo's they passed the deli counter that displayed the artfully arranged antipasto ingredients and desserts. There was also a "show kitchen" that was separated from the dining room by a long white counter. A striped awning and white tile floor provided the visual division between the two areas. All final preparation of the food was done in the "show kitchen" to allow the customers to see for themselves "just how fresh the food is." The dining room was off to the left and down two steps. A very simple white decor gave the feeling of a modern, elegant restaurant.

Background

Peter Schore, the other co-owner, held a Bachelors and a Master of Science degree in Hotel and Restaurant Management. Prior to opening Andiamo's, he was a food and beverage manager of a major, international hotel chain and had been a teacher at a culinary school. In order to fulfill his dream of opening a restaurant,

Schore purchased an inn outside Ithaca, New York where people would "take a Sunday drive to go and eat."

Schore wanted to start another, more commercial venture in a city or large, suburban area. After vacationing in Italy for three months, he decided to open a restaurant featuring northern Italian cuisine. Schore chose Ithaca for three reasons: He resided there, he liked the town, and he wanted the restaurant to be a neighborhood place for fine food at moderate prices. After weeks of searching, Schore discovered a location that was exactly what he wanted. He was most surprised when informed that a Mr. Quinn had recently approached the owner to discuss a similar proposition.

John Quinn had owned and operated a successful soup and salad-style restaurant in Ithaca for seven years. He recognized that the latest trend in gourmet pasta restaurants was uniformly popular elsewhere in the country and believed that an ethnic restaurant of that type would also prosper in the Ithaca area.

Schore and Quinn agreed to join forces and combine their talents to develop Andiamo's. Since both of the principal partners recognized that a co-manager setup could be potentially problematic, they agreed to the following division of responsibilities:

1. Quinn would be in charge of all record-keeping, advertising/promotion, cost control and maintenance, as well as the general supervision of the front of the house.
2. Schore would manage the back of the house to include food purchasing, storage, preparation, and presentation.
3. Each of the co-owners would function as manager 50 percent of the time (20 to 30 hours a week).

Getting Open

Andiamo's was started with a budget of $57,000. The white china was second-hand, the

---

[7]Adapted from Robert C. Lewis, *Cases in Hospitality Marketing and Management,* pp. 169–179. Copyright © 1989 John Wiley & Sons, New York. Reprinted by permission of John Wiley & Sons, Inc. Helaine Rockett researched and contributed to this case. Names and location have been disguised.

furniture was purchased at auction, and most of the equipment was used merchandise. Plumbing, electrical, and equipment hookup problems increased expenses to $118,000.

Quinn and Schore recognized that different meal periods would attract different customers, so they attempted to target their advertising to capture the appropriate markets. A brainstorming session produced the following consensus:

Meal Period	Target Market
Lunch	In-town and regional
Dinner	businesses
Afternoon snack	Remote areas
Brunch	Students, shoppers, locals
Late-night snack	Remote areas
Takeout	Students, locals
	Locals

Type of Media
13 local newspapers within a 30-mile radius
1 free Valley newspaper
New York Times
New York Magazine
Local radio station

In October, Andiamo's literally "just opened the doors." Two weeks prior to the opening, Quinn and Schore had placed advertisements in three area newspapers with an ad simply stating "Andiamo's." One week before the opening the ad was amended to read "Andiamo's–Fine Italian Cuisine."

Arrangements had been made to host a press party and a grand opening party for Ithaca's Chamber of Commerce members, but the "endless hours" involved in opening the restaurant, as well as a cash shortage, necessitated that plans for these events be scrapped. The co-owners did visit the admissions offices of the surrounding colleges, the local conference center, and all of Ithaca's downtown merchants to familiarize them with Andiamo's and to invite them for a complimentary cocktail.

Andiamo's served much the same menu for lunch and dinner, although the luncheon portions were smaller and the prices lower. Besides the appetizer and full dinner menu, there was also a separate pasta menu. Both beer and wine, but not liquor, were available, with a rather extensive Italian wine list with selections ranging from $10 to $35 per bottle.

Andiamo's Concept

Andiamo's was conceived as an establishment that served only "the freshest possible food made from scratch." It was intended to be a moderately priced restaurant in a neighborhood setting. The owners insisted they were "not interested in making a fast buck or a tremendous return," that they just wanted "to do reasonably well."

Operations

A year later, in October, Mark Jaslow became the Manager of Andiamo's. He had been employed as a cook in New York City for the previous six years and was just finishing his Hotel and Restaurant Management degree at Cornell University. Mark was originally hired as the Cashier/Assistant Manager seven weeks before. Upon his promotion, the co-owners retired from active management and assumed their new roles as "directors of investment and operations," and also as restaurant consultants.

Mark described the business level in the previous spring and summer as "booming." From November on, however, business began to decline. In an effort to improve the bottom line, manpower hours, laundry expenses, and advertising dollars were either decreased or, in the latter case, eliminated entirely. Lunch was eventually discontinued in December when advertisements for luncheon specials failed to significantly impact business. The owners decided that the amount of overhead simply exceeded the amount of sales revenue.

Jaslow staffed two to three waitpersons and no busperson on weekdays, and four waitpersons and one busperson on weekends. Andiamo's also employed a full-time chef and sous chef, and a part-time pasta maker and baker. All employees had been employed at Andiamo's for over one year and all were efficient, according to Jaslow.

Andiamo's could accommodate 76 patrons at the 22 tables in the restaurant. Jaslow stated that in a good week the average turnover rate was less than once on Sundays and weeknights, two times on Fridays, and three times on Saturdays. The average check for dinner was $18 per person and about 20 percent of the total was beer or wine.

According to Jaslow, close to 90 percent of the guests were repeat customers, and ten percent had been recommended by friends. The clientele was described as mostly upper-middle class couples in the $30,000–$40,000 income bracket from the surrounding cities within half an hour of Ithaca. Based on the menu, clientele, and atmosphere, Mark classified the restaurant as "gourmet."

In its first full year of operation, the restaurant averaged $9,500 per week in sales volume, with $6,000 coming in on the weekend nights. Food, beverage, and advertising costs are shown on the abbreviated income statement (Table 13-4-1).

Marketing

When asked his views on the marketing/advertising scenario, Quinn stated, "I feel our market is within a half-hour drive of Ithaca. Because of easy accessibility to Route 81, we see Andiamo's as capturing the transient vacationer who might be enroute to ski, camp, or fish. People from the city heading to the country want to stop in a somewhat cosmopolitan, interesting town."

The major problem, according to Schore, was how to divert those travelers from the superhighway and into Ithaca. "We could never afford to construct a billboard on Route 81, so I decided to attend a Chamber of Commerce meeting to determine how Ithaca is promoting itself." At the meeting, Schore discussed his

TABLE 13-4-1   Abbreviated Income Statement

Sales		
Food		
Served	$387,822	
Takeout	12,688	
Food Sales	400,510	
Wine & Beer	98,600	
Total Sales		$499,110
Cost of Sales		
Food	$111,075	
Wine & Beer	40,525	
Total Cost of Sales		$151,600
Advertising	$ 11,411	
Promotion	2,400	
		$ 13,811
Other Costs		
Total Other Operating Costs		$290,939
Total Costs		$456,350
Profit Before Occupation Cost		42,760
Occupation Costs		48,332
Profit (loss) Before Depreciation		(6,072)

concerns with the members and was instrumental in the creation of the Ithaca Publicity Committee. This committee drafted a marketing proposal and designed a brochure to distribute to ski areas, campgrounds, tourist agencies, and other tourist spots. The committee members visited local merchants and sold $200 advertising blocks to finance the brochure. In return, the merchants were promised valuable exposure. Table 13-4-2 shows the framework of the marketing plan.

Competition

There were 45 restaurants in Ithaca ranging from McDonald's to gourmet operations. Schore believed that the direct competition for Andiamo's were those which were medium-priced and had a somewhat unique atmosphere. He identified seven restaurants in the area as competition:

Type of Menu	Atmosphere	Price
Vegetarian	cafe	low
Cheese raclette	traditional	medium
American-mixed	inn	medium-high
American-mixed	traditional	medium
Chinese oriental	medium	high
Seafood	traditional	medium
Vegetarian	traditional	low-medium

Mark identified as competition three different restaurants that were within the Ithaca town lines:

Type of Menu	Atmosphere	Price
French	traditional	high
Italian	ethnic	medium
American	cafe	medium-high

Advertising

Advertising continued through most of the first year until all ads were eventually cancelled in November. Seventy-five percent of the ads simply stated "Andiamo's" and included a description of its food with the address and hours of operation. The remaining 25 percent of the ads were more informative, with specific details about the food and often a unique "gimmick" to attract customers to the establishment. One "gimmick," run in a free newspaper with a circulation of 29,000, was a coupon ad—only ten coupons were redeemed.

In February of Andiamo's second year of operation, an informal, unscientific study was conducted, taking in 25 residents within a ten-mile radius of Ithaca. The study revealed that none of the respondents recognized the name "Andiamo's," nor did they know what it was or where it was located.

TABLE 13-4-2   Chamber of Commerce Marketing Plan

CAMPAIGN OBJECTIVES

To attract more people downtown for shopping, dining, and entertainment

BY

Projecting "Main Street Ithaca" as a vibrant business community with traditional and contemporary elements that blend to give "Main Street Ithaca" broad appeal.

Target Markets

- Area Residents
- Residents of Major Highway Communities
- Colonial America buffs
    Shaker Community
    Historical New York
- Business Conference and Workshop Attendees
    Hotel and Motel Conference Centers
    Convention Bureaus
    Major Corporations
    University Centers
- Academic Travelers
    Prospective Students and Parents
    Visiting Parents
    Academic Conferences
    Returning Alumni
- Cultural Event Attendees
    Theater at Colleges and University Chamber Concerts
    Regional Theater, Orchestras, etc
- Summer Camp
    Staff
    Visiting Parents
- Antiques Buyers and Collectors
- Skiing Area Patrons
- Craftspeople and Buyers
- Country Inn Devotees

PROMOTIONAL CAMPAIGN

Develop Identity through consistently used logo—"Main Street Ithaca"

Press Releases widely distributed to announce "Main Street Ithaca" campaign and enumerate reasons to visit Ithaca.

Brochure/Business Directory distributed within two-hour driving radius to:

- Other Chambers of Commerce
- Tourist Booths
- College Visitors and Conferences
- Hotels and Motels
- Cultural Events
- Summer Camps
- Recreational Areas

(continued)

TABLE 13-4-2   (continued)

- Historical Areas
- Mailing to: Ad Respondants
    Area Resident Mailing List
    College Mailings
    Special-nterest Lists

Advertising Campaign promoting "Main Street Ithaca" with brochure request element.

- Local Media—Large ads with elements of Directory alternating with smaller institutional identification ads.
- New York, New England, and Northeast periodicals and newspapers and other media in two-hour driving distance. Also special interest periodicals, general tourism guides and periodicals.

PRELIMINARY BUDGET

Brochure Development, Production and Mailing: Ad Layouts	$ 9,000
Local and Regional Media Advertising	11,500
National Travel and Special Interest Publications	12,500
Approximate First-year Budget	$33,000

UNDERWRITING THE CAMPAIGN

MIX OF

1. *Directory Listing* of businesses on Main Street (Market to State Streets) and side streets (one block north and south of Main)

Category

Name   Address   Phone Number

        One-line description
        100 participants @ $200 ($4 per week)

2. *Corporate and Institutional Sponsers*

    Listing under Sponsors
    $200 Minimum   No Maximum
    Open to all businesses first year under sponsorship of Downtown Business Association.

BREAK-EVEN RETURN

$20,000 50 weeks = $400 per week or $80 per day

CHAPTER 14

The Communications Mix: Sales Promotions, Merchandising, Public Relations, and Publicity

This chapter will discuss four more elements of the communications mix: sales promotions, merchandising, public relations, and publicity. The reader should keep in mind the definition and discussion of the communications mix umbrella from the beginning of Chapter 13, as well as that relating to communications strategy and research.

Principles and Practices of Sales Promotion

Sales promotions are marketing communications that serve specifically as incentives to stimulate sales on a short-term basis. Sales promotions can also be effectively used to stimulate trial purchases. In hospitality, they are frequently used to bring in business during off-periods.

When McDonald's offers reduced prices on Ninja Turtle toys with a purchase of a Kid's Meal, that's a sales promotion. When Palm Springs hotels offer 50 percent off during the summer months, that's a sales promotion. When restaurants offer coupons, that's a sales promotion.

One of the most common forms of promotion in the tourism and hotel industries is packaging —a bundling of any combination of travel, rooms, meals, sight-seeing, and so forth in one all-inclusive price. These kinds of packages, however, are directed at specific market segments and have been discussed in Chapter 6.

Sales promotion involves the development of creative ideas aimed at producing business, or creating a customer, in support of the total marketing effort. Sales promotions must be in tune with overall objectives and must complement other elements of both the communications mix and the marketing mix.

While they should provide customer satisfaction, sales promotions, by definition, are not likely to build long-term customer loyalty in themselves. Obviously, there is nothing wrong with them if they do; it is just that they rarely work that way.

Consider, for example, that Sears department stores have a warehouse sale on appliances—returned merchandise, slightly damaged goods, and so on—a true promotion. You buy a refrigerator for half-price, but do you now feel compelled (loyal) to go to Sears to buy a microwave oven at the regular price? Isn't the same thing true of a special weekend rate at a hotel at one-third the regular rate?

Sears also guarantees that you can return any merchandise for any reason, no questions asked. Sears customers pay for that privilege, although the cost is hidden in the purchase price. It is not, however, a promotion; it is a policy designed to build customer loyalty, and it does.

Now suppose that Sears has a permanent warehouse sale "promotion" on all merchandise. All other things being equal, you go to Sears. Now Walmart, K-Mart, and 15 other large chains do likewise. Where is your "loyalty" now?

We usually think of sales promotions as short-term, of the moment. The frequent-traveler "point" programs that many hotel companies have instituted, however, are largely designed to be long-term—that is, to keep the customer coming back. In this sense, frequent-traveler programs become part of the augmented product, albeit they are also sales promotions. Regardless, the principles of promotion as discussed here apply just as well to frequent-traveler programs.

Although sales promotions are short-term oriented they may succeed in the long term; that is, they may develop repeat business. Long-term promotions, however, rarely succeed in the long term. The reason for this is because long-term promotions do become part of the product—that is, they are no longer promotions as originally intended. They become, instead, something you are forced to give customers, or something that customers come to expect, and something that customers must pay for whether or not they want it. Because frequent-traveler programs are such a prevalent example of this, we will discuss them in more detail than in our earlier brief mentions.

Frequent-Traveler Programs

Frequent-traveler programs are patterned after those originated by the airlines. This type of promotion was adapted to the hospitality industry by Holiday Inn in the late 1970s and has now expanded industry-wide. Almost all major hotel affiliations offer frequent-traveler programs of some kind, at least in North America. Most of these are tie-in promotions that offer benefits both inside and outside the hotels, such as free room stays, upgrades, car rentals, and airline mileage, the latter becoming increasingly more popular (Figure 14-1). The car rental companies and the airlines reciprocate. Other plans give away U.S. savings bonds, console pianos, or selections from a full gift catalog. Most plans award "points" to obtain these benefits (Figure 14-2) although some, as in Figure 14-1, offer mileage in lieu of points. The choice is the traveler's. Points are usually based on dollars spent, sometimes just on rooms, and sometimes also on food and beverages, which help keep guests in the hotel. Frequent-traveler programs have also added promotions within the augumented product. "Double points" for certain hotels or time periods promote awareness, trial, or increased usage within the framework of the normal frequent-traveler programs. The latter are true short-term promotions that fill short-term needs for individual properties.

Other benefits of these programs, sometimes called corporate rate programs, are more simply termed "privileges" and include guaranteed and preferred rates, guaranteed rooms, speedy check-out, express check-in, free room upgrades, complimentary cocktails and newspapers, free stays for spouses in rooms, and other amenities (Figure 14-3). These privileges are offered in the context of benefit marketing and do not come under the category of true promotions. They are part of the augmented product for members, and most are at little or no additional cost to the hotel.

Although there is much overlap between the two types of programs, from a marketing viewpoint they should be separated. The purpose of both programs is, purportedly, to cultivate the loyal customer, the one who will return to the same property or chain. That is a justifiable purpose for the added benefits programs, but not for long-term frequent-traveler point programs, which is why they are not truly promotions and may be self-defeating and costly in the long term.

"I'D LIKE TO PUT YOU 5,000 MILES CLOSER TO YOUR NEXT FREE TICKET. AND WITH NEW MARRIOTT MILES℠ I CAN."

Bill Marriott

Stay with us and watch the miles build up on American Airlines®, British Airways, Continental, Northwest, TWA and USAir. Add 5,000 miles for every 5 stays—whether you fly or not. To join, call 1-800-FOR-MILES.

Marriott
HOTELS · RESORTS · SUITES

WE MAKE IT HAPPEN FOR YOU.

You must be a member of a frequent flyer program to play. Earn 500 frequent flyer miles for every stay. *Plus*, 2,500 miles after every fifth stay, for a total of 5,000 miles for every 5 stays. With TWA (international hotels only) & Continental earn up to 10,000 miles for every 5 stays. Marriott Honored Guest Awards points will not be awarded for Marriott Miles stays. Marriott's Courtyard, Residence Inn, and Fairfield Inn hotels do not participate in Marriott Miles. To earn frequent flyer miles in Marriott Miles, check-in must occur between May 1, 1993 and June 30, 1994. ©1993 Marriott Corp.

Courtesy of Marriott Corporation

FIGURE 14-1   Offering airline mileage for hotel stays

RAMADA BUSINESS CARD AWARDS		RAMADA BUSINESS CARD GIFT CERTIFICATE	SERVICE MERCHANDISE GIFT CERTIFIC/
AWARD LEVEL	**TRAVEL AWARD**		
7,500		$5	$5
10,000	50% off 2-Night Weekend Stay at any Ramada in the U.S. or Canada. Includes one free day with a two-day minimum rental at all U.S. Alamo locations (compact through standard size car).	$10	$10
15,000	FREE 1-Night Stay Anytime at any Ramada in the U.S. or Canada. Includes one free day with a two-day minimum rental at all U.S. Alamo locations (compact through standard size car).	$25	$25
25,000	FREE 2-Night Weekend Stay at any Ramada in the U.S. or Canada. Includes two free days with a three-day minimum rental at all U.S. Alamo locations (compact through standard size car).	$50	$50
50,000	FREE 3-Consecutive-Night Stay at any Ramada in the U.S. or Canada. Includes three free days at all U.S. Alamo locations (compact through standard size car).	$100	$100
75,000	FREE 5-Consecutive-Night Stay at any Ramada in the U.S. or Canada. Includes five free days at all U.S. Alamo locations (intermediate size car only).	$150	$150
100,000	FREE 3-Consecutive-Night Stay (must include a Saturday night) at any Ramada in the U.S. or Canada and FREE round-trip airfare for one in the U.S. or Canada. Includes three free days at all U.S. Alamo locations (intermediate size car only).	$200	$200
125,000	FREE 3-Consecutive-Night Stay (must include a Saturday night) at any Ramada in the U.S. or Canada and FREE round-trip airfare for two in the U.S. or Canada. Includes three free days at all U.S. Alamo locations (intermediate size car only).	$250	$250
150,000	FREE 5-Consecutive-Night Stay (must include a Saturday night) at any Ramada in the U.S., Canada or the Caribbean and FREE round-trip airfare for one in the U.S., Canada or the Caribbean. Includes five free days at all U.S. Alamo locations (intermediate size car only).	$300	$300
175,000	FREE 5-Consecutive-Night Stay (must include a Saturday night) at any Ramada in the U.S., Canada or the Caribbean and FREE round-trip airfare for two in the U.S., Canada or the Caribbean. Includes five free days at all U.S. Alamo locations (luxury car only).	$350	$350
200,000	FREE 7-Consecutive-Night Stay (must include a Saturday night) at any Ramada in the U.S., Canada or the Caribbean and FREE round-trip airfare for one in the U.S., or the Caribbean. Includes seven free days at all U.S. Alamo locations (luxury car only).	$400	$400
250,000	FREE 7-Consecutive-Night Stay (must include a Saturday night) at any Ramada in the U.S., Canada or the Caribbean and FREE round-trip airfare for two in the U.S., Canada or the Caribbean. Includes seven free days at all U.S. Alamo locations (luxury car only).	$500	$500
300,000	FREE 7-Consecutive-Night Stay at any Ramada and FREE round-trip international airfare for one. Includes seven free days at all U.S. Alamo locations (luxury car only) or $150 toward rental in the U.K. (compact B-E only).	$600	$600
350,000	FREE 7-Consecutive-Night Stay at any Ramada and FREE round-trip international airfare for two. Includes seven free days at all U.S. Alamo locations (luxury car only) or $150 toward rental in the U.K. (compact B-E only).	$700	$700
400,000	FREE 7-Consecutive-Night Stay at any Ramada and FREE round-trip business-class international airfare for one. Includes seven free days at all U.S. Alamo locations (luxury car only) or $150 toward rental in the U.K. (compact B-E car only).	$800	$800
450,000	FREE 7-Consecutive-Night Stay at any Ramada and FREE round-trip business-class international airfare for two. Includes seven free days at all U.S. Alamo locations (luxury car only) or $150 toward rental in the U.K. (compact B-E car only).	$900	$900
500,000	FREE 10-Consecutive-Night Stay at any Ramada and FREE round-trip business-class international airfare for two. Includes ten free days at all U.S. Alamo locations (luxury car only) or $250 toward rental in the U.K. (compact B-E car only).	$1,000	$1,000

FIGURE 14-2   Award level "points" for Ramada Business Card customers

The airlines have been at it longer, so it is easiest to explain what we are saying by looking at their programs. Although the airlines' plans have been touted by the airlines as great successes, it is difficult to know whether that is really the case. Pan American World Airways, now extinct, reported losing $45 to $50 million after some colossal blunders when its plan was first inaugurated. *Business Week* reported that "most carriers lose as many fliers to rivals' programs as they attract to their own."[1] However, airlines that have tried dropping the plans have felt an immediate loss in business and have had to reinstate them. Today, anywhere from eight to twelve percent of the passengers on any given flight are flying free on frequent-flyer miles. To our knowledge, no one has yet researched how many of these would otherwise be "paying" passengers, and there are billions of accumulated free miles yet unused. In the meantime, the airlines are hemorrhaging money. Contrarily, Southwest Airlines, the only airline in the United States that is showing a consistent profit over the last few years, does not have a frequent-flyer program. Instead, it offers low fares and a customer-driven culture.

For the airlines, and in some hotel situations, free flights/rooms are an opportunity

[1]Anon., "Does the Frequent-Flier Game Pay Off for Airlines?", *Business Week*, August 27, 1984, pp. 74–75.

Just Remember, You're Here On Business.

Stay At An Omni Hotel In:

Atlanta, GA
Baltimore, MD
Boston, MA
Chapel Hill, NC
Charleston, SC
Charlotte, NC
Charlottesville, VA
Chicago, IL
Cincinnati, OH
Dallas, TX
Detroit, MI
Durham, NC
Evanston, IL
Indianapolis, IN
Jacksonville, FL
Lake George, NY
Memphis, TN
Miami, FL
Minneapolis, MN
New Orleans, LA
New York, NY
Newport News, VA
Norfolk, VA
Orlando, FL
Philadelphia, PA
Providence, RI
Richmond, VA
San Diego, CA
San Mateo, CA
Tampa, FL
Virginia Beach, VA
Washington, DC
Cancun, Mexico
Ixtapa, Mexico
Hong Kong
Singapore

*Where You Want To Be
When You Have To Be Away.*

Who says work can't be enjoyable?

When you stay at any of 41 Omni Hotels Worldwide, you'll find every convenience for doing business. Including the best business locations. But you'll also find everything required for pleasant living. Like big, comfortable rooms, gourmet dining and gracious, attentive service.

Plus as a Select Guest Club member, you can enjoy additional privileges such as priority room availability, accommodation upgrades, evening turn-down service, complimentary coffee and the morning paper delivered with your wake-up call, express check-out and more.

Everything you'll need to conduct your business and rejuvenate your spirit. All for less than you'd expect from an Omni Hotel.

So next time you set out on business, remember Omni Hotels. Then we'll do our best to make you forget why you're here.

OMNI HOTELS®

For Reservations Call Your Travel Agent Or

1-800-THE-OMNI

©1991 Omni Hotels

Courtesy of Omni Hotels

FIGURE 14-3   Benefit marketing for frequent guest members

*Guest room
discount certificates*

*Express check-out
& late check-out*

Guest room upgrades

Dining discounts

*Complimentary daily USA Today
and morning coffee*

Airport shuttle service

A FEW OF THE REASONS WHY OUR FREQUENT GUESTS ARE SO FREQUENT.

If you travel the West often, perhaps you should join the growing number of Red Lion's Frequent Guest Dividends members. In addition to our regular amenities like 500 Alaska Airlines miles for every stay, you'll enjoy an array of exclusive services and privileges. And although your benefits are available to you every time you stay, you'll find them anything but routine. In fact, many are seldom found in programs without membership fees. So call for an application today or visit a Red Lion soon—because with privileges like these on every stay, why frequent anyplace else?

RED LION HOTELS & INNS
800-232-1287

FIGURE 14-3   (continued)

cost. Tony Carpenter, Vice President–Operations for Hilton International's U.S. brand, Vista Hotels, reported, "The great unknown factors are how much of the business would you have gotten anyway? And how much loyalty is generated?"[2] In other situations, such as merchandise and airline mileage awards, hotels have simply added to their cost basis. In the same article in which Carpenter's comment appeared, Mark Lomano, the Director of Leisure-time Industry Research for Laventhol and Horwath at the time, stated, "Once you start giving something to a hotel guest, it's very difficult to take it away..."—that is, it has become part of the product offering. Additionally, it costs major users like Marriott up to $100 million a year just to manage its program. We believe that long-term "promotions" of this kind do not work well for hotels for four major reasons.

In the first place, hotel guests have many more options than airline flyers. This means that they can belong to everyone's program and still stay where they want, depending on where they are at any given time. They can switch back and forth so that everyone wins and everyone loses and the net gain or loss remains the same. Furthermore, the hotel guest is far more fickle than the air traveler and is known to choose hotels by individual property rather than by chain. This, of course, is what the programs are designed to overcome, but they don't help much when the benefits are similar everywhere.

The second reason is that, for hotels, different factors pertain. While the airlines are running their programs, they also engage in fare wars resulting in lower prices. This has attracted many new flyers into the market, but each airline matches the prices of the others on the same route. These new flyers do not fly very often, and thus they are more prone to stay with one or two airlines, build up their points, and take free flights that they might not take otherwise.

Hotels also cut rates to compete, but still lose customers to lower-priced properties that may also offer frequent-traveler benefits. Instead of expanding the market, the hotel industry has pushed it into lower price brackets. These customers are more price-conscious than they are point-conscious (see Figure 14-4).

The third reason is that the hotel industry, in large part, has a problem understanding its market. The heavy sales orientation is more prone to giving customers what they don't necessarily want, rather than finding out what they really do want. This loses them customers regardless of any frequent-stay points.

The fourth reason is that staying in one hotel or another is very different from flying one airline or another. The elements of product and service vary far more in hotels than they do in airplanes, not to mention the duration of stay. The frequent hotel customer is far more likely to choose a hotel because it fills specific needs, than to choose an airline where schedule is the main determining factor. The frequent hotel traveler is also, most likely, a frequent flyer who already has more travel points than time to use them, including free hotel stays.

This is not to say that frequent travelers don't stay at hotels to accumulate points. Many do, and they also get free prizes, take free flights, and have free vacations. The question is, what are the hotels getting back at a very high cost? One 400-room Marriott hotel that we know of averages eight to ten percentage points of its occupancy as free guests with Marriott points.

As a group, the hotel industry is giving away something to get the customer it already has, or should have, while trading customers with other frequent-guest programs, winning some and losing some, and spending millions of dollars to do it. At the same time it punishes non-frequent travel members (90-plus percent of the market) by making them pay the bill. Then, like the airlines, the industry complains about not being able to get the rates needed to make a profit. It flies in the face of reality to construe this as a successful promotion.

With a growing realization that frequent-traveler programs may be actually costing more

---

[2]Reported in David Martindale, "Hotels and Frequent Flyers: The Changing Relationship," *Frequent Flyer,* August, 1986, pp. 67–68.

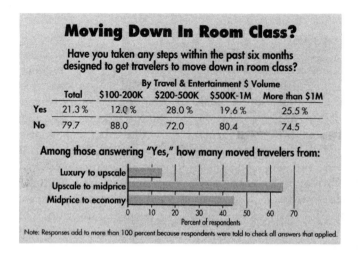

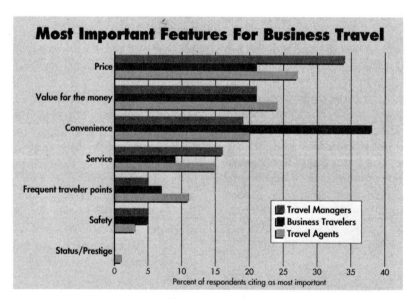

Source: Budget Rent a Car Corp. survey of 400 travel agents, 100 travel managers, and 200 business travelers, *Business Travel News,* March 7, 1994, p. 20. Reprinted by permission of *Business Travel News.*

FIGURE 14-4 Surveys of travelers on moving down in room class and on most important features for business travel

than the benefits obtained from them, many airlines and hotels have scaled back their programs and made them more restrictive. Also, major hotel companies are now pushing frequent-flyer miles as an incentive, as opposed to points toward free hotel rooms (Figure 14-1).

Sales Promotions and Marketing Needs

Sales promotions, we have said, are designed to fulfill a marketing need. It follows, then, that the first thing to be done is to define that need.

There are any number of needs for promotions—to create new business, to create awareness, and to create trial purchase are common ones. Some others are to increase demand in slow periods, to take business from the competition, or to meet the competition in its own promotional efforts. Whatever the reason, there is one major caveat with regard to promotions: They should be tied to something positive, such as a new or better facility, a new product, or a special time or offering.

Promotions tied to negative features—for instance, lack of business when it is expected to be good—tend to backfire. An example of this is restaurant "twofers." (two menu items for the price of one). Twofers are designed to generate business by bringing in new customers. In the best situations they succeed in doing this, but the customers they bring in may not be from the designated target market and few of them may ever return.[3]

Although there may be a temporary increase in business, it is obtained at a cost: If food cost percentage is 35 percent, it is now 70 percent. At the same time, regular customers who would normally pay the full price are also dining at half-price. The net gain is minimal, if not negative. This does not mean that twofers cannot be useful for other purposes, such as creating awareness or trial purchase. Usually they will work best at low-priced, family, or fast-food restaurants, rarely at upscale restaurants. Tom Feltenstein states,

> The trick is to discount in such a way that you do not sabotage the integrity of your menu. Disguise the lure so that it's perceived as something other than an attempt to discount mainline items.
>
> ...In the consumer's mind, there is always a correlation between product and price.... But over time, discounting is bound to raise questions in the consumer's mind about the integrity of your pricing structure.... If you must discount...[and] there are times when discounting is a sound pro-

motional technique—then put together a separate package to your regular offering, that will engender no recognizable negative effect on your customer's perception of the value and price of your menu.

> ...[Once] you get the customer in the store, remember it is going to take more than a cents-off coupon to bring him or her back.[4]

Guidelines for Sales Promotions

There are some general guidelines for promotions that should apply to most cases. The first of these is to define the real purpose of the promotion. That seems obvious enough, but often this guideline is violated. The result is that, after the fact, it is found that even the successful promotion does not meet its objectives.

Be Single-Minded   It is well to keep the purpose single-minded and not try to accomplish too many things at one time. Is the purpose to create new business, awareness, or trial; to increase demand in a slow period; to take away business; to meet the competition; or to sell specialties? Trying to do more than one or two of these things tends to diffuse the promotion, confuse the market, and accomplish none of them. Figures 14-5 and 14-6 are examples of single-mindedness, whereas Figure 14-7 shows a restaurant promoting "everything under the sun."

Define the Target Market   Is the target market first-time users, heavy users, nonusers? What benefits does it seek? What are the demographic and psychographic characteristics? The promotion must specifically focus on the needs of the target market.

What Specifically Do You Want to Promote?   This is not necessarily the tangible item that you may be promoting. For example, you may want to promote a new decor or atmosphere in the lounge, but the promoted tangible item could be a special drink. A hotel might

---

[3]See, e.g., "Fine-Dining Coupons Flop," *Nation's Restaurant News*, June 13, 1988, p. 1, 7, which states, "Fine-dining operations across the nation are complaining that coupons and restaurant profits mix like horseradish and heavy cream. 'It's a mistake,' operators said, 'thinking that frugal coupon diners can be converted to regular, upscale patrons.'"

[4]Tom Feltenstein, "How to Discount Your Product Without Sabotaging Your Image," *Nation's Restaurant News*, November 9, 1987, p. F20.

In celebration of our 75th Anniversary, we're offering you a special package that reduces the cost of your conference up to 50%. It includes:

Save up to 50% when you meet at The Broadmoor

· Exceptional room rates of $60 per person, per night, double occupancy

· Discounted greens fees (golf can be played here year-round) of $25 per person, per day (cart not included)

· Free welcome cocktail reception

· 25% off published banquet prices (excluding alcoholic beverages)

· Free standard audiovisual support

· Discounts of up to 50% with our travel partners (air and car rental; based on availability; holiday restrictions apply). And more!

Package applies to meetings held between November 12, 1993 and April 10, 1994, subject to availability. To book yours, call our Sales and Conferences office at 1-800-633-7711.

THE BROADMOOR
COLORADO SPRINGS
P. O. Box 1439, Colorado Springs, CO 80901

EUROPEAN GRANDEUR IN THE COLORADO ROCKIES.

FIGURE 14-5   A single-minded hotel promotion

want to promote its rooms on weekends; the tangible promotional feature could be free breakfast in bed with champagne. Gimmicks usually don't work (Figure 14-8).

What Is the Best Way to Promote It?   It is not just necessary to give something away or charge a lower price. You may even want to promote higher quality at a higher price. You could offer an additional service, a package price, a future incentive. Before you give some-

thing away, or charge less, think carefully about what you will get in return.

Make Sure You Can Fulfill the Demand
This is a critical point. Many customers are alienated and lost forever—the opposite intention of the promotional objective—by failure to deliver on the promotion. If you are promoting lobster dinner specials, don't run out of lobsters even at the risk of having to let some spoil. If you're offering weekend packages, pro-

FIGURE 14-6   A single-minded restaurant promotion

vide the rooms even if you have to upgrade. The worst thing that can happen is that you'll have a happier customer. At a minimum, do as the retail stores do and provide rainchecks, where customers can use the promotion at a later date; then, when customers collect on them, give something better, just to compensate for the inconvenience. Too many promotions end up losing customers, rather than winning them, because management forgets

FIGURE 14-7   Promoting everything but the kitchen sink

why it is having the promotion in the first place.

Make Sure Reality Meets Expectations Do this for the same reasons as those just mentioned: Grand-opening promotions that aren't "ready" lose customers instead of winning them. (Recall the restaurant example in Chapter 13.) Don't embellish on what you have to offer; stick to the facts. If you don't have it, don't say it. Also, don't be "picky" on other items. Some managements try to make up for what they are losing on the promotion in other ways, only to create an upset customer.

Communicate Your Promotion and All Related Aspects to the Market Promotional literature or ads are sometimes so confusing and/or presume so much knowledge on the customer's part that the customer ignores the ad or gets irritated. Specify clearly all pertinent in-

formation, such as price, quality, procedure, place, dates, time, and any other necessary detail. When customers ask for "it," give it to them; don't play games and say, "There are no more of those left." If you're promoting "children free in the same room," don't hassle with the customer as to whether the child is under 16 or not, or charge $15 for a cot—both are no-win situations.

Communicate It to Your Employees This is critical. Promotions break down too often over failure to do this: Management runs an ad in the local paper about a forthcoming promotion and simply assumes that the employees who have to implement it will know exactly what it's all about and how to handle it. A restaurant we know once ran a promotion of free movie tickets with certain special dinners. None of the waiters or waitresses knew anything

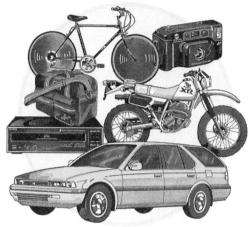

Come stay the night at any Journey's End
Hotel, Motel or Suite across Canada

—————— AND ENTER ——————

JOURNEY'S END

THANKS A MILLION™

SLEEPSTAKES

AT 120 PARTICIPATING PROPERTIES ACROSS CANADA

MATCH'N WIN INSTANTLY*!

*OVER $350,000 IN INSTANT PRIZES
AVAILABLE TO BE WON!*

INSTANT WIN PRIZES

FIRST PRIZE	1	Pair of **HONDA** dual purpose motorcycles.
SECOND PRIZE	12	**SONY** CD players from **Granada**.
THIRD PRIZE	100	**MINOLTA** 35mm Camera Packages.
FOURTH PRIZE	100	**RALEIGH** Mountain Bikes.
FIFTH PRIZE	1,000	**STRADELLINA** "Fiesta" Travel Totes.
SIXTH PRIZE	6,000	Free night's accommodation at any Canadian **Journey's End** property.

PLUS

Enter the Journey's End "Thanks A Million" Sleepstakes
for your chance to Win a Grand Prize Honda Accord Wagon!

*Look for Match'N Win details on poster displayed in the lobby

FIGURE 14-8   A gimmick sales promotion

about it when diners asked for their tickets, and management was "out of town." The result was a disaster. Front-desk clerks at hotels have the same problem with weekend specials, not to mention reservationists at 800 numbers, who often don't know what it is they are supposed to be promoting.

Finally, Measure the Results   Do this not just in terms of bodies or of dollars. Did the promotion meet its objectives? What were the benefits, gains, losses? Will it work again? If it didn't work, why didn't it? Will there be a lasting effect, or was it a one-shot deal? Some of the best promotion results are nothing more than good will, which will pay off in the future.

Sales promotions can be communicated via advertising, direct mail, tent cards, publicity, personal selling, telemarketing, and various other means. Promotions can be persuasive marketing tools when used wisely and appropriately.

Developing Sales Promotions

The use of sales promotions in the hospitality industry centers on creation of demand. A promotion is the development and execution of an event outside the normal day-to-day business.

The purpose of a sales promotion is twofold: to increase the satisfaction of the guest while increasing revenues for the hospitality establishment. If the guest is extremely satisfied with a promotion but the costs are so high that money is lost, then the promotion is unsuccessful. Similarly, if the hotel or restaurant makes a great deal of money but the customers feel slighted, then the promotion is equally unsuccessful.

Normally, there are two types of sales promotions: those centered around established events and those created entirely on their own. A promotion created around an established event might be a Mother's Day brunch, a Bastille Day food offering, a hotel package for Valentine's Day, a Sunday brunch, or Christmas shopping (Figure 14-9). In these cases hospitality establishments have an opportunity to create excitement for customers and build their volumes. Participation can vary from flying in a French chef to cook for Bastille Day to placing a corned beef sandwich on the menu for St. Patrick's Day.

The second type of sales promotion—that created independently of an established event—is more difficult to develop and execute. A good example comes from the Hilton Hotel in New Orleans. The Hilton, a large convention hotel,

REDWOODS SUNDAY BRUNCH

available Sunday's from 12:00 noon to 2:30 p.m

We invite you to enjoy what Torontonians call "The best Buffet in the City".
Our spectacular Sunday Brunch Buffet includes frittata station as well
as a wide assortment of chilled salad items, freshly prepared
Chef's entrées and a full selection of scrumptious desserts

. . . . adults 22.95   . . . . children 13.95

Sunday's Kids under 10 eat free from our Children's Menu when accompanied by a Parent!

Coming Soon . . .

CHRISTMAS SHOPPER'S BUFFET

Starting Monday, December 3rd through Friday, December 21st, enjoy our ever popular Christmas
Shopper's Buffet! This spectacular all you can eat buffet features Hot and Cold Chef's specialties,
a delicatessen counter and of course our pastry chef's decadent, rich Christmas dessert buffet.
Served Monday to Friday from 12:00 noon to 3:00 p.m.. the Shopper's Buffet is only $19.95.
Your host will gladly reserve you a table. Reservations are a must to avoid being disappointed.

For the Comfort of Other Patrons We Kindly Request that You Refrain
From the Smoking of Cigars and Pipes
In the Dining Room

Applicable Taxes and Gratuity Not Included   11/90

THE REDWOODS

FIGURE 14-9   Established event promotions

was experiencing flat sales of better-quality wines sold by the bottle. A newly-hired food and beverage manager, with a good knowledge of wines, decided to try selling the better wines by the glass, instead of by the bottle; after all, most of the hotel's guests were conventioneers, and not likely to purchase an expensive bottle of wine. Wines by the glass were offered in one of the restaurants as a test promotion. Within a month the better quality wines were outselling the cheaper house wines by four to one. Customers were looking for better wines but did not want to purchase the whole bottle.

The sales promotion was then instituted in all the food and beverage outlets. The first step was to train all food and beverage servers about the wine and the promotion. Other hotel employees were also informed and recruited into the promotion in novel ways. Bellpersons were given business cards that they could give to guests for a free glass of wine. Housekeepers also put these cards in guestrooms during turndown service and front desk employees were given wine labels to show to interested guests. In the restaurants, wine displays and table tents were set up in addition to a menu flap that was devoted to wines by the glass.

The hotel was provided all promotional materials by the winery and the local wholesaler, who also gave a quantity discount for the purchase of the wine. This sales promotion was a resounding success and, in this case, both the customers and the hotel were beneficiaries of an excellent promotion. The hotel was able to build on this promotion to develop a regular feature of better wines by the glass.

There are many, many variations of promotions. In fact, the number is limited only by the imagination. Table 14-1 describes ten different promotions reported by an industry newsletter.

TABLE 14-1   Promotional Ideas

Chocolate and Ice Cream Lovers Sweeten Weekend Sales at Upscale Florida Hotel

The First Annual Ice Cream & Chocolate Lovers Hyattfest may have ended Tampa's July quiet forever. Jennifer Regen, P.R. Director of the 525-room Hyatt Regency Tampa, calls it a smash. *"We had over 2,000 people in the hotel over three days; we sold over 250 room-nights,"* reports Regen. On Sunday, the public got into the Taste Fair for $3 and 1,500 attended. The package, $69 for one night or $99 for two, included admission to the Taste Fair both days. Regen invited Muhammad Ali's new chocolate chip cookie firm to take a booth, and Ali himself attended, providing publicity punch. *The event made a rare first-year profit.*

Free Harbor Cruise Tickets Help New England Lodge Fill Rooms on Sunday Night

Unless your property is different from most, Sunday night business is usually the slowest of the week. In West Yarmouth, Mass., the Tidewater Motor Lodge offers guests who either stay or check in Sunday night free Hyannis Harbor Cruise tickets. *"It definitely increases activity,"* says Manager Don Lake. Ads appear in the *Boston Globe* and require that the ad be presented to get the bonus. *In summer, Lake estimates that 10 to 15 guests per week take advantage of the offer.* And, Lake pays only for the tickets that are used. The cruise operator tallies how many rides his guests have taken and he receives a bill.

Beach Hotel in Mexico Wins Rave Reviews, Publicity by Offering Cooking Classes

Last year, the 1,020-room Acapulco Princess Hotel began offering cooking class packages to a limited number of 20 guests during low summer season. *It has proven so successful that there's now a waiting list* of those who want to book this year. Public Relations Manager Judy Blatman reports that enrollees learn how to prepare red snapper Mexicana, carne asada Tampiqueña and Kahlua truffles, among other dishes. The package also includes tours of the hotel kitchen and a trip to Acapulco's fish market. The hotel has also reaped free publicity—*articles on the classes appeared in 75 newspapers and magazines.*

Downtown Hotel Carves Weekend / Holiday Niche by Appealing to Culture Seekers

The 107-room Juliana Hotel in downtown San Francisco has built up a strong business clientele, but like many properties needs to fill in around the weekend and holidays. It found the solution by deciding to become identified with the arts and cultural community. Last December, *the hotel sold 75 packages with 2-for-1 tickets to the S.F. Ballet's "Nutcracker,"* and began promoting weekend packages for "second tier" (lesser known) music and stage groups. The groups mention the Juliana in their mailings and program. *Weekend/holiday occupancy is up about 15%,* reports Sales Manager Kathy Hansen.

Local Radio Broadcasts from Your Property Can Help Boost Room Sales, Catering

It pays to have radio broadcasts air from your property. There are two shows originating from Atlanta's 521-room Stouffer Waverly Hotel, one named Big Band Friday Night and the other a remote disc-jockey session from the lobby during Sunday brunch. *About 40% of the hotel's business is locally oriented* and its Marketing Director, Bill Maguire, estimates the broadcasts contributed toward *weekend occupancy gains of 10% a year since the radio shows began* three years ago. In addition to boosting room sales, Maguire believes the broadcasts help local residents remember the hotel for weddings, parties, and gala receptions.

Source: The Newsletter Group, Inc., 1552 Gilmore St., Mountain View, Cal. 94040.

Designing the Successful Sales Promotion

What, then, are the steps that need to be taken to ensure a successful promotion?

Identify the Gap   The purpose of the sales promotion from the management perspective is to increase revenues. It makes sense to plan promotions when the facility is not at capacity; the idea is to create new demand. A promotion should be designed to build revenues during known slack times or sell products that are traditionally in low demand. Examples are shown in Figures 14-10 and 14-11.

Design the Sales Promotion   There are two areas to address when designing the promotion: that of the customer and that of time. Normally, the customer should be considered before putting any type of promotion together. However, management might design a promotion because of excess inventory. Perhaps some wine was bought in too large a quantity and needs to be sold. A wine promotion is created, regardless of the needs of a customer, but the promotion itself is designed to satisfy needs.

The promotion must be consistent with the positioning of the restaurant or hotel. A disco promotion at the Ritz is not in keeping with the positioning of the hotel; a caviar promotion at a family restaurant is equally inappropriate.

The second important aspect in the design of the promotion is the timing and planning. For example, we have seen a restaurant manager decide, the week before Thanksgiving, that a turkey promotion is needed to get business.

Last-minute flyers are produced, an advertisement is hurried to the newspaper, and a menu is created. Servers are warned as they come to work that day, and the entire promotion is executed in an unprofessional manner.

The proper delivery of a promotion includes the integration of a variety of items in the communications mix. Advertising, merchandising, and public relations all need time to be coordinated. Those promotions that do not have the proper timing and planning are usually a failure.

Throughout the design of the promotion, a clear and concise message must be put forth to the customer. While this may not be as necessary for promotions centered around established events, promotions that are attempting to present a novel concept have to be clear. A St. Patrick's Day promotion can be easily understood by most customers because the event carries with it a certain level of expectation, but a novel promotion may have to be explained to customers and also to all employees.

Analyze the Competition   Competition should be analyzed before a sales promotion is developed. If all of the restaurants in town are offering a turkey dinner for Thanksgiving, what will make this promotion different? A close watch on competitive activity can give the promotion designer a head start on potential problems.

Allocate the Resources   No sales promotion will be successful if customers are unaware of the activity. A major reason for the failure of a promotion is underestimating the resources

We Pick The Village. You Save The Money

Take a **Wild Card Vacation** to a surprise destination in a Club Med "Romance or Friendship" village. For singles and couples. It's fun, fresh, interesting and simple: Book a whole week in the Caribbean or Mexico. One week prior we will confirm the surprise destination. Of course we will offer a financial reward for your spontaneity and spirit of adventure, you'll pay only **$1199** for your vacation*.

*Applicable only for January departures from Montreal and Toronto.

Club Med
"If only the real world were this real"

For more information or reservations call your travel agent or Club Med at (416) 960-3279 or 1-800-268-1160 toll free.

Call for departure dates. Subject to space availability. May change/expire any time. Amendments/cancellation policy applies. May not be combined with any other offer. Other restrictions may apply.

FIGURE 14-10   A "take a chance" sales promotion to fill empty spaces

Afternoon Tea Fashion Show

Rena Koh – *Winner of Hong Kong Fashion Week*
"Best Collection Award 1993"

June 25, 1993

3:00pm

HK$140 + 10%

The Lobby Lounge
Kowloon Shangri-La
For Reservations please call 721 2111 ext. 8911, 8912

Courtesy of Kowloon Shangri-La

FIGURE 14-11   An upscale sales promotion to fill "dead time"

needed to bring in customers. Just putting the corned beef sandwich on the blackboard of the restaurant may not be enough exposure to have a successful St. Patrick's Day promotion.

All parts of the communications mix should be evaluated for their ability to bring customers to a promotion. Public relations, advertising, and even direct sales can be used to get the message to potential participants. Direct mail can be a cost-effective way to deliver the promotion. In hotels, traditional merchandising methods, such as table tents, signage in the elevators, and employee buttons, can carry the theme of the promotion.

Establish Goals   How should success be judged? If a sales promotion is to satisfy both the customer and the manager, how many extra rooms, or covers, or cases of wine can reasonably be expected to be sold? Goals should be set in advance for evaluating the promotion at the conclusion of the event. Goals need to be realistic, and a measurement form should exist before the promotion takes place.

Understand the Break-Even Point   It is imperative to understand the economic consequences of the sales promotion before its execution. In following the steps outlined above, there may be too many resources allocated to the promotion to ever make meeting the goals financially feasible.

A promotion might use a $500 full-page advertisement in the local paper to reach the maximum number of potential customers. If the promotion was slated for a Thursday evening in a restaurant that normally sells 75 covers, a realistic goal for a successful promotion might well be 125 customers on the night of the event. However, if the average check for the event is planned at $15, with a gross profit margin of $4.50, the additional profit would be $225, obtained at a cost of $500.

Break-even analysis should be conducted early in the sales promotional planning. We saw one supposedly great promotion developed by a hotel team that at its most successful point—and success was widely anticipated—would have lost $100,000. The greatest "success" of this promotion, had it been carried out, would have been its failure. Both overallocation and underallocation of resources must be carefully analyzed in relation to the success of the promotion.

Pricing is an important factor in sales promotions and not just because of profits. Is the promotion so expensive to the customer that there will be little demand for the product, or is it so inexpensive that the market will be apprehensive of the quality?

Execute the Sales Promotion   This stage of the promotion is as important as all the others. Execution includes delivery of the product to the customer in the framework of the created expectation. Promotion delivery is more critical than normal delivery because the customer is excited and anticipatory. The promotion has created a demand. Demand has created a spe-

cial reason to use the product, and customer expectations are unusually high.

Proper execution includes employee participation. The entire staff needs to understand the promotion and its specific involvement. When a bartender shows up for work in the middle of an Oktoberfest without knowing the service steps involved, trouble can be anticipated. Employee involvement, perhaps even in the design stages of the promotion, will increase the chances for optimal delivery of the correct product.

Execution also means maintaining the proper inventory of goods to be sold. If the restaurant runs out of bratwurst during the Oktoberfest and has to substitute hamburgers, the customers' expectations will not be met. Part of the planning process of the promotion is the development of goals. Purchasing should be based on the attainment of these goals, at minimum. It is more desirable to have some waste than not to fulfill expectations.

Evaluate   All sales promotions should have an evaluation mechanism installed. Were the goals met? Were resources optimally allocated?

While these questions are certainly relevant and necessary, they constitute only half of the equation designated for success; the second half consists of the following questions: Were the customers satisfied? Were there any unusual complaints? Do comments reflect any information that might be useful for future promotions? All of these questions should be addressed in the evaluation process to allow a total assessment of the event.

When all feedback has been analyzed, the next stage is formulating the next promotion. Perhaps this particular promotion can be held monthly or yearly. What other promotions can be developed to fill in gap periods or to sell slower-moving products? The process of promotional development begins all over again.

Principles and Practices of Merchandising

Merchandising is primarily in-house marketing designed to stimulate purchase behavior through means other than personal selling or purchase of time or space in media. In a sense, merchandising is marketing to the captive customer once the customer comes into the hotel or restaurant to purchase a room or a meal. Many customers will buy nothing other than the basic product. The goal of merchandising is to provide opportunities for customers to purchase related or auxiliary products and services.

The Goal of Merchandising

The goal of merchandising, however, should not be just to stimulate sales; it also has the more long-term goal of increasing customer satisfaction. When the pastry cart is wheeled to the restaurant table at the end of the meal, the goal is to have customers order pastry and increase the check average. It is also to have customers feel even more satisfied because they have finished their meal in a very pleasing manner. If hotel guests order room service, they add to their overall bill. Also, we hope, their stay has been made just a little bit better and we have a few more satisfied customers.

Like everything else, we approach merchandising from a marketing perspective—fulfilling customers' needs and wants and solving their problems. If we are able to do this, the higher check averages and the larger bills will follow as night follows day. If, instead, we put all the emphasis on the increased revenue, we are likely to fall into the same old trap of forgetting about the customer.

The Basic Rules of Merchandising

The opportunities for merchandising in a hotel or restaurant are almost endless and, like sales promotions, are limited only by the imagination. There are a few rules that affect all merchandising that, again, are not unlike those for sales promotions.

Purpose   All merchandising should have a purpose. The commonly expressed purpose—"to increase sales"—is true, but not sufficient. Instead, let's say that the overall purpose is to increase customer satisfaction. Of course, we could also say the purpose is to fulfill needs and wants and solve problems. Much of merchandising does that, but in this case we go a little beyond the basic marketing concept.

Sometimes, just knowing that something is available, and can be had if wanted, will establish the need or want and/or increase satisfaction even when that thing is not consciously needed or wanted. A good example is the year-round swimming pool in an urban hotel. Proportionally, very few guests use these pools, but research has shown that they like the idea that the pools are there to use if they wish. A positive, however, is turned into a negative when the pool is not open at reasonable times when people want to use it, as sometimes is the case, usually for operational convenience.

The same sense of availability may be true of pastry carts in restaurants for all those people "on a diet." It is human nature to want to feel that we can have something if we want it; merchandising creates that feeling and increases satisfaction.

The other reason we go beyond the basic marketing concept is that merchandising is much involved in the *creation* of wants. Marketing does not do a great deal to create basic needs, but it can create wants. Restaurant diners might feel a need for chocolate after dinner (might even want it, in fact), but repress that need because it's "fattening." Along comes the pastry cart with all those chocolate goodies; now they really want it! The same is true of after-dinner drinks and flambé desserts. Restaurants have tremendous merchandising opportunities. The most powerful one, sometimes neglected, is the menu itself, which can range from the mundane and blasé to exciting and provocative.

By the same token, hotel guests do need to eat; and, merchandising can make them want to eat in one of the hotel's restaurants. Cards are put up in the elevators, signs in the lobby, and information on the desk in the room. Today, in many hotels, guests also see and hear about the in-house restaurants on the television in their room. In many European hotels, merchandising is practiced upon check-in, when the desk clerk asks if the guests would like a dinner reservation made for them.

All merchandising ploys need to have their purpose understood. One purpose, as we mentioned, is to create the feeling, "If you want it, we have it." Another might be to create excitement, as with an exotic drink, a flambé dessert, or a "spinning salad bowl," which, corny as it was, made Don Roth's Blackhawk Restaurant in Chicago famous. Another purpose might be entertainment, such as that provided by in-room movies, or even sensuality, as provided by late-evening adult movies. Other possible purposes are convenience (room service), relaxation (aperitifs), contentment (after-dinner cognac), or information (in-room directories).

Notice that most merchandising increases the tangibility of the product/service mix and establishes consumer expectations, as well as persuading customers to purchase. Merchandising is designed to boost sales, increase check averages, and do all those other good things, but its purpose should be based on the consumer. What will it do for customers to make them feel more satisfied? If it does that, they will spend the money.

A merchandising technique used by Marriott in some of its hotels, which can also be used in restaurants, occurs when you are first seated at your dining room table. A waiter or waitress immediately approaches with a basket of house wines, offered by the glass. The customer has immediate service, and a need identified by the customer has been served. Even if there is a delay in ordering the meal, instant satisfaction has been created. Marriott also uses the same approach at breakfast, as do Le Meridien in Paris and others: You are immediately greeted by a server with a pot of coffee in one hand and a pitcher of fresh orange juice in the other.

Compatibility and Consistency   Merchandising efforts should be compatible and consistent with the rest of the marketing effort in terms of quality, style, tone, class, and price. They should reinforce the basic product/service mix, since these efforts themselves are part of the augmented product. Hotels that have an eye on the growing family-vacation travel market should consider opening a child care center where parents can leave their children with trained, licensed professional staff. Holiday Inn's Sunspree Resorts offer 24-hour child care service. However, this market and this service may not be compatible in a hotel with a strong, transient business-traveler base.

Practicality   The rule here is: If you can't do it right, don't do it. Failure to follow this rule results in lost customers, not satisfied ones. The child care center is an example where serious problems can result if the service is not offered in a professional way.

Visibility   Let the customer know about it and how to get it. Elevator cards merchandising restaurants often fail to say where the restaurants are or what hours they are open. In today's modern hotels, wherein restaurants might be anywhere, finding a restaurant can literally be a mind-boggling experience.

Management seems to assume that everyone else knows what *it* knows about the hotel's layout. In-room directories get hidden in bottom drawers. Once found, some are so confusing that the guest either turns to the telephone or gives up. We have even seen directories with full pages on the swimming pool and health club facilities but no indication of how to get there or what to wear on your way. Many people don't use pools simply because they are too embarrassed to go there in a bathing suit and don't want to change in dressing rooms. The Royal Garden in Trondheim, Norway solved this customer problem by identifying a "swimming pool/health club" elevator specifically for that purpose. The Stouffer Orlando and Palm Springs Resorts have done likewise.

On the other hand, visibility doesn't mean total clutter. Some restaurant tables, or hotel desk tops, have so many table tents, flyers, and brochures on them that there isn't room for anything else or it's too confusing to find what you want.

Simplicity   Make it easy to understand and easy to obtain. Make it clear how much it will cost, how long it will take, when it is available, or any other information that will make it unnecessary for the customer to have to make additional inquiry. Customers tend just to give up when they have to go through too much effort to purchase a service. Placing a red heart next to "heart-healthy" menu items, for example, provides quick information to health-conscious customers and increases sales of those items.

Knowledgeable Employees Be sure that everyone knows about it—what it is, how it works, how you get it, what you do with it, and so forth. The keys to the success of any in-house promotion are the knowledgeable employees who publicize it to the customers.

Merchandising is just one more marketing tool for creating and keeping customers. It is also a communications tool because it says to the customer, "Here is what else we can do for you." Wisely used, merchandising is a powerful tool; it is a revenue-producer and, more important, a customer-satisfier. Too often, it becomes a "customer-annoyer." Figure 14-12 shows examples of hotel in-room merchandising.

Examples of Good Merchandising

Examples of good merchandising techniques abound. One case in point is Business Centers within some hotels. These Business Centers offer a variety of secretarial support services such as typing and dictation, together with copying, fax machines, and computer terminals. The Business Centers are usually located somewhat off the lobby, with a separate room in which to work. These services do cost money for the guests, and hotels can make a profit on them, but more importantly, they fill a need of the traveling businessperson and create a better guest experience.

Another example of good merchandising in a business-related restaurant is the offering of a "45-minute guaranteed lunch" to cater to the limited time of working people. While no additional charge is made for this service, the restaurant has differentiated itself from its competitors by satisfying a need through merchandising.

The emergence of pizza on finer hotels' room service menus is a merchandising opportunity that fills a need of many customers. Many people do not want a full, heavy meal in their room. Some just want to watch television and have something "fun," as if they were at home. The pizza (merchandised often with alcoholic beverages, as in one of the in-room pieces in Figure 14-12) fulfills the needs of customers while putting money into the hotels' cash registers.

This type of merchandising can only increase revenues. Rarely would you find a customer ordering a lower-priced pizza instead of a steak. Price does not become the deciding factor; instead, the product becomes the reason for the purchase. Those customers who really wanted pizza in the first place might have called for a delivery from outside or gone out of the hotel; either way, the money would have been spent outside the hotel or not at all. More important, once again, you have satisfied a customer by fulfilling a need.

Too much merchandising is designed to "get the buck" rather than to satisfy the customer. In fact, there are too many cases where it "gets the buck" once, but loses the customer. This seems to happen most often with price-gouging. The customer pays but never returns, or never buys again.

The inclusion of "mini-bars" in guestrooms both satisfies customers and increases hotel profits. Minibars are self-contained units containing beer, wine, mixed drinks, and soft drinks together with snacks for the guest to eat. An inventory is taken of the unit's contents before the guest checks in, and all items consumed are posted to the bill. The probability is low that a guest would call room service for one beer. With a minibar in the room, customers can open a beer at their convenience while watching television or reading. Both the hotel and the customers benefit from this merchandising opportunity.

Again, however, improper merchandising can lose customers. Too many mini-bar contents are overpriced, and customers are not particularly pleased when they have to pay the high prices. Instead, many buy outside and use the mini-bar as a refrigerator. This is an opportunity lost.

Merchandising is marketing to the "captured" customer. Unless your hotel or restaurant is alone on a desert island, don't translate

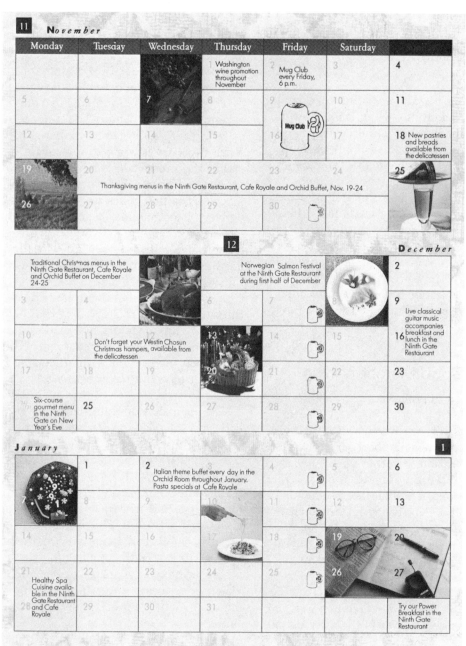

Courtesy of Westin Chosun Hotel

FIGURE 14-12 In-room hotel merchandising pieces

FIGURE 14-12   (continued)

capture into captivity. Even on a desert island, you may never see that customer again. Instead, translate capture into opportunity: "Here's an opportunity to make the customer even more satisfied."

Public Relations and Publicity

Public relations and publicity, although they are two separate components of the communications mix, are grouped together here because of their potential for "free" use in the media. For either one, instead of buying space in a newspaper or time on a radio station, the organization obtains it gratis, provided the media think the organization is newsworthy or of interest. In that sense, the organization does not control the placement of the information.

Every organization exists in a community, large or small, that has a direct or indirect influence on its success. It wants to have a positive image in the community and to be seen as a contributor to the overall well-being of society. Effective public relations is the management tool to present the product/service to the media and the community in the best light.

Although publicity can derive from public relations, the difference is that publicity constitutes only the information the media freely and without influence choose to use. Thus, publicity may be positive or negative. Public relations, on the other hand, attempts to control publicity, to "plant" information in the press, or to create a favorable image for reasons other than its formal product. In politics this is called "spin control."

Public relations, as well as publicity, also occurs through word-of-mouth. While much of this may be started by the media, other aspects may be spontaneous. For example, a restaurant makes a special effort to employ disabled people. This fact may never strike the media, but the word gets around and the restaurant is looked upon as doing good for the community. This reflects positively on other aspects of the restaurant.

To the listening public, public relations and publicity may be the most believable forms of the communications mix. A salesperson pitching a product, or a slick advertising campaign, may be subject to skepticism from consumers. When an independent source, such as a newspaper, writes about the product in an unbiased setting, credence is lent to the message unmatched by any other media format. A potential customer for a restaurant is more likely to try the veal specialty recommended by a restaurant reviewer than to try the same dish touted by a full-page ad proclaiming its excellence. A negative review can also totally counteract a full-page ad.

Public Relations

Public relations is the planned management of the media's and the community's perception. Although the press certainly cannot be told what to publish, a public relations effort can steer the story toward the best features of the product and away from negative images. Public relations efforts are designed to create stories that capture the attention of writers, with the hope that the writers will, in turn, communicate "the good news" to the desired readers, or target market. Figure 14-13 is an example of a P.R. news release worth evaluating.

We can demonstrate these points with some examples. Natural disasters, such as hurricanes and floods, create negative images that have a harmful effect on the hospitality and tourism industries in the affected region. A delicate balance exists between promoting a hotel or restaurant and not appearing callous to the human suffering that has resulted from such a disaster. After being hit by a major hurricane, hotel marketers in the affected area are put to the test. One hotel, the Doubletree, opened 11 days after a hurricane and publicized its decision to set aside ten percent of its available rooms as complimentary lodging for families who had lost their homes. The hotel Mayfair House created positive press by housing 300 displaced tourists for free immediately after the disaster. After the Mississippi River flooded Des Moines, Iowa in 1993, most hotels lost their water supply, but the Holiday Inn in West Des Moines still had water and made arrangements for guests from other hotels to take showers there.

OMNI ✿ BERKSHIRE PLACE

PHILIP GEORGAS
MANAGING DIRECTOR,
OMNI BERKSHIRE PLACE HOTEL,
NEW YORK,
AND REGIONAL VICE PRESIDENT OF OPERATIONS

With the opening of The Berkshire Place Kaffee, Philip Georgas, Managing Director of the Omni Berkshire Place Hotel and Regional Vice President of Operations for Omni Hotels, introduces a new concept in coffee enjoyment at the noted chain's New York property.

In his present capacity, Mr. Georgas is charged with overall management responsibilities for the Omni Berkshire Place in New York and has regional responsibilities for the newly acquired Omni Colonnade Hotel of Coral Gables and The Omni Chicago.

Mr. Georgas' career at Omni spans 20 years. In addition to serving as opening General Manager for the Berkshire Place Hotel in 1978, his positions in the northeast have included Vice President and Managing Director of the Park Central Hotel in New York, Managing Director of the Omni Parker House in Boston, and General Manager of the Philadelphia Omni.

He studied at Ealing Technical College in London and the Institut International de Glion in Montreux, Switzerland and attended the advanced management program at Cornell University's School of Hotel Administration.

Of European background and as an avid coffee drinker, Mr. Georgas has witnessed the phenomenal growth of coffee houses throughout the United States. "Our location and set-up is ideal" states Georgas. "The Berkshire Place Kaffee provides a unique relaxed setting in which to enjoy a wide variety of freshly roasted exotic coffees and international accompaniments."

#

21 East 52nd Street at Madison Avenue, New York, New York 10022   (212) 753-5800   Telex: 710/581-5256   FAX: (212) 754-5037

Courtesy of Omni Berkshire Place Hotel

FIGURE 14-13   A public relations release

Another example is that of McDonald's, a company widely acclaimed for its public relations efforts. For McDonald's, public relations is a major part of the marketing strategy. Ronald McDonald homes for families of ill children at nearby hospitals are nationally famous. When disaster strikes anywhere near a McDonald's, some of the first people on the scene are McDonald's employees with coffee and hamburgers for the unfortunate and for workers on the scene. When a man went berserk a few years ago in a McDonald's in California and shot and killed customers, McDonald's immediately closed the store and provided financial aid to the victims' families. When the company wanted to reopen the store a few months later, the townspeople strongly opposed it. McDonald's quickly complied by closing the store permanently. McDonald's, in essence, "created" these stories and gained a great deal of positive publicity from its public relations efforts.

In such cases and more often in less-serious situations, public relations is used to formulate an image in the consumer's mind of what the company or product represents. Public relations-engendered publicity enabled McDonald's to capitalize on a possibly negative image in the California tragedy. Having Ronald McDonald homes has nothing to do with the production of hamburgers, but the story is "created," sending the message that the company cares for children (and perhaps, one thinks subliminally, "cares" the same about preparing food). McDonald's is a "good guy" in a bad situation.

Doing Public Relations

Negative public relations happens as a result of bad publicity. Other public relations—the good kind—we try to make happen. Because the public views the editorial press as more credible than paid advertising, public relations can be far more effective.

Public relations is not there just to deal with negative happenings or simply to create positive happenings. Instead, public relations is an ongoing task and an important part of marketing planning. In this capacity, public relations plays the following roles:

> [I]mproving awareness, projecting credibility, combating competition, evaluating new markets, creating direct sales leads, reinforcing the effectiveness of sales promotion and advertising, motivating the sales force, introducing new products, building brand loyalty, dealing with consumer issues and in many other ways.[5]

Public relations also creates images for the local, public, and financial communities as well as for the firm's employees. It creates favorable attitudes toward a firm, its products, and its efforts.

Public relations creates pre-opening publicity for hotels and restaurants through news releases that the media will carry. The result is that the press attends a grand opening, or "ribbon-cutting." It invites dignitaries who make news and in whom the press and the public are interested. It sends out news releases about who slept or ate there. On an ongoing basis, it keeps the press, and hence the public, informed as to what is happening at the property or with the firm. Pre-opening public relations is extremely important in getting a hotel or a restaurant off to a good start. At this point we are not only marketing an intangible product but also one that does not yet exist. Several marketing objectives must be met during this time, including creating name recognition, establishing an image, building excitement, and cementing positive ties to the local community.[6] Pre-opening public relations must begin at least a year in advance and gather momentum as opening day approaches. Table 14-2 shows a sample timetable for pre-opening public relations.

Large companies or properties usually have their own public relations firms or agencies, hired on monthly retainers to maintain favorable publicity for the organization. Even these large companies, however, as well as smaller ones that cannot afford P.R. agencies, must practice public relations in-house on an ongoing basis. Doing this involves employee relations. It also involves relationships with taxi drivers and local police, attitudes toward the press, competitive relationships, members of the distribution channels (such as airlines, travel agencies, tour operators), purveyors (who can be excellent carriers of good tidings), shareholders, bankers, and all manner of other "publics" with which the firm interacts.

Hotel and restaurant managers should belong to the local Rotary, Chamber of Commerce, community task forces, and other groups. One could almost say that everything management does has some aspect of public relations in it. Even the employees of the firm may be excellent public relations elements; in fact, for some firms they may be the most important of all. What your employees say about you and the

[5]R. Haywood, *All About PR,* London: McGraw-Hill, 1984. Excerpted from Francis A. Buttle, *Hotel and Food Service Marketing,* London: Holt, Rinehart and Winston, 1986, p. 400.

[6]Karen W. Escalera., "A PR Primer for the Hotel Opening: The Case of the Vista International," *Cornell Hotel and Restaurant Administration Quarterly,* May 1984, pp. 70–81.

TABLE 14-2   Sample Timetable for Pre-opening Public Relations for a Hotel

This schedule begins six months before the hotel opening, at which time the announcement of construction plans and the groundbreaking ceremony will have been completed.

150–180 days before opening

1. Hold meeting to define objectives and to coordinate public relations effort with advertising; establish timetable in accordance with scheduled completion date.
2. Prepare media kit.
3. Order photographs and renderings.
4. Begin preparation of mailings and develop media lists.
5. Contact all prospective beneficiaries of opening events.
6. Reserve dates for press conferences at off-site facilities.

120–150 days before opening

1. Send announcement with photograph or rendering to all media.
2. Send first progress bulletin to agents and media (as well as corporate clients, if desired).
3. Begin production of permanent brochure.
4. Make final plans for opening events, including commitment to beneficiaries.

90–120 days before opening

1. Launch publicity campaign to national media.
2. Send mailings to media
3. Send second progress bulletin.
4. Arrange exclusive trade interviews and features in conjunction with ongoing trade campaign.
5. Begin trade announcement.

60–90 days before opening

1. Launch campaign to local media and other media with a short lead time; emphasize hotel's contribution to the community, announcement of donations and beneficiaries, etc.
2. Send third and final progress bulletin with finished brochure.
3. Commence "behind-the-scenes" public tours.
4. Hold "hard-hat" luncheons for travel writers.
5. Set up model units for tours.

30–60 days before opening

1. Send pre-opening newsletter (to be continued on a quarterly basis).
2. Hold soft opening and ribbon-cutting ceremony.
3. Hold press opening.
4. Establish final plans for opening gala.

The month of opening

1. Begin broadside mailing to agents.
2. Hold opening festivities.
3. Conduct orientation press trips.

Source: Jessica D. Zive, "Public Relations for the Hotel Opening," *Cornell Hotel and Restaurant Administration Quarterly,* May, 1981, p. 21. Copyright © Cornell University. Used by permission. All rights reserved.

way you operate reflects heavily on the image that will be created in the public's mind. Public relations serves well in times of need as a defensive weapon; more importantly, it is a continuous and ongoing offensive weapon.

Planning Public Relations

The same rules that apply in planning public relations efforts govern the rest of the communications mix. These include purpose, target market (in this case, the target market may not be the customer at all, but might be the financial community, the industry, employees, intermediaries), setting of tactics, integration with the product/service, and the firm's overall marketing efforts.

Purpose The purpose of a specific public relations effort must be established before any further planning occurs. The purpose must be definitive and quantifiable. For example, a restaurant might be under a new management that has to overcome a perception in the marketplace of slow service. In this case, it is unlikely that an advertising campaign would really convince anyone that the service was better. Improving the customers' perception of the restaurant's service would be the purpose of the public relations campaign. The quantifiable measurement, as in advertising, would be the increased number of covers. The subjective measurement would be the change in perception of the service.

A hotel might have a perception in the marketplace of being too expensive for local customers, and might thus be unused by them. The purpose of the public relations effort would be to dispel the perception by improving the price/value relationship image for the local marketplace. The success of this program can be measured by increased usage of guestrooms by local customers or in increased restaurant or lounge business outside of usual occupancy trends.

In both these situations, market research should be used to correctly evaluate customer perception, both before and after. Only then can the public relations effort be correctly focused.

Target Markets When planning public relations, one must consider the benefit to the customer in the target market. Choosing a target market for a public relations effort is as important as choosing the correct market for any advertising campaign. You must ask, "How will the target market be influenced to perceive the product?" This involves not only short-term benefits, but long-term ones as well, because hotels and restaurants are a major part of the community in which they exist. They are the most public of all commercial enterprises, so much so that they often become "public places" where people meet. It is these same people, as well, who answer such questions from out-of-towners as "Where should I stay?" or "Where's a good place to eat?"

Public relations will influence local responses even when the people themselves have never stayed or eaten at the property. Public relations creates an image in the mind of the consumer and reinforces that image in many ways. After the purpose and quantifiable measure have been established, gaining an understanding of the needs of the customer (target market) is the next step.

Choosing Targeted Media In addition to identifying a target audience comes the task of reaching these customers. While geographic location of the customers needs to be understood, the correct media to reach that geographic area must be analyzed as well. While a computer trade journal may appear to be a good place to advertise for a corporate meeting, such a journal may not be where a potential vacationer would be reading an article on the benefits of staying in a hotel.

While "selling stories" may sound unusual, good public relations experts will have a network of editors to whom they can do just that, by calling upon them personally. This relationship with decision-makers of a media channel can be critical to breaking a story. For this reason, public relations is becoming more of a science and less of a "hit or miss" communications effort.

The public relations expert will push a story much as a salesperson sells a product. Calls are made to the editors, they are wined and dined, and thank-you notes and flowers are sent in appreciation of the placement of the story or press release. A press release is a document giving the salient points of a story in a generic industry-wide format. A press release usually contains the contact name of the public relations professional who wrote the story, background information on the facility, and the body copy of the story. It is then "pitched" or sold to the media.

Personal contacts are what differentiates a good public relations firm from a poor one. Anyone can write stories and send them to papers and broadcast media, but only a true professional has the contacts to follow up until the article is printed.

Positioning   A cohesive message must be developed before a public relations campaign is launched. Ideally, the public relations message will integrate with the other forms of the communications mix. If the advertising message is telling customers that service is the main advantage of the product, the public relations stories should also center on that theme. If food quality is the spearhead of the marketing effort, stories on the chefs and their background will augment this effort.

The positioning must also be kept within the framework of the purpose of the public relations effort. If a public relations effort is undertaken to change the customer's perception of slow service, then the positioning should also follow this generic format. It is very easy to be distracted during a public relations campaign and to begin many activities unrelated to the purpose or positioning of the product. Positioning is where the "spin" is put on the story.

Developing Tactics

Before the public relations subset is employed, it is important to begin to develop stories on the product itself. Creating a story is usually much more expensive than presenting the existing product to the editors. The following subject titles represent good starting points in a public relations campaign.

Personnel   Numerous stories can be submitted based upon the employees who work every day in a hotel or restaurant. The Clarion Hotel in New Orleans received much media attention when an off-duty bellman chased and apprehended the attacker of a foreign tourist who had ventured into an unsafe area of the city.

For restaurants, a background on the chef can provide an interesting story. If the chef has won any awards or trained outside of the country, the local media are often willing to convey the story to their readers.

Customers   Sometimes customers become a story in themselves. A couple celebrating their thirtieth anniversary, now checking back into the same room they occupied on their honeymoon, can generate empathetic interest. A customer who eats regularly in a restaurant conveys an image of consistency that might cause readers to try the product. When celebrities or politicians dine in a restaurant or stay in a hotel, the public has a natural curiosity.

Positioning becomes an important element in using customers as a lead story for a hotel or restaurant. Be sure, however, that the customer being featured is the right representative for the desired target market. Publicizing that the latest-rage rock band is staying at the Pierre Hotel in New York could drive away customers seeking to have a quiet and inconspicuous stay in Manhattan.

History   A story line developed around the hotel building, neighborhood, owner's or manager's background can also provide a format of interest to the public. The Vista Hotel in New York City created a "Heritage and History" package that combined visits to the many ethnic neighborhoods of Lower Manhattan, where the hotel is located, with trips to the Statue of Liberty and Ellis Island (the historic immigration gateway) just across the bay.

Publicity

When "natural" stories like the above have been fully developed, other methods need to be employed to keep the press interested in the restaurant or hotel. Publicity now needs to be "created" so that editors will continue to have something to write about.

The creation of events is not as simple as it may sound. The purpose of the event needs to be established together with a target medium, and an evaluation of the event needs to follow. Publicity, in this sense, is like promotions, except that publicity is aimed specifically at the media to generate public relations. Promotions can be held without publicity; publicity is best held with promotions.

Publicity differs from promotions in the preparation for the event. Targeted audiences (readers) are researched, and the appropriate editors and radio or TV station managers are invited. Again, the personal relationship developed by the public relations expert is critical for successful attendance by the right people.

The event must be organized so that everything goes perfectly. If a promotion is not executed well, the hotel or restaurant is at risk for all of the patrons exposed to the event, plus any other potential customers who hear of it by word-of-mouth. While this might be catastrophic, it is nothing compared to the potential lost business that one editor could produce by writing negatively in a newspaper with a circulation of 100,000 readers.

At the event, press releases with background information are made available to the press. A prepared press release will answer questions such as the number of seats available in the restaurant, the name of the manager, and so on. The public relations professional will "work the event" by attending and "pitching" the points personally to the attendees. The end of the actual promotion signals the beginning of the placement work for the public relations effort. Thank-you notes and flowers are sent to remind the attendees of the importance of the event. Follow-up calls are made to cajole the writers to place the story in the best light, and to the editors for the actual placement. Having a story placed in a newspaper or on radio/television is not the only measure of success. Where the placement occurs is also vital to the maximization of the readership. The physical placement of the story is as important as getting the story into the media.

After all of this work is finished, the last stage of the public relations/publicity effort is the evaluation. Have more customers been generated? Was perception in the marketplace altered to the satisfaction of the management team? The evaluation process is as important as any other phase of the effort. Restaurant covers and rooms sold can be tracked at the property, but changes in customer perception are more difficult to measure. Further market research should be employed to better understand the impact.

Guidelines

Additional guidelines for public relations have been suggested by another expert, Joe Adams, President of the Adams Group Inc., a national public relations firm.

- P.R. is not free. This is the most common mistake hotels make. If you don't budget, don't expect results.
- Use top P.R. talent. P.R. titles are often bestowed on people who have no training or experience in public relations. You can usually buy the services of a good P.R. firm for what it costs to hire one experienced individual.
- Have a written plan. If you can write it down, you can make it happen.
- P.R. people must understand your marketing plan. You can't expect results unless you let them in on your plans and objectives. Make sure they understand that P.R. is a marketing tool.
- Demand regular reports on P.R. results. A consistent, ongoing P.R. program should provide consistent, ongoing results.
- If it doesn't sell it's not creative. It takes innovative ideas to get deserved P.R. coverage.
- Remember: Great public relations depends upon creative management.[7]

---

[7]Joe Adams, "Good P.R. Plan Can Be Potent Marketing Tool for Hotels," *Hotel & Motel Management,* June 8, 1987, p. 60.

Summary

This chapter offers a foundation and a methodology for successful execution of sales promotions, merchandising, and public relations programs. The most common reason for failure in delivering these subsets of the communications mix is lack of planning. Sales promotions usually have short-term objectives. They must be conducted for a specific target market and both employees and customers must be aware of the product/service being promoted. Different products have to be promoted in different ways but, eventually, results must be measured. Merchandising is primarily in-house marketing and the planning process includes assessing the needs of the customer and then providing the product to the customer in a cost-effective manner. With a strong planning process in place, and a good evaluation mechanism, both revenues and customer satisfaction can be maximized.

It is evident that the public relations effort of a hospitality entity is a very effective element of the communications mix. It may be the most effective element in that it is the most believable for the consumer. A potential customer is more likely to be convinced by reading or hearing a third party's praise for a product than by an advertising campaign.

The public relations campaign should be focused and quantifiable within the objectives of targeted positioning and purpose. Publicity remains a subset of the public relations umbrella, to be utilized after all "natural" stories have been highlighted by press coverage. Understanding the customer is the core of both the public relations effort and of marketing in general. In the next chapter we continue with the last element of the communications mix, personal selling. We shall devote an entire chapter to that subject because of the predominance of its use in the hospitality industry.

Discussion Questions

1. Develop a hypothetical promotion to sell more Portuguese wine in a restaurant using all of the steps outlined for a successful sales promotion.
2. Discuss the basic rules of merchandising using a real-life example.
3. Develop an example of good merchandising for a hotel or restaurant using at least two of the other communications mixes.
4. What are the components of a good public relations plan? Discuss how you might apply them to a local restaurant.
5. Discuss the similarities and differences between sales promotions and merchandising.
6. Contrast public relations and publicity and discuss the implications of each.
7. In the 1990s, a major role of public relations will be to deal with unexpected crises that result in bad publicity. Discuss how hospitality organizations can create positive public relations when faced with natural disasters such as floods, hurricanes, and earthquakes.
8. Develop a pre-opening public relations plan for a restaurant using Table 14-2 as a guide.
9. Develop the promotion for Sunday brunch in Case 14-1. Do a break-even analysis.
10. Evaluate the frequent-traveler program in Case 14-2. What's good about it? What isn't? What are the pitfalls?
11. Analyze Case 14-3. Why didn't the plan work? What would you do about it? How did Hugues Jaquier solve the coffee and orange juice problem?
12. Analyze Antoine Berberi's situation in Case 14-4. Did he have a good strategy? What should he do now?

✔ Case 14-1
Promoting Sunday Brunch

John Elder, Director of Sales for the Hilton Inn in Pittsfield, Massachusetts, looked over his brunch cover statistics with dismay. Total Sunday brunch covers at the 175-room hotel had steadily declined over the past two years, from 5,012 to 4,574 to 3,935—a 21.5 percent decline. Something, he thought, needs to be done.

A number of new restaurants had recently opened in Pittsfield and begun to penetrate the lucrative brunch market. Tom Harding, Food and Beverage Director of the hotel, felt that this competition was the major cause of the decline. The Hilton Inn had often served 150 for Sunday brunch in the past. These figures were now reached only on special occasions such as Mother's Day. Tom felt that there was potential to do 250 covers, which was about the room's capacity for brunch.

Sunday brunch was served in the Emerald Room, located on the fourteenth and top floor of the Hilton Inn. The view from any seat in the restaurant was spectacular, offering views of the Berkshire Mountains from all four sides. The food presentation was traditional, a full all-you-can-eat buffet with salads, breakfast items, a carving station, and well arranged with ice carvings and other attractive presentations.

The profit margin on Sunday brunch was slim, presently about ten percent of the $14.95 selling price, based on current sales. Beverage sales, however, raised the average check to $17.50, and the contribution margin on beverages was 65 percent. Tom figured he could double the present number of covers with the same labor force and fixed costs and make a margin on the additional food covers of 50 percent, plus the beverage margin. He also figured that above that number, to maximum capacity, the profit margin would be about 40 percent after adding additional labor, plus the beverage margin.

The target market for Sunday brunch was both in-house guests and local customers. Research disclosed that the local customers lived within a ten-mile radius, had household incomes of $40,000-plus, and were an average age of 45. Many younger couples were frequent brunch-goers as well. Middle-age customers with small children at home were not targeted.

The executive committee of the hotel decided they should reintroduce Sunday brunch to the local community. It believed that many of the customers who had been to the brunch were merely trying other restaurants. It was decided that a promotion, lasting about six months, was needed to induce new trial or repurchase by former customers.

After some brainstorming, "The Get Rich Quick Brunch at the Emerald Room of the Hilton Inn" was developed. The idea was that each customer would have an opportunity to win a lottery. A lottery ticket would be given to each customer, and there would be a weekly minimum payout. Legal ramifications of the promotion were researched and found acceptable.

John Elder and Tom Harding felt comfortable that the promotion would work. After convincing the executive committee of this, they were assigned to work out the details.

John and Tom had decided that lottery tickets, given to each brunch customer, would be valued at $1; but they wondered, should this be included in the current brunch price, charged for as an extra, or the brunch price raised $1 to cover it? How much should the weekly payout be? How would they promote the lottery, and how much would it cost? What were the merchandising opportunities? Could they get some local P.R. and publicity? Tom brought the Lotus program up on his computer screen, as John started working out the communications details.

✔ Case 14-2
The Real Road Warrior[8]

Prime Motor Inns wanted to establish the Howard Johnson chain as the preferred brand and most attractive franchise investment in midpriced lodging. To accomplish this, and to increase brand loyalty and market share, the Real Road Warrior frequent-traveler program was established. The program was also intended to maximize use of the nationwide 800 reservation system by requiring reservations be made through it. It was aimed at the primary target market, the frequent business-traveler, to better serve that market's needs. The program was to run for one calendar year, although prizes could be redeemed until December 15th of the following year.

The image of the Road Warrior was Howard Johnson's recognition of the business traveler's trying and sometimes exhausting days. Nights away from home, packing and unpacking suitcases, and long days on the road were not elements of an easy lifestyle. Howard Johnson wanted to reward these "warriors" for their daily battles.

The Road Warrior program emphasized three unique qualities. First, a traveler could earn prizes quicker than any other hotel's program through its low-scale point system. Second, the program was designed to be easily understood by eliminating complicated point structures, confusing merchandise catalogs, and a lot of fine print. Finally, it offered prizes that would be very attractive to the business traveler. These were chosen to more accurately match the wants of customers than those offered by the competition.

The program gave out "Real Rewards" based on a simple point system—ten points for each night stayed at any Howard Johnson property at full corporate or rack rate. Travelers became a member of the Road Warrior Travel Club by filling out an application. He or she was then identified with a personal ID number, deter-

mined by their social security number, which was to be used when making reservations. A permanent reservation record was established on the 800 number computer system to provide for personalized reservation service.

The Road Warrior Travel Club offered members both reservation system benefits, through a quicker reservation and pre-registration at check-in, and travel and merchandise awards. Members were also considered to be Howard Johnson's most important customers and would always receive friendly, warm, and helpful service. In addition, a Road Warrior emergency kit was available. This kit included items for unexpected needs, such as aspirin, toothbrush, septic stick, nylons, nail polish, saline solution, and more. They were available at no charge upon request at the front desk.

Promoting the Program

Howard Johnson used various means of advertising to promote awareness of the Road Warrior program. This was done primarily with television during sports events and with full-page ads in the national newspaper, *USA Today*. Travel agents were also made aware of the program and encouraged to promote it by special commissions paid for each booking.

At individual properties the promotion was announced by front desk staff to people paying rack or corporate rate. All employees wore a pin visible on their uniforms, which read, "Welcome to the Home of the Road Warrior." Applications, prominently displayed in each guestroom and at the front desk, were in the form of pamphlets that described and explained everything there was to know about the Road Warrior program. The panels of this pamphlet are shown in Exhibit 14-2-1.

Getting Started

The Road Warrior program got off to a shaky start. The following two instances were typical:

---

[8]Michelle Mayzer and Laila Mourey researched and contributed to this case.

EXHIBIT 14-2-1 Howard Johnson Road Warrior brochure

BETTER THAN THE COMPETITION

Other hotel programs offer weed-eaters, bathrobes, and theme parks. They obviously don't understand the Road Warrior. Compare for yourself.

	HOWARD JOHNSON	HOLIDAY	RAMADA	
30 nights	Two Weekend Nights OR Pierre Cardin Leather Valet Bag	A Mini-Workbench (1,900 Points)	50% Off Weekend/ 1 Rent-A-Car Upgrade (10,000 Points)	One Night Weekend/ $25 Savings
60 nights	Four Weekend Nights OR PANASONIC* Portable CD Player	Lawn Trimmer PLUS A Wallet (3,300 Points)	Sunglasses OR Mask/Snorkel Set (30,000 Points)	Three Nights OR $50 Savings
90 nights	Six Weekend Nights OR Portable Telephone for your Car on the Road	Two Nights Lodging in Philadelphia, Theme Park Admissions PLUS A Toaster (5,400 Points)	Tennis Racket OR His/Her Robes (50,000 Points)	Five N... OR $17...
120 nights	WEEK'S VACATION IN HONOLULU, HAWAII FOR 2: Air travel* and Six Nights Hotel Stay**	One Restricted Round Trip Airline Ticket (6,600 Points)	Two Nights and Two Admissions at WALT DISNEY WORLD Resort® OR Disneyland (Not Including Airfare) (60,000 Points)	
MEMBERSHIP FEE	NO FEE	$10.00	NO FEE	

— Sample competitive awards and point levels selected from current published brochures.
*Round trip coach air travel from Los Angeles or San Francisco to Honolulu.
**Lodging and all applicable taxes for one standard room.
Special air fares available on connecting United Airlines Flights.

APPLY TODAY

Get ready to claim your rewards. Fill out the simple attached application and return it to the front desk of any Howard Johnson property, or stamp it and drop it in the nearest mailbox. In about four weeks, you'll receive a membership card and brochure describing the Howard Johnson Road Warrior Travel Club in detail. Be ready to start earning real rewards when you stay at Howard Johnson Hotels, Suites, or Lodges.

HOWARD JOHNSON
Hotels, Suites & Lodges

For Reservations Call
1-(800)-654-2000

©1999 Howard Johnson
A Prime Motor Inns Company

Printed in U.S.A.

Howard Johnson is proud to be the Home of the Road Warrior.

AT LAST—
REAL REWARDS...

FOR REAL ROAD WARRIORS

HOWARD JOHNSON

Air travel via United Airlines.

EASY TO UNDERSTAND

In other hotel programs, baffling point structures, confusing merchandise catalogs, and fine print can drive you crazy. Howard Johnson makes the Road Warrior Travel Club easy to understand. We base your rewards on how many nights you spend at full corporate rates or full room rates, at 10 points per night – it's that simple.

You will receive a monthly statement summarizing how many nights you've spent in Howard Johnson Hotels, Suites and Lodges. You can begin earning rewards for your nights at Howard Johnson on January 1, 1990 and keep piling up points through December 31, 1990. Through December 15, 1991, you can collect any reward you've earned. It's easy, straightforward, and very, very rewarding.

Paradise! A reward from Howard Johnson.

WHAT YOU GET WHEN YOU JOIN THE ROAD WARRIOR TRAVEL CLUB

The Road Warrior Travel Club Card

This personalized card identifies you as a special traveler at Howard Johnson Hotels, Suites and Lodges. Simply use your personal ID number when making reservations, or present your membership card when you check in, and your Travel Club status will be automatically updated.

A Permanent Reservation Record

Road Warrior Travel Club Members get fast, easy and personalized reservation service because the Howard Johnson reservations computer has a permanent record of your vital information. Call our Reservation Center at 1-800-654-2000.

A Real Reward Program

You work hard for your rewards. As a member of the Road Warrior Travel Club, you're entitled to real rewards that go with your lifestyle. Here's what we offer:

# POINTS	YOUR REWARDS
150 (15 nights)	Free* Weekend Night at any Howard Johnson Property
300 (30 nights)	Two Free* Weekend Nights at any Howard Johnson Property OR Pierre Cardin Leather Valet Bag
450 (45 nights)	Three Free* Weekend Nights at any Howard Johnson Property
600 (60 nights)	Four Free* Weekend Nights at any Howard Johnson Property OR PANASONIC® Portable CD Player
750 (75 nights)	Five Free* Weekend Nights at any Howard Johnson Property
900 (90 nights)	Six Free* Weekend Nights at any Howard Johnson Property OR Portable Telephone for your Car on the Road
1050 (105 nights)	Seven Free* Weekend Nights at any Howard Johnson Property
1200 (120 nights)	ONE WEEK VACATION IN HAWAII FOR TWO: Six Nights' Hotel Stay* and Coach Air Travel from Los Angeles or San Francisco (Special air fares available on connecting flights from other United Airline cities.)

*Lodging and all applicable taxes for one standard room.
— Weekend night (either Friday, Saturday, or Sunday) rewards subject to availability and must be reserved not more than 60 days in advance.
— Weekend night rewards only are transferable.
— Other restrictions may apply. See General Rules and Conditions.
— Members earn points for overnight stays at Howard Johnson at full room rate or full corporate rate as listed in the Howard Johnson Directory or Reservations System, from January 1, 1990 through December 31, 1990.
— Members may collect any rewards through December 15, 1991.

You deserve six nights in Hawaii for two.

When your work takes you on the road, every day can be a battle. Early mornings, late nights and living out of a suitcase are not for the meek. At Howard Johnson, we respect your lifestyle. That's why we created a reward program designed especially for the traveler like you: the Road Warrior Travel Club.

BIG REWARDS

As a Road Warrior, you work hard and you deserve a reward that is worth your effort. And Howard Johnson can deliver a Week's Vacation for Two in HAWAII: six nights' hotel stay and air travel from Los Angeles to Honolulu and back.

Imagine unwinding on a tropical beach and recharging in the Pacific surf, experiencing the exotic sights and sounds of Oahu. Simply join the Road Warrior Travel Club and you could earn this Hawaii vacation by staying at Howard Johnson.

Mr. Jones had recently joined the Road Warrior Travel Club. He called a Howard Johnson Motor Lodge for a reservation because he couldn't remember the 800 number. The desk clerk took his reservation as well as his ID number and gave him a confirmation number. The clerk was then supposed to access the 800 number and repeat the information into the system computer. However, not having been trained to use the 800 system, instead he left a note in the shift book to inform someone who was trained to enter the reservation. When Mr. Jones arrived at the hotel, the clerk on duty had no knowledge that he was a Road Warrior. He found that he was not pre-registered and his registration procedure was no different than anyone else's.

Mrs. Smith approached the front desk to check out after spending a night at a Howard Johnson hotel. She noticed the Road Warrior pamphlet and inquired about the program, which the desk clerk described. She started to fill out the application and asked if the past night's stay would count toward the prize points. The desk clerk was not sure if the program was retroactive but said he would ask someone. In any event, she would have to pay the corporate rate, which was $7 more. This annoyed Mrs. Smith, a regular customer. She continued to fill out the form hoping to find a way around this difference. When she got to the social security number line, she asked why it was necessary and who had access to it. The clerk explained with the only answer he knew, that it was needed for her personal ID number. Aggravated, Mrs. Smith threw down the pen and handed back the pamphlet, saying, "I don't look like a Road Warrior anyway. I'm not a barbarian, I'm a businesswoman!"

Howard Johnson management was not unaware of these problems. "We just have to get these people trained better," they said, "and we've got a sure winner."

✔ Case 14-3
Merchandising Power Breakfasts

Le Meridien Hotel in Boston was located on the edge of the city's financial district. Its Cafe Fleuri served "power breakfasts," a term given to breakfast meetings of businesspeople who got together to negotiate "deals." Power breakfasts had come to replace the three-martini lunch as the social/business setting where power brokers "wheel and deal." Wheeling and dealing was the name of the game in the financial districts of cities like Boston and New York where most big deals were made. Of course, for every big deal there were a hundred little ones that also got

EXHIBIT 14-3-1   Cafe Fleuri breakfast menu

FRESH FRUITS, JUICES, AND CEREALS

Papaya or mango juice $3.15
Freshly squeeze orange or grapefruit juice $3.25
Apple, grape, tomato or prune juice $2.95
Half grapefruit $3.50
Seasonal melon $4.00
Yogurt with fresh fruit $5.50
Fruit salad or fresh berries $5.25
Cold cereal, oatmeal, porridge, or granola $3.00
Cereal with fresh fruit $5.00
Muesli cereal $3.75

OUR
CREATIVE SPECIALTIES

Smoked salmon plate with
condiments and toast
$13.25

Scrambled eggs with tomato
and basil
$8.25

Blueberry or strawberry crêpes
$7.50

Omelette of smoked salmon
$9.25

Omelette of onions, peppers,
tomato, and prosciutto
$8.50

Toasted bagel with cream cheese
$3.50

*With smoked salmon $9.50

LE PARISIEN

Juice of your choice
Breakfast pastries
Coffee, decaffeinated coffee, tea,
hot chocolate, milk or skim-milk
$8.25

LE JAPONAIS

Misochiru soup
Yaki Nori (seaweed)
Japanese pickles
Broiled salmon with vegetables
Steamed rice
Green tea
Please allow 30 min. for preparation
$17.00

Croissants or muffins $3.75
Danish $3.25
White or whole wheat toast $2.25
Six grain toast $2.50

JACQUES MANIÈRE
LOW CALORIE BREAKFAST

Plain yogurt with
fresh fruits
Omelette with steamed
turkey breast and mushrooms
Plain toast
1/2-oz. of butter
295 calories
$12.50

OMELETTES, EGGS
AND GRIDDLE

Two eggs, any style $5.00
With ham, bacon or sausage $7.50
Mushroom omelette $7.25
Eggs benedict $8.50
Ham and cheese omelette $7.50
Banana or blueberry
pancakes $8.50
Pancakes, French toast
or waffles with maple syrup $6.25
*With strawberries and whipped
cream $2.15
*With ham, bacon or sausage $3.75

BEVERAGES

Coffee, decaffeinated coffee,
tea, hot chocolate,
milk or skim-milk $1.95

Additional charge
The 5% State Tax will be added to your bill. Gratuity not included.
Please refrain from cigar and pipe smoking.

Le
MERIDIEN
BOSTON

250 Franklin Street, Boston, MA 02110 617 451-1900   5/89/1M

Courtesy of Le Meridien Boston

EXHIBIT 14-3-2   Julien breakfast flyer

**MAKE IT YOUR BUSINESS
TO BREAKFAST.
AT JULIEN.**

Served Monday through Friday
from 7:00 — 10:00 AM
Parisien Breakfast $9.50
Julien Breakfast $15.00

PUT THE NEW JULIEN BREAKFAST
ON YOUR AGENDA.

For More Information:
Please call (617) 451-1900

Julien Breakfast
$15.00
Freshly squeezed orange or grapefruit juice
The Julien Baker's Basket with assorted
jellies and preserves

Your choice of one of the following:

• • • •

•Brittany-style crêpes with sauteed apples
and strawberries
•Daily low calorie specialty inspired by
Chef Jacques Maniere
•Julien French toast
•Scrambled egg with Vermont ham and fresh herbs
or with bacon and sausage
•Shirred eggs with asparagus tips and
Nova Scotia grave lax
•Soft boiled eggs with toasted French bread
•Three egg omelette with onions, peppers and mushrooms
•Half melon in season
•Fresh fruit compote puree, salad of fresh fruits
or seasonal berries
•Yoplait yogurt or Petits Suisses with fresh fruits
•Hot Red River cereal, nutril grain, granola, Swiss muesli

• • • •

European blend coffee, selection of loose teas,
Swiss hot chocolate,
milk, skim millk, half and half, decaffeinated coffee,
espresso, decaffeinated espresso, cappuccino

• • • •

Parisien Breakfast
$9.50
Freshly squeezed orange or grapefruit juice
The Julien Baker's Basket with assorted jellies
and preserves
European blend coffee, selection of loose teas,
Swiss hot chocolate,
milk, skim milk, half and half, decaffeinated coffee,
espresso, decaffeinated espresso, cappuccino

Courtesy of Le Meridien Boston

negotiated. For this purpose, Le Meridien was ideally located, and Cafe Fleuri was the ideal spot to be.

In fact, for Hugues Jaquier, General Manager of Le Meridien, the success of breakfast in Cafe Fleuri had become a problem. Cafe Fleuri seated 180. Each morning, from Monday to Friday, it served 250 to 300 covers, with an average check of $14.50. (The breakfast menu is shown in Exhibit 14-3-1.) This was no small feat since power breakfast eaters were not prone to quick turnover. In fact, 90 percent of these breakfasts were served to "locals" from the surrounding business community who had "staked out" their own tables so that even Le Meridien hotel guests had a hard time getting into the restaurant.

Many hotel guests, however, were accommodated with a buffet breakfast served in a Le Meridien ballroom. This arrangement handled 100 to 400 breakfasts each morning from Mon-

EXHIBIT 14-3-3   Letter left after turn-down service

Le
MERIDIEN
BOSTON

Dear Guest,

As you may already know, the Julien Restaurant is one of the most
renowned dining rooms in all of Boston.

Which is why it gives me great pleasure to let you know that we have
recently introduced the Julien breakfast. Available weekday mornings,
the Julien breakfast is designed for professionals who appreciate not
only a healthy start, but a quite and civilized one as well -- with
freshly-squeezed juice, daily newspapers, wireless telephone, and
whatever else you need to get your day off to a productive beginning.

If you would like to sample Boston's newest business breakfast
firsthand, our captain will be more than happy to reserve a table for
you. Simply call the Julien (extension 7120) or our Concierge
(extension 3) for reservations.

In the meantime, I thank you for your patronage and wish you a most
pleasant stay in the Boston area.

Sincerely,

Francois Chockaert
Food & Beverage Director

Courtesy of Le Meridien Boston

day through Friday. Power breakfast people, however, didn't want a buffet. They wanted to be waited on as they whispered and negotiated and grabbed at every rhetorical opportunity. The buffet breakfast concept, moreover, was not popular with some hotel guests, who preferred a quick juice-and-coffee breakfast and thus had to wait to get into Cafe Fleuri.

There was another problem. The entrance to Cafe Fleuri was a small waiting space that accommodated only about 15 or 20 at a time, standing room only. This small space made it difficult for people waiting for a table. From this space one could look down over a railing upon the escalator by which people ascended to Cafe Fleuri. At the bottom of the escalator was a fairly large, empty space that was a combina-tion entryway, coming from the hotel lobby in one direction and from the street side entrance of the hotel in the other. Because many came into this area from both directions, they were uncertain of whether to proceed up the escalator to wait for Cafe Fleuri seating, or to go elsewhere.

The Proposed Solution

Le Meridien Hotel was also the location of a famous French dinner restaurant, called Julien, arguably the best French restaurant in Boston. It was on the same level as Cafe Fleuri but separated from it by a short walkway. Julien seated 90 and was far more distin-guished in its decor than Cafe Fleuri. Tables

EXHIBIT 14-3-4   Guest "welcome back" letter

Le MERIDIEN
BOSTON

Hugues Jaquier
Managing Director
Directeur Général

Dear [gender] [last]:

Once more, I am delighted to welcome you back to Boston and, of course, to the Meridien.

In case you weren't aware of it, I also wanted to take this opportunity to let you know that we are now serving breakfast in our Julien restaurant. Available weekday mornings, from 7 am until 10 am, the Julien breakfast is geared for professionals like yourself who appreciate not only a healthy start, but a quiet and civilized one as well - with freshly-squeezed juice, daily newspapers, wireless phones and whatever else you need to begin your day.

If you would like to sample what I'm sure will become Boston's most popular business breakfast, our captain will be more than happy to reserve a table for you. Simply call the Julien (extension 7120) or our Concierge (extension 3) for reservations.

In the meantime, I thank you for your continued patronage and, as always, I hope that you will contact me personally if there is any way in which I may be of assistance to you.

                Most sincerely,

                Hugues Jaquier

HJ:eml

Courtesy of Le Meridien Boston

EXHIBIT 14-3-5   Julien breakfast newspaper ad

Courtesy of Le Meridien Boston

EXHIBIT 14-3-6   Julien breakfast letter to major accounts

Hugues Jaquier
Managing Director
Directeur Général

September 13, 1989

Ms. Canice H. McGarry
Organization Development
Massachusetts Housing Finance Agency
50 Milk Street
Boston MA 02109

Dear Ms. McGarry,

I am pleased to announce that, beginning on Monday,
September 18, we will introduce breakfast service
in the Julien Restaurant.

Designed to meet the demands of our business
clientele, the Julien breakfast - served from 7:00
am until 10:00 am, Monday through Friday - will
provide a quiet, private setting and a prix fixe
menu including such specialties as Brittany-style
crepes with fresh fruit; Julien French toast; a
wide selection of egg dishes; and lighter fare
including yogurts, cereals and daily low-calorie
dishes inspired by Jacques Maniere.

I would like to invite you and a friend to be my
guests for a complimentary breakfast in the Julien
on whatever weekday morning is most convenient for
you between September 18 and 29. Please make your
reservation at least 24 hours in advance, by
calling the Julien Restaurant, and present this
letter upon your arrival.

In the meantime, thank you for your continued
interest in our hotel and I look forward to seeing
you very soon.

                    Sincerely,

                    Hugues Jaquier

HJ:eml

Courtesy of Le Meridien Boston

were farther apart and chairs were high-back, offering far more privacy. The room was warmly decorated with wood, the carpet thicker, and the lighting more discreet. "All in all," thought Hugues Jaquier, "Julien lends itself far better to power breakfasts; especially as it now sits idle during that time. If this room could be used for breakfast, it wouldn't solve my juice-and-coffee customer problem, but it would certainly take some pressure off Cafe Fleuri. And my customers would love it!"

From June through August the concept of a Julien breakfast was developed and preparation was made for a September 15 opening. The idea was to have a health-oriented breakfast for well-to-do businesspeople. It was to be good value at a low price with 100 percent fresh product, low calories, and top-quality service. Latest editions of the world financial press would be available for perusal.

First, the menu was developed and intentionally priced to be no higher than that in Cafe Fleuri. It was put on the back of a flyer to be used in-house and in mailings (Exhibit 14-3-2). Also for in-house, posters were made for the lobby and elevators, with the same Ken Maryanski-drawn caricatures that were used in all Le Meridien advertising. In addition, breakfast at Julien was to be featured on the in-house TV channel, and a letter was to be left on pillows after turn-down service (Exhibit 14-3-3). A similar letter was prepared as a "welcome back" for regular guests (Exhibit 14-3-4).

Externally, commercials were prepared for radio stations WEEI and WRKO. Print ads were prepared for the *Boston Business Journal,* the *Boston Business Magazine,* and the *Boston Globe* (Exhibit 14-3-5). A letter was also sent to major corporate offices (Exhibit 14-3-6) and to chief executives of financial companies, with a personal invitation from Hugues Jaquier. Finally, press invitations were sent out.

The planning was perfect and the execution flawless. "We've got a sure hit," said Hugues as he stood at the entrance to Julien on opening morning, September 15. "All I've got to do now is figure out what to do with my juice-and-coffee customer."

Four months later, in January, Hugues had figured out what to do with juice-and-coffee customers and, if nothing else, had accommodated some of these guests who wanted to get out and away quickly. This did not, however, relieve much of the pressure on Cafe Fleuri, and the covers in Julien were averaging only 15 to 20 each morning.

✔ Case 14-4
Hilton International / Toronto[9]

"The average room rate is $10 to $12 lower than last year. We really have to drop our rates to maintain occupancy, and we haven't even been able to do that."

Antoine Berberi, Front Office Manager at the Hilton International in Toronto, reflected on the state of Toronto's hotel market. The predicted slump in the economy had arrived, and the Hilton was facing the consequences. Its room rates had been the lowest in the city among comparable first-class hotels, yet occupancy was down from last year. Antoine hoped that the existing price war would not intensify in the coming spring season.

The Toronto Hilton

The 600-room Toronto Hilton was located in the heart of the city's entertainment and business area. It provided direct access to major business towers through a three-and-a-half-mile underground shopping mall walkway. Facilities included a heated indoor/outdoor swimming pool with sauna, a health club, 24-hour room service, covered underground parking, and convention and meeting facilities for groups up to 1,100. Standard amenities included color cable TV, AM/FM radios, first-run movies, mini-bars, alarm clocks, oversized beds, and individual climate-controlled rooms. The hotel also operated three restaurants and two lounges.

The Environment

Canada was in a recession, especially in the province of Ontario. The Goods and Services Tax (GST) of seven percent, imposed by former prime minister Brian Mulroney, had added to the burden. Occupancies had suffered a precipitous plunge from 75 percent to 58 percent citywide, in the past four years, although average room rates continued to rise, going from $90 to $103 in the same period of time. The hotel in-

dustry was not optimistic that the market would rebound in the near future. Additionally, 750 more rooms would be added to the 16,000-room supply, including a new 450-room Marriott two blocks north of the Hilton.

Antoine did not expect the Marriott to compete directly for the same markets as the Hilton, the latter being better located in the financial district for most business travelers. The Marriott, attached to a major shopping complex, would be more likely to appeal to tourists and out-of-towners than business travelers. Regardless, Marriott was known for grabbing market share, and Antoine was concerned with what its tactics would be. Rather than guess, he believed that all he could do was wait until it opened. More serious, at the moment, was what the Sheraton right around the corner was doing.

The Hilton's main competitors had already cut their room rates by as much as 50 percent. Table 14-4-1 shows these competitors and the winter specials each was promoting.

Pricing Strategy at the Hilton

The previous fall, with both winter and more recession materializing, Hilton management felt that its conservative clientele (40 percent group, 30 percent tourists, 30 percent individual business travelers) would not relish paying room rates over $100. It decided to lower rates below rack before the competition did it first. Rack rates ranged from $122 to $229 single and $142 to $249 double, depending on the type of accommodations.

Input was obtained from the International Sales Office and all members of the executive committee. It was agreed that the winter special would be $89 per room, single or double occupancy. A variety of promotional packages was also designed (Table 14-4-2). Since only about one percent of all daily occupied rooms ever sold at rack rate, this tactic was not seen by management as being a particularly radical move.

---

[9]Helen D'Olveira researched and contributed to this case.

Now What?

In February, the Toronto Hilton had the highest occupancy rate among its major competitors (Table 14-4-3) although its occupancy was five percentage points below the previous year. In late March, the Royal York cut its rates to $79 per room, single or double. In response, Hilton management decided to forego a planned spring increase to $99 and decided to maintain the $89 rate until at least the end of June.

In an attempt to combat the low rate, Antoine developed a reservation call strategy for direct calls (about 30 percent of calls came through the international Hilton 800 number) and trained all the Hilton reservationist accordingly. Reservationists receiving a call first asked a number of questions to help identify tastes and, hence, room rates that the caller might find acceptable, such as:

Are you a corporate client?
Will you be attending a convention while in town?
Will you be arriving on a weekday?
How many nights would you like to stay?
How many people will be staying in the room?

Would you like to reserve for any other times or at another Hilton?

Each day Antoine set a minimum daily rate, based on anticipated occupancy, that was conveyed to all reservationists. Reservationists were encouraged to quote the rack rate, but were allowed to quote a lower rate down to the minimum daily rate. Management approval was required to go lower than the minimum. If management was not available, however, reservationists were entrusted to use their discretion in quoting lower rates acceptable to the caller. Antoine believed this flexibility contributed greatly to the relatively high occupancies that Hilton enjoyed in the city. He found no indication that the flexibilty was abused. In fact, reservationists seemed to like the responsibility.

As spring approached, Antoine was not sure what price reaction to expect from his competitors. He concerned himself with maintaining the relatively high occupancy rate he had successfully established in the winter season. Finally, there was still the nagging thought of the Marriott opening in the fall with its special opening prices. Antoine decided to call a strategy meeting to formulate some plan to deal with these issues.

TABLE 14-4-1   Toronto First-Class Hotels' Winter Specials

Hotel	Room Rate (single/double)	Inclusive	Daily Rate	Valet Parking	In & Out Privileges
				Parking	
Sheraton	$105	Room & Full American Breakfast	$18	Included	NA
L'Hotel	$89	Room Only	$16	Included	Yes
Hilton	$89	Room & Continental Breakfast/Cup of Hot Chocolate/Passport*	$10	NA	Yes
Westin Harbour Castle	$80	Room Only	$16.25	Included	Yes
Royal York	$79	Room & Coffee or Tea & Morning Newspaper	$17 $25	NA or Included	NA Yes

*"Passport" refers to a special coupon booklet, distributed to eligible guests and containing discounts valid for a variety of stores and restaurants in the city.

TABLE 14-4-2   Promotional Packages at the Toronto Hilton

Package Name	Date	Available	Rate	Amenities	TA Code	Restrictions/ Comment
Warm Winter	1/7 to 4/15	Monday thru Sunday	$89 Single/ Double $20 Extra	Room, Cup of Hot Chocolate	11111	Mugs to the first 500 staying on this rate.
Interline Special Staff Rate	2/5 to 5/31	Monday thru Sunday	$60 Single/ Double $20 Extra	Room Only	88622	Subject to availability. Must be airline employee & have airline ID.
Travel Alerts Bounce Back & Romance Break	2/5 thru 4/31	Monday thru Sunday	BB $89 HM $211	See Packages as Outlined Above	88620	Based on availability at time of booking.
Enroute Hotel Clearing Center	3/8 to 6/1	Monday thru Sunday	$5 Off Minimum Rate of Day	Room Only	7777	Calls must come through hotel savings hotline.
Doubleheader Baseball Package	4/13 to 9/28	Friday Nights Only	$139 / Double $20 Extra	Room & 2 Field-level Tickets	"Base MDD"	Subject to availability. $35 advance deposit. 2 tickets/ room only.
American Express Dinner for 2	2/4 thru 7/31	Friday to Sunday	$89	Room, Continental Breakfast & Dinner	999999	Must be requested. Must have coupon for dinner on Friday.
Bounce Back (BB)	10/1 to 4/30	Monday thru Sunday	$89 Single/ Double $20 Extra	Room & Continental Breakfast	80000	Arrivals on Fridays only. "BB" in specials.
Bounce Back (BT)	Same As Above	Monday thru Sunday	$89 Single/ Double $20Extra	Room & Continental Breakfast	80000	Arrivals Thursday. Must stay thru Saturday.
Bounce Back (Junior Suite)	Same As Above	Same As Bounce Back Regular	$158 Single/ Double $20 Extra	Room & Continental Breakfast	80000	Guaranteed Junior Suite. "BB" in specials.
Bounce Back (Executive Floor)	Same As Above	Thursday thru Sunday	$150 Single/ Double $20 Extra	Room & Continental Breakfast	80000	Thursday arrivals. Must stay into weekend. "BB" in specials.

TABLE 14-4-2 (continued)

Package Name	Date	Available	Rate	Amenities	TA Code	Restrictions/ Comment
Toronto Doubles Your Adventure	11/15 to 3/31	Monday thru Sunday	$89 Single/ Double $20 Extra	Room Only	88888	Guest receives passport at check-in.
Romance Break (Regular Room) (RP)	10/1 to 4/30	Monday thru Sunday	$211 incl. Tax & Gratuities	Room & Wine & Gift & 2 American Breakfasts	90000	Guaranteed king-size bed. $170 for extra night. "HM" in package plan.
Romance Break (Junior Suite) (R1)	Same As Above	Same As Above	$239 incl. Taxes & Gratuities	Same As Above	90000	Guaranteed Junior Suite. $210 for extra night. "HJ" in package plan.
Romance Break (Executive Floors) (RP)	Same As Above	Same As Above	$257 incl. Taxes & Gratuities	Same As Above	90000	Guaranteed room on Executive Floor.
Hilton Gold Card Members (Weekdays)	10/1 thru 4/30	Sunday thru Thursday	$114 Single/ Double $20 Extra	Room & Food & Beverage Discounts	56	$229 for extra night. Must give card number, time of booking. Can book up to 10 rooms.
Hilton Gold Card Members (Weekend)	Same As Above	Friday thru Sunday	$81 Single/ Double $20 Extra	Same As Above	56	Only available Friday & Saturday. See above re. card.
Senior HH (SH)	10/1 to 12/31	Monday thru Sunday	$88 Single/ Double $20 Extra	Room Only	75000	Please put "HH" in specials.

All packages are subject to availability at time of booking and are exclusive of taxes

TABLE 14-4-3   February Occupancy Rates for Toronto First-Class Hotels

Hotel	Number of Rooms	Occupancy Rates
Hilton	601	67%
L'Hotel	587	42%
Royal York	1,438	48%
Sheraton	1,398	59%
Westin Harbour Castle	964	57%

CHAPTER 15

The Communications Mix: Personal Selling[1]

Personal selling is the direct interaction between a seller and a prospective buyer for the purpose of making the sale. Personal selling may be one of the more challenging aspects of the communications mix because it relies heavily on an individual's ability to meet with a customer face-to-face. While public relations communicates through stories and the media, advertising through copy and artwork, and merchandising through in-house promotions, the salesperson communicates through direct oral presentation to the customer.

Obviously, every employee should be a salesperson for his or her organization. In this chapter, however, we will discuss selling from the perspective of hospitality organizations that specifically designate people to carry out the direct sales function.

Organized personal selling is not universally used in the hospitality industry. Rarely will you meet a salesperson from the local Pizza Hut, McDonald's, or even Motel 6. On the other hand, full-service hotels and restaurants with extensive catering facilities will employ salespeople as an essential part of their communications mix.

Whether or not personal selling is used by an organization depends on several factors, including the complexity of the products and services offered, the quantities in which they are purchased, and the price that is paid. In the fast-food or budget hotel organization wherein the products and services are relatively simple, the customer knows what they are; they are usually purchased by individuals or small groups in relatively small quantities; and the price is low. For the buyer it is a low-risk, low-involvement purchase. Hiring a salesperson would not be cost-effective or even necessary. The interaction between the buyer and seller is easy and straightforward.

Contrast this with the 1,600-room Hilton in New Orleans. One salesperson may book a group of 500 rooms for three nights at $150 per room-night. This is $225,000 worth of room-night business alone, negotiated between the salesperson and a meeting planner. In addition, there are food and beverage functions, hospitality suites, general session, and break-out rooms, representing possibly another $100,000, and hundreds of other details to be worked out. The same is true of a resort such as The Broadmoor in Colorado Springs, in which high-risk purchases are made, with high involvement on the part of the buyer. The products and services

[1]We are grateful to Ursula Geschke, Sales Manager, Guest Quarters, Atlanta and Susan Morris, National Account Executive, Marriott International, 1994, for major contributions to this chapter.

are complex and need much explanation and confirmation before a contract is signed. A good salesperson will decrease the risk factor by offering assurance and providing examples.

The nature of a complex hospitality product and service lends itself to a heavy emphasis on the personal selling effort. Chains like Marriott, Hyatt, and Holiday Inn employ national and international sales managers to represent the entire chain to large accounts that have ongoing needs for hotels. Table 15-1 shows how the product offering establishes the need for a sales force.

Emphasis on Personal Selling

In each of the four subheadings of Table 15-1, the application to the hospitality product can be seen to lend itself to the direct sales portion of the communications mix. Buying the *Product* requires a major commitment on the purchaser's part. Even a small, three-day meeting of only 30 people in a suburban hotel can easily exceed a $10,000 expenditure. Assistance is necessary in application; that is, customers' goals must be understood, and they must be helped to achieve them. Personal demonstration and trial are common, such as site inspections, trial stays, and booking a small meeting before a large one. *Pricing* for meetings and group bookings is normally negotiated. *Distribution* channels, as outlined in Chapter 16, are short and direct, and intermediaries require training and assistance. Under *Communication,* advertising is inadequate and too expensive to reach and fulfill the needs of the buyer, including explaining the benefits. Finally, the marketplace sees the salesperson as an integral

---

TABLE 15-1   Characteristics of the Marketing Mix That Support Emphasis on Personal Selling

Personal selling is generally a significant tool when...

Product
The product requires that the customer receive application assistance (e.g., with computers and pollution control systems).
The product requires that the customers receive personal demonstrations and trials (e.g., with private aircraft and totally new products).
The product purchase decision requires a major commitment on the purchaser's part.

Pricing
The final price is negotiated, not fixed (e.g., with real estate, automobiles, and many industrial goods). The final price and quantity purchased allow an adequate margin to support selling expenses (traditional department stores vs. discounters).

Distribution
Distribution channels are short and direct.
Channel intermediaries require training and assistance.

Communication
Advertising media do not reach the intended markets effectively.
Information sought by potential customers cannot be provided entirely through advertising and sales promotion (e.g., with life insurance).
The size and dispersion of the market make advertising too expensive.
The firm's promotional budget is small and sales per customer are high.
The market sees personal selling as an essential part of the product.

Source: William Lazer and James D. Culley, *Marketing Management,* p. 752. Copyright 1983 by Houghton Mifflin Company. Used by permission.

TABLE 15-2   Characteristics of the Communications Mix

Communications Mode	Personal Selling: Direct & Face-to-face	Advertising: Indirect and Nonpersonal	Publicity: Usually Indirect and Nonpersonal	Sales Promotion: Usually Indirect and Nonpersonal
Communicator's control over the situation	High	Low	Moderate to low	Moderate to low
Amount of feedback	Much	Little	Little	Little to moderate
Speed of feedback	Immediate	Delayed	Delayed	Varies
Message flow	Two-way	One-way	One-way	Mostly one-way
Control over message content	Yes	Yes	No	Yes
Sponsor identified	Yes	Yes	No	Yes
Speed in reaching large audiences	Slow	Fast	Usually fast	Fast
Message flexibility	Tailored to prospect	Uniform and unvaried	No direct control over message	Uniform and varied

Source: Carl McDaniel, Jr. and William R. Darden, *Marketing,* Newton, Mass.: Allyn & Bacon, 1987, p. 526. Used with permission.

part of the product. As hotels in the same product class have become, essentially, a basic commodity, it is through salespeople that a competitive edge can be gained.

All the rules of the communications mix apply to sales. However, there are differences between the characteristics of personal selling and the other components of the communications mix, as seen in Table 15-2.

There are several advantages to using personal selling. These include:[2]

1. Personal selling can be used to tangibilize and describe products and services in greater detail.
2. Personal selling can be used to introduce and differentiate the product.
3. The sales pitch can be tailored to suit the customer's needs and solutions to customer's specific problems can be offered.
4. Prospective buyers can be identified and qualified before directing personal selling

resources; thus communications mix dollars may be more effectively spent.
5. Personal selling can reduce risk and is more effective in getting customers to close the deal and sign the contract.
6. Personal selling is the only part of the communications mix that permits direct feedback from the customer.
7. Personal selling provides an excellent opportunity for relationship marketing.

The Sales Process

There are several steps in the personal sales process. These include prospecting, qualifying prospects, the sales approach, handling objections, closing of the sale, and follow-up. The sales process also has two other very important aspects that must be kept in mind during the sales interaction: how to sell the product, given unique client needs, and what to sell. The successful sales team knows not only how to sell, but what to sell most efficiently.

[2]Adapted from Charles W. Lamb, Jr., Joseph F. Hair, Jr., and Carl McDaniel, *Principles of Marketing,* Cincinnati: South-Western Publishing Co., 1992, p. 496.

Prospecting

Prospecting is the term used for finding new customers. Prospecting leads to making sales calls, in person or by phone, on prospective customers who are not currently using the product. Prospecting is more difficult than calling on existing customers because new customers don't know the product, although they may certainly have some perception of it. New customers need to be convinced that the product they are currently using does not satisfy their needs, and they need to be convinced as well that your product would. One axiom goes like this:

> If you want to sell your product to our company, be sure your product is accompanied by a plan that will so help our business that we will be more anxious to buy than you are to sell.

It is highly unlikely that a meeting planner will "create" a meeting just because of your facility. The meeting either will already exist, having occurred before at a competitor's hotel, or will have been partially developed and waiting to be placed in a facility.

New customers are the competitors' existing customers (and vice versa!). In direct sales, the most common way to get new customers is to take them away from competitors. In almost all cases, new customers are currently using a competitor's product and have to be convinced (sold) to use yours. Prospecting has evolved over the past decade as the real challenge for selling in a competitive marketplace.

"Cold calling" used to be the main method to drum up new business. One technique was for a sales team to "blitz" an area or office building by making calls, unannounced, on companies within the buildings.[3] This method is still in place in some organizations, but is not generally recommended. Few like to have a salesperson walk in "cold" and ask to speak to the person who books meetings or banquets (incidentally, not the way to do it if you do cold call). Many salespeople do not like cold calling, nor do they like

the risk of rejection that comes with it either. On the other hand, some individual salespeople use cold calling, not necessarily "blitz," to successfully set up appointments and obtain pertinent information.[4]

More sophisticated methods of generating leads, or prospects, have emerged. Many sales directors are recognizing the cost of sales calls and realizing that sending salespeople out on calls without appointments is an expensive way to do business. Depending on the experience of the salesperson, the location, the account, and other variables, a sales call can cost $25 to $500 or more, after salary, benefits, office space, secretarial support, collateral, and travel are factored in as part of the cost of doing business. At even $50 per call, the salesperson becomes an expensive resource, not to be used without a well-devised plan. Direct mail and telemarketing (which also may be called cold calling), or sometimes a combination of both, are used effectively to set up sales calls in advance, and make for concentrated sales efforts. Once a face-to-face rapport is established, salespeople often revert back to the telephone since they have little time for too many face-to-face calls.

Qualifying Prospects

In this step, the salesperson determines if prospects are qualified to make the purchase—can they afford it, do they have the authority to make it, and just how serious are they? Qualifying is done during prospecting, for example, telemarketing, or as a follow-up to direct mail or advertising responses.

Direct mail responses can also be effective in qualifying prospects because only those who are genuinely interested in the service will bother to respond to the solicitation (except when you offer great incentive awards!). A mailing list is purchased, and a mailing piece is developed and mailed with a response card and, often, some

---

[3]"Blitz" implies multiple calls more or less at random; the preferred term today is "concentrated sales effort."

[4]For a positive view on cold calling and how to do it successfully, see Jeffrey H. Gitomer, *The Sales Bible,* pp. 94–108. New York: William Morrow, 1994. Gitomer's recommended opening line is, "Can you help me?"

kind of incentive. For example, a facility may want to increase its share of a certain market, such as medical meetings. Certain parameters that fit the property, such as size of meeting and geographic preference, are established. A direct mail piece is created to generate a response for more information. A sales manager or telemarketer would then follow up the lead, to determine the customer's needs. Figure 15-1 illustrates stages of this process, when Marriott Suites in Atlanta was converted to a Guest Quarters.

Telemarketing is another, more direct method, to generate and qualify leads. This time the prospect is phoned. The telemarketer may just find out if there is a need for the facility and then turn the lead over to the sales manager for professional follow-up. Many travel managers are besieged by sales managers and telemarketers on a daily basis, however, and keep their voice mail on to screen the unwanted invasion of calls. Yet, on the other hand, sales managers play an important part in fulfilling a travel manager's responsibilities since frequent contact keeps them apprised of the best "deals" with the best product.

Advertising to meeting planners is a common practice for large hotels, resorts, and hotel chains. Media presumably read by these people—such as *Successful Meetings, Meetings and Conventions,* and *Corporate Meetings and Incentives*—are used for advertising. Such ads

GUEST QUARTERS®
SUITE HOTELS

M E M O R A N D U M

▶ To: Audrey A. Mintz

▶ From: Jack P. Ferguson

▶ Date: November 9, 1992

▶ Re: Guest Quarters Suite Hotel/Atlanta Perimeter

Audrey:

As we reviewed this morning, the top priority in the NSO Telemarketing Department this week is to qualify the 588 accounts in the FIDELIO system that indicate travel into the Atlanta market. The created questionnaire for this project should accomplish what we want to uncover for the property from the standpoint of:

TRANSIENT, GROUP, EXTENDED STAY, SOCIAL, INCENTIVE/GIFT CERTIFICATE and what **TRAVEL AGENCY** they utilize in their Atlanta area hotel needs.

Audrey, the notes on the PROFILE need to be neat and clear as these will be used by our sales team for the Concentrated Sales Effort the week of December 14-18, 1992.

Additionally, use the updated FACT SHEET about the Hotel to verbally walk the customer through the facilities.

JFP/sd
Attachments: ATLANTA PROFILE/ATLANTA FACT SHEET

cc: S. Pletcher
     B. Bitner
     G. Sims
     L. Craig
     J. Mazur
     N. Billia

ATLANTA

Courtesy Guest Quarters Suite Hotels

FIGURE 15-1   Creating a direct marketing, telemarketing, and sales campaign

We would like to introduce you to our Guest Quarters® Suite Hotel Atlanta Perimeter. Now first class service with the room to enjoy it comes to the Atlanta Perimeter. A full service hotel with spacious suites *at the rate of an ordinary room.* Guest Quarters' reputation for service and superior value is unmatched in the hospitality industry.

In introducing you to this new Guest Quarters property we want you to know more about both our all suite hotel and the many money-saving programs and opportunities we are making available to you and your travelling guests and clients.

On Tuesday, December 15, Wednesday, December 16, and Thursday, December 17, selected members of our sales and marketing team will be coming to the Atlanta Perimeter to help tell you about our programs. To express our appreciation for your time we are going to give you a new Polaroid Instamatic Camera, Free. It's our gift to you and it's right in time for the holiday season.

What's more, you could win a Free vacation (5 days/4 nights) at our Guest Quarters at Walt Disney World® Village.

Please fill out and mail or FAX (404) 668-0008 the attached card to us in order that we can arrange a convenient time to meet with you and deliver your camera.

We look forward to meeting you and to introducing you to a first class all suite hotel in the Atlanta Perimeter.

You'll come back to GUEST QUARTERS®
SUITE HOTEL
ATLANTA PERIMETER

GUEST QUARTERS SUITE HOTELS

M E M O R A N D U M

▶ To: Kellie A. McShane-Harris

▶ From: Jack P. Ferguson

▶ Date: December 1, 1992

▶ Re: **Atlanta Concentrated Sales Effort - December 14-18, 1992**

Kellie:

As you are aware, the Atlanta project is well underway. On Thursday, December 3, 1992, we need to PRINT labels for all Atlanta area contacts for the sales solicitation during the concentrated sales effort. These accounts/contacts will be called on during the concentrated sales effort over the above dates. The PRINT labels are to be sent by AIRBORNE to Gary Sims on Thursday night.

Prior to the sales call the contact will receive both an announcement of Guest Quarters/ Atlanta Perimeter and will be telemarketed to see if we can arrange a specific date/time during the week of December 7th. The <u>goal</u> is to establish as many appointments as possible.

All hard copy PROFILES will be sent to Atlanta with Mary Kay for use by the sales team during the sales effort. At the end of the concentrated sales effort, Mary Kay will bring the PROFILES back to NSO/PHL for keypunch update. For those which are HOT, she will make a copy and give it to Laurie Craig.

As discussed, please <u>order</u> 2,000 labels, so we may have some for backup.

JPF/ug

cc: B. Bitner
     M.K. Ayscue
     A.A. Mintz
     G. Sims/L. Craig

ATLANTA16

FIGURE 15-1 (continued)

may (Figure 15-2) or may not (Figure 15-3) provide incentives or direct solicitations to respond for further information. Responses are followed up with new information; for example, sending brochures listing meeting room specifications, facilities, etc. (Figure 15-4). Some properties even send out videos to provide more graphic and direct presentations (Figure 15-5). Eventually, a personal sales call, or at least a telephone call, may be in order. As shown in Figure 15-6, it can take many prospects to get a few customers.

The Sales Approach

The sales approach, or communicating personally with customers, is a difficult skill to master. In the 1970s and 1980s, when the demand for guestrooms exceeded the supply, the selling process was simple—it was order-taking. A salesperson would simply answer the phone, or call back customers who had telephoned earlier, and take their orders. The sales process for the 1990s is very different. In most markets supply far exceeds demand and telephones no longer

GUEST QUARTERS®
SUITE HOTELS

NATIONAL SALES OFFICE

TO: Gary Sims/Laurie Craig, Guest Quarters/Atlanta

FROM: Jack Ferguson

DATE: December 3, 1992

SUBJECT: Atlanta Mailing Labels

Gary and Laurie:

Enclosed are the 784 mailing labels for the concentrated sales effort mailing which will be dropped on or before Monday, December 7th. Our telemarketing department will be working from the mailing list to set up as many appointments for the week of December 14th, 1992, concentrating on Tuesday, December 15th, Wednesday, December 16th, and Thursday, December 17th. We will use the shoulder days Monday, December 14th and Friday, December 18th only when the customer can not take advantage of any other day.

We still have more keypunching from MPI and the labels from the list we received from Laurie at the beginning of the week. (Out internal code for these new entries is AA1). When Mary Kay comes to Atlanta she will have PROFILES against these contacts. If we can telemarket them prior to the 14th, the PROFILE will be completed.

Laurie, I'll see you in Chicago. Gary, call me on Monday should you have any questions.

cc: Steve Pletcher
      Bob Bitner
      Mary Kay Ayscue
      Audrey Mintz
      Kellie McShane-Harris
      NSO Team

Folcroft East Business Park
101 Henderson Drive
Sharon Hill, PA 19079
(215) 532-6410 FAX (215) 532-1267
For nationwide reservations call 1-800-424-2900

FIGURE 15-1   (continued)

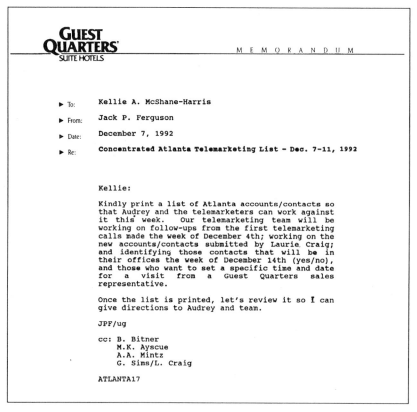

GUEST QUARTERS
SUITE HOTELS

M E M O R A N D U M

▶ To: Kellie A. McShane-Harris

▶ From: Jack P. Ferguson

▶ Date: December 7, 1992

▶ Re: **Concentrated Atlanta Telemarketing List – Dec. 7-11, 1992**

Kellie:

Kindly print a list of Atlanta accounts/contacts so
that Audrey and the telemarketers can work against
it this week. Our telemarketing team will be
working on follow-ups from the first telemarketing
calls made the week of December 4th; working on the
new accounts/contacts submitted by Laurie Craig;
and identifying those contacts that will be in
their offices the week of December 14th (yes/no),
and those who want to set a specific time and date
for a visit from a Guest Quarters sales
representative.

Once the list is printed, let's review it so I can
give directions to Audrey and team.

JPF/ug

cc: B. Bitner
    M.K. Ayscue
    A.A. Mintz
    G. Sims/L. Craig

ATLANTA17

FIGURE 15-1   (continued)

ring by themselves. A good sales process is what makes the telephones ring.

There is a right way to sell and a wrong way to sell, yet it is still a very personal skill. Many salespeople in the hospitality industry think they are selling by knocking on office doors without appointments (cold calling) and leaving behind a brochure. Today, good salespeople get "inside the buyer's head."

Theodore Levitt has chronicled this progression. In past practice, and perhaps still too often today, the seller tried to unload onto a buyer what the seller decided to offer. "This was the basis for the notion that a salesperson needs charisma, because it was charisma that made the sale rather than the product selling itself." Over time, selling progressed to where the seller "penetrates the buyer's domain to learn about his needs, desires, fears, and the like, and then designs and supplies the product in all its forms. Instead of trying to get the buyer to want what the seller has, the seller tries to have what the buyer will want. The 'product' is no longer merely an item but a whole bundle of value satisfactions." The progression process is from need to benefit to feature for the buyer.[5]

"Today, successful selling is more about long-term relationships between sellers and buyers. It is not just that once you get a customer you want to keep him. It is more a matter of what the buyer wants. He wants a vendor who will keep his promises [deliver the promises made to him], who'll keep supplying and stand behind what he promised."[6] Thus, there becomes an interdependence between the seller and the buyer.

It is this lesson that was learned by Ritz-Carlton Hotel Company in 1992 when it hired a research firm to study its relationships with meeting planners. The research showed that

---

[5]Theodore Levitt, "Relationship Management," in Theodore Levitt, *The Marketing Imagination,* New York: The Free Press, 1986, pp. 111–126.

[6]*Ibid.*

A WORD TO MEETING PLANNERS
FROM THE CARIBE HILTON...

WINNER OF THE FIRST AMERICAN EXPRESS DESTINATION QUALITYsm AWARD

"YES, WE HAVE IT ALL"

□ 668 beautiful rooms, each with an ocean view
□ Executive Floors with private concierge and express check-in/check-out
□ A 10,000-square-foot ballroom
□ The largest hotel Exhibition Center in the Caribbean
□ A beautiful auditorium; 3 Executive Business Center boardrooms; 7 conference rooms; and 21 meeting and banquet rooms

Whatever you want or need, just ask. The answer is almost certain to be, "yes."

"YES, WE DO IT BETTER"

Recently, 23 of the best hotels in the Caribbean competed for the American Express Destination Quality Award. The Caribe Hilton won. And we're not resting on our laurels. We've invested an additional $45,000,000 to insure that The Caribe Hilton will continue setting the standard for quality and service.

"YES, WE'RE COMPETITIVE AND FLEXIBLE"

We want to win you over. So, we're ready to work with you every step of the way. Just bring us your budget...or, an offer from another hotel...and let us show you what we can do for your meeting. We're sure your reaction will be, "Yes!"

"YES, A SPECIAL *AMENITIES PLUS* OFFER"

As a bonus, plan a meeting anytime in 1993 or 1994, book before March 31, 1994 and you can choose one of several high-value amenities, such as a free cocktail party or complimentary suite.* Should you consider holding your next meeting or conference at The Caribe Hilton and Casino? "Absolutely!" Call Michael O'Connor at Hilton International Sales at **1-800-544-3214**. Ask about our hotels in Ponce and Mayaguez.

*subject to availability

CARIBE

PONCE
AND CASINO
PONCE, PUERTO RICO

AND CASINO
SAN JUAN, PUERTO RICO

MAYAGUEZ
AND CASINO
MAYAGUEZ, PUERTO RICO

FIGURE 15-2   Incentive offer to meeting planners

FIGURE 15-3   Meeting planner solicitation without special incentive

where Ritz-Carlton was falling down was after the sale and before the event, a period of sometimes a year or more. Buyers felt, "Now, that they've got my business they don't care about me," when there was no contact from the hotel until just before the event. Buyers wanted an ongoing relationship during the interim that told them their business was appreciated.

Similarly, some companies, such as Marriott and Hyatt, have national account managers who work only a few major accounts, such as IBM and Hewlett Packard. These people "live" with these companies so as to get inside their culture and fully understand their needs when planning a meeting or event. This is a good example of relationship selling.

What to Sell[7]

The art of selling begins, like marketing, by understanding the needs of the customers. This is critical for a successful sale. Once again, the idea is to solve customers' problems. First, one must determine what they are; sometimes this calls for an interpretation. For example, a customer might say, "I need a good hotel close to the airport for my meeting" (i.e., one of the customer's problems is convenience). The salesperson's property might not be near the airport and the sale might be lost. Possibly, however, the sale might be saved by offering pickup and transportation, overcoming the distance by offering the convenience. In any event, the salesperson must determine the real problem in order to address it.

Sometimes a customer will express an opportunity, not a need. The salesperson has to understand the subtle difference. While a need is a customer want or desire that can be satisfied by the hospitality entity, an opportunity is a statement of a problem, without the expressed desire to solve the problem. Let's look at the difference:

"I need a hotel with a location near the airport." *(need)*

[7]The methodology for selling described here was developed by Learning International of Stamford, Connecticut and adapted for the hospitality industry.

"The hotel we use now is too far from the airport." *(opportunity)*

In the first statement the problem is explicit. The first statement expresses the desire to solve the problem. The second sentence is an opportunity that calls for further interpretation.

Suppose the salesperson responds by telling the customer how close their hotel is to the airport. The customer then might reply:

"That's nice, but it doesn't matter. My boss lives on the other side of town and doesn't want to travel all the way to the airport. I personally think the hotel we use now is out of the way, but what can you do?"

What the salesperson interpreted as an opportunity, was actually not a conscious need. By addressing a perceived opportunity with a benefit not important to the customer, he becomes disinterested. The location of the hotel was a problem for the meeting planner, but not one that he had a desire to solve. It is not uncommon for a salesperson to sell to an opportunity, rather than to a need.

Probing

How do you insure that you are not selling just to an opportunity? By asking the right questions of the customer. Asking the customer questions is defined as probing.

Probing comes in two forms, open probes and closed probes. Open probes encourage the customer to speak freely, to elaborate on problems. Closed probes limit the customer response to a yes or no answer, or a limited range provided by the salesperson. An example of open probes might be:

"Tell me about what is important to you when you select a restaurant?" or "What is the nature of your conference?"

In both cases, the customer is encouraged to discuss freely her or his feelings (and hopefully reveal some needs). The other probe is called a closed probe. The closed probe may sound like this:

"Is location important to you?" or "Do you prefer chain or independently run restaurants?"

The customer can answer yes or no to the first question, and has a limited option for the second question.

Let's go back to differentiating between needs and opportunities. In order to confirm that an opportunity is a need, then a closed probe is appropriate. Let's review the selling example already presented:

Salesperson: "Tell me a little bit about your meetings." *(open probe)*

Customer: "Oh, we have had many lately, but the hotel we use now is too far from the airport." *(opportunity)*

Salesperson: "Is an airport location important to you in choosing a hotel?" *(closed probe)*

Customer: "Not really, my boss lives on the other side of town and doesn't want to change now."

The salesperson has avoided talking about something the customer did not need. The salesperson would then open-probe further, until a customer need or a new opportunity was identified. In some cases, however, the salesperson might address the objective by further probes (why the boss won't change) and suggest a probable solution, before going on to new opportunities.

Once the need has surfaced, the salesperson has to support the need. Supporting is done in two stages: first, by acknowledging the need and, then, introducing the appropriate benefits and features to the customer. Acknowledging the need tells the customer that the salesperson understands the problem to be solved, who then introduces the solution (benefit and feature). An acknowledging statement by the salesperson may be: "I understand your concern for a large ballroom—rear screen projection can take up quite a bit of room."

Benefits and Features

Once the needs of the customer have been established through a series of probes, the customer is introduced to the product benefits and features. A feature is a tangible or intangible subset of the product the customer will buy. It is a characteristic of the service being offered. It is also important to recognize those features

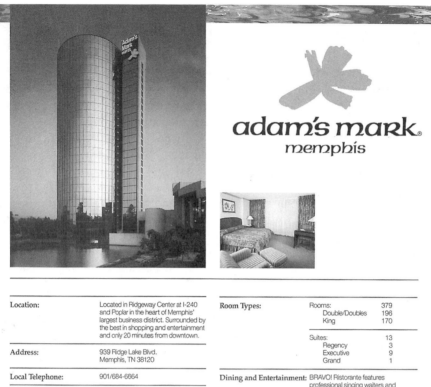

Location:	Located in Ridgeway Center at I-240 and Poplar in the heart of Memphis' largest business district. Surrounded by the best in shopping and entertainment and only 20 minutes from downtown.
Address:	939 Ridge Lake Blvd. Memphis, TN 38120
Local Telephone:	901/684-6664
Fax:	901/762-7411
Reservations:	Consult your local travel agent or call 800-444-ADAM (2326) for reservations at any Adam's Mark Hotel
Airport Transportation:	Free shuttle to and from Memphis International Airport, only 15 minutes. Easy access to I-240 and convenient to I-40 and I-55.
Guest Services:	Fax, copy, and typing service available 7:30 a.m.–4:30 p.m. Same day laundry service, health club, outdoor pool, access to local health club (nominal fee); gift shop, personal checks cashed, and free parking. Wheelchairs available upon request.
Accommodations:	Remote control T.V., complimentary ESPN, & CNN, direct dial telephone and wake up service.

Room Types:	Rooms:	379
	Double/Doubles	196
	King	170
	Suites:	13
	Regency	3
	Executive	9
	Grand	1

Dining and Entertainment: BRAVO! Ristorante features professional singing waiters and waitresses serving Authentic regional Italian and mediterranean specialties with show tunes, opera and operetta on the side. Open daily serving breakfast and lunch, with a themed lunch buffet Monday through Friday. SATCHMO's lounge features live entertainment nightly. Room service available from 6:30 a.m. to 12:00 mid-night.

Locations:

Charlotte
Clearwater Beach, FL
Houston
Indianapolis
Kansas City
Memphis
Philadelphia
St. Louis
Tulsa

Courtesy of Adam's Mark Hotels

FIGURE 15-4   Specifications for meeting planners

that differentiate the product from the rest of the competition. These distinctive features should be especially emphasized if they are important to the customer.

The most important thing to remember is that customers do not buy features; they buy benefits. A benefit is the value of the feature to the customer and should be mentioned first to get attention. Unless the benefit is clearly explained, the customer may not understand why the feature is important. A feature might be a ballroom with high ceilings, the benefit to the customer might be that they can produce a high tech show because the room's high ceilings can

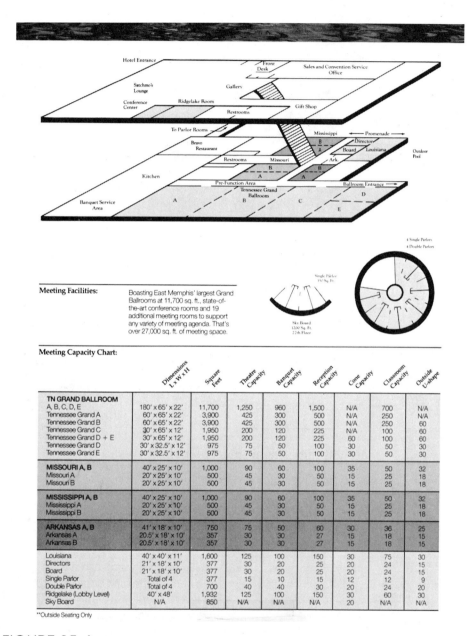

Meeting Facilities: Boasting East Memphis' largest Grand Ballrooms at 11,700 sq. ft., state-of-the-art conference rooms and 19 additional meeting rooms to support any variety of meeting agenda. That's over 27,000 sq. ft. of meeting space.

Meeting Capacity Chart:

	Dimensions L x W x H	Square Feet	Theatre Capacity	Banquet Capacity	Reception Capacity	Cone Capacity	Classroom Capacity	Outside U-shape
TN GRAND BALLROOM								
A, B, C, D, E	180' x 65' x 22'	11,700	1,250	960	1,500	N/A	700	N/A
Tennessee Grand A	60' x 65' x 22'	3,900	425	300	500	N/A	250	N/A
Tennessee Grand B	60' x 65' x 22'	3,900	425	300	500	N/A	250	60
Tennessee Grand C	30' x 65' x 12'	1,950	200	120	225	N/A	100	60
Tennessee Grand D + E	30' x 65' x 12'	1,950	200	120	225	60	100	60
Tennessee Grand D	30' x 32.5' x 12'	975	75	50	100	30	50	30
Tennessee Grand E	30' x 32.5' x 12'	975	75	50	100	30	50	30
MISSOURI A, B	40' x 25' x 10'	1,000	90	60	100	35	50	32
Missouri A	20' x 25' x 10'	500	45	30	50	15	25	18
Missouri B	20' x 25' x 10'	500	45	30	50	15	25	18
MISSISSIPPI A, B	40' x 25' x 10'	1,000	90	60	100	35	50	32
Mississippi A	20' x 25' x 10'	500	45	30	50	15	25	18
Mississippi B	20' x 25' x 10'	500	45	30	50	15	25	18
ARKANSAS A, B	41' x 18' x 10'	750	75	50	60	30	36	25
Arkansas A	20.5' x 18' x 10'	357	30	30	27	15	18	15
Arkansas B	20.5' x 18' x 10'	357	30	30	27	15	18	15
Louisiana	40' x 40' x 11'	1,600	125	100	150	30	75	30
Directors	21' x 18' x 10'	377	30	20	25	20	24	15
Board	21' x 18' x 10'	377	30	20	25	20	24	15
Single Parlor	Total of 4	377	15	10	15	12	12	9
Double Parlor	Total of 4	700	40	40	30	20	24	20
Ridgelake (Lobby Level)	40' x 48'	1,932	125	100	150	30	60	30
Sky Board	N/A	850	N/A	N/A	N/A	20	N/A	N/A

**Outside Seating Only

FIGURE 15-4 (continued)

accommodate complicated audiovisual requirements. A feature might be a good location; the benefit to the customer may be that the attendees of the meeting do not have far to drive from their offices.

To sell the potential customer on buying the product, the good salesperson will attempt to match the benefits and features to the customer's objectives and needs. Features that may not provide any benefit to the customer should be excluded from the presentation. A primary mistake made in direct sales is to misunderstand the needs of the customer, while simultaneously presenting features and benefits of the product that are unimportant.

One of the authors, training a salesperson on the selling process, encountered the following scenario:

Watch Guest Quarters raise it to an art.

It's sad, really, that doing the same thing over and over again doesn't often produce excellence, but merely predictability.

You might arrange your meeting through a big convention hotel, and settle for their routine best. Or, you can insist on something special, like Guest Quarters®.

At Guest Quarters Suite Hotels, we pride ourselves in hosting only smaller business meetings. And we treat each one like it was the most important event we've ever held. Because we believe that every occasion, and every client that we serve, is one of a kind.

Every Guest Quarters Suite Hotel has conference rooms to handle your small meeting. Plus Executive Suites for more private conferences. Our meeting coordinators will help plan everything, from flowers and special menus to all the necessary audio-visual equipment. Whatever the size, our meeting and catering services will please the most sophisticated tastes. Your guests stay in spacious suites, with all the amenities you expect in a first-class hotel. Plus business services like photocopying, fax machines, couriers, overnight shipping and typing. We also offer rentals of personal computers, VCRs and cellular telephones. All to help increase your, and your guests, productivity.

Small meetings. Short notice.

We even offer a "Meetings-In-A-Minute" program, specifically designed to expedite meeting arrangements for groups of fewer than fifty guests on short notice (from one to thirty days). We understand your need for the very best—brief notice or not, and our "Meetings-In-A-Minute" manager can provide excellent suggestions, and helpful tips, while confirming arrangements with just one phone call. We've even designed a "Meetings-In-A-Minute" checklist for you.

Call For Our Free Videotape.

Watch us raise meetings to an art on our video, "Small Business Meetings The Guest Quarters Way." We think it conveys what makes us, and our guests, special. Call today toll-free, or contact me personally, to order your free copy. And watch us make your next small business meeting perfect the first time.

GUEST QUARTERS®
SUITE HOTELS

Courtesy of Guest Quarters Suite Hotels

FIGURE 15-5   A video offer for graphic presentations

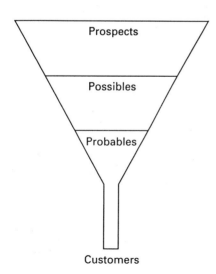

FIGURE 15-6   Many prospects, but few customers

Salesperson: "Tell me what is important to you when you choose a hotel for your meetings." *(open probe)*

Customer: "I want a hotel that can handle a large check-out all at once. *(need)* The last hotel we went to took one-and-a-half hours for our guests to pay their bills!"

Salesperson: "Was the problem the billing or the time to get *through the line?" (closed probe)*

Customer: "The time to get through the line."

Salesperson: "I can see why it is important for the group to check out effortlessly. At our hotel, we have video check-out to make leaving the hotel easier."

In this case, the salesperson was doing fine (satisfying the needs of the customer), until she introduced a feature (video check-out), without clearly articulating the benefit. The customer thought that the hotel had a video camera in the lobby to record check-outs. The customer was perplexed as to how this would ease the check-out process. The correct presentation would have been:

Salesperson: "I can see why it is important for the group to check out effortlessly. At our hotel, there is no waiting in line at all. *(benefit)* Attendees can call their bill up on their in-room television and check out right there! *(advantage)* We have video check-out to make leaving the hotel easier." *(feature)*

Once the feature was translated into the value for the customer, the customer accepted the benefit.

Like this example, it is sometimes necessary to translate the features of the facility into the benefits because, while customers may have some idea of the feature being sold, they may be skeptical, have a misunderstanding, or have the wrong impression from previous experience. For example, a health club may not seem to be in need of translation into benefits, but there is a big difference in the quality of health clubs in hotels. One of the authors stayed one night in a hotel with a "health club" that was a converted guestroom that smelled badly and sported one 15-year-old weight machine and a broken stationary bicycle. The following evening, at a different hotel, the health club had 5,000 sq.ft. of space with spas, Jacuzzis, state-of-the-art training equipment, personal instructors, etc. If a health club is relevant to the customer, then the benefits should be explained.

The same holds true for other generic hotel features. A concierge in a Le Meridien Hotel may be sophisticated, multilingual, and resourceful. A concierge in a Ramada Inn may be the manager's secretary. Both are marketed as concierge services, with very different benefits to customers. Convention services in one hotel may be a staff of ten, in another the bellman may also set the room. Translating what the features do for the customer is important in the sales process once you have determined what is important to the customer. Figure 15-7 shows a sample benefits/features form to be used in the selling process.

Once the need has surfaced, and been supported, other needs are sought to which the

salesperson can respond, by further probing. When it seems that you have uncovered all the needs, and responded to them, it may be time to close the sale.

Customer Attitudes

The salesperson can have an easy customer, like those in the scenarios outlined earlier in this chapter or, more likely, difficult customers. Recognizing customer attitudes is important for the successful selling effort.

The most common attitudes encountered on a sales call are skepticism or misunderstanding, indifference, and objection. Skepticism is evident when a customer doubts the benefit introduced to satisfy the need. A customer may say, "I do not think that your food is as good as you say it is." The salesperson would overcome skepticism or misunderstanding in a customer by introducing a "proof source," something that proves to the customer that the benefit introduced is as presented by the salesperson. A testimonial letter from another satisfied customer may be the proof needed to convince the skeptical customer that the food is actually as good as the salesperson says it is. A restaurant review from a local food critic may also be a good proof source. An independent source, in writing, may be all that is needed to convince the skeptical customer.

A more difficult customer attitude is indifference. When a customer is satisfied with another facility, or has internal options, the customer is considered indifferent. The customer may say, "I am already using the banquet facilities at the Fontainbleau Hotel" (i.e., "Why should I change?"). This customer is indifferent and not open to considering alternatives. The salesperson must provide him or her with a reason to consider options. If the customer has alternative internal options—for example, meetings rooms at the office—such a customer might see no need to have meetings at a hotel. In this case, the hotel salesperson would emphasize the benefits of not having office distractions during a meeting. By meeting off-site, attendees stay focused.

The solution for handling an indifferent customer is to probe for unrealized needs—unreal-

Objective-Benefit-Feature (OBF) Chart

Market Segment: _____

Customer Industry/Organization: _____

Customer Title/Job Function: _____

General Customer Needs (by Priority):

1. _____   4. _____

2. _____   5. _____

3. _____   6. _____

Customer Objectives	Benefits	Features

FIGURE 15-7   A sample benefits/features form for selling

ized needs that may well be the weakness of a competitor. Let's stay with the Fontainbleau example. The well-prepared salesperson would know the weakness of the competition, in this case the small size of the parking facility. The salesperson knows that there are never enough parking spaces at this hotel; he would probe to determine if there was a need to satisfy this problem.

The sales conversation might go like this (but probably not this easily!):

Customer: "I appreciate you coming by to see me, but I do not see the reason for the call. I am using the Fontainbleau for my banquets, and I am satisfied at this time." (expressing indifference)

Salesperson: "I see. Do you mind if I ask you some questions anyway?"

Customer: "Go ahead."

Salesperson: "I know that you hold some very large functions. Is it important for you to have enough parking for all of your quests?" *(closed probe for unrealized needs)*

Customer: "As a matter of fact, it is. At the last meeting the speaker was late to the podium because she couldn't find a place to park." *(expressing an opportunity)*

Salesperson: "Then having enough parking for your guests is critical for a successful banquet?" *(closed probe to determine need)*

Customer: "Certainly."

The salesperson has now uncovered a need and addressed that need by supporting it.

The final customer attitude is one of objection. Objection occurs when there is a real problem with your product offering that cannot be changed. If the customer wants a hotel near the airport, and yours is not, then you are dealing with an objection. If the customer wants a restaurant with a private dining area for a group, and yours does not have one, then you are dealing with an objection. Or, the objection that cannot be changed may be on the customer's side. For example, corporate mandates and prescribed hotel lists may dictate that travelers will not be reimbursed if they use your hotel.

Objections are very hard to overcome. It is important to view objections as positive customer feedback rather than as personal reverses during the sales process. Anticipating specific objections is the best way to prepare for them. The strategy for solving the objection is to present benefits already accepted, that outweigh the objection presented, or verify why the objection is important and figure out an alternative. Although the customer many want an airport location, the fact that your hotel is newly renovated, with a better pool and more flexible meeting space, may outweigh the location objection; or the fact that it is nearer the office, allowing most attendees who drive easier access.

A restaurant customer desiring a private room for a meal may be presented with more parking facilities, better food, and billing privileges. After all, customers make trade-offs between the different attributes of a product or service and choose the one that offers the best bundle of benefits. After reviewing the entire "buy" decision, the restaurant customer may be convinced to choose the restaurant without the private dining room. The focus, once again, should be on the objective and needs of the customer. You either overcome the objection by providing a solution acceptable to the customer *or* agree that it cannot be overcome, hoping that the "pros" of using your facility will outweigh the "cons."

Closing

The close, or signed contract, should come naturally without having to ask for it. If you've done a good job selling, and if you've handled all objections, the client may tell you he is ready to sign. Asking prematurely for a close puts too much pressure on the buyer and may lose the sale. Closing a sales call entails asking the customer for a commitment. Hence, a sales call close might be getting to meet the decision-maker's boss on the next visit, having the customer visit the hotel, or making a presentation to the board that will make the decision.

The ultimate closing occurs when the salesperson "asks for the business." (This entire process, of course, does not necessarily take place in one meeting.) At this point, the salesperson summarizes all of the benefits accepted by the customer, and then asks for the customer's commitment.

It should be apparent that the sales approach is a difficult one at best. With many new facilities in each market, the selling process is now more competitive than ever. The salesperson who has the correct selling skills, and uses them on the sales call, will close on a larger portion of business.

Follow-up

One of the most common complaints of meeting planners in the hospitality industry is that the person who made the sale is not around when the services are actually being performed. A convention or meeting may be booked in a hotel two to ten years in advance. The promises made by someone who may no longer be at the property, or who may be out trying to sell to another account, still should be kept when the event takes place. Too often, operations says, "We can't do that." Or, human error in incorrectly tracing a file can cause untold havoc. To create good word-of-mouth communications and to get customers to come back, follow-up is extremely important. Often, it is the convention or conference services manager who does this (Figure 15-8); working closely with this person may be as important to the salesperson as working with the customer.

Thus, the role of the professional salesperson is evolving. The "order taker" of the 1970s became the "order getter" in the 1980s. In the 1990s, when strategic marketing is a more common practice, successful salespeople will have to be relationship managers. This is especially important in service businesses where trust, credibility, and confidence that promises will be kept, form an essential part of the relationship between the buyer and the sales representative.

Of course, the working relationship of the salesperson with operations is also critical, as noted above. Customers sometimes ask the impossible—but, sometimes the impossible can be accomplished with the right knowledge and working relationship.

Sales Management

The management of an effective sales force entails integrating a variety of skills. Proper account management, organization of the sales team, development of personnel, and motivation of the workforce, all combine to make a sales team efficient. The skills necessary to manage the selling process are very different from the skills needed to sell. The best salesperson in an organization may be promoted to sales director and fail. The gap between good selling skills and good management skills is a wide one.

Account Management

The management of customers is called account management. The method of managing the sales process is called the account management system. The account management system balances the resources of the sales team with the profile of the customer base. The account management system allows the sales team to manage its customer accounts like a portfolio of stocks, spending time on the customers that will produce the most business, while balancing many smaller accounts in case one large account is lost.

The foundation of the account management system is the sales equation:

Past Customers + New Customers = Goals.

Past customers (or repeat guests) provide some of the business, and new customers provide the rest. If the products and services delivered are what the customer expects, new customers will become past customers, making everyone's job easier. First, past customers need to be analyzed and prioritized in terms of the business they provide. An example of this prioritization process is:

Category	Potential Rooms
A	500 +
B	100 to 499
C	less than 100

The past customer base is then placed into each category, and each customer account should be called according to its potential business. Customers who provide the most business are called on more than customers who provide less business. The account management system makes sure, however, that the smaller potential customers do get called on a regular basis.

Calculations are then made as to the total number of calls that the sales team needs to make to their past customers. These steps are indicated as follows:

Category	Number of Customer Accounts	Number of Calls per Year	Total Calls per Year
A	150	12	1,800
B	300	6	1,800
C	500	2	1,000
Total	950		4,600

The Westin Hotels in Singapore offer one of the largest and most comprehensive meeting and convention facilities in South East Asia.

THE WESTIN STAMFORD & THE WESTIN PLAZA
Singapore

Tel: (65)338-8585 Fax: (65)336-8783

FIGURE 15-8 The conventions services manager "completes the sale" on premise

This calculation shows that there needs to be 4,600 sales calls per year to properly cover the past customer base. Next, the call schedule is calculated, including new customers:

Position	Number of Calls per Week	Annualized
Director of Sales	20	960
Sales Manager #1	40	1,920
Sales Manager #2	40	1,920
Sales Manager #3	40	1,920
Total		6,720

With the past customers prioritized, and the resources allocated, the sales equation is again utilized to determine if the sales department has the proper perspective on their past and

Past Customers	+	New Customers	= Goals
4,600	+	2,120	= 6,720
68.5%		31.5%	100%

new customers:

The goals are derived from the resources available. Past customers are calculated from the account management system. New customers, or the prospecting effort, are calculated by subtracting the past customers from the goals. If the goals are less than or equal to the past customers, then new customers (prospecting) are being neglected.

For a mature property—one that has been in the marketplace for at least three years within the same product class and positioning—the above is the ideal model for the allocation of resources. The sales team should focus about 70 percent of its time on past customers, and the remaining 30 percent should be dedicated to finding new customers. In new hotels, restaurants, and catering facilities, the sales equation may be the reverse; with a small customer base the need for prospecting is intensified. Also, in some organizations, an account manager helps to maintain accounts so that the salesperson can be out creating new ones. The sales equa-

tion can be used to focus a sales team on its priorities.

The next step of the account management system is to assign revenue potential to each of the accounts. The following example continues the hotel scenario, with the understanding that room-nights could easily translate to restaurant covers, airline seats, or other hospitality sales units. Room-night revenue potential for each account is determined so the sales team can begin to develop the appropriate action steps needed to fill the gaps in revenues:

Category	Number of Accounts	Room-nights
A	150	75,000
B	300	90,000
C	500	30,000
Total	950	195,000

From this calculation, the director of sales can determine that, if all of the past customers on the account management system are called regularly, the hotel can potentially book 195,000 rooms from past customers. In most cases the goal, or budget, is higher than that. Let's look again at the sales equation in terms of room-nights:

Past Customers	+ New Customers =	Goals
195,000	+ 15,000	= 210,000

Now the selling task is clearer. Set the parameters and call goals, make sales calls on all of the past customers, and the hotel should sell 195,000 rooms. The goal, however, is 210,000 rooms. Therefore the sales team has to prospect, or find, 15,000 new room-nights.

Lowest Common Denominator (LCD)
Selling 210,000 rooms in one year may seem like an awesome task and, without making the task smaller, it is! So, the next step of the account management system is the breaking down of large tasks into smaller ones, or the *lowest common denominator* (LCD). The following model illustrates how LCD works:

210,000 Rooms Sold
15,000 New Rooms
7,500 New Customers
150 New Accounts
3 New Accounts per Week

195,000 past customers
two-night stay
50 rooms per year/avg. customer
48 weeks per year
3 sales managers

1 New Account per week opened per sales manager

The sales team can "go out and sell" 210,000 rooms for the year. Without applying LCD to the problem, the results are usually unfocused. The sales team becomes very busy trying to sell 210,000 rooms, but many times not productively. However, the sales team, after working through the LCD system, can define its strategy: to manage the account management system and open one new account per sales manager per week.

Sales Action Plan

The marketing plan is the overall vision for the upcoming year. It encompasses all of the marketing activities, including advertising, public relations, direct mail, and other communication vehicles. The sales action plan narrows the broader vision of the marketing plan and assigns detailed tasks to the sales managers. The sales action plan allows the sales team to take the marketing plan and step it down to the execution phase of the process. It enables the sales team to execute the portion of the marketing plan for which they are responsible. A typical sales action plan is shown in Table 15-3.

The sales action plan follows all of the phases of the account management system: calling on past customers and new customers. Goals are established through LCD for bookings and new accounts. The salesperson can clearly see what needs to be done on a monthly, weekly, and daily basis.

The sales action plan is formatted to accommodate 12 weeks of work. Each quarter, a new sales action plan is written to reflect the next 12-week period's work. This planning process allows the sales team to be flexible, to change activities to reflect market conditions. The umbrella marketing plan is written to give the direction and overall focus for the sales team.

Within the next 12 months, many assumptions made during the formation of the marketing plan may change. The quarterly sales action plan allows the team to adjust its course quickly.

The quarterly plan may also be broken down further into a weekly plan. Figure 15-9 shows a sample format by the week, by the day, and the weekly productivity.

Organization of the Sales Team

The size of the sales force is determined by the number of sales calls that should be made on a yearly basis. Staffing the sales office should result from a mathematical calculation of sales calls needed to satisfy current customers and those needed to find a reasonable amount of new customers. This is different from the practice in which a salesperson is added only when sales are down, and is eliminated when sales are up. In those situations, resources may be overallocated or underallocated. On a mathematical basis, a salesperson will usually handle between 250 and 350 accounts a year, depending on the market mix of the property.

Once staffing guidelines are established, salespeople are usually organized by geographic territory, market, event type (e.g., weddings), and/or product line. For example, in terms of potential customers for a hotel, the city of Cleveland can be divided in half. In order to keep the sales process orderly, one sales representative may be assigned to the east side while another is assigned to the west side.

Product lines are assigned by the type of service within the hotel that the salesperson represents. There are three types of product offerings sold through direct sales: group, transient, and catering. The group product line is for customers who purchase a number of rooms

TABLE 15-3   A Sales Action Plan

NAME: Mary Jones   Quarter: 3rd

SALES EQUATION\SALES CALLS

PAST CUSTOMERS	+	PROSPECTING	=	GOALS
100	+	60	=	160 MONTH
25	+	15	=	40 WEEK
5	+	3	=	8 DAY

BOOKING GOALS

480 MONTH	120 WEEK	30 DAY

NEW ACCOUNTS OPENED

20 MONTH	5 WEEK	1 DAY

PROSPECTING RESOURCES

*Meeting planner directories, convention & visitors bureau leads,
referrals from current customers, newspaper leads, etc.*

Action Plan by Week

Week 1 Sales calls to Hartford _____
Week 2 Make appts. for trade show _____
Week 3 Attend trade show_____
Week 4 Develop direct mail for groups_____
Week 5 Sales calls to Boston_____
Week 6 Send direct mail to planners _____
Week 7 Local sales calls _____
Week 8 Local sales calls _____
Week 9 Follow up leads from direct mail_____
Week 10 Follow up leads from direct mail_____
Week 11 Follow up leads from direct mail_____
Week 12 Develop next quarter sales action plan _____

at the same time. The group salesperson may or may not sell the function space simultaneously. A bus tour would be considered a group but would have no need for function space. A corporation might have the same number of guestroom requirements as the bus tour but have extensive meeting space needs. Depending on the size of the hotel, there may be more than one group salesperson; for example, there may be a need for a separate convention salesperson if this is a major market for the hotel.

Transient salespeople sell to customers who have a need to book guestrooms on an individual basis. The catering salesperson normally handles meetings and social events like weddings that don't require a large number of sleeping rooms. This person sells the ballroom space for functions with food and beverage, if possible.

Different organizations, of course, have different organizational structures and duty assignments. One company may have its *outside* sales force out of the office and cold calling four

SALES TEAM ACTIVITY REPORT

Name _____   Week Ending _____

Guest Quarters

SALES ACTIVITY AND RESULTS									
ACTION STEPS	DAY	MONDAY	TUES.	WED.	THUR.	FRIDAY	TOTALS		
	DATE						WEEK	MTD	
PERSONAL SALES CALLS	OBJECTIVE								
	RESULT								
TELEPHONE SALES CALLS	OBJECTIVE								
	RESULT								
NEW ACCOUNT DEVELOPMENT	OBJECTIVE								
	RESULT								
INTER HOTEL REFERRALS	OBJECTIVE								
	RESULT								
WHOLESALE/VOLUME ACCOUNTS SIGNED	OBJECTIVE								
	RESULT								
SALES CONTACT TOTALS	OBJECTIVES								
	RESULTS								

SEE BACK PAGE FOR PRODUCTIVITY QUOTAS AND RESULTS

KEY ACCOUNT ACTIVITY AND RESULTS			
ORGANIZATION	OBJECTIVE	RESULT	ACTION STEP

FIGURE 15-9   A sales action plan format

days a week, with one day in the office writing call reports. Sales leads get passed to *inside* sales people who close sales and maintain accounts. Another company may have sales managers who spend half their time inside and half outside. Leads are generated, pursued, and finalized. An inside support person, an account manager, is available to maintain accounts. Other companies may have variations of these two approaches.

WEEKLY PLAN

PRIORITIES FOR THIS WEEK:	RESULTS
1.	
2.	
3.	
4.	
5.	

DAY: DATE:

	SCHEDULED ACTIVITY	OBJECTIVE	RESULTS	ACTION STEP
8 AM				
9 AM				
10 AM				
11 AM				
12 NOON				
1 PM				
2 PM				
3 PM				
4 PM				
5 PM				
EXPENSES:				

DAY: DATE:

	SCHEDULED ACTIVITY	OBJECTIVE	RESULTS	ACTION STEP
8 AM				
9 AM				
10 AM				
11 AM				
12 NOON				
1 PM				
2 PM				
3 PM				
4 PM				
5 PM				
EXPENSES:				

DAY: DATE:

	SCHEDULED ACTIVITY	OBJECTIVE	RESULTS	ACTION STEP
8 AM				
9 AM				
10 AM				
11 AM				
12 NOON				
1 PM				
2 PM				
3 PM				
4 PM				
5 PM				
EXPENSES:				

FIGURE 15-9   (continued)

It takes a very disciplined effort to keep an effective sales organization on a focused track. The director of sales needs to cue in salespeople as to when business is most needed. For example, weddings may book a ballroom a year in advance. Large groups, such as an Elks Club convention, may also want the ballroom for the same weekend, but also will reserve a large portion of sleeping rooms. If a wedding with a few overnight rooms was already booked for the

WEEKLY PRODUCTIVITY REPORT

Name _____   Week Ending _____

DEFINITE BOOKINGS

ORGANIZATION	NEW	EXISTING	DATES	RATES	COVERS/ SUITE NIGHTS	CATERING / SUITE REVENUE

CANCELLED DEFINITES

TENTATIVE BOOKINGS

ORGANIZATION	NEW	EXISTING	DATES	RATES	COVERS/ SUITE NIGHTS	CATERING / SUITE REVENUE

CANCELLED TENTATIVES

PRODUCTIVITY SUMMARY

DEFINITES		COVERS/ SUITE NIGHTS	AVERAGE RATE	CATERING/ SUITE REVENUE	CATERING/ SUITE REV. QUOTA	TENTATIVES		COVERS/ SUITE NIGHTS	AVERAGE RATE	CATERING/ SUITE REVENUE	CATERING/ SUITE REV. QUOTA
	MONTHLY/WEEKLY TOTALS						MONTHLY WEEKLY TOTALS				
	QUOTAS						QUOTAS				

FIGURE 15-9   (continued)

ballroom, the Elks Club business might be lost. Conversely, if the wedding was turned away and the Elks Club did not choose the hotel, the ballroom might be empty on that date. Such decisions are made on a daily basis.

Product Line Management   Most hotel sales offices are structured to sell the three distinct products that we have discussed: transient programs for the individual traveler, such as Marriott's Honored Guest Awards, Sheraton's

S.E.T., and Omni's E.S.P. programs; the group product that offers the customer the opportunity to purchase both sleeping rooms and function facilities for a meeting; and the catering product for the customer who needs function or meeting space without guestrooms (the term for this last type of business is *freestanding*).

Many customer accounts have a need for more than one product, and in some cases a need for all three. For example, a planner at IBM might have occasion to need transient guestrooms, group space, and freestanding function space in the same hotel. Many present methods, however, divide the sales effort and provide for three different salespeople to represent the three products in the same hotel.

Most other industries do not operate in this manner. For instance, you can buy an entire range of automobiles or insurance coverage from the same person. Why, then, does the hotel industry make the same IBM customer talk to three different representatives to buy very similar products in the same location? The industry has been slow to react to the customer in this regard. The customer experience of trying to purchase various hotel products from the same hotel can easily mean negotiating with six to seven salespeople in one year.

The product line approach to sales, in which one sales representative services all three products for the same customer (sometimes called "one-stop shopping"), is a method to gain competitive edge over sales offices organized in the traditional format. Figure 15-10, in fact, shows how Marriott has developed one-stop shopping for IBM.

This is not to say that the current transient salesperson should be out selling weddings—that would result in utter chaos. It means that customers who have a need for more than one hotel product should be handled by the same salesperson in order to offer continuity to the customer during the sales process. Those customers who have only a need for one product (e.g., a wedding) should be handled in the regular manner, in the case of a wedding by the catering salesperson. The difficulty with the product line approach, and one which has slowed its acceptance, is that each salesperson

Just One Number Plans Your Next Meeting

1-800-4-IBM-113
(1-800-442-6113)

Marriott.

To reach a Marriott professional dedicated to assisting you with planning IBM conferences requiring 10 or more guestrooms, please call:

1-800-4-IBM-113 (Phone)
(1-800-442-6113)
1-703-506-2637 (Fax)

Marriott Hotels • Resorts • Suites
Courtyard by Marriott • Residence Inn by Marriott
Fairfield Inn by Marriott

FIGURE 15-10   One-stop shopping for IBM at Marriott

must be familiar with all the hotel's products and how to sell them.

Development of Personnel

The development of personnel is critical to the success of a sales organization. If the wrong people are hired, business will be lost. If good salespeople leave to go to a competitor for better opportunities, which frequently happens, there is additional opportunity to lose business. If a position remains open for any length of time, necessary sales calls to existing and new customers will not be made. Companies need to be conscious of this problem and address the reasons for it. Through better selection and training Ritz-Carlton reduced its sales force turnover from 40 percent to 10 percent, once they had identified the problem that salespeople well-trained by other hotel chains did not necessarily fit into the Ritz-Carlton mode.

Other reasons for high turnover include the "move up and out" philosophy. Promotions often involve relocation. If a salesperson is unwilling to relocate, the only other way to further a career is to move to another hotel. Also, salespeople are highly visible, not only to their clients but also in networking functions. This high exposure provides increased opportunities to move to other positions.

Development of an effective sales staff begins with recruitment. There should be an ongoing effort to locate and know the best salespeople in the marketplace. While new talent can be solicited at the college graduate level, there is still a void at the experienced salesperson level. Organizations such as Hotel Sales and Marketing Association International are good forums for getting to know the better salespeople in an area.

Training is critical to the development of salespeople. Although there are many existing sales training programs, the challenge is to use them. At least one month of training is necessary for new salespeople to minimally learn the product and understand the needs of customers. Even seasoned salespeople need to be constantly trained through role-playing and sales meetings, to keep their skills sharp. Training also indicates the level of commitment that the company has toward the individual development of a salesperson's career.

Ethics All salespeople must develop a code of ethics, both personally and through the company. There will be situations when ethical dilemmas will be encountered, and salespersons should adhere to guiding principles that allow

them to conduct their business with honesty and integrity. Several of these ethical issues are shown in Table 15-4.

Another perspective on ethics is provided by Thomas McCarthy, a 40-year hotel marketer who now provides hotel sales seminars. McCarthy asked a group of hotel sales and marketing people if they thought the following situations were ethical:

1. You offer one company, which has an average of ten reservations a month, a $100 rate. The company accepts. On the same day you offer another company the same rate for the same number of reservations. The prospect says it's too high, so you offer a $90 rate.
2. A hotel has a weekend policy that, if walk-ins ask for the weekend rate, they get it for $69; if they don't ask, they are charged $85.
3. A report indicates that an association has signed a contract with another hotel for next year's meeting. Your boss tells you to call the association and offer 50 percent off the other hotel's rate if it will break the contract and come to your hotel.

Results: 1) 37 percent said the action was unethical; 2) 60 percent said the practice was unethical; and 3) 67 percent said the request was unethical. All three practices are common. McCarthy offers the following two questions to answer when quoting rates:

1. If the public knew about this policy, what would be the reaction?

    If the reaction would be negative, there's something wrong with the policy.
2. If someone asked why one customer got a lower rate, could it be explained in a way that a logical person would accept and understand?

    If not, the practice is probably unethical.

    Apply these two questions to the three scenarios above and see what you think.[8]

---

[8]Thomas T. McCarthy, "Fair Rates Improve Profits and Image," *Hotel & Resort Industry,* January, 1994, pp. 12–13.

TABLE 15-4   Ethical Issues in Personal Selling

The Salesperson's Company
Misrepresentation of call reports.
Misrepresentation of expense accounts.
Use of company assets for personal benefit.
Conflict-of-interest situations.
Disclosure of proprietary company information.
Disparagement of the company.

The Salesperson's Customers and Prospects
Misrepresentation of yourself.
Misrepresentation of your company.
Misrepresentation of your products or services.
Use of high-pressure selling tactics.
Inappropriate gift-giving.
Disclosure of proprietary customer information.

The Salesperson's Competitors
Disparagement of a competitor's company.
Disparagement of a competitor's product or service.
Disparagement of a competitor's sales representative.

Source: John I. Coppett and William A. Staples, "Professional Selling: a relationship management process," Cincinnati: South-Western Publishing Co., 1990, p. 365

Motivation

Salespeople need to be consistently motivated to be effective. While this may be true of all job categories, it is especially true of salespeople, who represent the product on a daily basis.

Unlike their counterparts in the operations aspect of the hotel business, salespeople are usually paid salary plus commission or performance bonus. Normally, the operations people are paid a bonus based on the financial progress of the property and, one hopes, customer feedback. Salespeople are paid on their productivity, based upon quotas. Quotas are developed based upon the territory, the market, and the product sold. This quota is normally derived from the budget that the hotel has set for the sales team for that year. Once quotas are established, the salespeople are paid for achievement over and above the quota. Some incentives are paid monthly, and others quarterly or yearly. It is likely that the more immediate the gratification, the more motivated the salesperson will be.

Productivity, of course, is not the easiest thing to measure because it is not simply a matter of room-nights sold and/or revenue gained. To put this in perspective we cite from an article by Eric Orkin, consultant to the hotel industry in yield management:

In the hotel industry, we use averages to understand how we are doing and to help make decisions. But the premise is unsound: there is no average room night.

Consider the following one month's sales *chart:*

Sales Manager	Room-nights Sold	Average Rate	Total Revenue
Alan	600	$100	$60,000
Barry	583	$103	$60,000
Cathy	700	$ 85.71	$60,000
Debra	680	$ 99	$67,320

| | High-demand Days | | Medium-demand Days | | Low-demand Days | |
	Room-nights	ADR	Room-nights	ADR	Room-nights	ADR
Alan			600	$100		
Barry	583	$103				
Cathy	250	$103	250	$ 97	200	50
Debra	680	$ 99				

Who did the best job? Debra is the revenue leader with a good ADR. Barry has the highest ADR but the lowest room-night volume. Alan is in the middle. Cathy has the highest room-night volume but may be "giving away" the rooms.

Now consider the expanded sales chart at the top of the page.

The picture of efficiency and productivity now changes. Debra is selling high-demand room-nights at discount. Barry may be missing opportunities on off-peak days. Alan is okay. Cathy is the star; she is selling low-demand, as well as high-demand days; her ADR is justified because many of her room-nights would otherwise have remained unfilled.[9]

Orkin's point is, "If you use averages to measure performance, people will make decisions to improve the averages whether or not the numbers are good for the hotel.... The value of a room-night is a reflection of the probability that it can be sold and the rate it can command." If salespeople are motivated by goals, then those goals must be measured by measures other than averages.

Other forms of motivation, such as incentive trips and merchandise, are becoming part of the motivational toolbox of sales organizations. These are also based upon quotas and may be used when there is a short-term sales gap that needs to be filled. For an example, see Figure 15-11.

Sales and Operations

"Sales sells and operations provides" is an expression that describes what is often seen as the relationship between sales and operations. As previously mentioned, that relationship is a critical one and needs further explanation here, because a conflict between sales and operations can be incredibly damaging to a hotel's relationship marketing effort. In fact, this situation represents a real need for internal marketing, discussed in Chapter 2.

Knowledge of the product and capabilities of the organization is essential to successful selling. Constant and continuous communications between sales and operations are imperative to effective marketing for a hospitality organization. If what the salesperson sells cannot be delivered, the hotel will in most cases eventually lose the customer (and the salesperson!). It is natural for a salesperson to want to make promises in order to make the sale.

Salespeople have two difficulties in this regard, which they need to overcome. One is perception. Operations people see salespeople largely when they are in-house entertaining clients (e.g., having lunch, giving tours) and see their job as a "cushy" one. The second one is that salespeople have no direct authority over operations people, yet they need to make certain that their promises are executed properly. This can cause friction in the lines of authority needed to get the job done and keep promises to customers.

A thorough knowledge of the product and the capabilities of the organization will go a long way toward keeping these promises from creating unreasonable expectations for the customer. If the salesperson is not sure that the hotel can deliver, then he or she should confirm with operations before making the promise. This not only provides a confirmation, it also gets operations into the act so that there is

---

[9]Eric Orkin,"Breaking the law of averages," *Lodging Hospitality,* February, 1994, pp. 24–25.

$$

HOW TO MAKE MORE MONEY AND SCORE BIG BROWNIE POINTS WITH THE D.O.S.

1ST WAY! For every actual group roomnight in February booked after 1/11/94, you will receive $2.00

Minimum rate Monday-Thursday $79
Minimum rate Friday-Sunday $69

Example: Computerland Group 10 roomnights for 3 nights at a rate of $89 = $60 for Sales Manager

2ND WAY! Whoever exceeds 300 actual group room nights in the month of February will receive $100 BONUS on top of the "1st Way" promotion!

Cathy/Tracy: If you <u>exceed</u> the budgeted GQ Club goal of 300 roomnights in February, you will both receive $100

Get on your mark, set . . . Book 'em DANNO!!!!!

(* Please note the rate restriction of $99 over Super Show)

Amy <u>will</u> be accepting bribes for any inquiry calls!
Simply put your name and offer in a sealed envelope and return ASAP.

$$

FIGURE 15-11   Motivating to fill a short-term sales gap

more likelihood that someone will follow through.

If both parties are truly tuned in to solving the customer's problems, and each party fully understands the problems of the other, satisfactory resolution is most always possible. This is both internal and relationship marketing practiced at their best. It is the marketing and management leadership of the property or the company that sets the tone and that should make sure that it happens. The salesperson must go back to dissatisfied customers and ask for their business once more.

Summary

The sales process is becoming more complex in the competitive marketplaces of the 1990s. The selling process is not unlike the marketing process; understanding the needs of the customer is the primary focus of the sales organization. Understanding the needs of the customers is the foundation of selling. The selling process involves the skilled use of probing, supporting, and closing to manage the sale. Different customer attitudes—skepticism, indifference, and objection—are encountered on each sales call. All three are handled with professional selling skills.

Having the ability to sell is only half of the selling process. Planning the sales function is also important. Tools such as an account management system, LCD, and a sales action plan all assist the sales manager to focus on what is important. Maintaining a balance of resources to call on past and new customers is critical to the success of the entire organization.

Finding new customers has become a difficult task; each hospitality entity is vying for a smaller base of customers to fill expanding numbers of hotel rooms and meeting space. New methods to find customers, through direct mail and telemarketing, have replaced "cold calling" as methodologies for generating leads.

A sales organization needs to have a clear definition of the markets that it wants to attract and a recognition that it needs to penetrate competitors' businesses in order to increase its own. Additionally, the organization has to be knowledgeable and consistent about its goals through the sales organization and be prepared to sell the customer with appropriate features and benefits. The sales office that organizes the sales team carefully and develops and motivates its people effectively will be the most productive. As the marketplace absorbs more new hotels and demand remains stagnant, the competitive fight for the same business will intensify. Those who establish a strong plan based on the components discussed in this chapter will have the competitive edge necessary to win fair market share.

Discussion Questions

1. Describe the correct selling scenario for a customer who responds to your questions like this: "I am currently using a facility with which I am very satisfied."
2. Develop three proof sources for a banquet facility.
3. For an account management system, create a call schedule and a sales equation, given the following information:

Account Base Category	Number of Files
A	100
B	250
C	300

Positions: Director of Sales, Sales Manager #1

4. Break down the above task to its lowest common denominator.
5. Compose a benefits and features chart for a hotel and discuss how you would use it to address a specific target market.
6. Discuss the needs and difficulties in organizing a sales force by territory and by product line.
7. In Case 15-1, write a sales action plan for prospecting, calculate the correct mix of customers, and do an LCD format for new accounts/room-nights.
8. In Case 15-2, what is your reaction to the corporate order? How would you deal with it?
9. In Case 15-3, what would you do to win back the ABC Pharmaceutical Company's account?

✔ Case 15-1
Raise the Goal!

John Brady returned to his office to figure out what to do next. As Sales Manager of a large resort in Florida, he was responsible for the group market. Up to now, he thought he was doing well, making calls on his customers and booking business.

At a sales meeting prior to his return to the office, the director of sales had increased John's goals. Apparently, the corporate office of the hotel company was displeased with his results and had held a meeting with the director of sales. Now it was John's problem.

John's first thought was to look at his account management system. It looked like this for the current year:

Category	Number of Accounts	Room-nights	Average Rate
A	75	12,000	
B	75	5,000	
C	200	10,000	
Total	350	27,000	$70.91

John's previous goal for the year had been 25,000 room-nights, which he had been achieving on a consistent basis. Now, his goal has been raised to 30,000 room-nights, at a $75 average rate. He calculated what he had to do for the upcoming year, with his sales equation:

Room-nights			
Past Customers	+ New Customers	= Goals	
27,000	+ 3,000	= 30,000	

Clearly, John needed to find more rooms for the upcoming year. Of his 350 accounts, the breakdown by subsegment is as follows:

Group Files

Segment	# Files	Average Rate	Number of Rooms	Booking Lead Time
Corporate	150	$100	10,000	3 mos.
Tours	150	$50	15,000	6 mos.
Associations	50	$80	2,000	1 year
Total	350	$70.91	27,000	

John was constrained by time and felt he could only call on 350 accounts a year. If he had to make more calls, his prospecting time would be reduced to nothing. John had to get back to his director of sales within a week to let him know what he was going to do about increasing his quotas for the upcoming year.

✔ Case 15-2
Raise the Numbers![10]

The Plaza Royal Hotel was built in 1929. The hotel had been successful as a top-of-the-line property and over the years had developed a loyal clientele. In recent years, however, major competition had entered the market and was seriously threatening the hotel's market share. These new properties included those operated by Hilton International, Sheraton, and Four Seasons, among others. In the face of this competition, management recognized that the property had deteriorated and was in need of major refurbishing if it was going to maintain its market status.

The company commenced a three-year, $100 million renovation program that would completely refurbish all 1,200 rooms as well as the lobby, food and beverage outlets, meeting rooms, and back-of-the-house service areas. Rather than take the risk of losing customers to competitors, who might not return when the renovations were completed, it was decided to remain open and keep in operation any rooms or portions of the hotel that did not have to be shut down for construction.

By the following year, 600 rooms had been renovated but not without considerable difficulty. Customers were often forced to step over piles of lumber, around construction equipment, and through mazes of boxes, to get to their rooms. This had caused a considerable amount of dissatisfaction and numerous customer complaints. In fact, it was known that a number of regular customers had decided to go elsewhere, at least for the duration of the renovation period. Many, however, said they would return when it was finished.

At the same time, the economy had taken a downturn. Hotel occupancies, citywide, had dropped. This caused even more intense competition among hotels for the existing business. With another one to two years to go with its

renovation program, Plaza Royal management was struggling to maintain its forecasts. Of particular concern was the corporate market, and the sales staff was working hard to maintain the hotel's share of this segment.

Corporate group room-nights were estimated to finish the year with 33,500. Corporate transient room-nights would be about 90,000. Because of the renovation program and resultant periodic loss of meeting space, the next year's forecast for corporate group room-nights was lowered to 30,000. The corporate transient forecast was raised to 95,000 to compensate for this loss.

The sales department wasn't too sure just how it was going to meet these projections. The projected corporate rate was to remain at $114 per night. This compared to a $108 rate at the Sheraton, and a $150 rate at the Four Seasons. Hilton's corporate rate ranged from $104 to $120, and it had vowed to keep these rates throughout the next year, in view of the economy. These three hotels were perceived as the major competition for the corporate market in the city.

The Plaza Royal sales staff had little difficulty competing with its $114 rate for the newly renovated rooms. In fact, the refurbishing was so successful that it felt it could probably obtain even higher rates for those rooms. However, there would be only 600 of them to sell for much of next year and they couldn't always guarantee them. Further, even though the rooms were very satisfying, customers still had the problem of ongoing construction in public areas and hallways, along with the attendant dust, confusion, and noise.

For some customers, the quality rooms at $114 were worth the trade-off of the renovation confusion. For others, it was not. Worse, however, was the situation when a customer was placed in an unrenovated room and still had to endure the renovation mess. These customers were becoming increasingly difficult to keep.

In November the sales staff scheduled an all-day meeting to plan its strategy for the next

---

[10]Adapted from Robert C. Lewis, *Cases in Hospitality Marketing and Management*, pp. 143–144. Copyright © 1989 John Wiley & Sons, New York. Reprinted by permission of John Wiley & Sons, Inc. Vicki Tindle contributed the information for this case.

year; namely, how to maintain even 30,000 corporate group nights and how to increase corporate transient nights by 5,000. Also on the agenda was a longer-term consideration: How were they to keep and/or get back the customers being lost because of the renovations, after the renovations were completed?

The director of sales began the meeting by reading a memo she had just received from the corporate office. They weren't very pleased, she read, about the forecast projecting a loss in corporate group nights, or the increase in corporate transient nights of only 5,000. However, they were somewhat persuaded that perhaps these figures were realistic in view of the renovations going on. To make up for the loss of revenue, however, they wanted the corporate rate for next year to be set at $128 per night.

✔ Case 15-3
Winning Back the Customer[11]

For the past four years, the 438-room Marriott Hotel in Somerset, New Jersey had hosted the training meetings of ABC Pharmaceutical Company. These meetings were held throughout the calendar year, for periods of one to three weeks, as ABC trained its salespeople. ABC had very specific requirements for its meetings, as shown in Table 15-3-1. For the Marriott this business represented some 4,000 room-nights a year, plus ancillary business that came from other divisions of ABC. Thus the Marriott sales department was shocked to learn that ABC was going to take its next year's business to the nearby Hilton Hotel.

Mike Ellman, Director of Sales at the Marriott, immediately tried to establish the reason for ABC's move to Hilton. Although the reason was never made totally clear, Mike learned that there had been some billing mistakes. ABC found it a hassle to get these mistakes corrected, and some of them continued to occur. ABC also seemed to feel that, given the volume of business, Marriott's rates were too high. Finally, ABC seemed to have the impression that Marriott management and staff took the business of ABC for granted after the first two years. ABC felt their trainees were treated like second-class citizens, and there was poor response to problems.

After a year at the Hilton, ABC took its business to the nearby Holiday Inn and indicated some dissatisfaction with the Hilton. Hearing of this, Marriott's Mike Ellman decided to make another try for the business and visited the ABC Sales Training Director, Mr. Smith, to determine his needs. In September Mike made a proposal to ABC, as shown in Exhibit 15-3-1. After delivering the proposal, Mike called Mr. Smith three times, but no calls were returned. On the fourth call, he spoke to Mr. Smith, who denied receiving the messages that Mike had

TABLE 15-3-1   Corporate Training School Characteristics

- Dates are committed and rates negotiated in the fall for the following year.
- Number of trainees each session ranges from 8 to 20 individuals.
- Guestrooms are often double occupancy and need to be clustered together near a study/hospitality room.
- Trainees tend to be young, single, aggressive, athletic—a mix of male and female.
- Proximity of the hotel to the company's training facility, where the training is actually conducted, and means of transportation to the facility are very important.
- Expenses are paid for by the company, which tends to be very price-sensitive.
- There are minimal catering requirements.

called. He told Mike that ABC was returning to the Hilton, that he did not feel that the Marriott was truly interested in the business, and that the rate was unrealistic based on the volume of business.

In March of the following year, Susan Morris, a Sales Manager at the Somerset Marriott, took over the ABC account. At the time Susan called ABC to introduce herself, told them that ABC had been the Marriott's first major client and would never be taken for granted. Until August, Susan had various contacts with ABC's Mr. Smith at other meetings at the Marriott that he attended. In August, Susan received a message to call ABC regarding bidding for the next year's business. Her account activity log for the rest of the year read as follows:

August 6 Left message to call me back.
August 9 Set up appointment with Jones, #2 person. Told me they were taking bids from Marriott, Hilton, Holiday Inn, and Ramada.

[11]The details of this case were contributed by Susan Morris when she was Director of Marketing at the Somerset Marriott.

EXHIBIT 15-3-1   New proposal for ABC business by Mike Ellman

> **Marriott**
> HOTELS·RESORTS
>
> Somerset Marriott
>
> 110 Davidson Avenue
> Somerset, New Jersey 08873
> (201) 560-0500
>
> Mr. A. Smith
> Director, Sales Training
> ABC Company
> New Jersey
>
> Dear Mr. Smith:
>
> Thank you for your time at your office the other day. I appreciate you filling me in on ABC Company training needs for 1987.
>
> We at the Somerset Marriott are very excited about the possibility of hosting your 1987 Sales Training Program. At this time I can offer you the following:
>
> Sleeping Rooms - $79.00 per room per night (single or double occupancy). This rate will apply to your Sales Training Program.
>
> For your Relocating Managers - I can offer you a rate of $70.00 per room, per night, based on a minimum stay of fourteen (14) consecutive nights.
>
> Study Center/Work Room - $75.00 per day
>
> As I mentioned in your office we would be able to offer your in-house trainees a discount in our restaurant, but we can discuss that further at a later date.
>
> Mr. Smith, this is purely a "nuts and bolts" proposal that I do not feel fully describes how much the Somerset Marriott and I want to be your host in 1987. I can personally commit to you that my hotel will do the best job for you, for your people, and for your company. I would like to have ABC Company training business back. Hopefully, you will give us a chance.
>
> If you have any further questions or concerns, please do not hesitate to call. I look forward to speaking with you again.
>
> Yours truly,
>
> SOMERSET MARRIOTT HOTEL
>
> M. Ellman
>
> Michael Ellman
> Director of Sales
> SM:cr

August 10 Met with Jones. Reviewed needs of ABC. Discussed benefits of Marriott. Had "good vibes."

August 12 Delivered proposal (Exhibit 15-3-2). Neither Smith nor Jones available to see me.

August 13 Telephoned to see if proposal received and if any questions/concerns. Neither one available.

August 14 Dropped off Marriott Somerset signature chocolate, postcard, and notes. Neither one available.

August 17 Left message to call back.

August 19 Left message to call back.

August 28 Found out from Jones that business was going to Hilton. Basically, they felt that all was going well there, so why change?

September 4 Sent follow-up letter to Jones and received note from Smith (Exhibit 15-3-3). Thoughts: ABC unwilling to take risk? What incentive or motivation can we offer? Do they have trust in Susan Morris? Do they have trust in Marriott?

December 18 Sent Christmas card to Smith.

The next year, Susan Morris, now Director of Sales for the Somerset Marriott, renewed her

EXHIBIT 15-3-2   New proposal for ABC business by Susan Morris

Marriott
HOTELS·RESORTS

Somerset Marriott

110 Davidson Avenue
Somerset, New Jersey 08873
(201) 560-0500

Mr. R. Jones
Assistant Director, Sales Training
ABC Company
New Jersey

RE: 1988 ABC Company Sales Training Schools

Dear Bob:

It was a pleasure to meet with you recently regarding the possibility of
the Somerset Marriott Hotel hosting the ABC Company Sales Training Schools
in 1988.

Thank you very much for inviting us to bid for your Training Program. In
response to your request for accommodations and a Resource Room at the
Somerset Marriott, there are several objectives that I would like to
address:

<u>Objective #1:</u> To provide an environment conducive to the Training Schools
            while keeping the costs reasonable.

Marriott Hotels are well-renowned for their excellence, both in terms of
the quality of our facilities and the level of service we provide. The
Somerset Marriott Hotel is no exception. To assist you in maintaining the
budget designated for the 1990 Training Schools, we are pleased to extend
the following rates:

Single/Double Occupancy $75.00 (regularly $107.00/$122.00)
Resource Room $75.00 (regularly $109.00)

As you can see, we are offering ABC Company Sales Training a very
significant discount.

I understand that, upon occasion, there are ABC Company Managers who are
relocating to this area. We are glad to extend a $75.00 rate to these
individuals (minimum stay: 30 days).

<u>Objective #2:</u> A hassle-free Training School that flows smoothly.

It is our ambition to look after all of the logistics of the Training
Schools so that you may focus on the <u>purpose</u> of the training. By this we
mean that we will ensure that the following details are looked after:

1.   Welcome letters explaining the services and facilities
     available to attendees are presented upon check-in (sample enclosed).

efforts. Her account activity log reported the following:

August 18 Met with Smith re. the 1989 bid for business. When I mentioned our rate quotes for the two previous years, he was surprised and actually checked his files. He had the impression they were higher. He stated that his goal for trainees was to ensure they would be able to rest, enjoy, and have a hassle-free stay.

August 25 Delivered proposal. Same as previous year except raised rate $1. Competi-

tion has changed with the introduction of Embassy Suites to the scene.

September 6 Called to find out decision.

September 12 Left message.

September 16 Smith called to say that they had chosen Embassy, liked size of the rooms. (Note: Embassy rooms have a bedroom and sitting room so that two people sharing have some privacy. Price is the same as standard hotel room. Amenities include two televisions, VCR, refrigerator, sink, and microwave. Room rate includes breakfast and evening cocktail reception,

EXHBIT 15-3-2 (continued)

Page 2.

2. Wake-up calls are timely.
3. Messages and mail are received promptly.
4. Attendees' rooms are located in the vicinity of the Resource Room.
5. Bills are presented in a comprehensive format and on a timely basis. Recognizing that this is a problem that you have encountered in the past, I have enclosed a sample Master Bill. Please note that we provide a one page summary of the room, tax, and incidentals incurred by each attendee.

Objective #3: Treat the Attendees like VIP's.

Your attendees will feel very well accommodated in our guest rooms. The rooms have two (2) double beds as well as radios, alarm clocks, HBO, in-room movies, climate control, and spacious washrooms. Furthermore, we are commencing the renovations of one-third of our guest rooms in December and we have already started to redo some hallways.

Attendees may have breakfast in our bright and cheery King's Wharf Restaurant or enjoy a light, continental breakfast in our lounge. Both breakfast and dinner menus are enclosed so that you may see the variety and the low prices that are offered.

Recognizing that there will be opportunity for those attending the Training Schools to relax, we offer several alternatives. At the end of the day, attendees may soothe their weary muscles or do a full work-out in our Health Club complete with exercise rooms, hydrotherapy pool, and saunas. We also have an indoor/outdoor pool, shuffle board, and two (2) tennis courts that are lit at night. For those looking for a different kind of relaxation, there is nightly entertainment in our Main Brace Lounge.

Bob, we hope that this letter has given you an indication of how we at the Somerset Marriott Hotel can help make the 1988 Training Schools the most successful yet. We trust that we will receive your utmost consideration and look forward to a favorable reply. If everything meets with your approval, please sign and return the enclosed copy of the proposal to my attention no later than August 31, 1987.

We are hopeful of establishing a long term relationship between the Somerset Marriott and ABC Company. I hope to meet with you to further discuss our proposal. In the meantime, if you have any questions or concerns, please give me a call.

Best regards,

SOMERSET MARRIOTT HOTEL

Susan Morris
Sales Manager
SM:cr

cc: A. Smith, Director of Sales Training

but Smith says not interested in these. Drawbacks are one restaurant, one lounge with no entertainment or dancing. Room service hours restricted. Health club facilities and hours very limited. All bills are generated in Atlanta so local hotel cannot respond to problems efficiently. No washers or dryers for guest use, no bell staff, no telephone operators, no concierge.)

November 18 Sent Thanksgiving card.

December 16 Sent Christmas card.

The following year, Susan Morris' account activity log recorded the following:

March 7 Called Smith and he actually answered his telephone! Strange conversation. Said he didn't understand why I bothered calling him; it was obvious we did not need his business; our quotes were totally out of line (I repeated quotes of $75 and $76 and asked if that was out of line); accused me of trying to find out what he was paying at Embassy; was surprised by our rates, thought they were higher; thought all of ABC's business (we host other meetings) should be pulled out of Marriott.

March 8 Sent Smith letter of response (Exhibit 15-3-4).

April 11 Smith's secretary booked a meeting at Marriott for June because, she said, we have hosted similar meetings, successfully, for sister companies of ABC. Smith not involved in planning this.

June 13 Meeting went well. Spoke to Smith 2–3 times. At one point he said, "You really want my business, don't you?" After the meeting, called and sent him a letter requesting feedback. Silence.

July 15 Sister company to ABC, whose business we did host, informed me that parent company was pressuring them to use Hyatt, which was owned by parent company. Double the commute time from their facilities, didn't want to go there. I offered price incentive to stay at Marriott, offered to provide even lower rate if both companies came to Marriott. This put a different slant on the bidding process and the competition.

October 17 ABC going to Hyatt next year.

EXHBIT 15-3-3 Note received from Mr. Smith of ABC Company

Thank you for your thoughtfulness.

Susan —
Thank you very much for the Marriott Chocolates! A beautiful touch. I'm sure that by now you're aware we will not be using your facilities next year for our schools but appreciate all your efforts + attention to detail in the regard.

Thanks again —

Andrew Smith

EXHIBIT 15-3-4   Follow-up letter to phone call

Marriott.
HOTELS·RESORTS

Somerset Marriott

110 Davidson Avenue
Somerset, New Jersey 0887 1
(201) 560-0500

Mr. A. Smith
Director, Sales Training
ABC Company
New Jersey

Dear Mr. Smith:

Just a note to say thanks for the time that you extended me on
the telephone recently as we discussed the ABC Company Sales
Schools. I am pleased that the Embassy Suites is working out
well for you. They really do have a great product, especially
the oversized rooms which provide trainees with a little more
breathing space. Maybe we need to start knocking down walls at
the Marriott!!

I was disappointed to hear that you have the impression that the
Somerset Marriott does not want your business. It is difficult
not to take your comments personally, as I feel that I have
worked very hard for the last two years to get to know the needs
of the Sales Schools and to put together proposals that respond
to those needs. You mentioned that our pricing has not been in
the same ballpark as other hotels. I have enclosed copies of our
bids for the last two years...I did not realize that our quotes
of $75.00 and $76.00 respectively, were out of line.

Mr. Smith, I would like to apologize if you have found my efforts
to be overzealous, or if I have in any way led you to think that
the Marriott does not want your business. Quite to the contrary,
I have tried to show our enthusiasm by keeping in touch with you,
putting together competitive proposals, and demonstrating our
service by ensuring that the ABC Company Management Meetings go
off without a hitch.

I would like to request that you keep us on your list of hotels
to be considered for the 1990 Sales Training Schools. I have not
given up hope that one of these years, you and I will sign a
contract together.

In the meantime, if I can be of assistance, I am at your service.

Best regards,

SOMERSET MARRIOTT HOTEL

Susan Morris
Director of Sales
SM:cr

CHAPTER 16

Channels of Distribution

By definition, channels of distribution are a set of independent organizations involved in the process of making a product or service available for use or consumption. Most companies that produce goods or services need assistance in distributing their products to the end-user, the consumer. Goods-producing firms such as Procter & Gamble, Ford Motor Company, and Coca-Cola must somehow arrange to distribute their product—that is, get it to where the consumer can buy it. Consumers do not have to go to the bottling plant each time they want a drink of soda, nor do they have to travel to Detroit to purchase a car.

In the same sense, hospitality companies like Sheraton, McDonald's, and American Airlines need distribution systems through which their customers can find their products and services. There is a growing need in the hospitality industry to utilize channels of distribution as never before. In the past, when the demand for hotel rooms and restaurants exceeded the supply, customers managed to find their way to the product offered. This is not the case today, with the proliferation of new hospitality products, all vying for the same customer.

How Distribution Channels Work

In the usual manufactured goods situation, the producer of the goods uses a wholesaler or a broker to assist in the distribution of the product. A wholesaler is a business unit that buys, or takes on consignment, merchandise from the producer and sells it to the retailer. A broker serves a similar function but may or may not actually acquire the merchandise. The retailer is the point of sale where the consumer can purchase the product. Wholesaler, broker, and retailer are all part of the distribution system.

Companies have found it necessary to utilize these separate channels of distribution not only because of the prohibitive costs of developing their own distribution systems but also because distributors can get closer to the customer. Ford Motor Company, for example, distributes through its retailers, the local car dealerships, which sell Ford cars to the public. To purchase the real estate, construct the facilities, staff the organizations, and market the cars would be a tremendous burden on Ford's resources.

Procter & Gamble, on the other hand, works through brokers and wholesalers to get its product to the retailers, of which there are tens of thousands worldwide. Coca-Cola distributes through franchisees who buy syrup in bulk, make and bottle the final product, and deliver it to innumerable retailers. Variations of such distribution systems are endless. Some systems are vertically integrated: In these, retailers are owned by the manufacturer and sell only that company's products. An example would be

Tandy Corporation, which owns Radio Shack, the only stores that sell its product.

In conventional distribution systems, however, the retailer carries many brands, including those of competing companies. Control of the channel lies in the strength of the product being sold. If an item is in very high demand, the producer of this product may be able to set the terms of the channel. If the producer is offering a very strong product, it may manipulate the retailer into carrying and merchandising other and weaker products as well. When the product is weak, the wholesalers and retailers will dictate the terms of the channel to the consumer. The same principles apply to the hospitality industry, only in reverse.

Hospitality Distribution Channels

Although the principles are the same, the channels of distribution for the hospitality industry differ significantly from those used for manufactured goods. For one reason, the hospitality product is normally not "moved" to the consumer like a bottle of soda or a tube of toothpaste. For another, the product is often sold in conjunction with another product, such as airline tickets or charter tours. Finally, because of the unusually high perishability of the hospitality product, many traditional channels simply would not work.

In distribution channels of the hospitality industry, a separate wholesaler or retailer rarely takes physical possession of the product to be marketed and delivered to the end-consumer at a later date. (They may, however, take nominal possession, such as a wholesaler who purchases a block of rooms or airline seats to be packaged and sold to the ultimate consumer at a markup.) In hospitality, the manufacturer is not only the retailer, but manufacturer and seller of the product (delivers the service) simultaneously. The problem, then, is not how to distribute the product to the retailer, but how to get the customer to the retail outlet—that is, make it convenient. Thus arises the need for a different kind of distribution system to broaden the

base of customers and sell the product more efficiently.

Although there are thousands of hotels and food-service outlets all over the world carrying many familiar brand names, most of these are not owned by the companies whose names they bear. The industry is really three different businesses: one is development, building, and ownership; another is management; and a third is franchising. Some companies do all three. As well, they may be a franchisor (they sell the use of their name), a franchisee (they buy the use of another's name), or both.

One example is the Embassy Suites in Palm Beach, Florida. This hotel, built by a developer from the Midwest, is managed by Servico Management of Florida, which also owns and operates other hotels under different franchise names (Figure 16-1) and carries the Embassy Suites name as a franchise affiliation. Servico, however, does not franchise its own name. Major hotel companies such as Hilton, Sheraton, and Marriott are primarily hotel managers who operate hotels for owners who could be a partnership, trust, bank, insurance company, or some combination of these. They also franchise their names to others. In 1993, in fact, Marriott Corporation divided into two companies: Marriott International, Inc. manages hotels and resorts and franchises its name to those owned, and sometimes managed, by others; Host Marriott, Inc. is a real estate company that buys and owns properties, usually managed by Marriott International.

From an operator's point of view, it is critical to the successful distribution of a brand name to be in the right geographical areas, as opposed to specific desirable locations for a specific hotel or restaurant. These are often defined as primary, secondary, and tertiary markets. There are 15 so-called primary cities in the United States, including Boston, New York, Los Angeles, and Chicago. Secondary markets include Hartford, Connecticut, Salt Lake City, Utah, Portland, Oregon, and San Antonio, Texas. Finally, there are tertiary markets such as Des Moines, Iowa, Lexington, Kentucky, Boise, Idaho, and Spokane, Washington. The ranking depends on the size of the market and its buy-

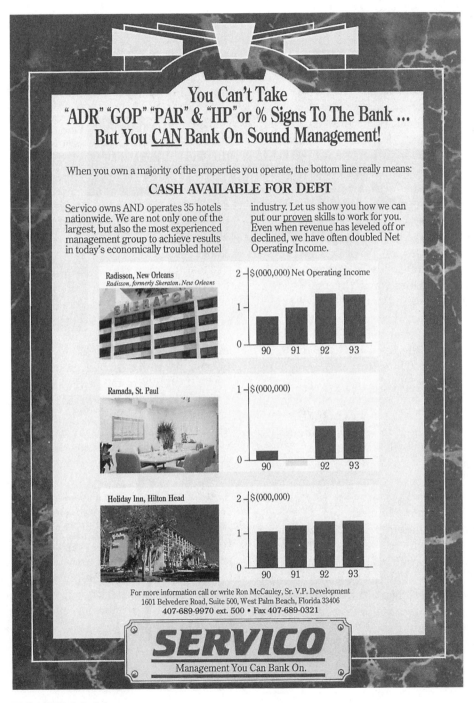

FIGURE 16-1   An owning and management company

ing power. There are also, of course, many smaller or even isolated market areas.

The same is true internationally. Primary international locations are Paris, Frankfurt, London, Tokyo, and Singapore. Secondary ones are Brussels, Amsterdam, Lisbon, Madrid, and Kyoto. In the tertiary category are Cologne, Marseilles, Athens, Stockholm, and Dusseldorf.

Resort locations likewise abound, from the Rocky Mountains to Florida to Honolulu to Bali, to the Cote d'Azur in France, Phuket in Thailand, the Costa del Sol in Spain, and the Fiji Islands. Having a property in Buenos Aires or Mexico City may be as important to a hotel company as it is for a fast-food chain to have a position on the New Jersey Turnpike.

Upscale hotel chains usually strive to be in the primary markets first, and then move into the other markets. Middle-tier, economy-tier, and restaurant chains, however, may do it the other way around. Certainly McDonald's is in about every conceivable level of market. Pizza Hut is not far behind. The point, of course, is to distribute the product to the right markets—first, by being there, and second, by being able to capture the same customer in another place. In order to increase the number of customers in the distribution system, it is necessary to offer the product in a variety of marketplaces where the customer either is or goes. Having a presence in the correct marketplace is critical to the success of a distribution channel.

A case in point is the Marriott Marquis Hotel in New York City, which opened in the mid-1980s, a rather late and expensive entry into the New York market. Marriott wanted to capture large conventions from the existing network of Hilton and Sheraton hotels. Major convention planners could buy the Hilton or Sheraton product in New York City, Chicago, and Las Vegas, among others. The Marriott product had a market presence in the corporate business segment, but its hotels were not large enough in size and meeting space to attract the really major conventions and associations. The Marriott Marquis in Atlanta was the first step into this distribution system, but no major player in the convention circuit can maximize its customer base without a hotel in New York City. Thus, the individual profit and loss statement of the New York City hotel was of lesser importance than that hotel's contribution to the overall Marriott convention network nationwide. The channel of distribution of convention hotels to national associations was very important to Marriott.

Budget and middle-tier hotel chains and food-service chains behave likewise in pursuing different markets—Days Inn is in India, Best Western is worldwide, Howard Johnson is in Israel, Jordan, Egypt, Turkey, Cyprus, and Greece under a management contract agreement, and McDonald's and Pizza Hut are worldwide, all adding to the distribution system of these chains.

Hospitality companies may use several different methods to distribute their products and services. These include their own channels—owning (wholly or partially), managing (through management contracts), and franchising. In 1994 Hilton Hotels wholly owned 13 hotels, partially owned 15, managed 23, and franchised 227 hotels. All of them bear the Hilton name. In addition, hotels use the channels of others. They may join consortia or affiliations, hire sales representatives, or join reservations systems to provide customers with greater access. Finally, firms use various intermediaries such as incentive houses, travel agents, and tour operators to increase their distribution networks. In any case, the major issue of distribution is where to be found, so the customer can reach you. We will first discuss distribution systems that are similar to those used by manufacturers: company-owned/-managed or franchised properties. We will then discuss some unusual distribution channels used in the hospitality industry.

Owning and/or Managing

Owning and managing provide the brand name with the best integrity from a product delivery point of view. If a company both owns and manages a facility, the product has a better chance of being consistently maintained and presented to customers in the network. Expansion, however, comes harder when a firm owns and manages all its facilities. The need for capital increases the financial drain and risk, and the opportunities for expansion may overtake the need to own and deliver the product. From a distribution standpoint, the need to expand the name brand identity usually outstrips the financial resources of the company.

Every hospitality company that wants to expand its product offerings geographically must eventually decide (1) to make slower progress by owning (at least partially) and managing each unit, (2) to manage without owning, or (3) to franchise its name to be managed by others.

Managing

In order to maintain the quality standards of the product name in the channel of distribution, managing is next-best to both owning and managing. In many cases, companies manage for a fee while the physical property is owned by others. The fee, however, is not always the sole objective of the managing company. As discussed above, being in the right places in the distribution channel can be equally or more important. For example, Westin's or Inter-Continental's presence in Singapore in the 1980s, at the time their new hotels were built by Asian investors, would probably have been sheer folly from an ownership perspective. Four Seasons, in 1994, wholly owned only one of the hotels it managed, had a 50 percent and 25 percent interest in two others, was a minority owner (3.4–24 percent) in nine others, had a 19.9 percent interest in a partnership that owned ten others, and managed 16 hotels with no ownership interest.[1]

Ritz-Carlton, in 1994, managed 30 hotels with its name on them. It owned three, had equity in ten, and no equity in the rest, which it managed for, typically, 5 percent of gross revenue, even if a hotel was unprofitable (at least half of them at the time), plus a percentage of earnings if it was.[2]

Currently, by contrast with the 1980s, lenders usually require some sort of equity position on the part of the management company. The reason for this is the increasing risk factor of hospitality enterprises. In the past, tax laws were so advantageous for the investor that the cash flow or actual business value of the facility was often not as important as the tax breaks. This situation was mutually beneficial for some time. The investor would provide the money for the facility, anticipating large tax write-offs in the short term and watching the value of the real estate grow in the long term, exclusive of the actual performance of the hotel. Simultaneously, management companies found a way to increase the presence of their brand name in important marketplaces without utilizing their own capital.

As with all "good deals," the economic laws of supply and demand eventually took over. Many marketplaces were overbuilt, with too many hotel rooms or restaurant seats in the same product class available for a marginally growing demand. The Stamford, Connecticut area turned into this kind of a situation when five upscale hotels were built based on the same feasibility study.

In addition, the tax advantages of such relationships were largely eliminated in the United States by legislation enacted in 1986. Taxes and oversupply combined have eliminated much of the no-equity management of hotels. (By "no-equity" deals, we mean the management of a hotel without significant capital investment on the part of the managing company.) Typically, the management company is paid a fee based on gross sales of the facility, with bonuses applied for performance over a mutually agreed-upon profit margin. These constraints will slow growth of new hotels in the future and, eventually, allow the demand for the product to rise to meet the supply and the average room rate to catch up with the consumer price index. Figure 16-2 graphically shows these changes in the U.S. market from 1990 to 1994 (projected).

In the last few years, there has been a tremendous shakeout among management companies. With management companies at little financial risk, many investors were saddled with

---

[1]Alison L. Cowan, "Four Seasons' Sour Footnotes," *New York Times*, January 24, 1994, p. D4.

[2]James S. Hirsch, "Of Luxury and Losses: Many Ritz Hotels are in the Red," *Wall Street Journal*, April 22, 1994, pp. B1, B2.

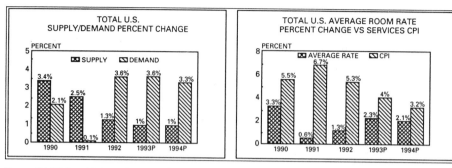

Source: *Hotel & Resort Industry,* January, 1994, p. 16, with courtesy of Smith Travel Research.

FIGURE 16-2   Changes in the U.S. market, 1990–1994

nonperforming assets in overbuilt markets. In the early 1990s, many of these investors defaulted on their loans, forcing many hotels into receivership; and, with the failure of many banks and savings and loan institutions, the U.S. government ended up owning many hotels. In fact, there was a period when failed hotel investments were the major part of the assets taken over by the Resolution Trust Corporation (the government entity that took over failed banks and their assets). Capital monies were practically unavailable, compromising management companies' abilities to keep some products in their portfolios.

For example, there may be a Hilton Hotel in a tertiary marketplace. A group of local investors may have provided the money to build the facility; Hilton manages the operation. As the marketplace becomes overbuilt and the tax incentives dry up, cash flow stagnates or dwindles. As the product becomes older in its life cycle, refurbishment becomes necessary to keep it competitive. The original investors can no longer depend on the asset itself to be self-supporting. Even if the hotel is covering its mortgage payments, it is unlikely that additional money has been set aside from operating funds for necessary refurbishment after the normal five- or six-year life cycle.

Hilton would now have to make a decision. Although its name is on the facility, and Hilton customers are becoming less satisfied with the product, the owners may be unable or unwilling to fund the necessary renovation. If the hotel is important enough to the Hilton distribution system, Hilton may choose to provide the funds itself, waiting until the supply/demand imbalance corrects itself and the hotel again becomes profitable. Hilton's other option is to withdraw from the contract and forfeit this marketplace in its distribution system and the related fees generated from the hotel. Four Seasons Hotels, as one example, has financed refurbishments of hotels it manages but doesn't own, choosing not to manage a deteriorated product that carries its name.

Management companies are also changed by owners. For example, CP Hotels held the management contract for L'Hotel in Toronto but failed to meet earnings projections called for in the contract. The owners went to court and threw out CP. Commonwealth Hospitality was brought in as the new management company with a Holiday Inn Crowne Plaza franchise. Also in Toronto, when the Sutton Place Hotel managed by Kempinski went into receivership, the lenders brought in Le Meridien as the managment company.

Finally, to cover all the bases, there are management companies like Servico, mentioned earlier, that own and manage nothing but franchises; that is, the management company's name (such as that shown in Figure 16-3) does not appear in the hotel name. Unlike, for example, Marriott International, which we could say is in the hotel business (i.e., it wishes to perpetuate its name as a brand or chain and manages hotels owned by others but with its name),

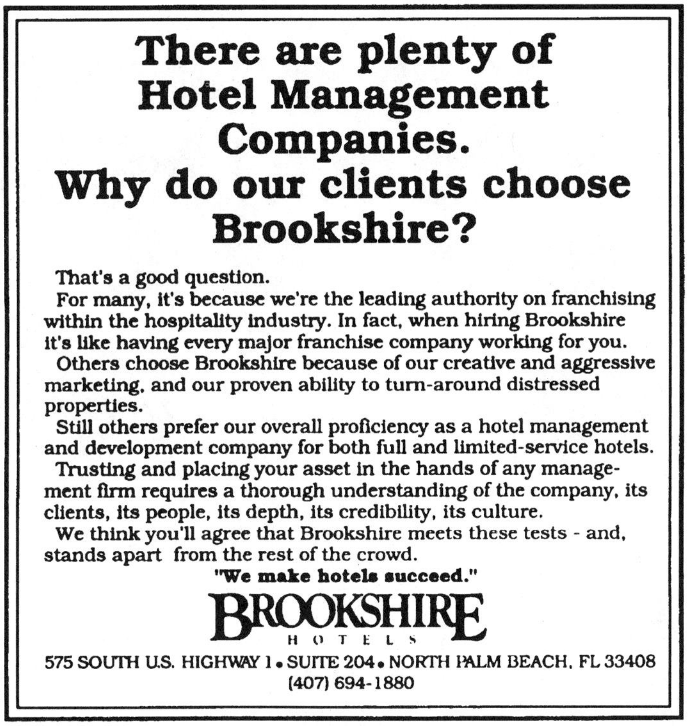

There are plenty of Hotel Management Companies. Why do our clients choose Brookshire?

That's a good question.

For many, it's because we're the leading authority on franchising within the hospitality industry. In fact, when hiring Brookshire it's like having every major franchise company working for you.

Others choose Brookshire because of our creative and aggressive marketing, and our proven ability to turn-around distressed properties.

Still others prefer our overall proficiency as a hotel management and development company for both full and limited-service hotels.

Trusting and placing your asset in the hands of any management firm requires a thorough understanding of the company, its clients, its people, its depth, its credibility, its culture.

We think you'll agree that Brookshire meets these tests - and, stands apart from the rest of the crowd.

"We make hotels succeed."

BROOKSHIRE
HOTELS

575 SOUTH U.S. HIGHWAY 1 • SUITE 204 • NORTH PALM BEACH, FL 33408
(407) 694-1880

FIGURE 16-3   Strictly a hotel management company

these companies are strictly in the hotel *management* business. Their names don't appear on the hotels, and they own neither the hotels nor the franchise. Instead, the owner buys the franchise and hires the management company to manage it. Interstate Hotels Corporation of Pittsburgh is the largest franchise manager of Marriott hotels. It also manages New York's Palace Hotel, owned by the Sultan of Brunei.

Franchising

Franchising is a commonly used method for a hospitality entity to increase its distribution network, both to create more revenue and to obtain the geographic presence discussed above. Franchising is also a common method of distribution for nonhospitality companies from Avis Rent-a-Car, Midas Mufflers, and H&R Block tax services to 7-11 convenience stores. Coca-Cola and Pepsi Cola franchise by allowing bottling plants to utilize their mixtures and then distribute their product. This method of distribution has been in common usage since what was called the franchise boom of the 1960s.

Franchising is the usage of a company name by someone else for the purpose of selling that product or service. Briefly, a company creates a product or service. It then offers other companies or persons the opportunity to use the name to market the offering in a variety of geographic areas. The amount of control a franchisor (the parent company) has over the franchisee (the company that buys the name to distribute the product or service) varies as widely as the franchising options available.

There is always a contract between the franchisee and franchisor that outlines the terms of the relationship. Items such as marketing support, revenues to the franchisor (usually determined as a percentage of sales), and duration of the agreement are covered. Territorial rights are also negotiated at the same time. A franchisee might obtain rights to a two-mile zone, five-

Here's an opportunity for those who don't believe one size fits all.

Plazas • Hotels • Park Square Inns • Lodges • HoJo Inns

1-800-I-GO-HOJO

RAMADA LIMITEDS • INNS • HOTELS • RESORTS • PLAZA HOTELS

1-800-2-RAMADA

1-800-325-2525

1-800-800-8000

1-800-2-RAMADA

1-800-437-PARK

Different hotel properties have unique marketing needs. That's why Hospitality Franchise Systems has five national chains designed to address these individual requirements. Whatever industry segment you want to be in, from economy to upper mid-scale, HFS has a brand to fit your needs.

And unlike some other brands, each HFS chain has its own strategic marketing programs, its own national advertising and its own 1-800 number.

And HFS is the world's largest hotel franchisor, with purchasing power that's unmatched in the industry. These economies of scale produce more cost effective media buys, more extensive marketing support and great prices on your supplies. So choose HFS as your next franchisor. We can make your property a success, whether it's in Portland, Maine, or Portland, Oregon.

HOSPITALITY
FRANCHISE
SYSTEMS, INC.

For more information concerning franchise opportunities, call HFS at 201-428-9700.

Courtesy of Hospitality Franchise Systems, Inc.

FIGURE 16-4   The world's largest franchise company in 1994

state area, or an entire country, in which no other franchisee of the same product or service can operate. For example, separate franchisees in India have acquired exclusive rights to the Days Inn, Choice International, and Sheraton names in that country.

Until recently the leader in franchising for hotels was Holiday Inn Worldwide Corporation with its Holiday Inn, Crowne Plaza, Holiday Inn Express, Garden Court, and SunSpree Resort brands. By 1994, however, Hospitality Franchise Systems (HFS) had acquired five major brand names and become the world's largest franchise hotel company (Figure 16-4). In the fast-food segment of the hospitality industry, the world leader is McDonald's; other familar names proliferate (Figure 16-5). These compa-

nies and many others recognize that their ability to distribute their products' names and identities throughout the world is limited by the amount of capital available. Methodically, they have offered their names and services to potential franchisees.

Major companies need to expose their products to more customers, in effect creating brand-loyal consumers who will buy their product wherever it is available. Their rationale is that the more places the customer can buy the product, the more often that customer will become a new customer of the same product in another marketplace. This distribution of the brand name by franchising has become integral to the growth of many major restaurant and hotel chains. There are, however, notable

Look What's Happening At

A "Quality Full-Service Restaurant" for the '90s!
We are now selecting our franchise business partners for the future:

• We hold the highest market share in the family segment of 14.5%
• Have been in business for more than 40 years with more than 1500 restaurants
• Can offer multi-restaurant development to qualified candidates
• Will have financing to offer to qualified applicants
• Do you meet the financial criteria?
*$750,000 net worth
*$250,000 liquid assets
If you are looking for a major opportunity to grow with a leader, please call
1-800-304-0222
to find out about your future with Denny's.

Denny's is committed to providing the best possible service to all customers regardless of race, creed, or national origin.

Join Pizza Inn® And You'll Be Rolling In Dough.

▲With 30 years of franchising experience, Pizza Inn supports over 425 restaurants operating in 20 states and 10 countries. ▲Pizza Inn is proud to rank #1 in Sales Growth per unit by <u>Restaurant News</u> Top 100 Chain List during 1993. ▲We are seeking franchisees for both Full Service and Delivery/Carryout stores.

FRANCHISE SUPPORT INCLUDES:

▲ Comprehensive Training
▲ Grand Opening Support
▲ Complete Marketing Services
▲ On-going Operations Assistance
▲ New Product Development
▲ Volume Purchasing

**Please call now:
800-2-THE-INN**

Pizza Inn.

5050 Quorum, Suite 500, Dallas, TX 75240
Minimum net worth of $150M. Minimum liquid assets of $75M.

FIGURE 16-5 Food-service franchisors

Strong Reservations

Being a Holiday Inn franchisee means even more than having instant name recognition, a glowing reputation, and a loyal following on your side. It means knowing up-front that a large number of roomnights are going to be booked. By us. For you. ► ► ►

Holiday Inn Worldwide was the first chain in the industry to implement a toll-free, reservation number, 1-800-HOLIDAY. Today that memorable number and those of our 24 Worldwide Reservation Offices are dialed more than 400,000 times a week.

Each of those calls, no matter where it originates, is managed by the sophisticated Holidex 2000 reservation system.

Over 30% of the total annual occupancy of Holiday Inn hotels is booked through the Holidex reservation system. That's more than 20,000,000 roomnights. In terms of income, the figure reaches beyond one billion dollars a year.

In addition to this steady flow of advance business, Holidex 2000 is also equipped to give you valuable hotel marketing/management tools.

Such things as yield management, market segmentation, demand pricing, night audit, and folio management, as well as recording guest profile information.

Best Known

It's no secret that partnering with a known commodity is a much more assured investment than going with an unknown. Taking that basic rule of smart business into account, consider the even stronger advantage of investing in the best known. ► ► ►

Guests choose Holiday Inn hotels because they know—and trust—our name. Our heritage has more than a little to do with that. But the largest share of the credit must go to the most aggressive, comprehensive marketing and advertising program in the industry.

We invest $100 million each year to keep the Holiday Inn name in the public eye. And it is worth every cent. Holiday Inn has a top-of-mind awareness level six times that of any other chain.

Becoming a Holiday Inn franchisee puts you in the world's most prestigious marketing league. We have developed strategic partnerships with companies like AT&T, Coca-Cola, Procter and Gamble, Hertz, American Express, and Northwest Airlines. Shared efforts with these respective industry giants increase the advertising clout of Holiday Inn Worldwide and crystalizes to key audiences our long-held position as the hospitality industry's standard bearer.

Perfect Partner

We're all in this together. Your success is our success. And vice versa. That's why, when all is said and done, nothing means more to the strength of the chain than the time and energy we devote to internal programs designed to be of real help to you and the operation of your hotel. ► ► ►

Holiday Inn Worldwide has always been at its best when it comes to supporting franchisees.

We stay abreast of all the challenges facing hotel owners and operators. We know what services are needed to enhance your daily operations and ultimately help improve your profitability.

Courtesy of Holiday Inns, Inc.

FIGURE 16-6   Franchisor services provided by Holiday Inn Worldwide

Through our unique, five-component Franchise Service Delivery System, we have those services in place to support every aspect of your operation. The five services are closely linked in order to provide you all the synergistic benefits. They are:

(1) Immediate personal attention for each hotel and owner provided by an assigned **Franchise Service Manager.** This is your direct link to Holiday Inn Worldwide for any and all questions you may have. (2) On-site employee training delivered by a highly qualified team of **Road Scholars** who travel North America, visiting each Holiday Inn two times a year. (3) Time-sensitive, expertly conducted, off-site **Executive Training** courses for general managers and hotel managers. (4) The very attentive **New Unit Opening Assistance Team** to bring tailored orientation and training programs to your property. (5) A consulting program called **Strategic Revenue Management** that ensures the future competitiveness and effectiveness of the Holidex 2000 reservation system and identifies changes that will give franchisees higher revenue potential. For example, trends in yield management and analyses of reservations center data.

The Franchise Service Delivery System was designed with one goal in mind, to help you succeed at the property level today, tomorrow, and far into the future.

Repeated Success

Holiday Inn Worldwide has developed innovative marketing programs pinpointing key market segments that mean the most to your business. Pursuing those segments in highly focused ways builds loyalty and can help increase revenues. A case in point, Priority Club was innovated expressly for the business traveler. ▶ ▶ ▶

Where would any hotel chain be without business travelers? They are a profit-margin requirement. In a successful effort to claim and keep our share (almost 60% of the Holiday Inn system's business), we created the Priority Club frequent traveler program.

Priority Club was the first and is one of the largest programs of its type in the industry. Today, almost 3.5 million members stay at Holiday Inn hotels on a consistent basis, enjoying the special hotel-level benefits associated with membership while earning points for travel and merchandise awards.

Just how important is that to you? Consider these points.

• 26% of Priority Club stays are incremental to the system. That is, the customers would have chosen different hotel brands without the program.

• Priority Club generates 2.6 points of incremental occupancy and $57,000 in incremental profit annually to a typical Holiday Inn.

• Priority Club members account for more than 10% of our system occupancy.

• Priority Club helped Holiday Inn hotels earn a 50% market share premium over the hotel industry for frequent business travelers.

And things can only get better. Because, as unique as it might seem for our industry, Priority Club is fully funded. We already hold in reserve enough capital to pay off every award if every member were to redeem their points at one time. That's a critical advantage for our owners. Even if that complete redemption scenario ever developed, they wouldn't face any out-of-pocket expenses. Ask the competition if this holds true for their programs.

FIGURE 16-6 (continued)

exceptions, such as Hyatt (until very recently), Westin, and Hilton International Hotels, which have not franchised so that they can have better control of daily operations. Just about all major restaurant chains do franchise.

In the United States in 1994, over two-thirds (and counting) of all hotels were branded, most by franchising. Hotels switch brands in search of the latest guest preference; some are forced to switch for falling below a chain's standards. In Canada, in 1994, only 13 percent of hotels with 20 or more rooms were branded, but 44 percent of guestrooms were. Percentages are even lower in other countries, but change continues. In general, properties with more rooms to fill increasingly feel the need for affiliation.

From a distribution standpoint there are two main advantages to being a franchisee. First, it automatically positions a hotel or restaurant in the marketplace where customers already have an image—for instance, McDonald's or a Days Inn. Without a known name, customers have a more difficult time determining the position and eventual product delivery of the facility. Second, for a lodging property, franchising often provides an immediate reservations network. Primarily for this reason, but also for drive-by recognition, independent properties are becoming unique in roadside and commercial markets in North America. Some claim that, with globalization, the lone hotel not connected to an international system will be lost among the flags.

The branding trend is also proliferating with resorts, and in other countries, both by management contracts and by franchising. Forte and Accor, for example, are branding properties all over Europe, while Choice International CEO Robert Hazard maintains the publicly stated ambition to have a brand name on every hotel property in the world. With 3,000 branded properties in 1994, Choice International's objective is to have 10,000 by the year 2000.

Traditionally, the franchisor provides the following services with its name affiliation (see Figure 16-6 for an actual example):

Technical Knowledge Each franchise operator does not have to reinvent the wheel. Although there are differences in each local mar-ketplace, many of the components of a business are generic. The franchisor provides the procedures for the business.

Managerial Techniques In some cases, the franchisee lacks management skills. Although procedures may need to be adapted to the local situation, they need not be developed from scratch each time a franchise is sold. Training and procedure manuals are made available by the franchisor. Some franchisors provide full, mandatory training programs for their operators. An example of this is McDonald's Hamburger University.

Marketing Support The phrase "the sum of the parts is greater than the whole" can be applied here. A franchisee pays a percentage of revenues toward the franchisor's marketing efforts. Each franchisee may market his or her product locally, but being part of a larger organization enables penetration into many cost-prohibitive geographic areas. Local marketing may have to follow guidelines to provide continuity with the rest of the product line, but it may not. For example, Figure 16-7 shows Holiday Inn advertising for its entire product line, company-owned and franchised, which includes six different products, from the budget Holiday Express to the upscale Crowne Plaza. (Earlier in this text, Figure 9-15 showed a franchisee's ad portraying a Holiday Inn as a luxury property—which, by corporate definition, it is not.)

Financial Support Connection with a successful franchisor is sometimes the key to obtaining financing for a business. Lending institutions are more willing to lend money to a project with national affiliation than to a local entity. The ability of a local operator to obtain business from outside marketplaces is greatly enhanced by a national or regional affiliation.

Safeguards This broad-based category is a catch-all for the support services offered by the franchisor to the franchisee. It includes such things as legal matters, safety regulations, and insurance issues.

Auditing Most franchises have specific guidelines for operation of their businesses.

WE'RE ALL
AROUND THE

WORLD

AND JUST AROUND
THE CORNER.

Wherever you travel you can count on
finding the warm welcome and friendly
service of a Holiday Inn® hotel. From San
Francisco to Springfield, from Rome to
Beijing, we're ready and waiting to make
you feel at home. In fact, we're in over
1,700 locations in more than 50 countries.
Which means we'll always be near. No
matter how far you go.

STAY WITH SOMEONE YOU KNOW.®

FOR RESERVATIONS CALL THE HOLIDAY INN WORLDWIDE RESERVATION OFFICE NEAREST YOU.

Courtesy of Holiday Inns, Inc.

FIGURE 16-7   Holiday Inn advertises its product line under the
brand name

Some are more stringent than others. The level of service needed to maintain a Days Inn franchise is different from that of a Holiday Inn Crowne Plaza or a Sheraton franchise. Normally, there is a systematic evaluation of the franchise to ensure that the customer is receiving the appropriate product and service.

Reservation System   For hotels, a major advantage of franchising is the reservations network. Being a member of a nationwide or world-wide chain can make the difference between a 50 percent occupancy and a 70 percent occupancy. The franchise affiliation automatically positions a hotel in the local marketplace. Simultaneously, it exposes the hotel to brand-loyal customers.

Traditionally, in North America, a toll-free 800 number is provided for the benefit of the customer. This is a great advantage for other intermediaries such as travel agents, as well as the individual customer. Radisson was the first hotel company to offer an international 800 number, globally toll-free. International lines are staffed 24 hours a day by reservation agents fluent in major languages. Callers in each country dial a local number that is answered by highly trained sales representatives who speak the national language of the caller.

Marriott uses different 800 numbers for its product line, all of which also carry the Marriott name. Choice International, on the other hand, maintains a policy of using one 800 number for all seven of its brands and 13 products (Figure 16-8), none of which carries the Choice name. Choice claims that one 800 number makes it easier for the customer to switch (and for them to switch the customer). We're not so sure. On one call for a reservation in the New York City area, an agent took 13 minutes to explain all the options, including three different brand products at the identical price. Other multiple franchisors, like HFS, use different 800 numbers for each brand, as was shown in Figure 16-4.

Other marketing support from a franchise relationship may include a national sales force that sells the product name to large consumer markets. These salespeople provide coverage in marketplaces where it would not be cost-effective for the local property to enter. The purpose is to sell all of the hotels in the chain to customers who have a need for more than one location.

For example, the accounting firm of Peat Marwick Main may need to have training meetings in Dallas, Tulsa, and Jacksonville. Because Peat Marwick Main is based in New York City, it is more cost-effective to have a member of a hotel chain's national sales organization call on this customer, representing all three locations (which may be managed by three different hotel companies under the same franchise umbrella), than it is for the individual hotels to send their own sales representatives. In many instances, the customers also prefer to deal with one sales representative rather than having to listen to three different sales pitches.

Franchising companies are recognizing the need to provide greater services to their franchisees. As the competition increases for expansion, it is critical to maintain the expansion of the number of franchises. To do this, additional services such as special toll-free numbers for travel agents, one-stop shopping for group book-

Hotel Brands			
Sleep Inns:	limited-service, economy hotels	Rodeway Inns:	limited and full service, upper-price economy hotels
Comfort Inns and Suites:	upper economy, limited-service hotels and all-suite hotels	Econo Lodges:	limited-service, mid-priced, economy hotels
Quality Inns Hotels and Suites:	mid-priced, full-service inns and limited-service all-suite hotels	Friendship Inns:	lower economy, limited-service hotels
Clarion Hotels, Suites, Resorts, and Carriage House Inns:	upscale hotels, all-suite hotels, resorts and boutique inns		

FIGURE 16-8   Choice International's seven brands and 13 products

"Travelodge is a family operation," says Babu, "by that, I mean they treat us like family. We value their personal treatment, and their professionalism."

"The people we deal with

has become more effective."

"Our staff is very important to our success," adds Babu. "I collect all the comment cards left by guests in our properties, and honestly, I've rarely seen a nega-

for Travelodge, and for Hitesh and me. You see, I want my son to be as successful a businessman as I've become. And I know, with Travelodge, he has a great chance."

"When it comes to the family business, my son and I prefer to deal with professionals. Not fair-weather friends."

From 1972 to 1987, Babu Patel owned and operated five independent lodging properties in Vancouver, British Columbia. In '87, he bought an independent property in Portland, Oregon and converted it to a Travelodge franchise. That same year, his son, Hitesh, joined him in the business. In the years since, they've built two additional Travelodges, and are now planning their fourth.

at Travelodge are very responsive," adds Hitesh, "whether it's our Regional Sales Manager, who's worked with us to land a lot of commercial contracts, or the people in the Reservations Center, which Travelodge and parent company, Forte Hotels, are making more effective with a new $15-million system."

"And thanks to the training videotapes and manuals from Travelodge," says Hitesh, "our staff

tive comment. That says a lot about our staff *and* why we received Travelodge's 'Operator-of-the-Year' Award for properties with 75 rooms or less."

"I was excited to accept the award at this year's Annual Conference in Las Vegas." says Babu, "and my excitement grew as I saw the unveiling of aggressive systemwide positioning plans for Travelodge. I would have to say the future looks very bright

If you'd like to know more about becoming a franchisee with Travelodge, whose parent company, Forte Hotels, is the largest and most profitable worldwide lodging chain, write to Gregory C. Plank, Senior Vice President of Franchise Development, Forte Hotels, Inc., 1973 Friendship Dr., El Cajon, CA 92020 or call 619-448-1884.

STAY SATISFIED

FIGURE 16-9   Travelodge advertises for franchisees

ings, and centralized commission disbursement for travel agents, all attempt to differentiate the franchise in the eyes of customers and investors. In the 1990s, there is intense competition

among hotel companies to attract good franchisees under their umbrellas (Figure 16-9). In 1992, for example, for the economy segment alone, 565 independent hotels in the United

States converted to franchises while 343 hotel left franchises to become independent. In addition, 500 hotels switched from one chain to another.[3]

Franchising also provides immediate positioning for a restaurant. Pricing, quality of food and beverage, and general ambience are all preconceived by the sign outside the establishment. Restaurant franchises are usually more tightly regulated by the franchisor than are their lodging counterparts. Variations in quality of product in fast-food stores such as McDonald's or Dunkin' Donuts are few, whereas there are a myriad of product and service experiences for travelers at Choice International or Sheraton franchises. Of course, fast-food operations have managed to successfully create a uniform level of service through simplification and technology, while hotels still must provide a higher level of service through human interaction.

Most customers cannot differentiate between the corporate-owned and managed hotel or restaurant, and that of a franchise. A sales representative of a franchisee in the East is somewhat at the mercy of another franchisee and different management company in the Midwest or Europe. Often, sales representatives meet resistance because of problems encountered by customers using the franchise located in a different area and managed by a different company.

Philosophies of Franchising

Hospitality companies have different philosophies of franchising. Marriott, for example, franchises a relatively small amount of full-service hotels for a company its size, but widely franchises its Courtyard and Fairfield Inn products. Contrarily, Holiday Inn has franchised over 85 percent of its product line. There are also some companies, such as Westin, Four Seasons, Stouffer, Fairmont, Oberoi of India, and Shangri La of Hong Kong, that do not franchise at all. Forte Hotels franchises its Travelodge

brand but not most of its other product lines. The philosophy of the latter companies is that the level of service they are attempting to deliver can be maintained only by direct control.

As mentioned earlier, franchising can result in a wide variety of product offerings to the consumer. McDonald's has done an excellent job of maintaining its standards; few can tell whether McDonald's or a franchisee is running any given restaurant under that name. Similarly, Marriott has maintained strong control over franchisees, keeping a similar product in front of the customers. Hilton and Sheraton have been less fortunate. There is a big difference between the company-managed St. Regis Sheraton in New York City, one of Sheraton's so-called "luxury collection," and the franchised Sheraton Inn in Bordentown, New Jersey.[4] A similar discrepancy exists between Hilton's Waldorf-Astoria in Manhattan and the franchised Berkshire Hilton Inn in Pittsfield, Massachusetts.

During the course of business cycles, companies may change direction on their decision to franchise. In the beginning, Marriott chose not to franchise its Courtyard by Marriott concept. Given the low amount of capital investment available for new construction, Marriott changed its mind. Hyatt recently changed direction and started to look for franchisees in 1994. Omni Hotels has come full circle; upon acquisition of the brand name in the early 1980s, no franchising was done. In the late 1980s and early 1990s, franchisees were pursued. The current direction is back to owned and managed properties.

A newcomer may obtain initial success in the distribution network through franchising. Radisson Hotel Corporation, originally operating with a relatively unknown name, was quickly able to amass a network of close to 100 hotels with about 50 percent of them franchised. By marketing the chain as a "collection" of hotels, Radisson was telling the customer up

---

[3]"Economy Lodging Redefines Itself," *Lodging,* November, 1993, p. 94.

[4]In 1993 Sheraton announced plans to launch a three-star division in Asia Pacific, dropping the Sheraton name in favor of a new name with the suffix, "By Sheraton." Initial emphasis was in China where the company identified 29 possible locations.

Fastest growing, upscale hotel company with more than 290 locations in 25 countries.

Resorts, hotels, inns and condos at 40 locations in 7 countries and the Hawaiian Islands.

Limited-service, country-style charm with 35 locations in the U.S. and Canada.

Family-style dining in country-modern decor with more than 245 locations in 3 countries.

A success phenomenon along with Dalts Grill with more than 225 locations in 7 countries.

For Development Information Call:

Radisson Hotels International: (612) 540-8185   Country Hospitality Corporation: (612) 449-1350
Colony Hotels & Resorts: (612) 449-1350   T.G.I. Friday's Inc.: (214) 450-5445

Carlson Hospitality Group℠

FIGURE 16-10   Carlson Hospitality's product line

front that the physical product might be different upon check-in, while the services inside were presumably the same. By adopting this concept, Radisson directly addressed one of the pitfalls of franchising, namely, that the product is not always the same. Carlson Hospitality Group, a division of Carlson Companies, Inc., the parent of Radisson, also manages, markets, and franchises Colony Hotels & Resorts, Country Lodging (by Carlson), Country Kitchen, T.G.I. Friday's, around the globe (Figure 16-10), plus two cruise ships.

Caveat

The examples we have given are intended to be illustrative only of the complexity of the owning, managing, and franchising "maze." The "reflagging" phenomenon (i.e., brand switching) that is occurring makes what is true today, false tomorrow (Figure 16-11). Figure 16-12 shows another example of the branding phenomenon. Wellesley Inns and AmeriSuites are Prime proprietary brands that Prime plans to expand aggressively; the other brands are franchises that Prime manages.

Other Distribution Channels

Strategic alliances between hotels and food-service companies are becoming common, especially in the economy hotel sector where many properties have no food and beverage outlets of their own and, thus, will link up with a food-service operator either in the property or close by. There are, of course, numerous ways to distribute the food-service product away from its place of production. Home or office delivery has become common. Other companies are also becoming more innovative, as shown in Figures 16-13 and 16-14. We anticipate seeing this trend continue and grow stronger.

Consortia, Affiliations, Reservations Companies, and Representation Companies

These four nomenclatures represent different distribution systems for hotel companies that can, at the same time, be both quite different

The Signs, They Are A-changing

Since May, new corporate flags wave over these and other hotels as owners and operators re-align their brand affiliations.

Old Brand/New Brand	City	Rooms
Bucksburn Moat House/ Holiday Inn Crowne Plaza	Aberdeen, Scotland	93
Bristol Moat House/Holiday Inn Crowne Plaza	Bristol, England	132
Caversham Hotel Reading/ Holiday Inn	Reading, England	112
Stouffer Riverview Plaza/ Adam's Mark	Mobile, Alabama	375
Econo Lodge/Holiday Inn Express	Greensboro, North Carolina	140
Carambola Beach Resort Rockresort (shuttered)/Radisson	St. Croix, US Virgin Islands	157
Clarion Inn/Sheraton Inn	Napa, California	191
Boston Vista Waltham/Westin	Waltham, Massachusetts	347
Newark Airport Vista/Hilton	Newark, New Jersey	375
Metrodome Hilton/Sheraton	Minneapolis, Minnesota	269
Lake Arrowhead Hilton/ Independent	Lake Arrowhead, California	261
Marriott/Hilton	Gaithersburg, Maryland	301
Renaissance/Hilton	East Brunswick, New Jersey	405
Exel Inn/Comfort Inn	Dallas/Fort Worth Airport	152
Ramada Inn/Courtyard by Marriott	Austin, Texas	98
Holiday Inn Crowne Plaza/ Ramada Plaza	Stamford, Connecticut	377

Source: Company reports, compiled by HOTELS.

Source: *Hotels*, October, 1993, p. 24. Courtesy of *Hotels*.

FIGURE 16-11   Changing flags—a continuous process

and quite similar. In general, we can say that none of the companies in these categories owns, manages, or franchises, although there are exceptions to that as well. Also, some companies that own, manage, and/or franchise *affiliate* with other companies that do likewise.

Perhaps, if we could generalize, we could say that these companies represent distribution channels that are *external* to companies that are in the hotel *operations* business. They are,

in fact, marketing tools and very important ones in the distribution process, especially internationally. A given hotel or hotel chain may be involved with all four.

In general, a *consortium* is a group of individual properties with different names that carry a common designation that groups them into the same product class. An *affiliation* is a group of hotels that carry the same common name, not necessarily in the same product class, or affiliate with another group, also with a same common name. *Reservations companies'* members carry their own names, or chain names, but use a common reservation system, as well as their own. *Representation companies* market and have sales offices to represent different properties under different names. All four categories have their own reservations systems.

Consortia

A consortium of hotels is a loosely-knit group of independently-owned and -managed properties with different names, a joint-marketing distribution purpose, and a common consortium designation. Some, however, may belong to chains. The hotel name is primary. Examples of consortia include Leading Hotels of the World and Preferred Hotels & Resorts Worldwide, each of which represents a number of upscale hotels, and Logis de France, which represents almost 4,700 family-run hotels of varying sizes in the one- and two-star categories in France. Tying these properties together is a joint-marketing effort aimed at similar target markets at different times and places. What also ties them together, and differentiates them from strictly reservations networks, is that there usually is some measure of control placed upon the membership.

The purpose of the consortium is to open a channel of distribution by maximizing combined marketing resources while retaining individual and independent management and products. Preferred Hotels, headquartered in the United States, is a marketing organization consortium of over 100 hotels in North America, Europe, the Middle East, and Asia. Preferred

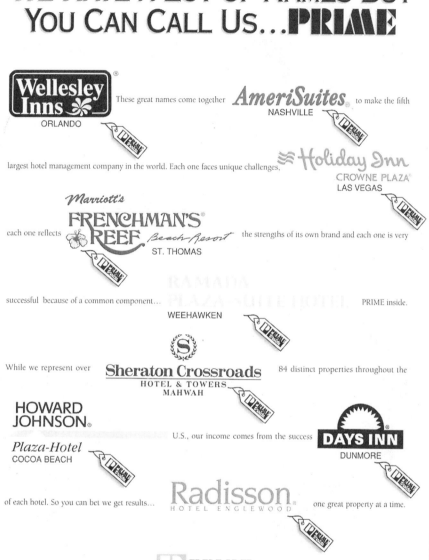

FIGURE 16-12 Prime Hospitality manages multiple brands including its own

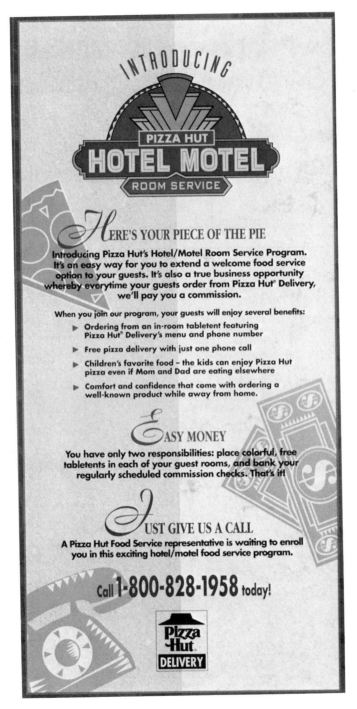

FIGURE 16-13   Pizza Hut extends its distribution to hotels

FIGURE 16-14   K-Paul's distributes "anywhere"

has a global reservations network and provides its members with a variety of marketing programs and services. The advantage to the property represented by Preferred is its ability to retain independent ownership and, therefore, individuality while obtaining worldwide representation in a product class. Its hotels are evaluated by an independent third party and must have an 80 percent score to pass (Figure 16-15). Preferred Hotels maintains very high standards within its membership grouping, and Preferred's hotel customers, in turn, realize that they are not buying a standardized product line (i.e., the traveler need not be wary of the potential experience). Preferred consortium members benefit not only from referrals, but also from advertising, public relations, sales, and direct marketing programs, a reduced credit card fee from American Express, toll-free reservation numbers worldwide, and inclusion in airlines' global distribution systems used by travel agents.

Consortia are far more abundant in Europe than in the United States. As an example, consider Inter Nor Hotels in Norway, which operates somewhat differently than Preferred.

Each Inter Nor hotel is independently named, owned, and managed. The collateral of each hotel carries the names of the others. Most promotions take place in all hotels simultaneously. Reservations are easily made from one to the other. Each hotel is labeled an Inter Nor hotel as if it were, in fact, a member of a unified chain. There is a "corporate" office in Oslo, which suggests and administers marketing programs for the "chain," evaluates the performance of each unit, arranges seminars to improve marketing and management, and, in general, acts in many ways like the corporate office of a hotel chain.

The services of this type of consortium do not end there; it may hook up with other consortia both to provide interchange reservations systems and to broaden the entire network. Inter Nor, for example, hooks up with Danway in Denmark, Arctia Hotels in Finland, Icelandic Hotels in Iceland, and Sara Hotels in Sweden, each of which is also a consortium. These arrangements provide a distribution network of over 100 hotels that not only reserve with each other but also combine on promotions.

"WHEN A HOTEL DOESN'T MEASURE UP, INSTEAD OF FIRING THE MANAGER, WE FIRE THE HOTEL."

We admit it's not standard operating procedure at the major hotel chains.

But then Preferred Hotels® and Resorts Worldwide is not a hotel chain.

We're an association of independent hotels.

It's our job to set and maintain the highest possible standards for a group of the finest hotels and resorts around the world. We're very strict when it comes to our standards. And very unforgiving with member hotels and resorts that don't adhere to them.

Admittedly, this is not an attractive concept to the great majority of hotels.

In fact, it's enough to keep all but the very best from applying. Which perhaps explains why, in a world of more than 300,000 hotels and resorts, at present only 105 are Preferred. They represent the very finest accommodations available anywhere at any price.

Interestingly, they are not necessarily the most expensive hotels in their market.

Ask your travel agent if there's a Preferred hotel where you plan to visit.

Or if you would like a directory listing our 105 current members, please call us at 1-800-447-5773.

PREFERRED
HOTELS & RESORTS
WORLDWIDE

©1992 Preferred Hotels® & Resorts Worldwide. All rights reserved.

Courtesy of Preferred Hotels & Resorts Worldwide

FIGURE 16-15 Preferred Hotels & Resorts maintains rigorous standards

THE PREFERRED
CONCEPT

To earn Preferred recognition, potential

member hotels must possess outstanding

credentials. Then they must submit to

two surprise inspections in which they

will be evaluated on more than 900

different criteria. Fewer than 10% of all

prospects survive this ordeal. In fact, so

rigorous is the evaluation that many four-

star hotels decline to apply.

Yes, our standards are high. Some might

argue that they are too high. Yet, to our

way of thinking, when a hotel displays the

Preferred plaque, it must be a hotel that

the most demanding and discriminating

traveller would prefer over all others.

It must represent true value and real quality.

RESERVATION
INFORMATION

For instant reservations at any Preferred Hotel
or Resort, contact your
professional travel planner or call:

North America
United States, Canada, Puerto Rico
1-800-323-7500
Apollo/Gemini/Sabre/SystemOne/
Worldspan (Pars & Datas II): PH

Asia · Pacific
Abacus, Axess: PH
Australia	02-247-65-37
Hong Kong	800-3365
Japan	03-3591-0585
Korea	0078-65-1-6547
Singapore	738-95-76
Thailand	001-800-65-6587

Europe
Amadeus, Galileo: PH
Austria	0660-83-73
Denmark	80-01-7191
France	0590-93-50
Germany	0130-86-00-33
Italy	1678-7-34-18
Netherlands	06-022-01-92
Spain	900-99-49-74
Sweden	020-79-55-56
Switzerland	155-11-18
United Kingdom	0-800-89-33-91

South America
Colombia	980-12-0995
Mexico	800-538-3600

Preferred Hotels & Resorts Worldwide
1901 South Meyers Road, Suite 220
Oakbrook Terrace, Illinois 60181 U.S.A.

FIGURE 16-15   (continued)

Relais & Chateaux is a Paris-based consortium with over 400 members in 30 countries, including the United States. Its collateral, published in several different languages, describes the consortium as follows:

> ...our objectives and procedures do not correspond to a fashion (fashion becomes outdated) but to a need—your's—we have no desire to change except for the better.... "The Relais & Chateaux do not form a chain, but a product." ...[O]ur clients are not interested in a chain. They look for a product with clearly defined differences, even if the presentation differs from one place to another....

Because a consortium does not exercise direct control over its properties, a major problem with consortia can be a disparity among its properties, both physically and in the way they are managed. Although properties are carefully screened for membership and there is really no desire for look-alikes, problems may still arise.

These differences among properties are not, of course, unique; many chains also have them, as we have pointed out. The franchise systems of Hilton and Sheraton are full of them, as are Holiday, Ramada, Wyndham, and many others. This is also true of restaurants, such as Ponderosa, Bennigan's, and Friendly's.

The problem that arises, in any case, is the one of customer expectations and perceptions. While the consortium network is a powerful one in the distribution system, it is also one that must be treated with great care. A chain can blame only itself if one of its units breaks down; a consortium, on the other hand, outside of flagrant protocol violation, must suffer its "wayward children." Such sufferance can be difficult. Conversely, the consortium distribution system represents the maintenance of individuality in a world of chain "sameness," with the advantage of chain marketing clout.

Affiliations

Many people consider Best Western a hotel chain. In fact, this worldwide organization is an affiliation of some 3,400 individually-owned properties in 47 countries, under a common umbrella. The hotel *name* is secondary in most cases but, as with consortia, each hotel is different. The variety of product offered to the customer is significant. The overall theme of the affiliation is the price-value relationship of the hotels. Best Western, in any marketplace, will tend to offer a clean room for the lowest price. The Best Western affiliation is a very successful channel of distribution. Although standards are lower than those for up-market counterparts, the strong sense of value in all marketplaces keeps customers coming back. Best Western, the largest such organization in the world under a common name, constantly seeks to add new members worldwide. It does not hesitate, however, to drop members that fail to live up to established standards. Best Western also painstakingly tries to differentiate itself from traditional franchised hotel chains (Figure 16-16).

Some hotel companies affiliate with other hotel companies for joint-marketing and distribution endeavors like the Inter Nor example given above. Radisson Hotels affiliated with Mövenpick Hotels International of Switzerland and SAS International Hotels of Oslo, until they had their own properties in Europe. These affiliations included joint sales and advertising efforts as well as marketing and reservations connections. Even Mövenpick restaurants throughout Europe carried listings of all the Radisson Hotels. Figure 16-17 shows an affiliation of these two chains in Beijing.

Golden Tulip Hotels, a subsidiary of KLM Royal Dutch Airlines, is another example of an affiliation that also serves as a reservations network with other chains such as Ashok of India.

Reservations Companies

Reservations companies are companies that offer member hotels a reservations service in all key areas of the world. These companies usually print an annual directory listing all member hotels but, apart from that, little sales and marketing is done on behalf of the members. The company itself, however, will spend a lot of effort and funds on promoting its company name and image to encourage travel agents and hotels to use its central reservations offices.

There is much overlap among consortia, affiliations, and reservations systems. Unlike consortia, however, reservations companies do not post entry requirements other than, perhaps, that the properties be within a certain product class range. A charge is assessed by the reservations company for each reservation made. Further, there is no significant central control that polices the properties.

The largest and most comprehensive reservation service is that of Utell International, in some ways also a representation company since it also has a sales staff. Utell has a central reservations system, worldwide sales offices, and connections to 450,000 travel agent terminals as well as all global distribution systems. Utell connects 6,500 hotels in over 140 countries, covering everything from tourist class to deluxe and from small independents to interna-

BEST WESTERN INTERNATIONAL

MORE THAN A FRANCHISE   A non-profit association dedicated solely to make profits FOR its member hotels, not FROM them. Fees not based on gross rooms revenue!

MORE THAN A HOTEL CHAIN   The world's largest chain with 3,400 Hotels, Resorts & Motor Hotels in 47 countries!

MORE THAN A RESERVATIONS SYSTEM   The best comprehensive support services — Business Builders & Cost Savers!

MORE THAN A FLAG   Super-power sales & marketing programs indispensable for success!

MORE THAN A SIGN   The symbol of reliability and value recognized the world over!

MORE THAN A CONTRACT   An annually renewable agreement you can cancel any time without penalty!

MORE THAN A "DEAL"   Irrefutably the greatest value in the industry!

MORE THAN EVER ...
THE TIME TO CALL IS NOW
For all the facts on *The Ultimate Affiliation*, call (602) 957-5867

Best Western
WORLDWIDE LODGING

FIGURE 16-16   Best Western advertises for affiliates

Beijing-Airport
MÖVENPICK Radisson
HOTEL

CINA

Categorìa ★★★★

Indirizzo:
Xiao Tianzhu Village
Shunyi County
P.O. Box 6913
Beijing /Repubblica popolare
di Cina
Telefono 01/900 02 86
900 80 41
Telefax 01/500 15 35
Telex 222 986 bamrh

Aeroporto:
Beijing Capital Airport,
5 minuti in bus pendolare

Sito:
All'aeroporto, a 25 minuti dal
centro città (bus pendolare)

Camere: 427
di cui 30 duplex
+ 48 suites junior

Ristoranti:
• Ristorante Mövenpick
(specialità europea)
• Chop Sticks
(cucina asiatica)
• Boulevard Lounge
• «Sproose Goose»
(Pub-Bar con animazione)

Conferenze:
Posti per 100 persone
Posti pranzo: 100 persone

Fitness/Sport:
Tennis, squash, ginnasio,
biciclette, solarium, massaggio,
campo di golf nelle vicinanze

Acquisti:
Arcata di negozi di souvenirs,
articoli d'arte ecc.

Banchetti:
Numero di sale: 4
Posti per 100 persone

47

FIGURE 16-17 Mövenpick and Radisson affiliate
for wider distribution

tional chains. Members pay, for each reservation, a fee to the airline reservation system (e.g., Sabre), Utell, and the travel agent that makes it, as well as a monthly fee to Utell.

Utell offers UtellVision, a unique visual display system that gives a picture of a hotel's rooms, its facilities and location in relation to major business and leisure venues, as well as

Courtesy of Utell International

FIGURE 16-18   Utell offers a "visual imagery" reservations system

rates and methods of payment (Figure 16-18). It accepts international currency deposits and pays travel agencies in their own currencies. In 1994, Utell booked over two million hotel reservations for five million room-nights worth over $800 million. Utell also offers "labelling service" for other systems such as Golden Tulip; that is, when you call Golden Tulip, what you really get is a Utell agent. Over 95 percent of Utell's business is travel agent-based.

FIGURE 16-19   Small inns combine to offer a reservation system

Figure 16-19 illustrates a reservations sytem for small inns. These kinds of distribution channels are becoming essential for just about every kind of lodging property in today's global marketplace.

Consortia and affiliations also have central reservations networks, and some share a reservations system, such as Golden Tulip with Utell. A hotel is assessed a charge by the reservations system for each reservation made.

Many hotel chains, of course, operate their own reservations systems as well. Among the largest and most successful are Holiday's Holidex and the systems of Sheraton's Reservatron, Hilton's Hiltron, Marriott's Marsha, Hyatt's Hyatt Spirit, and Radisson's Pierre. For the small chain or independent hotel, however, or for the company that wants to attract an international market from countries where it does not have properties or a reservation system, it is usually more cost-effective for them to hook up with a reservations/representation

One easy phone call reaches 250 hotels in Spain

And, everything else the country has to offer. Marketing Ahead is the specialist of quality tourism to Spain. And we make it so easy for you...just one phone call. From 3 star to 5 star, we represent and can put you in touch with more than 250 hotels in Spain. The right hotels for your clients, whether it be weekend or long-term, luxury or budget travel. Call us, we'll tailor the perfect travel package for your clients' needs.

Some of the hotels we represent:

PARADORES OF SPAIN -
(Representation In the Northeast, Mid West and West Coast of the United States)
SEVILLA - Hotel Inglaterra, Hotel Palacio Casa de Carmona
GRANADA - Hotel Alhambra Palace, Hotel La Bobadilla

BARCELONA - Derby Hotels, Hotel Colon, Hotel Condes de Barcelona
MADRID - Hotel Arosa, Hotel Suecia, Hotel Carlos V
IBIZA - Hotel La Hacienda
AVILA - Hotel Palacio Valderrabanos
SAN SEBASTIAN - Hotel Londres e Inglaterra
GALICIA - Gran Hotel La Toja

marketing ahead
Specializing in Quality Tourism to Spain

800-223-1356
433 fifth Avenue • new york, ny 10016 • (212) 686-9213 • (212) 686-0271 FAX

FIGURE 16-20   A region-specific reservation company

company to supplement their own systems. An example, a region-specific representation company, is shown in Figure 16-20.

Representation Companies

A representation ("rep") company is a channel of distribution that brings a hotel to a marketplace. These companies market a hotel to a customer base for a fee and are hired to act as sales organizations for independent properties that may have limited sales or reservations networks of their own. Major chains may also use rep firms to enhance their regional sales efforts. Rep firms have their own sales forces and represent a number of hotels through regional offices in different geographical areas.

Representation companies go much further than reservations companies in promoting their member hotels. Apart from the worldwide reservations network and link to all global distribution systems, they will, for instance, have a sales force actively selling their member hotels; they will print an annual directory featuring all hotels, with detailed information on their services and facilities, and print other marketing collateral such as special programs, newsletters, and flyers. They will also undertake aggresive public relations and advertising campaigns on behalf of their member hotels. Once a firm has been engaged, it uses all of the normal communications mix, such as direct sales, direct mail, advertising, and public relations, to get customers to buy certain hotels. Sales calls are the most utilized form of the communications mix, followed by direct mail.

Steigenberger Reservation Service (SRS), based in Frankfurt, is a case in point. SRS has over 330 members worldwide, 26 SRS sales offices, and four branding concepts. They are linked by a sophisticated reservations network and 11 reservation centers in 28 countries. Sales offices supply detailed information concerning all affiliated hotels.

Supranational, a very active sales and marketing company, is another example. Supranational's purpose is to unify the reservations network without sacrificing the identity of the individual property or chain. It represents 19 hotel companies, as well as a number of independent, rigorously-selected properties around the world (Figure 16-21). In total Supranational represents over 600 hotels in over 300 destinations in 50 countries and has 23 reservations offices worldwide. Thistle Hotels in the United Kingdom, Reso Hotels in Sweden, Delta Hotels in Canada, and Omni Hotels in the United States are members of this system. Supranational's selling point for customers is that, by calling the reservations office of the local hotel company of any of the member chains, it can book reservations directly anywhere in the world in any of the member chains' properties. A customer in Sweden can call the Reso Hotels reservations office in Stockholm and make a reservation at the Omni Hotel in New York City. Additionally, Supranational has an active sales force in all key markets, and each member hotel group is responsible for selling and marketing Supranational hotels in its local market; that is, each member of the system attempts to market its counterparts, in hopes that the counterparts are doing the same for them. A 4 percent commission on revenue is paid to the partner when this occurs. Supranational is a nonprofit organization operated by hoteliers for hoteliers.

Supranational also publishes a wide range of marketing programs, including directories with international hotel classifications, newsletters, "city savers," spotlight flyers, guaranted U.S. dollar programs, and incentive programs. Figure 16-22 shows some of its efforts. Its global distribution system, called SUPROS, is considered to be among the most cost-effective and advanced in the industry. It links into all the major airlines' systems and, all told, it has direct links to 240,000 travel agents.

A good rep firm also offers services to consumers, such as meeting planners, in prescreening hotels to be sure they will meet the consumers' needs, checking for space availability, negotiating the most attractive rates, and providing other information about hotels.

Representative firms either operate on a retainer basis or are paid a fee when the group checks out of the hotel. Once a hotel has retained the services of a representation company, the rep firm prints a brochure on the facility and markets it in clusters with other hotels in its network. Sales representatives of rep companies operate in much the same way as a hotel's sales department. They maintain a client base and files, and make sales calls to convince customers to use a facility in their portfolio rather than an alternative. Having a franchise does not preclude the use of a representation firm; some franchise operators like the opportunity of having as many people selling their hotels as possible.

A representation firm can be more cost-effective for a hotel company than establishing individual sales offices in feeder cities. A feeder city represents a geographic area from which business is derived, but where a company may or may not have a property of its own. For example, Chicago is a major feeder city for

We spend a long time selecting the hotels we recommend so that you don't have to.

At Supranational our reputation has been built on a rigorous hotel selection programme to ensure that member hotels meet our exacting standards.

● Supranational offers you a choice of over 600 business and resort hotels worldwide.

● Instant and written confirmation on your reservations.

● Guaranteed commission payments.

● A reliable, professional service from Supranational's 22 reservation offices around the world, with toll free numbers at most locations.

● Instant availability and room rates.

● Available on all major airline systems, Access code–SX.

For a free directory or reservations call:
AUSTRIA (662) 832 166
BELGIUM (078) 114 596 (Toll free)
DENMARK 8030 1031 (Toll free)
FINLAND (90) 131 001

FRANCE 0505 0011 (Toll free)
GERMANY 0130 6969 (Toll free)
GREAT BRITAIN (071) 937 8033
HOLLAND (020) 643 5734 (Toll free)
HUNGARY (361) 183 018

IRELAND (01) 605 000
ITALY 1678 13013 (Toll free)
JAPAN (03) 3545 9571
NORWAY (02) 171 700
S. AFRICA 0800 119000 (Toll free)

SPAIN–BARCELONA 900 300 684 (Toll free)
SPAIN–MADRID 900 100 149 (Toll free)
SWEDEN (08) 720 8880
SWITZERLAND (01) 715 1616
CRS ACCESS CODE: 'SX'

SUPRANATIONAL
HOTELS

Courtesy of Supranational Hotels

FIGURE 16-21   Supranational bases its reputation on product quality

New York City, as are Los Angeles, Paris, and London.

If Chicago was a major feeder city for a hotel in Phoenix, it might not be cost-effective for the Phoenix hotel to have a sales representative make frequent sales trips to Chicago. Also, setting up a regional office to call on customers can be very expensive. Instead, a representation

HOTEL CLASSIFICATION

The classification system adopted within this directory has been developed by the Publishers of the Official Hotel Guide. We hope it assists you in selecting your hotel.

Superior Deluxe An exclusive and luxury hotel, often palatial offering the highest standards of service, accommodation and facilities. Elegant and luxurious public rooms – A prestige address – Establishments in this category are among the world's top hotels.

Deluxe An outstanding property offering many of the same features as Superior Deluxe – May be less grand and offer more reasonable rates than the Superior Deluxe properties, yet in many instances may be just as satisfactory – Safe to recommend to most discriminating clients.

Moderate Deluxe Basically a Deluxe hotel, but with qualifications – In some cases, some accommodation or public areas may offer a less pronounced degree of luxury than that found in fully Deluxe properties – In other cases, the hotel may be a well-established famous name, depending heavily on past reputation – The more contemporary hotels may be heavily marketed to business clients, with fine accommodation and public rooms offering Deluxe standards in comfort, but with less emphasis on atmosphere and/or personal service.

Superior First An above average hotel May be an exceptionally well-maintained older hotel, more often a superior modern hotel specifically designed for the first class market, with some outstanding features – Accommodation and public areas are expected to be tastefully furnished and very comfortable – may be good value, especially if it is a commercial hotel – May be recommended to average clients and in most cases will satisfy the discriminating ones.

First An average, comfortable hotel with standardised rooms, amenities and public areas – Dependable but usually nothing special – May have superior executive level or wing May be safely recommended to average clients not expecting Deluxe facilities or special services – Should also be satisfactory for better groups.

Moderate First Essentially a First Class establishment with comfortable but somewhat simpler accommodation and public areas – May be lacking in some features (e.g. restaurant) – Some of the rooms or public areas while adequate, may tend to be basic and functional – Usually suitable for cost-conscious clients.

Superior Tourist Primarily a budget property with mostly well-kept, functional accommodation, some up to First Class standards – Public rooms may be limited or non-existent – Often just a place to sleep, but may have some charming or intimate features – May be good value – Should satisfy individuals (sometimes even discriminating ones) or groups on a budget.

Tourist Strictly a budget operation with some facilities or features of Superior Tourist Class, but usually no (or very few) First Class rooms – Should not be recommended to fussy or discriminating clients.

Unclassified Hotels (*) It is the policy of the Official Hotel Guide to classify hotels based on a comprehensive body of information encompassing a selection of reliable sources and contacts. If, however, that information is insufficient, incomplete or in any way ambiguous, a hotel may be listed without a classification, but this in no way reflects negatively on the property.

Courtesy of Supranational Hotels

FIGURE 16-22 Supranational hotel classifications and promotion efforts

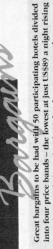

CITY SAVER Bonanza

SPECIAL LIMITED PERIOD OFFER!

FOR YOUR CLIENTS AND FOR YOU

Supranational Hotels' massive worldwide promotion, running from October 1st 1993 to 31 March 1994, offers your clients the chance to make huge savings on their city-centre hotel rooms, and you the opportunity to make excellent commission *and* win valuable prizes ... including the FIRST PRIZE OF TWO ROUND THE WORLD AIRLINE TICKETS!

- **ROOMS FROM JUST US$89.00**
  including service, tax and breakfast
- **50 SUPERB CITY CENTRE HOTELS**
  including Paris, London, San Francisco and Toronto
- **AVAILABLE EVERY DAY OF THE WEEK**
  unlike rival promotions which are only available at weekends
- **UNIVERSAL FLAT COMMISSION**
  paid in US dollars at higher than usual rates
- **TRAVEL RELATED BONUSES**
  to speed you along your way to winning the Big Round the World Trip for 2

Hotel Miguel Angel, Madrid

The Regency Hotel, London

CITY SAVER Bargains

Great bargains to be had with 50 participating hotels divided into four price bands – the lowest at just US$89 a night rising to US$119, US$149 and US$199 for the top properties.

Among the best bargains are the Hotel Emperador in Madrid and Hotel Eden in Amsterdam, both at US$89, Villa Florence in San Francisco and the Regency Hotel in London at US$119, and the Maritim Hotel in Cologne for US$149.

- **ALL RATES INCLUDE SERVICE, TAX AND BREAKFAST**
- **DOUBLE ROOM FOR SINGLE OCCUPANCY**
- **LATE CHECK-OUT**
- **AUTOMATIC UPGRADE** *(SUBJECT TO AVAILABILITY)*
- **FREE NEWSPAPER**

CITY SAVERS THAT EARN YOU MONEY...

- **COMMISSION SET AT US$10, $13, $16 AND $22 PER ROOMNIGHT FOR EACH BAND RESPECTIVELY**
- **COMMISSION PAYABLE WITHIN 21 DAYS OF GUESTS' DEPARTURE**

...AND SPECIAL BONUS PRIZES

During the promotion, agents booking more than 20 roomnights in any one month will receive a specially designed and branded leather luggage tag. At the end of March 1994, those who have booked a total of over 80 nights will receive a money belt; over 100 nights an alarm clock; and over 120 nights a special travel bag.

And, of course, there's the special
BONUS FIRST PRIZE OF A TRIP AROUND THE WORLD FOR 2

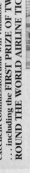

The Maritim Hannover Airport Hotel

The Hotel Alexander, Paris

FIGURE 16-22 (continued)

firm is retained in the feeder city and makes local calls, the most cost-effective method to build the channel of distribution.

Representation companies differ from normal wholesalers and retailers in the consumer goods channels of distribution in that they do not take even nominal possession of the goods. These firms do not buy blocks of hotel space and then resell. The client hotel does not pay for what it doesn't receive, but inventory can go unused if the representation firm is not successful.

On the surface, representation firms, generally located in major metropolitan centers, seem to offer a lucrative support system to the marketing distribution effort. This is usually the case. Sometimes, however, there are disputes as to where the booking originated. For example, a hotel might have an IBM account in its file system when its representative firm uncovers a piece of business from the same company through a different contact. The question arises as to whether the firm should be paid for the booking. Details like this need to be worked out before the representation agreement is consummated. If handled properly, this channel of distribution can be an effective addition to distribution efforts.

Incentive Houses

Incentive houses, companies that specialize in handling strictly incentive reward travel, are an excellent example of a strong channel of distribution. As discussed in Chapter 7, many organizations and firms have incentive contests to reward top-performing employees, salespeople, dealers, or retailers. Travel rewards are a popular form of incentive.

Major corporations often have their own in-house travel departments or individuals to handle incentive arrangements. Many companies have used travel agents. More and more, however, both large and small companies are relying on incentive houses, such as Carlson Marketing Group, to organize their trips. (Carlson Marketing Group is one of the leading incentive travel providers, with offices in 30 major cities in the United States and in 20 countries worldwide.)

The reason companies are turning to incentive houses is that incentive travel is a special case. For companies that frequently use this kind of reward, there is a constant need for destinations that are new, different, and exciting—in other words, that offer a real incentive. Second, there is a real need for the trip to be letter-perfect. Keeping up with all this, on a worldwide basis, is expensive and time-consuming.

Incentive houses, because of their collective accounts, can parcel out the costs of their expertise. Almost always, a representative from the incentive house will have visited and thoroughly inspected the destination, the hotels, the restaurants, and the ground services, before putting together the incentive package. The incentive house then "sells" it to the company and helps the company to "sell" it to those who will seek the reward.

For upscale hotels, particularly in resort areas or foreign destinations, it can be a real boost to the distribution channel to be on the incentive houses' lists. In these cases, a property (and incentive planners deal with individual properties as opposed to chains to be certain of the product) does not simply buy an incentive house's services. In effect, it earns them by doing things right. By contrast with consortia, reservations networks, rep firms, and travel agents, the incentive house's service is paid for by the customer, not the hotel.

In incentive reward situations, each channel member is integrally dependent on the others for performance. The incentive house has the corporate customer base. If customers are dissatisfied with the trip, they may choose another incentive house for the next program. Each channel member has to make sure that everything goes as promised. For example, if the ground transportation is an hour late in picking up a group at the airport, the entire trip can be spoiled and future business lost, not only to another incentive house, but to another destination.

Travel Agents

In a channel of distribution a travel agent is an intermediary who makes reservations for a variety of hospitality needs. The travel agent is compensated in the form of a commission, usually based upon the rate of the service purchased. As a rule of thumb in most cases, a 10 percent commission is paid to travel agents who book cruises and hotel rooms, while airlines and rental car firms pay a lesser rate. Travel agencies also form consortia, using the strength of many individual agencies to combine marketing and negotiating clout as a channel member. As a channel of distribution, the travel agent is second to none. Table 16-1 shows the status of travel agents in 1993.

In the less-recent past, the travel agent was primarily oriented toward the individual traveler, be it for business or pleasure. This practice has been changing, and agents are handling more meetings and group itineraries each year. The travel agency also is more of a full-service channel whereby hotel-booking may be incidental to the airline and ground transportation already arranged. Because of this, travel agencies are actively soliciting corporate meeting accounts, especially when they have previously handled the company's individual business travel. By promising more clout in negotiating

rates, the travel agency role in meeting planning is bound to increase.

The Travel Agent Role

The travel agent is faced with a blizzard of changing conditions in the marketplace. Airlines, collectively, are reported to change fares as many as 80,000 times a day. To recommend a hotel, the agent needs knowledge of location, rates, amenities, dining, entertainment, parking, ground transportation, recreation facilities, and more. The technology of the industry is changing at a furious pace in an attempt to keep up with all this information. Thus, the travel agent relies heavily on systems we have previously discussed, plus some others.

Agencies that were on manual systems only a short time ago, now have sophisticated database equipment to manage their bookings. (Almost 100 percent in the United States, but not so in Europe and Asia, as shown in Table 16-1.) Figure 16-23 shows one example of such sophistication. Other automated systems are, in fact, largely reservation terminals provided by the airlines (e.g., Apollo by United Airlines and Sa-

TABLE 16-1   A Brief Review of Travel Agencies

There are 32,000 travel agencies in the United States and 3,000 in Canada. The vast majority are single-location offices accounting for two-thirds of travel bookings. The mega-agencies account for just 25%. In the United States, 96% of all agencies are automated. They make $10.5 billion yearly in hotel bookings, half of which are CRS transactions.

The European agency market consists of 40,000 agency locations, producing $9 billion in hotel bookings. Six countries account for 75% of these agencies: the UK, Germany, France, Italy, Spain, and Sweden. Mega-agencies dominate and tend to specialize in either business or leisure/passage travel. Only 40% of agencies are automated. In the UK, 22% of agents are automated. Germany is one of Europe's most technologically advanced—70% are equipped with Amadeus' Start System. Only 13% of hotel bookings in Europe are made via CRS.

The Asia/Pacific market consists of 13,000 agencies doing $20 billion in hotel sales. Four central markets—Japan, Hong Kong, Australia, and Korea—account for 80% of all travel activity. The Japanese market is dominated by mega-agencies. Four account for half of the travel business. Japan Travel Bureau is the world's largest travel agency, followed by Kintetsu, Nippon Travel Agency, and Tokyo Travel. Automation is clearly on the rise, yet few hotel bookings are conducted through CRS. While 97% of Japanese agencies have CRS systems, only 30–40% outside Japan have access to CRS.

Source: Chris Schulz, *Hotels,* November, 1993, p. 82. Courtesy of *Hotels.*

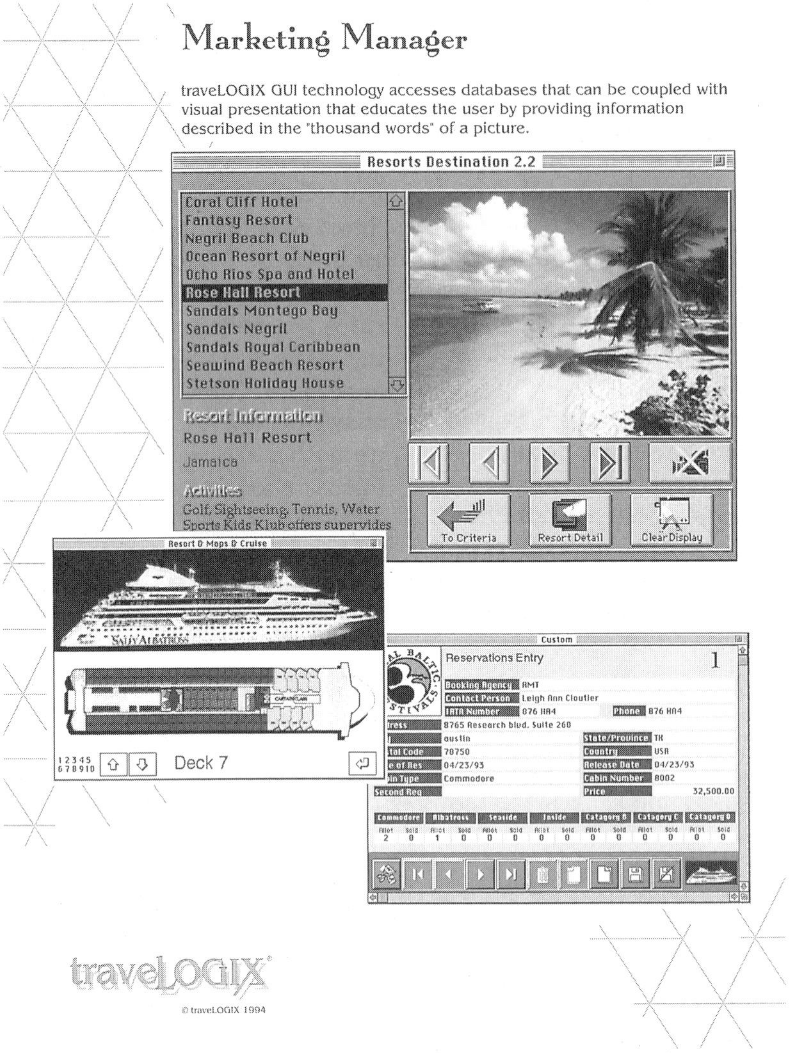

FIGURE 16-23 TraveLOGIX's CRS technology

bre by American Airlines), creating a direct link between travel agents and the airlines controlling this distribution channel. Figure 16-24 is a sample directory page from the Sabre system. Like the hotel systems, these have been called central reservations systems (CRS), but are now being called global distribution systems (GDS). Table 16-2 shows GDS computer screen data that travel agents would view for the Roger Smith Hotel in New York City.

Rates change at an unparalleled frequency in the history of travel. The proliferation of hotels offering thousands of packages, incentives, and varying rate structures to varying people at varying times, makes booking a difficult task at best.

The rental car industry has followed suit with the airlines and hotels, offering special promotions and incentives every day. Many of these promotions have conditions attached to them, such as booking an airline seat 30 days in advance, with cancellation penalty clauses. Add to all this the overlapping frequent-traveler awards (and the traveler's perplexity over a

SABRE ASSOCIATES RFERENCE 1994

HOTELS

ITT Sheraton

SHERATON HOTELS
Y/HHL/ZSI

SIGNATURE INNS .... Y/HHL/USJ
SKYLINE HOTELS .... Y/HHL/HSY
SLEEP INNS .... Y/HHL/ZQI
SMALL LUXURY HOTELS .... Y/HHL/XLX
SONESTA HOTELS .... Y/HHL/ZSO
SOUTHERN PACIFIC HTLS .... Y/HHL/USP
SOUTHERN SUN HTLS .... Y/HHL/HSU
S.R.S. HOTELS .... Y/HHL/XSR
STAKIS HOTEL GROUP .... Y/HHL/HBS
STERLING INTL .... Y/HHL/QWR
STOUFFER HOTELS .... Y/HHL/XST
SUMMERFIELD SUITES .... Y/HHL/QSS

SUMMIT INTERNATIONAL Y/HHL/XLQ
SUMMIT INTERNATIONAL HOTELS

SUPRANATIONAL LTD Y/HHL/HSX
Supranational Hotels

SUSSE CHALET .... Y/HHL/CEH
SWALLOW HOTELS .... Y/HHL/ZUK
SWISSOTEL .... Y/HHL/QSL
THISTLE HOTELS .... Y/HHL/QTX
TRAVAMERICA .... Y/HHL/TVH
TREFF HOTELS .... Y/HHL/TTX
TRUST INTL HOTELS .... Y/HHL/ETR
TURKEY DIRECT INTL .... Y/HHL/HTY

HOTELS

TRAVELODGE HOTELS Y/HHL/ZTL
Travelodge

ULTIMATE RESORTS .... Y/HHL/VUR

UTELL INTERNATIONAL Y/HHL/ZUI
UTELL INTERNATIONAL

VACATION NETWORK .... Y/HHL/ZVN
THE VAGABOND INNS .... Y/HHL/XVA
VENTURE INNS .... Y/HHL/ZVI
VIDAFEL RESORTS .... Y/HHL/QVV
VILLAGE RESORTS .... Y/HHL/ZVR
VILLAS BY MARRIOTT .... Y/HHL/HMB

VIP RESERVATIONS Y/HHL/ZVP
VIP RESERVATIONS INC.
CRS CODE: VP ... all Airlines ... Hotels ... Resorts
- *LOCATIONS IN MORE THAN 45 COUNTRIES*
- *INSTANT CONFIRMATIONS...Direct Link ALL Airlines*
- *GUARANTEED COMMISSION...Payment Programs through CitiCorp World Travel Payment Program*

WESTIN HOTELS .... Y/HHL/QWI
WESTMARK HOTELS .... Y/HHL/QWM
WICHITA INN SUITES .... Y/HHL/HWS
WORLD HOTELS .... Y/HHL/UWW
WYNDHAM HOTELS .... Y/HHL/QWY

INSURANCE

MUTUAL OF OHAMA Y/EXT/QMU
Mutual of Omaha Insurance Company

VOYAGEUR .... Y/EXT/VOY

LIMOUSINE SERIVCES

BOSTON COACH .... Y/EXT/UBC
CAMELOT BARTHROPP .... Y/EXT/QCB
CAREY INT'L LIMOUSINE .... Y/EXT/CYC
GOTHAM LIMOUSINE .... N*/GOTHAM
NIPPON TRAVEL AGENCY .... Y/EXT/NPN
N*/LIMO SERVICE NJ
N*/LIMO SERVICE LAX
N*/LIMO SERVICE RDU
N*/LIMO SERVICE SJU

NATIONAL TOURISM OFFICES

ANTIGUA .... N*/ANTIGUA
AUSTRALIA .... N*/AUSTRALIA
AUSTRIA .... N*/AUSTRIA
BAHAMAS .... N*/BAHAMAS
BARBADOS .... N*/BARBADOS
BARBUDA .... N*/BARBUDA
BELGIUM .... N*/BELGIUM
BERMUDA .... N*/BERMUDA
BRITAIN .... N*/BRITAIN
CHINA .... N*/CHINA
CURACAO .... N*/CURACAO
DENMARK .... N*/DENMARK
FINLAND .... N*/FINLAND
FRANCE .... N*/FRANCE
GERMANY .... N*/GERMANY
HAMBURG .... N*/HAMBURG
HOLLAND .... N*/NETHERLANDS
ITALY .... N*/ITALY
JAMAICA .... N*/JAMAICA
MALTA .... N*/MALTA
MEXICO .... N*/MEXICO
MARTINIQUE .... N*/MARTINIQUE
NETHERLANDS .... N*/NETHERLANDS
NEVIS .... N*/NEVIS
NEW ZEALAND .... N*/NEW ZEALAND
PHILIPPINES .... N*/PHILIPPINES
PORTUGAL .... N*/PORTUGAL
SAINT KITTS .... N*/ST KITTS
SAINT MARTIN .... N*/ST MARTIN
SINGAPORE .... N*/SINGAPORE
SPAIN .... N*/SPAIN
SWEDEN .... N*/SWEDEN
SWITZERLAND .... N*/SWITZERLAND
THAILAND .... N*/THAILAND
UNITED KINGDOM .... N*/BRITAIN

FIGURE 16-24 Page from a Sabre system directory

myriad of choices, whether to take airline, hotel, or car rental points) and you have an incredibly complex problem for the ordinary traveler. A good travel agent tries to ease this burden and may well earn his or her commission on this basis alone.

For some time, travel agents were considered necessary evils by both the airline and hotel

TABLE 16-2   GDS Hotel Information on Computer Monitor

```
HOD19789
PW19789 ROGER SMITH                          AIRPORT - LGA 501
        LEXINGTON AVE                        CURRENCY - USD/2
        NEW YORK NY 10017
        FONE 212-755-1400
        FAX  212-319-9130
   HOD*/*R   TO DISPLAY RATE GRID ONLY
   HOD*/-R   TO DISPLAY HOTEL INFORMATION W/O RATE GRID


RAC A1D       A2T       B1D       B2T       C1D       C2T
RAC AJS       AS1       AS2


EXTRAS/OPTS- RA 20.00 RC 20.00 CR    .00  EX 20.00
             FAM-Y MEAL-Y TAX-20
LOCATION- NEW YORK NY
          MIDTOWN MANHATTAN ON EASTSIDE
          NEAR UNITED NATIONS, ROCKEFELLER CENTER, FIFTH
          AVENUE,THEATERS,GRAND-CENTRAL STATION.


COMMUNICATIONS-
          TELEX   NOT AVAIL FAX   212-319 9130 OR 212 758 4061


TRANSPORTATION-
          TAXI LIMOUSINE
          PRIVATE AIRPORT TRANSFER RATES ARE AS FOLLOWS-
          HOTEL TO LAGUARDIA USD 30.00.ONE WAY
          HOTEL TO KENNEDY USD 45.00 ONE WAY
          HOTEL TO NEWARK USD 55.00 ONE WAY
          ALL RATES QUOTED ARE SUBJECT TO CHANGE
          FOR ARRIVALS ONLY PLEASE ADD USD 5.00 SUPPLEMENT.
          PLEASE REQUEST IN SI-FIELD WITH COMPLETE FLIGHT DETAILS.


POLICY-
          CHECK-IN 2PM  /  CHECK-OUT  1PM.
          MAXIMUM 4 PERSONS PER ROOM.
          CHILDREN UNDER 16 YRS FREE IN ROOM WITH PARENTS.
          CONTINENTAL BREAKFAST INCLUDED IN RATE.
          10% COMMISSION PAID WITHIN 48HRS OF GUEST DEPARTURE.
          TAXES ARE NOT INCLUDED IN RATE.


DEPOSIT/GUARANTEE-
          AX-CB-DC-MC-VS-DS CREDIT CARD GUARANTEE
          ACCEPTABLE WITH VALID EXPIRATION DATE AND
          CARDHOLDER NAME.


CANCELLATION/REVISION-
          MUST CANCEL OR REVISE BEFORE 4PM ON DAY OF ARRIVAL
          TO AVOID PENALTY.


CORPORATE RATE-
          SELL  FROM AVAILABILITY AND INCLUDE GUESTS COMPANY
          NAME AND CITY IN SI-FIELD.


FACILITIES-
          -136 OVERSIZE ROOMS INCLUDING 26 SUITES.  ALL ROOMS
           HAVE REFRIGERATORS AND COFFEE MAKERS /-SUITES ALL
           FEATURE KITCHENETTES.
```

TABLE 16-2 (continued)

```
                  -VIP FLOOR 9TH FEATURES MARBLE BATHROOMS WITH
                   JACUZZI, HEATED TOWEL RACKS, BATHROBES.
                  -PERMANENT AND ROTATING ART EXHIBITS BY MAJOR AND UP
                   AND COMING CONTEMPORARY ARTISTS.
                  -ROOFTOP TERRACE AND PENTHOUSE SUITE AVAILABLE FOR PRIVATE FUNCTIONS.
                  -NEARBY EXCELSIOR HEALTH CLUB AVAILABLE TO ADULT
                   GUESTS FEATURES LAP POOL, AEROBIC MACHINES/CLASSES,
                   WEIGHT EQUIPMENT, SUNDECK, COMPLIMENTARY BREAKFAST
                   FROM 7AM TO 11AM.
                  -LILYS RESTAURANT AND BAR-WHIMSICAL, SURPRISING,
                   ELEGANT, WAP-V.  FLAMBOYANT, ENERGETIC, PLAYFUL-SERVES
                   NEW AMERICAN ART CUISINE IN A CASUAL SETTING FROM 6AM
                   TO 10PM.

SERVICES-
                  -COMPLIMENTARY CONTINENTAL BREAKFAST BUFFET INCLUDED
                   IN RATE.
                  -24 HOUR ROOM SERVICE.
                  -ART EXHIBITIONS IN PUBLIC SPACE.
                  -WEEKDAY NEW YORK TIMES.
                  -PHOTOCOPY/SECRETARIAL SERVICE.
                  -EXERCISE AT NEARBY EXCELSIOR CLUB.
                  -CABLE TV WITH FREE.HBO/VIDEO RENTALS.
                  -WEEKEND PASSES TO MUSEUM OF MODERN ART OR GUGGENHEIM.
                  -FAMILY PLAN INCLUDES GIFTS FOR CHILDREN
                  -VALET PARKING.
                  -BABYSITTING.
                  -OVERNIGHT LAUNDRY SERVICE.

ATTRACTIONS-
                   ST. PATRICKS CATHEDRAL........... 4 BLOCKS
                   UNITED NATIONS................... 4 BLOCKS
                   CHRYSLER BUILDING................ 3 BLOCKS
                   MUSEUM OF MODERN ART............. 8 BLOCKS
                   THEATER DISTRICT/TIMES SQUARE.... 5 BLOCKS
                   JACOB JAVITS CONVENTION CENTER... 1 MILE
                   MADISON AVE. SHOPPING............ 2 BLOCKS
                   GRAND CENTRAL TERMINAL........... 3 BLOCKS
                   CENTRAL PARK.....................15 BLOCKS
                   GUGGENHEIM MUSEUM.............. 2.5 MILES

INDEXES-      C   11W  0 LGA
              C    0   0 NYC
              C   17NW 0 JFK
              S   18NE 0 EWR
          NY C   0N   0 CENTRAL PARK
          NY C   0W   0 ST PATRICKS CATHEDRAL
          NY C   0E   0 UNITED NATIONS
          NY C   0S   0 CHRYSLER BUILDING
          NY C   0W   0 MUSEUM OF MODERN ART
          NY C   2N   0 GUGGENHEIM MUSEUM
          NY C   0SW  0 TIMES SQUARE
          NY C   0S   0 GRAND CENTRAL STATION

QLW.QLW*AOB 1705/13DEC93 873602
```

industries. Managers felt that commissions were being paid for bookings that would have been received regardless. Supply-and-demand changes in the industry, however, have brought a new significance to the role of this intermediary. Ritz-Carlton Hotels, for example, has set a goal of having 50 percent of its reservations come through travel agents by 1996, up from its previous 15 percent in 1991. Over 50 percent of Radisson's bookings already come from travel agents.

It is contended that travel agents account for an annual $11 billion in hotel sales from the United States: 25 percent of domestic hotel occupancies, 50–80 percent of resort occupancies, 85–90 percent of international hotel sales, and nearly 100 percent of cruises.[5]

Working with Travel Agents

The travel agent needs clear, concise information on the product, and cooperation with the delivery of the product. The hotel company that can provide the least-complicated products to the travel agent, and deliver them to the customer, will get the most bookings. The more agents have to decipher very difficult booking procedures, the less likely they are to recommend the facility in the future.

All rates and information furnished to travel agencies on a property need to be as current as possible. Travel agencies have their own customer bases, and will be blamed by their customers for poor service at a facility that they recommended. As one example, the fact that a hotel plans lengthy renovations should be communicated to travel agents before they hear it from their customers. The short-term loss of revenue from the agents' not booking the facility during the renovation period will appear small when compared with the possible customer dissatisfaction and loss of future bookings.

Cooperation with the agent consists also of paying commissions on a timely basis. The agency has performed the desired service of bringing the product through the channel of distribution. For that service, it needs to be paid. Because most agencies are small, cash flow is very important to their survival. A company or hotel can very quickly get the reputation of being slow or of not paying on commissions. Agencies will go out of their way to avoid recommending the property if they are not receiving their commissions. Contrarily, agents are quick to recommend those who pay commissions promptly.

Further, cooperation with travel agents includes upgrading their important clients at no extra charge, offering complimentary stays to allow them to experience the product firsthand, doing special promotions to gain their loyalty and, in general, working with them in every way possible. To fail to do this is to bite the hand that feeds you. Hospitality companies today often market directly to the travel agent (Figure 16-25).

The hospitality company that does the best job utilizing this channel of distribution will be the one that gets the lion's share of their business. A familiarization trip (commonly referred to as a "fam trip") is a popular method used to expose the hotel product to intermediaries in the channel of distribution. A fam trip is just that; the hotel has a group of travel agents visit the facility to familiarize them with the features and benefits. Word-of-mouth advertising is the most believable form of communication. If travel agents are impressed with a facility during a fam trip, they will convey their enthusiasm to customers, and bookings will increase.

Travel agents are also reached through other distribution channels. Advertising in travel agent publications (e.g., *Travel Weekly*) is one such channel, but usually not a particularly strong one. Travel agents don't have time to read these carefully. Direct mail is another channel that has begun to suffer from information overload. The best channels, without a doubt, make information readily available to travel agents when they need it. Computer technology is doing this for some; for others, there are worldwide publications such as *Hotel & Travel Index* and *Official Hotel Guide* (Figure 16-26) that list, in summary fashion, basic details about hotels—but only the computer or a phone call can provide up-to-the-minute rates.

---

[5]Melinda Bush, "The Travel Agency Market is Key," *HSMAI Marketing Review*, Winter, 1994, p. 11.

PANAMA CANAL
TO THE MEXICAN RIVIERA AND CARIBBEAN

- 10 day cruises on the Cunard Crown Dynasty from Acapulco to Ft. Lauderdale or 11 day cruises from Ft. Lauderdale to Acapulco

- Ports include Puerto Caldera, Ocho Rios, Cozumel and Grand Cayman

- Early booking savings extended to sailing date for cruises through March 1994

- For cruises after March 1994, book 4 months prior and receive a 15% discount

- With these savings 10 day fares range from $1,270 to $4,212 including roundtrip economy air

- Combine two cruises and save up to 50% on the second cruise

- Or, book a group of as few as 10 passengers and qualify for discounts up to 35%

For a free brochure call 1-800-962-1130
Reservations: 1-800-5-CUNARD
In Canada: 1-800-268-3705
For Sales Assistance and
Group Information: 1-800-223-0764
Fax: 1-718-786-0038
In Western U.S.: 1-800-228-6449

CUNARD CROWN

Lose yourself in the experience, not in the crowd.

For ten days out of the year

the sun should revolve around your clients.

Savings are based on retail rates published in brochure and cannot be combined with any other discount or special offer. Rates are per person, double occupancy, subject to availability and dependent on departure date. Port and handling charges are $150 per person extra. Free roundtrip economy air from 91 U.S. and Canadian cities. See brochure for full details. Cunard Crown Dynasty is registered in Panama. ©1993 Cunard.

Z50

Courtesy of Cunard

FIGURE 16-25   Marketing directly to the travel agent

FIGURE 16-26   A hotel guide for travel agents

Travel agents are as important worldwide as they are in the United States. In major destination areas such as Singapore, Hong Kong, and Manila, many agents operate as "inbound" agents—that is, they deal primarily with people coming into the country as opposed to those going out. This means setting up ground arrangements, hotel bookings, local tours, and so forth.

In North America, travel agencies are becoming fewer in number but larger in size, because size is needed to handle the large accounts and negotiate the best arrangements, a necessary ability for being the agent of choice. Further, by banding together in consortia, groups of agencies have been able to bargain collectively with travel suppliers to gain access to preferred rates or other customer benefits. These are subsequently used as enticements to lure and retain commercial clientele, who could not obtain the same benefits. Through the control of information, agents exert great influence in all segments of the travel market.

Although nearly all U.S. travel agencies possess automated ticketing systems, they process only about 20 percent of their room reservations via those systems. However, this percentage is increasing as the speed of a transaction becomes increasingly critical to an agency's profitability. Figure 16-27 is an ad offering a CRS systems access code, while Figure 16-28 offers hotel reservations through seven global distribution systems.

In fact, travel agents do not sell airline seats, hotel rooms, or rental cars—they sell time. A 10 percent commission on a $100 room is $10. A travel agent can access this hotel room through a GDS in three to seven seconds. If that same travel agent had to look up the property in a directory, dial the 800 number, be put on hold, speak to an agent, and then confirm the booking, they would make the same $10 for ten minutes worth of work. In today's highly competitive environment, agencies that take ten minutes for a $10 commission will not be in business very long.

The Travel Agency Future

Ironically, the technology that allows agencies to have access to an increasing volume of information is the same technology that threatens their existence. Once the technology is adapted to personal computers, the channel of distribution will become increasingly direct to the consumer. The new information highways being developed today may eliminate portions of the travel agent's business.

Already, for example, one can personally fax a request through TravelFax, an automated booking system that can book flights, hotel rooms, and rental cars and fax back a confirmed travel itinerary in about an hour. While not offering the travel agent's expertise, TravelFax and personal computer-based reservation systems such as MailLink, PC Link, and Eaasy Sabre are catching on with business travelers who like the security of making their own reservations and don't want to spend a lot of time on the telephone.

There are already close to two million subscribers to Eaasy Sabre, the PC-based reservation service of AMR Corp., the parent company of American Airlines. Eaasy Sabre is accessed through public data networks such as CompuServe, Prodigy, and America OnLine, and gives access to most of the information available to travel agents using the industrial-strength Sabre computerized reservation system. Using Eaasy Sabre provides the added convenience of having tickets sent to you through a travel agent, delivered by overnight courier, or available to be picked up at the airport.

MailLink is an electronic mail-based version of TravelFax; PC Link is for stand-alone PC users. Both provide artificial intelligence software that takes a role in finding suitable travel arrangements. Their software actually scans the schedules for the user and proposes several choices that fit his or her parameters.

As of this writing, these systems are not yet a substitute for the experienced travel agent when booking complicated and/or international itineraries or making special requests at hotels. Rather, they are designed to complement the services of a travel agent when using routine bookings. The future, however, may tell a different story.

Another phenomenon that is occurring in the travel agent world is the "super" travel agent. For example, American Express has become through acquisitions the world's largest travel agency, with nearly twice the volume of its nearest competitor. In 1993, American Express sold more than $8 billion of airline, hotel, car rental, and cruise bookings.[6] American Express also operates as a full-service tour operator

---

[6]James S. Hirsch, "American Express, the Sleeping Giant, Wakes and Spooks the Travel Industry," *Wall Street Journal*, February 24, 1994, p. B1.

Eventually you'll know IT backwards!

A Systems Access Code worth remembering

Mount Charlotte Thistle Hotels, the UK's second largest hotel chain, makes it easier than ever to book your clients into our hotels.

Now one CRS code, TI, gives you access to over 110 hotels in the UK, incorporating 39 Thistle properties, and in London include Whites overlooking Kensington Gardens, The Tower Thistle with views across the Thames and the Mount Royal in Oxford Street.

Outside London, your choice is even greater with quality four star hotels including The Arden Thistle in Stratford upon Avon, the King James Thistle in Edinburgh: Luxury country house hotels, New Hall near Birmingham, Audleys Wood on the outskirts of the New Forest in Hampshire - we have the hotels, the choice is yours.

Johnstounburn House, Nr Edinburgh   The Arden Thistle, Stratford upon Avon   Whites (A Thistle Hotel), London   Royal Horseguards Thistle, London

TI gives you real time availability with the most up to date rates - details on special offers and instant confirmation of your reservation.

TI, another aspect of our commitment to enhance our service to you and your clients.

For reservations access TI or call Toll Free 1-800 847 4358

MOUNT CHARLOTTE
THISTLE HOTELS
OF BRITAIN

FIGURE 16-27   A hotel chain provides CRS access to agents

(Figure 16-29). American Express corporate charge cards generate reams of travel data on everything from a client's favorite carrier to his most frequented destination; this information is used when it bids for a company's travel account. Clients benefit from the company's massive purchasing power and its technological sophistication.

FIGURE 16-28 Hotel reservations through seven global distribution systems

Tour Operators and Wholesalers

Tour operators differ from their counterparts in channel management options in that they take nominal possession, or secure an allotment, of the hotel inventory to sell it to the public. Tour operators may also take nominal possession of the food and beverage product, by making reservations in a number of outlets at anticipated tour destination points, and they may arrange for ground transportation, side trips, historical site visits, etc. There are two types of tour operators: wholesalers, or tour brokers, and "ad hoc" tour operators. (The word *tour* should not necessarily be construed as meaning groups.)

FIGURE 16-29 American Express as a full-service tour operator

Generally, they all work through travel agent retailers, but these channels book as many, or more, individuals and couples.

The wholesaler or broker "blocks" space and then uses various combinations of the communications and distribution mixes to market the facilities to individual and group consumers. Brochures featuring a tour, or multiple tours, and all related accommodations are printed and distributed to travel agents or mailed to existing and potential customers, usually on request. The consumer picks up a brochure at a travel agency (an example, Figure 16-30), or responds to an ad.

Advertising in the print media is also a common practice to attract tour customers. Consider, for example, the Liberty Travel ad in Figure 16-31. The part shown is less than half of a full-page ad that Liberty Travel runs weekly on the back page of the Sunday *New York Times* Travel Section with various destinations and promotions. The small box for five Hyatt hotels in the Caribbean is paid for by Hyatt. The rest of the page is paid for by American Airlines, other advertised destinations, and Liberty Travel. Hyatt spends about 2 percent of its Caribbean wholesaler revenue on this type of advertising, for a wholesale market that is 30 percent of total rooms and 40 percent of FIT business for Hyatt in this destination. This activity, for Hyatt, does not really fall into the realm of advertising as discussed in Chapter 13, for nothing in the ad is stated but the name, location, and price. The activity flows through the distribution channels of the wholesaler, in this case GoGo Tours, and the retailer, in this case, Liberty Travel. GoGo Tours does millions of dollars of business in the Caribbean, as well as elsewhere. It takes an allotment of rooms from Hyatt, for example, at 20 percent off Hyatt's gross rate, in different rate categories, with cutoff time periods to sell them. Other wholesalers work on a "sell and report" basis, that is, they report sales only after they are made, free of a cutoff time. The hotel advises sellout periods. GoGo's inventory appears in the computers of 170 Liberty Travel agencies. GoGo also sells rooms for American Express under its private label, as was shown in Figure 16-29. The rooms are sold by travel agents at their regular rates, as if they called the hotel directly. Hyatt, of course, has paid GoGo a commission. GoGo pays a commission to the travel agent. Hyatt pays for the ad and has its own reservations system that books the rooms. Of course, other Hyatt advertising or experience complements this channel.[7]

The wholesaler market includes people using a variety of transportation options. The wholesaler negotiates with the airlines, cruise lines, railroads, hotels, car rental firms, and bus companies to develop travel options to be resold as a total package. (Figure 16-32 shows some examples.) Groups come from every realm of the spectrum, from a high school hockey team to an upscale corporate trip to the Super Bowl, to individual travelers. Wholesalers negotiate the best possible deals from the suppliers and then sell at a price to include their profit margins. Figure 16-33 shows a hotel advertising directly to tour operators.

International wholesalers exist both domestically and abroad. Domestic wholesalers under the umbrella of, for instance, "Visit USA," are called inbound operators; they handle tours and groups organized overseas, and manage their travel needs while in the United States. Their outbound counterparts handle the reverse travel internationally. This is true of all countries serving international markets. Figure 16-34 is an example of outbound and inbound tour cooperation between wholesalers in France and a travel agency in Canada.

"Ad hoc" groups are organizations already formed that want to book a tour to a previously-visited or new destination. An example of an ad hoc group is a Lions Club tour to the Ozarks in Arkansas, or an archaeology club to Mexico. The tour operator again takes possession of the inventory of hotel rooms and restaurant seats, but the risk is much lower because a solid booking is already in place.

The tour operator needs the full cooperation of channel members to be successful. Ad hoc groups are the least complicated to administer. Wholesale tours, on the other hand, are very risky; some hotels and restaurants have strict cancellation guidelines and, if the tour doesn't

---

[7]Special thanks to Ellen Krentzman Schuster, Divisional Director of Sales, Hyatt Resorts Caribbean, for clarifying this process for us.

ARISTOS IXTAPA 3★

This centrally located, 225-room hotel is attractively situated on the beach of Bahia El Palmar, just 20 minutes from the airport and across the street from Ixtapa's main shopping district. The lobby is decorated with a distinctive colonial flair and the hotel's Mexican patio is the centre of ongoing fiestas. We think this beachfront property is an excellent holiday value!

Facilities:

Large swimming pool with waterfall and bridge • Children's water slide
• 2 restaurants • Snack bar • Bar • 2 lit tennis courts • Golf course nearby
• Watersports available on the beach • Boutique • Gift shop • Square Garden
Mexican Patio • Safety deposit boxes

Your Accommodation:

OCEANVIEW ROOM: 2 double beds • Air conditioning • Ceiling fan
• Telephone • Satellite color tv • Bathroom with tub and shower
• Enclosed balcony

IXTAPA MEXICO

KIDS UP TO AGE 16 STAY FREE!
(Pay airfare and tax)
(Pay airfare and tax) when sharing room with 2 adults

MEAL DEAL $66 US

(per person) Includes: 7 Breakfasts and 3 Dinners. (Buffet or a-la-carte)
Tax and tips not included
Book with your Travel Agent and pay at Aristos Ixtapa.

FIGURE 16-30 A tour operator (Alba Tours) and wholesaler brochure page

694

FIGURE 16-31   Hyatt joins forces for wholesaler and retailer business

sell, the wholesaler can end up holding a large, perishable inventory.

Good channel management can work two ways. If a wholesale tour broker is attempting to coordinate a tour series to a destination, the hotels and restaurants should remain flexible to help in the development of the distribution network. The fall foliage season in New England may not be the time to help a channel member create a new series, since demand for the hotel product at that time exceeds the supply of hotel rooms. If the wholesaler is attempting to bring in business in a less-busy time, such as spring, every attempt should be made to encourage the effort. Short-term decisions regarding cancellation clauses could prejudice an active channel member in the future.

The other side of the coin is that, in times when business is slow, the tour operator will wield clout to obtain the lowest possible rates. In heavy destination areas such as the Algarve

coast in Portugal, where extensive overbuilding has occurred, British tour operators have bargained for tens of thousands of room-nights to bring room rates down to ridiculously low levels.

Strategies for Distribution Channels

There are two major strategies for increasing usage of the product in a distribution channel: the "push" strategy and the "pull" strategy. In the pull strategy, inducements are offered to make the consumer want to "pull" the product down the channel. Examples of pull strategies in the hospitality industry are the frequent-traveler programs. With these promotions, the customer presumably has an increased desire for the product and seeks the appropriate distribution channel.

FIGURE 16-32 A wholesaler combines all travel elements

ORLANDO

THE REAL MAGIC
IS SELECTING A HOTEL LIKE THIS
AT A REASONABLE RATE

You Deliver The Guests, We'll Deliver As Promised

Next time you're booking a Central Florida tour, don't leave anything to chance. Book a **Sure Tour** at the Clarion Plaza Hotel. We'll provide confirmation in one working day, *guaranteed* group room rates, group pre-registration and pre-key, complimentary room and meals for tour escort and driver, and much more! Located in the middle of the attraction action, this exceptional vacation destination features: • Complete guest services • Location 1 mile from Sea World, 10 minutes from Walt Disney World® Resort, 5 minutes from Universal Studios • 5 restaurants & lounges • 24-hour deli • Nightclub with live entertainment • Large, tropical heated pool • Game Room • Ample parking for buses • And much more!

Contact our sales office at 1-800-366-9700

Clarion Plaza Hotel
Orlando

9700 International Dr., Orlando, FL 32819-8114 • (407) 352-9700 • FAX (407) 351-9111

FIGURE 16-33   A hotel advertises to tour operators

The push strategy acts in the opposite way, by giving the incentive to the channel member (e.g., the travel agent) to sell the product to the consumer. An example of a push strategy would be to offer a 20 percent commission on all bookings made during a low-demand time period. At twice the normal commission, the travel agent has a reason to push one product over another that may be offering a lower commission. Certain incentives, such as free rooms, free airfare

FIGURE 16-34   Outbound/inbound tour cooperation

to destinations, and in some instances cash bonuses, have come into use. As competition for channel members' business becomes more intense, we expect the incentives of the push strategy to increase proportionately.

Promotional Tie-ins

This category of strategies is the catch-all for the burgeoning attempts of the industry to expand its market base through intermediaries. Under this umbrella lies the couponing utilized by restaurants and hotels alike. The numerous dining clubs sprouting up throughout the country present a good example of the promotional tie-in channel of distribution. In this method, a number of restaurants participate in a dining club, whereby the intermediary organization prints, markets, and distributes coupons representing everything from a free dessert to a two-for-one dinner offering. Hotel companies have been represented by various coupon organizations, primarily selling a 50 percent discount off rack or corporate rate to their members, often but not necessarily on weekends and during slow periods. With today's rampant discounting, this, like some car rental discounts, is often not

a good deal. One can often negotiate for less, but the coupon buyer/customer usually doesn't know this.

Another area of tie-ins for hotels involves the airlines. A majority of airline customers eventually become hotel customers. Hotels work with the airlines to arrange specific marketing packages to mutual destinations. Now, the channel of distribution grows longer. After the hotel enters an agreement for distribution with an airline, a second channel member, the travel agent or tour operator, moves in. Each intermediary, while offering new customers, takes a commission.

Hotel and rental car companies are increasingly integrating with the airline reservations systems (Figure 16-35). By combining technology, these channel members present a unique opportunity to the customers (in this case, travel agents) to take advantage of "one-stop shopping." Through direct access to global distributions systems, agents can make the flight arrangements, get a rental car, and book a sleeping room without ever using the telephone, as we have shown.

None of this channel participation is without cost. Without constant supervision and evaluation, channels of distribution can sometimes

Aston gives your clients the credit they deserve.

New! Aston guests can earn $50 or more in credit toward their Budget Rent a Car in Hawaii.

Beginning January 1, 1994 Aston and Budget Rent a Car will offer even greater vacation values for your clients. Just book your clients at one of Aston's 27 condominium resorts and hotels in Hawaii—and they'll receive an Aston Car Certificate good for up to $50 per week in credit for their Budget Rent a Car.

The longer they stay the more they receive.

This certificate will be validated for $10 in credit for every day of their stay, for up to five consecutive days. That gives them up to $50 in credit each week to use toward their Budget car rental. Your clients can also receive additional certificates for every week of their stay. Ask for Budget's car rental rate for Aston's guests and save on convertibles, luxury sedans, jeeps, vans and more— and explore the island at their leisure.

Budget
The Smart Money is on Budget.

Certificate must be used in conjunction with Budget's Aston rate. Certificate must be validated and is good for a maximum of $10 per rental day up to 5 days or $50 per week, per certificate. Offer subject to car availability, limitations, blackout periods, and rental requirements. Cannot be combined with any packages, other discounts, or special offers.

US & Canada 800-922-7866
From Hawaii call 800-321-2558
FAX 808-922-8785 • Airline Systems Access Code AH

Ask for Aston's Special Car Certificate

ASTON
Hotels & Resorts

FIGURE 16-35   A promotional tie-in for Aston Hotels & Resorts

become cost-prohibitive. For example, "super-saver" room rates could indeed bring in less than the cost of the channel of distribution. At $49, the commissions paid to the airline network, the travel agent, the contribution to the advertising, the contribution to the frequent-traveler plan, and the franchise fee could bring the net revenue to below the cost of providing the service!

Pitfalls of Channel Promotions

One of the major problems in the hospitality in-dustry's attempts at channel distribution lies in the execution of promotional tie-ins. In essence, the burden of execution may be on the most un-likely candidate, the employees. Think for a mo-ment of a supermarket. Within the confines of the store there are at least 5,000 different items available for purchase. Many of the strongest channel managers in the world are represented there—Procter & Gamble and Pepsi Cola, to name just two. Most of the products have made their way down some channel of distribution to be on the shelf, available for purchase.

Once in the store, there are hundreds of dif-ferent promotions on a daily basis. Some soap companies are offering two bars for the price of one, a cereal maker offers trips to Ireland, and a barbecue sauce company offers a free grill if you participate. The supermarket clerk does not need an M.B.A. to be qualified to handle these promotions. Somehow, the consumer goods industry has offered thousands of promotions and giveaways under one roof, yet the check-out clerk has no direct participation. Check-out lines are rarely encumbered with questions on different promotions. Most of the administration of the programs is handled at the host company's designated places of redemption.

Now, think how the hospitality industry has done the opposite. When a hotel company distributes coupons or has giveaways or special promotion programs, the desk clerk is the one who has to decipher all the different options and be prepared to encounter a myriad of customer inquires. For example, a desk clerk in one day must handle the frequent-traveler program that the hotel sponsors; administer a 50 percent discount program that the sales office has arranged; be knowledgeable about the award levels of the airline with which the hotel has a tie-in on a fly/stay package; understand group, corporate, and other discount rates; try to "up-sell" to higher-priced rooms; deal with the amenities offered those in the hotel's "club" plan; and, in his or her spare time, check in the lonely guest who is not associated with any of the above. We have not mentioned that this clerk must "keep smiling"—yet this clerk is one of the lowest-paid employees in the hotel who, when you look closely, may be the one most responsible for guest satisfaction.

Poor channel management compounds this problem. To publish a booklet outlining the procedures for each program currently in place, and to expect each concerned employee to be able to remember and handle them, is a simplistic and myopic answer to a bigger problem. Additionally, the tremendous turnover in the front office staff of most hotels makes difficult the training involved to keep each clerk cognizant of the programs. The answer lies in shorter, simpler channels of distribution for the promotional tie-ins that are simultaneously managed at a location other than that of the point of sale.

The choice options for channels in the hospitality industry having been described, a process needs to be established to select the correct member(s). Frequently, a corporate marketing department will develop a great promotion and give it to an airline, and the channel begins. If the plan is not well thought out, the program can roll out of control. Eventually, the customer is disappointed by the confusion and lack of delivery, and the local units of the company become frustrated by the myriad of options and the lack of information to help execute the programs.

To begin, a set of distribution objectives needs to be established by the company. One way to phrase the question would be, "If we are to be successful at the end of this channel, what would the results be?" The overall objective of any channel of distribution should be to create a customer; more specifically, an objective might be to have a larger share of airline customers.

Influences on Channels

The next step is to determine the influences on the channel strategies. What airlines can or will we do business with? The decision process might be narrowed down by the number of flights that go to cities where the chain has hotels. A thorough analysis of competitive hotels' channels would be needed to determine what they offer to both the channel member and the customers themselves.

Included in the influences on channel strategies is the corporate organization. Who is going to monitor and evaluate the programs offered? Is there need for additional staffing, or perhaps a combining of departments, to ensure that the channel is working as smoothly as possible?

At this point, it is necessary to realistically assess the strength of the product or promotion being driven through the channel. If the product is weak or redundant to other similar products, potential channel members such as travel agents and airlines may not be anxious to distribute the product, or at the very least, may not put forth a strong effort to make it successful.

For example, if a hotel develops a fly/ drive/stay package with an airline and rental car agency that is not differentiated from the hundreds of other similar products in the marketplace, the intermediaries (in this case, the airline and rental car agency) would really not have any reason to aggressively market the package. If a competitive hotel was offering its corporate rate to an airline's customers, would the same offer be enough to differentiate the product in the eyes of the channel member? Would there be enough of an incentive for the airline to aggressively market the offering? If not, the product needs to be enhanced enough to get the support of the airline and to provide a productive channel. Being clearly superior to the competition will make the success of any channel more probable.

Selecting the Channel of Distribution

Selecting the distribution channels is the next step. The length of the channel needs to be analyzed. In no uncertain terms, shorter is better; the longer the channel of distribution, the more potential problems arise for the management of that channel.

By "shorter" or "longer," we are referring to the number of intermediaries in the channel. Each intermediary has to make a profit and each one involves some measure of coordination. Therefore, the fewer middlemen involved, the more profit and the less chance for errors. At some point there may seem to be a need to add on channels. If the new intermediary can be reasonably expected to bring in more customers at a profit for the originator, the channel should probably be expanded. If the channel member cannot deliver the needed number of customers and profit, the decision should be negative.

Vertical Integration

When a company becomes its own supplier of products, it becomes vertically integrated. This type of distribution needs a large amount of capital to be successful, and this strategy should be considered only if the potential for success is somewhat assured. A good example in

the hospitality industry is the Carlson Companies, Inc.

Carlson consists of three groups: the Carlson Travel Group, an international network of travel agencies and tour operators; the Carlson Marketing Group, a promotional and incentive group; and the Carlson Hospitality Group (shown in Figure 16-10), which includes hotels and restaurants and the Radisson Diamond cruise ships. Both the Carlson Travel Group and the Marketing Group feed reservations to the hotels and the cruise ships. All customers of the Carlson Travel Network are encouraged to stay in Radisson Hotels in all of the relevant destinations. If a customer has a firm preference for an alternative hotel, the travel agency will certainly book that reservation. In a vertically integrated channel of distribution such as this, the company becomes its own source of business.

Channel Management

Good channel management stems from the formulation of a good working relationship among channels from the start. All agreements pertaining to the workings of the channel should be in writing and should be updated as conditions periodically change. There is rarely an all-win situation. If a channel member is not deriving some reasonable value from the network, that member will not participate actively, and distribution will eventually become more difficult and more costly.

For example, a hotel could develop a good working relationship with a representation firm for marketing their property. The rep firm then markets the hotel through sales calls, brochures, direct mail, and so on. A booking results, and a commission becomes due. If the hotel begins to dispute the validity of the origination of the bookings, or delays the payment, the relationship within the channel of distribution becomes ineffective. The representation firm will not be anxious to market the facility in the future, and will spend its time selling more cooperative hotels. This becomes a no-win situation. The hotel is dissatisfied with the productivity of the channel member, and the rep firm will move on to more lucrative endeavors.

Each channel member seeks to create customers for a profit, but without some give-and-take on a regular basis by all channel members, the system becomes tedious and disruptive. Hospitality firms that have carefully selected their partners, and are managing them well, will be consistently increasing their customer base while others are looking for new channel members.

Evaluation of the Channel

This step is critical for the continued success of any program. If a hospitality entity is unable to tell how many bookings a rep firm produced, or how many coupons were turned in from the dining guide, then intelligent channel management is impossible. Often, channel members can report the statistics. If unit management is unable at least to spot check these numbers, the channel member will be in control when it comes time to negotiate the next agreement.

For example, the hotel that engages in a channel agreement with an airline sets an objective. The objective needs to be set in a quantitative format, to be used in the evaluation process. The success of the channel of distribution might be defined as raising the productivity of the airline reservation service from 100 rooms per month to 120 per month.

It is also beneficial to understand the break-even point of the channel. In the above example, it might take an additional ten rooms per month to cover the additional commissions and some combined advertising costs. After a predetermined amount of time, the channel is evaluated. If it is producing less than 110 rooms per month, careful consideration might be given to either increasing the marketing support for the program or dropping the channel member completely.

Evaluation is more than just a tally of dinner covers or room-nights. A channel may be driving the volume, but if the customer is unhappy, the effort is not only shortsighted but dangerous.

A dining guide, for example, can market a two-for-one dinner promotion in a number of different ways. If customers expect two lobsters for the price of one when making reservations, and find out the promotion applies only to chicken menu items, they will be sincerely disappointed. If the hotel guests were expecting deluxe accommodations, and agreement with the channel member was to offer run-of-the-house rooms, the guests who get the inferior rooms will not be happy with their purchase. They may not be unhappy enough to complain, but still worse, they may be unhappy enough not to come back.

The marketing-driven company with good channel-management skills will ensure its customer satisfaction throughout the process. If a channel member is producing customers who are consistently unhappy, it would be better never to have used that distribution method in the first place.

Motivation and Recruitment of Channel Members

In channel management, two ongoing factors are needed to ensure continued success: motivation and recruitment. It must be recognized that most channel members are carrying many similar products into the marketplace. Travel agents have a variety of hotels and airfares from which to choose. The representation firms have several hotels in their portfolio that match the needs of their customers. The number of promotional tie-ins available to both the consumers and the channel members is mind-boggling. Franchising options for the developers and independent managers are plentiful.

Motivation   Some type of motivation must be continuously offered by the channel leader. Unless the product offered is so desirable that there are several channel members bidding on the rights to carry it, motivational techniques are necessary.

The "push" strategies mentioned earlier are the primary source of motivational support for channel members. Incentive trips for outstanding travel agents or the best franchisee in the system will go a long way toward smoothing operating channels of distribution. Many companies in the consumer goods and industrial products industries have full-time staff members who do nothing but organize and implement channel incentives in order to keep members interested in their products.

Incentives need not be in the form of travel. Consumer goods such as appliances and televisions can make the bonus system easier to attain, and they provide short-term gratification for participants. The drawback of the magnificent incentive trip to Europe may be that it takes a year to win, and only a very few employees will ever have a chance to collect the prize.

Although the motivational options available are almost unlimited, an area that also needs attention is that of top management. All of the sales representatives can win trips and toasters, but the president of the company is often ignored. Travel agency owners do not need toasters and trips; what they need is the personal attention that allows their views to reach someone important. An invitation to dinner by a senior executive of the hospitality company may buy more loyalty than 1,000 toasters. Too often, in the rush to motivate a channel member, the owner of the business is left out of the process.

Recruitment   The second ongoing task for the channel manager is to recruit potential new channel members. If this task is not organized and planned, the channel is in perpetual danger. Unfortunately, the danger is subtle because a company may not realize that it is exposed until a member drops out.

A travel agency may be one of your best producers in the Florida market, for example. It sends an unusually high number of guests to your hotel because it has done a good job marketing your facility, and it has built up a good clientele. One day the travel agent calls and says it is dropping your facility in favor of your competition down the street. Immediately the reservations slip and business starts falling.

This scenario is very realistic for a number of managers. First, the competitor had a good recruitment program in place and replaced its channel member with yours, thereby improving

its distribution network overnight. Second, without having had a good recruitment program of its own, your hotel now has to begin the process of finding a strong replacement channel member. As you are now in dire need, the negotiations will swing in favor of the potential new channel member.

There will always be times when a channel member leaves and/or needs to be replaced. This is part of doing business. However, a good channel manager will have alternatives ready and pre-screened according to the criteria mentioned earlier in the chapter.

Recruitment is also necessary to provide alternatives to channel members who are not performing satisfactorily. It is far easier to deal with an unsatisfactory situation once you have other options than to have to recruit channel members when at a disadvantage.

Summary

Channels of distribution are methods of marketing a hospitality entity that are gaining greater use in an increasingly competitive environment. In a business where the product is perishable and where production and consumption are simultaneous, we need to find many ways to allow customers to easily purchase our products and services.

Management contracts and franchising allow a firm to enter markets without incurring large capital investment and financial risk. However, these firms lose operational control by lending their names to franchisees all over the world.

Consortia, affiliations, reservations networks, and representation firms provide greater access to our products and services, especially in faraway places. Incentive houses, travel agents, and tour operators are intermediaries who can also distribute our services to customers.

The backbone of any channel of distribution is channel management. The distribution method of marketing that has been so critical and successful for the consumer and industrial goods industries has new significance for the hospitality industry.

Any marketing-driven organization will take the time to evaluate its current distribution system and organize a cohesive plan for improvement. A competent channel manager should then be assigned to monitor and consistently reevaluate the network to obtain the maximum benefits to the company. This channel manager may take the form of the director of sales, the general manager, or the resident manager at the unit level of the hotel. The corporate marketing office should assume responsibility for chain-wide agreements. Finally, the satisfaction of the consumer is the true test of a channel's success. Without this, none of the steps outlined above is productive or needed.

For most hotels, at least, channel management is a far more productive and critical part of the marketing mix today than advertising.

Discussion Questions

1. Discuss the advantages and disadvantages of franchising as a method of increasing the channels of distribution.

2. Discuss the similarities and dissimilarities between consortia, affiliations, reservations companies, and representation firms.

3. Why are channels of distribution inherently different for the hospitality industry than for goods industries?

4. Describe the difference between a push and a pull strategy. When might it be best to use one instead of the other?

5. What are the most important criteria for choosing a channel member and why? Discuss the ramifications.

6. Describe the ways, means, and significance of motivating channel members.

7. Cases 16-1 and 16-2 describe the pitfalls of hotel and restaurant franchises, respectively, under different market conditions. Analyze these cases. What were the opportunities? What happened? Is this a bad signal for franchising?

8. In Case 16-3, what would you do to get a larger share of the Japanese market in Nice?

✔ Case 16-1
The Sheraton Parc Central

The partners of Hotelgroup 2000 met in the L'Affair room of the Sheraton Parc Central in St. Bartholomew, Florida. All of the partners were successful local businesspeople—doctors, lawyers, and local merchants who had banded together to form Hotelgroup 2000 and to build the Parc Central. This day they were meeting to determine the future of the hotel.

Background

"How can we miss?" had said John Martin, a well-known chiropractor and President of Hotelgroup 2000, eight years before. Property values were skyrocketing, and the cash flow of the project really didn't matter, he had claimed. The value of the asset would cover any shortfall in revenues. Anyway, the Japanese would probably buy the hotel in a few years and everyone would have a sizeable profit.

Hotelgroup 2000 had made all the right moves. It had hired a reputable management company from Miami. The Sheraton name brand, which it had franchised, was a "home run," guaranteeing business even in bad times. The hotel was a success. Occupancy rose to 80 percent in the second year, with a $90 average room rate. Sheraton's reservation system and marketing programs were providing almost 25 percent of the business. Mrs. Martin had become the marketing consultant and interior decorator.

Within a few years, however, competition began to recognize the strong demand for hotel rooms in the area. Soon Marriott Courtyard, Hilton, and Omni began to build and operate hotels nearby. Parc Central business levels fell monthly and yearly, until occupancy reached 65 percent, with an ADR of $75, and Hotelgroup was unable to meet its obligations to the bank. The partners, once proud of their community contribution, now were upset with the financial ramifications of their hotel icon. When they had to write personal checks to cover the cash shortfalls (called a cash call),

they felt they'd had enough. It was time to take action.

Decision, Decision

The first decision made by Hotelgroup 2000 was to fire its management company. Despite initial successes in an underbuilt market, it had become the lightning rod for the hotel's problems, and the group blamed it for its problems. Changing management companies, however, did not significantly alter the situation. Hotelgroup 2000 had a fresh set of faces to yell at, but in the end the results did not change.

In fact, the new management committee of Hotelgroup 2000 had a different problem. Since recent financial performance had been so poor, Hotelgroup 2000 decided not to fund the renovation portion of the budget even though the Parc Central was beginning to show the wear and tear of its history.

Sheraton told the group that, in order to keep the Sheraton franchise, the hotel would require $2 million in capital funding—Sheraton promised no more business or a higher rate for doing this and claimed this input was necessary just to maintain existing business levels.

Hotelgroup 2000 was then approached by two new prospective franchisors. Holiday Inn suggested a repositioning of the hotel, but only after a $1 million renovation. This, Holiday claimed, would mean the hotel could achieve a 68 percent occupancy with a $69 ADR. About 30 percent of the total occupancy would come from Holidex, the corporate equivalent of Sheraton's Reservatron system.

Next, Choice Hotels approached the owners with an option to join the Quality Inn system without any further renovations. Forecasts were that there was an opportunity to achieve a 62 percent occupancy with a $60 ADR. The Quality franchise, it said, would make a 20 percent contribution to the overall occupancy of the property.

Mr. Martin had assembled the partners to decide what to do. Unfortunately, most of the local businesses also had been hit by the recession. Hotelgroup 2000 partners wanted answers. The prestige of owning a Sheraton Hotel had long since vanished. "How can we salvage or make money from this enterprise?" asked the partners, in desperation.

✔ Case 16-2
Savage House Pizza Parlours[8]

After many months of negotiations, Attsami Pizza House, Ltd. purchased three Savage House Pizza Parlour restaurants. The principals borrowed $150,000 from Old National Bank in Spokane, Washington, as a down payment. They also signed a note to the prior owners for $420,000. At the time, that was the entire debt of Attsami Pizza House, Ltd.

The restaurants were to be supervised by Dennis Guenther, the operating partner, who was also actively involved in managing two Perkins' Family restaurants for the company. John Temple was hired to oversee the day-to-day operation of the Savage House Pizza restaurants.

Savage House restaurants were what you might call "taverns" that sold extremely good pizza. They were dark and dingy, with a lot of barn wood on the walls, somewhat worn, torn carpet on the floors, lots of pool tables and games, and very old, mostly dirty, restrooms. They did serve, however, an excellent pizza and they had, by normal standards, very good volume for pizza and beer restaurants.

The new ownership simply ran the restaurants as efficiently as they could. They remained fairly profitable, with about the same volume of business. Six months later they added a fourth restaurant, in a shopping center in another area of town, but with lighter wood, brighter carpets, and a more upbeat or modern decor. This restaurant immediately started doing a fairly high volume and was quite profitable.

As a result, a decision was made to clean up the other restaurants by remodeling, painting, installing new carpets, and brightening to make them have more of a family-type atmosphere. Attsami borrowed money to complete the redecorating. That increased debt, but instead of sales increasing, they declined.

The least-profitable and lowest-volume store had its lease come due. Rather than leave and take the equipment somewhere else, the store was converted into a Chuckie Cheese children's-type pizza restaurant. At the time, that concept was becoming popular. Changing the concept improved sales only slightly and again added to the overhead, with not enough of a corresponding increase in sales to cover the additional cash flow requirements.

A problem at one store seemed to be the lack of parking. The building next door was purchased, demolished, and 23 car parks replaced it. Volume failed to increase, but monthly overhead went up significantly. Management was frustrated. Cleaning up an operation through remodeling and adding lighting, parking, and changing the theme and decor seemed a sure way to increase sales. In no case, at no time, did any of these things have a positive effect on volume, however. Quite to the contrary, they had a very negative impact on profits.

The Franchise Solution

Soon thereafter, Godfather's Pizza came into the Spokane market with a tremendous expansion and marketing program that ate away at the Savage House restaurants' volume. Watching the success of the Godfather's Pizza units and their ability to market their product, the principals of Attsami Pizza got together and decided that what they needed was to affiliate with a national franchise that would help with the marketing effort. Numerous franchises were researched.

Roundtable Pizza, which at that time was a regional California-based (more specifically, San Francisco) pizza chain, was chosen. It had been very successful with its marketing efforts and had about 250 units, mostly in northern California. Roundtable also had an extremely good product, considered critical because Savage House had a reputation of having one of the better pizzas in town.

Negotiations with Roundtable led to an area franchisee agreement. Three Savage Houses

---

[8]We are grateful to Professor Denney Rutherford, Ph.D., Washington State University, Pullman, WA, for the use of this case.

were converted to Roundtables, and a new store was opened in the Spokane Valley. The Chuckie Cheese store was closed and litigation entered into on the remaining years of the lease.

The decision to expand into the Valley was based on reasoning that this would provide fairly good geographical coverage of the Spokane area, and that the added sales would contribute dollars to the marketing effort. As it turned out, however, this store was not in a particularly good location and never did generate the sales that had been forecasted.

Immediately upon converting from Savage House to Roundtable, sales volumes took another drastic drop. In retrospect, it appeared most likely that people didn't know what a Roundtable Pizza restaurant was; they were simply going somewhere else where they "knew" a name and product.

The restaurants continued to operate, but not profitably. A substantial amount of money was borrowed from the Perkins' operations until local purveyors' bills could no longer be paid. Aware that survival was in question, the company attempted without success to sell the restaurants.

Conclusion

After about a year, the original owners of Savage House foreclosed on the two remaining res-

taurants that they had sold to Attsami. Six months after that, the other two stores were closed because of declining sales and inability to pay the bills. That triggered numerous lawsuits against both Attsami Pizza House, Ltd., the corporation, and the three principals. There were some leases and loans that all three had signed, and there was a great deal of purveyor debt that Dennis Guenther had signed as Operations Manager. Dennis had been quite successful with the Perkins' Family operations, and never in his wildest dreams did he feel that a restaurant he operated would have financial problems. So, whenever a personal signature was required, he was quick to guarantee payment. He eventually filed for bankruptcy, as did the corporation, not long afterward.

Attsami Pizza House, Ltd. was no longer a corporation doing business in Washington. Of the two restaurants that reverted to the original owners, one was still operating and one was closed. Of the two that were closed, one reopened as a pizza restaurant but soon closed; the other was converted to an Italian restaurant and continued to operate. Dennis Guenther was now completely involved in the operation of the Perkins' Family restaurants, with absolutely no intention of ever expanding outside the Perkins' franchise. With his complete attention given to Perkins', its volumes increased drastically and profit improved considerably.

✔ Case 16-3
The Japanese Market in Nice[9]

Le Meridien, a 314-room hotel at 1 Promenade des Anglais, on the waterfront in Nice, France, had an average room rate of 700 ff. The hotel was one of 58 worldwide properties of Meridien Hotels, a wholly-owned subsidiary of Air France. Nearby, at 37 Promenade des Anglais, also on the waterfront, stood the Negresco, a 158-room hotel with an average room rate of 1,100 ff. It was an independently-owned hotel and a member of Leading Hotels of the World.

The Negresco had a large Japanese clientele.

In fact, 75 percent of the Japanese market went to this hotel while the other 25 percent went to lower-rated hotels. Le Meridien, in an attempt to cut into this market, began offering a Japanese welcome tea and breakfast, a Japanese room setup, a Japanese receptionist, a welcome letter, and a Japanese "passport" offering special privileges. Six months later, 75 percent of the Japanese market still went to the Negresco. What could Le Meridien do to capture more of this market?

---

[9]Marcel Levy, GM of Le Meridien Nice at the time, contributed the facts for this case.

PART VI
The International Market

CHAPTER 17

International Marketing

There are few industries in the world that can match the global nature of the hospitality industry. This industry provides goods and services to people away from home and it is only natural that, as international borders collapse (e.g., the European Community) and international trade accelerates (e.g., the North American Free Trade Agreement), this industry will continue to grow.

As we have previously pointed out, many hospitality corporations have a global presence with locations in many countries. In the hotel industry, Accor hotels are in 64 countries, Sheraton in 61, Holiday Inn in 57, Hilton International in 47, Meridien in 35, Hyatt in 34, Forte in 33, and Best Western and Inter-Continental in 51 countries each.[1] Some other, better-known hotel companies operating in numerous international arenas include Marriott, Choice, Days, Howard Johnson, Ritz-Carlton (all U.S.-based); Four Seasons and Delta (Canada); Penta (Germany), Sol (Spain), Mövenpick (Switzerland), SAS (Belgium); Taj and Oberoi (India); Peninsula and New World/Renaissance (Hong Kong); and ANA, Tokyu, and Nikko (Japan).

In addition, many restaurant chains, especially in the fast-food category, have also gone international, such as McDonald's (66 countries—4,400 of 13,400 outlets and 40 percent of 1992 revenues), Burger King, Ruth's Chris Steakhouse, and Pizza Hut (440 units in Australia alone).

In short, the hospitality industry has gone international. This means it is necessary not only to understand the national markets in which one locates, but also to understand the international traveler, who comes from many diverse geographical locations and cultures.

Throughout this text we have provided examples of marketing situations in international arenas. We have done this not so much because these examples become different in an international context, but because they are similar. The basic principles of marketing are no different wherever you go—they always involve the needs and wants and solutions of problems of customers. Likewise, the concepts of positioning, segmentation, and marketing-planning or strategy are no different. What changes, of course, are the consumers. International marketing does not involve any changes in marketing concepts; instead, it involves understanding the changes in consumers.

We do not minimize other factors that vary from country to country. Distribution systems, political influences, and even the way of doing

---

[1]Hotels 325, *Hotels,* July, 1994, p. 43.

business will affect the marketing of hospitality from one country to another. These factors, however, impose constraints upon marketing (or, in some cases, remove them), rather than alter basic marketing principles.

Examination of the international hospitality industry shows that the greatest differences do not reflect differences in basic marketing, but differences in culture, and the need for marketers to recognize differences. When McDonald's first opened in Moscow in 1990, they served 35,000 customers a day. It can be argued that, for a business that has such a high demand, no advertising or promotion was necessary. McDonald's realized that Russians ate with utensils and were not accustomed to picking up food in their hands. So McDonald's created brochures and tray liners explaining *how* to eat a hamburger, not *why* to buy one.[2]

Burger King also had similar experiences, in the South American marketplace:

Consider Burger King's experience in adjusting to Venezuelan tastes and preferences at its restaurants in Caracas. The hamburger buns don't come with sesame seeds on them anymore, the Venezuelans kept brushing them off. Catsup is sweeter, and milk shakes are sweeter and creamier. The menu includes soft ice cream—which is everyone's favorite dessert in Latin America. Latins are late diners, so Caracas Burger Kings stay open as late as 1:30 A.M.[3]

These are not differences in marketing. Rather, they point out the necessity of knowing your market. You might think, obviously, anyone would know this? Then, why did the largest company in the world, General Motors, promote the Chevrolet Nova in Spain and Puerto Rico? (*No va* in Spanish means "It doesn't go.")

Burger King also realized that mere adaptation to cultural differences does not mean that one gets to know the market. Burger King originally served wine in its restaurants in France, but customers tended to linger and visit over

glasses of wine. This slowed table turnover and adversely impacted revenues, so wine was removed from the menu. Conversely, Disney did not allow any alcohol to be served in its newest theme park, EuroDisney. The French were outraged at not being able to have a glass of wine with their meals. Eventually, Disney changed its policy.

The main thrust of this chapter, then, is not to tell you that the essence of marketing internationally is different, but to reemphasize that you have to know your market and that the way that you do marketing may be different.

Having said that, we immediately revert to a defensive position. No company should be so naive as to not find out what "No va" means in Spanish. But what do you do when your customer mix originates in the following countries, as does that of Hilton International's property in Sao Paulo, Brazil: United States, Canada, Mexico, Belgium, England, France, Germany, Holland, Italy, Portugal, Spain, Sweden, Switzerland, Latin America, the Caribbean, Australia, China, Japan, and Africa, not to mention "others," the Brazilians? This is the challenge that faces hospitality firms that have an international focus.

The International Hospitality Industry

In the 1960s and '70s, U.S. hotel companies abroad almost always aimed at the higher-priced end of the market. Even Ramada and Holiday Corp., in general, did not aim at the same market level abroad as they did in the United States. There was good reason for this. These companies, traditionally, had targeted the international traveler abroad; in many cases, at least initially, this was largely the U.S. business traveler on an expense account. Inter-Continental, having begun as a subsidiary of Pan American Airways, located its first hotels at major destination points of the airline. When Hilton International became a subsidiary of Trans World Airlines, Hilton followed the same practice.

---

[2]Charles Lamb, Joseph Hair, and Carl McDaniel, *Principles of Marketing,* Cincinnati: South-Western Publishing Co., 1992 , p. 647.

[3]Robert Gross and Duane Kujawa, *International Business: Theory and Managerial Applications,* Boston: Irwin, 1992, p. 327.

These companies were able to stay more or less "above" the economic uncertainties of the countries in which they operated. Labor and operating costs were usually much lower than in the United States, while rates charged were based on U.S. levels. Foreign business travelers also accepted these rates, because those who traveled possessed either expense accounts or ample means. The North American tourist abroad paid the price to "feel at home away from home" (Figure 17-1).

As the economies of many countries grew stronger, particularly those of developing nations that had not previously introduced their own upscale hotel chains, the situation began to change. Essentially, two things happened. The first was that foreign developers began to invest. Many at first brought in North American companies to manage their properties. Eventually, they developed their own chains, also initially in the upscale market.

The second thing that happened was that the traveler changed. Persons of lower income or not on expense accounts began to travel, both abroad and in their own countries. These people resisted the high prices of the upscale hotels and searched for alternatives. North Americans especially felt that they no longer had to stay at an "American" hotel. The result was that many of these hotels had to learn to adjust to the local economy. An example is the Hilton International in Paris, a hotel once priced and geared to the U.S. market; when the U.S. market fell apart, management realized that it had shut out much of the European market. Today, in countries like Korea, Brazil, and India, domestic travelers account for 40 percent or more of hotel occupancy at many hotels.

Hilton International was affected by other economic forces in Sao Paulo, Brazil, where the local currency devalued at an incredibly high inflation rate. The economy weakened and international travelers no longer came to Sao Paulo in the same numbers. Hilton was forced to turn to the Brazilian market—but this also had suffered. Companies in Rio de Janeiro, Brazil had persuaded airlines to add more morning and evening flights to Sao Paulo, a one-hour flight, so that business travelers could return in

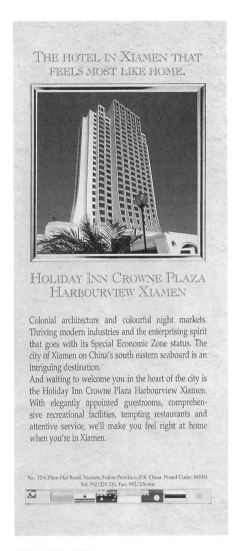

FIGURE 17-1 Holiday Inn wants Americans to feel at home in China

the same day. At the same time, new hotels opened with wealthy, prestige-seeking owners who were willing to cut prices in order to obtain business.

The collapse of the oil market in the mid-1980s had the same effect in the Middle East. International hotel companies, not just American ones, found themselves with fewer customers. Although international hotel companies have always had to grapple with the intricacies of monetary exchange rates, in the later '80s they suddenly had to confront them at the local level. The environment forced these companies to seek more national customers of the countries in which they operate, and such customers are less able to pay. Thus, the Maurya Sheraton in New Delhi, a five-star hotel that thrived on the diplomatic market due to its proximity to major embassies, decided to go after the "second level" of business traveler with a flexible rate policy.

Hotel companies of countries other than the United States also tended to enter foreign markets at the upper end of the scale. It was difficult to find major companies that did otherwise. An exception was Accor of France. This company took its two- and three-star concepts into neighboring European countries and Asia, as well as the United States, under the names of Ibis (Figure 17-2) and Novotel (Figure 17-3), and bought Motel 6, a U.S. budget chain. Accor's strategy, as it turned out, was a forerunner of the future as economic conditions continued to change. Days Inn and Choice International budget properties are now worldwide, Holiday Inn has Garden Courts in Europe (Figure 17-4) and Africa, and Holiday Express in India, and Country Lodging by Carlson is now expanding globally.

There are still many countries without sufficient satisfactory middle-tier hotel accommodations to serve the market, countries as diverse as Finland and India. Residents of these countries, as well as international travelers who visit them in increasing numbers, must often choose between top-rate hotels or less-than-desirable facilities. Many companies are moving to take advantage of these opportunities. Vietnam is emerging as a lucrative destination that needs to be developed—estimates are that it will take $20 billion in foreign investment there to create a satisfactory infrastructure to support a high level of tourism.

The prospects for the international hospitality industry for the late 1990s appear to be quite favorable. World tourism as measured by arrivals grew at a 3.2 percent rate from 1990 to 1994 and is expected to grow by 4.4 percent

from 1995 to 2000.[4] According to the World Travel and Tourism Council, gross output generated by travel and tourism for 1994 is expected to be $3.4 trillion and it is expected to double to $7.9 trillion by the year 2005.[5]

Asia is a special case because it has been economically less-developed for so long. Strong economic growth coupled with political stability in most Asian countries are the major reasons for the strong growth surge. Higher disposable incomes of the Asian population, increased leisure time, and relaxation of travel restrictions have added to these promising and continuing trends. Table 17-1 shows some Asian growth statistics from 1982 to 1992; Table 17-2 lists statistics on hotel development in 1994.

Aiding and abetting these trends is vast improvement in the distribution system in Asia. Seventeen thousand travel agency outlets across the Asia/Pacific control upwards of $26 billion in sales each year, a figure that is increasing. The market is presently controlled by small to mid-sized independents. Especially in Hong Kong and the Philippines, nearly 70 percent are single-location offices; in Indonesia less than 20 percent are single-office independents. Although 70 percent of Asian agencies use CRS systems, only 7 percent of hotel reservations are made that way. Most are still made by telephone or fax directly with local reservations offices or hotels.[6]

These trends indicate that there will be opportunities for international hospitality marketers, but these opportunities will not come without risks and challenges. While most marketing decisions relevant to marketing principles remain the same, it is the forces of the geographic environment—economic, social and cultural, political and legal, and demographic forces of particular regions—in which these decisions are made that remain unique, determine the outcome, and make international marketing different from marketing in one's home country.

---

[4]World Tourism Organization, Madrid. Cited in *Hotels*, January, 1994, p. 40.

[5]*Ibid.*

[6]Survey Research Hong Kong, Asia Regional Travel Industry Survey for *Hotel & Travel Index/ABC International Edition*, 1994, a publication of Reed Travel Group, Secaucus, N.J.

Welkom bij Ibis

Of U nu zakelijk of privé onderweg bent, U kunt altijd op een comfortabel en ontspannen verblijf in Hotel Ibis Rotterdam/ Vlaardingen rekenen.

- gratis parkeren.
  - Free car park.
  - Kostenloser Parkplatz.

- Ons lunchbuffet biedt U een keur aan heerlijke gerechten.
  - Our lunchbuffet offers a delicious choice of well prepared dishes.
  - Das Lunchbuffet bietet eine erstklassige Auswahl an wunderbare Gerichten.

- De vriendelijke receptie medewerkers staan 24 uur per dag voor U klaar.
  - The friendly reception staff is available 24 hours a day.
  - Das freundliche Empfangspersonal heißt Sie 24 Stunden am Tag willkommen.

Welcome to Ibis

Wether your stay is for business or for pleasure, you will have a thoughly relaxed stay at the Hotel Ibis Rotterdam/Vlaardingen.

- Geniet ontspannen van een drankje in de Lobby bar.
  - Enjoy a relaxing drink at the Lobby bar.
  - Genießen Sie einen entspannenden Drink in der Lobby bar.

- De zalen zijn multifunctioneel en goed ingericht.
  - Conference facilities are flexible and well equipped.
  - Flexible und gut ausgestattete Konferenzeinrichtungen

Willkommen bei Ibis

Ganz gleigh, ob Sie geschäftlich oder privat unterwegs sind, Sie können immer einen erholsamen Aufenthalt im Hotel Ibis Rotterdam/ Vlaardingen genießen.

- De kamers zijn comfortabel en modern.
  - All the bedrooms are comfortable and modern.
  - Alle Gästezimmer sind komfortabel und modern.

- 'Le Restaurant' biedt U een uitstekend diner in een vriendelijke atmosfeer.
  - Le 'Restaurant' offers you an excellent dinner in a friendly atmosphere.
  - 'Le Restaurant' bietet Sie eine erlesene Speise und gemütliche Atmosphäre.

FIGURE 17-2 Accor takes its two-star product to Rotterdam

717

novotel

brussels off grand 'place

GRASMARKT 120 RUE MARCHE AUX HERBES
BRUXELLES - 1000 - BRUSSEL
TEL: (02) 514 33 33 - TELEX. 20.377 - TELEFAX: (02) 511 77 23

NOVOTEL BRUSSELS off GRAND 'PLACE

Au cœur de Bruxelles historique, un NOVOTEL tout neuf, habillé de style espagnol 16ème siècle. Une véritable prouesse architecturale sur l'Esplanade de l'Europe! Cent mètres, et vous êtes à la Grand'Place, au terminal Sabena ou à la gare Centrale, Manneken Pis, la Monnaie, la Bourse, l'Ilôt Sacré et le Palais des Congrès... tout est tout près. A moins de 500 m des 136 chambres confortablement équipées de salle de bains, TV couleur, radio, mini-bar, téléphone, climatisation d'air. De son bar et de son restaurant (ouvert de 6 à 24h.). De ses salles de réunion. Et un parking public couvert à 20 mètres de l'hôtel.

NOVOTEL BRUSSELS off GRAND 'PLACE

In het hart van historisch Brussel verrijst een gloednieuw NOVOTEL in 16e eeuwse Spaanse stijl. Een architectuuraal hoogstandje op de Esplanade van Europa! En slechts honderd meter verwijderd van de Grote Markt, de Sabena-terminal en het Centraal Station... Manneken Pis, de Munt, de Beurs, 'Ilôt Sacré" en het Congrespaleis liggen bij manier van spreken vlak om de hoek. Dat wil zeggen op minder dan 500 m van de 136 comfortabele kamers (badkamer, kleurentelevisie, mini-bar, radio, telefoon en airconditioning). U vindt er een bar en een restaurant (open van 6 tot 24 uur), zalen en een overdekte publieke parking, op 20 m afstand van het hotel.

NOVOTEL BRUSSELS off GRAND 'PLACE

Im Herzen des historischen Brüssel finden Sie ein ganz neues NOVOTEL im spanischen Stil des 16 Jahrhunderts. Ein architektonisches Glanzstück auf der Esplanade von Europa. Nur hundert Meter vom Grand'Place entfernt, ganz in der Nähe von Sabena, Zentralbahnhof, Manneken Pis, Münztheater, Börse, Altstadt und dem Kongreßpalast... alles in unmittelbarer Nähe. 136 Zimmer komfortabel ausgestattet mit Bad, Farbfernsehen, Radio, mini-Bar, Telefon, Klimaanlage in Ihrem NOVOTEL. Die NOVOTEL Bar und das Restaurant sind von 6 bis 24 Uhr geöffnet. Konferenzräume stehen zu Ihrer Verfügung. Ein öffentliches Parkhaus ist ca. 20 Meter vom Hotel entfernt.

NOVOTEL BRUSSELS off GRAND 'PLACE

In the very heart of historical Brussels, a brand-new NOVOTEL decorated in 16th century Spanish style. An architectural masterpiece on the Esplanade of Europe! Right next to the Grand'Place, the Sabena air terminal, and Central Station. The Manneken Pis, Monnaie Opera House, Bourse, Ilot Sacré, and the Brussels Conference Centre (Palais des Congrès)... everything is just around the corner. Less than a block from 136 comfortable rooms (with bath, colour TV, radio, mini-bar, telephone, air-conditioning), NOVOTEL'S bar and restaurant (open from 6:00 a.m. to midnight), and meeting rooms, and an in-door public parking accomodation, hardly 20 yards away from the hotel.

FIGURE 17-3 Accor takes its three-star product to Brussels

FIGURE 17-4 Holiday Inn takes its two-star product to France

Economic Environments

Of all environmental concerns, the economic environment may be the most universally critical to the company doing business in foreign lands. It is the economic environment that opens doors to opportunities, and also closes them. This is because countries differ greatly in areas of growth rate, consumer consumption, level of economic development, and discretionary income.

The Macroeconomy

Every nation's economy is at a certain stage of economic development at any given time. West-ern Europe, Japan, and the United States are fully industrialized, while Korea, Malaysia, Brazil, and Argentina are developing at a fast pace. On the other hand, the economies of India and China are less-developed but on the verge of taking off. These different stages of economic development often determine the kinds of opportunities available for hospitality firms.

When the macroeconomic environment of a country is in high gear, companies from other nations see opportunities to enter new markets. For a goods company (e.g., Proctor & Gamble) major marketing decisions (assuming a "market" exists) center on the name and communication and distribution strategies. For a hotel company the situation is more complex. First

TABLE 17-1   Asian Growth in Visitor Arrivals and Hotel Rooms 1982–1992

Country	1992 Arrivals	Increase from 1982	Country	Total Rooms 1992	Increase from 1982
Malaysia	6,016,209	677%	China	351,044	245%
China	4,006,427	424	Thailand	205,009	177
Indonesia	3,064,161	418	Macau[a]	4,633	117
Macau	1,884,417	190	Indonesia[b]	45,245	113
South Korea	3,231,081	182	South Korea	43,739	104
Hong Kong	6,986,163	169	Guam	5,584	98
Gaum	876,742	169	Hong Kong	33,534	93
Thailand	5,136,443	132	Malaysia	55,809	93
Singapore	5,989,940	103	Singapore[c]	24,573	74
Japan	3,581,540	100	Japan[d]	124,168	61
Philippines	1,152,952	42	Taiwan	15,018	27
Fiji	278,534	37	Philippines	15,769	25
Taiwan	1,873,327	32	Fiji	4,562	19
Total	**44,077,936**	**171%**	**Total**	**928,687**	**139%**

[a]3-star and above.
[b]Classified rooms assigned a 1-5 star rating.
[c]Gazetted hotels registered with the Singapore Tourism Promotion Board.
[d]Western style.
Source: Tourism offices of respective countries, compiled by Global Hospitality Resources, Inc., San Diego. Published in *Hotels*, April, 1994, p. 47.

comes finding a developer. Contract negotiations and site location can easily take a year or more. Construction to opening can easily take three years or more. Hyatt, for example, spent 13 years to "build" a hotel in Jerusalem as its developer periodically ran out of funds. McDonald's, which can open a restaurant in the United States in a few months for a cost of approximately $1 million, spent almost ten times that amount, and many years, before they could open their first unit in Russia.

In the meanwhile, the macroeconomic environment probably changes continually, sometimes slowly if not drastically. If the economy declines, the market picture changes as well and the marketing plan has to be altered accordingly. High-priced goods and services tend to suffer more in a declining economy. Conversely, McDonald's and Burger King have done well in international markets in spite of weak economies. The long-term perspective must be kept in mind.

Currency fluctuations also greatly affect the travel market. For example, when the U. S.

dollar strengthens, travel "reverses," and more Americans go to Canada and abroad; when the dollar weakens, more foreigners come to the United States. This is not a one-way street, of course. It is the relative strength of one currency against another that is the critical factor.

The number of airline seats that arrive every day, or "lift' into a destination, is another of the elements affecting the international travel market. The foreign tourist market for many areas may be not much larger than the number of arriving passengers on airline seats, regardless of the number of hotel rooms. In many parts of the world, the number of flights is a consequence of political and economic actions as much as they are of business practice.

The Microeconomy

On the other side of the coin exists the microeconomic environment. This environment is concerned with use of the product, awareness levels, and the competitive situation. A good example is Singapore where, in the early 1980s,

TABLE 17-2 Planned Hotel Development in Asia in 1994

Company/Headquarters	Rooms Existing Under Development	Hotels Existing Under Development
Prince Hotels (48 IC)*	19,055	51
Tokyo	1,373	5
Tokyo Hotel Group (62 IC)*	18,196	73
Pan Pacific	1,968	6
Tokyo/Costa Mesa, California		
Holiday Inn Worldwide	15,962	50
Atlanta	2,185	12
Fujita Kanko (IC)*	15,799	70
Tokyo	0	0
ITT Sheraton	14,166	37
Boston	1,035	3
Hyatt International	14,078	36
Chicago	2,457	6
Hilton International	13,113	27
London	312	2
New World Hotels/Renaissance	13,110	32
Hotels & Resorts	3,128	8
Hong Kong/Miami		
Shangri-La International	12,407	24
Hong Kong	3,241	7
Southern Pacific (36 IC)*	11,984	69
Sydney	775	4
ANA Hotels International (27 IC)*	11,341	36
Tokyo	503	2
Nikko Hotels International JAL (11 IC)*	9,382	24
Tokyo	2,533	6
Accor, Asia Pacific	8,882	53
Paris	3,263	13
Dai-ichi Hotels (36 IC)*	8,204	42
Tokyo	0	0
Westin	7,416	15
Seattle	661	2
New Otani (19 IC)*	6,541	21
Tokyo	0	0
Inter-Continental	5,795	9
London	733	2
Shanghai Jin Jiang Group (11 IC)*	5,620	13
Shanghai, China	500	1
Miyako Hotels (IC)*	5,152	17
Tokyo	252	1
Rihga Royal (15 IC)*	5,149	17
Osaka	621	26

*IC = in country

Source: Global Hospitality Resources Inc., San Diego. Published in *Hotels*, April, 1994, p.48.

the economy was booming; both tourism and international business travel were on the increase. Inter-Continental, another Sheraton, and Westin entered the market with over 2,000 rooms; Mandarin, New Otani from Japan, Peninsula from Hong Kong, and others also opened new hotels. By the time most of these hotels were built (and others were still building or had construction halted), the macroeconomy had softened. The microeconomy now presented a totally different picture. Rate-cutting practices became intense and consumers could almost name their own price for hotel rooms. It was the 1990s before the situation showed real improvement, occupancy caught up, and a new hotel-building binge began. In Hong Kong, this binge has been almost continuous, in spite of recent hotel closings, due to the ability of their owners to get higher, more profitable rents for their hotels as office buildings.

A country's economic policies affect international companies. In India, for example, a previous government mandated that a foreign company could only hold less than 50 percent equity in an Indian business. It was because of this that McDonald's, Coca-Cola, and IBM all withdrew from India. In the mid-1990s, India moved toward economic liberalization, and all these firms reentered India—a market, by the way, where average annual individual income is $400, but where the middle class is larger than the entire population of the United States. India is home to about one of every six people in the world.

In some cases there is also government competition. For years, Russia only had rubles as a currency. Rubles had no value on the open market, so international companies had a difficult time doing business and getting paid for it. Pepsi Cola solved this problem by taking its "profits" out of the country in units of Stolichnaya vodka, which it, in turn, sold outside of Russia for hard currency.

In the final analysis, any company seeking to penetrate an international market must carefully weigh all the economic considerations. Each country requires of a company specific strategic approaches and marketing plans that must fit that company's resources, culture, and capabilities. The long-term economic environment is the primary consideration. Although many developing countries offer inducements such as tax incentives and low-cost employment, they may still be very unstable for market entry.

Food-service companies entering international markets deal almost totally with the local consumer. Although there are obvious exceptions—there are restaurants in Paris and other cities geared to Americans or Britons—these generally are not the purpose of entry for a foreign firm. This means that understanding the "local" population demographics, wage levels, disposable income, standards of living, and other economic factors is of prime importance. The conventional wisdom of the home-base country usually does not apply. In Australia, for example, Kentucky Fried Chicken is considered expensive dining.

For hotel companies seeking to expand abroad there are two considerations. One concerns the local economic climate: The geographical customer mix and that portion of room-nights sought from the domestic market are very important.

The other consideration is the international travel market: Will it be sought, where will it come from, and what economic factors will affect it? Regardless of its decision, the international hotel company will still have to confront the local market for its food and beverage outlets as well as a portion of its meetings business. Although hotel dining and drinking is not necessarily fashionable in the United States or countries like France and England, in some countries, such as India, hotels are where almost all "better" dining takes place. Hotel companies need to understand this market as well, and its economic impacts.

Social and Cultural Environment

Although the economic environment will probably have the greatest impact upon major international marketing decisions, it is certainly the cultural environment that will most deeply affect marketing behavior. Culture is the common set of values shared by most citizens in any country—its personal beliefs and aspirations, assumptions and attitudes, interpersonal relationships, and social structure.

Communications between host population and entering company representatives are often difficult, not only because of differing spoken languages but also because of misunderstood nonverbal communications such as body language. A simple greeting can take on many different forms in different cultural contexts. Dealing with written communications can be especially difficult. Coca-Cola, when written in Chinese characters, means "bite the wax tadpole." In India, any advertising campaign slogan has to be effectively translated into any or all of 14 *national* languages.

Negotiation practices also vary in different cultures. Americans and Europeans tend to be more direct, while negotiations in the Pacific Rim nations often include long evenings of dining, drinking, and entertaining. Hospitality marketers need to be keenly aware of cultural norms, those of both the *countries* in which they operate and the nationalities or countries of their *customers*. It is sensible practice to have management personnel from the native country who understand at least that country's culture. Without this understanding, a firm may have great difficulty in succeeding in a foreign market.

Knowing the Local Market

Establishing a hotel in a foreign land requires giving up some preconceived notions. The astute company will first go into the marketplace and determine the cultures, social customs, dining-out habits, and other environmental elements of the host population, and do a competitive analysis.

Sofitel initiated research in the local markets they planned to enter in the United States to determine local restaurant needs and wants. Hyatt International has steered away from the "grande salon" dining room concept and, instead, installed smaller Italian, steak, and seafood concepts in its hotels. These outlets operate as individual profit centers with their own chef and manager, in contrast to the traditional F&B

manager and executive chef organizational chart.

Of course, all this is no different from knowing your market wherever you are—it just takes a little more effort. If you want to learn from guest complaints, it will be difficult for you in Asian cultures wherein smiling and being pleasant, and never disagreeing, are emphasized.

Consider some problems of doing business in Islamic societies. When an Inter-Continental hotel was built in Saudi Arabia in the holy city of Mecca, Christians customarily were not allowed inside the holy city. Construction had to be supervised from a distance via television cameras. Obstacles arose managing a property where only Moslems were allowed and where the entire workforce was required to be Moslem, and none female.

One does not have to go to the Islamic holy city of Mecca to find such strong cultural influence. Five times a day, wherever they are in the world, Moslems pray while facing Mecca. Hotels catering to the Moslem market—and there are many in the Middle East and South Asia—provide in each room a directional indicator oriented toward Mecca.

In Moslem countries such as Kuwait, alcoholic beverages are totally banned. This is no idle gesture. Incoming airplanes are boarded to be certain that their liquor stock is locked and secured. Imagine developing weekend packages for a hotel in Kuwait, when Cairo with all its nightclubs is just a short flight away! In India, four of five people are Hindu and eat no beef—a cultural factor that McDonald's responds to by using a non-beef substitute "spiked" for Indian tastes.

Values important to one culture may mean little to another. Conflicts sparked by differing values become even more intense, however, in an industry that sells very personal services to a diversified clientele. Different cultures reflect different beliefs, attitudes, motivations, moralities, perceptions, and rituals. Preconceived notions of what the hotel guest wants may conflict with the guest's own notions in *any* country; they can result in disaster when marketing to *other* cultures. Thus, cultural differences have a tremendous basic impact upon marketing mix decisions in international operations.

In Thailand, for example, most business dealings are transacted among friends. So, a new element of the marketing mix is your friends, clients, and guests, to increase your business. In most of the Western world, kickbacks are illegal, but in some parts of Asia, people may think you strange if you refuse to accept them. Attracting and retaining skilled labor is a huge challenge in Asia and Africa. Hotel GMs are constantly looked to for guidance by the rank and file as "providers for" their families. Training, motivating, and compensating staff is much different elsewhere than it is in the U.S. and Europe.

There are interesting social changes taking place in many countries. One major change is in the levels of domestic travel by many more nations' own citizens. This phenomenal broadening of numbers of travelers, having occurred for some time in the United States, is really only beginning in some European and most Asian countries. In Scandinavia, whose people once routinely took holidays in southern Europe to enjoy warmer temperatures, increasing numbers of people stay closer to home. With high discretionary income and long vacation periods, many Scandinavians are now more often traveling, staying in hotels, and eating out in their own countries. Eastern European countries, long closed to foreign travel, are now hosting millions of western Europeans, relatively a short trip for most from the western nations.

Political, Regulatory, and Legal Environments

It is clear that political, regulatory, and legal environments of countries other than one's own will differ from each other, and often radically. These elements are intertwined with economic and cultural differences. Sometimes local custom will require that "who you know" or who you pay "extra to" will determine when, or even *if*, a project will get done—or, in the worst cases, whether you will get bombed (see Case 17-2). It

may take economic influence to get the political influence to get around the regulatory barriers. Sometimes, wherein competitors know "someone higher" than you do—well, that's the system!

In Abu Dhabi, United Arab Emirates, the same company (Abu Dhabi National Hotels Company) owned all the five-star competing hotels until 1993 (when the Forte Grand opened), each managed by different companies. The owning company tells the hotels what they will charge, where they will be positioned, and what markets, or groups, each will serve.

In Al Khobar, Saudi Arabia, alcoholic beverages are restricted. The city, like the country, is dry, and women's lives are also restricted. The shops do well because of their tax-free status but the hotels suffer because it is a short ride across the bridge to Bahrain, where liquor flows freely and women are allowed to work. Visa restrictions on "quick trips" have curtailed this traffic, but Le Meridien, the most beautiful hotel in Al Khobar, and others, face a difficult competitive situation.

Tax control, price control, and labor restrictions are other influences that can become difficult when doing business in unfamiliar countries. Problematic political and regulatory environments, however, are not limited to developing countries; they occur in almost all countries, including Spain, Italy, and France. Rioting in the streets of Paris over wages for students certainly affects the decisions of foreign travelers to go to this destination. All such problems impact marketing strategies and tactics.

Despite perceived difficulties, companies from all countries with expanding economies will increasingly go abroad. Domestic markets get overbuilt, currency exchange rates fluctuate, and the need to continually expand the customer base and revenues, all lead in one direction—international.

Demographic Environments

Many Americans are familiar with demographic shifts taking place in the United States—Generation X, the aging of the baby boomers, the increasing purchasing power of senior citizens—demographic trends actually shaping the populations of every nation. The size of a country's population, its per-capita income or purchasing power of citizens, all are important factors in every country and must be evaluated. Even though China and India are the world's most populous countries, for example, only about 10 percent of the population can actually afford to purchase services offered by the hospitality industry. Still, such data show that these markets have a huge potential. Mathematically, 10 percent of India's population represents a market of almost 100 million people.

What this means is that an international company like Sheraton, Hyatt, Days Inn, Holiday Inn, or Accor can no longer simply assume a management contract in, say, Taipei, bring in a European management staff, and set up business for the international traveler. To be successful today, these companies must understand the local population and trends, and a host of other environmental factors.

The International Marketing Mix

Products and Services

Many product/service decisions are ones that must be made when the hotel is being designed. Hilton International and Inter-Continental Hotels virtually exported American-type hotels. Today, says S.C. Jain,

> [The] product decision must be made on the basis of careful analysis and review. The nature, depth, and breadth of the product line; the possibilities of new product development and product innovation; the importance attached to product design (the adaptation and customization of products to suit local conditions vis-a-vis standardization); the decision on foreign R&D; and a planned screening and elimination of unsuccessful products bear heavily on success in foreign markets.[7]

Yet Theodore Levitt appears to have argued to the contrary when he says, "High-touch products [hotels and restaurants] are as globalized as high-tech, and the globally-oriented company should seek global standardization. It digresses from this mode only at its peril."[8]

It is clear that marketers should carefully consider Levitt's thesis on standardization vs. customization to local markets and preferences when developing product/service strategies in foreign markets. We have already given numerous examples of product differences in different countries, and have cited cases of the product not being adapted to the local market. The question of standardization vs. customization is a complex one. As with all product decisions, however, the answer should lie in the needs and wants of the marketplace and the degrees of difference among the markets being served.

There are pitfalls in either case. Hilton International's standardization of product helped it to establish a common image worldwide so that Americans, first, and then other international travelers became accustomed to it and bought Hilton when available. This standardized product, however, did not match the conditions in every market. Holiday Inn, by contrast, in foreign markets in which it has adapted the product has been more successful than in those where it has not. Fast-food firms have been quick to adapt internationally. In Australia, KFC has delivery service and a "smorgasbar" deli case; Pizza Hut has spicy sauces, barbecue and all-you-can-eat dessert bars; and Sizzler includes pumpkin soup on its menu. All of these are adaptations popular in the host country.

Each international expansion requires designing the product line for the location and the markets to be served. Products such as hotels and restaurants likewise need to be adapted to different countries and cultures. The product objectives for each country and market must be clearly delineated and related to the local situation as well as to the overall corporate objectives.

---

[7]Subhash C. Jain, *International Marketing Management*, Boston: Kent Publishing, 1984, p. 345.

[8]Theodore A. Levitt, "The Globalization of Markets," *Harvard Business Review*, May/June, 1983, pp. 92–102. Copyright © by the President and Fellows of Harvard College; all rights reserved.

Presentation Mix

Recall that the presentation mix consists of all elements used to increase the tangibility of the products and services. These include location, physical plant, atmosphere, employees, customers, and price. In international markets, the issue of standardization versus customization arises. Since most hospitality ventures have local investors and partners, the presentation mix elements have to be worked out between the hospitality firms and the local owners.

New locations are extremely expensive and difficult to obtain in most major international cities. The cost of good locations in Hong Kong, Tokyo, or even Bombay is greater than in New York City!

> The bureaucracies in these countries send developers through a maze of permits, licenses and complicated, inefficient approval processes. City planners make unreasonable demands and each new agency that enters the process has a chance to impose new restrictions. Tales abound of building requirements changed three or four times and multiple duplications of effort. Even when the rules are clear, they may be bent either way—for you and, sometimes, against you. Prague city government upset the Ritz-Carlton Hotel Co. in January 1993 by offering a site to Four Seasons Hotels and Resorts without adhering to the required bidding process.[9]

Physical plants need to be designed with the target markets in mind, with modifications made to account for local trends. Take the case of hotel restaurants. In most U.S. cities, hotel restaurants have a difficult time competing with their independent counterparts and hotel food and beverage services may be quite limited. In Africa and Asia, as we have noted, the opposite pertains and the best restaurants are often inside the upscale hotels.

Atmospherics, needless to say, are greatly, but not always, influenced by local mores and traditions in international locations. Amazingly enough, there are still properties like a Holiday Inn in Kuala Lumpur, Malaysia, where one can

easily believe he is in a Holiday Inn in Des Moines, Iowa. Pan Pacific, an upscale division of Tokyu Hotel Group, seems to do likewise (Figure 17-5) in a Kuala Lumpur hotel ad. Perhaps this hotel ad view does not look like Des Moines, but does it look any less like Seattle or New York City? Consider, instead, the Oberoi in Goa, India (Figure 17-6), a Portuguese settlement, or Bali, Indonesia (Figure 17-7) or Cairo, Egypt (Figure 17-8), or Forte Heritage hotels in the United Kingdom (Figure 17-9). Consider, as well, the case of Forte's Grand Hotel in Abu Dhabi, opened in 1993:

> This hotel entered a well-established market of international hotel chains and independents, mostly owned by the aforementioned Abu Dhabi National Hotels Company. It used the presentation mix to get an edge in the market.
>
> The Forte Grand is the tallest building in the city and easily spotted on the road from the airport. Its design is unmistakable—a lean ellipse of sheer blue glass. The local market in Abu Dhabi is important because government laws allow alcoholic licenses only in hotel outlets. Consequently, hotels compete to attract local residents as well as international travelers.
>
> The designer arrived at a feel that is understated European with the opulence of Arabian motifs and furnishings. The lobby reflects the local tradition of *majlis*—an open meeting place—with Arabic seating areas on a sweep of marble. The overall effect is one of clear coolness, important in a climate that can reach daytime temperatures of 110°F (43°C) and 100 percent humidity. All bedrooms have natural lighting, a sea view, and a comfortable window seat spanning an arc of glass.
>
> The hotel has an eclectic group of eight F&B outlets including a revolving rooftop restaurant where every diner gets a spectacular view of the city and the sea. The rest includes a piano bar, an American bar, a Lebanese restaurant, and an Italian restaurant. In its first six months the hotel achieved a 58 percent occupancy, all of which came from the other hotels. The ultimate question, of course, is will it keep these customers.[10]

The human elements of the presentation mix, employees and customers, are affected by

---

[9]"All's not quiet on the Eastern Front," *Hotel and Motel Management,* March 7, 1994, pp. 14–15.

[10]Abstracted from "Hotel Design—Forte Means Business in Abu Dhabi," *Hotels,* April, 1994, pp. 62–65.

This Is Just The View From Our Elevator.

30th floor view

18th floor view

6th floor view

If you're impressed with the view from our lifts, then we're sure you'll be pleasantly surprised when you step out of them.

Because our view (nice as it is) is surpassed by the courteous service

and high standards that you would expect from the Pan Pacific.

But please, don't just take our word for it. Experience it for yourself. And while you're at it, enjoy the view.

THE PAN PACIFIC HOTEL
Kuala Lumpur

Jalan Putra, P.O. Box 11468, 50746 Kuala Lumpur, Malaysia. Tel: 03-442 5555, 442 6555.
For reservations in North America, use the access code "PF". Or Call (800) 327-8585 toll free.

FIGURE 17-5   Pan Pacific fails to differentiate its geographic location

the economic, social, and cultural environments of the country. The level of economic development has a major impact on how customers and employees view the hospitality in-dustry. When Kentucky Fried Chicken (now KFC) opened their first unit in Beijing, it be-came the most fashionable place to "dine out." Employees who worked there felt great pres-

FIGURE 17-6   Oberoi positions to its environment in Goa

FIGURE 17-7   Oberoi positions to its environment in Bali

tige in their positions as fast-food workers and the managers made more money than most Chinese physicians.

In the Abu Dhabi Forte Grand Hotel, men-tioned above, the general manager personally interviewed 2,200 of the 24,000 applicants, in 14 countries, to obtain 311 permanent staff, who were then trained for four months.

FIGURE 17-8   Oberoi positions to its environment in Cairo

Pricing

Pricing is a very complex variable of the marketing mix in the international marketplace. There are two main reasons for this beyond the usual complexities of pricing: fluctuating monetary exchange rates and unscrupulously competitive pricing tactics.

First, on a daily basis monetary exchange rates fluctuate, radically during either national or international economic cycles, and affect every international visitor as well as local guests.

The president of one international hotel company with worldwide properties once said to one of the authors, "We're not in the hotel business; we're in the monetary exchange business." While this statement was not to be taken literally, it demonstrates the concerns of a company operating internationally. Probably, one of the greatest problems in the international segment is pricing both for the native of a host country and for the international traveler, each of whom may have totally different perspectives on the price/value relationship. What is the dollar worth against other world currencies? It depends. Table 17-3 provides a factual answer to this question as of August 3, 1994, figures probably very different than they will be the day you read this chapter.

French hotels quote "straight" rates; in other words, for the ordinary traveler the rack rate (or rate posted with the government by law) is usually the rate you pay.[11] Thus France, or any other country, becomes either a bargain or costly, depending on the exchange rate between

---

[11]This is also true in much of Europe. Many European countries also use an official or unofficial rating system based on the "number of stars system." There is minimum overlap in the rates between hotels with different star ratings. The ratings also indicate the physical facilities available. Thus, customers know pretty well what the property offers, and at what rate range, when they choose a one-, two-, three-, four-, or five-star hotel, which have different meanings than in the U.S. Examples in Paris of a five-star hotel are the Ritz; four-star, Le Meridien; three-star, Novotel; and two-star, Ibis. One-star properties are close to being hostels. There are efforts, however, to adopt a uniform rating system, such as that used by Supranational to rate hotels and mentioned in Chapter 16. Just about all hotels and restaurants in Europe add a 10 to 15 percent service charge.

FIGURE 17-9   Forte Heritage hotels maintain tradition

that country and the one you are coming from at the time you travel.

Traveling with exchange rates in mind is tricky business. Consider the following scenario: In the past, an American could book a room in an American company-operated hotel in Acapulco through an American travel agency for $80 per night, or could go to Mexico, exchange dollars for pesos, go to the hotel, and obtain the same room for $40. What may seem

TABLE 17-3   Exchange Rates of U.S. Dollar, August 3, 1994

Country	U.S. $ equiv.		Currency per U.S. $	
	Wed.	Tues.	Wed.	Tues.
Argentina (Peso)	1.01	1.01	.99	.99
Australia (Dollar)	.7313	.7327	1.3674	1.3648
Austria (Schilling)	.09021	.08982	11.09	11.13
Bahrain (Dinar)	2.6522	2.6522	.3771	.3771
Belgium (Franc)	.03083	.03076	32.43	32.51
Brazil (Real)	1.1037528	1.0893246	.91	.92
Britain (Pound)	1.5420	1.5355	.6485	.6513
30-Day Forward	1.5408	1.5343	.6490	.6518
90-Day Forward	1.5387	1.5322	.6499	.6527
180-Day Forward	1.5360	1.5295	.6510	.6538
Canada (Dollar)	.7207	.7198	1.3875	1.3893
30-Day Forward	.7200	.7191	1.3888	1.3906
90-Day Forward	.7188	.7178	1.3913	1.3931
180-Day Forward	.7158	.7148	1.3971	1.3989
Czech. Rep. (Koruna)				
Commercial rate	.0351593	.0351593	28.4420	28.4420
Chile (Peso)	.002417	.002417	413.72	413.72
China (Renminbi)	.115221	.115221	8.6790	8.6790
Colombia (Peso)	.001226	.001226	815.62	815.62
Denmark (Krone)	.1615	.1606	6.1929	6.2275
Ecuador (Sucre)				
Floating rate	.000456	.000456	2192.02	2192.02
Finland (Markka)	.19303	.19178	5.1804	5.2144
France (Franc)	.18561	.19476	5.3875	5.4125
30-Day Forward	.18545	.18459	5.3923	5.4173
90-Day Forward	.18526	*.18441*	5.3978	5.4228
180-Day Forward	.18513	.18428	5.4015	5.4265
Germany (Mark)	.6346	.6317	1.5758	1.5830
30-Day Forward	.6343	.6314	1.5766	1.5&38
90-Day Forward	.6343	.6314	1.5766	1.5838
180-Day Forward	.6352	.6323	1.5744	1.5816
Greece (Drachma)	.004206	.004179	237.75	239.30
Hong Kong (Dollar)	.12945	.12946	7.7250	7.7245
Hungary (Forint)	.0098522	.0098746	101.5000	101.2700
India (Rupee)	.03212	.03212	31.13	31.13
Indonesia (Rupiah)	.0004619	.0004619	2165.02	2165.02
Ireland (Punt)	1.5246	1.5145	.6559	.6603
Israel (Shekel)	.3298	.3298	3.0320	3.0320
Italy (Lira)	.0006371	.0006305	1569.51	1586.17

TABLE 17-3   (continued)

Country	U.S. $ equiv.		Currency per U.S. $	
	Wed.	Tues.	Wed.	Tues
Japan (Yen)	.009965	.009965	100.35	100.35
30-Day Forward	.009987	.009987	100.13	100.13
90-Day Forward	.010030	.010030	99.70	99.70
180-Day Forward	.010110	.010110	98.91	98.91
Jordan (Dinar)	1.4725	1.4725	.6791	.6791
Kuwait (Dinar)	3.3565	3.3565	.2979	.2979
Lebanon (Pound)	.000596	.000596	1676.50	1676.50
Malaysia (Ringolt)	.3893	.3868	2.5750	2.5850
Malta (Lira)	2.7027	2.7027	.3700	.3700
Mexico (Peso)				
Floating rate	.2966039	.2955956	3.3715	3.3830
Netherland (Guilder)	.5652	.5626	1.7692	1.7774
New Zealand (Dollar)	.6003	.6013	1.6658	1.6631
Norway (Krone)	.1453	.1"7	6.8807	6.9098
Pakistan (Rupee)	.0328	.0328	30.53	30.53
Peru (New Sol)	.4696	.4696	2.13	2.13
Philippines (Peso)	.03812	.03812	26.23	26.23
Poland (Zloty)	.00004380	.00004395	22833.01	22752.00
Portugal (Escudo)	.006222	.006201	160.73	161.26
Saudi Arabia (Riyal)	.26664	.26664	3.7504	3.7504
Singapore (Dollar)	.6636	.6638	1.5070	1.5065
Slovak Rep.(Koruna)	.0315557	.0316356	31.6900	31.6100
South Africa (Rand)				
Commercial rate	.2747	.2740	3.6400	3.6495
Financial rate	.2198	.2193	4.5500	4.5600
South Korea (Won)	.0012460	.0012456	802.60	802.80
Spain (Peseta)	.007704	.007671	129.80	130.36
Sweden (Krona)	.1297	.1294	7.7112	7.7250
Switzerland (Franc)	.7508	.7476	1.3320	1.3376
30-Day Forward	.7509	.7477	1.3318	1.3374
90-Day Forward	.7515	.7484	1.3306	1.3362
180-Day Forward	.7534	.7502	1.3273	1.3329
Taiwan (Dollar)	.037682	.037682	26.54	26.54
Thailand (Baht)	.04005	.04005	24.97	24.97
Turkey (Lira)	.0000319	.0000321	31361.61	31199.78
United Arab (Dirham)	.2723	.2723	3.6725	3.6725
Uruguay (New Peso)				
Financial	.199860	.199860	5.00	5.00
Venezuela (Bolivar)	.00590	.00590	169.57	169.57

frustrating, or even devious to the American consumer, becomes a major headache for the operator who is trying to make a profit while serving markets with totally different monetary values.

The same scenario is repeated worldwide, one way or another, in various international markets. It is no wonder that the tourist is bewildered, but it is no less a wonder that the hotel company has a difficult problem on its hands. Now consider the same scenario as taking place when the market mix of the hotel comes from many different countries, each with its own rate of exchange against the currency of the host country and each rate of exchange affected by the prevailing inflation rate in each country.

Second, pricing tactics by locally-owned competitors can send rate structures into a tailspin. Consider the pricing tactics of "unscrupulous" competitors. Many international hotel owners are primarily profit-driven, not to mention high-rate-oriented. When business is good, everyone gets top price. When business is bad, however, many local owners operating in their own countries, as well as some foreign chains, will do anything to get business—which here means cutting room rates. With "deep pockets" for survival, these hotels discount to a level at which their international counterparts, who need to show a profit, cannot compete.

Pricing a hotel room in the international market can be extremely risky, yet pricing is a marketing tool that cannot be ignored. Discounting when there simply isn't enough demand for the supply, as in Singapore in the 1980s, ends up being self-defeating for all. As an alternative destination, Singapore competes with Hong Kong, and its discount pricing helped to stabilize Hong Kong prices.

In the food and beverage areas a somewhat different situation exists. In much of Europe and in parts of Asia, "eating out" approximates a national pastime (at least for the middle and upper classes), far more so than in the United States. This causes high demand and the prices reflect it. Even so-called moderate restaurants can be expensive, and some of the better ones are simply exorbitant. The natives seem to accept it, but for Americans, to whom eating out is often something to do "before, during, or after" and in more of a hurry, such high prices can come as quite a shock. Where hotel dining is more customary, the percentage sources of revenues can change quite drastically, as shown in Table 17-4.

Communications Mix

Communications in the international arena are also affected by cultural differences. Coordination of communications efforts with other elements of the marketing mix in foreign markets is more difficult. The quality and the availabil-

TABLE 17-4   Source of Hotel Revenues in Different Countries

Country	Sources of Revenues (Ratio to Total Sales)			
	Rooms	Food	Beverage	Other
United States	66.8%	19.6%	5.9%	7.7%
France	63.5	22.1	8.0	6.4
Germany	53.8	26.9	13.0	6.3
United Kingdom	47.9	31.7	13.5	6.9
Mexico	55.8	22.6	11.2	10.4
Australia	55.4	24.5	12.3	7.8
Hong Kong	48.6	29.7	7.7	14.0

Source: Hotels, June, 1993, p. 52

FIGURE 17-10   Holiday Inn in Brussels prints "Dallas" copy in five languages

ity of the means and the media vary from country to country and affect the usefulness and success of various techniques.

Global advertising (i.e., advertising using similar copy in different countries) is practiced by many international hotel companies and often fails to differentiate—rooms, business centers, F&B outlets, etc.—as we have shown. The Holiday Inn at Brussels Airport, for example, prints its collateral in five languages but uses nearly the same advertising copy as a Holiday Inn in Dallas (Figure 17-10). The target market, the business traveler, actually is the same, assuming no cultural differences. On the other hand, there is nothing wrong with a common theme. Le Meridien carries out its Ken Maryan-

ski caricature theme worldwide, thus immediately identifying its properties (Figure 17-11).

Cultural barriers, however, make implementing a global campaign problematic. In a survey of 100 American advertisers, these barriers were defined as follows:

19 percent said their biggest mistake abroad was failure to allow for cultural differences.

79 percent develop distinctly different media plans in each country to reflect cultural and linguistic differences.

57 percent redesign the product or the packaging for each individual overseas market.

40 percent believe that universal advertising

When it comes to large conferences, we'll never head the professional organiser's list....

Le
MERIDIEN
LONDON

FIGURE 17-11   Le Meridien has a constant theme internationally

rises above cultural differences only on rare occasions.

Results from a separate study of marketers in the European Economic Community confirmed similar attitudes and concerns.[12]

Because of this, and because of the need to communicate with numerous and dissimilar markets, there tends to be more emphasis on personal selling at the unit level, and less sell-ing at the national level. Corporate hotel sales-people seem to spend their lives on airplanes and in foreign cities. There is also a greater use of representation firms and consortia than in the United States.

With some exceptions in Europe, most inter-national chain hotel properties are new and modern, offer the same basic services, and make the same claims and promises in the same product class. It is truly difficult, as it is in the United States, to differentiate one from the other in advertising copy. Thus, many com-panies, like airlines, stress the destination and

[12]Reported in "Differences, Confusion Slows Global Marketing Bandwagon," *Marketing News,* January 16, 1987, p. 1.

HOTEL MERIDIEN

At Le Meridien Phuket
there's sometimes nothing to do.

There's no hurry, no rush. When you're ready for a little gentle scuba diving, or sailing, or fishing, everything's there.

Until then, just lie by the huge free-form pool and soak up the sun. Sip a long cool drink on your private balcony overlooking the Andaman Sea. Or take an evening stroll to be lulled by the sound of waves on sand.

When you're ready for dinner, the exotic delights of fresh-caught seafood await you. Or Thai specialities with real local flavour. Or finest continental cuisine.

Later you'll be free to attend one of our celebrated theme night celebrations. An added dimension that's earnt Le Meridien Phuket a reputation for inventive incentives.

And more ways to do nothing than anywhere in Asia.

For information and reservations call Chris Reynolds on **312 222 9200**.

Le
MERIDIEN
PHUKET
THAILAND

PREDICTABLY WONDERFUL. WONDERFULLY UNPREDICTABLE.

As befits a storybook island, we've created a storybook resort. Nestled in a private cove, with lush gardens, bright architecture, 4 restaurants and a full menu of sports. It's a place where the senses can be soothed—or delightfully stirred. For reservations and information, call 800-543-4300 or your travel agent.

Le MERIDIEN
L'Habitation Le Domaine
SAINT MARTIN

Over 50 hotels and resorts worldwide. In North America: Boston, Chicago, Montreal, Nassau-Bahamas, New Orleans, New York, Newport Beach, San Diego, St. Martin, Vancouver

FIGURE 17-11   (continued)

put the emphasis on the brand name. The strategy in these cases is largely one of awareness and reminder.

The older hotels that have charm, warmth, or historic atmosphere (Figures 17-12, 17-13, 17-14) are, of course, advertised differently than the newer Hyatts, Hiltons, or Sheratons. The attributes of the older hotels are rarely if ever captured in modern hostelries or in their ads. In some cases, however, these attributes may be used to advantage in advertising. A more real example is the ad for a *pousada* in Portugal, illustrated in Figure 17-15. (*Pousadas* are small inns housed in historic buildings, castles, palaces, and monasteries that reflect the history and cultural traditions of the region in which they are located.) In other countries attempts are made to mix the new with the old (Figure 17-16) or with the panorama (Figure 17-17).

Delightfully French.

Le Grand Hotel Inter-Continental Paris   Carlton Inter-Continental Cannes   Hotel Inter-Continental Paris

Uniquely Inter·Continental.

Paris. Where Chopin came to compose, Picasso to paint and James Joyce
to write *Ulysses*. And Cannes. Where Cole Porter came to be inspired, the Vanderbilts
to play and the Duke and Duchess of Windsor to be among friends. Truly, there are no two
destinations in Europe more rewarding. Nor three grand French hotels so uniquely
experienced in handling all of your incentive program needs.

Our unique blend of deluxe accommodations, outstanding meeting and recreational
facilities, historic salons, superb restaurants, exemplary personal service and
custom-tailored programs is your assurance of the ultimate reward you seek.

Inter-Continental's Paris and Cannes Ultimate Incentives. The ultimate in motivational
travel rewards complete with suggested group and individual sightseeing tours and excursions,
program suggestions, unique theme parties, hotel fact sheets and more.
All uniquely designed for your needs by Inter-Continental Hotels.

**For more information and Ultimate Incentive brochures,
call toll-free 800-327-1177**

INTER·CONTINENTAL®HOTELS

FIGURE 17-12   Inter-Continental emphasizes French history and charm

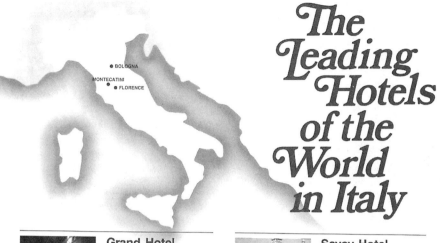

The Leading Hotels of the World in Italy

Grand Hotel Baglioni

Via Indipendenza, 8 - 40121 BOLOGNA
Tel. (051) 225445 - Fax 234840 - Telex 510242

118 rooms, 7 suites, fully airconditioned.
Conference facilities for up to 120 persons.
5 min. from railway station - 20 min from
G. Marconi airport.
"I Carracci" restaurant, Caffé Baglioni Bar.
All major credit cards.
18-hole golf course, hairdresser, beauty salon and
swimming pool available nearby.
Limousine airport transfer on request.

Savoy Hotel

Piazza della Repubblica, 7 - 50123 FLORENCE
Tel. (055) 283313 - Fax 284840 - Telex 570220

97 rooms, 4 suites, fully airconditioned;
convention facilities up to 150 persons.
40 min. from Pisa airport, 5 min. from rail station.
Credit cards: AC, AE, DC, EC, VS.
Restaurant, Snack Bar, American Bar; Cocktail
Bar with musical entertainment in the evening;
beauty parlour. 18-hole golf course 20 min. from
hotel.

Grand Hotel & La Pace

Via della Torretta, 1 - 51061 MONTECATINI TERME
Tel. (0572) 75801 - Fax 78451 - Telex 570004

150 rooms, 20 suites, fully airconditioned;
conference facilities for up to 220 persons.
40 kms. from Florence; 50 kms. from Pisa;
transfer on request.
Open April through October.
Credit cards: AE, DC, EC, MC.
Indoor and open-air restaurants; cocktail terrace;
sauna; hydro and manual massages; mud baths;
dieticians; revitalizing centre; physiotherapists;
health and beauty treatments; gymnasium;
swimming pool; solarium; clay tennis court.

Hotel Villa Medici

Via Il Prato, 42 - 50123 FLORENCE
Tel. (055) 238-1331 - Fax 2381336 - Telex 570179

83 rooms, 10 suites, 6 singles, fully
airconditioned; convention facilities.
5 min. from rail station, 40 min. from Pisa airport.
Credit cards: AC, AE, DC, EC, MC, VS.
New Lorenzo de Medici restaurant with summer
garden dining; Cocktail Bar with piano music in
the evening. Garden swimming pool; Beauty
salon, barbershop.

Hotel Villa San Michele

Via Doccia, 4 - 50014 FIESOLE (Florence)
Tel. (055) 59451 - Fax 598734 - Telex 570643

26 rooms, most with Jacuzzi, 2 suites.
Open March through November. Courtesy
sheduled shuttle bus to/from down-town Florence
(15 min.). Designed by Michelangelo, this ancient
monastery has been transformed into a hotel of
unsurpassed beauty.
Situated on the hill of Fiesole it enjoys a
spectacular view over the town. Open air dining
in the antique Loggia and intimate restaurant.
Large park. Outdoor heated swimming-pool open
June to September (extended in favourable weather).
Major Credit cards.

Hotel Regency

Piazza Massimo D'Azeglio, 3 - 50121 FLORENCE
Tel. (055) 245247 - Fax 2342937 - Telex 571058

38 rooms, 5 suites, fully airconditioned.
Gourmet Restaurant Relais le Jardin.
All major credit cards.
Tennis nearby; golf 13 kms.; private garden;
garage.
The most delightful hotel in Rome, Hotel Lord
Byron has a twin-sister in Florence.
Overlooking a quiet park in one of the finest
quarters of Florence, the Regency in earlier times was
the elegant townhouse of a noble family, today a
prestigious very exclusive hotel for those who
appreciate contemporary comfort and traditional
hospitality.

The Leading Hotels of the World

FIGURE 17-13   Traditional hotels in Italy

The decision on whether to standardize advertising worldwide or to adapt it to each country and/or each market is a difficult one. The very diversity of the countries and the markets calls on the one hand for diversity in advertising; on the other hand, total diversity would be prohibitively expensive and thus calls for standardization. Nevertheless, each hotel has its own specific collateral and does its own advertising to specific markets; in these cases, every attempt at differentiation should be made. In all cases, advertising by whatever medium should be consistent with the corporate image, should position the establishment in its desired marketplace, and should be a cost-effective method for communicating with the market.

The Obvious Choice

For more than 230 years Hotel d'Angleterre has remained the number one hotel in Copenhagen.

It's majestic presence in the centre of Copenhagen's King's Square makes the Hotel d'Angleterre simply the best address in Copenhagen.

130 comfortable and elegant rooms and suites

are all equipped with cable-TV, radio, mini-bar, bathrobes and hairdryers.

La Brasserie, Copenhagen's answer to Cafe de la Paix.

Le Restaurant offers an unforgettable evening with unique French food and superb service.

Banquet and Conference facilities for up to 600 people.

FIGURE 17-14 A classic hotel in Copenhagen

Distribution

By and large, external distribution channels are more heavily relied upon by international hotel companies in foreign lands than in their own home countries. The reasons for this extend from the previous discussion. Markets are drawn from many geographical areas, with many cultural differences as well as different needs and wants. Reaching these markets fully and efficiently by advertising and/or direct selling is cost-prohibitive.

In local markets hotel companies need someone who knows the market, knows its needs and wants, how to reach it, how to communicate with it, and how to sell it. Only a few countries enjoy full toll-free telephone dialing; thus, companies in other countries depend more on consortia, referral agencies, travel agencies, wholesalers, and brokers for business. As one example, Sol Hotels in Spain relies on wholesalers for 95 percent of their rooms sales in their resort properties. Most hotels on the Algarve coastline in Portugal, or the beach resort areas in Turkey, do likewise.

Consider Southeast Asia: Huge numbers of tourists come to this part of the world as part of tours or on individual travel packages from Europe, North America, Australia, and Japan. Consider Europe, where the largest outside markets are North America and Japan. Consider South America, which draws its bulk business from North America and Europe.

While wholesale distribution channels are essential to international markets, they also cause problems. First of all, tour operators want bargain rates for their clients and have the clout to get them. Second, they want commissions. Third, they often make promises that are difficult for properties to fulfill and for which the hotels will subsequently be blamed. Fourth, they can be manipulative. For example, some wholesalers will boycott a hotel if that hotel does business with another wholesaler. When the wholesaler cannot deliver all the business that the hotel needs, the hotel is in a difficult position.

Nevertheless, heavy use of distribution channels is necessary and a fact of life in international markets. Channel members are brought to see and be sold on the destination. In this process expenses are incurred that have to be absorbed. Even when channel members come on personal pleasure trips, large discounts are granted as a matter of routine.

International franchising is also used by multinational companies to increase their dis-

FIGURE 17-15 Marketing historic charm in Portugal

Variations on a theme

A Thai reward.

Enjoy the service. Savour the food. Get into the party mood.

The mood is Thai. Or anything you want your theme party to be.

Company incentives at the Central Plaza Bangkok. Memorable. Eventful. Rewarding.

The Central Plaza is uniquely located. Fifteen minutes downtown, fifteen minutes from the airport. Nestled in the midst of the most exciting shopping in the world.

Think up a theme. We'll give it variety.

THE CENTRAL PLAZA BANGKOK

1695 Phaholyothin Road, Bangkhen, Bangkok 10900 Thailand Phone: 66 (2) 541-1234 Telex: 20173 CENTEL TH Telefax: 66 (2) 541-1087

FIGURE 17-16   Mixing the new with the old in Bangkok

tribution network. McDonald's, Burger King, Dairy Queen, and Denny's all have international franchisees. Although these franchisees essentially maintain the product line of the franchisor, they may make local adaptations. For example, Denny's serves ginger pork and curried rice in Japan; McDonald's serves wine in France and beet-root in Austria (and actually sells the catsup for its hamburgers); and Dairy Queen offers a type of bread called *roti,* and a fried vegetable and meat dish in the Middle East. Many well-known hotel companies franchise internationally as well, as we have discussed.

Segmentation

Segmentation takes on a different perspective for the hotel company in the international arena. The potential market is so diverse that special care must be taken in regard to customer mix. For the individual restaurant, segmentation strategies are developed in much the same way as in the home country. The hotel restaurant will likewise segment, both by its in-house market and by the local market it wishes to attract.

Home-based hotels in countries other than the United States, at least those in major cities, have long had to deal with wide geographic segmentation. These hotels may segment locally, as many do throughout Europe outside the major cities. Groupe Accor's Formule1, Ibis division, and the Novotel division segment on the lower and middle portions of the French market. Its upper-end Sofitel division segments primarily on the international market. In some small countries, such as Singapore, the upscale hotels are almost totally dependent on the international market. In the United States relatively few hotels segment on the international market. However, as international tourism into the U.S. grows rapidly in the 1990s, many hotels in gateway cities such as New York, Los Angeles, and Miami actively seek out foreign visitors.

When a hotel company strays to foreign lands, the picture changes. The company must first seek geographic definition of its markets. The Nikko in New York City and the New Otani in Los Angeles initially sought to capture the

Pearl-Continental Hotel, Bhurban

Nestled in the midst of natural grandeur, at an elevation of over 2000 metres, is the Pearl-Continental Hotel, Bhurban. The hotel set against a breath-taking backdrop of the Kashmir Valley at the foothills of the Himalayas is an hour and a half scenic drive away from Islamabad.

The hotel provides 200 elegantly furnished rooms, including 16 suites, with private terraces. It offers complete health facilities with swimming pools, squash and tennis courts, a well-equipped gym with spa, jacuzzi, sauna and steam bath. Guests can enjoy outdoor activities from trekking to horse-back riding or golf on the adjacent nine- hole golf course.

FIGURE 17-17   Mixing the new with the panorama—the Pearl-Continental Hotel in Bhurban, Pakistan

Japanese market. More specifically, they segmented on both the Japanese business market and the Japanese pleasure travel market. Other companies, like those from France, did not necessarily target a particular nationality; instead, they hoped to attract from a number of segments. When these companies or American companies locate in other parts of the world, however, they all seek a diverse international clientele.

International hotel marketers must first make conscious decisions about the geographic segments they wish to attract. Many of these segments are not mutually compatible. The Japanese market, Taiwanese market, Australian market, ASEAN (Association of South East Asia Nations) market, German market, European market, and North American market, all have special significance for hotels in ASEAN countries (Philippines, Singapore, Malaysia, Thailand, Indonesia, and Brunei). This is true whether the hotels are operated by companies of the native country, United States, Hong Kong, Japan, or any other country. This situation is even more apparent in Hong Kong where, like Singapore, very few guests will be national residents.

It is also possible, of course, for some of these hotels to have guests from over 20 different countries at one time or another, as we have previously shown. Resources would be spread too thin, however, if a hotel made concentrated efforts to appeal to all of them. Many hotels purposefully avoid the stigma of being a "one-origin" hotel, its clientele predominantly from one nation.

A case in point is the Oberoi hotel in Bombay, which tried to shed the image of catering primarily to the international traveler while its rival, the Taj hotel, skimmed off the cream of the Indian market. Another case is a former Holiday Inn in Antwerp, Belgium, that wanted to dispel the image of being an "American" hotel, especially when the American market weakened. Focusing too narrowly on a major share of just one market can be misleading and counterproductive when you consider that no one geographic market segment is large enough to maintain necessary occupancy.

Fine-Tuning Segments

It can be a mistake to segment on very broad geographical areas as well. All Europeans are clearly not the same, nor are all Moslems, and not all Americans. Thus, some international hotel companies are beginning to fine-tune their segmentation strategies with a global perspective. This could mean, for example, focusing on a certain level of business executive regardless of geographic origin, as was shown in Figure 17-10. This segment, composed of diverse cultures, is more difficult and expensive to reach, and difficult to service, but increasingly global communication media and distribution channels are easing the task.

A good example of this is the Century Park Sheraton in Singapore, an All Nippon Airways (ANA)-managed hotel. The prime market for this hotel is the business traveler. Main sources of this market are Japan, the United States, United Kingdom, and Europe. All this hotel's business travelers have essentially the same needs—a business center, a location near the business area, dining and entertainment facilities, and a good communication infrastructure. Although each ethnic or national group may have different priorities, their needs remain the same. The Century Park segments as follows:

Sheraton—business generated by the Sheraton reservations system.
Corporate—business generated by companies located in Singapore.
Diplomatic—business generated by local diplomatic missions.
Crew—airline crew rooms booked by contract, travel agency, and airline personnel, and business generated by airline reservations systems.

By carefully targeting these markets, the hotel was able to maintain its image even in bad times by refusing tour groups. The Century Park is a good example of one hotel's avoiding the trap that some other Singapore hotels fell into by not utilizing careful segmentation strategies.

Fine-tuning follows the pattern of good segmentation strategy—that is, complementary target markets. Le Meridien Etoile at Porte Maillot in Paris, a 1,000-room hotel, had considerable segmentation difficulties with its mixture of executives and tour groups. The company took over another hotel, at Montparnasse in a commercially less-desirable (for the businessperson) location in Paris, where it booked most of its tour

TABLE 17-5   Hotel Dimensions and Benefit Segments of Business Travelers in Scandinavia

Dimensions on Which Hotels are Evaluated

Efficient core service: The efficiency and friendliness of service, quiet rooms and good reception, and other intangible benefits.

Business services: Variety of business services offered as well as working possibilities in rooms, and office options.

Restaurants and image: Restaurants and nightclub image, business customer clientele, and interior decors.

Accessibility: Location of the hotel.

Benefit Segments of Business Customers

Indifferents: Regard core service and business services as unimportant, indifferent by contrast with other dimensions.

High business service and access: Business services and location critical, restaurant and image insignificant.

Core service: Basic services important; location, restaurant and image unimportant.

High access and core service: Location and core services important: business services, restaurant, and image of no importance.

High business services and restaurants: Business services and restaurants important, other dimensions unimportant.

High restaurant and core services: Don't value business services.

Source: K. E. K. Moller, J. R. Lehtinen, G. Rosenqvist, and K. Storbacka, "Segmenting Hotel Business Customers: A Benefit Clustering Approach," in T. Bloch, et al. (eds.), *Services Marketing in a Changing Environment, Chicago:* American Marketing Association, 1985, pp. 74–75.

groups. This move considerably enhanced the position of the Porte Maillot property.

One way to fine-tune is to look at the business market as something other than one vast market. Kristian Moller and his colleagues researched over 700 business travelers in Scandinavia on "regular" hotel usage—that is, congresses, conventions, and seminars were excluded. Using a benefit-clustering approach, they were able to show that business travelers do not evaluate hotels homogeneously. The research defined six meaningful and homogeneous segments based on four underlying dimensions. The four dimensions and the six subjectively-labeled segments that were identified are shown in Table 17-5.

It is informative to note some of the conclusions of Moller and his colleagues:

[A] striking feature is the number of segments regarding business services as clearly unimportant—covering 47% of respondents.

...[B]oth business service oriented segments differ from the other segments by including a larger share of top and middle management personnel, who also travel more than the average business customers. Moreover, they do more work during their stay at the hotel. The High Business Services & Restaurant & Image segment has some additional, fairly unique, features. Its members are keen on hotel advice...using the "right" hotels, and it has a high share of U.S. and UK visitors...it has more loyal patronizing behavior than other segments, and its members are more favorable towards international "luxury" chains...they also exhibit a more active recreation pattern.[13]

It is also worth noting that SAS Hotels of Brussels was particularly successful in using psychographic segmentation, concentrating on

[13]K. E. K. Moller, J. R. Lehtinen, G. Rosenqvist, and K. Storbacka, "Segmenting Hotel Business Customers: A Benefit Clustering Approach," in T. Bloch, et al. (eds.), *Services Marketing in a Changing Environment,* Chicago: American Marketing Association, 1985, pp. 72–76. Published by the American Marketing Association.

the efficiency-minded segment. In Stavanger, Norway, SAS operates an "efficient" business-persons' hotel without the usual flourish of varied restaurants and lounges usually associated with upscale hotels.

The pitfalls of concentrated segmentation are more acute with international markets. Some geographical markets collapse overnight, as occurred with the fall of the North American market in Europe due to terrorism activities in 1986. The same thing happened in Florida in the 1990s with the German market, as foreign tourists were the victims of violent crimes that received tremendous publicity. Of course, there is no way to foresee these types of events but being forewarned means not depending on one segment too heavily.

Globalization of Markets

Somewhat contrary to segmentation practice, Theodore Levitt considered that the era of multinational marketing must move to one of "globalization of markets." Levitt argued,

> ...Though companies always customize for specific segments, success in a world whose wants become more homogenized requires of such companies strategic and operating modes that search for opportunities to sell to similar segments throughout the globe to achieve the scale economies that keep their costs competitive.
>
> Seldom these days is a segment in one country unique to that country alone. It is found everywhere, [and is] thus available to sellers from everywhere. Small local segments in this fashion become globally standardized, large, and therefore subject to global competition, especially price competition...the successful global corporation does not abjure customization or differentiation for the requirements of markets that differ in product preferences, spending patterns, shopping preferences.... But the global corporation accepts and adjusts to these differences only reluctantly, only after relentlessly testing their immutability—after trying in various ways to circumvent and reshape them.[14]

Does Levitt argue against segmentation? If a country, or even a segment within that country is not homogeneous, can the world be one homogeneous marketplace? Does this apply to the hospitality industry? Is a hotel room, or a restaurant meal, basically the same worldwide with minor modifications? Should the marketer adjust only after testing the waters? Or, contrarily, why did a new, conventional Holiday Inn Crowne Plaza in Salzburg, Austria lose $2.3 million at 27 percent occupancy the first year it was open in 1993? Certainly, this is how Hilton International and Inter-Continental started, but others have not necessarily followed. We leave this discussion to the reader because the final chapter has yet to be written and Levitt's comments have been controversial. We include them here because they clearly come under the category of environmental scanning in the international arena.

Positioning

Closely related to segmentation is the issue of positioning. Relative to what we have already stated, most hotel companies that went abroad sought to position in the high-upper end of the market. Perhaps this was a given when these companies were among the first to enter markets such as Singapore and Hong Kong.

Because it is easy to look at Singapore with hindsight, let's look at Hong Kong with foresight, since the situation will no doubt be different by the time the British crown colony reverts to Chinese sovereignty in 1997. Hong Kong has long been a top hotel market. Not only does the city achieve high occupancy but it contains some of the best world-class hotels. Every aspect of service is primed to perfection by intense competition.

Hong Kong hotelkeeping has been recognized as the modern state of the art. This is the city where guests of the Mandarin and Peninsula Hotels are met at the airport by Rolls Royces, and a Holiday Inn has eight specialty cuisine restaurants. Every hotel is aware that the customer has many similar choices. As a result, hotels maintain continuous staff training, qual-

[14]Theodore A. Levitt, "The Globalization of Markets," *Harvard Business Review,* May/June, 1983, pp. 92–102. Copyright © by the President and Fellows of Harvard College; all rights reserved.

ity of food and beverage, and refurbishing. In spite of this situation, the hotel community has, relatively speaking, maintained reasonable rack rates.

When Singapore was in the same situation, rack rates increased drastically, building proliferated, and occupancy fell. In 1987, Singapore occupancy averaged below 50 percent during a number of months, and discount rates made the city a bargain for the tourist.

In mid-1987, Hong Kong had 21,000 hotel rooms. Eighteen new projects were under development, and hotel capacity increased to 29,000 rooms by 1990 and to 33,500 in 1992. Building continues. Most of the present rooms and almost all of the new ones are in the top end of the market. Also developed was the massive Hong Kong Convention and Exhibition Centre, which contains a 600-room Grand Hyatt.

Just about all major international hotel chains are in the Hong Kong market. These include two Holiday Inns, Hilton International, Omni, Peninsula, Renaissance, Inter-Continental, two Hyatts, Meridien, Sheraton, Shangri-La, Nikko, and Regent, as well as top Hong Kong companies. Despite the increase in supply, occupancy was expected to increase to 89 percent in 1994, up from 86 percnet in 1993, reflecting the strength of the Hong Kong economy.[15] Can this continue, or will Hong Kong suffer the short-term fate of Singapore, a country of about the same size?

When international companies applied the same "top end of the market" positioning strategy in markets such as London and Paris the situation was different. These cities had individual (some are now chain or consortium members), classic hotels that held sway in the deluxe market category with a product that couldn't be duplicated, such as the Connaught and Dorchester in London and the Bristol and Ritz in Paris. Many of the new hotels were forced into down-market positions when they found they couldn't compete for the same customer.

In essence, positioning at the upper end of the market is no longer a given in foreign marketplaces. As inevitably happens, the competi-

tion moves in and there are too few non-price sensitive customers to go around. Positioning opportunities should be the first stage of market analysis for any hospitality company seeking to penetrate foreign marketplaces. This is exactly what Group Sol, Spain's largest hotel company has done. In 1994, it announced plans to build 60 small, economy motels in Germany targeted at business travelers. Sol hotels are primarily vacation-oriented but they are already well-known in Germany, from where most of Spain's tourists originate.

Branding

Brand names also need to be considered for positioning in international markets. There are essentially three different common practices: single name, multi-names, and individual names.

Perhaps the most common practice is to use a single name, as do Sheraton and Meridien. The purpose in this case is to create immediate identity. As Sheraton proclaimed in one ad:

> Knowing where you're going is knowing where to stay. In Sana'a [the capital of Yemen, in the Middle East], and around the world, that can only mean Sheraton Hotels. Where the art of hospitality finds new expressions of excellence. And sensitivity to the needs of the business and leisure traveler results in a superior guest experience. So when you come to Sana'a come to Sheraton to stay.

Perhaps one of the more perplexing brand name situations occurs with Hilton. In the United States, the name Hilton is used. Overseas, however, the Hilton name is not allowed to be used by the same company because of previous business transactions. Therefore, the name Conrad is used to represent Hilton-managed hotels overseas. To confuse issues further, Hilton International (a totally different company) uses its brand name overseas and uses the name Vista in the United States. Hilton International hotels are generally more upscale than U.S. Hilton hotels. It is not unusual for a European or Asian to reserve at a Hilton hotel, such as at New York's John F. Kennedy International Airport, when coming to the United

[15]*Hotels,* January, 1994, pp. 43–44.

States, unaware of the separate companies, and to be quite shocked by the property.

The multi-name practice is followed by Groupe Accor to differentiate its product line. The corporate name is never used. To many people in the 60-plus foreign countries in which Accor operates, perhaps even in France, Sofitel, Novotel, and Ibis may be perceived as three separate and distinct chains, as distinct as its Motel 6 acquisition in the United States.

A company that maintained individual names on its hotels, and still does for some (as shown in Figure 17-9), was Trusthouse Forte of England. Customers could stay at the Compleat Angler (Marlow, England) for a country inn; the Wynnstay (Machynlleth, Wales) for a small-town hotel; the Old England (Bowness-on-Windermere, England) for a lakeside resort; the Post House (Edinburgh, Scotland) for an outside-the-city hotel; the Strand Palace (London) for a touristy group hotel; or the George V (Paris), the Dom (Cologne), the Plaza Athenee (New York), the Ritz (Madrid), or the Sandy Lane (Barbados) for top-of-the-line luxury hotels—all without knowing they were in a Trusthouse Forte property, unless they recognized the small but ubiquitous "thf" initials. Case 9-3 illustrated how Forte developed product line brands to try to overcome the confusion.

Somewhat similarly, Mövenpick, a Swiss company, uses its name alone, and in combination, to position its four-, three-, and two-star brands in Yemen, Belgium, and Switzerland to an Italian market (see Figure 17-18).

Marketing Research

Marketing research is no less important internationally than it is domestically. It may be even more important. The problems of doing marketing research, however, multiply when applied internationally.

Consumers in other parts of the world are not as accustomed to answering research questions as are Americans. In some countries there may be outright refusal. Sampling methods can be grossly distorted for lack of adequate representative sampling frames. Telephone listings, street directories, census tract and block data, and social and economic characteristics of the population are frequently inaccurate, if available at all.

Mailing is expensive and may not reach the intended destination. Return postage-paid incentives are of little use in countries that don't honor them (most countries don't); or, if you distribute them indiscriminately to hotel guests, you don't know what country they will be mailed from. Telephoning is expensive because of the lack of WATS lines or their equivalent. Both personal interviewing and written questionnaires present serious language problems even when conducted or written by natives of the area. In such marketing research, where scrupulous wording is essential to accuracy, the translation from one language to another can be less than precise. When questions are needed in multiple languages, the problem is compounded, as Sheraton learned when it translated a survey questionnaire into 14 languages.

In spite of all these problems, marketing research is needed but is done less in the international hospitality industry. Its frequency is increasing, however. Reliance on guest comment cards is surely inadequate, if not grossly misleading, under most circumstances. Although it is difficult and expensive to research broad markets, it is not impossible to research one's own customers. The Century Park Sheraton in Singapore redesigned its rooms based on feedback from customer research. Focus groups with customers are certainly feasible and should be conducted more frequently. Feedback from employees on a regular basis can also be revealing.

Customs and regulations may even enhance the process in some ways. Hotel guests in many countries are required to provide information when registering, at which Americans in the United States would probably balk. Additional information can be obtained at this time. Government agencies and tourism boards also collect substantial information. Governments have the power—and sometimes use it—to randomly sample departing visitors on cruise ships or airlines before they can leave the country.

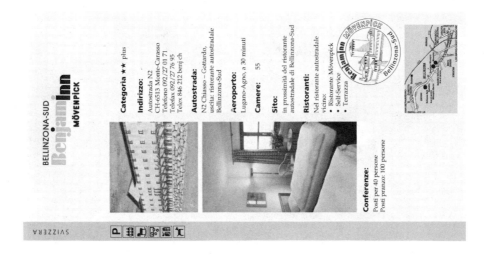

FIGURE 17-18 Mövenpick positions its product line with different names

747

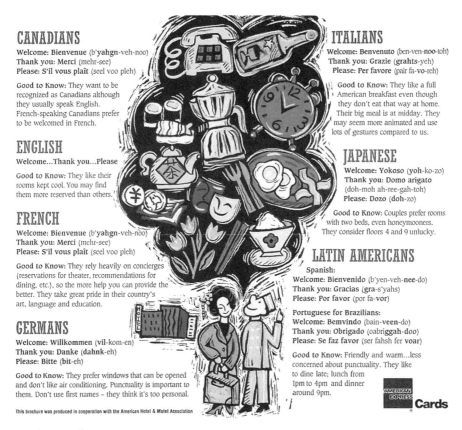

CANADIANS
Welcome: Bienvenue (b'yahgn-veh-noo)
Thank you: Merci (mehr-see)
Please: S'il vous plaît (seel voo pleh)

Good to Know: They want to be
recognized as Canadians although
they usually speak English.
French-speaking Canadians prefer
to be welcomed in French.

ENGLISH
Welcome...Thank you...Please

Good to Know: They like their
rooms kept cool. You may find
them more reserved than others.

FRENCH
Welcome: Bienvenue (b'yahgn-veh-noo)
Thank you: Merci (mehr-see)
Please: S'il vous plaît (seel voo pleh)

Good to Know: They rely heavily on concierges
(reservations for theater, recommendations for
dining, etc.), so the more help you can provide the
better. They take great pride in their country's
art, language and education.

GERMANS
Welcome: Willkommen (vil-kom-en)
Thank you: Danke (dahnk-eh)
Please: Bitte (bit-eh)

Good to Know: They prefer windows that can be opened
and don't like air conditioning. Punctuality is important to
them. Don't use first names – they think it's too personal.

This brochure was produced in cooperation with the American Hotel & Motel Association

ITALIANS
Welcome: Benvenuto (ben-ven-noo-toh)
Thank you: Grazie (grahts-yeh)
Please: Per favore (pair fa-vo-reh)

Good to Know: They like a full
American breakfast even though
they don't eat that way at home.
Their big meal is at midday. They
may seem more animated and use
lots of gestures compared to us.

JAPANESE
Welcome: Yokoso (yoh-ko-zo)
Thank you: Domo arigato
(doh-moh ah-ree-gah-toh)
Please: Dozo (doh-zo)

Good to Know: Couples prefer rooms
with two beds, even honeymooners.
They consider floors 4 and 9 unlucky.

LATIN AMERICANS
Spanish:
Welcome: Bienvenido (b'yen-veh-nee-do)
Thank you: Gracias (gra-s'yahs)
Please: Por favor (por fa-vor)

Portuguese for Brazilians:
Welcome: Bemvindo (bain-veen-do)
Thank you: Obrigado (oabriggah-doo)
Please: Se faz favor (ser fahsh fer voar)

Good to Know: Friendly and warm...less
concerned about punctuality. They like
to dine late; lunch from
1pm to 4pm and dinner
around 9pm.

AMERICAN EXPRESS **Cards**

Courtesy of American Express

FIGURE 17-19   Understanding the very basics of international travelers

In today's increasingly competitive international marketplace, it is shortsighted for any international hospitality firm *not* to be doing some legitimate research—at a minimum, to learn basic customer courtesies and preferences like those shown in Figure 17-19.

Summary

International hospitality marketing is fraught with both conceptual and practical complexities. Many firms jump into the international arena, or international locations, without a full awareness of the consequences. This can result in misjudged or lost opportunities and many costly mistakes. Environmental forces vary from one nation to another, and international hospitality firms must be attuned to these differences, including differences in the economic, cultural, social, legal, regulatory, and demographic environments.

Customer and market needs have to be identified and understood before planning the hospitality marketing mix on the international level. Although there may be many similarities in the needs of international travelers, products and services still have to be adapted to the local environment. Cultural differences play a major role in hospitality marketing because of the reliance on people to provide most of the services. Communications also have to be modified to suit the culture and language of the locale.

Globalization of markets leads to important decisions regarding market segmentation and positioning. Hospitality firms such as Sheraton and McDonald's have to balance standardization with the needs of foreign environments. This is complicated by the myriad of local laws and regulations regarding transfer of foreign exchange and import restrictions.

All of this calls for even greater insight into strategic and marketing planning than when operating domestically. Many errors made by hospitality firms in foreign waters can be avoided with better analysis and planning. This goes far beyond the usual cursory feasibility study on which many firms rely. It has been shown conclusively, over and over again, that location and the "ultimate in facilities and physical plant" are insufficient for lasting success in the international marketplace. Hospitality firms have realized that there are opportunities in foreign markets, but international business is long-term oriented, and an investment abroad may take many years before desired yields are returned.

Discussion Questions

1. Obtain a copy of *The Wall Street Journal* or other major newspaper and locate the foreign exchange rates. Compare these rates with those in Table 17-3. Assuming that hotel room rates have otherwise stayed constant in their native currency, calculate the impact on different markets traveling to different countries.

2. A hotel in a Southeast Asian capital city was confronted with a unique marketing problem. This hotel refused to follow the common and accepted practice of its competitors in freely allowing prostitutes in the hotel. As a result, it suffered a drastic loss in market share. How would you deal with this problem?

3. Why is segmentation so difficult in properties that target international markets? Discuss ways that markets could be segmented to overcome these difficulties.

4. Discuss Levitt's concept of globalization. Do you agree or disagree? How does it apply to the hospitality industry?

5. Describe the economic, social, cultural, and legal differences that affect the decisions of Kentucky Fried Chicken in China?

6. Discuss how the North American Free Trade Agreement will affect the hospitality industries of Canada, Mexico, and the United States.

7. In Case 17-1, consider the international environment and how it is impacting the Plaza Hotel as an independent. What should Plaza management do?

8. In Case 17-2, how would you advise Arun Chatterjee? Should he "wait out" the environment? What can he do about it? Should he pay extortion bribes? What should he do about his employees and service? Should he open another restaurant in Lithuania? Finally, what can he do to increase demand?

9. In Case 17-3, analyze the market for the Quality Inn product. What are the opportunities, the pitfalls? How should A.K. Dave and Associates proceed?

10. In Case 17-2 and/or Case 17-3, analyze the environmental impacts that have been discussed in the chapter.

✔ Case 17-1
The Plaza Hotel in Buenos Aires[16]

Alex Fiz, Assistant Operations Manager of the Plaza Hotel, looked at the memo that he had just received from the hotel's general manager. It was brief and to the point: "What's happening? We are losing market share and there are two more competitors coming next year. How are we going to position ourselves in this environment?"

Background

The Plaza Hotel was an independent hotel located in the heart of the city of Buenos Aires, close to the business district, shops, restaurants and theaters. The Plaza was an historic, grand hotel with superb service and attention to details (Exhibit 17-1-1). Built in 1910, the hotel was a classical building that had been maintained in first-class condition. It offered a traditional, luxurious, old-fashioned image compared to the luxurious modern style offered by its competition. It was the only member of Leading Hotels of the World in Argentina.

Buenos Aires, sometimes called "the Paris of South America," had 13 million inhabitants and was the capital city of Argentina. It was famous for its nightlife and cosmopolitan atmosphere. However, the city had only a small tourism market with an unusually short stay average. Most tourists stopped there only on their way to other tourist destinations. From a corporate point of view, it was an "interesting" city but, being "far away from everything" made it difficult for the city to attract businesses. Market demand was not growing nearly as fast as the hotel supply.

Since it first opened and until 1978, the Plaza did not have direct competition. Between 1978 and 1991, however, three new hotels entered the market: the Sheraton, Libertador Kempinski, and the Alvear Palace (Exhibits 17-1-2 to 17-1-4). In spite of this, the Plaza was able to maintain its position and occupancy at the top of the market. Then, in 1992, a luxury

[16]We are grateful to Alex Fiz for the information used in developing this case.

EXHIBIT 17-1-1   The Plaza Hotel in Buenos Aires

EXHIBIT 17-1-2   The Sheraton Buenos Aires

HOTEL

IN BUENOS AIRES, MAKE IT SHERATON.

LOCATION   Overlooking Rio de la Plata in the heart of the business district and near the Florida Street shopping district. Near museums and government offices and 20 miles from Ezeiza International Airport.

FEATURES   The modern 24-story tower with 757 guest rooms includes 37 suites and 2 presidential suites, as well as the elegant rooms of The Towers. All rooms have individual air conditioning and TV.

RECREATION   Amenities include outdoor swimming pool, health club with sauna, 2 lighted tennis courts, shopping arcade, etc.

DINING/ENTERTAINMENT   Enjoy international specialties in the elegant atmosphere of El Aljibe restaurant; visit our Italian restaurant. La Pampa coffee shop is open 24-hours and you can enjoy cocktails at both the Atalaya rooftop lounge and the lobby bar.

CONFERENCES   14 meeting rooms accommodate 10 to 2,000.

No charges for stages, blackboards, or bulletin boards.

RATES*   U.S. Dollars
Valid from May 1 to December 31, 1992
Main Building
Single $205, Double $225
Suites Single/Double $515
Towers
Single $275, Double $295
Suites Single/Double $580
Extra Person: US $30 + 18% tax in Main Building; no charge for extra person in Towers.

*All rates subject to 18% tax. All rates and tax subject to change without notice. Not all rates listed are available at all times. Please call for details.

RESERVATIONS   For reservations at any ITT Sheraton Hotel, call (800) 325-3535. For travel agents only call (800) 334-8484. Use your ARC/IATA number every time you call. The ITT Sheraton CRT code is SI. Apollo 813, Sabre 486, SystemOne 260, Pars, Datas II.

This is an ITT Sheraton Club International Hotel.

Sheraton Buenos Aires
HOTEL & TOWERS

ITT Sheraton

EXHIBIT 17-1-3   The Hotel Libertador Kempinski

HOTEL LIBERTADOR
Kempinski Buenos Aires

LOCATION/DESCRIPTION: strategically located in the heart of the Argentine capital, walking distance from the business and government areas and only a few meters from the exclusive shops on Florida St. 45 min. by car from Ezeiza International Airport and 15 min. from J. Newbery domestic airport. A magnificent 22 story hotel, with superb service and all the comfort of its newly renovated facilities.

ACCOMMODATIONS: 191 rooms, 12 Junior Suites and 3 Presidential Suites, designed to offer the guests all the comfort and care they expect and deserve.

SPECIAL FEATURES: Year-round rooftop swimming pool, sauna, solarium, fitness center and massage. 24-hour room service and concierge. In-house travel agent service for tours and connections. Parking garage next to the hotel.

CONFERENCE FACILITIES: Eight different size meeting rooms, which can accommodate in total up to 1,600 participants. Individually, they can suit the needs of meetings from 30 to 700.

RESTAURANT: "La Pérgola" with its distinguished cuisine, is the ideal place for an informal breakfast, business lunch or candle-light dinner. The recently inaugurated "Maximilian" lobby bar offers the opportunity to enjoy the "Happy Hour" with its varied cocktails and hors d'oeuvres in a comfortable elegant and relaxed atmosphere.

RATES: Standard $170 (single), $185 (double)
Deluxe $180 (single), $215 (double)
Standard Jr. Suite $344 (single), $369 (double)
Deluxe Jr. Suite $384(single), $409 (double)
Presidential Suite $640

All rates are plus tax (18%) and subject to modifications. 10% Travel Agent Commission Paid Promptly.

Av. Córdoba y Maipú - (1054) Buenos Aires, Argentina
Tel.: (541) 322-2095/8395/9236 - Telex: 24264 - Fax: (541) 322-9703

Reservation offices: CANADA/USA: 1 800 426 3135 - GERMANY: 0130-3339
GREAT BRITAIN: 0800-89-8588 - FAR EAST: 00852-877-3777
Reservation systems: general access to Kempinski:
SABRE KI Y/HIL/QKI 17419. APOLLO KI MKE 9796.
PARS KI G/HTL/KIQ KI E81 - UTELL - DATAS II: DL (U) 4184)
SYSTEM ONE: EA (U) 4184) - SAHARA: XS (U) BUE 4184)

Kempinski Hotels are ⊕ **Lufthansa** Hotels

EXHIBIT 17-1-4   The Alvear Palace Hotel

BUENOS AIRES 👑 *ARGENTINA*

FONTANARROSA & ASOCIADOS

60 ANNIVERSARY

The Alvear Palace Hotel makes the traveler feel like a king. Not only for its splendid decoration and luxury but also for its personalized service.

Two restaurants, tea room, cocktail lounge, 160 rooms and suites.

Meeting and conventions facilities for up to 1.500 guests.

In the heart of Bs. As. the best suggestion and hospitality awaits the traveler at the Alvear Palace Hotel.

YOU DON'T HAVE TO WEAR A CROWN TO STAY AT THE PALACE.

ROOM RATES	
Single	U$S 220
Double	U$S 250
Junior Suite	U$S 290
De Luxe Suite	U$S 390
Diplomatic Suite	U$S 450
Governor Suite	U$S 710
Presidential Suite	U$S 1.100

Buffet breakfast is included, served at our winter garden.
18% Tax not included.
10% Travel Agent commission, paid promptly and accurately.

RESERVATIONS
Utell International
800 44-UTELL
1-(402) 498-0574
LRI 800 223-0888
1 - (212) 545-2222.

All rates and taxes are subject
Credit Cards: We accept American Express, Diners, Visa, MasterCard and JCB.
CRS Numbers:
AA (16583) UA (21118)
PM (07166) EA (BUEALV)
DL (7166) JL (6003)
XS (BUE 7166)

ALVEAR PALACE HOTEL

A SUMMIT INTERNATIONAL HOTEL

1891 Alvear Ave. - (1129) Buenos Aires - Argentine
Phones: (54-1) 804-4031/45 - TLX 18674 ALPCH AR - Fax: (54-1) 804-0034

Park Hyatt opened in a renovated turn-of-the-century mansion (Exhibit 17-1-5). And, recently, a luxurious, modern Caesar Park with atrium lobby, operated by Westin, opened in the same area (Exhibit 17-1-6).

All six of these hotels were located close to each other in the center of the city, although some had specific location advantages that attracted certain markets (Exhibit 17-1-7). The Plaza was seriously threatened by the two

EXHIBIT 17-1-5   The Park Hyatt Hotel

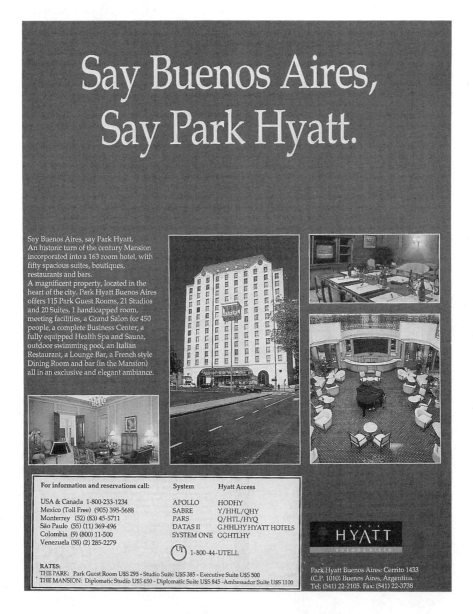

Say Buenos Aires, Say Park Hyatt.

Say Buenos Aires, say Park Hyatt.
An historic turn of the century Mansion
incorporated into a 163 room hotel, with
fifty spacious suites, boutiques,
restaurants and bars.
A magnificent property, located in the
heart of the city. Park Hyatt Buenos Aires
offers 115 Park Guest Rooms, 21 Studios
and 20 Suites, 1 handicapped room,
meeting facilities, a Grand Salon for 450
people, a complete Business Center, a
fully equipped Health Spa and Sauna,
outdoor swimming pool, an Italian
Restaurant, a Lounge Bar, a French style
Dining Room and bar (in the Mansion)
all in an exclusive and elegant ambiance.

For information and reservations call:

USA & Canada 1-800-233-1234
Mexico (Toll Free) (905) 395-5688
Monterrey (52) (83) 45-5711
São Paulo (55) (11) 369-496
Colombia (9) (800) 11-500
Venezuela (58) (2) 285-2279

System	Hyatt Access
APOLLO	HODHY
SABRE	Y/HHL/QHY
PARS	Q/HTL/HYQ
DATAS II	G.HHLHY HYATT HOTELS
SYSTEM ONE	GGHTLHY

1-800-44-UTELL

RATES:
THE PARK: Park Guest Room U$S 295 - Studio Suite U$S 385 - Executive Suite U$S 500
THE MANSION: Diplomatic Studio U$S 650 - Diplomatic Suite U$S 845 - Ambassador Suite U$S 1100

HYATT

Park Hyatt Buenos Aires: Cerrito 1433
(C.P. 1010) Buenos Aires, Argentina.
Tel: (541) 22-2105. Fax: (541) 22-3738

newer hotels and began losing customers to both of them, as well as Sheraton, including top-suite customers to Hyatt. The Caesar Park was cutting rates to create awareness. All of these hotels competed head-on for the same corporate clientele.

The situation would become even more competitive with an Inter-Continental and a Crowne Plaza, due to open in the near future, adding more supply in the highly competitive Buenos Aires market. Inter-Continental pricing was expected to be very aggressive and include "price-dumping" to create awareness.

The Plaza Hotel

The Plaza Hotel had 300 rooms, including 30 suites, 215 deluxe, and 55 standard. The suites

EXHIBIT 17-1-6   The Westin Caesar Park Hotel

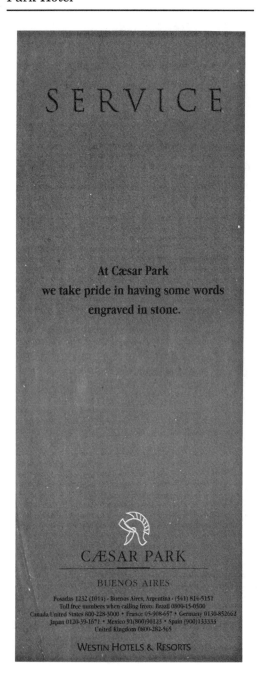

were priced at $500 but usually sold at the corporate rate of $185.[17] The hotel's approximate occupancies, with the desired rate for each segment, was as follows.

Rack Rate (deluxe)	10%	$240
Corporate	35%	$185
Agencies	10%	$160
Groups	30%	$150
Honeymoon	4%	$225
Local Market	6%	$100
Complimentary	5%	

Eighty percent of the Plaza's business was repeat. Having been a very loyal clientele, however, it was beginning to diminish. Thirty percent of business was from the United States, 40 percent from Europe, 15 percent from South America, and 15 percent from the Far East and "Other." The local market was very difficult to attract because it could not afford the prices.

Leading Hotels of the World delivered 35 percent of the Plaza's business and 10 percent came from the Utell International network. The rest of the business was direct. The biggest customer was Coca-Cola, three blocks away, which booked 2,000 room-nights a year.

Alex Fiz looked at the other information he had collected to show the last three months' figures, which were typical of the market situation (Table 17-1-1). He noted that the high-level customers were going to the Hyatt and Caesar Park and that Sheraton's high occupancy and low ADR were greatly affected by its seven floors of crew rooms at $62 a night. He also noted that the other locally-owned and -operated hotel, Alvear Palace, had a large portion of the government market, which paid full rates.

Alex knew that the Plaza had to maintain a 60 percent occupancy at an ADR of $130 just to break even. That break-even point was perilously close, and he realized that some new strategies were needed, especially with Inter-Continental and Crowne Plaza opening soon.

---

[17]All prices in the case are given in U.S. Dollar currency.

EXHIBIT 17-1-7   Buenos Aires with hotel locations

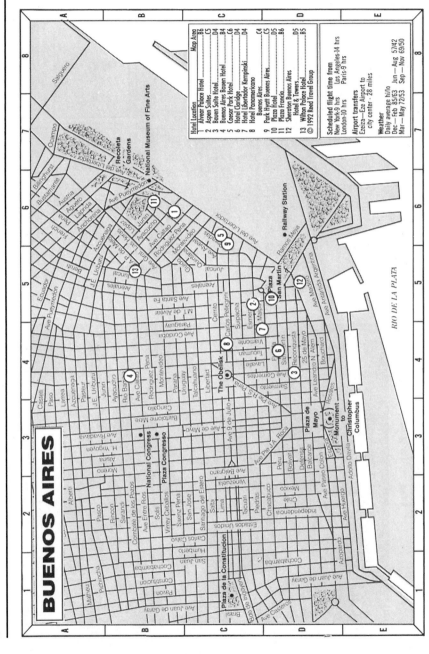

BUENOS AIRES

Hotel Location	Map Area
1 Alvear Palace Hotel	B6
2 Aspen Suites	C5
3 Bauen Suite Hotel	D4
4 Buenos Aires Bauen Hotel	B4
5 Caesar Park Hotel	C6
6 Hotel Claridge	D4
7 Hotel Libertador Kempinski	D4
8 Hotel Panamericano	C4
9 Park Hyatt Buenos Aires	C5
10 Plaza Hotel	D5
11 Plaza Francia	B6
12 Sheraton Buenos Aires Hotel & Towers	D5
13 Wilton Palace Hotel	B5

© 1992 Reed Travel Group

Scheduled flight time from
New York-9 hrs   Los Angeles-14 hrs
London-10 hrs   Paris-9 hrs

Airport transfers
Ezeiza–Eze Airport to
city center - 28 miles

Weather
Daily average hi/lo
Dec— Feb 85/63   Jun — Aug 5/7/42
Mar — May 72/53   Sep — Nov 69/50

National Museum of Fine Arts

Recoleta
Gardens

Railway Station

Plaza
San Martin

The Obelisk

Plaza de
Mayo

National Congress

Plaza Congresso

Plaza de la Constitución

Monument
to
Christopher
Columbus

RIO DE LA PLATA

TABLE 17-1-1   Buenos Aires Market Information

Hotel	Rooms	Rack$ Sgl.	Rack$ Dbl.	April Occ.%	April ADR$	May Occ.%	May ADR$	June Occ.%	June ADR$	June REVPAR$
Plaza	300	240	240	63.9	142	52.2	143	54.6	142	77.53
Kempinski	203	180	215	48.7	110	41.1	126	34.7	116	40.25
Libertad										
Sheraton	757	205	225	84.5	107	84	112	85.1	105	89.36
Caesar Park	170	295	295	51.1	223	34.8	225	46.2	198	91.48
Hyatt	163	295	295	68	227	63.1	225	65.4	229	149.77
Alvear Palace	248	220	250	64.5	182	55	186	67	175	117.25

✔ Case 17-2
The Bengal Tiger Restaurant[18]

Arun Chatterjee looked at the wreckage of his restaurant in Vilnius, Lithuania. A wild fight had erupted the night before during which chairs were broken, windows were smashed, and flatware was destroyed. A large amount of alcohol was stolen. A call to the local police resulted only in their condolence, "At least you are alive!" Two days before, Arun's head waiter had been viciously attacked and beaten by a gang of thugs while on his way home from work. In a previous incident, Chatterjee's car was firebombed while in the parking lot of the restaurant.

Arun Chatterjee was born in a small fishing village near Bombay, where he developed a knowledge of Indian miniature paintings. By buying these cheaply and selling them to upscale tourists in India, he had been able to gather a sizeable sum of money. Arun had relatively little formal education, but had studied Indian painting extensively in the libraries and in the Prince of Wales Museum of Bombay.

Chatterjee initially went to London, where he became a successful trader of art. He would go to the Oxfam charity's secondhand shop and purchase jewelry after newly-donated items were stocked and then resell the items in various flea markets for tremendous profits. Eventually, he decided that the best use of his capital would be to invest in a restaurant in one of the newly-developing nations of the former Soviet Union. A chance meeting with a Lithuanian expatriate led him to decide to move to Lithuania, where he wished to start the first authentic Indian restaurant in Vilnius.

Arun Chatterjee became a member of a group of British investors (known as Alpha Investments) that planned to start a series of Indian restaurants in several large Lithuanian cities, including Klaipeda and Kaunas. The investors seemed correct in recognizing an unmet demand for exotic food in former Soviet nations.

Acts of violence, however, forced Chatterjee to recognize that running a business in a country with a strong and relatively uncontrolled protection racket would require some important decisions. Chatterjee pondered whether he was correct in refusing to buy the suggested 10 percent "protection insurance" from representatives of the mob. Was coming to a country of the former Soviet Union at this time a major mistake? Should Alpha Investments open other restaurants in Lithuania? Would customers continue to come?

Background

Vilnius was Lithuania's capital and largest city, situated on several hills that border the Neris River, the longest river in the country. The city was established over 500 years ago by people who had lived in the area for over a thousand years. About 51 percent of Vilnius's current 600,000 population was ethnic Lithuanian whose ancestry dated back 1,500 years. The remaining 49 percent of the people were of mainly Polish, Russian, Ukrainian, and Byelorussian descent.

Lithuania became independent for the first time in over a half-century in the early 1990s with the breakup of the Soviet Union. When a part of the Soviet Union (1940–1991) Lithuanians were not allowed to own or operate private businesses. The country was now experiencing an entrepreneurial "rebirth," with many individuals starting and successfully operating small or family businesses. While very few of these entrepreneurs had formal business training, many had all the requisite "know-how" from years of experience in operating in an underground economy. Some lingering Soviet values and attitudes about the "evil" of private property and profit-making still existed, however. Moreover, the establishment of a free market in a country steeped in Leninist dictum

---

[18]We are grateful to Professors Paul P. Poppler, Charles Wankel, and Justin P. Carey, all of St. John's University, Jamaica, New York, for the use of this case.

presented budding entrepreneurs with many economic, sociocultural, and political challenges.

The lack of formal business education and the private economic infrastructure (e.g., a uniform commercial code, established business media, standard accounting practices, and international commercial banking connections) meant that entrepreneurs often made many decisions with incomplete or unreliable information. As a result, businesses typically ran without long-term strategies and often focused on opportunities of the moment. Economic transactions had almost always been consummated in a hard currency such as the U.S. Dollar or German Deutschmark, since inflation of the Lithuanian Lita had run between 12 and 15 percent per month after independence was gained. Trust was at a low ebb and businesspeople often conducted business functions at a personal level. For instance, formal advertising and marketing techniques generally were not well understood or used. Employee recruitment was typically conducted through personal networks.

Business legislation in Lithuania was often ambiguous and contradictory. At times it seemed impossible to comply with the full gamut of laws. Legislators in the Parliament focused on political agendas that differed from the interests of small businesses. Underpaid government clerks and bureaucrats frequently were corrupt and very often expected payments to assist in correctly completing forms or to assure that the paperwork was dispatched properly. Government employees were still largely communist-era appointees who often disliked or mistrusted entrepreneurs.

Many new systems of accounting and other business practices were being introduced in Lithuania. These systems were more likely to help the larger enterprises, particularly former Soviet state enterprises, than the entrepreneur. Business legislation was often amended by the ministries charged with enforcement. Thus, one ministry's interpretation of a specific tax might not be the same as another ministry's interpretation. As a result, most businesspeople were hesitant to discuss financial matters since so many things were in a state of fluctuation. To complicate matters, various syndicates of organized crime emerged, and the entrepreneur was often confronted with the decision either to ignore or comply with implied or real threats. It was estimated that 30 percent of all private economic activity in Lithuania was conducted on the black market; 30 percent was controlled by gangs or mafias, and 40 percent was conducted honestly.

Chatterjee, like many others in Lithuania, believed that the corruption and organized crime of the moment were passing phenomena, something like a rite of passage. Chatterjee heard many people argue that, just as the United States had passed through an era of gangsters (such as Chicago gangsters of the 1930s), so also would Lithuania emerge from what the Lithuanians understood to be a typical phase of capitalistic development. Soon, it was argued, the people of Lithuania would enjoy the prosperity of the West.

The average monthly wage in Lithuania was roughly equivalent to US$60. While inflation had subsided from the wild rates of 180–200% per year in the early 1990s, people still found that their wages barely covered monthly housing and food requirements. The typical Lithuanian at this time did not have much in the way of monthly personal disposable income.

A Seedbed of Change

The Lithuanian marketplace was very much in transition away from communism. Many joint ventures with German, Dutch, Finnish, Danish, Swedish, Australian, Canadian, and American firms had been established. Notable investments were made in telecommunications, hotel and restaurant management, financial consulting, computer equipment, retailing, and building supplies.

Many Western business associations, such as the International Rotary Club and the International Executive Service Corps, were active in the country. Western financial consulting firms, such as KPMG Peat Marwick, were assisting in the development of viable privatization schemes in state industrial and agricultural enterprises. Western universities, including St.

John's University and DePaul University, were providing support for program and curricula development, training, educational facility development, and student recruitment. Through these contacts and programs many Lithuanian entrepreneurs were learning that they had to take responsibility for satisfying the customer rather than just placating bosses. Under communism, for instance, patrons of restaurants would regularly expect rude or indifferent treatment, few and poorly-prepared menu items, and sometimes capricious changes in the prices charged. These old ways were rapidly being displaced as entrepreneurs began to learn the values of a customer-driven market economy.

Vilnius Restaurants

There were predominantly three types of restaurants in Vilnius in the early 1990s: inexpensive state-run establishments, privately-owned/traditional Lithuanian establishments, and upscale continental establishments. The state-run restaurants were characterized by a dark decor and dim lighting, carryovers of the Soviet mentality of conserving electricity. The customer often found that these restaurants were dank, smokey, and cold. Plates were usually chipped and mismatched, flatware was poorly cleaned, and linens often smudged and frayed. Entrees typically included meat that was very fatty and covered with a pasty gravy. Accompaniments typically included greasy potatoes, boiled cabbage, cucumbers, and tomatoes. Complete meals were approximately three to four U.S. dollars. The clientele of the state-run restaurants were often state employees, lower-middle class Lithuanians with some disposable food income, and sometimes racketeers.

Privately-owned restaurants had a variety of forms and themes. One of these specialized in pizza and other Italian dishes. Another was Chinese, offering authentic Hunan and Mongolian dishes. Still another was noted as a Greek restaurant, featuring variations of traditional Greek dishes such as gyro plates. Private Lithuanian restaurants with Lithuanian cuisine, such as The Black and Red and The Old Barron, offered home-cooked dishes prepared in traditional Lithuanian fashion. These restaurants tended to have clean dishes, clean linens, and higher-quality ingredients. Patrons of the privately-owned restaurants included higher-status government officials, bankers, lawyers, and businesspeople. A full meal in these kinds of restaurants typically cost between six and ten U.S. dollars.

There were two restaurants that might be called upscale continental. The Stikilai was the most prestigious. Because of television commercials Lithuanians were very familiar with its French provincial dining room and fabulous desserts. Few, however, could hope to pay the more than the US$20 per person that such a dinner cost. Clientele included government officials, racketeers, traveling businessmen, and foreign visitors. Patrons of the Stikilai were offered fresh crayfish and other exotica that could not be easily found elsewhere in Lithuania or in other Baltic and neighboring nations. A second prestigious restaurant, the Idabasar, offered traditional German cuisine. It was noted for high-quality hearty soups, salads, meat dishes, and a exceptionally well-stocked beer and wine cellar. It catered to the same kind of clientele as the Stikilai. Significantly, both the Stikilai and the Idabasar had armed security people at the ready.

The Bengal Tiger

Arun Chatterjee spent about a half of a year gathering information and convincing acquaintances in London to invest in the Lithuanian venture. Eventually, with his Alpha Investors partners, US$50,000, and an initial business plan, he set out for Vilnius.

Chatterjee hired a local management consultant to help locate a suitable site for the restaurant. The site chosen was an available commercial building within walking distance of some international hotels, although the location was not on a busy street. Chatterjee found no end to the number of forms and problems that the government bureaucrats presented to him. However, Chatterjee steadfastly refused to pay bribes to various representatives of groups offering protection. For approximately the first five months of operation, the start-up business proceeded without any unusual events.

Finding reliable suppliers was initially tricky. Chatterjee found that he needed to personally oversee the delivery of the raw materials once a contract was completed and the goods dispatched (due to pilferage). Chatterjee eventually found that three of his initial ten food and spice suppliers were trustworthy and fairly reliable. Beyond these suppliers, he found that some spices, decorations, foodstuffs, and tools still had to be imported from India. Chatterjee wanted to create an authentic India restaurant, and native Lithuanian suppliers could not completely supply the materials for achieving this objective.

Whenever possible and within the limits of authenticity, Chatterjee subcontracted locally for certain supplies. For instance, he found a local creamery that promised to make a certain amount of yogurt in Indian style. Similarly, he contacted a local butcher whom he convinced to provide lamb at a negotiated price. Since Western bank credit-card and check-writing systems were not in place, Chatterjee found that he had to pay contracts in cash. Through contacts with a local banker, Chatterjee's consultant secured an arrangement to allow Chatterjee to use bank drafts in his monetary transactions; this alleviated, to a large degree, the problem of having cash for payments.

Chatterjee found that he had to spend more time training employees than anticipated. In addition to the time and expense for on-the-job training in cooking, table-waiting, and customer relations, Chatterjee found it necessary to work with the employees on such things as work punctuality, teamwork (cooperation), and respect for the company's plant and equipment. Chatterjee also found that workers initially failed to understand the concepts of costs and profits. For instance, when a tool was broken, the notion that the cost of replacing the tool would affect profitability, and ultimately employee wages, was not immediately understood by the workers.

Chatterjee also found that workers sometimes capriciously took time off from work.

Training time was necessary to inculcate the importance of completing work cycles and shift times. Thus, Chatterjee found that certain business values concerning work and customers had to be taught, beyond the task assignments. By the end of his second quarter of operation, Chatterjee had a core of employees who understood that employment in a customer-driven market economy was not a protected social right, as under the Soviet system, but a matter of understanding customer needs and responding to those needs.

Chatterjee developed a menu containing a variety of curry and other authentic Indian dishes. In addition, the Bengal Tiger offered ten regional specialties. The average meal was about US$15 per person; this included a complete traditional meal with tea and dessert. The restaurant was a moderate success for the first three months, gradually picking up during the second quarter of the first year. The clientele grew to include prominent politicians, bureaucrats, businessmen, travelers, and successful racketeers.

Extortion

A clean-cut man with a business-like manner appeared at the Bengal Tiger during the sixth month of its operation. The man explained to Chatterjee that he represented a private security firm and that the success of the Bengal Tiger meant that the restaurant needed to be protected. He noted that, without such protection, at any moment a wild donnybrook could break out in the main dining room and lay to waste much of the furnishings and property. Even worse, hooligans might torch the business itself if "protection" was not arranged. The man made it clear that, for a price of 10 percent of average monthly profits, he could arrange for security such that none of these "tragic" events would occur.

Chatterjee politely refused the man's offer, arguing that police protection was sufficient. Two nights later, Chatterjee's car was set ablaze in the parking lot just 20 minutes before closing time. Chatterjee considered this incident an isolated event since car theft and destruction were relatively common in Vilnius if a car was left isolated for a long period of time.

Exactly seven days after the strange man's visit, the fight that caused much physical damage occurred just after the lunch hour rush. Chatterjee was out of town, in London arranging for future furnishing supplies; his head waiter, Arvydis, called to tell him about the disaster. Chatterjee ordered the restaurant closed indefinitely and told the waiter that he would be in Vilnius in three days; at that time damage assessment would be conducted and plans made.

When he arrived in Vilnius, Chatterjee was shocked to find that Arvydis had been savagely beaten by a gang of thugs after being asked for a match on a street near the Bengal Tiger. Severely beaten about the face, Arvydis would be in the hospital for over a week.

That evening, as Chatterjee surveyed the damage, he was again accosted by the man offering security. Chatterjee was shocked to find that the man had copies of Chatterjee's bank records and the government tax forms that he just filed. This security firm was clearly run by organized crime with the collaboration of government and bank officials. Chatterjee feared for his safety and the safety of his employees. He later heard of a bombing of the city's only Chinese restaurant during the week he was in London.

Chatterjee had come to Lithuania with a dream of a chain of Indian restaurants. Should he close the restaurant and return to London? Should he attempt to hire security guards not associated with the racketeers? Should he try to find assistance from the police and government? Should he hire the security services of the stranger who suggested that the Bengal Tiger needed protection? If not, how would he market a restaurant that, along with its employees, was constantly threatened with physical damage and destruction?

✔ Case 17-3
Quality Inns India[19]

Uttam Dave hadn't sleep well lately. His job as Vice-President at Quality Inns India (QII) was to oversee management contracts, overall corporate development, and franchise development. QII had been in business for three years but was having trouble attracting franchisees. Uttam Dave wanted desperately to know why.

Background

Quality Inns India (QII) was a joint venture between A.K. Dave and Associates (AKDA) and Quality International Inc. (QI), from which it held master franchise rights in India to set up a network of two-, three-, and four-star hotels throughout India. AKDA offered professional, technical, and management consultancy services to independent entrepreneurs in the hospitality industry. It had been established ten years before and had undertaken over 100 assignments for both private and government organizations. The objectives of AKDA were:

1. To serve the cause of Indian tourism by assisting individual two-, three-, and four-star hotels to achieve international standards in planning, design, and operations.
2. To provide independent entrepreneurs the entire range of technical expertise available only to large hotel chains, but at reasonable cost.

Quality International Inc., a division of Choice International, was one of the world's largest and fastest-growing hotel chains. At this time it had more than 1,000 hotels in 17 countries with three brand names that were licensed to QII (Exhibit 17-3-1). QI was known for its marketing innovation and aggressiveness, high standards, and adaptability in different cultural environments. Robert Hazard, the President and CEO, was once quoted as saying that QI's mission was "to make profit for the entre-preneurs—developer and licensee—who join us as our partner for profit. The licensee is the reason for our existence, he drives our system, and he plays the tune we all dance to."

It had taken AKDA three years to get the joint venture with QI approved by the Secretariat of Industrial Approvals, when it took roughly six to eight months for other companies. "Nothing talks like money does in India," according to A.K. Dave. Refusing to abide by this principle, QII had lost the competitive advantage of being the first to attract an international chain to cater to the lower end of the market, by not being the first to get it up and running.

Changing Trends

The overall growth rate in Indian tourism had been 15 percent per year for the past ten years in spite of infrastructural shortcomings. The number of tourist arrivals was expected to more than double in the next ten years, from its present level of 1,500,000. Foreign tourist arrivals accounted for over 60 percent of total hotel occupancy. The approximate ratios of country origin and purpose of visit are as follows:

Country of Origin

United Kingdom	16.4%
United States	12.8%
Sri Lanka	7.9%
France	6.9%
West Germany	6.4%
Canada	4.2%
Italy	4.1%
Japan	3.8%
Australia	3.5%
United Arab Emirates	3.0%
Other	31.0%

Purpose of Visit

Pleasure	45%
Business	30%
Friends and Relatives	11%
Other (pilgrimage, studies)	14%

---

[19]Prabal K. Gupta researched and contributed to this case. We are grateful to Uttam Dave for use of the information.

EXHIBIT 17-3-1   Quality Inn brands in the master franchise for India

Explained

Quality International has made its name worldwide by offering three distinct brands — Comfort, Quality and Clarion — to make it easy for you to choose the perfect hotel to fit all your needs and your budget.

Comfort Inns offer first rate accommodations at no-frills prices. If you want excellent value without paying for the extras you don't need, try one of the 500 Comfort Inns worldwide.

Mid-priced Quality Inns feature large, comfortable, well-appointed rooms with complete facilities at affordable prices. Enjoy a delicious meal, hold a meeting or take a refreshing swim at a Quality Inn.

Luxurious Clarion Hotels and Resorts offer fine restaurants, lounges, meeting facilities, recreational facilities and that special class found only at the world's best hotels.

It was predicted that the ratio of foreign to domestic tourists would change dramatically in the future, when there would be ten domestic tourists for every one foreign tourist—40 percent on business travel and 60 percent on leisure travel. The expected growth in domestic tourism would be due to a number of factors: a trend toward reduced working hours, an increase in the number of double-income households, a rise in the level of female employees who will take more holidays, and a higher priority placed on recreation and leisure.

India had also had a number of prosperous agricultural years that had contributed to economic and political stability. Satisfactory monsoon seasons (the rainy season critical to agriculture) had led to price stability and a general mood of satisfaction. Unless rocked by opposition efforts or external political interventions, relative prosperity and growth was expected on all fronts. New political leadership was inclined to pursue and nurture already initiated growth efforts. The recent growth in GDP (*gross domestic product*) of nine percent and an all-around business buoyancy augered well for the hotel industry. The recent accent on export profitability and import liberalization also supported increased domestic and foreign travel. Major collaborators in this effort were the United States, United Kingdom, Germany, Switzerland, Japan, France, and Italy.

There were, however, rising tensions between the Indian government and the Sikhs, who were threatening civil war in their bid for an independent motherland. Tensions were also increasing between India and its immediate neighbours, Pakistan, Sri Lanka, and Nepal.

India's Hotel Industry

Close to 30 percent of India's hotel room supply was five-star or five-star deluxe properties, but only 8 percent were four-star. Thirty-five percent were two- or three-star properties, although they were inconsistent, often of poor quality, and far below the standards set for similarly-rated hotels in Western Europe and North America. Six percent of the rooms were a very inferior one-star, while another 21 percent were awaiting classification.

One-half of the total rooms supply was concentrated in only four major metropolitan cities: New Delhi, Calcutta, Bombay, and Madras. There was a shortage of rooms in the two-, three-, and four-star class, especially in the state capitals and smaller cities. There was a need for quality accommodations that were clean and comfortable and catered to the price-conscious traveler. Thus, QII saw major segments in the middle and lower parts of the market.

The Indian government was encouraging the development of two-, three-, and four-star hotels in India. It was becoming easier to obtain land for the purposes of developing hotels within these star classes, and airline capacities were increasing to facilitate tourism. There was an increased realization by the government of the need to declare/accept tourism as a high-growth industry. With gradual enhancement of concessions, for example, allocation of hotel sites was being constantly recommended and sanctioned. Due to the trade deficit imbalance, the tourism industry was being recognized as a high foreign exchange earner. Major thrust areas identified were a move from culture-oriented tourism to holiday and leisure tourism; development of trekking, winter sports, wildlife, and beach tourism; allocation of charter flights primarily from Canada, the United Kingdom, and West Germany; and increased airline capacity allowed to major international airlines.

Foreign chains were permitted to own up to 51 percent equity in hotel investments in India, and nonresident Indians up to 74 percent. Approval had been granted to allow overseas borrowing of up to 50 percent of a project's cost. If foreign exchange earnings exceeded 50 percent, a 20 percent rebate in interest was allowed. Fifty percent of foreign exchange income was allowed as an income tax deduction, and the balance was exempted if it was put in a reserve fund for investment in tourism. There were also interest rebates on institutional loans, and a subsidy was provided for lower-star category hotels. A number of other rebates and incentives were established to encourage development of the tourism infrastructure.

Competition

When the QII joint venture was established, there were four major players in the industry. Taj Hotels, Oberoi, and Welcomgroup had concentrated at the top end of the market. Only Taj and Welcomgroup had ties with international companies (Inter-Continental and Sheraton), which offered operating and marketing assistance. ITDC (Ashok Hotels), the fourth major competitor, had proven to be inconsistent and, as with most Indian public sector companies, had a poor image. The breakdown of rooms for these four chains was as follows:

Chain	Number of Hotels	Number of Rooms
Taj	25	4,060
Oberoi	15	2,320
Welcomgroup	18	2,300
ITDC	37	4,022

Other companies had since entered the market, or were planning to after arranging alliances with Indian companies. With financial incentives formalized and sanctioned by the government, major Indian hotel chains and industrial companies had "gone shopping" for international hotel chain affiliations. In the upper end of the market these were Asian Hotels (Hyatt International), Bharat Hotels (Holiday Inn), and Pure Drinks Company (Le Meridien).

Others focused their attention downwards to the lower and middle tiers of the hotel market. The two-, three-, and four-star hotels in India were typically small or medium-sized, widely dispersed, independently owned and managed, and devoid of an image and identity, with no access to international marketing. They tended to be lacking in quality and consistency of product and service. The recent interest from the government, however, in developing the lower tiers of the hotel industry prompted other leading hotel companies to expand their product and enter the two-, three-, and four-star market. Already, in the economy sector, East India Hotels (Oberoi) had formed an alliance with Novotel of France, and Mahindra Ugine Steel Company had bought master rights for Days Inn. The financial incentives and benefits were significant, and companies like Hilton, Marriott, and Club Med had expressed interest.

Internationally, there was a trend toward economy travel, and the middle and upper-middle income segments of foreigners were the largest and fastest-growing ones. It was estimated that India would have over 300 hotels in these segments within the next five years.

Quality Inns India

The joint venture collaboration with Quality International was intended to be the vehicle for QII to extend international franchises, marketing, and technology to new hotels in the economy and middle tiers and ensure in them high standards of management and operation. QII's specific objective was that, in addition to growth and increased revenue, this expansion would provide the benefits of increased brand recognition and a larger global market share. Franchising was particularly attractive because it required substantially lower capital than ownership. Having established itself as a premier consultancy firm in India, A.K. Dave and Associates wanted to expand its horizons to hotel chain operations. A corporate office was opened in New Delhi and sales offices in Bombay, Bangalore, Madras, and Calcutta.

AKDA management made a conscious effort to stay away from the major metropolitan cities for sites, in view of prevailing high land prices that they felt would make an economy class hotel unfeasible. From past experience and new studies, several state capitals, places of tourism interest, and pilgrimage spots were identified as needing efficient and no-frills hotels at reasonable rates. Hotels would be 70 to 200 rooms with moderate food and beverage facilities.

Prospective franchisees were informed of QII franchise opportunities through direct mailings, advertisements in leading magazines and papers, and other media announcements. Table 17-3-1 shows the Franchise, Marketing, and Management Service Packet sent to prospective franchisees. Quality International fees to the franchisee were US$150 a room, annually, and three percent of gross room revenue, of which 25 percent would be spent in India. AKDA fees to the franchisee were 1.5 percent of the project cost excluding land and finance charges, three percent of gross food and beverage revenue, and 10 percent of GOP before interest and depreciation as a management and operation fee. By ruling of the Central Financial Institution, however, the managment and operation fee was to be subordinated to interest payments.

Three years had passed since the joint venture was formed, but it had failed to make much headway. Only two hotels had been franchised, these being conversions that had been marketed by AKDA prior to the formation of QII. They were doing reasonably well, but that was hardly enough. QII was facing incoming competition from other chains and needed to reach some closures.

Uttam Dave looked at the papers before him, particularly the results of a recent survey on acceptance of an international franchise expansion (Table 17-3-2), looking for a clue. If he could just get one franchise sold, things would improve. He was sure of it. But *how*?

TABLE 17-3-1 Franchise, Marketing, and Management Services Agreement

As a Member, your Hotel will receive a wide range of services, both national and international, from which it will derive several tangible benefits.

A. SERVICES AT INTERNATIONAL LEVEL

International Franchise and Brand Name	International Franchise and Brand Name of Quality International, which will make your hotel internationally "visible."
International Sales Promotion	Increased sales for your Hotel through international marketing, group advertising and sales promotion through Quality International's Sales Offices in the United States, Canada, Mexico, Belgium, United Kingdom, West Germany, Switzerland, The Netherlands, Ireland, France, Spain, Japan, Australia, and New Zealand. Unlike other international hotel chains in India, no additional prorated costs of international advertising have to be paid over and above the franchise fees.
Worldwide Reservations	Instant Reservations access through Quality's SUNBURST worldwide satellite-linked computerized Reservations System that interfaces with 257 Airlines, Travel Agent networks and automated hotel reservations databases. Also, referred reservations from over 1,150 hotels in 16 countries.
Promotional Literature	Publicity through listing in the various directories, brochures, and promotional literature distributed worldwide by Quality International (e.g., Travel and Vacation Directory, Corporate Rate Directory, Group Tour Rate Directory, and other directories, Regional and Country brochures, etc.)
International Trade Marts	Publicity and sales promotion through participation by Quality International in over 60 prominent travel trade marts worldwide.
Public Relations	Quality International will promote the image, identity and awareness of the Member Hotels internationally through public relations efforts to various market segments by organizing press publicity, familiarization tours, etc.
Technology Transfer and Training	Quality International will ensure an on-going transfer of "state-of-the-art" technology for hotel management and operations systems and procedures to the Member Hotels, resulting in international standards of management and operations. Quality International will also provide annual training to managerial and supervisory personnel of Member Hotels.
Competitive Advantage	The International Franchise will immediately give your hotel a strong competitive edge over other hotels in your city.
Higher Tariffs, Revenues and Profits	By virtue of its international name and image, your hotel would be able to charge higher tariffs, thereby generating higher revenues and profits.

(continued)

TABLE 17-3-1   (continued)

Confidence for Financial Institutions	The franchise will generate confidence amongst Financial Institutions that loans given and investments made will be well-managed.

B. SERVICES AT THE NATIONAL LEVEL

All-India Sales Promotion	Matching the international efforts, in India Quality Inns India will promote the sales of your hotel by marketing and sales promotion through well-staffed Sales offices at Delhi, Bombay, Madras, Bangalore, and Calcutta. The will result in high occupancies, turnover, and profit. *In addition, Quality International will spend 25% of its own fees in India itself, promoting the chain and the Member hotels.*
All-India Reservations	Quality Inns India will provide Instant Reservations facilities from five centres at Delhi, Bombay, Calcutta, Madras, and Bangalore, and referred reservations from other Indian Member Hotels. The availability of such a reservations network in India will result in ease of bookings for travel agents, companies, and individuals and will result in higher occupancies.
Advertising	Quality Inns India will provide Group Advertising featuring members of the group and will supervise the Member Hotel's own advertising campaigns to ensure stipulated standards. This will result in widespread awareness of your hotel.
Marketing and Sales Promotion Plans	Quality Inns India will prepare a long-term Strategic Marketing Plan based on a careful analysis of the segments which can be drawn to the hotel, taking into account the facilities and amenities that the hotel offers. Annually, Quality Inns India will also develop a sales promotion, publicity, and advertisement action plan and ensure its implementation throughout the year.
Marketing and Sales Programs	Quality Inns India, on its own and jointly with Quality International, will develop a variety of specialized marketing and sales promotion programmes such as group tours, packages, sales blitzes, and other special promotions that are all designed to boost the occupancies of Member Hotels.
Promotional Literature	The Member Hotels will be included in the marketing brochures and other publicity material of Quality Inns India, which will be distributed widely among travel agents, business houses, and institutions.
Public Relations	Quality Inns India will promote the image, identity, and awareness of the Member Hotels, through public relations efforts to various market segments by organizing press publicity, familiarization tours, etc.
Liaison with Travel Trade	Quality Inns India jointly, with Quality International will organize visits of travel agents, tour operators, and travel writers, Indian and foreign, for popularising the hotel and its services. Quality Inns India will also participate in Travel Trade Shows in India.

TABLE 17-3-1   (continued)

Management and Operations Services	Quality Inns India will provide management services for the day-to-day management and operations of the Member Hotels to stipulated international standards. These services will include installation of management and operating policies, systems, and procedures, day-to-day supervision, and provision of managerial and supervisory personnel. Quality Inns India has Departments of Franchise Development, Marketing, Reservations, Management and Operations, for providing support to Member Hotels. Quality International will ensure a constant transfer of technology for hotel management and operations systems and procedures to Quality Inns India.
Targets and Budgets	Quality Inns India will develop sales targets and operating budgets for the Front Office Manager, Sales Manager, Food and Beverage Manger, and the General Manager of the Hotel to achieve.
Reports	Owners of Member Hotels will be kept fully informed on all aspects of the Hotel's operations. They will receive copies of the Weekly and Monthly reports on the operations of the Hotel. They will also receive copies of relevant correspondence between Quality Inns India Headquarters and the managerial personnel at the Hotel. Quality Inns India will also furnish monthly reports to the Owners on the Marketing and Sales efforts carried out on behalf of the Member Hotel and the response received. Other hotel chains do not follow this practice.
Training	As soon as possible, a Training Centre will be established for training of employees of the Quality Inns India Member Hotels. It will be equipped with training films and other materials supplied by Quality International and experts will come once a year to train the managerial staff. Quality Inns India will train employees of the Member Hotels on a regular basis to ensure standards of service and operations.
Technical Services for Hotel Projects	With inputs from Quality International, Quality Inns India will provide new hotel projects Technical Services of an international standard at reasonable terms. Unlike other international hotel chains in India, no foreign exchange payments will have to be made for this.
Conclusion	The services and benefits that will be provide by Quality Inns India to your hotel, as detailed above, are far wider in scope than those offered by Indian hotel chains, as they encompass both national and international services. Yet the fee structure is competitive when compared to that of other Indian and International chains.

Note: Brochures on any of the three brands—Quality, Comfort, and Clarion—are available on request.

TABLE 17-3-2   Survey of Factors Determining Acceptance of an Internation Franchise in a Host Country

Factor	Mean
Political stability	3.8
Substantial-size middle class	3.8
High level of economic growth	3.6
Substantial disposable income	3.5
Considerable urbanization	3.4
High level of population growth	3.1
High levels of education	2.9
Substantial consumer mobility	2.8
Substantial proportion of women working outside the home	2.4
Large number of small businesses	2.3
High level of auto ownership	2.1
Widespread use of English	2.1
Relatively short workweeks	1.2

Note: For each factor, respondents assigned a value from 0 to 5, with 5 indicating the most importance and 0 the least importance. The number of respondents per factor ranged from 380 to 389. Factors are ranked by means in descending order.

Source: Walker, International Franchise Association study.

CHAPTER 18

International Tourism Marketing[1]

In this chapter the focus of the book shifts from the marketing of individual hospitality organizations to that of public sector organizations. First, current trends in international tourism and the factors that contribute to these trends are briefly discussed. Second, we discuss types of marketing activities that national tourism organizations (NTOs) perform in the marketing of countries, and subsets of countries, as tourist destinations. The concepts that have been presented in the first seventeen chapters are no different when applied to tourism; rather, they are applied here to the larger public entity that collaborates with individual organizations, not the individual organizations themselves.

The chapter repeats, briefly, the issues of environmental impacts, applied in global contexts, and then discusses the marketing of destinations. Because these are not new concepts in this text, the chapter is a short one. The more detailed explanation and application, however, are contained in four longer cases at the end of

the chapter, a better way to present material applied to international tourism than to repeat concepts in the text.

International Tourism Today

Tourism has grown enormously and its influence has spread widely since World War II, and especially since 1960. International tourist arrivals increased at a phenomenal annual growth rate of 6.5 percent from 1960 to 1992, as shown in Figure 18-1, a trend that is continuing. The World Tourism Organization (WTO) projects that international arrivals will reach over 700 million by the year 2000. International recessions in 1982–1983 and 1991 caused slight declines, but recovery was swift and strong. In more recent years, the rate of growth in international tourism receipts has exceeded the growth rate of tourist arrivals, which is indicative of an increase in per capita expenditures by international tourists.

The fastest-growing destinations in recent years have been outside the traditionally stronger continents of North America and Europe. Most parts of Asia, Oceania, Africa, and

[1]We are grateful to Professor Kye-Sung (Kaye) Chon, Ph.D., William F. Harrah College of Hotel Administration, University of Nevada/Las Vegas, for writing and contributing this chapter, as well as Case 18-4.

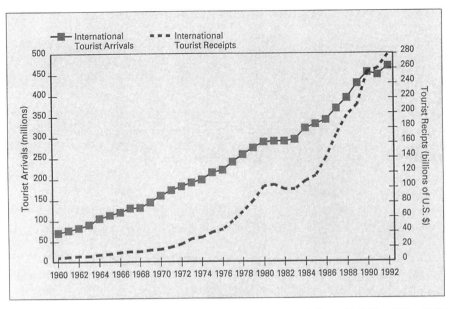

Source: Kye-Sung Chon, *Welcome to Hospitality: An Introduction,* Cincinnati: South-Western Publishing, 1994, p. 57. Data from World Tourism Organization

FIGURE 18-1 World tourism growth 1960–1992

South America have recently experienced rates of growth significantly above the world average. Possible explanations for the rapid growth of tourism in these regions would include the fast economic growth, relatively stable political environment, ability to finance infrastructure development, aggressive marketing efforts by NTOs, and an increase of tourism demand worldwide. The following sections discuss in more detail the general environmental factors that continue to influence the growth of international tourism.

Economic Environment

Consumption patterns in international tourism, including total visitor volume, are largely dependent upon the economic conditions in the market of the countries or regions in which prospective visitors live. Developed and growing economies sustain large numbers of trips away from home for business purposes of all kinds. Business meetings, attendance at conferences and trade shows, and travel on government business are all important parts of the travel

and tourism industry. The influence of economic conditions is even more obvious in leisure travel where, in many countries with advanced and developed economies, average disposable income per capita has grown to a size large enough to enable a majority of the population to take vacation trips in foreign lands.

Tourism from and within Asia, for example, showed an unprecedented growth in the 1980s, stemming from the very fast economic growth in many countries in the region; and it continues in the 1990s. Economic growth in newly industrialized countries also makes it possible for these countries to fund infrastructure development, thus increasing the capacity to accommodate international tourists. At the same time, the relatively stable political and social climate in most Asian countries, combined with the rapid growth of the industrial and service sectors, contributes to a rapid development of personal disposable income and private consumption, thus considerably improving many Asians' ability to travel.

The Japanese market in particular has shown remarkable growth since the value of the

FIGURE 18-2   NTOs promote through source country outlets

yen rose sharply against other currencies. Further, riding on a favorable economy in Japan, the Japanese government in 1987 launched the "Ten Million Program," which aimed at doubling the number of Japanese overseas travelers from the 1986 level of 5.5 million to 10 million by the end of 1991. The Ten Million Program was achieved in 1990, one year before the target year. This strong trend is continuing throughout the 1990s.

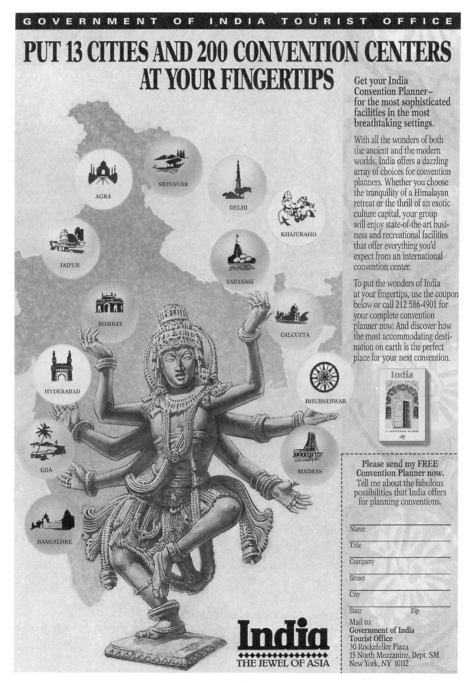

FIGURE 18-2   (continued)

FIGURE 18-2   (continued)

Technological Environment

Technology and travel are natural partners. The rapid growth of travel and tourism in the last 20 years has been fostered by technological developments, principally in air transport through the development and refinement of the jet engine, more sophisticated aircraft design, and improved systems. The world's three largest aircraft manufacturers (MacDonald Doug-

las, Boeing, and Lockheed) all introduced wide-bodied passenger airplanes, such as the DC-10, Boeing 747, and Tri-star L-1011, in the 1970s. These companies, along with Airbus of France, have continuously modified planes to fly longer distances with better fuel economy. The original Boeing 747 had to make a refueling stop at an intermediate location in making a direct flight from New York to Tokyo. The Boeing 747-400,

Ladies at Ascot Races, Berkshire

History... We celebrate many centuries' worth. It shows in our graceful palaces, stately manors, craggy castles, and fine museums.

Capacity... We roll out the red carpet and "beat retreats" for groups of 4 to 40,000.

State-of-the-Art Conference Centres and Accommodation... From the great exhibition halls of London, Birmingham, Edinburgh and Glasgow to quiet country retreats, there's a modern meeting place and a comfortable hotel to meet your most exacting demands.

Diversity... From the beaches of Brighton to the Highlands of Scotland, from the stages of Stratford to the Whisky Trail, there are a thousand crowning opportunities to explore.

Language... We speak yours. Only the accents—and some colourful colloquialisms—are different.

Tradition... We specialise in royal rituals, pomp and pageantry—and impeccable, unobtrusive service. It's the royal treatment in every way. Why settle for less?

Business Travel Department
British Tourist Authority
551 Fifth Avenue
New York, NY 10176-0799
Tel: (212)986-2266, Fax: (212)986-1188

BRITAIN
*where business
becomes pleasure*

FIGURE 18-2   (continued)

the newer version of the original jumbo jet, makes the same flight nonstop.

Wide use of computer technology has brought to the travel industry another leap forward. Computer software has been designed to cover a wide range of activities undertaken by the travel trade (e.g., information retrieval, reservation, ticketing, invoicing, etc.), as was discussed in Chapter 16. There is strong evidence to suggest that future developments will result

IF THEY'RE VERY, VERY, VERY GOOD,
THEY CAN GO TO HEAVEN.

If there is a place on this earth that is the ultimate reward, it is the magical island of Bermuda.

Say the word, and your top performers perform even better. Sales contests exceed goals. And no wonder.

Our pristine island is wonderfully civilized. Our pink beaches will put them in the clouds. Our business amenities rate with the best.

And with Bermuda less than 2 hours from the East Coast, the trip over won't jangle their nerves.

What's more, should you hold a meeting, our tax treaty lets you receive the same divine benefits as if the meeting were held stateside—and the entire trip could cost you less than many U.S. destinations.

It's our little corner of heaven. And we'd love to share it. Call Dianne Carlson at 800-223-6106 ext. 213.

B E R M U D A

FIGURE 18-3 Building positive destination images

in a revolution in the distribution and marketing of the various travel and tourism services throughout all segments of the industry.

Political/Legal Environment

Government interest in tourism has stemmed primarily from its economic significance, particularly employment earnings and tax potentials. Tourism demand, however, is also largely influenced by legislative actions at various levels of government and intergovernment agencies (e.g., World Tourism Organization [WTO] and International Air Transport Association [IATA]). As well, international politics play a significant role in the volume of travel and tourism business. For example, 35 percent of U.S. travelers with reservations to Europe canceled their flights following a series of terrorist activities in Europe and elsewhere in 1985–

FIGURE 18-3   (continued)

1986. Likewise, as illustrated in Case 18-4, the Gulf War had a profound effect on Thailand's tourism industry in terms of canceled reservations.

The air transport industry was liberalized in most tourist-generating countries in the 1980s. The deregulation of the airline industry in North America generated a significant increase in intercontinental flights, which, in turn, positively contributed to the growth of world tourism. The adoption of an "open sky" policy in Asian countries resulted in a substantial increase in air traffic within Asia and fostered the introduction of new carriers like Eva Airways (Taiwan) and Asian Airlines (South Korea).

Relaxed travel restrictions and increasing leisure time and income of residents in newly industrialized countries contributed significantly to a growth of tourism within and from Asia. In the past, both the Taiwanese and South Korean governments restricted or limited overseas travel by their citizens. With rapid eco-

FIGURE 18-3 (continued)

nomic growth and an increase in consumer disposable income, the concept of leisure travel became widespread in these countries, and their governments gradually lifted overseas travel bans. Once, for example, the Korean government prevented its citizens from obtaining a passport for "sightseeing" purposes. Previously, to obtain a passport for pleasure travel, an applicant had to be at least 50 years old in 1983, 40 in 1987, and 30 in 1988. In 1989, the government eliminated all age restrictions on the issu-

ance of passports to its citizens. The Taiwanese government followed the same course. The number of outbound tourists from Taiwan increased more than threefold in four years. The number of South Korean outbound travelers increased fivefold during the same period.

Sociocultural Environment

Social and cultural considerations involve the beliefs, values, attitudes, opinions, and life-

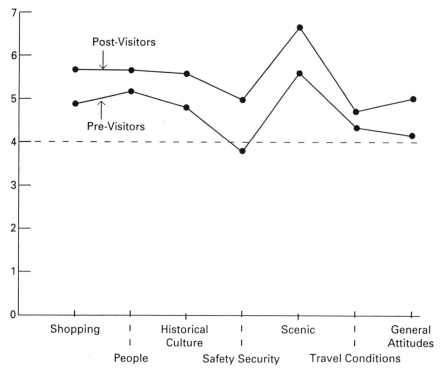

Source: Kye-Sung Chon, "Perceptual Differences of Korea as a Tourist Destination Between Pre-visit and Post-visit American Tourists," unpublished Master's theses, Las Vegas: University of Nevada, 1985.

FIGURE 18-4   Korea's image in the minds of pre-visit and post-visit Americans

styles of those in the market environment, as developed from their cultural, ecological, demographic, religious, educational, and ethnic conditioning. For example, while Japanese and Koreans share similar cultural heritages, these two national groups are very different in travel behavior. Japanese travelers like to travel in groups, most likely with their work colleagues. Koreans like to travel with friends, seldom with co-workers; Koreans also prefer FIT packages rather than group packages.

A key element in the tourism marketing process is the significant demographic shifts affecting the population, particularly in selecting target markets. In 1970, 24 percent of the U.S. population was between 25 and 45 years of age. By 1990, this age group accounted for 33 percent of the population, a 38 percent increase. Another continuing phenomenon is the growth rate of the over-60 segment, a group that likes

to travel. Other countries have had similar demographic shifts. Moreover, as social attitudes change, so too do the leisure patterns of consumers. Popularity of "ecotourism" in recent years is one good example.

The Role of NTOs

At the national level, governments promote their countries in the international tourist market through *national tourism organizations* (NTOs). The United States Travel and Tourism Administration (USTTA), under the Department of Commerce, is the NTO for the United States. In some countries, such as Mexico and Canada, government leaders have recognized the importance of tourism to a nation's economy and have elevated the status of the NTO to cabinet level, instituting a Ministry of Tour-

TABLE 18-1   Destination Image Modification and Travel
Decision Making

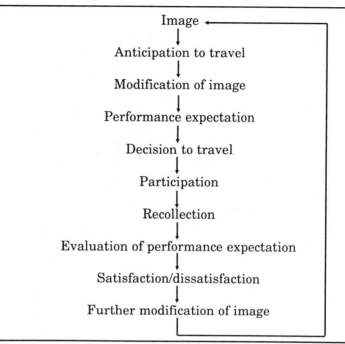

Source: Adapted from Kye-Sung Chon, "The Role of Destination Image in
Tourism: A Review and Discussion," *The Tourist Review,* 33(2), 1990, pp. 2–9.

ism. Regardless of their position in governments, NTOs have similar objectives: They promote their countries through publicity campaigns, conduct research, and develop plans for destinations. Due to increased competition in world tourism, NTOs today spend much more on their tourism marketing budget than they did in the 1980s. A significant part is spent to publicize a country as a destination, through outlets in major source countries, to create public awareness and to promote positive images (Figure 18-2).

Importance of Image Promotion

A destination's image is a major factor influencing a traveler's decision to visit a country. Every exposure to anything related to a destination helps in forming an image of that place; books, movies, television, postcards, songs, photographs, news stories, and advertising, all con-

tribute. Favorable images, of course, greatly improve the chance of increasing tourist traffic. For example, Austria became a popular vacation destination for many Americans as a result of the favorable images portrayed in the movie *The Sound of Music,* while Kenya enjoyed a substantial increase in tourism after the movie *Out of Africa.*

On the other hand, negative images can also have a profound impact. The "war image" of Korea associated with the television drama *M.A.S.H.,* even 25 years after the Korean War, was a detrimental factor for Korea in promoting the country as a tourist destination for North Americans in the 1970s. One of the difficulties in promoting India as a tourist destination has been the image of poverty that people associate with the country; the scenic beauty and many cultural attractions are often overshadowed by negative scenes of starving people and squalor. Negative images increase the challenge for

FIGURE 18-5   A state tourism bureau promotion

FIGURE 18-6   A province tourism bureau promotion

NTO marketers to promote a country's tourism overseas.

Images of a destination are so important that states and countries spend millions of dollars to build positive images of their destinations (Figure 18-3). Some researchers postulate that a tourist's experience is nothing but a constant modification of the destination image. As shown in Table 18-1, a tourist makes a destination choice based on a previously-held image of the destination. The tourist's *actual* experience in the destination provides comparison with the previous image, a "reality check," and determines the tourist's level of satisfaction or dissatisfaction with the overall experience. The following example illustrates this process:

Ken is a 21-year-old college student from Pittsburgh who decides to take a vacation over spring break and reads brochures for spring travel pack-

FIGURE 18-7   A county tourism bureau promotion

ages to Cancun, Mexico. He has never been to Mexico and is excited about the idea of going to Cancun. At this point, Ken's image of Cancun is mainly based on two things: the written information from the tour package brochure and his previous knowledge about Mexico acquired through books, mass media, and friends. Ken's image of the destination is most important here because his expectations of Cancun (and also Mexico in general) are based on his images of the area.

Spring break comes and Ken travels to Cancun. He participates in water sports and also meets new friends. When he returns home, he goes through a "recollection" stage in which he evaluates his overall experience, including a comparison of his expectations and his actual experiences. When the actual experiences live up to the expectations (based on images of the destination), there is satisfaction; if the actual experiences do not live up to expectations, there is dissatisfaction. Depending on his level of satisfaction or dissatisfaction, Ken will decide whether to return to Cancun, as well as other places in Mexico, in the future. More important, he'll talk about his experiences with his friends, which will, in turn, help his friends form images of Cancun and Mexico.

Planners with vision look no further.

You need look no further than the Lake Geneva Region. Look no further than the beauty and the cosmopolitan spirit that have long drawn knowledgeable people, from movie stars to corporate executives. Here your meeting will be implemented with famous Swiss efficiency. For more information use the magazine inquiry card or write to: Lake Geneva Region, P.O. Box 742, Radio City Station, New York, NY 10101 or **call 1-800-335-LAKE(5253)**

Look no further. **Lake Geneva Region. Switzerland.**

FIGURE 18-8   A region tourism bureau promotion

The primary images of a destination as perceived by a tourist have a lot to do with the tourist's ultimate satisfaction or dissatisfaction.

Research indicates that an initial impression (or image) of a destination is hard to change. That is, everything that happens, good or bad, is ultimately based on the original image. In a study that attempted to determine the image of South Korea as a tourist destination of American visitors, pre- and post-visit surveys were administered American tourists visiting the country. The country's image was measured in seven areas: shopping opportunities, friendliness of the Korean people, historical and cul-

At Big Sky, You're Just Far Enough Away From Yellowstone To Sleep Soundly.

The Yellowstone area is home to some of North America's most imposing wildlife. Fortunately, it's also home to one of the West's most accommodating convention sites. Big Sky Resort.

Big Sky offers over 1,000 comfortable guest accommodations, plus more than 43,000 square feet of function space in the Yellowstone Conference Center.

So call 1-800-548-8096 for planning assistance or further information about Big Sky. Where your next meeting can be as wild or as tame as you want it to be.

©1992 Big Sky Montana

BIG SKY
MONTANA
A BOYNE USA RESORT

FIGURE 18-9   An area tourism bureau promotion

tural attractions, safety and security concerns, scenic attractions, travel conditions, and the tourists' general attitudes toward the country. Post-visitors rated each of the seven areas more favorably. Interestingly enough, however, the pattern of perception for each of the seven areas remained similar to the perception held by pre-visitors. (Figure 18-4 shows these results.) This helped to confirm that a destination's image, once established in the mind of the public, is hard to change.[2]

Marketing Functions of NTOs

Historically, the principal marketing role of NTOs has been seen in fairly narrow promotional terms—creating and communicating overall appealing destination images and messages to the target market. Traditional NTO functions are changing, however, as today's in-

ternational tourism industry becomes more competitive and tourists become increasingly more sophisticated in their destination choice behavior. Tourism industry leaders in many countries recognize the importance of collaboration between the public and private sectors. They launch and implement various collaborative marketing programs.

As described in Case 18-4, Thailand's tourism industry in the early 1990s was adversely affected by the Persian Gulf War, the spread of AIDS in the country, and political unrest that occurred in early 1992. To offset the adverse publicity, the Tourism Authority of Thailand (TAT), in collaboration with airlines, hotels and tour operators, launched "The World Our Guest" program, a massive familiarization trip campaign aimed at travel intermediaries. More than 11,000 individual tourists and travel agents were invited to Thailand and given free hotel rooms, airline tickets, meals, and tours. The promotion was declared by TAT to be an unqualified success.

The marketing activities of an NTO are mainly centered around the promotion of the

---

[2]Kye-Sung Chon, "Perceptual Differences of Korea as a Tourist Destination Between Pre-visit and Post-visit American Tourists," unpublished Master's theses, Las Vegas: University of Nevada, 1985.

FIGURE 18-10   A city tourism bureau promotion

country as a whole. Subsets, however, are common. States (Figure 18-5), provinces (Figure 18-6), counties (Figure 18-7), regions (Figure 18-8), areas (Figure 18-9), cities (Figure 18-10), and other smaller parts of a country participate in similar activities to promote their unique destinations, as described in Case 18-1 and implied in Case 18-2.

A natural extension of such efforts is a "facilitation role" that typically includes collecting, analyzing, and disseminating market research data; establishing a representation in the markets of origin; participating in trade shows; organizing and coordinating familiarization trips; and supporting the private sector in the production and distribution of literature. For example, the USTTA conducted an analysis of the pleasure travel market potential for 15 major countries of origin; the analysis involved looking at nine important travel market characteristics that relate to volume of travel and associated spending:

Total number of potential travelers
Incidence rate of long-haul adult pleasure travelers

Actual number of visitors
Potential for more visitors
Potential for additional market penetration
Current receipts from pleasure travelers
Per-capita pleasure traveler receipts
Total potential receipts
Potential for additional pleasure travel
    receipts

The analysis included the process of assigning each item a mathematical weight relative to its importance and ranking each of the target countries according to each item. The results were the final ranking of the most important target markets, as shown in Table 18-2.

In the top eight countries, the USTTA already had field office representation; therefore, USTTA reasoned, the next countries in which to open its field offices would be those on the list that follow Italy—Brazil, Hong Kong, and South Korea. Because Hong Kong would undergo a major political change in the upcoming years, Brazil and South Korea were actually considered first.

Summary

The growth and traffic patterns of international tourism are largely influenced by environmental trends related to economic, technological, political, and sociocultural factors of the world. In order to make sound marketing decisions, an NTO or its subset needs to constantly monitor any changes occurring in the environment and take a pro-active posture in its marketing programs. Because of the importance of building positive destination images, in the future NTOs and their subsets will continue to play an important image building and image communication role in the market place. At the same time, they will play a greater role as facilitators for market research and as collaborators of marketing efforts by the private sector of the tourism industry.

TABLE 18-2   USTTA's Market Potential of 15 Target Countries

Country	Rank
Japan	1
Germany	2
Canada	3
Mexico	4
France	5
Australia	6
United Kingdom	7
Italy	8
Brazil	9
Hong Kong	10
South Korea	11
Singapore	12
Switzerland	13
Venezuela	14
Netherlands	15

Source: "Analysis: The Potential of International Pleasure Travel Markets to the USA," Washington, D.C.: Department of Commerce, United States Travel and Tourism Administration, 1993.

Discussion Questions

1. Choose a little-known or remote destination of the world. Research and discuss the environmental influences that impact tourism in that destination.
2. Choose a destination in the world that has a negative image for you. What created this image? Research and show what this destination could do to overcome it. If it does, can it meet expectations?
3. From the anecdote on Ken and Cancun, trace the model in Table 18-1. What might have gone wrong? Gone right? Trace the impact.
4. Describe how you would promote your own home town. What research would you do?
5. In Case 18-1, why did the Creole Christmas idea succeed?
6. In Case 18-2, what can Aristos Politis do to reach his goal? Sort out his marketing plan including target markets, positioning, promotion, and distribution.

7. In Case 18-3, analyze the Fiji Island situation. Should the World Bank loan money? How, where, and why?

8. In Case 18-4, analyze all the environmental impacts on Thai tourism. What caused the rise and the fall in the tourism markets in a strategic sense?

✔ Case 18-1

Creole Christmas in New Orleans

The month of December is traditionally a slow season for the hotel industry in non-resort destinations in the United States. Families spend the holidays at home, and very little convention and commercial activity takes place. December hotel occupancy in U.S. cities is usually well below 50 percent, with the national average hovering around the 45–48 percent range.

New Orleans, Louisiana, a popular tourist destination famous for its jazz, French Quarter, and Creole history, was no exception. Each December, vacant rooms and empty restaurant seats meant revenues lost forever. Industry employees also had little to cheer about during this holiday month, as labor hours were reduced, and some even faced the prospect of being laid off. Indeed, in the past, many New Orleans hotels had shut down completely during the middle half of December. A group of tourism industry executives decided to try to do something about the situation.

The Idea

The idea of a Christmas promotion for New Orleans originated as a result of the success of another festival held in the city's French Quarter: the first French Quarter Festival, held in 1985, when the Mayor of New Orleans, with the support of tourism and city officials, decided to throw a "block party" in the French Quarter. The second weekend in April was dedicated to this Festival, with the objective of reacquainting residents and visitors with the cultural heart and soul of New Orleans. This event turned out to be a resounding success. Buoyed by the resounding success of the Festival, a group of French Quarter businesspeople informally bandied about the idea of doing something similar in the off-season, specifically during December.

Although this was welcomed as a good idea by the city and its tourism industry, there were no resources available to bring it to fruition. Some businesses, residents, and hospitality companies decided, however, to fund a small and informal Christmas celebration. This effort resulted in a Christmas tree in Jackson Square in the French Quarter and carol singing by the volunteer Mardi Gras Chorus—a local barbershop quartet. The success of this December French Quarter Festival provided the impetus to make it an annual event. A shoestring budget of donations from hospitality organizations provided a full-time coordinator's salary for six months. The event was again successful due mainly to the coordinator's organizational skills, an army of volunteers, and support from merchants, residents, and the hospitality industry in this part of New Orleans.

Six French Quarter hospitality organizations supported the coordinator's salary for another six months so that she could formally coordinate the Christmas festival. These efforts resulted in the first Creole Christmas Festival, bringing together, in a unique package, the diverse Christmas holiday events, traditional and new, that occur in and around New Orleans: carol singing in Jackson Square; Christmas Eve bonfires along the Mississippi River; Creole cooking demonstrations; tours of majestic nineteenth-century homes, trimmed in traditional Christmas style, and special appearances by the Creole Santa Claus, "Papa Noel"; Christmas in the Oaks, an elaborate Christmas lighting display in 200-year-old oak trees in City Park; and numerous other special events. The period ranged from the waning days of the convention season (around December 7th) to the beginning of the Sugar Bowl festivities (December 28th).

Organizing an Annual Event

The coalition of tourism industry executives lobbied City Hall for support for an annual event. French Quarter Festival, Inc., a nonprofit corporation of the City of New Orleans, was formed to handle the administrative responsibility for both the Creole Christmas and the French Quarter Festivals. The official coordinator of these festivals and one employee were the only full-time people on the payroll, assisted by as many as 300 volunteers from the community. Office space was donated by the City of New Orleans. The Festival committee consisted of 67 representatives of the hospitality industry, retailers, residents, and French Quarter preservationists.

Financial resources were obtained from a variety of sources, both cash and in-kind donations, but originally they came from a core group of French Quarter hospitality executives who literally pulled whatever they could afford from their own pockets. Creole Christmas expenses exceeded income in the first two years, and surpluses from the French Quarter Festival (held in April each year) were used to subsidize it. This caused a debate as to the viability of Creole Christmas, given the lack of a formal financial structure. Tourism and hospitality industry leaders persisted, however, and developed a more formal method of financing the Creole Christmas promotion. Since the direct beneficiary of the Creole Christmas festival was the hospitality industry, it was natural that this industry provide a majority of the cash financial support. Hotels were assessed a fee of $1.50 per room, with a minimum of $250 and a maximum of $1,500. Restaurants were assessed a fee of $1 per seat, with a $150 minimum and a maximum of $500. Other tourism organizations, such as tour and travel companies, were assessed a flat fee. In return, all these companies were acknowledged in the Creole Christmas promotional brochures, where they could list their rates and telephone numbers.

In-kind donations included the printing of brochures by a major New Orleans corporation, free mailing lists provided by a major credit card company, and advertising provided through the Greater New Orleans Marketing Committee (a joint private and public entity whose mission was to promote New Orleans to leisure travelers). The Greater New Orleans Tourist and Convention Commission (GNOTCC) and the Louisiana Office of Tourism also included Creole Christmas in their promotional campaigns. In addition, various hospitality organizations pitched in to host familiarization trips for travel writers and tour operators. Costs of mailing brochures to 10,000 potential visitors were borne by the Greater New Orleans Marketing Committee.

Advertising

Community leaders realized the importance of tourism promotion, both at the city and state levels. A multi-pronged promotional campaign of Creole Christmas was conducted, the centerpiece of the campaign being a brochure that showed a calendar of events for each day of the season (December 1–31). Included in the brochure were listings of participating restaurants with their respective dinner menus and prices. Several local tour operators were also listed to provide information on package tours, and a separate insert was included listing hotel information and the "Papa Noel" rates, which were a 40–50 percent discount off rack rates. Restaurants offered special Christmas season dinners at attractive prices. Potential visitors could obtain this brochure by calling a toll-free number or by writing directly. Along with the Creole Christmas brochure, each respondent received a coupon book, a Christmas in New Orleans brochure, and a promotional piece from the Aquarium of the Americas in New Orleans. Several hotels ran "piggyback" advertising during this marketing campaign.

Free billboard advertising was provided by a billboard advertiser and several radio stations outside the vicinity of New Orleans had Creole Christmas package "giveaways," which helped provide free air time for the event. Direct mailings were sent to 35,000 credit card holders in the area around New Orleans, including Mississippi, Florida, and Alabama. The Greater New Orleans Marketing Committee provided $75,000 worth of promotion on Cable TV, in newspapers, and on the radio, while the Louisiana Office of Tourism included Creole Christmas in their November advertising campaign on Louisiana tourism.

Two major familiarization trips were also conducted, one for travel writers and another for tour operators. The latter included trips to

Lafayette, Alexandria, Natchitoches in Louisiana, and Natchez, Mississippi—all cities trying to promote Christmas season tourism. Local New Orleans tourist magazines carried details of holiday events and several new local events, such as the Christmas in New Orleans Parade and Christmas in the Oaks. Decorated streetcars generated even greater local awareness.

What began as a celebration generally confined to the French Quarter, in later years became a city-wide celebration of Christmas in New Orleans. The Christmas in New Orleans Parade with Mardi Gras-style floats was a natural addition. Thousands of miniature lights and ornaments adorned the magnificent oak trees in New Orleans' City Park and came to attract over 300,000 visitors. Creole Christmas expanded to include a combination of a variety of events and attractions packaged together into a unique festival.

Performance Evaluation

In order to assess the economic success of the Creole Christmas Festival, surveys of participating hotels and restaurants were conducted. Hotels were asked to provide a breakdown of rooms occupied each day at the special Creole Christmas package rate and also the number of guests occupying those rooms. Hotels also provided the total number of rooms occupied and lists of number of guests during that period. Data from responding hotels were used to estimate the numbers of rooms sold for all hotels listed in the Creole Christmas brochure.

In the first year, 9,696 rooms were sold at the special Creole Christmas rate; in the second year, 17,916 rooms were sold. These numbers do not include rooms sold to tour operators and wholesalers as part of package tours. A remarkable and consistent increase continued: Total rooms sold increased from 62,915 in the second year, to 116,893 in the fourth year, and to 251,327 in the sixth year. These numbers reflect the effectiveness of the additional promotional efforts in later years. Hotel occupancies in the city for this period increased from 32.2 percent to 56.6 percent. Data from participating restaurants, with dramatic increases in meals served, also showed a pattern similar to the hotels.

The success of the Creole Christmas Festival in New Orleans can be attributed to the cooperation shown by all segments of the hospitality industry, the Mayor's Office, and the merchants and residents of the French Quarter. It is also likely that hard economic times, both for the City of New Orleans and its hospitality industry, provided the foundation upon which this diverse coalition was built. However, it was the persistence of a few hospitality industry executives, with organizational support from a cash-strapped City Hall and many New Orleans volunteers, that enhanced the success of the Creole Christmas and French Quarter Festivals.

The economic success of Creole Christmas may be further attributed to the clear goals of the event organizers and a concerted effort by all the constituents to reverse the negative effects of seasonality. The Festival continues today and provides a healthy boost to the hospitality industry of New Orleans.

✔ Case 18-2
Tourism in Corfu[3]

Aristos Politis was working at his desk when the phone rang. It was the general manager of the Corfu Hotel.

"Aristos, I have your preliminary report here in front of me and I'm a little concerned."

Aristos Politis put down his pen and sat back.

"Really, sir. What seems to be the problem?"

"Well, Aristos," began the general manager, "for one thing, I think your numbers were pulled out of a hat! How are we ever going to achieve a 65,000,000 Drachmas (Drs) GOP this year? That's totally unrealistic! And then there's the timing problem. You're supposed to be formulating a long-term marketing strategy and a marketing plan for this year. Well, it's April already, and we haven't seen your final report yet. Our season starts in ten days, Aristos, or have you forgotten that this is a real business, and not a textbook one?"

Aristos Politis listened to the tirade in frustration. He had been given this very large task only a month ago, and very little information had been available for him to use. He knew, however, that the general manager was more concerned about the end result than the means to that end, and would not accept any excuses.

Aristos spoke to the general manager with more confidence than he felt.

"Sir, I will have my analysis complete and on your desk one week from today. With it will be a complete marketing plan for the year, and you will see that a GOP of 65,000,000 Drs is, indeed, realistic."

As Aristos looked at the piles of paper around him he groaned. One week to analyze all this, and to convince his superiors that his projected GOP was valid. What on earth would he put in the marketing plan?

Background

Although Odysseus met Nausika there on his way back to Ithaca after the Trojan Wars, it was not until the 1950s that tourism played a major role in the Corfu economy. Until then, agriculture had been the main industry on this beautiful Greek island, one of the Ionian Islands off the northwest coast of Greece (Exhibit 18-2-1).

Tourists arrived on the island either by air or water. Aristos Politis had found that information on the number of tourist arrivals was scarce, and he had only been able to locate arrival figures for the previous year: Arrivals at the Corfu airport had totalled 713,408; 80 percent of these were international tourists, 90 percent of whom arrived on a charter flight. The majority of all international arrivals (73 percent) were from the United Kingdom; another 9 percent came from West Germany.

Corfu had two ports. The domestic port linked Corfu to mainland Greece with a ferryboat that arrived every hour during the daytime. The international port received large cruise ships from Italy and beyond. A breakdown of arrivals by air and by sea for each month is shown in Table 18-2-1. Table 18-2-2 shows the breakdown percentage, by country, of international arrivals.

The Corfu Hotel

The Corfu Hotel was a 250-room seasonal resort hotel located on Corfu. It had been in operation for nine years and had always been considered a four-star resort. Like most other hotels on the island, the Corfu Hotel was open from April until October, due mainly to the climate. The average rack rate for the previous year, in high season, was approximately 7,500 Drs[4] for a single room and 11,700 Drs for a double; in low season, 5,400 Drs and 8,000 Drs, respectively. Average daily rate per room-night for the year was only 4,900 Drs; occupancy was 58 percent.

The Corfu Hotel had begun experiencing a decline in performance two years before. The previous year's performance was the worst ever. Table 18-2-3 indicates the revenue and GOP

---

[3]Antonios Manessis researched and contributed to this case.

[4]At the time of the case, $1 U.S.=164 Drachmas.

EXHIBIT 18-2-1   Location of Corfu

figures for the hotel, both in actual figures and adjusted for inflation, for all nine years of operation. The monthly occupancy for the previous year is shown in Table 18-2-4, and is compared to the average occupancy of each month over nine years of operation.

The reasons for this dramatic decline in performance were not clear in the mind of Aristos, who had not been working at the hotel the previous year. Aristos was hired in March as a marketing consultant. Before that, "marketing" was not a word in the everyday vocabulary of management. Management had always been profit-oriented, and financial goals had been paramount. Now, feeling that "marketing" was becoming popular, management felt it had nothing to lose by hiring a marketing consultant.

The first thing that Aristos became acutely aware of was that the Corfu Hotel did not have detailed records on its customers. Guest history files were nonexistent. Nor was there any customer segmentation report. Customer feedback was in the form of comment cards, yet no systematic analysis of this data existed.

Aristos Politis discovered, however, that about 85 percent of the hotel's occupancy was made up of tours. He also noticed that only about 50 percent of the bed-nights allotted to the various tour groups were realized, and less than 54 percent of the room-nights, in the last two years, had resulted in actual bookings. Table 18-2-5 shows a summary of tour operator performance at the Corfu Hotel for the past two years. It also shows the rooms allotted for the present year.

Corfu as a Destination

Aristos then made a preliminary observation of the external environment. The existing market was segmented by point of entry to Corfu. The domestic terminal of the airport was dominated by Greek citizens coming for business (one-third) and Corfiots coming back home (another one-third); the remaining one-third was one-

EXHIBIT 18-2-1 (continued)

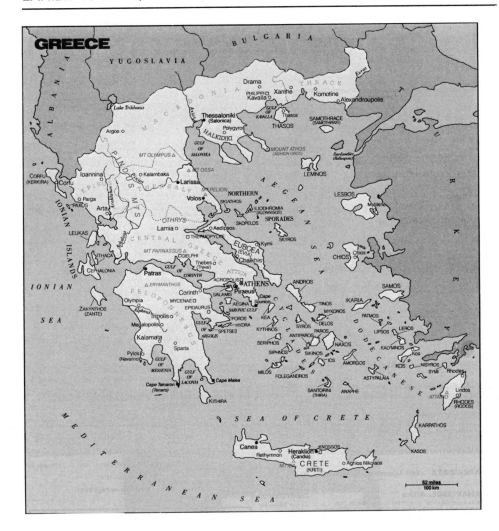

half international travelers (some on vacation and some on business) and one-half Greek families on vacation (visiting friends or relatives or coming directly from Salonica in northeast Greece). The domestic ferry carried 80 percent Greek citizens, mostly traveling by car, and 20 percent international travelers, also with cars.

The international cruises and large ferries from Italy, Patras, and beyond carried 30 percent Italians and 14 percent each Germans and Americans. Most Italians and Germans traveled by car; most Americans were college student backpackers. The other 42 percent were a mixture, as shown in Table 18-2-2.

The other environmental change that Politis

noted was the change in destinations targeted by UK tour operators. A large number had started to promote Turkey as a "sun spot" destination. Tourism in the UK was almost completely run by tour operators and travel agents, and tourists were primarily influenced by their policies. One report on tourism by the EC Commission had stated, "Tour operators seem to maintain the ability to launch tourist destinations and make them become fashionable resorts."

Empirical data supported this statement. For example, in Greece five years before, more than 35 percent of all British arrivals went to Corfu, more than 30 percent of all German arrivals went to Crete, and more than 45 percent

TABLE 18-2-1   Arrivals on the the Island of Corfu by Month

Month	Int'l. Air	Domestic Air	Int'l. Sea	Domestic Sea	Total
January	7,439	1,835	4,351	4,934	18,559
February	7,439	1,839	4,351	4,934	18,559
March	10,873	2,682	6,360	7,212	27,127
April	41,776	10,302	24,443	27,709	104,220
May	64,094	15,806	37,487	42,514	159,901
June	73,251	18,064	42,842	48,587	182,744
July	109,877	27,098	64,263	72,880	274118
August	111,022	27,379	64,932	73,640	276,973
September	77,830	19,195	45,520	51,624	194,169
October	48,643	11,997	28,450	32,265	121,355
November	10,301	2,540	6,025	6,832	25,698
December	9,731	2,399	5,691	6,454	24,275
Total	572,276	141,132	334,705	379,585	1,427,698

TABLE 18-2-2   International Arrivals on the Island of Corfu by Percentage of Origin

Country	By Air %	By Sea %	Total %
UK	73.5	4.9	56.5
Germany	8.8	15.4	10.5
Netherlands	3.6	1.3	3.1
France	2.1	4.3	2.6
Ireland	1.6	1.5	1.5
Italy	1.2	30.9	8.5
Belgium/Luxembourg	.8	.6	.7
Denmark	.7	2.0	1.0
Austria	2.8	2.5	2.7
Sweden	1.3	4.1	2.0
Switzerland	1.1	1.9	1.3
Finland	.8	.8	.8
Other Europe	.3	1.9	1.1
Total Europe	98.6	72.1	92.3
Total Asia	.3	.9	.5
Total America	.7	19.8	5.1
Total Oceania	.3	6.6	1.9
Total Africa	.1	.6	.2
Total	100	100	100

TABLE 18-2-3   Revenue and GOP, Actual and Adjusted for Inflation (Thousands of Drachmas)

Year	Actual Revenue	Actual GOP	Adjusted Revenue	Adjusted GOP	% GOP
1	107,501	22,392	107,501	22,392	20.8
2	130,870	34,589	108,157	28,585	26.4
3	120,386	25,244	85,153	17,878	20.9
4	197,394	39,240	123,680	24,586	19.9
5	256,228	64,595	143,224	36,107	25.2
6	298,756	81,819	147,972	40,524	27.4
7	303,296	79,057	138,935	36,215	26.1
8	231,775	36,516	100,335	15,807	15.7
9	219,659	16,565	89,147	6,723	7.5

of all Swedish arrivals went to Rhodes. Tour operators identified destinations already successful with individual tourism, as in the case of Corfu, and then "programmed" its development as a tour destination. By so doing they caused regional biases through their distribution systems and created the phenomenon of dependence of the destination on their bookings. At the same time, the large tour groups tended to drive away individual tourism.

As a result, small enterprises in southern European destinations had weak bargaining power when selling their product to wholesale tour operators, and thus became dependent upon them. This was especially true of hotels on Corfu in their relationship with UK tour operators. Thus, the decision by the tour operators to promote Turkey was especially detrimental to the island, as well as all southern European resort destinations that had relied on this business.

Competition

Little information was available to Aristos Politis about the competition. The total supply on the Island of Corfu, including villas and apartments, was 13,469 rooms, 83 percent were hotel rooms, with 1,075 in the five-star deluxe category. In the A class (four-star) there were 28 hotels with 3,800 rooms. There were also 41 B hotels (3,100 rooms), 91 C hotels (2,600 rooms), 22 D hotels (420 rooms), and 20 E hotels (200 rooms). Aristos was able to locate some rack rate information from the *Hotel and Travel Index* about other resorts on the island that he considered competitive; this information is shown in Table 18-2-6.

TABLE 18-2-4   Previous Year's Occupancy Compared to Nine-year Average

Month	Previous Year*	Nine-year Average
April	75.4%	53.5%
May	60.0	66.8
June	45.6	75.6
July	58.1	83.5
August	91.7	98.7
September	43.2	78.4
October	33.5	75.3
7-month average	58.21%	72.36%

*177 days and 25,671 room-nights

TABLE 18-2-5   Previous Two Years' Tour Operator Performance and Current Year Allotments

| Operator | Country | Past Two Years | | Present |
		Alotted	Bookings	Allotment
Airtours Int.	UK	3,502	120	
Charitos Travel	Netherlands	10,712	4,699	15,708
International	UK	3,468	3,543	1,870
Martin Rooks	UK	8,446	4,647	
Plotin Corfu		10,094	765	
Portland	UK	51,500	36,507	
Tui	Germany	5,800	1,891	
Meander		162	162	
Horizon	UK	24,926	13,681	
Tjaereborg	UK	14,350	6,162	
Manos Holidays	UK			1,870
Sunair	UK	2,789	616	
Olympic Holidays	UK	10,712	4,122	
Global Air	UK	4,532	1,400	
Grecian	UK	4,120	2,211	
La Palma Cruises		3,168	0	
Allsun		2,060	0	
BBI		14	14	
Super Travel		462	462	
Nur (Neckerman)	Germany			18,700
Pondos Travel	Netherlands			748
Comitours	Italy			7,667
Sunspots				2,805
Sunhellas				1,122
Alltour (Haritos)	Germany			3,740
Pondos-Sonenreisen	Germany			4,862
Supertravel				3,740
Dido Travel (Pilos)	Austria			5,610
Greek Skies				5,610
Total Bed-nights		160,817	81,002	74,052
Total Room-nights		84,600	45,050	37,026

Marketing Plan

Aristos Politis looked at all the information he had collected since he had been hired one month before. He also read parts of an article by the British writer Gerald Durrell that he had saved some years before (Table 18-2-7). He knew that his arguments would be critical in convincing upper management that a solid marketing plan would benefit the hotel, which had, until now, been concerned only with profits. Aristos knew that he had been hired only in a last-ditch effort to reverse the decline in performance, and that his superiors had little faith in "marketing," per se. Aristos Politis needed to convince the general manager that marketing was necessary, not trendy. He had a feeling that he would have to start by convincing the GM that the Corfu Hotel could, in fact, attain a GOP of 65,000,000 Drs. It was up to him to show them how.

TABLE 18-2-6   Similarly-Rated, Competitive Resort Hotels and Their Rack Rates

Hotel	No. Rooms	Single Low	Single High	Double Low	Double High
Deluxe					
Corfu Palace	106	15,500	21,000	22,000	31,000
Hilton	274	10,300	19,300	16,300	26,600
Astir	308	10,500	17,500	16,000	39,000
Miramare	149	5,600	15,100	9,700	28,700
Kontokali	238	7,600	10,100	11,700	17,600
A Category					
Chandris	550	8,700	12,200	11,700	13,500
Ermones	272	6,500	11,900	9,600	17,300
Divani Palace	165	10,400	14,300		
Kerkyra Golf	240	7,000	10300	10000	13500
Grecotel DA	260	5,350	10,100	8,800	16,000
Elaea	198	6,200	10,000	8,400	14,880
Ag. Gordios	223	5,600	9,100	10,400	16,500
Glyfada	242	8,100	9,300	13,000	16,400
Yaliskari	227	5,600	9,100	10,100	16,500
Grecotel CO	252	5,100	8,800	8,500	13,700
Margarona	118	7,600	8,500	10,600	13,400
Nissaki BCH	239	4,200	8,300	6,500	18,800
Regency	185	5,000	7,500	7,400	12,800
Corfu Hotel	250	5,400	7,500	8,000	11,700
Alexandros	91	5,500	7,500	7,750	10,900
Eva Palace	174	6,100	7,200	8,900	10,300
B Category					
Park Hotel	196	4,400	7,100	6,600	10,200
Paleokastri	163	4,600	6,100	7,300	8,400
Roda	360	5,400	8,200		
Potamaki	140	3,600	5,100	5,500	8,200
Messongi	828	3,000	4,000	4,000	5,200
Aeolos	324	5,000	9,000	7,770	10,900

TABLE 18-2-7   Commentary on Corfu by Gerald Durrell

I have had a most extraordinary affair of the heart. It started when I was eight years old, and I fell deeply and irrevocably in love with a ravishing creature who was mature and beautiful....Her name was Kerkyra, the island of Corfu. Going back to her recently was like paying a visit to the most beautiful woman in the world suffering from an acute and probably terminal case of leprosy—commonly called tourism....I have been back many times and suffered as I watched her demise.

Tourism is a curious modern disease. It attacks the shoeless man, the man of meager wealth, and the bloated man of affluence, whereupon it becomes an epidemic like the Black Death that stalked through Europe in the Middle Ages. It now ranges all over the world. The people of Corfu were blessed with a magnificent, magical inheritance, an island of staggering beauty, probably one of the most beautiful islands in the whole of the Mediterranean. What they have done with it is vandalism beyond belief.

...Tourists [in those days] were a mixed and unlovely bunch—as indeed they are today, for the species does not appear to have changed but just increased in numbers. There were two color varieties— bright scarlet and peeling or fish-belly white. They seemed mainly composed of anemic English and Germans....These were the horrors of tourism in 1935.

...Returning in the early sixties, I could see the signs that warned of what the future had in store. A few hotels, apparently designed by Salvador Dali aided by an inmate of the Corfu lunatic asylum, had sprung up along one of Corfu's greatest assets, her lovely seacoast. There these monsters crouched along her shoreline like decaying teeth.

...[Today], I know it would be foolish and untruthful to say that there is nothing left of the beauty of Corfu, but what there is, is rapidly vanishing. The beauty that is left hardly compensates for having your terrace, your breakfast, and your guests drenched with insecticide from low-flying planes. It hardly compensates for a half-mile-long, six-feet-wide coastal slick of suntan oil (smelling like every stale beach resort)....[N]ature, once destroyed, can never be re-created, and nature is just as much part of the cultural heritage of a country as its monuments or cathedrals.

Source: Excerpted from *European Travel & Life*, July/August, 1988

✔ Case 18-3
Fiji Islands: Tourism Development Strategy[5]

The timing could not have been worse. Teresa Lauder (Knowlton Mathieson Consultants, Auckland, New Zealand) received a letter from Mr. Stephane Somfich (Executive Vice-President, International Finance Corporation—World Bank, Washington, D.C.) informing her that Knowlton Mathieson had been given approval to proceed with Phases 1 and 2 of the Tourism Assessment and Strategic Recommendations for the Fiji Islands. Somfich had requested that a preliminary opportunities assessment and strategy for development be completed in six weeks time.

The only person in the office sufficiently knowledgeable about the process of conducting a strategic assessment was Colin Brookes, a junior partner. For years, Teresa's firm had been pursuing projects sponsored by the World Bank, but to no avail. As Teresa had learned from others, the World Bank was both a high-profile client and one difficult to please.

Mr. Berenado Rhunibado (Honourable Minister for Tourism, Civil Aviation and Energy in Suva, Fiji) had expressed his position regarding the project in a prior conversation with Teresa:

> ...Local supplies of capital are insufficient to meet total capital requirements. Whether or not Fiji can achieve its tourism targets will depend substantially on the ability of the country to attract foreign capital to its tourist industry.

Many of Fiji's hotels, resorts, and attractions were not up to international standards. Fijians were very hospitable, but there was growing concern that tourism had caused an increased incidence of alcoholism, drug addiction, crime, and traffic congestion.

"I mention these points," said Teresa to Colin, "only to encourage you to consider the complexities of island tourism. Here is my file. I have set aside a few hours next Monday so that we can meet to thrash out the details. Come prepared to express your thoughts about (1) the current issues and underlying constraints, as well as the challenges and opportunities that the Fijian visitor industry needs to address; and (2) a framework that concentrates on the components as well as the procedures for developing a thorough strategic assessment."

Fiji and International Tourism

Fiji's visitor industry was the largest in the South Pacific region (see Exhibit 18-3-1 for location and major islands) and, with the decline of sugar prices, it had become increasingly important to the economy. In 1989 Fiji received about 60 percent of total visitor arrivals to the South Pacific islands. The spending associated with 250,000 visitors accounted for 12 percent of gross domestic product (GDP), 25 percent of foreign exchange earnings, and provided employment, directly or indirectly, to 20,000 people. The National Development Plan targeted 400,000 annual visitors within four years, but political upheavals and other factors scotched that objective. Visitor arrivals rose to 279,000 in 1990 and the value of their gross expenditures increased to F$335.9 million. Average daily expenditure was US$110. Actual arrivals for 1991 were expected to fall to 259,000 and were expected to drop again in subsequent years. This was well above arrivals in neighboring islands such as New Caledonia (82,000), Solomon Islands (10,000), Vanautu (24,000), Papua New Guinea (49,000), but much below the Philippines (1,076,000). (Exhibit 18-3-2 shows Fiji's position and neighbors in the South Pacific.) Obviously, a recovery was contingent on finding a long-term solution to the problems.

From a global perspective, there were over 450 million worldwide international arrivals in 1990—a 1.6 percent increase from 1989 and a 4.1 percent annual growth rate from 1980. Receipts amounted to US$250 billion, a 4.8 percent increase from 1989, for an 8.4 percent av-

[5]We are grateful to Professor K. Michael Haywood, University of Guelph, and Laurel J. Walsh, International Strategies Inc., Boston, for contributing this case.

EXHIBIT 18-3-1 Location of Fiji and its major islands

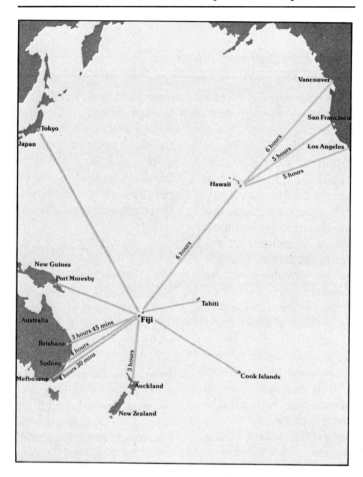

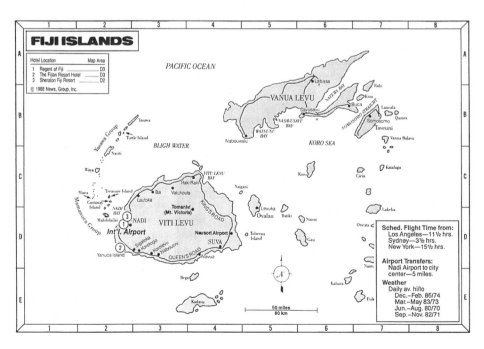

EXHIBIT 18-3-2   Fiji's position in the South Pacific

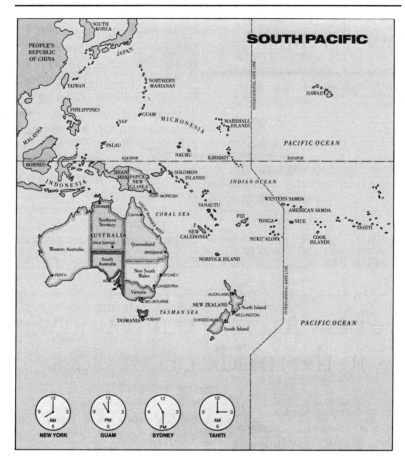

erage annual growth rate since 1980. East Asia and the Pacific represented the region with the biggest gain in international arrivals and receipts. Market share of arrivals in this region rose from 7.01 percent in 1980 to 19.94 percent in 1990. Receipts increased from 7.31 percent to 15.87 percent during the same period (World Tourism Organization, 1990).

With sustained economic development, absence of conflict and acts of terrorism, total worldwide international tourist arrivals of 615 million and 700 million were forecast for 1995 and 2005, respectively. Global receipts (at 1989 value) from international tourism were expected to rise by 8 percent a year, reaching more than US$527 billion in the year 2000. Regions recording higher-than-average growth of arrivals were

expected to be Asia/Oceania, the Americas, and Africa, all at the expense of Europe, the share of which was forecast as falling from 62 percent in international arrivals in 1989 to 53 percent by the year 2000. Asia/Oceania's share of international tourist arrivals was expected to show the greatest increase and was forecasted to rise from 14.7 percent in 1989 to 21.9 percent in 2000, while the region's rise in receipts was likely to be even more significant—from 19.5 percent in 1989 to 30.5 percent in 2000 (World Tourism Organization, 1991).

Tourism and Fiji

Mass tourism did not develop in Fiji until the late 1960s, when there were only 15,000 annual arrivals. For five years there was rapid growth. Fiji's first downward slump in tourism began with the global energy crisis in the 1970s. Cyclones, Fiji's dollar appreciation against the Australian dollar, longer-range aircraft overflying the islands, and political unrest caused continuing problems until the mid-1980s, when growth resumed, peaked in 1990, and then turned downward again. The global recession did nothing to help the situation.

Approximately 90 percent of Fiji's arrivals were by plane. The remainder were by boat and cruise ship, but these sea arrivals had suffered too and were only one-half of what they had been five years before. Most cruise ship passengers stayed two to three days.

Fiji's primary source and longer-average-stay markets (10–11 days) were Australia and New Zealand; these tended to be younger markets with families. Foreign carriers joined forces with travel wholesalers who distributed Fiji's product in these source markets. The growth potential of these two short-haul, price-sensitive markets was low because Fiji had already achieved considerable penetration and other destinations were being used more. In fact, these markets may have peaked in 1987, and they had been on a downward trend since.

The North American market was stagnant, with actual declines occurring in visitation rates. This market was a more senior one, generally traveling in couples. Many of these tourists were on multi-country group package tours and sought destinations comparable to Hawaii. Average length of stay was 5–7 days, short compared to the European markets (7–9 days), which were also relatively stagnant.

The Japanese market, on the other hand, tended to be younger and appeared to be increasing, although not rapidly. Single-destination, short-duration travel patterns (4–5 days) characterized this market. The fact that neighboring destinations in the Pacific received a substantial and growing volume of Japanese visitors demonstrated the potential. It was reported, however, that Fiji lacked the amenities and standards considered essential by this market. Table 18-3-1 shows a breakdown by major markets.

Tourism Supply—Hotels

Fiji's 125 visitor accommodations provided 4,365 rooms in 1990. Hotels ranged from the 300-room, chain-operated hotels (Regent, Hyatt, Sheraton, Shangri-La, Travelodge), to smaller, owner-operated resorts, typically on the outer islands, to budget hotels on the main islands. The upscale resorts were mainly dependent on international visitors and were targeted toward upper- and mid-market segments. Many North American visitors and Japanese honeymooners traveling on independent trips tended to select such resorts.

Over the last three years, 16 new resorts had been developed—mainly small, offshore resorts on the west coast of Viti Levu catering to the middle and upper sections of the market. Half were open for business, the others still under construction. Two vacant hotel properties were reopened during this period, and some major upgrading and expansion work had been undertaken at existing resorts. These developments would add 600 rooms to the total. Average annual occupancy rates hovered around the 50 percent mark.

It was estimated that 1,200 additional, mainly up-market hotel rooms would be required to accommodate an 80 percent desired increase in visitor levels in the medium term. Investment proposals valued at approximately US$1.2 billion, and involving more than 8,000 rooms, had been put forward by the private sector and approved by government. While not all were likely to be implemented, a doubling of existing capacity was possible in the medium term.

Tourism Supply—Attractions

The Fiji Islands were endowed with a glorious climate and varied sea- and landscapes. It was a popular destination for game fishing, sailing, and scuba diving; numerous boats and charters operated off the main islands. Various small cruise boats offered two- and three-day package tours to the outer islands; this activity showed the potential for expansion. Two domestic airlines operated among the islands.

EXHIBIT 18-3-3   Structure of the Fiji tourist industry

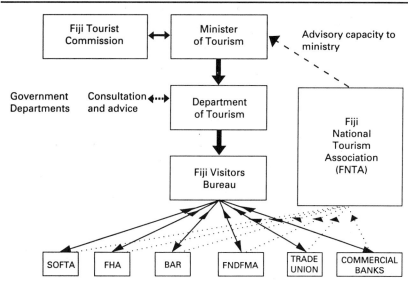

Source: Tourism Council of the South Pacific

Fiji's climate was ideal for golf, especially popular with Japanese visitors. Although there were a number of golf courses, it would take upgrading to international standards to position Fiji in the upscale golf market.

About 17 percent of visitors participated in organized island tours. The low demand was attributed to a combination of a lack of overall marketing, limited tourist spending power, and a lack of developed activities. There was a consensus that the industry needed to develop more tourist activities. The island had potential for festivals, special events, marine life exhibits, and man-made attractions, all of which would enhance the destination and ensure higher retention of the visitor dollar. Some progress was being made.

Tourism Supply—Transportation

Fiji was accessible from most parts of the world, via either the local Air Pacific or Air New Zealand, Quantas, and Polynesian Airlines. A reduction in airline capacity on the North American routes remained a most serious problem, not only for Fiji, but for the region as a whole. Continental Airlines' withdrawal (due largely to

a dispute with Australian authorities and Quantas) resulted in reduced seat capacity and the loss of promotion and sales support. In effect, this action reversed a strong growth trend in the North American market. Restoration and maintenance of withdrawn schedules and capacity on the trans-Pacific routes were vital for Fiji and the rest of the South Pacific region. Indeed, Fiji was the only gateway for the redistribution of visitor traffic flows to other island countries. The practical implication of Fiji's strategically-important location was the promotion of regional tour packages using Fiji as a hub. Fiji had no departure tax and the government lacked strong aviation policies.

The Fiji Visitor Industry

The Fiji government had taken an active interest in the tourist industry, providing incentives to interested parties and regulations to ensure proper functioning. The government had also been concerned about the impact of tourism on Fiji's society as a whole. The development of tourism ventures had been limited to carefully-chosen areas of the country, but potential investors had shown interest in developing other ar-

EXHIBIT 18-3-4   Strategic planning model for tourism development

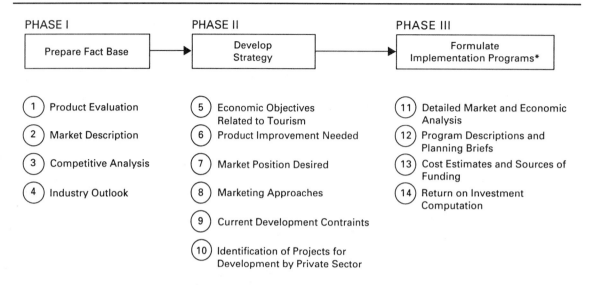

PHASE I — Prepare Fact Base
1. Product Evaluation
2. Market Description
3. Competitive Analysis
4. Industry Outlook

PHASE II — Develop Strategy
5. Economic Objectives Related to Tourism
6. Product Improvement Needed
7. Market Position Desired
8. Marketing Approaches
9. Current Development Contraints
10. Identification of Projects for Development by Private Sector

PHASE III — Formulate Implementation Programs*
11. Detailed Market and Economic Analysis
12. Program Descriptions and Planning Briefs
13. Cost Estimates and Sources of Funding
14. Return on Investment Computation

* These will be related to specific projects for implementation by the private sector.

Source: Arthur D. Little, Inc. Washington, D.C.

eas. The government always tried to seek the approval of the local inhabitants before giving the go-ahead for hotel and resort construction. Priority was always given to landowners who wished to develop tourism ventures, financed with the help of the Fiji Development Bank and Hotel Aid Assistance from the Ministry of Tourism. Table 18-3-2 provides a profile of the country.

The Fiji National Tourist Association (FNTA) played an important role in advising the government on behalf of the various organizations that it represented. Exhibit 18-3-3 shows its composition and Table 18-3-3 explains its structure.

Conclusion

Aware of Teresa Lauder's anxiety, Colin Brookes reassured her that he was up to the task. But as she left his office, he began to wonder. Was the traditional strategic-planning model appropriate in this situation (Exhibit 18-3-4)? Could he produce a document that would assist all stakeholders in developing strategies that could master the present and preempt the future? Would it persuade the World Bank to put up the money?

TABLE 18-3-1   Visitor Arrivals by Major Market

Market	1990	1991 (est.)
Australia	103,535	86,600
New Zealand	29,432	30,600
USA	36,928	31,800
Canada	18,438	15,200
United Kingdom	16,733	16,500
Germany	(a)	9,800
Other Europe	27,211	16,400
Japan	21,619	27,800
Other Asia	(b)	7,400
Pacific Islands	17,528	16,200
Other Countries	7,532	800
Total	278,966	259,100

Note: (a) included in Other Europe; (b) included in Other Countries.
Cruise ship passenger arrivals not included
Source: Bureau of Statistics, Fiji

TABLE 18-3-2   Fiji Islands: A Profile of the Country

Fiji is located in the South Pacific 3,000 kilometers (1,875 miles) east of Australia and about 1,930 km (1,200 miles) south of the equator. It comprises 322 islands (18,333 square kilometers or 7,078 square miles), 105 of which are uninhabitable. Each island is quite distinctive. The two largest are Viti Levu and Vanua Levu with extinct volcanoes rising abruptly from the sea. There are thousands of streams and rivers in Fiji, the largest being the Kioa River on Viti Levu, navigable for 148 km (80 miles). Mt. Victoria, also on Viti Levu, is the country's highest peak, at 1,322 m (4,430 ft). The Great Sea Reef is located between Viti Levu and Vanua Levu. The Astrolabe Reef south of Viti Levu offers spectacular coral reefs and diving. There is another 19-mile reef located southeast of Vanua Levu.

People

Native Fijians are a mixture of Polynesian and Melanesian stock. The estimated population is 735,985, 48.8% Indian and 46% mixed Polynesian and Melanesian people. Most of the population lives in rural areas. The main languages are Fijian and Hindi. English is the official language and is widely spoken. The majority of Fijians are Christian (Methodist and Roman Catholic), while the majority of Indo-Fijians are Hindu. A strictly fundamentalist Methodist version of Christianity is enshrined in the Fijian Constitution. Constitution.

Climate

Fiji enjoys a South Sea tropical climate. Maximum summer temperatures (January, February) average 30C (86F) and the mean minimum is 23C (73F). The winter average maximum (July, August) is 26C (79F) and the mean minimum is 20C (68F). The temperatures are much cooler in the uplands of the interior of the larger islands. A cooling trade wind blows from the east-south-east for most of the year.

Social Profile

International cuisine is available, but local Fijian and Indian cooking prevails. The Fijian *lovo* feast of meats, fish, and vegetables cooked in covered pits is served in a number of hotels and restaurants. Local beers, imported wines, and distilled products are available. Throughout Fiji the drinking of *yaqona* (pronounced "yanggona") or *kava* is common. It is made from the root of the pepper plant and, although it has become a social drink, the *yaqona* drinking ceremony is still important in the Fijian tradition.

Major hotels and resorts have live bands and music during the evening, and there are a number of nightclubs. Most of Fiji's social life, however, is in private clubs, in which visitors can obtain temporary membership through hotels. Fijian entertainment (*mokeo*) is offered by the hotels on a rotating basis.

Fully-equipped fishing launches operate from a number of hotels. Swimming, waterskiing, snorkeling, diving, and sailing are common resort-based activities. Dangerous reef waves prevent surfing. There are two 18-hole and numerous 9-hole golf courses. Tennis and volleyball are popular on-shore activities, as is horseback riding.

There are a number of major festivals and special events celebrated annually in Fiji. Visitors may not appreciate, however, the elaborate symbolism of the ritual codes that are suggestive of ethnic antagonism between Indians and Fijians.

Business Profile

The economy is largely agricultural, sugar being the main product. Together with tourism, these two industries comprise 90% of Fiji's foreign export earnings. Copra, once the second most important

(continued)

TABLE 18-3-2   (continued)

product, has been overtaken by gold, fish, and timber. Low-grade copper deposits have been discovered, although it is not clear whether they will be exploited. There are a number of light industrial enterprises, and the government is looking to develop exports by offering tax incentives. Textiles have started to develop under these incentives, and it is hoped that shipping services (repair yards and boat building), as well as the timber industry, will develop along the same lines. Fiji's largest trading partners are Australia, New Zealand, the U.S., and the U.K.

Fijians own 83% of the land as communal property, which may not be leased without consent of the Native Land Trust Board, the government agency that administers leases of native land.

History and Government

As the rivalry of the European imperial powers spread in the Pacific during the late nineteenth century, Fiji fell under British control. The British brought in a large number of workers from India to develop a plantation economy. By the 1960s Indian descendants formed the majority community on the islands, leading to social tensions between them and the indigenous Fijians. Fiji gained independence from Britain in the early 1970s. In the elections of April, 1987, Indians won a majority in Parliament for the first time. This was a trigger for an army coup d'tat to ensure the preservation of native Fijian rights. There was an interim military government, pending a new Constitution. Constitutional reforms were discussed and approved by the Great Council of Chiefs, comprised of the country's hereditary leaders, after which negotiations began in September 1987 involving leaders of all parties. The resulting state of affairs led to another coup at the end of that month, and several key aides were removed.

A new Constitution came into force in July, 1990, allowing for a bicameral legislature comprising a 70-seat House of Representatives and a Senate of Chiefs with 34 appointed members. The seats in the House are divided along ethnic lines, with 37 seats elected by ethnic Fijians, 27 by Indians, and the remainder by others.

TABLE 18-3-3   Components of the Structure of the Fijian Tourist Industry

1. *Fiji Tourist Commission*

Established by government ordinance, the Commission consists of the Minister responsible for tourism and two other ministers appointed by the Prime Minister. Its main role is to set broad policies by which the whole tourist industry is to function, taking into account at all times the cultures and customs of the people of Fiji.

2. *Minister of Tourism*

The role of the Minister of Tourism (a combined portfolio with Civil Aviation and Energy) is to decide on specific policies of the tourist industry, including civil aviation and bilateral air agreements, in consultation with the Tourist Commission and the FNTA. Similarly with the Hotel Licensing Board and the Director of the Department of Tourism, the Minister decides on the issuing of licences to build hotels and resorts.

3. *Department of Tourism*

Reporting directly to the Minister of Tourism, this department coordinates and implements the policies handed down by the decision-making bodies. It conducts research aimed at improving the operation of the tourist industry, including development of education and training programs for personnel at all levels of the industry.

The following tourism objectives were outlined in the Department of Tourism's National Development Plan:

   a) Ensure that tourism is in harmony with national development policies.
   b) Increase the use of local agricultural and other produce in hotels, to enhance linkages with the rest of the economy.
   c) Provide greater opportunities for local entrepreneurs to invest in hotels and related industries, and employ local people at senior- and middle-management levels.
   d) Encourage small-scale secondary activity of local entrepreneurs by providing basic infrastructure, physical resources, and credit.
   e) Increase the level of tourism awareness among the local people and visitors to Fiji.
   f) Ensure that adverse effects on local customs and cultures are avoided.

4. *Fiji Visitors Bureau*

The FVB is a statutory body, headed up by a General Manager. Its primary role is to promote and market Fiji as a potential tourist destination, mainly in Australia, New Zealand, the United States, and Japan.

5. *Sector Organizations*

Directly under the FVB come the various sector organizations that make up the Tourist Industry:

   a) SOFTA (Society of Fiji Travel Agents).
   b) FHA (Fiji Hotel Association), consisting of independent hotel owners.
   c) BAR (Board of Airline Representatives) from government and other airlines.
   d) FNDFMA (Fiji National Duty Free Merchants Association), consisting of independent merchants.
   e) Trade Unions (of hotel employees).
   f) Commercial Banks (banking center centre within Fiji).

(continued)

TABLE 18-3-3   (continued)

Each sector sends two representatives to sit on the FNTA (Fiji National Tourism Association). The FNTA works in an advisory capacity to the Minister of Tourism.

6. *FNTA (Fiji National Tourism Association)*

The FNTA is made up of: (a) two representatives from each of SOFTA, FHA, BAR, FNDFMA, trade unions, and commerce/banks; (b) the town clerk; (c) the FNTA's chairman; (d) the FNTA's secretary. The role of the FNTA is to work together with the Ministry of Tourism on behalf of the various organizations it represents. It has the potential to create better conditions for the bodies it represents, and for the improvement of the tourist industry as a whole.

✔ Case 18-4
Thailand Tourism[6]

Thailand, a nation of more than 55 million people, is today one of the developing world's most dynamic economies. A favorable economic climate in the 1980s propelled the Thai economy into achieving one of the highest growth rates in the world, with an average annual increase of 10 percent in the Gross Domestic Product (GDP) from 1986 to 1990. Tourism played an ever-increasing and crucial role in the growth and development of the economy and was Thailand's largest source of foreign exchange earnings. Strong marketing efforts by both the public and private sector were credited for the rapid growth of tourist arrivals from 1.85 million in 1980 to 5.3 million in 1990. Table 18-4-1 shows the changes in arrivals from 1976 to 1991.

Thailand's tourism industry, however, faced new challenges in 1991. While the government had pushed both tourism growth and export industry growth to improve the economy, it did so at the expense of the long-term health of tourism. As the economy grew, pollution and traffic worsened and were not addressed; an AIDS problem and political unrest also added to problems. As the government was promoting tourism, it was not addressing the issues that would eventually lead to the challenges the tourism industry now faced.

Tourism Development in Thailand

Tourism development and promotion in Thailand attracted the attention of the Thai government in 1979 when tourism was included in the Fourth National Economic and Social Development Plan (1972–1981) as an integral part of its national economic development policy. The plan was aimed at strengthening the Thai economy in the areas of international trade, investment, and tourism to boost foreign exchange earnings and to create and expand employment opportunities. The success of the policy was evident

when tourism became the fastest-growing and most important sector of the Thai economy. Along with the increase in arrivals, tourism income increased more than three-and-a-half times, from $1.2 billion in 1985 to $4.3 billion in 1990.

The success of tourism promotion in Thailand from 1987 to 1988 rested largely on the high level of cooperation between the public and private sector. In celebration of the 60th birthday of King Rama IX and his status as the longest-reigning monarch of the Chakri dynasty, the year 1987 was declared as "Visit Thailand Year." As part of the celebration, festivals, fairs, processions, and cultural displays were organized throughout the country. A diversity of tourist experiences in national parks and historical sites was provided. The scope of activities was expanded to promote the cultural heritage, history, folk arts and crafts, and natural environment of Thailand. Special tour packages were also introduced, combining several Thai destinations: Bangkok plus Chiang Mai, the principal northern city in the mountains; and Pattaya or Phuket, eastern and southern coastal resort areas, the latter being an island approximately the size of Singapore. Exhibit 18-4-1 shows the location and areas of Thailand. International marketing efforts created a strong presence at trade shows in the main tourist markets of Europe, North America, Asia, and Australia. The marketing campaign continued in 1988–1989 with the promotion of the "Thailand Arts and Crafts Year." These marketing efforts were fruitful, as evidenced by the increase of visitor arrivals over these years.

Asia and Pacific markets represented about 60 percent of all arrivals in Thailand in 1990 with over 3.1 million tourists, an increase of almost 12 percent over the previous year. Taiwan and South Korea markets provided the largest growth rates, largely due to the lifting of overseas travel restrictions in those two countries. Visitor arrivals from Australia, Japan, and Singapore continued to grow during the

---

[6]This case was contributed by Professor Kye-Sung (Kaye) Chon, Ph.D., University of Nevada/Las Vegas.

EXHIBIT 18-4-1   The location of Thailand in Southeast Asia

period. European visitors increased more than 11 percent over 1989. This increase coincided with the relative decline of European arrivals in Mediterranean destinations. Tourist arrival statistics are shown in Table 18-4-2.

The rapid growth and success of the Thai tourism industry was attributed to a number of factors. The prosperity and high economic growth rate of Asian countries was a major one in encouraging regional travel. Asian economic growth recorded the world's largest average annual expansion at 5.5 percent. As a result, Asian tourists from newly-industrialized countries like South Korea and Malaysia traveled in greater numbers.

At the same time, tourists from West Germany and Japan, Thailand's major markets for many years, recorded increases in arrivals as their countries continued to lead in world economic performance. A rising trend in long-haul travel in Europe and North America, spurred by larger and more fuel-efficient jet aircraft that facilitated nonstop travel, increased Thailand's role as a popular commercial aviation hub. Thailand also occupied an advantageous geographical location because it was a convenient stopover or transit point between Europe, Australia, and the Far East. Accordingly, new air links were established with other airlines that created new markets in Canada, Finland, Spain, and Switzerland.

Along with the expansion of the tourism sector, there was a corresponding boom in the lodging industry. Average occupancy rates in Thailand increased from about 60 percent in 1986 to 87 percent in 1990. At the same time, average room rates more than tripled, from about $30 in 1986 to $114 in 1990, but posed no threat to demand due to a shortage of rooms. Thus, through special incentives the Thai government introduced policies that promoted hotel construction in order to encourage investment in the lodging industry. Hotel industry statistics are shown in Table 18-4-3.

In an effort to lengthen the visitor's stay, tour operators diversified their package tours by combining trips to remote border areas with trips into Indochina. Consequently, the number of repeat visitors returning to Thailand increased from 1.8 million out of 3.5 million total visitors in 1987 to 2.3 million out of 4.8 million in 1989. Overall, about 47 percent of all tourists to Thailand were repeat visitors. Germany, Switzerland, Australia, Malaysia, and Singapore provided the bulk of repeat visitors. Repeat visitors were attracted by the opportunities to travel upcountry and experience the diverse attractions of northern and southern cultural and historical sites, jungle treks, beaches, and scuba-diving.

Challenges

After four years of extensive tourism growth from 1987 to 1990, the Thai tourism industry started experiencing difficulties that led to lower arrivals and depressed market conditions in 1991 and 1992. The rapid expansion had brought forth mass tourism, resulting in the deterioration and disorderliness of the tourism industry. The Persian Gulf War and world economic recession in North America and Europe, as well as political unrest, pollution, high prices, competition, and hotel room oversupply, disrupted tourism. Fairly expensive airfares and hotel room rates, especially in Bangkok, made European packages to Thailand 20 percent more expensive than those to alternative destinations such as Singapore. In addition, the country's tourism industry failed to market itself aggressively after the successful campaigns that took place from 1987 to 1990.

Thailand's woes continued with the airplane crash and pillaging of a Lauda Air 767 in late May 1991, attracted widespread media and public attention in key markets. Together with an ongoing image problem over AIDS, the sex industry, and environmental neglect at some destinations, Thailand's positive tourist image began to decline in the minds of visitors, primarily from the negative publicity. Consequently, tourists were avoiding Thailand in favor of Singapore, Malaysia, and Indonesia (especially Bali). From 1989 to 1991, visitor arrivals in Indonesia increased from 1.6 million to 2.2 million, while the visitor arrivals in Malaysia increased from 3.9 million to 7.5 million.

Another major contributing factor in Thailand's slide was the winding down of Thailand's economic and investment boom. Overall, the effects of various constraints led to a decline in tourist arrivals in 1991, by about 4 percent, to 5.1 million.

Environmental Impacts

The Persian Gulf War was a severe blow to European and Middle East airlines since it forced the suspension of services to Thailand and rerouted others. Flight cancellations from Europe and Asia reached 20 percent and 15 percent, respectively, in the first three months of 1991 alone. As many as 20 percent of tour operators in Thailand went out of business, and the cancellations cost the tour trade at least $20 million in lost bookings. European inbound tourism received the brunt of the decrease. The impact was heightened by a terrorist warning in Thailand that affected arrivals from North America, Australia, and the United Kingdom. The overall impact was a 35 percent cancellation of visitors from Japan, Europe, and North America. Occupancy rates declined; for example, the occupancy rate for Bangkok's five luxury hotels (Oriental, Regent, Dusit Thani, Hilton, and Shangri-La) dropped in January 1991 to about 60 percent, from 85 percent for the same period in 1990.

Socioculture The spread of AIDS in Thailand, primarily among Thai citizens, coincided with the boom in international tourism toward the late 1980s. Thailand found itself saddled with an image of a "sexual paradise," an image problem only heightened when connected with AIDS and prostitution—the risk of contracting AIDS discouraged many tourists from visiting Thailand. More than 300,000 Thais were thought to be HIV positive, and this figure was expected to increase rapidly. Facing a downfall in tourist arrivals, the Thai tourism authorities minimized the existence and threat of the disease so that Thailand would not lose its attractiveness as a tourist destination—in other words, they sensed no threat from AIDS and did not take any restrictive or preventive measures to protect those at risk.

Overbuilding The effects of overbuilding were more strongly felt in Bangkok than in the rest of the country. Lower occupancies and average room rates were the result. The arrival slump could hardly have come at a worse time. From 1990 to 1992, the supply of rooms in Bangkok doubled to almost 40,000 rooms, while the average hotel occupancy rate in the city was below 60 percent.

Bangkok hotel prices had risen 250 percent between 1987 and 1990. Higher occupancies had prompted hotels to break their contracts with tour operators and turn away leisure guests in favor of full-fare business guests. As a result of the excess supply and downfall in tourist arrivals, room rates fell by 25 percent in Bangkok in 1991 while the decline nationwide was up to 50 percent.

Ecology The ravaging of Thailand's environment by rapid industrialization contributed to problems of pollution in cities, resorts, and beaches. The air in Bangkok became highly polluted. European tour cancellations were attributed to the high level of pollution in Bangkok and at some resorts such as Pattaya. A report of the National Environment Board said that coral reefs around some of the country's main islands were being damaged by litter and boats dragging their anchors. Additionally, tourists were spending more time in the northern city of Chiang Mai, or in the resort island of Phuket or Ko Samui in the south, to avoid the traffic congestion in Bangkok.

Economy International investors were seeking alternatives to Thailand in Southeast Asia for their investments, citing inability of successive Thai administrations to correct severe infrastructure defects, especially Bangkok's rapidly deteriorating traffic network.

Political Since the fall of the absolute monarchy in 1932, Thailand had experienced ten successful coups, a number of failed ones, and 14 new constitutions. Another bloodless military coup in late February, 1991 resulted in the overthrow of the government. Tourists from Japan, Taiwan, and Hong Kong, who were highly conscious of political instability, chose other destinations. Coupled with the Persian Gulf War, tourist arrivals from Asia fell by 20 percent.

The pro-democracy uprising in late May 1992 resulted in a major blow to the Thai economy and tourism industry. As a result of the uprising, the National Economic and Social Development Board (NESDB) revised its pre-May projection of GDP growth from 7.9 percent to 7.6 percent for 1992. The most immediate effect, however, was on the tourism industry, likely to incur a potential loss of millions of dollars in tourism revenues. Tourism revenue, which in 1991 brought in $4.48 billion, fell to $4.28 billion from a previously-estimated $5 billion.

Overall Impact The severest blow came from canceled bookings by Japanese tourists, who constituted the lion's share of Thailand's tour market. Cancellations by Japanese, who comprised the second largest group of arrivals after Malaysia in 1991, ran as high as 40 percent. Airlines were also affected. Singapore Airlines cancelled a number of flights and Thai Airways cancelled more than 200 scheduled flights during the crisis. Many Thai professionals even boycotted the airline to protest its military ties.

In the lodging industry, Bangkok's premier hotels reported occupancies of 20 percent to 30 percent, down from normal occupancy rates of about 60 percent. Pattaya hotels were less than 30 percent full, while occupancies of hotels in Chiang Mai and Phuket ranged between 30 percent and 35 percent. Average occupancy for the nation as a whole was far below 60 percent for 1992. Prices and average rates fell rapidly.

Despite the crisis, new hotels continued to open and worsened the over building situation. The 700-room Sol Twin Towers and the 420-room Royal Garden Riverside opened in June of 1992, adding another 1,000 rooms to the supply in Bangkok. New hotels such as the luxurious Sukhotai, Grand Hyatt Erawan, and Mansion Kempinski were under pressure to discount rooms, following the lead of other hotels in Bangkok, as a way of surviving the slack season and building market share. For example, the Grand Hyatt Erawan cut its listed room rates by 30 percent, while the Sukhotai, which had an occupancy of less than 30 percent, discounted its rooms by 40–50 percent.

The political unrest, however, was instrumental in arousing the nation and drawing the world's attention to the magnitude of the problems facing Thailand—and the need to take immediate action. The eventual price Thailand would have to pay to restore its image and credibility hinged on an orderly, timely, and wholehearted commitment to resolve the current problems and revive the ailing tourism industry through vigorous marketing and promotion.

Marketing Strategies for a Turnaround

The most important aspect of the tourism revival campaign was the cooperation between the private and public sector, a cooperative effort that had been absent since the highly successful "Visit Thailand Year" in 1987. The Tourist Authority of Thailand (TAT), the NTO of Thailand, embarked on a tourism recovery program to restore the tourism industry. TAT's first objective, aimed at the high-spending Japanese tourists, was to assure them that Thailand was safe to visit. Advertising and promotion in major tourist markets was also aimed at restoring confidence among tourists that Thailand was a safe and stable country.

The second objective addressed the problems of pollution, cheating, touting, and tourist hijacks that had become rampant and gained notoriety. Familiarization trips to Thailand for the foreign press and travel agents were conducted by Thai tourism representatives to encourage travel to Thailand. TAT also increased its presence in Japan, South Korea, and Taiwan by opening three new sales offices in 1992. Airlines, travel agents, and hoteliers restructured low-cost holiday packages to entice visitors. To avoid sparking rate wars, hotels emphasized value by offering free upgrades and complimentary extra room-nights.

Promotion A major public relations and promotional campaign, called "The World Our Guest," was developed in August 1992 to coincide with the 60th birthday of Queen Sirikit. An estimated 11,000 visitors to Thailand were given free hotel rooms, airline tickets, meals, and tours as part of the promotion, which was declared an unqualified success by the TAT. The campaign was intended to kick-start Thailand's declining tourism industry.

Image-Changing Due to the AIDS crisis, the government attempted to change the tourist image by stressing the bargain shopping and cultural and natural attractions of Thailand, rather than sexual attractions. Even the new Thai Prime Minister, Chuan Leek-Pai, who was elected in September 1992, vowed to restore Thailand's image abroad by taking steps to clean the environment and to address the AIDS issue. His new cabinet of numerous financial advisers reflected the emphasis on economic development as a top priority.

TAT increased its cooperation with the national tourism authorities of the Association of Southeast Asian Nations (ASEAN) to promote multi-destination travel. The inauguration of "Visit ASEAN Year 1992" was an example of cooperative marketing by the tourism agencies of the six-member ASEAN countries: Thailand,

TABLE 18-4-1   International Tourist Arrivals in Thailand (1976–1991)

Year	Arrivals (000)	% Change
1976	1,098	—
1977	1,220	11.12
1978	1,453	19.10
1979	1,591	9.47
1980	1,858	16.80
1981	2,015	8.44
1982	2,218	10.06
1983	2,191	−1.24
1984	2,346	7.11
1985	2,438	3.90
1986	2,818	15.58
1987	3,482	23.59
1988	4,230	21.47
1989	4,809	13.68
1990	5,299	10.18
1991	5,100	−3.75

Source: Tourism Authority of Thailand

Malaysia, Indonesia, Brunei, Philippines, and Singapore. Furthermore, the year 1992 was designated as "Women's Visit Thailand Year" in order to encourage more women to visit a country where the ratio of male tourists was unusually high. The opening of the Bangkok national convention center, in Bangkok, with a seating capacity of 10,000 (the largest in Asia) in its main hall, also spurred hotels to improve servicing of meetings and conferences in order to attract business travelers and market Thailand as a convention site.

Distribution The signing of a Cambodian Peace Treaty in October 1992 was a positive step that provided Thailand the opportunity to market itself as the gateway to Indochina for tourists desiring to visit Vietnam, Cambodia, or Laos. Tour operators combined tour packages that included trips to Indochina, such as Cambodia, to visit the historical and religious Angkor Wat. Since Indochina, especially Vietnam, was in the development stages of exploratory visits for overseas investments and tourism, Thailand benefited significantly by having direct access to Indochina's emerging markets.

Conclusion

Thailand's experience showed that tourism demands self-discipline, planning, and marketing to be successful. Whether or not Thailand will fulfill its promise as Asia's biggest holiday destination and regain its former stature will also depend upon the depth of commitment from the tourism industry, and the lessons learned about the results of inadequate planning.

TABLE 18-4-2   Tourist Arrivals in Thailand by Major Origins (1986–1990)

	1986	1987	1988	1989	1990
United States	196.4	235.8	257.6	340.0	367.8
Canada	36.7	44.2	56.2	61.6	69.0
N. America	233.1	280.0	313.8	401.6	436.8
% Change		+20.1%	+12.1%	+28.0	+8.8%
Germany	119.4	148.4	190.3	222.1	243.1
United Kingdom	147.2	184.4	279.6	200.3	227.9
France	100.4	131.6	157.3	187.0	197.4
Italy	52.0	65.9	86.4	92.5	108.1
Switzerland	38.1	45.1	60.1	75.3	81.1
Netherlands	34.0	41.5	50.8	54.1	63.5
Sweden	27.5	35.9	48.8	54.1	67.4
Europe	518.6	602.8	873.3	885.4	988.5
% Change		+16.2%	+44.9%	+1.3%	+11.6
Malaysia	652.9	765.2	867.6	736.0	751.6
Japan	259.4	341.9	449.1	555.6	652.3
Taiwan	111.2	194.7	188.7	399.7	503.2
Hong Kong	84.0	132.3	154.4	395.7	382.8
Singapore	194.1	240.0	248.5	290.4	335.7
Australia	94.7	110.7	138.4	218.9	252.2
South Korea	30.6	37.1	65.4	111.6	147.7
India	119.5	117.6	127.5	120.0	128.2
Asia/Pacific	1546.4	1939.5	2239.6	2827.9	3153.7
% Change		+25.4%	+15.5%	+26.3%	+11.5%

Source: Tourism Authority of Thailand

TABLE 18-4-3   Thailand Hotel Industry Statistics (1986–1990)

	1986	1987	1988	1989	1990
Number of Rooms	117,000	124,000	136,000	148,000	169,000
Average Room Rates (in US$)	$30.00	$62.10	$84.84	$101.26	$114.57
Average Occupancy	60.8%	82.6%	90.1%	87.1%	85.9%

Source: Tourism Authority of Thailand; World Tourism Organization

Glossary

Ad hoc group A tour group of customers, headed for a specific destination, that stays enroute at a hotel overnight. The enroute stay is a stopover and not part of the reason for the tour.

Account Management System Methodology for managing customer accounts in a sales office.

Airline market Housing of airline employees and crew members by a hotel on a contractual basis, normally over a period of at least one year. Also known as "base business."

Area of Dominant Influence (ADI) Specific geographic population bases determined by television audience but also used by newspaper and magazine media for distribution coverage.

Atmospherics In a positive sense, the conscious designing of a concept to create certain effects in buyers; the effort to design buying environments to produce specific emotional effects in the buyer that will enhance purchase probability. May also be negative.

Attitudes Affective component of the belief-attitude-behavior triad; emotional responses toward beliefs.

Augmented product The totality of all benefits received or experienced by the customer when purchasing the product.

Average check The method of tracking the spending habits of food customers, derived by dividing the total money collected within a meal period by the number of customers served. Some establishments include liquor purchased in the calculation.

Average Room Rate (ARR) The method to track the spending habits of rooms customers, derived by dividing the total money collected for room rent on a given day by the number of rooms sold; also called Average Daily Rate (ADR). Establishments may or may not include complimentary rooms, out-of-order rooms, and day-use rooms in the calculation.

Behavioral differences The ways in which one segment (customer) behaves differently from another. Can lead to conflict among segments.

Belief Something we think is fact (something we believe) about an object, for whatever reason or derivation. A belief is cognitive.

Benefits Serve the needs and wants of the consumer; what a feature can do for the customer; the reason that a customer needs or uses the feature or product.

Bimodal or strongly-skewed life cycle Two possible configurations of the product life cycle when it does not always follow a bell-shaped curve.

Break-even pricing Pricing to cover at least fixed costs beyond variable cost per unit.

Bus tour Travelers arriving at a hospitality establishment by motorcoach, as part of a total tour package.

Business purpose To create and keep a customer.

Business traveler Customer who utilizes a hospitality product because of a need to conduct business in the particular destination. This person usually travels alone or with a limited number of individuals.

Business Center A service offered by the hotel that includes some of the following: fax, secretarial services, copiers, conference rooms, computers, shipping, etc.

Cannibalized market An offering by the same company of a similar product to the same customer in the same market; giving the consumer an alternative to the existing hotel or restaurant, under the same ownership, when a customer gained is also a customer lost.

Cash flow pricing A strategy to maximize short-run revenues to generate cash.

Catering salesperson Handles meetings, banquets, and social events (such as weddings) that require few sleeping rooms.

Channels of distribution The means used to get the product to the customer; in hospitality it often means creating awareness and availability in order to get the customer to the product, often through other entities.

Chapter 11 bankruptcy The court protection of an existing business entity from its creditors. When a business is no longer viable and/or solvent, the courts will assist in the reorganization and/or the orderly distribution of assets to creditors. Chapter 11 is voluntary on the part of the organization to gain protection before it is forced into involuntary bankruptcy, usually so it can continue to operate. United States only.

Close Gaining a verbal or written commitment from the customer.

Closed probe A communications method used during a sales call to direct customers who may not be aware of their needs or cannot express those needs well.

Closing The customer makes a commitment to buy.

Cognitive dissonance A theory that recognizes a customer's potential uncertainty after the purchase decision has been made. A customer may believe that his or her choice of product was wrong, incorrect, or a mistake.

Collateral A term used in advertising to include brochures, fliers, cocktail napkins, matchbooks, and other promotional materials.

Communications mix The variety of methods used to tell the consumer about a product, including advertising, merchandising, promotions, public relations, and direct selling.

Communication strategy The purpose, or desired effect, of the communication to the marketplace before it has been decided how to say it.

Comparative group A target market that a customer may try to emulate. For example, teenagers may consider a rock band as a comparative group and make their product choices accordingly.

Compensatory models The purchase decision model that assumes the willingness to trade one feature for another in order to make the buy decision.

Competitive intelligence Includes information-gathering beyond industry statistics and trade gossip and involves close observation of competitors to learn what they do and why they do it.

Competitive strategy The firm chooses its competition and when and where it will compete. The firm then targets all its marketing forces towards the identified competitor(s).

Conceptitis A word we have coined to describe those people who are afflicted with total immersion in design concepts with little or no regard for how the customer will use the product.

Conference Center hotel A hotel that specializes in the meetings market.

Conjunctive model Consumers might establish a minimum acceptable level for each important product attribute and make a choice only if each attribute equals or exceeds the minimum level.

Consortium A loosely knit group of independently owned and managed hotels (or other companies such as travel agencies) with a joint marketing distribution process.

Construct validity Measuring what you think you are measuring; for example, ensuring the behavior pattern being measured is actually significant to the customer's buy decision.

Consumer demand Consists of the existing, latent, and incipient demand of consumers having a need for a specific product.

Contribution margin pricing A version of markup pricing that can be used to price a product. A margin is assigned to an offering above the variable cost to establish the price. The contribution is to fixed cost after the variable cost has been covered, even when there is no absolute profit.

Control The feedback loop of the marketing system, which includes research and marketing intelligence that tells if the system is working right.

Convention or conference services manager Hotel personnel assigned to handle conventions and conferences and their needs while at the hotel.

Core product What the customer is really buying, often abstract and intangible attributes.

Cost percentage or markup pricing Favored by the restaurant industry, this method features either a dollar markup on the variable ingredient-cost of the item, a percentage markup based on the desired ingredient cost percentage, or a combination of both.

Cost-plus pricing Establishing the total cost of a product, including overhead, plus a predetermined gross profit margin.

Cottage industries Small companies and businesses supply a major product offering and/or sell directly to the consumer.

Cover Generic term applied to a meal served; for instance, 20 customers in a restaurant are 20 covers.

Customized product The design of a product to fit the specific needs of a particular target market.

Data collection, external The assembling of information from environmental sources—such as currency rates, international terrorism, population growth, demographics, and

so on—that may indicate trends that affect the purchase decisions of customers.

Data collection, internal The assembling of information within the context of the hospitality establishment—such as average room rate, menu preferences, and so on—that may indicate trends that affect the purchase decisions of customers.

Data collection, primary The assembling of information directly from the consumer, as in consumer research.

Data collection, secondary The assembling of information from other sources that have collected it for another purpose.

Demand analysis An analysis of a market to determine whether it is ready, willing, and able to buy a specific product.

Demographic segmentation Customer definition based on geographic location, income, race, age, nationality, and so on.

Descriptive data Information that tells us who and what, but not why.

Descriptive quantitative research Research that tells us how many, how often, and what percentage, such as how old people are, their sex, or their income; provides means, standard deviations, and other statistics.

Designated Market Area (DMA) Developed by the A.C. Nielsen, a research company, these are geographic areas serviced by television stations. Data include demographic characteristics that can be used for reaching specific audiences; also used generically as a target merket area.

Determinant attributes Attributes that determine choice.

DEWKS Acronym for couples of dual employment, with kids; about 50 percent of U.S. married couples.

Differentiation The ability to convey to a customer a tangible or intangible advantage of one product over a competitive one.

DINKS Acronym for couples with a double income, no kids; about 18 percent of U.S. married couples.

Director of Marketing (as commonly applied) Within the hierarchy of a hospitality entity's organizational chart, the department head responsible for producing revenues, usually through the utilization of the communications mix. This position is normally found in larger hotels and restaurant chains. The Director of Marketing reports to the General Manager and oversees the position of Director of Sales, if applicable.

Director of Sales In smaller hospitality entities, the same job description as Director of Marketing applies. In larger organizations, this position reports to the Director of Marketing and heads the direct sales effort.

Disjunctive model The consumer establishes a minimum level of expectation based on only one or a few attributes.

Distribution strategy The process by which a hotel determines its options for channels of distribution.

Edifice/Oedipus complex An emphasis on the edifice or building as the primary selling point in the product and/or communications mix. When used pejoratively, the hotel structure fails to differentiate itself from other hotels in both a physical and positioning sense, thus losing any possible differentiation in the customer's mind. In Greek mythology, Oedipus was banished from the kingdom as a child; as an adult he returned and, ignorant of his heritage, murdered his father and wed his mother. In psychology, the term *Oedipus complex* is used to define a male who has a fixation for his mother. In the sense described above, the term "edifice complex" is used colloquially as a play on words to mean *not* recognizing the real reason people buy hotel rooms because of a fixation on the physical property.

Elasticity The economic model that establishes the relationship between pricing of a product and demand for the product.

Environmental scanning The analysis of trends that may affect both the production and the purchase of a product by the customer.

Expatriate Person who lives and works in a country not of his or her own origin or nationality.

Expectancy-value model Assumes that people have a measurement of belief about the existence of an attribute and that each attribute has an importance weight relative to the other attributes.

Expectation pricing Pricing according to what it is believed people expect to pay, regardless of intrinsic value.

External information Data gathered from distribution members such as suppliers, vendors, and local, state, and national agencies and associations.

Facilitating goods Tangible goods that accompany an intangible product or service to facilitate its purchase; for instance, airport limo service or an 800 reservation phone number.

Family life cycle Spans the basic stages of life (e.g., single, married, married with children, married with grown children, widowed), and how these stages affect the purchasing decision.

Feasibility study The thorough evaluation and determination of a business venture and its ability to perform in a marketplace. Market feasibility indicates market demand; financial feasibility indicates financial performance.

Feature A tangible or intangible component of a product that is offered to solve the customer's problem.

Fern bars A trendy concept of the 1970s that features an atmosphere filled with plants, brass, and glass.

Focus group An assemblage of typical customers used to discuss and critique products (typically determined by the use of screening techniques). A moderator normally leads the discussion of five to ten people.

Food and Beverage (F&B) The term applied to the department within a hotel that manages the food and beverage products.

Foreign or Free Independent Traveler (FIT) A visitor from another country, or simply any individual without a preset itinerary such as a package or tour; variously used in the industry.

Formal product The basic product customers think they are buying, such as a hotel room or a meal, as opposed to the core product.

Franchisee An organization or person that purchases a brand name to distribute the product or service.

Franchising A method for a hospitality entity to increase its distribution network, both to create more revenue and to obtain increased geographic presence. Management of the hospitality entity that is franchised is not retained by the parent company.

Franchisor The parent company of a franchising distribution network.

Freestanding A slang term for a customer who needs function or meeting space without accompanying guestrooms. This term can also be applied to food and beverage outlets not associated, or positioned not to be associated, with a host hotel.

Frequent-flyer programs Programs that reward the airline passenger for repeated patronage with free mileage credit toward future flights and other awards such as rental cars and hotel rooms.

Frequent traveler By industry definition, a traveler who spends at least ten nights per year in a hotel room for any number of reasons; also called frequent guest.

Frequent-traveler programs Emulation of frequent-flyer programs that offer free hotel rooms, upgrades, and other benefits and prizes for repeat patronage.

Functional strategies The "what" of the strategic system; that is, "what" we are going to do specifically within the marketing mix to reach the customer.

General Manager (GM) This position is normally the head of the individual hospitality entity, such as a restaurant or hotel.

Global Distribution Systems (GDS) These are the electronic booking processes by which hotel, car, and airline reservations services are made worldwide.

Goods Tangible, physical factors over which management has direct control; or, in other industries, manufactured goods.

Grazing restaurants A concept of restaurants where the customers are offered a variety of foods throughout the day and night; the customer is allowed to walk up to many food stations in the restaurant, sampling more than just one entree—hence the term *grazing*. Also used as a customer behavior where the customer may "nibble" at any time rather than at set meal periods.

Ground services Ancillary services such as transportation, tours, sight-seeing, etc., at a destination for arriving travelers.

Group product line For customers who purchase a number of rooms, catering, and related services.

Group market segment Five or more single attendees at a meeting whose purpose is business and/or pleasure, usually within the facilities of the hotel.

Group salesperson The member of the hotel sales force who handles the needs of customers booking ten or more hotel rooms at a time, and generally accompanying meeting space.

Hassle-free A common industry term that describes a customer's experience as being without any problems or hang-ups.

Heterogeneity Variation and lack of uniformity in a service being performed; also, variation of consumers in the marketplace.

Hospitality marketing mix Contains four major submixes: product/service mix, presentation mix, communications mix, and distribution mix.

Hospitality product The goods and services offered by the hospitality entity. The goods and services include guestrooms, food, beverages, health clubs, pools, and so on, and all services, whether included in the price or priced separately.

Importance attributes Items that are important to the consumer in making a choice of product, or in consuming the product, but are not necessarily determinant.

Inbound operator A channel of distribution that handles international travel to the host country from all locations outside the country; also handles ground services when the traveler arrives.

Incentive houses Companies that specialize in handling the needs of organizations that reward their employees with travel.

Incipient demand Demand for which even the customer does not yet recognize there is a need (i.e., the demand is in its embryonic stage.)

Incongruities Discrepancies between what is and what ought to be.

Inferential quantitative research This method allows the extrapolation of findings from a survey sample to a larger population base; for this sample, each person in the population being studied must have an equal chance of being selected in the sample.

Innovators A consumer term identifying those who are the first to try a new product.

In-plants Travel agencies that are located on the premises of a customer.

Intangible Unable to be perceived by the sense of touch; used in marketing as unable to be perceived by the five senses or easily grasped conceptually.

Intention The conative stage of the buying process—what people intend to do.

Internal information Data collected from sources within the organization, such as occupancy, average room rate, average check, number of covers, frequently-ordered menu items, and so on.

Internal marketing Applying the philosophies and practices of marketing to people who serve the external customers so that (1) the best possible people can be employed and retained, and (2) they will do the best job of serving the customer. Management emphasis is equally on the employee, the customer, and the job as it is on the product.

Internal marketing concept Organization's internal market of employees can be influenced effectively and motivated to customer-consciousness, market orientation, and sales-mindedness by a marketing-like internal approach and by using marketing-like activities internally.

Internal Rate of Return (IRR) The method of determining the percentage of profit needed for projects funded with existing cash.

Internal validity Reported research findings that are free from bias and are valid in their conclusions.

Judgmental sample A nonprobability sample using a specified variation. Subjects are "screened" to ensure they meet criteria specified.

Latent demand A consumer need for which no suitable product is available to satisfy the need (e.g., fast-food before McDonald's).

Leader Someone who has followers.

Lowest Common Denominator (LCD) The The sales process by which large tasks are broken down into the smallest (most manageable) pieces of work to be completed by a salesperson.

Loss leaders Items that are offered to customers at low (loss) prices to create traffic, and the potential purchase of a more desirably priced item; for example, a soup special may be priced at 50 cents in the hope that the customer will also order a sandwich.

Macro competition Anything that is competing for the same consumer's dollar that you are, regardless of the product similarity; for instance, a new car might compete with an extended vacation.

Market demand The measurement of the amount of demand in the marketplace. See *Demand analysis*.

Market positioning Creating an image of a product in the marketplace in the consumer's mind.

Market segmentation Assumes a heterogeneity in the marketplace and a divergent demand. Segmentation divides the market into various segments, with homogeneity along one or more common dimensions.

Market share The determination of a hospitality entity's actual success rate in attracting customers. Once a determination of total supply for the product is made, each competing business has a "fair" market share; that is, its proportion of the total supply. Its proportion of actual sales is its "actual" market share. The market share establishes who has sold more or less than their fair share of the available supply.

Marketing Communicating to and giving the target market what they want, when they want it, where they want it, and at a price they are willing to pay.

Marketing concept   The theory that the customer has a choice and does not have to buy a product, or your product—hence the need to market or attract the customer to the product.

Marketing mix   Traditionally, the "Four Ps"—product, price, place, and promotion; in hospitality the product/service, presentation, communication, and distribution that directly affects the consumer.

Marketing opportunity   Exists when the needs (problems) of the customer are not being satisfied, or could be enhanced.

Marketing orientation   The philosophy, foundations, and practices of marketing as evidenced in the philosophy of the firm.

Marketing-oriented management   The philosophy that customer needs are primary to all processes; for example, when designing a product before the sale, when delivering a product after the sale, and while the customer consumes the product.

Marketing plan   Working document that the hospitality enterprise develops for action during the forthcoming year. A situation analysis and all phases of the communications mix should be addressed as needed.

Marketing system   Makes marketing orientation and marketing concept work. Comprises leadership, opportunity, planning, and control.

Maslow's hierarchy   Higher-level needs do not become primary until lower-level needs have been fulfilled.

Master strategy   Shapes objectives after developing and weighing alternatives; specifies where the firm is going and is the framework of the marketing effort. Normally a long-term planning process.

Micro competition   Any business that is competing for the same customers in the same product class; that is, is a direct competitor with a similar product in a similar context.

Mission statement   The statement that delineates the total perspectives or purpose of a business. It states why the business exists, the competitors, the marketplace, and how the business serves its constituents.

Multiple brand strategy   The strategy of a firm that crosses over a variety of levels of con-

sumer needs for the same product; for example, Marriott Hotels offers five brands of hotels, from deluxe J.W. Marriotts for the non-price-sensitive guest to the Fairfield concept for the price-sensitive budget traveler.

New markets   The attempt to increase the customer base of a business by developing new markets through the solicitation of current nonusers, or fulfilling unfulfilled, latent, or incipient demand.

Non-contact employees   Those employees who have little or no direct contact with the customers; dishwashers and laundry workers are two examples of non-contact employees.

No-equity deals   The management of a hospitality entity without significant capital investment on the part of the managing company.

Noncompensatory models   When the customer perceives no trade-off of attributes (e.g., conjunctive or disjunctive models); for example, some customers would not accept a double-bed guestroom in lieu of a promised king-bed guestroom even if the price were much lower.

Nonprobability sample   Everyone in the population does not have an equal chance of being selected; includes judgmental, quota, or convenience samples.

Nontargeted prospecting   Using list of potential clients to make "cold" calls (i.e., calls with no advance contact).

Normative beliefs   The thought process that certain individuals or groups should conform to a particular behavior.

Objective positioning   The process of creating an image about a product that reflects its physical characteristics and functional features.

Odd-numbered pricing   A pricing methodology employed to create a perception of a lower price by charging, for example, $6.99 rather than $7.00.

Open probe   A question phrased by a salesperson to encourage a customer to speak freely.

Opening specials A pricing methodology used as inducement to try the product in the initial phases of the product life cycle; also called introductory pricing.

Operations orientation A work ethic within a hospitality entity that focuses on the internal mechanism of the organization rather than the customer. Sometimes, similarly, called the F&B mentality because of that department's historical emphasis on controlling cost and running a smooth operation before consideration of customers' needs or wants.

Opportunity analysis Matching product strengths to opportunity while avoiding threats caused by product weaknesses.

Organizational customer A customer who buys the hospitality product for groups of secondary customers with a common purpose.

Outbound operator A channel of distribution that handles international travel from the host country to all points of destination outside the country.

Package market Offering to consumers a combination of room and amenities for an inclusive price.

Penetration pricing A company drastically reduces prices to initially create awareness and trial of product, eventually stealing customers and building volume.

Perception What is real to the consumer; that is, what the consumer perceives or believes.

Perceptual mapping Process that helps to determine the positioning strategy relative to the competition by "mapping" competitive positions or product attributes.

Perishability A characteristic of a product that indicates the length of time available for sale to a customer, after which it perishes. An automobile may have a perishability of a year before a new model is introduced—even then it can be sold at a reduced price; a hotel room-night has one day, after which it can't even be given away.

Perpetuability A word we have coined to describe the characteristic and ability to perpetuate repeated sales of the same product, e.g., a hotel room or an airline seat. Although

the room-night has perished, the same product can be sold the following day.

Personal constructs Devices that individuals use to interpret or make sense out of what they confront. Personal constructs are on a bipolar continuum; for instance, good–bad.

Physical plant The term for the actual building and its components that house the hospitality entity.

Physical supports Materials necessary for the production of a service (e.g., a reservations system). From this support, both the contact personnel and the customer will draw services.

Planning Defining what has to be done and allocating the resources to do it.

Porte cochere A covered carriage entrance at the front of a building.

Positioning The consumer's mental perception of a product, which may or may not differ from the actual physical characteristics of a product or brand.

Positioning strategy The planning by the hospitality entity to maintain, enhance, or change the consumer's mental perception of the product.

Presentation mix All elements used by the firm to increase the perception of the product/service mix in the mind of the consumer.

Presentation strategy The idea that the presentation mix must be consistent with the product/service and the overall master strategy.

Press release A document prepared for the press providing the salient points of a story that the hospitality entity would like published.

Price A statement of value, usually in monetary terms, that can be used to express the cost of a good or service.

Price lining This technique clumps prices together so that a perception of substantially increased quality is created (e.g., $79, $99, and $119 rooms).

Price skimming The pricing of a product at the high end of the scale to create a perceived value, skim off the top of the market, and then eventually reducing the price to include a larger number of potential consumers.

Pricing objective   The desired results of a pricing strategy, which should be consistent with the hospitality entity's other marketing objectives.

Primary reference groups   Small, usually intimate groups whose behavior patterns may directly influence individuals within the group.

Proact   Opposed to react; act before the event rather than afterward (commonly used in strategy vernacular).

Probing   Method to determine the needs of the customer through a series of inquiries.

Product   An offering of a business entity as it is perceived by both present and potential customers; a bundle of benefits designed to satisfy the needs and wants, and solve the problems of specified target markets. A product is composed of both tangible and intangible elements; it may be as concrete as a chair or a dinner plate, or as abstract as a feeling. The utility of a product derives from what it does for the customer.

Product awareness   Whether consumers are familiar with a product or even know it exists.

Product differentiation   Perceived difference in a product when compared with others.

Product life cycle   The description of the various stages that a product experiences during its tenure in the market; these phases include an introduction or embryonic stage, growth stage, mature stage, and stage of decline.

Product orientation   An organizational approach to marketing that focuses on the product itself and assumes that the product will sell itself; for instance, emphasis on atrium lobbies or swimming pools as the product the customer is buying (related to *Edifice complex*).

Product parity   The competition is selling the same thing, or the consumer perceives no difference between offerings.

Product strategy   Deals with the benefits the product provides, the problems it solves, and how it differentiates from the competition.

Production line orientation   An organizational approach based on how fast, how many, and how cheaply to produce a product to get it to the market in bulk at the lowest possible price.

Product/service   The totality of what hospitality companies offer their customers, including goods, services, and environment.

Product/service mix   Combination of products and services, whether free or for sale, aimed at satisfying the needs of the target market.

Profit center concept   The idea of breaking a larger organization into smaller, more manageable pieces by assigning profit contribution goals to individual departments.

Profit Impact of Marketing Strategy (PIMS)   Program that is a computerized cross-sectional study based on about 200 pieces of data supplied by more than 450 companies in more than 3,000 businesses. This program has shown that the profitability of a business is affected by 37 basic factors that explain more than 80 percent of the profitability variation among the businesses.

Proprietary research   When research is conducted for a particular organization for the specific use of that organization as opposed to general use.

Prospecting   The methodology used in finding new customers; an example would be making sales calls on customers who are not currently using the product.

Psychographers   People who correlate factors into relatively homogeneous categories using classification terms for consumers' lifestyles, such as homebodies, traditionalists, swingers, and so on.

Psychographic segmentation   Lifestyle patterns combine the virtues of demographics with the way people live, think, and behave in their everyday lives to divide them into market segments, i.e., by their attitudes, interests, and opinions (AIO).

Psychological pricing   Pricing strategy utilized to elicit consumer reactions such as perceived quality or value.

Public relations   The organized attempt by a business to get favorable stories concerning their product or services carried by the media.

Publicity   The format used in public relations to "create" a story. Stories are created through organized promotions.

Pull strategy Inducements are offered to make the consumer want to purchase a product or "pull" the product down the channel of distribution.

Push strategy Inducements are offered to the channel member to sell or "push" the product down the channel of distribution.

Probability sample One in which every member of the population has an equal chance of being selected.

Qualitative research The process of obtaining information on consumer attitudes and behavior on a subjective basis. This research is largely exploratory in nature and the findings cannot be generalized to a larger population. An example is the use of focus groups.

Quantitative research The process of obtaining information on consumer attitudes and behavior on an objective basis. This research is factual in nature and the findings sometimes can be generalized to a larger population.

Rack rates Regular published rates for hotel rooms, almost always discounted except in periods of very high demand.

Reference groups/Referents Groups that form small pockets of influence that affect consumers.

Relationship marketing The emphasis on retaining existing customers through building good relationships.

Reliability In research, findings can be projected to a larger population if it is the intent of the researcher to do so; also, if the study is repeated, similar findings will emerge.

Repositioning Changing the position or image of a product to consumers in the marketplace.

Representative firm Channel of distribution that brings a hotel to a marketplace, they market a hotel to a customer base for a fee.

Research design The process of establishing the total objectives and method of research to be conducted.

Research problem The designation of the problem of the research; that is, stating what the research is going to answer (not necessarily the same as the management problem).

Research purpose What you intend to do with the findings; what kind of business decisions you plan to make after you have the results.

Reservation networks Central reservations systems that serve multiple companies or properties.

Retail market Middlemen such as travel agents who sell directly to the consumer; a member of the distribution mix.

Return on Assets (ROA) The ratio of profits to assets that is generated by a business.

Return on Investment (ROI) The ratio of profits to investment that is generated by a business.

Revenue management See *Yield management.*

Run-of-the-house room The generic term for the random assignment of guestrooms to customers. Customers are not promised a certain type of room before their arrival at the hotel.

Sales equation The mathematical process by which the past customers, new customers, and budget expectations are calculated

Sales action plan Format to organize and manage a sales department to create and maximize dales.

Salient attributes Those attributes that readily come to mind when you think of a product or product class.

Sample A group derived from the population at large; from it we hope to learn the characteristics of many based on a few.

Segmentation The dividing of a large customer base into smaller homogeneous categories, based on a variety of applicable factors.

Selective acceptance The theory that customers accept only information that they choose to accept, that they select from a variety of information only what is applicable.

Selective attention The theory that customers attend to only what is of particular interest to them.

Selective comprehension The theory that customers will try to comprehend, digest, and evaluate something only if they are still interested in it after attending to and accepting it.

Selective retention The theory that customers retain in memory for future reference only what suits their particular interest after attention, acceptance, and comprehension.

Selling orientation To practice "hard sell" techniques; the emphasis is on selling what you have to offer and persuading the customer to buy, rather than on the needs of the customer.

Service Nonphysical, intangible attributes that management controls (or should), including friendliness, efficiency, attitude, professionalism, responsiveness, and so on.

Service augmentation The marketing strategy to add to a generic product by enhancing services; for instance, the perception of a hotel room may be enhanced by the availability of a shoe-shine service.

Share of mind Marketing jargon associated with positioning; it means that the positioning has been established in the consumer's mind.

Simultaneous production and consumption Unique service characteristic whereby consumption depends on participation of the seller and the seller requires the participation of the buyer.

SMERF A market segment that covers the social, military, ethnic, religious and fraternal customer base.

Soft opening Product introduction begins a few days to a few weeks before the official opening.

Standard Metropolitan Statistical Area (SMSA) Area that the government defines as a large economic area in terms of supposed economic boundaries. Government produces data on these areas such as population, ethnic mix, income, and so on.

Standard product The attempt to provide a similar experience to the customer despite different locations or managers; for example, McDonald's offers a standard hamburger throughout the United States.

Strategic Business Unit (SBU) Units of a business that have a common market base. Each SBU serves a clearly defined product-market base with its own strategy.

Strategic marketing Long-term view of the market and the business to be in; marketing management stresses running that business and seeks to optimize objectives within the constraints established by the strategy.

Strategic planning Developing a plan for how to get from here (situation analysis) to there (objectives). It is concerned with setting business objectives, the match between products and markets, the choices of competition, the allocation of resources, and planning ahead to reach the objectives.

Strategic thinking Synthesis as opposed to analysis in strategic planning.

Subjective norm People's perception of the social pressures put on them to perform or not perform in a particular way.

Subjective positioning The perceived image that does not necessarily belong to the product or brand, but is the property of the consumer's mental perceptions.

Suitcase party Customers come to a hotel with their suitcases packed, and during the evening, an exotic weekend away is awarded randomly, and the couple is whisked away to their destination.

Tactics The step-by-step procedure of executing the details of a strategic plan.

Target marketing The marketing strategy to aim a product or service at one portion of a specific market segment.

Target markets Homogeneous markets that allow for more detailed analysis and evaluation of potential customers of a segment.

Technology orientation Belief that success in the marketplace is a result of the finest technological development. This thought process is similar to the business philosophy exemplified by Polaroid for many years. Also akin to atrium lobbies with lakes and waterfalls.

Tour series Prearranged link of stopovers for customers traveling by bus, usually carrying a theme.

Transient salespeople The salesperson who is designated to sell to organizations that have a need to book guestrooms on an individual basis.

Trial This stage of product introduction attempts to get the consumer to try a product.

Two-fer Restaurant promotion that offers two meals or drinks for the price of one.

Vertical integration Company becomes its own supplier of products (for instance, Holiday Inns had a subsidiary that sold hotel furnishings) or its own distributor (for instance, Radisson Hotels and Carlson Travel Agency belong to the same company).

Walked customers Resulting from overbooking hotel rooms, customers' reservations are not honored and they are sent to a different hotel.

Wholesale tour operator Middlemen who create hospitality packages, such as group tours, and sell to the customer through retail agents. A member of the distribution mix.

Word-of-mouth advertising The marketing strategy that satisfied customers are the best form of communication. Satisfied customers will tell potential customers of their experience, thus increasing the customer base.

Yield management The concept of maximizing the revenue yield by raising or lowering prices depending upon the demand. Better called *revenue management*.

INDEX

Aaker, David A., 358n
Abbey, James, 469n
Abu Dhabi National Hotels
    Company, 723, 725
Accor hotels. *See* Groupe Accor
Action plans, 115–117; sales,
    627, 628
Adam's Mark Hotel, Memphis,
    specifications for meeting
    planners, 618–619
ADI (area of dominant
    influence), 308
ADR (average daily rate), 348
Advertising, 528–546; and
    collateral, 544–546; current
    use of, 538–542; defined, 528;
    evaluating, 542–544; failure
    to differentiate, 530; goals,
    528; management in, 4; for
    increasing loyalty, 212; in the
    international market,
    733–734; and Marriott ad,
    531–534; objectives of, 528,
    531; roles of, 528;
    standardizing, 737
Affiliations, 670; ads for, 671,
    672
AH&MA (American Hotel &
    Motel Association), 144, 273
Airlines, crew market, 243,
    273–275

Aizen, Icek, 209n
Alabama, ad, 782
Alba Tours, ad, 694
Albrecht, Karl, 170n
Allentuck, Andrew, 504n
All-inclusive resorts, 105;
    Sandals resort ad, 231
All-suite hotel concept, 305,
    404; and augmented product,
    398–399; hotels using, 305;
    and product segmentation,
    305; purpose of, 305; sample
    list of, 305
Alonzo, Vincent, 263n
Alpert, Mark, 400n
Amenities, hotel: amenities
    programs, 148; amenities
    wars, 161–162; amenity
    creep, 219; bathroom
    amenities, 413
American Express, 689–690,
    693; ad, 692, 748
AMS (actual market share),
    109–111, 164
Ananth, F.J., 232n
Arrowwood Resort Conference
    Center, ad, 266
Ashok Group, 79; ad, 80
Association, convention, and
    trade show markets, 243;
    annual expenditures in

hospitality establishments,
    268; and food and beverage
    service, 269; and hotel
    unions, 269; needs of, 267;
    purpose, 269; planning and
    coordinating, 269; price
    sensitivity of delegates to, 271
Aston Hotels & Resorts, ad, 699
Astor Chocolate Corporation,
    ad, 6
Atmospherics, 437–443; defined,
    437; and international
    marketing, 725; as a
    marketing tool, 437–440;
    planning, 440–443; and
    presentation mix, 427
Atrium lobbies, 167; ad for, 441
Augmented product, and
    marketing mix, 397–399

Baby boomers, expectations of,
    148
Banff Springs Hotel, Alberta,
    Canada, 152, 435, 436
Bass Plc. of England, 11n, 150
Behavioral differences, 320
Belief–attitude–intention triad,
    208–209
Bell, Martin L., 463n
Bell, Russell A., 258n

Benchmark Hospitality, Inc., and conference center descriptions, 264–265

Benefit bundle, 437

Berkshire Hilton Inn, 662

Bermuda, ad, 777

Berry, L.L., 48n, 51n

Best Western, 670; ad, 671

Boca Raton Hotel and Club, Florida, 149

Bodett, Tom, 450

Borden, Neil, 393, 393n

Boston Park Plaza Hotel & Towers, ad, 300

Brand name(s): demand and situational analysis, 75; and franchising, 655, 657; and multi-name practice, 746; positioning in international markets, 745–746

Breakers Hotel, Palm Beach, Florida, 105

Break-even point, and the sales promotion, 576

Break-even pricing, 477, 478, 479

Brennan, Denise M., 355n

Bristol Hotel, Paris, 404

Britain, ad, 776

Broadmoor Hotel, Colorado Springs, 607; ad, 568

Brookshire Hotels, ad, 653

Buck Hill Inn, Poconos, Pennsylvania, ad, 110

Budget motel chains: and industrialization of service, 38, 39; and market opportunity, 155

Building loyalty, 49–54

Bundling of goods and services, 228

Burger King, 139, 140; and ADI, 308; in South America, 714

Bush, Melinda, 686n

Business mission statement, 69

Business purpose, 5

Business traveler market segment, 215–222; complexity of, 216; needs of, 216

Buyers. See Customer(s); Consumers

Buying decision process: and alternative comparison, 208–209; and alternative

evaluation, 208; and attitudes, 208; and behavior, 209; and beliefs, 205; and choice intentions, 209; and outcomes, 209; and perceptions, 204–205, 209; and search process, 203; and selective acceptance, 204; and selective attention, 203; and selective comprehension, 204; and selective retention, 204; and stimuli selection, 203–204

Cambridge Suites, ad, 464

Canadian Pacific Hotels & Resorts (CP Hotels), 81, 152, 652; Deerhurst, 544–545; Royal York, ad, 745

Cancun, Mexico, 784

Caneel Bay, Virgin Islands, 431

Car rental industry, 682

Carlson Companies, Inc., 701; Carlson Hospitality Group, 663, ad, 663; Carlson Marketing Group, 680

Carlzon, Jan, 16–17, 17n

Carpenter, Tony, 565

Central Plaza Hotel, Bangkok, ad, 740

Cerromar Beach Hotel, 344

Chacko, Harsha E., 279n

Check-in, using technology to enhance, 142

Choice International Hotels, 79, 81, 139, 146, 232; ad, 166, 367, 406, 660; brand positioning, 368; product line, 147. See also Quality Inns

Chon, Kye-Sung, 780, 781, 786n

Ciga Hotels, 144

Claremont Resort and Conference Center, ad, 260

Clarion Hotels, 79, 146; Clarion Plaza Hotel, Orlando, ad, 432, 697

Cleanliness, and selection of hotels by business travelers, 217

Cloisters Hotel, Sea Island, Georgia, 105

Club Med, 86, 229, 356, 437, 475, 574; ad, 230, 574; Eleuthera, Bahamas, 105

Coca-Cola, 647; research, 208

Colonnade Hotel, Boston, ad, 219

Comfort Inns, 79, 146, 483. See also Choice International Hotels; Quality Inns

Commonwealth Hospitality, 652

Communication, to the target market, 3

Communications mix, 505–547; and advertising, 528–546; and advertising agencies, 86; coordination of, 116; and database marketing, 525–528; definition of, 85, 505; and difference from presentation mix, 505; elements of, 505–506; and Howard Johnson's case, 518–519; and international marketing, 732–737; and methods, 86; and principles and practices of merchandising, 576–582; and public relations and publicity, 582–589; and research, 512–517; and rules of persuasion, 511; and sales promotions, 559–576; and strategy, 507–511; and target markets, 511–512; and word-of-mouth communication, 506–507, 517–519. See also Advertising; Communications mix research; Merchandising; Promotions; Personal selling; Publicity; Public relations

Communications mix research, and customer complaints, 522–525

Communications strategy, ad, 87; adopting the process model, 511–512; and communication tactics, 507; determining objectives of, 501–512

Company policies, conflict with ability of employees to satisfy customers, 44–46

Competition: beating the, 109, 165–166; definition of, 105; effective market positioning, 166; micro, 158–166; and services, 161; and situational analysis, 75

Competitive analysis, 156–158; and beating the competition, 109, 165–166; and choosing the right competition, 158; and competitive intelligence, 162, 164; and competitive intensity, 161–162; and computation of fair market share, 110, 164; and conceptitis, 159; and hypothetical demand, 111; and market opportunities, 155–156; and marketing research, 169–170; and micro competition, 158–166; and pricing in international markets, 728–732

Competitive environment, changes in, 139

Competitive intelligence, 162; and market share, 164

Competitive intensity, 161–162

Competitive marketing, strategies for, 166

Competitive positioning, 363–366; and hotel restaurants, 365–366; and hypothetical perceptual map, 364

Competitive pricing, 480–481

Competitive strategy, 79, 81

Competitive strategy, rethinking of, 159–160

Computer databases, 325–326

Computerized information systems, and concierge service, 140; and consumer needs, 140–143

Conceptitis, 159

Concierge floors, 148, 217

Conference center hotels, 155

Conference center, compared with hotels, 262; and corporate meetings, 261–263; descriptions, 264–265

Connaught Hotel, London, UK, 745

Conrad Hotels, ad, 536

Consortia, 664, 667, 669–670; defined, 664; differences among, 670; examples of, 664;

purpose, 664; and travel agents, 681

Consumer(s): mental evaluation process, 215; networks in Europe, 667; and price search, 486–487; stages, model of, 512. See also Customer(s)

Consumer price index (CPI), 465

Consumerism, and sociocultural change, 150. See also Sociocultural changes

Contribution to fixed costs, and volume objectives, 473

Contribution margin pricing, 477

Convention centers, 271–273; ad, 272

Convention and visitors bureaus (CVBs), 273; ad, 274

Conventions, ads soliciting, 270, 271

Cooper, Simon, Delta Hotels & Resorts, 46

Core product, 396–397; atmospherics as, 437

Corporate culture, and corporate travel market, 256

Corporate meetings market, 243; and hotel's problems with, 261

Corporate meeting planners, and the corporate meetings market, 259–261; and site selection criteria, 246–247

Corporate rates, 217

Corporate travel buyers, procedures of, 256, 258

Corporate travel market, 254–259; and understanding travel patterns, 258

Corporate travel planner, compared with corporate meeting planner, 254

Cost, control, 4

Cost pricing, 476–480; and break-even analysis, 478–479; and break-even pricing, 477, 478, 479; and contribution margin pricing, 477; and cost percentage or markup pricing, 476–477; one dollar per thousand, 477, 480

Couples Resort, Jamaica, 105

Courtyard by Marriott. See Marriott

Cowan, Alison L., 651n

CRS (central or computer reservations systems), 498, 682

Cunard Crown, ad, 687

Cunningham, Mark W., 450n

Customer: as basis for pricing, 449–451; creating and keeping, 4, 5; expectations of, 8–10; and hospitality, 3; hotel amenities war, 161; importance of, 14–16; judgment, 31; in marketing, 3,4; as marketing tool, 445–448; and micro competition, 158; perception of value, 5; problem-solving, 7–10; retaining, 5; service fluctuation of, 35

Customer base, and volume objectives, 473

Customer behavior: and application of the theories, 200; and the buying decision process, 202–214; characteristics of, 200–214; and customer markets, 199–234; and gaps between consumers' problems and solutions, 210; and perceptions, 34; premises, 199–200; and price, 217. See also Buying decision process

Customer comments, keeping logs on, 107

Customer complaints: and research, 522–525; solving, 524–525; and word-of-mouth communication, 35, 519–522

Customer expectations, 8–10; creation of, 34, 35; employees and, 46; and incongruities, 166–167; and opportunities, 167; satisfaction of, 44

Customer needs and wants: anticipating needs of, 40, 41; impossibility of anticipating all, 44, 45; and micro competition, 161; and segmentation, 301–308

Customer mix, positioning, 445–448

Customer objectives, 474–476

Customer perceptions, 395–396; and the product/service mix, 396; selectivity of, 396

Customer pricing: and expectation pricing, 484–485; objectives of, 470–476; and the price/value relationship, 483–484; and psychological pricing, 485–486; and the target market, 483–486

Customer problems: core product, 396–397; and marketing research, 170; trade-off model, 8–10

Customer profile and situational analysis, 75

Customer satisfaction: and competitive tactics, 161; definition of, 46; and employee empowerment, 45; and services, 161

Customer service, appropriate treatment in, 38

Customer types, 215–235; and the business traveler, 215–222; and dealing with the business segment, 220–222; and the free independent traveler (FIT), 234; and the pleasure traveler market, 222–227

Customization, 403–404

Dallas Convention and Visitors Bureau, ad, 272

Database marketing, 525–528; components of, 526; and customized databases, 526; and proprietary databases, 526; and using the database, 527–528

Data collection, in market research design, 178–179

Days Inn: competitive strategy of, 79; research, 296

Decision-making process, of consumer, 8

Default sample, 178

Default strategy, 66

Delta Hotels & Resorts, 46, 146: ad, 85, 142

Demand: brand, 75; capabilities of meeting, 306–307; generic, 75; types of consumer, 156

Demand analysis, 306–307; price and, 481; and price elasticity, 482

DeMico, P., 232n

Denny's Restaurants, 740; ad, 655

Department of Commerce, USTTA, 788n

Descriptive quantitative research, 172, 174

Desensitization of consumer to price, 475

Desired consumer response, 78

Dev, Chekitan, 450n

DEWKS, 148

Diamond, Michael, 148

Differentation, 291–201; defined, 291. See also Market differentiation

Differentiation, Segmentation, and Target Marketing. See Market segmentation

DINKS, 148

Discounting, in poor economy, 37

Distribution channels, 647–704; and affiliations, 664, 670; and channel management, 701–703; company-managed, 648; company-owned and -managed, 650–651; and concierges, 87; and consortia, 664, 667, 669–670; defined, 647; and distribution systems, 647–648; elements of, 86; evaluation of, 702; and franchising, 653–663; and the hospitality industry, 648–650; and importance of geographical areas, 648–649; and incentive houses, 680; and influences on strategies, 700–701; and international marketing, 738–739; managing, 651–653; and motivation and recruitment of channel members, 702–703; and promotional pitfalls, 699–700; and promotional tie-ins, 698–699; and representation companies, 675–680; and reservations networks, 670–675; and restaurants, 87; selecting, 701; strategies for, 695–701; and tour operators and wholesalers, 691–695; and travel agents, 680–690; and vertical integration, 701

Distribution mix, definition of, 86

DMA (designated market area), 308

Domino's Pizza, 155

Dorchester Hotel, London, UK, 745

Doubletree Hotels, 582; ad, 534, 616

Dowling, William Q., 353, 354

Downsizing, 244

Drucker, Peter F., 5, 5n, 29n, 166, 166n, 167, 167n, 468, 468n

Dunfey Hyannis Hotel, Cape Cod, 442

Dunkin' Donuts, 148

Dunn, Victoria, 276n

Eaasy Sabre reservation system, 689

Ecological concerns of guests, CP Hotels, 152

Ecological trends, environmental analysis of, 75

Econolodge, 146, 344

Economic environment, in international marketing, 718–721; and the macroeconomy, 718–719; and the microeconomy, 719, 721

Economic impacts, and environmental scanning, 146

Ecotourism, and Belize, 151

Electronic door locks and security, 149

Embassy Suites, 256, 406, 441; ad, 353, 441; Palm Beach, Florida, 648

Emmett, Paul, 408

Employee(s): and attitudes, 44; and management practices,

44; as marketing tool, 44; as part of presentation mix, 443–445; and relations with customers, 44; empowerment, 45; motivating, 46

Environment, defined, 30

Environmental analysis: purpose of, 75; trends, 75

Environmental scanning, 137–139; and competitive analysis, 155, 156–158; and consumer demand, 139; and ecological impacts; and economic impacts, 146; fads, 139; and identification of competition, 139; as leadership tool, 138; and linking to corporate strategy, 154; and macro competition, 139–140; and major task of, 153; and marketing research, 169–170; and micro competition, 158–166; and opportunities, 155; and political impacts, 143, 144; reasons for growing importance of, 137, 180; and regulatory impacts, 150–151; and the single woman traveler, 148; and sociocultural impact, 146–150; and technological impacts, 140–143; and threats, 155, 156; and types of environment, 140–155

Equatorial Hotel, Penang, ad, 270

Escalera, Karen W., 584n

Essex House, New York, 81

European Economic Community, 734

Exchange rates of U.S. Dollar, table of, 730–731

Expectation pricing, 484–485

Expectations. See Customer expectations

Expense accounts, and 1986 tax bill, 151

Fairfield Inns, 81, 146. See also Marriott

Fairmont Hotels, 483; ad 471

"Fam" trip, 686

Farnsworth, Martha, 312

Fast food: chain manuals, 3; operation, 68

Feedback loops and functional strategies, 87, 88

Feltenstein, Tom, 413n, 567, 567n

Ferrell, O.C., 15n

Fidelio Software, ad, 143

Financial objectives of pricing, 471–472

Fishbein, Martin, 209n

FIT (free independent traveler), 234

Fitzgerald, Thomas, 41

FMS (fair market share), 109–111, 164

Focus groups, 171–172

Foote, Nelson, 400

Formule1 hotels, 81. See also Groupe Accor

Forte Hotels, 8, 144, 658, 746; ad, 433; Forte Grand, 723, 725, 727; Forte Heritage, 725, 729

"Four Ps," 82; and communication mix, 85; and the marketing mix, 393–394, 395, 427

Four Seasons Hotels, 37, 222, 428–429, 475, 651; ad, 42–43, 430–431

Franchising, 653–663; and auditing, 658–659; and branding, 655, 657; defined, 653; exceptions to, 658, 663; and financial support, 658; international, 738–739; and local adaptations, 740; and managerial techniques, 658; and marketing support, 658; philosophies of, 662–663; and the reservation system, 659; safeguards, 658; and technical knowledge, 658

France, Nice, ad, 787

Franco's Italian Restaurant, ad, 570

Frequent-traveler programs: and giveaways, 148; and problems in the hotel industry, 565–566; and pull strategies, 695; and relationship marketing, 49, 82

Friendship Inns, 146

Functional Strategies, 82–87. See also Strategic Marketing

Garvey, Joe, 313n

GDS (global distribution systems), 682, 691; hotel information, 684–685

General Mills, restaurants, 366

Generic demand and situational analysis, 75

Generic organizational market, 243–245

Geographic segmentation, 308–309

Girardeau, Freddie, 404

Gitomer, Jeffrey H., 610n

Global advertising, 733–734

Globalization in hospitality industry, 144

Globalization of markets, vs. segmentation, 744

Grisanti's Restaurant, ad, 538

Golden Tulip Hotels, 670, 673–674

Goods: defined, 30; functional differences between services and, 41

Goods marketing, as compared with hospitality marketing, 394

Green Suites International, ad, 153

Greenbriar Hotel, White Sulphur Springs, W. Virginia, 105, 411, 434–435

Gross, Robert, 714n

Group tour and travel market, 276–277

Groupe Accor, 79, 81, 139, 146, 371, 658, 688, 713, 716, 746; brochure, 717; Formule1, 81, 146, 740; Ibis, 81, ad, 415; Motel 6, 81, 450, 716; and multi-name practice, 746; Novotel, 81, 716, ad, 718; Sofitel, 81, 722, 740, ad, 310

Group market, 243

Group tour and travel market, 243

Gubbins, J.J., 263

Guest databases, 140, 143

Guest Quarters Suite Hotels, 45; ad, 318–319, 464; Guest message on empowerment, 45

Hair, Joseph, 714n, 609n
Haley, Russell I., 316, 316n
"Happy hours," banning of, 151
Hayes, Robert H., 103n
Haywood, K. Michael, 165n, 584n
Hazard, Robert, 146, 166, 301, 303, 367, 369, 658
Helmsley Hotels, ad, 206, 207
Helyar, John, 150n
Heterogeneity of service, 37–39
Hilton, 81, 106, 109, 232, 571–572, 650, 651; ad, 214, 347; and brand name problem, 734–746; Chicago, 344; image problem, 370; New Orleans, 607; promotion, 581
Hilton International, 414, 713, 714, 715; ad, 354, 615
Hirsch, James S., 651n, 689n
Holiday Inn, 76, 106, 144, 150, 155, 167, 216, 356, 400, 443, 658, 659, 662, 713, 716, 733; ad, 370, 659, 715; and amenities, 220; brochure page, 733; and comment cards, 522; Crowne Plaza, 109, 652, 658, 744; ad, 664, 715; Garden Court, ad, 718; Holiday Express, 658; Hong Kong, 744; mission statement, 71; and positioning ad, 370; standards manual, Sunspree Resort, 316n; Weisbaden, 151
Holiday Inn Worldwide Corporation, 150, 655; franchisor services, 656–657
Homestead Hotel, Hot Springs, Virginia, 105, 411, 434–435
Hospitality Franchise Systems, 79, 367, 369, 517; ad, 654
Hospitality industry, marketing and management in, 3. See also Hotels; Restaurants
Hospitality marketing, difference from goods marketing, 394. See also Services marketing.

Hospitality marketing mix, 394–395. See also Hospitality marketing; Hospitality product
Hospitality product: additional services, 40, 41; aspects of service component of, 34–41; components, 30–31
Hospitality service, potential gaps in, 211–212
Hospitality services, differences from other services, 54
Hotel amenities. See Amenities, hotel
Hotel & Travel Index, 686
Hotel D'Angleterre, Copenhagen, ad, 738
Hotel del Coronado, California, 105
Hotel Nikko, San Francisco, ad, 36
Hotel Plaza II, Toronto, ad, 480
Hotels: and affiliations, 670; classification of, 678; and representation companies, 675–680; and reservation systems, 674–675; and tangibilizing the intangible, 350, 351; and tier structure, 146. See also Hospitality industry; and under names of specific hotels and hotel chains
Houston, Franklin S., 16n
Houstonian Hotel, ad, 531
Howard Johnson, 79, 155, 205–206, 356, 368, 400, 411, 476, 517; ad, 371, 520; advertising caption, 400; chronology of failure, 76, 77; and confusing brand name image, 371; and differentiation, 294; and environmental change, 76; Ground Round, 76; handling of opportunities and threats, 76; Park Square Inn, 476; repositioning campaign, 518–519
Howey, R.M., 232n
Hyatt Hotels, 82, 109, 144, 155, 166, 294, 313, 348, 400, 662, 713, 719; ad, 138, 221, 257,

402, 403, 695; and anticipating customers' future needs, 138; Hyatt International, 722; Hyatt Regency, 105; and international marketing, 719; joint advertising, 693; and positioning, 344

Ibis hotels, 79, 81, 415. See also Groupe Accor
Image, and effective positioning, 350
Incentive organizational customer market, 243; and the incentive buyer, 244; and the incentive market, 263–267
Incentive planners, and the incentive trip, 266–267
India: ad, 774; failure of hotel strategy in, 76
Indifference price, 484
Industrialization of service, 38
Industry change, 166
InnLink, ad, 674
Intangible products, as services, 40, 41
Intangible services, 34, 35; and pricing decisions, 35
Inter-Continental Hotels, 81, 651; ad, 15, 537, 736
Internal marketing, 41–46; and the creation and keeping of employees, 41; culture, 48; definition of, 41
Internal positioning analysis, 371–375
International Air Transport Association, 777
International Hotel Association, 1992 Environmental Award, 151
International marketing, 713–749; and American hotel chains, 716; and Asia, 710, 716, 719; and basic marketing principles, 713; and branding, 745–746; changes in, 715; and cultural differences and values, 714, 722; and demographic environments, 723–724; and distribution,

738–739; economic environments in, 718–721; and economic policies, 721; and fine-tuning segments, 742–744; and foodservice companies, 721; and foreign hotel companies, 716; and government competition, 721; and hotel chains, 721; hotel companies, 713, 721; and the international hospitality industry, 714–717; and knowing the local market, 722–723; and marketing research, 746–748; and middle tier accommodations, 716; and political, regulatory and legal environments, 723; and positioning, 744–746; prospects, 716; restaurant chains in, 713; and segmentation, 740; and the social and cultural environment, 721–723

International marketing mix, 724–728; and communications mix, 732–737; and pricing, 728–732; and products and services, 724–725

International tourism marketing, 771–788; ad, 773–778, 782–787; and the challenge for NTO marketers, 782–783; and destination image modification and travel decision making, 780; and the economic environment, 772–774; facilitation role in, 787; and the importance of image promotion, 781, 783–786; and Korea's image, 781; and language problems, 234; and marketing functions of NTOs, 786–788; and marketing relationships, 234; and number of international travelers, 232; and the political/legal environment, 777–779; and presentation, 725–727; and the role of NTOs, 780–788; and the sociocultural environment, 779–780; and the

technological environment, 775–777; and USTTA market potential chart, 788; and world tourism growth chart, 772

Inter Nor Hotels, Norway, 667

Interstate Hotels Corporation, Pittsburgh, 653

Inventory management, 36–37

ITC-Welcomgroup, ad, 255

Jain, Subhash C., 84, 84n, 146, 146n, 400, 400n, 406, 406n, 413, 413n, 724, 724n; environmental scanning model, 154

Journey's End Hotels, 325; ad, 321, 571

Judgmental sample, 178

Kahneman, D., 503n

Kelly, Robert E., 48n

Kentucky Fried Chicken (KFC), 144, 721, 724, 726

Kimes, Sheryl E., 504, 504n

Knetsch, J.L., 503n

Korea, ad, 773

Kotler, Philip, 16n

Koss, Laura, 470n

Kraft General Foods, 69; mission statement and strategies to achieve it, 72–74

Krim, Karen, 467n

Kroc, Ray, 3, 17, 155, 429

Lafayette Hotel, Boston, ad, 448

Laguna Beach resort, Phuket, Thailand, 151

Lamb, Charles, 609n, 714n

Lana'i Rock Resorts, 508, 510, 511; ad, 508

Langton, Bryan, 150

La Quinta Inns, 508, 510, 511; ad, 355, 509

Lavidge, Robert J., 511–512, 511n, 518

Lead times, for hotel contract signing, 248, 249

Leadership marketing, 16–17

Lehtinen, J.R., 743n

Leisure-time, industry research, 565

Leisure market, 222–227

Leisure travelers, and the group tour and travel market, 276–277

Le Meridien Hotels, 81, 347, 652, 578; ad, 250, 260, 313, 349, 734, 735; Boston, 228; Montparnasse, Porte Maillot, Paris, 742

Lettuce Entertain You Enterprises Inc., 296; ad, 297

Leven, Michael, 40, 150, 161

Levitt, Theodore, 38, 49, 49n, 299–300, 299n, 300n, 396, 468, 468n, 614n, 724, 724n, 744, 744n

Lewis, R. C., 11n, 19n, 39n, 161n, 244n, 313n, 317n, 362n, 374n, 482n, 523n, 524n; hotel choice attributes, 224

L'Hôtel, Toronto, 152

Lieberman, W., 500n

Lifestyle, and environmental analysis, 75

Lima, Tony, 296n

Little Dix Bay, Virgin Gorda, ad, 436

Location: as a marketing tool, 435–437; diminishing importance of, 434–435

Lomano, Mark, 565

Lovelock, Christopher H., 343n, 358; positioning model, 360

Lutece, 344, 483

Luxury market, 83

Macroeconomy, 146, 718–719

MailLink reservation system, 689

Makens, James C. 498n

Malaysia, ad, 779

Malcolm Baldridge National Quality Award, 294, 295

Mall-intercept, 178

Management: and strategic marketing planing, 68; in service business, 3; practices, 44–46

Manapany Hotel, Saint Barths, ad, 436

Mandarin Hotel, Hong Kong, 744; Bangkok, ad, 294

Manuals, operations, 10–11

Market(s): analysis and segmentation chart, 323; creation of new, 155; drawbacks, 295; opportunities, 155–156; research, 88

Marriott, Bill, 531, 534

Market demand pricing, 481–483

Market differentiation, 291–301; of anything, 296, 299–301; bases of, 292–293; concrete examples of, 294; and difference from segmentation, 301; and food-service establishments, 296; guidelines, 302; of intangibles, 293; as a marketing tool, 293–296; and Peabody Hotel, 291–292; and the Plaza and Waldorf-Astoria hotels, 293; vs. segmentation, 303

Market feasibility studies, 169

Market mix, and positioning, 354

Market positioning, 343–416; analytic questions, 375; areas affected by, 354; checklist for strategies, 362; and competitive positioning, 363–366; and consistency, 355; defensive, 166; definition, 82; and definition of subjective positioning, 355; and determinance, 362–363; developing strategy, 360; development of strategies for, 79, 81, 82; and differentiation, 350; and differentiation among salient, determinant, and importance product attributes or benefits, 360; and effective positioning, 350–356; and essential criteria, 350; to exploit industry change, 166; of hotels in Hong Kong, 744–745; and Howard Johnson, 368–369; and

internal positioning analysis, 371–375; and international marketing, 744–746; as key to growth, 166; and multiple brand positioning, 366–371; and objective positioning, 343–345; and perception of competition, 158–161; pitfalls of, 343; and positioning approaches, 361; and positioning checklist, 366; and positioning maps, 371; and positioning statements of the past, 352; relationship to other operational strategies, 67; relationship to target markets, 82; and truth in advertising, 369; vital role of, 353

Market repositioning, 356–358; art of, 358; defined, 356; and developing positioning strategies, 358; examples of, 356–387; and new segments, 356; and Ramada Hotel San Francisco repositioning ad, 357; and reasons for, 356

Market research: and factors most likely to be associated with successful new products, 414; and public relations, 586

Market segments, example of incompatible, 442

Market segmentation: and all-suite hotels, 305; and commercially meaningful segments, 300; definition of, 326; and determining needs and wants of the marketplace, 305–306; guidelines, 302; and intangible positioning, 347–349; in international markets, 740–744; matching the market and one's capabilities, 78, 306–307; and objective of differentiation, 326; and positioning, 326; procedure for, 358; process of, 301, 305–308; relationship to marketing strategies and programs, 323; and relativity, 348; selecting target markets

from identified segments, 307–308; and strategy, 320–322; and subjective positioning, 346–347; and tailoring the product to the wants and needs of the target market, 307–308; and tangible positioning, 347; tests for, 322; variables, 308–320; vs. differentiation, 301, 303. See also Market segmentation variables; Market segments mix; Target marketing

Market segmentation variables: and benefit segmentation, 316–318; and demographic segmentation, 309–313; and price segmentation, 308–310; and psychographic segmentation, 310–313; and usage segmentation, 313–316

Market share: and competitive intelligence, 164; and hypothetical example of, 164–165

Marketing: budget as tool of, 120; concept of, 3–8; definition of, 3; differentiation, 10; experience based, 17; foundations and practices, 3; goal of, 10; inescapability of interaction between marketing and production, 4, 39, 40; inseparability of management and, 54; internal, 41–46; knowledge-based and experience-based, 17; leadership, 3, 16–17; nontraditional techniques in, 4, 54; objectives as part of master strategy, 75; orientation, 4; perceptions and, 235; practising the concept of, 16; services, 29; strategic, as distinct from marketing management, 65; strategies for, 51–54; validity of, 16, 17; as warfare, 180. See also Services(s) marketing; Distribution channels; Strategic marketing; and

entries beginning with
Marketing
Marketing budget, 117–120
Marketing concept, 14–16; and conceptitis, 159–161; and customer's needs and wants, 350
Marketing management: definition of, 65; vs. strategic planning, 65
Marketing mix: and action plans, 115; and the augmented product, 397–399; and the communications mix, 395; definition, 82, 393; and developing new products/services, 413–414; and the distribution mix, 395; and the "Four Ps," 82, 393–394; and functional strategies, 82–87; and the presentation mix, 83–85, 394–395, 427–451; and the product/service mix, 394, 395–404; and submixes of, 394; traditional, 416
Marketing planning: and action plans, 115–117; and analysis of property needs, 108–109; annual, 103; appropriateness of, 104; and budget categories, 117–118; and competitive information needed in, 106; components of competitive analysis, 108; and creating a new use for the product, 109; creation of new business, 109; and data analysis, 107–108, 111; data collection, 104–107; definition, 104; development of, 104; external impacts on, 105; establishing the context of, 104; failure of annual, 65; importance of industry trends on, 104–105; importance of internal data collection in, 107; importance of objectivity in, 105; and internal analysis questions, 112; and major strategic errors, 158; and market analysis, 111–112; and the marketing budget,

117–120; and marketing controls, 120; and the marketing forecast, 117; and mission statement, 112; and necessity for flexibility, 103; necessity of gathering and analysing information, 110; objectives of, 113; operational integration of, 104; and opportunity analysis, 111–112; and public relations, 584; and retaining customers, 115; requirements for, 103–104
Marketing opportunities. *See* Opportunities
Marketing research, 169–180; appropriateness of, 179–180; and data analysis, 179; definition, 171; and environmental scanning, 168–169; formal, 171; and inferential quantitative research, 174; and international tourism, 746–748; and interpretation of data, 172–173; and marketing decisions, 180; need for, 174–175; and primary data, 171; purpose of, 171; qualitative, 171–172; quantitative, 172, 174; and secondary data, 171
Marketing research design, 175–179; and data collection, 178–179; and establishing the research purpose, 175; and expected information results, 177; flowchart of the research process, 176; and identifying the research problem, 176; methods of, 177–179; reliability and validity of, 179; and research objectives, 176–177
Marketplace. *See* Market
Marriott: 13, 31, 32, 33, 69, 74, 81, 82, 139, 146, 407, 565, 648, 653, 660, 662; ad, 140, 216, 233, 252–253, 304, 356, 363, 366, 373, 398, 399, 438, 443, 501, 517, 535, 561; Allie's, 69, 74; Check-out, 141;

Copley Place, 69; Courtyard by Marriott, 146, 156, 303, 366, 399; Fairfield Inn, 69, 366, and image, 370; Long Wharf, Boston, 69; Marriott Host/Travel Plazas, 170; Marriott International, Inc., 648, 652; Marriott Marquis Hotel, N.Y.C., 650, and Atlanta, 650; master strategy, 69, 74; mission statements, 69; "one-stop shopping," 632; and positioning, 373; research, 201n; Residence Inns, 69, 366; Roy Rogers, 69; Toronto Eaton Centre, 13
Martindale, David, 565n
Maslow, 200, 200n; hierarchy of needs, 201
Master strategy, 69, 74–76; facets of, 75; long-range perspectives of, 74; of Marriott, 69, 74; and situation analysis, 74
Mature traveler, 231–232
Mayfair House, 582
McCarthy, E. Jerome, 393, 393n
McCarthy, Thomas T., 633, 633n
McDaniel, Carl, 609n, 714n
McDonald, Ronald, 294
McDonald's, 1, 81, 82, 84, 105, 139, 166, 208, 398, 400, 407, 408, 410, 429, 483, 559, 583–584, 647, 650, 655, 658, 662, 722, 740, 749; and ADI, 308, 317; and food in India, 722; and international marketing, 719; Red Square, Moscow, 144, 407, 714
McKenna, Regis, 17, 17n
McKinsey & Co., 469
Mercadente, Blaise, 318n, 465n
Merchandising, 576–582; basic rules of, 577–578; compatibility and consistency, 578; goal of, 577; good, 579, 582; and knowledgeable employees, 579; and simplicity, 578–579; and visibility of offering, 578
Meridien Hotels. *See* Le Meridien Hotels
Merrill Lynch, 311

Mexico, ad, 778

Micro competition; avoidance of overgeneralizing, 158; and choosing the right competition, 158–161; and competitive intelligence, 162–164; and conceptitis, 159; defined, 158

Microeconomy in international marketing; 719, 721

Microtel, ad, 163

Millenium Hotel, N.Y.C., 435

Mirage Hotel, Las Vegas, 439; ad, 515

Mission statement(s), 68, 112; corporate, 69; criteria of an effective, 70; Holiday Inn, 71; Kraft General Foods, 72–74; Marriott, 69; and objectives, 68–69

Moller, K.E. Kristian, et al., 317n; 743

Moreo, P., 232n

Morgan, Michael S., 317n

Morris, Susan V., 523n, 524n

Moss, Nan K., 217

Motel 6, 81, 144, 294, 306, 450
See also Groupe Accor

Motorcoach tour market, 277–278; defined, 277

Mount Charlotte Thistle Hotels, UK, ad, 690

Mövenpick, 670, 746; ad, 569; brochure page, 672, 745; comment card, 173

Muller, Christopher, 74n

Multiple brand positioning, 366–371; examples of, 371

Myers, James, 400n

Nassikas, Jim, 296, 348

National Restaurant Association (NRA), 140, 140n, 144, 272

National Tour Association, 277

Nebel, Eddystone C., 279n, 524, 524n

New Otani Hotel, Los Angeles, 740; Singapore, 294

Nikko Hotel, ad, 36, 740

Nightingale, Michael, 11n, 39n

Nonprobability sample, 178

Nontraditional marketing, 4; components of, 30–31; culmination of, 393; and marketing of services, 32, 33; physical plant, 429; and services vs. goods, 29–30

Novotel. See Groupe Accor hotels

NTOs (national tourism organizations), 771, 773, 780; and marketing functions, 786–788

Oberoi Hotels, 83, 725; brochure pages, 727, 728; in Bombay, 742

Objectives: and mission statement of marketing plan, 68, 69; and situational analysis, 76

Objective positioning, 343–345; and unique features, 345

Occupancy: forecasting, 118; turnover and volume objectives, 473

Odd-numbered pricing, 485

Official Hotel Guide, 686, ad, 688

Ogilvy, David, 352, 352n

Olive Garden Restaurants, 344

Omni Hotels, 81, 144, 356, 357, 563, 662; ad, 563; Omni Berkshire Place, NYC, 442; public relations release, 583

Opening specials, 474

Operational strategies, 78–79, 81–82

Operations, 4; orientation, 10–11, problems created by, 37; usage rules as elements of, 40

Opportunities: competitive analysis and, 169; defined, 180; and environmental analysis, 75; and knowing your market, 167; and market research, 170; and solutions, 167; and sources of new markets, 166–167; successes and failures, 169

Opportunity analysis: defined, 76; and environmental changes, 76; and marketing research, 169–170

Opryland Hotel, Nashville, Tennessee, 45; ad, 271; differentiation at, 294

Organization, and situational analysis, 76

Organizational customer: buying process, 245–254; and needs assessment, 245, 248, 249

Organizational planner: and conference centers, 261–263; and controlling costs, 258–259; and convention centers and convention and visitors bureaus, 271–273; and the "Copley Connection," 251–253; and the corporate meetings market, 259–261; and the corporate travel market, 254–259; decision making by, 244; defined, 243; and discounts, 256–257; and evaluation of results, 254; and executing the meeting, 254; and the generic organizational market, 243–245; and goals-setting, 250; and group and individual needs, 244–245; and the group tour market, 276–277; and the incentive market, 263–267; and incentive planners, 266; and motorcoach tour travelers, 277–278; and resolving conflicts, 251; and site selection criteria, 246–247; and target market segments, 243; and tasks of corporate meeting planner, 245–254; and understanding travel patterns, 258. See also Association, Convention, and Trade Show Markets

Organizational values and situational analysis, 75

Orientations: management, 10–11; marketing, 16

Orkin, Eric, 634–635, 635n

Ortt, Terry, 325

Package market segments, 227–231; advantages for customers, 228–229;

advertisements for, 227, 228, 230, 341; and Club Med, 229; defined, 227; and fulfillment of promises, 229; and hotels offering weekend packages, 227

Packaging, of promotions, 559

Palace Hotel: New York, 653; Tokyo, ad, 345

Pan Pacific Hotel, ad, 13, 446, 726

Pannell Kerr Forster (PKF), 117n, 201n, 217n, 220n

Parasuraman, A., Zeithaml, V.A., and Berry, L.L., gap model, 210

Parker Meridien, New York, 81

Partlow, Charles, 46n

PC Link reservation system, 689

Peabody Hotels, 445; ad, 292; and differentiation, 291–292; Orlando, Florida, 45

Pearl–Continental Hotel, Pakistan, ad, 741

Penetration pricing, 481

Peninsula Hotel, Hong Kong, 294, 744; New York, ad, 539

People's Express Airlines, 481

PepsiCo, 155; restaurants, 366

Perceived value, 484

Perceptual map(s): and competitive positioning, 364; and restaurant attributes, 374

Perishability of services, 35–37

Personal interviews, 172

Personal selling: closing, 623; customer attitude, 621–623; follow-up, 623–624; probing, 617–621; prospecting, 610–613; sales approach, 613–614

Personnel, policies and internal marketing concept, 46

Phillips Seafood Restaurant, ad, 532

Philosophy, marketing, 3–4

Physical plant, 428–434; defined, 428; and developing the physical plant package, 428–429; and nontraditional marketing, 439

Pierre Hotel, New York, 587

Pizam, Abraham, 374n

Pizza Hut, 140, 650, 724; ad, 666

Pizza Inn, ad, 655

Plaza Hotel, New York City, 293

Pleasure traveler market, 222–227; and growth potential, 223; importance of hotel attributes compared with business travelers, 224; and international travelers, 232; and the mature traveler, 231; and the package market, 227–231; resorts and, 226–227

Plog, Stanley, 276, 276n

Plummer, Joseph, 310–311, 311n

PMS (property management systems), 140, 498, 527

Point of marginal expensiveness (PME), 467

Policies, and situational analysis, 76

Ponderosa Steak House, 344

Population, defined in research, 177

Porter, Michael E., 159, 159n, 166, 166n

Portman, John, 167, 440

Positioning. See Market positioning

Pousadas, 736

Preconference meeting, 251

Preferred Hotels & Resorts Worldwide; 219, 664, 667; ad, 88, 668–669

Premier Resorts & Hotels, ad, 691

Presentation mix: and atmospherics, 437–443; and customers, 84, 445; definition, 83, 85, 427; and employees, 84, 443–445; and location, 84, 434–437; and international marketing, 725–727; and physical plant and atmosphere, 84, 428; and price, 427, 449–451; and pricing strategy, 84

Presentation substrategy, 83–85. See also Presentation mix

Price: establishment of, 4; elasticity, 482; price-lining, 485; and range, 217; skimming, 474; tangibility of, 30

Price sensitivity measurement (PSM), 465–467

Price/value relationship, 4, 483–484; and customer pricing, 484

Pricing, 463–487; basis of, 463, 469–480; cost-oriented, 476; competitive information needed for, 480–481; and customer objectives, 474–476; and hotel room pricing, 465–469; and hotelier views of discounting versus value-added services, 470; and integration of product and price, 463–464; in international markets, 728–732; and market demand, 481–483; mistakes in, 486–487; practices, 465–469; psychological, 485–486; and restaurant pricing, 465; and usage, 482–483; and yield management, 498–504. See also Cost pricing

Pricing decisions, difficulty of, 35

Pricing objectives, 470–476; financial, 471–472; volume, 472–474

Pricing strategy: and discounting, 485; five major categories of, 469; and price-quoting, 486; and the rate-sensitive customer, 486

Pride, William M., 16n

Prime Hospitality Corp., ad, 665

Prime Motor Inns, 476, 517, 518

Princess Hotels: Acapulco, ad, 514; Southampton, Bermuda, ad, 513

Probability sample, 178

Proctor & Gamble, 647; ad, 7

Product(s); classification as goods or services, 29, 30; components of hospitality, 30; death spiral, 412; defined, 395; differentiation, 166; factors most likely to be associated with successful new, 414; major elements of hospitality, 30; strategy, 78, 81

Product life cycle (PLC), 405–406; decline stage of, 411–412; graph of stages in, 405; and the growth stage, 408–409; and locating products in their life cycles, 412; and mature stage, 409–411; nature of, 405; stages of, 406–413

Product differentiation, defined, 299

Product segmentation, 301–305

Product/service mix, 83–84, 395–404; ad illustrating product/service strategy, 83; complexity of, 399–400; and the core product, 396–397; and customer perceptions, 396; and customization, 403–404; definition, 82; and designing the hospitality product, 396; developing new services, 413–414; from point of view of target market, 405; and the international marketing mix, 724–725; and making the product decision, 404–405; and merchandising, 578

Product/service: ad illustrating strategy of, 83; orientation, 11; and standard products, 400–403; and standard products with modifications, 402–403; and situational analysis, 76

Product strategy, 79

Professional Convention Management Association (PCMA), 146

Profit, and marketing, 4–5

Promotion (sales): definition of, 559; and delivering on promises, 568–569; designing, 574–576; developing, 571–576; and distribution channel strategies, 698–699; employee awareness of 699; and frequent-traveler programs, 560–566; guidelines for, 567–571; and hotels, 565–566; and ideas for promotions, 573; and marketing needs, 566–567;

principles and practices of, 559–576

Public information, and competitive intelligence, 162–164

Public relations: compared with publicity, 582; definition, 582; and development of tactics, 587–588; doing, 584–585; and evaluation, 588; guidelines, 588; and news releases, 584; and perception of target markets, 586; planning, 586–587; and positioning of product, 587; and publicity, 587–588; and the press release, 587, 588; and sample timetable, 585; and selection of media, 586–587

Québec, ad, 783

QSC, quality, service, cleanliness, 1

Qualitative research: advantage of, 172; forms of, 172; problems with, 172; reasons for, 172

Quality, consumers' measurement of, 38

Quality Inns, 79, 146, 166, 303, 356, 367, 368; and Comfort Inns, 303; and Quality Royale, 303. See also Choice International Hotels

Quantitative research, 172, 174

Queens Moat Houses, England, 144

Questionnaire design for market research, 179–180

Rack rate, 217, 258

Radisson Hotels International, 144, 662, 663, 670; ad, 83, 145, 157, 293, 672

Raise the numbers, 104

Ramada, 79, 356; ad, 225, 357, 367; and business card awards, 562

Random sample, 178

Range of acceptable price (RAP), 467

Red Lion Hotels & Inns, ad, 564

Red Lobster, 158, 344

Red Roof Inn, 107

Regent Hotels, 528; Beverly Wilshire, ad, 346, 529; Melbourne, ad, 529

Regulatory environment, and environmental scanning, 150–151

Relais & Chateaux, 669

Relationship marketing, 5, 46–54; applicability of, 46; and core services, 51; and customer loyalty, 49, 51; and customized services, 51; defined, 46, 49; and internal marketing, 54; in manufacturing industries, 46; and ongoing relationships, 49; and pricing, 51; and service augmentation, 51

Renaghan, Leo M., 82n, 83, 85n, 394, 394n, 395n, 416

Renaissance Hotels, 159, 356; ad, 160, 314

Representation companies, 675–680; defined, 675–676

Research methods: flowchart, 176; and population, 177; reliability and validity, 179; samples of, 177–178

Reservation companies, 670–675

Reservation systems, and labeling service, 673

Reso Hotels of Sweden, 144

Resource(s), and situational analysis, 75

Restaurant(s): and atmospherics, 481; creative advertising, 299; designating market of, 65; and salad bar, 167; and tangibilizing the intangible, 352

REVPAR, 165

Revson, Charles, 8

Risk loop, 88

Ritz-Carlton Hotels, 46, 79, 81, 82, 84, 166, 344, 475, 483, 614, 616, 651, 745; ad, 47, 295, 351; and differentiation, 294; and target marketing, 324; and travel agents, 686

RockResorts on Lana'i, Hawaii, 508

Rodeway Hotels, 146, 406
Roger Smith Hotel, New York City, 293, 682; GDS hotel information, 684–685
Rosenquist, G., 743n
Ross, Elliot B., 469, 469n
Royal Classic Hotels, Denmark, 144
Royal Monceau Hotel, Paris, ad, 87
Rutherford, Denney G., 254, 254n, 269, 269n

Sabre system, directory, 683
Sales management: account management, 624, 626, 627; action plans, 627
Salespeople: ethics, 633–634; motivation, 634–635; personal development, 632–633; relationship with, in goods and services marketing compared, 39
Sales organizations, 627–632; relationships with other departments, 635–636
Salience, determinance, and importance, 360–363
Sambo's Restaurants, 306
Sameness of restaurant advertising, 298
Sample, types of, 177–178
Sandals Resorts, ad, 231
SAS International Hotels; Brussels, 743; Oslo, Norway, 670; merchandising, 581
SBU. See Strategic business unit
Scandinavia, research on business travelers in, 743
Scandinavian Airways System, 16–17
Seal, Kathy, 245n
Sears, 559, 560
Segmentation. See Market segmentation
Seller-buyer relationship. See Relationship marketing
Selling, orientation, 11
Service(s): as aspect of marketing, 31; as process, 49; defined, 30; fluctuations in, 37; functional differences

between goods and, 41; in hospitality industry, 3; room 30, 31; quality of, 44
Service(s) marketing, compared with manufactured goods marketing, 29–30
Service sector, 29
Servico Management of Florida, 648, 652; ad, 649
Sharpe, John, 48n
Sheraton, 170, 473n, 525, 647, 648, 713, 716, 749; ad, 14, 171, 213, 255, 372; image problem, 370; Century Park, Singapore, 742, 746; Sheraton Boston, 144, ad, 540; Sheraton Inn, Bordentown, New Jersey, 81, 662; Sheraton Inn, Westchester County, 81; Sheraton New York Hotel & Towers, 81, 140; St. Regis Sheraton, 81, 662, ad, 449
Shangri-La Hotel, Kowloon, promotion, 575
Shansby, J. Gary, 358n
Shaw, Margaret, 244n, 250n, 263n
Shure, Peter, 275n
Signature Inns, Inc., ad, 54
Simultaneity of production and consumption, 39–40, 44
Singapore, ad, 775
Single-product companies, 79
Site selection criteria, 246–247
Situational analysis, elements of, 75
Skydome Hotel, Toronto, 152
Sleep Inns, 79, 146. See also Choice International Hotels
SMSAs, standard metropolitan statistical areas, 308
SMERF market, 243; defined, 275–276
"Smile training," 44
Smith Travel Research, 652
Sociocultural changes, and environmental analysis, 75; and environmental scanning, 146
Sociocultural environment, trends in, 148
Sofitel, 81, 722, 740; ad, 310. See also Groupe Accor

Sol Hotels, Spain, 144, 738, 745
Southerst, John, 325n
Southwest Airlines, 481; ad, 162
SRI International, 311–313; VALS 2, 312
Stanford Court Hotel, San Francisco, 296, 348, 429, 475; ad, 350
Stanhope Hotel, New York, 82
Starhotels, weekend package ad, 227
Stark, Steven J., 519n
Statler, E.M., 434, 435
Statler Hotel chain, 434
Steigenberger Hotels, Germany, 151
Steigenberger Reservation Service (SRS), Frankfurt, 676
Steiner, Gary A., 511–512, 511n, 518
Storbacka, K., 743n
Stouffer Hotels & Resorts, 49, 53, 81, 140, 356; ad, 50, 226
Strategic business unit (SBU), 65, 69, 70; definition of, 69; and mission statements, 69; and objectives, 69
Strategic framework, 67
Strategic marketing: and alternative courses of action, 89; concept of, 66, 68; definition, 65; as distinct from marketing management, 65; functional strategies, 82–87; mission statement, 68; and strategy evaluation, 89; and strategy selection, 89; system, 68, 69, 74–76; systems model, 67
Strategic planning, 89; and strategic business units (SBUs), 69; and situational analysis, 66; and unit managers, 89; using the systems model of, 76–78
Strategic thinking, 68
Strategy, concept of, 66; competitive, 79
Subjective positioning, defined, 346–347, 355
Suite hotel chains, 155. See All-suite hotels

Supranational hotels: ad, 677, 679; brochure page, 678; and network members of, 676; promotion, 679

Sutton Place Hotel, Toronto, 652

Switzerland, Lake Geneva area, ad, 785

Systems perspective, 68

Taco Bell, 146, 465; research, 317–318

Tactics, marketing strategy and, 66

Tailoring the product to the wants and needs of the target market, 307–308

Tandy Corporation, 648

Tangibilizing the intangible: ads, 350, 432, 433; in advertising, 293; and presentation mix, 427; and price, 295–296; and product differentiation, 293. See also Atmospherics; Presentation

Target market(s): and communications strategy, 511–512; and pricing, 482, 483; segments of, 243; selecting from identified segments, 307–308; stages, 511–512; strategy, 78. See also Market segmentation; Target marketing

Target marketing, 322–326; and computer databases, 325; defined, 322; and multi-segment targeting, including examples, 324; and the Ritz Carlton, 324; strategies for selecting, 322–324; and target markets of one, 325–326

Taylor, Stephen P., 357, 357n

Technological change, and environmental analysis, 75

Telemarketing, 611, 613, 614

Thai Wah Group, Thailand, 151

Thailand, 723; ad, 268

Thaler, 503n

The Newsletter Group, Inc., 573n

Threat, and environmental analysis, 75

Tier structure in hotel industry, 146

Tokyu Hotel Group, 725

Tour operators: advertising for, 693; defined, 691; as hotel advertisers, 82; and wholesalers, 691–695

Tourism Authority of Thailand (TAT), 786

Tourism Canada, 171

TQM, total quality management, 411, 444

Trade-off model, consumer, 8, 18

Trade show markets. See Association, convention, and trade show markets

Traditional marketing, 4; limitations of, 416

Travel agents, 680–690; and automated ticketing systems, 681–682; and changing conditions in the marketplace, 682; cooperating with, 686, 688–689; defined, 681; future of, 689–691; marketing to, 686–688; and push strategy, 697; review of, 681; and relationship with hotels, 683, 686; role of, 681–683, 686; wholesaler ad, 695

TravelFax reservation system, 689

Travel Industry Association, 234

Travelodge, 144, 439; ad, 661

TraveLOGIX, CRS technology, 682

Travers, Kenneth, 465, 467n

"Twofers," 49, 148, 474

Umbreit, W. Terry, 254, 254n, 269, 269n

Upselling, 155

United Stated Travel and Tourism Administration (USTTA), 780

U.S. Travel Data Center, 171, 215, 216n, 217n, 222n, 223n, 232n

Utell International, 670, 672–674; ad, 673

Valle's Steak House, 411

Value, perception, 5

Values & lifestyles (VALS) psychograhic segmentation tool, 311–312

Venture Inns of Canada, 81; ad, 278

Victoria Station restaurants, 411

VingCard, ad, 149

Visibility factor, 485

Vista Hotels, 565, 587

Volume, objectives of pricing, 472; sensitivity, 472

Waldorf-Astoria, New York City, 293, 358, 435, 662; ad, 359

Watkins, Ed, 368n

wee-bag-it, 167; ad, 168

Wendy's, 79, 139, 146, 166

Westendorp, Peter H., 465

Westin, 81, 109, 144, 400; ad, 12, 218, 252–253, 401, 533, 625; Chosun, merchandising, 580

Whattaburger, 155

Wilson, Kemmons, 155

Withiam, Glenn, 368n, 503n

Windsor Court, New Orleans, 293, 439; ad, 439

Word-of-mouth communication, 82, 517–519; and advertising, 532; behavior of hotel complainants, 523; and buyers of services, 35; and customer complaints, 519–522

WTO (World Tourism Organization), 716n, 771, 777

Yesawich, Peter, 301, 301n, 367; classification strategy, 302, 303

Yield management, 498–504; calculation of yield, 503; and the customer, 504; defined, 498–499, 500; and demand forecasting, 500; effective use of, 500; and pricing, 500, 503, 504; and why hotels are different, 499–500

Zemke, Ron, 170n

Zive, Jessica D., 585

World Maps

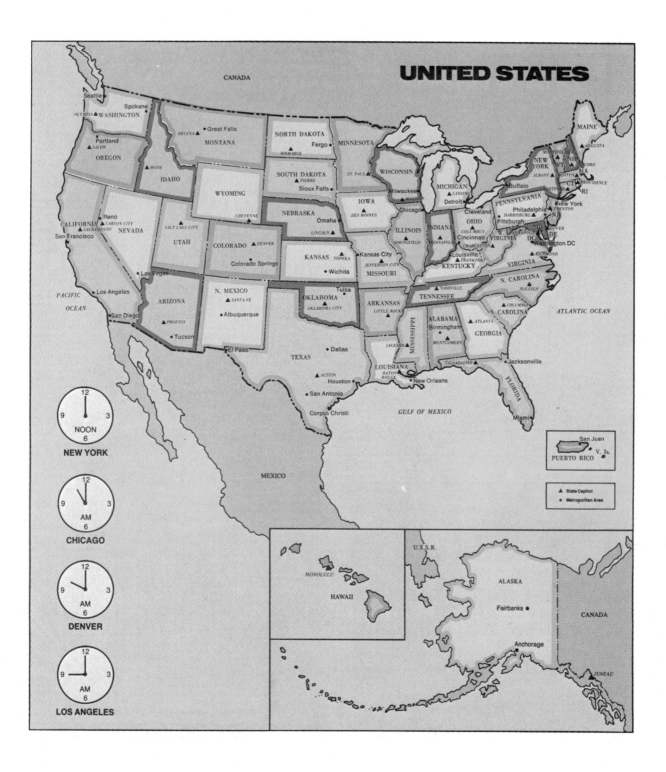

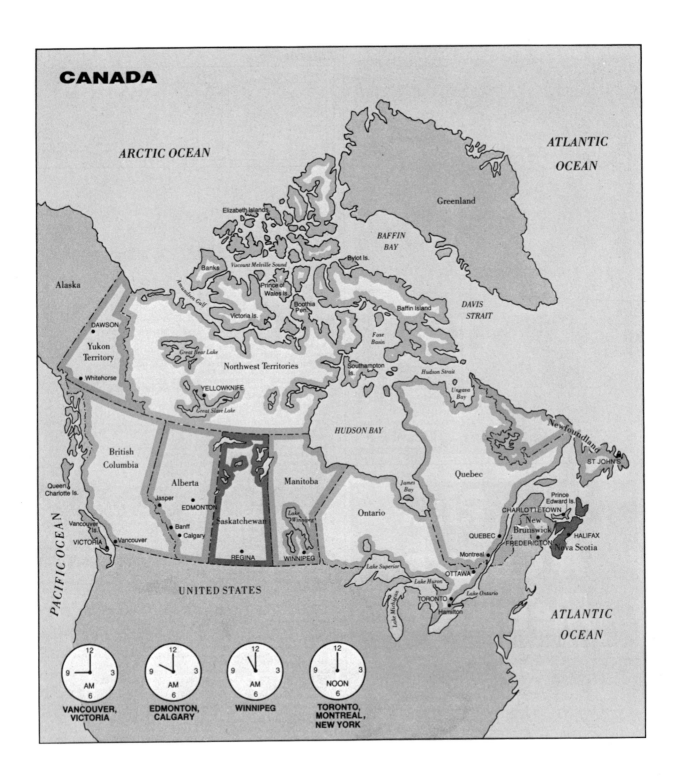

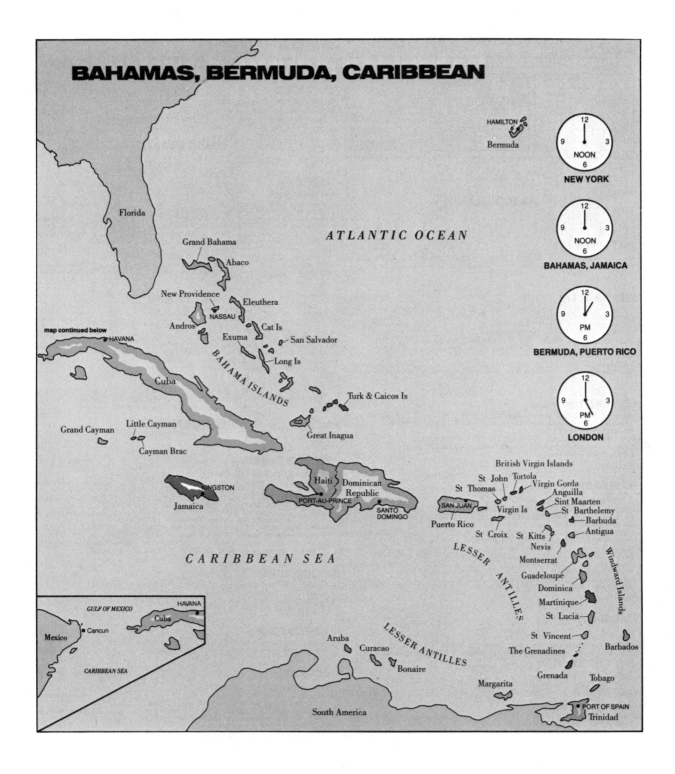

BAHAMAS, BERMUDA, CARIBBEAN

HAMILTON
Bermuda

ATLANTIC OCEAN

Florida

Grand Bahama
Abaco
New Providence
Eleuthera
NASSAU
Andros
Cat Is
Exuma
San Salvador
Long Is

map continued below
HAVANA

BAHAMA ISLANDS

Cuba

Grand Cayman
Little Cayman
Cayman Brac

Turk & Caicos Is

Great Inagua

KINGSTON
Jamaica
Haiti
Dominican
Republic
PORT-AU-PRINCE
SANTO
DOMINGO

British Virgin Islands
St John
Tortola
St Thomas
Virgin Gorda
Anguilla
Sint Maarten
SAN JUAN
St Barthelemy
Virgin Is
Barbuda
Puerto Rico
Antigua
St Croix
St Kitts
Nevis
Montserrat
LESSER ANTILLES
Guadeloupe
Dominica
Windward Islands
Martinique
St Lucia
St Vincent
The Grenadines
Barbados
Grenada
Tobago

CARIBBEAN SEA

GULF OF MEXICO
HAVANA
Cuba
Mexico
Cancun
CARIBBEAN SEA

Aruba
LESSER ANTILLES
Curacao
Bonaire

Margarita

PORT OF SPAIN
Trinidad

South America

NEW YORK — 12 NOON

BAHAMAS, JAMAICA — 12 NOON

BERMUDA, PUERTO RICO — PM

LONDON — PM

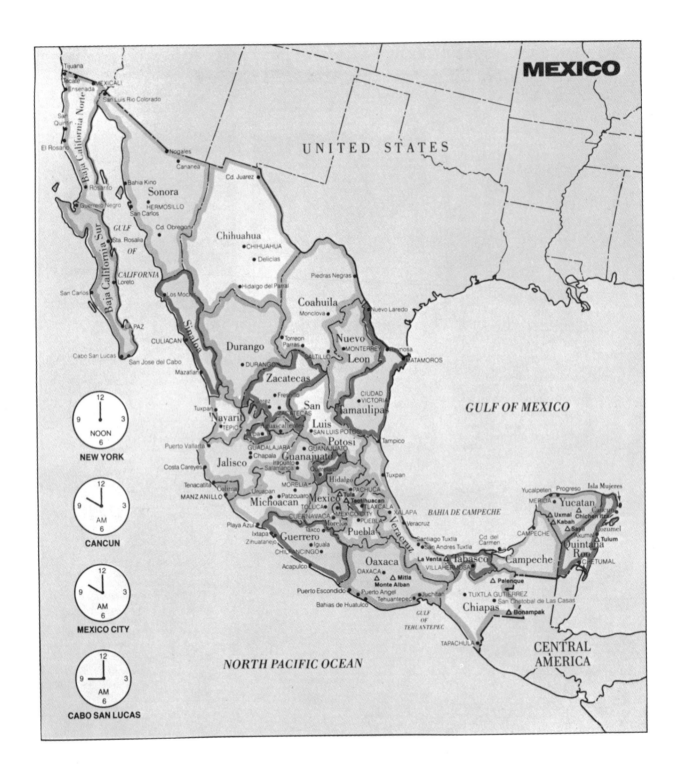

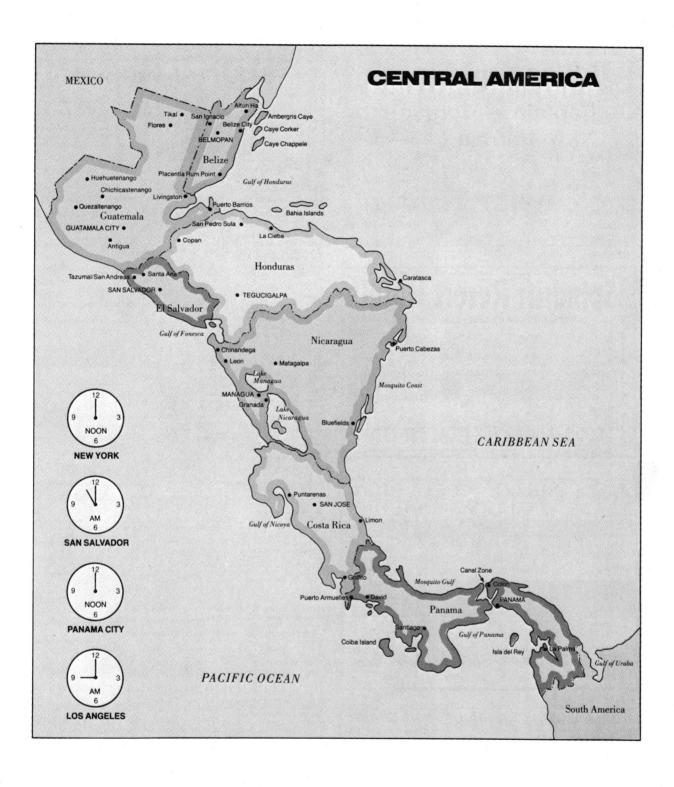

CENTRAL AMERICA

MEXICO

Tikal
San Ignacio
Altun Ha
Ambergris Caye
Flores
Belize City
Caye Corker
BELMOPAN
Caye Chappele

Belize

Huehuetenango
Placentia Rum Point
Gulf of Honduras
Chichicastenango
Livingston
Quezaltenango
Puerto Barrios
Guatemala
Bahia Islands
GUATAMALA CITY
San Pedro Sula
La Cieba
Antigua
Copan

Honduras

Tazumal/San Andreas
Santa Ana
Caratasca
SAN SALVADOR
TEGUCIGALPA

El Salvador

Gulf of Fonseca
Nicaragua
Chinandega
Puerto Cabezas
Leon
Matagalpa
Lake Managua
Mosquito Coast
MANAGUA
Granada
Lake Nicaragua
Bluefields

CARIBBEAN SEA

Puntarenas
SAN JOSE
Limon
Gulf of Nicoya
Costa Rica

Canal Zone
Mosquito Gulf
Golfito
Colon
Puerto Armuelles
David
PANAMA
Panama
Santiago
Gulf of Panama
Coiba Island
Isla del Rey
La Palma
Gulf of Uraba

PACIFIC OCEAN

South America

NEW YORK
12 3 6 9 NOON

SAN SALVADOR
12 3 6 9 AM

PANAMA CITY
12 3 6 9 NOON

LOS ANGELES
12 3 6 9 AM

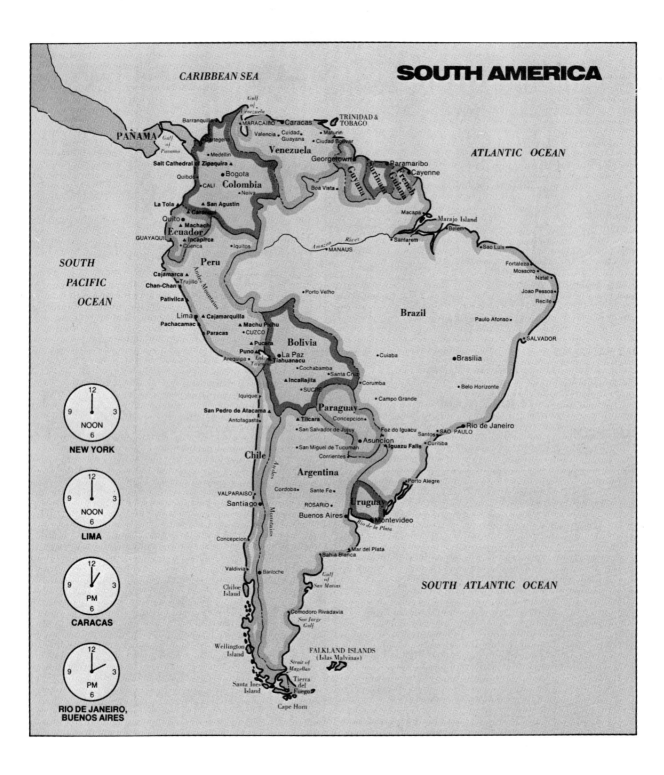

SOUTH AMERICA

CARIBBEAN SEA

Gulf of Venezuela

Barranquilla
MARACAIBO   Caracas
Valencia   Ciudad Guayana
PANAMA   *Gulf of Panama*
Cartagena

TRINIDAD & TOBAGO
Maturin
Ciudad Bolivar

ATLANTIC OCEAN

Medellin
Salt Cathedral at Zipaquira ▲
Quibdo
▲ San Agustin
Venezuela
Georgetown

Paramaribo
Cayenne

• Bogota
CALI   **Colombia**
Neiva

Boa Vista

Guyana
Surinam
French Guiana

La Tola
▲ San Agustin
▲ Carapan
Quito •
▲ Machachi
Ecuador
▲ Incapirca
GUAYAQUIL •
• Cuenca

Macapa
• Marajo Island
Belem
Santarem

• Iquitos
Amazon   River
MANAUS

Peru
Sao Luis

Cajamarca •
▲ Trujillo
Chan-Chan •

Fortaleza
Mossoro
Natal

Pativilca

Andes Mountains

• Porto Velho

Joao Pessoa
Recife

Lima • ▲ Cajamarquilla
Pachacamac • ▲ Paracas
Brazil
Paulo Afonso •

▲ Machu Pichu
▼ CUZCO
▲ Pucara

SALVADOR

Puno ▲
Arequipa •
Lake Titicaca
▲ La Paz
Tiahuanacu
Bolivia

• Cuiaba

• Brasilia

• Cochabamba
• Santa Cruz

▲ Incallajita
▲ SUCRE

• Corumba

• Belo Horizonte

▲ San Pedro de Atacama
Antofagasta •
Paraguay
Concepcion •
• Campo Grande

• Campo Grande

▲ Tilcara
• San Salvador de Jujuy
Foz do Iguacu
Santos
SAO PAULO
• Rio de Janeiro

Chile
• San Miguel de Tucuman
Asuncion •
Iguazu Falls
Curitiba
Corrientes

Andes

Argentina
Porto Alegre

VALPARAISO •
Cordoba •
Sante Fe •
ROSARIO •
Uruguay

Santiago •
Buenos Aires
Montevideo
Rio de la Plata

Mountains

Concepcion •

• Mar del Plata
Bahia Blanca

Valdivia •
• Bariloche

Gulf of San Matias

SOUTH ATLANTIC OCEAN

Chiloe Island

Comodoro Rivadavia
San Jorge Gulf

Wellington Island

FALKLAND ISLANDS
(Islas Malvinas)

Strait of Magellan

Santa Ines Island
Tierra del Fuego

Cape Horn

SOUTH
PACIFIC
OCEAN

NEW YORK
12 NOON 3 6 9

LIMA
12 NOON 3 6 9

CARACAS
12 PM 3 6 9

RIO DE JANEIRO, BUENOS AIRES
12 PM 3 6 9

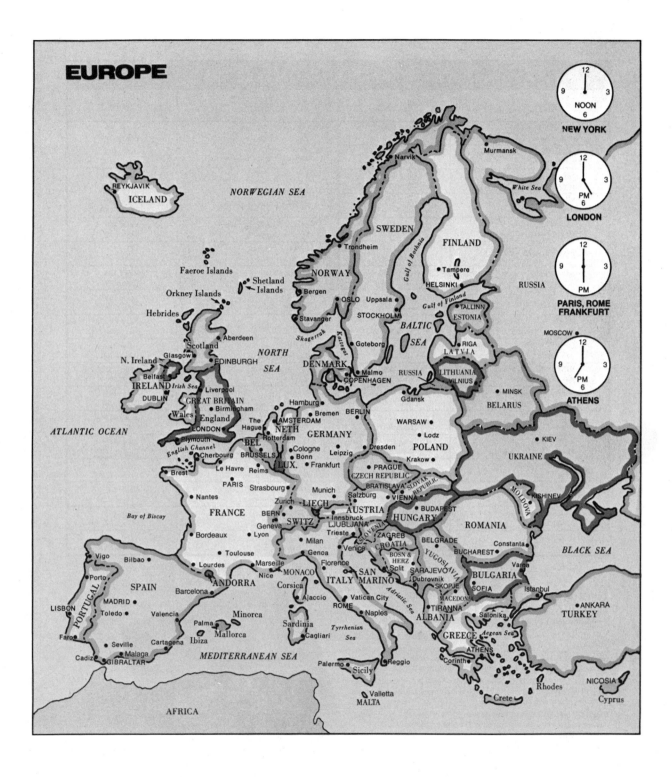

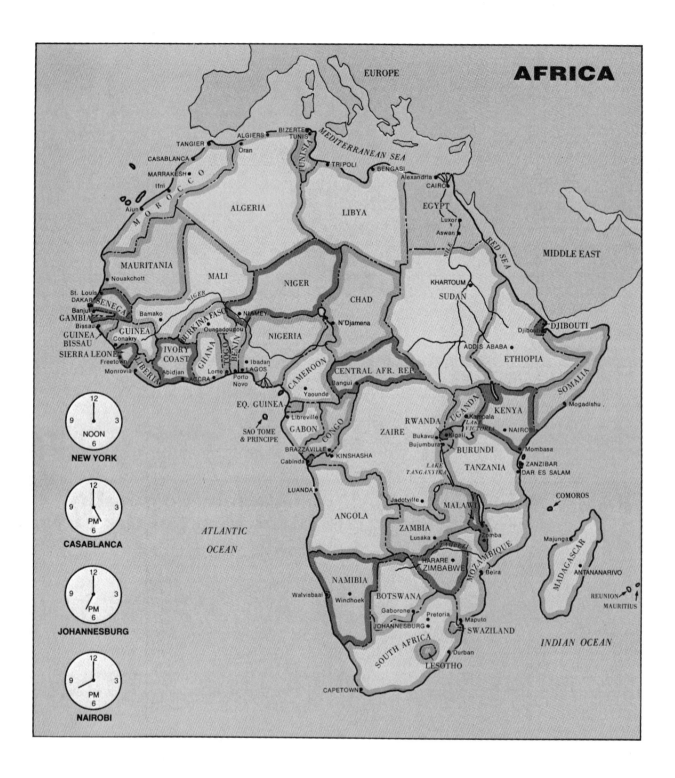

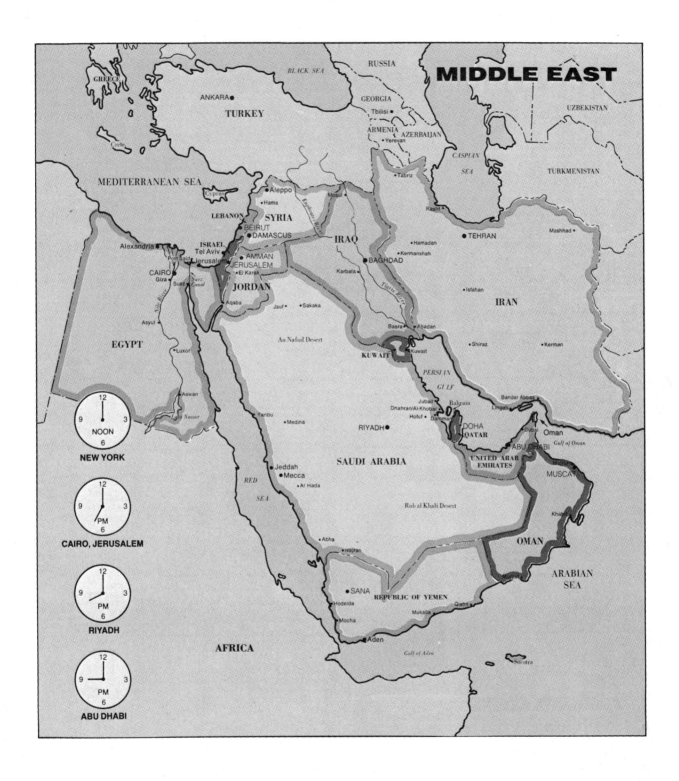

MIDDLE EAST

GREECE

BLACK SEA

RUSSIA

TURKEY

ANKARA

GEORGIA

Tbilisi

UZBEKISTAN

ARMENIA

AZERBAIJAN

Yerevan

CASPIAN
SEA

TURKMENISTAN

Crete

Tabriz

Rasht

MEDITERRANEAN SEA

Cyprus

Aleppo

Hama

Mosul

Euphrates River

TEHRAN

Mashhad

LEBANON

SYRIA

BEIRUT

DAMASCUS

IRAQ

Hamadan

Kermanshah

Alexandria

ISRAEL
Tel Aviv

Jerusalem

AMMAN

BAGHDAD

Tigris River

Isfahan

IRAN

CAIRO

Port Said

JERUSALEM

Karbala

Giza

Suez

Suez Canal

El Karak

JORDAN

Aqaba

Jauf

Sakaka

Basra

Abadan

Shiraz

Kerman

EGYPT

Nile River

Asyut

An Nafud Desert

KUWAIT

Kuwait

Luxor

PERSIAN

GULF

Aswan

Lake Nasser

Bandar Abbas

Jubail

Bahrain

Lingah

Dhahran/Al-Khobar

Yanbu

Medina

Hofuf

Dammam

DOHA

Dubai

Oman

Gulf of Oman

RED

SEA

Jeddah

Mecca

RIYADH

QATAR

ABU DHABI

UNITED ARAB
EMIRATES

Al Hada

SAUDI ARABIA

MUSCAT

Rub al Khali Desert

Khabura

Abha

OMAN

Najran

ARABIAN

SEA

AFRICA

SANA

REPUBLIC OF YEMEN

Qishn

Hodeida

Mukalla

Mocha

Muscat

Aden

Gulf of Aden

Socotra

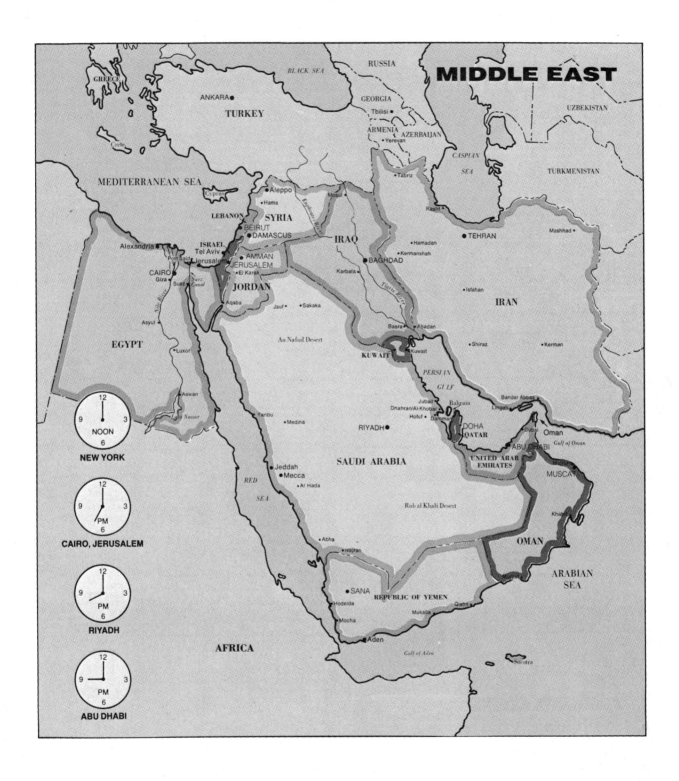

NOON

NEW YORK

PM

CAIRO, JERUSALEM

PM

RIYADH

PM

ABU DHABI

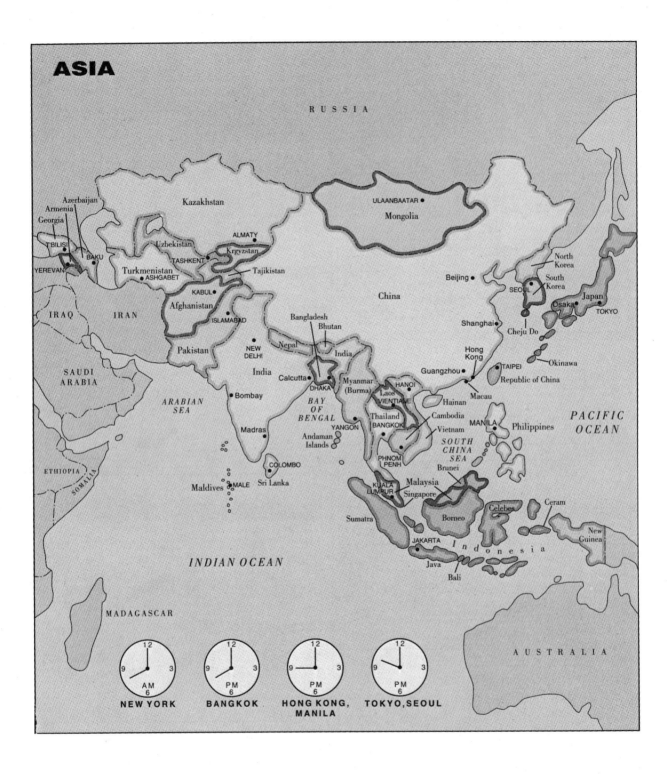

ASIA

RUSSIA

Kazakhstan

Azerbaijan
Armenia
Georgia
T'BILISI
YEREVAN
BAKU
Turkmenistan
ASHGABET
Uzbekistan
ALMATY
TASHKENT
Krgyzstan
Tajikistan
ULAANBAATAR
Mongolia

IRAQ
IRAN
KABUL
Afghanistan
ISLAMABAD
Pakistan
NEW
DELHI
Nepal
Bangladesh
Bhutan
India
China
Beijing
North
Korea
SEOUL
South
Korea
Osaka
Japan
TOKYO
Shanghai
Cheju Do

SAUDI
ARABIA

ARABIAN
SEA
Bombay
Calcutta
DHAKA
Myanmar
(Burma)
HANOI
Laos
VIENTIANE
Hong
Kong
Guangzhou
Macau
TAIPEI
Republic of China
Okinawa

ETHIOPIA
SOMALIA

Madras
BAY
OF
BENGAL
YANGON
Thailand
BANGKOK
Cambodia
Vietnam
MANILA
Philippines
Hainan
SOUTH
CHINA
SEA

PACIFIC
OCEAN

Andaman
Islands
PHNOM
PENH
Brunei
Maldives
MALE
COLOMBO
Sri Lanka
KUALA
LUMPUR
Malaysia
Singapore
Celebes
Ceram
New
Guinea

INDIAN OCEAN
Sumatra
Borneo
JAKARTA
Indonesia
Java
Bali

MADAGASCAR

AUSTRALIA

NEW YORK
12
AM
6
9
3

BANGKOK
12
PM
6
9
3

HONG KONG,
MANILA
12
PM
6
9
3

TOKYO, SEOUL
12
PM
6
9
3

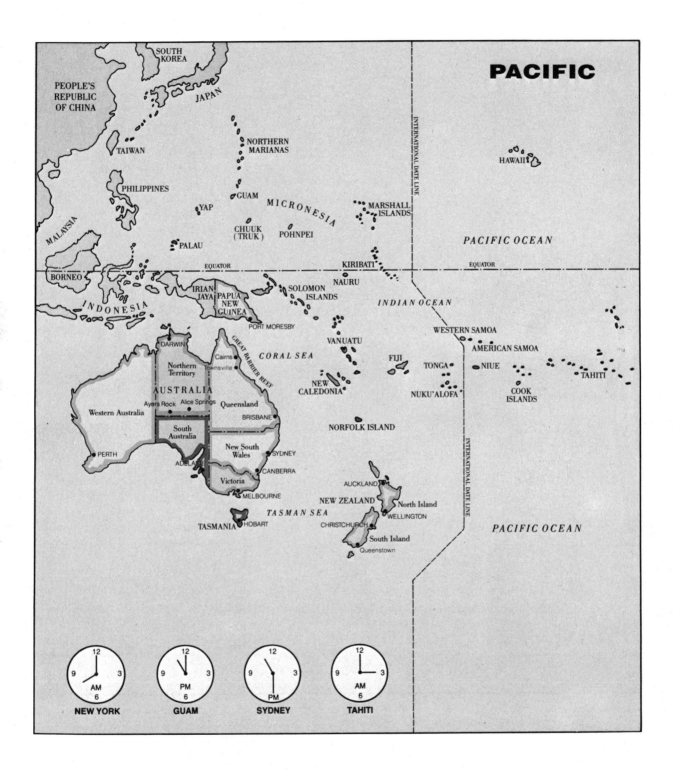

PACIFIC

ARCTIC OCEAN

180°
160°W
140° West Longitude
80°N
80°W
60°W
40°W
20°W

Arctic Circle
Alaska (U.S.)

Kalaallit Nunaat
(Greenland)
(DENMARK)

ICELAND

60°N

CANADA

NORTH

AMERICA

UNITED STATES

UNITED
KINGDOM

IRELAND NET

SWITZ

ANDORR

40° North Latitude

PACIFIC

OCEAN

CASE 9-1 Hotel Inter-
Continental / Toronto
Pages 377-378

ATLANTIC

OCEAN

Azores
(PORT.)

PORTUGAL SPA

GIBRALTAR

MOROCCO

Midway Island
(U.S.)

Bermuda
(U.K.)

CASE 2-1 Sojourn
in Jamaica
Pages 56-58

Western
Sahara
(MOROCCO)

Tropic of Cancer

MEXICO

CUBA

BAHAMAS

20°N

Hawaii (U.S.)

DOMINICAN
REPUBLIC

Puerto Rico (U.S.)
Virgin Is. (U.S./U.K.)

ANTIGUA AND BARBUDA

MAURITANIA

MA

JAMAICA

HAITI

ST. KITTS
AND NEVIS
ST. LUCIA

Guadeloupe (FR.)
DOMINICA
Martinique (FR.)
BARBADOS

CAPE
VERDE

GAMBIA SENEGAL

GUATEMALA

BELIZE

GUINEA-
BISSAU

GUINEA

BU

HONDURAS

NICARAGUA

GRENADA

ST. VINCENT AND THE GRENADINES

SIERRA
LEONE

IVORY
COAST

EL SALVADOR

COSTA
RICA

PANAMA

VENEZUELA

TRINIDAD AND TOBAGO

GUYANA
SURINAME

LIBERIA

EC

French Guiana (FR.)

SAO TOME AND PRII

0° Equator

COLOMBIA

PACIFIC

KIRIBATI

Galápagos I.
(ECUADOR)

ECUADOR

PERU

SOUTH

AMERICA

Tokelau (N.Z.)

WESTERN
SAMOA

American
Samoa (U.S.)

BRAZIL

TONGA

Cook Islands
(N.Z.)

BOLIVIA

20°S

PARAGUAY

Tropic of Capricorn

French
Polynesia
(FRANCE)

ATLANTIC

OCEAN

Easter Island
(CHILE)

CHILE

URUGUAY

PACIFIC

OCEAN

ARGENTINA

CASE 17-1
The Plaza Hotel
in Buenos Aires
Pages 750-756

40°S

Falkland Islands
(U.K.)

South Georgia
(U.K.)

60°S

Antarctic Circle

ANTARCTICA

80°S

180°
160°W
140°W
120°W
100°W
80°W
60°W
40°W
20°W

© 1995 GeoSystems Global Corp.